E.D.H.S.

2006-09

SECOND CANADIAN EDITION

ACCOUNTING PRINCIPLES

▶ JERRY J. WEYGANDT Ph.D., C.P.A.

Arthur Andersen Alumni Professor of Accounting
University of Wisconsin—Madison
Madison, Wisconsin

▶ DONALD E. KIESO Ph.D., C.P.A.

KPMG Peat Marwick Emeritus Professor of Accountancy
Northern Illinois University
DeKalb, Illinois

▶ PAUL D. KIMMEL Ph.D., C.P.A.

University of Wisconsin–Milwaukee
Milwaukee, Wisconsin

▶ BARBARA TRENHOLM M.B.A., F.C.A.

University of New Brunswick
Fredericton, New Brunswick

 JOHN WILEY AND SONS CANADA, LTD.

To our students — past, present, and future

National Library of Canadian Cataloguing in Publication Data
Main entry under title:
    Accounting principles

2nd Canadian ed. (in 1 vol.)
Includes index.
ISBN 0-470-83199-5

  1. Accounting. I. Weygandt, Jerry

HF5635.A3778 2002   657'.044   C2002-901332-1

Production Credits

Publisher: John Horne
Publishing Services Director: Karen Bryan
Editorial Manager: Karen Staudinger
Senior Marketing Manager: Janine Daoust
New Media Editor: Elsa Passera
Publishing Services/Permissions Co-ordinator: Michelle Marchetti
Design & Typesetting: Appleby Color Lab
Cover Design: Interrobang Graphic Design
Cover Photo: Steve Satushek/Image Bank
Printing & Binding: Tri-Graphic Printing Limited

Printed and bound in Canada
10 9 8 7 6 5 4 3 2 1

John Wiley & Sons Canada, Ltd.
22 Worcester Road
Etobicoke, Ontario M9W 1L1
Visit our website at: www.wiley.com/canada

ABOUT THE AUTHORS

Second Canadian Edition

Barbara Trenholm, MBA, FCA is a professor of accounting at the Faculty of Administration, University of New Brunswick, Fredericton, New Brunswick. She has received recognition for the quality of her teaching as a recipient of the National Post's Leaders in Management Education award, the Academy of Business Administration's Global Teaching Excellence Award, and the University of New Brunswick's Allan P. Stuart Excellence in Teaching Award. A recent edition of *The Maclean's Guide to Canadian Universities & Colleges* named her one of UNB's most popular professors.

She has also been active in professional accounting bodies such as the Canadian Institute of Chartered Accountants, the New Brunswick Institute of Chartered Accountants, the Canadian Academic Accounting Association, the American Accounting Association, the Institute of Internal Auditors, and the Atlantic School of Chartered Accountancy. Barbara is currently serving as a member of the Canadian Institute of Chartered Accountants Board of Directors and is a past president of the New Brunswick Institute of Chartered Accountants. In addition to her involvement with her profession, she also has an extensive record of service in leadership roles in the university and the community.

She has published widely in the field of accounting standard setting and explored various director and auditor liability issues in journals including *Accounting Horizons, International Journal of Production Economics, CAmagazine, CGA Magazine,* and *CMA Magazine.* She is also the Canadian author of Kimmel, Weygandt, Kieso, and Trenholm, *Financial Accounting: Tools for Business Decision-Making,* published by John Wiley & Sons Canada, Ltd.

U.S. Edition

Jerry J. Weygandt, PhD, CPA, is the Arthur Andersen Alumni Professor of Accounting at the University of Wisconsin—Madison. He has published many articles in the area of financial accounting, which have appeared in *Accounting Review, Journal of Accounting Research, Journal of Accountancy,* and other professional journals. He is a member and past president of the American Accounting Association and a member of the Wisconsin Society of Certified Public Accountants. In addition, he has been actively involved with the American Institute of Certified Public Accountants and has been a member of the Accounting Standards Executive Committee of that organization. Professor Weygandt has received the American Accounting Association's Outstanding Educator Award, the Chancellor's Award for Excellence in Teaching, the Wisconsin Institute of CPA's Outstanding Educator's Award and its Lifetime Achievement Award.

Donald E. Kieso, PhD, CPA, has served as chair of the Department of Accountancy and is currently the KPMG Peat Marwick Emeritus Professor of Accountancy at Northern Illinois University. Professor Kieso is a recipient of NIU's Teaching Excellence Award and four Golden Apple Teaching Awards. He has served as Secretary-Treasurer of the American Accounting Association. Professor Kieso is currently serving as a member of the Board of Directors of several corporations and universities. He has served as a charter member of the national Accounting Education Change Commission. He is a recipient of the Outstanding Accounting Educator Award from the Illinois CPA Society, the FSA's Joseph A. Silvoso Award of Merit, the NIU Foundation's Humanitarian Award for Service to Higher Education, and the Distinguished Service Award from the Illinois CPA Society.

Paul D. Kimmel, PhD, CPA, is an Associate Professor at the University of Wisconsin—Milwaukee. He is the recipient of the UWM School of Business Advisory Council Teaching Award, the Reggie Taite Excellence in Teaching Award, a three-time winner of the Outstanding Teaching Assistant Award at the University of Wisconsin, and a recipient of the Elijah Watts Sells Award for Honorary Distinction for his results on the CPA exam. He is a member of the American Accounting Association and has published articles in *Accounting Review, Accounting Horizons, Issues in Accounting Education* and the *Journal of Accounting Education* as well as other journals. His research interests include accounting for financial instruments and innovation in accounting education. He has published papers and given numerous talks on incorporating critical thinking into accounting education, and helped prepare a catalogue of critical thinking resources for the Federated Schools of Accountancy.

STUDENT OWNERS MANUAL

STUDENT LETTER TO STUDENTS

Student,

I would like to congratulate you on your decision to study accounting. Whether you are planning on pursuing a career as an accountant or fulfilling a business or other degree requirement, you will discover how vital a strong basic knowledge of accounting is for everyone interested in building a career in business or commerce or even using the concepts on a personal level. At the end of this *Accounting Principles* course you will have gained a very strong understanding of the fundamentals of accounting and a good foundation for all your remaining accounting and/or business courses. To help you be successful during this course, I would like to share some tips I used:

- Read! Success will come easier if you take the time to read the chapter before class. This will give you a general understanding of the concepts and procedures being introduced and will allow you to focus on the professor's main lecture points.

- Make use of textbook study aids. The list of Study Objectives and Preview will help you understand what the chapter is about and the Before You Go On exercises will tell you whether you have understood and learned the material in each section. This may sound like a lot of effort but the time spent doing these will shorten your studying time for exams and enable you to understand each subsequent chapter more quickly.

- Do your homework!!! Read what is required before you read the exercise or problem itself. This will allow you to pick out the relevant information and lessen the chance of using information that is not required. If you are able to complete the problems in the chapter, you will have a good understanding of the material. I cannot stress enough the importance of doing the homework; it will be the difference between a passing and failing grade.

- Read Accounting in Action. These will give you a good understanding of how what is being taught in each chapter is used in the "real world".

- Stay current. In this course each lesson builds on the previous lesson. Falling behind will affect how you are able to grasp the new lessons. Avoid this struggle by staying on top of your homework and reading.

I hope your experience with this course will be as rewarding as my own and will result in you pursuing further accounting studies.

Best of Luck,

April Wheeler

April Wheeler
Ottawa, Ontario

HOW TO USE THE STUDY AIDS IN THIS BOOK

Concepts for Review, listed at the beginning of each chapter, are the accounting concepts you learned in previous chapters that you will need to know in order to understand the topics you are about to cover. Page references are provided if you need to review before reading the chapter.

The **Feature Story** helps you picture how the chapter topic relates to the real world of accounting and business. Throughout the chapter, references to the Feature Story will help you put new ideas in context, organize them, and remember them. Many feature stories end with the **Internet address** of the company cited in the story. The exercise called **A Look Back at Our Feature Story** toward the end of the chapter helps you pull together the ideas learned in the chapter.

> **Concepts for Review**
>
> Before studying this chapter, you should understand or, if necessary, review:
>
> **a.** *How to close revenue, expense, and drawings accounts. (Ch. 4, pp. 158–159)*
> **b.** *The steps in the accounting cycle. (Ch. 4, pp. 163–164)*

Taking Stock— from Backpacks to Bicycles

VANCOUVER, B.C.—Backpacks and jackets sporting the jagged peaks of the Mountain Equipment Co-op logo are a familiar sight on Canadian cam-

...sts. This system provides continu-...s and up-to-date information, iden-...ying merchandise that has been sold ...d merchandise still on hand avail-...le to be sold. MEC uses this infor-...ation to ensure a smooth flow of ...ar into its stores from its suppliers ...d to minimize stock outages.

Unlike most retail operations, ...EC is not out to make a profit. As a ...op, it exists to serve its members.

"But we have to stay fiscally healthy to do that," points out Ms. Jumani. "If we go bankrupt, we won't be serving anyone." Accounting for inventory— from backpacks to bicycles—is an important part of MEC's fiscal fitness routine.

www.mec.ca

THE NAVIGATOR ✔

- Understand *Concepts for Review* ☐
- Read *Feature Story* ☐
- Scan *Study Objectives* ☐
- Read *Preview* ☐
- Read text and answer *Before You Go On*
  p. 58 ☐ p. 62 ☐ p. 72 ☐ p. 75 ☐
- Work *Demonstration Problem* ☐
- Review *Summary of Study Objectives* ☐
- Answer *Self-Study Questions* ☐
- Complete assignments ☐

CHAPTER · 2

THE RECORDING PROCESS

The Navigator is a learning system designed to help guide you through each chapter and help you succeed in learning the material. It consists of (1) a checklist at the beginning of each chapter, which outlines text features and study skills you will need, and (2) a series of check boxes that prompts you to use the learning aids in the chapter and set priorities as you study.

Study Objectives at the beginning of each chapter provide you with a framework for learning the specific concepts and procedures covered in the chapter. Each study objective reappears at the point within the chapter where the concept is discussed. You can review all the study objectives in the **Summary** at the end of the chapter.

► STUDY OBJECTIVES ◄

After studying this chapter, you should be able to:

1. *Explain what an account is and how it helps in the recording process.*
2. *Define debits and credits and illustrate how they are used to record business transactions.*
3. *Describe the basic steps in the recording process.*
4. *Explain what a journal is and how it helps in the recording process, and journalize business transactions.*
5. *Explain what a ledger is and how it helps in the recording process.*
6. *Explain what posting is and how it helps in the recording process.*
7. *Explain the purpose of, and prepare, a trial balance.*

The **Preview** links the feature story with the major topics of the chapter. It also graphically outlines the major topics and subtopics that will be discussed. This narrative and visual preview gives you a mental framework upon which to arrange the new information you are about to learn.

Study Objectives reappear in the margins at the point that the topic is discussed. End-of-chapter questions, exercises and problems are keyed to study objectives.

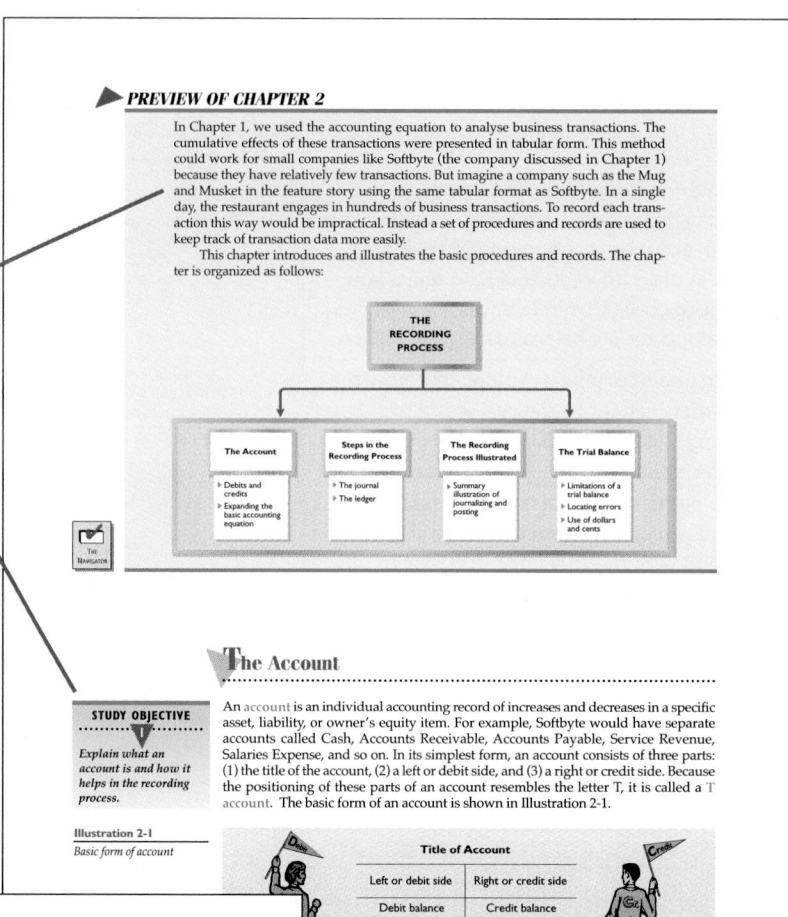

► **PREVIEW OF CHAPTER 2**

In Chapter 1, we used the accounting equation to analyse business transactions. The cumulative effects of these transactions were presented in tabular form. This method could work for small companies like Softbyte (the company discussed in Chapter 1) because they have relatively few transactions. But imagine a company such as the Mug and Musket in the feature story using the same tabular format as Softbyte. In a single day, the restaurant engages in hundreds of business transactions. To record each transaction this way would be impractical. Instead a set of procedures and records are used to keep track of transaction data more easily.

This chapter introduces and illustrates the basic procedures and records. The chapter is organized as follows:

THE RECORDING PROCESS

The Account	Steps in the Recording Process	The Recording Process Illustrated	The Trial Balance
► Debits and credits ► Expanding the basic accounting equation	► The journal ► The ledger	► Summary illustration of journalizing and posting	► Limitations of a trial balance ► Locating errors ► Use of dollars and cents

▼ The Account

STUDY OBJECTIVE

▼

Explain what an account is and how it helps in the recording process.

Illustration 2-1
Basic form of account

An account is an individual accounting record of increases and decreases in a specific asset, liability, or owner's equity item. For example, Softbyte would have separate accounts called Cash, Accounts Receivable, Accounts Payable, Service Revenue, Salaries Expense, and so on. In its simplest form, an account consists of three parts: (1) the title of the account, (2) a left or debit side, and (3) a right or credit side. Because the positioning of these parts of an account resembles the letter T, it is called a T account. The basic form of an account is shown in Illustration 2-1.

	Title of Account	
Left or debit side		Right or credit side
Debit balance		Credit balance

T Account

$1,000 a year, or $83 per month. Accordingly, amortization for the month of October is recognized by the following adjusting entry:

Oct. 31	Amortization Expense	8	3	
	Accumulated Amortization—Office Equipment			83
	To record monthly amortization.			

$$A = L + OE$$
$$-83 \qquad\qquad -83$$

The following shows the accounts after the adjusting entry has been posted:

Office Equipment		Amortization Expense	
10/1 5,000		10/31 Adj. 83	

Accumulated Amortization— Office Equipment	
	10/31 Adj. 83

The balance in the Accumulated Amortization account will increase $83 each month. After journalizing and posting the adjusting entry at November 30, the balance will be $166. At December 31, the balance of the accumulated amortization will be $249, and so on.

Statement Presentation. A contra account is offset against a related account on the income statement or balance sheet. On the balance sheet, it can be a **contra asset account** (offset against an asset) or a **contra liability account** (offset against a liability). We will discuss contra income statement accounts in Chapter 5.

Accumulated Amortization—Office Equipment is a contra asset account that is related to the asset account Office Equipment. Its normal balance is a credit—the opposite of the normal debit balance of its related account, Office Equipment. The Accumulated Amortization account is used instead of crediting (decreasing) the Office Equipment account directly in order to **show both the original cost of the equipment and the portion of the cost that has been allocated to expense to date.** In the balance sheet, Accumulated Amortization—Office Equipment is deducted from the related asset account as follows:

Office equipment		$5,000
Less: Accumulated amortization—office equipment		83
Net book value		$4,917

The difference between the cost of any amortizable asset and its accumulated amortization is called the net book value (or simply **book value**) of that asset. In Illustration 3-7, the book value of the equipment at the balance sheet date is $4,917. You should realize that the book value and the market value (the price at which it could be sold in the marketplace) of the asset are usually different. The reason the two are different is that amortization is a means of **cost allocation**, not a matter of **valuation**. That is, amortization does not attempt to show what an asset is worth. It shows only its unallocated cost.

Amortization expense identifies the portion of the asset's cost that has expired in October. As in the case of other adjustments for prepaid expenses, **if this adjusting entry is not made, total assets, owner's equity, and net income will be overstated and amortization expense will be understated.**

If the company owns additional equipment, such as delivery or store equipment,

Alternative terminology
Amortization is also called depreciation.

Helpful hint Increases, decreases, and normal balances of contra accounts are the *opposite of the accounts they relate to.*

Illustration 3-7
Balance sheet presentation of accumulated amortization

Alternative terminology
Net book value is sometimes called *carrying value.*

The **Accounting Equation** has been inserted in the margin next to key journal entries throughout the text. This feature helps you understand the impact of each accounting transaction on the financial statements.

Alternative Terminology familiarizes you with other commonly used terms.

Helpful Hints in the margins help clarify concepts being discussed.

Key Terms and concepts are printed in blue where they are first explained in the text. They are defined again in the end-of-chapter glossary.

Colour Illustrations visually reinforce important concepts.

---

customers have a good selection. But such an inventory policy may incur excessive carrying costs (e.g., investment, storage, insurance, taxes, obsolescence, and damage). On the other hand, low inventory levels lead to stockouts, lost sales, and disgruntled customers.

In addition to the gross profit and profit margins, discussed earlier in this chapter, there is the inventory turnover ratio. It assesses the efficiency by which a company sells its inventories. The inventory turnover ratio measures the number of times, on average, inventory is sold during the period. It is calculated by dividing cost of goods sold by average inventory. Whenever a ratio compares a balance sheet figure (e.g., inventory) to an income statement figure (e.g., cost of goods sold), the balance sheet figure must be averaged. Average balance sheet figures are determined by adding beginning and ending balances together and dividing by two. Averages are used to ensure that the balance sheet figures (which represent end-of-period amounts) cover the same period of time as the income statement figures (which represent amounts for the entire period).

Illustration 5-17 calculates the inventory turnover ratio for The Second Cup. The Second Cup did not separately disclose its cost of goods sold in its 2000 financial statements. It did, however, disclose its cost of goods sold in a prior year. The Second Cup's inventory turnover ratio for a prior year was as follows:

Cost of Goods Sold	÷	Average Inventory	=	Inventory Turnover
$37,605,000	÷	$\dfrac{\$6,439,000 + \$605,000}{2}$	=	10.7 times

Illustration 5-17
Calculation of inventory turnover ratio

Generally, the greater the number of times per year the inventory turns over, the more efficiently sales are being made. It is informative to convert the inventory turnover ratio into a period of time, describing the age of the inventory. This ratio, called days sales in inventory, is calculated by dividing 365 days by the inventory turnover ratio, as illustrated for The Second Cup.

Days In Year	÷	Inventory Turnover	=	Days Sales in Inventory
365 days	÷	10.7	=	34 days

Illustration 5-18
Calculation of days sales in inventory

...ios to those of other companies—even those in
...Cup's reasons for no longer giving this infor-
...aningful when compared to results from other

...has too much or too little inventory on hand?
...E5–11.

THE NAVIGATOR

Action Plan

• Determine the types of accounts needed. Eszter will need asset accounts for each different type of asset she invests in the business, and liability accounts for any debts she has.
• Understand the types of owner's equity accounts: Only owner's capital will be needed when Eszter begins the business. Other owner's equity accounts will be added later.

Solution

Eszter would likely need the following accounts to record the transactions that prepare her beauty salon for opening day: Cash (debit balance), Supplies (debit balance), Equipment (debit balance), Accounts Payable (credit balance), Note Payable (credit balance) if she borrows money, and E. Schwenke, Capital (credit balance).

Related exercise material: BE2–1, BE2–2, BE2–3, E2–1, E2–2, and E2–3.

THE NAVIGATOR

Steps in the Recording Process

In practically every business, the basic steps in the recording process are:
1. Analyse each transaction in terms of its effect on the accounts.
2. Enter the transaction information in a journal (book of original entry).
3. Transfer the journal information to the appropriate accounts in the ledger (book of accounts).

Although it is possible to enter transaction information directly into the accounts without using a journal or ledger, few businesses do so.

The actual sequence of events in the recording process begins with the transaction. Evidence is provided by a **business document** such as a sales slip, cheque, bill, or cash register tape. This evidence is analysed to determine the effect of the transaction on specific accounts. The transaction is then entered in the journal. Finally, the journal entry is transferred to the correct accounts in the ledger. The sequence of events in the recording process is shown below:

STUDY OBJECTIVE 3
Describe the basic steps in the recording process.

Illustration 2-9
The recording process

The Recording Process

Analyse each transaction | Enter transaction in a journal | Transfer journal information to ledger accounts

The basic steps in the recording process occur repeatedly in every business whether a computerized or manual accounting system is used. However, the first step—the analysis of each transaction—must be done by people even when a computerized system is used. Determining what to record is the most critical point, and for most businesses the most expensive step, in the accounting process. There are more examples of this step in this and later chapters.

The basic difference between a computerized and a manual accounting system is found in the next two steps in the recording process—entering and transferring information. In computerized systems, the input and subsequent processing of the

Accounting Cycle Tutorial—Recording Business Transactions

Infographics, a special type of illustration, pictorially link concepts to the real world and provide visual reminders of key concepts.

A **CD icon** at various places through the book refers you to the interactive CD that came with your textbook. On the CD, you will find an accounting cycle tutorial, additional demonstration problems, key terms matching activities, additional interpreting financial statement cases, and other helpful resources.

Before You Go On sections follow each key topic. **Review It** questions prompt you to stop and review the key points you have just studied. If you cannot answer these questions, you should go back and read the section again.

Review It questions marked with The Second Cup icon ask you to find information in The Second Cup's 2000 annual report, which is featured in Appendix A at the end of the text.

Brief **Do It** exercises ask you to put your newly acquired knowledge to work. They outline an **Action Plan** necessary to complete the exercise, and the accompanying **Solution** helps you see how the problem should be solved. (The Before You Go On section is keyed to similar exercises.)

---

474   CHAPTER 10 ▶ *Capital Assets*

Before You Go On . . .

▶ Review It

1. What is the relationship, if any, of amortization to (a) cost allocation, (b) asset valuation, and (c) cash accumulation?
2. What are the formulas for calculating annual amortization under each of the amortization methods—straight-line, declining-balance, and units-of-activity?
3. How do the effects of the methods on annual amortization and net income differ over the useful life of the asset?
4. Are revisions of periodic amortization made to prior periods or future periods? Explain.

▶ Do It

On January 1, 2002, Iron Mountain Ski Company purchased a new snow grooming machine for $50,000. The machine is estimated to have a five-year life with a $2,000 residual value. It is also expected to have a total useful life of 6,000 hours. It was used 1,000 hours during 2002 and 1,200 hours during 2003. How much amortization expense would Iron Mountain Ski record in each of 2002 and 2003 using each of the following methods of amortization: (a) straight-line, (b) double declining-balance, and (c) units-of-activity?

Action Plan

- Amortization is an allocation concept.
- Under straight-line amortization, an equal amount of the amortizable cost (cost less residual value) is allocated to each period.
- Under declining-balance amortization, more amortization is allocated in the early years than in the later years. Apply double the straight-line rate of amortization to the net book value. Residual values are ignored in this method.
- Under units-of-activity amortization, determine an amortizable cost per unit. Multiply this amount by the actual usage in each period to determine amortization expense.

Solution

	2002	2003
Straight-line	$ 9,600	$ 9,600
Double declining-balance	20,000	12,000
Units-of-activity	8,000	9,600

(a) Straight-line: ($50,000 − $2,000) ÷ 5 years = $9,600
(b) Double declining-balance: 100 ÷ 5 years = 20% straight-line rate
    2002: $50,000 × 20% × 2 = $20,000
    2003: ($50,000 − $20,000) × 20% × 2 = $12,000
(c) Units-of-activity: ($50,000 − $2,000) ÷ 6,000 hours = $8.00 per hour
    2002: 1,000 × $8.00 = $8,000
    2003: 1,200 × $8.00 = $9,600

Related exercise material: BE10–5, BE10–6, BE10–7, BE10–8, E10–3, E10–4, E10–5, and E10–6.

...es During Useful Life

...seful life of a capital asset, a company may incur costs for ordinary ...ons, or improvements. Ordinary repairs are costs to *maintain* the oper-...y and expected life of the unit. They are usually fairly small amounts ...quently. Motor tune-ups and oil changes, painting of buildings, and ...f worn-out gears on machinery are examples. Such repairs are debited ...Maintenance) Expense as they occur. Because they are immediately ...a expense against revenues, these costs are referred to as operating

...s and improvements are costs incurred to *increase* the operating effi-...tive capacity, or expected useful life of a capital asset. They are usually ...d occur less often. Additions and improvements increase the company's ...productive facilities and are generally debited to the appropriate

---

Intangible Capital Assets ▪ 483

Copyrights

Copyrights, granted by the Canadian Intellectual Property Office, give the owner an exclusive right to reproduce and sell an artistic or published work. Copyrights extend for the life of the creator plus 50 years. Generally, the useful life of a copyright is significantly shorter than its legal life.

The cost of a copyright consists of the **cost of acquiring and defending it**. The cost may only be the fee paid to register the copyright. Or, it may amount to a great deal more if a copyright infringement suit is involved.

Helpful hint The first Canadian copyright was issued in 1841 to protect *Canada's Spelling Book.*

▶ Accounting in Action ▶ ℰ-Business Insight

On-line music company MP3.com recently paid US$53.4 million to Universal Music Group, the world's largest record company, to settle a copyright infringement lawsuit. A judge had previously ruled that MP3.com wilfully violated copyrights of music companies when it copied their songs from CDs and made them available free on its website. MP3.com has also reached settlements with the four other major music companies—Warner Music Group, BMG, EMI, and Sony Music Entertainment—and has arranged licensing deals with each of them. The overall amount of the settlements has not been disclosed, but is believed to be in the US$170 million range.

The MP3.com decision comes as lawyers, Internet entrepreneurs, and the global entertainment industry are embroiled in a war over copyright and compensation. Forrester Research estimates that record labels lose $3.1 billion annually in music sales to piracy and other methods of digital distribution.

Source: Steven Chase, "Web Music Scofflaws Take Hard Hit," *The Globe and Mail,* September 7, 2000, A1.

Trademarks and Trade Names

A trademark or trade name is a word, phrase, jingle, or symbol that identifies a particular enterprise or product. Trade names like President's Choice, Benetton, KFC, Nike, Nissan, Sony, Sunkist, Kleenex, Coke, Big Mac, the Blue Jays, and TSN create immediate product identification. They also enhance the sale of the product. The creator may obtain exclusive legal right to the trademark or trade name by registering it with the Canadian Intellectual Property Office. This registration provides continuous protection. It may be renewed every 15 years, as long as the trademark or trade name is in use.

In most cases, companies continuously renew their trademarks or trade names. In such cases, as long as the trademark or trade name continues to be marketable, it will have an indefinite useful life. **Intangible assets with indefinite useful lives are not amortized.** Instead, their values are tested annually for impairment, as explained earlier in this chapter.

If the trademark or trade name is **purchased**, its cost is the purchase price. If the trademark or trade name is developed internally rather than purchased, the cost includes legal fees, registration fees, design costs, successful legal defence costs, and other expenditures directly related to securing it.

▶ International note
A panel of international judges recently ranked the world's top 50 corporate logos. The Michelin man ranked first as "a fabulous piece of corporate iconography, and probably the first example of a liquid identity." Nike's swoosh symbol was ranked 4th, Coca-Cola's symbol 9th.

▶ Accounting in Action ▶ ℰ-Business Insight

Domain names are a good example of a trade name. Buying domain names is a hot market these days. Canada's domain name system has strict regulations to ensure that dot.ca web addresses are granted to legitimate organizations and holders of registered trademarks. While the cost of registration is negligible, if a company has to purchase its name from a cybersquatter—people who register

---

Accounting in Action boxes give you more glimpses into the real world of accounting by discussing actual challenges faced by accountants. Each type of issue—business, ℰ-business, ethics, or international—is identified by its own icon. New to this edition, ℰ-business Insights describe how ℰ-business technology has expanded the services provided by accountants.

International Notes introduce international issues and similarities or differences in accounting practice.

Ethics Notes help sensitize you to the real-world ethical dilemmas of accounting.

---

286   CHAPTER 6 ▸ *Inventory Costing*

▸**Ethics note**

Inventory fraud increases during recessions. Such fraud includes pricing inventory at higher amounts than its actual value, or claiming to have inventory when no inventory exists. Inventory fraud is usually done to over-state ending inventory, thereby understating cost of goods sold, which results in higher income.

net income. An understatement in cost of goods sold will produce an overstatement in net income. An overstatement in cost of goods sold will produce an understatement in net income.

Since the ending inventory of one period becomes the beginning inventory of the next period, **an error in ending inventory of the current period will have a reverse effect on net income of the next period**. This is shown in Illustration 6-18. Note that the $3,000 understatement of ending inventory in 2002 will result in an understatement of beginning inventory in 2003 and an overstatement of net income in 2003 of the same amount.

Condensed Income Statements

	2002		2003	
	Incorrect	Correct	Incorrect	Correct
Sales		$80,000	$80,000		$90,000		$90,000
Beginning inventory	$20,000		$20,000		$12,000		$15,000	
Cost of goods purchased	40,000		40,000		68,000		68,000	
Cost of goods available for sale	60,000		60,000		80,000		83,000	
Ending inventory	12,000		15,000		23,000		23,000	
Cost of goods sold		48,000	45,000		57,000		60,000
Gross profit		32,000	35,000		33,000		30,000
Operating expenses		10,000	10,000		20,000		20,000
Net income		$22,000	$25,000		$13,000		$10,000

($3,000) $3,000
Net income   N   et income
understated   overstated

The combined net income for two years is correct because the errors cancel each other out.

Illustration 6-18

Effects of inventory errors on income statements of two successive years

Over the two years, total net income is correct. The errors offset one another. Notice that total income using incorrect data is $35,000 ($22,000 + $13,000). This is the same as the total income of $35,000 ($25,000 + $10,000) using correct data. Nevertheless, the distortion of the year-by-year results can have a serious impact on financial analysis and management decisions.

Note that an error in the beginning inventory does not result in a corresponding error in the ending inventory. The correctness of the ending inventory depends entirely on the accuracy of taking and costing the inventory at the balance sheet date.

Balance Sheet Effects

...rors on the balance sheet can be determined by using the basic account- **Assets = Liabilities + Owner's Equity**. In the following illustration, U ...tement, O is for overstatement, and NE is for no effect.

...ure of Error	Assets	=	Liabilities	+	Owner's Equity
... ending inventory	U	=	NE	+	U
...nding inventory	O	=	NE	+	O

...beginning inventory have no impact on the balance sheet, if ending ...orrectly calculated in the current period. Understating ending inven- ...will understate net income, as we saw in Illustration 6-17. If net income ..., then owner's equity will be understated (because net income is part ...uity).

Statement Presentation of Receivables ◂ 439

The Second Cup's acid test ratio, shown in Illustration 9-10, means that $0.60 of assets are available to be quickly converted into cash to cover every $1 of current liabilities. Whether this is a strong or weak ratio depends on many factors, including the industry average. In this particular case, The Second Cup's acid test ratio is exactly equal to the industry average of 0.6:1.

A high acid test ratio is not necessarily indicative of a strong liquidity position either. The acid test ratio might be artificially high if there are many slow-paying customers for whom an adequate allowance for doubtful accounts has not been provided.

The receivables turnover is a useful measure for assessing a company's efficiency in converting its credit sales into cash. Often, the amount of credit sales is not available to the general public. In such instances, total sales can be used as a substitute for comparison. Total sales was used to calculate the receivables turnover for The Second Cup in Illustration 9-11. In this calculation, we used The Second Cup's total revenue, not system-wide sales. System-wide sales are the sales reported by all Second Cup franchise operations. These franchise operations are owned by individuals, not The Second Cup. Total revenues is the amount that has been earned specifically by the corporate entity The Second Cup Ltd.

Whenever a ratio compares a balance sheet figure (e.g., accounts receivable) to an income statement figure (e.g., sales), the balance sheet figure must be averaged. Average balance sheet figures are determined by adding beginning and ending balances together and dividing by 2. The rationale for using averages is to ensure that the balance sheet figures (which represent the end-of-period amounts) cover the same period of time as the income statement figures (which represent amounts for the entire period).

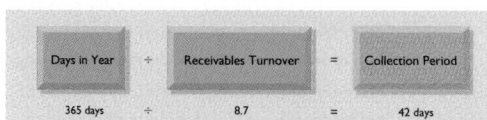

Illustration 9-11

Calculation of receivables turnover

Net Credit Sales	÷	Average Accounts Receivable	=	Receivables Turnover
$20,844	÷	$2,294 + $2,494 / 2	=	8.7 times

The result indicates an accounts receivable turnover ratio of 8.7 times per year for The Second Cup. The higher the turnover ratio is, the more liquid the company's receivables are.

It is informative to convert the receivables turnover ratio into the number of days it takes the company to collect its receivables. This ratio, called the collection period, is calculated by dividing 365 days by the receivables turnover ratio, as illustrated for The Second Cup below.

Illustration 9-12

Collection period

Days in Year	÷	Receivables Turnover	=	Collection Period
365 days	÷	8.7	=	42 days

This means that The Second Cup collects its receivables, on average, in approximately 42 days. The collection period is frequently used to assess the effectiveness of a company's credit and collection policies. The general rule is that the collection period should not greatly exceed the credit term period (i.e., the time allowed for payment).

One technique for determining the meaning of the information on financial statements is **ratio analysis**. Throughout this text, you will analyse key financial ratios using data from The Second Cup's financial statements. Chapter 19 addresses the topic of financial analysis in detail.

Financial statements appear throughout the book. Those from real companies are often identified by a logo or related photo. Numbers or categories are frequently highlighted in coloured type to draw your attention to key information.

THE FORZANI GROUP LTD.
Notes to the Financial Statements (partial)
January 30, 2000
(in thousands)

Illustration 4-13
Capital assets section

Capital assets	Cost		Accumulated Amortization	Net Book Value
Land	$	638		$ 638
Building	5	,813	$ 954	4,859
Building on leased land		3,143	599	2,544
Furniture, fixtures, equipment, and automotive		44,434	24,069	20,365
Leasehold improvements		61,868	24,435	37,433
Trademarks		259	208	51
		$116,155	$50,265	$65,890

Current Liabilities

Current liabilities are listed first in the liabilities and owner's equity section of the balance sheet. Current liabilities are obligations that are reasonably expected to be paid from current assets or through the creation of other current liabilities. As in the case of current assets, the time period for payment is one year or the operating cycle, whichever is longer. Current liabilities include (1) debts related to the operating cycle, such as accounts payable and salaries payable, and (2) other short-term debts, such as notes payable, interest payable, income taxes payable (owed by corporations), sales taxes payable, and current maturities of long-term liabilities (payments to be made within the next year on long-term debt).

Current liabilities are often listed in order of currency. That is, the liabilities that come due first are listed first. However, for many companies, the arrangement of items within the current liabilities section is the result of custom rather than a prescribed rule. The current liabilities section from Sears Canada's balance sheet is as follows:

SEARS CANADA INC.
Balance Sheet (partial)
December 30, 2000
(in millions)

Illustration 4-14
Current liabilities section

SEARS

Current liabilities	
Accounts payable	$ 974.6
Accrued liabilities	440.3
Income and other taxes payable	109.3
Principal payments on long-term obligations due within one year	152.5
	53.3
	1,730.0

one year are classified as long-term liabilities.
...de (1) bonds payable, (2) mortgages payable,
..., and (5) obligations under employee pension
...rm debt that matures after one year as a single
...ey show the details of the debt in the notes that
...Sleeman Breweries reported long-term obliga-
...e sheet, with the following selected information

Before You Go On . . .
▶**Review It**

1. What is the purpose of an adjusted trial balance?
2. How is an adjusted trial balance prepared?

Related exercise material: BE3–10, BE3–11, E3–11, and E3-12.

THE NAVIGATOR

▶ **A Look Back at Our Feature Story**
....

Refer to the feature story about Seneca College and answer the following questions:
1. Why should Seneca be concerned about the period in which revenue is recognized?
2. What journal entry was most likely made when students paid for their summer courses in March? What adjusting entry should be made to record the tuition revenue at the end of the summer session?
3. What other types of adjusting entries do you believe Seneca College might make?

Solution

1. As a not-for-profit institution, Seneca College must operate within its government subsidies and its own budget. It must know what revenues are attributable to each operating/accounting period. Assignment of revenues to the proper operating periods (namely, to the periods they are earned in) is necessary in order to make operating/accounting periods (years) comparable.
2. Ron Currie probably used the account Unearned Tuition Revenue, because tuition was received in advance of the summer semester courses. The original journal entry was likely debit Cash and credit Unearned Tuition Revenue. If so, the adjusting entry would be debit Unearned Tuition Revenue and credit Tuition Revenue.
3. (a) Accrued expenses: ...
   (b) Accrued revenues: unpaid tuition, lab fees, interest, government grants
   (c) Prepaid expenses: insurance, supplies
   (d) Unearned revenues: lab fees, theatre tickets, athletic tickets
   (e) Estimates: amortization

THE NAVIGATOR

DEMONSTRATION PROBLEM

Julie Szo opens the Green Thumb Lawn Care Company on April 1. At April 30, the trial balance shows the following balances for selected accounts:

Prepaid Insurance	$ 3,600
Equipment	28,000
Note Payable	20,000
Unearned Revenue	4,200
Service Revenue	1,800

Additional Demonstration Problem

Analysis reveals the following additional data about these accounts:
1. Prepaid insurance is the cost of a 12-month insurance policy, effective April 1.
2. Amortization on the equipment is $500 per month.
3. The note payable is dated April 1. It is a six-month, 4% note.
4. Seven customers paid for the company's six-month lawn-service package of $600, beginning in April. These customers were serviced in April.
5. Lawn services performed for other customers but not billed at April 30 totalled $1,500.

Instructions

Prepare the adjusting entries for the month of April. Show calculations.

The last **Before You Go On** exercise in each chapter takes you back for a critical look at the chapter-opening feature story.

Demonstration Problems review the chapter material. These sample problems provide you with **Action Plans** that list the strategies needed to solve the problem and **Solutions**. The **CD icon** tells you there is an additional demonstration problem you can work through on the CD that came with your textbook.

Glossary • 79

Summary of Study Objectives

1. *Explain what an account is and how it helps in the recording process.* An account is an individual accounting record of increases and decreases in a specific asset, liability, or owner's equity item.

2. *Define debits and credits and illustrate how they are used to record business transactions.* Assets, drawings, and expenses are increased by debits (left-hand side of the account) and decreased by credits (right-hand side of the account). Liabilities, owner's capital, and revenues are increased by credits (right-hand side of the account) and decreased by debits (left-hand side of the account).

3. *Describe the basic steps in the recording process.* The basic steps in the recording process are as follows: (a) analyse each transaction in terms of its effect on the accounts, (b) enter the transaction information in a journal, (c) transfer the journal information to the appropriate accounts in the ledger.

4. *Explain what a journal is and how it helps in the recording process, and journalize business transactions.* The first accounting record of a transaction is entered in a journal, and the data are later transferred to the general ledger. A journal (a) discloses in one place the complete effect of a transaction, (b) provides a chronological record of transactions, (c) prevents and helps locate errors

because the debit and credit amounts for each entry can be easily compared, and (d) provides an explanation of the transaction and reference to the source document, where applicable.

5. *Explain what a ledger is and how it helps in the recording process.* The entire group of accounts maintained by a company is called the ledger. The ledger keeps in one place all the information about changes in each of the specific account balances.

6. *Explain what posting is and how it helps in the recording process.* Posting is the procedure of transferring journal entries to the ledger accounts. This phase of the recording process accumulates the effects of journalized transactions in the individual accounts.

7. *Explain the purpose of, and prepare, a trial balance.* A trial balance is a list of accounts and their balances at a given time. Its primary purpose is to prove the equality of debits and credits after posting. A trial balance also uncovers certain types of errors in journalizing and posting, and is useful in preparing financial statements.

GLOSSARY

Account A record of increases and decreases in a specific asset, liability, or owner's equity item. (p. 54)

Chart of accounts A list of accounts and the account numbers which identify their location in the ledger. (p. 65)

Compound entry An entry that involves three or more accounts. (p. 62)

Credit The right side of an account. (p. 55)

Debit The left side of an account. (p. 55)

Double-entry system A system that records the dual effect of each transaction in appropriate accounts. (p. 55)

General journal The book of original entry in which transactions are recorded when they are not recorded in other specialized journals. (p. 60)

General ledger A ledger that contains accounts for all assets, liabilities, equities, revenues, and expenses. (p. 63)

Key Term Matching Activity

Journal An accounting record in which transactions are recorded in chronological (date) order. (p. 60)

Journalizing The entering of transaction data in the journal. (p. 60)

Ledger A book of final entry that contains all accounts for the company or specialized accounts supporting other ledgers. (p. 63)

Posting The procedure of transferring journal entries to the ledger accounts. (p. 64)

T account A form of account resembling the letter T with the title above the ho
left of the vertical lin

Trial balance A lis
given time, usually
(p. 73)

The **Summary of Study Objectives** relates the study objectives to the key points in the chapter. It gives you another opportunity to review as well as to see how all the key topics within the chapter are related.

The **Glossary** defines all the terms and concepts introduced in the chapter. Page references help you find any terms you need to study further. The **CD icon** tells you that there is a Key Term Matching Activity on the CD that came with your textbook that will help you master the terms and concepts.

Self-Study Questions • 129

Note: All **asterisked** Questions, Exercises, and Problems below relate to material contained in Appendix 3A.

SELF-STUDY QUESTIONS

Chapter 3 Self-Test

Answers are at the end of the chapter.

(SO 1) K **1.** The time period assumption states that:
  a. revenue should be recognized in the accounting period in which it is earned.
  b. expenses should be matched with revenues.
  c. the economic life of a business can be divided into artificial time periods.
  d. the fiscal year should correspond with the calendar year.

(SO 2) K **2.** The principle which states that efforts (expenses) should be recorded in the same period as the related accomplishments (revenues) is the:
  a. matching principle.
  b. cost principle.
  c. time period assumption.
  d. revenue recognition principle.

(SO 3) K **3.** Which of the following statements about the accrual basis of accounting is false?
  a. Expenses are recorded when goods or services are used or consumed.
  b. Revenue is recognized in the period in which it is earned.
  c. The accrual basis is in accordance with generally accepted accounting principles.
  d. Revenue is recorded only when cash is received, and expenses are recorded only when cash is paid.

(SO 4) K **4.** Adjusting entries are made to ensure that:
  a. expenses are matched to revenues in the period in which the revenue is generated.
  b. revenues are recorded in the period in which they are earned.
  c. balance sheet and income statement accounts have correct balances at the end of an accounting period.
  d. All of the above.

(SO 5) K **5.** Which of the following is not a type (or category) of adjusting entry?
  a. Prepaid expenses
  b. Accrued revenues
  c. Estimates
  d. Earned revenues

(SO 6) AP **6.** The trial balance shows Supplies $1,350 and Supplies Expense $0. If $600 of supplies are on hand at the end of the period, the adjusting entry is:
  a. Supplies   600
       Supplies Expense   600
  b. Supplies   750
       Supplies Expense   750
  c. Supplies Expense   750
       Supplies   750
  d. Supplies Expense   600
       Supplies   600

(SO 6) K **7.** Adjustments for unearned revenues:
  a. decrease liabilities and increase revenues.
  b. increase liabilities and increase revenues.
  c. increase assets and increase revenues.
  d. decrease revenues and decrease assets.

(SO 7) K **8.** Adjustments for accrued revenues:
  a. increase assets and increase liabilities.
  b. increase assets and increase revenues.
  c. decrease assets and decrease revenues.
  d. decrease liabilities and increase revenues.

(SO 7) AP **9.** Kathy Kiska earned a salary of $400 for the last week of September. She will be paid in October. The adjusting entry for Kathy's employer at September 30 is:
  a. No entry is required.
  b. Salaries Expense   400
       Salaries Payable   400
  c. Salaries Expense   400
       Cash   400
  d. Salaries Payable   400
       Cash   400

(SO 8) K **10.** Accumulated Amortization is:
  a. an expense account.
  b. an owner's equity account.
  c. a liability account.
  d. a contra asset account.

(SO 9) K **11.** Which of the following statements concerning the adjusted trial balance is *incorrect*?
  a. An adjusted trial balance proves the equality of the total debit balances and the total credit balances in the ledger, after all adjustments are made.
  b. The adjusted trial balance provides the primary basis for the preparation of financial statements.
  c. The adjusted trial balance lists the account balances divided into assets and liabilities.
  d. The adjusted trial balance is prepared after the adjusting entries have been journalized and posted.

(SO 10) AP *12. The trial balance shows Supplies $0 and Supplies Expense $1,350. If $600 of supplies are on hand at the end of the period, the adjusting entry is:
  a. Supplies   600
       Supplies Expense   600
  b. Supplies Expense   750
       Supplies   750
  c. Supplies   750
       Supplies Expense   750
  d. Supplies Expense   600
       Supplies   600

Self-Study Questions are a practice test, keyed to Study Objectives, that give you an opportunity to check your knowledge of important topics. Answers appear on the last page of the chapter. (Keyed to Study Objectives and Bloom's Taxonomy.)

The level of cognitive skill required to solve the question, exercise, or problem have been classified following Blooms's Taxonomy. Each assignment is coded with a letter indicating the level of cognitive skill needed. You will find more information about Bloom's and this coding system later in this Preface.

The **web icon** tells you that there is an additional Self-Test on the Weygandt website <www.wiley.com/canada/weygandt2>.

Questions allow you to explain your understanding of concepts and relationships covered in the chapter. (Keyed to Study Objectives and Bloom's Taxonomy.)

QUESTIONS

(SO 1) C   1. (a) How does the time period assumption affect an accountant's analysis of business transactions?
(b) Explain the terms *fiscal year, calendar year,* and *interim periods.*

(SO 2) C   2. Identify and describe two generally accepted accounting principles that relate to adjusting the accounts.

(SO 2) C   3. Pierce Dussault, a lawyer, accepts a legal engagement in March, performs the work in April, and is paid in May. If Dussault's law firm prepares monthly financial statements, when should it recognize revenue from this engagement? Why?

(SO 2) C   4. In completing the engagement in question 3, Dussault incurred $2,000 of salary expenses specifically related to this engagement in March, $2,500 in April, and none in May. How much expense should be deducted from revenue in the month the revenue is recognized? Why?

(SO 3) C   5. Why do accrual basis financial statements provide more useful information than cash basis statements?

(SO 3) C   6. Should the balance in total owner's equity equal the balance in the Cash account? Explain why or why not.

(SO 4) C   7. "Adjusting entries are needed to respect the cost principle of accounting." Do you agree? Explain.

(SO 4) C   8. Why might a trial balance not contain up-to-date and complete financial information?

(SO 5) C   9. Distinguish among the three categories of adjusting entries, and identify the types of adjustments applicable to each category.

(SO 6) K   10. What is the debit/credit effect of a prepaid expense adjusting entry?

(SO 6) K   11. What is the debit/credit effect of an unearned revenue adjusting entry?

(SO 7) K   12. A company received cash from a customer. It debited the Cash account, but it did not credit any revenue account. Name two other accounts that the company might have used to record a cash receipt from a customer.

(SO 7) K   13. A company fails to recognize revenue earned but not yet received. Which accounts are involved in the [...]nts selected, indicate [...]r credited in the entry.

[...]tility expense that has [...]icate which account is [...] the adjusting entry.

(SO 7) AP   15. A company makes an accrued revenue adjusting entry for $900 and an accrued expense adjusting entry for $600. Which financial statement items were overstated or understated prior to these entries? Explain.

(SO 7) AP   16. On January 9, a company pays $5,000 for salaries, of which $1,700 was reported as Salaries Payable on December 31. Give the entry to record the payment.

(SO 6,7) C   17. For each of the following items before adjustment, indicate the type of adjusting entry (prepaid expense, unearned revenue, accrued revenue, accrued expense, estimate) that is needed to correct the misstatement. If an item could result in more than one type of adjusting entry, indicate each of the types.
(a) Assets are understated.
(b) Liabilities are overstated.
(c) Liabilities are understated.
(d) Expenses are understated.
(e) Assets are overstated.
(f) Revenue is understated.

(SO 8) C   18. "Amortization is a valuation process that results in the reporting of the market value of the asset." Do you agree? Explain.

(SO 8) C   19. Explain the difference between amortization expense and accumulated amortization.

(SO 8) AP   20. Shen Company purchased equipment for $12,000. By the current balance sheet date, $7,000 had been amortized. Indicate the balance sheet presentation of the data.

(SO 6,7, 8) K   21. One half of the adjusting entry is given below. Indicate the account title for the other half of the entry.
(a) Salaries Expense is debited.
(b) Amortization Expense is debited.
(c) Interest Payable is credited.
(d) Supplies is credited.
(e) Accounts Receivable is debited.
(f) Unearned Revenue is debited.

(SO 6,7, 8) C   22. "An adjusting entry may affect more than one balance sheet or income statement account." Do you agree? Why or why not?

(SO 9) C   23. Why is it possible to prepare financial statements directly from an adjusted trial balance?

(SO 10) C   *24. The Alpha Company debits Supplies Expense for all purchases of supplies, and credits Rent Revenue for all rental payments received in advance. For each type of adjustment, state which account should be debited and which should be credited.

Brief Exercises ◂ 131

BRIEF EXERCISES

BE3–1   The ledger of the Yap Company includes the following accounts. Explain why each account may require adjustment.
1. Prepaid Insurance   3. Unearned Revenue   5. Rent Receivable
2. Accumulated Amortization   4. Interest Payable

Indicate why adjusting entries are needed.
(SO 4) C

BE3–2   The Spahn Advertising Company's trial balance at December 31 shows Advertising Supplies $8,700, and Advertising Supplies Expense $0. On December 31, there is $1,500 of supplies on hand. Prepare the adjusting entry at December 31. Using T accounts, enter the balances in the accounts, post the adjusting entry, and indicate the adjusted balance in each account.

Prepare and post adjusting entry for supplies.
(SO 6) AP

BE3–3   On July 1, 2003, Bere Co. pays $10,000 to Hindi Insurance Co. for a two-year insurance contract. Both companies have fiscal years that end December 31. For Bere Co., journalize and post the entry on July 1, and the adjusting entry on December 31.

Prepare and post adjusting entries for prepaid expense.
(SO 6) AP

BE3–4   Using the data in BE3–3, journalize and post the entry on July 1 and the adjusting entry on December 31, 2003, for Hindi Insurance Co.

Prepare and post adjusting entries for unearned revenue.
(SO 6) AP

BE3–5   The bookkeeper for the deVos Company asks you to prepare the following adjusting entries at December 31:
1. Interest on notes receivable of $300 is accrued.
2. Services provided but unbilled total $1,400.
3. Salaries of $900 earned by employees have not been recorded.

Prepare adjusting entries for accruals.
(SO 7) AP

BE3–6   At the end of its first year, the trial balance of the Tai Woo Company shows Equipment $25,000, and zero balances in Accumulated Amortization—Equipment, and Amortization Expense. Amortization for the year is estimated to be $5,000. Prepare the adjusting entry for amortization at December 31, post the adjustments to T accounts, and indicate the balance sheet presentation of the equipment at December 31.

Prepare and post adjusting entries for amortization, show balance sheet presentation.
(SO 8) AP

BE3–7   Indicate the impact of each of the following transactions on cash and net income. The first transaction has been completed for you as an example.

Transaction	Cash	Net Income
(a) Purchased supplies on hand for cash, $100.	–$100	$0
(b) Recorded the use of $50 of the supplies purchased in (a) in an adjusting journal entry.		
(c) Performed services on account, $1,000.		
(d) Received $800 from customers in payment of their account in (c).		
(e) Purchased office equipment for cash, $500.		
(f) Recorded amortization of office equipment for the period, $50.		

Identify the impact each of the following transactions has upon cash and net income.
(SO 3, 6, 7, 8) AP

BE3–8   The Riko Company has the following adjustment data at December 31. Indicate (a) the type of adjustment (prepaid expense, accrued revenue, and so on), and (b) the status of the accounts before adjustment (overstated or understated).
1. Supplies of $600 are on hand. The unadjusted balance in the Supplies account is $800.
2. Services provided but unbilled total $900.
3. Interest of $200 has accrued on a note payable.
4. Rent collected in advance totalling $800 has been earned.
5. Amortization of $100 is estimated on the office equipment.

Identify types of adjusting entries and account relationships.
(SO 6, 7, 8) C

BE3–9   The trial balance of the Hoi Company includes the following balance sheet accounts. Identify the accounts that require adjustment. For each account that requires adjustment, indicate (a) the type of adjusting entry required (prepaid expense, unearned revenue, accrued revenue, accrued expense, or amortization), and (b) the related account in the adjusting entry.
Accounts Receivable   Interest Payable
Prepaid Insurance   Unearned Service Revenue
Equipment   Interest Receivable
Supplies   Rent Payable

Analyse accounts in a trial balance.
(SO 6, 7, 8) C

Brief Exercises help you focus on one Study Objective at a time. They help you build confidence in your basic skills and knowledge. (Keyed to Study Objectives and Bloom's Taxonomy.)

Exercises help you continue to build your confidence. (Keyed to Study Objectives and Bloom's Taxonomy.)

Certain exercises or problems marked with an icon ✏️ help you practise business **writing skills**.

---

132   **CHAPTER 3** ► *Adjusting the Accounts*

Prepare income statement from adjusted trial balance.
(SO 9) AP

BE3–10   The adjusted trial balance of the Klar Company at December 31, 2003, includes the following accounts: S. Klar, Capital, $15,600; S. Klar, Drawings, $6,000; Service Revenue, $38,400; Salaries Expense, $13,000; Insurance Expense, $2,000; Rent Expense, $4,000; Supplies Expense, $500; and Amortization Expense, $1,000. Prepare an income statement for the year.

Prepare statement of owner's equity from adjusted trial balance.
(SO 9) AP

BE3–11   A partial adjusted trial balance data for the Klar Company is presented in BE3–10. The balance in S. Klar, Capital, is the balance as at January 1, 2003. Prepare a statement of owner's equity for the year.

Prepare adjusting entry for supplies in alternative way.
(SO 10) AP

***BE3–12**   Refer to BE3–2. Assume that instead of debiting purchases of advertising supplies to the Advertising Supplies account, Spahn Advertising debits purchases of supplies to the Advertising Supplies *Expense* account. Spahn Advertising Company's trial balance at December 31 shows Advertising Supplies $0 and Advertising Supplies Expense $8,700. On December 31, there is $1,500 of supplies on hand.
(a) Prepare the adjusting entry at December 31. Using T accounts, enter the balances in the accounts, post the adjusting entry, and indicate the adjusted balance in each account.
(b) Compare the adjusted balances in BE3–2, when an asset account was originally debited, with the adjusted balances in this brief exercise, when an expense account was originally debited. Does it matter whether an original entry is recorded to an asset account or an expense account?

Prepare transaction and adjusting entry for unearned revenue in alternate ways.
(SO 6, 10) AP

***BE3–13**   Paboudjian Apartments receives one month's rent in advance for the month of May, $600, from a tenant.
(a) Assuming the company records all prepayments in balance sheet accounts:
    1. Prepare the original journal entry Paboudjian should record when it receives the rent on May 1.
    2. Prepare the adjusting journal entry Paboudjian should record at the end of May, when the month's rent has been earned.
(b) Assuming the company records all prepayments in income statement accounts:
    1. Prepare the original journal entry Paboudjian should record when it receives the rent on May 1.
    2. Prepare the adjusting journal entry Paboudjian should record at the end of May, when the month's rent has been earned.
(c) Compare and comment upon the ending account balances for each alternative, (a) and (b).

EXERCISES
··

Distinguish between cash and accrual bases of accounting.
(SO 3) C
✏️

E3–1   The 1997–1998 Government of Canada accounts recorded a $2.5 billion expense for the Millennium Scholarship Fund, even though the first Millennium scholarships weren't awarded until the year 2000! The government—accused by the opposition of cooking the books to minimize the current budgetary surplus—staunchly maintained that it was appropriate to record these financial charges in the books in the year the program was announced.

Instructions
(a) What is the difference between the accrual and cash bases of accounting?
(b) With respect to recording the $2.5 billion expense for the Millennium scholarships, is the government using the cash basis of accounting, the accrual basis of accounting, or some other basis of accounting? Explain why the government believed it was appropriate to record the scholarship expense in the year the program was announced.
(c) Prior to 2001, the federal government used the cash basis of accounting for many of its transactions. In 2001, the government moved all of its accounting systems to the accrual basis. Write a letter to your Member of Parliament explaining what effect you think the adoption of the accrual basis of accounting will have on the government accounts.

Determine income using cash and accrual bases. Comment on usefulness.
(SO 3) AP

E3–2   In its first year of operations, Brisson Company earned $26,000 in service revenue. Of this revenue, $4,000 was on account and the remainder, $22,000, was received in cash from customers.
The company incurred operating expenses of $15,000. Of these expenses, $13,500 was paid in cash. At year end, $1,500 was still owing on account. In addition, Brisson prepaid $2,500 for insurance coverage that would not be used until its second year of operations.

---

136   **CHAPTER 3** ► *Adjusting the Accounts*

Prepare adjusting entries and income statements.
(SO 6, 7, 8, 9) AP

E3–11   The income statement of Virmani Co. for the m[...] based on Service Revenue $5,500, Wages Expense $2[...] Expense $600. In reviewing the statement, you discov[...]
1. Insurance of $300 that expired during July was e[...]
2. Supplies expense includes $500 of supplies that [...]
3. Amortization of $150 on equipment was omitte[...]
4. Accrued but unpaid wages of $300 at July 31 we[...]
5. Services provided but unrecorded totalled $900.[...]

Instructions
(a) Prepare the adjusting entries at July 31, 2003.
(b) Prepare a revised income statement, after the ad[...]

Prepare financial statements from adjusted trial balance.
(SO 9) AP

E3–12   The adjusted trial balance for the Lim Compa[...]

Instructions
Prepare the income statement and statement of owne[...] at August 31, 2003.

Prepare and post transaction and adjustment entries, using alternative treatment of prepayments.
(SO 10) AP

***E3–13**   At the Devereaux Company, prepayments are debited to expense when paid, and unearned revenues are credited to revenue when received. During January of the current year, the following transactions occurred:
Jan. 2 Paid $2,400 for fire insurance protection for the year.
    10 Paid $1,700 for supplies.
    15 Received $5,100 for services to be performed in the future.
On January 31, it is determined that $1,500 of the service revenue has been earned, and that there is $800 of supplies on hand.

Instructions
(a) Journalize and post the January transactions. Use T accounts.
(b) Journalize and post the adjusting entries at January 31.
(c) Determine the ending balance in each of the accounts.

PROBLEMS: SET A
··

Match adjusting entry type.
(SO 5) K

P3–1A   Adjusting entries can be classified into the following types:
1. Prepaid expenses   3. Accrued expenses   5. Estimates (amortization)
2. Unearned revenues   4. Accrued revenues

Instructions
Match the type of adjusting entry with the adjusting journal entry transaction described below by inserting the appropriate number in the space provided. If an adjusting entry is not required, leave the space blank.
_____ (a) Record interest on note payable.
_____ (b) Record interest on note receivable.
_____ (c) Allocate cost of capital asset over its useful life.
_____ (d) Record revenue that has been earned but not billed or collected.
_____ (e) Record revenue that has been earned that was previously received in advance.
_____ (f) Record hiring of employees.
_____ (g) Record salaries owed.
_____ (h) Record supplies used.

Prepare original and adjusting journal entries for prepayments.
(SO 6) AP

P3–2A   Ouellette & Associates began operations on January 1, 2002. Its fiscal year end is December 31, and it only prepares financial statements and adjusts its accounts annually. Selected transactions during 2002 follow:
1. On January 1, 2002, bought office supplies for $4,500 cash. A physical count at December 31, 2002, revealed $900 of supplies was still on hand.
2. Bought a $3,600 one-year insurance policy for cash on September 1, 2002. The policy came into effect on this date.

Each **Problem** helps you pull together and apply several concepts of the chapter.

Two sets of problems—**Set A** and **Set B**—are keyed to the same study objectives and cognitive level. These provide additional opportunities to apply concepts learned in the chapter.

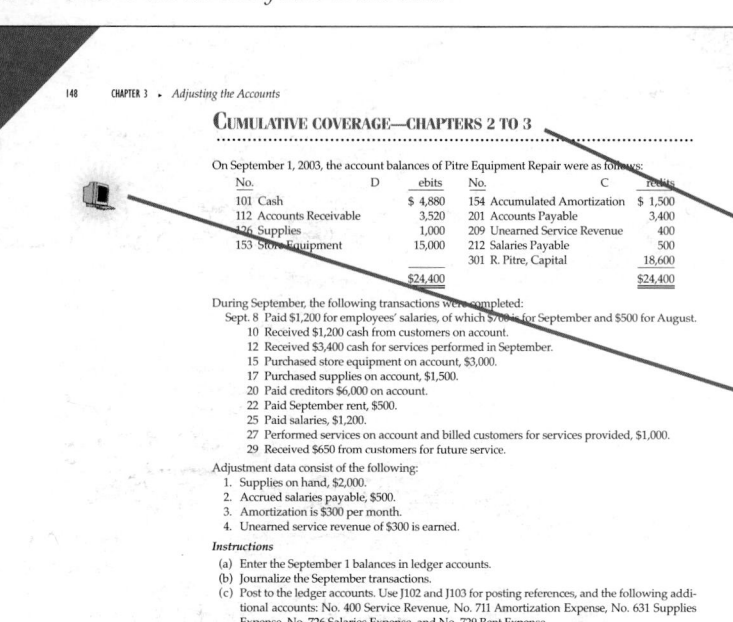

In selected chapters, a **Cumulative Coverage Problem** follows the A and B problem sets. The cumulative coverage problem pulls together, and uses, topics you have learned over several chapters.

General Ledger Problems, identified by this icon, are selected problems that can be solved using the *General Ledger Software Package*.

The **Broadening Your Perspective** section helps you pull together various concepts covered in the chapter and apply them to real-life business decisions.

The **Financial Reporting Problem** familiarizes you with the format, content, and uses of financial statements prepared by The Second Cup Ltd., which is presented in Appendix A at the end of the text.

Interpreting Financial Statements asks you to apply the concepts you have learned to specific situations faced by actual companies. The **CD icon** tells you there is an additional case on the CD that came with your textbook to help you master the material.

Accounting on the Web cases ask you to visit websites where you can find and analyse information related to the chapter topic. Case details are found on the Weygandt website <www.wiley.com/canada/weygandt2>.

At the book's website, you will also find many other valuable resources and activities, including interactive quizzes, a Checklist of Key Figures, and PowerPoint slides.

Collaborative Learning Activities prepare you for the business world, where you will be working with many people, by giving you practice in solving problems with colleagues.

Communication Activities ask you to engage in real-life business situations using your writing, speaking, or presentation skills.

Through the **Ethics Case**, you will reflect on ethical situations an accountant typically confronts.

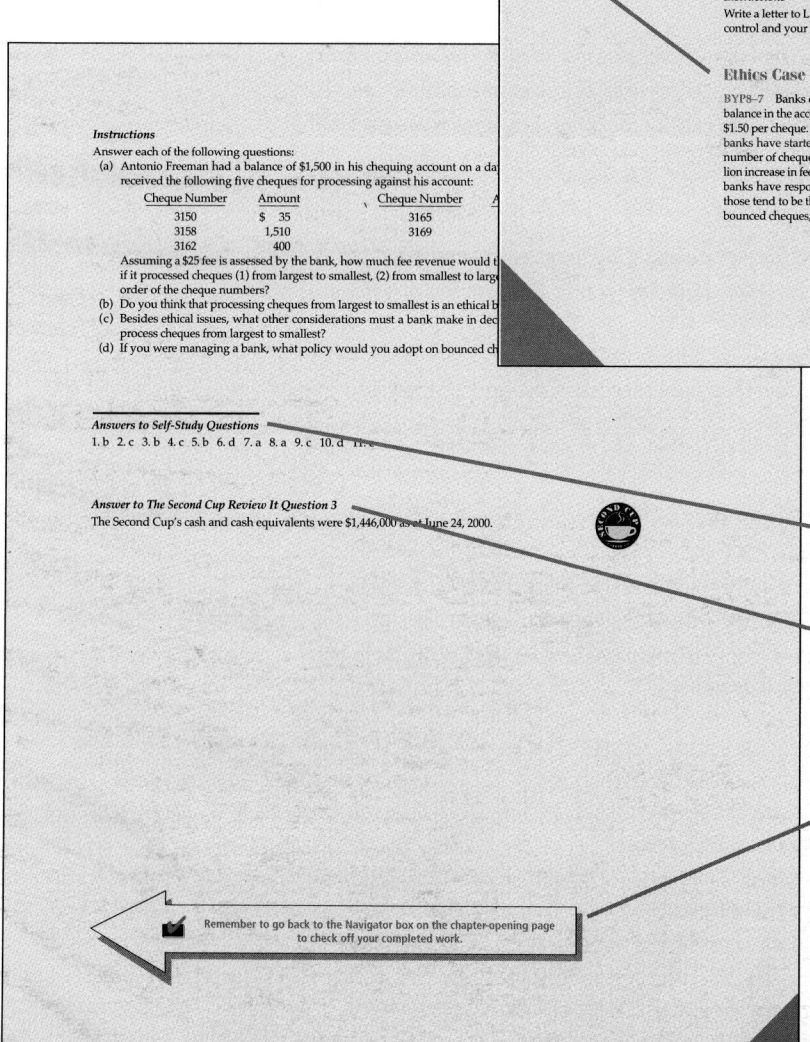

418   **CHAPTER 8** ► *Internal Control and Cash*

Instructions
Identify the internal control features outlined in management's report. Explain how each of these features strengthens internal control within TELUS.

Accounting on the Web

BYP8–4   Internal control and governance are tightly linked. The management of a company, including the board of directors, must ensure that effective control exists in the organization. This problem reviews a well-known Canadian retailer that demonstrate good corporate governance and control practices.

Instructions
Specific requirements of this Internet case are available on the Weygandt website.

CRITICAL THINKING

Collaborative Learning Activity

BYP8–5   From your employment or personal experiences, identify situations in which cash was received and disbursed.

Instructions
In groups of five or six students, do the following:
 (a) Identify the internal control principles used for cash receipts in the situations you have selected.
 (b) Identify the internal control principles used for cash disbursements in the situations you have selected.
 (c) Identify any weaknesses in internal control related to these cash receipts and disbursements.

Communication Activity

BYP8–6   As a new auditor for the public accounting firm of Rawls, Keoto, and Landry, you have been assigned to review the internal controls over the mail cash receipts of Avalon Company. Your review reveals the following: cheques are promptly endorsed "For Deposit Only" but no list of the cheques is prepared by the person opening the mail. The mail is opened either by the cashier or by the employee who maintains the accounts receivable records, depending upon who is less busy. Mail receipts are deposited in the bank weekly by the cashier.

Instructions
Write a letter to L. S. Osman, owner of the Avalon Company, explaining the weaknesses in internal control and your recommendations for improving the system.

Ethics Case

BYP8–7   Banks charge fees of up to $25 for "bounced" cheques—that is, cheques that exceed the balance in the account. It has been estimated that processing bounced cheques costs a bank roughly $1.50 per cheque. Thus, the profit margin on a bounced cheque is very high. Recognizing this, some banks have started to process cheques from largest to smallest. By doing this, they maximize the number of cheques that bounce if a customer overdraws an account. One bank projected a $14-million increase in fee revenue as a result of processing the largest cheques first. In response to criticism, banks have responded that their customers prefer to have large cheques processed first, because those tend to be the most important. At the other extreme, some banks will cover their customers' bounced cheques, effectively extending them an interest-free loan while their account is overdrawn.

Instructions
Answer each of the following questions:
 (a) Antonio Freeman had a balance of $1,500 in his chequing account on a da... received the following five cheques for processing against his account:

Cheque Number	Amount	Cheque Number	
3150	$ 35	3165	
3158	1,510	3169	
3162	400		

Assuming a $25 fee is assessed by the bank, how much fee revenue would t... if it processed cheques (1) from largest to smallest, (2) from smallest to larg... order of the cheque numbers?
 (b) Do you think that processing cheques from largest to smallest is an ethical b...
 (c) Besides ethical issues, what other considerations must a bank make in dec... process cheques from largest to smallest?
 (d) If you were managing a bank, what policy would you adopt on bounced ch...

Answers to Self-Study Questions
1. b 2. c 3. b 4. c 5. b 6. d 7. a 8. a 9. c 10. d 11. c

Answer to The Second Cup Review It Question 3
The Second Cup's cash and cash equivalents were $1,446,000 as at June 24, 2000.

Remember to go back to the Navigator box on the chapter-opening page to check off your completed work.

Answers to Self-Study Questions provide feedback on your understanding of concepts.

Answers to *Review It* Questions based on The Second Cup financial statements provide feedback on your search for information in The Second Cup Annual Report.

After you complete your assignments, it's a good idea to go back to **The Navigator** checklist at the start of the chapter to see if you have used all the study aids of the chapter.

THE USE OF BLOOM'S TAXONOMY

Bloom's Taxonomy, which was developed in 1956 by Benjamin Bloom, is a classification framework that you can use to develop your skills from the most basic to the most advanced competence levels: Knowledge, comprehension, application, analysis, synthesis, and evaluation. These levels are hierarchical in nature in that performance at each level requires mastery of all prior levels.

Questions, exercises, and problems at the end of each chapter of this text have been classified by the knowledge level required in answering each one. Below you will learn what your role is in each of the six skill levels and how you can demonstrate mastery at each level. Key word clues will help you recognize the skill level required for a particular question. You will also find an example from the text which will help illustrate each skill level.

(K) Knowledge (Remembering)

Student's role: "I read, listen, watch or observe, I take notes and am able to recall information, ask and respond to questions."

Student demonstrates knowledge by: stating who, what, when, why, and how in the same form in which they learned it.

Key words clues: define, identify, label, name, etc.

Example from *Accounting Principles*: "What is the basic accounting equation?"

(C) Comprehension (Understanding)

Student's role: "I understand the information or skill. I can recognize it in other forms and I can explain it to others and make use of it."

Student demonstrates comprehension by: giving an original example of how the information would be used.

Key words clues: describe, distinguish, give example, compare, differentiate, explain, etc.

Example from *Accounting Principles*: "Indicate whether each of the following items is an asset, liability or part of owner's equity."

(AP) Application (Solving the Problem)

Student's role: "I can apply my prior knowledge and understanding to new situations."

Student demonstrates knowledge by: solving problems independently. Recognition of when the information or skill is needed and uses it to solve new problems or complete tasks.

Key word clues: calculate, illustrate, prepare, complete, use, produce, etc.

Example from *Accounting Principles*: "Determine total liabilities if assets equal $94,000 and owner's equity equals $62,000."

(S) Synthesis (Creating)

Student's role: "I use all knowledge, understanding, and skills to create alternatives. I can convey this information to others effectively."

Student demonstrates knowledge by: acting as a guide to others, designing, creating.

Key word clues: relate, tell, write, categorize, devise, formulate, generalize, create, design.

Example from *Accounting Principles*: "Prepare a memo to the president, clearly addressing his question as to why the balance sheet lists the company's assets at less than their true value."

(E) Evaluation (Appraisal)

Student's role: "I am open to and appreciative of the value of ideas, procedures, and methods and can make well-supported judgements, backed up by knowledge, understanding, and skills."

Student demonstrates knowledge by: formulating and presenting well-supported judgement, displaying consideration of others, examining personal options, making wise choices.

Key word clues: appraise, assess, criticize, critique, decide, evaluate, judge, justify, recommend.

Example from *Accounting Principles*: "A company is suffering declining sales of its principal product, non-biodegradable plastic cartons. The president instructs his controller to lengthen the estimated asset lives in order to reduce the amortization expense and increase net income. Identify the stakeholders in this situation. Discuss whether the suggested change is unethical or simply a shrewd business practice. What should the controller do?"

HOW DO YOU LEARN BEST?

This questionnaire aims to find out something about your preferences for the way you work with information. You will have a preferred learning style. One part of that learning style is your preference for the intake and the output of ideas and information. Circle the letter of the answer that best explains your preference. Circle more than one if a single answer does not match your perception. Leave blank any question that does not apply.

1. You are about to give directions to a person who is staying with you. She is staying in a hotel in town and wants to visit your house later. She has a rental car. Would you
   V) draw a map on paper?
   R) write down the directions (without a map)?
   A) tell her the directions?
   K) pick her up at the hotel in your car?

2. You are staying in a hotel and have a rental car. You would like to visit friends whose address you do not know. Would you like them to
   V) draw you a map on paper?
   R) write down the directions (without a map)?
   A) tell you the directions by phone?
   K) pick you up at the hotel in their car?

3. You have just received a copy of your itinerary for a world trip. This is of interest to a friend. Would you
   A) call her immediately and tell her about it?
   R) send her a copy of the printed itinerary?
   V) show her on a map of the world?
   K) share what you plan to do at each place you visit?

4. You are going to cook something as a special treat for your family. Do you
   K) cook something familiar without need for instructions?
   V) thumb through the cookbook looking for ideas from the pictures?
   R) refer to a specific cookbook where there is a good recipe?
   A) ask for advice from others?

5. A group of tourists has been assigned to you to find out about national parks. Would you
   K) drive them to a national park?
   R) give them pamphlets or a book on national parks?
   V) show them slides and photographs?
   A) give them a talk on national parks?

6. You are about to purchase a new CD player. Other than price, what would most influence your decision?
   A) The salesperson telling you what you want to know.
   K) Listening to it.
   R) Reading the details about it.
   V) Its distinctive, upscale appearance.

7. Recall a time in your life when you learned how to do something like playing a new board game. (Try to avoid choosing a very physical skill, e.g., riding a bike.) How did you learn best? By
   V) visual clues—pictures, diagrams, charts?
   A) listening to somebody explaining it?
   R) written instructions?
   K) doing it?

8. You have an eye problem. Would you prefer that the doctor
   A) tell you what is wrong?
   V) show you a diagram of what is wrong?
   K) use a model to show what is wrong?

9. You are about to learn to use a new program on a computer. Would you
   K) sit down at the keyboard and begin to experiment with the program's features?
   R) read the manual that comes with the program?
   A) telephone a friend and ask questions about it?

10. You are not sure whether a word should be spelled "dependent" or "dependant." Do you
    R) look it up in the dictionary or check the grammar software?
    V) see the word in your mind and choose the best way it looks?
    A) sound it out in your mind?
    K) write both versions down?

11. Apart from price, what would most influence your decision to buy a particular book?
    K) You have used a copy before.
    R) Quickly reading parts of it.
    A) A friend talking about it.
    V) The way it looks is appealing.

12. A new movie has arrived in town. What would most influence your decision to go or not to go?
    A) You heard a radio review of it.
    R) You read a review of it.
    V) You saw a preview of it.

13. Do you prefer an instructor who likes to use
    R) textbook, handouts, readings?
    V) flow diagrams, charts, graphics?
    K) field trips, labs, practical sessions?
    A) discussion, guest speakers?

Count your choices:

☐ ☐ ☐ ☐
V A R K

Now match the letter or letters you have recorded most to the same letter or letters in the Learning Styles Chart on the following page. You may have more than one learning style preference—many people do. Next to each letter in the Chart are suggestions that will refer you to different learning aids throughout this text.

LEARNING STYLES CHART

 VISUAL

WHAT TO DO IN CLASS	WHAT TO DO WHEN STUDYING	TEXT FEATURES THAT MAY HELP YOU	WHAT TO DO PRIOR TO EXAMS
• Pay close attention to charts, drawings, and handouts your instructor uses. • Underline and highlight. • Use different colours. • Use symbols, flow charts, graphs, different arrangements on the page, white space.	Convert your lecture notes into "page pictures." To do this: • Use the "What to do in class" strategies. • Reconstruct images in different ways. • Redraw pages from memory. • Replace words with symbols and initials. • Look at your pages.	The Navigator Feature Story Preview Infographics/Illustrations Photos Accounting in Action Accounting Equation Analyses Key Terms in blue Words in bold Demonstration Problem/Action Plan Questions/Exercises/Problems Financial Reporting Problem Interpreting Financial Statements Accounting on the Web	• Recall your "page pictures." • Draw diagrams where appropriate. • Practise turning your visuals back into words.

 AURAL

WHAT TO DO IN CLASS	WHAT TO DO WHEN STUDYING	TEXT FEATURES THAT MAY HELP YOU	WHAT TO DO PRIOR TO EXAMS
• Attend lectures and tutorials. • Discuss topics with students and instructors. • Explain new ideas to other people. • Use a tape recorder. • Leave spaces in your lecture notes for later recall. • Describe overheads, pictures, and visuals to somebody who was not in class.	You may take poor notes because you prefer to listen. Therefore: • Expand your notes by talking with others and with information from your textbook. • Tape record summarized notes and listen. • Read summarized notes out loud. • Explain your notes to another "aural" person.	Preview Infographics/Illustrations Accounting in Action Review It/Do It/Action Plan Summary of Study Objectives Glossary Demonstration Problem/Action Plan Self-Study Questions Questions/Exercises/Problems Financial Reporting Problem Accounting on the Web Collaborative Learning Activity Communication Activity Ethics Case	• Talk with the instructor. • Spend time in quiet places recalling the ideas. • Practise writing answers to old exam questions. • Say your answers out loud.

Source: Adapted from VARK pack. © Copyright Version 2.0 (2000) held by Neil Fleming, Christchurch, New Zealand and Charles Bonwell, Green Mountain Falls, Colorado, USA. This material may be used for faculty or student development if attribution is given. It may not be published in either paper or electronic form without consent of the authors. There is a VARK web site at <www.active-learning-site.com>.

READING/WRITING

WHAT TO DO IN CLASS	WHAT TO DO WHEN STUDYING	TEXT FEATURES THAT MAY HELP YOU	WHAT TO DO PRIOR TO EXAMS
• Use lists and headings. • Use dictionaries, glossaries, and definitions. • Read handouts, textbooks, and supplemental library readings. • Use lecture notes.	• Write out words again and again. • Reread notes silently. • Rewrite ideas and principles into other words. • Turn charts, diagrams, and other illustrations into statements.	The Navigator Feature Story Study Objectives Preview Review It/Do It/Action Plan Summary of Study Objectives Glossary Self-Study Questions Questions/Exercises/Problems Writing Problems Financial Reporting Problem Interpreting Financial Statements Accounting on the Web Collaborative Learning Activity Communication Activity	• Write exam answers. • Practise with multiple choice questions. • Write paragraphs, beginnings and endings. • Write your lists in outline form. • Arrange your words into hierarchies and points.

KINESTHETIC

WHAT TO DO IN CLASS	WHAT TO DO WHEN STUDYING	TEXT FEATURES THAT MAY HELP YOU	WHAT TO DO PRIOR TO EXAMS
• Use all your senses. • Go to labs, take field trips. • Listen to real-life examples. • Pay attention to applications. • Use hands-on approaches. • Use trial-and-error methods.	You may take poor notes because topics do not seem concrete or relevant. Therefore: • Put examples in your summaries. • Use case studies and applications to help with principles and abstract concepts. • Talk about your notes with another "kinesthetic" person. • Use pictures and photographs that illustrate an idea.	The Navigator Feature Story Preview Infographics/Illustrations Review It/Do It/Action Plan Summary of Study Objectives Demonstration Problem/Action Plan Self-Study Questions Questions/Exercises/Problems Financial Reporting Problem Interpreting Financial Statements Accounting on the Web Collaborative Learning Activity Communication Activity	• Write practice answers. • Role-play the exam situation.

For all learning styles: Be sure to use the Student Navigator CD to enhance your understanding of the concepts and procedures of the text. In particular, use the writing handbook, interactive navigator, accounting cycle tutorial, additional demonstration problems, key term matching activities, and interpreting financial statement cases.

SPECIAL STUDENT SUPPLEMENTS THAT HELP YOU GET THE BEST GRADE YOU CAN

Student Navigator CD

 Included with this text is an interactive CD packed with a learning styles assessment, an accounting cycle tutorial, demonstration problems complete with action plans and solutions, key term matching exercises, a database of annual reports, a writing handbook, a "surviving the group project" handbook, career information, and much more.

The Accounting Principles Website <www.wiley.com/canada/weygandt2>

 This resource and learning tool serves as a launching pad to numerous activities, resources, and related sites. On the website, you'll find learning styles charts designed to help you discover how they learn best, study skills and tools, interactive quizzing, an on-line glossary, Accounting on the Web cases, additional demonstration problems, and other useful references. In addition, there are links to companies discussed in the text and items available for downloading such as a Checklist of Key Figures and PowerPoint slides.

A Reader's Guide to Accounting Principles: Strategies for Successful Reading and Supplemental Glossary

Reading strategies for increased comprehension and retention include a number of techniques for handling, understanding, and remembering difficult vocabulary. A supplemental dictionary of commonly used business terms and idioms complements the accounting terms defined in the end-of-chapter glossaries.

Student Study Guide–Volume 1: Chapters 1-11 and Volume 2: Chapters 12-19

The Student Study Guide is a comprehensive review of accounting and a powerful tool for you to use in the classroom. Each chapter includes a preview of the chapter, study objectives, and a summary of key points in the chapter. A demonstration problem is included, in addition to other opportunities for students to prac-

tise their knowledge and skills through true/false, multiple-choice, matching questions related to key terms, and exercises linked to study objectives. Solutions to these questions, exercises, and problems explain the hows and whys so you get immediate feedback.

Working Papers

Working Papers are partially completed accounting forms for end-of-chapter exercises and problems. Journals, ledgers, T accounts, and other required working papers have been predetermined and included for each textbook assignment, so that you can redirect limited time to important accounting concepts rather than formatting.

Mark's Music Practice Set

This practice set exposes you to a real world simulation of maintaining a complete set of accounting records for a business. Business papers add a realistic dimension by enabling you to handle documents, cheques, invoices, and receipts that you would encounter in a small proprietorship. This practice set reinforces key concepts from Chapters 1 through 4 and allows you to apply the information you have learned. It is an excellent way to see how these concepts are all brought together to generate the accounting information that is essential in assessing the financial position and operating results of a company.

Accounting Software

 The General Ledger Software is an interactive program that allows you to solve selected end-of-chapter problems, which are identified by a computer icon (pictured at right), using a computerized accounting system. You can record and post journal entries, generate trial balances, financial statements, as well as a variety of other reports. In addition, proprietorships or corporations can be created from scratch. This software also allows you to complete the Mark's Music practice set on the computer.

TO THE INSTRUCTOR

In the previous edition of *Accounting Principles*, we sought to create a book about business that made the subject clear and fascinating to students. And, that is still our passion: to provide a link between accounting principles, student learning, and the real world.

Student Empowerment and Success

In our effort to create an even more effective text, we surveyed the market and talked personally to instructors and students. We heard again and again that the biggest challenges students face are becoming motivated, learning how to study, and managing their tasks. We were gratified to learn that our first edition has helped empower students to meet these challenges and has been rated highly in consumer satisfaction by both instructors and students. We have responded to this information by making the pedagogical framework of the Second Canadian Edition of *Accounting Principles* even stronger and the presentation even clearer. We continue to give students the tools and the motivation they need to succeed in subsequent accounting courses and in their future business careers.

Goals and Features of the Second Canadian Edition

The revision of *Accounting Principles* provided an opportunity to improve a textbook that had already set high standards for quality. Users and reviewers continue to comment positively on the writing style, the use of real-world examples, the many pedagogical features, and the fact that the textbook is not only about accounting but about business as well.

The primary purpose of this revision was to maintain these successful features and improve on them. We gathered four consistent messages from our developmental research:

- Some topics are beyond the scope of the introductory accounting. We've carefully evaluated all topics regarding their suitability for, and relevance to, beginning accounting students. Those topics more suitable for an advanced course in accounting were deleted from this edition. Added, were features and topics more relevant to today's electronic and @-business environment.
- A textbook should be as pedagogically effective as possible. *The Navigator,* our guide to the learning process, is a leader in pedagogical effectiveness. In addition, we had an expert in Bloom's Taxonomy review the wording of our study objectives and add

cognitive level coding to the end-of-chapter material. Students (and instructors) can now easily determine if the assignment is at the knowledge (K), comprehension (C), application (AP), analysis (AN), synthesis (S), or evaluation (E) level.

- The book continues to involve students in the learning process and ensure they understand the *why* as well as the *how*. Our Student Navigator CD, integrated throughout the text, empowers students to succeed by teaching them how to study, what to study, and why they study.
- This edition continues, and expands, the inclusion of user-oriented material to demonstrate the relevance of accounting to all students, no matter their area of study. These learning activities are designed to develop many skills that will be of use to students in other courses, in their careers, and in their personal lives. These include financial statement analysis skills, international awareness, and the ability to use the Internet. We have also, with the permission of CGA-Canada, added end-of-chapter material from their examinations, because students told us they wished to gain experience with professional accounting examination questions. In addition, to give students the opportunity to follow an extended real-world example, we have integrated references to The Second Cup Ltd.'s financial statements throughout the book.

Simplified Presentation

As in the first edition, we continue to simplify and condense the textual material. To achieve this goal, the text was reviewed and carefully edited to ensure the clarity and exposition. The changes that were made can be characterized into four types:

Organizational Changes. The most significant organizational change is the relocation of the inventory chapter from Chapter 9 to Chapter 6. The coverage of inventory in Chapter 5 emphasizes the perpetual inventory accounting system. It is followed immediately by the periodic inventory system coverage and cost flow assumptions, in Chapter 6. This back-to-back inventory coverage was recommended by many first edition adopters. We believe students will benefit from the closer proximity of these two topics.

We also reorganized and expanded the Broadening Your Perspective section of the end-of-chapter material. The Broadening Your Perspective section focuses on two areas: (1) financial reporting and analysis and (2) critical thinking. The financial reporting and analysis section includes a financial reporting problem using the information presented in The Second Cup's annual report, one or more interpreting financial statements cases and accounting on the web cases. The critical thinking section includes one or more of each of the following: collaborative learning activity, communication activity, and ethics case.

Additions. In response to demand, we added more infographics to visually depict complex topics. We also added accounting equation analyses to each journal entry, so that students could comprehend the impact of each transaction on the financial position of the company. We included a new type of accounting in action box, **℮**-business insights, to inform students about relevantt **℮**-business situations.

In addition, we expanded the end-of-chapter material, including adding an alternate problem set. The second set of problems provides additional coverage to that offered in the first set. This will provide further practice for students, allowing an instructor to demonstrate one problem in class and assign another, or alternate assigned problems in different terms. Some of these problems are exact alternates to those included in the first set. Others extend the problem in Set A or present the same topic in a different way.

In a very few cases, we added new material to the textbook. These topics had to pass a strict test to warrant their inclusion. They were added only if they represented a major concept, issue, or procedure that a beginning student should understand.

Condensations and Deletions. We either condensed or deleted material that was better suited for more advanced level courses, along with concepts and procedures that are little used. We made these decisions after gathering a great deal of information from instructors on how they teach the course and what they think beginning accounting students need to know.

Updates. This edition was subject to comprehensive updating to ensure that it is relevant and fresh. Updating involved replacing numerous Accounting in Action boxes, end-of-chapter material, real-world examples cited in the text, infographic illustrations, and chapter-opening feature stories.

Proven Pedagogical Framework

Accounting Principles has always provided tools to help students learn accounting concepts and procedures and apply them to the real world. The second Canadian edition places increased emphasis on the processes students go through as they learn.

Learning How to Use the Text

A **Student Owner's Manual** begins the text to help students understand the value of the text's pedagogy and how to use it.

- After becoming familiar with the pedagogy, students can take a **Learning Styles Quiz** to help them identify how they learn best (visually, aurally, through reading and writing, kinesthetically, or through a combination thereof). They then get tips on in-class and out-of-class learning strategies, as well as help in identifying the text pedagogy that would be most useful to them when they study.
- **Concepts for Review**, listed at the beginning of each chapter, identify concepts covered previously that will apply in the chapter to come. In this way, students see the relevance to the current chapter of concepts covered earlier.
- Chapter 1 contains notes that explain each pedagogical element the first time it appears.
- Finally, **The Navigator** pulls all the learning aids together into a learning system designed to guide students through each chapter and help them succeed in learning the material. It consists of (1) a checklist at the beginning of the chapter, which outlines text features and study skills they will need, and (2) a series of check boxes that prompt students to use the learning aids in the chapter and set priorities as they study. At the end of the chapter, students are reminded to return to The Navigator to check off their completed work. The Navigator from Chapter 2 is shown below.

THE NAVIGATOR	✔
■ Understand *Concepts for Review*	☐
■ Read *Feature Story*	☐
■ Scan *Study Objectives*	☐
■ Read *Preview*	☐
■ Read text and answer *Before You Go On* p. 58 ☐ p. 62 ☐ p. 72 ☐ p. 75 ☐	
■ Work *Demonstration Problem*	☐
■ Review *Summary of Study Objectives*	☐
■ Answer *Self-Study Questions*	☐
■ Complete assignments	☐

Understanding the Context

- The **Feature Story** helps students picture how the chapter topic relates to the real world of accounting and business. It also serves as a running example in the chapter and is the topic of a series of review questions called **A Look Back at Our Feature Story**, toward the end of the chapter.
- **Study Objectives** form a learning framework for the text, with each objective being repeated in the margin at the appropriate place in the main body of the chapter and in the **Summary**. Further, end-of-chapter assignment material is linked to the Study Objectives.
- A chapter **Preview** links the chapter opening feature story to the major topics of the chapter. First, an introductory paragraph explains how the feature story applies to the topics that will be discussed. Then a graphic outline of the chapter provides a visual road map, useful for seeing the big picture as well as the connections between subtopics.

Learning the Material

- **Financial statements** appear regularly throughout the book. Those from real companies are usually identified by a logo or related photo. Often, numbers or categories are highlighted in coloured type to draw students' attention to key information.
- **Key ratios**, using data from The Second Cup's 2000 annual report, are examined in appropriate spots throughout the text. Integration of ratios enables students to see two important pieces of information about financial data: how they are presented in financial statements as well as how they are analysed by users of financial information. In addition, Chapter 19 includes a complete presentation on financial statement analysis.
- The **Accounting Equation** appears in the margin next to key journal entries throughout the text. This feature reinforces the students' understanding of the impact of an accounting transaction on the financial statements.
- **Key terms** and concepts are printed in blue where they are first explained in the text and are defined again in the end-of-chapter glossary.
- **Accounting in Action** boxes give students insight into how real companies practise accounting. The boxes cover business, ethics, and international issues. Of particular interest are the new **℮**-business insight boxes reporting on how business technology has expanded the services provided by accountants.
- **Colour photographs and illustrations** support and reinforce the concepts of the text.

- **Infographics** are a special type of illustration that helps students visualize and apply accounting concepts to the real world.
- **Before You Go On** sections occur at the end of each key topic and often include two parts: *Review It* serves as a learning check within the chapter by asking students to stop and answer questions about the material just covered. *Review It* questions marked with The Second Cup icon send students to find information in The Second Cup's annual report (featured in Appendix A at the end of the text). These exercises help cement students' understanding of how topics covered in the chapter are reported in real-world financial statements. Answers appear at the end of the chapter. A demonstration problem, in sections called *Do It*, gives immediate practice of the material just covered. Solutions are provided to help students understand the reasoning involved in reaching an answer. The last **Before You Go On** exercise takes students back for a critical look at the chapter-opening feature story.
- **Helpful Hints** in the margins offer students succinct examples that clarify the concept under discussion.
- **Alternative Terminology** presents synonymous terms, since terminology may differ in common usage.
- **International Notes** also found in the margins of each chapter, provide a helpful and convenient way for instructors to expose students to international issues in accounting.
- **Ethics Notes** help to sensitize students to the real-world ethical dilemmas of accounting.

Putting It Together

- **Demonstration Problems** give students the opportunity to refer to a detailed solution to a representative problem as they do assignments. **Action Plans** list strategies to assist students in understanding the solution and establishing a logic for approaching similar types of problems. Additional demonstration problems, complete with action plans and solutions, are available on the interactive Student Navigator CD.
- The **Summary of Study Objectives** relates the study objectives to the key points of the chapter. It gives students another opportunity to review as well as to see how all the key topics within the chapter are related.
- The **Glossary** defines all concepts and terms, highlighted in blue type, introduced in each chapter. A key term matching activity is available on the interactive Student Navigator CD.

Developing Skills Through Practice

- **Self-Study Questions** are a practice test that gives students an opportunity to check their knowledge of important chapter topics. With questions keyed to the Study Objectives, students can go back and review sections of the chapter in which they find they need further work. Additional self-tests are available on the Weygandt website.
- **Brief Exercises** help build students' confidence and test their basic skills. Each exercise generally focuses on one of the **Study Objectives**.
- Each of the **Exercises** focuses on one or more **Study Objectives**. These tend to take a little longer to complete and present more of a challenge to students than **Brief Exercises**. These **Exercises** help instructors and students make a manageable transition to the more challenging problems.
- **Problems** stress the application of the concepts presented in the chapter. Certain problems, marked with a pencil icon ✎═▷, help build business writing skills. **Cumulative Coverage Problems** tie together concepts from more than one chapter, where appropriate.
- Each **Self-Study Question, Question, Brief Exercise, Exercise**, and **Problem**, has a description of the concept covered and is keyed to Study Objectives. The end-of-chapter material has been written to guide students from the simpler level of cognitive ability (knowledge and comprehension) to the more complex (such as evaluation, which includes critical thinking and creative problem solving). The level of cognitive skill each assignment requires has been classified following **Bloom's Taxonomy**. A fuller explanation of **Bloom's Taxonomy** and its application in *Accounting Principles* is found on page xviii of this preface.

Expanding and Applying Knowledge

Broadening Your Perspective is a unique section at the end of each chapter that offers a wealth of resources to help instructors and students pull together what has been learned in the chapter. This section offers problems and projects for those instructors who want to broaden the learning experience by bringing in more real-world decision-making and critical thinking activities. The elements of the Broadening Your Perspective section are described below.

Financial Accounting and Reporting

- A **Financial Reporting Problem** directs students to study various aspects of the financial statements of The Second Cup Ltd.'s annual report, which is featured in Appendix A at the end of the text.
- **Interpreting Financial Statements** ask students to read parts of financial statements and interpret that information in light of concepts presented in the chapter. Additional interpreting financial statement cases are available on the interactive Student Navigator CD.
- **Accounting on the Web** cases guide students to the Student Resources section of the Weygandt website where they can find web cases and hyperlink to other websites to analyse information related to the chapter topic.

Critical Thinking

- The **Collaborative Learning Activity** helps build decision-making skills by analysing accounting information in a less structured situation. These cases require evaluation of a manager's decision or lead to a decision among alternative courses of action. As collaborative activities, they promote teamwork.
- **Communication Activities** ask students to engage in real-world business situations using writing, speaking, or presentation skills.
- **Ethics Cases** describe typical ethical dilemmas and ask students the analyse the situation, identify the stakeholders, and the ethical issues involved, and decide on an appropriate course of action.

ACKNOWLEDGEMENTS

During the course of development of *Accounting Principles*, Second Canadian Edition, the authors benefited greatly from the feedback from instructors and students of accounting principles courses throughout the country, including many users of the First Edition of this text. The constructive suggestions and innovative ideas helped focus this revision on the needs of the students. In addition, the input and advice of the reviewers and ancillary authors and the throughness and accuracy of the proofers provided valuable feedback throughout the development of this revision.

Reviewers

Maria Belanger, Algonquin College
Bryan J. Bessner, Devry Institute of Technology
Dave Bopara, Toronto School of Business
Vern Gibson, British Columbia Institute of Technology
Donna P. Grace, Sheridan College
Elizabeth Hicks, Douglas College
Bob Holland, Nova Scotia Community College
Valerie Kinnear, Mount Royal College
Barbara Klein, Yorkdale Secondary School
Dieter Loerick, John Abbott College
John Mitchell, Sault College
Joe Pidutti, Durham College
Carole Reid Clyne, Centennial College
Doug Ringrose, Grant MacEwan Community College
David J. Sale, Kwantlen University College
Helen Vallee, Kwantlen University College
Karin Vickars, Capilano College

Ancillary Authors, Contributors, and Proofers

Vaneeta Dabas, West Humber Collegiate
Cécile Ashman, Algonquin College
Carole Bowman, Sheridan College
Tashia Batstone
Susan Cohlmeyer, Memorial University
Elizabeth D'Anjou
Elizabeth Hicks, Douglas College
Carmel A. Robbins, Southern Alberta Institute of Technology
Joanne Hinton, University of New Brunswick
Zofia Laubitz
Gary Lubin
Janet Pierce
David Schwinghamer, Collège Ahuntsic
Enola Stoyle
Barbara Trenholm, University of New Brunswick

Accuracy

We have made every effort to ensure that this text is error-free. *Accounting Principles* has been extensively reviewed and proofed at three different production stages prior to publication. In addition, the ancilliary authors read the draft text. As well, the end-of-chapter material has been independently solved by at least three individuals, in addition to the authors. We would like to express our sincere gratitude to every one who spent countless hours ensuring the accuracy of this text and the solutions to the end-of-chapter material.

Publications

We would like to thank The Second Cup Ltd., for permitting the use of The Second Cup Ltd. 2000 Annual Report as our specimen financial statements. We would also like to acknowledge the co-operation of many Canadian and international companies that allowed us to include extracts from their financial statements in the text and end-of-chapter material. The participation of the Certified General Accountants Association of Canada in allowing selected examination questions to be reproduced in the end-of-chapter material is very much appreciated. Articles from *The National Post, Globe and Mail, CAmagazine, CMA Magazine, CGA Magazine,* and numerous other sources have been useful in providing interesting Accounting in Action boxes.

A Final Note of Thanks

I consider myself privileged to be able to work with the outstanding US author team of Jerry Weygandt, Don Kieso, and Paul Kimmel. They have been generous in sharing their extensive teaching and writing experiences with me.

I appreciate the exemplary support and professional commitment given me by Wiley Canada's president Diane Wood, publisher John Horne, publishing services director Karen Bryan, editorial manager Karen Staudinger, new media editor Elsa Passera, publishing services/permissions co-ordinator Michelle Marchetti, senior marketing manager Janine Daoust, director of sales and marketing Maureen Talty, and sales managers Carolyn Wells and Darren Lalonde. I wish to also thank Wiley's dedicated sales representatives who work tirelessly to service your needs. In addition, I owe a debt of gratitude to Bill McGrath and Robert Oviatt of Appleby Color Lab and Jan Brooks of Jan Brooks Creative Design for their design expertise and contributions to this project.

It would not have been possible to write this text without the understanding of my employer, colleagues, students, family, and friends. Together, they provided a creative and supportive environment for my work.

Suggestions and comments from all users—instructors and students alike—of this textbook are encouraged and appreciated.

Barbara Trenholm
trenholm@unb.ca
Fredericton, New Brunswick
November 2001

BRIEF CONTENTS

CHAPTER • 1 ▶ **A**CCOUNTING IN ACTION

CHAPTER • 2 ▶ **T**HE RECORDING PROCESS

CHAPTER • 3 ▶ **A**DJUSTING THE ACCOUNTS

CHAPTER • 4 ▶ **C**OMPLETION OF THE ACCOUNTING CYCLE

CHAPTER • 5 ▶ **A**CCOUNTING FOR MERCHANDISING OPERATIONS

CHAPTER • 6 ▶ **I**NVENTORY COSTING

CHAPTER • 7 ▶ **A**CCOUNTING INFORMATION SYSTEMS

CHAPTER • 8 ▶ **I**NTERNAL CONTROL AND CASH

CHAPTER • 9 ▶ **A**CCOUNTING FOR RECEIVABLES

CHAPTER •10 ▶ **C**APITAL ASSETS

CHAPTER •11 ▶ **C**URRENT LIABILITIES

CHAPTER •12 ▶ **A**CCOUNTING PRINCIPLES

CHAPTER •13 ▶ **A**CCOUNTING FOR PARTNERSHIPS

CHAPTER •14 ▶ **C**ORPORATIONS: ORGANIZATION AND SHARE CAPITAL TRANSACTIONS

CHAPTER •15 ▶ **C**ORPORATIONS: DIVIDENDS, RETAINED EARNINGS, AND INCOME REPORTING

CHAPTER •16 ▶ **L**ONG-TERM LIABILITIES

CHAPTER •17 ▶ **I**NVESTMENTS

CHAPTER •18 ▶ **T**HE CASH FLOW STATEMENT

CHAPTER •19 ▶ **F**INANCIAL STATEMENT ANALYSIS

Appendix A Specimen Financial Statements: The Second Cup Ltd.
Appendix B Present Value Concepts

CONTENTS

CHAPTER · 1 ▶ ACCOUNTING IN ACTION   **1**
Brewing Up Success at The Second Cup

What Is Accounting?   **2**
Who Uses Accounting Information   3
Brief History of Accounting   5
Distinguishing between Bookkeeping
    and Accounting   6
Accounting and You   6
The Accounting Profession   7

The Building Blocks of Accounting   **9**
Ethics—A Fundamental Business Concept   9
Generally Accepted Accounting Principles   10
Assumptions   11
Basic Accounting Equation   14

Using the Building Blocks   **17**
Transaction Analysis   18
Summary of Transactions   22
Financial Statements   24
Using the Information in the Financial Statements   27

CHAPTER · 2 ▶ THE RECORDING PROCESS   **52**
No Such Thing As a Perfect World

The Account   **54**
Debits and Credits   55
Expanding the Basic Accounting Equation   58

Steps in the Recording Process   **59**
The Journal   60
The Ledger   63

The Recording Process Illustrated   **66**
Summary Illustration of Journalizing
    and Posting   71

The Trial Balance   **73**
Limitations of a Trial Balance   74
Locating Errors   74
Use of Dollars and Cents   75

CHAPTER · 3 ▶ ADJUSTING THE ACCOUNTS   **100**
Fiscal Year Ends, But Classes Move On

Timing Issues   **102**
Selecting an Accounting Time Period   103
Fiscal and Calendar Years   103
Recognizing Revenues and Expenses   103

Accrual versus Cash Basis of Accounting   **104**

The Basics of Adjusting Entries   **406**
Types of Adjusting Entries   106
Adjusting Entries for Prepayments   107
Adjusting Entries for Accruals   111
Adjusting Entries for Estimates   116
Summary of Basic Relationships   118

The Adjusted Trial Balance and Financial Statements   **120**
Preparing the Adjusted Trial Balance   120
Preparing Financial Statements   121

APPENDIX 3A ▶ Alternative Treatment of Prepaid Expenses and Unearned Revenues   **124**

CHAPTER · 4 ▶ COMPLETION OF THE ACCOUNTING CYCLE   **154**
Breezing Through Month End With Style

Using a Work Sheet   **156**

Closing the Books   **158**
Preparing Closing Entries   158
Posting Closing Entries   161
Preparing a Post-Closing Trial Balance   163

Summary of the Accounting Cycle   **163**
Reversing Entries — An Optional Step   164
Correcting Entries — An Avoidable Step   165

Classified Financial Statements   **166**
Standard Balance Sheet Classifications   167
Classified Balance Sheet Illustrated   170

Using the Information in the
Financial Statements 171

APPENDIX 4A ▶ *Using a Work Sheet in an Electronic World*   **175**

APPENDIX 4B ▶ *Reversing Entries*   **179**

CHAPTER · 5 ▶ ACCOUNTING FOR MERCHANDISING OPERATIONS   **206**
Taking Stock—From Backpacks to Bicycles

Merchandising Operations   **208**
Operating Cycles 209
Inventory Systems 210

Recording Purchases of Merchandise   **212**
Subsidiary Inventory Records 213
Freight Costs 214
Purchase Returns and Allowances 215
Discounts 215

Recording Sales of Merchandise   **216**
Sales 216
Sales Taxes 217
Sales Returns and Allowances 217
Discounts 218
Freight Costs 218

Completing the Accounting Cycle   **220**
Adjusting Entry 220
Closing Entries 221
Post-Closing Trial Balance 222
Summary of Merchandising Entries 222

Merchandising Financial Statements   **223**
Multiple-Step Income Statement 223
Single-Step Income Statement 227
Classified Balance Sheet 228
Using the Information in the Financial Statements 228

APPENDIX 5A ▶ *Sales Taxes*   **233**

APPENDIX 5B ▶ *Using a Work Sheet for a Merchandising Operation*   **237**

CHAPTER · 6 ▶ INVENTORY COSTING   **262**
No Coffee, Just Great Service at University Bookstore

Inventory Basics   **264**
Determining Inventory Quantities 265

Periodic Inventory System   **268**
Recording Sales of Merchandise 268
Recording Purchases of Merchandise 269
Comparison of Entries—Perpetual vs. Periodic 270
Cost of Goods Sold 270

Income Statement Presentation 272
Completing the Accounting Cycle 273

Inventory Costing Under a Periodic Inventory System 275
Using Actual Physical Flow Costing
–Specific Identification 277
Using Assumed Cost Flow Methods
–FIFO, Average Cost, and LIFO 277
Financial Statement Effects of Cost Flow Methods 281
Selection of Cost Flow Method 283

Inventory Errors   **285**
Income Statement Effects 285
Balance Sheet Effects 286

Statement Valuation and Presentation   **287**
Valuing Inventory at the Lower of Cost and Market 287
Classifying Inventory 289
Presentation 289

APPENDIX 6A ▶ *Inventory Cost Flow Methods in Perpetual Inventory Systems*   **291**

APPENDIX 6B ▶ *Estimating Inventories*   **296**

CHAPTER · 7 ▶ ACCOUNTING INFORMATION SYSTEMS 320
Helping the Helpers: Accounting Systems Are for Everyone

Basic Concepts of Accounting Information Systems 322
Principles of Accounting Information Systems 322
Developing an Accounting System 323
Manual vs. Computerized Systems 324

Subsidiary Ledgers   **325**
Example 326
Advantages of Subsidiary Ledgers 327

Special Journals   **328**
Sales Journal 329
Cash Receipts Journal 332
Purchases Journal 335
Cash Payments Journal 337
Effects of Special Journals on General Journal 340

APPENDIX 7A ▶ *Special Journals in a Periodic Inventory System*   **343**

APPENDIX 7B ▶ *Sales Taxes*   **344**

CHAPTER · 8 ▶ INTERNAL CONTROL AND CASH   **370**
Minding the Money in Moose Jaw

Internal Control   **372**
Principles of Internal Control 373
Limitations of Internal Control 377

Cash Controls   379
   Internal Control over Cash Receipts   379
   Internal Control over Cash Disbursements   382

Use of a Bank   385
   Making Bank Deposits   386
   Electronic Funds Transfer   386
   Writing Cheques   386
   Bank Statements   388
   Reconciling the Bank Account   390

Reporting Cash   394
   Using the Information in the
      Financial Statements   395

CHAPTER · 9 ▶ ACCOUNTING FOR RECEIVABLES   420
How Long Should the Cheque Be in the Mail?

Types of Receivables   422

Accounts Receivable   423
   Recognizing Accounts Receivable   423
   Valuing Accounts Receivable   424
   Disposing of Accounts Receivable   431

Notes Receivable   434
   Calculating Interest   435
   Recognizing Notes Receivable   435
   Valuing Notes Receivable   435
   Disposing of Notes Receivable   436

Statement Presentation of Receivables   438
   Using the Information in the
      Financial Statements   438

CHAPTER · 10 ▶ CAPITAL ASSETS   458
On the Books, Your Classroom May Be Worthless

Tangible Capital Assets   460

Property, Plant, and Equipment   461
   Determining the Cost of Property,
      Plant, and Equipment   461
   Amortization   464
   Expenditures During Useful Life   474
   Disposals of Property, Plant,
      and Equipment   475

Natural Resources   478
   Amortization   479

Intangible Capital Assets   481
   Patents   482
   Copyrights   483
   Trademarks and Trade Names   483
   Franchises and Licences   484
   Goodwill   484
   Research and Development Costs   485
   Other Intangible Assets   485

Statement Presentation of Capital Assets   486
   Using the Information in the
      Financial Statements   487

CHAPTER · 11 ▶ CURRENT LIABILITIES   512
Does Size Matter?

Accounting for Current Liabilities   514

Definitely Determinable Liabilities   515
   Operating Line of Credit   515
   Notes Payable   516
   Sales Taxes Payable   517
   Payroll and Employee Benefits   518
   Unearned Revenues   520
   Current Maturities of Long-Term Debt   521

Estimated Liabilities   522
   Property Taxes   522
   Product Warranties   523

Contingent Liabilities   525
   Recording Contingent Liabilities   525
   Disclosure of Contingent Liabilities   525

Financial Statement Presentation   526

APPENDIX 11A ▶ Payroll Accounting   529

CHAPTER · 12 ▶ Accounting Principles   560
The Big Question

The Conceptual Framework of Accounting   562
   The Objective of Financial Reporting   563
   Qualitative Characteristics of Accounting
      Information   564
   Elements of Financial Statements   566
   Recognition and Measurement Criteria   566

Assumptions   567
   Going Concern Assumption   567
   Monetary Unit Assumption   568
   Economic Entity Assumption   568
   Time Period Assumption   568

Principles   569
   Revenue Recognition Principle   569
   Matching Principle (Expense Recognition)   573
   Full Disclosure Principle   574
   Cost Principle   575

Constraints in Accounting   576
   Cost-Benefit Constraint   577
   Materiality Constraint   577
   Summary of Conceptual Framework   577

International Accounting Standards   578
   Differences in Standards   578
   Uniformity in Standards   579

CHAPTER • 13 ► Accounting For Partnerships   **602**

Partners Come and Go, But the Beat Goes On

Partnership Form of Organization   **604**

Characteristics of Partnerships   604
Organizations with Partnership Characteristics   607
Advantages and Disadvantages of Partnerships   608
Partnership Agreement   608

Basic Partnership Accounting   **609**

Forming a Partnership   609
Dividing Net Income or Net Loss   610
Partnership Financial Statements   614

Admission and Withdrawal of Partners   **615**

Admission of a Partner   616
Withdrawal of a Partner   620

Liquidation of a Partnership   **624**

No Capital Deficiency   624
Capital Deficiency   626

CHAPTER • 14 ► Corporations: Organization and Share Capital Transactions   **646**

Student Savvy Pays Off for Research in Motion

The Corporate Form of Organization   **648**

Characteristics of a Corporation   649
Forming a Corporation   652
Ownership Rights of Shareholders   652
Share Issue Considerations   654
Corporate Capital   657

Accounting for Common Share Issues   **659**

Issuing No Par Value Shares for Cash   659
Issuing Stated Value Shares for Cash   660
Issuing Par Value Shares for Cash   660
Issuing Shares for Services or Noncash Assets   661
Reacquisition of Shares   661

Preferred Shares   **663**

Dividend Preference   664
Convertible Preferred   664
Redeemable and Retractable Preferred   665
Liquidation Preference   666

Statement Presentation of Shareholders' Equity   **666**

Presentation   666
Using the Information in the Financial Statements   667

CHAPTER • 15 ► Corporations: Dividends, Retained Earnings, and Income Reporting   **688**

Standing on Guard for High-Tech Business

Dividends   **690**

Cash Dividends   691
Stock Dividends   693
Stock Splits   695

Retained Earnings   **698**

Retained Earnings Restrictions   698
Prior Period Adjustments   699
Statement of Retained Earnings   701
Reporting Shareholders' Equity   702

Corporation Income Statements   **704**

Corporate Income Tax   704
Presentation of Non-Typical Items   706

Using the Information in the Financial Statements   **709**

Earnings Performance   709
Dividend Record   711

CHAPTER • 16 ► Long-Term Liabilities   **734**

Confederation Bridge is Attractive to Both Travellers and Bondholders

Bond Basics   **736**

Why Issue Bonds?   736
Types of Bonds   738
Issuing Procedures   739
Bond Trading   740
Determining the Market Value of Bonds   741

Accounting for Bond Issues   **742**

Issuing Bonds at Face Value   742
Discount or Premium on Bonds   743
Issuing Bonds at a Discount   744
Issuing Bonds at a Premium   748
Issuing Bonds Between Interest Dates   751

Accounting for Bond Retirements   **753**

Redeeming Bonds at Maturity   753
Redeeming Bonds Before Maturity   753

Accounting for Other Long-Term Liabilities   **755**

Long-Term Notes Payable   755
Lease Liabilities   757

Statement Presentation and Analysis of Long-Term Liabilities   **759**

Using the Information in the Financial Statements   759

CHAPTER • 17 ► Investments   **782**

Students Learn and Earn

Why Corporations invest   **784**

Temporary and Long-Term Investments   **786**
Temporary Investments   786
Long-Term Investments   787

Accounting for Debt Investments   **787**
Temporary Debt Investments   787
Long-Term Debt Investments   788

Accounting for Equity Investments   **790**
Holdings of Less Than 20%   791
Holdings of Between 20% and 50%   792
Holdings of More Than 50%   794

Valuation and Reporting of Investments   **796**
Temporary Investments   796
Long-Term Investments   797
Financial Statement Presentation   797
Comprehensive Balance Sheet   798
Income Statement   800

CHAPTER • 18 ► The Cash Flow Statement   **820**

Looking for the Big Picture in Small Business Loans

The Cash Flow Statement: Purpose and Format   **822**
Purpose of the Cash Flow Statement   823
Meaning of Cash Flows   823
Classification of Cash Flows   823
Significant Noncash Activities   824
Format of the Cash Flow Statement   825
Usefulness of the Cash Flow Statement   825
Preparation of the Cash Flow Statement   826

SECTION 1 ► Indirect Method   **829**
First Year of Operations—2002   829
Second Year of Operations—2003   835

SECTION 2 ► Direct Method   **842**
First Year of Operations—2002   842
Second Year of Operations—2003   848

Using the Information in the Financial Statements   **854**
Cash Current Debt Coverage   855
Cash Return on Sales   855
Cash Flow Per Share   856
Cash Total Debt Coverage   857

APPENDIX 18A ► Using a Work Sheet to Prepare the Cash Flow Statement — Indirect Method   **860**

CHAPTER • 19 ► Financial Statement Analysis   **888**

Just Fooling Around

Basics of Financial Statement Analysis   **890**
Need for Comparative Analysis   890
Tools of Financial Statement Analysis   891

Horizontal Analysis   **892**
Balance Sheet   893
Income Statement   893
Statement of Retained Earnings   894

Vertical Analysis   **895**
Balance Sheet   895
Income Statement   896
Intercompany Comparisons   896

Ratio Analysis   **898**
Liquidity Ratios   899
Profitability Ratios   904
Solvency Ratios   912
Summary of Ratios   914

Limitations of Financial Analysis   **916**
Estimates   917
Cost   917
Alternative Accounting Methods   917
Atypical Data   917
Diversification of Firms   917

Appendix A—-Specimen Financial Statements: **A1**
The Second Cup Ltd.

Appendix B—-Present Value Concepts   **B1**

Before studying this chapter, you should understand or, if necessary, review:

a. *How to use the study aids in this book. (Student Owner's Manual, pp. vii-xvii)*
b. *How you learn best. (Student Owner's Manual, pp. xix-xxi)*
c. *The student supplements that accompany this text. (Student Owner's Manual, p. xxii)*

THE
NAVIGATOR

The Navigator learning system encourages you to use the learning aids in the chapter and set priorities as you study.

The Feature Story helps you picture how the chapter topic relates to the real world of accounting and business. You will find references to the story throughout the chapter and in the "A Look Back at Our Feature Story" exercise toward the end of the chapter.

Brewing Up Success At The Second Cup

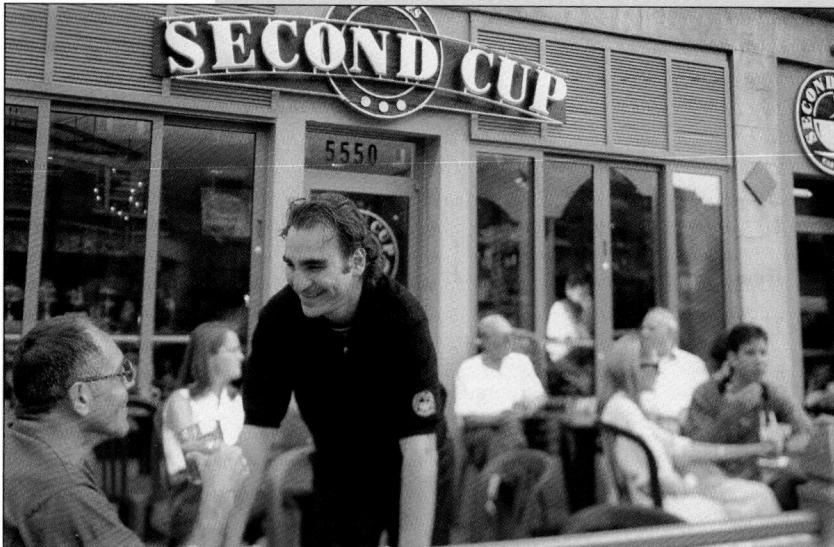

TORONTO, Ont.—No organization can hope to do a drop of business without sound accounting information. Take The Second Cup, for instance.

In 1975, Tom Culligan and Frank O'Dea opened the original Second Cup retail outlet at Scarborough Town Centre, a large mall in eastern Toronto. It sold only whole-bean coffee, but its numbers were successful enough that Culligan and O'Dea soon opened other locations and began to sell brewed coffee and related merchandise.

By 1988, The Second Cup had grown to 120 locations and was bought by Toronto restaurant entrepreneur Michael Bregman. In 1993, Bregman incorporated The Second Cup Ltd.

Today, with its almost 400 locations across the country, The Second Cup is the largest specialty coffee retailer in Canada. It has a major presence not only in its franchised cafés but through partnerships with companies such as Kraft Canada, Air Canada, Delta Hotels, and Cara Operations, generating system-wide sales of over

$170 million in 2001.

Stop for a moment and think of all the decisions that needed to be made over 25 years for one small coffee-bean store to grow this much.

To make these decisions, The Second Cup's management, like that of other companies, relied in large part on accounting information. But management isn't the only user of this information. Most of The Second Cup's owners (shareholders) used the financial information in the annual report to decide whether or not to invest in the company. And this same information was used by potential lenders (creditors) to know if a loan was a good risk.

It's a warm summer evening. The patio of the Danforth Avenue Second Cup is bustling. Trendy young couples, families with strollers, and business people are among the patrons lingering at the sidewalk tables over a cappuccino or an iced latté. The Second Cup has come a long way since 1975, and one can safely say that its accounting information has been as much a part of the company's success as its brewed coffee and coffee beans.

THE
NAVIGATOR

www.secondcup.com

THE NAVIGATOR ✔

■ Understand *Concepts for Review* ☐

■ Read *Feature Story* ☐

■ Scan *Study Objectives* ☐

■ Read *Preview* ☐

■ Read text and answer *Before You Go On*
  p. 9 ☐   *p. 17* ☐   *p. 23* ☐   *p. 28* ☐

■ Work *Demonstration Problem* ☐

■ Review *Summary of Study Objectives* ☐

■ Answer *Self-Study Questions* ☐

■ Complete assignments ☐

CHAPTER · 1

ACCOUNTING IN ACTION

Study Objectives give you a framework for learning the specific concepts covered in the chapter.

▶ STUDY OBJECTIVES ◀

After studying this chapter, you should be able to:

1. *Explain what accounting is.*
2. *Identify the users and explain the uses of accounting.*
3. *Demonstrate an understanding of why ethics is a fundamental business concept.*
4. *Explain the meaning of generally accepted accounting principles and the cost principle.*
5. *Explain the meaning of the going concern, monetary unit, and economic entity assumptions.*
6. *State and utilize the basic accounting equation and explain the meaning of assets, liabilities, and owner's equity.*
7. *Calculate the effect of business transactions on the basic accounting equation.*
8. *Understand what the four financial statements are and how they are prepared.*

THE NAVIGATOR

The opening story about The Second Cup Ltd. highlights the importance of having good financial information to make effective business decisions. Regardless of one's pursuits, the need for financial information is inescapable. You cannot earn a living, spend money, buy on credit, make an investment, or pay taxes without receiving, using, or giving financial information. Good decision-making depends on good information.

This chapter shows you that accounting is the system used to provide useful financial information. The chapter is organized as follows:

The **Preview** outlines the major topics and subtopics you will see in the chapter.

ACCOUNTING IN ACTION

What Is Accounting?	**The Building Blocks of Accounting**	**Using the Building Blocks**
▸ Who uses accounting information? ▸ Brief history of accounting ▸ Distinguishing between bookkeeping and accounting ▸ Accounting and you ▸ The accounting profession	▸ Ethics—a fundamental business concept ▸ Generally accepted accounting principles ▸ Assumptions ▸ Basic accounting equation	▸ Transaction analysis ▸ Summary of transactions ▸ Financial statements ▸ Using the information in the financial statements

THE NAVIGATOR

What Is Accounting?

Accounting is an information system that **identifies**, **records**, and **communicates** the economic events of an organization to interested users. Economic events are activities related to the production and distribution of goods and services in an organization. Let's take a closer look at these activities:

1. **Identifying economic activities** involves selecting those events that are **evidence of economic activity by a particular organization**. The sale of coffee by Second Cup, the delivery of telephone service by Bell Canada, and the payment of salaries by major league sports teams are examples of economic events.
2. Once identified, economic events are **recorded** to provide a history of the financial activities of the organization. Recording consists of keeping a **systematic chronological diary of events measured in dollars and cents**. In recording, economic events are also **classified** and **summarized**.
3. This identification and recording of activities is only useful if the information is **communicated** to interested users. The information is communicated through accounting reports, the most common of which are called **financial statements**. To make the financial information meaningful, accountants report the recorded

data in a standardized way. Information resulting from similar transactions is accumulated and totalled. Because the transactions are grouped together, they are said to be reported **in aggregate**.

For example, all sales transactions of Second Cup are accumulated over a certain period of time and reported as one amount in its financial statements. By presenting the recorded data in aggregate, the accounting process simplifies a multitude of transactions and makes a series of activities understandable and meaningful. This simplification can result in the loss of detail, though. The Second Cup's financial statements are highly condensed and some would argue that the presentation is oversimplified. The Second Cup is not alone in this reporting practice, however. Most companies report condensed information for simplicity, but also to avoid revealing significant details to their competitors.

A vital part of communicating economic events is the accountant's ability and responsibility to **analyse** and **interpret** the reported information. Analysis involves the use of ratios, percentages, graphs, and charts to highlight significant financial trends and relationships. Interpretation involves **explaining the uses, meaning, and limitations of reported data**.

The accounting process may be summarized as follows:

References throughout the chapter tie the accounting concepts that you are learning to the story that opened the chapter.

Illustration 1-1

Accounting process

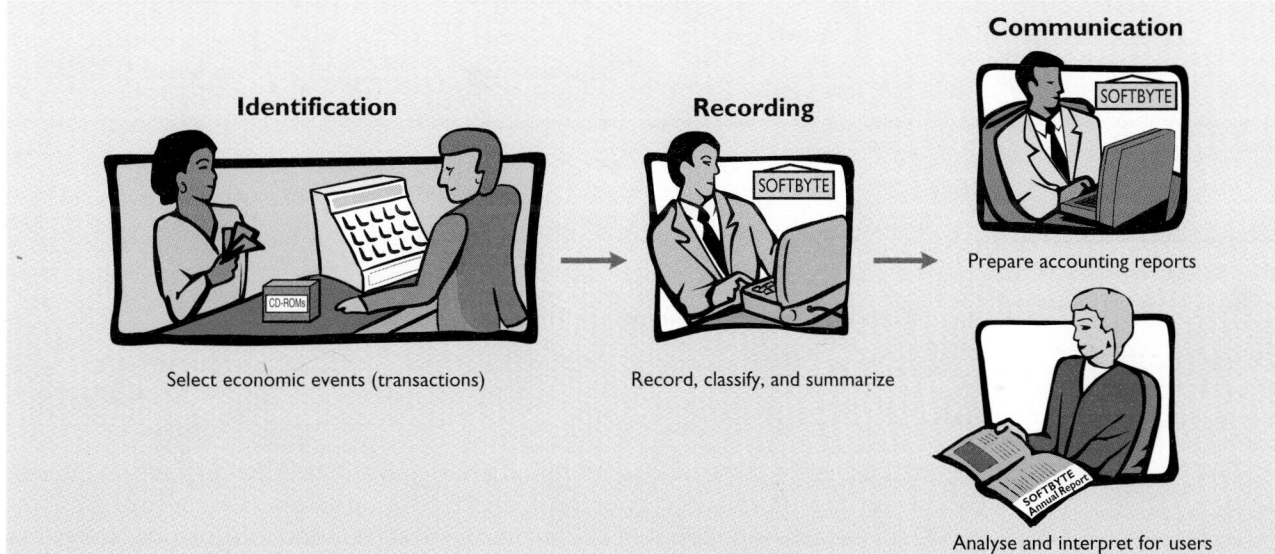

Identification

Select economic events (transactions)

Recording

Record, classify, and summarize

Communication

Prepare accounting reports

Analyse and interpret for users

Accounting must consider the needs of the users of financial information. Therefore, accountants need to know who these users are, and something about their needs for information.

Who Uses Accounting Information?

Because it communicates financial information, accounting is often called the **language of business**. The information a user of financial information needs depends upon the kinds of decisions that user makes. The differences in the decisions divide the users of financial information into two broad groups: internal users and external users.

STUDY OBJECTIVE
••••••••• **2** •••••••••
Identify the users and explain the uses of accounting.

Internal Users

Internal users of accounting information are those who plan, organize, and run a business. These include **marketing managers, production supervisors, finance directors, and company officers**. In running a business, internal users must answer many important questions, as shown in Illustration 1-2.

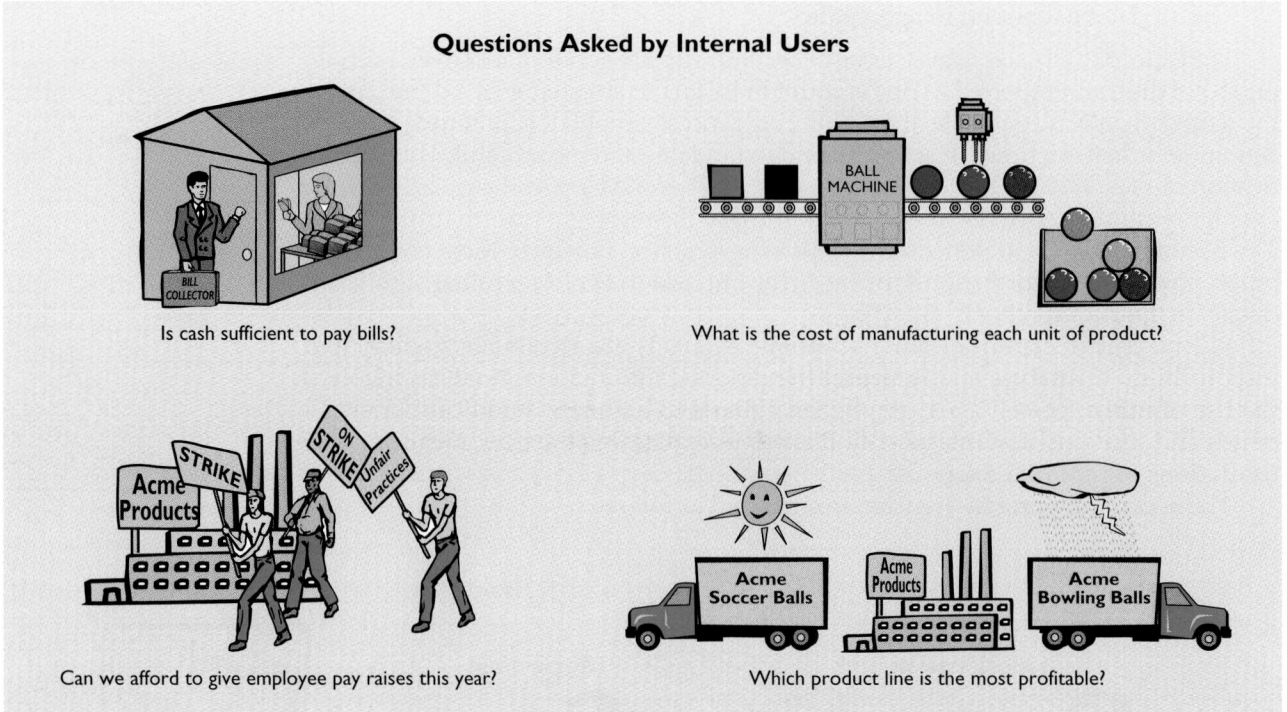

Questions Asked by Internal Users

Is cash sufficient to pay bills?

What is the cost of manufacturing each unit of product?

Can we afford to give employee pay raises this year?

Which product line is the most profitable?

Illustration 1-2

Questions asked by internal users

To answer these and other questions, users need detailed information on a timely basis. For internal users, accounting provides **internal reports**. Examples are financial comparisons of operating alternatives, projections of earnings from new sales campaigns, and forecasts of cash needs for the next year.

External Users

External users are those who work for other organizations but who have an interest in and need for information about the financial position and performance of the company. There are several types of external users of accounting information. **Investors** (owners) use accounting information to make decisions to buy, hold, or sell their shares. **Creditors**, such as suppliers and bankers, use accounting information to evaluate the risks of granting credit or lending money. Some questions that investors and creditors may ask about a company are shown in Illustration 1-3.

The information needs and questions of other external users vary considerably. **Taxing authorities**, such as the Canada Customs and Revenue Agency, want to know whether the company respects the tax laws. **Regulatory agencies**, such as provincial securities commissions, want to know whether the company is operating within prescribed rules. **Customers** are interested in whether a company will continue to honour product warranties and support its product lines. **Labour unions** want to know whether the owners can pay increased wages and benefits. **Economic planners** use accounting information to forecast economic activity.

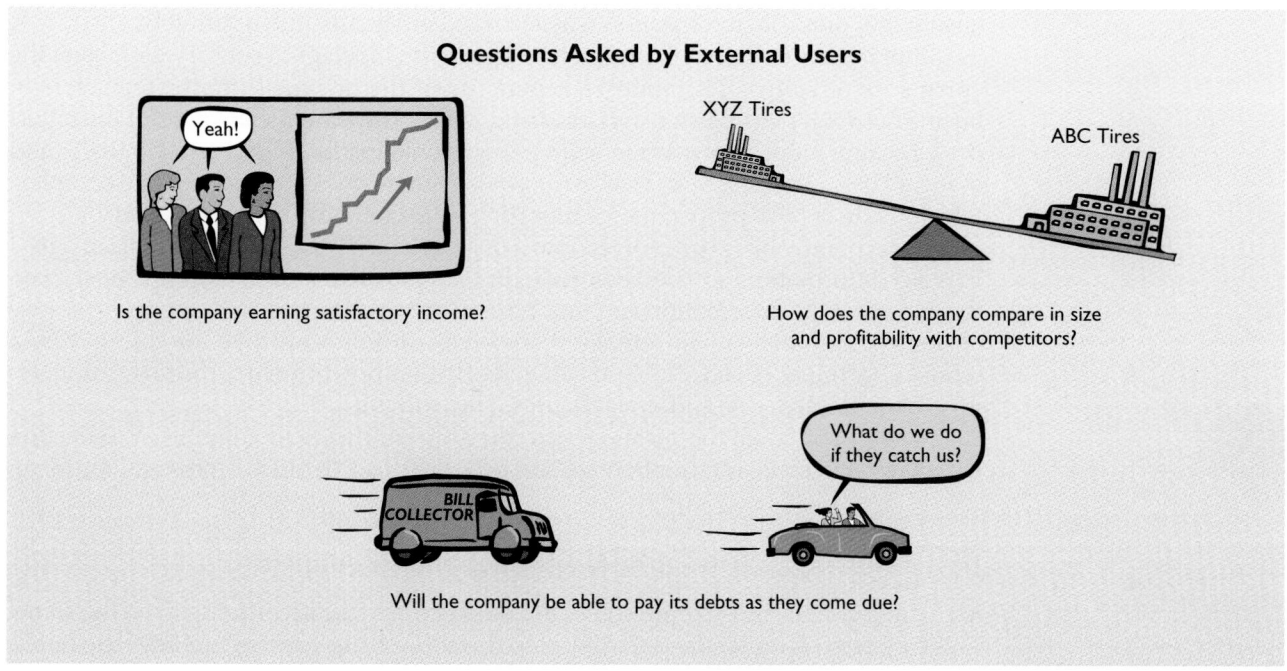

Questions Asked by External Users

Is the company earning satisfactory income?

How does the company compare in size and profitability with competitors?

Will the company be able to pay its debts as they come due?

Illustration 1-3

Questions asked by external users

►Accounting in Action ► *International Insight*

 When the chief engineer of Irkutsk Energo, a public utility in Moscow, addressed a gathering of international investors, he provided them with all kinds of financial information about the company. The reason? Russians desperately need foreign investment. Foreign investors, in the past, had been reluctant to invest because Russian firms were secretive—and sometimes deceptive—about their financial affairs. Times change, and companies such as Irkutsk Energo are enjoying share price surges after providing candid accounting information. Good accounting information may help Russia solve some of its economic problems.

Source: Neela Banerjee, "Russian Concerns Find Glasnost Pays," *Wall Street Journal,* June 9, 1995, A6.

Throughout this textbook, you will find Accounting in Action examples like this. These examples illustrate important and interesting information from real accounting situations in business. Different icons highlight each type of issue: a globe, as here, for international insights, scales for ethics insights, a lightbulb and city skyline for business insights, and an **℮** over the globe surrounded by a gear wheel for e-business insights.

International Insight   **Ethics Insight**   **Business Insight**   **℮-Business Insight**

Brief History of Accounting

The **origins of accounting** are generally attributed to the work of Luca Pacioli, an Italian Renaissance mathematician. Pacioli was a close friend and tutor to Leonardo da Vinci. He was also a contemporary of Christopher Columbus. In his text *Summa de Arithmetica, Geometrica, Proportioni et Proportionalita,* Pacioli described a system to ensure that financial information was recorded efficiently and accurately.

With the beginning of the **industrial age** in the nineteenth century and, later, the emergence of large corporations, a separation of the owners from the managers of businesses took place. As a result, the need to report the financial status of the enterprise became more important to ensure that managers acted in the company's (and owners') best interests. Also, transactions between businesses became more complex, which made better approaches for reporting financial information necessary.

Our economy has now evolved into a post-industrial age—the **information age**—in which information services are products. Globalization and the Internet have been the drivers of the information age, and business now changes at a faster pace because of them. Companies must remake themselves rapidly, and they are doing it by a whole assortment of actions: rightsizing, worker empowerment, process reengineering, mergers, alliances, and novel financial instruments.

Responding to all these changes, accounting continues to adapt itself, reflecting the types of financial information needed in today's fast-paced business environment.

Distinguishing between Bookkeeping and Accounting

Many individuals mistakenly consider bookkeeping and accounting to be the same. This confusion is understandable because **the accounting process includes the bookkeeping function**. However, accounting also includes much more. Bookkeeping usually involves only the **recording of economic events**. It is therefore just one part of the accounting process. Accounting, however, involves the **entire process** of identifying, recording, and communicating economic events. Accounting requires a higher level of expertise and judgement than bookkeeping, because economic events must be identified and measured, effectively communicated, and then interpreted meaningfully to help users in their decision-making.

Thanks to computers, much of the detail work that is part of the bookkeeping process is now performed electronically, rather than manually. Businesses of all sizes are finding that computers have made the entire recording process more efficient. However, you will need to know the procedures used in a manual accounting system in order to understand the operations a computer performs.

Now that you know the difference between bookkeeping and accounting, you should also know that accounting may be further divided into financial accounting and managerial accounting. Financial accounting is the field of accounting that provides economic and financial information for investors, creditors, and other external users. Managerial accounting provides economic and financial information for managers and other internal users. Financial accounting is the focus of this text.

Accounting and You

One question frequently asked by students of accounting is, "How will the study of accounting help me?" It should help you a great deal, because a working knowledge of accounting is desirable for virtually every field of endeavour. Some examples of how accounting is used in other careers include:

General management.   Imagine running Bombardier, the Toronto Hospital for Sick Children, a Second Cup franchise, or the Vancouver Canucks. You would need to understand accounting data in order to make wise business decisions.

Finance.   Do you want to be a banker, an investment analyst, or a stock broker? These fields rely heavily on accounting. In all of them, you will regularly examine financial statements to understand the financial standing of your customer. It is difficult to get a good job in finance without an adequate foundation in accounting.

Marketing.   Marketing specialists use their knowledge and understanding of consumers and competition to develop strategies that help an organization meet its performance objectives. Whether the organization has a profit or a social objective, its marketing specialists must be sensitive to costs and benefits. Accounting helps them quantify and understand these costs and benefits.

Information technology.   Accounting is an information business. Knowing how to create, communicate, understand, and act upon accounting information will help you cope with information technology and e-commerce. Your career may include the preparation, selection, or implementation of financial software. You could specialize in hardware, databases, telecommunications, or office productivity tools and project management. More Canadians now work in the information technology industry than in banking, mining, forestry, or automobile assembly.

►**A**ccounting in **A**ction ► ℮ -*Business Insight*

 E-business involves much more than simply selling goods over the Internet. According to Lou Gerstner, IBM's CEO, "e-business is all about cycle time, speed, globalization, enhanced productivity, reaching new customers, and sharing knowledge across institutions for competitive advantage." Many accountants are involved in designing and implementing computer systems, including systems for e-business. In fact, e-business consulting has been one of the greatest growth areas for large accounting firms.

Accounting is even useful for occupations you might think completely unrelated, such as doctor, lawyer, social worker, teacher, engineer, architect, or entrepreneur. For your more personal needs, a knowledge of accounting will help you prepare a household budget, decide whether to borrow money to purchase a car, judge how quickly you can afford to repay your student loan, determine how to invest your savings, and plan for retirement. For almost any endeavour, you will find that a working knowledge of accounting is relevant.

The Accounting Profession

There are three primary organizations that provide precertification professional accounting education and experience. You may choose to become a **chartered accountant** (CA) with the Canadian Institute of Chartered Accountants, a **certified general accountant** (CGA) with the Canadian Certified General Accountants Association, or a **certified management accountant** (CMA) with the Society of Management Accountants of Canada. Large numbers of these professional accountants apply their expertise in three major fields: public accounting, managerial accounting, and not-for-profit accounting. If you would like to communicate with one or more of these organizations and learn about their programs of study, the Weygandt website includes addresses and hotlinks for these three bodies. It also includes other Internet business sites of interest to students.

Careers in Accounting

This **CD Icon** informs you of additional resources available on the CD that came with your text.

Public Accounting

In public accounting, you offer services to the general public in much the same way as a doctor attends patients and a lawyer serves clients. A major portion of public accounting involves auditing. In this area, a qualified professional accountant examines information and expresses an opinion as to whether or not it fairly reflects the economic events that occurred during the accounting period. Audited financial statements are examined to determine whether they are fairly presented in accordance with an appropriate disclosed basis of accounting, which is normally **generally accepted accounting principles**. In the opening story, audited financial statements would be required by Second Cup's investors and creditors before they decide whether or not to invest in the company or loan money to it.

Taxation is another major area of public accounting. The work performed by tax specialists includes tax advice and planning, preparing tax returns, accounting for Provincial Sales Tax (PST) and Goods and Services Tax (GST) or Harmonized Sales Tax (HST), and representing clients before government agencies such as the Canada Customs and Revenue Agency.

A third area in public accounting is business advisory services. Business advisory services range all the way from the installation of basic computerized accounting systems, to helping small businesses plan for succession, to managing human resources and executive remuneration, to advising on acquisitions and dispositions.

In Canada, the top five public accounting firms are KPMG, Deloitte & Touche, Ernst & Young, PricewaterhouseCoopers, and Grant Thornton.

Private Accounting

Instead of working in public accounting, you might choose to work in private accounting, also known as managerial accounting. Working as an employee of a business enterprise, you might be involved in one or more of the following activities:

1. **General accounting.** Recording daily transactions and preparing financial statements and related information.
2. **Cost accounting.** Determining the cost of producing specific products.
3. **Budgeting.** Helping management quantify goals concerning revenues, costs of goods sold, and operating expenses.
4. **Accounting information systems.** Designing both manual and computerized accounting information systems.
5. **Income tax accounting.** Preparing tax returns and doing tax planning for the company.
6. **Internal auditing.** Reviewing the company's operations to evaluate their compliance with management policies and efficiency.

You can see that in certain companies, private accountants can perform as wide a variety of duties as public accountants.

Not-for-Profit Accounting

Like businesses that exist to make a profit, not-for-profit organizations also need sound financial reporting and control. To decide whether they should continue supporting such organizations and events as the United Way, the Red Cross, and the CIBC Run for the Cure, donors want information about how well the organization or event has met its financial objectives. Hospitals, colleges, and universities must also make decisions about allocating funds and reporting financial decisions. Municipal, provincial, and federal government units provide financial information to legislators, citizens, employees, and creditors.

►Accounting in Action ► *International Insight*

Volunteer auditors each donated a minimum of 10 days evaluating processes, devising warehousing procedures, ensuring safety, and monitoring the cash operations of such things as food stands, parking lots, and ticket sales at the Sydney 2000 Olympic Summer Games. The volunteers spent most of their time verifying if users were licensed to rent the Olympic logo—the most protected trademark in the world. For these Games, the price of becoming an Olympic sponsor and using the five rings on company products cost anywhere from $10 million to $40 million. If companies had been allowed to use the trademark without permission, millions of dollars would have been lost for the International Olympic Committee (IOC). The IOC estimates that sponsorship revenues account for about one-third of its total revenues, second only to revenue from television rights.

Before You Go On . . .

►*Review It*

1. What is accounting?
2. Who uses accounting information?
3. What is the difference between bookkeeping and accounting?
4. How will you be able to use your accounting knowledge?

Related exercise material: BE1–1.

Before You Go On questions at the end of major text sections offer an opportunity to stop and re-examine the key points you have studied. Related exercise material directs you to Brief Exercises (BE) and Exercises (E) with similar study objectives.

THE
NAVIGATOR

The Building Blocks of Accounting

Every profession develops a body of theory that consists of principles and assumptions. Accounting is no exception. Just as a doctor follows certain standards to treat a patient's illness, an accountant follows certain standards to report financial information. For these standards to work, a fundamental business concept is followed—ethical behaviour.

Ethics—A Fundamental Business Concept

Wherever you make your career—accounting, marketing, management, finance, government, or elsewhere—your behaviour and actions will affect other people and organizations. The standards of conduct by which one's actions are judged as right or wrong, honest or dishonest, fair or unfair, are ethics. Imagine trying to carry on a business or invest money if you could not trust the individuals you dealt with. If managers, customers, investors, co-workers, and creditors all consistently misled you, effective communication and economic activity would be impossible. Information would have no credibility.

STUDY OBJECTIVE
3

Demonstrate an understanding of why ethics is a fundamental business concept.

Fortunately, most individuals in business are ethical. Their actions are both legal and responsible. The organization's interests are considered when they make decisions. However, in some situations, public officials, business executives, and respected leaders act unethically and sometimes even illegally. For example, MLAs have been convicted for falsifying expense accounts, a former mutual fund manager was indicted for insider trading, a military leader resigned due to an unaccountable absence of cash in his budget, and executives have been dismissed and sent to jail for violating environmental legislation.

The three professional accounting bodies described earlier have extensive rules of conduct to guide the behaviour of their members with each other and the public.

Many companies today have also adopted codes of conduct that outline their commitment to ethical behaviour in internal and external relationships.

▶Accounting in Action ▸ *Ethics Insight*

 Canadian business is recognized around the world as being ethically, socially and environmentally responsible. An International Code of Ethics for Canadian Business was adopted in 1997 by a group of companies wanting to demonstrate their commitment to ethical business practices. It has been endorsed by the Minister of Foreign Affairs and most of Canada's leading business associations.

In adopting this Code, companies commit to doing business around the world in the same way they do business in Canada. The following is a relevant excerpt from the Code:

"Concerning business conduct, we will:
• Not make illegal and improper payments and bribes and will refrain from participating in any corrupt business practices.
• Comply with all applicable laws and conduct business activities in a transparent fashion.
• Ensure contractors', suppliers' and agents' activities are consistent with these principles."

Illustration 1-4

Steps used to analyse ethical dilemmas

To sensitize you to ethical situations and to give you practice at solving ethical dilemmas, we have included three types of ethics materials: (1) **marginal notes** that provide helpful hints for developing ethical sensitivity, (2) **ethics in accounting boxes** that highlight ethical situations and issues, and (3) in the end-of-chapter material, an **ethics case** that simulates a business situation. When you analyse these ethical situations, you should apply the steps outlined in Illustration 1-4.

Solving an Ethical Dilemma

1. Recognize an ethical situation and the ethical issues involved.

Use your personal ethics or an organization's code of ethics to identify ethical situations and issues.

2. Identify and analyse the principal elements in the situation.

Identify the *stakeholders*—persons or groups who may be harmed or benefited. Ask the question: What are the responsibilities and obligations of the parties involved?

3. Identify the alternatives, and weigh the impact of each alternative on various stakeholders.

Select the most ethical alternative, considering all the consequences. Sometimes there will be one right answer. Other situations involve more than one possible solution. These situations require an evaluation of each and a selection of the best alternative.

Generally Accepted Accounting Principles

STUDY OBJECTIVE
············ ▼ 4 ············

Explain the meaning of generally accepted accounting principles and the cost principle.

The accounting profession has developed a set of standards that are generally accepted and universally practised. This common set of standards is called generally accepted accounting principles (GAAP). These standards—developed over time in response to tradition, experience, and user needs—recommend how to report economic events.

The Canadian Institute of Chartered Accountants (CICA) has the primary responsibility for the development and issuance of generally accepted accounting principles in Canada. GAAP, as published in the *CICA Handbook*, has legal status for companies that adhere to the regulations of the *Canada Business Corporations Act* and the provincial securities commissions. It is important to understand that standards are not static. They should, and do, change over time to ensure that their primary purpose—the provision of information that is relevant to decision-making—continues to be met.

Internationally, accounting standards can vary from country to country. Most countries have their own standard-setting body. One group, the International Accounting Standards Board, has been working to reduce the differences in accounting practices across countries. This, in turn, improves the ability of investors, creditors, and others to make informed resource allocation and policy decisions.

►Accounting in Action ► *International Insight*

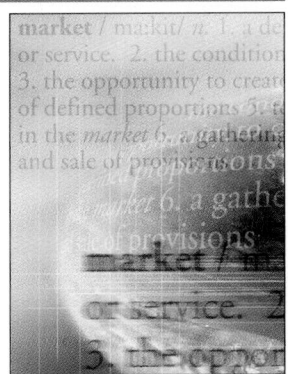

Canada is teeming with foreign culture and products—Microsoft, Samsung, Wal-Mart, The Gap, McDonald's, NIKE, and Toyota, just to name a few. Foreign-controlled companies—mostly American, some from Britain and Japan—accounted for 31.5% of the $1.3 trillion in corporate revenue generated in Canada in a recent year.

Canadians have also become more global. More than 220 Canadian companies are listed on at least one stock exchange outside of Canada. Canadian companies are expanding foreign operations, selling to foreign interests, and merging with companies located in other countries to better compete in the global marketplace.

What does this mean to the users of financial information? One must understand not only the differences in reporting requirements, but also important economic, legal, political, and cultural issues before well-informed business decisions can be made.

We need to have a good understanding of generally accepted accounting principles in order to prepare and understand accounting information. Many generally accepted accounting principles will be introduced as you progress through the text. In this chapter, we learn about the cost principle. In later chapters, we will introduce the revenue recognition principle (Chapter 3), the matching principle (Chapter 3), and the full disclosure principle (Chapter 12). Chapter 12 explores these principles, and the underlying assumptions and constraints of accounting, in greater detail.

One of the basic principles is the cost principle. This principle states that assets should be recorded at their original historical cost. **Cost is the value exchanged at the time something is acquired.** If you buy a house today, the cost is the amount you pay for it, say $125,000. If the house is appraised in two years at $130,000, the appraised amount is its **fair market value**—the value determined by the market for homes at that time. At the time of acquisition, cost and fair market value are the same. In later periods, cost and fair market value may vary, but **the cost amount continues to be used**.

To see the importance of the cost principle, consider the following example. At one time, Greyhound had 128 bus stations throughout North America with a cost of approximately $200 million. The current market value of the stations is approximately $1 billion. Under the cost principle, the bus stations are recorded and reported at $200 million, not $1 billion. Until the bus stations are actually sold, estimates of market values are too subjective.

As the Greyhound example indicates, cost has an important advantage over other valuations. It is reliable. Cost is definite and verifiable. The values exchanged at the time something is acquired can be objectively measured. Users can rely on the information supplied as they know it is based on fact. However, critics argue that cost is often not relevant. They believe market values provide more useful information. Despite its shortcomings, cost continues to be used in financial statements because of its reliability.

Assumptions

In developing generally accepted accounting principles, certain basic assumptions are made. These assumptions provide a foundation for the accounting process. One assumption that underlies the cost principle is the **going concern assumption**. Two other important assumptions are the **monetary unit assumption** and the **economic entity assumption**.

Going Concern Assumption

Implicit in the decision to record Greyhound's bus stations at cost, rather than at market, is the going concern assumption. Going concern assumes the firm will continue to operate in the foreseeable future. In spite of numerous business failures, companies have a fairly high continuance rate (they stay in business year after year).

Historical cost is the most appropriate value at which to record assets such as Greyhound's bus stations because the stations were acquired for use in the business, rather than for resale. What has relevance to the company is the amount they gave up to acquire these assets, not an estimate of their current worth. The going concern assumption presumes that the company will operate long enough to utilize these assets for their intended purpose and to fulfill its commitments. The going concern assumption and cost principle are modified if the company is expected to discontinue operations. In such cases, the lower of the cost and estimated market value is used as the most relevant value for decision-makers.

Monetary Unit Assumption

The monetary unit assumption requires that only transaction data that can be expressed in terms of money be included in the accounting records. This assumption enables accounting to quantify (measure) economic events. In Canada, we use the dollar to record these transactions. In Europe, the Euro is used. In Japan, the yen is used.

This assumption does prevent some relevant information from being included in the accounting records. For example, the health of the owner, the quality of service, and the morale of employees would not be included because they cannot be quantified in terms of money.

An important part of the monetary unit assumption is the added assumption that the unit of measure remains sufficiently constant over time. In other words, inflation (a rise in prices) or deflation (a drop in prices) is ignored when adding, subtracting, or comparing dollars of different years. Assume a company purchases land in 1962 for $100,000 and that land in a similar location and of the same size cost $400,000 in 2002, 40 years later. If a second lot of land were purchased in 2002, the land account for the company would show a total cost of land of $500,000. The fact that these dollars had different value (or purchasing power) throughout the years is overlooked. Although inflation was once a significant accounting issue, for the last five years, inflation has averaged less than 2.5%. Inflation is considered a non-issue for accounting purposes in Canada.

Economic Entity Assumption

An economic entity can be any organization or unit in society. It may be a business enterprise (such as Bombardier), a governmental unit (such as the Province of Alberta), a municipality (such as the City of Toronto), a native band council (such as the Kingsclear Indian Band), a school board (such as the Burnaby School Board), a curling championship event (such as the Labatt's Brier), or a club (such as the Hamilton Rotary Club). The economic entity assumption requires that the activities of the entity be kept separate and distinct from the activities of its owner, and all other economic entities.

To illustrate, if Ellen Gélinas, owner of Ellen's Boutique, charges any of her personal living costs as expenses of the Boutique, then the economic entity assumption is violated. Similarly, the economic entity assumption assumes that the activities of Second Cup and Swiss Chalet, both owned by Cara Operations, can each be segregated into separate economic entities for accounting purposes.

▶Accounting in Action ▸ *Ethics Insight*

A violation of the economic entity assumption contributed to the incarceration of Bruce McNall, former co-owner of the Toronto Argonauts football team, Los Angeles Kings hockey team, and other interests in the entertainment and sports world. Creditors and investors were angered to learn that company invoices, inventories, other assets, and income tax returns were falsified to help support McNall's $300,000-a-month glamorous personal lifestyle that included a Maserati, a Rolls-Royce, and an Aston Martin.

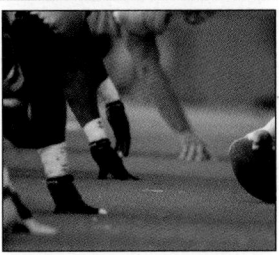

The economic entity assumption is generally discussed regarding a business enterprise, which may be organized as a proprietorship, partnership, or corporation.

Proprietorship. A business owned by one person is a proprietorship. The owner is generally the operator of the business. Small service businesses (hair stylists, service stations, and bookkeepers), farms, and small retail stores (antique shops, corner grocery stores, and book stores) are often proprietorships. Usually only a relatively small amount of money (capital) is necessary to start in business as a proprietorship. The owner (the proprietor) receives any profits, suffers any losses, and is personally liable for all debts of the business. There is no legal distinction between the business as an economic unit and the owner. However, the records of the business activities are kept separate from the personal records and activities of the owner, in accordance with the economic entity assumption. Proprietorships represent the largest number of businesses in Canada, yet they are typically the smallest in size.

Partnership. A business owned by two or more persons associated as partners is a partnership. In most aspects, a partnership is similar to a proprietorship, except that more than one owner is involved. Typically, a partnership agreement (written or oral) defines such terms as initial investments, duties of each partner, division of net income (or net loss), and settlement to be made upon death or withdrawal of a partner. Each partner generally has unlimited personal liability for all debts of the partnership, regardless of which partner created the debt. Similar to an owner in a proprietorship, a partner's personal assets may be sold to repay the partnership debt. **Like a proprietorship, the partnership activities must be kept separate from the personal activities of the partners for accounting purposes.** Partnerships are often used to organize service-type businesses, including professional practices (lawyers, doctors, architects, and accountants).

Corporation. A business that is organized as a separate legal entity under federal or provincial corporation law is a corporation. Its ownership is divided into transferable shares. The owners of the shares (shareholders) enjoy **limited liability**. They are not personally liable for the debts of the corporate entity. Shareholders **may sell all or part of their shares to other investors at any time.** Easy changes of ownership add to the attractiveness of investing in a corporation. Because ownership can be transferred without dissolving the corporation, the corporation enjoys an **unlimited life**.

Although the combined number of proprietorships and partnerships in Canada is more than the number of corporations, the revenue produced by corporations is far greater. Most of the largest enterprises in Canada—for example, Bell Canada, Ford Motor Company of Canada, George Weston, Nortel Networks, Alcan Aluminium, and Loblaw—are corporations. The annual revenue of each of these corporations

Helpful hint Principles and assumptions will be discussed throughout the text. Those discussed so far are shown in bold:

Principles
Cost
Revenue recognition
Matching
Full disclosure

Assumptions
Going concern
Monetary unit
Economic entity
Time period

ranges from $7 billion to $22 billion. These corporations are publicly traded. That is, their shares are listed on Canadian stock exchanges. Public corporations commonly distribute their financial statements to shareholders, creditors, other interested parties, and the general public upon request.

Other companies are private corporations, which do not issue publicly traded shares. Some of the largest private companies in Canada include McCain Foods, Irving Oil, the West Edmonton Mall, and Palliser Furniture. Along with proprietorships and partnerships, these companies seldom distribute their financial statements publicly.

Basic Accounting Equation

STUDY OBJECTIVE
••••••••• 6 •••••••••

State and utilize the basic accounting equation and explain the meaning of assets, liabilities, and owner's equity.

Other essential building blocks of accounting are the categories into which economic events are classified. The two basic elements of a business are what it owns and what it owes. **Assets** are the resources owned by a business. The Second Cup has total assets of approximately $18.6 million. **Liabilities and owner's equity** are the rights or claims against these resources. Claims of those to whom money or other obligations are owed (creditors) are called **liabilities**. Claims of owners are called **owner's equity**. The Second Cup has liabilities of $16.9 million and owner's equity of $1.7 million. This relationship of assets, liabilities, and owner's equity can be expressed as an equation as follows:

Illustration 1-5

The basic accounting equation

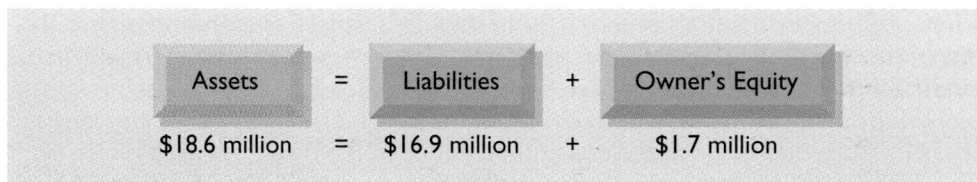

Assets	=	Liabilities	+	Owner's Equity
$18.6 million	=	$16.9 million	+	$1.7 million

Accounting Cycle Tutorial—Analysing Business Transactions

This equation is referred to as the basic accounting equation. Assets must equal the sum of liabilities and owner's equity. Because creditors' claims are paid before ownership claims if a business is liquidated, liabilities are shown before owner's equity in the basic accounting equation.

The accounting equation applies to all **economic entities** regardless of size, nature of business, or form of business organization. It applies to a small proprietorship such as a corner grocery store as much as it does to a large corporation such as Second Cup. The equation provides the underlying framework for recording and summarizing the economic events of a business enterprise.

Let's look at the categories in the basic accounting equation in more detail.

Assets

As noted earlier, assets are the resources owned by a business. They are used to carry out activities such as the production and distribution of merchandise. Every asset has the capacity to provide future services or benefits. In a business enterprise, that service potential or future economic benefit eventually results in cash inflows (receipts) to the enterprise.

For example, Campus Pizza owns a delivery truck that provides economic benefits because it is used to deliver pizzas. Other assets of Campus Pizza are tables, chairs, a CD player, a cash register, an oven, dishes, silverware, inventory, supplies, and, of course, cash.

Liabilities

Liabilities are claims against assets. That is, **liabilities are existing debts and oblig-ations**. For example, businesses of all sizes usually borrow money and purchase merchandise inventory and supplies on credit. Campus Pizza, for instance, purchases pizza ingredients and beverages on credit from suppliers. These obligations are called accounts payable. Campus Pizza also has a note payable to the Bank of Montreal for the money borrowed to purchase its delivery truck. Campus Pizza may also have wages payable to employees, GST payable and PST payable to the federal and provincial governments, and property taxes payable to the municipality. All of these persons or entities to which Campus Pizza owes money are called its **creditors**.

A creditor who is not paid may legally force the liquidation of a business. In that case, the law requires that creditor claims be paid before ownership claims.

Owner's Equity

The ownership claim on total assets is known as owner's equity. It is equal to total assets minus total liabilities. To find out what belongs to owners, we subtract creditors' claims (the liabilities) from assets. The remainder—owner's equity—is the owner's claim on the assets of the business. Since the claims of creditors must be paid before ownership claims, the owner's equity is often called **residual equity**. If the equity is negative—that is, if total liabilities exceed total assets—the term **owner's deficiency** (or deficit) describes the shortage.

Increases in Owner's Equity.   In a proprietorship, owner's equity is increased by owner's investments and revenues.

Investments by Owner.   Investments by owner are the assets the owner puts into the business. Investments may be in the form of cash or capital assets (e.g., vehicle, computer) that are contributed by the owner.

Revenues.   Revenues result from business activities performed to earn income. Generally, revenues result from the sale of merchandise inventory, the performance of services, the rental of property, and the lending of money.

Revenues normally result in an increase in an asset and an increase in owner's equity. They may arise from different sources and are identified by various names, depending on the nature of the business. Campus Pizza, for instance, has two categories of sales revenues—pizza sales and beverage sales. Common sources of revenue include sales, fees, services, commissions, and rent.

Decreases in Owner's Equity.   In a proprietorship, owner's equity is decreased by owner's drawings and expenses.

Drawings.   An owner may withdraw cash (or other assets) for personal use. These withdrawals could be recorded as a direct decrease of owner's equity. It is generally considered preferable to use a separate classification called drawings so the total withdrawals for the accounting period can be determined.

Expenses.   Expenses are the costs of assets consumed or services used in the process of earning revenue. They are decreases in owner's equity that result from operating the business. Like revenues, expenses take many forms and are identified by various names, depending on the type of asset consumed or service used. For example, Campus Pizza recognizes (records) the following expenses: cost of ingredients (meat, flour, cheese, tomato paste, mushrooms, etc.), cost of beverages, wages expense, utility expense (electric, gas, and water expense), telephone expense, delivery expense (gasoline, repairs, licences, etc.), supplies expense (napkins, detergents, aprons, etc.), rent expense, insurance expense, interest expense, and property tax expense.

In summary, the principal sources (increases) of owner's equity are (1) investments by the owner, and (2) revenues. Decreases in owner's equity are a result of (1) withdrawals of assets by the owner, and (2) expenses.

These relationships are shown in Illustration 1-6.

Illustration 1-6

Increases and decreases in owner's equity

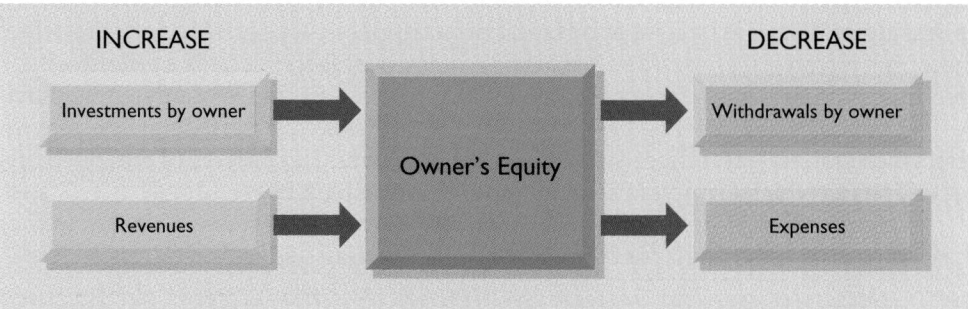

Net income results when revenues exceed expenses. Conversely, a **net loss** occurs when expenses exceed revenues. For information purposes, the components of owner's equity—investments by the owner, revenues, withdrawals, and expenses—are separately identified for the reporting period.

Accounting Equation Distinctions by Type of Business Organization

Previously, you were introduced to the three forms of business organizations—proprietorship, partnership, and corporation. In the early chapters of this text, we focus primarily on the proprietorship form of organization. Partnerships will be discussed in more detail in Chapter 13, and corporations in Chapter 14. Until that time, you need only a general understanding of the accounting distinctions between these types of organization. Accounting for assets, liabilities, revenues, and expenses is the same, regardless of the form of business organization. The primary distinction between the forms of organization is found in (1) the terminology used to name the equity section, and (2) the accounting and reporting of the owner's investments and withdrawals.

In a proprietorship, the company is owned by one person and the equity is termed **owner's equity**. In a partnership, reflective of the two or more owners, the equity is termed **partners' equity**. In the corporate form of business organization, the owners are the shareholders and the equity is called **shareholders' equity**. In an earlier example, when the assets, liabilities, and equity were reported for The Second Cup, the equity was identified as owner's equity for simplicity. Technically, since The Second Cup is a corporation, this equity should have been called *shareholders'* equity.

You have learned that in a proprietorship, owner's equity is increased by owner's investments and revenues, and decreased by owner's drawings and expenses. In a partnership, each partner's equity is similarly increased by the investments of the partner and their proportionate share of partnership revenues, and decreased by the drawings of each partner and their proportionate share of partnership expenses. In both proprietorships and partnerships, equity is reported for each owner in a one-line capital account.

It is not practical to do this for a corporation, where thousands of owners may exist. In a corporation, the investments by the shareholders (owners) are made by purchasing shares. These investments are aggregated and called **share capital**. They are the first portion of shareholders' equity. The second portion of shareholders' equity is reported as **retained earnings**. Retained earnings represent the accumulated earnings of the company that have been retained (i.e., not paid out to shareholders). Payments to the shareholders are called **dividends**. Illustration 1-7 shows how equity is reported for each different type of business organization.

Proprietorship		Partnership		Corporation	
Owner's equity:		Partners' equity:		Shareholders' equity:	
V. Buré, capital	$50,000	M. Wu, capital	$ 75,000	Share capital	$500,000
		A. Scholten, capital	75,000	Retained earnings	350,000
		Total partners' equity	$150,000	Total shareholders' equity	$850,000

Illustration 1-7

Reporting equity by type of business organization

Before You Go On . . .

►Review It

1. Why is ethics a fundamental business concept?
2. What are generally accepted accounting principles? Give an example.
3. Explain the going concern, monetary unit, and economic entity assumptions.
4. What is the basic accounting equation?
5. What are assets, liabilities, and owner's equity?
6. Distinguish the types of equity for each form of business organization.

►Do It

Classify the following items as investment by owner (I), owner's drawings (D), revenues (R), or expenses (E), and indicate whether these items increase or decrease owner's equity: (1) Rent Expense, (2) Service Revenue, (3) Drawings, and (4) Salaries Expense.

Action Plan

- Review the rules for changes in owner's equity: Investments and revenue increase owner's equity. Expenses and drawings decrease owner's equity.
- Understand the sources of revenue: the sale of merchandise, performance of services, rental of property, and lending of money.
- Understand what causes expenses: the consumption or use of assets or services.
- Recognize that drawings are withdrawals of cash or other assets from the business for personal use.

Solution

1. Rent Expense is classified as an expense (E). It decreases owner's equity.
2. Service Revenue is classified as revenue (R). It increases owner's equity.
3. Drawings are classified as owner's drawings (D). The decrease owner's equity.
4. Salaries Expense is classified as an expense (E). It decreases owner's equity.

Related exercise material: BE1–2, BE1–3, BE1–4, BE1–5, E1–1, E1–2, E1–3, and E1–4.

THE NAVIGATOR

◢Using the Building Blocks
....

Transactions are the economic events of an enterprise that are recorded. Transactions may be external or internal. **External transactions involve economic events between the company and some outside party.** For example, the purchase of cooking equipment by Campus Pizza from a supplier, the payment of monthly rent to the landlord, and the sale of pizzas to customers are all external transactions. **Internal transactions are economic events that occur entirely within one company.** The use of cooking and cleaning supplies is an internal transaction for Campus Pizza.

A company may carry on many activities that do not in themselves represent business transactions. Hiring employees, answering the telephone, talking with customers, and placing an order for merchandise with a supplier are examples. Some of these activities, however, may lead to a business transaction. Employees will earn

STUDY OBJECTIVE
..........**7**..........

Calculate the effect of business transactions on the basic accounting equation.

salaries, and merchandise will be delivered by the supplier. Each transaction must be analysed for its effect upon the components of the basic accounting equation and recorded in the accounting process. This analysis must identify the specific items affected and the amount of change in each item.

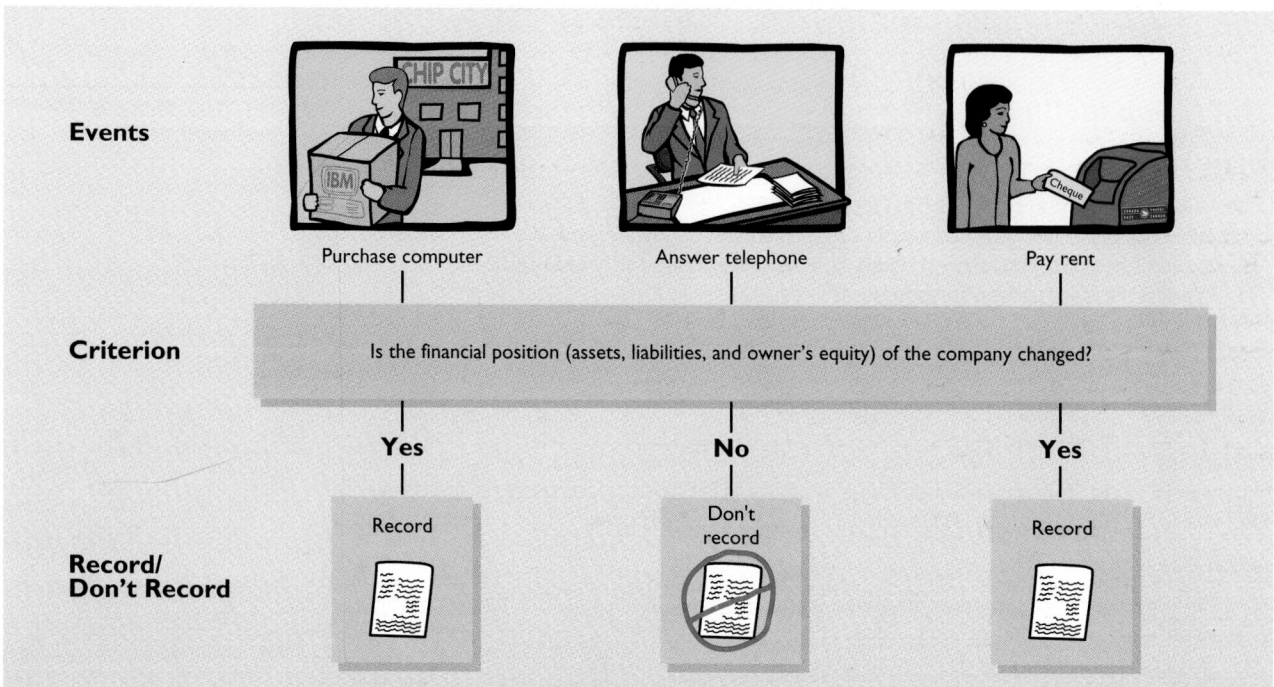

Illustration 1-8

Transaction identification process

The equality of the basic accounting equation must always be preserved. Therefore, each transaction must have a dual effect on the equation. For example, if an asset is increased, there must be a corresponding:

1. Decrease in another asset, or
2. Increase in a liability, or
3. Increase in owner's equity.

Two or more items could be affected when an asset is increased. For example, as one asset is increased by $10,000, another asset could decrease by $6,000, and a liability could increase by $4,000. Any change in a liability or ownership claim requires a similar analysis.

Transaction Analysis

The following examples are business transactions for a computer programming business during its first month of operations. You should study these transactions until you are sure you understand them. They are not difficult, but they are important to your success in this course. The ability to analyse transactions in terms of the basic accounting equation is essential for an understanding of accounting.

Transaction (1): Investment by Owner.   Marc Doucet decides to open a computer programming service. On September 1, 2002, he invests $15,000 cash in the business, which he names Softbyte. This transaction results in an equal increase in assets and owner's equity. In this case, there is an increase in the asset Cash, $15,000, and an

When a specific **account title** is used, the account name is capitalized.

equal increase in the owner's equity, M. Doucet, Capital, $15,000. The effect of this transaction on the basic equation is:

	Assets	=	Liabilities	+	Owner's Equity	
					M. Doucet, Capital	
	Cash	=				
(1)	+ $15,000	=			+ $15,000	Investment

Observe that the equality of the basic equation has been maintained. Note also that the source of the increase in owner's equity (investments) is indicated. Why does this matter? Because investments by the owner do not represent revenues. They are excluded when determining net income. Therefore, it is necessary to make clear that the increase is an investment rather than revenue from operations.

Transaction (2): Purchase of Equipment for Cash. Softbyte purchases computer equipment for $7,000 cash. This transaction results in an equal increase and decrease in total assets, though the composition of assets changes. Cash is decreased by $7,000, and the asset Equipment is increased by $7,000. The specific effect of this transaction and the cumulative effect of the first two transactions are:

		Assets			=	Liabilities	+	Owner's Equity
								M. Doucet, Capital
	Balance	Cash	+	Equipment	=			
	Old	$15,000						$15,000
(2)		− 7,000		+ $7,000				
	New	$ 8,000	+	$7,000	=			$15,000

$$\$15,000$$

Observe that total assets are still $15,000, and that Doucet's equity also remains at $15,000, the amount of his original investment.

Transaction (3): Purchase of Supplies on Credit. Softbyte purchases $1,600 of computer paper and other supplies expected to last several months from the Chuah Supply Company. Chuah Supply agrees to allow Softbyte to pay this bill next month (in October). This transaction is referred to as a **purchase on account**, or a **credit purchase**. Assets are increased because of the expected future benefits of using the paper and supplies. Liabilities are increased by the amount due to Chuah Supply Company. The asset Supplies is increased by $1,600, and the liability Accounts Payable is increased by the same amount. The effect on the equation is:

			Assets				=	Liabilities	+	Owner's Equity
								Accounts		M. Doucet,
	Balance	Cash	+	Supplies	+	Equipment	=	Payable	+	Capital
	Old	$8,000				$7,000				$15,000
(3)				+ $1,600				+ $1,600		
	New	$8,000	+	$1,600	+	$7,000	=	$1,600	+	$15,000

$16,600	$16,600

Total assets are now $16,600. This total is matched by a $1,600 creditor's claim and a $15,000 ownership claim.

Transaction (4):   Services Provided for Cash.   Softbyte receives $1,200 cash from customers for programming services it has provided. This transaction represents Softbyte's principal revenue-producing activity. Recall that revenue increases owner's equity. Cash is increased by $1,200, and M. Doucet, Capital, is increased by $1,200. The new balances in the equation are:

			Assets			=	Liabilities	+		Owner's Equity	
							Accounts		M. Doucet,		
Balance	Cash	+	Supplies	+	Equipment	=	Payable	+	Capital		
Old	$8,000		$1,600		$7,000		$1,600		$15,000		
(4)	+1,200								+ 1,200		**Service Revenue**
New	$9,200	+	$1,600	+	$7,000	=	$1,600	+	$16,200		
			$17,800					$17,800			

The two sides of the equation balance at $17,800. The source of the increase in owner's equity is indicated as service revenue. Service revenue is included in determining Softbyte's net income.

Transaction (5):   Purchase of Advertising on Credit.   Softbyte receives a bill for $250 from the local newspaper for advertising the opening of its business. It postpones payment of the bill until a later date. This transaction results in an increase in liabilities and a decrease in owner's equity (because the cost of the advertising is an expense). The cost of advertising is an expense, as opposed to an asset, because the benefits have already been used. This expense is included in determining net income, and ultimately capital. The specific items involved are Accounts Payable and M. Doucet, Capital. The effect on the accounting equation is:

			Assets			=	Liabilities	+		Owner's Equity	
							Accounts		M. Doucet,		
Balance	Cash	+	Supplies	+	Equipment	=	Payable	+	Capital		
Old	$9,200		$1,600		$7,000		$1,600		$16,200		
(5)							+ 250		– 250		**Advertising Expense**
New	$9,200	+	$1,600	+	$7,000	=	$1,850	+	$15,950		
			$17,800					$17,800			

The two sides of the equation still balance at $17,800. Owner's equity is decreased when the expense is incurred, and the specific cause of the decrease (advertising expense) is noted. Expenses do not have to be paid in cash at the time they are incurred. When payment is made at a later date, the liability Accounts Payable will be decreased and the asset Cash will also be decreased [see Transaction (8)].

Transaction (6):   Services Rendered for Cash and Credit.   Softbyte provides $3,500 of programming services for customers. Cash of $1,500 is received from customers, and the balance of $2,000 is billed to customers on account. This transaction results in an equal increase in assets and owner's equity. Three specific items are affected: Cash is increased by $1,500, Accounts Receivable is increased by $2,000, and M. Doucet, Capital, is increased by $3,500. The new balances are as follows:

			Assets					=	Liabilities	+	Owner's Equity	
			Accounts						Accounts		M. Doucet,	
Balance	Cash	+	Receivable	+	Supplies	+	Equipment	=	Payable	+	Capital	
Old	$ 9,200						$7,000		$1,850		$15,950	
(6)	+ 1,500		+$2,000								+ 3,500	Service Revenue
New	$10,700	+	$2,000	+	$1,600	+	$7,000	=	$1,850	+	$19,450	
				$21,300						$21,300		

Why increase owner's equity by $3,500 when only $1,500 has been collected? The reason is that the assets resulting from the earning of revenues do not have to be in the form of cash. Owner's equity is increased when revenues are earned. In Softbyte's case, revenues are earned when the service is provided. When collections on account are received at a later date, Cash will be increased and Accounts Receivable will be decreased [see Transaction (9)].

Transaction (7): Payment of Expenses. Expenses paid in cash for September are store rent, $600, salaries of employees, $900, and utilities, $200. These payments result in an equal decrease in assets and owner's equity. Cash is decreased by $1,700 in total ($600 + $900 + $200) and M. Doucet, Capital, is decreased by the same amount (because the rent, salaries, and utilities are all expenses). The effect of these payments on the equation is:

			Assets					=	Liabilities	+	Owner's Equity	
			Accounts						Accounts		M. Doucet,	
Balance	Cash	+	Receivable	+	Supplies	+	Equipment	=	Payable	+	Capital	
Old	$10,700		$2,000		$1,600		$7,000		$1,850		$19,450	
(7)	− 600										− 600	Rent Expense
	− 900										− 900	Salaries Expense
	− 200										− 200	Utilities Expense
New	$9,000	+	$2,000	+	$1,600	+	$7,000	=	$1,850	+	$17,750	

The two sides of the equation now balance at $19,600. Three lines are required in the analysis to indicate the different types of expenses that have been paid.

Transaction (8): Payment of Accounts Payable. Softbyte pays its $250 *National Post* advertising bill in cash. Remember that the bill was previously recorded in Transaction (5) as an increase in Accounts Payable and a decrease in owner's equity. This payment on account decreases the asset Cash by $250 and also decreases the liability Accounts Payable. The effect of this transaction on the equation is:

			Assets					=	Liabilities	+	Owner's Equity
			Accounts						Accounts		M. Doucet,
Balance	Cash	+	Receivable	+	Supplies	+	Equipment	=	Payable	+	Capital
Old	$9,000		$2,000		$1,600		$7,000		$1,850		$17,750
(8)	− 250								− 250		
New	$8,750	+	$2,000	+	$1,600	+	$7,000	=	$1,600	+	$17,750
				$19,350						$19,350	

Observe that **the payment of a liability related to an expense that has previously been recorded does not affect owner's equity**. This expense was recorded in Transaction (5) and should not be recorded again.

Transaction (9):   Receipt of Cash on Account.   The sum of $600 in cash is received from a few of the customers who have previously been billed for services in Transaction (6). This transaction does not change total assets, but it does change the composition of those assets. Cash is increased by $600, and Accounts Receivable is decreased by $600. The new balances are:

Balance				Assets					=	Liabilities	+	Owner's Equity
	Cash	+	Accounts Receivable	+	Supplies	+	Equipment	=		Accounts Payable	+	M. Doucet, Capital
Old	$8,750	+	$2,000	+	$1,600	+	$7,000	=		$1,600	+	$17,750
(9)	+ 600		− 600									
New	$9,350	+	$1,400	+	$1,600	+	$7,000	=		$1,600	+	$17,750
				$19,350						$19,350		

Note that **a collection on account for services previously billed and recorded does not affect owner's equity.** Revenue was already recorded in Transaction (6) and must not be recorded again.

Transaction (10):   Withdrawal of Cash by Owner.   Marc Doucet withdraws $1,300 in cash from the business for his personal use. This transaction results in an equal decrease in assets and owner's equity. Both Cash and M. Doucet, Capital, are decreased by $1,300, as shown below:

Balance				Assets					=	Liabilities	+	Owner's Equity	
	Cash	+	Accounts Receivable	+	Supplies	+	Equipment	=		Accounts Payable	+	M. Doucet, Capital	
Old	$9,350	+	$1,400	+	$1,600	+	$7,000	=		$1,600	+	$17,750	
(10)	−1,300											− 1,300	Drawings
New	$8,050	+	$1,400	+	$1,600	+	$7,000	=		$1,600	+	$16,450	

Observe that the effect of a cash withdrawal by the owner is the opposite of the effect of an investment by the owner. Also note, **owner's drawings are not expenses.** Expenses are incurred for the purpose of earning revenue. Drawings do not generate revenue. They are a *disinvestment*. Like owner's investments, drawings are excluded in determining net income.

Summary of Transactions

The transactions of Softbyte are summarized in Illustration 1-9 to show their cumulative effect on the basic accounting equation. The transaction number, the specific effects of the transaction, and the balances after each transaction are indicated.

	Cash	+	Accounts Receivable	+	Supplies	+	Equipment	=	Accounts Payable	+	M. Doucet, Capital	
(1)	+ $15,000										+ $15,000	Investment
(2)	− 7,000						+ $7,000					
	8,000					+	7,000	=			$15,000	
(3)					+ $1,600				+ $1,600			
	8,000			+	1,600	+	7,000	=	1,600	+	15,000	
(4)	+ 1,200										+ 1,200	Service Revenue
	9,200			+	1,600	+	7,000	=	1,600	+	16,200	
(5)									+ 250		− 250	Advertising Expense
	9,200			+	1,600	+	7,000	=	1,850	+	15,950	
(6)	+ 1,500		+ $2,000								+ 3,500	Service Revenue
	10,700	+	2,000	+	1,600	+	7,000	=	1,850	+	19,450	
(7)	− 600										− 600	Rent Expense
	− 900										− 900	Salaries Expense
	− 200										− 200	Utilities Expense
	9,000	+	2,000	+	1,600	+	7,000	=	1,850	+	17,750	
(8)	− 250								− 250			
	8,750	+	2,000	+	1,600	+	7,000	=	1,600	+	17,750	
(9)	+ 600		− 600									
	9,350	+	1,400	+	1,600	+	7,000	=	1,600	+	17,750	
(10)	− 1,300										− 1,300	Drawings
	$ 8,050	+	$1,400	+	$1,600	+	$7,000	=	$1,600	+	$16,450	

Assets = Liabilities + Owner's Equity

$18,050 $18,050

Illustration 1-9

Tabular summary of Softbyte transactions

The illustration demonstrates some significant facts:
1. Each transaction must be analysed in terms of its effect on:
   (a) the three components (assets, liabilities, and owner's equity) of the basic accounting equation, and
   (b) specific items within each component.
2. The two sides of the equation must always be equal.
3. The causes of each change in the owner's capital account must be indicated in the owner's equity column.

There! You made it through transaction analysis. If you feel a bit shaky on any of the transactions, it might be a good idea to get up, take a short break, and come back again for a 10- to 15-minute review of the transactions. Make sure you understand them before moving on to the next section.

Before You Go On . . .

▶Review It

1. Give an example of an external transaction. Give an example of an internal transaction.
2. If an asset increases, what are the three possible effects on the basic accounting equation? What are the possible effects if a liability increases?

▶Do It

A tabular analysis of the transactions made by Virmari & Co., a public accounting firm, for the month of August is shown on the following page. Describe each transaction that occurred for the month.

	Assets		=	Liabilities	+	Owner's Equity		
	Cash	+	Office Equipment	=	Accounts Payable	+	A. Virmari Capital	
1.	+ $25,000						+ $25,000	Investment
2.			+ 7,000		+ 7,000			
3.	+ 8,000						+ 8,000	Service Revenue
4.	− 850						− 850	Rent Expense

Action Plan

- Analyse the tabular analysis to determine each transaction.
- Keep the accounting equation in balance.

Solution

1. The owner invested $25,000 of cash in the business
2. The company purchased $7,000 of office equipment on credit.
3. The company received $8,000 of cash in exchange for services performed.
4. The company paid $850 for this month's rent.

Related exercise material: BE1–6, BE1–7, BE1–8, E1–5 and E1–6.

Financial Statements

STUDY OBJECTIVE

⬤⬤⬤⬤⬤⬤⬤⬤⬤⬤⬤⬤ 8 ⬤⬤⬤⬤⬤⬤⬤⬤⬤⬤⬤⬤

Understand what the four financial statements are and how they are prepared.

After transactions are identified, recorded, and summarized, four financial statements are prepared from the summarized accounting data:

1. An income statement presents the revenues and expenses and resulting net income or net loss for a specific period of time.
2. A statement of owner's equity summarizes the changes in owner's equity for a specific period of time.
3. A balance sheet reports the assets, liabilities, and owner's equity at a specific date.
4. A cash flow statement summarizes information about the cash inflows (receipts) and outflows (payments) for a specific period of time.

Helpful hint   The income statement, statement of owner's equity, and cash flow statement are all for a *period* of time. The balance sheet is at a *point* in time.

Each statement provides management, owners, and other interested parties with relevant financial data.

The financial statements of Softbyte and their interrelationships are shown in Illustration 1-10. The statements are interrelated: **(1) Net income of $2,750 shown on the income statement is added to the beginning balance of owner's capital in the statement of owner's equity. (2) Owner's capital of $16,450 at the end of the reporting period shown in the statement of owner's equity is reported on the balance sheet. (3) Cash of $8,050 on the balance sheet is reported on the cash flow statement.**

The essential features of Softbyte's four financial statements are briefly described in the following sections.

Income Statement

Alternative terminology
The income statement is sometimes called the *statement of earnings* or *statement of operations*.

Softbyte's income statement reports the revenues and expenses for a specific period of time. The income statement is prepared from the data appearing in the owner's equity column of Illustration 1-9. The heading of the statement identifies the company, the type of statement, and the time period covered by the statement. The primary focus of the income statement is reporting the profitability of the company's operations over a specified period of time (a month, a quarter, a year). To indicate that it applies for a period of time, the income statement is dated **For the Month Ended September 30, 2002.**

On the income statement, revenues are listed first, followed by expenses. Finally, net income (or net loss) is determined. Note that investment and withdrawal transactions between the owner and the business are not included in the measurement of net income. For example, the cash withdrawal by Marc Doucet from Softbyte is not there.

They are not included because they are not business expenses, as explained earlier.

Illustration 1-10

Financial statements and their interrelationships

SOFTBYTE
Income Statement
For the Month Ended September 30, 2002

Revenues		
Service revenue		$4,700
Expenses		
Salaries expense	$900	
Rent expense	600	
Advertising expense	250	
Utilities expense	200	
Total expenses		1,950
Net income		$2,750

SOFTBYTE
Statement of Owner's Equity
For the Month Ended September 30, 2002

M. Doucet, Capital, September 1		$ 0
Add: Investments	$15,000	
Net income	2,750	17,750
		17,750
Less: Drawings		1,300
M. Doucet, Capital, September 30		$16,450

SOFTBYTE
Balance Sheet
September 30, 2002

Assets		
Cash		$ 8,050
Accounts receivable		1,400
Supplies		1,600
Equipment		7,000
Total assets		$18,050

Liabilities and Owner's Equity		
Liabilities		
Accounts payable		$ 1,600
Owner's equity		
M. Doucet, Capital		16,450
Total liabilities and owner's equity		$18,050

SOFTBYTE
Cash Flow Statement
For the Month Ended September 30, 2002

Cash flows from operating activities		
Cash receipts from customers	$ 3,300	
Cash payments to suppliers and employees	(1,950)	
Net cash provided by operating activities		$ 1,350
Cash flows from investing activities		
Purchase of equipment	$ (7,000)	
Net cash used by investing activities		(7,000)
Cash flows from financing activities		
Investments by owner	$15,000	
Drawings by owner	(1,300)	
Net cash provided by financing activities		13,700
Net increase in cash		8,050
Cash, September 1		0
Cash, September 30		$ 8,050

Statement of Owner's Equity

Softbyte's statement of owner's equity reports the changes in owner's equity for a specific period of time. Data for the preparation of the statement of owner's equity are obtained from the owner's equity column of the tabular summary (Illustration 1-9) and from the income statement. The heading of this statement identifies the company, the type of statement, and the time period covered by the statement. The time period is the same as that covered by the income statement. It is therefore dated **For the Month Ended September 30, 2002.** The beginning owner's equity amount is shown on the first line of the statement. Then the owner's investments, net income, and the owner's drawings are identified. The information in this statement indicates the reasons why owner's equity has increased or decreased during the period.

What if Softbyte reported a net loss in its first month? The loss would reduce owner's capital. There would be no addition of net income, and the loss would be reported as a deduction, along with drawings.

Balance Sheet

Alternative terminology
The balance sheet is sometimes called the *statement of financial position.*

Softbyte's balance sheet reports the assets, liabilities, and owner's equity at a specific date. The balance sheet is prepared from the column headings and the month-end data shown in the last line of the tabular summary (Illustration 1-9). The heading of a balance sheet must identify the company, the statement, and the date. The balance sheet is like a snapshot of the company's financial condition at a specific moment in time (usually the end of a quarter or year). To indicate that the balance sheet is at a specific point in time, it is dated **September 30, 2002.** Sometimes, the words "as at" precede the balance sheet date. Observe that the assets are listed at the top, followed by liabilities and owner's equity. Total assets must equal total liabilities and owner's equity. In the Softbyte balance sheet, only one liability, accounts payable, is reported. In most cases, there will be more than one liability.

Cash Flow Statement

Alternative terminology
The cash flow statement is sometimes called the *statement of changes in financial position.*

Softbyte's cash flow statement provides information about the cash receipts and cash payments for a specific period of time. To aid investors, creditors, and others in their analysis of cash, the cash flow statement reports the following: (1) the cash effects of a company's operations during a period, (2) the cash inflows and outflows from investing transactions (e.g., purchase and sale of capital assets), (3) the cash inflows and outflows from financing transactions (e.g., borrowing and repayment of debt), (4) the net increase or decrease in cash during the period, and (5) the cash amount at the end of the period.

Reporting the sources, uses, and change in cash is useful because investors, creditors, and others want to know what is happening to a company's most liquid resource, its money. The cash flow statement provides answers to the following simple but important questions:

1. Where did the cash come from during the period?
2. What was the cash used for during the period?
3. What was the change in the cash balance during the period?

Softbyte's cash flow statement, provided in Illustration 1-10, covers the same period of time as the income statement. As shown in the statement, cash increased by $8,050 during the year. Net cash flow from operating activities increased cash by $1,350. Cash flow from investing activities decreased cash by $7,000. Cash flow from financing activities increased cash $13,700. At this time, you do not need to know how these amounts are determined. Chapter 18 will examine the cash flow statement in detail.

Using the Information in the Financial Statements

Illustration 1-10 introduced the financial statements for Softbyte. Every set of financial statements is accompanied by explanatory notes and supporting schedules that are an integral part of the statements. Public corporations issue their financial statements and supplementary materials within an annual report. The **annual report** is a document that includes useful non-financial information about the company, as well as financial information.

Non-financial information may include a management discussion of the company's mission, goals and objectives, market position, and people involved in the company. Financial information may include a review of current operations and a summary of historical key financial figures and ratios, in addition to comparative financial statements. Public company financial statements are usually audited and have the auditors' report attached to them. A statement of management responsibility for the statements is also attached.

A vital element in communicating economic events is the accountant's ability and responsibility to **analyse** and **interpret** the reported information. Analysis involves the use of ratios, percentages, graphs, and charts to highlight significant financial trends and relationships. Interpretation involves **explaining the uses, meaning, and limitations of reported data**.

Included in Appendix A at the end of this textbook is the annual report from The Second Cup Ltd. Briefly examine Appendix A to see what kind of information Second Cup includes in its annual report. Then look more specifically at Second Cup's financial statements. Carefully examine the format and content of each financial statement outlined earlier in Illustration 1-10. What similarities can you find between the financial statements in Illustration 1-10 and the more complicated financial statements for The Second Cup Ltd.? We will continue to refer to The Second Cup's financial statements to illustrate selected topics. By the end of this course, you'll be surprised at how much you understand about these and other financial statements.

► **International note**

The average annual report runs about 44 pages. Foreign reports tend to run a bit longer. An Italian bank once produced an annual report that ran a record 302 pages!

►Accounting in Action ► *@-Business Insight*

 A research study by the CICA examines the impact of technology on financial reporting and the issues the accounting profession needs to consider as a result. "Technology is challenging the very nature of financial reporting in two significant ways," says the author of the study, Gerry Trites. "The increasing use of the Internet, as well as its multimedia capability and capacity for interactive communication, is challenging the boundaries, framework and even the fundamental role of financial reporting in society. Technology in general is changing the way financial information is communicated to investors, creditors, and other interested parties."

For example, the thought of putting a company's annual financial statements on the Web would have been viewed as frivolous and ineffective just a few years ago. Today, most companies are doing that and more. They are going beyond financial statements and offering many other types of financial and non-financial information pertinent to understanding the financial affairs of a business.

Source: Gerald Trites, *The Impact of Technology on Financial and Business Reporting,* CICA Research Report, 1999.

For **Review It** questions
marked with this "Second
Cup" icon, you need to use
The Second Cup's
Annual Report.

Before You Go On . . .

▸*Review It*

1. What are the income statement, statement of owner's equity, balance sheet, and cash flow statement?
2. Explain how The Second Cup's financial statements are interrelated: identify specific accounts and amounts. The answer to this question is provided at the end of the chapter.
3. What information is normally found in an annual report?

Related exercise material: BE1–9, BE1–10, BE1–11, BE1–12, E1–7, E1–8, E1–9, E1–10, E1–11, E1–12, E1–13, E1–14, E1–15, and E1–16.

▸*A Look Back at Our Feature Story*

A Look Back exercises refer
to the chapter opening story.
These exercises help you
analyse the story's real-world
situation in terms of the
accounting topic of the
chapter.

Refer to the opening story about The Second Cup Ltd., and answer the following questions:
1. If you were interested in investing in The Second Cup Ltd., what would the balance sheet and income statement tell you?
2. Would you request audited financial statements? Explain.
3. Will the financial statements show the market value of the company? Explain.

Solution

1. The balance sheet reports the assets, liabilities, and owner's equity of the company. The balance sheet is like a snapshot of the company's financial condition at a point in time. The income statement presents the revenues and expenses and resulting net income (or net loss) for a specific period of time. The income statement should give you a good indication of the profitability of the company.
2. You should request audited financial statements—statements that a public accountant has examined and for which he or she has expressed an opinion about whether or not the presentation is fair and in accordance with generally accepted accounting principles. You should not make decisions without having audited financial statements.
3. The financial statements will not show the market value of the company. One important principle of accounting is the cost principle, which states that assets should be recorded at cost instead of market value. Cost has an important advantage over other valuations. It is reliable.

DEMONSTRATION PROBLEM

**Additional
Demonstration Problem**

The **Demonstration
Problem** is a final review
before you work on the
assignment material. The
problem-solving strategies in
the margins give you tips about
how to approach the problem.
The solutions show both the
form and the content of
complete answers.

Raman Balakrishnan opens his own law office on July 1, 2003. During the first month of operations, the following transactions occur:
1. Invests $10,000 in cash in the law practice.
2. Pays $800 for July rent on office space.
3. Purchases office equipment on account, $3,000.
4. Provides legal services to clients for cash, $1,500.
5. Borrows $700 cash from a bank on a note payable.
6. Provides legal services to client on account, $2,000.
7. Pays monthly expenses: salaries, $500; utilities, $300; and telephone, $100.

Instructions

(a) Prepare a tabular summary of the transactions.
(b) Prepare the income statement, statement of owner's equity, and balance sheet at July 31 for Raman Balakrishnan, Barrister & Solicitor.

Solution to Demonstration Problem

(a)

Trans-action	Cash	+	Accounts Receivable	+	Equipment	=	Note Payable	+	Accounts Payable	+	Balakrishnan, Capital	
(1)	+ $10,000					=					+ $10,000	Investment
(2)	− 800					=					− 800	Rent Expense
	9,200					=					9,200	
(3)					+ $3,000	=			+ $3,000			
	9,200	+			3,000	=			3,000	+	9,200	
(4)	+ 1,500										+ 1,500	Fees Earned
	10,700	+			3,000	=			3,000	+	10,700	
(5)	+ 700						+$700					
	11,400	+			3,000	=	700	+	3,000	+	10,700	
(6)			+ $2,000								+ 2,000	Fees Earned
	11,400	+	2,000	+	3,000	=	700	+	3,000	+	12,700	
	− 500										− 500	Salaries Expense
	− 300										− 300	Utilities Expense
	− 100										− 100	Telephone Expense
	$10,500	+	$2,000	+	$3,000	=	$700	+	$3,000	+	$11,800	

Assets = Liabilities + Owner's Equity

$15,500 $15,500

(b)

RAMAN BALAKRISHNAN
Barrister & Solicitor
Income Statement
For the Month Ended July 31, 2003

Revenues		
Fees earned		$3,500
Expenses		
Rent expense	$800	
Salaries expense	500	
Utilities expense	300	
Telephone expense	100	
Total expenses		1,700
Net income		$1,800

RAMAN BALAKRISHNAN
Barrister & Solicitor
Statement of Owner's Equity
For the Month Ended July 31, 2003

Raman Balakrishnan, Capital, July 1		$ 0
Add: Investments	$10,000	
Net income	1,800	11,800
Raman Balakrishnan, Capital, July 31		$11,800

Action Plan

- Assets must equal liabilities plus owner's equity after each transaction.
- Investments and revenues increase owner's equity.
- Withdrawals and expenses decrease owner's equity.
- The income statement shows revenues and expenses for a period of time.
- The statement of owner's equity shows the changes in owner's equity for the same period of time as the income statement.
- The balance sheet reports assets, liabilities, and owner's equity at a specific date.

RAMAN BALAKRISHNAN
Barrister & Solicitor
Balance Sheet
July 31, 2003

Assets

Cash	$10,500
Accounts receivable	2,000
Equipment	3,000
Total assets	$15,500

Liabilities and Owner's Equity

Liabilities	
Note payable	$ 700
Accounts payable	3,000
Total liabilities	3,700
Owner's equity	
Raman Balakrishnan, Capital	11,800
Total liabilities and owner's equity	$15,500

◣ Summary of Study Objectives

1. Explain what accounting is. Accounting identifies, records, and communicates the economic events of an organization to interested users.

2. Identify the users and explain the uses of accounting. The major users and uses of accounting are as follows: (a) Management uses accounting information to plan, control, and evaluate business operations. (b) Investors (owners) decide whether to buy, hold, or sell their financial interests on the basis of accounting data. (c) Creditors (suppliers and bankers) evaluate the risks of granting credit or lending money on the basis of accounting information. Other groups that use accounting information are taxing authorities, regulatory agencies, customers, labour unions, and economic planners.

3. Understand why ethics is a fundamental business concept. Ethics are the standards of conduct by which one's actions are judged as right or wrong. If you cannot depend on the honesty of the individuals you deal with, effective communication and economic activity will be impossible and information will have no credibility.

4. Explain the meaning of generally accepted accounting principles and the cost principle. Generally accepted accounting principles are a common set of standards used to prepare and report accounting information. The cost principle states that assets should be recorded at their historical (original) cost.

5. Explain the meaning of the going concern, monetary unit, and economic entity assumptions. The going concern assumption presumes that a business will continue operations for enough time to use its assets for their intended purpose and to fulfill its commitments. The

monetary unit assumption requires that only transaction data that can be expressed in terms of money be included in the accounting records. The economic entity assumption requires that the activities of each economic entity be kept separate from the activities of its owner and other economic entities.

6. State and utilize the basic accounting equation and explain the meaning of assets, liabilities, and owner's equity. The basic accounting equation is:

Assets = Liabilities + Owner's Equity

Assets are resources owned by a business. Liabilities are creditorship claims on total assets. Owner's equity is the ownership claim on total assets.

7. Calculate the effect of business transactions on the basic accounting equation. Each business transaction must have a dual effect on the accounting equation. For example, if an individual asset is increased, there must be a corresponding (1) decrease in another asset, (2) increase in a liability, and/or (3) increase in owner's equity.

8. Understand what the four financial statements are and how they are prepared. An income statement presents the revenues and expenses of a company for a specific period of time. A statement of owner's equity summarizes the changes in owner's equity that have occurred for a specific period of time. A balance sheet reports the assets, liabilities, and owner's equity of a business at a specific date. A cash flow statement summarizes information about the cash inflows (receipts) and outflows (payments) for a specific period of time.

GLOSSARY

Accounting The process of identifying, recording, and communicating the economic events of an organization to interested users of the information. (p. 2)

Accounting equation Assets = Liabilities + Owner's Equity. (p. 14)

Annual report Information provided annually by a company to its shareholders and other interested parties concerning its operations and financial position. It includes the financial statements and auditors' report, in addition to information and reports by management. (p. 27)

Assets Resources owned by a business. (p. 14)

Assumptions Basic assumptions (going concern, monetary unit, economic entity, and time period) underlie the financial accounting structure. (p. 11)

Auditing The examination of financial statements by a qualified professional accountant in order to express an opinion as to whether or not they are presented fairly in accordance with generally accepted accounting principles. (p. 7)

Balance sheet A financial statement that reports the assets, liabilities, and owner's equity at a specific date. (p. 24)

Bookkeeping A part of accounting that involves only the recording of economic events. (p. 6)

Business advisory services An area of public accounting that involves assisting management in a wide variety of financial planning, information, and control initiatives. (p. 8)

Cash flow statement A financial statement that provides information about the cash inflows (receipts) and cash outflows (payments) of an entity for a specific period of time. (p. 24)

Corporation A business organized as a separate legal entity under corporation law, with ownership divided into transferable shares. (p. 13)

Cost principle An accounting principle which states that assets should be recorded at their original historical cost. (p. 11)

Drawings Withdrawal of cash or other assets from an unincorporated business for the personal use of the owner. (p. 15)

Economic entity assumption An assumption that economic events can be identified with a particular unit of accountability. (p. 12)

Economic events Activities related to the production and distribution of goods and services in an organization. (p. 2)

Ethics The standards of conduct by which one's actions are judged as right or wrong, honest or dishonest, fair or unfair. (p. 9)

Expenses The cost of assets consumed or services used in the process of earning revenue. (p. 15)

Financial accounting A field of accounting that provides information for external users such as investors and creditors. (p. 6)

Generally accepted accounting principles (GAAP) An accepted set of standards that indicate how to report economic events. (p. 10)

Going concern assumption An assumption which states that the entity will continue operations for enough time to use its assets for their intended purpose and to fulfill its obligations. (p. 12)

Income statement A financial statement that presents the revenues and expenses and resulting net income (or net loss) for a company for a specific period of time. (p. 24)

Investments by owner The assets put into the business by the owner. (p. 15)

Liabilities Creditorship claims on total assets. (p. 15)

Managerial accounting A field of accounting that provides information for managers and other internal users. (p. 6)

Monetary unit assumption An assumption which states that only transaction data that can be expressed in terms of money may be included in the accounting records. (p. 12)

Net income The amount by which revenues exceed expenses. (p. 16)

Net loss The amount by which expenses exceed revenues. (p. 16)

Owner's equity The ownership claim on total assets. (p. 15)

Partnership An association of two or more persons to carry on as co-owners of a business for profit. (p. 13)

Private corporation A limited company whose shares are not listed on a stock exchange and are not available to a public investor. (p. 14)

Proprietorship A small business owned by one person. (p. 13)

Public corporation A limited company whose shares are publicly traded and available for purchase by the general public. (p. 14)

Revenues The increase in owner's equity that results from business activities performed to earn income. (p. 15)

Statement of owner's equity A financial statement that summarizes the changes in owner's equity for a specific period of time. (p. 24)

Taxation An area of public accounting that involves tax advice, tax planning, and preparing tax returns. (p. 8)

Transactions The economic events of the enterprise recorded by accountants. (p. 17)

SELF-STUDY QUESTIONS

Chapter 1 Self-Test

Answers are at the end of the chapter.

(SO 1) C   1. The accounting process does *not* include:
    a. identification.
    b. verification.
    c. recording.
    d. communication.

(SO 2) C   2. One of the following statements about users of accounting information is incorrect. The incorrect statement is:
    a. Management is an internal user.
    b. Taxing authorities are external users.
    c. Creditors are external users.
    d. Regulatory authorities are internal users.

(SO 2) K   3. The public accountant generally provides the following services:
    a. auditing, taxation, and business advisory services.
    b. auditing, budgeting, and business advisory services.
    c. auditing, budgeting, and cost accounting.
    d. internal auditing, budgeting, and business advisory services.

(SO 3) K   4. Ethics are the standards of conduct by which one's actions are judged to be:
    a. decent or indecent.
    b. successful or unsuccessful.
    c. profitable or unprofitable.
    d. right or wrong.

·(SO 4) K   5. Generally accepted accounting principles:
    a. are unwritten, but generally understood by accountants.
    b. may be found in the regulations which form part of the *Income Tax Act*.
    c. are similar to the basic laws of nature, and thus do not change.
    d. constitute accepted accounting theory and practice.

(SO 3) K   6. The cost principle states that:
    a. assets should be recorded at cost and adjusted when their market value changes.
    b. activities of an entity should be kept separate and distinct from those of its owner.
    c. assets should be recorded at their original cost.
    d. only transaction data capable of being expressed in terms of money should be included in the accounting records.

THE NAVIGATOR

7. Which of the following statements about basic (SO 5) C   assumptions is incorrect?
    a. Basic assumptions are the same as accounting principles.
    b. The economic entity assumption states that there should be a particular unit of accountability.
    c. The monetary unit assumption enables accounting to measure economic events.
    d. An important part of the monetary unit assumption is the stable monetary unit assumption.

8. As at December 31, Stoneland Company has assets of (SO 6) AP $3,500 and owner's equity of $2,000. What are the liabilities for Stoneland Company as at December 31?
    a. $1,000.
    b. $1,500.
    c. $2,000.
    d. $2,500.

9. Net income will result during a time period when: (SO 6) C
    a. assets exceed liabilities.
    b. assets exceed revenues.
    c. expenses exceed revenues.
    d. revenues exceed expenses.

10. The effects on the basic accounting equation of per- (SO 7) C   forming services on account are:
    a. increased assets and decreased owner's equity.
    b. increased assets and increased owner's equity.
    c. increased assets and increased liabilities.
    d. increased liabilities and increased owner's equity.

11. Genesis Company buys a $10,000 machine on credit. (SO 7) C   This transaction will affect the:
    a. income statement only.
    b. balance sheet only.
    c. income statement and statement of owner's equity only.
    d. income statement, statement of owner's equity, and balance sheet.

12. The financial statement that reports assets, liabilities, (SO 8) K   and owner's equity is the:
    a. income statement.
    b. statement of owner's equity.
    c. balance sheet.
    d. cash flow statement.

QUESTIONS

(SO 1) C   1. "Accounting is ingrained in our society and it is vital to our economic system." Do you agree? Explain.

(SO 1) C   2. Identify and describe the steps in the accounting process.

(SO 2) C   3. (a) Who are internal users of accounting data?
(b) How does accounting provide relevant data for these users?

(SO 2) C   4. What uses of financial accounting information are made by the following external users: (a) investors and (b) creditors?

(SO 2) C   5. "Bookkeeping and accounting are the same." Do you agree? Explain.

(SO 3) AN   6. Why are ethics important to the accounting profession?

(SO 4) AP   7. Ouellette Travel Agency purchased land for $75,000 cash on December 10, 2002. At December 31, 2002, the land's value had increased to $95,000. What amount should be reported for land on Ouellette's balance sheet at December 31, 2002? Would your answer differ if the land value declined to $65,000? Explain.

(SO 5) C   8. What is the monetary unit assumption? What impact does inflation (rising prices) have on the monetary unit assumption?

(SO 5) K   9. What is the economic entity assumption?

(SO 5) C   10. What are the three basic forms of business organization for profit-oriented enterprises?

(SO 5) AP   11. Martha Ross is the owner of a successful printing shop. Recently, her business has been increasing, and Martha has been thinking about changing the organization of her business from a proprietorship to a corporation. Identify the differences in accounting for equity if Martha were to incorporate her business.

(SO 6) K   12. What is the basic accounting equation?

(SO 6) C   13. (a) Define assets, liabilities, and owner's equity.
(b) What items affect owner's equity?

(SO 6) K   14. Which of the following items are liabilities of Gilt Jewellery Store?
(a) Cash
(b) Accounts payable
(c) Drawings
(d) Accounts receivable
(e) Supplies
(f) Equipment
(g) Salaries payable
(h) Service revenue
(i) Rent expense

(SO 6) AP   15. Can a business enter into a transaction in which only the left side of the basic accounting equation is affected? If yes, give an example.

(SO 7) AP   16. Are the following events recorded in the accounting records? Explain your answer in each case.
(a) The owner of the company dies.
(b) Supplies are purchased on account.
(c) An employee is terminated.
(d) The owner of the business withdraws cash from the business for personal use.

(SO 7) AP   17. Indicate how the following business transactions affect the basic accounting equation:
(a) Paid cash for janitorial services.
(b) Purchased equipment for cash.
(c) Invested cash in the business.
(d) Paid an account payable in full.

(SO 7) AN   18. In February 2003, Paul Dumas invested an additional $10,000 in his business, Dumas's Pharmacy, which is organized as a proprietorship. Dumas's accountant, Donna Wortham, recorded this receipt as an increase in cash and revenues. Is this treatment appropriate? Why or why not?

(SO 8) AP   19. A company's net income appears directly on the income statement and the statement of owner's equity. It is also included indirectly in the company's balance sheet. Do you agree? Explain.

(SO 8) C   20. Below are some items found in the financial statements of Kaustev Sen, M.D. Indicate in which financial statement(s) the items would appear.
(a) Service revenue
(b) Equipment
(c) Advertising expense
(d) Accounts receivable
(e) Kaustev Sen, Capital (ending balance)
(f) Wages payable

(SO 8) AP   21. Schwinghamer Enterprises had a capital balance of $168,000 at the beginning of the period. At the end of the accounting period, the capital balance was $198,000.
(a) If there were no additional investments or withdrawals during the period, what is the net income for the period?
(b) Assuming an additional investment of $18,000 but no withdrawals during the period, what is the net income for the period?

(SO 8) AP   22. Summarized operations for the King Co. for the month of July are as follows:
Revenues earned: for cash, $35,000;
on account, $70,000.
Expenses incurred: for cash, $26,000;
on account, $40,000.
Indicate the following for King Co.: (a) total revenues, (b) total expenses and (c) net income for the month of July.

(SO 8) C   23. What kind of information is presented in the notes to the financial statements? In the annual report?

BRIEF EXERCISES

....

Identify users of accounting information.
(SO 2) K

BE1–1   Match each of the following five decisions with the most appropriate decision-maker listed in (a) to (e):
1. Determine whether the company complied with income tax regulations.
2. Determine whether the company can pay its obligations.
3. Determine whether a marketing proposal will be cost-effective.
4. Determine whether the company's net income will result in an increase in drawings.
5. Determine how the company should finance its operations.

_____ (a) Owner

_____ (b) Marketing managers

_____ (c) Creditors

_____ (d) Chief Financial Officer

_____ (e) Canada Customs and Revenue Agency

Describe forms of business organization.
(SO 5) AP

BE1–2   Match each of the following forms of business organization with a set of characteristics: proprietorship (P), partnership (PP), corporation (C).

_____ (a) Simple to set up; founder retains control

_____ (b) Shared control; increased skills and resources

_____ (c) Easier to transfer ownership and raise funds; no personal liability

Solve basic accounting equation.
(SO 6) AP

•BE1–3   Presented below is the basic accounting equation. Determine the missing amounts:

	Assets	=	Liabilities	+	Owner's Equity
(a)	$80,000		$50,000		?
(b)	?		$45,000		$70,000
(c)	$94,000		?		$62,000

Solve basic accounting equation.
(SO 6) AP

• BE1–4   Use the accounting equation to answer each of the following questions:
(a) The liabilities of Logan Company are $90,000 and the owner's equity is $240,000. What is the amount of Logan Company's total assets?
(b) The total assets of Pereira Company are $170,000 and its owner's equity is $80,000. What is the amount of its total liabilities?
(b) The total assets of Yap Co. are $600,000 and its liabilities are equal to two-thirds of its total assets. What is the amount of Yap Co.'s owner's equity?

Solve basic accounting equation.
(SO 6) AP

•BE1–5   At the beginning of the year, Lam Company had total assets of $700,000 and total liabilities of $500,000. Answer the following questions:
(a) If total assets increased by $150,000 during the year and total liabilities decreased by $80,000, what is the amount of owner's equity at the end of the year?
(b) During the year, total liabilities increased by $100,000 and owner's equity decreased by $70,000. What is the amount of total assets at the end of the year?
(c) If total assets decreased by $90,000 and owner's equity increased by $120,000 during the year, what is the amount of total liabilities at the end of the year?

Determine effect of transactions on basic accounting equation.
(SO 7) AP

• BE1–6   Presented below are six business transactions. List the letters (a) through (f), with columns for assets, liabilities, and owner's equity. For each column, indicate whether the transactions increased (+), decreased (–), or had no effect (NE) on assets, liabilities, and owner's equity:
(a) Purchased supplies on account.
(b) Received cash for providing a service.
(c) Paid expenses in cash.
(d) Invested cash in the business.
(e) Cash withdrawn by owner.
(f) Received cash from a customer who had been billed previously for services provided.

Determine effect of transactions on owner's equity.
(SO 7) AP

BE1–7   Three transactions are presented below. Mark each transaction as affecting owner's investment (I), owner's drawings (D), revenue (R), expense (E), or not affecting owner's equity (NA):

_____ (a) Received cash for services performed.

_____ (b) Paid cash to purchase equipment.

_____ (c) Paid employee salaries.

BE1–8 Classify each of the following items as owner's drawings (D), revenue (R), or expense (E)

_____ (a) Costs incurred for advertising

_____ (b) Commission earnings

_____ (c) Insurance paid

_____ (d) Amounts paid to employees

_____ (e) Services performed

_____ (f) Rent received

_____ (g) Utilities incurred

_____ (h) Cash distributed to owner

Determine effect of transactions on owner's equity.
(SO 7) AP

BE1–9 Balance sheet items for Yung Company at December 31, 2002, are in alphabetical order below. Prepare a balance sheet.

Accounts payable	$80,000
Accounts receivable	71,000
Cash	40,500
Kim Yung, Capital	31,500

Prepare a balance sheet.
(SO 8) AP

BE1–10 Indicate whether each of the following items is an asset (A), liability (L), or part of owner's equity (OE).

_____ (a) Accounts receivable

_____ (b) Salaries payable

_____ (c) Equipment

_____ (d) Office supplies

_____ (e) Capital invested

_____ (f) Notes payable

_____ (g) Drawings

Identify balance sheet elements.
(SO 8) C

BE1–11 Indicate whether the following items would appear on the income statement (IS), balance sheet (BS), and/or statement of owner's equity (OE).

_____ (a) Notes payable

_____ (b) Advertising expense

_____ (c) Harrison, Capital (ending balance)

_____ (d) Cash

_____ (e) Fees earned

_____ (f) Interest receivable

_____ (g) Service revenue

_____ (h) Harrison, Drawings

Identify elements of financial statements.
(SO 8) AP

BE1–12 The **Calgary Exhibition and Stampede Limited** was established in 1886 to produce "The Greatest Outdoor Show on Earth." The Stampede has the following selected accounts included in its financial statements. In each case, identify whether the item would appear on the balance sheet (BS) or income statement (IS).

_____ (a) Accounts receivable

_____ (b) Inventories

_____ (c) Food services expense

_____ (d) Share capital

_____ (e) Building

_____ (f) Stampede revenue

_____ (g) Horse racing revenue

_____ (h) Accounts payable and accrued liabilities

_____ (i) Cash and short-term deposits

_____ (j) Administration, marketing, and park services expenses

Identify elements of financial statements.
(SO 8) AP

Exercises

....

E1–1 Presented below are the assumptions and principles discussed in this chapter:

1. Cost principle
2. Monetary unit assumption
3. Going concern assumption
4. Economic entity assumption

Identify accounting assumptions and principles.
(SO 4, 5) C

Instructions

Identify by number the accounting assumption or principle that is described below. Do not use a number more than once.

_____ (a) Is the rationale for why capital assets are not reported at liquidation value. (*Note*: Do not use the cost principle.)

_____ (b) Indicates that personal and business record-keeping should be separately maintained.

_____ (c) Assumes that the dollar is the "measuring stick" used to report on financial performance.

_____ (d) Indicates that market value changes after purchase are not recorded in the accounts.

Identify assumption or principle that has been violated.
(SO 4, 5) C

E1–2   Marietta Company had three major business transactions during 2002:
(a) Land with a cost of $208,000 is reported at its market value of $260,000.
(b) The owner of Marietta, George Winston, purchased a truck for personal use and charged it to his drawings account.
(c) Marietta wanted to make its 2002 net income look worse than it really was, so it reported its figures in inflation-adjusted dollars, rather than actual dollars.

Instructions

In each situation, identify the assumption or principle that has been violated, if any, and discuss what should have been done.

Classify items as assets, liabilities, and shareholders' equity, and prepare accounting equation.
(SO 6) AP

E1–3   The following items were taken from the balance sheet of **NIKE, Inc.** NIKE is the world's #1 shoe company, selling its products in 110 countries.

Instructions

(a) Classify each of these items as an asset (A), liability (L), or owner's (shareholders') equity (OE) item (all items are in millions of U.S. dollars).

_____	Cash	$ 108.6	_____	Inventories	$1,396.6
_____	Accounts receivable	1,674.4	_____	Income taxes payable	28.9
_____	Share capital	265.4	_____	Property, plant, and equipment	1,153.1
_____	Notes payable	480.2	_____	Retained earnings	2,996.2
_____	Other assets	1,064.7	_____	Accounts payable	584.6
_____	Other liabilities	1,042.1			

(b) Determine NIKE's accounting equation by calculating the value of total assets, total liabilities, and total shareholders' equity.

Classify accounts as assets, liabilities, and owner's equity.
(SO 6) AP

E1–4   Ace Cleaners has the following balance sheet items:

_____	(a) Accounts payable		_____	(e) Accounts receivable
_____	(b) Cash		_____	(f) Notes payable
_____	(c) Cleaning equipment		_____	(g) Salaries payable
_____	(d) Cleaning supplies		_____	(h) Ace, Capital

Instructions

Classify each item as an asset, liability, or owner's equity.

Analyse effect of transactions.
(SO 7) AP

E1–5   Selected transactions for Lush Lawn Care Company are listed below:
1. Made cash investment to start business.
2. Paid monthly rent.
3. Purchased equipment on account.
4. Billed customers for services performed.
5. Withdrew cash for owner's personal use.
6. Received cash from customers billed in transaction 4.
7. Incurred advertising expense on account.
8. Purchased additional equipment for cash.
9. Received cash from customers when service was rendered.

Instructions

List the numbers of the above transactions and describe the effect of each transaction on assets, liabilities, and owner's equity. For example, the first answer is (1) Increase in assets and increase in owner's equity.

Analyse effect of transactions on assets, liabilities, and owner's equity.
(SO 7) AN

E1–6   Wong Computer Company entered into the following transactions during May 2003:
1. Purchased computer terminals for $19,000 from Digital Equipment, on account.
2. Paid $4,000 cash for May rent of storage space.
3. Received $15,000 cash from customers for contracts billed in April.
4. Provided computer services to Brieske Construction Company for $3,000 cash.
5. Paid NB Power $11,000 cash for energy usage in May.
6. Mr. Wong invested an additional $32,000 in the business.
7. Paid Digital Equipment for the terminals purchased in transaction 1 above.
8. Incurred advertising expense for May of $1,000, on account.

Instructions

Indicate with the appropriate letter whether each of the transactions above results in:

(a) an increase in assets and a decrease in assets.
(b) an increase in assets and an increase in owner's equity.
(c) an increase in assets and an increase in liabilities.
(d) a decrease in assets and a decrease in owner's equity.
(e) a decrease in assets and a decrease in liabilities.
(f) an increase in liabilities and a decrease in owner's equity.
(g) an increase in owner's equity and a decrease in liabilities.

(*Note:* Some letters may be used more than once, or not at all.)

E1–7 Here is a list of words or phrases discussed in this chapter:

1. Accounts payable
2. Creditor
3. Balance sheet
4. Proprietorship
5. Corporation
6. Owner's capital
7. Accounts receivable
8. Audit

Match words with descriptions.
(SO 5, 6, 8) K

Instructions

Match each word or phrase with the best description below.

_____ (a) An examination of financial statements to determine whether they are presented in accordance with generally accepted accounting principles

_____ (b) A business enterprise that raises money by issuing shares

_____ (c) The portion of owner's equity that results from receiving investments from the owner

_____ (d) Obligations to suppliers of goods

_____ (e) Amounts due from customers

_____ (f) A party to whom a business owes money

_____ (g) A financial statement that reports assets, liabilities, and owner's equity at a specific date

_____ (h) A business that is owned by one individual

E1–8 The 2002 summaries of balance sheet and income statement data for the proprietorships Wyatt Company and Maxim Enterprises are presented below. Two items are missing from each summary.

Analyse financial statement items.
(SO 6, 8) AN

	Wyatt Company	Maxim Enterprises
Beginning of year:		
Total assets	$ 95,000	$125,000
Total liabilities	80,000	(c)
Total owner's equity	(a)	95,000
End of year:		
Total assets	160,000	180,000
Total liabilities	120,000	50,000
Total owner's equity	40,000	130,000
Changes during year in owner's equity:		
Investments	(b)	25,000
Drawings	24,000	(d)
Total revenues	215,000	100,000
Total expenses	175,000	85,000

Instructions

Determine the missing amounts.

E1–9 The Depeau Company had the following assets and liabilities on the dates indicated:

Determine net income (or loss).
(SO 6, 8) AP

December 31	Total Assets	Total Liabilities
2001	$400,000	$250,000
2002	460,000	320,000
2003	590,000	400,000

Depeau began business on January 1, 2001, with an investment of $100,000.

Instructions

From an analysis of the accounting equation and the change in owner's equity during the year, calculate the net income (or loss) for:

(a) 2001, assuming Depeau's drawings were $15,000 for the year.
(b) 2002, assuming Depeau made an additional investment of $50,000 and had no drawings in 2002.
(c) 2003, assuming Depeau made an additional investment of $10,000 and had drawings of $20,000 in 2003.

Analyse transactions and calculate net income.
(SO 7, 8) AP

E1–10 An analysis of the transactions made by Bourque & Co., a public accounting firm, for the month of August 2003 is shown below.

	Cash	+	Accounts Receivable	+	Supplies	+	Office Equipment	=	Accounts Payable	+	Bourque, Capital	
1.	+ $12,000										+ $12,000	Investment
2.	– 2,000						+ $5,000		+ $3,000			
3.	– 750				+ $750							
4.	+ 2,600		+ $3,400								+ 6,000	Fees Earned
5.	– 1,500								– 1,500			
6.	– 2,000										– 2,000	Drawings
7.	– 650										– 650	Rent Expense
8.	+ 450		– 450									
9.	– 2,900										– 2,900	Salaries Expense
10.									+ 500		– 500	Utilities Expense

Instructions

(a) Describe each transaction that occurred in the month.
(b) Determine how much owner's equity increased for the month.
(c) Calculate the amount of net income for the month.

Prepare financial statements.
(SO 8) AP

E1–11 An analysis of transactions for Bourque & Co. is presented in E1–10.

Instructions

Prepare an income statement and statement of owner's equity for August, and a balance sheet at August 31, 2003.

Prepare income statement and statement of owner's equity.
(SO 8) AP

E1–12 The following information relates to Serg Co. for the year ended December 31, 2002:

Serg, Capital, January 1, 2002	$48,000	Serg, Drawings	5,000
Service revenue	55,000	Salaries expense	28,000
Rent expense	10,400	Utilities expense	3,100
Interest expense	1,700	Advertising expense	1,800

Instructions

After analysing the data, prepare an income statement and a statement of owner's equity for the year ended December 31, 2002.

Correct incorrectly prepared balance sheet.
(SO 8) AN

E1–13 Clare Gardner is the bookkeeper for Otago Company. Clare has prepared the balance sheet of Otago Company, as follows:

OTAGO COMPANY
Balance Sheet
December 31, 2002

Assets		Liabilities	
Cash	$20,500	Accounts payable	$20,000
Supplies	8,000	Accounts receivable	(10,000)
Equipment	46,000	Otago, Capital	67,500
Otago, Drawings	3,000	Total liabilities and	
Total assets	$77,500	owner's equity	$77,500

Instructions

Prepare a correct balance sheet.

E1–14 Judy Cumby is the sole owner of Deer Park, a public camping ground near Gros Morne National Park. Judy has compiled the following financial information as at December 31, 2002:

Calculate net income and prepare balance sheet.
(SO 8) AP

Revenues during 2002, camping fees	$160,000	Revenues during 2002, general store	$40,000
Expenses during 2002	150,000	Cash on hand	20,000
Supplies on hand	2,500	Original cost of equipment	115,500
Market value of equipment	140,000	Notes payable	60,000
Accounts payable	11,000	Capital, January 1, 2002	17,000

Instructions

(a) Determine Judy's net income from Deer Park for the year ended December 31, 2002.

(b) Prepare a balance sheet for Deer Park as at December 31, 2002.

E1–15 Financial information for the October 2003 operations of the Atlantic Cruise Company is presented below:

Prepare income statement.
(SO 8) AN

Maintenance expense	$ 80,000
Property tax expense (on dock facilities)	10,000
Salaries expense	142,000
Advertising expense	3,500
Ticket revenue	325,000
Food, fuel, and other operating expenses	20,500

Instructions

Prepare the income statement for the month of October 2003 for the Atlantic Cruise Company.

E1–16 Information related to the proprietorship of Lorraine Ring, lawyer, for the year ended January 31, 2003, is presented below:

Prepare statement of owner's equity.
(SO 8) AN

Legal fees earned	$360,000
Total expenses	205,000
Assets, February 1, 2002	85,000
Liabilities, February 1, 2002	62,000
Assets, January 31, 2003	168,000
Liabilities, January 31, 2003	70,000
Drawings	?

Instructions

Prepare the statement of owner's equity for Lorraine Ring's legal practice, for the year ended January 31, 2003, after determining the missing amount for drawings.

PROBLEMS: SET A

P1–1A Financial decisions often depend more on one type of financial statement than others. Consider each of the following hypothetical situations independently:

Identify users and uses of financial statements.
(SO 2) AP

(a) The North Face is considering extending credit to a new customer. The terms of the credit would require the customer to pay within 30 days of receipt of the goods.

(b) An investor is considering investing in WestJet Airlines. The investor plans on holding the investment for at least five years.

(c) Caisse D'Economie Base Montréal is thinking about extending a loan to a small company. The company would be required to make interest payments at the end of each year for five years, and to repay the loan at the end of the fifth year.

Instructions

In each situation, state whether the individual would depend mostly on the information provided by the income statement, the balance sheet, or the cash flow statement. Provide a brief justification for your choice.

P1–2A The president of Richelieu Motors received a draft income statement from his controller for the year ended December 31, 2002. "Suzanne," he said to the controller, "the statement indicates that a net income of $2 million was earned last year. You know the value of the company is more than $2 million greater than it was this time last year."

"You're probably right," replied Suzanne. "You see, there is an assumption and a generally

Discuss accounting assumptions and GAAP related to value.
(SO 4, 5) S

accepted accounting principle that sometimes keep reported operating results from reflecting the change in value of a company."

Instructions

Prepare a short memo explaining what the controller is referring to.

Identify assumption or principle violated.
(SO 4, 5) AN

P1–3A   A number of accounting reporting situations are described below:

1. Dot.com Company believes its people are its most significant assets. It estimates and records their value on its balance sheet.
2. Barton Co. is carrying its land at its current market value of $100,000. The land had an original cost of $75,000.
3. Steph Wolfson, president of the Classic CD Company, bought a computer for her personal use. She paid for the computer with company funds and debited the Computers account.

Instructions

For each of the above, list any assumption or principle that has been violated and explain why the situation violates this assumption or principle.

Analyse transactions and calculate net income.
(SO 6, 7) AN

P1–4A   On April 1, Merle Peper established the Peper Travel Agency. The following transactions were completed during the month:

Apr. 1 Deposited $15,000 cash in the Canadian Imperial Bank of Commerce, in the name of the agency.
   2 Paid $400 cash for April office rent.
   2 Purchased office equipment for $2,500 cash.
   7 Incurred $300 of advertising costs, on account.
   8 Paid $600 cash for office supplies.
  11 Earned $9,000 for services rendered: cash of $1,000 is received from customers, and the balance of $8,000 is billed to customers on account.
  15 Withdrew $200 cash for personal use.
  25 Paid the amount due in the April 7 transaction.
  30 Paid employees' salaries, $2,200.
  30 Received $8,000 in cash from customers who were billed in the April 11 transaction.

Instructions

(a) Prepare a tabular analysis of the transactions using the following column headings: Cash, Accounts Receivable, Supplies, Office Equipment, Accounts Payable, and Merle Peper, Capital.
(b) From an analysis of the column Capital Merle Peper, calculate the net income or net loss for April.

Analyse transactions and prepare financial statements.
(SO 7, 8) AN

P1–5A   Julie Szo operates a law office under the name Julie Szo, Barrister & Solicitor. On July 31, 2003, the balance sheet showed Cash $4,000; Accounts Receivable $1,500; Supplies $500; Office Equipment $5,000; Accounts Payable $4,200; and Julie Szo, Capital $6,800. During August the following transactions occurred:

Aug. 4 Collected $1,400 of accounts receivable.
   7 Paid $2,700 cash on accounts payable.
   8 Earned fees of $6,400, of which $3,000 is collected in cash and the balance is due in September.
  12 Purchased additional office equipment for $1,000, paying $400 in cash and the balance on account.
  15 Paid salaries, $2,500; rent for August, $900; and advertising expenses, $350.
  20 Withdrew $550 in cash for personal use.
  26 Received $2,000 from the Bank of Montreal—money borrowed on a note payable.
  29 Incurred utility expenses for the month on account, $250.

Instructions

(a) Beginning with July the 31 balances, prepare a tabular analysis of the August transactions. The column headings should be as follows: Cash + Accounts Receivable + Supplies + Office Equipment = Notes Payable + Accounts Payable + Julie Szo, Capital.
(b) Prepare an income statement for August, a statement of owner's equity for August, and a balance sheet at August 31, 2003.

Analyse transactions and prepare balance sheet.
(SO 7, 8) AN

P1–6A   The following events relate to Jeannie LeTourneau, a Manitoba law school graduate:

1. On March 4, 2003, she spent $10 on a Lucky Seven Lottery ticket.
2. On March 7, she won $240,000 in the lottery and immediately quit her job as a legal assistant.
3. On March 10, she decided to open her own law practice, and deposited $75,000 of her winnings in a business chequing account.

4. On March 14, she purchased a new condominium with a downpayment of $100,000 from her personal funds plus a home mortgage of $200,000.

5. On March 16, Ms. LeTourneau signed a rental agreement for her law office space, commencing on April 1, 2003. She had to pay a $2,000 cash damage deposit (from her business cash). It will be fully refundable when she vacates the premises, provided they are in good condition. (*Hint*: This deposit should be treated as a company asset.) The monthly rental payments are to be made in advance on the first business day of each month. The first payment of $1,000 is due April 1.

6. On March 20, she hired a receptionist. He will be paid $500 per week, and will report to work on April 1.

7. On March 25, she purchased a computer and related equipment for her law practice for $3,000 cash plus a $4,000 note payable due in six months.

8. On March 27, she purchased $1,500 of office supplies, on account (to be paid in one month).

9. On March 31, she purchased office furniture for her law practice. The total cost of $5,000 was paid in cash.

Instructions

(a) Use the accounting equation to analyse the effects of the transactions on Jeannie LeTourneau's law practice.

(b) Prepare a balance sheet for Jeannie LeTourneau's law practice as at March 31, 2003.

P1–7A The following selected data from the 2002 financial statements for Jatou Trading Company are in random order:

Use financial statement relationships to determine missing amounts.
(SO 6, 8) AN

Liabilities at the end of the year	$ 940,000
Investment by the owner during the year	23,000
Assets at the beginning of the year	1,235,000
Drawings by the owner during the year	64,000
Net income for the year	59,000
Capital at the beginning of the year	250,000
Total revenue for the year	749,000

Instructions

Determine the amount of each of the following items:
(a) Liabilities at the beginning of the year
(b) Total expenses for the year
(c) Capital at the end of the year
(d) Assets at the end of the year

P1–8A On June 1, Ann Okah started Natural Cosmetics Co., a company that provides individual skin care treatment to clients at their residence. She invested $27,200 cash in the business. Listed below, in alphabetical order, are the assets and liabilities of the company at June 30, and the revenues and expenses for the month of June:

Prepare financial statements.
(SO 7, 8) AP

Accounts payable	$ 1,200	Gas and oil expense	$ 800
Accounts receivable	4,000	Notes payable	13,000
Advertising expense	500	Service revenue	6,500
Cash	12,000	Supplies expense	1,200
Cosmetic supplies on hand	2,400	Utilities expense	300
Equipment	25,000		

Ann made no additional investment in June, but withdrew $1,700 in cash for personal use during the month.

Instructions

(a) Prepare an income statement and statement of owner's equity for the month of June, and a balance sheet at June 30, 2003.

(b) Indicate how the financial statements in (a) would be affected by the following additional data: (1) $800 of fees were earned but not billed or collected at June 30, and (2) $100 of gas and oil expense was incurred but not recorded or paid.

Determine financial statement amounts, prepare a statement of owner's equity, and comment.
(SO 7, 8) AN

P1–9A Financial statement information for four different companies is as follows:

	Baker Lake Company	Come By Chance Company	Georgian Bay Company	Edmonton Company
January 1, 2002:				
Assets	$ 75,000	$ 90,000	(g)	$150,000
Liabilities	50,000	(d)	75,000	(j)
Owner's equity	(a)	60,000	45,000	90,000
December 31, 2002:				
Assets	(b)	120,000	180,000	(k)
Liabilities	55,000	62,000	(h)	80,000
Owner's equity	45,000	(e)	110,000	140,000
Owner's equity changes in year:				
Investment	(c)	8,000	10,000	15,000
Drawings	10,000	(f)	12,000	10,000
Total revenues	350,000	400,000	(i)	500,000
Total expenses	335,000	385,000	360,000	(l)

Instructions

(a) Determine the missing amounts.

(b) Prepare the statement of owner's equity for Baker Lake Company.

(c) Write a memorandum explaining (1) the sequence for preparing financial statements, and (2) the interrelationship of the statement of owner's equity with the income statement and balance sheet.

Analyse transactions and prepare balance sheet.
(SO 7, 8) AP

P1–10A The Loonie Bin Coin Shop's balance sheet at April 29, 2003, consisted of the following items (listed here in alphabetical order):

Accounts payable	$ 10,000	Furnishings (store)	$ 48,000
Accounts receivable	7,000	Land	36,000
Building	110,000	Long-term debt payable	107,000
Capital	137,000	Notes payable	22,000
Cash	12,000	Office and store supplies	4,000
Equipment (office)	59,000		

On the following day, April 30, these transactions and events occurred:

1. Paid $3,000 of the amount owed on accounts payable.
2. Purchased equipment for $15,000. Paid $1,000 in cash and signed a short-term note for the balance.
3. A professional real estate appraiser estimated the value of the land at $40,000.
4. Sold some surplus office equipment for $5,000 in cash, which was the same as the original acquisition cost of the equipment.
5. Made a payment of $7,000 on the long-term debt.

Instructions

Prepare, in good form, a balance sheet for the Loonie Bin Coin Shop, as at April 30, 2003. Show supporting calculations for all new amounts.

P1–11A Michel Carrier organized the Multi-Media Consulting Co. on March 1, 2003. The owner's equity column of the tabular summary for the month of March contained the following recorded data:

Prepare income statement and statement of owner's equity.
(SO 8) AP

Transaction	Amount	Description
1.	$15,000	Investment
4.	750	Rent expense
6.	3,250	Fees earned
8.	400	Advertising expense
11.	1,000	Salaries expense
12.	2,100	Fees earned
15.	250	Utilities expense
18.	500	Drawings
20.	3,200	Fees earned
22.	200	Repair expense
24.	1,000	Advertising expense
27.	300	Drawings
29.	1,100	Fees earned
32.	900	Salaries expense
34.	200	Property tax expense
36.	150	Utilities expense

All data were properly recorded except the following:
- In transaction 22, $50 of the repair expense was applicable to Michel's personal residence.
- In transaction 34, $150 was applicable to business property; the remainder was applicable to the owner's personal residence.

Instructions

(a) Prepare an income statement for the month of March.
(b) Prepare a statement of owner's equity for March.

PROBLEMS: SET B
••

P1–1B Financial decisions often depend more on one type of financial statement than on others. Consider each of the following hypothetical situations independently:

Identify users and uses of financial statements.
(SO 2) AP

(a) An Ontario investor is considering investing in Bally Total Fitness Company, which operates 13 fitness centres in the Toronto area. The investor plans on holding the investment for at least three years.
(b) Bombardier is considering extending credit to a new customer. The company would require the customer to pay within 60 days of receipt of the goods.
(c) The Laurentian Bank is considering extending a loan to a small company. The company would be required to make interest payments at the end of each month for five years, and to repay the loan at the end of the fifth year.

Instructions

In each situation, state whether the individual would depend mostly on the information provided by the income statement, balance sheet, or cash flow statement. Provide a brief justification for your choice.

P1–2B The president of Montiero Company received a draft balance sheet from her controller for the year ended December 31, 2002. "Sergio," she said to her controller, "the statement shows total assets of $2 million. You know the value of the company's assets is far more than $2 million."

Discuss accounting assumptions and GAAP related to value.
(SO 4, 5) S

"You're right," replied Sergio. "You see, there is an assumption and a generally accepted accounting principle that prohibit the recording of assets on the books at their market value."

Instructions

Prepare a short memo explaining what the controller is referring to.

Identify assumption or principle violated.
(SO 4, 5) AN

P1–3B   A number of accounting reporting situations are described below:
1. In preparing its financial statements, Karim Corporation tried to estimate and record the impact of the recent death of its president.
2. Paradis Company recently purchased a power boat. It plans on inviting clients for outings occasionally, so the boat was paid for with company funds, and recorded in the company's records. Marc Paradis's family will use the boat whenever it is not being used to entertain clients. It is estimated that the boat will be used by the family about 75 percent of the time.
3. Because of a "flood sale," equipment worth $300,000 was purchased for only $200,000. The equipment was recorded for $300,000 on the company's books.

Instructions

For each of the above, list any assumption or principle that has been violated. Explain why the situation described violates the assumptions or principles.

Analyse transactions and calculate net income.
(SO 6, 7) AN

P1–4B   Kumar's Repair Shop was started on May 1 by U. Kumar. A summary of the May transactions is presented below:

May 1 Invested $15,000 cash to start the repair shop.
   2 Purchased equipment for $5,000 cash.
   5 Paid $400 cash for May office rent.
   7 Purchased $500 of supplies on account.
   9 Received $4,100 in cash from customers for repair service.
  15 Withdrew $500 cash for personal use.
  15 Paid part-time employee salaries, $1,000.
  23 Paid utility bills, $140.
  28 Provided repair service on account to customers, $400.
  30 Collected cash of $120 for services billed on May 28.

Instructions

(a) Prepare a tabular analysis of the transactions, using the following column headings: Cash, Accounts Receivable, Supplies, Equipment, Accounts Payable, and U. Kumar, Capital. Revenue is called Service Revenue.
(b) From an analysis of the U. Kumar, Capital column, calculate the net income or net loss for May.

Analyse transactions and prepare financial statements.
(SO 7, 8) AP

P1–5B   Bruce Smith opened Smith Veterinary Clinic in Saskatoon, on August 1, 2003. On August 31, the balance sheet showed Cash $9,000; Accounts Receivable $1,700; Supplies $600; Office Equipment $6,000; Accounts Payable $3,600; and B. Smith, Capital $13,700. During September the following transactions occurred:

Sept. 1 Paid $3,100 cash on accounts payable.
    4 Collected $1,300 of accounts receivable.
    8 Purchased additional office equipment for $2,100, paying $800 in cash and the balance on account.
   17 Earned revenue of $5,900, of which $2,500 is paid in cash and the balance is due in October.
   19 Withdrew $600 cash for personal use.
   25 Received $7,000 from the Western Bank—money borrowed on a note payable.
   30 Paid salaries, $700; rent for September, $900; and advertising expense, $300.
   30 Incurred utility expenses for the month on account, $170.

Instructions

(a) Prepare a tabular analysis of the September transactions beginning with the August 31 balances. The column headings should be as follows: Cash + Accounts Receivable + Supplies + Office Equipment = Notes Payable + Accounts Payable + B. Smith, Capital.
(b) Prepare an income statement for September, a statement of owner's equity for September, and a balance sheet at September 30, 2003.

Analyse transactions and prepare income statement and balance sheet.
(SO 7, 8) AP

P1–6B   Jessica Bell started her own consulting firm, Bell Consulting, on May 1, 2003. The following transactions occurred during the month of May:

May 1 Bell invested $4,000 cash in the business.
   2 Paid $800 for office rent for the month.
   3 Purchased $500 of supplies on account.
   5 Paid $50 to advertise in the *County News*.
   9 Received $1,000 cash for services provided.
  12 Withdrew $700 cash for personal use.

15 Performed $3,000 of services on account.
17 Paid $2,500 for employee salaries.
20 Paid for the supplies purchased on account on May 3.
23 Received a cash payment of $2,000 for services provided on account on May 15.
26 Borrowed $5,000 from the bank on a note payable.
29 Purchased office equipment for $2,400.
30 Paid $150 for utilities.

Instructions

(a) Show the effects of each transaction on the accounting equation.
(b) Prepare an income statement for the month of May.
(c) Prepare a balance sheet at May 31, 2003.

P1–7B The following selected data from the 2002 financial statements for the Ojibway Trading Company are in random order:

Use financial statement relationships to determine missing amounts.
(SO 6, 8) AN

Liabilities at the end of the year	$ 910,000
Investments by the owner during the year	30,000
Assets at the beginning of the year	1,265,000
Drawings by the owner during the year	74,000
Net income for the year	56,000
Capital at the beginning of the year	245,000
Total revenue for the year	687,000

Instructions

Determine the amount of each of the following items:
(a) Liabilities at the beginning of the year
(b) Total expenses for the year
(c) Capital at the end of the year
(d) Assets at the end of the year

P1–8B On September 1, Emily Jackson started Specialty Cosmetics Co., by investing $10,000 cash in the business. The alphabetical list below shows the assets and liabilities of the company at September 30, and the revenues and expenses for the month of September:

Prepare financial statements.
(SO 7, 8) AP

Accounts payable	$1,800	Equipment	$20,000
Accounts receivable	5,000	Notes payable	15,000
Advertising expense	600	Service revenue	5,900
Cash	9,000	Supplies expense	1,500
Cosmetic supplies	2,700	Utilities expense	1,300

Emily invested an additional $10,000 on September 20, and withdrew $2,600 in cash for personal use during the month.

Instructions

(a) Prepare an income statement and statement of owner's equity for the month of September, and a balance sheet at September 30, 2003.
(b) Indicate how the financial statements in (a) would be affected by the following additional data: (1) Fees of $900 were earned but not billed or collected at September 30. (2) Gas and oil expense of $300 was incurred but not recorded or paid.

*Determine financial statement
amounts, prepare a statement of
owner's equity, and comment.*
(SO 7, 8) AP

P1–9B   Financial statement information for four different companies is as follows:

	Montreal Company	Calgary Company	Edmonton Company	Vancouver Company
January 1, 2002:				
Assets	$80,000	$110,000	(g)	$170,000
Liabilities	50,000	(d)	75,000	(j)
Owner's equity	(a)	60,000	50,000	90,000
December 31, 2002:				
Assets	(b)	145,000	200,000	(k)
Liabilities	55,000	65,000	(h)	80,000
Owner's equity	58,000	(e)	130,000	180,000
Owner's equity changes in year:				
Investments	(c)	15,000	10,000	15,000
Drawings	25,000	(f)	14,000	20,000
Total revenues	350,000	420,000	(i)	520,000
Total expenses	320,000	385,000	350,000	(l)

Instructions

(a) Determine the missing amounts.
(b) Prepare a statement of owner's equity for Calgary Company.
(c) Write a memorandum explaining (1) the sequence for preparing financial statements, and (2) the interrelationship of the statement of owner's equity with the income statement and balance sheet.

*Analyse transactions and pre-
pare balance sheet.*
(SO 7, 8) AP

P1–10B   The Franc d'Or Coin Shop's balance sheet at June 29, 2003, consisted of the following items (which are listed here in alphabetical order):

Accounts payable	$ 11,000	Equipment (store)	$ 24,000
Accounts receivable	6,000	Land	40,000
Building	120,000	Long-term debt payable	111,000
Capital	189,000	Merchandise inventory	110,000
Cash	13,000	Notes payable	20,000
Equipment (office)	12,000	Office and store supplies	6,000

On the following day, June 30, these transactions and events occurred:
1. Paid $4,000 of the amounts owed on accounts payable.
2. Purchased office equipment for $5,000, paid $1,500 in cash, and signed a short-term note for the balance.
3. A professional real estate appraiser estimated the value of the land at $150,000.
4. Sold some surplus store equipment for $4,500 in cash, which was the same as the original acquisition cost of the equipment.
5. Made a payment of $8,000 on the long-term debt.

Instructions

Prepare, in good form, a balance sheet for the Franc d'Or Coin Shop as at June 30, 2003. Show supporting calculations for all new amounts. (*Hint:* Merchandise inventory is an asset, representing goods on hand for sale.)

*Prepare income statement and
statement of owner's equity.*
(SO 8) AP

P1–11B   Theresa Nash organized Nash Consulting Co. on January 1, 2003. The owner's equity column of the tabular summary for the month of January contained the following recorded data:

Transaction	Amount	Description
1.	$12,000	Investment
4.	800	Rent expense
6.	3,750	Service revenue
8.	450	Advertising expense
11.	1,200	Salaries expense
12.	2,300	Service revenue
15.	300	Utilities expense
18.	600	Drawings
20.	3,700	Service revenue
22.	250	Repair expense

24.	1,100	Advertising expense
27.	400	Drawings
29.	1,200	Service revenue
32.	1,000	Salaries expense
34.	250	Property tax expense
36.	180	Utilities expense

All data were properly recorded except the following:

- In transaction 32, $500 of the salary expense was paid to Theresa Nash herself.
- In transaction 34, $150 was applicable to business property, and the remainder to the owner's personal residence.

Instructions

(a) Prepare an income statement for the month of January.

(b) Prepare a statement of owner's equity for January.

Broadening Your Perspective

FINANCIAL REPORTING AND ANALYSIS

Financial Reporting Problem

BYP1–1   The actual financial statements of **The Second Cup Ltd.**, as presented in the company's *2000 Annual Report*, are contained in Appendix A (at the back of the textbook).

Instructions

Refer to The Second Cup's financial statements and answer the following questions:

(a) How many notes to the financial statements are presented for The Second Cup? How many pages of the annual report do these notes occupy? How many pages do the financial statements themselves occupy?

(b) Notice that the dates on the financial statements are June 24, 2000, and June 30, 1999. (The company's 1998 financial statements were dated June 27.) What is The Second Cup's fiscal year end?

(c) Who are the auditors for The Second Cup Ltd.?

(d) What were The Second Cup's total assets as at June 24, 2000? June 30, 1999?

(e) What is the amount of change in The Second Cup's net earnings (loss) from 1999 to 2000?

(f) What amount of cash and cash equivalents did The Second Cup have on June 24, 2000? June 30, 1999?

(g) Refer to the five-year financial review which is included in the annual report. What was the percentage change in systemwide sales from 1996 to 2000?

Interpreting Financial Statements

Additional Cases

BYP1–2   Corel Corporation is an innovative Canadian software company. The company's products, which include CorelDRAW® and WordPerfect®[1], are used by more than 50 million people worldwide. Corel's 2000 annual report included the following excerpt from its corporate profile statement:

> With over 1,300 employees in two locations and sales offices worldwide, Corel is one of the world's top software developers. The Company's corporate headquarters in Ottawa, Canada, is home to its business and graphics development teams. Its Dublin, Ireland, office handles software localization, along with a portion of the Company's technical support and customer service. ... Recognized the world over, Corel's award-winning products ship in over 15 languages through a network of more than 160 distributors in over 60 countries.

COREL CORPORATION
Balance Sheet
As at November 30
(in thousands of US$)

	2000	1999
Assets		
Current assets		
Cash and cash equivalents	$127,430	$ 18,021
Restricted cash	1,136	
Accounts receivable		
Trade	28,620	54,770
Other	773	3,954
Inventory	3,117	13,567
Income taxes recoverable		5,135
Future tax asset	479	1,642
Prepaid expenses	1,050	2,042
Total current assets	162,605	99,131
Investments	11,996	2,873
Capital assets	42,471	49,697
Other assets	1,515	
Total assets	$218,587	$151,701

Instructions

(a) What do you think the most important economic resources (assets) would be for a software development company such as Corel? Where would these be recorded on the balance sheet? At what value (if any) should they be shown?

(b) Does the balance sheet tell you what Corel Corporation is worth? What information does the balance sheet give you about the value of the Company?

(c) Why do you think a Canadian company such as Corel would prepare its financial statements in U.S. dollars?

---

[1] Corel, CorelDraw, WordPerfect, and the Corel logo are registered trademarks of Corel Corporation or Corel Corporation Limited.

Accounting on the Web

BYP1–3   This case views the websites of professional accounting organizations and firms, amongst others, to learn about career opportunities. We'll find out the educational and experience requirements for accounting and related careers, and read about the exciting lives of prominent accountants in sports, entertainment, industry, business, and government.

Instructions

Specific requirements of this Internet case are available on-line on the Weygandt website.

CRITICAL THINKING

Collaborative Learning Activity

BYP1–4   Patsy and Perry Ross, local golf stars, opened the Long-Shot Driving Range on May 1, 2003, by investing $10,000 of their cash savings in the business. A caddy shack was constructed for cash at a cost of $4,000, and $1,800 was spent on golf balls and golf clubs. The Rosses leased five acres of land at a cost of $1,000 per month and paid the first month's rent. During the first month, advertising costs totalled $750, of which $150 was unpaid at May 31. Members of the high school golf team were paid $400 for retrieving golf balls. All fees from customers were deposited in the company's bank account. On May 15, Patsy and Perry withdrew $800 in cash for personal living expenses. A $100 utility bill was received on May 31, but it was not paid. On May 31, the balance in the company's bank account was $7,550.

Patsy and Perry weren't sure how they did in their first month of operations. Their estimates of profitability ranged from a loss of $2,450 to net income of $3,100.

Instructions

With the class divided into groups, answer the following:
(a) How could the Rosses have concluded that the business operated at a loss of $2,450? Was this a valid way to determine net income?
(b) How could the Rosses have concluded that the business operated at a net income of $3,100? (*Hint*: Prepare a balance sheet at May 31.) Was this a valid way to determine net income?
(c) Without preparing an income statement, determine the actual net income for May.
(d) What were the fees earned in May? (*Hint:* You can determine this either by (1) preparing an income statement, and using your answer from part (c) and the information about expenses, and then inserting the missing amount for fees earned [revenue], or (2) by analysing the changes in cash and inserting the missing amount for fees [cash receipts].)

Communication Activity

BYP1–5   Israel Unger is the owner of Mount Company. Israel has prepared the following balance sheet:

MOUNT COMPANY
Balance Sheet
For the Month Ended December 31, 2002

Assets

Equipment	$21,500
Cash	9,000
Supplies	2,000
Accounts payable	(6,000)
Total assets	$26,500

Liabilities and Owner's Equity

Unger, Capital	$21,000
Accounts receivable	(3,000)
Unger, Drawings	(2,000)
Notes payable	10,500
Total liabilities and owner's equity	$26,500

Instructions

Explain to Israel, in a memo, why the original balance sheet is incorrect and what should be done to correct it.

Ethics Case

BYP1–6   After numerous campus interviews, Stephane Pelli, a graduating student at the University of New Brunswick, Fredericton, received interview offers from two large firms located in Saint John, New Brunswick. Both firms offered to cover his out-of-pocket expenses (travel, hotel, and meals). He scheduled the interviews for both firms on the same day, one in the morning and one in the afternoon.

At the conclusion of each interview, Stephane submitted to each firm his total out-of-pocket expenses for the trip: use of private vehicle $70 (280 kilometres at $0.25), hotel $120, meals $36, plus parking and tips $18, for a total of $244. He believes this approach is appropriate. If he had made two trips, his cost would have been two times $244. He is also certain that neither firm knew he had visited the other on that same trip.

Within a few days, Stephane received two cheques in the mail, each for $244.

Instructions
(a) Who are the stakeholders (affected parties) in this situation?
(b) What are the ethical issues in this case?
(c) What would you do in this situation?

Answers to Self-Study Questions
1. b 2. d 3. a 4. d 5. d 6. c 7. a 8. b 9. d 10. b 11. b 12. c

Answer to Review It Question 2

The net earnings of $972,000 on the Statement of Operations (also known as the Income Statement) are included on the Statement of Retained Earnings (Deficit) to determine the ending deficit of $60,657,000. In fact, these two statements are combined as one for presentation purposes. The ending deficit amount of $60,657,000 is reported on the Balance Sheet. The cash and cash equivalents of $1,446,000 on the balance sheet is also shown on the Cash Flow Statement as the ending balance.

Remember to go back to the Navigator box on the chapter-opening page
to check off your completed work.

Concepts for Review

Before studying this chapter, you should understand or, if necessary, review:

a. *What assets, liabilities, owner's capital, owner's drawings, revenues, and expenses are. (Ch. 1, pp. 14–16)*
b. *Why assets equal liabilities plus owner's equity. (Ch. 1, p. 14)*
c. *What transactions are, and how they affect the basic accounting equation. (Ch. 1, pp. 18–23)*

THE NAVIGATOR

No Such Thing As a Perfect World

SURREY, B.C.—When she got a job doing the accounting for Forster's Restaurants, Tanis Anderson had almost finished her Business Administration degree at Simon Fraser University. But even after Tanis completed her degree requirements, her education still continued—this time, in the real world.

Tanis's responsibilities include paying the bills, tracking food and labour costs, and managing the payroll for The Mug and Musket, a popular destination restaurant in Surrey, B.C. "My title is Director of Finance," she laughs, "but really that means I take care of whatever needs doing!"

The use of judgement is a big part of the job. As Tanis says, "I learned all the fundamentals in my business classes, but school prepares you for a perfect world, and there is no such thing."

She feels fortunate that her boss understands that her job is a learning experience as well as a responsibility. "Sometimes he's let me do something he knew perfectly well was a mistake so I can learn some-

thing through experience," she admits.

On the other hand, some tasks, like recording transactions, she finds easier to do in the real world than they were in school. "Our computer software, *Simply Accounting*, really helps," she explains. "Recording transactions using the software, after you've learned how to do it by hand, is like boiling water in a microwave

instead of on a campfire. It's fast and easy." It also makes repairing mistakes much easier. "If I goof up an entry," says Tanis, "I can just go back and fix it, without making fifteen adjustments."

THE NAVIGATOR

THE NAVIGATOR ✔

- Understand *Concepts for Review* ☐
- Read *Feature Story* ☐
- Scan *Study Objectives* ☐
- Read *Preview* ☐
- Read text and answer *Before You Go On*
  p. 58 ☐   p. 62 ☐   p. 72 ☐   p. 75 ☐
- Work *Demonstration Problem* ☐
- Review *Summary of Study Objectives* ☐
- Answer *Self-Study Questions* ☐
- Complete assignments ☐

CHAPTER • 2

THE RECORDING PROCESS

▶ STUDY OBJECTIVES ◀

After studying this chapter, you should be able to:

1. *Explain what an account is and how it helps in the recording process.*
2. *Define debits and credits and illustrate how they are used to record business transactions.*
3. *Describe the basic steps in the recording process.*
4. *Explain what a journal is and how it helps in the recording process, and journalize business transactions.*
5. *Explain what a ledger is and how it helps in the recording process.*
6. *Explain what posting is and how it helps in the recording process.*
7. *Explain the purpose of, and prepare, a trial balance.*

THE NAVIGATOR

In Chapter 1, we used the accounting equation to analyse business transactions. The cumulative effects of these transactions were presented in tabular form. This method could work for small companies like Softbyte (the company discussed in Chapter 1) because they have relatively few transactions. But imagine a company such as the Mug and Musket in the feature story using the same tabular format as Softbyte. In a single day, the restaurant engages in hundreds of business transactions. To record each transaction this way would be impractical. Instead a set of procedures and records are used to keep track of transaction data more easily.

This chapter introduces and illustrates the basic procedures and records. The chapter is organized as follows:

THE
NAVIGATOR

The Account

···

STUDY OBJECTIVE
········ 1 ········

Explain what an account is and how it helps in the recording process.

An account is an individual accounting record of increases and decreases in a specific asset, liability, or owner's equity item. For example, Softbyte would have separate accounts called Cash, Accounts Receivable, Accounts Payable, Service Revenue, Salaries Expense, and so on. In its simplest form, an account consists of three parts: (1) the title of the account, (2) a left or debit side, and (3) a right or credit side. Because the positioning of these parts of an account resembles the letter T, it is called a T account. The basic form of an account is shown in Illustration 2-1.

Illustration 2-1

Basic form of account

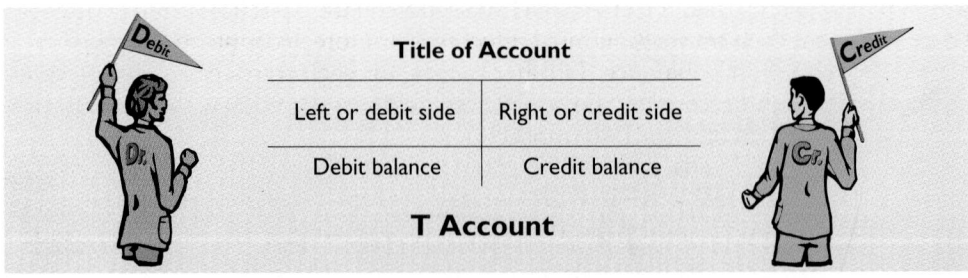

This form of account will be used throughout the book to explain basic accounting relationships.

Debits and Credits

The term **debit** means left. The term **credit** means right. They are commonly abbreviated Dr. for debit and Cr. for credit.[1] These terms are directional signals. They indicate which side of a T account to record on. Entering an amount on the left side of an account is called **debiting** the account. Making an entry on the right side is called **crediting** the account.

The custom of having debits on the left side of an account and credits on the right side (like the custom of driving on the right-hand side of the road) is an accounting custom, or rule. It has been adopted in this and other countries. **This rule applies to all accounts.** When the totals of the two sides are compared, an account will have a **debit balance** if the total of the debit amounts exceeds the credits. Conversely, an account will have a **credit balance** if the credit amounts exceed the debits.

The recording of debits and credits in an account is shown in Illustration 2-2 for the cash transactions of Softbyte. The data are taken from the cash column of the tabular summary in Illustration 1-9.

STUDY OBJECTIVE
·········· **2** ··········
Define debits and credits and illustrate how they are used to record business transactions.

Illustration 2-2

Tabular summary compared to account form

Tabular Summary		Account Form		
Cash		**(Debits)**	Cash	**(Credits)**
$15,000			15,000	7,000
−7,000			1,200	600
1,200			1,500	900
1,500			600	200
−600				250
−900				1,300
−200		Balance	8,050	
−250		**(Debit)**		
600				
−1,300				
$ 8,050				

In the tabular summary, every positive item represents a receipt of cash. Every negative amount represents a payment of cash. Notice that in the account form the increases in cash are recorded as debits, and the decreases in cash are recorded as credits. Having increases on one side and decreases on the other helps in determining the totals of each side of the account, as well as the balance in the account. The account balance, a debit of $8,050, indicates that Softbyte has $8,050 more increases than decreases in cash.

Debit and Credit Procedure

In Chapter 1, you learned the effect of a transaction on the basic accounting equation. Remember that each transaction must affect two or more accounts to keep the basic accounting equation in balance. In other words, for each transaction, **debits must equal credits** in the accounts. The equality of debits and credits is the basis for the double-entry system of recording transactions.

Under the **double-entry system**, the dual (two-sided) effect of each transaction is recorded in appropriate accounts. This universally used system provides a logical method for recording transactions. It also offers a way of proving the accuracy of the

Helpful hint Debits must equal credits for each transaction.

---

[1]These terms and their abbreviations come from the Latin words *debere* (Dr.) and *credere* (Cr.).

recorded amounts. If every transaction is recorded with equal debits and credits, then the sum of all the debits to the accounts must equal the sum of all the credits.

Assets and Liabilities.   In the Softbyte illustration, increases in Cash—an asset account—were entered on the left side, and decreases in Cash were entered on the right side. We know that both sides of the basic equation (assets = liabilities + owner's equity) must be equal. To maintain this equality, increases and decreases have to be recorded opposite each other. Thus, increases in assets must be entered on the left or debit side, and decreases in assets must be entered on the right or credit side. Increases in liabilities must be entered on the right or credit side, and decreases in liabilities must be entered on the left or debit side.

Debits to a specific asset account should exceed the credits to that account. Credits to a liability account should exceed debits to that account. Thus, asset accounts normally show debit balances, and liability accounts normally show credit balances.

The effects that debits and credits have on assets and liabilities and the normal balances are as follows:

> **Helpful hint** Be careful here. Even though increases and decreases in the Cash account are recorded as debits and credits, respectively, for some accounts, debits are not increases and credits are not decreases.

Illustration 2-3

Debit and credit effects—assets and liabilities

Assets				Liabilities	
Debit for increase	Credit for decrease			Debit for decrease	Credit for increase
Normal Balance					Normal Balance

Knowing the normal balance in an account may help you trace errors. In automated systems, the computer is programmed to find these normal balance exceptions and to print out error or exception reports. In manual systems, careful visual inspection of the accounts is required to detect variations from normal balances. For example, a credit balance in an asset account such as Land or a debit balance in a liability account such as Wages Payable would likely indicate recording errors. Occasionally, an abnormal balance may be correct. The Cash account, for example, will have a credit balance when a company has overdrawn its bank balance. This happens often when a company has an operating line of credit. We will learn more about using credit in Chapter 11.

> **Helpful hint** The normal balance for an account is always on the increase side.

Owner's Equity.   As indicated in Chapter 1, owner's equity is increased by owner's investments and revenues. It is decreased by owner's drawings and expenses. Separate accounts are kept for each of these types of transactions.

Owner's Capital.   Investments by owners are credited to the owner's capital account. Like liability accounts, the owner's capital account is increased by credits and decreased by debits. For example, when cash is invested in the business, the Cash account is debited and Owner's Capital is credited.

The rules of debit and credit for the owner's capital account and the normal balance in this account are as follows:

Illustration 2-4

Debit and credit effects—owner's capital

Owner's Capital	
Debit for decrease	Credit for increase
	Normal Balance

As liabilities and owner's equity are on the same side of the accounting equation, the rules of debit and credit are the same for these two types of accounts.

Owner's Drawings.   An owner may withdraw cash or other assets for personal use. Withdrawals could be debited directly from Owner's Capital to indicate a decrease in owner's equity. However, it is preferable to establish a separate account, called Owner's Drawings. The separate account makes it easier to determine the total withdrawals for the accounting period and to prepare the statement of owner's equity. The **drawings account decreases owner's equity**. Owner's drawings are recorded by debits and the account has a normal debit balance. Credits to an owner's drawings account are unusual, but might be used to correct a withdrawal recorded in error, for example.

The rules of debit and credit for the Drawings account and the normal balance are as follows:

Owner's Drawings	
Debit for increase	Credit for decrease
Normal Balance	

Illustration 2-5

Debit and credit effects—owner's drawings

Revenues and Expenses.   Remember that the ultimate purpose of earning revenues is to benefit the owner of the business. When revenues are earned, owner's equity is increased. Accordingly, **the effect of debits and credits on revenue accounts is identical to their effect on owner's capital**. Revenue accounts are increased by credits and decreased by debits.

Expenses have the opposite effect: **expenses decrease owner's equity**. As a result, expenses are recorded as debits. Since expenses are the negative factor in calculating net income, and revenues are the positive factor, it is logical that the increase and decrease sides of expense accounts should be the reverse of revenue accounts. Thus, expense accounts are increased by debits and decreased by credits.

Credits to revenue accounts should exceed the debits. Debits to expense accounts should exceed credits. Thus, revenue accounts normally show credit balances. Expense accounts normally show debit balances.

The effect of debits and credits on revenues and expenses and the normal balances are as follows:

Revenues		**Expenses**	
Debit for decrease	Credit for increase	Debit for increase	Credit for decrease
	Normal	Normal	

Illustration 2-6

Debit and credit effects—revenues and expenses

►Accounting in Action ► *Business Insight*

The Blue Jays baseball organization has the following major revenue and expense accounts:

Revenues	**Expenses**
Home admissions	Players' salaries
Radio, over-the-air television and pay television	Team travel, lodging, and meals
Concessions and publications	Team uniforms and equipment
Licensing royalties	Stadium rental
Stadium advertising	Game and other club promotions
Souvenir operations	Administration

Expanding the Basic Accounting Equation

Illustration 2-7

Expanded basic equation and debit/credit rules and effects

You have already learned the basic accounting equation. Illustration 2-7 expands this equation to show the accounts that form owner's equity. In addition, the debit/credit rules and effects on each type of account are illustrated. Study this diagram carefully. It will help you to understand the fundamentals of the double-entry system. Like the basic equation, the expanded basic equation must always be in balance (total debits equal total credits).

The normal balance of each account is on its increase side. Illustration 2-8 summarizes the normal balances of each type of account included in the expanded accounting equation.

Illustration 2-8

Normal account balances

	Normal Balance (Increase)
Balance sheet accounts:	
Assets	Debit
Liabilities	Credit
Owner's Capital	Credit
Statement of owner's equity account:	
Owner's Drawings	Debit
Income statement accounts:	
Revenues	Credit
Expenses	Debit

Before You Go On . . .

▸ Review It

1. What do the terms "debit" and "credit" mean?
2. What are the debit and credit effects on assets, liabilities, and owner's equity?
3. What are the debit and credit effects on revenues, expenses, and the owner's drawings accounts?
4. What are the normal balances for The Second Cup's Accounts Receivable, Income Taxes Payable, and Product Sales accounts? The answer to this question is provided at the end of this chapter.

▸ Do It

Eszter Schwenke has just rented space in a shopping mall in which she will open and operate a beauty salon, called Hair It Is. Long before opening day and before purchasing equipment, hiring employees, and remodelling the space, Eszter is advised to set up a double-entry set of accounting records to record all of her business transactions.

Name the balance sheet accounts that Eszter will need for recording the transactions that open her business. Indicate whether the normal balance of each account is a debit or a credit.

Action Plan

- Determine the types of accounts needed. Eszter will need asset accounts for each different type of asset she invests in the business, and liability accounts for any debts she has.
- Understand the types of owner's equity accounts: Only owner's capital will be needed when Eszter begins the business. Other owner's equity accounts will be added later.

Solution

Eszter would likely need the following accounts to record the transactions that prepare her beauty salon for opening day: Cash (debit balance), Supplies (debit balance), Equipment (debit balance), Accounts Payable (credit balance), Note Payable (credit balance) if she borrows money, and E. Schwenke, Capital (credit balance).

Related exercise material: BE2–1, BE2–2, BE2–3, E2–1, E2–2, and E2–3.

Steps in the Recording Process

In practically every business, the basic steps in the recording process are:
1. Analyse each transaction in terms of its effect on the accounts.
2. Enter the transaction information in a journal (book of original entry).
3. Transfer the journal information to the appropriate accounts in the ledger (book of accounts).

Although it is possible to enter transaction information directly into the accounts without using a journal or ledger, few businesses do so.

The actual sequence of events in the recording process begins with the transaction. Evidence is provided by a **business document** such as a sales slip, cheque, bill, or cash register tape. This evidence is analysed to determine the effect of the transaction on specific accounts. The transaction is then entered in the journal. Finally, the journal entry is transferred to the correct accounts in the ledger. The sequence of events in the recording process is shown below:

STUDY OBJECTIVE

3

Describe the basic steps in the recording process.

Illustration 2-9

The recording process

The Recording Process

Analyse each transaction

Enter transaction in a journal

Transfer journal information to ledger accounts

The basic steps in the recording process occur repeatedly in every business whether a computerized or manual accounting system is used. However, the first step—the analysis of each transaction—must be done by people even when a computerized system is used. Determining what to record is the most critical point, and for most businesses the most expensive step, in the accounting process. There are more examples of this step in this and later chapters.

The basic difference between a computerized and a manual accounting system is found in the next two steps in the recording process—entering and transferring information. In computerized systems, the input and subsequent processing of the

Accounting Cycle Tutorial—Recording Business Transactions

information consist of file merging and report generation. These steps occur invisibly. To understand how computerized systems do this, we need to understand manual approaches to processing accounting data.

The Journal

Transactions are initially recorded in chronological (date) order in a journal before being transferred to the accounts. Thus, the journal is referred to as the book of original entry. For each transaction, the journal shows the debit and credit effects on specific accounts. Companies may use various kinds of journals, but every company has the most basic form of journal, a general journal. Whenever we use the term "journal" in this textbook without a modifying adjective, we mean the general journal.

The journal makes several significant contributions to the recording process:
1. It discloses, in one place, the complete effect of a transaction.
2. It provides a chronological record of transactions.
3. It helps to prevent and locate errors, because the debit and credit amounts for each entry can be easily compared.
4. It provides an explanation of the transaction and, where applicable, identifies the source document.

Journalizing

Entering transaction data in the journal is known as journalizing. Separate journal entries are made for each transaction. A complete entry consists of the following: (1) the date of the transaction, (2) the accounts and amounts to be debited and credited, and (3) a brief explanation of the transaction.

*In the margins next to key journal entries are **equation analyses.** They summarize the effects of the transactions on the three elements of the accounting equation (A=L+OE).*

To illustrate the technique of journalizing, the first two transactions of Softbyte are journalized in Illustration 2-10. Typically, a general journal has spaces for dates, account titles and explanations, references, and two money columns (debit and credit). As the illustration shows the first page of Softbyte's general journal, it is numbered J1.

Softbyte's first two transactions were (1) September 1, Marc Doucet invested $15,000 cash in the business, and (2) computer equipment was purchased for $7,000 cash.

Illustration 2-10

Technique of journalizing

A	= L	+	OE
+15,000			+15,000

A	= L	+	OE
+7,000			
–7,000			

GENERAL JOURNAL				J1
Date	Account Titles and Explanation	Ref.	Debit	Credit
2002 Sept. 1	Cash		15,000	
	M. Doucet, Capital			15,000
	Invested cash in business.			
1	Equipment		7,000	
	Cash			7,000
	Purchased equipment for cash.			

The standard form and content of journal entries are as follows:
1. The date of the transaction is entered in the Date column. The date recorded should include the year, month, and day of the transaction.
2. The debit account title (the account to debit) is entered first at the extreme left margin of the column headed Account Titles and Explanation. The credit account title (the account to credit) is entered on the next line, indented under the line above. The indentation decreases the possibility of confusing the debit and credit amounts.
3. The amounts for the debits are recorded in the Debit (left) column and the amounts for the credits are recorded in the Credit (right) column.

4. A brief explanation of the transaction is given on the line below the credit account title. This explanation also provides an important reference to the source document (invoice number, cheque number, etc.), if applicable.
5. A space is left between journal entries. The blank space separates individual journal entries and makes the entire journal easier to read.
6. The column titled Ref. (which stands for reference) is left blank when the journal entry is made. This column is used later, when the journal entries are transferred to the ledger accounts. At that time, the ledger account number is placed in the Reference column to indicate where the amount in the journal entry was transferred to.

Computerized journals and manual journals serve the same purpose. The format of the computerized journal may vary slightly from that described above, but the content is the same with few exceptions. Computerized systems often require an account number rather than an account name to be entered. The account name is automatically inserted by the computer for you. We will discuss account numbers in more detail later in this chapter. Automatic error checks ensure that only legitimate account numbers are used and that debits and credits balance for each transaction.

It is important to use correct and specific account titles in journalizing. Since the accounts appear later in the financial statements, inaccurate account titles lead to incorrect financial statements. Some flexibility exists initially in selecting account titles. The main criterion is that each title accurately describe the content of the account. For example, the account title used for delivery trucks may be Delivery Equipment, Delivery Trucks, or Trucks. Once a company chooses the specific title to use, all transactions involving the account should be recorded under that account title. In assignments, when specific account titles are given, they should be used. When account titles are not given, you may select account titles that identify the nature and content of each account. The account titles used in journalizing should not contain explanations (such as Cash Paid or Cash Received).

►Accounting in Action ► *Business Insight*

Can you imagine the chaos if transactions were distributed among account titles that sounded similar? That's what happened to one company when its bookkeeper set up four different computer accounts for Vehicle Expense. In addition to the original account, Vehicle Expense, the bookkeeper added Automobile Expense, Car Expense, and Vehicule (the French spelling) Expense. Vehicle expenses were recorded haphazardly throughout all four accounts. When the manager performed a computer search to determine the amount spent to date for Vehicle Expense, the computer displayed only the balance in the Vehicle Expense account, not the total vehicle expenditures. The manager ended up overspending her Vehicle Expense budget and was very unhappy when the end-of-period accounting procedures revealed this problem.

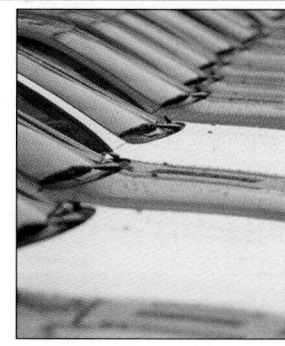

If an entry involves only two accounts, one debit and one credit, it is considered a simple entry. Some transactions, however, use more than two accounts in journalizing. When three or more accounts are required in one journal entry, the entry is referred to as a **compound entry**. To illustrate, assume that on October 2 Softbyte purchases a delivery truck costing $34,000 by paying $8,000 cash and the balance on a note to be paid later. The compound entry is as follows:

Illustration 2-11

Technique of journalizing

A	=	L	+	OE
+34,000		+26,000		
– 8,000				

GENERAL JOURNAL					J2
Date	Account Titles and Explanation	Ref.	Debit	Credit	
2002 Oct. 2	Delivery Equipment		34,000		
	Cash			8,000	
	Note Payable			26,000	
	Purchased truck for cash and note payable.				

In a compound entry, the total debit and credit amounts must equal. Also, the standard format requires that all debits be listed before the credits.

Before You Go On . . .

▸Review It

1. What is the sequence of steps in the recording process?
2. What contribution does the journal make to the recording process?
3. What is the standard form and content of a journal entry made in the general journal?
4. How does a manual journal entry differ from a computerized journal entry?

▸Do It

In establishing her beauty salon, Hair It Is, Eszter Schwenke engaged in the following activities:
1. May 1: Opened a bank account in the name of Hair It Is and deposited $20,000 of her own money in this account as her initial investment.
2. May 3: Purchased equipment on account (to be paid in 30 days), for a total cost of $4,800.
3. May 5: Interviewed three persons for the position of stylist.

In what form (type of record) should Eszter record these three activities? Prepare the entries to record the transactions.

Action Plan

- Understand which activities need to be recorded and which do not. The ones that have economic effects should be recorded in a journal.
- Analyse the effects of the transactions on asset, liability, and owner's equity accounts.

Solution

Each transaction that is recorded is entered in the general journal. The three activities would be recorded as follows:

1. May 1	Cash		20,000		
	E. Schwenke, Capital			20,000	
	Invested cash in the business.				
2.	3	Equipment	4,800		
		Accounts Payable		4,800	
		Purchased equipment on account.			
3.	5	No entry because no transaction has occurred.			

Related exercise material: BE2–4, BE2–5, BE2–6, E2–4, and E2–5.

The Ledger

The entire group of accounts maintained by a company is called the ledger. The ledger keeps in one place all the information about changes in each account.

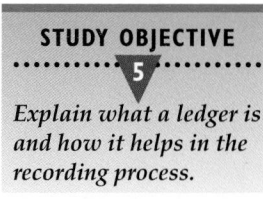

Companies may use various kinds of ledgers, but every company has a general ledger. A general ledger contains all the assets, liabilities, and owner's equity accounts. Selected accounts are shown in Illustration 2-12. A business can use a loose-leaf binder or card file for the ledger. Each account is kept on a separate sheet or card, if a manual accounting system is used. In a computerized accounting system, each account is kept in a separate file. Whenever we use the term "ledger" in this textbook without a modifying adjective, we mean the general ledger.

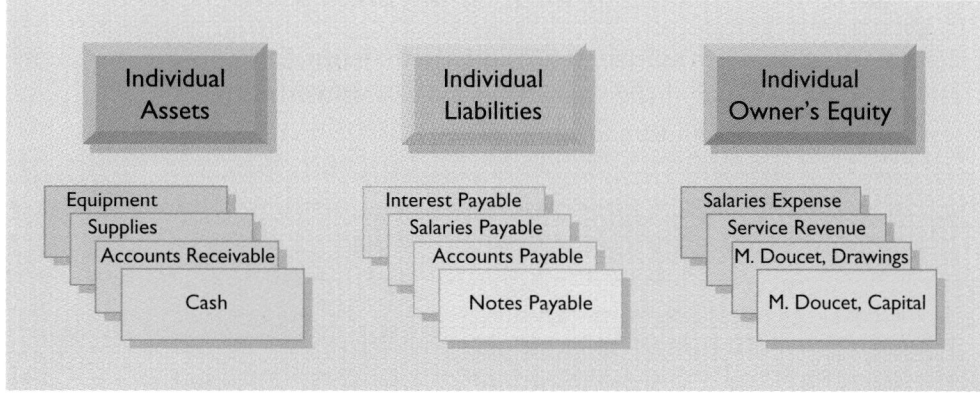

Illustration 2-12

The general ledger

The ledger should be arranged in the order in which accounts are presented in the financial statements, beginning with the balance sheet accounts. The asset accounts come first, followed by liability accounts, owner's capital, owner's drawings, revenues, and expenses. Of course, in a computerized system, the accounts can easily be rearranged in any order desired. Each account is numbered for easier identification.

The ledger provides management with a summary of transactions and the balance in each account. For example, the Cash account shows the amount of cash that is available to meet current objectives. Amounts due from customers can be found by examining Accounts Receivable. Amounts owed to creditors can be found by examining Accounts Payable.

Standard Form of Account

The simple T account form used in accounting textbooks is often very useful for illustrations. However, in reality, the account forms used in ledgers are much more structured. A form widely used in both manual and electronic systems is shown in Illustration 2-13, using data from Softbyte's Cash account.

Illustration 2-13

Three-column account

Cash						No. 101
Date		Explanation	Ref.	Debit	Credit	Balance
2002						
Sept.	1			15,000		15,000
	1				7,000	8,000
	3			1,200		9,200
	9			1,500		10,700
	17				600	10,100
	17				900	9,200
	17				200	9,000
	20				250	8,750
	25			600		9,350
	30				1,300	8,050

This form is often called the three-column form of account because it has three money columns—debit, credit, and balance. The balance in the account is determined after each transaction. Note that the explanation space and reference columns make it possible to provide information about the transaction.

Posting

STUDY OBJECTIVE
••••••••• **6** •••••••••

Explain what posting is and how it helps in the recording process.

The procedure of transferring journal entries to the ledger accounts is called **posting**. Posting involves the following steps:

1. **General Ledger**—In the ledger, enter the following in the appropriate columns of each affected account: the date, journal page, and debit or credit amount shown in the journal.
2. **General Journal**—In the reference column of the journal, write the account numbers to which the debit and credit amounts were posted.

These steps are shown in Illustration 2-14 using the first journal entry of Softbyte.

Illustration 2-14

Posting a journal entry

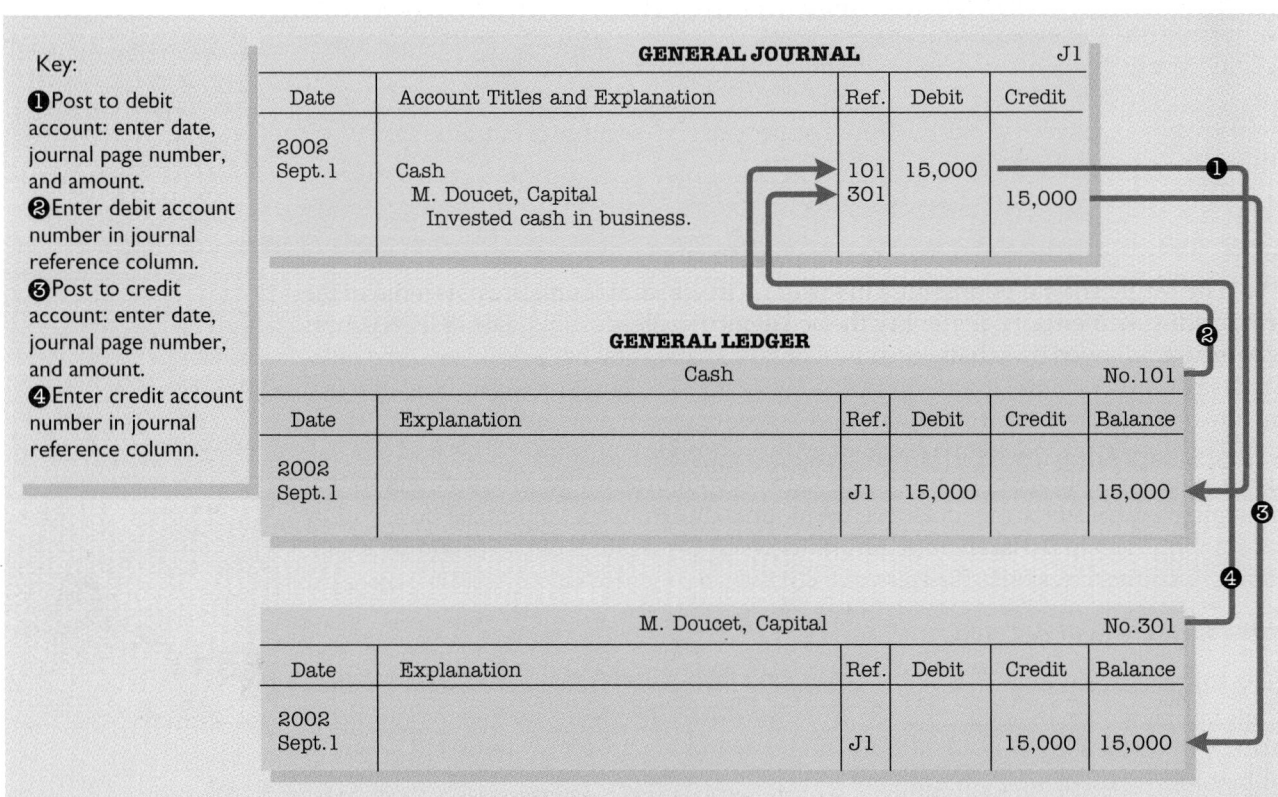

The **reference column in the journal** serves several purposes. The numbers in this column indicate the entries that have been posted. After the last entry has been posted, this column should be scanned to see that all postings have been made. The references also show the account numbers to which the amounts have been posted. The **reference column of a ledger account** indicates the journal page from which the transaction was posted.

The explanation space of the ledger account is rarely used because an explanation already appears in the journal. It is used only when detailed analysis of account activity is required.

Posting should be performed in chronological order. That is, all the debits and credits of one journal entry should be posted before proceeding to the next journal entry. Postings should be made on a timely basis—normally monthly—to ensure that the ledger is up to date.

In a computerized accounting system, posting usually occurs simultaneously after each journal entry is prepared. Obvious errors in the recording process (e.g., unbalanced entries or the use of non-existent accounts) are detected by the system and are not processed until corrected. Because the initial entry is so important, many systems search for more subtle errors, such as unreasonable dollar amounts or account balances (e.g., debit balance when the account has a normal credit balance) for specific accounts.

Chart of Accounts

The number and type of accounts used differ for each enterprise. The number of accounts depends on the amount of detail desired by management. The management of one company may want one account for all types of utility expense. Another may keep separate expense accounts for each type of utility expenditure such as gas, electricity, and water. Similarly, a single proprietorship like Softbyte has fewer accounts than a corporation like The Second Cup. Softbyte may be able to manage and report its activities in 20 to 30 accounts, while The Second Cup requires hundreds of accounts to keep track of its activities.

Helpful hint A good chart of accounts tells you a lot about the organization, such as:
 1. Is it a proprietorship, partnership, or corporation?
 2. Is it decentralized and, if so, how?
 3. Is it a merchandising, manufacturing, service, or not-for-profit company?

The first step in designing an accounting system—whether computerized or manual—is to create a **chart of accounts**. The chart of accounts extablishes the framework for the entire database of accounting information. The chart of accounts lists the accounts and the account numbers which identify their location in the ledger. The numbering system used to identify the accounts usually starts with the balance sheet accounts and follows with the income statement accounts.

►Accounting in Action ► *Business Insight*

The numbering system used to identify accounts can be quite sophisticated, or relatively simple. For example, at Goodyear (a tire and rubber company) an 18-digit system is used. The first three digits identify the division or plant. The second set of three-digit numbers contains the following account classifications:

100–199	Assets	300–399	Revenues
200–299	Liabilities and Owner's Equity	400–599	Expenses

Other digits describe the location of a specific plant, product line, region of the country, and so on.

In this and the next two chapters, we will explain the accounting for a proprietorship named Pioneer Advertising Agency (a service enterprise). Accounts 100–199 indicate asset accounts, 200–299 indicate liabilities, 300–399 indicate owner's equity accounts, 400–499, revenues, and 600–999, expenses. The chart of accounts for Pioneer Advertising Agency (C. R. Byrd, owner) is shown in Illustration 2-15. Accounts shown in red are used in this chapter; accounts shown in black are explained in later chapters.

You will notice that there are gaps in the numbering system of the chart of accounts for Pioneer Advertising. Gaps are left to permit the insertion of new accounts as needed during the life of the business.

Illustration 2-15

Chart of accounts

Pioneer Advertising Agency
Chart of Accounts

Assets	Owner's Equity
101. Cash	301. C. R. Byrd, Capital
112. Accounts Receivable	306. C. R. Byrd, Drawings
129. Advertising Supplies	
130. Prepaid Insurance	Revenues
151. Office Equipment	400. Service Revenue
152. Accumulated Amortization—	
Office Equipment	Expenses
Liabilities	611. Advertising Supplies Expense
200. Notes Payable	711. Amortization Expense
201. Accounts Payable	722. Insurance Expense
209. Unearned Revenue	726. Salaries Expense
212. Salaries Payable	729. Rent Expense
230. Interest Payable	905. Interest Expense

▼The Recording Process Illustrated

Illustrations 2-16 through 2-25 show the basic steps in the recording process, using the October transactions of the Pioneer Advertising Agency. Its accounting period is one month. A basic analysis and a debit/credit analysis precede the journalizing and posting of each transaction. For simplicity, the T account form is used in the illustrations instead of the standard account form. Study these transaction analyses carefully. **The purpose of transaction analysis is first to identify the type of account involved, and then to determine whether a debit or a credit to the account is required.** You should always do this type of analysis before preparing a journal entry. It will help you understand the journal entries discussed in this chapter, as well as more complex journal entries to be described in later chapters.

Keep in mind that every journal entry affects one or more of the following items: assets, liabilities, owner's capital, owner's drawings, revenues, or expenses. By becoming skilled at transaction analysis, you will be able to recognize quickly the impact of any transaction on these items.

Illustration 2-16

Investment of cash by owner

Helpful hint To correctly record a transaction, you must carefully analyse the event and translate that analysis into debit and credit language.

1. Determine what types of accounts are involved.

2. Determine what items increased or decreased and by how much.

3. Translate the increases and decreases into debits and credits.

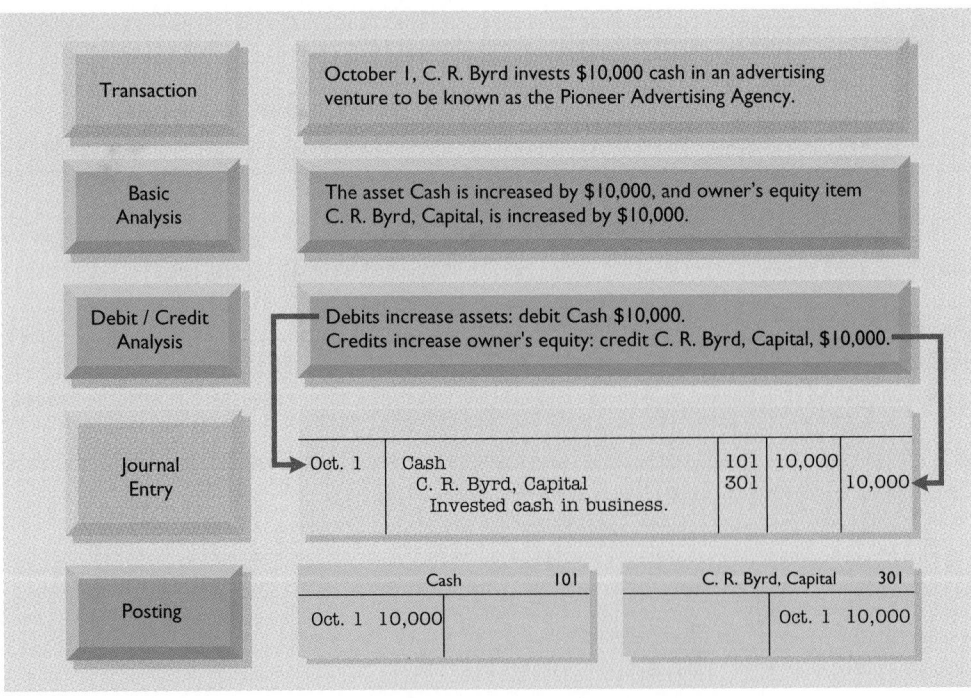

Illustration 2-17
Purchase of office equipment

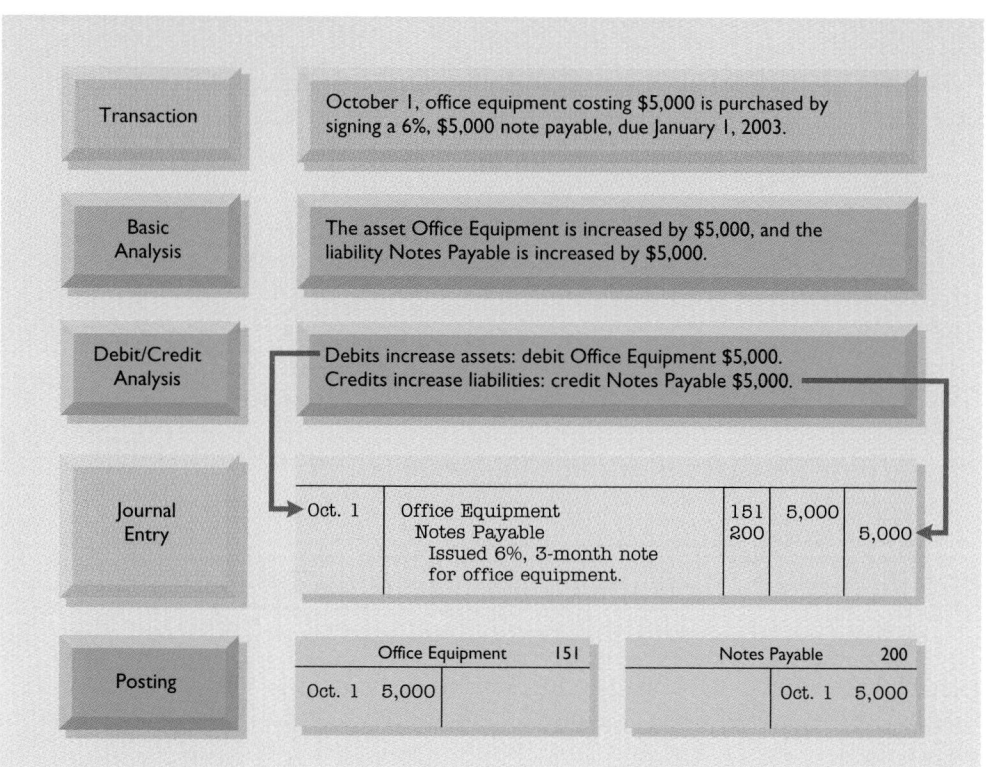

Transaction	October 1, office equipment costing $5,000 is purchased by signing a 6%, $5,000 note payable, due January 1, 2003.
Basic Analysis	The asset Office Equipment is increased by $5,000, and the liability Notes Payable is increased by $5,000.
Debit/Credit Analysis	Debits increase assets: debit Office Equipment $5,000. Credits increase liabilities: credit Notes Payable $5,000.

Oct. 1	Office Equipment	151	5,000	
	Notes Payable	200		5,000
	Issued 6%, 3-month note for office equipment.			

Posting

Office Equipment	151		Notes Payable	200
Oct. 1 5,000				Oct. 1 5,000

Illustration 2-18
Receipt of cash for future service

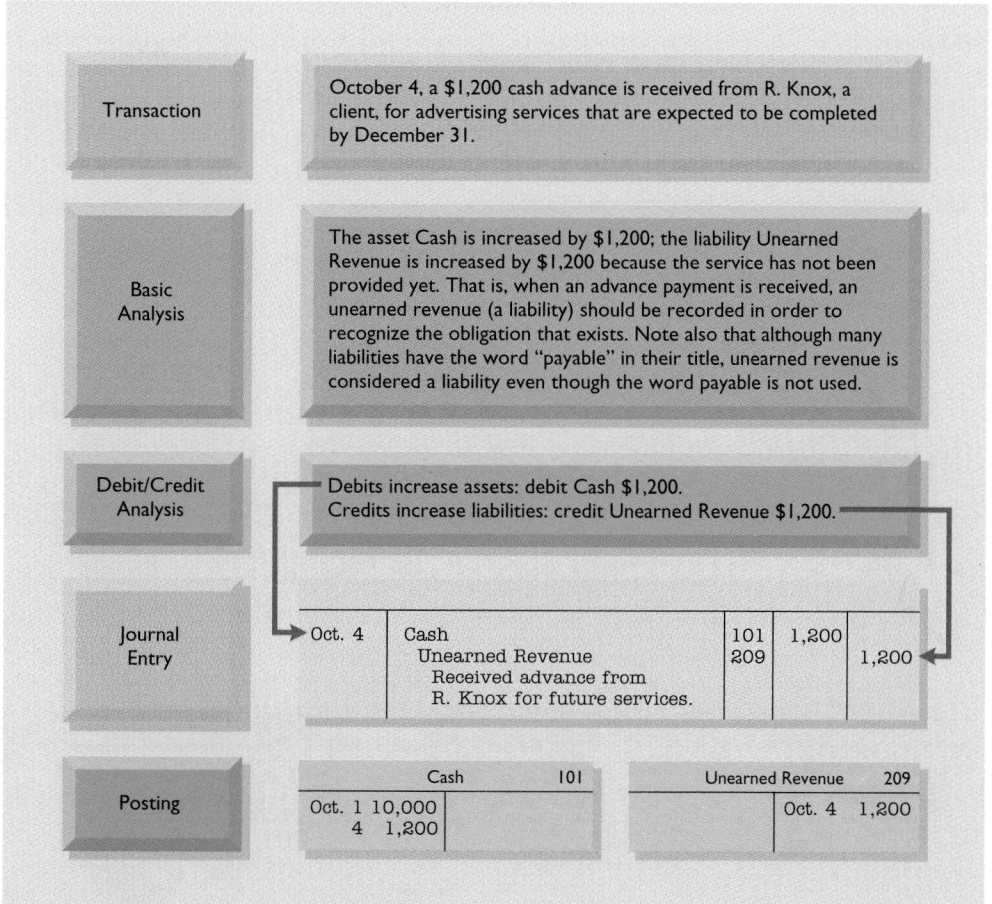

Transaction	October 4, a $1,200 cash advance is received from R. Knox, a client, for advertising services that are expected to be completed by December 31.
Basic Analysis	The asset Cash is increased by $1,200; the liability Unearned Revenue is increased by $1,200 because the service has not been provided yet. That is, when an advance payment is received, an unearned revenue (a liability) should be recorded in order to recognize the obligation that exists. Note also that although many liabilities have the word "payable" in their title, unearned revenue is considered a liability even though the word payable is not used.
Debit/Credit Analysis	Debits increase assets: debit Cash $1,200. Credits increase liabilities: credit Unearned Revenue $1,200.

Oct. 4	Cash	101	1,200	
	Unearned Revenue	209		1,200
	Received advance from R. Knox for future services.			

Posting

Cash	101		Unearned Revenue	209
Oct. 1 10,000				Oct. 4 1,200
4 1,200				

Illustration 2-19

Payment of monthly rent

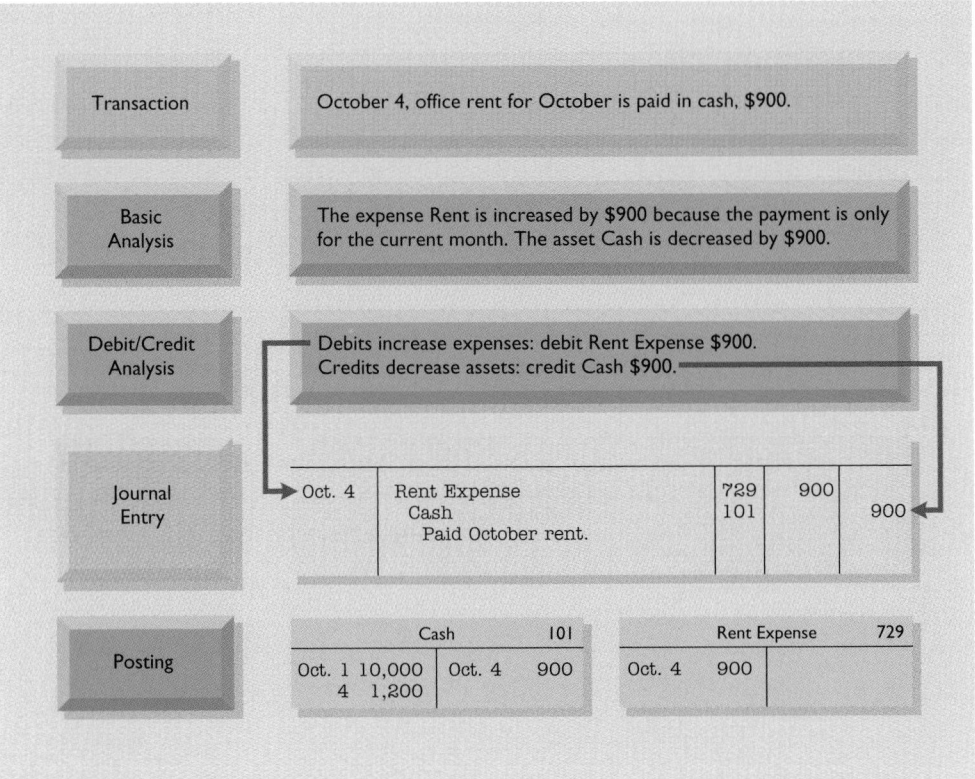

Illustration 2-20

Payment for insurance

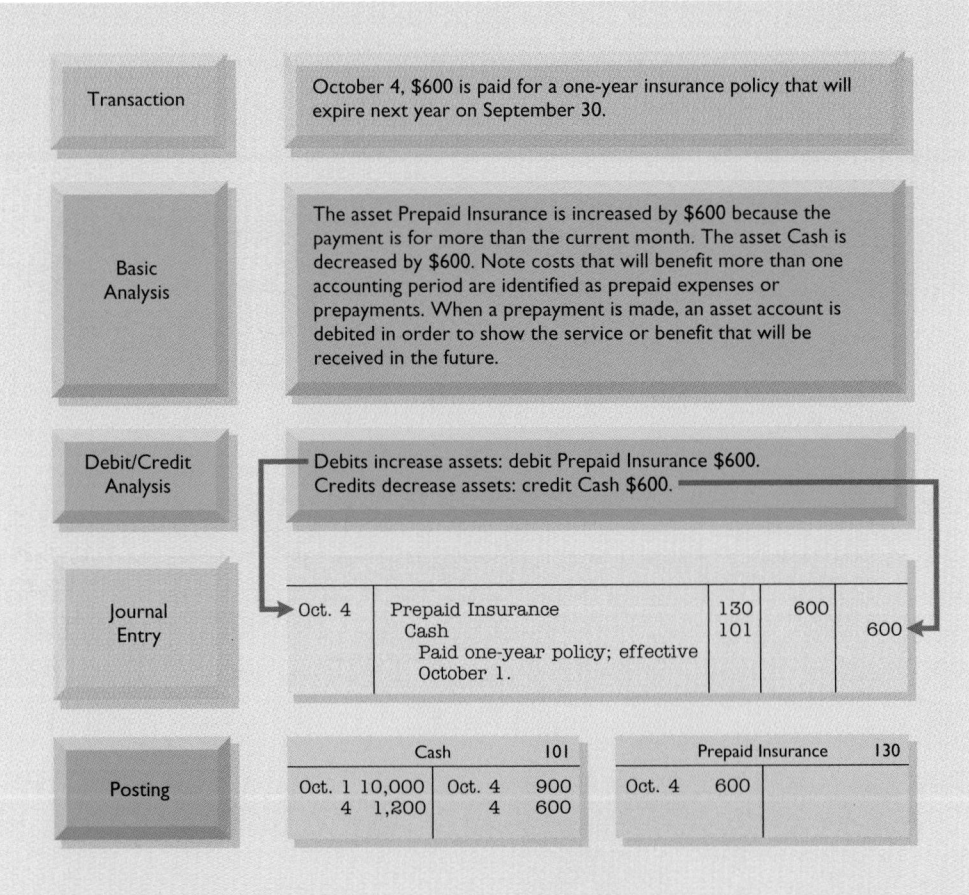

Illustration 2-21

Purchase of supplies on credit

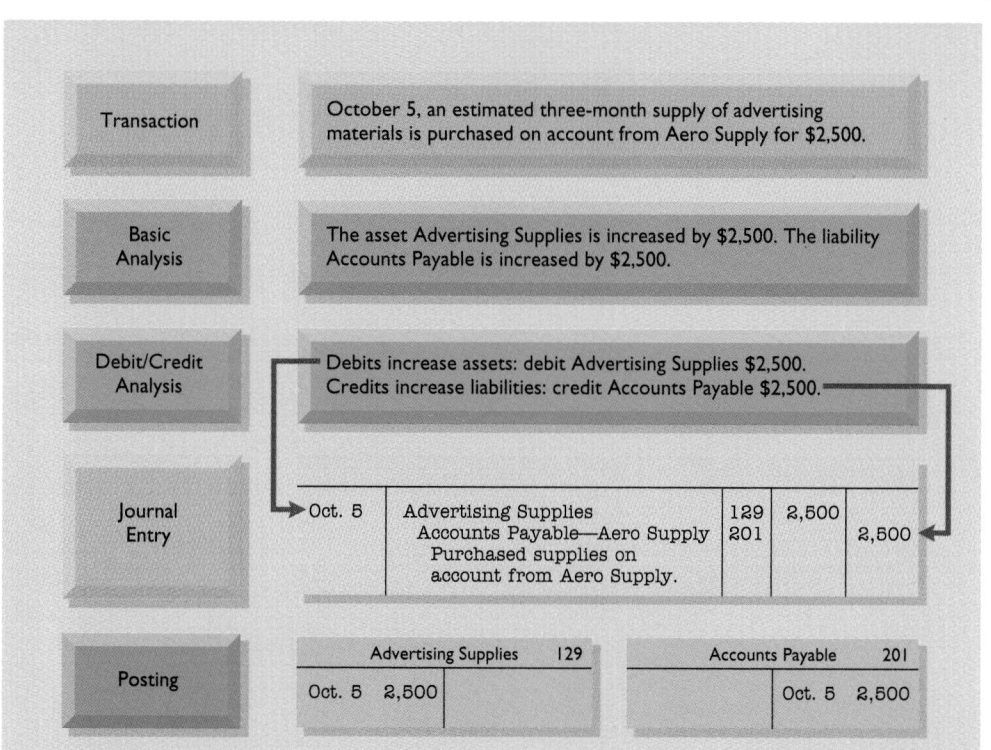

Transaction	October 5, an estimated three-month supply of advertising materials is purchased on account from Aero Supply for $2,500.			
Basic Analysis	The asset Advertising Supplies is increased by $2,500. The liability Accounts Payable is increased by $2,500.			
Debit/Credit Analysis	Debits increase assets: debit Advertising Supplies $2,500. Credits increase liabilities: credit Accounts Payable $2,500.			

Journal Entry

Oct. 5	Advertising Supplies	129	2,500	
	Accounts Payable—Aero Supply	201		2,500
	Purchased supplies on account from Aero Supply.			

Posting

Advertising Supplies 129		Accounts Payable 201	
Oct. 5 2,500			Oct. 5 2,500

Illustration 2-22

Hiring of employees

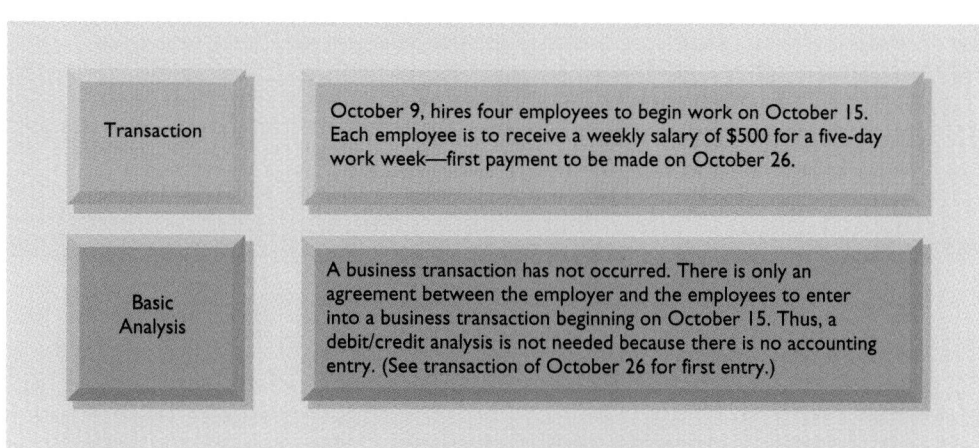

Transaction	October 9, hires four employees to begin work on October 15. Each employee is to receive a weekly salary of $500 for a five-day work week—first payment to be made on October 26.
Basic Analysis	A business transaction has not occurred. There is only an agreement between the employer and the employees to enter into a business transaction beginning on October 15. Thus, a debit/credit analysis is not needed because there is no accounting entry. (See transaction of October 26 for first entry.)

Illustration 2-23

Withdrawal of cash by owner

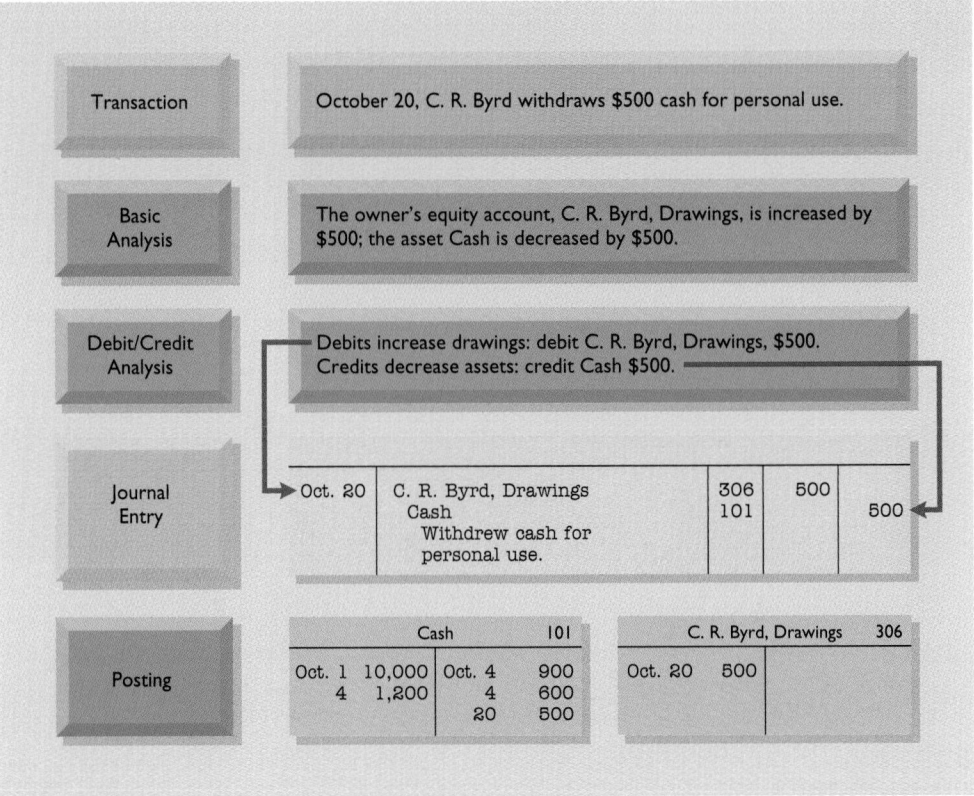

Illustration 2-24

Payment of salaries

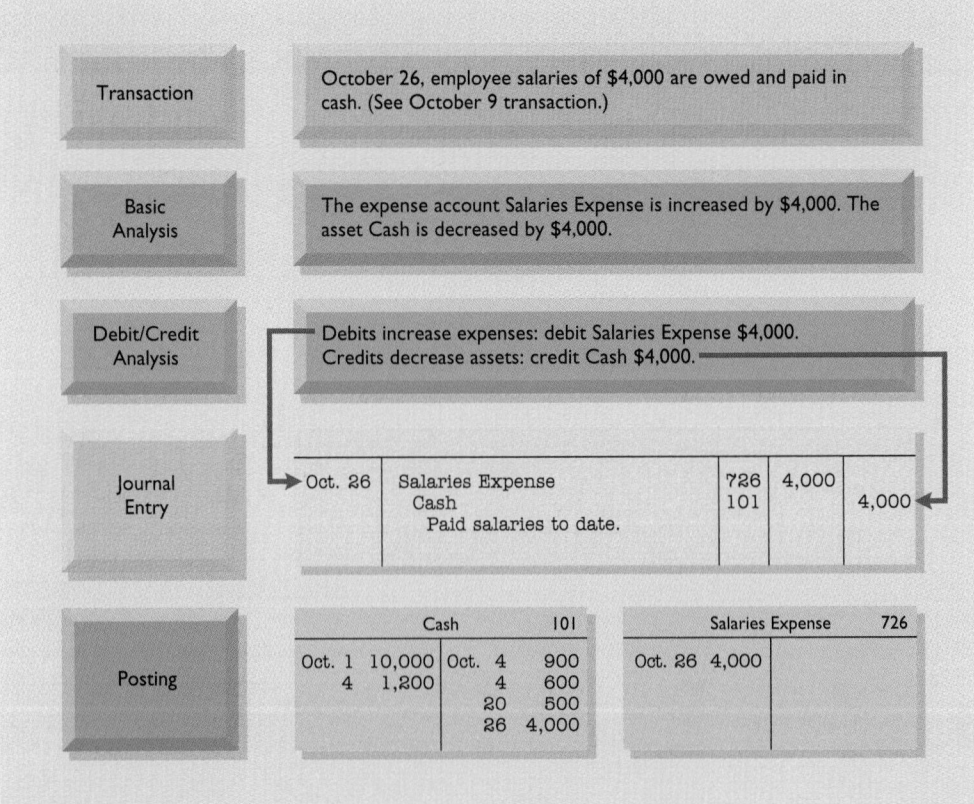

Illustration 2-25

Receipt of cash for service revenue

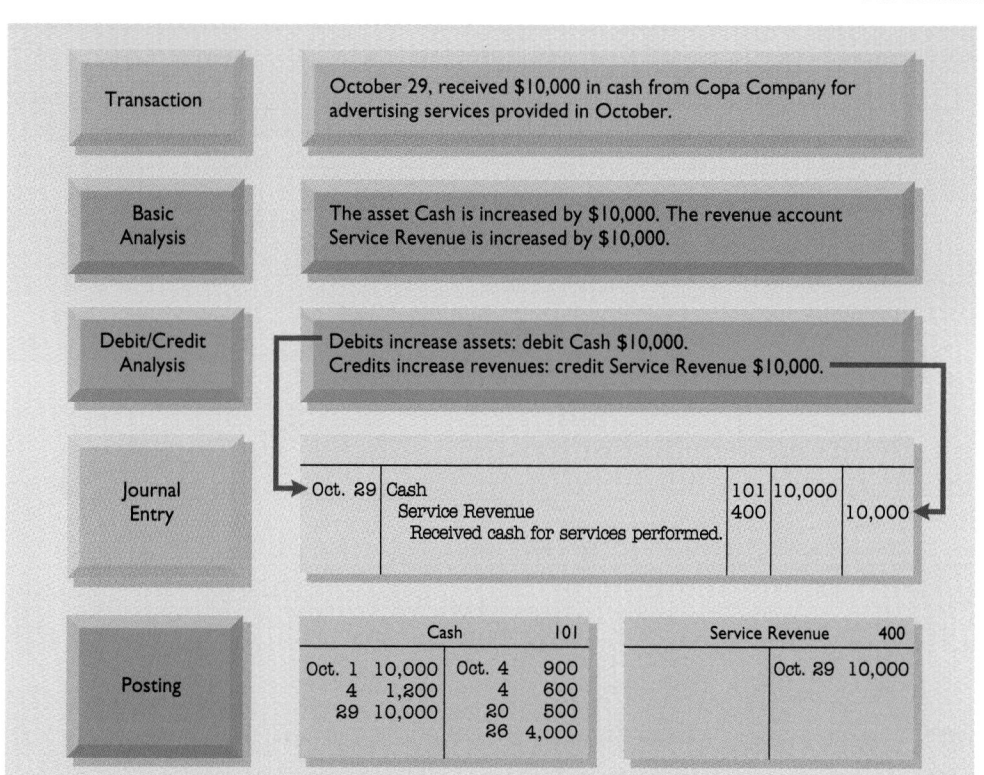

Summary Illustration of Journalizing and Posting

The journal for Pioneer Advertising Agency for October is shown in Illustration 2-26. The ledger is shown in Illustration 2-27 with all balances in colour.

Illustration 2-26

General journal entries

	GENERAL JOURNAL			J1
Date	Account Titles and Explanation	Ref.	Debit	Credit
2002				
Oct. 1	Cash	101	10,000	
	C. R. Byrd, Capital	301		10,000
	Invested cash in business.			
1	Office Equipment	151	5,000	
	Notes Payable	200		5,000
	Issued 6%, 3-month note for office equipment.			
4	Cash	101	1,200	
	Unearned Revenue	209		1,200
	Received advance from R. Knox for future services.			
4	Rent Expense	729	900	
	Cash	101		900
	Paid October rent.			
4	Prepaid Insurance	130	600	
	Cash	101		600
	Paid one-year policy; effective October 1.			
5	Advertising Supplies	129	2,500	
	Accounts Payable—Aero Supply	201		2,500
	Purchased supplies on account from Aero Supply.			
20	C. R. Byrd, Drawings	306	500	
	Cash	101		500
	Withdrew cash for personal use.			
26	Salaries Expense	726	4,000	
	Cash	101		4,000
	Paid salaries to date.			
29	Cash	101	10,000	
	Service Revenue	400		10,000
	Received cash for services performed.			

Illustration 2-27

General ledger

GENERAL LEDGER

			Cash		No. 101
Date	Explanation	Ref.	Debit	Credit	Balance
2002					
Oct. 1		J1	10,000		10,000
4		J1	1,200		11,200
4		J1		900	10,300
4		J1		600	9,700
20		J1		500	9,200
26		J1		4,000	5,200
29		J1	10,000		15,200

		Advertising Supplies			No. 129
Date	Explanation	Ref.	Debit	Credit	Balance
2002					
Oct. 5		J1	2,500		2,500

		Prepaid Insurance			No. 130
Date	Explanation	Ref.	Debit	Credit	Balance
2002					
Oct. 4		J1	600		600

		Office Equipment			No. 151
Date	Explanation	Ref.	Debit	Credit	Balance
2002					
Oct. 1		J1	5,000		5,000

		Notes Payable			No. 200
Date	Explanation	Ref.	Debit	Credit	Balance
2002					
Oct. 1		J1		5,000	5,000

		Accounts Payable			No. 201
Date	Explanation	Ref.	Debit	Credit	Balance
2002					
Oct. 5		J1		2,500	2,500

		Unearned Revenue			No. 209
Date	Explanation	Ref.	Debit	Credit	Balance
2002					
Oct. 4		J1		1,200	1,200

		C. R. Byrd, Capital			No. 301
Date	Explanation	Ref.	Debit	Credit	Balance
2002					
Oct. 1		J1		10,000	10,000

		C. R. Byrd, Drawings			No. 306
Date	Explanation	Ref.	Debit	Credit	Balance
2002					
Oct. 20		J1	500		500

		Service Revenue			No. 400
Date	Explanation	Ref.	Debit	Credit	Balance
2002					
Oct. 29		J1		10,000	10,000

		Salaries Expense			No. 726
Date	Explanation	Ref.	Debit	Credit	Balance
2002					
Oct. 26		J1	4,000		4,000

		Rent Expense			No. 729
Date	Explanation	Ref.	Debit	Credit	Balance
2002					
Oct. 4		J1	900		900

Before You Go On . . .

▸*Review It*

1. How does journalizing differ from posting in a manual system? In a computerized system?
2. What is the purpose of (a) the ledger, and (b) a chart of accounts?

▸*Do It*

In the week that followed her successful grand opening of Hair It Is, Eszter Schwenke collected $1,280 in cash for hairstyling services, and paid $400 in wages and $92 for utilities. The opening balance in the Cash account was $20,000. Eszter recorded these transactions in a general journal and posted the entries to the general ledger.

(a) Record and post these transactions.
(b) Explain the purpose and process of journalizing and posting these transactions.

Action Plan

- Analyse the transactions. Determine the accounts affected and whether the transaction increases or decreases the account.
- Record the transaction in the general journal using debits and credits. Remember that credits are indented slightly and shown to the right.
- Posting involves transferring the journalized debits and credits to specific accounts in the ledger.
- Determine the ending balances by netting the total debits and credits.

Solution

(a)

May	Cash		1,280	
	Hairstyling Service Revenue			1,280
	Received cash for services.			
	Wages Expense		400	
	Utilities Expense		92	
	Cash			492
	Paid cash for services.			

Cash		Hairstyling Service Revenue	Wages Expense	Utilities Expense
20,000	492	1,280	400	92
1,280				
20,788				

(b) The purpose of journalizing is to record every transaction in chronological order. Journalizing involves dating every transaction, measuring the dollar amount of each transaction, identifying or labelling each amount with account titles, and recording (in a standard format) equal debits and credits. Posting involves transferring the journalized debits and credits to the affected accounts in the ledger.

Related exercise material: BE2–7 and E2–6.

THE
NAVIGATOR

The Trial Balance

A **trial balance** is a list of accounts and their balances at a specific time. A trial balance is normally prepared monthly, and at least at the end of each accounting period. The accounts are listed in the order in which they appear in the ledger, with debit balances listed in the left column and credit balances in the right column.

The primary purpose of a trial balance is to prove (check) that the debits equal the credits after posting. If the debits and credits do not agree, the trial balance can uncover errors in journalizing and posting. In addition, it helps one prepare the financial statements, as will be explained in the next two chapters.

To prepare a trial balance:
1. List the account titles and their balances, using separate columns for debits and credits.
2. Total the debit and credit columns.
3. Ensure the two columns are equal.

The trial balance prepared from the ledger of Pioneer Advertising Agency is presented below:

Illustration 2-28

A trial balance

PIONEER ADVERTISING AGENCY Trial Balance October 31, 2002		
	Debit	Credit
Cash	$15,200	
Advertising Supplies	2,500	
Prepaid Insurance	600	
Office Equipment	5,000	
Notes Payable		$ 5,000
Accounts Payable		2,500
Unearned Revenue		1,200
C. R. Byrd, Capital		10,000
C. R. Byrd, Drawings	500	
Service Revenue		10,000
Salaries Expense	4,000	
Rent Expense	900	
Totals	$28,700	$28,700

Helpful hint To total or sum a column of figures can be referred to as *to foot the* column. The column is then said to be *footed*.

Note that the total debits of $28,700 equal the total credits of $28,700. Account numbers are sometimes shown to the left of the account titles in the trial balance.

Limitations of a Trial Balance

Although a trial balance reveals many types of errors which can be made in the bookkeeping process, **a trial balance does not prove that all transactions have been recorded or that the ledger is correct**. Numerous errors may exist even though the trial balance columns agree. For example, the trial balance may balance in the following cases: (1) a transaction is not journalized, (2) a correct journal entry is not posted, (3) a journal entry is posted twice, (4) incorrect accounts are used in journalizing or posting, or (5) offsetting errors are made in recording the amount of a transaction. In other words, as long as equal debits and credits are posted, even to the wrong account or in the wrong amount, the total debits will equal the total credits when the trial balance is prepared.

Locating Errors

▸ *Ethics note*

Auditors differentiate errors from irregularities when evaluating the accounting system. An error is the result of an unintentional mistake. As such, it is neither ethical nor unethical. An irregularity, on the other hand, is an intentional misstatement, which is generally viewed as unethical.

The procedure for preparing a trial balance is relatively simple. However, if the trial balance does not balance, locating an error in a manual accounting system can be time-consuming, tedious, and frustrating. Errors generally result from mathematical mistakes, incorrect postings, or simply transcribing data incorrectly. Errors in a computerized system usually involve the initial recording rather than some mechanical error in the posting or preparation of a trial balance.

What do you do if you are faced with a manual trial balance that does not balance? First determine the amount of the difference between the two columns of the trial balance. After this amount is known, the following steps are often helpful:
1. If the error is an amount such as $1, $100, or $1,000, recalculate the trial balance columns. Recalculate the account balances.
2. If the error is divisible by two, scan the trial balance to see whether a balance equal to half the error has been entered in the wrong column.
3. If the error is divisible by nine, retrace the account balances on the trial balance to see whether they are incorrectly copied from the ledger. For example, if a

balance was $12 but was listed as $21, a $9 error has been made. Reversing the order of numbers is called a **transposition error**.

4. If the error is not divisible by two or nine, scan the ledger to see whether an account balance in the amount of the error has been omitted from the trial balance. Scan the journal to see whether a posting in the amount of the error has been omitted. Check your additions.

▶Accounting in Action ▸ *Business Insight*

If you've ever made an arithmetic error in your cheque book, you may take some comfort from an accountant's mistake at Fidelity Investments, the world's largest mutual fund investment company. The accountant failed to include a minus sign while doing a tax calculation, which made a $1.3 billion loss look like a $1.3 billion gain. No one expects that kind of mistake at a firm like Fidelity, with sophisticated computer systems and top investment managers. In explaining the mistake to shareholders, Fidelity's manager, J. Gary Burkhead, wrote: "Some people have asked how, in this age of technology, such a mistake could be made. While many of our processes are computerized, the requirements of the tax code are complex and dictate that some steps must be handled manually by our tax managers and accountants, and people can make mistakes." Evidently so. That's why it pays to do a "reasonableness check." Someone at Fidelity must have had a sense that the year's results shouldn't have been as rosy as the accounting numbers first indicated.

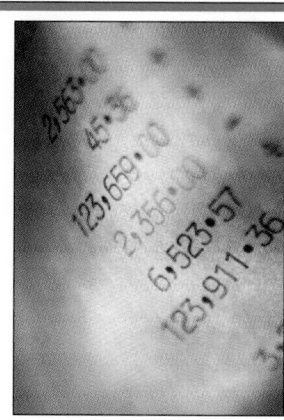

Use of Dollars and Cents

In the interests of simplicity, we have not included cents in the dollar figures we record in journal entries, general ledger accounts, and trial balances. Avoiding cents in entries will save you time and effort without inhibiting the understanding of the accounting process. In reality, it is important to understand that cents should be, and are, used in the formal accounting records. Cents are important, and quickly add up to dollars!

Dollar signs do not appear in the journals or ledgers. Dollar signs are used only in the trial balance and the financial statements. Generally, a dollar sign is shown only for the first item in the column, and for the total of that column. A single line is placed under the column of figures to be added or subtracted. The total amount is double-underlined to indicate the final sum.

Before You Go On . . .
▶*Review It*

1. What is a trial balance, and what is its primary purpose?
2. How is a trial balance prepared?
3. What are the limitations of a trial balance?

Related exercise material: BE2–8, BE2–9, E2–7, E2–8, E2–9, and E2–10.

THE
NAVIGATOR

▶ *A Look Back at Our Feature Story*

Refer back to the feature story about the Mug and Musket at the beginning of the chapter. Answer the following questions:

1. What accounting entries would Tanis likely make to record each of the following: (a) the receipt of cash from customers in payment of their bills, (b) purchases of food supplies, and (c) payment of wages for the waiters?
2. How did Tanis's job as Director of Finance help her studies as she finished her Business Administration degree?

Solution

1. Tanis would likely make the following entries:
   (a) Cash

        Food Sales

            Receipt of payment for food services.

   (b) Food Supplies Expense

        Cash

            Purchased food supplies.

   Periodically, the unused food would be counted and an entry made to record the food remaining (Food Supplies).

   (c) Salaries (or Wages) Expense

        Cash

            Paid waiters' wages.

THE
NAVIGATOR

2. As a result of her accounting position, Tanis was able to relate the subject matter as well as much of the assignment material in her business courses to a real-world context. From her job, she knew how bills were paid; how supplies were determined; how employees were hired, managed, evaluated, and paid; and much more.

**Additional
Demonstration Problem**

DEMONSTRATION PROBLEM

Nge Aung opened the Campus Laundromat on September 1, 2002. During the first month of operations, the following transactions occurred:

Sept. 1 Invested $20,000 cash in the business.
    2 Paid $1,000 cash for store rent for the month of September.
    3 Purchased washers and dryers for $25,000, paying $10,000 in cash and signing a $15,000 6-month, 5% note payable.
    6 Paid $1,200 for a one-year insurance policy.
  10 Received bill from *The Daily News* for advertising the opening of the laundromat, $200.
  20 Withdrew $700 cash for personal use.
  30 Cash receipts for laundry fees for the month were $6,200.

The chart of accounts for the company is the same as the one for Pioneer Advertising Agency on page 64 except for the following: No. 153 Laundry Equipment and No. 610 Advertising Expense.

Instructions

(a) Journalize the September transactions. (Use J1 for the journal page number.)
(b) Open ledger accounts and post the September transactions.
(c) Prepare a trial balance at September 30, 2002.

Solution to Demonstration Problem

(a)

GENERAL JOURNAL   J1

Date		Account Titles and Explanation	Ref.	Debit	Credit
2002					
Sept.	1	Cash	101	20,000	
		Nge Aung, Capital	301		20,000
		Invested cash in business.			
	2	Rent Expense	729	1,000	
		Cash	101		1,000
		Paid September rent.			
	3	Laundry Equipment	153	25,000	
		Cash	101		10,000
		Notes Payable	200		15,000
		Purchased laundry equipment for			
		cash and 6-month, 5% note payable.			
	6	Prepaid Insurance	130	1,200	
		Cash	101		1,200
		Paid one-year insurance policy.			
	10	Advertising Expense	610	200	
		Accounts Payable—*Daily News*	201		200
		Received bill from *The Daily News*			
		for advertising.			
	20	Nge Aung, Drawings	306	700	
		Cash	101		700
		Withdrew cash for personal use.			
	30	Cash	101	6,200	
		Service Revenue	400		6,200
		Received cash for laundry services.			

Action Plan

- Separate journal entries are made for each transaction.
- In journalizing, make sure debits equal credits.
- In journalizing, use specific account titles taken from the chart of accounts.
- Provide an appropriate description of each journal entry.
- Arrange the ledger in statement order, beginning with the balance sheet accounts.
- Post in chronological order.
- Numbers in the reference column indicate the amount has been posted.
- The trial balance lists accounts in the order in which they appear in the ledger.
- Debit balances are listed in the left column of the trial balance, credit balances in the right column.

(b)

GENERAL LEDGER

Cash — No. 101

Date	Explanation	Ref.	Debit	Credit	Balance
2002					
Sept. 1		J1	20,000		20,000
2		J1		1,000	19,000
3		J1		10,000	9,000
6		J1		1,200	7,800
20		J1		700	7,100
30		J1	6,200		13,300

Prepaid Insurance — No. 130

Date	Explanation	Ref.	Debit	Credit	Balance
2002					
Sept. 6		J1	1,200		1,200

Laundry Equipment — No. 153

Date	Explanation	Ref.	Debit	Credit	Balance
2002					
Sept. 3		J1	25,000		25,000

Notes Payable — No. 200

Date	Explanation	Ref.	Debit	Credit	Balance
2002					
Sept. 3		J1		15,000	15,000

Accounts Payable — No. 201

Date	Explanation	Ref.	Debit	Credit	Balance
2002					
Sept. 10		J1		200	200

Nge Aung, Capital — No. 301

Date	Explanation	Ref.	Debit	Credit	Balance
2002					
Sept. 1		J1		20,000	20,000

Nge Aung, Drawings — No. 306

Date	Explanation	Ref.	Debit	Credit	Balance
2002					
Sept. 20		J1	700		700

Service Revenue — No. 400

Date	Explanation	Ref.	Debit	Credit	Balance
2002					
Sept. 30		J1		6,200	6,200

Advertising Expense — No. 610

Date	Explanation	Ref.	Debit	Credit	Balance
2002					
Sept. 10		J1	200		200

Rent Expense — No. 729

Date	Explanation	Ref.	Debit	Credit	Balance
2002					
Sept. 2		J1	1,000		1,000

(c)

CAMPUS LAUNDROMAT
Trial Balance
September 30, 2002

	Debit	Credit
Cash	$13,300	
Prepaid Insurance	1,200	
Laundry Equipment	25,000	
Notes Payable		$15,000
Accounts Payable		200
Nge Aung, Capital		20,000
Nge Aung, Drawings	700	
Service Revenue		6,200
Advertising Expense	200	
Rent Expense	1,000	
Totals	$41,400	$41,400

Summary of Study Objectives

1. *Explain what an account is and how it helps in the recording process.* An account is an individual accounting record of increases and decreases in a specific asset, liability, or owner's equity item.

2. *Define debits and credits and illustrate how they are used to record business transactions.* Assets, drawings, and expenses are increased by debits (left-hand side of the account) and decreased by credits (right-hand side of the account). Liabilities, owner's capital, and revenues are increased by credits (right-hand side of the account) and decreased by debits (left-hand side of the account).

3. *Describe the basic steps in the recording process.* The basic steps in the recording process are as follows: (a) analyse each transaction in terms of its effect on the accounts, (b) enter the transaction information in a journal, (c) transfer the journal information to the appropriate accounts in the ledger.

4. *Explain what a journal is and how it helps in the recording process, and journalize business transactions.* The first accounting record of a transaction is entered in a journal, and the data are later transferred to the general ledger. A journal (a) discloses in one place the complete effect of a transaction, (b) provides a chronological record of transactions, (c) prevents and helps locate errors because the debit and credit amounts for each entry can be easily compared, and (d) provides an explanation of the transaction and reference to the source document, where applicable.

5. *Explain what a ledger is and how it helps in the recording process.* The entire group of accounts maintained by a company is called the ledger. The ledger keeps in one place all the information about changes in each of the specific account balances.

6. *Explain what posting is and how it helps in the recording process.* Posting is the procedure of transferring journal entries to the ledger accounts. This phase of the recording process accumulates the effects of journalized transactions in the individual accounts.

7. *Explain the purpose of, and prepare, a trial balance.* A trial balance is a list of accounts and their balances at a given time. Its primary purpose is to prove the equality of debits and credits after posting. A trial balance also uncovers certain types of errors in journalizing and posting, and is useful in preparing financial statements.

THE NAVIGATOR

GLOSSARY

Account A record of increases and decreases in a specific asset, liability, or owner's equity item. (p. 54)

Chart of accounts A list of accounts and the account numbers which identify their location in the ledger. (p. 65)

Compound entry An entry that involves three or more accounts. (p. 62)

Credit The right side of an account. (p. 55)

Debit The left side of an account. (p. 55)

Double-entry system A system that records the dual effect of each transaction in appropriate accounts. (p. 55)

General journal The book of original entry in which transactions are recorded when they are not recorded in other specialized journals. (p. 60)

General ledger A ledger that contains accounts for all assets, liabilities, equities, revenues, and expenses. (p. 63)

 Key Term Matching Activity

Journal An accounting record in which transactions are recorded in chronological (date) order. (p. 60)

Journalizing The entering of transaction data in the journal. (p. 60)

Ledger A book of final entry that contains all accounts for the company or specialized accounts supporting other ledgers. (p. 63)

Posting The procedure of transferring journal entries to the ledger accounts. (p. 64)

T account A form of account resembling the letter T with the title above the horizontal line. Debits are shown to the left of the vertical line, credits to the right. (p. 54)

Trial balance A list of accounts and their balances at a given time, usually at the end of the accounting period. (p. 73)

SELF-STUDY QUESTIONS

Answers are at the end of the chapter.

(SO 1) K   1. Which of the following statements about an account is true?
   a. The left side of an account is the credit or decrease side.
   b. An account is an individual accounting record of increases and decreases in specific asset, liability, and owner's equity items.
   c. There are separate accounts for specific assets and liabilities but only one account for owner's equity items.
   d. In its simplest form, an account consists of two parts.

(SO 2) K   2. Debits:
   a. increase both assets and liabilities.
   b. decrease both assets and liabilities.
   c. increase assets and decrease liabilities.
   d. decrease assets and increase liabilities.

(SO 2) K   3. A revenue account:
   a. is increased by debits.
   b. is decreased by credits.
   c. has a normal balance of a debit.
   d. is increased by credits.

(SO 2) K   4. Accounts that normally have debit balances are:
   a. assets, expenses, and revenues.
   b. assets, expenses, and owner's capital.
   c. assets, liabilities, and owner's drawings.
   d. assets, owner's drawings, and expenses.

(SO 3) K   5. Which of the following is not part of the recording process?
   a. Analysing transactions
   b. Preparing a trial balance
   c. Entering transactions in a journal
   d. Posting transactions

(SO 4) K   6. Which of the following statements about a journal is false?
   a. It is not a book of original entry.
   b. It provides a chronological record of transactions.
   c. It helps to locate errors because the debit and credit amounts for each entry can be readily compared.
   d. It discloses in one place the complete effect of a transaction.

(SO 5) K   7. A ledger:
   a. contains only asset and liability accounts.
   b. should show accounts in alphabetical order.
   c. is a collection of the entire group of accounts maintained by a company.
   d. is a book of original entry.

(SO 6) C   8. Posting:
   a. normally occurs before journalizing.
   b. transfers ledger transaction data to the journal.
   c. is an optional step in the recording process.
   d. transfers journal entries to ledger accounts.

(SO 7) C   9. A trial balance:
   a. is a list of accounts with their balances at a given time.
   b. proves the accuracy of journalized transactions.
   c. will not balance if a correct journal entry is posted twice.
   d. proves that all transactions have been recorded.

(SO 7) C   10. A trial balance will not balance if:
   a. a correct journal entry is posted twice.
   b. the purchase of supplies on account is debited to Supplies and credited to Cash.
   c. a $100 cash drawing by the owner is debited to Owner's Drawings for $1,000 and credited to Cash for $100.
   d. a $450 payment on account is debited to Accounts Payable for $45 and credited to Cash for $45.

QUESTIONS

(SO 1) C   1. Describe a T account.

(SO 2) C   2. The terms "debit" and "credit" mean increase and decrease, respectively. Do you agree? Explain.

(SO 2) C   3. Jos Arcelus, a fellow student, contends that the double-entry system means each transaction must be recorded twice. Is Jos correct? Explain.

(SO 2) C   4. Kim Nouyen, a beginning accounting student, believes debit balances are favourable and credit balances are unfavourable. Is Kim correct? Discuss.

(SO 2) K   5. State the rules of debit and credit and identify the normal balance for (a) asset accounts (b) liability accounts, and (c) owner's equity accounts.

(SO 2) K   6. What is the normal balance for each of the following accounts?

(a) Accounts Receivable   (e) Service Revenue
(b) Cash   (f) Salaries Expense
(c) Owner's Drawings   (g) Owner's Capital
(d) Accounts Payable

(SO 2) K   7. Decide if each of the following accounts is an asset, a liability, or an owner's equity account and if it would have a normal debit or credit balance:
(a) Accounts Receivable   (d) Owner's Drawings
(b) Accounts Payable   (e) Supplies
(c) Equipment   (f) Unearned Revenue

(SO 2) C   8. For the following transactions, indicate the account debited and the account credited:
(a) Supplies are purchased on account.
(b) Cash is received on signing a note payable.
(c) Employees are paid salaries in cash.

(SO 2) C 9. Indicate whether the following accounts generally will have (a) debit entries only, (b) credit entries only, or (c) both debit and credit entries:
1. Accounts Payable   4. Owner's Drawings
2. Accounts Receivable 5. Salaries Expense
3. Cash   6. Service Revenue

(SO 3) C 10. Ben Benoit, a fellow student, is unclear about the basic steps in the recording process. Briefly explain the steps, in the order in which they occur.

(SO 4) K 11. (a) When entering a transaction in the journal, should the debit or the credit be written first?
(b) Which should be indented, the debit or the credit?

(SO 4) C 12. Explain what is meant by a compound journal entry and give an example.

(SO 4) AP 13. Journalize the following business transactions:
(a) Doris Wang invests $9,000 in her business.
(b) Insurance of $800 is paid for the year.
(c) Supplies of $1,500 are purchased on account.
(d) Cash of $7,500 is received for services rendered.

(SO 4, 5) AP 14. (a) Can business transaction debits and credits be recorded directly in the ledger accounts?
(b) What are the advantages of first recording transactions in the journal, and then posting to the ledger?

(SO 5, 6) AP 15. (a) What is a ledger?
(b) What is a chart of accounts, and why is it important?

(SO 6) AP 16. The account number is entered as the last step in posting the amounts from the journal to the ledger. What is the advantage of this step?

(SO 7) AP 17. What is a trial balance? What are its purposes?

(SO 3, 4, 5, 6, 7) AP 18. Kap Shin is confused about how accounting information flows through the accounting system. He believes the flow of information is as follows:
(a) Debits and credits are posted to the ledger.
(b) The business transaction occurs.
(c) Information is entered in the journal.
(d) Financial statements are prepared.
(e) A trial balance is prepared.
Show Kap the proper flow of information.

(SO 7) S 19. Two students are discussing the use of a trial balance. They wonder if the following errors would prevent the trial balance from balancing. Consider each error separately.
(a) The bookkeeper debited Cash for $600 and credited Wages Expense for $600 for payment of wages.
(b) Cash collected on account was debited from Cash for $900 and credited to Service Revenue for $90.
· What would you tell them?

BRIEF EXERCISES

BE2–1 For each of the following accounts indicate (a) the effect of a debit or credit on the account, and (b) the normal balance:
1. Accounts Payable
2. Advertising Expense
3. Service Revenue
4. Accounts Receivable
5. J. Takamoto, Capital
6. J. Takamoto, Drawings
7. Prepaid Insurance
8. Office Equipment
9. Rent Expense
10. Unearned Revenue
11. Advertising Supplies
12. Notes Payable

Indicate debit and credit effects and normal balance.
(SO 2) K

BE2–2 Transactions for the Ing Company for the month of June are presented below. Identify the accounts to be debited and credited for each transaction.
June 1 D. Ing invests $2,000 cash in a small welding business.
2 Buys equipment on account for $900.
3 Pays $500 to landlord for June rent.
12 Bills T. Sargeant $300 for welding work done.

Identify accounts to be debited and credited.
(SO 2) K

BE2–3 A. Fisher has the following transactions during August of the current year. Indicate (a) the basic analysis, and (b) the debit/credit analysis, as illustrated in the chapter.
Aug. 1 Opens an office as a financial advisor, investing $6,000 in cash.
4 Pays insurance in advance for six months, $1,800.
16 Receives $900 from clients for services rendered.
27 Pays secretary $500 salary.

Indicate basic and debit/credit analysis.
(SO 2) K

BE2–4 M. Therriault, a fellow student, is unclear about the steps in the recording process. Identify and briefly explain the steps in the order in which they occur.

Identify and explain steps in recording process.
(SO 3) C

BE2–5 Using the data in BE2–2, journalize the transactions.

Journalize transactions.
(SO 4) AP

BE2–6 Using the data in BE2–3, journalize the transactions.

Journalize transactions.
(SO 4) AP

Post journal entries to T accounts.
(SO 6) AP

BE2–7 Selected transactions for the Glasson Company are presented in journal entry form below. Post the transactions to T accounts.

GENERAL JOURNAL   J1

Date	Account Titles and Explanation	Ref.	Debit	Credit
May 5	Accounts Receivable		3,200	
	Service Revenue			3,200
12	Cash		2,400	
	Accounts Receivable			2,400
15	Cash		2,000	
	Service Revenue			2,000

Prepare trial balance.
(SO 7) AP

BE2–8 From the ledger balances given below, prepare a trial balance for the Beirsdorf Company at June 30, 2003. All account balances are normal.

Accounts Payable	$ 5,000	Service Revenue	$6,000
Cash	4,800	Accounts Receivable	3,000
Beirsdorf, Capital	20,000	Salaries Expense	4,000
Beirsdorf, Drawings	1,200	Rent Expense	1,000
Equipment	17,000		

Prepare correct trial balance.
(SO 7) AP

BE2–9 An inexperienced bookkeeper prepared the following trial balance that does not balance. Prepare a correct trial balance, assuming all account balances are normal.

BOURQUE COMPANY
Trial Balance
December 31, 2002

	Debit	Credit
Cash	$16,800	
Prepaid Insurance		$ 3,500
Accounts Payable		3,000
Unearned Revenue	2,200	
Lea Bourque, Capital		15,000
Lea Bourque, Drawings		4,500
Service Revenue		25,600
Salaries Expense	18,600	
Rent Expense		2,400
Totals	$37,600	$54,000

EXERCISES

••

Identify debits and credits and their effect on normal balances, and classify accounts.
(SO 2) K

E2–1 Selected accounts for Poitras Company follow:
1. Accounts Payable
2. Accounts Receivable
3. Cash
4. H. Poitras, Drawings
5. Interest Revenue
6. Office Equipment
7. Prepaid Insurance
8. Rent Expense

Instructions
(a) Indicate the normal balance of each of the above accounts.
(b) Identify whether a debit or credit is necessary to *decrease* the normal balance of each of the above accounts.
(c) Indicate the financial statement in which each account appears.

Identify accounts, debits, credits, and normal balances.
(SO 2) K

E2–2 Selected transactions for L. Visser, an interior decorator, in her first month of business are as follows:

Mar. 3 Invested $8,000 cash in the business.
  6 Purchased used car for $4,000 cash, for use in the business.
  7 Purchased supplies on account for $500.
  12 Billed customers $1,800 for services performed.

21 Paid $200 cash for advertising the launch of the business.
25 Received $700 cash from customers billed on March 12.
28 Paid creditor $300 cash on account.
31 Withdrew $500 cash for owner's personal use.

Instructions

For each transaction indicate:
(a) The basic type of account debited and credited (asset, liability, owner's equity)
(b) The specific account debited and credited (Cash, Rent Expense, Service Revenue, etc.)
(c) Whether the specific account is increased or decreased
(d) The normal balance of the specific account

Use the following format, in which transaction 1 is given as an example:

	Account Debited				Account Credited			
Trans-action	(a) Basic Type	(b) Specific Account	(c) Effect	(d) Normal Balance	(a) Basic Type	(b) Specific Account	(c) Effect	(d) Normal Balance
Mar. 3	Asset	Cash	Increase	Debit	Owner's Equity	L. Visser, Capital	Increase	Credit

E2–3 The information below is for Gardiner Real Estate Agency:

Analyse transactions.
(SO 2) AP

Oct. 1 Lynn Gardiner begins business as a real estate agent with a cash investment of $15,000.
   2 Hires an administrative assistant at a salary of $960 per month.
   3 Buys office furniture for $1,900, on account.
   6 Sells a house and lot to B. Rollins. Fees due from Rollins, $3,200 (not paid by Rollins at this time).
  10 Receives cash of $140 as fee for renting an apartment.
  27 Pays $700 on the balance indicated in the transaction of October 3.
  30 Pays the administrative assistant $960 in salary for October.

Instructions

Prepare the debit/credit analysis for each transaction, as illustrated in the chapter.

E2–4 Data for L. Visser, interior decorator, are presented in E2–2.

Journalize transactions.
(SO 4) AP

Instructions

Journalize the transactions.

E2–5 Transaction data for Gardiner Real Estate Agency are presented in E2–3.

Journalize transactions.
(SO 4) AP

Instructions

Journalize the transactions.

E2–6 Selected transactions for the Basler Company during its first month in business are presented below:

Prepare journal entries and post.
(SO 4, 6) AP

Sept. 1 Invested $12,000 cash in the business.
   5 Purchased equipment for $10,000, paying $4,000 in cash and the balance on account.
  25 Paid $3,000 cash on the balance owed for equipment.
  30 Withdrew $500 cash for personal use.

Basler's chart of accounts shows the following: Cash No. 101, Equipment No. 157, Accounts Payable No. 201, Shirley Basler, Capital, No. 301, and Shirley Basler, Drawings, No. 306.

Instructions

(a) Journalize the transactions.
(b) Post the transactions to the accounts in the ledger.

Journalize transactions from account data and prepare trial balance.
(SO 4, 7) AP

E2–7 The ledger for Fortin Co. is presented below:

Cash			No. 101
10/1	5,000	10/4	400
10/10	650	10/12	1,500
10/10	5,000	10/31	250
10/20	500	10/30	300
10/25	2,000	10/31	500

Accounts Receivable			No. 112
10/6	800	10/20	500
10/20	940		

Supplies		No. 126
10/4	400	

Furniture		No. 149
10/3	2,000	

Notes Payable		No. 200
	10/10	5,000

Accounts Payable			No. 201
10/12	1,500	10/3	2,000

A. Fortin, Capital		No. 301
	10/1	5,000
	10/25	2,000

A. Fortin, Drawings		No. 306
10/30	300	

Service Revenue		No. 400
	10/6	800
	10/10	650
	10/20	940

Store Wages Expense		No. 628
10/31	500	

Rent Expense		No. 729
10/31	250	

Instructions

(a) Reproduce the journal entries for the transactions for the month of October, and provide explanations for each.

(b) Determine the October 31 balance for each account. Prepare a trial balance at October 31, 2003.

Post journal entries and prepare trial balance.
(SO 6, 7) AP

E2–8 Selected transactions from the journal of L. Meche, investment broker, are presented below:

Date	Account Titles and Explanation	Ref.	Debit	Credit
2003				
Aug. 1	Cash		2,600	
	L. Meche, Capital			2,600
10	Cash		2,400	
	Service Revenue			2,400
12	Office Equipment		4,000	
	Cash			1,000
	Notes Payable			3,000
25	Accounts Receivable		1,400	
	Service Revenue			1,400
31	Cash		900	
	Accounts Receivable			900

Instructions

(a) Post the transactions to T accounts.

(b) Prepare a trial balance at August 31, 2003.

Analyse errors and their effect on trial balance.
(SO 6, 7) AN

E2–9 The bookkeeper for Allain Equipment Repair made a number of errors in journalizing and posting:

1. A credit posting of $400 to Accounts Receivable was omitted.
2. A debit posting of $750 for Prepaid Insurance was debited to Insurance Expense.
3. A collection on account of $100 was journalized and posted as a debit to Cash $100 and a credit to Service Revenue $100.
4. A credit posting of $300 to Property Taxes Payable was made twice.
5. A cash purchase of supplies for $250 was journalized and posted as a debit to Supplies $2,500 and a credit to Cash $2,500.
6. A debit of $465 to Advertising Expense was posted as $645.

Instructions

For each error, indicate (a) whether the trial balance will balance. If the trial balance will not balance, indicate (b) the amount of the difference, and (c) the trial balance column that will have the larger total. Consider each error separately. Use the following form, in which error 1 is given as an example:

Error	(a) In Balance	(b) Difference	(c) Larger Column
1.	No	$400	Debit

E2–10   The accounts in the ledger of Express Delivery Service contain the following balances on July 31, 2003:

Prepare trial balance.
(SO 7) AP

Accounts Payable	$ 7,396	Insurance Expense	$ 523
Accounts Receivable	8,642	Notes Payable	18,450
T. Weld, Capital	44,636	Prepaid Insurance	1,968
Cash	?	Repair Expense	961
Delivery Equipment	49,360	Salaries Expense	4,428
T. Weld, Drawings	700	Salaries Payable	815
Gas and Oil Expense	758	Service Revenue	10,610

Instructions

Prepare a trial balance, with the accounts arranged as illustrated in the chapter, and fill in the missing amount for Cash.

PROBLEMS: SET A

● ●

P2–1A   Yee Company has the following accounts:

Identify increases, decreases, normal balances, and types of accounts.
(SO 2) K

Account	(1) Type of Account	(2) Financial Statement	(3) Normal Balance	(4) Increase	(5) Decrease
1. Cash	Asset	Balance sheet	Debit	Debit	Credit
2. Accounts Receivable					
3. Drawings					
4. Interest Expense					
5. Land					
6. Office Supplies					
7. Salary Expense					
8. Service Revenue					

Instructions

Complete the table by identifying (1) the type of account (e.g., asset, liability, owner's equity, revenue, expense), (2) what financial statement it is presented on, (3) the normal balance of the account, (4) whether the account is increased by a debit or credit, and (5) whether the account is decreased by a debit or credit. The first one is done for you as an example.

P2–2A   The Bucket Club Miniature Golf and Driving Range was opened on May 1 by Amod Phatarpeker. The following selected events and transactions occurred during May:

Journalize a series of transactions.
(SO 2, 4) AP

May 1   Invested $45,000 cash in the business.

   3   Purchased Lee's Golf Land for $38,000 cash. The price consists of land, $23,000; building, $9,000; and equipment, $6,000. (Make one compound entry.)

   5   Advertised the opening of the driving range and miniature golf course, paying advertising expenses of $1,600.

   6   Paid $1,480 cash for a one-year insurance policy.

  10   Purchased golf clubs and other equipment for $1,600 from Woods Company, payable in 30 days.

  18   Received golf fees of $800 in cash.

  19   Sold 100 coupon books for $15 each. Each book contains 10 coupons that entitle the holder

        to one round of miniature golf or to hit one bucket of golf balls.
   25 Withdrew $500 cash for personal use.
   30 Paid salaries of $600.
   30 Paid Woods Company in full.
   31 Received $500 of fees in cash.

Amod uses the following accounts: Cash; Prepaid Insurance; Land; Buildings; Equipment; Accounts Payable; Unearned Golf Fees; Amod Phatarpeker, Capital; Amod Phatarpeker, Drawings; Golf Fees Earned; Advertising Expense; and Salaries Expense.

Instructions

Journalize the May transactions.

Journalize transactions, post, and prepare trial balance.
(SO 4, 6, 7) AP

P2–3A Maria Rojas is a licensed architect. During the first month of operation of her business, the following events and transactions occurred:

 Apr. 1 Invested $15,000 cash.
   1 Hired a secretary-receptionist at a salary of $1,200 monthly.
   2 Paid office rent for the month, $800.
   3 Purchased architectural supplies on account from Halo Company, $1,500.
   10 Completed blueprints on a carport and billed client $900 for services.
   11 Received $500 cash advance from R. Welk for the design of a new home.
   20 Received $1,500 cash for services completed and delivered to P. Donahue.
   30 Paid secretary-receptionist for the month, $1,200.
   30 Paid $600 to Halo Company on account.

Maria uses the following chart of accounts: No. 101 Cash, No. 112 Accounts Receivable, No. 126 Supplies, No. 201 Accounts Payable, No. 209 Unearned Revenue, No. 301 Maria Rojas, Capital, No. 400 Service Revenue, No. 726 Salaries Expense, and No. 729 Rent Expense.

Instructions

(a) Journalize the transactions.
(b) Post to the ledger accounts.
(c) Prepare a trial balance as at April 30, 2003.

Journalize transactions, post, and prepare trial balance.
(SO 4, 6, 7) AP

P2–4A The trial balance of Speedy Laundry on September 30 is shown below:

SPEEDY LAUNDRY
Trial Balance
September 30, 2003

Account No.		Debit	Credit
101	Cash	$ 7,500	
112	Accounts Receivable	2,200	
126	Supplies	1,700	
157	Equipment	8,000	
201	Accounts Payable		$ 4,000
209	Unearned Revenue		700
301	Jane Kent, Capital		14,700
	Totals	$19,400	$19,400

The October transactions were as follows:

 Oct. 5 Received $800 cash from customers on account.
   10 Billed customers for services performed, $5,500.
   15 Paid employee salaries, $1,200.
   17 Performed $400 of services for customers who paid in advance in August.
   20 Paid $1,600 to creditors on account.
   22 Received $200 for services provided for cash (i.e., not on account).
   26 Purchased supplies on account, at a cost of $300.
   29 Withdrew $500 for personal use.
   31 Paid utilities, $600.

Instructions

(a) Enter the opening balances in the ledger accounts as at October 1. Write "Balance" in the explanation space and insert a check mark (√) in the reference column. Provision should be made for the following additional accounts: No. 306 Jane Kent, Drawings, No. 426 Laundry Revenue, No. 726 Salaries Expense, and No. 732 Utilities Expense.

(b) Journalize the transactions.

(c) Post to the ledger accounts.

(d) Prepare a trial balance as at October 31, 2003.

P2–5A   The Starlite Theatre, owned by Lee Baroni, is unique as it shows only triple features of sequential theme movies. As at February 28, the ledger of Starlite showed the following: No. 101 Cash, $16,000; No. 140 Land, $42,000; No. 145 Buildings (concession stand, projection room, ticket booth, and screen), $18,000; No. 157 Equipment, $16,000; No. 201 Accounts Payable, $12,000; and No. 301 L. Baroni, Capital, $80,000. During the month of March, the following events and transactions occurred:

Journalize transactions, post, and prepare trial balance.
(SO 4, 6, 7) AP

Mar. 2 Acquired three *Star Wars* movies (*Star Wars, The Empire Strikes Back*, and *The Return of the Jedi*) to be shown for the first three weeks of March. The film rental was $9,000. Of that amount, $3,000 was paid in cash and $6,000 will be paid on March 10.

   3 Ordered the first three *Scream* movies to be shown the last 10 days of March. The film rental fee will cost $300 per night.

   9 Received $6,500 cash from admissions.

   10 Paid balance due on *Star Wars* movies rental and $3,000 on February 28 accounts payable.

   11 Starlite Theatre contracted with Brewer Company to operate the concession stand in the future. Brewer is to pay 15% of gross concession receipts (payable on the last day of each month) for the right to operate the concession stand.

   12 Paid advertising expenses, $800.

   20 Received $7,200 cash from admissions.

   21 Received the *Scream* movies and paid the rental fee of $3,000 ($300 × 10 nights).

   31 Paid salaries of $3,800.

   31 Received statement from Brewer showing gross receipts from concessions of $8,000 and the balance due to Starlite Theatre of $1,200 ($8,000 x 15%) for March. Brewer paid one-half the balance due and will remit the remainder on April 5.

   31 Received $12,500 cash from admissions.

In addition to the accounts identified above, the chart of accounts shows the following: No. 112 Accounts Receivable, No. 405 Admission Revenue, No. 406 Concession Revenue, No. 610 Advertising Expense, No. 632 Film Rental Expense, and No. 726 Salaries Expense.

Instructions

(a) Enter the beginning balances in the ledger as at March 1. Insert a check mark (√) in the reference column of the ledger for the beginning balance.

(b) Journalize the March transactions.

(c) Post the March journal entries to the ledger. Assume that all entries are posted from page 2 of the journal.

(d) Prepare a trial balance as at March 31, 2003.

P2–6A   Bablad Brokerage Services was formed on May 1, 2003. The following transactions took place during its first month:

Journalize transactions, post, and prepare trial balance and financial statements.
(SO 4, 6, 7) AP

May 1 Jacob Bablad invested $120,000 cash in the company.

   5 Hired two employees to work in the warehouse. They will each be paid a salary of $1,000 per month.

   5 Signed a two-year rental agreement on a warehouse. Paid $36,000 cash in advance for the first year. (*Hint*: The portion of the cost related to May 2003 ($3,000) is an expense for this month.)

   8 Purchased furniture and equipment costing $70,000. A cash payment of $20,000 was made immediately. The remainder will be paid in six months.

   9 Paid $3,000 cash for a one-year insurance policy on the furniture and equipment. (*Hint*: The portion of the cost related to May 2003 ($250) is an expense for this month.)

   12 Purchased office supplies for $1,000 cash.

   15 Purchased more office supplies for $2,000 on account.

   20 Total revenues earned to date were $30,000—$10,000 cash and $20,000 on account.

   22 Paid $800 to suppliers on account.

26 Collected $5,000 from customers on account.
30 Received utility bills in the amount of $400, to be paid next month.
30 Paid the monthly salaries of the two employees, totalling $2,000.

Instructions

(a) Prepare journal entries to record each of the events listed.
(b) Post the journal entries to T accounts.
(c) Prepare a trial balance as at May 31, 2003.
(d) Prepare an income statement and a statement of owner's equity for Bablad Brokerage Services for the month ended May 31, 2003, and a balance sheet as at May 31, 2003.

Journalize transactions, post, prepare trial balance, and determine elements of financial statements.
(SO 4, 6, 7) AP

P2–7A   Leo Mataruka owns and manages a computer repair service, which had the following trial balance on December 31, 2002 (the end of its fiscal year):

CYBERDYNE REPAIR SERVICE
Trial Balance
December 31, 2002

	Debit	Credit
Cash	$10,000	
Accounts Receivable	15,000	
Repair Parts Inventory	13,000	
Prepaid Rent	3,000	
Shop Equipment	21,000	
Accounts Payable		$19,000
Leo Mataruka, Capital		43,000
Totals	$62,000	$62,000

Summarized transactions for January 2003 were as follows:

1. Advertising costs, paid in cash, $500.
2. Additional repair parts inventory acquired on account, $2,000.
3. Miscellaneous expenses, paid in cash, $2,000.
4. Cash collected from customers on account, $13,000.
5. Cash paid to creditors on account, $15,000.
6. Repair parts used during January, $4,000. (*Hint*: Debit this to Repair Parts Expense.)
7. Repair services performed during January: for cash, $4,000; on account, $9,000.
8. Wages for January, paid in cash, $3,000.
9. Rent expense for the month of January recorded. However, no cash was paid. A rent payment had been made for three months, in advance, on December 1, 2002, in the amount of $4,500.
10. Leo's January drawings, $5,000.

Instructions

(a) Explain why the December 31, 2002, balance in the Prepaid Rent account is $3,000. (Refer to the Trial Balance and item 9.)
(b) Open T accounts for each of the accounts listed in the trial balance, and enter the opening balances for 2003.
(c) Prepare journal entries to record each of the January transactions.
(d) Post the journal entries to the accounts in the ledger.
(e) Prepare a trial balance as at January 31, 2003.
(f) Determine the total assets as at January 31, 2003. (It is not necessary to prepare a balance sheet. Simply list the relevant amounts from the trial balance, and calculate the total.)
(g) Determine the net income or loss for the month of January 2003. (It is not necessary to prepare an income statement. Simply list the relevant amounts from the trial balance, and calculate the amount of the net income or loss.)

Prepare financial statements from trial balance.
(SO 7) AP

P2–8A   Refer to the trial balance prepared in part (e) of P2–7A.

Instructions

Based upon the data in P2–7A, prepare:

(a) An income statement for Cyberdyne Repair Service for the month ended January 31, 2003.
(b) A statement of owner's equity for the month ended January 31, 2003.
(c) A balance sheet as at January 31, 2003.

P2–9A You are presented with the following alphabetical list of accounts and balances (in thousands) for Kia Taggar Enterprises at June 30, 2003:

Prepare trial balance and financial statements.
(SO 7) AP

Accounts receivable	$ 500	Land	$ 800
Taggar, Capital	800	Long-term debt	1,200
Cash	180	Notes payable, current	1,000
Equipment	1,200	Operating expenses	870
Insurance expense	130	Prepaid insurance	90
Interest expense	225	Service revenue	2,000
Long-term investment	495	Supplies	510

Instructions

(a) Prepare a trial balance, sorting each account balance into the debit column or the credit column.

(b) Prepare a balance sheet as at June 30, 2003, and an income statement and statement of owner's equity for the year ended June 30, 2003, for Kia Taggar Enterprises.

P2–10A As the accountant for Coho Company, you are disappointed to learn that the column totals of the December 31, 2002, trial balance do not balance. The Machinery account has a debit balance of $31,200. In your analysis of transactions, you have determined that a correctly recorded purchase of a machine for $7,000 was posted with a $7,000 debit to the Machinery account and a $7,000 debit to Accounts Payable.

Answer questions about trial balance error and identify source documents.
(SO 3, 7) AN

Instructions

(a) Answer the following questions:
  1. Is the balance of the Machinery account overstated, understated, or correctly stated?
  2. Is the balance of the Accounts Payable account overstated, understated, or correctly stated?
  3. Is the debit column total of the trial balance overstated, understated, or correctly stated?
  4. Is the credit column total of the trial balance overstated, understated, or correctly stated?
  5. If the credit column total of the trial balance is $360,000 before correcting the error, what is the total of the debit column?

(b) Which of the following items are likely to serve as source documents for journal entries?
  1. Invoice from supplier   4. Sales ticket
  2. Income statement   5. Balance sheet
  3. Utility bill   6. Trial balance

Source: Adapted from Certified General Accountants Association of Canada, *Financial Accounting 1 Examination*, June 1998, Question 2.

P2–11A The owner of a small auto repair company prepared the following trial balance (in thousands of dollars):

Identify errors and prepare correct trial balance.
(SO 7) AN

MEHTA AUTOMOTIVE SERVICES
Trial Balance
For the Year Ended December 31, 2002

	Debit	Credit
Machinery and Equipment		$ 89
Accounts Payable	$ 38	
Prepaid Rent		5
Cash	24	
Capital	42	
Wages Expense	76	
Advertising Expense		30
Prepaid Insurance	3	
Miscellaneous Expenses	49	
Note Payable	45	
Service Revenue		202
Drawings	20	
Accounts Receivable		31
	$297	$357

Instructions

(a) Identify the errors in the trial balance presented above. Be specific.

(b) Prepare a corrected trial balance for Mehta Automotive Services.

P2–12A   The trial balance of Winau Co. shown below does not balance:

WINAU CO.
Trial Balance
June 30, 2003

	Debit	Credit
Cash		$ 2,840
Accounts Receivable	$ 3,231	
Supplies	800	
Equipment	3,000	
Accounts Payable		2,666
Unearned Fees	1,200	
T. Winau, Capital		9,000
T. Winau, Drawings	800	
Fees Earned		2,380
Salaries Expense	3,400	
Office Expense	910	
	$13,341	$16,886

Each of the listed accounts has a normal balance in the general ledger. An examination of the ledger and journal reveals the following errors:

1. Cash received from a customer on account was debited for $570 and Accounts Receivable was credited for the same amount. The actual collection was for $750.
2. The purchase of a computer printer on account for $340 was recorded as a debit to Supplies for $340 and a credit to Accounts Payable for $340.
3. Services worth $890 were performed on account for a client. Accounts Receivable was debited for $890 and Fees Earned was credited for $89.
4. A debit posting to Salaries Expense of $600 was omitted.
5. A payment on account for $206 was credited to Cash for $206 and credited to Accounts Payable for $260.
6. The withdrawal of $400 cash for Winau's personal use was debited to Salaries Expense for $400 and credited to Cash for $400.

Instructions

Prepare a correct trial balance. Show calculations for each new amount.

PROBLEMS: SET B

....

*Identify increases, decreases,
normal balances, and types of
accounts.*
(SO 2) K

P2–1B   Kobiashi Company has the following accounts:

	(1)	(2)	(3)	(4)	(5)
Account	Type of Account	Financial Statement	Normal Balance	Increase	Decrease
1. Cash	Asset	Balance sheet	Debit	Debit	Credit
2. Accounts Payable					
3. Kobiashi, Capital					
4. Kobiashi, Drawings					
5. Office Equipment					
6. Office Supplies					
7. Rent Expense					
8. Service Revenue					

Instructions

Complete the table by identifying (1) the type of account (e.g., asset, liability, owner's equity, revenue, expense), (2) what financial statement it is presented on, (3) the normal balance of the account, (4) whether the account is increased by a debit or credit, and (5) whether the account is decreased by a debit or credit. The first one is done for you as an example.

P2–2B The Adventure Park was started on April 1 by Al Rossy. The following selected events and transactions occurred during April:

Journalize a series of transactions.
(SO 2, 4) AP

Apr. 1 Rossy invested $50,000 cash in the business.
  4 Purchased land costing $30,000 for cash.
  8 Incurred advertising expenses of $1,800 on account.
  11 Paid salaries to employees, $1,500.
  12 Hired park manager at a salary of $4,000 per month, effective May 1.
  13 Paid $1,500 cash for a one-year insurance policy.
  17 Withdrew $600 cash for personal use.
  20 Received $5,700 in cash for admission fees.
  25 Sold 100 coupon books for $25 each. Each book contains 10 coupons that entitle the holder to one admission to the park.
  30 Received $5,900 in cash for admission fees.
  30 Paid $700 on account for advertising expenses incurred on April 8.

Al Rossy uses the following accounts: Cash; Prepaid Insurance; Land; Accounts Payable; Unearned Admissions Revenue; Al Rossy, Capital; Al Rossy, Drawings; Admissions Revenue; Advertising Expense; and Salaries Expense.

Instructions

Journalize the April transactions.

P2–3B Lisa Heins is a CGA. During the first month of operation of her accounting practice, the following events and transactions occurred:

Journalize transactions, post, and prepare trial balance.
(SO 4, 6, 7) AP

May 1 Heins invested $32,000 cash.
  2 Hired a secretary-receptionist at a salary of $1,000 per month.
  3 Purchased $1,200 of supplies on account from Read Supply Company.
  7 Paid office rent of $900 cash for the month.
  11 Completed a tax assignment and billed client $1,100 for services rendered.
  12 Received a $3,500 advance on a management consulting engagement.
  17 Received cash of $1,200 for services completed for Arnold Co.
  31 Paid secretary-receptionist $1,000 salary for the month.
  31 Paid 40% of balance due Read Supply Company.

Lisa uses the following chart of accounts: No. 101 Cash; No. 112 Accounts Receivable; No. 126 Supplies; No. 201 Accounts Payable; No. 209 Unearned Revenue; No. 301 Lisa Heins, Capital; No. 400 Service Revenue; No. 726 Salaries Expense; and No. 729 Rent Expense.

Instructions

(a) Journalize the transactions.
(b) Post to the ledger accounts.
(c) Prepare a trial balance at May 31, 2003.

P2–4B The trial balance of Steiner Dry Cleaners at June 30 is shown below:

Journalize transactions, post, and prepare trial balance.
(SO 4, 6, 7) AP

STEINER DRY CLEANERS
Trial Balance
June 30, 2003

Account No.		Debit	Credit
101	Cash	$12,532	
112	Accounts Receivable	10,536	
126	Supplies	4,844	
157	Equipment	25,950	
201	Accounts Payable		$15,878
209	Unearned Revenue		1,730
301	C. Steiner, Capital		36,254
	Totals	$53,862	$53,862

The July transactions were as follows:

July 8 Collected $5,936 in cash related to June 30 accounts receivable.

9 Paid employee salaries, $2,100.

11 Received $4,325 in cash for services rendered.

14 Paid June 30 creditors $10,750 on account.

17 Purchased supplies on account, $554.

22 Billed customers for services rendered, $5,700.

30 Paid employee salaries of $3,114, utilities of $1,384, and repairs of $692, all in cash.

31 Withdrew $700 cash for personal use of owner.

Instructions

(a) Enter the opening balances in the ledger accounts as at July 1. Write "Balance" in the explanation space and insert a check mark (√) in the reference colomn. Provision should be made for the following additional accounts: No. 306 C. Steiner, Drawings; No. 428 Dry Cleaning Revenue; No. 622 Repair Expense; No. 726 Salaries Expense; and No. 732 Utilities Expense.

(b) Journalize the transactions.

(c) Post to the ledger accounts.

(d) Prepare a trial balance at July 31, 2003.

Journalize transactions, post, and prepare trial balance.
(SO 4, 6, 7) AP

P2–5B The Grand Theatre is owned by Fran Holley. At March 31, the ledger showed the following: No. 101 Cash, $6,000; No. 140 Land, $10,000; No. 145 Buildings (concession stands, projection room, ticket booth, and screen), $8,000; No. 157 Equipment, $6,000; No. 201 Accounts Payable, $2,000; No. 275 Mortgage Payable, $8,000; and No. 301 Fran Holley, Capital, $20,000. During April, the following events and transactions occurred:

Apr. 2 Paid film rental of $800 on first movie.

3 Ordered two additional films at $500 each.

9 Received $1,800 cash from admissions.

10 Made $2,000 payment on mortgage and $1,000 on accounts payable.

11 Grand Theatre contracted with Thoms Company to operate the concession stand in the future. Thoms is to pay 17% of gross concession receipts (payable monthly) for the right to operate the concession stand.

12 Paid advertising expenses, $300.

20 Received one of the films ordered on April 3 and was billed $500. The film will be shown in April.

25 Received $5,200 cash from admissions.

29 Paid salaries, $1,600.

30 Received statement from Thoms showing gross concession receipts of $1,000 and a balance due to the The Grand Theatre of $170 ($1,000 x 17%) for April. Thoms paid one-half of the balance due and will remit the remainder on May 5.

30 Prepaid $700 rental on special film to be run in May.

In addition to the accounts identified above, the chart of accounts shows the following: No. 112 Accounts Receivable; No. 136 Prepaid Rentals; No. 405 Admission Revenue; No. 406 Concession Revenue; No. 610 Advertising Expense; No. 632 Film Rental Expense; and No. 726 Salaries Expense.

Instructions

(a) Enter the beginning balances in the ledger as at April 1. Insert a check mark (√) in the reference column of the ledger for the beginning balance.

(b) Journalize the April transactions.

(c) Post the April journal entries to the ledger. Assume that all entries are posted from page 1 of the journal.

(d) Prepare a trial balance at April 30, 2003.

Journalize transactions, post, and prepare trial balance and financial statements.
(SO 4, 6, 7) AP

P2–6B Rowland Brokerage Services was formed on September 1, 2003. The following transactions took place during its first month:

Sept. 1 Bob Rowland invested $125,000 cash in the company.

1 Hired two employees to work in the warehouse. They will each be paid a salary of $1,800 per month.

5 Paid rent for the warehouse for the month of September, $3,750.

8 Purchased furniture and equipment costing $75,000. A cash payment of $25,000 was made immediately. The remainder is on account.

10 Paid $320 cash for the month's insurance on the furniture and equipment.

12 Purchased office supplies for $1,100 cash.

19 Purchased more office supplies for $1,900 on account.

24 Total revenues earned to date were $40,000 ($15,000 cash and $25,000 on account).

26 Paid $750 to suppliers on account.

29 Collected $6,500 from customers on account.

30 Received utility bills for the month of September in the amount of $450, to be paid next month.

30 Paid the monthly salaries of the two employees, totalling $3,600.

Instructions

(a) Prepare journal entries to record each of the events.

(b) Post the journal entries to T accounts.

(c) Prepare a trial balance as at September 30, 2003.

(d) Prepare an income statement and a statement of owner's equity for Rowland Brokerage Services for the month ended September 30, 2003, and a balance sheet as at September 30, 2003.

P2–7B Gary Hobson owns and manages a computer repair service which had the following trial balance at March 31, 2003 (the end of its fiscal year):

Journalize transactions, post, prepare trial balance, and determine elements of financial statements.
(SO 4, 6, 7) AP

SOFT-Q REPAIR SERVICE
Trial Balance
March 31, 2003

	Debit	Credit
Cash	$ 7,000	
Accounts Receivable	12,000	
Repair Parts Inventory	15,000	
Prepaid Rent	3,200	
Shop Equipment	21,000	
Accounts Payable		$21,000
Gary Hobson, Capital		37,200
Totals	$58,200	$58,200

Summarized transactions for April 2003 were as follows:

1. Advertising costs, paid in cash, $900.
2. Additional repair parts inventory acquired on account, $3,200.
3. Miscellaneous expenses, paid in cash, $2,100.
4. Cash collected from customers on account, $9,000.
5. Cash paid to creditors on account, $8,000.
6. Repair parts used during April, $3,000. (*Hint*: Debit this to Repair Parts Expense.)
7. Repair services performed during April: for cash, $3,000, on account, $9,000.
8. Wages for April, paid in cash, $4,000.
9. Recorded the rent expense pertaining to the month of April. However, no cash was paid. A rent payment had been made for three months, in advance, on March 1, 2003, in the amount of $4,800.
10. Gary's drawings during April were $1,000.

Instructions

(a) Explain why the March 31, 2003, balance in the Prepaid Rent account is $3,200. (Refer to the Trial Balance and item 9 above.)

(b) Open T accounts for each of the accounts listed in the trial balance, and enter the opening balances for 2003.

(c) Prepare journal entries to record each of the April transactions.

(d) Post the journal entries to the accounts in the ledger.

(e) Prepare a trial balance as at April 30, 2003.

(f) Determine the total assets as at April 30, 2003. (It is not necessary to prepare a balance sheet. Simply list the relevant amounts from the trial balance, and calculate the total.)

(g) Determine the net income or loss for the month of April 2003. (It is not necessary to prepare an income statement. Simply list the relevant amounts from the trial balance, and calculate the net income or loss.)

Prepare financial statements from trial balance.
(SO 7) AP

P2–8B   Refer to the trial balance prepared in part (e) of P2–7B.

Instructions

Based on the data in P2–7B, prepare:

(a) An income statement for Soft-Q Repair Service for the month ended April 30, 2003.
(b) A statement of owner's equity for the month ended April 30, 2003.
(c) A balance sheet as at April 30, 2003.

Prepare trial balance and financial statements.
(SO 7) AP

P2–9B   The **Hudson's Bay Company** had the following alphabetical list of accounts and balances (in thousands of dollars), as at January 31, 2000:

Capital assets	$1,447,200
Cash in stores	8,480
Credit card receivables	483,940
Future income taxes payable	54,368
Income tax expense	96,369
Income taxes recoverable	25,445
Interest expense	79,140
Investments	49,264
Long-term debt	700,184
Long-term debt due within one year	151,695
Long-term receivables	29,348
Merchandise inventories	1,598,695
Operating expenses	7,024,207
Other accounts payable and accrued expenses	584,644
Other accounts receivable	127,522
Other assets	378,970
Other long-term liabilities	64,445
Prepaid expenses	44,606
Sales and revenue	7,295,751
Shareholders' (owner's) equity, February 1, 1999	2,169,490
Short-term borrowings	29,597
Short-term deposits	41,792
Trade accounts payable	384,804

Instructions

(a) Prepare a trial balance, sorting each account balance into the debit column or the credit column.
(b) Prepare an income statement for the year ended January 31, 2000, and a balance sheet as at January 31, 2000, for Hudson's Bay.

Answer questions about trial balance error and identify source documents.
(SO 3, 7) AN

P2–10B   As the accountant for Desjardins Company, you are disappointed to learn that the column totals of the December 31, 2002, trial balance do not balance. The debit column of the trial balance totals $350,000. In your analysis of the transactions, you have determined that a correctly recorded service, provided on account for a customer for $5,000, was posted with a $5,000 credit to the Accounts Receivable account and $5,000 credit to Service Revenue.

Instructions

(a) Answer the following questions:
   1. Is the balance of the Accounts Receivable account overstated, understated, or correctly stated? If the amount is incorrect, indicate by how much.
   2. Is the balance of the Service Revenue account overstated, understated, or correctly stated? If the amount is incorrect, indicate by how much.
   3. Is the debit column total of the trial balance overstated, understated, or correctly stated?
   4. Is the credit column total of the trial balance overstated, understated, or correctly stated?
   5   What is total of the credit column before correcting the error?
(b) Which of the following items are likely to serve as source documents for journal entries?
   1. Cheque
   2. Income statement
   3. Property tax bill
   4. Sales slip
   5. Balance sheet
   6. Trial balance
   7. Cash register tape

P2–11B The owner of a small engine repair company prepared the following trial balance (in thousands of dollars):

Identify errors and prepare correct trial balance.
(SO 7) AN

CHRISTOPHER'S SMALL ENGINE REPAIRS
Trial Balance
For the Year Ended December 31, 2002

	Debit	Credit
Machinery and Equipment		$ 91
Accounts Payable	$ 41	
Prepaid Rent	5	
Cash	29	
Capital	45	
Wages Expense	71	
Prepaid Insurance	25	
Miscellaneous Expenses	47	
Note Payable	50	
Service Revenue		202
Drawings	30	
Accounts Receivable		40
	$343	$333

Instructions

(a) Identify the errors in the trial balance presented above. Be specific.

(b) Prepare a corrected trial balance for Christopher's Small Engine Repairs.

P2–12B The trial balance of the Shawnee Company shown below does not balance:

Prepare correct trial balance.
(SO 5, 7) AN

SHAWNEE COMPANY
Trial Balance
May 31, 2003

	Debit	Credit
Cash	$ 5,850	
Accounts Receivable		$ 2,750
Prepaid Insurance	700	
Equipment	8,000	
Accounts Payable		4,600
Property Taxes Payable	560	
M. Flynn, Capital		11,700
Service Revenue	6,690	
Salaries Expense	4,200	
Advertising Expense		1,100
Property Tax Expense	1,100	
Totals	$27,100	$20,150

Your review of the ledger reveals that each account has a normal balance. You also discover the following errors:

1. Prepaid Insurance, Accounts Payable, and Property Tax Expense were each understated by $100.
2. Transposition errors were made in Accounts Receivable and Service Revenue. Based on postings made, the correct balances were $2,570 and $6,960, respectively.
3. A debit posting to Salaries Expense of $200 was omitted.
4. A $700 cash withdrawal by the owner was debited to M. Flynn, Capital for $700 and credited to Cash for $700.
5. A $520 purchase of supplies on account was debited to Equipment for $520 and credited to Cash for $520.
6. A cash payment of $250 for advertising was debited to Advertising Expense for $25 and credited to Cash for $25.
7. A collection from a customer for $210 was debited to Cash for $210 and credited to Accounts Payable for $210.

Instructions

Prepare a correct trial balance. (*Note:* The chart of accounts includes the following: M. Flynn, Drawings, and Supplies.) (*Hint:* It helps to prepare the correct journal entries for the transactions described and to compare them to the mistakes made.)

*B*roadening *Your Perspective*

FINANCIAL REPORTING AND ANALYSIS

Financial Reporting Problem

BYP2–1   The financial statements of The Second Cup Ltd. for 2000, in Appendix A at the back of this textbook, show the following selected accounts (stated in thousands of dollars):

Accounts payable and accrued liabilities	$ 2,718
Accounts receivable	2,294
Capital assets	1,768
Franchise revenue	19,021
Income taxes expense	4,058
Interest and other investment expense	13
Prepaid expenses and sundry assets	419

Instructions

(a) Answer the following questions:
  1. What is the increase side (i.e., debit or credit) and decrease side for each of the above accounts?
  2. What is the normal balance for each of these accounts?
(b) Identify the other account probably involved in the transaction, and the effect on that account, when:
  1. Accounts Receivable are decreased.
  2. Capital Assets are increased.
  3. Franchise Revenue is increased.
  4. Income Taxes Expense is increased.
  5. Interest and Other Investment Expense is increased.
  6. Prepaid Expenses and Sundry Assets are increased.

Interpreting Financial Statements

Additional Cases

BYP2–2   United Grain Growers (UGG) Limited is one of Western Canada's largest agri-business companies. Founded in 1906, the company provides production, marketing, and information services to farmers.

  The following list of accounts and amounts was extracted from UGG's financial statements. The accounts have been reorganized into alphabetical order.

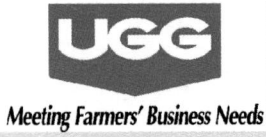

Meeting Farmers' Business Needs

UNITED GRAIN GROWERS LIMITED
Trial Balance
July 31, 2000
(in thousands)

Accounts receivable and prepaid expenses	$ 128,126
Accounts payable and accrued expenses	91,440
Bank and other loans	66,352
Capital assets	307,202
Cash	13,340
Cost of goods sold expense	1,576,718
Depreciation and amortization expense	26,380
Dividends payable	5,315
Income tax expense	2,313
Interest expense	17,350
Inventories	106,604
Long-term debt	210,051
Operating, general, and administrative expenses	154,250
Other assets	44,159
Other expense	595
Sales and revenue from services	1,779,789
Shareholders' (owner's) equity, August 1, 1999	224,090

Instructions

(a) Prepare a trial balance for UGG, with accounts reorganized in financial statement order as shown in the textbook.

(b) Present UGG's accounts and amounts in the form of the accounting equation: Assets = Liabilities + Shareholder's (Owner's) Equity.

Accounting on the Web

BYP2–3 Business ethics provide the necessary foundation for good corporate conduct. This case explores topical ethical issues facing business today and applies the ethical framework introduced in Chapter 1 to these issues.

Instructions

Specific requirements of this Internet case are available on the Weygandt website.

CRITICAL THINKING

•••

Collaborative Learning Activity

BYP2–4 Andrée Boudreau operates the Boudreau Riding Academy. The academy's primary sources of revenue are riding fees and lesson fees, which are provided in cash only. Andrée also boards horses for owners, who are billed monthly for boarding fees. In a few cases, boarders pay in advance of expected use.

The academy owns 10 horses, a stable, a riding corral, riding equipment, and office equipment. It employs stable helpers and an office employee, each of whom receives a weekly salary. At the end of each month, the mail brings bills for advertising, utilities, and veterinary services. Other expenses include feed for the horses and insurance.

Andrée Boudreau's only source of income is the academy. She makes periodic withdrawals of cash for her personal living expenses.

The Boudreau Riding Academy's chart of accounts is as follows:

Account Number	Account Title	Account Number	Account Title
101	Cash	301	A. Boudreau, Capital
112	Boarding Accounts Receivable	306	A. Boudreau, Drawings
126	Hay and Feed Supplies	410	Riding Fees Earned
130	Prepaid Insurance	411	Lesson Fees Earned
145	Building	420	Boarding Fees Earned
151	Office Equipment	610	Advertising Expense
157	Riding Equipment	626	Salaries Expense
170	Horses	722	Insurance Expense
172	Riding Corral	732	Utilities Expense
201	Accounts Payable	737	Veterinary Expense
205	Unearned Boarding Fees	738	Hay and Feed Expense

During the first month of operations, an inexperienced bookkeeper was employed. Andrée asks you to review the following nine journal entries (of the 50 entries made during the month). In each case, the explanation for the entry is correct.

May 1	Cash	15,000	
	A. Boudreau, Capital		15,000
	Invested $15,000 cash in business.		
5	Cash	250	
	Riding Fees Earned		250
	Received $250 cash for lesson fees.		

7	Cash	1,500	
	Boarding Fees Earned		1,500
	Received $1,500 for boarding of horses, beginning June 1.		
9	Hay and Feed Expense	1,700	
	Cash		1,700
	Purchased estimated two months' supply of hay and feed for $1,700 on account.		
14	Riding Equipment	80	
	Cash		800
	Purchased desk and other office equipment for $800 cash.		
15	Salaries Expense	400	
	Cash		400
	Issued cheque to Andrée Boudreau for personal use.		
20	Cash	145	
	Riding Fees Earned		154
	Received $154 cash for riding fees.		
31	Veterinary Expense	75	
	Accounts Payable		75
	Received bill of $75 from veterinarian for services rendered.		
31	Hay and Feed Expense	1,000	
	Cash		100
	Used $1,000 worth of hay and feed during the month.		

Instructions

With the class divided into groups, answer the following:
(a) Identify each journal entry that is correct. For each journal entry that is incorrect, prepare the entry that should have been made by the bookkeeper.
(b) Which of the incorrect entries would prevent the trial balance from balancing?
(c) What was the correct net income for May, assuming the bookkeeper reported net income of $4,500 after posting all 50 entries?
(d) What was the correct cash balance at May 31, assuming the bookkeeper reported a balance of $12,475 after posting all 50 entries?

Communication Activity

BYP2–5   Merry Maid Company offers home cleaning services. Two common transactions for the company are billing customers for services rendered and paying employee salaries. For example, on March 15, bills that totalled $6,000 were sent to customers, and $2,000 in salaries was paid to employees.

Instructions

Write a memo to your instructor that explains and illustrates the steps in the recording process for each of the March 15 transactions.

Ethics Case

BYP2–6   Vu Hung is the assistant chief accountant at Staples Company, a manufacturer of computer chips and cellular phones. The company presently has total sales of $20 million. It is the end of the first quarter. Vu is hurriedly trying to prepare a general ledger trial balance so that quarterly financial statements can be prepared and released to management and regulatory agencies. The total credits on the trial balance exceed the debits by $1,000.

In order to meet the 4 p.m. deadline, Vu decides to force the debits and credits into balance by adding the amount of the difference to the Equipment account. She chose Equipment because it is one of the larger account balances. Percentagewise, it will be the least misstated. She believes that the difference will not affect anyone's decisions. She wishes that she had more time to find the error, but realizes that the financial statements are already late.

Instructions

(a) Who are the stakeholders in this situation?

(b) What are the ethical issues involved?

(c) What are Vu's alternatives?

Answers to Self-Study Questions

1. b   2. c   3. d   4. d   5. b   6. a   7. c   8. d   9. a   10. c

Answer to Second Cup Review It Question 4

Accounts Receivable (asset)—debit; Income Taxes Payable (liability)—credit; Product Sales (revenue)—credit

Before studying this chapter, you should understand or, if necessary, review:

a. *The double-entry system. (Ch. 2, pp. 55–57)*
b. *How to increase or decrease assets, liabilities, and owner's equity accounts using debit and credit procedures. (Ch. 2, pp. 56–58)*
c. *How to journalize transactions. (Ch. 2, pp. 60–62)*
d. *How to post transactions to the general ledger. (Ch. 2, pp. 64–65)*
e. *How to prepare a trial balance. (Ch. 2, pp. 73–74)*

THE NAVIGATOR

Fiscal Year Ends, But Classes Move On

TORONTO, Ont.—In accounting, as in comedy, timing is everything. An organization's fiscal year end is like a punch line—everything leads up to it. Once it's gone, you start all over.

At Seneca College's dozen campuses in the northern half of Toronto and neighbouring York region, as at most schools, the bulk of students arrive in September and leave in April or May. But the College's books close on March 31, when its fiscal year ends.

"The reason goes back to 1967 and the provincial act establishing community colleges in Ontario," explains Ron Currie, Director of Finance for Seneca. "That's the government's year end."

No matter what date is selected for Seneca's fiscal year end, the college has to apply revenues in the year in which the service is performed. This is necessary to satisfy the revenue recognition and matching principles. For example, Seneca might collect tuition for the summer term in one accounting period, but provide teaching services in the next accounting period. "Typically," says Mr. Currie, "students pay in March for a summer semester course, so those prepayments get deferred on our balance sheet. Same with the student activity fees."

Seneca also teaches courses that are funded by grant money from the government, private industry, and trade and professional associations. The same principles apply. "Let's say XYZ Corporation came along and gave us $30,000 to run a program in March, April, and May," Mr. Currie elaborates, "we would defer two-thirds of it to the next year."

THE NAVIGATOR

www.senecac.on.ca

THE NAVIGATOR ✔

- Understand *Concepts for Review* ☐
- Read *Feature Story* ☐
- Scan *Study Objectives* ☐
- Read *Preview* ☐
- Read text and answer *Before You Go On*
  - p. 106 ☐ p. 111 ☐ p. 115 ☐
  - p. 120 ☐ p. 123 ☐ p. 127 ☐
- Work *Demonstration Problem* ☐
- Review *Summary of Study Objectives* ☐
- Answer *Self-Study Questions* ☐
- Complete assignments ☐

CHAPTER · 3

ADJUSTING THE ACCOUNTS

▶ STUDY OBJECTIVES ◀

After studying this chapter, you should be able to:

1. *Explain the time period assumption.*
2. *Distinguish between the revenue recognition principle and the matching principle.*
3. *Explain the accrual basis of accounting.*
4. *Explain why and distinguish when adjusting entries are needed.*
5. *Identify and distinguish between the major types of adjusting entries.*
6. *Identify and prepare adjusting entries for prepayments.*
7. *Identify and prepare adjusting entries for accruals.*
8. *Identify and prepare the adjusting entry for amortization.*
9. *Describe the nature and purpose of an adjusted trial balance and prepare.*
10. *Identify and prepare adjusting entries for the alternative treatment of prepayments. (Appendix 3A)*

THE NAVIGATOR

In Chapter 2, we examined the recording process up to, and including, the preparation of the trial balance. Before we prepare financial statements from the trial balance, however, additional steps are required. The timing mismatch between the tuition received by Seneca College for its summer classes and the costs incurred to offer these classes illustrates the type of situation that makes these additional steps necessary. For example, computer equipment purchased prior to March 31, the end of Seneca's fiscal year, will be used to keep student records and accounts for the summer session. What portion of the computer cost, if any, should be recognized as an expense of the current period? Before financial statements can be prepared, this and other questions related to the recognition of revenues and expenses must be answered. Once we know the answers, we can adjust the relevant account balances.

This chapter is organized as follows:

THE
NAVIGATOR

▼ Timing Issues

STUDY OBJECTIVE
·········· ▼ ··········

Explain the time period assumption.

No adjustments would be necessary if we could wait until a company ended its operations to prepare its financial statements. At that point, we could easily determine its final balance sheet and the amount of lifetime income it earned. The following anecdote illustrates one way to calculate lifetime income:

A grocery store owner from the old country kept his accounts payable on a spindle, accounts receivable on a note pad, and cash in a chocolate box. His daughter, having just passed the CGA Professional Applications exam, chided her father: "I don't understand how you can run your business this way. How do you know what your profits are?"

"Well," her father replied, "when I arrived in Canada 40 years ago, I had nothing but the pants I was wearing. Today, your brother is a doctor, your sister is a teacher, and you are a CGA. Your mother and I have a nice car, a well-furnished house, and a home by the lake. We have a good business and everything is paid for. So, you add all that together, subtract the pants, and there's your profit."

Selecting an Accounting Time Period

Although the grocer may be correct in his evaluation, it is impractical to wait so long for the results of operations. All entities—from the corner grocery, to a company like Second Cup, to your college or university—find that reporting the results of their activities frequently facilitates timely decision-making. For example, management usually wants monthly financial statements. Investors want to view the results of publicly traded companies at least quarterly. The Canada Customs and Revenue Agency wants annual financial statements filed with annual income tax returns. To meet these needs, **accountants make the assumption that the economic life of a business can be divided into artificial time periods**. This assumption is referred to as the time period assumption.

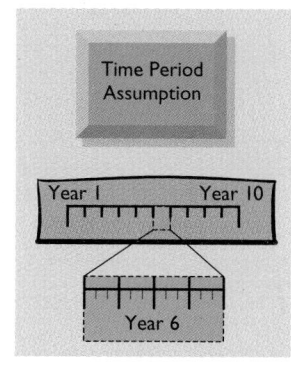

Many business transactions affect more than one of these arbitrary time periods. For example, the computer equipment purchased by Seneca College last year, the milking machine bought by Farmer Li two years ago, and the airplanes purchased by Air Canada five years ago are still in use today. We must therefore determine the relevance of each business transaction to specific accounting periods. This may involve subjective judgements and estimates.

Fiscal and Calendar Years

Both small and large companies prepare financial statements periodically in order to assess their financial condition and results of operations. **Accounting time periods are generally one month, one quarter, or one year.** Time periods of less than one year are called interim periods. Most large companies are required to report both quarterly and annually.

An accounting time period that is one year in length is referred to as a fiscal year. The accounting period used by many businesses coincides with the **calendar year** (January 1 to December 31). However, this need not be the case. Companies whose fiscal year differs from the calendar year include Mark's Work Wearhouse (last Saturday in January), Sun Ice (January 31), Cara Operations (Sunday closest to March 31), Andrés Wines (March 31), Second Cup (last Saturday in June), United Grain Growers (July 31), and CIBC (October 31). Seneca College's fiscal year is April 1 through March 31, which is typical of many universities and governments.

Helpful hint A business normally selects a fiscal year that ends when business activity is relatively low.

Recognizing Revenues and Expenses

Determining the amount of revenues and expenses to report in a specific accounting period can be difficult. To help in this task, accountants have developed two principles as part of generally accepted accounting principles: (1) the revenue recognition principle, and (2) the matching principle.

The revenue recognition principle states that **revenue must be recognized in the accounting period in which it is earned**. In a service enterprise, revenue is considered earned at the time the service is performed. To illustrate, assume that a dry cleaning business cleans clothing on June 30, and customers do not claim and pay for their clothes until the first week of July. Under the revenue recognition principle, revenue is earned in June when the service is performed, rather than in July when the cash is received. So at June 30, the dry cleaner would report a receivable on its balance sheet and revenue in its income statement for the service performed.

Accountants follow the approach of "let the expenses follow the revenues." That is, expense recognition depends on revenue recognition. In the preceding example, this principle means that the salary expense incurred to do the cleaning on June 30 should be reported in the income statement for the same period in which the service revenue is recognized.

The critical issue in expense recognition is the period when efforts are made to generate revenues. This may or may not be the same period in which the expense is paid.

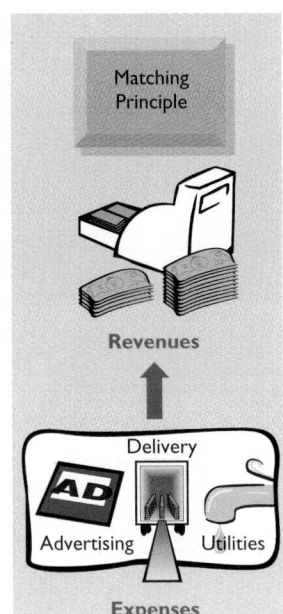

Illustration 3-1

GAAP relationships in revenue and expense recognition

If the salary incurred on June 30 is not paid until July, the dry cleaner would still report a salary expense on its June income statement and salaries payable on its June 30 balance sheet. The practice of expense recognition is called the **matching principle** because it matches efforts **(expenses) with accomplishments (revenues)**.

Once the economic life of a business has been divided into artificial time periods, the revenue recognition and matching principles can be applied. The time period assumption and revenue recognition and matching principles provide guidelines for when to report revenues and expenses. These relationships are shown in Illustration 3-1.

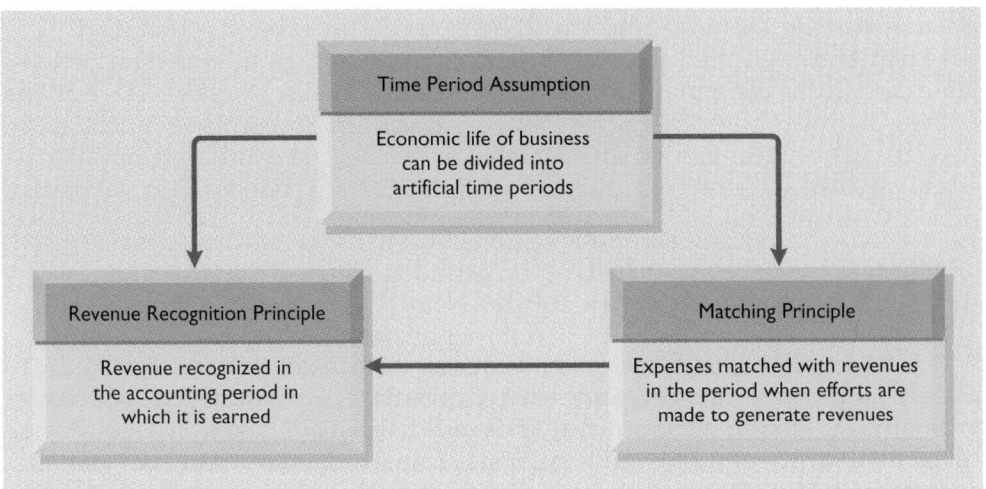

▶Accounting in Action ▶ *Business Insight*

Suppose you are a filmmaker like George Lucas and spend $11 million to produce a film such as *Star Wars*. Over what period should the cost be expensed? It should be expensed over the economic life of the film. But what is its economic life? The filmmaker must estimate how much revenue will be earned from box office sales, video sales, television, and games and toys—a period that could be less than a year or more than twenty years. This is the case for Twentieth Century Fox's *Star Wars*, originally released in 1977, and re-released in 1997. Domestic revenues total more than $500 million for *Star Wars* and continue to grow. This situation demonstrates the difficulty of properly matching expenses to revenues.

▶Accrual Versus Cash Basis of Accounting

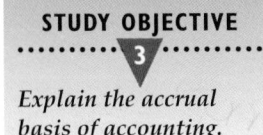

STUDY OBJECTIVE

3

Explain the accrual basis of accounting.

If you follow the revenue recognition and matching principles, you are using the **accrual basis of accounting**. Under the accrual basis, transactions that change a company's financial statements are recorded **in the periods in which the events occur**. For example, service revenue is recognized when it is earned, rather than when the cash is received. The critical event is the performance of the service, not the collection of cash. Expenses are recognized when services (e.g., salaries) or goods (e.g., supplies) are used or consumed, rather than when the cash is paid. This results in revenues that have been earned being matched with the expenses to earn these same revenues. As stated earlier, efforts are matched with accomplishments. Thanks to this practice, financial statements are more meaningful for decision-making.

An alternative to the accrual basis of accounting is the cash basis. Under the **cash basis of accounting**, revenue is recorded when cash is received, and expenses are recorded when cash is paid. The cash basis often leads to misleading financial statements. It fails to record revenue which has been earned if the cash has not been received. This violates the revenue recognition principle. In addition, expenses are not matched with revenues, which violates the matching principle. **The cash basis of accounting is not in accordance with generally accepted accounting principles.**

Although most companies use the accrual basis of accounting, some small companies use the cash basis of accounting. Farmers and fishermen also tend to use the cash basis of accounting. The cash basis of accounting is justified for these types of businesses because they have few receivables and payables. Accountants are sometimes asked to convert cash basis records to the accrual basis. As you might expect, extensive journal entries are required for this task.

Using a simple example, Illustration 3-2 shows the relationship between accrual-based numbers and cash-based numbers. Suppose you own a painting company and you paint a large building during year 1. In year 1, you incur total expenses of $50,000, which includes the cost of the paint and your employees' salaries. Now assume that you bill your customer $80,000 at the end of year 1, but you aren't paid until year 2. On an accrual basis, you report the revenue during the period earned—year 1. The expenses are recorded (matched) in the period in which the revenues are earned. Thus your net income for year 1 is $30,000. No revenue or expense from this project is reported in year 2. The $30,000 of income reported for year 1 provides a useful indication of profitability and of your efforts during that period.

If, instead, you were reporting on a cash basis, you would report expenses of $50,000 in year 1 and revenues of $80,000 in year 2. For year 1, you would report a loss of $50,000. For year 2, you would report net income of $80,000. Cash basis measures are not very informative about the results of your efforts during year 1 or year 2.

►*International note*

Although different accounting standards are often used in other countries, the accrual basis of accounting is followed by all major industrialized countries.

	Year One	Year Two
Activity	Purchased paint, painted building, paid employees	Received payment for work done in year 1
Accrual basis	Revenue $80,000 Expense 50,000 Net income $30,000	Revenue $ 0 Expense 0 Net income $ 0
Cash basis	Revenue $ 0 Expense 50,000 Net loss ($50,000)	Revenue $80,000 Expense 0 Net income $80,000

Illustration 3-2

Accrual versus cash basis accounting

►Accounting in Action ► *Business Insight*

After years of using modified cash-based accounting systems, the Government of Canada finally made sweeping changes in the type of financial information provided to decision-makers. Under the Financial Information Strategy, new financial systems implemented in 2001 generate full accrual accounting information similar to that used by the private sector. This information is also used in the day-to-day decision-making of department managers. This strategy helps government strengthen its management of business lines and increases its accountability to Parliament.

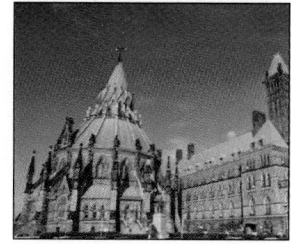

Before You Go On . . .

▶Review It

1. Why do we need to have a time period assumption?
2. What are the revenue recognition and matching principles?
3. What are the differences between the cash and accrual bases of accounting?

Related exercise material: E3–1 and E3–2.

THE NAVIGATOR

The Basics of Adjusting Entries

STUDY OBJECTIVE

4

Explain why and distinguish when adjusting entries are needed.

Accounting Cycle Tutorial—Making Adjusting Entries

For revenues to be recorded in the period in which they are earned, and for expenses to be matched with the revenues they generate, adjusting entries are made at the end of the accounting period. In short, **under the accrual basis of accounting,** adjusting entries **are needed to ensure that the revenue recognition and matching principles are followed**.

Adjusting entries make it possible to report the appropriate assets, liabilities, and owner's equity on the balance sheet. They also make it possible to report the proper net income (or loss) on the income statement for the period. However, the unadjusted trial balance—determined the first time transaction data are pulled together—may not contain up-to-date and complete data. This are true for the following reasons:

1. Some events are not journalized daily because it is not efficient to do so. Examples are the consumption of supplies and the earning of wages by employees.
2. Some costs are not journalized during the accounting period because they expire with the passage of time rather than through recurring daily transactions. Examples are rent, insurance, and amortization.
3. Some items may be unrecorded. An example is a utility service bill that will not be received until the next accounting period. The bill, however, covers services delivered in the preceding accounting period.

Adjusting entries are needed every time financial statements are prepared. We first analyse each account in the trial balance to see if it is complete and up-to-date. The analysis requires a thorough understanding of the company's operations and the interrelationship of accounts. Preparing adjusting entries is often a long process. For example, to accumulate the adjustment data, a company may need to count its remaining supplies. It may also need to prepare supporting schedules of insurance policies, rental agreements, and other contractual commitments. Adjustment data is often not available until after the end of the period in question. In such cases, the adjusting entries are still dated as at the balance sheet date. For these reasons, in some small companies, financial statements are prepared on an annual basis only.

Types of Adjusting Entries

STUDY OBJECTIVE

5

Identify and distinguish between the major types of adjusting entries.

Adjusting entries can be classified as prepayments, accruals, or estimates, as shown below:

Prepayments	Accruals	Estimates
1. Prepaid Expenses Expenses paid in cash and recorded as assets before they are used or consumed.	1. Accrued Expenses Expenses incurred but not yet paid in cash or recorded.	1. Amortization Allocation of the cost of capital assets to expense over their useful lives.
2. Unearned Revenues Revenues received in cash and recorded as liabilities before they are earned.	2. Accrued Revenues Revenues earned but not yet received in cash or recorded.	

Specific examples and explanations of each type of adjustment are given on the following pages. Each example is based on the October 31 trial balance of Pioneer Advertising Agency, reproduced in Illustration 3-3 from Chapter 2. We assume that Pioneer Advertising uses an accounting period of one month. Thus, monthly adjusting entries will be made. The entries will be dated October 31.

PIONEER ADVERTISING AGENCY Trial Balance October 31, 2002	Debit	Credit
Cash	$15,200	
Advertising Supplies	2,500	
Prepaid Insurance	600	
Office Equipment	5,000	
Notes Payable		$ 5,000
Accounts Payable		2,500
Unearned Revenue		1,200
C. R. Byrd, Capital		10,000
C. R. Byrd, Drawings	500	
Service Revenue		10,000
Salaries Expense	4,000	
Rent Expense	900	
	$28,700	$28,700

Illustration 3-3

Trial balance

Adjusting Entries for Prepayments

Prepayments are either prepaid expenses or unearned revenues. Adjusting entries are used to record the portion of the prepayment that is for the **expense incurred or the revenue earned** in the current accounting period. If an adjustment is needed for prepayments, the asset and liability are overstated and the related expense and revenue are understated until the adjustments are made.

For example, in the trial balance, the balance in the asset account Advertising Supplies shows only supplies purchased. This balance is overstated. The related expense account, Advertising Supplies Expense, is understated because the cost of supplies used has not been recognized. Thus the adjusting entry for prepayments will decrease a balance sheet account (Advertising Supplies) and increase an income statement account (Advertising Supplies Expense). The effects of adjusting entries for prepayments are shown in Illustration 3-4.

STUDY OBJECTIVE
.... **6** ....

Identify and prepare adjusting entries for prepayments.

Illustration 3-4

Adjusting entries for prepayments

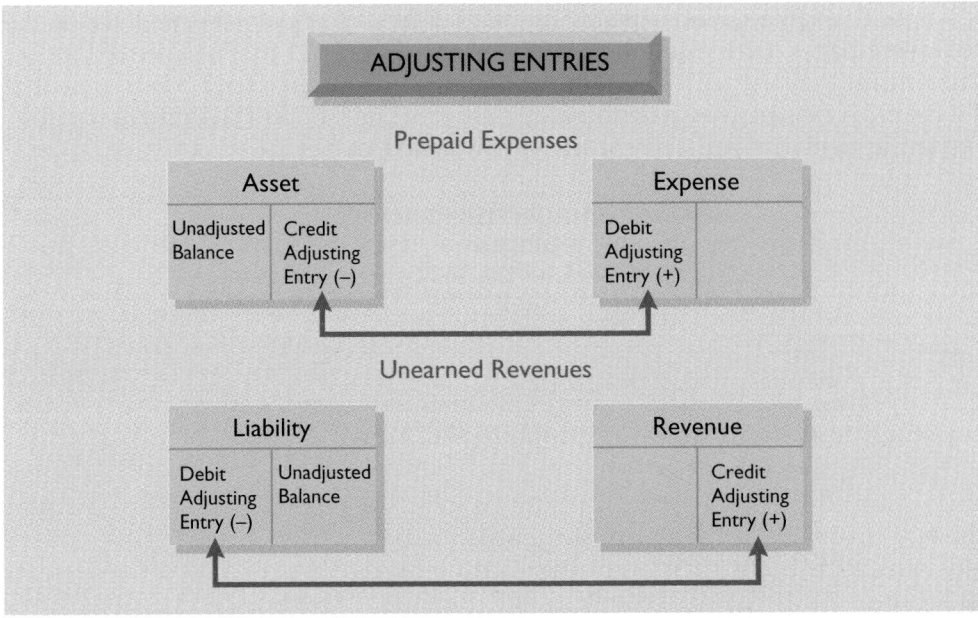

Helpful hint Remember that credits decrease assets and increase revenues. Debits increase expenses and decrease liabilities.

Prepaid Expenses

Alternative terminology Prepaid expenses are also called *deferred expenses* or *future expenses*.

Costs paid in cash and recorded as assets before they are used or consumed are called **prepaid expenses**. When a cost is incurred, an asset account is debited to show the service or benefit that will be received in the future. Prepayments often occur for insurance, supplies, advertising, and rent.

Prepaid expenses expire either with the passage of time (e.g., rent and insurance) or through use and consumption (e.g., supplies). It is not necessary (or practical) to record the expiration of these costs on a daily basis. Instead, these expirations are recorded when financial statements are prepared. At each statement date, adjusting entries are made for two purposes: (1) to record the expenses (expired costs) that apply to the current accounting period, (2) to show the unexpired costs in the asset accounts.

Prior to adjustment, assets are overstated and expenses are understated. **Thus, the prepaid expense adjusting entry results in a debit (increase) to an expense account and a credit (decrease) to an asset account.**

Supplies.   Businesses use various types of supplies. For example, an accounting firm will have office supplies such as pens, pencils, paper, and envelopes. An advertising firm will have advertising supplies such as graph paper, video film, and poster paper. Supplies are generally debited to an asset account when they are bought. During the course of operations, supplies are depleted. However, the amount of supplies used is only recorded during the adjustment process. At that point, a physical inventory (count) of supplies is taken. The difference between the balance in the supplies (asset) account and the cost of supplies actually remaining gives the supplies used (expense) for the period.

Pioneer Advertising Agency purchased advertising supplies costing $2,500 on October 5. A debit (increase) was made to the asset account Advertising Supplies. This account shows a balance of $2,500 in the October 31 trial balance. An inventory count at the close of business on October 31 reveals that only $1,000 of supplies is still on hand. Thus, the cost of supplies used is $1,500 ($2,500 – $1,000), and the following adjusting entry is made:

A	=	L	+	OE
–1,500				–1,500

Oct. 31	Advertising Supplies Expense	1,500	
	Advertising Supplies		1,500
	To record supplies used.		

After the adjusting entry is posted, the two advertising supplies accounts show the following:

Advertising Supplies				Advertising Supplies Expense		
10/5	2,500	10/31 Adj.	1,500	10/31 Adj. 1,500		
10/31 Bal.	1,000					

The asset account Advertising Supplies now shows a balance of $1,000, which is the cost of supplies remaining at the statement date. In addition, Advertising Supplies Expense shows a balance of $1,500, which is the cost of supplies used in October. **If the adjusting entry is not made, October expenses will be understated and net income overstated by $1,500. Also, both assets and owner's equity will be overstated by $1,500 on the October 31 balance sheet.**

►Accounting in Action ► *Business Insight*

The costs of product advertising on radio, television, and magazines are sometimes considered prepayments. As a manager for Procter & Gamble noted, "If we run a long ad campaign for soap, we sometimes report the costs as prepayments if we think we'll receive sales benefits from the campaign down the road." At present, whether these costs should be assets or expenses in the current period is a judgement call. Developing guidelines that are consistent with the matching principle is difficult because situations vary widely from company to company. The issue is important because expenditures for advertising can be substantial. Big advertising spenders include General Motors of Canada, the biggest Canadian advertiser, which spent $111.4 million in a recent year. BCE spent $94 million on advertising, Procter & Gamble spent $84 million, and Hudson's Bay Co. spent $72 million.

Source: Neilsen Media Services, Inc.

Insurance. Most companies have fire and theft insurance for merchandise and equipment, personal liability insurance for accidents suffered by customers on the company's premises, and automobile insurance for company cars and trucks. The term of coverage is usually one year. Insurance premiums (the cost of the insurance policy) are normally charged to the asset account Prepaid Insurance when they are paid. At the financial statement date, it is necessary to make an adjustment to debit (increase) Insurance Expense and credit (decrease) Prepaid Insurance for the cost that has expired during the period.

On October 4, Pioneer Advertising Agency paid $600 for a one-year fire insurance policy. The effective date of coverage was October 1. The premium was charged to Prepaid Insurance when it was paid. This account shows a balance of $600 in the October 31 trial balance. An analysis of the policy reveals that $50 ($600 ÷ 12) of insurance expires each month. Thus, the following adjusting entry is made:

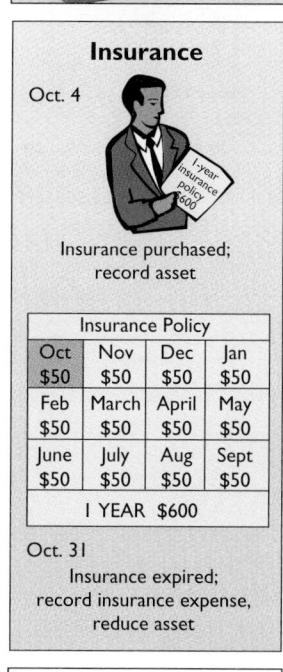

Oct. 31	Insurance Expense	50	
	Prepaid Insurance		50
	To record insurance expired.		

After the adjusting entry is posted, the accounts show the following:

Prepaid Insurance				Insurance Expense		
10/4	600	10/31 Adj.	50	10/31 Adj. 50		
10/31 Bal.	550					

The asset Prepaid Insurance shows a balance of $550. This amount represents the unexpired cost for the remaining 11 months of coverage (11 × $50). The $50 balance in Insurance Expense is equal to the insurance cost that has expired in October. **If this adjustment is not made, October expenses will be understated by $50 and net income overstated by $50. Also, both assets and owner's equity will be overstated by $50 on the October 31 balance sheet.**

Unearned Revenues

Revenues received in cash that have not yet been earned are called **unearned revenues**. Such items as rent, magazine subscriptions, and customer deposits for future service may result in unearned revenues. Airlines such as Air Canada treat receipts from the sale of tickets—often paid long before the flight date—as unearned revenue until the flight service is provided. Similarly, tuition received prior to the start of an academic session, as in the opening story about the summer session at Seneca College, is considered unearned revenue. Unearned revenues are the opposite of prepaid expenses. Indeed, unearned revenue on the books of one company is likely to be a prepayment on the books of the company that has made the advance payment. For example, if identical accounting periods are assumed, your landlord will have unearned rent revenue when you (the tenant) have prepaid your rent.

When a payment is received for services that will be provided in a future accounting period, an unearned revenue account (a liability) should be credited (increased) to recognize the obligation that exists. Unearned revenues become earned when the service is provided to the customer. It is not practical to make daily journal entries as the revenue is earned. Recognition of earned revenue is normally delayed until the end of the accounting period. Then an adjusting entry is made to record the revenue that has been earned and to show the liability that remains. In the typical case, liabilities are overstated and revenues are understated prior to adjustment. Thus, **the adjusting entry for unearned revenues results in a debit (decrease) to a liability account and a credit (increase) to a revenue account**.

Pioneer Advertising Agency received $1,200 on October 4 from R. Knox for advertising services that will be completed by December 31. The payment was originally credited (increased) to Unearned Revenue, an account that shows a balance of $1,200 in the October 31 trial balance. Analysis reveals that $400 of those fees was earned in October. So the following adjusting entry is made:

A	=	L	+	OE
		−400		+400

Oct. 31	Unearned Revenue	400	
	Service Revenue		400
	To record revenue for services provided.		

After the adjusting entry is posted, the accounts show:

Unearned Revenue					
10/31	Adj.	400	10/4		1,200
			10/31 Bal.		800

Service Revenue		
10/29		10,000
10/31 Adj.		400
10/31 Bal.		10,400

The liability Unearned Revenue now shows a balance of $800. This amount represents the remaining advertising services that will be performed in the future. At the same time, Service Revenue shows total revenue of $10,400 earned in October. **If this adjustment is not made, revenues and net income will be understated by $400 in the income statement. Also, liabilities will be overstated and owner's equity understated by $400 on the October 31 balance sheet.**

Before You Go On . . .

▶Review It

1. What are the purposes of adjusting entries?
2. What is the effect on assets, owner's equity, expenses, and net income if a prepaid expense adjusting entry is not made?
3. What is the effect on liabilities, owner's equity, revenues, and net income if an unearned revenue adjusting entry is not made?

▶Do It

The trial balance of Panos, Inc., on March 31, 2003, includes the following selected accounts before adjusting entries:

	Debit	Credit
Prepaid Insurance	$1,200	
Office Supplies	2,800	
Unearned Revenue		$9,200

An analysis of the accounts shows the following:

1. Insurance expires at the rate of $100 per month.
2. Supplies on hand at March 31 total $800.
3. One-half of the unearned revenue was earned in March.

Prepare the adjusting entries for the month of March.

Action Plan

- Make adjusting entries at the end of the period for revenues and expenses incurred in the period.
- Failure to adjust for prepayments leads to overstatement of the asset or liability and related understatement of the expense or revenue.

Solution

March 31	Insurance Expense	100	
	Prepaid Insurance		100
	To record insurance expired.		
	Office Supplies Expense	2,000	
	Office Supplies		2,000
	To record supplies used: $2,800 previously on		
	hand − $800 currently on hand = $2,000 used.		
	Unearned Revenue	4,600	
	Service Revenue		4,600
	To record revenue earned: $9,200 × 1/2 = $4,600		
	earned.		

THE
NAVIGATOR

Related exercise material: BE3–1, BE3–2, BE3–3, BE3–4, and E3–3.

Adjusting Entries for Accruals

The second category of adjusting entries is **accruals**. These adjustments record revenues earned, and related expenses, in the current accounting period that have not yet been recognized (recorded) through daily journal entries.

    If an accrual adjustment is needed, the revenue account (and the related asset account) are understated. The expense account (and the related liability account) are

STUDY OBJECTIVE
· · · · · · · · · · **7** · · · · · · · · ·

Identify and prepare adjusting entries for accruals.

also understated. Thus, the adjusting entry for accruals will **increase both a balance sheet and an income statement account**. Adjusting entries for accruals are shown in Illustration 3-5:

Illustration 3-5

Adjusting entries for accruals

Helpful hint For accruals, there may be no prior entry. The accounts that require adjustment may both have zero balances prior to adjustment.

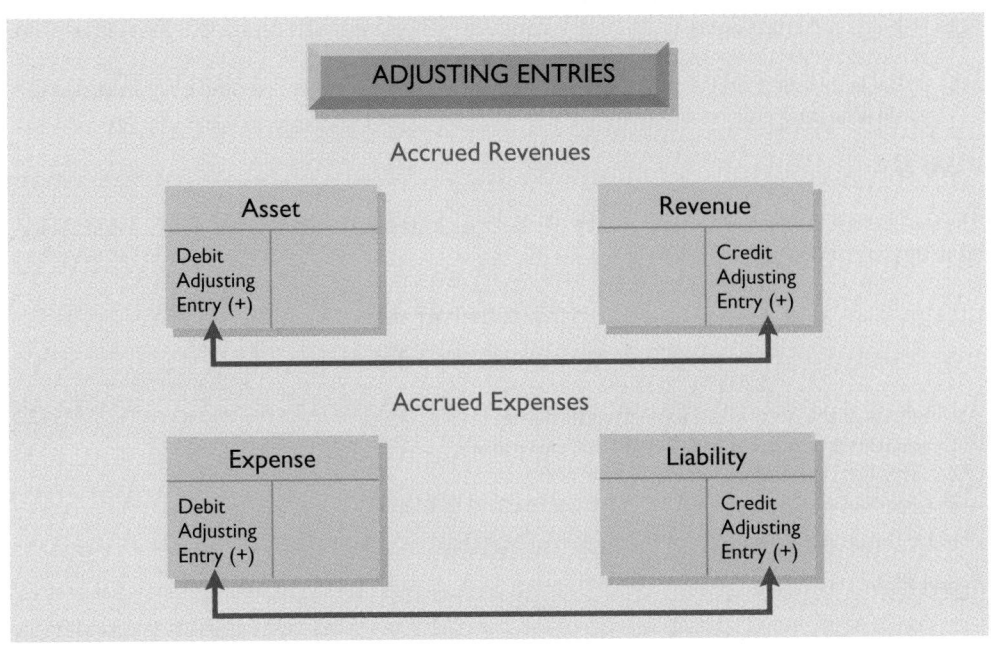

Accrued Revenues

Accrued Revenues

Oct. 31

My fee is $200

Receivable and revenue are recorded for unbilled services performed

Nov. 30
Cash is received; receivable is reduced

Revenues earned, but not yet received in cash or recorded at the statement date, are **accrued revenues**. Accrued revenues may accumulate (accrue) with the passage of time, as in the case of interest revenue and rent revenue. Or, they may result from services that have been performed but neither billed nor collected, as in the case of commissions and fees. The former are unrecorded because the earning of interest and rent does not involve daily transactions. The latter may be unrecorded because only a portion of the total service has been provided.

An adjusting entry is required for two purposes: (1) to show the receivable that exists at the balance sheet date, and (2) to record the revenue that has been earned during the period. Prior to adjustment, both assets and revenues are understated. Accordingly, **an adjusting entry for accrued revenues results in a debit (increase) to an asset account and a credit (increase) to a revenue account**.

In October, Pioneer Advertising Agency earned $200 in fees for advertising services that were not billed to clients until November. Because these services have not been billed, they have not been recorded. The following adjusting entry is made:

A	=	L	+	OE
+200				+200

Oct. 31	Accounts Receivable	200	
	Service Revenue		200
	To accrue revenue earned but not billed or collected.		

After the adjusting entry is posted, the accounts show the following:

Accounts Receivable			
10/31 **Adj.**	200		

Service Revenue			
		10/29	10,000
		10/31 Adj.	400
		10/31 **Adj.**	200
		10/31 Bal.	10,600

The asset Accounts Receivable shows that $200 is owed by clients at the balance sheet date. The balance of $10,600 in Service Revenue represents the total revenue earned during the month. **If the adjusting entry is not made, assets and owner's equity on the balance sheet, and revenues and net income on the income statement, will all be understated.**

In the November accounting period, the clients will be billed. The entry to record the billing should recognize that $200 earned in October was already recorded in the October 31 adjusting entry. To illustrate, bills that total $3,000 are mailed to clients on November 10. Of this amount, $200 represents revenues earned in October and recorded as Service Revenue in the previous month's (October 31) adjusting entry. The remaining $2,800 represents revenue earned in November. Thus, the following entry is made:

Nov. 10	Accounts Receivable	2,800	
	Service Revenue		2,800
	To record revenue for services provided.		

A	=	L	+	OE
+2,800				+2,800

This entry records the amount of revenues earned between November 1 and November 10. The subsequent collection of cash from clients (including the $200 earned in October) will be recorded as follows:

Nov. 30	Cash	3,000	
	Accounts Receivable		3,000
	To record collection of cash from clients.		

A	=	L	+	OE
+3,000				
−3,000				

Accrued Expenses

Expenses incurred but not yet paid or recorded at the statement date are called accrued expenses. Interest, rent, property taxes, and salaries can be accrued expenses. Accrued expenses result from the same causes as accrued revenues. In fact, an accrued expense on the books of one company is an accrued revenue for another company. For example, the $200 accrual of revenue by Pioneer is an accrued expense for the client that received the service.

Adjustments for accrued expenses are needed for two purposes: (1) to record the obligations that exist at the balance sheet date, and (2) to recognize the expenses that apply to the current accounting period. Prior to adjustment, both liabilities and expenses are understated. Therefore, **the adjusting entry for accrued expenses results in a debit (increase) to an expense account and a credit (increase) to a liability account.**

Accrued Interest. On October 1, Pioneer Advertising Agency signed a $5,000, three-month note payable, due January 1, 2003. The note requires interest to be paid at an annual rate of 6%. The amount of interest accumulation is determined by three factors: (1) the face value, or principal amount, of the note; (2) the interest rate, which is always expressed as an annual rate; and (3) the length of time the note is outstanding. The formula for calculating interest and its application to Pioneer Advertising Agency for the month of October is shown in Illustration 3-6.

Accrued Expenses

Oct. 31

Your bill will be $200

Expense and payable are recorded for unbilled services received

Nov. 30

Cash is paid; payable is reduced

Illustration 3-6

Formula for calculating interest

Helpful hint A simplified method of interest calculation is used in the illustration to aid comprehension. In reality, interest is calculated using the exact number of days in the interest period and year.

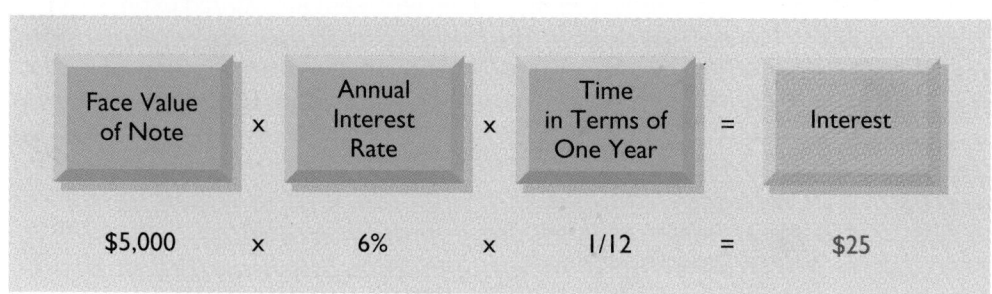

Face Value of Note	×	Annual Interest Rate	×	Time in Terms of One Year	=	Interest
$5,000	×	6%	×	1/12	=	$25

In this instance, the total interest due on the $5,000 note at its due date three months later is $75 ($5,000 × 6% × 3/12 months), or $25 for one month. **Interest rates are always expressed as an annual rate.** The time period must be adjusted for the fraction of the year the note is outstanding. The calculation of interest will be looked at in more depth in later chapters.

The accrued expense adjusting entry at October 31 is as follows:

A	=	L	+	OE
		+25		−25

Oct. 31	Interest Expense	25	
	Interest Payable		25
	To accrue interest on note payable.		

After this adjusting entry is posted, the accounts show:

Interest Expense			Interest Payable	
10/31 **Adj.**	25			10/31 **Adj.**	25

Alternative terminology
Accrued expenses are also called *accrued liabilities*.

Interest Expense shows the interest charges for the month of October. The amount of interest owed at the statement date is shown in Interest Payable. It will not be paid until the note comes due, on January 1, 2003. The Interest Payable account is used instead of crediting Note Payable to show the two types of obligations (interest and principal) in the accounts and statements. **If this adjusting entry is not made, liabilities and expenses will be understated. Net income and owner's equity will be overstated.**

Helpful hint Recognition of an accrued expense does not mean that a company is slow or deficient in paying its debts. The accrued liability may not be payable until after the balance sheet date.

Accrued Salaries. Some types of expenses, such as employee salaries and commissions, are paid after the work has been performed. At Pioneer Advertising, employees began work on October 15. They were last paid on October 26. The next payment of salaries will not occur until November 9. As shown in the calendar, three working days remain in October (October 29–31).

At October 31, the salaries for the last three days represent an accrued expense and a related liability to Pioneer Advertising. The four employees each earn a salary of $500 for a five-day work week, or $100 per day. Thus, accrued salaries for Pioneer Advertising at October 31 are $1,200 ($100 × 3 days × 4 employees). The adjusting entry is as follows:

A	=	L	+	OE
		+1,200		−1,200

Oct. 31	Salaries Expense	1,200	
	Salaries Payable		1,200
	To record accrued salaries.		

After this adjusting entry is posted, the accounts show the following:

Salaries Expense				Salaries Payable		
10/26		4,000			10/31 Adj.	1,200
10/31 Adj.	1,200					
10/31 Bal.	5,200					

After this adjustment, the balance in Salaries Expense of $5,200 (100 × 13 days × 4 employees) is the actual salary expense for October (the employees started work on October 15). The balance in Salaries Payable of $1,200 is the amount of the liability for salaries owed as at October 31. **If the $1,200 adjustment for salaries is not recorded, Pioneer's expenses and liabilities will be understated by $1,200. Net income and owner's equity will be overstated by $1,200.**

At Pioneer Advertising, salaries are payable every two weeks. The next payday is November 9, when total salaries of $4,000 will again be paid. The payment consists of $1,200 of salaries payable at October 31 plus $2,800 of salaries expense for November ($100 × 7 working days [for the period November 1–9] × 4 employees). The following entry is made on November 9:

Nov. 9	Salaries Payable	1,200	
	Salaries Expense	2,800	
	Cash		4,000
	To record November 9 payroll.		

A	=	L	+	OE
−4,000		−1,200		−2,800

This entry does two things: (1) It eliminates the liability for Salaries Payable that was recorded in the October 31 adjusting entry. (2) It records the proper amount of Salaries Expense for the period between November 1 and November 9.

Before You Go On . . .

►Review It

1. If an accrued revenue adjusting entry is not made, what is the effect on assets, owner's equity, revenues, and net income?
2. If an accrued expense adjusting entry is not made, what is the effect on liabilities, owner's equity, expenses, and net income?

►Do It

Calvin and Hobbs are the new owners of Micro Computer Services. At the end of August 2003, their first month of ownership, Calvin and Hobbs are trying to prepare monthly financial statements. The following information relates to August:

1. At August 31, Calvin and Hobbs owed their employees $800 in salaries that will be paid on September 1.
2. On August 1, Calvin and Hobbs borrowed $30,000 from a local bank on a five-year term loan. The annual interest rate is 5%.
3. Service revenue earned but not yet billed for August totalled $1,100.

Prepare the adjusting entries needed at August 31, 2003.

Action Plan

- Make adjusting entries at the end of the period for revenues earned and expenses incurred to generate these revenues in the period.
- Don't forget to make adjusting entries for accruals. Adjusting entries for accruals increase both a balance sheet and an income statement account.

Solution

1.	Aug. 31	Salaries Expense		800	
		Salaries Payable			800
		To record accrued salaries.			
	31	Interest Expense		125	
		Interest Payable			125
		To record accrued interest: $\$30,000 \times 5\% \times {}^{1}/_{12} = \$125$.			
	31	Accounts Receivable		1,100	
		Service Revenue			1,100
		To accrue revenue earned but not billed or collected.			

THE NAVIGATOR

Related exercise material: BE3–5, E3–4, and E3–5.

Adjusting Entries for Estimates

Estimates are required in accounting because we do not always know what will happen in the future. If the current period will be affected by these future events, subjective estimates must be made. Throughout this text, we discuss many estimates found in accounting (e.g., uncollectible accounts receivable, which are discussed in Chapter 9). One important estimate introduced in this chapter is the allocation of the cost of capital assets over their estimated future useful lives. This allocation is known as amortization.

Amortization

Amortization

Oct. 1

Office equipment purchased;
record capital asset

Office Equipment			
Oct $83	Nov $83	Dec $83	Jan $83
Feb $83	March $83	April $83	May $83
June $83	July $83	Aug $83	Sept $83
Amortization = $1,000/year			

Oct. 31
Amortization recognized;
record amortization expense
and accumulated amortization

A business usually owns productive facilities such as land, buildings, equipment, and vehicles. Each is recorded as an asset, rather than as an expense, in the year it is acquired, because these capital assets provide a service for a number of years. The time of service is referred to as the **useful life**.

According to the matching principle, a portion of the cost of a capital asset should be reported as an expense during each period of the asset's useful life. Amortization is the allocation of the cost of these types of assets to expense over their useful lives. All capital assets, **except land**, are amortized. Land is not amortized as it has an unlimited useful life.

Need for Amortization Adjustment.   From an accounting standpoint, acquiring productive facilities is essentially a long-term prepayment for services. The procedure for periodic adjusting entries for amortization is similar to the adjustment procedure for prepaid expenses: recognize the cost that has expired (become an expense) during the period, and report the unexpired cost (which is still an asset) at the end of the period.

At the time an asset is acquired, its useful life is not known with certainty. The asset may be useful for a longer or shorter time than expected, depending on such factors as actual use, deterioration due to elements, or obsolescence. Thus, it is important to recognize that **amortization is an estimate** rather than a factual measurement of the cost that has expired. A common procedure for calculating amortization expense is to divide the cost of the asset by its useful life. For example, if cost is $5,000 and useful life is expected to be five years, annual amortization is $1,000. Calculating amortization is examined in more detail in Chapter 10, including how amortization is affected by any residual value recovered through disposal of the asset at the end of its useful life.

For Pioneer Advertising, amortization on the office equipment is estimated to be

$1,000 a year, or $83 per month. Accordingly, amortization for the month of October is recognized by the following adjusting entry:

Oct. 31	Amortization Expense	83	
	Accumulated Amortization—Office Equipment		83
	To record monthly amortization.		

A	=	L	+	OE
−83				−83

The following shows the accounts after the adjusting entry has been posted:

Office Equipment	
10/1 5,000	

Amortization Expense	
10/31 Adj. 83	

Accumulated Amortization— Office Equipment	
	10/31 Adj. 83

The balance in the Accumulated Amortization account will increase $83 each month. After journalizing and posting the adjusting entry at November 30, the balance will be $166. At December 31, the balance of the accumulated amortization will be $249, and so on.

Statement Presentation. A contra account is offset against a related account on the income statement or balance sheet. On the balance sheet, it can be a **contra asset account** (offset against an asset) or a **contra liability account** (offset against a liability). We will discuss contra income statement accounts in Chapter 5.

Accumulated Amortization—Office Equipment is a contra asset account that is related to the asset account Office Equipment. Its normal balance is a credit—the opposite of the normal debit balance of its related account, Office Equipment. The Accumulated Amortization account is used instead of crediting (decreasing) the Office Equipment account directly in order to **show both the original cost of the equipment and the portion of the cost that has been allocated to expense to date.** In the balance sheet, Accumulated Amortization—Office Equipment is deducted from the related asset account as follows:

Office equipment	$5,000
Less: Accumulated amortization—office equipment	83
Net book value	$4,917

Alternative terminology
Amortization is also called *depreciation*.

Helpful hint Increases, decreases, and normal balances of contra accounts are the *opposite of the accounts they relate to.*

Illustration 3-7

Balance sheet presentation of accumulated amortization

The difference between the cost of any amortizable asset and its accumulated amortization is called the net book value (or simply **book value**) of that asset. In Illustration 3-7, the book value of the equipment at the balance sheet date is $4,917. You should realize that the book value and the market value (the price at which it could be sold in the marketplace) of the asset are usually different. The reason the two are different is that amortization is a means of **cost allocation**, not a matter of **valuation**. That is, amortization does not attempt to show what an asset is worth. It shows only its unallocated cost.

Alternative terminology
Net book value is sometimes called *carrying value.*

Amortization expense identifies the portion of the asset's cost that has expired in October. As in the case of other adjustments for prepaid expenses, **if this adjusting entry is not made, total assets, owner's equity, and net income will be overstated and amortization expense will be understated.**

If the company owns additional equipment, such as delivery or store equipment, or if it has a building, amortization expense is recorded on each of these items. Related accumulated amortization accounts are also established, such as Accumulated Amortization—Delivery Equipment, Accumulated Amortization—Store Equipment, and Accumulated Amortization—Building.

Summary of Basic Relationships

Illustration 3-8

Summary of adjusting entries

The three basic types of adjusting entries are summarized in Illustration 3-8. Take some time to study and analyse the adjusting entries shown in the summary. Be sure to note that **each adjusting entry affects one balance sheet account and one income statement account**.

	Type of Adjustments	Reason for Adjustments	Accounts Before Adjustments	Adjusting Entry
Prepayments	Prepaid expenses	Prepaid expenses, originally recorded in asset accounts, have been used.	Assets overstated; Expenses understated	Dr. Expense Cr. Asset
	Unearned revenues	Unearned revenues, initially recorded in liability accounts, have been earned.	Liabilities overstated; Revenues understated	Dr. Liability Cr. Revenue
Accruals	Accrued revenues	Revenues have been earned but not yet received in cash or recorded.	Assets understated; Revenues understated	Dr. Assets Cr. Revenue
	Accrued expenses	Expenses have been incurred but not yet paid.	Expenses understated; Liabilities understated	Dr. Expense Cr. Liability
Estimates	Amortization	Cost of capital asset must be allocated to expense over useful life.	Assets overstated; Expenses understated	Dr. Amortization Expense Cr. Accumulated Amortization

Helpful hint
1. Adjusting entries should not involve debits and credits to cash.
2. Evaluate whether the adjustment makes sense. For example, an adjustment to recognize supplies used should increase supplies expense.
3. Double-check all calculations.

Illustration 3-9

General journal showing adjusting entries

The journalizing and posting of adjusting entries for Pioneer Advertising Agency on October 31 are shown in Illustrations 3-9 and 3-10. All adjustments are identified in the ledger by the reference J2 because they have been journalized on page 2 of the general journal. A centre caption entitled Adjusting Entries may be inserted between the last transaction entry and the first adjusting entry to identify these entries. When reviewing the general ledger in Illustration 3-10, note that the adjustments are highlighted in colour.

	GENERAL JOURNAL			J2
Date	Account Titles and Explanations	Ref.	Debit	Credit
2002	Adjusting Entries			
Oct. 31	Advertising Supplies Expense	611	1,500	
	Advertising Supplies	129		1,500
	To record supplies used.			
31	Insurance Expense	722	50	
	Prepaid Insurance	130		50
	To record insurance expired.			
31	Unearned Revenue	209	400	
	Service Revenue	400		400
	To record revenue for services provided.			
31	Accounts Receivable	112	200	
	Service Revenue	400		200
	To accrue revenue earned but not billed or collected.			
31	Interest Expense	905	25	
	Interest Payable	230		25
	To accrue interest on note payable.			
31	Salaries Expense	726	1,200	
	Salaries Payable	212		1,200
	To record accrued salaries.			
31	Amortization Expense	711	83	
	Accumulated Amortization—Office Equipment	152		83
	To record monthly amortization.			

Illustration 3-10

General ledger after adjustment

GENERAL LEDGER

Cash — No. 101

Date	Explanation	Ref.	Debit	Credit	Balance
2002					
Oct. 1		J1	10,000		10,000
4		J1	1,200		11,200
4		J1		900	10,300
4		J1		600	9,700
20		J1		500	9,200
26		J1		4,000	5,200
29		J1	10,000		15,200

Accounts Receivable — No. 112

Date	Explanation	Ref.	Debit	Credit	Balance
2002					
Oct. 31	Adj. Entry	J2	200		200

Advertising Supplies — No. 129

Date	Explanation	Ref.	Debit	Credit	Balance
2002					
Oct. 5		J1	2,500		2,500
31	Adj. Entry	J2		1,500	1,000

Prepaid Insurance — No. 130

Date	Explanation	Ref.	Debit	Credit	Balance
2002					
Oct. 4		J1	600		600
31	Adj. Entry	J2		50	550

Office Equipment — No. 151

Date	Explanation	Ref.	Debit	Credit	Balance
2002					
Oct. 1		J1	5,000		5,000

Accumulated Amortization—Office Equipment — No. 152

Date	Explanation	Ref.	Debit	Credit	Balance
2002					
Oct. 31	Adj. Entry	J2		83	83

Notes Payable — No. 200

Date	Explanation	Ref.	Debit	Credit	Balance
2002					
Oct. 1		J1		5,000	5,000

Accounts Payable — No. 201

Date	Explanation	Ref.	Debit	Credit	Balance
2002					
Oct. 5		J1		2,500	2,500

Unearned Revenue — No. 209

Date	Explanation	Ref.	Debit	Credit	Balance
2002					
Oct. 4		J1		1,200	1,200
31	Adj. Entry	J2	400		800

Salaries Payable — No. 212

Date	Explanation	Ref.	Debit	Credit	Balance
2002					
Oct. 31	Adj. entry	J2		1,200	1,200

Interest Payable — No. 230

Date	Explanation	Ref.	Debit	Credit	Balance
2002					
Oct. 31	Adj. Entry	J2		25	25

C.R. Byrd, Capital — No. 301

Date	Explanation	Ref.	Debit	Credit	Balance
2002					
Oct. 1		J1		10,000	10,000

C.R. Byrd, Drawings — No. 306

Date	Explanation	Ref.	Debit	Credit	Balance
2002					
Oct. 20		J1	500		500

Service Revenue — No. 400

Date	Explanation	Ref.	Debit	Credit	Balance
2002					
Oct. 29		J1		10,000	10,000
31	Adj. entry	J2		400	10,400
31	Adj. entry	J2		200	10,600

Advertising Supplies Expense — No. 611

Date	Explanation	Ref.	Debit	Credit	Balance
2002					
Oct. 31	Adj. entry	J2	1,500		1,500

Amortization Expense — No. 711

Date	Explanation	Ref.	Debit	Credit	Balance
2002					
Oct. 31	Adj. Entry	J2	83		83

Insurance Expense — No. 722

Date	Explanation	Ref.	Debit	Credit	Balance
2002					
Oct. 31	Adj. Entry	J2	50		50

Salaries Expense — No. 726

Date	Explanation	Ref.	Debit	Credit	Balance
2002					
Oct. 26		J1	4,000		4,000
31	Adj. entry	J2	1,200		5,200

Rent Expense — No. 729

Date	Explanation	Ref.	Debit	Credit	Balance
2002					
Oct. 4		J1	900		900

Interest Expense — No. 905

Date	Explanation	Ref.	Debit	Credit	Balance
2002					
Oct. 31	Adj. Entry	J2	25		25

Many computer systems handle the adjusting process like any other transaction. The accountant inputs the adjustment at the time required. The main difference between adjusting entries and regular transactions is that with adjusting entries, part of the computer system may perform the required calculation (for items such as amortization or interest) before sending these figures to the journalizing process.

Such systems are also able to display information before and after changes were made. Management may be interested in such information to highlight the impact that adjustments have on the various accounts and financial statements.

Before You Go On . . .

▶ Review It

1. What are the three types of adjusting entries?
2. What is the purpose of amortization?
3. What journal entry is made to record amortization at the end of each accounting period?
4. Does net book value equal fair market value? Explain why or why not.
5. Using Second Cup's statement of operations (income statement), find the amount of depreciation and amortization expense recorded for 2000 and 1999 (use pro forma figures). The answer to this question is provided at the end of the chapter.

THE NAVIGATOR

Related exercise material: BE3–6, BE3–7, BE3–8, BE3–9, E3–6, E3–7, E3–8, E3–9, and E3–10.

The Adjusted Trial Balance and Financial Statements

STUDY OBJECTIVE

9

Describe the nature and purpose of an adjusted trial balance and prepare.

After all adjusting entries have been journalized and posted, another trial balance is prepared from the ledger accounts. This is called an adjusted trial balance. The procedures for preparing an adjusted trial balance are identical to those described in Chapter 2 for preparing a trial balance.

Preparing the Adjusted Trial Balance

An adjusted trial balance proves the equality of the total debit balances and the total credit balances in the ledger, after all adjustments have been made. The proof provided by an adjusted trial balance, like the proof contained in a trial balance, applies only to the mathematical accuracy of the ledger. **The adjusted trial balance provides all data that are needed for the preparation of financial statements.**

The adjusted trial balance for Pioneer Advertising Agency is presented in Illustration 3-11. It has been prepared from the ledger accounts shown in Illustration 3-10. The amounts affected by the adjusting entries are highlighted in colour in the adjusted trial balance columns. Compare these amounts to those in the unadjusted trial balance in Illustration 3-3.

Illustration 3-11

Adjusted trial balance

PIONEER ADVERTISING AGENCY
Adjusted Trial Balance
October 31, 2002

	Debit	Credit
Cash	$15,200	
Accounts Receivable	200	
Advertising Supplies	1,000	
Prepaid Insurance	550	
Office Equipment	5,000	
Accumulated Amortization—		
Office Equipment		$ 83
Notes Payable		5,000
Accounts Payable		2,500
Unearned Revenue		800
Salaries Payable		1,200
Interest Payable		25
C. R. Byrd, Capital		10,000
C. R. Byrd, Drawings	500	
Service Revenue		10,600
Advertising Supplies Expense	1,500	
Amortization Expense	83	
Insurance Expense	50	
Salaries Expense	5,200	
Rent Expense	900	
Interest Expense	25	
	$30,208	$30,208

Preparing Financial Statements

Financial statements can be prepared directly from the adjusted trial balance. The preparation of financial statements from the adjusted trial balance of Pioneer Advertising Agency and the interrelationship of data are presented in Illustrations 3-12 and 3-13.

As shown in Illustration 3-12, the income statement is prepared from the revenue and expense accounts. The statement of owner's equity is derived from the owner's capital and drawings accounts, and from the net income (or net loss) shown in the income statement. As shown in Illustration 3-13, the balance sheet is then prepared from the asset and liability accounts and the ending owner's capital balance, as reported in the statement of owner's equity.

Helpful hint Financial statements are prepared in the sequence stated in Chapter 1:
1. Income statement
2. Statement of owner's equity
3. Balance sheet

However, they are usually presented in the following order:
1. Balance sheet
2. Statement of owner's equity
3. Income statement

Illustration 3-12

Preparation of the income statement and statement of owner's equity from the adjusted trial balance

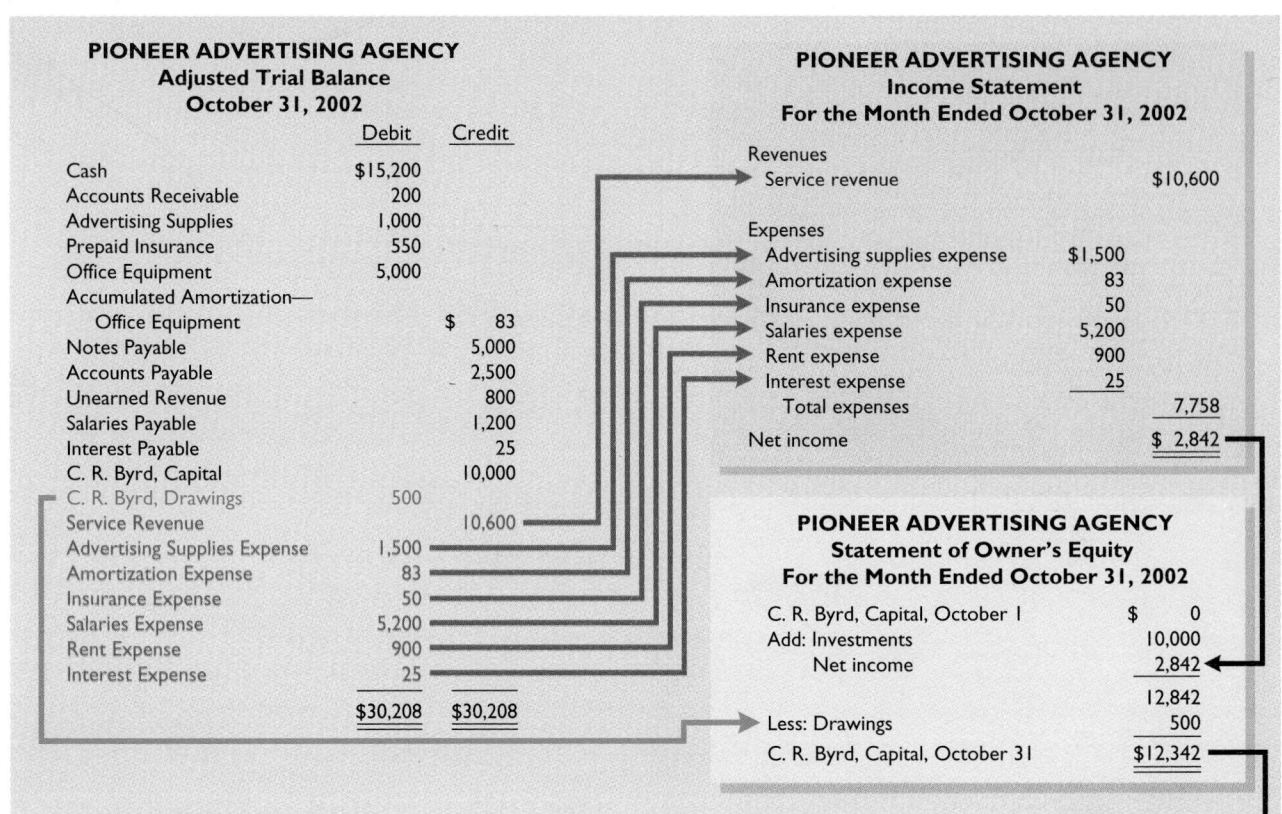

Illustration 3-13

Preparation of the balance sheet from the adjusted trial balance

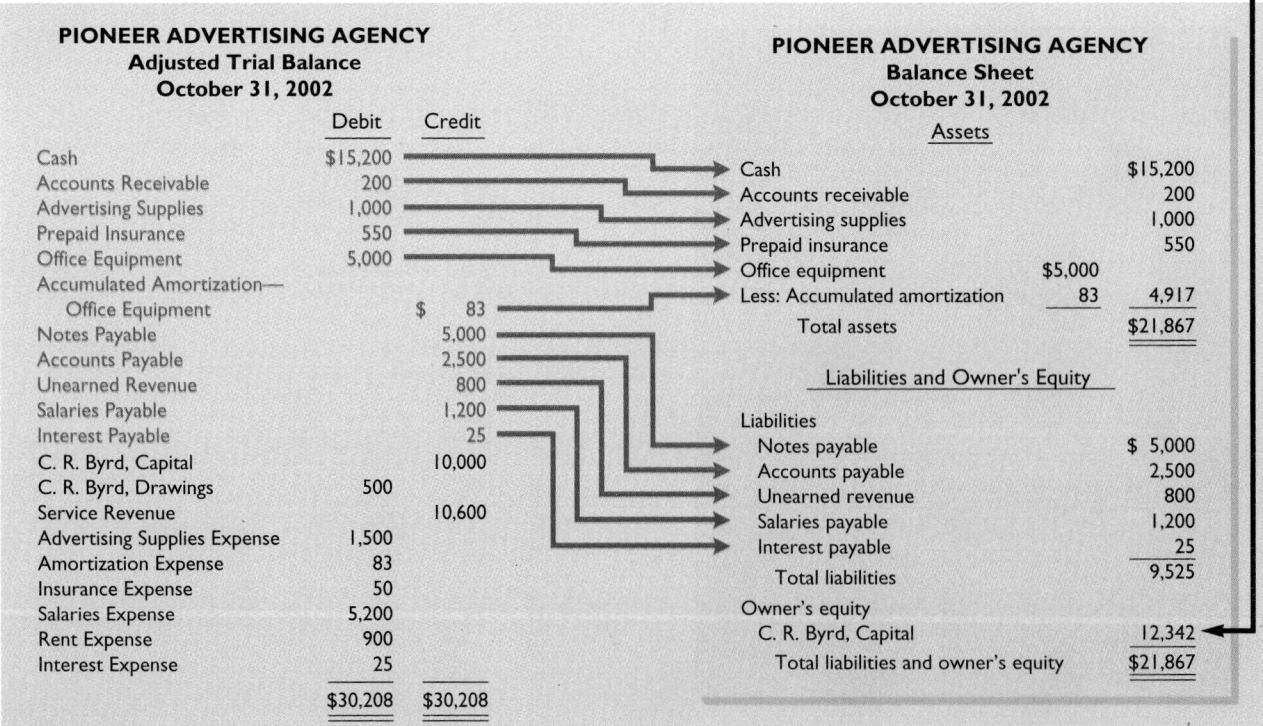

Before You Go On . . .

▶Review It

1. What is the purpose of an adjusted trial balance?
2. How is an adjusted trial balance prepared?

Related exercise material: BE3–10, BE3–11, E3–11, and E3-12.

▶ A Look Back at Our Feature Story

Refer to the feature story about Seneca College and answer the following questions:
1. Why should Seneca be concerned about the period in which revenue is recognized?
2. What journal entry was most likely made when students paid for their summer courses in March? What adjusting entry should be made to record the tuition revenue at the end of the summer session?
3. What other types of adjusting entries do you believe Seneca College might make?

Solution

1. As a not-for-profit institution, Seneca College must operate within its government subsidies and its own budget. It must know what revenues are attributable to each operating/accounting period. Assignment of revenues to the proper operating periods (namely, to the periods they are earned in) is necessary in order to make operating/accounting periods (years) comparable.
2. Ron Currie probably used the account Unearned Tuition Revenue, because tuition was received in advance of the summer semester courses. The original journal entry was likely debit Cash and credit Unearned Tuition Revenue. If so, the adjusting entry would be debit Unearned Tuition Revenue and credit Tuition Revenue.
3. (a) Accrued expenses: salaries, utilities, interest, professional fees
   (b) Accrued revenues: unpaid tuition, lab fees, interest, government grants
   (c) Prepaid expenses: insurance, supplies
   (d) Unearned revenues: lab fees, theatre tickets, athletic tickets
   (e) Estimates: amortization

DEMONSTRATION PROBLEM

Julie Szo opens the Green Thumb Lawn Care Company on April 1. At April 30, the trial balance shows the following balances for selected accounts:

Prepaid Insurance	$ 3,600
Equipment	28,000
Note Payable	20,000
Unearned Revenue	4,200
Service Revenue	1,800

Analysis reveals the following additional data about these accounts:
1. Prepaid insurance is the cost of a 12-month insurance policy, effective April 1.
2. Amortization on the equipment is $500 per month.
3. The note payable is dated April 1. It is a six-month, 4% note.
4. Seven customers paid for the company's six-month lawn-service package of $600, beginning in April. These customers were serviced in April.
5. Lawn services performed for other customers but not billed at April 30 totalled $1,500.

Instructions

Prepare the adjusting entries for the month of April. Show calculations.

Additional Demonstration Problem

Solution to Demonstration Problem

Action Plan

- Note that adjustments are being made for one month.
- Look at how the amounts are currently recorded in the accounts, before trying to determine what adjustments are necessary.
- Select account titles carefully. Use existing titles whenever possible.
- Make sure debits are made first and credits are indented.
- Check that debits equal credits for each entry.

THE NAVIGATOR

	GENERAL JOURNAL				J2
Date	Account Titles and Explanations	Ref.	Debit		Credit
	Adjusting Entries				
Apr. 30	Insurance Expense		300		
	Prepaid Insurance				300
	To record insurance expired:				
	$3,600 ÷ 12 = $300 per month.				
30	Amortization Expense		500		
	Accumulated Amortization—Equipment				500
	To record monthly amortization.				
30	Interest Expense		67		
	Interest Payable				67
	To accrue interest on notes payable:				
	$20,000 × 4% × 1/12 = $67.				
30	Unearned Revenue		700		
	Service Revenue				700
	To record service revenue: $600 ÷ 6 months.				
	= $100; $100 per month × 7 customers = $700.				
30	Accounts Receivable		1,500		
	Service Revenue				1,500
	To accrue revenue earned but not billed or collected.				

APPENDIX 3A ▸ *Alternative Treatment of Prepaid Expenses and Unearned Revenues*

STUDY OBJECTIVE

10

Identify and prepare adjusting entries for the alternative treatment of prepayments.

In our discussion of adjusting entries for prepaid expenses and unearned revenues, we illustrated transactions which already had entries in balance sheet accounts. In the case of prepaid expenses, the prepayment was debited to an asset account. In the case of unearned revenue, the cash received was credited to a liability account. **Recording your first entry in a balance sheet account facilitates internal control over assets and imitates the real flow of costs (i.e., from asset to expense).**

Some businesses use an alternative treatment, which is equally acceptable. At the time an expense is prepaid, it is debited to an expense account. At the time of a receipt for future services, it is credited to a revenue account. The circumstances that justify such entries and the different adjusting entries that may be required are described in the following sections. The alternative treatment of prepaid expenses and unearned revenues has the **same effect on the financial statements** as the procedures described earlier in this chapter.

▾ Prepaid Expenses

Prepaid expenses become expired costs through either the passage of time, as in the case of insurance, or through consumption, as in the case of advertising supplies. If, at the time of purchase, the company expects to consume the supplies before the next financial statement date, **it may be more convenient initially to debit (increase) an expense account rather than an asset account.**

Assume that Pioneer Advertising expects that all of the supplies purchased on October 5 will be used before the end of the month. A debit of $2,500 to Advertising Supplies Expense rather than to the asset account Advertising Supplies, on October 5, will eliminate the need for an adjusting entry on October 31, if all the supplies are used. At October 31, the Advertising Supplies Expense account will show a balance of $2,500, which is the cost of supplies used between October 5 and October 31.

But what if the company does not use all the supplies and an inventory of $1,000 of advertising supplies remains on October 31? Obviously, an adjusting entry is needed. The following adjusting entry is made:

Oct. 31	Advertising Supplies	1,000	
	Advertising Supplies Expense		1,000
	To record supply inventory.		

$$A = L + OE$$
$$+1,000 \qquad +1,000$$

After posting of the adjusting entry, the accounts show the following:

Advertising Supplies			Advertising Supplies Expense			
10/31 Adj.	1,000		10/5	2,500	10/31 Adj.	1,000
			10/31 Bal.	1,500		

After adjustment, the asset account, Advertising Supplies, shows a balance of $1,000, which is equal to the cost of supplies on hand at October 31. In addition, Advertising Supplies Expense shows a balance of $1,500, which is equal to the cost of supplies used between October 5 and October 31. If the adjusting entry is not made, expenses will be overstated and net income will be understated by $1,000 in the October income statement. Also, both assets and owner's equity will be understated by $1,000 on the October 31 balance sheet.

A comparison of the entries and accounts for advertising supplies is shown in Illustration 3A-1.

Illustration 3A-1

Adjustment approaches—a comparison

Prepayment Initially Debited to Asset Account (as in chapter)				Prepayment Initially Debited to Expense Account (as in appendix)			
Oct. 5	Advertising Supplies	2,500		Oct. 5	Advertising Supplies Expense	2,500	
	Accounts Payable		2,500		Accounts Payable		2,500
Oct. 31	Advertising Supplies Expense	1,500		Oct. 31	Advertising Supplies	1,000	
	Advertising Supplies		1,500		Advertising Supplies Expense		1,000

After posting of the entries, the accounts appear as follows:

(as in chapter) Advertising Supplies				(as in appendix) Advertising Supplies			
10/5	2,500	10/31 Adj.	1,500	10/31 Adj.	1,000		
10/31 Bal.	1,000						

Advertising Supplies Expense				Advertising Supplies Expense			
10/31 Adj.	1,500			10/5	2,500	10/31 Adj.	1,000
				10/31 Bal.	1,500		

Note that the **account balances under each alternative are the same** at October 31 (Advertising Supplies $1,000, and Advertising Supplies Expense $1,500).

Unearned Revenues

Unearned revenues become earned either through the passage of time, as in the case of unearned rent, or through providing the service, as in the case of unearned fees. Rather than crediting an unearned revenue (liability) account initially, a revenue account may be credited (increased) when cash is received for future services, and a different adjusting entry may be necessary.

To illustrate, assume that when Pioneer Advertising received $1,200 for future services on October 4, the services were expected to be performed before October 31. In such a case, Service Revenue would be credited. If revenue is in fact earned before October 31, no adjustment is needed. However, if at the statement date, $800 of the services has not been provided, an adjusting entry is required. The revenue account, Service Revenue, is overstated by $800, and the liability account, Unearned Revenue, is understated by $800. Thus, the following adjusting entry is made:

A	=	L	+	OE
		+800		−800

Oct. 31	Service Revenue	800	
	Unearned Revenue		800
	To record unearned revenue.		

After posting of the adjusting entry, the accounts show:

Unearned Revenue				Service Revenue			
		10/31 Adj.	800	10/31 Adj.	800	10/4	1,200
						10/31 Bal.	400

The liability account Unearned Revenue shows a balance of $800, which is equal to the services that will be provided in the future. In addition, the balance in Service Revenue equals the services provided in October. If the adjusting entry is not made, both revenues and net income will be overstated by $800 in the October income statement. On the October 31 balance sheet, liabilities will also be understated by $800, and owner's equity will be overstated by $800.

A comparison of the entries and accounts for service revenue and unearned revenue is presented in Illustration 3A-2:

Illustration 3A-2

Adjustment approaches— a comparison

Unearned Revenue Initially Credited to Liability Account (as in chapter)				Unearned Revenue Initially Credited to Revenue Account (as in appendix)			
Oct. 4	Cash	1,200		Oct. 4	Cash	1,200	
	Unearned Revenue		1,200		Service Revenue		1,200
Oct. 31	Unearned Revenue	400		Oct. 31	Service Revenue	800	
	Service Revenue		400		Unearned Revenue		800

After posting the entries, the accounts will show:

(as in chapter) Unearned Revenue				(as in appendix) Unearned Revenue			
10/31 Adj.	400	10/4	1,200			10/31 Adj.	800
		10/31 Bal.	800				

Service Revenue				Service Revenue			
		10/31 Adj.	400	10/31 Adj.	800	10/4	1,200
						10/31 Bal.	400

Note that the balances in the accounts are the same under the two alternatives (Unearned Revenue $800, and Service Revenue $400).

Summary of Additional Adjustment Relationships

The use of alternative adjusting entries requires additions to the summary of basic relationships for prepayments presented earlier in Illustration 3-8. The additions are shown in colour in Illustration 3A-3.

Illustration 3A-3

Summary of adjusting entries for prepayments

	Type of Adjustments	Reason for Adjustments	Accounts Before Adjustments	Adjusting Entry
Prepayments	Prepaid expenses	Prepaid expenses, initially recorded in asset accounts, have been used.	Assets overstated; Expenses understated	Dr. Expense Cr. Asset
		Prepaid expenses, initially recorded in expense accounts, have not been used.	Assets understated; Expenses overstated	Dr. Asset Cr. Expense
	Unearned revenues	Unearned revenues, initially recorded in liability accounts, have been earned.	Liabilities overstated; Revenues understated	Dr. Liability Cr. Revenue
		Unearned revenues, initially recorded in revenue accounts, have not been earned.	Liabilities understated; Revenues overstated	Dr. Revenue Cr. Liability

Alternative adjusting entries do not apply to accruals or estimates because no entries occur before these types of adjusting entries are made. Therefore, the entries shown in Illustration 3-8 for these two types of adjustments remain unchanged.

Before You Go On . . .

►Review It

1. Compare recording prepayments in balance sheet accounts versus recording them in income statement accounts. If an appropriate adjusting journal entry is made at the end of the period, does it matter which practice is followed?

*Related exercise material: *BE3–12, *BE3–13 and *E3–13.*

THE NAVIGATOR

Summary of Study Objectives

1. *Explain the time period assumption.* The time period assumption divides the economic life of a business into artificial time periods.

2. *Distinguish between the revenue recognition principle and the matching principle.* The revenue recognition principle states that revenue should be recognized (recorded) in the accounting period in which it is earned. The matching principle states that expenses should be recognized (recorded) when they make their contribution to revenues.

3. *Explain the accrual basis of accounting.* Accrual basis accounting means that events that change a company's financial statements are recorded in the periods in which the events occur, rather than in the periods in which the company receives or pays cash.

4. *Explain why and distinguish when adjusting entries are needed.* Adjusting entries are made at the end of an accounting period. They ensure that revenues are recorded in the period in which they are earned. Expenses are recognized in the period in which services or goods are used or consumed in order to match expenses with revenues.

5. *Identify and distinguish between the major types of adjusting entries.* The major types of adjusting entries are prepayments (prepaid expenses and unearned revenues), accruals (accrued revenues and accrued expenses), and estimates (e.g., amortization).

6. *Identify and prepare adjusting entries for prepayments.* Prepayments are either prepaid expenses or unearned revenues. Adjusting entries for prepayments are required at the statement date. They record the portion of the prepayment that applies to the expense or the revenue applicable to the current accounting period.

7. *Identify and prepare adjusting entries for accruals.* Accruals are either accrued revenues or accrued expenses. Adjusting entries for accruals record revenues and expenses applicable to the current accounting period that have not yet been recognized through daily journal entries.

8. *Identify and prepare the adjusting entry for amortization.* Amortization is the process of allocating the cost of a capital asset to expense over the periods the asset provides benefits. The journal entry is debit amortization expense and credit accumulated amortization, a contra asset account.

THE NAVIGATOR

9. *Describe the nature and purpose of an adjusted trial balance and prepare.* An adjusted trial balance shows the balances of all accounts, including those that have been adjusted, at the end of an accounting period. Its purpose is to show the effects of all financial events that have occurred during the accounting period.

10. *Identify and prepare adjusting entries for the alternative treatment of prepayments (Appendix 3A).* Prepayments may be initially debited (increased) to an expense account. Unearned revenues may be credited (increased) to a revenue account. At the end of the period, these accounts may be overstated. The adjusting entries for prepaid expenses are a debit (increase) to an asset account and a credit (decrease) to an expense account. Adjusting entries for unearned revenues are a debit (decrease) to a revenue account and a credit (increase) to a liability account. It doesn't matter which alternative is used to record and adjust prepayments, as the ending account balances should be the same under each alternative.

Glossary

 Key Term Matching Activity

Accrual basis of accounting   Accounting basis in which transactions that change a company's financial statements are recorded in the period in which the events occur. Revenues are recorded when earned. Expenses are recorded in the same period as the revenue to which they are related. (p. 104)

Accrued expenses   Expenses incurred but not yet paid in cash or recorded. (p. 113)

Accrued revenues   Revenues earned but not yet received in cash or recorded. (p. 112)

Adjusted trial balance   A list of accounts and their balances after all adjustments have been made. (p. 120)

Adjusting entries   Entries made at the end of an accounting period to ensure that the revenue recognition and matching principles are followed. (p. 106)

Amortization   The allocation of the cost of a capital asset to expense over its useful life in a rational and systematic manner. (p. 116)

Cash basis of accounting   Revenue is recorded when cash is received. An expense is recorded when cash is paid. (p. 104)

Contra account   An account that is offset against another account on the income statement or balance sheet. (p. 117)

Fiscal year   An accounting period that is one year in length. It does not need to coincide with the calendar year. (p. 103)

Interim periods   Accounting time periods of less than one year in duration. (p. 103)

Matching principle   The principle that efforts (expenses) should be matched with accomplishments (revenues). (p. 104)

Net book value   The difference between the cost of an amortizable asset and its accumulated amortization. That is, the unallocated or unexpired portion of the capital asset's cost. (p. 117)

Prepaid expenses   Expenses paid in cash and recorded as assets before they are used or consumed. (p. 108)

Revenue recognition principle   The principle that revenue should be recognized in the accounting period in which it is earned. (p. 103)

Time period assumption   An assumption that the economic life of a business can be divided into artificial time periods: normally, a month, quarter, or year. (p. 103)

Unearned revenues   Revenues received in cash and recorded as liabilities before they are earned. (p. 110)

Note: All **asterisked** Questions, Exercises, and Problems below relate to material contained in Appendix 3A.

SELF-STUDY QUESTIONS

Chapter 3 Self-Test

Answers are at the end of the chapter.

(SO 1) K   1. The time period assumption states that:
a. revenue should be recognized in the accounting period in which it is earned.
b. expenses should be matched with revenues.
c. the economic life of a business can be divided into artificial time periods.
d. the fiscal year should correspond with the calendar year.

(SO 2) K   2. The principle which states that efforts (expenses) should be recorded in the same period as the related accomplishments (revenues) is the:
a. matching principle.
b. cost principle.
c. time period assumption.
d. revenue recognition principle.

(SO 3) K   3. Which of the following statements about the accrual basis of accounting is false?
a. Expenses are recorded when goods or services are used or consumed.
b. Revenue is recognized in the period in which it is earned.
c. The accrual basis is in accordance with generally accepted accounting principles.
d. Revenue is recorded only when cash is received, and expenses are recorded only when cash is paid.

(SO 4) K   4. Adjusting entries are made to ensure that:
a. expenses are matched to revenues in the period in which the revenue is generated.
b. revenues are recorded in the period in which they are earned.
c. balance sheet and income statement accounts have correct balances at the end of an accounting period.
d. All of the above.

(SO 5) K   5. Which of the following is not a type (or category) of adjusting entry?
a. Prepaid expenses
b. Accrued revenues
c. Estimates
d. Earned revenues

(SO 6) AP   6. The trial balance shows Supplies $1,350 and Supplies Expense $0. If $600 of supplies are on hand at the end of the period, the adjusting entry is:

a. Supplies	600	
Supplies Expense		600
b. Supplies	750	
Supplies Expense		750
c. Supplies Expense	750	
Supplies		750
d. Supplies Expense	600	
Supplies		600

(SO 6) K   7. Adjustments for unearned revenues:
a. decrease liabilities and increase revenues.
b. increase liabilities and increase revenues.
c. increase assets and increase revenues.
d. decrease revenues and decrease assets.

(SO 7) K   8. Adjustments for accrued revenues:
a. increase assets and increase liabilities.
b. increase assets and increase revenues.
c. decrease assets and decrease revenues.
d. decrease liabilities and increase revenues.

(SO 7) AP   9. Kathy Kiska earned a salary of $400 for the last week of September. She will be paid in October. The adjusting entry for Kathy's employer at September 30 is:
a. No entry is required.

b. Salaries Expense	400	
Salaries Payable		400
c. Salaries Expense	400	
Cash		400
d. Salaries Payable	400	
Cash		400

(SO 8) K   10. Accumulated Amortization is:
a. an expense account.
b. an owner's equity account.
c. a liability account.
d. a contra asset account.

(SO 9) K   11. Which of the following statements concerning the adjusted trial balance is *incorrect*?
a. An adjusted trial balance proves the equality of the total debit balances and the total credit balances in the ledger, after all adjustments are made.
b. The adjusted trial balance provides the primary basis for the preparation of financial statements.
c. The adjusted trial balance lists the account balances divided into assets and liabilities.
d. The adjusted trial balance is prepared after the adjusting entries have been journalized and posted.

*(SO 10) AP   *12. The trial balance shows Supplies $0 and Supplies Expense $1,350. If $600 of supplies are on hand at the end of the period, the adjusting entry is:

a. Supplies	600	
Supplies Expense		600
b. Supplies Expense	750	
Supplies		750
c. Supplies	750	
Supplies Expense		750
d. Supplies Expense	600	
Supplies		600

THE NAVIGATOR

QUESTIONS

(SO 1) C   1. (a) How does the time period assumption affect an accountant's analysis of business transactions?
(b) Explain the terms *fiscal year*, *calendar year*, and *interim periods*.

(SO 2) C   2. Identify and describe two generally accepted accounting principles that relate to adjusting the accounts.

(SO 2) C   3. Pierce Dussault, a lawyer, accepts a legal engagement in March, performs the work in April, and is paid in May. If Dussault's law firm prepares monthly financial statements, when should it recognize revenue from this engagement? Why?

(SO 2) C   4. In completing the engagement in question 3, Dussault incurred $2,000 of salary expenses specifically related to this engagement in March, $2,500 in April, and none in May. How much expense should be deducted from revenue in the month the revenue is recognized? Why?

(SO 3) C   5. Why do accrual basis financial statements provide more useful information than cash basis statements?

(SO 3) C   6. Should the balance in total owner's equity equal the balance in the Cash account? Explain why or why not.

(SO 4) C   7. "Adjusting entries are needed to respect the cost principle of accounting." Do you agree? Explain.

(SO 4) C   8. Why might a trial balance not contain up-to-date and complete financial information?

(SO 5) C   9. Distinguish among the three categories of adjusting entries, and identify the types of adjustments applicable to each category.

(SO 6) K   10. What is the debit/credit effect of a prepaid expense adjusting entry?

(SO 6) K   11. What is the debit/credit effect of an unearned revenue adjusting entry?

(SO 7) K   12. A company received cash from a customer. It debited the Cash account, but it did not credit any revenue account. Name two other accounts that the company might have used to record a cash receipt from a customer.

(SO 7) K   13. A company fails to recognize revenue earned but not yet received. Which accounts are involved in the adjusting entry? For the accounts selected, indicate whether they would be debited or credited in the entry.

(SO 7) K   14. A company fails to recognize a utility expense that has been incurred but not paid. Indicate which account is debited and which is credited in the adjusting entry.

(SO 7) AP   15. A company makes an accrued revenue adjusting entry for $900 and an accrued expense adjusting entry for $600. Which financial statement items were overstated or understated prior to these entries? Explain.

(SO 7) AP   16. On January 9, a company pays $5,000 for salaries, of which $1,700 was reported as Salaries Payable on December 31. Give the entry to record the payment.

(SO 6, 7) C   17. For each of the following items before adjustment, indicate the type of adjusting entry (prepaid expense, unearned revenue, accrued revenue, accrued expense, estimate) that is needed to correct the misstatement. If an item could result in more than one type of adjusting entry, indicate each of the types.
(a) Assets are understated.
(b) Liabilities are overstated.
(c) Liabilities are understated.
(d) Expenses are understated.
(e) Assets are overstated.
(f) Revenue is understated.

(SO 8) C   18. "Amortization is a valuation process that results in the reporting of the market value of the asset." Do you agree? Explain.

(SO 8) C   19. Explain the difference between amortization expense and accumulated amortization.

(SO 8) AP   20. Shen Company purchased equipment for $12,000. By the current balance sheet date, $7,000 had been amortized. Indicate the balance sheet presentation of the data.

(SO 6, 7, 8) K   21. One half of the adjusting entry is given below. Indicate the account title for the other half of the entry.
(a) Salaries Expense is debited.
(b) Amortization Expense is debited.
(c) Interest Payable is credited.
(d) Supplies is credited.
(e) Accounts Receivable is debited.
(f) Unearned Revenue is debited.

(SO 6, 7, 8) C   22. "An adjusting entry may affect more than one balance sheet or income statement account." Do you agree? Why or why not?

(SO 9) C   23. Why is it possible to prepare financial statements directly from an adjusted trial balance?

(SO 10) C   *24. The Alpha Company debits Supplies Expense for all purchases of supplies, and credits Rent Revenue for all rental payments received in advance. For each type of adjustment, state which account should be debited and which should be credited.

BRIEF EXERCISES

··

BE3–1 The ledger of the Yap Company includes the following accounts. Explain why each account may require adjustment.

    1. Prepaid Insurance   3. Unearned Revenue   5. Rent Receivable

    2. Accumulated Amortization   4. Interest Payable

Indicate why adjusting entries are needed.
(SO 4) C

BE3–2 The Spahn Advertising Company's trial balance at December 31 shows Advertising Supplies $8,700, and Advertising Supplies Expense $0. On December 31, there is $1,500 of supplies on hand. Prepare the adjusting entry at December 31. Using T accounts, enter the balances in the accounts, post the adjusting entry, and indicate the adjusted balance in each account.

Prepare and post adjusting entry for supplies.
(SO 6) AP

BE3–3 On July 1, 2003, Bere Co. pays $10,000 to Hindi Insurance Co. for a two-year insurance contract. Both companies have fiscal years that end December 31. For Bere Co., journalize and post the entry on July 1, and the adjusting entry on December 31.

Prepare and post adjusting entries for prepaid expense.
(SO 6) AP

BE3–4 Using the data in BE3–3, journalize and post the entry on July 1 and the adjusting entry on December 31, 2003, for Hindi Insurance Co.

Prepare and post adjusting entries for unearned revenue.
(SO 6) AP

BE3–5 The bookkeeper for the deVos Company asks you to prepare the following adjusting entries at December 31:

1. Interest on notes receivable of $300 is accrued.
2. Services provided but unbilled total $1,400.
3. Salaries of $900 earned by employees have not been recorded.

Prepare adjusting entries for accruals.
(SO 7) AP

BE3–6 At the end of its first year, the trial balance of the Tai Woo Company shows Equipment $25,000, and zero balances in Accumulated Amortization—Equipment, and Amortization Expense. Amortization for the year is estimated to be $5,000. Prepare the adjusting entry for amortization at December 31, post the adjustments to T accounts, and indicate the balance sheet presentation of the equipment at December 31.

Prepare and post adjusting entries for amortization, show balance sheet presentation.
(SO 8) AP

BE3–7 Indicate the impact of each of the following transactions on cash and net income. The first transaction has been completed for you as an example.

Transaction	Cash	Net Income
(a) Purchased supplies on hand for cash, $100.	–$100	$0
(b) Recorded the use of $50 of the supplies purchased in (a) in an adjusting journal entry.		
(c) Performed services on account, $1,000.		
(d) Received $800 from customers in payment of their account in (c).		
(e) Purchased office equipment for cash, $500.		
(f) Recorded amortization of office equipment for the period, $50.		

Identify the impact each of the following transactions has upon cash and net income.
(SO 3, 6, 7, 8) AP

BE3–8 The Riko Company has the following adjustment data at December 31. Indicate (a) the type of adjustment (prepaid expense, accrued revenue, and so on), and (b) the status of the accounts before adjustment (overstated or understated).

1. Supplies of $600 are on hand. The unadjusted balance in the Supplies account is $800.
2. Services provided but unbilled total $900.
3. Interest of $200 has accrued on a note payable.
4. Rent collected in advance totalling $800 has been earned.
5. Amortization of $100 is estimated on the office equipment.

Identify types of adjusting entries and account relationships.
(SO 6, 7, 8) C

BE3–9 The trial balance of the Hoi Company includes the following balance sheet accounts. Identify the accounts that require adjustment. For each account that requires adjustment, indicate (a) the type of adjusting entry required (prepaid expense, unearned revenue, accrued revenue, accrued expense, or amortization), and (b) the related account in the adjusting entry.

          Accounts Receivable   Interest Payable

          Prepaid Insurance   Unearned Service Revenue

          Equipment   Interest Receivable

          Supplies   Rent Payable

Analyse accounts in a trial balance.
(SO 6, 7, 8) C

Prepare income statement from adjusted trial balance.
(SO 9) AP

BE3–10   The adjusted trial balance of the Klar Company at December 31, 2003, includes the following accounts: S. Klar, Capital, $15,600; S. Klar, Drawings, $6,000; Service Revenue, $38,400; Salaries Expense, $13,000; Insurance Expense, $2,000; Rent Expense, $4,000; Supplies Expense, $500; and Amortization Expense, $1,000. Prepare an income statement for the year.

Prepare statement of owner's equity from adjusted trial balance.
(SO 9) AP

BE3–11   A partial adjusted trial balance data for the Klar Company is presented in BE3–10. The balance in S. Klar, Capital, is the balance as at January 1, 2003. Prepare a statement of owner's equity for the year.

Prepare adjusting entry for supplies in alternative way.
(SO 10) AP

*BE3–12   Refer to BE3–2. Assume that instead of debiting purchases of advertising supplies to the Advertising Supplies account, Spahn Advertising debits purchases of supplies to the Advertising Supplies *Expense* account. Spahn Advertising Company's trial balance at December 31 shows Advertising Supplies $0 and Advertising Supplies Expense $8,700. On December 31, there is $1,500 of supplies on hand.

(a) Prepare the adjusting entry at December 31. Using T accounts, enter the balances in the accounts, post the adjusting entry, and indicate the adjusted balance in each account.

(b) Compare the adjusted balances in BE3–2, when an asset account was originally debited, with the adjusted balances in this brief exercise, when an expense account was originally debited. Does it matter whether an original entry is recorded to an asset account or an expense account?

Prepare transaction and adjusting entry for unearned revenue in alternate ways.
(SO 6, 10) AP

*BE3–13   Paboudjian Apartments receives one month's rent in advance for the month of May, $600, from a tenant.

(a) Assuming the company records all prepayments in balance sheet accounts:
1. Prepare the original journal entry Paboudjian should record when it receives the rent on May 1.
2. Prepare the adjusting journal entry Paboudjian should record at the end of May, when the month's rent has been earned.

(b) Assuming the company records all prepayments in income statement accounts:
1. Prepare the original journal entry Paboudjian should record when it receives the rent on May 1.
2. Prepare the adjusting journal entry Paboudjian should record at the end of May, when the month's rent has been earned.

(c) Compare and comment upon the ending account balances for each alternative, (a) and (b).

EXERCISES

• •

Distinguish between cash and accrual bases of accounting.
(SO 3) C

E3–1   The 1997–1998 Government of Canada accounts recorded a $2.5 billion expense for the Millennium Scholarship Fund, even though the first Millennium scholarships weren't awarded until the year 2000! The government—accused by the opposition of cooking the books to minimize the current budgetary surplus—staunchly maintained that it was appropriate to record these financial charges in the books in the year the program was announced.

Instructions

(a) What is the difference between the accrual and cash bases of accounting?

(b) With respect to recording the $2.5 billion expense for the Millennium scholarships, is the government using the cash basis of accounting, the accrual basis of accounting, or some other basis of accounting? Explain why the government believed it was appropriate to record the scholarship expense in the year the program was announced.

(c) Prior to 2001, the federal government used the cash basis of accounting for many of its transactions. In 2001, the government moved all of its accounting systems to the accrual basis. Write a letter to your Member of Parliament explaining what effect you think the adoption of the accrual basis of accounting will have on the government accounts.

Determine income using cash and accrual bases. Comment on usefulness.
(SO 3) AP

E3–2   In its first year of operations, Brisson Company earned $26,000 in service revenue. Of this revenue, $4,000 was on account and the remainder, $22,000, was received in cash from customers.

The company incurred operating expenses of $15,000. Of these expenses, $13,500 was paid in cash. At year end, $1,500 was still owing on account. In addition, Brisson prepaid $2,500 for insurance coverage that would not be used until its second year of operations.

Instructions

(a) Calculate the first year's net income under the cash basis of accounting. Calculate the first year's net income under the accrual basis of accounting.

(b) Which basis of accounting (cash or accrual) provides the most useful information for decision-makers?

E3–3 The following information is available regarding Hallal Company:

1. On its December 31, 2001, balance sheet, the company had prepaid rent of $20,000 ($4,000 per month), which covered the period January 1–May 31, 2002.

2. On May 1, 2002, it negotiated a new lease agreement that covered a three-year period at a rent of $5,000 per month, effective June 1, and immediately paid a "security deposit" of $5,000. This amount will be refunded to the company after the termination of the lease (subject, of course, to the premises being in reasonable condition when vacated).

3. On June 1, 2002, Hallal Company paid the rent for the first six months of the new lease ($30,000) in advance.

4. On December 1, the $30,000 rent payment for the next six months (i.e., for the period December 1, 2002–May 31, 2003) was due. However, because of an administrative error, this was not actually paid until January 2, 2003.

Analyse transactions, prepare journal entries, and determine amounts to be presented in the financial statements.
(SO 6) AP

Instructions

(a) Prepare general journal entries to record each of the four transactions. If no entry is required, state "no entry required."

(b) Prepare any adjusting journal entries required to update the rent accounts at December 31, 2002.

(c) How much rent expense should be reported on the company's income statement for the year ending December 31, 2002?

(d) Indicate what (if anything) should be reported on Hallal Company's balance sheet as at December 31, 2002, with respect to rent. Be specific.

E3–4 Selected accounts of the Nie Company are shown below:

Journalize basic transactions and adjusting entries.
(SO 6, 7) AP

Supplies Expense				Salaries Payable		
7/31	500				7/31	1,200

Supplies					Unearned Revenue			
7/1 Bal.	1,100	7/31	500	7/31	900	7/1 Bal.	1,500
7/10	200					7/20	700

Accounts Receivable				Service Revenue		
7/1 Bal.	500				7/14	3,000
					7/31	900
Salaries Expense					7/31	500
7/15	1,200					
7/31	1,200					

Instructions

After analysing the accounts, journalize (a) the July transactions, and (b) the adjusting entries that were made on July 31. July transactions were all for cash.

Analyse adjusted data.
(SO 6, 7) AP

E3–5 A partial adjusted trial balance of the Thietke Company at January 31, 2003, shows the following:

THIETKE COMPANY
Adjusted Trial Balance
January 31, 2003

	Debit	Credit
Supplies	$ 700	
Prepaid Insurance	2,400	
Salaries Payable		$ 800
Unearned Revenue		750
Supplies Expense	950	
Insurance Expense	400	
Salaries Expense	1,800	
Service Revenue		2,000

Instructions

Answer the following questions, assuming the company's fiscal year begins January 1:
  (a) If the amount in Supplies Expense is the January 31 adjusting entry, and $850 of supplies was purchased in January, what was the balance in Supplies on January 1?
  (b) If the amount in Insurance Expense is the January 31 adjusting entry, and the original insurance premium was for one year, what was the total premium, and when was the policy purchased?
  (c) If $2,500 of salaries was paid in January, what was the balance in Salaries Payable at December 31, 2002?
  (d) If $1,600 was received in January for services performed in January, what was the balance in Unearned Revenue at December 31, 2002?

Identify types of adjustments and account relationships.
(SO 6, 7, 8) AP

E3–6 The McLean Company accumulates the following adjustment data at December 31:
  1. Services provided but unbilled total $600.
  2. Store supplies of $300 have been used.
  3. Utility expenses of $225 are unpaid and unrecorded.
  4. Unearned revenue of $260 has been earned.
  5. Salaries of $800 are unpaid and unrecorded.
  6. Prepaid insurance that totals $350 has expired.
  7. Amortization of $500 is estimated.

Instructions

For each of the above items indicate (a) the type of adjustment (prepaid expense, unearned revenue, accrued revenue, accrued expense, or amortization), and (b) the status of the accounts before adjustment (overstatement or understatement).

Prepare adjusting entries from selected account data.
(SO 6, 7, 8) AP

E3–7 The ledger of Bourque Rental Agency on March 31 of the current year includes the following selected accounts before adjusting entries have been prepared:

	Debit	Credit
Prepaid Insurance	$ 3,600	
Supplies	2,800	
Equipment	24,000	
Accumulated Amortization—Equipment		$ 6,400
Notes Payable		20,000
Unearned Rent Revenue		9,300
Rent Revenue		60,000
Wage Expense	14,000	

An analysis of the accounts shows the following:
  1. The equipment is amortized at the rate of $400 per month.
  2. One-third of the unearned rent was earned during the quarter.
  3. Interest of $500 is accrued on the notes payable.
  4. Supplies on hand total $850.
  5. Insurance expires at the rate of $300 per month.

Instructions

Prepare the adjusting entries at March 31, assuming that adjusting entries are made quarterly.

E3–8 Kay Ong, D.D.S., opened a dental practice on January 1, 2003. During the first month of operations, the following transactions occurred:

Prepare adjusting entries.
(SO 6, 7, 8) AP

1. Performed services for patients who had dental plan insurance. At January 31, $750 of these services was earned but not yet billed to the insurance companies.
2. Utility expenses incurred but not paid prior to January 31 totalled $520.
3. Purchased dental equipment on January 1 for $60,000, paying $20,000 in cash and signing a $40,000, three-year note payable. The equipment is amortized at the rate of $1,000 per month. Interest on the note is $250 per month.
4. Purchased a one-year malpractice insurance policy on January 1 for $12,000.
5. Purchased $1,600 of dental supplies. On January 31, determined that $500 of supplies was on hand.

Instructions

Prepare the adjusting entries at January 31.

E3–9 The trial balance for the Pioneer Advertising Agency is shown in Illustration 3-3. Replace the adjusting entries shown in the text at October 31, with the following adjustment data:

Prepare adjusting entries.
(SO 6, 7, 8) AP

1. Advertising supplies on hand at October 31 total $1,400.
2. Expired insurance for the month is $100.
3. Amortization for the month is $50.
4. Unearned revenue in October totals $600.
5. Services provided but unbilled at October 31 are $300.
6. Interest expense accrued at October 31 is $70.
7. Accrued salaries at October 31 are $1,500.

Instructions

Prepare adjusting entries for the items above.

E3–10 The trial balances before and after adjustment for the Lim Company at the end of its fiscal year are as follows:

Prepare adjusting entries from analysis of trial balances.
(SO 6, 7, 8) AP

LIM COMPANY
Trial Balance
August 31, 2003

	Before Adjustment		After Adjustment	
	Dr.	Cr.	Dr.	Cr.
Cash	$10,400		$10,400	
Accounts Receivable	8,800		9,400	
Office Supplies	2,300		700	
Prepaid Insurance	4,000		2,500	
Office Equipment	14,000		14,000	
Accumulated Amortization—Office Equipment		$ 3,600		$ 4,800
Accounts Payable		5,800		5,800
Salaries Payable		0		1,100
Unearned Rent Revenue		1,500		700
E. Lim, Capital		15,600		15,600
Service Revenue		34,000		34,600
Rent Revenue		11,000		11,800
Salaries Expense	17,000		18,100	
Office Supplies Expense	0		1,600	
Rent Expense	15,000		15,000	
Insurance Expense	0		1,500	
Amortization Expense	0		1,200	
Totals	$71,500	$71,500	$74,400	$74,400

Instructions

Prepare the adjusting entries that were made.

Prepare adjusting entries and income statements.
(SO 6, 7, 8, 9) AP

E3–11 The income statement of Virmani Co. for the month of July 2003 shows net income of $1,400 based on Service Revenue $5,500, Wages Expense $2,300, Supplies Expense $1,200, and Utilities Expense $600. In reviewing the statement, you discover the following:

1. Insurance of $300 that expired during July was omitted.
2. Supplies expense includes $500 of supplies that are still on hand at July 31.
3. Amortization of $150 on equipment was omitted.
4. Accrued but unpaid wages of $300 at July 31 were not included.
5. Services provided but unrecorded totalled $900.

Instructions

(a) Prepare the adjusting entries at July 31, 2003.
(b) Prepare a revised income statement, after the adjustments. Show all your calculations.

Prepare financial statements from adjusted trial balance.
(SO 9) AP

E3–12 The adjusted trial balance for the Lim Company is given in E3–10.

Instructions

Prepare the income statement and statement of owner's equity for the year, and the balance sheet at August 31, 2003.

Prepare and post transaction and adjustment entries, using alternative treatment of prepayments.
(SO 10) AP

*E3–13 At the Devereaux Company, prepayments are debited to expense when paid, and unearned revenues are credited to revenue when received. During January of the current year, the following transactions occurred:

Jan. 2 Paid $2,400 for fire insurance protection for the year.
   10 Paid $1,700 for supplies.
   15 Received $5,100 for services to be performed in the future.

On January 31, it is determined that $1,500 of the service revenue has been earned, and that there is $800 of supplies on hand.

Instructions

(a) Journalize and post the January transactions. Use T accounts.
(b) Journalize and post the adjusting entries at January 31.
(c) Determine the ending balance in each of the accounts.

PROBLEMS: SET A

· ·

Match adjusting entry type.
(SO 5) K

P3–1A Adjusting entries can be classified into the following types:

| 1. Prepaid expenses | 3. Accrued expenses | 5. Estimates (amortization) |
| 2. Unearned revenues | 4. Accrued revenues | |

Instructions

Match the type of adjusting entry with the adjusting journal entry transaction described below by inserting the appropriate number in the space provided. If an adjusting entry is not required, leave the space blank.

_____ (a) Record interest on note payable.
_____ (b) Record interest on note receivable.
_____ (c) Allocate cost of capital asset over its useful life.
_____ (d) Record revenue that has been earned but not billed or collected.
_____ (e) Record revenue that has been earned that was previously received in advance.
_____ (f) Record hiring of employees.
_____ (g) Record salaries owed.
_____ (h) Record supplies used.

Prepare original and adjusting journal entries for prepayments.
(SO 6) AP

P3–2A Ouellette & Associates began operations on January 1, 2002. Its fiscal year end is December 31, and it only prepares financial statements and adjusts its accounts annually. Selected transactions during 2002 follow:

1. On January 1, 2002, bought office supplies for $4,500 cash. A physical count at December 31, 2002, revealed $900 of supplies was still on hand.
2. Bought a $3,600 one-year insurance policy for cash on September 1, 2002. The policy came into effect on this date.

3. On November 15, Ouellette received a $1,200 advance cash payment from a client for accounting services expected to be provided in the future. As at December 31, all of these services had been performed.

4. On December 15, the company rented out excess office space for a six-month period *starting on this date*, and received a $460 cheque for the first month's rent.

Instructions

For each of the above situations, prepare the journal entry for the original transaction and any adjusting journal entry required at December 31, 2002. If no journal entry is required, write "No journal entry required."

P3–3A Your examination of the records of a company that uses the cash basis of accounting tells you that the company's reported income in 2003 is $35,190. If this firm had followed accrual basis accounting practices, it would have reported the following year-end balances:

Convert income from cash to accrual basis. (SO 3, 6, 7) AP

	2002	2003
Accounts receivable	$2,500	$3,400
Supplies on hand	1,160	1,300
Unpaid wages owing	2,400	1,200
Other unpaid amounts	1,600	1,440

Instructions

Determine the company's net income on an accrual basis for 2003. Show all your calculations in an orderly fashion.

P3–4A The following data are taken from the comparative balance sheets of Breakers Billiards Club, which prepares its financial statements using the accrual basis of accounting:

Record transactions on accrual basis; convert revenue to cash receipts. (SO 3, 7) AP

December 31	2002	2001
Fees receivable from members	$12,000	$ 9,000
Unearned fees revenue	17,000	22,000

Fees are billed to members based upon their use of the club's facilities. Unearned fees arise from the sale of gift certificates which members can apply to their future use of club facilities. The 2002 income statement for the club showed that fee revenue of $153,000 was earned during the year.

Instructions

(*Hint*: You will find it helpful to use T accounts to analyse these data in sequence, as missing information must first be determined before moving on. Post your journal entries as you progress, rather than waiting until the end.)

(a) Prepare journal entries for each of the following events that took place during 2002:
1. Fees receivable from 2001 were all collected.
2. Gift certificates outstanding at the end of 2001 were all redeemed.
3. An additional $30,000 worth of gift certificates was sold during 2002. Some of these were used by the recipients during the year. The remainder were still outstanding at the end of 2002.
4. Fees for 2002 were billed to members.
5. Fees receivable for 2002 (i.e., those billed in item 4 above) were partially collected.

(b) Determine the amount of cash received by the club with respect to fees during 2002.

P3–5A The following independent situations for the Theatre Brunswick for the year ended December 31, 2002, may require an original journal entry, an adjusting journal entry, or both.

Prepare original and adjusting journal entries. (SO 6, 7) AP

1. Office supplies on hand at the Theatre Brunswick amounted to $640 at the beginning of the year. On July 1, additional office supplies were purchased for cash at a cost of $1,560. At the end of the year, a physical count showed that supplies on hand amounted to $740.
2. At the beginning of January, the theatre borrowed $10,000 from the Bank of Montreal at an annual interest rate of 6%. The principal and interest are to be repaid in two years' time.
3. Upon reviewing its books on December 31, 2002, it was noted that the telephone bill for the month of December had not yet been received. A call to NBTel yielded the information that the telephone bill was $400.
4. On January 1, 2002, the theatre purchased a used truck for use in its business for $18,000, paying cash in full. Annual amortization is estimated at $3,600.
5. Every Friday, the total payroll for the theatre is $3,000 for employee wages earned during a five-day week (Monday through Friday, inclusive). This year, December 31 falls on a Wednesday. Wages were paid (and recorded) on Friday, December 26. No adjusting entry has yet been recorded for the period from December 26 through December 31.

Instructions

Prepare the journal entry (or entries) required to record (a) the original transaction, and (b) the year-end adjusting entry, if required.

Prepare adjusting entries.
(SO 6, 7) AP

P3–6A A review of the ledger of Greenberg Company at December 31, 2002, produces the following important data for the preparation of annual adjusting entries:

1. Prepaid Advertising has a balance of $13,200. This consists of payments on two advertising contracts. The contracts provide for monthly advertising in two trade magazines. The terms of the contracts are as follows:

Contract	Date	Amount	Number of Magazine Issues
A650	May 1	$ 6,000	12
B974	Sept. 1	7,200	24
		$13,200	

The first advertisement runs in the month in which the contract is signed.

2. Unearned Rent Revenue has a balance of $369,000. The company began subleasing office space in its new building on November 1. Each tenant (nine in total) is required to make a $5,000 security deposit, which is refundable after the lease has been satisfactorily ended. At December 31, the company had the following rental contracts that were paid in full for the entire term of the lease:

Date	Term (in months)	Monthly Rent	Number of Leases	Total Rent Paid
Nov. 1	6	$4,000	5	$120,000
Nov. 1	6	8,500	4	204,000
				$324,000

3. Notes Payable has a balance of $80,000. This consists of a note for one year at an annual interest rate of 8%, dated June 1.

4. Salaries Payable has a balance of $0. There are eight salaried employees. Salaries are paid every Friday for a five-day (Monday–Friday) work week. Five employees receive a salary of $700 per week, and three employees earn $500 per week. December 31 is a Tuesday.

Instructions

Prepare the adjusting entries at December 31, 2002. Show all your calculations.

Prepare accrual-based income statement from cash-based information.
(SO 3, 6, 7, 8) AP

P3–7A During the first week of January 2003, Angela Smith began an office design business, Exotic Designs. She kept no formal accounting records; however, her record of cash receipts and disbursements was accurate. The business was an instant success. In fact, it was so successful that she required additional financing to keep up. She approached her bank for a $10,000 loan and was "put on hold" until she brought a balance sheet and income statement prepared on an accrual basis.

Knowing very little about accounting, she engaged you to prepare the statements requested by the bank. She supplied you with the following information for the year ended December 31, 2003:

	Receipts	Disbursements
Investment by owner	$30,000	
Equipment		$18,400
Supplies		12,200
Rent payments		9,600
Insurance premium		1,800
Advertising—all ads completed		3,600
Wages of assistant		18,400
Telephone		980
Payments to owner		24,000
Design revenue received	61,500	
	91,500	88,980
Cash balance		2,520
	$91,500	$91,500

Additional information:

1. The equipment has an estimated 10-year life.
2. Supplies on hand on December 31 were $1,800.
3. Rent payments included $750 per month rental and a $600 deposit refundable at the end of the two-year lease.

4. Insurance premium was for a two-year period expiring on December 31, 2004.
5. Wages earned the last week in December and to be paid in January 2004 amounted to $400.
6. Design revenue earned but not yet collected amounted to $3,800.
7. Angela Smith used her personal automobile for business purposes, 12,000 km, at 30 cents per km. She was not paid for use of her car, but would like to be paid for it.

Instructions

Prepare an accrual-based income statement for the year ended December 31, 2003. Prepare the December 31, 2003, balance sheet.

Source: Adapted from Certified General Accountants of Canada, *Financial Accounting 1 Examination*, December 1995, Question 3.

P3–8A Image.com has the following information available at November 30, its year end, to assist with the preparation of its adjusting journal entries:

Identify effects of adjusting journal entries.
(SO 6, 7, 8) AP

1. The balance in the Prepaid Insurance account at November 30 is $1,200, representing a payment made on July 1 for a 12-month insurance policy.
2. The balance in the Supplies account at November 30 was $1,000. Supplies on hand are $800.
3. Unearned service revenue of $750 is earned.
4. Accrued salaries payable are $500.
5. Accrued interest receivable is $100.
6. Amortization for the year is $1,200.

Instructions

Indicate the effect that each of the adjusting journal entries will have on the company's financial statement if Image.com *fails* to make the entry. Indicate whether, and by how much, the financial statement classification will be understated (U), overstated (O), or not affected (NA) in the table provided below. The first one is done for you as an example.

Adjusting Entry	Balance Sheet						Income Statement				
	Assets	=	Liabilities	+	Owner's Equity		Revenues	–	Expenses	=	Net Income
1.	$500 O		NA		$500 O		NA		$500 U		$500 O
2.											
3.											
4.											
5.											
6.											

P3–9A The trial balance before adjustment of Atlantic Tours at the end of its first month of operations follows:

Prepare adjusting entries, post, and prepare adjusted trial balance.
(SO 6, 7, 8, 9) AP

ATLANTIC TOURS
Trial Balance
June 30, 2003

	Debit	Credit
Cash	$ 3,000	
Prepaid Insurance	7,200	
Office Equipment	1,800	
Buses	140,000	
Notes Payable		$ 62,000
Unearned Fees		15,000
Eldon Kaplan, Capital		70,000
Fees Earned		15,900
Salaries Expense	9,000	
Advertising Expense	800	
Gas and Oil Expense	1,100	
	$162,900	$162,900

Other data:
1. The insurance policy has a one-year term that began June 1, 2003.
2. The monthly amortization is $50 on office equipment and $2,300 on buses.
3. Interest of $300 accrues on the notes payable each month.

4. Deposits of $1,500 each were received for advance tour reservations from 10 school groups. At June 30, four of these deposits have been earned.
5. Bus drivers are paid a combined total of $400 per day. At June 30, three days' salaries are unpaid.
6. A senior citizens' organization that had not made an advance deposit took a Coastal tour on June 30 for $1,200. This group was not billed for services rendered until July 3.
7. Additional advertising costs of $500 have been incurred, but the bills have not been received by June 30. (Use an Accounts Payable account.)

Instructions

(a) Journalize the adjusting entries at June 30, 2003.
(b) Prepare a ledger. Enter the trial balance amounts and post the adjusting entries.
(c) Prepare an adjusted trial balance at June 30, 2003.

Prepare adjusting entries, post, and prepare adjusted trial balance and financial statements.
(SO 6, 7, 8, 9) AP

P3–10A The Highland Cove Resort opened for business on June 1, 2003, with eight units. Its trial balance before adjustment on August 31 is as follows:

HIGHLAND COVE RESORT
Trial Balance
August 31, 2003

	Debit	Credit
Cash	$ 19,600	
Prepaid Insurance	5,400	
Supplies	3,300	
Land	25,000	
Cottages	125,000	
Furniture	26,000	
Accounts Payable		$ 6,500
Unearned Rent Revenue		6,800
Mortgage Payable		80,000
Keath Yhap, Capital		100,000
Keath Yhap, Drawings	5,000	
Rent Revenue		80,000
Salaries Expense	51,000	
Utilities Expense	9,400	
Repair Expense	3,600	
	$273,300	$273,300

Other data:

1. Insurance expires at the rate of $450 per month.
2. A count of supplies on August 31 shows $1,000 of supplies on hand.
3. Annual amortization is $6,250 on cottages and $5,200 on furniture.
4. Unearned rent of $5,000 was earned prior to August 31.
5. Salaries of $400 were unpaid at August 31.
6. Rentals of $800 were due from tenants at August 31.
7. The mortgage interest rate is 8% per year. The mortgage was taken out on August 1.

Instructions

(a) Journalize the adjusting entries on August 31 for the three-month period June 1–August 31.
(b) Prepare a ledger, enter the trial balance amounts, and post the adjusting entries.
(c) Prepare an adjusted trial balance at August 31.
(d) Prepare an income statement and a statement of owner's equity for the three months ending August 31, and a balance sheet as at August 31, 2003.

Prepare adjusting entries and financial statements.
(SO 6, 7, 8, 9) AP

P3–11A The adjusted and unadjusted trial balances of the Yount Advertising Agency as at December 31, 2002, are shown in the table on the following page:

YOUNT ADVERTISING AGENCY
Trial Balance
December 31, 2002

	Before Adjustment		After Adjustment	
	Dr.	Cr.	Dr.	Cr.
Cash	$ 11,000		$ 11,000	
Accounts Receivable	20,000		21,500	
Art Supplies	8,400		5,000	
Prepaid Insurance	3,350		2,500	
Printing Equipment	60,000		60,000	
Accumulated Amortization		$28,000		$35,000
Accounts Payable		5,000		5,000
Interest Payable		0		150
Note Payable		5,000		5,000
Unearned Advertising Revenue		7,000		5,600
Salaries Payable		0		1,300
T. Yount, Capital		25,500		25,500
T. Yount, Drawings	12,000		12,000	
Advertising Revenue		58,600		61,500
Salaries Expense	10,000		11,300	
Insurance Expense			850	
Interest Expense	350		500	
Amortization Expense			7,000	
Art Supplies Expense			3,400	
Rent Expense	4,000		4,000	
Totals	$129,100	$129,100	$139,050	$139,050

Instructions

(a) Journalize the annual adjusting entries that were made.

(b) Prepare an income statement and a statement of owner's equity for the year ended December 31, 2002, and a balance sheet at December 31.

(c) Calculate the annual interest rate on the note. The note payable has been outstanding for 10 months.

(d) Determine the balance in Salaries Payable on December 31, 2001. The company paid $13,500 in salaries in 2002.

P3–12A In P3–2A, when journal entries were originally recorded, prepaid expenses were debited to an asset account, and unearned revenues were credited to a liability account. This problem repeats P3–2A, assuming an alternative treatment of the original journal entry.

Prepare original and adjusting journal entries for prepayments using alternative treatment. (SO 10) AP

Instructions

Prepare the journal entry for the original transaction and any adjusting journal entry required at December 31, 2002, for each of the situations outlined in P3–2A. If no journal entry is required, state "No journal entry required."

P3–13A The Global Graphics Company was organized on January 1, 2003, by Jill Batke. At the end of the first six months of operations, the trial balance contained the following accounts in alphabetical order:

Prepare adjusting entries, adjusted trial balance, and financial statements, using alternative treatment of prepayments. (SO 7, 8, 9, 10) AP

GLOBAL GRAPHICS COMPANY
Trial Balance
June 30, 2003

	Debits		Credits
Accounts Receivable	$14,000	Accounts Payable	$9,000
Advertising Expense	1,900	Jill Batke, Capital	25,000
Cash	9,500	Consulting Revenue	5,000
Equipment	45,000	Graphic Revenue	52,100
Insurance Expense	1,800	Note Payable	17,000
Rent Expense	1,500		
Salaries Expense	30,000		
Supplies Expense	2,700		
Utilities Expense	1,700		
	$108,100		$108,100

Analysis reveals the following additional data:

1. The $2,700 balance in Supplies Expense represents supplies purchased in January. At June 30, there was $1,500 of supplies on hand.
2. The note payable was issued on February 1. It is an 8%, six-month note.
3. The balance in Insurance Expense is the premium on a one-year policy that is dated March 1, 2003.
4. At June 30, consulting revenue of $1,000 was unearned.
5. Graphic revenue earned but unbilled at June 30 totals $2,000.
6. Amortization is $9,000 per year.

Instructions

(a) Journalize the adjusting entries at June 30. (Adjustments are recorded every six months.)
(b) Prepare an adjusted trial balance.
(c) Prepare an income statement and statement of owner's equity for the six months ended June 30, and a balance sheet at June 30, 2003.

PROBLEMS: SET B

Match adjusting entry type.
(SO 5) K

P3–1B   Adjusting entries can be classified into the following types:

1. Prepaid expenses	3. Accrued expenses	5. Estimates (amortization)
2. Unearned revenues	4. Accrued revenues	

Instructions

Match the type of adjusting entry with the adjusting journal entry transaction described below by inserting the appropriate number in the space provided. If an adjusting entry is not required, leave the space blank.

_____ (a) Record interest on overdue account payable.

_____ (b) Record interest earned on overdue account receivable.

_____ (c) Allocate cost of equipment over its useful life.

_____ (d) Record revenue owed by customer for services provided.

_____ (e) Record fees that have been earned that were previously received in advance.

_____ (f) Record signing of lease for rental space.

_____ (g) Record property taxes due.

_____ (h) Record expiration of rent at the end of the month.

Prepare original and adjusting journal entries for prepayments.
(SO 6) AP

P3–2B   Burke Bros. began operations on January 1, 2002. Its fiscal year end is December 31. It only prepares financial statements and adjusts its accounts annually. Selected transactions during 2002 follow:

1. On January 1, 2002, bought office supplies for $2,800 cash. A physical count at December 31, 2002, revealed $500 of supplies was still on hand.
2. Bought a $3,600 one-year insurance policy for cash on August 1, 2002. The policy came into effect on this date.
3. On November 15, Burke received a $1,200 advance cash payment from three clients for services expected to be provided in the future. As at December 31, services had been performed for two of the clients ($400 each).
4. On December 15, the company paid $4,500 rent in advance for the month of January 2003.

Instructions

Prepare the journal entry for the original transaction and any adjusting journal entry required at December 31, 2002, for each of the above situations.

P3–3B Your examination of the records of a company that follows the cash basis of accounting tells you that the company's reported cash basis income in 2002 is $43,900. If the company had followed accrual basis accounting practices, it would have reported the following year-end balances:

Convert income from cash to accrual basis.
(SO 3, 6, 7, 8) AP

	2002	2001
Accounts payable	$ 1,500	$ 2,200
Accounts receivable	3,600	2,700
Accumulated amortization	22,000	20,000
Prepaid insurance	1,550	1,310
Unearned revenues	1,360	1,500

Instructions

Determine the company's net income, on an accrual basis, for 2002. Show all your calculations.

P3–4B The following selected data are taken from the comparative financial statements of the Hammer Curling Club. The club prepares its financial statements using the accrual basis of accounting.

Record transactions on accrual basis; convert revenue to cash receipts.
(SO 3, 7) AP

September 30	2002	2001
Dues receivable from members	$ 15,000	$ 11,000
Unearned ticket revenue	20,000	25,000
Dues revenue	148,000	132,000

Dues are billed to members based upon their use of the club's facilities. Unearned ticket revenues arise from the sale of tickets to events.

Instructions

(*Hint*: You will find it helpful to use T accounts to analyse these data in sequence, as missing information must first be determined before moving on. Post your journal entries as you progress, rather than waiting until the end.)

(a) Prepare journal entries for each of the following events that took place during 2002:
 1. Dues receivable from members for 2001 were all collected.
 2. Unearned ticket revenue at the end of 2001 was all earned.
 3. In 2002, $35,000 of additional tickets was sold for cash. Some of these were used by the purchasers during the year. The remaining tickets are for an upcoming event in 2003.
 4. Dues for the 2002 fiscal year were billed to members.
 5. Dues receivable for 2002 (i.e., those billed in item 4 above) were partially collected.
(b) Determine the amount of cash received by the club from the above transactions during the year.

P3–5B The following independent situations for the Theatre Dupuis for the year ended December 31, 2002, may require an original journal entry, an adjusting journal entry, or both.

Prepare original and adjusting journal entries.
(SO 6, 7) AP

 1. Office supplies on hand at Theatre Dupuis amounted to $300 at the beginning of the year. During the year, additional office supplies were purchased for cash at a cost of $1,500. At the end of the year, a physical count showed that supplies on hand amounted to $500.
 2. At the beginning of June, the theatre borrowed $4,000 from La Caisse Populaire Desjardins at an annual interest rate of 8%. The principal and interest are to be repaid in a year's time.
 3. Upon reviewing the books on December 31, 2002, it was noted that the utility bill for the month of December had not yet been received. A call to Hydro-Québec revealed that the utility bill was $1,400.
 4. On January 1, 2002, the theatre purchased a truck for use in its business for $38,000, paying cash in full. Annual amortization is estimated to total $10,000 for this truck.
 5. The total payroll for the theatre is $3,000 every two weeks for employee wages earned during a six-day week. This year, December 31 falls on a Tuesday. Wages were paid (and recorded) on Saturday, December 28. Assume the six-day workweek is from Monday through Saturday. No adjusting entry has yet been recorded for the period from December 30 through December 31.

Instructions

Prepare the journal entry (or entries) required to record (a) the original transaction, and (b) the year-end adjusting entry, if required.

Prepare adjusting entries.
(SO 6, 7) AP

P3–6B   A review of the ledger of the Hashmi Company at December 31, 2002, produces the following data pertaining to the preparation of annual adjusting entries:

1. Prepaid Insurance has an unadjusted balance of $15,400. The company has separate insurance policies on its buildings and its motor vehicles. Policy B4564 on the building was purchased on July 1, 2002, for $9,600. The policy has a term of two years. Policy A2958 on the vehicles was purchased on January 1, 2002, for $5,800. This policy also has a term of two years.

2. Unearned Subscription Revenue has a balance of $49,000. The company began selling magazine subscriptions in 2002. The selling price of a subscription is $50 for 12 monthly issues. A review of subscription contracts reveals the following:

Subscription Date	Number of Subscriptions
October 1	200
November 1	300
December 1	480
	980

3. Salaries Payable has a balance of $0. There are eight salaried employees, each of whom is paid every Friday for the current week. Five employees receive a salary of $600 each per week, and three employees earn $700 each per week. December 31 is a Wednesday. Employees do not work weekends. All employees worked the last three days of December.

Instructions

(a) Prepare a calculation to show why the balance (before adjustments) in the Prepaid Insurance account is $15,400.

(b) Prepare the adjusting entries at December 31, 2002. Show all your calculations.

Prepare accrual-based income statement from cash-based information.
(SO 3, 6, 7, 8) AP

P3–7B   During the first week of November 2002, Danielle Charron opened a ski tuning and repair shop, The Radical Edge, on a busy ski hill. She didn't do any bookkeeping, but she kept careful track of all her cash receipts and cash payments. She supplies you with the following information at the end of the ski season, April 30, 2003:

	Cash Receipts	Cash Payments
Investment by Danielle Charron	$20,000	
Payment for repair equipment		$ 9,200
Rent payments		1,225
Newspaper advertising paid		375
Utility bills paid		970
Part-time helper's wages paid		2,600
Cash receipts from ski and snowboard repair services	32,150	
Subtotals	52,150	14,370
Cash balance		37,780
Totals	$52,150	$52,150

You learn that the repair equipment has an estimated useful life of eight years. The company rents space at a cost of $175 per month on a one-year lease. The lease contract requires payment of the first and last months' rent in advance, which Danielle paid. The part-time helper is owed $120 at April 30, 2003, for unpaid wages. At April 30, 2003, customers owe The Radical Edge $650 for services they have received but have not yet paid for.

Instructions

(a) Prepare an accrual basis income statement for the six months ended April 30, 2003.

(b) Prepare the April 30, 2003, balance sheet.

Identify effects of adjusting journal entries.
(SO 6, 7, 8) AP

P3–8B   Gear.com has the following information available at December 31, its year end, to assist with the preparation of its adjusting journal entries:

1. The balance in the Prepaid Insurance account at December 31 is $1,200, representing a payment made on October 1 for a 12-month insurance policy.

2. The balance in the Prepaid Rent account at December 31 was $1,000. This represented rent for the month of December that was paid December 1.

3. The balance in the Unearned Rent Revenue account at December 31 was $750. This represented rent for the month of December that was received December 1.

4. Services rendered at the end of December but not yet billed to customers totalled $2,000.

5. Accrued interest payable is $250.
6. Amortization for the year is $1,000.

Instructions

Indicate the effect that each of the above adjusting journal entries will have on the company's financial statements if Gear.com *fails* to make the entry. Indicate whether, and by how much, the financial statement classification will be understated (U), overstated (O), or not affected (NA) in the table provided. The first one is done for you as an example.

	Balance Sheet				Income Statement			
Adjusting Entry	Assets	=	Liabilities	+ Owner's Equity	Revenues	–	Expenses	= Net Income
1.	$300 O		NA	$300 O	NA		$300 U	$300 O
2.								
3.								
4.								
5.								
6.								

P3–9B The Orosco Security Service began operations on January 1, 2002. At the end of the first year of operations, the trial balance before adjustment shows the following:

Prepare adjusting entries, post, and prepare adjusted trial balance.
(SO 6, 7, 8, 9) AP

OROSCO SECURITY SERVICE
Trial Balance
December 31, 2002

	Debit	Credit
Cash	$ 12,400	
Accounts Receivable	3,200	
Prepaid Insurance	3,600	
Automobiles	58,000	
Notes Payable		$ 45,000
Unearned Revenue		2,500
C. Orosco, Capital		18,000
Service Revenue		84,000
Salaries Expense	57,000	
Repair Expense	6,000	
Gas and Oil Expense	9,300	
Totals	$149,500	$149,500

Other data:
1. Services provided but unbilled total $2,500 at December 31.
2. Insurance coverage began January 1 under a two-year policy.
3. Automobile amortization is $15,000 for the year.
4. Interest of $5,400 accrued on notes payable for the year.
5. $1,000 of the unearned revenue has been earned.
6. Drivers' salaries total $500 per day. At December 31, three days' salaries are unpaid.
7. At December 31, repairs to automobiles total $650, but bills have not been received. (Use Accounts Payable.)

Instructions

(a) Journalize the annual adjusting entries at December 31, 2002.
(b) Prepare a ledger. Enter the trial balance amounts and post the adjusting entries.
(c) Prepare an adjusted trial balance at December 31, 2002.

*Prepare adjusting entries, post,
and prepare adjusted trial balance and financial statements.*
(SO 6, 7, 8, 9) AP

P3–10B   The Super Motel opened for business on May 1, 2003. Its trial balance before adjustments on May 31 is as follows:

SUPER MOTEL
Trial Balance
May 31, 2003

	Debit	Credit
Cash	$ 2,500	
Prepaid Insurance	1,800	
Supplies	1,900	
Land	15,000	
Lodge	70,000	
Furniture	16,800	
Accounts Payable		$ 4,700
Unearned Rent Revenue		3,600
Mortgage Payable		35,000
Sara Sutton, Capital		60,000
Rent Revenue		9,200
Salaries Expense	3,000	
Utilities Expense	1,000	
Advertising Expense	500	
Totals	$112,500	$112,500

Other data:
1. The 12-month insurance policy was purchased May 1.
2. A physical count of supplies shows $1,000 remaining on May 31.
3. Annual amortization is $3,500 on the lodge and $3,360 on the furniture.
4. The 8% mortgage began May 1.
5. Unearned rent of $1,500 has been earned.
6. Rent revenue of $800 earned in May will not be billed until the first week of June. This transaction has not yet been recorded.
7. Salaries of $300 are accrued and unpaid at May 31.

Instructions

(a) Journalize the adjusting entries on May 31.
(b) Prepare a ledger. Enter the trial balance amounts and post the adjusting entries.
(c) Prepare an adjusted trial balance at May 31.
(d) Prepare an income statement and statement of owner's equity for the month of May and a balance sheet at May 31.

*Prepare adjusting entries and
financial statements.*
(SO 6, 7, 8, 9) AP

P3–11B   The Irabu Co. was organized at July 1, 2003. Quarterly financial statements are prepared. The unadjusted and adjusted trial balances as at September 30 are shown below:

IRABU CO.
Trial Balance
September 30, 2003

	Unadjusted Dr.	Unadjusted Cr.	Adjusted Dr.	Adjusted Cr.
Cash	$ 6,700		$ 6,700	
Accounts Receivable	400		1,000	
Prepaid Rent	1,500		900	
Supplies	1,200		1,000	
Equipment	15,000		15,000	
Accumulated Amortization—Equipment				$ 350
Note Payable		$ 5,000		5,000
Accounts Payable		1,510		1,510
Salaries Payable				400
Interest Payable				50
Unearned Rent Revenue		900		600
Yosuke Irabu, Capital		14,000		14,000
Yosuke Irabu, Drawings	600		600	
Commission Revenue		14,000		14,600

Rent Revenue		400		700
Salaries Expense	9,000		9,400	
Rent Expense	900		1,500	
Amortization Expense			350	
Supplies Expense			200	
Utilities Expense	510		510	
Interest Expense			50	
Totals	$35,810	$35,810	$37,210	$37,210

Instructions

(a) Journalize the adjusting entries that were made.

(b) Prepare an income statement and a statement of owner's equity for the three months ending September 30 and a balance sheet at September 30.

(c) If the note bears interest at 12%, how many months has it been outstanding?

*P3–12B   In P3–2B, when journal entries were originally recorded, prepaid expenses were debited to an asset account, and unearned revenues were credited to a liability account. This problem repeats P3–2B, assuming instead that prepaid expenses are debited originally to an expense account, and unearned revenues credited originally to a revenue account.

Prepare original and adjusting journal entries for prepayments, using alternative treatment. (SO 10) AP

Instructions

Prepare the journal entry for the original transaction and any adjusting journal entry required at December 31, 2002, for each of the situations outlined in P3–2B, assuming this alternative treatment of prepaid expenses and unearned revenues.

*P3–13B   The Royal Graphics Company was organized on July 1, 2002, by Jan Bejar. At the end of the first six months of operations, the trial balance contained the following accounts:

Prepare adjusting entries, adjusted trial balance, and financial statements, using alternative treatment of prepayments. (SO 7, 8, 9, 10) AP

ROYAL GRAPHICS COMPANY
Trial Balance
December 31, 2002

	Debits		Credits
Cash	$ 8,600	Note Payable	$ 18,000
Accounts Receivable	13,000	Accounts Payable	11,000
Equipment	48,000	Jan Bejar, Capital	22,000
Supplies Expense	3,300	Graphic Fees Earned	55,500
Insurance Expense	2,100	Consulting Fees Earned	7,600
Salaries Expense	33,000		
Advertising Expense	1,700		
Rent Expense	2,500		
Utilities Expense	1,900		
	$114,100		$114,100

Analysis reveals the following additional data:

1. The $3,300 balance in Supplies Expense represents supplies purchased in July. At December 31, $1,500 of supplies had been used.

2. The note payable was issued November 1. It is a 10% three-month note.

3. The balance in Insurance Expense is the premium on a one-year policy that is dated September 1, 2002.

4. Consulting fees are credited to revenue when received. At December 31, consulting fees of $1,600 are unearned.

5. Amortization is $2,200 per year.

6. Utilities of $200 are owed at December 31.

Instructions

(a) Journalize the adjusting entries at December 31. (Adjustments are recorded every six months.)

(b) Prepare an adjusted trial balance.

(c) Prepare an income statement and statement of owner's equity for the six months ended December 31, and a balance sheet at December 31, 2002.

CUMULATIVE COVERAGE—CHAPTERS 2 TO 3

On September 1, 2003, the account balances of Pitre Equipment Repair were as follows:

No.		Debits	No.		Credits
101	Cash	$ 4,880	154	Accumulated Amortization	$ 1,500
112	Accounts Receivable	3,520	201	Accounts Payable	3,400
126	Supplies	1,000	209	Unearned Service Revenue	400
153	Store Equipment	15,000	212	Salaries Payable	500
			301	R. Pitre, Capital	18,600
		$24,400			$24,400

During September, the following transactions were completed:

Sept. 8 Paid $1,200 for employees' salaries, of which $700 is for September and $500 for August.
10 Received $1,200 cash from customers on account.
12 Received $3,400 cash for services performed in September.
15 Purchased store equipment on account, $3,000.
17 Purchased supplies on account, $1,500.
20 Paid creditors $6,000 on account.
22 Paid September rent, $500.
25 Paid salaries, $1,200.
27 Performed services on account and billed customers for services provided, $1,000.
29 Received $650 from customers for future service.

Adjustment data consist of the following:
1. Supplies on hand, $2,000.
2. Accrued salaries payable, $500.
3. Amortization is $300 per month.
4. Unearned service revenue of $300 is earned.

Instructions

(a) Enter the September 1 balances in ledger accounts.
(b) Journalize the September transactions.
(c) Post to the ledger accounts. Use J102 and J103 for posting references, and the following additional accounts: No. 400 Service Revenue, No. 711 Amortization Expense, No. 631 Supplies Expense, No. 726 Salaries Expense, and No. 729 Rent Expense.
(d) Prepare a trial balance at September 30.
(e) Journalize and post adjusting entries.
(f) Prepare an adjusted trial balance.
(g) Prepare an income statement and a statement of owner's equity for September, and a balance sheet at September 30, 2003.

*B*roadening Your Perspective

FINANCIAL REPORTING AND ANALYSIS

Financial Reporting Problem

BYP3–1   The financial statements and accompanying notes of **The Second Cup Ltd.** are presented in Appendix A at the end of this textbook.

Instructions

Answer the following questions, with reference to The Second Cup's consolidated financial statements and the notes to its consolidated financial statements:

(a) What title does The Second Cup use for its income statement?
(b) What different types of revenues were reported by The Second Cup?

(c) Notice that only a few selected expenses are shown on the company's income statement. Why do you think The Second Cup presents its data in this manner?

(d) Does The Second Cup report any prepayments on its balance sheet? If so, identify each item that is a prepaid expense or unearned (deferred) revenue. Indicate what other account title would likely be used in preparing adjusting entries for these accounts.

(e) Does The Second Cup report any accruals on its balance sheet? If so, identify each item that is an accrued revenue or accrued expense. Indicate what other account title would likely be used in preparing adjusting entries for these accounts.

Interpreting Financial Statements

BYP3–2   Cott Corporation, headquartered in Pointe-Claire, Quebec, is the fourth largest soft drink company in the world. It produces and distributes sports drinks, bottled water, and fruit-flavoured sparkling water in Canada, the U.S., the UK, Continental Europe, Japan, Australia, and Ireland.

Additional Cases

Until October 31, 1998, Cott Corporation included on its balance sheet a long-term asset called Prepaid Contract Costs. An excerpt from the management discussion and analysis accompanying Cott's fiscal 1997 financial statements noted the following:

COTT CORPORATION
Management Discussion and Analysis (partial)
January 25, 1997

Prepaid Contract Costs

The Corporation has relatively few customers when compared with the customer base of the national brand soft drink manufacturers, making it relatively more vulnerable to the loss of one or more customers. The risk that the Corporation will lose any single customer can be mitigated by entering into long-term contracts only with the payment of an up-front fixed amount of money ... The contracts entered into generally provide: (i) that the Corporation will be the exclusive supplier of premium retailer brand soft drinks; and (ii) for minimum annual volume targets to be achieved by the customers. Since these amounts are paid with the objective of realizing a revenue stream over a period of more than one year, the Corporation elects to capitalize these amounts as prepaid contract costs and amortizes them over the term of the related contracts.

Effective October 31, 1998, Cott changed its accounting policy and is no longer capitalizing its prepaid contract costs. Instead, it is recording these costs as expenses when incurred.

Instructions

(a) Assume that the up-front contract payment costs paid by Cott for fiscal 1997 totalled $29,743,000. Prepare the journal entry Cott would have made to record this payment.

(b) Cott amortized its Prepaid Contract Costs in the same way it amortized its capital assets. Assume its amortization expense for fiscal 1997 was $26,349,000. Prepare the journal entry Cott would have made to record the amortization of its Prepaid Contract Costs.

(c) Since the Prepaid Contract Costs were incurred to earn revenue, do you believe the amortization expense recorded above should be reported as a reduction of sales revenue or as an expense? Explain your reasoning.

(d) In fiscal 1998 and subsequent years, Cott decided not to capitalize these costs any longer. It is now expensing these costs as Prepaid Expenses when incurred.
  1. Discuss the reasoning Cott might have used in making this change from capitalizing prepaid costs to expensing prepaid costs. Use the revenue recognition and matching principles to support your reasoning.
  2. Redo the journal entries you made in (a) and (b) above, now that Cott is expensing these contract costs rather than capitalizing them.

BYP3–3   Laser Recording Systems, founded in 1981, produces laser disks for use in the home market. Sales have increased approximately 15% per year since the 1980s. The following is an excerpt from Laser Recording Systems' financial statements (all dollars in thousands):

> ### LASER RECORDING SYSTEMS
> #### Management Discussion (partial)
>
> Accrued liabilities increased to $1,642 at January 31, from $138 at the end of the previous fiscal year. Compensation and related accruals increased $195 due primarily to increases in accruals for severance, vacation, commissions, and relocation expenses. Accrued professional services increased by $137 primarily as a result of legal expenses related to several outstanding contractual disputes. Other expense increased $35, of which $18 was interest payable.

Instructions

(a) Can you tell from the discussion whether Laser Recording has prepaid its legal expenses and is now making an adjustment to the asset account Prepaid Legal Expenses, or whether the company is recording the legal expense using an accrued expense adjustment?

(b) Five types of possible adjustments are discussed in the chapter. For each of the adjustments Laser Recording mentions, state what kind of adjustment it is. How is net income ultimately affected by each of the adjustments?

(c) What journal entry did Laser Recording make to record the accrued interest?

Accounting on the Web

BYP3–4   A financial decision-maker should never rely solely on the financial information reported in an annual report. It is important to know the latest financial news. This problem demonstrates how to search for financial news on the web.

Instructions

Specific requirements of this Internet case are available on the Weygandt website.

CRITICAL THINKING
••

Collaborative Learning Activity

BYP3–5   RV World was organized on April 1, 2002, by Michel Cormier. Michel is a good manager but a poor accountant. From the trial balance prepared by a part-time bookkeeper, Michel prepared the following income statement for the quarter that ended March 31, 2003:

RV WORLD
Income Statement
For the Quarter Ended March 31, 2003

Revenues		
Campground rental fees		$95,000
Operating expenses		
Advertising	$ 5,200	
Wages	29,800	
Utilities	900	
Amortization	800	
Repairs	4,000	
Total operating expenses		40,700
Net income		$54,300

Michel knew that something was wrong with the statement because net income had never exceeded $20,000 in any one quarter. He asks you to review the income statement and other data.

You first look at the trial balance. In addition to the account balances reported above in the income statement, the ledger contains the following additional selected balances at March 31, 2003:

Supplies	$ 5,200
Prepaid Insurance	7,200
Note Payable	12,000

You then make inquiries and discover the following:
1. Campground rental fees include advance rentals for summer-month occupancy, in the amount of $30,000.
2. There was $1,300 of supplies on hand at March 31.
3. Prepaid insurance resulted from the payment of a one-year policy on January 1, 2003.
4. The mail in April 2003 brought the following bills: advertising for the week of March 24, $110; repairs made March 10, $260; and utilities for the month of March, $180.
5. There are four employees who receive wages that total $400 ($100 each) per day. At March 31, two days' wages have been incurred but not paid.
6. The note payable is a three-month 8% note dated January 1, 2003, and due on April 1, 2003.

Instructions

With the class divided into groups, do the following:
(a) Prepare a correct income statement for the quarter ended March 31, 2003.
(b) Explain to Michel (1) the generally accepted accounting principles that he did not recognize in preparing his income statement, and (2) their effect on his results.

Communication Activity

BYP3–6   In reviewing the accounts of the Marylee Co. at the end of the year, you discover that adjusting entries have not been made.

Instructions

Write a memorandum to Mary Lee Virgil, the owner of Marylee Co., that explains the following: the nature and purpose of adjusting entries, why adjusting entries are needed, and how her financial statements could be affected by the lack of adjustments. Give specific examples that are related to the various types of adjusting entries.

Ethics Case

BYP3–7   Die Hard Company is a pesticide manufacturer. Its sales declined greatly this year due to the passage of legislation that outlawed the sale of several of Die Hard's chemical pesticides. In the coming year, Die Hard will have new, environmentally safe chemicals to replace these discontinued products. Sales in the next year are expected to greatly exceed those of any previous year. The drop in sales and profits appears to be a one-year aberration. But even so, the company president fears that a large dip in the current year's profits could cause a significant drop in the market price of Die Hard's shares, and make the company a takeover target.

To avoid this possibility, the company president calls in Carole Chiasson, the company's controller, to discuss this period's year-end adjusting entries. He urges her to accrue every possible revenue and to defer as many expenses as possible when preparing this period's December 31 year-end adjusting entries. He says to Carole, "We need the revenues this year, and next year can easily absorb expenses deferred from this year." Carole didn't record the adjusting entries until January 17, but she dated the entries December 31 as if they were recorded then. Carole also made every effort to comply with the president's request.

Instructions

(a) Who are the stakeholders in this situation?
(b) What are the ethical considerations of (1) the president's request, and (2) Carole's dating the adjusting entries December 31?
(c) Can Carole accrue revenues and defer expenses and still be ethical?

Answers to Self-Study Questions

1. c 2. a 3. d 4. d 5. d 6. c 7. a 8. b 9. b 10. d 11. c 12. a

Answer to The Second Cup Review It Question 5

Second Cup reported depreciation of capital assets of $621,000 and $430,000, and amortization of goodwill of $300,000 and $300,000 for the years ended June 24, 2000, and June 30, 1999, respectively.

Remember to go back to the Navigator box on the chapter-opening page to check off your completed work.

Concepts for Review

Before studying this chapter, you should understand or, if necessary, review:

a. *How to apply the revenue recognition and matching principles. (Ch. 3, pp. 103–104)*
b. *How to make adjusting entries. (Ch. 3, pp. 106-118)*
c. *How to prepare an adjusted trial balance. (Ch. 3, pp. 120–121)*
d. *How the balance sheet, income statement, and statement of owner's equity are connected. (Ch. 3, pp. 121–122)*

THE NAVIGATOR

Breezing Through Month End With Style

WINNIPEG, Man.—Owned and operated by the Gorenstein family of Winnipeg, Moulé has four gallery-style retail stores across Canada. Each one features gifts, jewellery, and other treasures from around the world. They have been crafted by talented artists working in glass, ceramics, metal, and other media. Founded in 1987, Moulé also designs and manufactures a signature line of soft, feminine, and sophisticated women's apparel. The clothing is sold in Moulé stores and distributed across North America.

Month end finds its chief operations officer, Laurie Gorenstein, running off extra reports on the DacEasy computer software he uses for accounting. "I receive all the invoices from the stores at month end, do a second count, and check it against the figures in the computer. Then I run the general ledger and the trial balance."

"My accountant checks them," he continues, "and we make any updates or corrections necessary—such as a cheque posted to the wrong account—

with an adjusting or correcting entry. It usually comes out pretty smoothly." Monthly financial statements follow.

"So it really is pretty easy," confides Mr. Gorenstein. Once a year, the load gets a little heavier when the books are closed. At this point, he's very glad of the care taken to find discrepancies

and to make adjustments at month end. If errors are left undetected, "then they come back to haunt you months later and you can spend forever trying to sort them out."

THE NAVIGATOR

THE NAVIGATOR

✔

- Understand *Concepts for Review* ☐
- Read *Feature Story* ☐
- Scan *Study Objectives* ☐
- Read *Preview* ☐
- Read text and answer *Before You Go On*
  p. 166 ☐ p. 172 ☐ p. 179 ☐ p. 181 ☐
- Work *Demonstration Problem* ☐
- Review *Summary of Study Objectives* ☐
- Answer *Self-Study Questions* ☐
- Complete assignments ☐

CHAPTER · 4

COMPLETION OF THE ACCOUNTING CYCLE

▶ STUDY OBJECTIVES ◀

After studying this chapter, you should be able to:

1. Describe the purpose of a work sheet.
2. Demonstrate the process of closing the books.
3. Describe and produce a post-closing trial balance.
4. State the steps in the accounting cycle.
5. Explain and demonstrate the approaches to preparing correcting entries.
6. Identify and prepare the various sections of a classified balance sheet.
7. Illustrate measures used to evaluate liquidity.
8. Prepare a work sheet (Appendix 4A).
9. Prepare reversing entries (Appendix 4B).

THE NAVIGATOR

In Chapter 3, we prepared financial statements directly from the adjusted trial balance. In this chapter we will explain the role of the remaining steps in the accounting cycle—especially the closing process. Once again, we will use the Pioneer Advertising Agency as an example.

Then we will consider correcting entries. It is easy to make errors because of the many details involved in the end-of-period accounting procedures. Locating and correcting errors can cost much time and effort, as Laurie Gorenstein notes in the opening story. We conclude by discussing the classification and use of balance sheets.

This chapter is organized as follows:

THE
NAVIGATOR

Using a Work Sheet

STUDY OBJECTIVE
··········· I ···········

Describe the purpose of a work sheet.

In our discussion in Chapter 3, we used an adjusted trial balance to arrive at the amounts used to prepare financial statements. Accountants frequently use a device known as a work sheet to determine these accounts. A **work sheet** is a multiple-column form that may be used in the adjustment process and in preparing financial statements. Work sheets can be prepared manually, but today most are done by accounting software or electronic spreadsheet programs.

Popular accounting software programs include ACCPAC, Simply Accounting, Quick Books, and DacEasy, which Laurie Gorenstein uses at Moulé. Spreadsheet programs include Excel and Quattro Pro. The advantage of an electronic work sheet over a manually prepared one is the capability it provides to change selected data easily. When data are changed, the computer updates your calculations instantly. An automated work sheet program can also substantially reduce the time needed for the end-of-period procedures.

As its name suggests, the work sheet is a working tool for the accountant. **A work sheet is not a permanent accounting record**; it is neither a journal nor a part of the general ledger. The work sheet is merely a device used to make it easier to prepare adjusting entries and financial statements. In small companies that have relatively few accounts and adjustments, a work sheet may not be needed. In companies with numerous accounts and many adjustments, it is almost indispensable.

The basic form of a work sheet and the procedure for preparing it (five steps) are shown in Illustration 4-1.

Illustration 4-1

Form and procedure for a work sheet

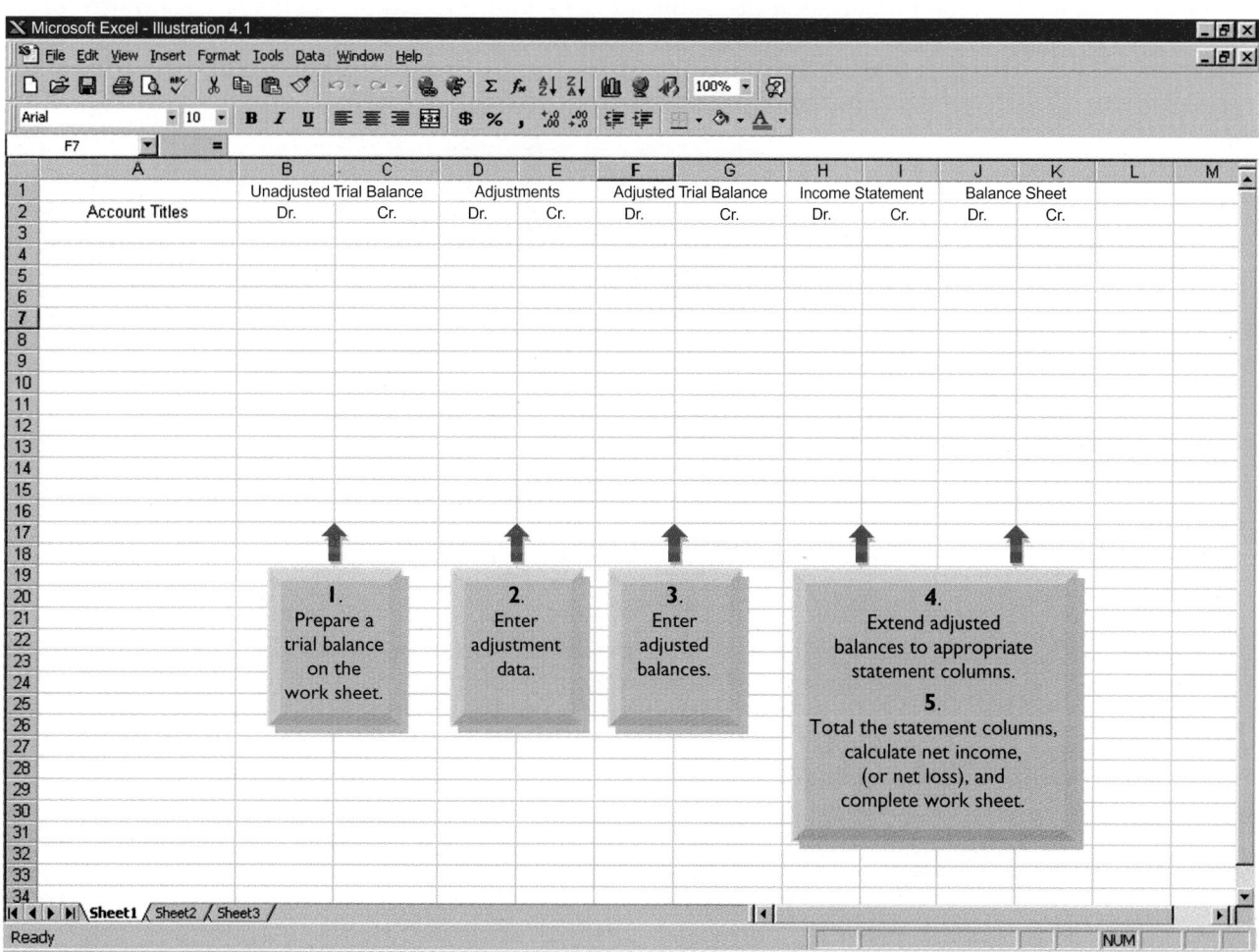

The steps required to prepare the work sheet must be performed in the proper sequence.

Although **the use of a work sheet is optional**, it is useful. Financial statements, for example, can be easily prepared from the work sheet, reducing errors. A work sheet also makes it easier to prepare interim (e.g., monthly or quarterly) financial information for internal use: adjusting entries can be prepared and entered in the work sheet, allowing interim financial statements to be developed.

◥ Closing the Books

At the end of the accounting period, the accounts are made ready for the next period. This is called closing the books. When closing the books, it is necessary to distinguish between temporary and permanent accounts. Temporary accounts relate to a single accounting period. They include all income statement accounts and the owner's drawings account. **All temporary accounts are closed.** In contrast, permanent accounts relate to one or more future accounting periods. They consist of all balance sheet accounts, including the owner's capital account. **Permanent accounts are not closed.** Instead, their balances are carried forward into the next accounting period. Illustration 4-2 identifies the accounts in each category.

Illustration 4-2

Temporary versus permanent accounts

Helpful hint   A contra asset account, such as accumulated amortization, is a permanent account also.

TEMPORARY	PERMANENT
These accounts are closed.	These accounts are not closed.
All revenue accounts	All asset accounts
All expense accounts	All liability accounts
Owner's drawings account	Owner's capital account

Preparing Closing Entries

**Accounting Cycle
Tutorial—Preparing
Financial Statements
and Closing Books**

At the end of the accounting period, the temporary account balances are transferred to the equity account of the owner of the proprietorship, Owner's Capital, by preparing closing entries. Closing entries formally record in the ledger the transfer of net income (or net loss) and the owner's drawings to the owner's capital account. This updates the owner's capital balance, as shown in the statement of owner's equity. **These entries produce a zero balance in each temporary account. These accounts are then ready to accumulate data in the next accounting period separately from the data of earlier periods.** Permanent accounts are *not* closed.

Journalizing and posting closing entries is a required step in the accounting cycle. This step is performed after financial statements have been prepared. In contrast to the steps in the cycle that you have already studied, closing entries are generally journalized and posted **only at the end of a company's annual accounting period**. Moulé, introduced in the chapter-opening story, closes its books once a year. This practice simplifies the preparation of annual financial statements, because all temporary accounts contain data for the entire year.

In preparing closing entries, each income statement account is usually closed directly to Owner's Capital, especially in computerized accounting systems. Some people believe this results in excessive detail in the permanent owner's capital account. Instead, they first close the revenue and expense accounts to another temporary account, **Income Summary**. The total net income or net loss is then transferred from this account to Owner's Capital. Either procedure is acceptable. We will demonstrate closing directly to Owner's Capital in this text, as it is more commonly done.

Closing entries are journalized in the general journal. A centre caption entitled Closing Entries may be inserted in the journal between the last adjusting entry and the first closing entry, to identify these entries. Then the closing entries are posted to the ledger accounts.

Closing entries may be prepared directly from (1) the adjusted balances in the general ledger or adjusted trial balance, (2) the income statement and statement of owner's equity, or (3) the work sheet, if available. If we used a work sheet, the data for the closing entries would appear in the income statement columns and in the drawings account in the balance sheet. Separate closing entries could then be prepared for each temporary account. However, the compound entries illustrated in the first two of the following three entries are more efficient:

1. Debit each individual revenue account for its balance, and credit Owner's Capital for total revenues.
2. Debit Owner's Capital for total expenses, and credit each individual expense account for its balance.
3. Debit Owner's Capital for the balance in Owner's Drawings, and credit Owner's Drawings for the same amount.

Helpful hint These entries assume that the temporary accounts have normal balances.

In Illustration 4-3, the three entries are shown in the diagram of the closing process for a proprietorship, using T accounts.

Illustration 4-3

Diagram of closing process

Closing Entries Illustrated

To illustrate the journalizing and posting of closing entries, we will assume that Pioneer Advertising Agency uses a manual accounting system. A computerized accounting system performs the entire closing process automatically when you are ready to start a new accounting period. For illustrative purposes, we have also assumed that the company has chosen October 31 as its fiscal year end. Pioneer Advertising's adjusted trial balance on October 31, first illustrated in Chapter 3 (Illustration 3-11), is reproduced in Illustration 4-4.

Illustration 4-4

Adjusted trial balance

PIONEER ADVERTISING AGENCY
Adjusted Trial Balance
October 31, 2002

	Debit	Credit
Cash	$15,200	
Accounts Receivable	200	
Advertising Supplies	1,000	
Prepaid Insurance	550	
Office Equipment	5,000	
Accumulated Amortization—		
Office Equipment		$ 83
Notes Payable		5,000
Accounts Payable		2,500
Unearned Revenue		800
Salaries Payable		1,200
Interest Payable		25
C. R. Byrd, Capital		10,000
C. R. Byrd, Drawings	500	
Service Revenue		10,600
Advertising Supplies Expense	1,500	
Amortization Expense	83	
Insurance Expense	50	
Salaries Expense	5,200	
Rent Expense	900	
Interest Expense	25	
	$30,208	$30,208

We will use the adjusted account balances shown here to prepare the three required closing entries. The temporary accounts involved in the closing process have been highlighted in red. Although the C. R. Byrd, Capital account is not a temporary account, it has been highlighted because it is involved in the closing process. **The capital account balance in the trial balance is the opening balance** (plus any investment made by the owner during the period), not the ending balance that appears in the statement of owner's equity and balance sheet. This permanent account is not closed but the net income (loss) and drawings for the period must be recorded to update the account to its ending capital balance.

The closing entries at October 31 are shown in Illustration 4-5.

Illustration 4-5

Closing entries journalized

		GENERAL JOURNAL			J3
Date		Account Titles and Explanation	Ref.	Debit	Credit
		Closing Entries			
2002		(1)			
Oct. 31		Service Revenue	400	10,600	
		C. R.Byrd, Capital	301		10,600
		To close revenue account.			
		(2)			
	31	C. R. Byrd, Capital	301	7,758	
		Advertising Supplies Expense	611		1,500
		Amortization Expense	711		83
		Insurance Expense	722		50
		Salaries Expense	726		5,200
		Rent Expense	729		900
		Interest Expense	905		25
		To close expense accounts.			
		(3)			
	31	C. R. Byrd, Capital	301	500	
		C. R. Byrd, Drawings	306		500
		To close drawings account.			

A couple of cautions in preparing closing entries: (1) Remember that **the reason for making closing entries is to bring the temporary accounts to zero balances**. Avoid unintentionally doubling the revenue, expense, and drawings account balances, rather than bringing them to zero. (2) Do not close owner's drawings with the expenses. **Owner's drawings are not an expense, and are not a factor in determining net income.**

Posting Closing Entries

Illustration 4-6

Posting closing entries—temporary accounts

The posting of the closing entries is shown in Illustration 4-6.

(Temporary Accounts Only)
GENERAL LEDGER

	C. R. Byrd, Drawings				No. 306
Date	Explanation	Ref.	Debit	Credit	Balance
2002					
Oct. 20		J1	500		500
31	Closing Entry	J3		500	0

	Insurance Expense				No. 722
Date	Explanation	Ref.	Debit	Credit	Balance
2002					
Oct. 31	Adjusting Entry	J2	50		50
31	Closing Entry	J3		50	0

	Service Revenue				No. 400
Date	Explanation	Ref.	Debit	Credit	Balance
2002					
Oct. 29		J1		10,000	10,000
31	Adjusting Entry	J2		400	10,400
31	Adjusting Entry	J2		200	10,600
31	Closing Entry	J3	10,600		0

	Salaries Expense				No. 726
Date	Explanation	Ref.	Debit	Credit	Balance
2002					
Oct. 26		J1	4,000		4,000
31	Adjusting Entry	J2	1,200		5,200
31	Closing Entry	J3		5,200	**0**

	Advertising Supplies Expense				No. 611
Date	Explanation	Ref.	Debit	Credit	Balance
2002					
Oct. 31	Adjusting Entry	J2	1,500		1,500
31	Closing Entry	J3		1,500	0

	Rent Expense				No. 729
Date	Explanation	Ref.	Debit	Credit	Balance
2002					
Oct. 4		J1	900		900
31	Closing Entry	J3		900	0

	Amortization Expense				No. 711
Date	Explanation	Ref.	Debit	Credit	Balance
2002					
Oct. 31	Adjusting Entry	J2	83		83
31	Closing Entry	J3		83	0

	Interest Expense				No. 905
Date	Explanation	Ref.	Debit	Credit	Balance
2002					
Oct. 31	Adjusting Entry	J2	25		25
31	Closing Entry	J3		25	0

Note: The temporary accounts for Pioneer Advertising Agency are shown here; the permanent accounts are shown in Illustration 4-7. Both permanent and temporary accounts are part of the general ledger. They are separated here to aid in learning.

The permanent accounts of Pioneer Advertising are shown in the general ledger in Illustration 4-7. The **permanent accounts** (assets, liabilities, and owner's capital) are not closed; the account balance is carried forward to the next period. Note that the balance in the owner's capital account represents the total equity of the owner at the end of the accounting period.

Stop and check your work after the closing entries are posted. (1) All **temporary accounts** (revenues, expenses, and owner's drawings) should have zero balances, as shown in Illustration 4-6. (2) The balance in the capital account should equal the ending balance reported in the statement of owner's equity and balance sheet.

(Permanent Accounts Only)

GENERAL LEDGER

Cash					No. 101
Date	Explanation	Ref.	Debit	Credit	Balance
2002					
Oct. 1		J1	10,000		10,000
4		J1	1,200		11,200
4		J1		900	10,300
4		J1		600	9,700
20		J1		500	9,200
26		J1		4,000	5,200
29		J1	10,000		15,200

Accounts Receivable					No. 112
Date	Explanation	Ref.	Debit	Credit	Balance
2002					
Oct. 31	Adjusting Entry	J2	200		200

Advertising Supplies					No. 129
Date	Explanation	Ref.	Debit	Credit	Balance
2002					
Oct. 5		J1	2,500		2,500
31	Adjusting Entry	J2		1,500	1,000

Prepaid Insurance					No. 130
Date	Explanation	Ref.	Debit	Credit	Balance
2002					
Oct. 4		J1	600		600
31	Adjusting Entry	J2		50	550

Office Equipment					No. 151
Date	Explanation	Ref.	Debit	Credit	Balance
2002					
Oct. 1		J1	5,000		5,000

Accumulated Amortization—Office Equipment					No. 152
Date	Explanation	Ref.	Debit	Credit	Balance
2002					
Oct. 31	Adjusting Entry	J2		83	83

Notes Payable					No. 200
Date	Explanation	Ref.	Debit	Credit	Balance
2002					
Oct. 1		J1		5,000	5,000

Accounts Payable					No. 201
Date	Explanation	Ref.	Debit	Credit	Balance
2002					
Oct. 5		J1		2,500	2,500

Unearned Revenue					No. 209
Date	Explanation	Ref.	Debit	Credit	Balance
2002					
Oct. 4		J1		1,200	1,200
31	Adjusting Entry	J2	400		800

Salaries Payable					No. 212
Date	Explanation	Ref.	Debit	Credit	Balance
2002					
Oct. 31	Adjusting Entry	J2		1,200	1,200

Interest Payable					No. 230
Date	Explanation	Ref.	Debit	Credit	Balance
2002					
Oct. 31	Adjusting Entry	J2		25	25

C. R. Byrd, Capital					No. 301
Date	Explanation	Ref.	Debit	Credit	Balance
2002					
Oct. 1		J1		10,000	10,000
31	Closing Entry	J3		10,600	20,600
31	Closing Entry	J3	7,758		12,842
31	Closing Entry	J3	500		12,342

> *Note:* The permanent accounts for Pioneer Advertising Agency are shown here; the temporary accounts are shown in Illustration 4-6. Both permanent and temporary accounts are part of the general ledger. They are separated here to aid in learning.

Illustration 4-7

Posting closing entries—permanent accounts

▶Accounting in Action ▸ ℮-Business Insight

Technology has dramatically changed the end-of-period accounting process. When Larry Carter became chief financial officer of Cisco Systems, a worldwide leader in connecting Canadians and others on the Internet, closing the accounts would take up to 10 days. Within four years, he got it down to two days. Now, he is aiming to be able to do a "virtual close"—closing within a day on any day.

This is not just showing off. Knowing exactly where you are all of the time, says Mr. Carter, allows you to respond faster than your competitors. But it also means that the 600 people who used to spend 10 days tracking transactions can now be more usefully employed on things such as mining data for business intelligence.

Source: "Business and the Internet," *The Economist,* June 26, 1999, 12.

Preparing a Post-Closing Trial Balance

After all closing entries have been journalized and posted, another trial balance, called a **post-closing trial balance**, is prepared from the ledger. The post- (or after-) closing trial balance is a list of permanent accounts and their balances after closing entries have been journalized and posted. **The purpose of this trial balance is to prove the equality of the permanent account balances that are carried forward into the next accounting period.** Since all temporary accounts will have zero balances, **the post-closing trial balance will contain only permanent (balance sheet) accounts**.

STUDY OBJECTIVE
· · · · · · · · · 3 · · · · · · · · ·

Describe and produce a post-closing trial balance.

To prepare a post-closing trial balance, we list the accounts and their balances. The post-closing trial balance for Pioneer Advertising, using the permanent accounts listed in Illustration 4-7, is shown below.

PIONEER ADVERTISING AGENCY Post-Closing Trial Balance October 31, 2002		
	Debit	Credit
Cash	$15,200	
Accounts Receivable	200	
Advertising Supplies	1,000	
Prepaid Insurance	550	
Office Equipment	5,000	
Accumulated Amortization—Office Equipment		$ 83
Notes Payable		5,000
Accounts Payable		2,500
Unearned Revenue		800
Salaries Payable		1,200
Interest Payable		25
C. R. Byrd, Capital		12,342
	$21,950	$21,950

Illustration 4-8

Post-closing trial balance

Helpful hint Total debits in a post-closing trial balance will not equal total assets on the balance sheet if contra accounts, such as accumulated amortization, are present. Accumulated amortization is deducted from assets on the balance sheet but added to the credit column in a trial balance.

A post-closing trial balance provides evidence that the journalizing and posting of closing entries has been properly completed. It also shows that the accounting equation is in balance at the end of the accounting period or the beginning of the next accounting period. The post-closing trial balance can be dated at the end of the period (October 31 as in Pioneer Advertising's case) or the beginning of the next period (November 1) to serve as an opening trial balance. We have chosen to do the former here.

As in the case of the trial balance, the post-closing trial balance does not prove that all transactions have been recorded or that the ledger is correct. For example, the post-closing trial balance will still balance if a transaction is not journalized and posted, or if a transaction is journalized and posted twice. That is why it is so important, as Laurie Gorenstein states in the opening story, to find and correct all errors before the books are closed.

Summary of the Accounting Cycle
· ·

The steps in the accounting cycle are shown in Illustration 4-9. You can see that the cycle begins with the analysis of business transactions and ends with the preparation of a post-closing trial balance. The steps in the cycle are performed in sequence and are repeated in each accounting period.

STUDY OBJECTIVE
· · · · · · · · · 4 · · · · · · · · ·

State the steps in the accounting cycle.

Illustration 4-9

Steps in the accounting cycle

Accounting Cycle Tutorial

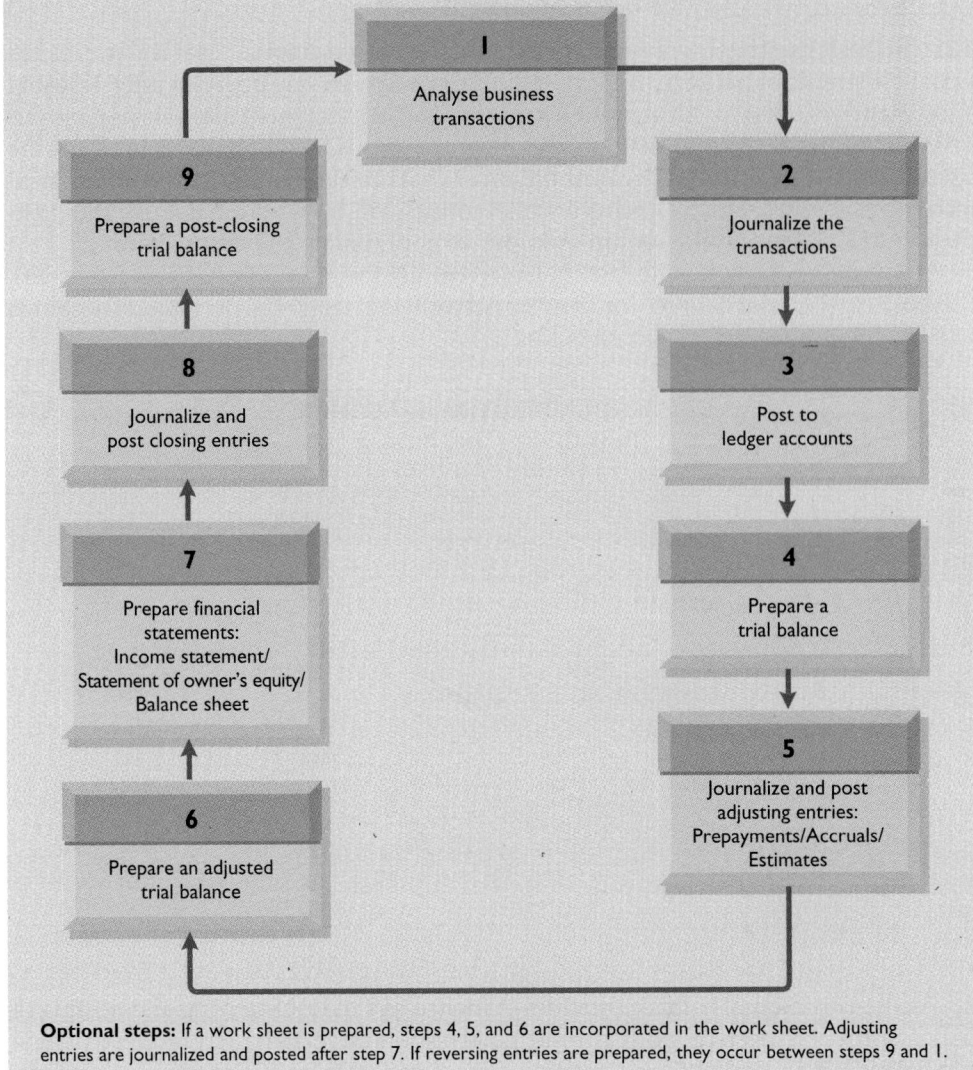

Optional steps: If a work sheet is prepared, steps 4, 5, and 6 are incorporated in the work sheet. Adjusting entries are journalized and posted after step 7. If reversing entries are prepared, they occur between steps 9 and 1.

Steps 1 and 2 may occur daily during the accounting period, as explained in Chapter 2. Steps 3 through 7 are performed on a periodic basis, such as monthly, quarterly, or annually. Steps 8 and 9, closing entries and a post-closing trial balance, are usually prepared only at the end of a company's **annual** accounting period.

There are also two optional steps in the accounting cycle. As you have seen, a work sheet may be used to prepare trial balances, adjusting entries, and financial statements. If a work sheet is used, adjusting entries are not formally recorded or posted until after the financial statements are prepared. In addition, reversing entries may be used, as the following section explains.

Reversing Entries—An Optional Step

Some accountants prefer to reverse certain adjusting entries at the beginning of a new accounting period. A reversing entry is made at the beginning of the next accounting period. It is the exact opposite of the adjusting entry made in the previous period. **The preparation of reversing entries is an optional bookkeeping procedure that is not a required step in the accounting cycle.** Accordingly, we have chosen to cover this topic in Appendix 4B at the end of the chapter.

Correcting Entries—An Avoidable Step

Unfortunately, errors may occur in the recording process. Errors should be corrected as soon as they are discovered by journalizing and posting correcting entries. If the accounting records are free of errors, no correcting entries are necessary. You should understand several differences between correcting entries and adjusting entries. First, adjusting entries are an integral part of the accounting cycle. Correcting entries, on the other hand, are unnecessary if the records have no errors. Second, **adjustments are journalized and posted only at the end of an accounting period. In contrast, correcting entries are made whenever an error is discovered.** Finally, adjusting entries always affect at least one balance sheet account and one income statement account. In contrast, correcting entries may involve any combination of accounts in need of correction. Both adjusting and correcting entries must be journalized and posted before closing entries.

STUDY OBJECTIVE

5

Explain and demonstrate the approaches to preparing correcting entries.

To determine the correcting entry, it is useful to compare the incorrect entry with the entry that should have been made. Doing this helps identify the accounts and amounts that should—and should not—be corrected. After comparison, a correcting entry is made to correct the accounts. This approach is illustrated in the following two cases:

Case 1. On May 10, a $50 cash collection on account from a customer is journalized and posted as a debit to Cash $50 and as a credit to Service Revenue $50. The error is discovered on May 20, when the customer pays the remaining balance in full.

Incorrect Entry (May 10)			Correct Entry (May 10)		
Cash	50		Cash	50	
Service Revenue		50	Accounts Receivable		50

A comparison of the incorrect entry with the correct entry that should have been made (but was not) reveals that the debit to Cash of $50 is correct. However, the $50 credit to Service Revenue should have been credited to Accounts Receivable. As a result, both Service Revenue and Accounts Receivable are overstated in the ledger. The following correcting entry is required:

	Correcting Entry		
May 20	Service Revenue	50	
	Accounts Receivable		50
	To correct entry of May 10.		

A	=	L	+	OE
−50				−50

Case 2. On May 18, office equipment that costs $450 is purchased on account. The transaction is journalized and posted as a debit to Delivery Equipment $45 and as a credit to Accounts Payable $45. The error is discovered on June 3, when the monthly statement for May is received from the creditor.

Incorrect Entry (May 18)			Correct Entry (May 18)		
Delivery Equipment	45		Office Equipment	450	
Accounts Payable		45	Accounts Payable		450

A comparison of the two entries shows that three accounts are incorrect. Delivery Equipment is overstated by $45; Office Equipment is understated by $450; and Accounts Payable is understated by $405 ($450 − $45). The correcting entry is as follows:

	Correcting Entry		
June 3	Office Equipment	450	
	Delivery Equipment		45
	Accounts Payable		405
	To correct May 18 entry.		

A	=	L	+	OE
+450		+405		
−45				

Instead of preparing a correcting entry, many accountants simply **reverse the incorrect entry and then record the correct entry**. Even though this approach will result in more entries and postings, it is an easier and often more logical procedure.

Before You Go On . . .

▶Review It

1. How do permanent accounts differ from temporary accounts?
2. What three different types of entries are required in closing the books?
3. What is the content and purpose of a post-closing trial balance?
4. What are the required and optional steps in the accounting cycle?
5. Distinguish between an adjusting and a correcting entry.

▶Do It

The work sheet for the Nguyen Company shows the following: H. Nguyen, Drawings, $5,000; H. Nguyen, Capital, $42,000; Service Revenue, $18,000; and Operating Expenses, $10,000. Prepare the closing entries at December 31.

Action Plan

• Make the first two entries to close revenues and expenses to owner's capital.
• Make the final entry to close owner's drawings to owner's capital.
• Determine the balance in each temporary account. Debit the revenue account(s), and credit the expense and drawings accounts in order to result in a zero balance in each account.
• Check your work after posting the closing entries. Do the temporary accounts have zero balances? Does the ending capital balance equal the balance reported on the statement of owner's equity and balance sheet?

Solution

Dec. 31	Service Revenue	18,000	
	H. Nguyen, Capital		18,000
	To close revenue to capital.		
31	H. Nguyen, Capital	10,000	
	Operating Expenses		10,000
	To close expenses to capital.		
31	H. Nguyen, Capital	5,000	
	H. Nguyen, Drawings		5,000
	To close drawings to capital.		

THE NAVIGATOR

Related exercise material: BE4–1, BE4–2, BE4–3, BE4–4, BE4–5, BE4–6, BE4–7, E4–1, E4–2, E4–3, and E4–4.

◤Classified Financial Statements

STUDY OBJECTIVE
⬤⬤⬤⬤⬤ 6 ⬤⬤⬤⬤⬤

Identify and prepare the various sections of a classified balance sheet.

The financial statements illustrated up to this point were simplified. We classified items as assets, liabilities, and owner's equity in the balance sheet, and as revenues and expenses in the income statement. However, **financial statements are more useful to management, creditors, and potential investors when the elements are classified into significant subgroups.** In the remainder of this chapter, we will introduce you to the primary balance sheet classifications. The classified income statement will be presented in Chapter 5.

Standard Balance Sheet Classifications

A classified balance sheet for a proprietorship generally contains the following standard classifications:

Assets	Liabilities and Owner's Equity
Current assets	Current liabilities
Long-term investments	Long-term liabilities
Capital assets	Owner's (shareholders') equity

Illustration 4-10

Standard balance sheet classifications

These sections help the financial statement user determine such matters as (1) the availability of assets to meet debts as they come due, and (2) the claims of short and long-term creditors on total assets. A classified balance sheet also makes it easier to compare companies in the same industry, such as The Second Cup and Starbucks. Each of the sections is explained below.

▶ *International note*

Other countries use a different format for the balance sheet. In the United Kingdom, for example, capital assets are reported first on the balance sheet. In addition, current liabilities are deducted from current assets and shown as net current assets.

Current Assets

Current assets are cash and other resources that will be realized within one year of the balance sheet date or the company's operating cycle, whichever is longer. They may be realized in cash or as items sold or consumed in the business. For example, accounts receivable are current assets because they will be realized in cash as the amounts are collected within the year. A prepayment such as supplies is a current asset because of the expected use or consumption of the supplies by the business within one year.

The operating cycle of a company is the average time that is required to go from cash to cash in producing revenues. The term "cycle" suggests a circular flow, which, in this case, starts and ends with cash. For example, in taxi companies, the operating cycle would tend to be short, since services are provided almost entirely on a cash basis. On the other hand, the operating cycle in a clothing company such as Moulé is longer. Orders are received for clothing produced in advance of the season, and delivery, billing, and collection may extend for several months. Most companies have operating cycles of less than one year. More will be said about operating cycles in later chapters.

In a service enterprise, it is customary to recognize four types of current assets: (1) cash, (2) short-term (temporary) investments (e.g., treasury bills, shares, and bonds), (3) receivables (e.g., notes receivable, accounts receivable, and interest receivable), and (4) prepaid expenses (e.g., rent, insurance, and supplies). A fifth category of current assets, inventories (merchandise available for sale), will be introduced when merchandising companies are discussed in Chapter 5.

Current assets are listed in the order of liquidity that is, in the order in which they are expected to be converted into cash. This arrangement is shown in the presentation used by Canada Post, in Illustration 4-11. Note that Canada Post has combined cash and cash equivalents on one line for reporting purposes. Canada Post's cash equivalents consist of short-term investments which will mature within 12 months or less. This is a common practice for many companies, since short-term investments, if readily marketable, are considered to be *nearly cash*.

CANADA POST CORPORATION Balance Sheet (partial) March 25, 2000 (in millions)	
Current assets	
Cash and cash equivalents	$ 631
Accounts receivable	372
Prepaid expenses	52
	$1,055

Illustration 4-11

Current assets section

A company's current assets are important in assessing the company's short-term debt paying ability, as explained later in the chapter.

Long-Term Investments

Like current assets, long-term investments are resources that can be realized in cash. However, the conversion into cash is not expected within one year or the operating cycle. This category, often just called *investments*, normally includes shares and bonds of other corporations that cannot be, or are not intended to be, converted into cash quickly. Note that these are investments (assets) acquired by the company. These are to be distinguished from investments (owner's equity) made by the owner in the company.

Most companies report long-term investments as a single amount in the balance sheet, and show the details in the accompanying notes. BCE, a global communications company, reported the following in a recent balance sheet, with further detail provided about the investments in a note to the financial statements:

Illustration 4-12

Long-term investments section

BCE INC. Balance Sheet (partial) December 31, 2000 (in millions)	
Assets	
Investments in significantly influenced and other companies	$1,648

BCE owns shares in telecommunication companies such as Teleglobe, Aliant, Bruncor, MT&T, and Nortel Networks.

Capital Assets

Capital assets are long-lived assets used in the operation of the business to produce and distribute products or provide services. Unlike current assets, which will be used or consumed in the current accounting period, capital assets provide benefits over many accounting periods. Capital assets can be tangible, with physical substance, or intangible, without physical substance. **Tangible capital assets** may include (1) property, plant, and equipment, and (2) natural resources, such as mineral deposits, oil and gas reserves, and timber. **Intangible capital assets** provide future benefits through the special rights and privileges they convey, rather than through any physical characteristics. Patents, copyrights, trademarks, and franchises are some examples of intangible assets.

Alternative terminology
Property, plant, and equipment are also known as *fixed assets*.

Although the order of listing capital assets can vary among companies, **capital assets are normally listed in the balance sheet in order of permanency.** Land is usually listed first because it has an indefinite life, followed by the asset with the longest useful life (normally buildings), and so on.

Since capital assets benefit future periods, their cost is matched to expense over these future periods through amortization, as we learned in Chapter 3. Assets which are amortized should be reported at their net book value (cost minus accumulated amortization). The Forzani Group is Canada's largest sporting goods retailer, operating under the banners Sport Chek, Sports Experts, and Forzani. In the following illustration, the company reports its capital assets at net book value on its balance sheet. It details the cost and accumulated amortization in a note to the financial statements. Except for land (the useful life of which is unlimited), all capital assets are amortized.

Illustration 4-13

Capital assets section

THE FORZANI GROUP LTD.
Notes to the Financial Statements (partial)
January 30, 2000
(in thousands)

Capital assets	Cost	Accumulated Amortization	Net Book Value
Land	$ 638		$ 638
Building	5,813	$ 954	4,859
Building on leased land	3,143	599	2,544
Furniture, fixtures, equipment, and automotive	44,434	24,069	20,365
Leasehold improvements	61,868	24,435	37,433
Trademarks	259	208	51
	$116,155	$50,265	$65,890

Current Liabilities

Current liabilities are listed first in the liabilities and owner's equity section of the balance sheet. Current liabilities are obligations that are reasonably expected to be paid from current assets or through the creation of other current liabilities. As in the case of current assets, the time period for payment is one year or the operating cycle, whichever is longer. Current liabilities include (1) debts related to the operating cycle, such as accounts payable and salaries payable, and (2) other short-term debts, such as notes payable, interest payable, income taxes payable (owed by corporations), sales taxes payable, and current maturities of long-term liabilities (payments to be made within the next year on long-term debt).

Current liabilities are often listed in order of currency. That is, the liabilities that come due first are listed first. However, for many companies, the arrangement of items within the current liabilities section is the result of custom rather than a prescribed rule. The current liabilities section from Sears Canada's balance sheet is as follows:

Illustration 4-14

Current liabilities section

SEARS CANADA INC.
Balance Sheet (partial)
December 30, 2000
(in millions)

Current liabilities	
Accounts payable	$ 974.6
Accrued liabilities	440.3
Income and other taxes payable	109.3
Principal payments on long-term obligations due within one year	152.5
Current portion of deferred credit	53.3
	1,730.0

Long-Term Liabilities

Obligations expected to be paid after one year are classified as long-term liabilities. Liabilities in this category can include (1) bonds payable, (2) mortgages payable, (3) notes payable, (4) lease liabilities, and (5) obligations under employee pension plans. Many companies report long-term debt that matures after one year as a single amount in the balance sheet. Then they show the details of the debt in the notes that accompany the financial statements. Sleeman Breweries reported long-term obligations of $74,524,000 on a recent balance sheet, with the following selected information detailed in a note:

Illustration 4-15

Long-term liabilities section

SLEEMAN BREWERIES LTD. Balance Sheet (partial) December 25, 1999 (in thousands)	
Long-term obligations	
Bank of Nova Scotia	$37,255
Bank of Montreal	39,000
Shaftebury	4,968
	81,223
Less amount due within one fiscal year (reported as a current liability)	6,699
	$74,524

Equity

As discussed briefly in Chapter 1, the content of the equity section varies with the form of business organization. In a proprietorship, there is one capital account under the heading **owner's equity**. In a partnership, there is a capital account for each partner under the heading **partners' equity**. For a corporation, **shareholders' equity** is divided into two sections: share capital (also known as capital stock) and retained earnings. Amounts invested in the business by the shareholders are recorded in one of the share capital accounts. Income kept for use in the business is recorded in the retained earnings account. The share capital and retained earnings accounts are combined and reported as shareholders' equity on the balance sheet. We'll learn more about these corporation equity accounts in later chapters.

As noted in Chapter 1, it is difficult to gain access to proprietorship and partnership financial statements. Public corporations, on the other hand, issue their financial statements for use by present and potential investors, among others. In its balance sheet, Andrés Wines Ltd., a corporation, reported its shareholders' equity section as follows:

Illustration 4-16

Shareholders' equity section

ANDRÉS WINES LTD. Balance Sheet (partial) March 31, 2000 (in thousands)	
Shareholders' equity	
Capital stock	$ 4,420
Retained earnings	60,607
	$65,027

Classified Balance Sheet Illustrated

Using the post-closing trial balance accounts in Illustration 4-8 at October 31, 2002, we can prepare the classified balance sheet shown in Illustration 4-17. Note that Pioneer Advertising only has one capital asset, office equipment. Pioneer Advertising rents its premises so it does not report other capital assets such as land or building. As discussed earlier in this chapter, if it did, it would present the longest lived capital asset (e.g., land) first. Also note that, for illustrative purposes, we have assumed that $1,000 of the notes payable is due currently and $4,000 is long-term.

The balance sheet is most often presented in **report form**, as in Illustration 4-17, with the assets shown above the liabilities and owner's equity. The balance sheet may also be presented in **account form**, with the assets section placed on the left and the liabilities and owner's equity sections on the right. The majority of Canadian companies use the report form of presentation on the balance sheet.

Illustration 4-17

Classified balance sheet in report form

PIONEER ADVERTISING AGENCY
Balance Sheet
October 31, 2002

Assets

Current assets		
Cash		$15,200
Accounts receivable		200
Advertising supplies		1,000
Prepaid insurance		550
Total current assets		16,950
Capital assets		
Office equipment	$5,000	
Less: Accumulated amortization	83	4,917
Total assets		$21,867

Liabilities and Owner's Equity

Current liabilities	
Notes payable	$ 1,000
Accounts payable	2,500
Unearned revenue	800
Salaries payable	1,200
Interest payable	25
Total current liabilities	5,525
Long-term liabilities	
Notes payable	4,000
Total liabilities	9,525
Owner's equity	
C. R. Byrd, Capital	12,342
Total liabilities and owner's equity	$21,867

Using the Information in the Financial Statements

Now that you are familiar with the components of the classified balance sheet, you should look more closely at Second Cup's balance sheet, reproduced in Appendix A at the end of this text. While you will note some variations of presentation, the format is very similar to other companies' reporting practices illustrated in this chapter.

Users of financial statements look closely at many relationships between the figures on the balance sheet. One important relationship is between current assets and current liabilities. The difference between current assets and current liabilities is called working capital. Working capital is important in order to evaluate a company's liquidity—it represents the company's ability to pay obligations that become due within the next year or operating cycle. When current assets exceed current liabilities at the balance sheet date, the likelihood for paying the liabilities is favourable. When the reverse is true, short-term creditors may not be paid.

The Second Cup's working capital is a negative $989,000, as shown in Illustration 4-18.

STUDY OBJECTIVE
••••••••• **7** •••••••••
Illustrate measures used to evaluate liquidity.

Illustration 4-18

Calculation of working capital

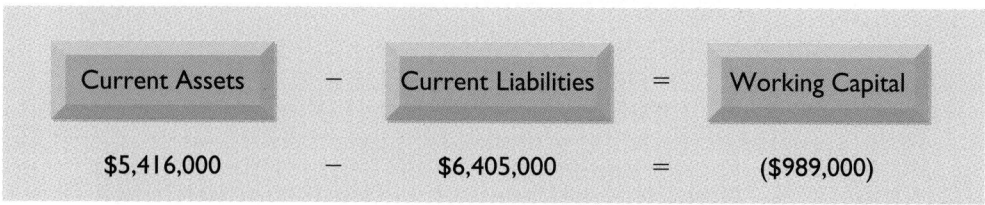

Current Assets	–	Current Liabilities	=	Working Capital
$5,416,000	–	$6,405,000	=	($989,000)

The relationship can also be expressed as a ratio, called the current ratio. The current ratio is calculated by dividing current assets by current liabilities. The current ratio for Second Cup for 2000 is as follows:

Illustration 4-19

Calculation of current ratio

Current Assets	÷	Current Liabilities	=	Current Ratio
$5,416,000	÷	$6,405,000	=	0.8:1

A current ratio of less than 1 to 1 (1:1) indicates that Second Cup does not have sufficient current assets on hand to cover current liabilities. Of course, not all the current liabilities have to paid at this point in time. Additional current assets may be generated in the future. Second Cup comments in its annual report that its working capital is lower than normal due to a special dividend paid to shareholders on May 31, 2000. Still, a negative working capital and a current ratio of 0.8:1 may be indicative of future liquidity problems and should be closely watched.

It is important to be aware that norms vary between companies and between industries. Ratios should never be interpreted without considering certain factors. The current ratio and other ratios should be assessed (1) in reference to general economic and industry conditions, (2) in connection with other specific financial information about the firm over time, and (3) in comparison with other firms in the same or related industries. We will discuss how to analyse ratios further in Chapter 19.

Before You Go On . . .

▶ Review It

THE
NAVIGATOR

1. What are the major sections in a classified balance sheet?
2. What is working capital? How might it be expressed as a ratio?
3. Using Second Cup's balance sheet, identify the components of its current assets and current liabilities at June 24, 2000. Can you tell if current assets and current liabilities are listed in order of liquidity, or in some other order? The answer to these questions is provided at the end of this chapter.

Related exercise material: BE4–8, BE4–9, E4–5, E4–6, E4–7, and E4–8.

▶ A Look Back at Our Feature Story

Refer to the feature story about Moulé, and answer the following questions:
1. Moulé uses a computer system; we have primarily focused on manual accounting systems. Does the accounting cycle seem to be any different in a computerized environment compared to a manual environment?
2. Why does Moulé close its books annually?
3. Mr. Gorenstein discussed adjusting and correcting the books with his accountant. When are adjusting entries usually prepared? Correcting entries? Would a cheque posted to the wrong account be fixed with an adjusting entry or a correcting entry?

Solution

1. The accounting cycle is the same for a computerized or manual environment.
2. Temporary accounts (revenues, expenses, and owner's drawings) are closed annually, to (1) make the records ready for the next fiscal year's postings, and (2) transfer the period's net income (loss) and drawings to update owner's capital.
3. Adjusting entries are journalized and posted at the end of the period, month end in this case. Correcting entries should be made whenever an error is found. It sounds as though Moulé's

accountant checks the books once a month. Adjusting and correcting entries are both executed monthly. That's fine as long as no one relies on incorrect balances in the interim. A correcting entry is required to fix the cheque that was recorded in the wrong account.

DEMONSTRATION PROBLEM

At the end of its first month of operations, the Paquet Answering Service has the following unadjusted trial balance, with the accounts presented in alphabetical order rather than in financial statement order:

**Additional
Demonstration Problem**

PAQUET ANSWERING SERVICE
August 31, 2003
Trial Balance

	Debit	Credit
Accounts Payable		$ 2,400
Accounts Receivable	$ 2,800	
Accumulated Amortization—Building		500
Accumulated Amortization—Equipment		1,000
Advertising Expense	400	
Amortization Expense	1,500	
Building	150,000	
Ryan Paquet, Capital		129,000
Cash	5,400	
Ryan Paquet, Drawings	1,000	
Equipment	60,000	
Insurance Expense	200	
Interest Expense	350	
Interest Payable		1,350
Land	50,000	
Notes Payable		140,000
Prepaid Insurance	2,200	
Salaries Expense	3,200	
Service Revenue		4,900
Supplies	1,000	
Supplies Expense	300	
Utilities Expense	800	
Totals	$279,150	$279,150

Action Plan
- Identify which accounts are balance sheet accounts and which accounts are income statement accounts.
- In preparing a classified balance sheet, know the contents of each of the sections.
- In journalizing closing entries, remember that there are only three entries, and that the drawings account is closed to owner's capital.
- Always check your work. Make sure that ending owner's capital in the general ledger equals the balance reported on the balance sheet.

Instructions

(a) Prepare a classified balance sheet for Paquet Answering Service at August 31, 2003. Assume
that $5,000 of the notes payable is currently due.
(b) Journalize the closing entries.

Solution to Demonstration Problem

(a)

PAQUET ANSWERING SERVICE
Balance Sheet
August 31, 2003

Assets

Current assets			
Cash			$ 5,400
Accounts receivable			2,800
Prepaid insurance			2,200
Supplies			1,000
Total current assets			11,400
Capital assets			
Land		$ 50,000	
Building	$150,000		
Less: Accumulated amortization—building	500	149,500	
Equipment	$ 60,000		
Less: Accumulated amortization—equipment	1,000	59,000	258,500
Total assets			$269,900

Liabilities and Owner's Equity

Current liabilities		
Notes payable		$ 5,000
Accounts payable		2,400
Interest payable		1,350
Total current liabilities		8,750
Long-term liabilities		
Notes payable		135,000
Total liabilities		143,750
Owner's equity		
Ryan Paquet, capital		126,150*
Total liabilities and owner's equity		$269,900

(b)

Aug. 31	Service Revenue	4,900	
	Ryan Paquet, Capital		4,900
	To close revenue account to capital.		
31	Ryan Paquet, Capital	6,750	
	Salaries Expense		3,200
	Amortization Expense		1,500
	Utilities Expense		800
	Interest Expense		350
	Advertising Expense		400
	Supplies Expense		300
	Insurance Expense		200
	To close expense accounts to capital.		
31	Ryan Paquet, Capital	1,000	
	Ryan Paquet, Drawings		1,000
	To close drawings to capital.		

*Ryan Paquet, Capital

Date	Explanation	Ref.	Debit	Credit	Balance
2003					
Aug.				129,000	129,000
31	Closing Entry			4,900	133,900
31	Closing Entry		6,750		127,150
31	Closing Entry		1,000		126,150

THE
NAVIGATOR

APPENDIX 4A ▸ *Using a Work Sheet in an Electronic World*

As discussed in the chapter, a work sheet is a multiple-column form that may be used in the adjustment process and in preparing financial statements. The five steps for preparing a work sheet are described in the next section. The steps must be performed in the sequence shown.

> **STUDY OBJECTIVE**
> ·········· ▼ ··········
> **8**
> *Prepare a work sheet.*

Steps in Preparing a Work Sheet

We will use the October 31 trial balance and adjustment data for Pioneer Advertising from Chapter 3 to illustrate the preparation of a work sheet. Each step of the process is described below, and demonstrated in Illustration 4A-1.

Step 1. Prepare a Trial Balance on the Work Sheet. All ledger accounts with balances are entered in the account title space. Debit and credit amounts from the ledger are entered in the trial balance columns. The work sheet trial balance for Pioneer Advertising Agency is shown in Illustration 4A-1 (Steps 1–3) and 4A-2 (Steps 1–5).

Step 2. Enter the Adjustments in the Adjustment Columns. When a work sheet is used, all adjustments are entered in the adjustment columns. In entering the adjustments, relevant trial balance accounts should be used. If additional accounts are needed, they should be inserted on the lines immediately below the trial balance totals.

In a manually prepared work sheet, each adjustment is cross-referenced (usually by letter) to make it easier to journalize the adjusting entry in the general journal. This has been done in Illustration 4A-1. **It is important to realize that year-end adjustments must still be journalized, but not until after the work sheet is completed and the financial statements have been prepared.** The books should not be filled with interim adjustments unless they need to show the adjusted information on a more timely basis.

The adjustments on Pioneer Advertising Agency's work sheet are the same as the adjustments displayed in Illustration 3-9. They are recorded in the adjustments columns of the work sheet as follows:
(a) An additional account, Advertising Supplies Expense, is debited $1,500 for the cost of supplies used, and Advertising Supplies is credited $1,500.
(b) An additional account, Insurance Expense, is debited $50 for the insurance that has expired, and Prepaid Insurance is credited $50.
(c) Unearned Revenue is debited $400 for fees, and Service Revenue is credited $400.
(d) Accounts Receivable is debited $200 for fees earned but not billed, and Service Revenue is credited $200.
(e) Two additional accounts relating to interest are needed. Interest Expense is debited $25 for accrued interest, and Interest Payable is credited $25.
(f) Salaries Expense is debited $1,200 for accrued salaries, and an additional account, Salaries Payable, is credited $1,200.
(g) Two additional accounts are needed. Amortization Expense is debited $83 for the month's amortization, and Accumulated Amortization—Office Equipment is credited $83.

Note in the illustration that after all the adjustments have been entered, the adjustment columns are totalled, in this case automatically by the computer. And the equality of the column totals is proven.

Step 3. Enter the Adjusted Balances in the Adjusted Trial Balance Columns. The adjusted balance of an account is obtained by combining the amounts entered in the first four columns of the work sheet for each account. For example, the Prepaid Insurance

Illustration 4A-1

Preparing a work sheet—Steps 1–3

Work Sheet Walkthrough

Microsoft Excel - Illustration 4A-1.xls

Account Titles	Unadjusted Trial Balance Dr.	Cr.	Adjustments Dr.	Cr.	Adjusted Trial Balance Dr.	Cr.	Income Statement Dr.	Cr.	Balance Sheet Dr.	Cr.
Cash	15,200				15,200					
Accounts Receivable			200 (d)		200					
Advertising Supplies	2,500			(a) 1,500	1,000					
Prepaid Insurance	600			(b) 50	550					
Office Equipment	5,000				5,000					
Notes Payable		5,000				5,000				
Accounts Payable		2,500				2,500				
Unearned Revenue		1,200	(c) 400			800				
C. R. Byrd, Capital		10,000				10,000				
C. R. Byrd, Drawings	500				500					
Service Revenue		10,000		(c) 400 / (d) 200		10,600				
Salaries Expense	4,000		(f) 1,200		5,200					
Advertising Supplies Expense			(a) 1,500		1,500					
Rent Expense	900				900					
Insurance Expense			(b) 50		50					
Interest Expense			(e) 25		25					
Interest Payable				(e) 25		25				
Salaries Payable				(f) 1,200		1,200				
Amortization Expense			(g) 83		83					
Accumulated Amortization—Office Equipment				(g) 83		83				
Totals	28,700	28,700	3,458	3,458	30,208	30,208				

1. Prepare a trial balance on the work sheet.

2. Enter adjustment data.

3. Enter adjusted balances.

account in the trial balance columns has a $600 debit balance and a $50 credit in the adjustments columns. These two amounts combine to result in a $550 debit balance in the adjusted trial balance columns. **For each account on the work sheet, the amount in the adjusted trial balance columns is equal to the account balance that will appear in the ledger after the adjusting entries have been journalized and posted.** The balances in these columns are the same as those in the adjusted trial balance in Illustration 4-4.

After all account balances have been entered in the adjusted trial balance columns, the columns are totalled and their equality is proven. The agreement of the column totals makes it easier to complete the work sheet. If these columns are not in agreement, the error(s) must be found before the computer program will allow you to proceed. If the errors are not found, the statement columns will not balance and the financial statements will be incorrect.

Step 4. Enter the Adjusted Trial Balance Amounts in the Appropriate Financial Statement Columns. The fourth step is to enter adjusted trial balance amounts in the income statement or balance sheet columns of the work sheet. Balance sheet accounts are entered in the appropriate balance sheet debit and credit columns. For instance, Cash is entered in the balance sheet debit column and Notes Payable is entered in the credit column. Because the work sheet does not have columns for the statement of owner's equity, the balance in Owner's Capital is entered in the balance sheet credit column. In addition, the balance in the owner's drawings account is entered in the balance sheet debit column because it is an owner's equity account with a debit balance.

The amounts in expense and revenue accounts such as Salaries Expense and Service Revenue are entered in the appropriate income statement columns. All of these extensions are shown in Illustration 4A-2. Before you turn to this illustration, study the accounts in Illustration 4A-1 and try to determine on your own which adjusted trial balance amounts would be extended to which financial statement columns.

Step 5. Total the Statement Columns, Calculate the Net Income (or Net Loss), and Complete the Work Sheet. Each of the financial statement columns must be totalled. The net income or loss for the period is then found by calculating the difference between the totals of the two income statement columns. If total credits exceed total debits, net income has resulted. In such a case, as shown in Illustration 4A-2, the words "Net income" are inserted in the account title space. The amount is then entered in the income statement debit column and the balance sheet credit column. **This balances the income statement columns and the balance sheet columns.** In addition, the credit in the balance sheet column indicates the increase in owner's equity that results from net income. Conversely, if total debits in the income statement columns exceed total credits, a net loss has occurred. In such a case, the amount of the net loss is entered in the income statement credit column and the balance sheet debit column.

After the net income or net loss has been entered, new column totals are determined. The totals shown in the debit and credit income statement columns will now match. The totals shown in the debit and credit balance sheet columns will also match. If either the income statement columns or the balance sheet columns are not equal after the net income or net loss has been entered, there is an error in the work sheet.

Helpful hint Every adjusted trial balance amount must appear in one of the four statement columns. Debit amounts go to debit columns and credit amounts go to credit columns.

Preparing Financial Statements from a Work Sheet

After a work sheet has been completed, all the data required to prepare the financial statements are at hand. The income statement is prepared from the income statement columns. The balance sheet and statement of owner's equity are prepared from the balance sheet columns.

Illustration 4A-2

Preparing a work sheet—Steps 1–5

Work Sheet Walkthrough

Microsoft Excel - Illustration 4A-2.xls

Account Titles	Unadjusted Trial Balance Dr.	Unadjusted Trial Balance Cr.	Adjustments Dr.	Adjustments Cr.	Adjusted Trial Balance Dr.	Adjusted Trial Balance Cr.	Income Statement Dr.	Income Statement Cr.	Balance Sheet Dr.	Balance Sheet Cr.
Cash	15,200				15,200				15,200	
Accounts Receivable			200 (d)		200				200	
Advertising Supplies	2,500			1,500 (a)	1,000				1,000	
Prepaid Insurance	600			50 (b)	550				550	
Office Equipment	5,000				5,000				5,000	
Notes Payable		5,000				5,000				5,000
Accounts Payable		2,500				2,500				2,500
Unearned Revenue		1,200	400 (c)			800				800
C. R. Byrd, Capital		10,000				10,000				10,000
C. R. Byrd, Drawings	500				500				500	
Service Revenue		10,000		400 (c) 200 (d)		10,600		10,600		
Salaries Expense	4,000		1,200 (f)		5,200		5,200			
Advertising Supplies Expense			1,500 (a)		1,500		1,500			
Rent Expense	900				900		900			
Insurance Expense			50 (b)		50		50			
Interest Expense			25 (e)		25		25			
Interest Payable				25 (e)		25				25
Salaries Payable				1,200 (f)		1,200				1,200
Amortization Expense			83 (g)		83		83			
Accumulated Amortization—Office Equipment				83 (g)		83				83
Totals	28,700	28,700	3,458	3,458	30,208	30,208	7,758	10,600	22,450	19,608
Net income							2,842			2,842
Totals							10,600	10,600	22,450	22,450

1. Prepare a trial balance on the work sheet.

2. Enter adjustment data.

3. Enter adjusted balances.

4. Enter adjusted balances in appropriate statement columns.

5. Total the statement columns, calculate net income, (or net loss), and complete work sheet.

Using a work sheet, accountants can prepare financial statements before adjusting entries have been journalized and posted. However, **the completed work sheet is not a substitute for formal financial statements**. Data in the financial statement columns of the work sheet are not properly arranged for statement purposes. Also, as noted earlier, the financial statement presentation for some accounts differs from their statement columns on the work sheet. A work sheet is basically a working tool of the accountant. It is not distributed to management or other parties.

Before You Go On . . .

►Review It

1. What are the five steps in preparing a work sheet?
2. How is net income or net loss shown in a work sheet?
3. How does a work sheet relate to preparing financial statements and adjusting entries?

► Do It

David Johnson is preparing a work sheet. Explain to David how the following adjusted trial balance accounts should be entered in the financial statement columns of the work sheet: Cash; Accumulated Amortization; Accounts Payable; D. Johnson, Drawings; Service Revenue; and Salaries Expense.

Reasoning

- Identify which accounts are income statement accounts and which are balance sheet accounts.
- Identify the normal (debit or credit) balances of each account.
- Enter the account balance in the appropriate debit or credit columns of either the income statement or the balance sheet.

Solution

Income statement debit column—Salaries Expense
Income statement credit column—Service Revenue
Balance sheet debit column—Cash; D. Johnson, Drawings
Balance sheet credit column—Accumulated Amortization; Accounts Payable

THE
NAVIGATOR

Related exercise material: *BE4–10, *BE4–11, *E4–9, and *E4–10.

APPENDIX 4B ► *Reversing Entries*

After the financial statements are prepared and the books are closed, it is often helpful to reverse some of the adjusting entries before recording the regular transactions of the next period. Such entries are called **reversing entries. A reversing entry is made at the beginning of the next accounting period and is the exact opposite of the adjusting entry made in the previous period.** The recording of reversing entries is an **optional** step in the accounting cycle.

> **STUDY OBJECTIVE**
> ·········▼9·········
> *Prepare reversing entries.*

The purpose of reversing entries is to simplify the recording of subsequent transactions related to an adjusting entry. As you may recall from Chapter 3, to bill the accounts in November after accruing amounts earned in October, you had to remember that an adjusting entry had been made. This prevented the $200 of service revenue from being recorded twice. Accounts Receivable and Service Revenue in November were recorded as $2,800, not the $3,000 amount billed in November. With reversing entries, the entire billing can be debited to Accounts Receivable and credited to Service Revenue. You don't have to remember what has gone on before. The use of reversing entries does not change the amounts reported in the financial statements. What it does is simplify the recording of future transactions.

Illustration of Reversing Entries

Reversing entries are most often used to reverse accruals: accrued revenues and accrued expenses. They are seldom needed for prepayments (prepaid expenses or unearned revenues) or for estimates. To illustrate the optional use of reversing entries for accrued revenues, we will use the unbilled services transactions for Pioneer Advertising Agency. The transaction and adjustment data were as follows:

1. October 31 (adjusting entry): Service revenue earned in October but not yet billed is $200. This will be billed November 10 and subsequently collected from clients.
2. November 10 (subsequent billing entry): Bills that total $3,000 are prepared and mailed to clients. Of this amount, $200 is related to services performed in October.

Illustration 4B-1

Comparative entries—not reversing versus reversing

The comparative entries when not using reversing entries and when using them are shown in Illustration 4B-1.

When Reversing Entries Are Not Used (as in the chapter)				When Reversing Entries Are Used (as in the appendix)		
Adjusting Entry				**Adjusting Entry**		
Oct. 31	Accounts Receivable	200		Oct. 31	Accounting Receivable	200
	Service Revenue		200		Service Revenue		200
Closing Entry				**Closing Entry**		
Oct. 31	Service Revenue	200		Oct. 31	Service Revenue	200
	C. R. Byrd, Capital		200		C. R. Byrd, Capital		200
Reversing Entry				**Reversing Entry**		
Nov. 1	No reversing entry is made			Nov. 1	Service Revenue	200
					Accounts Receivable		200
Subsequent Billing Entry				**Subsequent Billing Entry**		
Nov. 10	Accounts Receivable	2,800		Nov. 10	Accounts Receivable	3,000
	Service Revenue		2,800		Service Revenue		3,000

Helpful hint The differences between reversing entries and other entries:

1. Reversing entries are made only at the beginning of the next period.
2. Abnormal balances in expense (or revenue) accounts temporarily result after posting reversing entries.
3. Expense accounts are subsequently debited for the full payment, and revenue accounts credited for the amount billed.

Illustration 4B-2

Postings with reversing entries

The first two entries are the same whether or not reversing entries are used. The last two entries are different. The November 1 **reversing entry** eliminates the $200 balance in Accounts Receivable that was created by the October 31 adjusting entry. The reversing entry also creates a $200 debit balance in the Service Revenue account. As you have already learned, it is unusual for a revenue account to have a debit balance. The balance is correct in this instance. It anticipates that the entire amount of the first billing in the new accounting period will be credited to Service Revenue. This credit entry will eliminate the debit balance. The resulting credit balance in the revenue account will equal the revenue earned in the new accounting period ($2,800 in this example).

When reversing entries are made, all billing of revenue can be credited to the revenue account. This means that on November 10 (and for future billings), Service Revenue can be credited for the amount billed without considering any accrued revenues. Being able to make the same entry each time simplifies the recording process. Future transactions can be recorded as if the related adjusting entry had never been made.

The posting of the entries that result when reversing entries are used is shown in Illustration 4B-2, using T accounts.

Accounts Receivable			
10/31 Adjusting	200	11/01 Reversing	200
11/10 Billings	3,000		
Balance	3,000		

Service Revenue			
10/31 Closing	200	10/31 Adjusting	200
		Balance	0
11/01 Reversing	200	11/10 Billings	3,000
		Balance	2,800

Before You Go On . . .

►*Review It*

1. What is the purpose of reversing entries?

Related exercise material: *BE4–12 and *E4–11.

Summary of Study Objectives

1. *Describe the purpose of a work sheet.* The work sheet is a device used to make it easier to prepare adjusting entries and financial statements.

2. *Demonstrate the process of closing the books.* Closing the books occurs at the end of an accounting period by journalizing and posting the closing entries. In closing the books, separate entries are made to close revenues and expenses to owner's capital, and owner's drawings to owner's capital. Only temporary accounts (revenue, expense, and owner's drawings) are closed.

3. *Describe and produce a post-closing trial balance.* A post-closing trial balance contains the balances in permanent (balance sheet) accounts that are carried forward to the next accounting period. The purpose of this, as with other trial balances, is to prove the equality of these balances.

4. *State the steps in the accounting cycle.* The steps in the accounting cycle are (1) analyse business transactions, (2) journalize the transactions, (3) post to ledger accounts, (4) prepare a trial balance, (5) journalize and post adjusting entries, (6) prepare an adjusted trial balance, (7) prepare financial statements, (8) journalize and post closing entries, and (9) prepare a post-closing trial balance.

5. *Explain and demonstrate the approaches to preparing correcting entries.* One approach for determining the correcting entry is to compare the incorrect entry with the correct entry. After comparison, a correcting entry is made to correct the accounts. An equally acceptable alternative is to reverse the incorrect entry and then record the correct entry.

6. *Identify and prepare the various sections of a classified balance sheet.* In a classified balance sheet, assets are classified as current assets, long-term investments, and capital assets. Liabilities are classified as either current or long-term. There is also an owner's equity section, which varies with the form of business organization.

7. *Illustrate measures used to evaluate liquidity.* The excess of current assets over current liabilities is called working capital. This can also be expressed as a ratio (current assets ÷ current liabilities), and used to assess short-term liquidity.

8. *Prepare a work sheet (Appendix 4A).* The steps in preparing a work sheet are (1) prepare a trial balance on the work sheet, (2) enter the adjustments in the adjustments columns, (3) enter adjusted balances in the adjusted trial balance columns, (4) enter adjusted trial balance amounts in appropriate financial statement columns, and (5) total the statement columns, calculate net income (or net loss), and complete the work sheet.

9. *Prepare reversing entries (Appendix 4B).* A reversing entry is the direct opposite of the adjusting entry made in the preceding period. It is made at the beginning of a new accounting period to simplify the recording of later transactions related to the adjusting entry. In most cases, only accrued adjusting entries are reversed.

GLOSSARY

 Key Term Matching Activity

Capital assets Tangible (property, plant, and equipment and natural resources) and intangible long-lived resources that are used in the operations of the business. (p. 168)

Classified balance sheet A balance sheet that contains a number of classifications or sections. (p. 167)

Closing entries Entries made at the end of an accounting period to transfer the balances of temporary accounts (revenues, expenses, and drawings) to the permanent owner's equity account, Owner's Capital. (p. 158)

Closing the books The process of journalizing and posting closing entries, to update the capital account and prepare the temporary accounts for the next period's postings. (p. 158)

Correcting entries Entries to correct errors made in recording transactions. (p. 165)

Current assets Cash and other resources that are expected to be realized in cash or sold or consumed in the business within one year or the operating cycle, whichever is longer. (p. 167)

Current liabilities Obligations expected to be paid from current assets or through the creation of other current liabilities within the next year or operating cycle, whichever is longer. (p. 169)

Current ratio A measure of short-term debt paying ability determined by dividing current assets by current liabilities. (p. 171)

Liquidity The ability of a company to pay obligations that are expected to become due within the next year or operating cycle. (p. 171)

Long-term investments Resources not expected to be realized in cash within the next year or operating cycle. (p. 168)

Long-term liabilities Obligations expected to be paid after one year. (p. 169)

Operating cycle The average time required to go from cash to cash in producing revenues. (p. 167)

Permanent accounts Balance sheet accounts whose balances are carried forward to the next accounting period. (p. 158)

Post-closing trial balance A list of debit and credit balances of the permanent (balance sheet) accounts after closing entries have been journalized and posted. (p. 163)

Reversing entry An entry made at the beginning of the next accounting period that is the exact opposite of the adjusting entry made in the previous period. (p. 164)

Shareholders' equity The ownership claim of shareholders on total assets. It is to a corporation what owner's equity is to a proprietorship. (p. 170)

Temporary accounts Revenue, expense, and drawings accounts whose balances are transferred to owner's capital at the end of an accounting period. (p. 158)

Working capital The excess of current assets over current liabilities. (p. 171)

Work sheet A multiple-column form that may be used in the adjustment process and in preparing financial statements. (p. 156)

Note: All **asterisked** Questions, Exercises, and Problems below relate to material contained in the appendices to the chapter.

SELF-STUDY QUESTIONS

 Chapter 4 Self-Test

Answers are at the end of the chapter.

(SO 1) K   1. Which of the following statements regarding the work sheet is *incorrect*?
   a. The work sheet is essentially a working tool of the accountant.
   b. The work sheet is distributed to investors and other interested parties.
   c. The work sheet cannot be used as a basis for posting to ledger accounts.
   d. Financial statements can be prepared directly from the work sheet before journalizing and posting the adjusting entries.

(SO 2) K   2. An account that will have a zero balance after closing entries have been journalized and posted is:
   a. Service Revenue.
   b. Advertising Supplies.
   c. Prepaid Insurance.
   d. Accumulated Amortization.

(SO 2) K   3. To close an expense account, the expense account is:
   a. debited, and owner's capital credited.
   b. credited, and owner's capital debited.
   c. debited, and owner's drawings credited.
   d. credited, and owner's drawings debited.

(SO 2) K   4. After the closing entries have been posted, the balance in the owner's capital account should equal:
   a. the net income reported on the income statement.
   b. the opening capital balance reported on the statement of owner's equity.
   c. the ending capital balance reported on the statement of owner's equity and balance sheet.
   d. the opening capital balance plus any investments made by the owner during the period.

5. Which types of accounts will appear in the post-closing trial balance?   (SO 3) K
   a. Permanent (balance sheet) accounts
   b. Temporary (revenue, expense, and drawings) accounts
   c. All accounts
   d. None of the above

6. Which of the following is an optional step in the accounting cycle?   (SO 4) K
   a. Journalizing and posting closing entries
   b. Preparing an adjusted trial balance
   c. Preparing a post-closing trial balance
   d. Preparing a work sheet

7. Cash of $100 is received at the time a service is provided. The transaction is journalized and posted as a debit to Cash of $100 and a credit to Accounts Receivable of $100. Assuming the incorrect entry is not reversed, the correcting entry is: (SO 5) K
   a. debit Service Revenue $100 and credit Accounts Receivable $100.
   b. debit Accounts Receivable $100 and credit Service Revenue $100.
   c. debit Cash $100 and credit Service Revenue $100.
   d. debit Accounts Receivable $100 and credit Cash $100.

8. Current assets are listed: (SO 6) K
   a. by liquidity.
   b. by importance.
   c. by longevity.
   d. alphabetically.

(SO 7) AP 9. A company reports current assets of $10,000 and current liabilities of $8,000. Its current ratio is:
    a. $2,000.
    b. 80%.
    c. 1.25:1.
    d. Insufficient information is provided to calculate the ratio.

(SO 8) K *10. In a work sheet, net income is entered in the following columns:
    a. income statement (Dr.) and balance sheet (Dr.).
    b. income statement (Cr.) and balance sheet (Dr.).
    c. income statement (Dr.) and balance sheet (Cr.).
    d. income statement (Cr.) and balance sheet (Cr.).

*11. On December 31, the Mott Company correctly made (SO 9) AP an adjusting entry to recognize $2,000 of accrued salaries payable. On January 8 of the next year, total salaries of $3,400 were paid. Assuming the correct reversing entry was made on January 1, the entry on January 8 will result in a credit to Cash of $3,400, and the following debit(s):
    a. Salaries Payable $1,400, and Salaries Expense $2,000.
    b. Salaries Payable $2,000, and Salaries Expense $1,400.
    c. Salaries Expense $3,400.
    d. Salaries Payable $3,400.

THE NAVIGATOR

QUESTIONS

(SO 1) C 1. A work sheet is a permanent accounting record and its use is required in the accounting cycle. Do you agree? Explain.

(SO 1) C 2. Why is it necessary to prepare formal financial statements, if all of the data are in the statement columns of the work sheet?

(SO 2) C 3. How do closing entries differ from adjusting entries?

(SO 2) C 4. Identify the account(s) debited and credited in each of the three closing entries.

(SO 3) C 5. What are the content and purpose of a post-closing trial balance?

(SO 3) K 6. Which of the following accounts would not appear in the post-closing trial balance: (a) Interest Payable, (b) Equipment, (c) Amortization Expense, (d) Ben Alschuler, Drawings, (e) Unearned Revenue, (f) Accumulated Amortization—Equipment, and (g) Service Revenue?

(SO 3) K 7. Identify, in the sequence in which they are prepared, the three trial balances that are required in the accounting cycle.

(SO 4) C 8. The use of a work sheet affects two steps of the accounting cycle after the trial balance is prepared. What are the steps, and how are they affected by the work sheet?

(SO 4) K 9. Indicate, in the sequence in which they are made, the three required steps in the accounting cycle that involve journalizing.

(SO 5) C 10. How do correcting entries differ from adjusting entries?

11. What standard classifications are used to prepare a classified balance sheet? (SO 6) K

12. What is meant by the term "operating cycle"? (SO 6) K

13. Define current assets. What basis is used for arranging individual items within the current assets section? (SO 6) C

14. Distinguish between long-term investments and capital assets. (SO 6) C

15. How do current liabilities differ from long-term liabilities? (SO 6) C

16. (a) What is the term used to describe the owner's equity section of a corporation? (b) Identify the two owner's equity accounts in a corporation and indicate the purpose of each. (SO 6) K

17. What is liquidity? Identify one measure of liquidity. (SO 7) C

*18. If a company's revenues are $122,000 and its expenses are $113,000, in which financial statement columns of the work sheet will the net income of $9,000 appear? When expenses exceed revenues, in which columns will the difference appear? (SO 8) K

*19. Distinguish between a reversing entry and an adjusting entry. Are reversing entries required? (SO 9) C

*20. At December 31, interest payable totalled $4,500. On January 10, interest of $5,000 is paid. (a) Assuming that reversing entries are made at January 1, give the January 10 entry and indicate the Interest Expense account balance after the entry is posted. (b) Repeat part (a), assuming reversing entries are not made. (SO 9) AP

BRIEF EXERCISES

List steps in preparing work sheet.
(SO 1) K

BE4–1   The steps in using a work sheet are presented in random order below. List the steps in the proper order by placing numbers 1–5 in the blank spaces.

(a) _____   Total the statement columns, calculate net income (loss), and enter it on the work sheet.

(b) _____   Enter adjustment data.

(c) _____   Prepare a trial balance on the work sheet.

(d) _____   Enter adjusted balances.

(e) _____   Enter adjusted balances in appropriate statement columns.

Prepare closing entries.
(SO 2) AP

BE4–2   The ledger of the Khalifa Company contains the following balances: T. Khalifa, Capital $30,000; T. Khalifa, Drawings $2,000; Service Revenue $50,000; Salaries Expense $26,000; and Supplies Expense $4,000. Prepare the closing entries at December 31.

Post closing entries.
(SO 2) AP

BE4–3   Using the data in BE4–2, enter the balances in general ledger accounts. Post the closing entries, and balance the accounts.

Prepare and post closing entries.
(SO 2) AP

BE4–4   The income statement for the Edgebrook Golf Club for the month ending July 31 shows, Green Fees Earned $26,000; Salaries Expense $8,200; Maintenance Expense $2,500; and Members' Capital $50,000. Prepare the entries to close the revenue and expense accounts. Post the entries to the revenue, expense, and capital accounts, and complete the closing process for these accounts.

Identify post-closing trial balance accounts.
(SO 3) C

BE4–5   The following selected accounts (amounts in thousands of dollars) appear in the financial statements of **The Jean Coutu Group (PJC) Inc.**:

Accounts payable	$ 181,060
Accounts receivable	132,305
Amortization expense	40,455
Capital assets	185,028
Cash	5,861
Interest on long-term debt expense	12,143
Long-term debt	162,579
Other revenues	170,478
Prepaid expenses	3,414
Sales	2,118,892

Identify the accounts that would be included in a post-closing trial balance.

List steps in accounting cycle.
(SO 4) K

BE4–6   The required steps in the accounting cycle are listed below in random order. List the steps in the proper sequence by placing numbers 1–9 in the blank spaces.

(a) _____   Prepare a post-closing trial balance.

(b) _____   Prepare an adjusted trial balance.

(c) _____   Analyse business transactions.

(d) _____   Prepare a trial balance.

(e) _____   Journalize the transactions.

(f) _____   Journalize and post the closing entries.

(g) _____   Prepare the financial statements.

(h) _____   Journalize and post the adjusting entries.

(i) _____   Post to the ledger accounts.

Indicate impact of error on financial statements and prepare correcting entries.
(SO 5) AP

BE4–7   At Hébert Company, the following errors were discovered after the transactions had been journalized and posted:

1. A collection on account from a customer for $780 was recorded as a debit to Cash of $780 and a credit to Service Revenue of $780.

2. The purchase of office supplies on account for $1,730 was recorded as a debit to Equipment of $1,370 and a credit to Accounts Payable of $1,370.

   (a) Indicate the impact of each error on the balance sheet and income statement by stating whether assets, liabilities, owner's equity, revenue, expense, and net income are understated (U), overstated (O), or not affected (NA).

   (b) Prepare the correcting entries.

BE4–8 The adjusted trial balance of Reuben Company includes the following accounts: Accounts Receivable $12,500; Prepaid Insurance $3,600; Cash $18,400; Supplies $5,200; and Short-Term Investments $8,200. Prepare the current assets section of the balance sheet as at December 31, 2002, listing the accounts in proper sequence.

Prepare current assets section of balance sheet.
(SO 6) AP

BE4–9 These selected condensed data are taken from a recent balance sheet of **Bob Evans Farms**:

Cash	$ 8,241,000
Marketable securities	1,947,000
Accounts receivable	12,545,000
Inventories	14,814,000
Other current assets	5,371,000
Total current assets	$42,918,000
Total current liabilities	$44,844,000

Calculate (a) the working capital and (b) the current ratio for Bob Evans Farms.

Calculate working capital and current ratio.
(SO 7) AP

*BE4–10 The ledger of Coulombe Company includes the following unadjusted balances: Prepaid Insurance $4,000; Service Revenue $58,000; and Salaries Expense $25,000. Adjusting entries are required for (1) Expired insurance $1,200, (2) Services provided but unbilled and uncollected $900, and (3) Accrued salaries payable $800. (a) Enter the unadjusted balances and adjustments into a work sheet. (b) Complete the work sheet. *Note*: You will need to add additional accounts.

Prepare partial work sheet.
(SO 8) AP

*BE4–11 The following accounts appear in the adjusted trial balance columns of the work sheet for the Khanna Company: Accounts Payable; Accounts Receivable; Accumulated Amortization; Amortization Expense; H. Khanna, Capital; H. Khanna, Drawings; and Service Revenue. Indicate the financial statement column (income statement Dr., balance sheet Cr., etc.) to which each balance should be extended (recorded in).

Identify work sheet columns for selected accounts.
(SO 8) C

*BE4–12 At October 31, Orlaida Company made an accrued expense adjusting entry of $800 for salaries. Prepare the reversing entry on November 1 and indicate the balances in Salaries Payable and Salaries Expense after posting the reversing entry.

Prepare and post reversing entry.
(SO 9) AP

EXERCISES

E4–1 Selected T accounts for Eden Beauty Salon are presented below. All June 30 postings are from closing entries.

Prepare closing entries.
(SO 2) AP

Salaries Expense			
6/10	3,200	6/30	7,800
6/28	4,600		
Balance	0		

Service Revenue			
6/30	15,600	6/15	7,200
		6/24	8,400
		Balance	0

B. Eden, Capital			
6/30	12,800	6/1	12,000
6/30	2,500	6/30	15,600
		Balance	12,300

Supplies Expense			
6/12	800	6/30	1,500
6/24	700		
Balance	0		

Rent Expense			
6/1	3,500	6/30	3,500
Balance	0		

B. Eden, Drawings			
6/13	1,000	6/30	2,500
6/25	1,500		
Balance	0		

Instructions

(a) Prepare the closing entries that were made.
(b) Explain which account(s) from which financial statement(s) the ending balance of B. Eden, Capital should agree with.

Journalize and post closing entries and prepare post-closing trial balance.
(SO 2, 3) AP

E4–2   At the end of its fiscal year, the adjusted trial balance of Rafael Company is as follows:

RAFAEL COMPANY
Adjusted Trial Balance
July 31, 2003

No.	Account Titles	Debits	Credits
101	Cash	$ 14,940	
112	Accounts Receivable	8,780	
157	Equipment	15,900	
167	Accumulated Amortization		$ 5,400
201	Accounts Payable		6,220
208	Unearned Rent Revenue		1,800
301	R. Rafael, Capital		45,200
306	R. Rafael, Drawings	14,000	
404	Commission Revenue		63,100
429	Rent Revenue		6,500
711	Amortization Expense	4,000	
720	Salaries Expense	55,700	
729	Rent Expense	14,900	
	Totals	$128,220	$128,220

Instructions

(a) Prepare the closing entries, and post them to the appropriate accounts.
(b) Prepare a post-closing trial balance at July 31, 2003.

Journalize and post closing entries and prepare post-closing trial balance.
(SO 2, 3) AP

E4–3   The adjusted trial balance for Kwok Yuen Ho Company is presented in E4–9.

Instructions

(a) Journalize the closing entries at April 30.
(b) Post the closing entries.
(c) Prepare a post-closing trial balance at April 30, 2003.

Prepare correcting entries.
(SO 5) AP

E4–4   The Choi Company has an inexperienced accountant. During the first two weeks on the job, the accountant made the following errors in journalizing transactions. All incorrect entries were posted.

1. A payment on account of $830 to a creditor was debited to Accounts Payable $380, and credited to Cash $380.
2. The purchase of supplies on account for $500 was debited to Equipment $50, and credited to Accounts Payable $50.
3. A $400 withdrawal of cash for L. Choi's personal use was debited to Salaries Expense $400, and credited to Cash $400.
4. The purchase of $1,200 of office equipment with a three-year useful life was debited to Office Supplies.

Instructions

Prepare the correcting entries.

Prepare financial statements from adjusted trial balance.
(SO 6) AP

E4–5   The adjusted trial balance for Rafael Company is presented in E4–2.

Instructions

(a) Prepare an income statement and a statement of owner's equity for the year. Mr. Rafael did not make any capital investments during the year.
(b) Prepare a classified balance sheet at July 31, 2003.

Prepare financial statements from adjusted trial balance.
(SO 6) AP

E4–6   The adjusted trial balance for Kwok Yuen Ho Company is presented in E4–9.

Instructions

Prepare an income statement, a statement of owner's equity, and a classified balance sheet.

E4–7 The adjusted trial balance for Summit's Bowl-A-Drome Alley at December 31, 2002, contains the following accounts:

Prepare a classified balance sheet and comment on liquidity.
(SO 6, 7) AN

Debits		Credits	
Accounts Receivable	$ 14,520	Accounts Payable	$ 13,480
Amortization Expense	5,360	Accumulated Amortization—	
Building	128,800	Building	45,600
Cash	20,840	Accumulated Amortization—	
Equipment	62,400	Equipment	18,720
Insurance Expense	780	Bowling Revenues	14,180
Interest Expense	2,600	Interest Payable	2,600
Land	63,200	Mortgage Payable	93,600
Prepaid Insurance	4,680	T. Bolgos, Capital	115,000
	$303,180		$303,180

Instructions

(a) Prepare a classified balance sheet. Assume that $13,600 of the mortgage payable will be paid in the year 2003.

(b) Compare current assets and current liabilities and comment on the liquidity of the company.

E4–8 The **Québec Winter Carnival** is recognized as the world's biggest winter celebration, and is the world's third largest carnival (after those in Rio and New Orleans). The following data were taken from the Carnaval de Québec Inc.'s financial statements:

Calculate working capital and current ratio and comment on liquidity.
(SO 7) AN

	April 30, 2000	April 30, 1999	April 30, 1998
Current assets	$1,408,529	$1,064,667	$726,484
Current liabilities	568,035	401,111	315,589

Instructions

(a) Calculate the working capital and current ratio for each year.

(b) Discuss the Carnival's liquidity in 2000, compared to the prior two years.

*E4–9 The adjusted trial balance columns of the work sheet for Kwok Yuen Ho Company are as follows:

Prepare work sheet.
(SO 8) AP

KWOK YUEN HO COMPANY
Work Sheet (Partial)
For the Month Ended April 30, 2003

Account Titles	Adjusted Trial Balance Dr.	Cr.	Income Statement Dr.	Cr.	Balance Sheet Dr.	Cr.
Cash	15,052					
Accounts Receivable	7,840					
Prepaid Rent	2,280					
Equipment	23,050					
Accumulated Amortization		4,921				
Notes Payable		5,700				
Accounts Payable		5,972				
Ho, Capital		33,960				
Ho, Drawings	3,650					
Service Revenue		12,590				
Salaries Expense	9,840					
Rent Expense	760					
Amortization Expense	671					
Interest Expense	57					
Interest Payable		57				
Totals	63,200	63,200				

Instructions

Complete the work sheet.

Determine adjusting entries from work sheet data.
(SO 8) AP

*E4–10   Selected work sheet data for Blanchard Company are presented below:

Account Titles	Trial Balance Dr.	Trial Balance Cr.	Adjusted Trial Balance Dr.	Adjusted Trial Balance Cr.
Accounts Receivable	(1)		34,000	
Prepaid Insurance	26,000		18,000	
Supplies	9,000		(3)	
Accumulated Amortization		12,000		(5)
Salaries Payable				7,000
Service Revenue		88,000		94,000
Insurance Expense			(4)	
Amortization Expense			10,000	
Supplies Expense			4,000	
Salaries Expense	(2)		49,000	

Instructions

(a) Fill in the missing amounts.

(b) Prepare the adjusting entries that were made.

Prepare and post adjusting, closing, reversing, and subsequent entries.
(SO 2, 9) AP

*E4–11   On December 31, the unadjusted trial balance of Masterson Employment Agency shows the following selected data:

Accounts Receivable	$ 0	Commission Revenue	$92,000
Interest Expense	7,800	Interest Payable	0
Masterson, Capital	48,000		

Analysis shows that adjusting entries were made to (1) accrue $5,000 of commission revenue, and (2) accrue $2,000 of interest expense.

Instructions

(a) Prepare and post (1) the adjusting entries, and (2) the closing entries for the temporary accounts at December 31.

(b) Prepare and post the reversing entries on January 1.

(c) Prepare the entries to record (1) the collection of the $5,000 of accrued commissions on January 10, and (2) the payment of all interest owed on January 15.

(d) Post the entries from (c) to the appropriate accounts.

PROBLEMS: SET A

Prepare financial statements, closing entries, and post-closing trial balance.
(SO 2, 3, 6) AP

P4–1A   The adjusted trial balance for Gunter Company is shown below:

GUNTER COMPANY
Adjusted Trial Balance
December 31, 2002

Account No.	Account Titles	Dr.	Cr.
101	Cash	$ 6,600	
112	Accounts Receivable	13,500	
131	Prepaid Rent	3,500	
157	Equipment	26,000	
158	Accumulated Amortization		$ 5,600
201	Accounts Payable		13,300
212	Salaries Payable		3,000
301	N. Gunter, Capital		34,000
306	N. Gunter, Drawings	12,000	
400	Service Revenue		59,000
622	Repair Expense	1,800	
711	Amortization Expense	2,600	
726	Salaries Expense	35,000	
729	Rent Expense	12,200	
732	Utilities Expense	1,700	
	Totals	$114,900	$114,900

Instructions

(a) Prepare an income statement, statement of owner's equity, and classified balance sheet. Mr. Gunter made no additional investments during the year.
(b) Prepare the closing entries.
(c) Prepare general ledger accounts and post the closing entries.
(d) Prepare a post-closing trial balance.

P4–2A The following is Campus Cycle Shop's trial balance as at January 31, 2003, one month after the company began operations:

Prepare closing entries.
(SO 2) AP

CAMPUS CYCLE SHOP
Trial Balance
January 31, 2003

	Debit	Credit
Cash	$ 8,200	
Accounts Receivable	1,400	
Prepaid Insurance	400	
Land	50,000	
Building	90,000	
Accumulated Amortization—Building		$ 5,000
Equipment	25,000	
Accumulated Amortization—Equipment		500
Accounts Payable		4,000
Mortgage Note Payable, due 2010		95,000
Dude, Capital		66,000
Dude, Drawings	8,600	
Service Revenue		24,000
Amortization Expense	5,500	
Insurance Expense	400	
Interest Expense	800	
Salaries Expense	3,200	
Utilities Expense	1,000	
Totals	$194,500	$194,500

Instructions

(a) Prepare all closing journal entries necessary to close Campus Cycle Shop's temporary accounts at January 31, 2003, assuming it closes its books monthly.
(b) Calculate the ending balance of the Dude, Capital account after all closing entries are recorded and posted. Which balance on which financial statement(s) should this amount agree with?

P4–3A The following T accounts show the balances before the accounts were closed, and the closing entries which were posted to them:

Analyse account data and prepare closing entries.
(SO 2) AN

Repair Service Revenue	
	180,000
180,000	

J. Lecoure, Capital	
145,000	70,000
4,000	200,000

Repair Service Expense	
125,000	125,000

J. Lecoure, Drawings	
4,000	4,000

Other Expenses	
20,000	20,000

Other Revenue	
20,000	20,000

Instructions

Prepare, in general journal format, the closing entries that were made. (*Hint*: Notice that some of the amounts in the above T accounts are repeated several times. Think about which of them are related to one another in terms of the closing entries.)

*Prepare financial statements,
closing entries, and post-closing
trial balance.*
(SO 2, 3, 6) AP

P4–4A   The adjusted trial balance for Cormier Company, owned by Pierre Cormier, is as follows:

CORMIER COMPANY
Adjusted Trial Balance
December 31, 2002

Account No.	Account Titles	Dr.	Cr.
101	Cash	$ 13,600	
112	Accounts Receivable	15,400	
126	Supplies	1,500	
130	Prepaid Insurance	2,800	
151	Office Equipment	34,000	
152	Accumulated Amortization—Office Equipment		$ 8,000
200	Notes Payable		16,000
201	Accounts Payable		6,000
212	Salaries Payable		3,000
230	Interest Payable		500
301	P. Cormier, Capital		25,000
306	P. Cormier, Drawings	10,000	
400	Service Revenue		88,000
631	Supplies Expense	5,700	
711	Amortization Expense	4,000	
722	Insurance Expense	5,000	
726	Salaries Expense	40,000	
729	Rent Expense	14,000	
905	Interest Expense	500	
	Totals	$146,500	$146,500

Instructions

(a) Prepare an income statement, statement of owner's equity, and classified balance sheet. (*Note*: $10,000 of the notes payable becomes due in the year 2002.) Pierre did not make any additional investments in the business during the year.

(b) Prepare the closing entries.

(c) Open general ledger accounts and post the closing entries.

(d) Prepare a post-closing trial balance.

Analyse errors and prepare corrections.
(SO 5) AN

P4–5A   Bob Thebeau, CA, was hired by Campus TV Repair to prepare financial statements for April 2003. Thebeau accumulated all the ledger balances from the owner's records and found the following:

CAMPUS TV REPAIR
Trial Balance
April 30, 2003

	Debit	Credit
Cash	$ 5,000	
Accounts Receivable	3,200	
Supplies	3,800	
Equipment	10,600	
Accumulated Amortization		$ 1,350
Accounts Payable		2,100
Salaries Payable		800
Unearned Revenue		590
S. Morris, Capital		16,900
Service Revenue		5,450
Salaries Expense	3,300	
Advertising Expense	400	
Miscellaneous Expense	290	
Amortization Expense	500	
Repair Expense	100	
Totals	$27,190	$27,190

Bob Thebeau reviewed the records and found the following errors:

1. Cash received from a customer on account was recorded as $650 instead of $590.
2. The purchase on account of a computer that cost $3,300 was recorded as a debit to supplies and a credit to accounts payable for $3,300.
3. The computer in error 2 was purchased February 1, 2003, and is expected to have a three-year useful life. Amortization, estimated to be $275, has not been recorded.
4. A payment of $30 for advertising expense was entered as a debit to Miscellaneous Expense of $30 and a credit to Cash of $30.
5. The first salary payment this month was for $1,900, which included $800 of salaries payable on March 31. The payment was recorded as a debit to Salaries Expense of $1,900 and a credit to Cash of $1,900. (No reversing entries were made on April 1.)
6. A cash payment for a repair expense on equipment of $86 was recorded as a debit to Equipment $68 and a credit to Cash of $68.
7. Rent expense of $1,000 is owed, but has not yet been recorded.

Instructions

(a) Prepare an analysis of each error that shows (1) the incorrect entry, (2) the correct entry, and (3) the correcting entry.
(b) Prepare a correct trial balance.

P4–6A The following accounting errors were made in the records of XYZ Company, and were not discovered. Unless otherwise specified, assume the other side of each entry was correctly recorded and posted.

Determine impact of errors on financial statements.
(SO 5) AN

1. A $500 debit to Prepaid Rent was debited to Accounts Payable.
2. A $300 debit to Supplies was debited to Rent Expense.
3. A $400 credit to Cash was posted to the Cash account twice.
4. A debit to Utilities Expense of $92 was posted as a debit of $29.
5. A $580 credit to Service Revenue was posted as a $500 credit.
6. A $600 credit to Interest Income was posted to Interest Receivable as a debit.
7. A $250 debit to Advances from Customers was not posted.
8. A $300 advance from a customer was credited to Service Revenue.

Instructions

(a) For each item, indicate the effect of the error (understatement or overstatement) on expenses, revenues, assets, and liabilities. Use the following format to answer this question:

Item	Expenses	Revenue	Assets	Liabilities

(b) Determine the total amount of the understatement or overstatement of net income resulting from the above errors.

Source: Adapted from Certified General Accountants Association of Canada, *Financial Accounting 1 Examination,* March 1998, Question 2.

P4–7A Loblaw Companies Limited has the following selected accounts listed in a recent balance sheet:

Identify balance sheet classifications.
(SO 6) K

Accounts payable and accrued liabilities	Long-term debt
Accounts receivable	Long-term debt due within one year
Bank indebtedness	Prepaid expenses and other assets
Cash	Short-term bank loans
Fixed assets	Short-term investments
Inventories	Taxes recoverable

Instructions

Identify the classification of each balance sheet account listed above.

P4–8A Sleeman Breweries Ltd. is the largest craft brewer in Canada and the country's leading maker of premium beers. Founded in 1834, it produces all-natural bottled and draft beer marketed under its own name.

Calculate working capital and current ratio and comment on liquidity.
(SO 7) AN

The 1999 balance sheet of Sleeman Breweries showed current assets of $34,132,000 and current liabilities of $31,462,000, including a bank overdraft (negative cash balance) of $8,446,000. The 1998 balance sheet reported current assets of $23,573,000 and current liabilities of $24,774,000, including bank indebtedness of $2,547,000.

Instructions

(a) Calculate Sleeman's working capital and current ratio for each year.
(b) What do each of the measures calculated in (a) show? Comment on Sleeman's liquidity.

Prepare work sheet, financial statements, and adjusting and closing entries.
(SO 2, 6, 8) AP

*P4–9A　The trial balance columns of the work sheet for Lavigne Roofing at March 31, 2003, are as follows:

LAVIGNE ROOFING
Work Sheet
For the Month Ended March 31, 2003

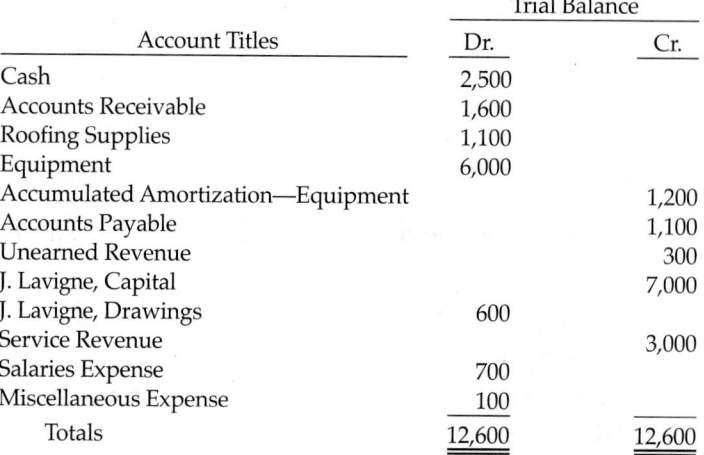

Account Titles	Trial Balance Dr.	Trial Balance Cr.
Cash	2,500	
Accounts Receivable	1,600	
Roofing Supplies	1,100	
Equipment	6,000	
Accumulated Amortization—Equipment		1,200
Accounts Payable		1,100
Unearned Revenue		300
J. Lavigne, Capital		7,000
J. Lavigne, Drawings	600	
Service Revenue		3,000
Salaries Expense	700	
Miscellaneous Expense	100	
Totals	12,600	12,600

Other data:

1. A physical count reveals $320 of roofing supplies on hand.
2. Amortization for March is $100.
3. Unearned revenue amounts to $200 (after adjustment) on March 31.
4. Accrued salaries are $400.
5. Accrued rent expense is $800.

Instructions

(a) Enter the trial balance on a work sheet and complete the work sheet.
(b) Prepare an income statement and statement of owner's equity for the month of March, and a classified balance sheet at March 31, 2003. J. Lavigne did not make any additional investments in the month of March.
(c) Journalize the adjusting entries from the adjustments columns of the work sheet.
(d) Journalize the closing entries from the financial statement columns of the work sheet.

Prepare work sheet, classified balance sheet, adjusting and closing entries, and post-closing trial balance.
(SO 2, 3, 6, 8) AP

*P4–10A　Water World Park has a fiscal year ending on September 30. Selected data from the September 30 work sheet are presented below:

WATER WORLD PARK
Work Sheet
For the Year Ended September 30, 2003

Account Titles	Trial Balance Dr.	Trial Balance Cr.	Adjusted Trial Balance Dr.	Adjusted Trial Balance Cr.
Cash	41,400		41,400	
Supplies	18,600		1,200	
Prepaid Insurance	31,900		3,900	
Land	80,000		80,000	
Building	500,000		500,000	
Accumulated Amortization—Building		125,000		150,000
Equipment	120,000		120,000	
Accumulated Amortization—Equipment		36,200		43,000
Accounts Payable		14,600		14,600
Unearned Admission Revenue		3,700		1,700
Mortgage Payable		350,000		350,000
M. Berge, Capital		159,700		159,700
M. Berge, Drawings	14,000		14,000	
Admission Revenue		302,500		304,500
Salaries Expense	105,000		105,000	
Repair Expense	30,500		30,500	
Advertising Expense	9,400		9,400	
Utilities Expense	16,900		16,900	

Property Taxes Expense	18,000		21,000	
Interest Expense	6,000		12,000	
Totals	991,700	991,700		
Insurance Expense			28,000	
Supplies Expense			17,400	
Interest Payable				6,000
Amortization Expense			31,800	
Property Taxes Payable				3,000
Totals			1,032,500	1,032,500

Instructions

(a) Prepare a complete work sheet.

(b) Prepare a classified balance sheet. (*Note*: In the next fiscal year, $50,000 of the mortgage payable is due for payment.)

(c) Journalize the adjusting entries, using the work sheet as a basis.

(d) Journalize the closing entries, using the work sheet as a basis.

(e) Prepare a post-closing trial balance.

*P4–11A A work sheet for Steam Carpet Cleaners, in which certain amounts have been removed and replaced by letters, is presented below.

Use work sheet relationships to determine missing amounts.
(SO 8) AN

STEAM CARPET CLEANERS
Work Sheet
January 31, 2003

Account Titles	Trial Balance Dr.	Trial Balance Cr.	Adjustments Dr.	Adjustments Cr.	Adjusted Trial Balance Dr.	Adjusted Trial Balance Cr.	Income Statement Dr.	Income Statement Cr.	Balance Sheet Dr.	Balance Sheet Cr.
Cash	(a)				1,200				1,200	
Accounts Receivable	4,400		(e)		5,000				5,000	
Cleaning Supplies	1,200			(i)	(m)				400	
Prepaid Insurance	(b)			(j)	1,650				1,650	
Equipment	7,000				7,000				7,000	
Accumulated Amortization		1,000		(k)		1,250				1,250
Accounts Payable		1,200				1,200				(x)
H. Kohl, Capital		10,000				10,000				10,000
H. Kohl, Drawings	(c)				900				900	
Service Revenue		6,000		(l)		(q)		(u)		
Rent Expense	200				200		200			
Salaries Expense	(d)		(f)		(n)		2,000			
Totals	18,200	18,200								
Amortization Expense			(g)		(o)		(s)			
Insurance Expense			150		150		150			
Cleaning Supplies Expense			(h)		(p)		(t)			
Salaries Payable				500		(r)				500
Totals			2,300	2,300	19,550	19,550	3,400	(v)	16,150	(y)
Net Income							3,200			(z)
Totals							6,600	(w)	16,150	16,150

Instructions

Determine the amounts that should appear in each of the spaces labelled (a) through (z) in the work sheet for Steam Carpet Cleaners. (*Hint*: You will not be able to determine the missing items in alphabetical order.)

*P4–12A The Farid Company had the following balances on its December 31, 2002, balance sheet:

Prepare and post subsequent transaction entries, with and without reversing entries.
(SO 9) AN

Interest receivable	$ 2,000
Prepaid insurance	5,000
Wages payable	36,000
Unearned sales revenue	40,000

During early 2003, $3,000 cash was collected for interest, and $90,000 was paid out for wages.

The company's insurance policy expired in 2003, and a premium of $8,000 was paid for a new one-year policy. Sales of $420,000 in 2003 included $40,000 of goods delivered to customers who had made advance payments during 2002.

Instructions

(a) Assuming that the company does not use reversing entries:
    1. Prepare journal entries to record the 2003 transactions noted above.
    2. Post your entries to T accounts, and calculate the balance in each account.
(b) Assuming that Farid uses reversing entries:
    1. Prepare the appropriate reversing entries on January 1, 2003, for the accrued interest and accrued wages.
    2. Prepare journal entries to record the transactions for 2003 noted above.
    3. Post your entries to T accounts, and calculate the balance in each account.

PROBLEMS: SET B

Prepare financial statements, closing entries, and post-closing trial balance.
(SO 2, 3, 6) AP

P4–1B The adjusted trial balance for Panaka Company is shown below.

PANAKA COMPANY
Adjusted Trial Balance
December 31, 2002

Account No.	Account Titles	Dr.	Cr.
101	Cash	$ 10,200	
112	Accounts Receivable	7,500	
130	Prepaid Insurance	1,800	
140	Land	100,000	
145	Building	150,000	
146	Accumulated Amortization—Building		$ 18,000
157	Equipment	28,000	
158	Accumulated Amortization—Equipment		8,600
201	Accounts Payable		12,000
212	Salaries Payable		3,000
301	O. Panaka, Capital		252,000
306	O. Panaka, Drawings	7,200	
400	Service Revenue		64,000
622	Repair Expense	3,200	
711	Amortization Expense	8,800	
722	Insurance Expense	1,200	
726	Salaries Expense	36,000	
732	Utilities Expense	3,700	
	Totals	$357,600	$357,600

Instructions

(a) Prepare an income statement, a statement of owner's equity, and a classified balance sheet. O. Panaka made an additional investment in the business of $4,000 during 2002.
(b) Prepare the closing entries.
(c) Open general ledger accounts and post the closing entries.
(d) Prepare a post-closing trial balance.

Prepare closing entries.
(SO 2) AP

P4–2B The following is the Radical Edge Sports Repair Shop's trial balance (presented in alphabetical order) as at September 30, 2003, one month after the company began operations.

RADICAL EDGE SPORTS REPAIR SHOP
Trial Balance
September 30, 2003

	Debit	Credit
Accounts Payable		$ 4,000
Accounts Receivable	$1,400	
Accumulated Amortization—Equipment		425
Amortization Expense	425	
Bachchan, Capital		8,300
Bachchan, Drawings	600	
Bank Loan Payable		15,000
Cash	8,200	
Equipment	25,000	
Insurance Expense	400	
Interest Expense	200	
Rent Expense	1,500	
Repair Service Revenue		14,000
Salaries Expense	3,200	
Supplies	600	
Supplies Expense	200	
Totals	$41,725	$41,725

Instructions
(a) Prepare all closing journal entries necessary to close the Radical Edge's temporary accounts at September 30, 2003, assuming it closes its books monthly.
(b) Calculate the ending balance of the Bachchan, Capital account after all closing entries are recorded and posted. Which balance on which financial statement(s) should this amount agree with?

Analyse account data and prepare closing entries.
(SO 2) AN

P4–3B The following T accounts show the balances before the accounts were closed, and the closing entries which were posted to them:

Other Revenue		Repair Service Revenue		R. Laporte, Capital	
30,000	30,000	170,000	170,000	135,000	800,000
				40,000	200,000

Repair Service Expense		R. Laporte, Drawings		Other Expenses	
110,000	110,000	40,000	40,000	25,000	25,000

Instructions
(a) Identify the normal account balance (debit or credit) of each of the above accounts.
(b) Prepare, in general journal format, the closing entries that were made. (*Hint*: Notice that some of the amounts in the above T accounts are repeated several times. Think about which of them are related to one another in terms of the closing entries.)

Prepare financial statements, closing entries, and post-closing trial balance.
(SO 2, 3, 6) AP

P4–4B   The adjusted trial balance for Shmi Skywalker Company is as follows:

SHMI SKYWALKER COMPANY
Adjusted Trial Balance
March 31, 2003

Account No.	Account Titles	Dr.	Cr.
101	Cash	$ 20,800	
112	Accounts Receivable	15,400	
126	Supplies	2,300	
130	Prepaid Insurance	4,800	
140	Land	50,000	
145	Building	150,000	
146	Accumulated Amortization—Building		$ 9,000
151	Office Equipment	44,000	
152	Accumulated Amortization—Office Equipment		18,000
200	Notes Payable		20,000
201	Accounts Payable		8,000
212	Salaries Payable		3,000
230	Interest Payable		1,000
275	Mortgage Payable		100,000
301	S. Skywalker, Capital		108,000
306	S. Skywalker, Drawings	12,000	
400	Service Revenue		109,000
610	Advertising Expense	12,000	
631	Supplies Expense	3,700	
711	Amortization Expense	15,000	
722	Insurance Expense	4,000	
726	Salaries Expense	39,000	
732	Utilities Expense	2,000	
905	Interest Expense	1,000	
	Totals	$376,000	$376,000

Instructions

(a) Prepare an income statement and statement of owner's equity for the year ended March 31, 2003, and a classified balance sheet as at March 31, 2003. Within a year, $10,000 of the notes payable and $15,000 of the mortgage payable become due. S. Skywalker did not make any additional investments in the business during 2003.

(b) Prepare the closing entries.

(c) Open general ledger accounts and post the closing entries.

(d) Prepare a post-closing trial balance.

Analyse errors and prepare corrections.
(SO 5) AN

P4–5B   Eric Mayers, CA, was hired by Interactive Computer Repair to prepare financial statements for March 2003. Mayers accumulated all the ledger balances from the owner's records and found the following:

INTERACTIVE COMPUTER REPAIR
Trial Balance
March 31, 2003

	Debit	Credit
Cash	$ 6,000	
Accounts Receivable	3,800	
Supplies	900	
Equipment	11,400	
Accumulated Amortization		$ 1,815
Accounts Payable		3,000
Salaries Payable		600
Unearned Revenue		935
H. Maurice, Capital		14,160
Service Revenue		6,450
Salaries Expense	2,900	

Advertising Expense	800	
Miscellaneous Expense	310	
Amortization Expense	700	
Repair Expense	150	
Totals	$26,960	$26,960

Eric Mayers reviewed the records and found the following errors:

1. Cash received from a customer on account was recorded as $750 instead of $570.
2. The purchase on account of a zip drive for an office computer that cost $375 was recorded as a debit to Supplies and a credit to Accounts Receivable for $375.
3. A payment of $50 for advertising expense was entered as a debit to Miscellaneous Expense of $30 and a credit to Cash of $30.
4. The first salary payment this month was for $1,800, which included $600 of salaries payable on February 28. The payment was recorded as a debit to Salaries Expense of $1,800 and a credit to Cash of $1,800. (No reversing entries were made on March 1.)
5. A cash payment for a repair expense on equipment of $90 was recorded as a debit to Equipment of $90 and a credit to Cash of $90.
6. Rent of $1,000 is overdue. The company has neither paid, nor recorded, this amount.

Instructions

(a) Prepare an analysis of each error that shows (1) the incorrect entry, (2) the correct entry, and (3) the correcting entry.
(b) Prepare a correct trial balance.

P4–6B The following accounting errors were made in the records of Fu Company, and were not discovered. Unless otherwise specified, assume the other side of each entry was correctly recorded and posted:

Determine impact of errors on financial statements.
(SO 5) AN

1. A $300 debit to Supplies was debited to Supplies Expense.
2. A $500 debit to Accounts Receivable was debited to Cash.
3. A $400 cash sale was posted to the Cash and Service Revenue accounts twice.
4. The amortization adjusting entry was recorded and posted as $29, rather than $92.
5. A $680 posting to Accounts Receivable and Service Revenue was posted erroneously as $600.
6. A $600 debit to Interest Expense was posted to Interest Revenue as a debit.
7. A $500 collection in advance was not posted to the Cash and Unearned Service Revenue accounts.
8. A $300 rent prepayment was debited to Rent Expense.
9. A $1,000 cash withdrawal by the owner was debited to Salaries Expense.

Instructions

(a) For each item, indicate the effect and amount of the error—understatement (U), overstatement (O), or no effect (NE)—on the income statement and balance sheet components. Use the following format in answering this question. The first one has been done for you as an example.

	Income Statement			Balance Sheet		
Item	Revenue	Expenses	Net Income	Assets	Liabilities	Owner's Equity
1.	NE	O $300	U $300	U $300	NE	U $300

(b) Determine the total amount of the understatement or overstatement resulting from the above errors.

P4–7B **Sobeys Inc.** has the following selected accounts listed in a recent balance sheet:

Identify balance sheet classifications.
(SO 6) K

Accounts payable and accrued charges	Investments and advances
Bank loans (short-term)	Long-term debt
Cash	Long-term debt due within one year
Marketable securities	Prepaid expenses
Income taxes payable	Property and equipment
Income taxes recoverable	Receivables
Inventories	

Instructions

Identify the classification of each balance sheet account listed above.

Calculate working capital and current ratio and comment on liquidity.
(SO 7) AN

P4–8B   **Sideware Systems Inc.,** headquartered in North Vancouver, develops and markets web-based e-business solutions.

Sideware's 1999 balance sheet reported current assets of $9,214,140 (including cash and cash equivalents of $8,558,482) and current liabilities of $956,873. The company reported a net loss of $7,992,669 in 1999. The 1998 balance sheet reported current assets of $1,070,353 and current liabilities of $278,738. Sideware reported a net loss of $2,409,390 in 1998.

Instructions

(a) Calculate Sideware's working capital and current ratio for each year.
(b) What do each of the measures calculated in (a) show? Comment on Sideware's liquidity.
(c) How can Sideware have such a large cash balance, yet report a net loss?

Prepare work sheet, financial statements, adjusting and closing entries.
(SO 2, 6, 8) AP

*P4–9B**   Allison Mason began operations as a private investigator on January 1, 2003. The trial balance columns of the work sheet for Mason P. I. at March 31 are as follows:

MASON P. I.
Work Sheet
For the Quarter Ended March 31, 2003

| | Trial Balance | |
Account Titles	Debit	Credit
Cash	11,400	
Accounts Receivable	5,620	
Supplies	1,050	
Prepaid Insurance	2,400	
Equipment	30,000	
Notes Payable		10,000
Accounts Payable		12,350
A. Mason, Capital		20,000
A. Mason, Drawings	600	
Service Revenue		13,620
Salaries Expense	2,200	
Travel Expense	1,300	
Rent Expense	1,200	
Miscellaneous Expense	200	
Totals	55,970	55,970

Other data:
1. Supplies on hand total $750.
2. Amortization is $1,500 per quarter.
3. Interest accrues on the six-month note payable, issued January 1, at a rate of 10%.
4. Insurance expires at the rate of $150 per month.
5. Services provided but unbilled at March 31 total $750.

Instructions

(a) Enter the trial balance on a work sheet and complete the work sheet.
(b) Prepare an income statement and statement of owner's equity for the quarter, and a classified balance sheet at March 31, 2003. Allison Mason did not make any additional investments in the business during the quarter ended March 31, 2003.
(c) Journalize the adjusting entries from the adjustments columns of the work sheet.
(d) Journalize the closing entries from the financial statement columns of the work sheet.

Prepare work sheet, classified balance sheet, adjusting and closing entries, and post-closing trial balance.
(SO 2, 3, 6, 8) AP

*P4–10B**   **Sherrick Management Services** began business on January 1, 2003, with a capital investment of $120,000. The company manages condominiums for owners (Service Revenue) and rents space in its own office building (Rent Revenue). The trial balance and adjusted trial balance columns of the work sheet at the end of the first year are as follows:

SHERRICK MANAGEMENT SERVICES
Work Sheet
For the Year Ended December 31, 2003

Account Titles	Trial Balance Dr.	Trial Balance Cr.	Adjusted Trial Balance Dr.	Adjusted Trial Balance Cr.
Cash	14,500		14,500	
Accounts Receivable	23,600		23,600	
Prepaid Insurance	3,100		1,600	
Land	56,000		56,000	
Building	106,000		106,000	
Equipment	48,000		48,000	
Accounts Payable		10,400		10,400
Unearned Rent Revenue		5,000		1,800
Mortgage Payable		100,000		100,000
R. Sherrick, Capital		120,000		120,000
R. Sherrick, Drawings	20,000		20,000	
Service Revenue		75,600		75,600
Rent Revenue		23,000		26,200
Salaries Expense	30,000		30,000	
Advertising Expense	17,000		17,000	
Utilities Expense	15,800		15,800	
Totals	334,000	334,000		
Insurance Expense			1,500	
Amortization Expense—Building			2,500	
Accumulated Amortization—Building				2,500
Amortization Expense—Equipment			3,900	
Accumulated Amortization—Equipment				3,900
Interest Expense			10,000	
Interest Payable				10,000
Totals			350,400	350,400

Instructions

(a) Prepare a complete work sheet.
(b) Prepare a classified balance sheet. (*Note*: In the next year, $10,000 of the mortgage payable is due for payment.)
(c) Journalize the adjusting entries.
(d) Journalize the closing entries.
(e) Prepare a post-closing trial balance.

Use work sheet relationships to
determine missing amounts.
(SO 8) AN

*P4–11B   A work sheet for Nohe's Carpet Cleaners, in which certain amounts have been removed and replaced by letters, is presented below:

NOHE'S CARPET CLEANERS
Work Sheet
April 30, 2003

Account Titles	Trial Balance Dr.	Cr.	Adjustments Dr.	Cr.	Adjusted Trial Balance Dr.	Cr.	Income Statement Dr.	Cr.	Balance Sheet Dr.	Cr.
Cash	(a)				1,300				1,300	
Accounts Receivable	4,200		(e)		5,200				5,200	
Cleaning Supplies	1,100			(i)	(m)				500	
Prepaid Insurance	(b)			(j)	1,360				1,360	
Equipment	7,160				7,160				7,160	
Accumulated Amortization		1,200		(k)		1,450				1,450
Accounts Payable		1,300				1,300				(x)
J. Nohe, Capital		9,000				9,000				9,000
J. Nohe, Drawings	(c)				1,100				1,100	
Service Revenue		7,000		(l)		(q)		(u)		
Rent Expense	220				220		220			
Salaries Expense	(d)		(f)		(n)		2,500			
Totals	18,500	18,500								
Amortization Expense			(g)		(o)		(s)			
Insurance Expense			160		160		160			
Cleaning Supplies Expense			(h)		(p)		(t)			
Salaries Payable				600		(r)				600
Totals			2,610	2,610	20,350	20,350	3,730	(v)	16,620	(y)
Net Income							4,270			(z)
Totals							8,000	(w)	16,620	16,620

Instructions

Determine the amounts that should appear in each of the spaces labelled (a) through (z) in the work sheet for Nohe's Carpet Cleaners. (*Hint*: You will not be able to determine the missing items in alphabetical order.)

Prepare and post subsequent
transactions entries, with and
without reversing entries.
(SO 9) AN

*P4–12B   The Friendly Food Company had the following balances on its December 31, 2002, balance sheet:

Rent receivable	$ 2,500
Prepaid insurance	4,800
Property taxes payable	3,000
Unearned service revenue	45,000

During early 2003, $4,000 cash was collected for rent, and $8,000 was paid out for property taxes.

The company's insurance policy expired in 2003, and a premium of $9,000 was paid for a new one-year policy. Services provided of $450,000 in 2003 included $45,000 of services to customers who had made advance payments during 2002.

Instructions

(a) Assume that the company does not use reversing entries:
   1. Prepare journal entries to record the transactions for 2003 noted above.
   2. Post your entries to T accounts and calculate the balance in each account.
(b) Assuming that The Friendly Food Company uses reversing entries:
   1. Prepare the appropriate reversing entries for January 1, 2003, for the accrued rent and accrued property taxes.
   2. Prepare journal entries to record the transactions for 2003 noted above.
   3. Post your entries to T accounts and calculate the balance in each account.

CUMULATIVE COVERAGE—CHAPTERS 2 TO 4

Lee Chan opened Lee's Window Washing on July 1, 2003. During July, the following transactions were completed:

July 1 Invested $18,000 cash in the business.
1 Purchased a used truck for $26,000, paying $3,000 cash and the balance on account.
1 Paid $500 rent for the month.
3 Purchased cleaning supplies for $900 on account.
5 Paid $1,200 on a one-year insurance policy, effective July 1.
12 Billed customers $2,500 for cleaning services.
18 Paid $3,000 of amount owed on truck, and $500 of amount owed on cleaning supplies.
20 Paid $1,200 for employee salaries.
21 Collected $1,400 from customers billed on July 12.
25 Billed customers $3,000 for cleaning services.
31 Paid gas and oil for the month on the truck, $250.
31 Withdrew $1,600 cash for personal use.

The chart of accounts for Lee's Window Washing contains the following accounts: No. 101 Cash; No. 112 Accounts Receivable; No. 128 Cleaning Supplies; No. 130 Prepaid Insurance; No. 157 Equipment; No. 158 Accumulated Amortization—Equipment; No. 201 Accounts Payable; No. 212 Salaries Payable; No. 301 Lee Chan, Capital; No. 306 Lee Chan, Drawings; No. 400 Cleaning Revenue; No. 633 Gas and Oil Expense; No. 634 Cleaning Supplies Expense; No. 711 Amortization Expense; No. 722 Insurance Expense; No. 726 Salaries Expense; No. 729 Rent Expense.

Instructions

(a) Journalize and post the July transactions. Use page J1 for the journal.
(b) Prepare a trial balance at July 31.
(c) Journalize and post the following adjustments:
   1. Earned but unbilled fees at July 31 were $1,500.
   2. Amortization on truck for the month was $700.
   3. One-twelfth of the insurance expired.
   4. An inventory count shows $600 of cleaning supplies on hand at July 31.
   5. Accrued but unpaid employee salaries were $400.
(d) Prepare an adjusted trial balance.
(e) Prepare the income statement and statement of owner's equity for July, and a classified balance sheet at July 31, 2003.
(f) Journalize and post the closing entries, and complete the closing process.
(g) Prepare a post-closing trial balance at July 31.

*B*roadening Your Perspective

FINANCIAL REPORTING AND ANALYSIS

Financial Reporting Problem

BYP4-1 The financial statements and accompanying notes of **The Second Cup Ltd.** are presented in Appendix A at the end of this book.

Instructions

Answer the following questions, using The Second Cup's financial statements and the notes which accompany them:

(a) How is Second Cup's balance sheet classified? What classifications does it use?
(b) What are the "cash equivalents" reported with cash in the current asset classification?
(c) The Second Cup's working capital and current ratio for the fiscal year 2000 are calculated in the chapter. Calculate its working capital and current ratio for the 1999 fiscal year (use the Pro Forma results). Compare them to the 2000 results.

Interpreting Financial Statements

BYP4–2   Future Shop Ltd. is one of North America's largest computer and electronics retailers. Established in 1982, the company has grown to over 83 stores in Canada. In addition, Future Shop sells its products on-line.

Future Shop's 1999 balance sheet showed current assets of $221.3 million and current liabilities of $253.9 million, including bank indebtedness (cash overdraft) of close to $24 million. Future Shop also recorded a net loss of $82.2 million in fiscal 1999. In 2000, Future Shop reported current assets of $226.2 million, current liabilities of $260.2 million, and net income of $23.7 million.

Instructions

(a) Calculate the working capital and current ratio for Future Shop for 2000 and 1999. Do you believe that Future Shop's creditors should be concerned about its liquidity? Explain why or why not.

(b) If you were a creditor of Future Shop's and noted that it did not have enough current assets to cover its current liabilities in 1999, what additional information might you request to help you assess its liquidity?

Additional Cases

BYP4–3   Fishery Products International (FPI) Limited is the world's largest seafood supplier. Headquartered in St. John's, Newfoundland, FPI produces and markets a full range of seafood products, which are marketed throughout North America, Southeast Asia, South America, and Europe. A simplified version of FPI's December 31, 1999, year-end adjusted trial balance follows:

FISHERY PRODUCTS INTERNATIONAL

FISHERY PRODUCTS INTERNATIONAL LIMITED
Trial Balance
December 31, 1999
(in thousands)

Account Titles	Debit	Credit
Cash	$ 916	
Accounts receivable	80,644	
Inventories	119,471	
Prepaid expenses	5,637	
Property, plant, and equipment	220,798	
Other long-term assets	14,057	
Accumulated amortization		$ 127,121
Short-term bank indebtedness		43,124
Accounts payable and accrued liabilities		37,252
Current portion of long-term debt		8,351
Long-term debt		62,323
Shareholders' equity		155,148
Dividends (similar to drawings)	1,822	
Sales revenue		708,911
Commission revenue		3,327
Cost of goods sold, administrative, and marketing expenses	678,580	
Amortization expense	9,883	
Interest expense	7,146	
Other expenses	2,506	
Income tax expense	4,097	
Totals	$1,145,557	$1,145,557

Instructions

(a) From the trial balance, prepare an income statement and a classified balance sheet as at December 31, 1999.

(b) FPI's current assets were $219,652,000 and current liabilities were $110,374,000 at December 31, 1998. Using the appropriate financial statement amounts you determined in (a), calculate FPI's 1999 and 1998 working capital and current ratio.

(c) Comment briefly on the change in FPI's liquidity over the last two years.

Accounting on the Web

BYP4–4 This case explores the advantages of e-commerce and the use of the Internet technology in financial processes.

Instructions

Specific requirements of this Internet case are available on the Weygandt website.

CRITICAL THINKING

· ·

Collaborative Learning Activities

BYP4–5 Everclean Janitorial Service was started two years ago by Jean-Guy Richard. Because business has been exceptionally good, Jean-Guy decided on July 1, 2002, to expand operations by acquiring an additional truck and hiring two more assistants.

To finance the expansion, Jean-Guy obtained a bank loan on July 1, 2002, for $25,000, with an interest rate of 10%. Of the loan amount, $10,000 is due on July 1, 2003. The balance is due on July 1, 2004. The terms of the loan require that the borrower have working capital of at least $10,000 at December 31, 2002. If these terms are not met, the entire amount of the bank loan will become due immediately.

At December 31, 2002, the accountant for Everclean Janitorial Service prepared the following balance sheet:

EVERCLEAN JANITORIAL SERVICE
Balance Sheet
December 31, 2002

Assets

Current assets		
Cash		$ 6,500
Accounts receivable		9,000
Janitorial supplies		5,200
Prepaid insurance		4,800
Total current assets		25,500
Capital assets		
Cleaning equipment (net)	$22,000	
Delivery trucks (net)	34,000	56,000
Total assets		$81,500

Liabilities and Owner's Equity

Current liabilities	
Notes payable	$10,000
Accounts payable	2,500
Total current liabilities	12,500
Long-term liability	
Notes payable	15,000
Total liabilities	27,500
Owner's equity	
Jean-Guy Richard, Capital	54,000
Total liabilities and owner's equity	$81,500

Jean-Guy presented the balance sheet to the bank's loan officer on January 2, 2003, confident that the company had met the terms of the loan. However, the loan officer was not impressed. She said, "We need financial statements which have been audited."

An auditor was hired and immediately realized that the balance sheet had been prepared from a trial balance and not from an adjusted trial balance. The adjustment data at the balance sheet date consisted of the following:

1. Earned but unbilled janitorial services were $5,000.
2. Janitorial supplies on hand were $2,500.
3. Prepaid insurance was a two-year policy dated January 1, 2002.
4. December expenses incurred but unpaid at December 31 were $300.
5. Interest on the bank loan was not recorded.
6. The amounts for capital assets were reported net of accumulated amortization of $4,000 for cleaning equipment and of $5,000 for delivery trucks, as at January 1, 2002. Amortization for 2002 was $2,000 for cleaning equipment and $5,000 for delivery trucks.

Instructions

With the class divided into groups, answer the following:
(a) Prepare a correct balance sheet.
(b) Were the terms of the bank loan met? Explain.

BYP4-6 The following adjustments were incorrectly omitted from the books of This Old Thing Company for the years 2002 and 2003:

	2002	2003

1. A number of costs (such as insurance and rent) were paid in advance during 2002, and debited to a prepaid expense account. These amounts were partially applicable to the last part of 2002 and partially to the first part of 2003. No adjusting entry was made for these costs at the end of 2002. This error was discovered in the middle of 2003, and the costs were expensed at that time.
2. In 2002, revenue was collected from customers in advance of the services being performed and recognized as having been earned that year. No adjusting entry was made; the services were provided during 2003.
3. No adjusting entry was made at the end of 2002 for accrued expenses owing (such as wages and taxes). These items were paid, and charged to appropriate expense accounts, during the year 2003.
4. There was no adjustment made at the end of 2002 for revenue which had been earned but not billed at the end of the year. However, the billings were made and the revenue was recorded early in 2003.

Instructions

With the class divided into groups, indicate what effect the item would have on the net income for each of 2002 and 2003, by entering either "U" for Understated, "O" for Overstated, or "NE" for No Effect in the column for each year.

Communication Activity

BYP4–7 The accounting cycle is important for understanding the accounting process.

Instructions

Write a memo to your instructor that lists and briefly explains each of the steps in the accounting cycle in the order in which they should be completed. Your memorandum should also discuss the optional steps in the accounting cycle.

Ethics Case

BYP4–8 As the controller of Breathless Perfume Company, you discover a significant misstatement that overstated net income in the prior year's financial statements. The misleading financial statements are contained in the company's annual report, which was issued to banks and other creditors less than a month ago.

After much thought about the consequences of telling the president, Eddy Lieman, about this misstatement, you gather your courage to inform him. Eddy says, "Hey! What they don't know won't hurt them. But, just so we set the record straight, we'll adjust this year's financial statements for last year's misstatement. We can absorb that misstatement better this year than last year anyway!

Just don't make that kind of mistake again."

Instructions

(a) Who are the stakeholders in this situation?

(b) What are the ethical issues in this situation?

(c) As a controller, what would you do in this situation?

Answers to Self-Study Questions

1. b 2. a 3. b 4. c 5. a 6. d 7. b 8. a 9. c *10. c *11. c

Answer to Second Cup Review It Question 3

Second Cup's current assets include Cash and Cash Equivalents, $1,446; Accounts Receivable, $2,294; Inventories, $107; Prepaid Expenses and Sundry Assets, $419; and Income Taxes Receivable, $1,150. Second Cup's current liabilities include Accounts Payable and Accrued Liabilities, $2,718; Current Portion, Long-Term Debt, $3,000; and Deposits, $687. All amounts are listed in thousands. Second Cup's current assets and current liabilities appear to be listed in order of liquidity, with the most current or liquid account listed first.

Remember to go back to the Navigator box on the chapter-opening page to check off your completed work.

Concepts for Review

Before studying this chapter, you should understand or, if necessary, review:

a. *How to close revenue, expense, and drawings accounts. (Ch. 4, pp. 158–159)*
b. *The steps in the accounting cycle. (Ch. 4, pp. 163–164)*

Taking Stock— from Backpacks to Bicycles

VANCOUVER, B.C.—Backpacks and jackets sporting the jagged peaks of the Mountain Equipment Co-op logo are a familiar sight on Canadian campuses. MEC has five retail stores across Canada and a huge market in catalogue sales around the world. It ships everything from climbing ropes to kayaks to bike helmets, to destinations as far away as Japan and South America.

Keeping track of the flow of these items is the responsibility of Fara Jumani, head of inventory costing at MEC and a part-time CGA student. "We have tens of thousands of items in inventory and we are adding new ones all the time," says Ms. Jumani. "Because we make a lot of our own clothing goods, we also have a lot of in-house inventory—fabric and supplies that will be used to make products."

Managing inventory is a challenge for all retailers. MEC uses a perpetual inventory system to track its merchandise inventory quantities and costs. This system provides continuous and up-to-date information, identifying merchandise that has been sold and merchandise still on hand available to be sold. MEC uses this information to ensure a smooth flow of gear into its stores from its suppliers and to minimize stock outages.

Unlike most retail operations, MEC is not out to make a profit. As a co-op, it exists to serve its members. "But we have to stay fiscally healthy to do that," points out Ms. Jumani. "If we go bankrupt, we won't be serving anyone." Accounting for inventory— from backpacks to bicycles—is an important part of MEC's fiscal fitness routine.

www.mec.ca

THE NAVIGATOR

- Understand *Concepts for Review* ☐
- Read *Feature Story* ☐
- Scan *Study Objectives* ☐
- Read *Preview* ☐
- Read text and answer *Before You Go On*
  p. 216 ☐ p. 219 ☐ p. 223 ☐ p. 228 ☐
  p. 229 ☐ p. 237 ☐ p. 239 ☐
- Work *Demonstration Problem* ☐
- Review *Summary of Study Objectives* ☐
- Answer *Self-Study Questions* ☐
- Complete assignments ☐

CHAPTER · 5

ACCOUNTING FOR MERCHANDISING OPERATIONS

▶ STUDY OBJECTIVES ◀

After studying this chapter, you should be able to:

1. Describe the differences between a service company and a merchandising company.
2. Explain and complete the entries for purchases under a perpetual inventory system.
3. Explain and complete the entries for sales revenue under a perpetual inventory system.
4. Explain and perform the steps in the accounting cycle for a merchandising company.
5. Distinguish between and be able to prepare both a multiple-step and a single-step income statement.
6. Explain the importance of and be able to calculate gross profit.
7. Calculate the inventory turnover and days sales in inventory ratios.
8. Describe and perform the accounting for sales taxes (Appendix 5A).
9. Prepare a work sheet for a merchandising company (Appendix 5B).

THE NAVIGATOR

The first four chapters of this text focused mostly on service companies like the fictional Pioneer Advertising. Other examples of service companies include Air Canada, Canada Post, College Pro Painters, and the Bank of Montreal. Mountain Equipment Co-op, as indicated in the opening story, buys (or makes) and sells goods rather than perform services to earn a profit. Merchandising companies that purchase and sell directly to consumers—such as MEC, Best Buy, Hudson's Bay, Indigo.ca, and Toys "R" Us—are called retailers.

The steps in the accounting cycle for a merchandising company are the same as the steps for a service enterprise. However, merchandising companies need additional accounts and entries in order to record merchandising transactions.

This chapter is organized as follows:

THE
NAVIGATOR

Merchandising Operations

STUDY OBJECTIVE
·········· **1** ··········
Describe the differences between a service company and a merchandising company.

Measuring net income for a merchandising company is basically the same as for a service company. That is, net income (or loss) results when expenses are matched with revenues. In a merchandising company, the primary source of revenues is the sale of merchandise. These revenues are referred to as **sales revenue**, or simply **sales**. Unlike expenses for a service company, expenses for a merchandising company are divided into two categories: (1) cost of goods sold, and (2) operating expenses.

The **cost of goods sold** is the total cost of merchandise sold during the period. This expense is directly related to the revenue earned from the sale of the goods. Sales revenue less cost of goods sold is called **gross profit**. For example, when a pocket calculator that costs $15 is sold for $25, the gross profit is $10.

After gross profit is calculated, operating expenses are deducted to determine net income (or net loss). **Operating expenses** are expenses that are incurred in the process of earning sales revenue. Examples of operating expenses are salaries, advertising, insurance, and amortization. The operating expenses of a merchandising company include many of the same expenses found in a service company.

Alternative terminology
Gross profit is also called *gross margin.*

The income measurement process for a merchandising company is diagrammed in Illustration 5-1. The items in the two blue boxes are only used by a merchandising company. They are not used by a service company.

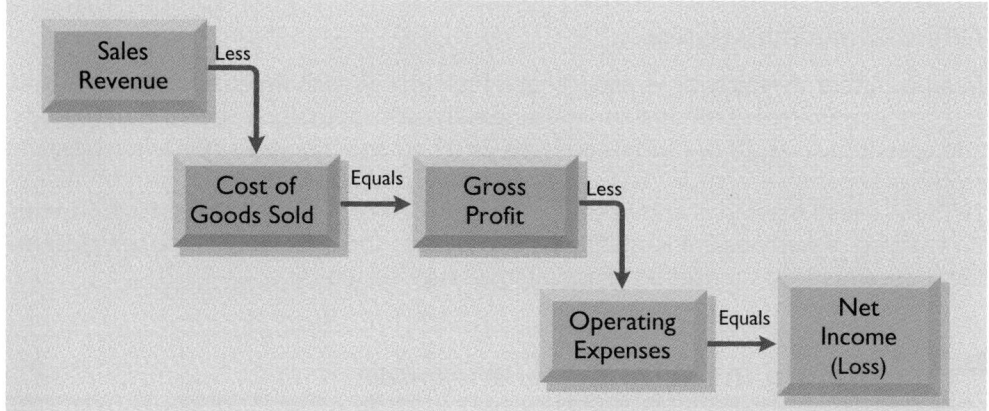

Illustration 5-1

Income measurement process for a merchandising company

Operating Cycles

While measuring income for a merchandising company is basically the same as for a service company, the operating cycles differ. As explained in Chapter 4, an operating cycle is the average time it takes to go from cash to cash in producing revenues. The normal operating cycle of a merchandising company is longer than that of a service company. The purchase of merchandise inventory and its eventual sale lengthens the cycle. The operating cycles of service and merchandising companies can be contrasted as shown in Illustration 5-2. Note that the added asset account for a merchandising company is an inventory account. It is usually titled Merchandise Inventory. Merchandise inventory is reported as a current asset on the balance sheet.

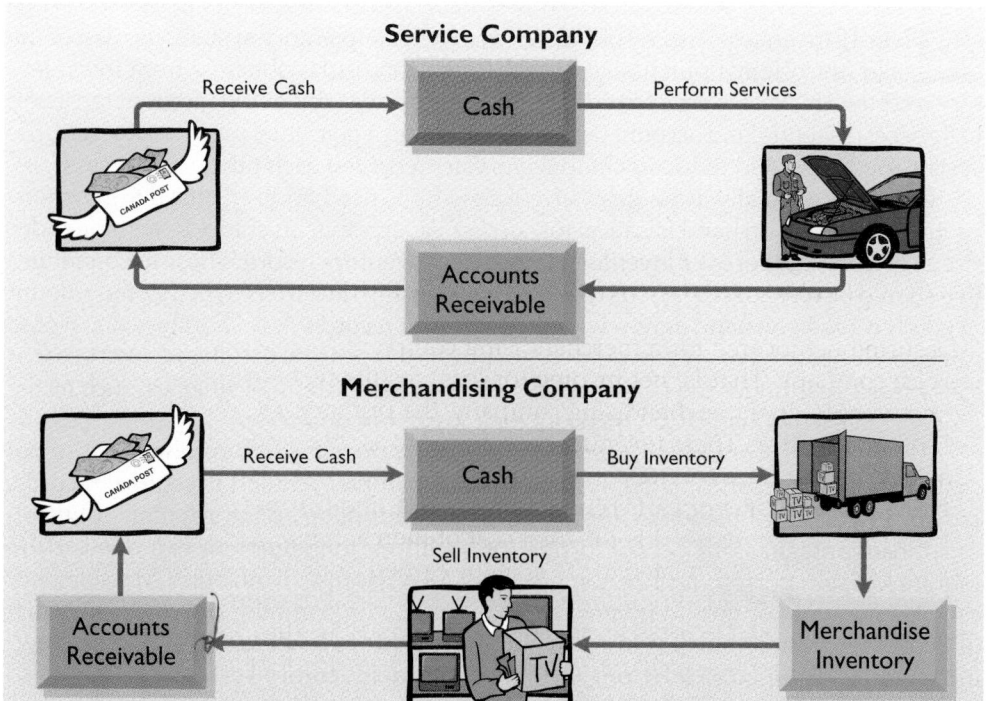

Illustration 5-2

Operating cycles for a service company and a merchandising company

Inventory Systems

A merchandising company keeps track of its inventory to determine what is available for sale (inventory) and what has been sold (cost of goods sold). One of two systems is used to account for inventory and cost of goods sold: a **perpetual inventory system** or a **periodic inventory system**.

Perpetual Inventory System

In a perpetual inventory system, detailed records of each inventory purchase and sale are maintained. This system continuously—perpetually—shows the quantity and cost of the inventory purchased, sold, and on hand. For example, a Ford dealership has separate inventory records for each automobile, truck, and van on its lot. With the use of bar codes and optical scanners, a grocery store can keep a daily running record of every box of Kraft Dinner that it buys and sells. That's also why Mountain Equipment Co-op uses a perpetual inventory system.

▶Accounting in Action ▸ *Business Insight*

Bar codes were invented in 1973 by George Laurer, primarily to speed up checkouts and reduce cashier errors in the grocery story industry. Although there are many bar code formats, the most common bar code in North America is the UPC (Universal Product Code). The UPC contains machine-readable symbols: the first digit is a system identifier, the next five or six digits are assigned manufacturer numbers, the following five or six digits are product numbers, and the last digit is a check digit. When a code is read by a bar code reader and transmitted to a computer, the computer finds the disk file item record(s) associated with that item number. In the disk file are the price, vendor name, quantity on hand, description, and so on. The computer does a "price look-up" by reading the bar code, and then it creates a register of the items and adds the price to the subtotal of groceries purchased. It also subtracts the quantity from the "on hand" total.

The invention of the bar code opened the door to the digital world. Now there's a bar code for virtually everything. From letters to Cokes, from fishes to smokes—it's got a bar code.

When an inventory item is sold under a perpetual inventory system, the cost of the goods sold (the original purchase cost of the merchandise) is obtained from the inventory records. This cost is transferred from the Merchandise Inventory account (an asset) to the Cost of Goods Sold account (an expense). Under a perpetual inventory system, the cost of goods sold and reduction in inventory are recorded each time a sale occurs.

Inventory is usually the largest current asset for a merchandiser. Effective inventory control over goods on hand is critical for success. A perpetual inventory system provides strong internal control over inventories. Since the inventory records show the quantities that should be on hand, the goods can be counted at any time to see whether the amount of goods actually on hand agrees with the inventory records. Any shortages uncovered can be investigated. For control purposes, a physical inventory count is always taken at least once a year under the perpetual inventory system. Many businesses, such as the Fredericton Direct Charge Co-Op, count their inventory quarterly.

A perpetual inventory system does result in more clerical work and additional costs, even with an automated system, to maintain the detailed inventory records. However, for many businesses, the advantages of this detailed information outweigh this disadvantage. With access to this information, management can answer the inquiries of salespersons and customers about merchandise availability. Management can also maintain optimum inventory levels, and avoid running out of stock. Much of Leon's Furniture's success in managing its inventory, as described on the following page, is attributed to its sophisticated perpetual inventory system.

►Accounting in Action ► *ℰ-Business Insight*

Perpetual inventory systems combined with high-tech advances have enabled integrated *just in time* inventory management systems for many retailers. S. El-Raheb, a principal with a Toronto-based consulting firm, explains: "If you buy a mattress at Leon's, it won't be in stock. The store will place an electronic order with the manufacturer, who makes it and ships it to their dock. Another truck is right there to pick up and deliver the piece, and all this takes place in less than 24 hours." Within the company, ordering, inventory control, billing, and accounting are seamless. The computer determines when and how many items to buy, prepares and submits the purchase order, issues the bill, and updates the inventory and accounting records.

Source: Olev Edur, "One-Keystroke Communication," *The Financial Post*, April 26, 1997, 58.

Periodic Inventory System

In a periodic inventory system, detailed inventory records of the goods on hand are not kept throughout the period. The cost of goods sold is **determined only at the end of the accounting period**—that is, periodically. A physical inventory count is taken to determine the quantity and cost of the goods on hand at the end of the accounting period. We will learn more about how to determine the quantity and cost of inventory later in this chapter and in the next chapter.

Once the cost of the goods on hand at the end of the period is determined, we can calculate the cost of the goods sold. To determine the cost of goods sold in a periodic inventory system, the following steps are necessary: (1) Determine the cost of goods on hand at the beginning of the accounting period (beginning inventory). (2) Add to it the cost of goods purchased. (3) Subtract the cost of goods on hand at the end of the accounting period (ending inventory).

Periodic inventory systems are widely used by companies that sell thousands of low-unit-value items (e.g., nails) that turn over rapidly. Periodic systems are also used by companies with homogeneous goods, such as sawmill companies, where it is not possible to separately identify each piece of lumber among others of the same size and grade. Many small businesses also use a periodic inventory system, because the cost of the detailed record keeping required for a perpetual inventory systems outweighs the benefit. They can adequately control merchandise and manage day-to-day operations without perpetual inventory records. Periodically, they count their merchandise to determine quantities on hand and establish costs for accounting purposes.

Illustration 5-3 compares the sequence of activities and the timing of the cost of goods sold calculation under the two inventory systems.

Illustration 5-3

Comparing periodic and perpetual inventory systems

Because the perpetual inventory system is widely used, we illustrate it in this chapter. The periodic system, still used by many small businesses, is described in the next chapter.

Recording Purchases of Merchandise

STUDY OBJECTIVE
•••••••••**2**•••••••••

Explain and complete the entries for purchases under a perpetual inventory system.

Purchases of inventory may be made for cash or on account (credit). The purchase is normally recorded by the purchaser when the goods are received from the seller. Every purchase should be supported by business documents that provide written evidence of the transaction. In larger companies, each order's origin is documented with a **purchase order**. A purchase order is a document used to place an order for goods (or services) with a supplier.

Cash purchases should be supported by a cash register receipt indicating the items purchased. Both cash purchases and credit purchases are also supported by a **purchase invoice**. This document indicates the total purchase price and other relevant information. However, the purchaser does not prepare a separate purchase invoice. Instead, the copy of the sales invoice sent by the seller becomes the purchase invoice for the buyer. In Illustration 5-4, the sales invoice prepared by Highpoint Electronic serves as both a sales invoice for the seller (Highpoint Electronic) and a purchase invoice for the buyer (Chelsea Video).

Illustration 5-4

Sales/purchase invoice

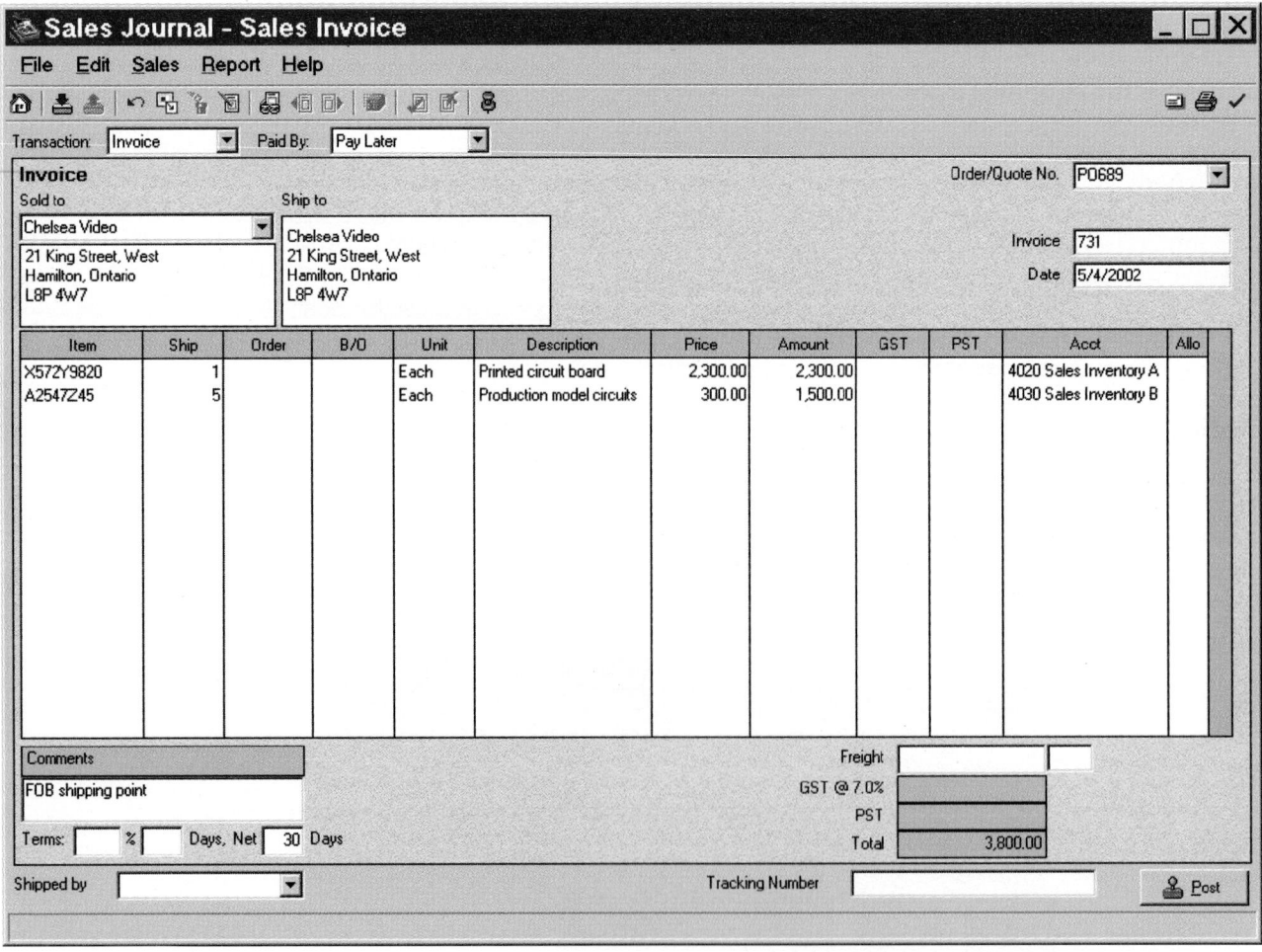

The purchaser, Chelsea Video, would make the following entry to record this information:

May 4	Merchandise Inventory	3,800			
	Accounts Payable		3,800		
	To record goods purchased				
	on account, terms n/30.				

A	=	L	+	OE
+3,800		+3,800		

Under a perpetual inventory system, when merchandise is purchased for resale to customers, the current asset account Merchandise Inventory is debited for the cost of the goods. Mountain Equipment Co-op, introduced in the feature story, debits Merchandise Inventory for the 9,000 different products it purchases or makes for resale. It maintains a separate **subsidiary account** for each different product it sells in order to track individual balances.

Not all purchases are automatically debited to Merchandise Inventory. Purchases of assets acquired for use and not for resale—such as supplies, equipment, and similar items—should be debited to specific asset accounts rather than to Merchandise Inventory. For example, Fara Jumani would debit the Supplies account for the supplies MEC purchases and uses to make shelf signs and labels. The fabric and supplies she purchases to make clothing for resale, however, are recorded differently. These are part of the cost of a product for resale and are debited to Merchandise Inventory.

Subsidiary Inventory Records

In a perpetual inventory system, the Merchandise Inventory account in the general ledger acts as a **control account** for all the subsidiary or individual inventory accounts. At all times, the control account balance equals the total of all the individual inventory account balances. We will learn more about how to record and balance subsidiary and control account transactions in Chapter 7. For now, we illustrate a subsidiary inventory record, using assumed product information, in Illustration 5-5.

Illustration 5-5

Subsidiary inventory record

The subsidiary inventory records are linked to purchases and sales. Unit quantities and costs are automatically updated at the time of each transaction.

Freight Costs

Alternative terminology
Other common shipping terms include *FCA* (free carrier), *CIF* (cost, insurance, freight) or *CPT* (carriage paid to).

The purchase agreement should indicate whether the seller or the buyer must pay the cost of transporting the goods to the buyer's place of business. When a carrier such as a railroad, trucking company, or airline is used, the transportation company prepares a freight bill (often called a bill of lading) in accordance with the purchase agreement. Freight terms may vary but generally say who pays the freight and who assumes the risk during transit. For example, the terms may be expressed as either **FOB shipping point** or **FOB destination**. The letters FOB mean **free on board**. FOB shipping point means that the goods are placed free on board the carrier by the seller, and the buyer pays the freight costs. Conversely, FOB destination means that the goods are placed free on board to the buyer's place of business, and the seller pays the freight. For example, the purchase invoice in Illustration 5-4 shown earlier in this chapter indicates that freight is FOB shipping point. Thus, the buyer (Chelsea Video) pays the freight charges. Illustration 5-6 illustrates these shipping terms.

Illustration 5-6

Terms of shipping

When the purchaser (buyer) pays for the freight costs, Merchandise Inventory is debited for the cost of the transportation. **Any freight paid by the purchaser is part of the cost of the merchandise purchased.** The reason is that the inventory cost should include any freight charges necessary to bring the goods to the purchaser. Freight costs paid by MEC on its kayaks and canoes, for example, form part of the cost of these products.

To illustrate the purchaser's journal entry to record the cost of shipping, assume that, upon delivery of the goods on May 4, Chelsea Video pays Acme Freight Company $150 for freight charges. The entry on Chelsea Video's books is:

A = L + OE				
+150	May 4	Merchandise Inventory	150	
−150		Cash		150
		To record payment of freight on goods purchased.		

▶ Accounting in Action ▸ *ℯ-Business Insight*

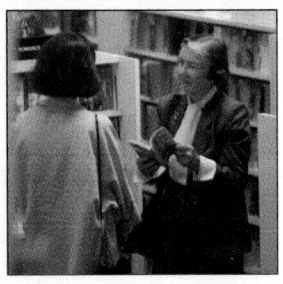

It can cost a lot to convert from traditional business to e-commerce. For example, when Chapters launched Chapters Online, it also had to launch a distribution centre, Pegasus Wholesale. The reason? It previously shipped large orders of books to its stores. Now it had to distribute tiny orders to individual customers. The distribution costs of on-line sales are surprisingly high—as much as 15% of sales.

Pegasus Wholesale, located in Brampton, has the largest, most technologically advanced book distribution centre in Canada. Pegasus fills more Internet orders than anyone else in Canada—not just for Chapters, new owner, Indigo, but for all major Canadian publishers.

Purchase Returns and Allowances

A purchaser may be dissatisfied with the merchandise received. The goods may be damaged or defective, of inferior quality, or perhaps they do not meet the purchaser's specifications. In such cases, the purchaser may return the goods to the seller. The purchaser receives a cash refund if the purchase was made for cash. Credit is granted if the sale was made on credit. Both types of return are known as a purchase return. Alternatively, the purchaser may choose to keep the merchandise if the seller is willing to grant an allowance (deduction) from the purchase price. This transaction is known as a purchase allowance.

Assume that Chelsea Video returned goods costing $300 to Highpoint Electronic on May 8. The entry by Chelsea Video for the merchandise returned is as follows: Chelsea Video increased Merchandise Inventory when the goods were originally pur-

May 8	Accounts Payable	300	
	Merchandise Inventory		300
	To record return of goods to Highpoint Electronic.		

A	=	L	+	OE
−300		−300		

chased. So, Chelsea Video decreases Merchandise Inventory when it returns the goods, or when it is granted an allowance.

Discounts

The terms of a credit purchase may include an offer of a quantity discount for a bulk purchase. A quantity discount provides a reduction in price dependent upon the volume of purchases. Quantity discounts are not recorded or accounted for separately. For example, Highpoint may offer a 10% price discount on orders of 25 or more items. Then, if 25 printed circuit boards were ordered, the price per board would be $2,070 ($2,300 x 90%) rather than $2,300. Only the $2,070 amount would be recorded by Chelsea Video.

Quantity discounts are not the same as purchase discounts, which are offered to customers for early payment of the balance due. Purchase discounts are noted on the invoice by the use of **credit terms** specifying the amount and time period for the purchase discount. They also indicate the length of time in which the purchaser is expected to pay the full invoice price. For example, credit terms might be stated as 1/10, n/30 (read "one ten, net thirty"). This means that a 1% cash discount may be taken on the invoice price (less any returns or allowances) if payment is made within 10 days of the invoice date (the discount period). Otherwise, the invoice price is due 30 days from the invoice date.

When the seller elects not to offer a discount for prompt payment, credit terms will specify only the maximum time period for paying the balance due. For example, the time period may be stated as n/30, n/60, or EOM (end of month). In the invoice in Illustration 5-4, credit terms are n/30. This means that payment is due within 30 days of the invoice date. There is no discount offered for early payment.

In contrast to quantity discounts, purchase discounts are recorded separately. The use of purchase discounts is not common in Canada except in specialized industries (e.g., the lumber brokerage industry). Accordingly, the accounting entries for purchase discounts are left to other accounting courses.

Before You Go On . . .

▶*Review It*

1. How does the measurement of net income in a merchandising company differ from that in a service company?
2. In what ways is a perpetual inventory system different from a periodic inventory system?
3. Under the perpetual inventory system, what entries are made to record purchases, freight costs, purchase returns and allowances, and quantity discounts?

Related exercise material: BE5–1, BE5–2, and E5–1.

THE NAVIGATOR

Recording Sales of Merchandise

Sales revenue, like service revenue, is recorded when it is earned. This is in accordance with the revenue recognition principle. Typically, sales revenue is earned when the goods are transferred from the seller to the buyer. At this point, the sales transaction is completed and the sales price has been established.

Sales may be made on credit or for cash. Every sales transaction should be supported by a **business document** that provides written evidence of the sale. **Cash register tapes** provide evidence of cash sales. A **sales invoice**, like the one shown in Illustration 5-4, can provide support for a credit or a cash sale. The original copy of the invoice goes to the customer. A copy is kept by the seller for use in recording the sale. The invoice shows the date of sale, customer name, sales price, total amount due, and other relevant information.

Sales

Two entries are made for each sale. The first entry records the sales revenue: Cash (or Accounts Receivable, if a credit sale) is increased by a debit, and Sales is increased by a credit for the selling (invoice) price of the goods. The second entry records the cost of the merchandise sold: Cost of Goods Sold is increased by a debit, and Merchandise Inventory is decreased by a credit for the cost of the goods. As a result, the Merchandise Inventory account will always show the amount of inventory that should be on hand.

To illustrate a credit sales transaction, Highpoint Electronic's $3,800 sale to Chelsea Video on May 4 (see Illustration 5-4) is recorded as follows. Assume the merchandise cost Highpoint Electronic $2,400 when it was originally purchased.

A	=	L	+	OE
+3,800				+3,800

May 4	Accounts Receivable	3,800	
	Sales		3,800
	To record credit sale per invoice #731 to Chelsea Video.		

A	=	L	+	OE
−2,400				−2,400

4	Cost of Goods Sold	2,400	
	Merchandise Inventory		2,400
	To record cost of merchandise sold per invoice #731 to Chelsea Video.		

For internal purposes, merchandisers may use more than one sales account, just as they use more than one inventory account. For example, Highpoint Electronic may keep separate sales accounts for its TV sets, VCRs, cassette players, CD players, and microwave ovens. By using separate sales accounts for major product lines, company management can monitor sales trends more closely and respond more strategically to changes in sales patterns. For example, if CD players are increasing while cassette player sales are decreasing, the company can re-evaluate its advertising and pricing policies on each of these items.

However, on its income statement presented to outside investors, a merchandiser would normally provide only a single sales figure—the sum of all of its individual sales accounts. This is done for two reasons. First, providing detail on individual sales accounts would add too much length to the income statement. Second, companies do not want their competitors to know the details of their operating results.

Sales Taxes

Sales taxes are collected by many organizations, including service and merchandising enterprises, on the services that they provide and the goods that they sell. Sales taxes may take the form of the **Goods and Services Tax (GST)** and the **Provincial Sales Tax (PST)**. The federal GST is assessed at a rate of 7% across Canada. Provincial sales tax rates vary throughout the provinces and territories. In the Atlantic provinces (except for PEI), GST and PST have been combined into one 15% tax called the **Harmonized Sales Tax (HST)**.

Although a company collects these sales taxes in conjunction with a sale, **sales taxes are not revenue to the company**. These monies are collected on behalf of the federal and provincial governments, and must be periodically remitted to them. Until then, they are a current liability of the company.

Sales taxes add much complexity to the accounting process. In addition, not all companies and their goods and services are taxable. Accounting transactions in this and other chapters are presented without the added intricacies of sales taxes. That is why Invoice No. 731, shown in Illustration 5-4, omitted sales taxes, which would normally be added to the invoice price.

For those students who wish to advance their understanding of this topic, sales taxes are discussed in more detail in Appendix 5A.

Sales Returns and Allowances

We now look at the "flipside" of purchase returns and allowances, which are sales returns and allowances recorded on the books of the seller.

Highpoint Electronic records a $300 credit for Chelsea Video's returned goods in two entries: (1) The first is an increase in Sales Returns and Allowances and a decrease in Accounts Receivable at the $300 selling price. (2) The second is an increase in Merchandise Inventory (assume a $140 original cost) and a decrease in Cost of Goods Sold. The entries are as follows:

May 8	Sales Returns and Allowances	300	
	Accounts Receivable		300
	To record credit granted to Chelsea Video		
	for returned goods.		

A	=	L	+	OE
−300				−300

8	Merchandise Inventory	140	
	Cost of Goods Sold		140
	To record cost of goods returned.		

A	=	L	+	OE
+140				+140

For a sales return or allowance on a cash sale, a cash refund is normally made. In such a case, Cash is credited instead of Accounts Receivable.

If the goods are returned because they are damaged or defective, the first entry stays the same. The second entry still credits Cost of Goods Sold (since the goods have not been sold), but the debit is to a loss (expense) account rather than to an asset account, Merchandise Inventory, if the inventory is no longer saleable. If the inventory can be repaired and resold, it is debited to Merchandise Inventory. Some companies maintain a separate Merchandise Inventory account to record used or damaged goods for resale.

Sales Returns and Allowances is a contra revenue account to Sales. The normal balance of Sales Returns and Allowances is a debit. A contra account is used instead of debiting sales to disclose the amount of sales returns and allowances in the accounts. This information is important to management. Excessive returns and allowances suggest inferior merchandise, inefficiencies in filling orders, errors in billing customers, and mistakes in delivery or shipment of goods. Also, a debit recorded directly to sales could distort comparisons between total sales in different accounting periods.

▶Accounting in Action ▸ *Business Insight*

Returned goods can represent as much as 15% of total sales volume. Most companies do a poor job of dealing with returned goods, often destroying perfectly good merchandise. A new piece of software changed this for the cosmetic company Estée Lauder. When boxes of Estée Lauder lipstick and other products are returned by a retailer, each bar code is scanned, and each item's expiration date and condition are determined. The item is then either scrapped or sorted for resale to employees, to "seconds" stores, or to poor countries. The system paid for its $1.5 million development cost in nine months because it enabled the company to resell two-and-one-half times as many items at less than half the cost of the old system. Estée Lauder plans to license its software to other retailers.

Source: "Cash from Trash," *The Economist*, February 6, 1999, 66.

Discounts

Quantity discounts and sale discounts given on sales prices affect the seller in addition to the purchaser. No separate entry is made to record a **quantity discount**. Merchandise is recorded at cost—the price actually paid—whether it is the full retail price, a sale price, or a volume discount price.

Like a purchase discount, the seller may offer the customer a cash discount for the prompt payment of the balance due. From the seller's point of view, this is called a sales discount. Neither sales discounts nor purchase discounts are common in today's business world. As mentioned earlier, further discussion of this topic is left to another accounting course.

Freight Costs

Freight terms—FOB destination and FOB shipping point—on the sales invoice indicate who assumes responsibility for shipping costs. If the term is FOB destination, the seller assumes the responsibility of getting the goods to their intended destination. **Freight costs incurred by the seller on outgoing merchandise are an operating expense to the seller.** These costs are debited to a Freight Out or Delivery Expense account. When the freight charges are paid by the seller, the seller will usually establish a higher invoice price for the goods to cover the expense of shipping.

In the sale of electronic equipment to Chelsea Video, the freight terms (FOB shipping point) indicate that Chelsea Video must pay the cost of shipping the goods from Highpoint Electronic's location in Toronto to Chelsea Video's location in Hamilton. The seller (Highpoint Electronic) makes no journal entry to record the cost of shipping, since this cost was incurred by Chelsea and not by Highpoint.

Before You Go On . . .

►Review It

1. Under a perpetual inventory system, what are the two entries that must be recorded at the time of each sale?
2. Why is it important to use the Sales Returns and Allowances account, rather than simply reduce the Sales account, when goods are returned?
3. What journal entry (if any) is recorded by the seller and the buyer when the shipping terms are FOB destination? FOB shipping point?

►Do It

On September 4, La Hoya Company buys merchandise on account from Junot Company. The selling price of the goods is $1,500, and the cost to Junot Company was $800. On September 8, goods with a selling price of $200 and a cost of $80 are returned and restored to inventory. Record the transaction on the books of both companies.

Action Plan

- Purchaser: Record purchases of inventory at cost. Reduce the Merchandise Inventory account for returned goods.
- Seller: Record both the sale and the cost of goods sold at the time of the sale. Record returns in a contra acccount, Sales Returns and Allowances, and reduce Cost of Goods Sold when merchandise is returned to inventory.

Solution

La Hoya Company (Purchaser)

Sept. 4	Merchandise Inventory	1,500	
	Accounts Payable		1,500
	To record goods purchased on account.		
8	Accounts Payable	200	
	Merchandise Inventory		200
	To record return of defective goods.		

Junot Company (Seller)

Sept. 4	Accounts Receivable	1,500	
	Sales		1,500
	To record credit sale.		
4	Cost of Goods Sold	800	
	Merchandise Inventory		800
	To record cost of goods sold on account.		
8	Sales Returns and Allowances	200	
	Accounts Receivable		200
	To record credit granted for receipt of returned goods.		
8	Merchandise Inventory	80	
	Cost of Goods Sold		80
	To record cost of goods returned.		

Related exercise material: BE5–3, BE5–4, BE5–5, E5–2, E5–3, E5–4, and E5–5.

▼Completing the Accounting Cycle

STUDY OBJECTIVE

·········▼·········

4

Explain and perform the steps in the accounting cycle for a merchandising company.

Up to this point, we have illustrated the basic entries for recording transactions related to purchases and sales in a perpetual inventory system. Now, it is time to consider the remaining steps in the accounting cycle for a merchandising company.

Each of the required steps described in Chapter 4 for a service company applies to a merchandising company. Use of a work sheet (an optional step) is shown in Appendix 5B to the chapter.

Adjusting Entry

A merchandising company generally has the same types of adjusting entries as a service company. But, for control purposes, a merchandiser using a perpetual inventory system may require one additional adjustment to make the recorded inventory agree with the actual inventory on hand.

Helpful hint In a perpetual inventory system, the physical count can occur at any time. It does not necessarily have to be at, or near, year end.

In a perpetual inventory system, the Merchandise Inventory account balance should equal the cost of the merchandise on hand (ending inventory) at all times. A **physical inventory count** adds an important control feature to the perpetual inventory system. Even though the Merchandise Inventory account provides a record of the inventory on hand, it only indicates what *should* be there, not what actually is there. If inventory errors have occurred, or if inventory has been stolen or damaged, it is important that management be aware of this at an early stage so that preventive controls can be put in place.

Taking a physical inventory involves the following:
1. Counting the units on hand for each item of inventory.
2. Applying unit costs to the total units on hand for each item of inventory.
3. Totalling the costs for each item of inventory to determine the total cost of goods on hand.

If Highpoint Electronic's accounting records show an ending inventory balance of $40,500 at the end of May and a physical inventory count indicates only $40,000 on hand, the following journal entry should be prepared. The inventory shortage increases the Cost of Goods Sold account. Although this inventory hasn't been *sold*, inventory losses are part of the cost of the goods.

May 31	Cost of Goods Sold		500	
	Merchandise Inventory			500
	To record difference between inventory records and physical units on hand.			

$$
\begin{array}{ccccc}
A & = & L & + & OE \\
-500 & & & & -500
\end{array}
$$

The non-existent inventory is removed from the Merchandise Inventory account so that accuracy is maintained and performance measures using inventory are not distorted.

▶ Accounting in Action ▸ *Ethics Insight*

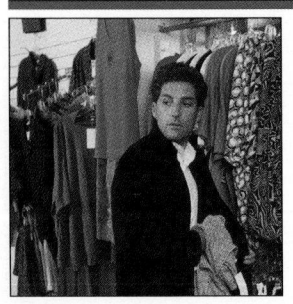

Inventory losses can be substantial. Shoplifting is a big crime in Canada. Canadian retailers lost $4.5 million every day in 1999 to customer and employee theft, according to the Retail Council of Canada (RCC). Stores estimate that they lose between 2% and 5% of their gross sales to shoplifting.

"The total losses suffered by Canadian retailers due to theft remains unacceptably high," commented Diane Brisebois, President and CEO of RCC. "As consumers, we all pay the price when customers and store employees steal. The good news is that more retailers are taking action." Many retailers have set up a loss-prevention department. They have also adopted procedures to stem their losses by developing strong inventory management controls through computerized point-of-sale systems.

Closing Entries

An adjusted trial balance, using assumed data, is shown below for Highpoint Electronic. The accounts used only by a merchandising company are highlighted in red.

Illustration 5-7

Adjusted trial balance

HIGHPOINT ELECTRONIC **Adjusted Trial Balance** **December 31, 2002**		
	Debit	Credit
Cash	$ 9,500	
Accounts Receivable	16,100	
Merchandise Inventory	40,000	
Prepaid Insurance	1,800	
Store Equipment	80,000	
Accumulated Amortization		$ 24,000
Accounts Payable		20,400
Salaries Payable		5,000
R. A. Lamb, Capital		83,000
R. A. Lamb, Drawings	15,000	
Sales		480,000
Sales Returns and Allowances	20,000	
Cost of Goods Sold	316,000	
Salaries Expense	45,000	
Rent Expense	19,000	
Utilities Expense	17,000	
Advertising Expense	16,000	
Amortization Expense	8,000	
Freight Out	7,000	
Insurance Expense	2,000	
Totals	$612,400	$612,400

For a merchandising company, like a service company, all temporary accounts (revenues, expenses, and drawings) are closed to the owner's capital account. In journalizing, the steps are as follows: (1) All temporary accounts with credit balances are debited. Sales is a new account that must be closed to the owner's capital account. (2) All temporary accounts with debit balances are credited. Three new accounts are included in this entry: Sales Returns and Allowances, a contra revenue account with a debit balance; Cost of Goods Sold; and Freight Out. (3) Drawings, a temporary account with a debit balance, is credited separately to the owner's capital account, as indicated in the following closing entries:

Dec. 31	Sales	480,000		A = L + OE	
	R. A. Lamb, Capital		480,000		−480,000
	To close accounts with credit balances.				+480,000
31	R. A. Lamb, Capital	450,000		A = L + OE	
	Sales Returns and Allowances		20,000		−450,000
	Cost of Goods Sold		316,000		+20,000
	Salaries Expense		45,000		+316,000
	Rent Expense		19,000		+45,000
	Utilities Expense		17,000		+19,000
	Advertising Expense		16,000		+17,000
	Amortization Expense		8,000		+16,000
	Freight Out		7,000		+8,000
	Insurance Expense		2,000		+7,000
	To close accounts with debit balances.				+2,000

A	=	L	+	OE
				−15,000
				+15,000

	Dec. 31	R. A Lamb, Capital	15,000	
		R. A. Lamb, Drawings		15,000
		To close drawings to capital.		

Post-Closing Trial Balance

After the closing entries are posted, a post-closing trial balance should be prepared. You will recall that the purpose of this trial balance is to ensure that debits equal credits in the permanent (balance sheet) accounts after all temporary accounts have been closed. The only new account in the post-closing trial balance is the current asset account, Merchandise Inventory.

Preparation of a post-closing trial balance does not differ from the process described in Chapter 4 and is not illustrated again here.

Illustration 5-8

Merchandising journal entries

Summary of Merchandising Entries

The entries for the merchandising accounts using a perpetual inventory system are summarized in Illustration 5-8.

	Transactions	Daily Recurring Journal Entries	Debit	Credit
Sales	Selling merchandise to customers.	Cash or Accounts Receivable	XX	
		Sales		XX
		Cost of Goods Sold	XX	
		Merchandise Inventory		XX
	Granting sales returns or allowances to customers.	Sales Returns and Allowances	XX	
		Cash or Accounts Receivable		XX
		Merchandise Inventory	XX	
		Cost of Goods Sold		XX
	Paying freight costs on sales, FOB destination.	Freight Out	XX	
		Cash		XX
	Receiving payment from customers.	Cash	XX	
		Accounts Receivable		XX
Purchases	Purchasing merchandise for resale.	Merchandise Inventory	XX	
		Cash or Accounts Payable		XX
	Paying freight costs on merchandise purchased, FOB shipping point.	Merchandise Inventory	XX	
		Cash		XX
	Receiving purchase returns or allowances from suppliers.	Cash or Accounts Payable	XX	
		Merchandise Inventory		XX
	Paying suppliers.	Accounts Payable	XX	
		Cash		XX

		Adjusting Entry	Debit	Credit
End of Period	Physical count determined that inventory in general ledger is higher than inventory actually on hand.	Cost of Goods Sold	XX	
		Merchandise Inventory		XX

		Closing Entries	Debit	Credit
	Close temporary accounts with credit balances.	Sales	XX	
		Capital		XX
	Close temporary accounts with debit balances (drawings closed separately).	Capital	XX	
		Sales Returns and Allowances		XX
		Cost of Goods Sold		XX
		Freight Out		XX
		Other expenses		XX
	Close drawings account.	Capital	XX	
		Drawings		XX

Before You Go On . . .

►Review It

1. Why is an adjustment to the Merchandise Inventory account sometimes necessary?
2. How do closing entries for a merchandising company differ from closing entries for a service company?
3. What merchandising account(s) will appear in the post-closing balance?

►Do It

The trial balance of the Yee Clothing Company at December 31 shows Merchandise Inventory $25,000; Yee, Capital $12,000; Sales $162,400; Sales Returns and Allowances $4,800; Cost of Goods Sold $110,000; Rental Revenue $6,000; Freight Out $1,800; Rent Expense $8,800; Salaries Expense $22,000; and Drawings $3,600. Prepare the closing entries for the above accounts.

Action Plan

- Close all temporary accounts with credit balances to Yee, Capital.
- Close all temporary accounts with debit balances (except drawings) to Yee, Capital.
- Close drawings separately to Yee, Capital.

Solution

Dec. 31	Sales	162,400	
	Rental Revenue	6,000	
	Yee, Capital		168,400
	To close accounts with credit balances.		
31	Yee, Capital	147,400	
	Sales Returns and Allowances		4,800
	Cost of Goods Sold		110,000
	Freight Out		1,800
	Rent Expense		8,800
	Salaries Expense		22,000
	To close accounts with debit balances.		
31	Yee, Capital	3,600	
	Drawings		3,600
	To close drawings account.		

Related exercise material: BE5–6, BE5–7, and E5–6.

THE
NAVIGATOR

Merchandising Financial Statements

Merchandisers use the classified balance sheet introduced in Chapter 4. In addition, two forms of income statement are widely used by merchandising companies. How merchandisers use them is explained below.

Multiple-Step Income Statement

The multiple-step income statement has its name because it shows the steps in determining net income (or net loss). It shows two main steps: (1) Cost of goods sold is subtracted from net sales to determine gross profit. (2) Operating expenses are deducted from gross profit to determine net income. These steps involve the company's principal operating activities. A multiple-step statement also distinguishes between **operating** and **non-operating** activities. This distinction provides users with more information about a company's income performance. The statement also highlights intermediate components of income and shows subgroupings of expenses.

STUDY OBJECTIVE
5

Distinguish between and be able to prepare both a multiple-step and a single-step income statement.

Net Sales

The multiple-step income statement begins by presenting sales revenues. As a contra revenue account, Sales Returns and Allowances is deducted from Sales in the income statement to arrive at **net sales**. The sales revenue section for Highpoint Electronic (using data presented in the adjusted trial balance in Illustration 5-7) is as follows:

Illustration 5-9

Calculation and presentation of net sales

HIGHPOINT ELECTRONIC Income Statement (partial) For the Year Ended December 31, 2002		
Sales revenue		
Sales		$480,000
Less: Sales returns and allowances		20,000
Net sales		460,000

This presentation discloses the key aspects of the company's principal revenue-producing activities. Many companies condense this information and report only net sales in their income statement.

Gross Profit

STUDY OBJECTIVE
▿ 6

Explain the importance of and be able to calculate gross profit.

From Illustration 5-1, you learned that cost of goods sold is deducted from sales revenue to determine **gross profit**. Sales revenue used for this calculation is net sales (which takes into account sales returns and allowances). On the basis of the sales data presented in Illustration 5-9 and cost of goods sold of $316,000, the gross profit for Highpoint Electronic is $144,000, calculated as follows:

Illustration 5-10

Calculation of gross profit

Net sales	$460,000
Cost of goods sold	316,000
Gross profit	144,000

A company's gross profit may also be expressed as a percentage, called the **gross profit margin**. This is done by dividing the amount of gross profit by net sales. For Highpoint Electronic, the gross profit margin is 31.3%, determined as follows:

Illustration 5-11

Gross profit margin formula and calculation

The gross profit margin is generally considered to be more useful than the gross profit amount. The margin expresses a more meaningful (relative) relationship between net sales and gross profit. For example, a gross profit amount of $1,000,000 may sound impressive. But, if it is the result of a gross profit margin of only 7%, it is not so impressive.

Gross profit represents the **merchandising profit** of a company. It is not a measure of the overall profitability, because operating expenses have not been deducted. The amount and trend of gross profit are closely watched by management and other interested parties. They compare current gross profit to amounts reported in past periods. They also compare the company's gross profit margin to the margin of competitors and to industry averages. Such comparisons provide information about the effectiveness of a company's purchasing and the soundness of its pricing policies.

Many companies, including The Second Cup Ltd., do not report gross profit separately on their income statement. Rather, they combine cost of goods sold with various operating expenses for reporting purposes. There are a number of reasons for this practice. There may be sensitive information which companies do not wish to make available to their competitors. Or, when considered on a consolidated or combined basis, gross profit may not be a meaningful number.

Operating Expenses and Net Income

Operating expenses are the third component in measuring net income for a merchandiser. As indicated earlier, these expenses are similar in merchandising and service companies. At Highpoint Electronic, operating expenses total $114,000 (from Illustration 5-7, $45,000 + $19,000 + $17,000 + $16,000 + $8,000 + $7,000 + $2,000). If there are no non-operating activities, the company's net income is determined by subtracting operating expenses from gross profit. Thus, net income is $30,000, as shown below:

Gross profit	$144,000
Operating expenses	114,000
Net income	$ 30,000

Illustration 5-12

Operating expenses in calculating net income

The net income is the "bottom line" of a company's income statement. Net income is often expressed as a percentage of sales, similar to the gross profit margin. The profit margin divides net income by net sales. Highpoint's profit margin is 6.5% ($30,000 ÷ $460,000).

Subgrouping of Operating Expenses. In larger companies, operating expenses are often subdivided into selling expenses and administrative expenses. Selling expenses are those associated with making sales. They include expenses for sales promotion. They also include expenses for completing the sale, such as delivery and shipping. Administrative expenses (sometimes called general expenses) relate to general operating activities such as personnel management, accounting, and store security.

When subgroupings are made, some expenses may have to be prorated (e.g., 70% to selling and 30% to administrative expenses). For example, if a store building is used for both selling and general functions, building expenses such as amortization, utilities, and property taxes will need to be allocated.

Any reasonable classification of expenses that serves to inform those who use the statement is satisfactory. The present tendency in statements prepared for management's internal use is to present detailed expense data grouped according to lines of responsibility.

Non-Operating Activities

Illustration 5-12 assumed that Highpoint Electronic had no activities other than those from primary operations. Most companies also have non-operating activities. **Non-operating activities** consist of (1) revenues and expenses from auxiliary operations and (2) gains and losses that are unrelated to the company's operations. The results of non-operating activities are shown in two sections: other revenues and gains and

other expenses and losses. For a merchandising company, these sections will typi-cally include the following items:

Illustration 5-13

Items reported in non-operating sections

Non-Operating Activities	
Other Revenues and Gains	Other Expenses and Losses
Interest from notes receivable and temporary investments	Interest expense on notes and loans payable
Dividend revenue from investments in share capital	Casualty losses from recurring causes such as vandalism and accidents
Rent revenue from subleasing a portion of the store	Losses from the disposal of capital assets
Gain from the disposal of capital assets	Losses from strikes

The non-operating activities are reported in the income statement immediately after the company's primary operating activities, appropriately subdivided into sell-ing and administrative expenses. These sections are shown in Illustration 5-14, using assumed data, for Highpoint Electronic.

HIGHPOINT ELECTRONIC
Income Statement
For the Year Ended December 31, 2002

Sales revenue			
Sales			$480,000
Less: Sales returns and allowances			20,000
Net sales			460,000
Cost of goods sold			316,000
Gross profit			144,000
Operating expenses			
Selling expenses			
Salaries expense		$45,000	
Advertising expense		16,000	
Amortization expense—store equipment		8,000	
Freight out		7,000	
Total selling expenses		76,000	
Administrative expenses			
Rent expense		$19,000	
Utilities expense		17,000	
Insurance expense		2,000	
Total administrative expenses		38,000	
Total operating expenses			114,000
Income from operations			30,000
Other revenues and gains			
Interest revenue		$3,000	
Gain on sale of equipment		600	
Total non-operating revenues and gains		3,600	
Other expenses and losses			
Interest expense		$1,800	
Casualty loss from vandalism		200	
Total non-operating expenses and losses		2,000	
Net non-operating revenue			1,600
Net income			$31,600

Left margin labels: Calculation of gross profit; Calculation of income from operations; Calculation of non-operating activities

When the two non-operating sections are included, the heading **Income from operations** (or Operating income) precedes them. It clearly identifies the results of the company's normal operations. Income from operations is determined by subtracting cost of goods sold and operating expenses from net sales.

In the non-operating activities sections, items are generally reported at the net amount. Thus, if a company received a $2,500 insurance settlement on vandalism losses of $2,700, the loss is reported at $200. Note, too, that the results of the two non-operating sections are netted. The difference is added to, or subtracted from, income from operations to determine net income. It is not uncommon for companies to combine these two non-operating sections into a single "Other revenues and expenses" section.

►Accounting in Action ► *Business Insight*

During a recent quarter, the income of computer chip maker Intel shot up 79%. But enthusiasm about the huge jump was dampened by the fact that many analysts were openly sceptical about the income figure. The analysts were concerned because in the ordinary income figure there were a variety of special items and "one-time" gains from sales of investments. The analysts would prefer that these items were reported separately under "Other revenues and expenses." In evaluating the company, many analysts simply ignore the investment gains.

Single-Step Income Statement

Another income statement format is the single-step income statement. The statement has this name because only one step, subtracting total expenses from total revenues, is required in determining net income (or net loss).

In a single-step statement, all data are classified under two categories: (1) revenues, and (2) expenses. The **revenues** category includes both operating revenues and other revenues and gains. The **expenses** category includes cost of goods sold, operating expenses, and other expenses and losses.

For a corporation, income tax expense is reported in a separate section. Income tax expense is reported separately whether a multiple-step or single-step income statement is used. Highpoint Electronic does not display any income tax expense because it is a proprietorship, not a corporation. In such cases, income tax is the responsibility of the owner, who pays for it personally, instead of the company.

A condensed single-step statement for Highpoint Electronic is shown in Illustration 5-15.

Illustration 5-15

Single-step income statement

HIGHPOINT ELECTRONIC Income Statement For the Year Ended December 31, 2002		
Revenues		
Net sales		$460,000
Interest revenue		3,000
Gain on sale of equipment		600
Total revenues		463,600
Expenses		
Cost of goods sold	$316,000	
Selling expenses	76,000	
Administrative expenses	38,000	
Interest expense	1,800	
Casualty loss from vandalism	200	
Total expenses		432,000
Net income		$ 31,600

There are two primary reasons for using the single-step format: (1) A company does not realize any type of profit or income until total revenues exceed total expenses, so it makes sense to divide the statement into these two categories. (2) The format is simpler and easier to read than the multiple-step format.

Classified Balance Sheet

In the balance sheet, merchandise inventory is reported as a current asset immediately following accounts receivable. Recall from Chapter 4 that items are listed under current assets in their order of liquidity. Merchandise inventory is less liquid than accounts receivable because the goods must first be sold before revenue can be collected from the customer. Illustration 5-16 presents the assets section of a classified balance sheet for Highpoint Electronic.

Illustration 5-16

Assets section of a classified balance sheet

Helpful hint   The $40,000 is the cost of the inventory on hand, not its expected selling price.

HIGHPOINT ELECTRONIC		
Balance Sheet (partial)		
December 31, 2002		
Assets		
Current assets		
Cash		$ 9,500
Accounts receivable		16,100
Merchandise inventory		40,000
Prepaid insurance		1,800
Total current assets		67,400
Capital assets		
Store equipment	$80,000	
Less: Accumulated amortization—store equipment	24,000	56,000
Total assets		$123,400

The remaining two financial statements, the statement of owner's equity and cash flow statement (to be discussed in Chapter 18) are the same as those of a service company. They are not shown in this chapter.

Before You Go On . . .

▸ **Review It**

1. What are non-operating activities and how are they reported in the income statement?
2. How does a single-step income statement differ from a multiple-step income statement?
3. How much inventory does The Second Cup Ltd. report in its 2000 and 1999 (pro forma) balance sheets? Does The Second Cup report its cost of goods sold on its income statement (statement of operations)? The answers to these questions are provided at the end of this chapter.

Related exercise material: BE5–8, BE5–9, BE5–10, E5–7, E5–8, and E5–9.

Using the Information in the Financial Statements

STUDY OBJECTIVE

▼ **7**

Calculate the inventory turnover and days sales in inventory ratios.

Inventory is of prime importance to a business. It is usually the largest current asset on the balance sheet (ending inventory) and the largest expense on the income statement (cost of goods sold). It affects the financial position of the business and is a significant component of working capital and the current ratio, which were introduced in Chapter 4.

Inventory management is a double-edged sword that requires constant attention. On one hand, management wants to have a variety and quantity of inventory on hand so customers have a good selection. But such an inventory policy may incur excessive carrying costs (e.g., investment, storage, insurance, taxes, obsolescence, and damage). On the other hand, low inventory levels lead to stockouts, lost sales, and disgruntled customers.

In addition to the gross profit and profit margins, discussed earlier in this chapter, there is the inventory turnover ratio. It assesses the efficiency by which a company sells its inventories. The **inventory turnover ratio** measures the number of times, on average, inventory is sold during the period. It is calculated by dividing cost of goods sold by average inventory. Whenever a ratio compares a balance sheet figure (e.g., inventory) to an income statement figure (e.g., cost of goods sold), the balance sheet figure must be averaged. Average balance sheet figures are determined by adding beginning and ending balances together and dividing by two. Averages are used to ensure that the balance sheet figures (which represent end-of-period amounts) cover the same period of time as the income statement figures (which represent amounts for the entire period).

Illustration 5-17 calculates the inventory turnover ratio for The Second Cup. The Second Cup did not separately disclose its cost of goods sold in its 2000 financial statements. It did, however, disclose its cost of goods sold in a prior year. The Second Cup's inventory turnover ratio for a prior year was as follows:

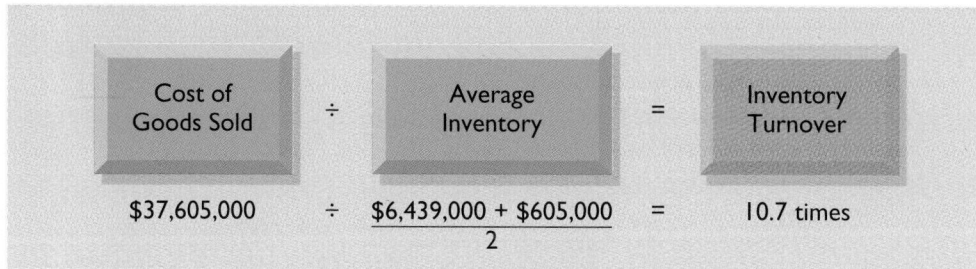

Illustration 5-17

Calculation of inventory turnover ratio

Generally, the greater the number of times per year the inventory turns over, the more efficiently sales are being made. It is informative to convert the inventory turnover ratio into a period of time, describing the age of the inventory. This ratio, called **days sales in inventory**, is calculated by dividing 365 days by the inventory turnover ratio, as illustrated for The Second Cup.

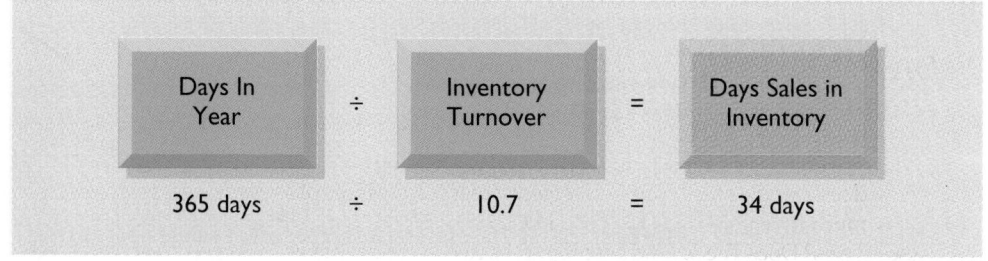

Illustration 5-18

Calculation of days sales in inventory

Be cautious in comparing these ratios to those of other companies—even those in the same industry. One of The Second Cup's reasons for no longer giving this information is that this ratio is not very meaningful when compared to results from other companies or divisions.

Before You Go On . . .

▶Review It

1. How can you tell whether a company has too much or too little inventory on hand?

Related exercise material: BE5–11, E5–10, and E5–11.

THE NAVIGATOR

▶ *A Look Back At Our Feature Story*

Refer back to the feature story about Mountain Equipment Co-op (MEC) and answer the following questions:

1. Why do you think MEC uses a perpetual inventory system?
2. What entry would MEC make when expedition backpacks are ordered? When backpacks are received? When paying shipping costs on backpack orders? When returning backpacks? When allowing customers to return backpacks? Assume all transactions are cash transactions.
3. In a perpetual inventory system, is it necessary to take a physical inventory count? Why? How often would you recommend that MEC count its inventory?

Solution

1. A perpetual inventory system provides MEC with information about the quantities and costs of products on hand, facilitating reordering decisions. The perpetual system, integrated with a point-of-sale (cash register) system, integrates accounting for the quantities of goods with the cost of the goods. It also allows MEC to determine inventory shortages, by comparing physical inventory counts of what is actually on hand to the accounting records.
2. No entry is made at the time the expedition backpacks are ordered. Probably an open purchase order file or memo record is used for keeping track of open (unfilled) purchase orders. When backpacks are received, MEC would record the purchases at invoice cost as follows:

Merchandise Inventory—Expedition Backpacks	XX	
Cash		XX
To record goods purchased.		

Shipping costs paid by MEC form part of the cost of the merchandise. MEC would record freight charges as follows:

Merchandise Inventory—Expedition Backpacks	XX	
Cash		XX
To record freight charges on purchases.		

When backpacks are returned to the supplier, MEC would prepare the following entry:

Cash	XX	
Merchandise Inventory—Expedition Backpacks		XX
To record returns.		

When MEC gives a refund for a returned backpack that is restored to inventory, the following entries would be made. The first entry is recorded at the backpack's selling price, the second at its cost.

Sales Returns and Allowances	XX	
Cash		XX
To record payment for returned goods.		
Merchandise Inventory—Expedition Backpacks	XX	
Cost of Goods Sold		XX
To return merchandise to inventory.		

3. A physical inventory count is required at least once a year. It would be useful to count inventory more often, at the end of each season. The physical inventory count would be compared to the records and any discrepancies would be adjusted.

   It is necessary to have an accurate record of your inventory in order to make good ordering and return decisions. Accurate ordering and efficient return practices are essential for MEC.

THE
NAVIGATOR

DEMONSTRATION PROBLEM

The adjusted trial balance data for the year ended December 31, 2002, for Dykstra Company are as follows:

Additional
Demonstration Problem

DYKSTRA COMPANY
Adjusted Trial Balance
December 31, 2002

	Debit	Credit
Cash	$ 14,500	
Accounts Receivable	15,100	
Merchandise Inventory	29,000	
Prepaid Insurance	2,500	
Land	150,000	
Building	500,000	
Accumulated Amortization—Building		$ 40,000
Equipment	95,000	
Accumulated Amortization—Equipment		18,000
Mortgage Payable—currently due		25,000
Accounts Payable		10,600
Property Taxes Payable		4,000
Mortgage Payable—long-term		530,000
Gene Dykstra, Capital		81,000
Gene Dykstra, Drawings	12,000	
Sales		627,200
Sales Returns and Allowances	6,700	
Cost of Goods Sold	353,800	
Salaries Expense	61,000	
Property Tax Expense	24,000	
Utilities Expense	18,000	
Advertising Expense	12,000	
Amortization Expense	29,000	
Freight Out	7,600	
Insurance Expense	4,500	
Interest Revenue		2,500
Interest Expense	3,600	
Totals	$1,338,300	$1,338,300

Instructions

(a) Prepare an income statement for the year ended December 31, 2002. Dykstra Company does not use subgroupings for operating expenses.

(b) Prepare a statement of owner's equity for Dykstra Company for the year ended December 31, 2002. No additional investments were made by Mr. Dykstra during the year.

(c) Prepare a classified balance sheet as at December 31, 2002.

Solution to Demonstration Problem

(a)

DYKSTRA COMPANY
Income Statement
For the Year Ended December 31, 2002

Sales revenues		
Sales		$627,200
Less: Sales returns and allowances		6,700
Net sales		620,500
Cost of goods sold		353,800
Gross profit		266,700
Operating expenses		
Salaries expense	$61,000	
Property tax expense	24,000	
Utilities expense	18,000	
Advertising expense	12,000	
Amortization expense	29,000	
Freight out	7,600	
Insurance expense	4,500	
Total operating expenses		156,100
Income from operations		110,600
Other revenues and gains		
Interest revenue	$ 2,500	
Other expenses and losses		
Interest expense	3,600	(1,100)
Net income		$109,500

(b)

DYKSTRA COMPANY
Statement of Owner's Equity
For the Year Ended December 31, 2002

Gene Dykstra, Capital, January 1, 2002	$ 81,000
Add: Net income	109,500
	190,500
Deduct: Drawings	12,000
Gene Dykstra, Capital, December 31, 2002	$178,500

(c)

DYKSTRA COMPANY
Balance Sheet
December 31, 2002

Assets

Current assets		
Cash		$ 14,500
Accounts receivable		15,100
Merchandise inventory		29,000
Prepaid insurance		2,500
		61,100
Capital assets		
Land		150,000
Building	$500,000	
Less: Accumulated amortization	40,000	460,000
Equipment	$ 95,000	
Less: Accumulated amortization	18,000	77,000
		687,000
Total assets		$748,100

Liabilities

Current liabilities	
Accounts payable	$ 10,600
Property taxes payable	4,000
Mortgage payable	25,000
	39,600
Long-term liabilities	
Mortgage payable	530,000
Total liabilities	569,600
Owner's Equity	
Gene Dykstra, Capital	178,500
Total liabilities and owner's equity	$748,100

APPENDIX 5A ▸ *Sales Taxes*

The general principle of collecting taxes on sales transactions is ingrained in the Canadian economy and affects most goods and services sold. It is, therefore, important for students of accounting to understand how sales taxes affect the accounts.

STUDY OBJECTIVE
............▾............
8

Describe and perform the accounting for sales taxes.

Although this is the first chapter in which sales taxes have been introduced, this does not mean that sales taxes affect only merchandising enterprises. Sales taxes affect both service and merchandising enterprises, as well as other organizations. They have been ignored until now to ensure that you have a good grasp of basic accounting concepts before adding the complexities of sales taxes.

As mentioned in the chapter, sales taxes may take the form of the Goods and Services Tax (GST), Provincial Sales Tax (PST), or Harmonized Sales Tax (HST). As an agent of the federal and provincial governments, a company is required to collect sales taxes on the sale of certain goods and services. The federal GST is assessed at the rate of 7% across Canada, whereas provincial sales tax rates vary. For example, in the Province of Ontario, 8% PST (in addition to the 7% GST) is collected on taxable goods and services. In the Province of Alberta, there is no PST, only the 7% federal GST. In Newfoundland and Labrador, Nova Scotia, and New Brunswick, the PST and GST have been combined into one 15% tax called the HST.

Helpful hint   In Quebec, provincial sales tax is known as the Quebec Sales Tax (QST)

Sales taxes are collected on most receipts, and paid on most disbursements. We will discuss sales taxes in the following sections.

▸Accounting in Action ▸ *@-Business Insight*

Internet-based transactions are creating tremendous opportunities for Canadian businesses to win new customers, reach global markets, and grow revenues, while achieving business efficiency. But borderless e-commerce and digital goods have resulted in sales tax chaos in this virtual environment. That's because tax laws were designed for the old economy. "The existing tax system is based on the concept of physical premise, which electronic trade eliminates," explains Pierre Bourgeois, tax partner for PricewaterhouseCoopers in Montreal.

For example, if a customer located in Canada makes a purchase on an American website whose server is located in Bermuda, who should tax this transaction? If a book, music, or software is downloaded, how do you determine whether sales tax is due or not—especially if the supplier doesn't even know where the customer is? They could be anywhere—in Montreal, New York, Beijing...or even on a plane. Or they could pretend to be.

The Canada Customs and Revenue Agency can't say exactly how much it is losing on Internet-related sales taxes. It just knows the figure is high. It is concerned about the situation and is trying to find solutions.

Source: René Lewandowski, "The Net Tax Nightmare," *CAmagazine*, March 2001, 18.

▸Sales Taxes Collected On Receipts
....

The GST is a 7% personal consumption tax that is collected on most goods and services provided in Canada. Some goods are exempted (e.g., residential rent and insurance). Others are taxed at a rate of 0% (zero-rated) (e.g., basic groceries and prescription drugs). For the most part, however, GST is collected every time a taxable good or service is provided.

Unlike the GST, which is a multi-stage tax imposed each time a good or service is sold, PST is a single-stage tax collected from final consumers on goods and services. There are very few exemptions available for PST. Groceries, residential rent, and insurance are a few items on which PST is not collected. PST regulations and exemptions vary by province.

We will use the transactions presented earlier in the chapter for Highpoint Electronic to illustrate the additional accounts required to record sales when sales taxes such as GST and PST are involved. As mentioned, PST and GST have been combined into a 15% HST in Nova Scotia, New Brunswick, and Newfoundland and Labrador. We will continue to refer to GST and PST throughout the following discussion, but if you live in these Atlantic provinces, substitute HST and the 15% rate whenever PST and GST are mentioned. Otherwise, the accounting is unchanged in the Atlantic provinces except that only one sales tax payable account (HST Payable) is required.

Illustration 5A–1

Sales/purchase invoice, with GST

Let's look now at the sales invoice prepared by Highpoint Electronic to document a sale to Chelsea Video, first shown in Illustration 5-4.

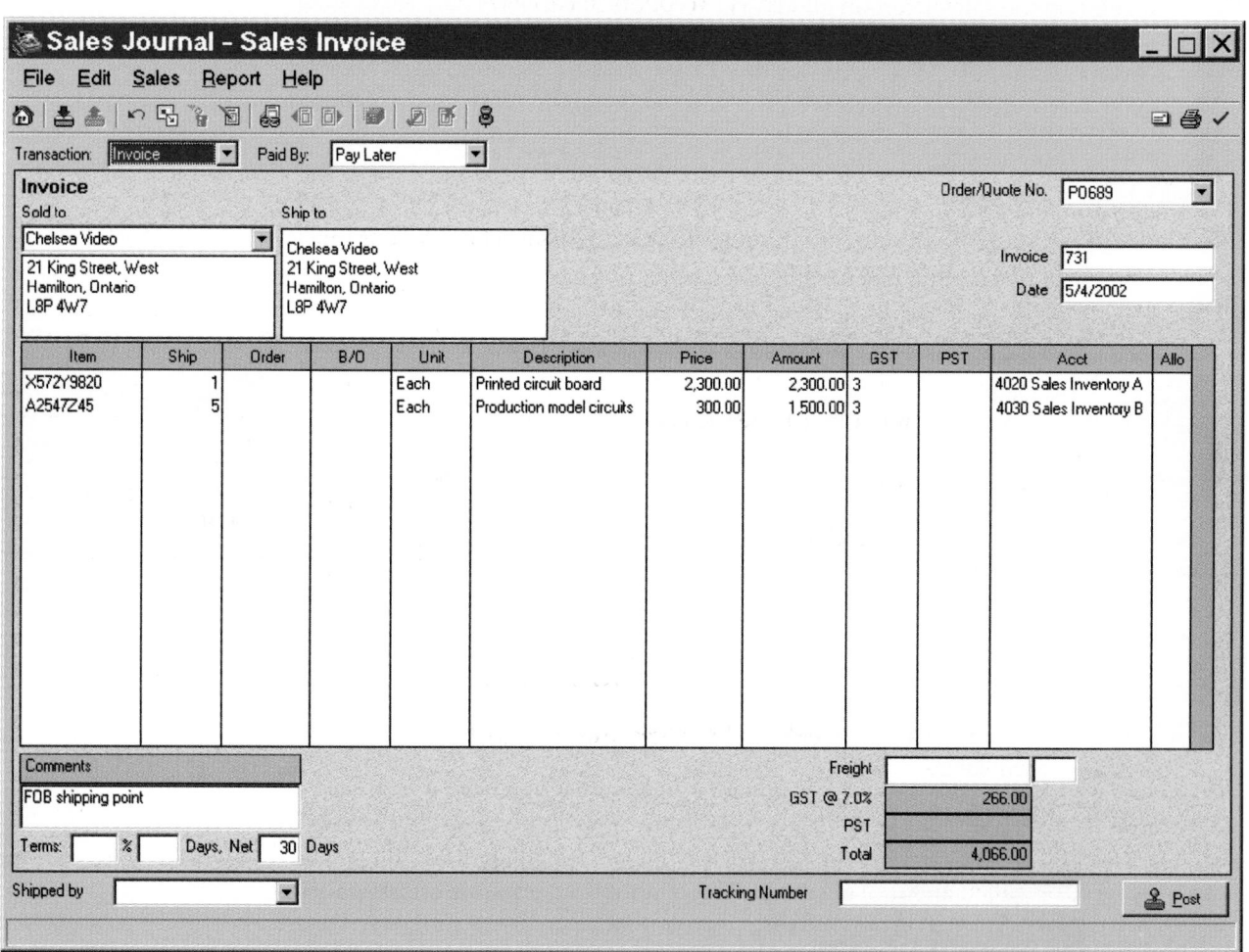

Seven percent GST ($266) is due on the sales price of $3,800. Including tax, the total invoice amount due is $4,066 ($3,800 + $266). No PST is payable by Chelsea Video since it is not the final consumer of the product purchased. Chelsea Video, as a retailer, has purchased goods from the wholesaler, Highpoint Electronic, to sell to final consumers.

As previously noted, sales taxes collected from customers are not revenue to Highpoint Electronic. They must be remitted to the Receiver General, the collection agency for the federal government for GST. The taxes are a current liability until remitted.

The following entries would be made by Highpoint Electronic to record this credit sale. The account we have added, in comparison to the entries presented on page 216, are highlighted in colour.

May 4	Accounts Receivable	4,066	
	Sales		3,800
	GST Payable		266
	To record credit sale per invoice #731.		

A	=	L	+	OE
+4,066		+266		+3,800

4	Cost of Goods Sold	2,400	
	Merchandise Inventory		2,400
	To record cost of merchandise sold per invoice #731 to Chelsea Video.		

A	=	L	+	OE
−2,400				−2,400

If the revenue arises from services provided by a service enterprise, rather than from goods sold by a merchandise enterprise, the same procedure is followed except that there is no second cost of goods sold entry. Accounts Receivable (or Cash) is debited, and the appropriate revenue and sales tax payable accounts are credited.

Sales Returns and Allowances

If a $300 sales return and allowance is granted, the seller's entry to record the credit memorandum will require a debit to the Sales Returns and Allowances account and a credit to the customer's Accounts Receivable account. The sales tax account must also be reversed, as tax is no longer owed.

May 8	Sales Returns and Allowances	300	
	GST Payable	21	
	Accounts Payable		321
	To record allowance for returned goods.		

A	=	L	+	OE
		−21		−300
		+321		

8	Merchandise Inventory	140	
	Cost of Goods Sold		140
	To record cost of goods returned.		

A	=	L	+	OE
+140				+140

Sales Taxes Paid On Disbursements

Businesses pay sales taxes on the goods and services they buy, just as they charge PST and GST on their sales.

Businesses pay GST on their purchases, but are able to recover the GST. Consequently, **when merchandise is purchased, the GST paid by a business is *not* part of the inventory cost**. The GST paid on purchases is debited to an account called GST Recoverable and is called an input tax credit. These input tax credits are offset against GST Payable. You will recall from our earlier discussion about recording sales that GST Payable results when GST is collected from customers at the time merchandise is sold.

The company does not receive a separate reimbursement from the government for GST Recoverable (paid on purchases). Nor does it remit a separate GST Payable amount (collected on sales) to the government. Instead, the company combines the two together, and is paid, or repays, the net difference. If there is a net debit balance (more GST paid than collected), the government will repay the company the GST. If there is a net credit balance (more GST collected than paid), the company must pay the difference to the government.

There will normally be a balance in the GST Recoverable or GST Payable account as reimbursement or repayment occurs in the next month, or the next quarter, depending on the size of the business. A net debit balance is reported as a current asset on the balance sheet. A net credit balance is reported as a current liability on the balance sheet. The two GST accounts are maintained separately in the general ledger for accounting purposes, but are usually combined for reporting purposes.

GST legislation is applied differently depending upon the type of organization and amount of revenue. For example, businesses with less than $30,000 of annual taxable sales can elect not to collect GST at all. If an organization does not collect GST from customers, GST paid is not recoverable. In this case, the GST paid is added to the cost of the good to which it relates.

PST, on the other hand, is paid only by the final consumer. Therefore, **retail businesses do not have to pay PST on any merchandise purchased for resale**.

Purchases of Merchandise

Neither GST nor PST forms part of the cost of goods purchased. GST is recoverable and PST is not paid on goods purchased for resale. The entry by the purchaser, Chelsea Video, to record the merchandise sold to it by Highpoint Electronic (see the invoice in Illustration 5A–1), follows:

```
A    =   L    +  OE
+3,800   +4,066
+266
```

May 4	Merchandise Inventory		3,800	
	GST Recoverable		266	
	Accounts Payable			4,066
	To record goods purchased on account, terms n/30.			

Helpful hint   Compare these entries made by Chelsea Video to those made earlier in the chapter, without sales tax, on pages 213 and 215.

Purchase Returns and Allowances

The entry by Chelsea Video for the $300 of merchandise returned on May 8 is as follows:

```
A    =   L    +  OE
−21     −321
−300
```

May 8	Accounts Payable		321	
	GST Recoverable			21
	Merchandise Inventory			300
	To record return of goods to Highpoint Electronic.			

To summarize, GST paid on purchases is normally recoverable and is recorded as a current asset, GST Recoverable. PST is not paid on purchases of merchandise for resale. Neither GST nor PST forms part of the cost of purchases. Returns and allowances require an adjustment of GST only, since PST was not paid on the original purchase.

Operating Expenses

Although PST is not charged on goods purchased for resale, it is charged to businesses that use taxable goods and services in their operations. For example, a business must pay PST when it buys office supplies. There are very few exemptions available to businesses for PST. GST must also be paid on most operating expenses incurred by businesses.

GST, however, continues to be recoverable, while PST forms part of the respective expense. Since PST is not recoverable, it becomes a cost of doing business and affects the prices charged to customers.

Using office supplies as an illustration, assume that Chelsea Video pays $1,000 to replenish its office supplies on May 1. PST of 8% and GST of 7% are collected by the retailer, Grand & Toy, from Chelsea Video for later remittance to the government.

May 1	Office Supplies ($1,000 + $80 PST)	1,080	
	GST Recoverable	70	
	Cash		1,150

A	=	L	+	OE
+1,080				
+70				
−1,150				

Sales tax law is intricate, and has added a great deal of complexity to accounting for the majority of transactions flowing through today's businesses. Fortunately, computers that are programmed to automatically determine and record the correct sales tax rate for each good or service provided have simplified matters somewhat.

Before recording sales tax transactions, however, it is important to understand all of the relevant sales tax regulations. Check the federal and provincial laws in your jurisdiction.

Before You Go On...

▸*Review It*

1. Explain how GST and PST affect revenues.
2. How does GST affect purchases of merchandise? PST?
3. Explain how GST and PST affect operating expenses.

Related exercise material: *BE5–12 and *E5–12.

THE NAVIGATOR

*A*PPENDIX 5B ▸ *Using a Work Sheet for a Merchandising Operation*

Three of the required steps in the accounting cycle can be made easier with the use of a work sheet. These steps, discussed in Chapter 4, are as follows: Step 4: prepare a trial balance, Step 5: journalize and post adjusting entries, and Step 6: prepare an adjusted trial balance. A work sheet also enables financial statements to be prepared before the adjusting entries are journalized and posted. To illustrate the use of a work sheet, we will assume that Highpoint Electronic uses one. The use of a work sheet is optional.

STUDY OBJECTIVE
•••••••••• 9 ••••••••••
Prepare a work sheet for a merchandising company.

▾Using a Work Sheet

The steps in preparing a work sheet for a merchandising company are the same as for a service enterprise. The work sheet for Highpoint Electronic is shown in Illustration 5B-1. The accounts unique to a merchandising company are highlighted in red.

Trial Balance Columns

Data for the trial balance are obtained from the general ledger balances of Highpoint Electronic at December 31. These balances are not shown in this chapter and have been assumed where required.

Account Titles	Unadjusted Trial Balance Dr.	Cr.	Adjustments Dr.		Cr.	Adjusted Trial Balance Dr.	Cr.	Income Statement Dr.	Cr.	Balance Sheet Dr.	Cr.
Cash	9,500					9,500				9,500	
Accounts Receivable	16,100					16,100				16,100	
Merchandise Inventory	40,500			(a)	500	40,000				40,000	
Prepaid Insurance	3,800			(c)	2,000	1,800				1,800	
Store Equipment	80,000					80,000				80,000	
Accumulated Amortization		16,000		(d)	8,000		24,000				24,000
Accounts Payable		20,400					20,400				20,400
R.A.Lamb, Capital		83,000					83,000				83,000
R.A.Lamb, Drawings	15,000					15,000				15,000	
Sales		480,000					480,000		480,000		
Sales Returns and Allowances	20,000					20,000		20,000			
Cost of Goods Sold	315,500		500	(a)		316,000		316,000			
Salaries Expense	40,000		5,000	(b)		45,000		45,000			
Rent Expense	19,000					19,000		19,000			
Advertising Expense	16,000					16,000		16,000			
Utilities Expense	17,000					17,000		17,000			
Freight Out	7,000					7,000		7,000			
Totals	599,400	599,400									
Salaries Payable				(b)	5,000		5,000				5,000
Insurance Expense			2,000	(c)		2,000		2,000			
Amortization Expense			8,000	(d)		8,000		8,000			
Totals			15,500		15,500	612,400	612,400	450,000	480,000	162,400	132,400
Net income								30,000			30,000
Totals								480,000	480,000	162,400	162,400

Key: (a) Adjustment to inventory on hand, (b) Salaries accrued, (c) Insurance expired, (d) Amortization expense

Illustration 5B-1

Work sheet for a merchandising company—perpetual inventory system

Adjustments Columns

Adjustment (a) was required to adjust the inventory recorded in the records to that actually on hand, as determined by a physical inventory count. Except for this one entry, a merchandising company generally has the same types of adjustments as a service company. As you see in the work sheet, adjustments (b), (c), and (d) are assumed for salaries, insurance, and amortization. These adjustments were also required for Pioneer Advertising Agency, as illustrated in Chapters 3 and 4.

After all adjustment data are entered on the work sheet, the equality of the adjustments column totals is established. The balances in all accounts are then extended to the adjusted trial balance columns.

Adjusted Trial Balance

The adjusted trial balance shows the balance of all accounts after adjustment at the end of the accounting period.

Income Statement Columns

The accounts and balances that affect the income statement are transferred from the adjusted trial balance columns to the income statement columns. For Highpoint Electronic, Sales, with a balance of $480,000, is shown in the credit column whereas the contra revenue account, Sales Returns and Allowances ($20,000), is shown in the debit column. Similarly, Cost of Goods Sold ($316,000) is extended to the debit column.

Finally, all the credits in the income statement column should be totalled and compared to the total debits in the related column. If the credits exceed the debits, the company has net income. In Highpoint Electronic's case, there was net income of $30,000. If the debits exceed the credits, the company reports a net loss.

Balance Sheet Columns

The major difference between the balance sheets of a service company and a merchandising company is inventory. For Highpoint Electronic, the ending inventory amount of $40,000 is shown in the balance sheet debit column. The information needed to prepare a statement of owner's equity is also found in these columns. That is, the beginning balance (including any owner's investments during the period) in the capital account of R. A. Lamb is $83,000. The drawings for R. A. Lamb are $15,000. Net income (as determined in the income statement columns) is entered as a credit in the balance sheet columns. If there had been a net loss (the total of the credits exceeds the total of the debit balances), it would be entered as a debit in the balance sheet columns.

Before You Go On . . .

►*Review It*

1. How does a work sheet for a merchandising company differ from a work sheet for a service company? In what ways is the work sheet similar for a merchandising company and a service company?

*Related exercise material: *BE5–13 and *E5–13.*

THE
NAVIGATOR

Summary of Study Objectives

1. *Describe the differences between a service company and a merchandising company.* A service company has service or fee revenue and operating expenses. A merchandising company has sales revenue, cost of goods sold, gross profit, and operating expenses.

2. *Explain and complete the entries for purchases under a perpetual inventory system.* The Merchandise Inventory account is debited for all purchases of merchandise and freight, if freight is paid by the purchaser. It is credited for purchase returns and allowances.

3. *Explain and complete the entries for sales revenue under a perpetual inventory system.* When inventory is sold, two entries are required: (1) Accounts Receivable (or Cash) is debited and Sales is credited for the selling price of the merchandise. (2) Cost of Goods Sold is debited and Merchandise Inventory is credited for the cost of the inventory items sold.

4. *Explain and perform the steps in the accounting cycle for a merchandising company.* Each of the required steps in the accounting cycle for a service company applies to a merchandising company. An additional adjusting journal entry may be required under a perpetual inventory system. The Merchandise Inventory account must be adjusted to agree with the physical count if any difference exists.

5. *Distinguish between and be able to prepare both a multiple-step and a single-step income statement.* A multiple-step income statement shows numerous steps in determining net income. Step 1 deducts cost of goods sold from net sales to determine gross profit. Step 2 deducts operating expenses, classified into selling and administrative categories, from gross profit to determine income from operations. Step 3 adds or deducts any non-operating activities to determine net income. In a single-step income statement, all data are classified under two categories (revenues or expenses), and net income is determined by one step.

6. *Explain the importance of and be able to calculate gross profit.* Gross profit is calculated by subtracting cost of goods sold from net sales. Gross profit represents the merchandising profit—what is left over after subtracting inventory cost to cover operating expenses—that contributes to the bottom line. The amount and trend of gross profit are closely watched by management and other interested parties.

7. *Calculate the inventory turnover and days sales in inventory ratios.* These ratios assess the efficiency with which inventory is converted into sales. Inventory turnover is calculated by dividing cost of goods sold by average inventory. Days sales in inventory is determined by dividing 365 days by the inventory turnover ratio.

8. *Describe and perform the accounting for sales taxes (Appendix 5A).* GST and PST on sales are collected by retailers on behalf of federal and provincial government collection agencies. After collection, these taxes are a current liability (GST/PST Payable) to the retailer until remitted to the respective collection agency. GST is recoverable when paid, and is recorded as a current asset (GST Recoverable). GST Recoverable is offset against GST Payable and any difference is remitted to or recovered from the

THE NAVIGATOR

federal government. PST is not paid on purchases of merchandise for resale. PST is part of the recorded cost when paid on other assets or expenses.

9. *Prepare a work sheet for a merchandising company (Appendix 5B).* The steps in preparing a work sheet for a merchandising company are the same as for a service company. The unique accounts for a merchandiser are Merchandise Inventory, Sales, Sales Returns and Allowances, Cost of Goods Sold, and Freight Out.

GLOSSARY

Key Term Matching Activity

Administrative expenses   Expenses that relate to general operating activities such as personnel management, accounting, and store security. (p. 225)

Contra revenue account   An account that is offset against a revenue account on the income statement. (p. 218)

Cost of goods sold   The total cost of merchandise sold during the period. (p. 208)

Days sales in inventory—The number of days inventory is on hand. It is calculated by dividing 365 days by the inventory turnover ratio. (p. 229)

FOB destination   Freight terms indicating that the seller will pay for the shipping costs of the goods. (p. 214)

FOB shipping point   Freight terms indicating that the seller will be responsible for the shipping costs of the goods only until they reach their shipping point. Since this is normally the seller's place of business (shipping point), there is no cost to the seller. The buyer pays freight costs from the shipping point to the destination of the buyer. (p. 214)

Goods and Services Tax (GST)   A 7% federal sales tax on goods and services. (p. 233)

Gross profit   The excess of net sales over the cost of goods sold (NS − CGS = GP). (p. 208)

Gross profit margin   Gross profit expressed as a percentage of net sales. It is calculated by dividing gross profit by net sales. (p. 224)

Harmonized Sales Tax (HST)   A 15% combined federal and provincial sales tax on goods and services that is applied in Nova Scotia, New Brunswick, and Newfoundland and Labrador. (p. 233)

Income from operations   Income from a company's principal operating activity, determined by subtracting operating expenses from gross profit (GP − OE = Income from operations). (p. 227)

Inventory turnover ratio   An indicator of how often a company is selling (turning over) its inventory. It is calculated by dividing cost of goods sold by average inventory. (p. 229)

Multiple-step income statement   An income statement that shows numerous steps to determine net income or net loss. (p. 223)

Net sales   Sales less sales returns and allowances. (p. 224)

Operating expenses   Expenses incurred in the process of earning sales revenues. They are deducted from gross profit in the income statement. (p. 208)

Other expenses and losses   A non-operating activities section of the income statement that shows expenses from auxiliary operations and losses unrelated to the company's operations. (p. 226)

Other revenues and gains   A non-operating activities section of the income statement that shows revenues from auxiliary operations and gains unrelated to the company's operations. (p. 225)

Periodic inventory system   An inventory system in which detailed records are not maintained. The cost of goods sold is determined only at the end of the accounting period. (p. 211)

Perpetual inventory system   A detailed inventory system in which the quantity and cost of each inventory item are maintained. The records continuously show the inventory that should be on hand. (p. 210)

Profit margin   Net income expressed as a percentage of net sales. It is calculated by dividing net income by net sales. (p. 225)

Provincial Sales Tax (PST)   A sales tax legislated by provincial governments levied on taxable goods and services. Rates vary by province. (p. 233)

Purchase discount   A discount, based on the invoice price less any returns and allowances, given to a buyer for early payment of a balance due. (p. 215)

Purchase returns (allowances)   The return (or reduction in price) of unsatisfactory purchased merchandise. It results in a debit to cash or accounts payable. (p. 215)

Quantity discount   A cash discount, reducing the invoice price, given to the buyer for volume purchases. (p. 215)

Sales discount   A reduction, based on the invoice price less any returns and allowances, given by a seller for prompt payment of a credit sale. (p. 218)

Sales returns and allowances   The return, or reduction in price, of unsatisfactory sold merchandise. It results in an account receivable credit or cash refund. (p. 217)

Sales revenue   The primary source of revenue in a merchandising company. (p. 208)

Selling expenses   Expenses associated with making sales. (p. 225)

Single-step income statement   An income statement that shows only one step in determining net income (or net loss). (p. 227)

Note: All **asterisked** Questions, Exercises, and Problems below relate to material contained in the appendices to the chapter.

SELF-STUDY QUESTIONS

Chapter 5 Self-Test

Answers are at the end of the chapter.

(SO 1) K   1. Gross profit will result if:
   a. operating expenses are less than net income.
   b. sales revenues is greater than operating expenses.
   c. sales revenues is greater than cost of goods sold.
   d. operating expenses are greater than cost of goods sold.

(SO 2) K   2. When goods are purchased for resale by a company using the perpetual inventory system:
   a. purchases are debited to Merchandise Inventory.
   b. purchases are debited to Sales.
   c. purchase returns are debited to Merchandise Inventory.
   d. freight costs are debited to Freight Out.

(SO 3) K   3. To record the cash sale of goods in a perpetual inventory system:
   a. only one journal entry is necessary to record the cost of goods sold and reduction of inventory.
   b. only one journal entry is necessary to record the receipt of cash and the sales revenue.
   c. two journal entries are necessary: one to record the receipt of cash and sale revenue, and one to record the cost of the goods sold and reduction of inventory.
   d. two journal entries are necessary: one to record the receipt of cash and reduction of inventory, and one to record the cost of the goods sold and sales revenue.

(SO 3) K   4. A contra sales account that normally has a debit balance is:
   a. Sales Returns and Allowances.
   b. Sales.
   c. Quantity Discounts.
   d. Cost of Goods Sold.

(SO 3) K   5. A credit sale on December 20 with terms of n/EOM is due to be collected by:
   a. December 31.
   b. January 10.
   c. January 20.
   d. January 31.

(SO 4) K   6. The steps in the accounting cycle for a merchandising company are the same as those for a service company *except*:
   a. an additional adjusting journal entry for inventory may be needed in a merchandising company.
   b. closing journal entries are not required for a merchandising company.
   c. a work sheet is required for a merchandising company.
   d. a multiple-step income statement is required for a merchandising company.

(SO 5) K   7. The multiple-step income statement for a merchandising company shows each of the following features *except*:
   a. gross profit.
   b. cost of goods sold.
   c. net sales.
   d. investing activities.

(SO 5) K   8. In a single-step income statement:
   a. gross profit is reported.
   b. cost of goods sold is not reported.
   c. sales revenue and other revenues and gains are reported in the revenues section of the income statement.
   d. operating income is reported separately.

(SO 6) AP   9. If sales revenue is $400,000, cost of goods sold is $310,000, and operating expenses are $60,000, the gross profit is:
   a. $30,000.
   b. $90,000.
   c. $340,000.
   d. $400,000.

(SO 7) AP   10. If sales are $500,000, cost of goods sold $350,000, and average inventory $35,000, the inventory turnover ratio is:
   a. 1.4 times.
   b. 10 times.
   c. 14 times.
   d. 36.5 days.

(SO 8) K   *11. When sales taxes are applied to a sales transaction, they should be:
   a. debited to an expense account.
   b. debited to a contra revenue account.
   c. credited to a liability account.
   d. credited to the Sales account.

(SO 9) K   *12. In a work sheet, Merchandise Inventory is shown in the following columns:
   a. adjusted trial balance debit and income statement credit.
   b. adjusted trial balance debit and balance sheet debit.
   c. income statement debit and balance sheet credit.
   d. income statement credit and balance sheet debit.

THE NAVIGATOR

QUESTIONS

(SO 1) C   1. How do the components of revenues and expenses differ between a merchandising company and a service company?

(SO 1) C   2. Explain the income measurement process in a merchandising company.

(SO 1) C   3. Why is the normal operating cycle for a merchandising company likely to be longer than that for a service company?

(SO 1) C   4. Distinguish between a perpetual and a periodic inventory system.

(SO 1) C   5. What types of businesses are most likely to use a perpetual inventory system?

(SO 2) C   6. Why are purchases of merchandise for resale recorded in a separate account from the purchases of other items, such as supplies or equipment? Wouldn't it make more sense to use one account, titled Purchases, to record all these purchases?

(SO 2, 3) C   7. Distinguish between FOB shipping point and FOB destination. What freight term will result in a debit to Merchandise Inventory by the purchaser? A debit to Freight Out by the seller?

(SO 3) K   8. (a) What is the primary source document for recording: (1) cash sales, (2) credit sales, and (3) sales returns and allowances? (b) Using XXs for amounts, give the journal entry for each of the transactions in part (a) for both the purchaser and the seller.

(SO 3) C   9. Explain why sales returns are not debited directly to the Sales account.

(SO 4) C   10. "The steps in the accounting cycle for a merchandising company are different from those in the accounting cycle for a service enterprise." Do you agree or disagree?

(SO 4) C   11. Song Yee wonders why a physical inventory count is necessary in a perpetual inventory system. After all, the accounting records show how much inventory is on hand. Explain why a physical inventory count is required in a perpetual inventory system.

(SO 4) K   12. What merchandising account(s) will appear in the post-closing trial balance?

(SO 5) AP   13. Ford Company reports net sales of $800,000, gross profit of $580,000, and net income of $300,000. What are its operating expenses, assuming it has no non-operating activities?

(SO 5) K   14. Identify the sections of a multiple-step income statement that relate to (a) operating activities, and (b) non-operating activities.

(SO 5) C   15. Distinguish between the groupings of operating expenses. What problem is created by these groupings?

(SO 5) C   16. How does the single-step form of income statement differ from the multiple-step form?

(SO 6) AP   17. Rudy Co. has sales revenue of $100,000, cost of goods sold of $70,000, and operating expenses of $20,000. What is its gross profit? Its gross profit margin? Its net income? Its profit margin?

(SO 7) K   18. Identify two ratios that help management determine whether or not there is sufficient inventory on hand.

(SO 7) C   19. Why is managing inventory critical to a company's success?

(SO 7) C   20. Would an increase in days sales in inventory from one year to the next year be viewed as an improvement or a deterioration in the company's efficiency in managing its inventory?

(SO 8) AP   *21. Goods with a cost of $600 are sold on credit for $900 plus 7% GST and 10% PST. Give the journal entry(ies) required to record this transaction.

(SO 8) AP   *22. Office furniture is purchased on account at a cost of $2,000 plus 7% GST and 8% PST. Give the journal entry to record this.

(SO 9) K   *23. Indicate the columns of the work sheet in which (a) merchandise inventory, and (b) cost of goods sold will be shown.

BRIEF EXERCISES

Calculate missing amounts in determining net income.
(SO 1) AP

BE5–1   The components in Deschenes Company's income statement are presented below. Determine the missing amounts.

	Sales	Cost of Goods Sold	Gross Profit	Operating Expenses	Net Income
(a)	$ 75,000	?	$ 31,500	?	$10,800
(b)	108,000	$70,000	?	?	29,500
(c)	?	71,900	109,600	$39,500	?

Journalize inventory transactions.
(SO 2) AP

BE5–2   Prepare the journal entries to record the following transactions on Rowen Company's books:
(a) On March 2, Hunt Company sold $900,000 of merchandise to Rowen Company, terms n/30. The cost of the merchandise sold was $600,000.
(b) On March 6, Rowen Company returned $130,000 of the merchandise purchased on March 2.

The cost of the returned merchandise was $90,000. The merchandise was returned to inventory for future resale.

(c) On March 31, Hunt Company received the balance due from Rowen Company.

BE5–3 From the information in BE5–2, prepare the journal entries to record these transactions on Hunt Company's books.

Journalize sales transactions.
(SO 3) AP

BE5–4 Keo Company buys merchandise for cash from Mayo Company on Novenber 12. The selling price of the goods is $900, and the cost of the goods is $700. Journalize the transaction on the books of both companies.

Journalize inventory transactions on buyer's and seller's books.
(SO 2, 3) AP

BE5–5 In March, Zina Company's first month of operations, it has the following transactions: March 3, purchased on account 20 units of Product X at $25 per unit; March 6, returned three units for credit; March 21, sold on account 15 units at $45 per unit. Journalize the three transactions. What are the quantity and cost of the inventory at the end of the month?

Journalize inventory transactions on buyer's and seller's books.
(SO 2, 3) AP

BE5–6 At its August 31 year end, the inventory records of Dren Company showed merchandise inventory of $98,000. The company determined, through a physical count, that its actual inventory on hand was $97,100. Record the necessary adjusting entry.

Prepare adjusting entry for merchandise inventory.
(SO 4) AP

BE5–7 Prasad Company has the following merchandise account balances at its July 31 year end: Sales $180,000; Sales Returns and Allowances $2,000; Cost of Goods Sold $100,000; Merchandise Inventory $40,000; and Prasad, Capital $150,000. Prepare the closing entries.

Prepare closing entries for merchandise inventory accounts.
(SO 4) AP

BE5–8 Hulda Company provides the following information for the month ended October 31, 2003: Sales on credit $300,000; Cash sales $100,000; Sales returns and allowances $30,000. Prepare the sales revenue section of the income statement.

Prepare sales revenue section of income statement.
(SO 5) AP

BE5–9 Explain where each of the following items would appear on (1) a multiple-step income statement, and (2) a single-step income statement: (a) Gain on sale of equipment, (b) Interest expense, (c) Cost of goods sold, and (d) Rent revenue.

Indicate income statement presentation.
(SO 5) C

BE5–10 Assume Cajon Company has the following account balances: Sales $500,000; Sales Returns and Allowances $15,000; Cost of Goods Sold $340,000; Selling Expenses $70,000; and Administrative Expenses $40,000. Calculate the following: (a) net sales, (b) gross profit, and (c) net income.

Calculate net sales, gross profit, and net income.
(SO 5, 6) AP

BE5–11 Ry Company reported net sales $550,000; cost of goods sold $300,000; and average inventory $25,000. Calculate the following ratios: (a) gross profit margin, (b) inventory turnover, and (c) days sales in inventory.

Calculate inventory ratios.
(SO 6, 7) AP

*BE5–12 Journalize the purchase on account of $8,000 of merchandise for resale, and $1,000 of supplies for use in the business. GST is 7% and PST is 10%.

Journalize inventory transactions, with sales taxes.
(SO 8) AP

*BE5–13 Indicate where the following items will appear on the work sheet presented below: (a) Cash, (b) Merchandise Inventory, (c) Sales, and (d) Cost of Goods Sold. The first one has been done for you as an example.

Identify work sheet columns for selected accounts.
(SO 9) K

Trial Balance		Adjustments		Adjusted Trial Balance		Income Statement		Balance Sheet	
Dr.	Cr.	Dr.	Cr.	Dr.	Cr.	Dr.	Cr.	Dr.	Cr.

Example:

Cash: Trial balance debit column; Adjusted trial balance debit column; and Balance sheet debit column.

EXERCISES

•••

Journalize inventory transactions.
(SO 2) AP

E5–1   Information related to Olaf Co. is shown below:
1. On April 5, purchased merchandise from DeVito Company for $18,000, terms n/30, FOB shipping point.
2. On April 6, paid freight costs of $900 on merchandise purchased from DeVito.
3 On April 7, purchased equipment on account for $26,000.
4. On April 8, returned damaged merchandise to DeVito Company and was granted a $3,000 purchase allowance.
5. On May 2, paid the amount due to DeVito Company in full.

Instructions

Prepare the journal entries to record these transactions on the books of Olaf Co.

Journalize inventory transactions on buyer's and seller's books.
(SO 3) AP

E5–2   Transactions related to Pippen Company are shown below:
1. On December 3, Pippen Company sold and shipped merchandise to Thomas Co. for $400,000, terms n/30, FOB shipping point. This merchandise cost Pippen Company $320,000.
2. On December 8, Thomas Co. was granted a sales allowance of $20,000 for defective merchandise purchased on December 3. No merchandise was returned.
3. On December 31, Pippen Company received the balance due from Thomas Co.

Instructions

(a) Prepare the journal entries to record these transactions on the books of Pippen Company.
(b) Prepare the journal entries to record these transactions on the books of Thomas Co.

Journalize inventory transactions.
(SO 2, 3) AP

E5–3   On September 1, Campus Bookstore had an inventory of 30 pocket calculators at a cost of $20 each. During September, the following transactions occurred:
Sept. 6 Purchased 60 calculators at $20 each from Digital Co. on account, terms n/30.
   10 Returned two calculators to Digital Co. for $40 credit because they did not meet specifications.
   12 Sold 26 calculators for $30 each to Campus News, terms n/30.
   14 Granted credit of $30 to Campus News for the return of one calculator that was not ordered.
   20 Sold 30 calculators for $30 each to Campus Testing Services, terms n/30.

Instructions

Journalize the September transactions.

Journalize inventory transactions.
(SO 2, 3) AP

E5–4   On September 1, Collegiate Office Supply had an inventory of 10 desk sets that cost $15 each. During September, the following transactions and events occurred:
Sept. 2 Purchased 90 desk sets at $15 each from Digital Inc., terms n/30.
    5 Received credit of $60 for the return of four desk sets purchased on September 2 that were defective.
    8 Sold 50 desk sets for $25 each to University Bookstore, terms n/30.
   12 Sold 30 desk sets for $25 each to Hilltop Card Shop, terms n/30.
   20 Purchased 15 desk sets at $16 each from Sterling Company, terms n/30.
   30 Counted inventory and found 30 desk sets actually on hand.

Instructions

Journalize the September transactions and events.

Prepare correcting entries.
(SO 2, 3) AN

E5–5   An inexperienced accountant for Churchill Company made the following errors in recording merchandising transactions:
1. A $150 cash refund to a customer for faulty merchandise was debited to Sales $150 and credited to Cash $150.
2. A $250 credit purchase of supplies was debited to Merchandise Inventory $250 and credited to Cash $250.
3. A $50 purchase return on account was recorded as a debit to Accounts Payable $50 and a credit to Sales $50.
4. A cash payment of $30 for freight on merchandise purchases was debited to Merchandise Inventory $300 and credited to Cash $300.

Instructions

Prepare correcting entries for each error.

E5–6 On June 10, Pele Company purchased $5,000 of merchandise from Duvall Company FOB shipping point, terms n/30. Pele paid freight costs to Hoyt Movers of $300 on June 11. Damaged goods totalling $500 were returned to Duvall for credit on June 12. On July 7, Pele paid Duvall Company in full. On July 15, Pete paid all of the remaining merchandise purchased from Duvall for $8,500 cash.

Prepare inventory entries and closing entries.
(SO 2, 4) AP

Instructions

(a) Prepare separate entries for each transaction on the books of Pele Company.
(b) Prepare closing entries on July 31 for the temporary accounts.

E5–7 The adjusted trial balance of Cecilie Company shows the following data pertaining to sales at the end of its fiscal year, October 31, 2003: Sales $900,000; Freight Out $12,000; Sales Returns and Allowances $24,000.

Prepare sales revenue section and prepare closing entries.
(SO 4, 5) AP

Instructions

(a) Prepare the sales revenue section of the income statement.
(b) Prepare closing entries for these accounts.

E5–8 Financial information is presented below for three different companies:

Calculate missing amounts.
(SO 5) AN

	Natural Cosmetics	Mattar Grocery	Allied Wholesalers
Sales	$90,000	(c)	$144,000
Sales returns	(a)	6,000	12,000
Net sales	74,000	94,000	(f)
Cost of goods sold	64,000	(d)	(g)
Gross profit	10,000	22,000	24,000
Operating expenses	6,000	(e)	18,000
Net income	(b)	10,000	(h)

Instructions

Determine the missing amounts.

E5–9 In its income statement for the year ended December 31, 2002, Chevalier Company reported the following condensed data:

Prepare multiple-step and single-step income statements.
(SO 5) AP

Administrative expenses	$ 435,000
Cost of goods sold	989,000
Interest expense	70,000
Interest revenue	45,000
Loss on sale of equipment	10,000
Net sales	2,359,000
Selling expenses	690,000

Instructions

(a) Prepare a multiple-step income statement.
(b) Prepare a single-step income statement.

E5–10 JetForm Corporation, headquartered in Ottawa, is a world leader in electronic forms. It has offices in more than 10 countries throughout the world.

In its income statement for the year ended April 30, 2000, JetForm reported the following condensed data (in thousands):

Prepare multiple-step and single-step income statements and calculate inventory ratios.
(SO 5, 6, 7) AP

Revenues from products and services	$94,317	Investment income	$ 2,868
Sales and marketing expenses	45,097	Other income	295
Cost of products and services	24,426	Amortization expense	10,300
General and administrative expenses	26,485	Gain on sale of assets	1,813
Income tax expense	1,086		

Instructions

(a) Prepare a single-step income statement.
(b) Prepare a multiple-step income statement.
(c) Calculate the gross profit margin, profit margin, inventory turnover, and days sales in inventory. Average inventory was $1,111,500. Are these ratios in any way misleading?

Calculate inventory ratios.
(SO 6, 7) AN

E5–11   This information is available for **Future Shop Ltd.**, Canada's largest computer and electronic retailer, for the years ended March 31, 2000, 1999, and 1998 (in thousands of dollars).

	2000	1999	1998
Inventory	$ 193,831	$ 160,092	$ 254,690
Sales	1,683,142	1,960,274	1,760,160
Cost of sales	1,298,606	1,546,723	1,370,773

Instructions

Calculate the inventory turnover ratio, days sales in inventory, and gross profit margin for Future Shop for 2000 and 1999. Comment on whether each ratio has improved or deteriorated over the last two years.

Journalize inventory transactions, with sales tax.
(SO 8) AP

*E5–12   Journalize the transactions in E5–4, assuming that Goods and Services Tax of 7% is applied to all purchases and sales. No provincial sales tax is collected or paid.

Complete work sheet and identify accounts for post-closing trial balance.
(SO 9) C

*E5–13   Presented below are selected accounts for Milia Company as reported in the work sheet at the end of May 2003:

Accounts	Adjusted Trial Balance Dr.	Adjusted Trial Balance Cr.	Income Statement Dr.	Income Statement Cr.	Balance Sheet Dr.	Balance Sheet Cr.
Cash	9,000					
Merchandise Inventory	80,000					
Sales		450,000				
Sales Returns	10,000					
Cost of Goods Sold	250,000					
Rent Expense	42,000					

Instructions

(a) Complete the work sheet by extending amounts reported in the adjusted trial balance to the appropriate columns in the work sheet. Do not total the columns.

(b) Identify the account(s) that would be in the post-closing trial balance.

PROBLEMS: SET A

Journalize and post inventory transactions.
(SO 2, 3) AP

P5–1A   On April 1, Varsity Auto Sales' new car inventory records show total inventory of $230,000, which consisted of the following:

Model	Units	Unit Cost
Custom Sedans	4	$24,000
Convertibles	3	26,000
Recreational Vans	2	28,000

During April, the following purchases and sales were made on account:

April 5 Purchased three custom sedans for $24,000 each.

   13 Purchased two recreational vans for $28,000 each.

   17 Sold four custom sedans for $28,500 each.

   20 Purchased two convertibles for $26,000 each.

   22 Returned one convertible purchased on April 20 for $26,000 credit.

   24 Sold three recreational vans for $34,000 each.

   28 Sold one convertible for $31,000.

Instructions

(a) Journalize the transactions. Use separate inventory accounts for each car model.

(b) Post the journal entries from part (a) to T accounts for Merchandise Inventory—Custom Sedans; Merchandise Inventory—Convertibles; Merchandise Inventory—Recreational Vans; and Cost of Goods Sold.

P5–2A Travel Warehouse distributes suitcases to retail stores and extends credit terms of n/30 to all of its customers. At the end of July, Travel's inventory consisted of 40 suitcases purchased at $30 each. During the month of July, the following merchandising transactions occurred:

Journalize inventory transactions.
(SO 2, 3) AP

July 1 Purchased 50 suitcases on account for $30 each from Suitcase Manufacturers, FOB destination, terms n/30. The appropriate party also made a cash payment of $100 for freight on this date.

　　　3 Sold 40 suitcases on account to Luggage World for $50 each.

　　　9 Paid Suitcase Manufacturers in full.

　　12 Received payment in full from Luggage World.

　　17 Sold 30 suitcases on account to The Travel Spot for $50 each.

　　18 Purchased 60 suitcases on account for $1,700 from Vacation Manufacturers, FOB shipping point, terms n/30. The appropriate party also made a cash payment of $100 for freight on this date.

　　20 Received $300 credit for 10 suitcases returned to Vacation Manufacturers.

　　21 Received payment in full from The Travel Spot.

　　22 Sold 40 suitcases on account to Vacations-Are-Us for $50 each.

　　30 Paid Vacation Manufacturers in full.

　　31 Granted Vacations-Are-Us $250 credit for five suitcases returned costing $150. The suitcases were in good condition and were restored to inventory.

Travel Warehouse's chart of accounts includes the following: No. 101 Cash; No. 112 Accounts Receivable; No. 120 Merchandise Inventory; No. 201 Accounts Payable; No. 401 Sales; No. 412 Sales Returns and Allowances; and No. 505 Cost of Goods Sold.

Instructions

Journalize the transactions for the month of July for Travel Warehouse.

P5–3A The Nisson Distributing Company completed the following merchandising transactions in the month of April 2003. At the beginning of April, Nisson's ledger showed Cash $9,000; and M. Nisson, Capital $9,000.

Journalize and post transactions, and prepare partial income statement and balance sheet.
(SO 2, 3, 5) AP

Apr. 2 Purchased merchandise on account from Kananaskis Supply Co. for $4,900, FOB destination, terms n/30.

　　　4 Sold merchandise on account for $5,000, FOB destination, terms n/30. This merchandise had cost Nisson Distributing $4,000.

　　　5 Paid $200 freight on April 4 sale.

　　　6 Received credit from Kananaskis Supply Co. for merchandise returned, $300.

　　14 Purchased merchandise for cash, $4,400.

　　16 Received refund from supplier on cash purchase of April 14, $500.

　　18 Purchased merchandise from Pigeon Distributors for $4,200, FOB shipping point, terms n/30.

　　20 Paid freight on April 18 purchase, $100.

　　23 Sold merchandise for cash, $6,400. The cost of this merchandise was $5,200.

　　26 Purchased merchandise for cash, $2,300.

　　27 Paid Kananaskis Supply Co. the amount due.

　　28 Received collections in full from customers billed on April 4.

　　29 Made refunds to cash customers for merchandise, $90. The returned merchandise had a cost of $60. The merchandise was returned to inventory for future resale.

　　30 Sold merchandise on account for $3,700, FOB shipping point, terms n/30. Nisson's cost for this merchandise was $3,000.

Nisson Distributing Company's chart of accounts includes the following: No. 101 Cash; No. 112 Accounts Receivable; No. 120 Merchandise Inventory; No. 201 Accounts Payable; No. 301 M. Nisson, Capital; No. 401 Sales; No. 412 Sales Returns and Allowances; No. 505 Cost of Goods Sold; and No. 644 Freight Out.

Instructions

(a) Journalize the transactions.

(b) Set up general ledger accounts, enter the beginning cash and capital balances, and post the transactions.

(c) Prepare a partial multiple-step income statement, up to gross profit, for the month of April 2003.

(d) Prepare the current assets section of the balance sheet at the end of April.

*Prepare financial statements and
closing entries.*
(SO 4, 5) AP

P5–4A   The unadjusted trial balance of World Enterprises for the year ending December 31, 2002, is shown below:

WORLD ENTERPRISES
Trial Balance
December 31, 2002

	Debit	Credit
Cash	$ 14,000	
Accounts Receivable	30,600	
Merchandise Inventory	27,500	
Prepaid Insurance	1,800	
Store Equipment	42,000	
Accumulated Amortization—Store Equipment		$ 9,000
Accounts Payable		34,400
Sales Taxes Payable		3,000
R. Roger, Capital		50,300
Sales		238,500
Sales Returns and Allowances	4,600	
Cost of Goods Sold	177,000	
Salaries Expense	31,600	
Rent Expense	6,100	
Totals	$335,200	$335,200

Other data:
1. Insurance expired, $800.
2. Amortization expense, $3,000.
3. Rent payable, $500.

Instructions

(a) Prepare a multiple-step income statement, statement of owner's equity, and balance sheet.
(b) Prepare the closing entries.

*Prepare financial statements, and
adjusting and closing entries.*
(SO 4, 5) AP

P5–5A   Daigle Department Store is located in midtown Metropolis. Over the past several years, net income has been declining because of suburban shopping centres. At the end of the company's fiscal year on November 30, 2003, the following accounts appeared in alphabetical order in its unadjusted and adjusted trial balances:

	Trial Balances	
	Unadjusted	Adjusted
Accounts Payable	$ 47,310	$ 47,310
Accounts Receivable	11,770	11,770
Accumulated Amortization—Delivery Equipment	15,680	19,680
Accumulated Amortization—Building	32,300	41,800
Amortization Expense—Delivery Equipment	0	4,000
Amortization Expense—Building	0	9,500
Building	125,000	125,000
B. Daigle, Capital	84,200	84,200
Cash	8,000	8,000
Cost of Goods Sold	633,220	633,220
Delivery Equipment	57,000	57,000
Delivery Expense	8,200	8,200
B. Daigle, Drawings	12,000	12,000
Insurance Expense	0	9,000
Interest Expense	8,000	8,000
Interest Revenue	5,000	5,000
Land	50,000	50,000
Merchandise Inventory	36,200	36,200
Mortgage Payable	96,000	96,000
Prepaid Insurance	13,500	4,500
Property Tax Expense	0	3,500
Property Taxes Payable	0	3,500
Salaries Expense	139,000	139,000
Sales	850,000	850,000

Sales Commissions Expense	8,000	12,750
Sales Commissions Payable	0	4,750
Sales Returns and Allowances	10,000	10,000
Utilities Expense	10,600	10,600

Analysis reveals the following additional data:

1. Salaries expense is 70% selling and 30% administrative.
2. Insurance expense is 50% selling and 50% administrative.
3. Amortization expense—building, utilities expense, and property tax expense are administrative expenses.
4. A mortgage payment of $6,000 is currently due.

Instructions

(a) Prepare a multiple-step income statement, a statement of owner's equity, and a classified balance sheet.
(b) Journalize the adjusting entries that were made.
(c) Journalize the closing entries that are necessary.

P5–6A You are provided with the following list of accounts from the adjusted trial balance for Swirsky Company:

Classify the accounts of a merchandising company.
(SO 5) K

Accounts Payable	Accounts Receivable
Accumulated Amortization—Office Building	Accumulated Amortization—Store Equipment
Advertising Expense	Amortization Expense—Office Building
Amortization Expense—Store Equipment	Cash
Swirsky, Capital	Freight Out
Swirsky, Drawings	Income Tax Expense
Income Tax Payable	Insurance Expense
Interest Expense	Interest Payable
Land	Merchandise Inventory
Mortgage Payable	Office Building
Prepaid Insurance	Salaries Expense—Office Staff
Salaries Expense—Store Staff	Salaries Payable
Sales Returns and Allowances	Store Equipment
Utilities Expense—Office	Utilities Expense—Store
Wages Payable	

Instructions

For each account, identify whether the account should be reported on the balance sheet, statement of owner's equity, or multiple-step income statement. Please specify where the account should be classified. For example, Accounts Payable would be classified under current liabilities on the balance sheet.

P5–7A An inexperienced accountant prepared the following condensed income statement for McGrath Company, a retail firm that has been in business for a number of years.

Prepare correct multiple-step and single-step income statements.
(SO 5) AP

MCGRATH COMPANY
Income Statement
For Year Ended December 31, 2002

Revenues		
Net sales	$740,000	
Other revenues	24,000	$764,000
Cost of goods sold		555,000
Gross profit		209,000
Operating expenses		
Selling expenses	$104,000	
Administrative expenses	69,000	173,000
Net earnings		$ 36,000

As a knowledgeable accountant, you review the statement and determine the following facts:

1. Net sales consist of sales $800,000, less delivery expense on merchandise sold $30,000 and sales returns and allowances $30,000.
2. Other revenues consist of rent revenue $40,000, less bonuses paid to sales staff $16,000.

3. Selling expenses consist of salespersons' salaries $80,000, amortization on office equipment $8,000, advertising $10,000, and sales commissions $6,000.

4. Administrative expenses consist of office salaries $27,000, owner's drawings $4,000, utilities $12,000, interest expense $2,000, and rent $24,000.

Instructions

(a) Prepare a correct, detailed multiple-step income statement.

(b) Prepare a correct, condensed single-step income statement.

Calculate inventory ratios and comment.
(SO 6, 7) AN

P5–8A IPSCO Inc., headquartered in Regina, Saskatchewan, produces steel mill and fabricated products for the oil and natural gas, manufacturing, agricultural, and transportation industries in Canada and the U.S.

Selected financial information related to IPSCO's inventories from its December 31 consolidated financial statements (in thousands of U.S. dollars) follows:

	2000	1999	1998
Inventories	$225,958	$212,382	$164,557
Sales	949,263	808,251	719,963
Cost of sales	764,198	615,827	547,767

Instructions

(a) Calculate the gross profit margin, inventory turnover, and the days sales in inventory for 2000 and 1999.

(b) Evaluate IPSCO's performance with respect to inventories.

Journalize inventory transactions, with sales taxes.
(SO 2, 3, 8) AP

*P5–9A Presented below are selected transactions for the Norlan Company during September of the current year.

Sept. 2 Purchased merchandise on account from Hillary Company at a cost of $60,000 plus 7% GST of $4,200; terms FOB shipping point, n/30.

4 Paid freight charges of $2,000 on the merchandise purchased from Hillary Company on September 2.

5 Returned damaged goods costing $7,000 purchased from Hillary Company. Received a credit for this, plus the applicable GST.

6 Sold merchandise costing $15,000 to Kimmel Company on account for $21,000 plus 7% GST of $1,470 and 5% PST of $1,050; terms FOB shipping point, n/30.

15 Made cash purchase of supplies costing $4,000 plus GST of $280 and PST of $200.

18 Made cash purchases of merchandise for $6,000 plus GST of $420.

22 Sold merchandise costing $20,000 to Waldo Company on account for $28,000 plus 7% GST and 5% PST; terms FOB destination, n/30.

27 Purchased delivery equipment on account for $30,000, FOB destination, plus 7% GST and 5% PST.

28 Paid Hillary Company the balance due for the September 2 transaction.

30 Received the balance due from Kimmel Company.

Instructions

Journalize the September transactions.

Journalize and post transactions, and prepare trial balance and partial income statement, with sales taxes.
(SO 2, 3, 5, 8) AP

*P5–10A Billy Jean Evert, a former professional tennis star, operates B. J.'s Tennis Shop at Meech Lake Resort. At the beginning of the current season, the ledger of B. J.'s Tennis Shop showed Cash $2,500, Merchandise Inventory $3,500, and B. J. Evert, Capital $6,000. The following transactions were completed during April 2003:

April 4 Purchased racquets and balls from Robert Co. for $600 on account plus GST of $42; terms FOB shipping point, n/30.

6 Paid freight charges of $60 on the Robert Co. purchase.

8 Sold merchandise on account to members for $900 plus GST of $63 and PST of $90; terms n/30. The merchandise sold had a cost of $630.

10 Received a credit of $40 plus the applicable 7% GST from Robert Co. for a damaged racquet that was returned.

11 Purchased tennis shoes from Niki Sports for $300 cash plus GST of $21.

14 Purchased tennis shirts and shorts from Martina's Sportswear for $700 on account plus GST of $49; terms FOB shipping point, n/60.

15 Received a cash refund of $50 plus the applicable 7% GST from Niki Sports for damaged merchandise that was returned.

17 Paid freight charges of $70 on the Martina's Sportswear purchase.

18 Made cash sales to members for $800 plus GST of $56 and PST of $80. The merchandise had a cost of $560.

20 Received $500 in cash from members in settlement of their accounts.

27 Granted a credit of $30 plus the applicable 7% GST and 10% PST to a member for tennis clothing that did not fit. The cost of the returned clothing was $25.

29 Paid Robert Co. the full amount due.

30 Sold merchandise to members for $1,000 on account plus 7% GST and 10% PST; terms n/30. The merchandise sold had a cost of $730.

30 Received cash payments on account from members, $1,200.

The chart of accounts for the tennis shop includes the following: No. 101 Cash; No. 112 Accounts Receivable; No. 114 GST Recoverable; No. 120 Merchandise Inventory; No. 201 Accounts Payable; No. 214 GST Payable; No. 215 PST Payable; No. 301 B. J. Evert, Capital; No. 401 Sales; No. 412 Sales Returns and Allowances; No. 505 Cost of Goods Sold.

Instructions

(a) Journalize the April transactions.

(b) Enter the beginning balances in the ledger accounts and post the April transactions.

(c) Prepare a trial balance at April 30, 2003.

(d) Prepare a partial multiple-step income statement for the month of April, up to gross profit.

*P5–11A The trial balance of Metis Wholesale Company contained the following accounts at December 31, the end of the company's fiscal year:

Complete work sheet, financial statements, adjusting and closing entries, and post-closing trial balance.
(SO 4, 5, 9) AP

METIS WHOLESALE COMPANY
Trial Balance
December 31, 2002

	Debit	Credit
Cash	$ 33,400	
Accounts Receivable	37,600	
Merchandise Inventory	92,400	
Land	92,000	
Buildings	197,000	
Accumulated Amortization—Buildings		$ 54,000
Equipment	83,500	
Accumulated Amortization—Equipment		42,400
Notes Payable		50,000
Accounts Payable		37,500
G. Metis, Capital		267,800
G. Metis, Drawings	10,000	
Sales		902,100
Cost of Goods Sold	712,100	
Salaries Expense	69,800	
Utilities Expense	9,400	
Repair Expense	5,900	
Gas and Oil Expense	7,200	
Insurance Expense	3,500	
Totals	$1,353,800	$1,353,800

Adjustment data:

1. Amortization is $10,000 on buildings and $9,000 on equipment.
2. Interest of $4,000 is due and unpaid on notes payable at December 31.
3. Merchandise inventory actually on hand at December 31, 2002, is $90,000.

Other data:

1. Salaries are 80% selling and 20% administrative.
2. Utilities expense, repair expense, and insurance expense are 100% administrative.
3. Gas and oil expense is a selling expense.
4. Amortization is an administrative expense.
5. The notes payable are due within the year.

Instructions

(a) Enter the trial balance on a work sheet and complete the work sheet.
(b) Prepare a multiple-step income statement and a statement of owner's equity for the year, and a classified balance sheet as at December 31, 2002.
(c) Journalize the adjusting entries.
(d) Journalize the closing entries.
(e) Prepare a post-closing trial balance.

Problems: Set B

▪▪

Journalize and post inventory transactions.
(SO 2, 3) AP

P5–1B   On June 1, Goldstar Boat Sales' boat inventory records show total inventory of $214,000 which consisted of the following:

Model	Units	Unit Cost
Jet Runners	4	$22,000
20' Skiffs	3	24,000
25' Power Boats	2	27,000

During June, the following purchases and sales were made on account:

June 5 Purchased two jet runners for $22,000 each.
   13 Purchased two skiffs for $25,000 each.
   17 Sold four jet runners for $26,500 each.
   18 Purchased two skiffs for $26,000 each.
   22 Returned one skiff purchased on June 18 for $26,000 credit.
   23 Sold two 25' power boats for $33,000 each.
   24 Sold three 20' skiffs (original cost $24,000) for $29,000.

Instructions

(a) Journalize the transactions. Use separate inventory accounts for each boat model.
(b) Post the journal entries from part (a) to T accounts for Merchandise Inventory—Jet Runners; Merchandise Inventory—20' Skiffs; Merchandise—25' Power Boats; and Cost of Goods Sold.

Journalize inventory transactions.
(SO 2, 3) AP

P5–2B   Dazzle Book Warehouse distributes hardback books to retail stores and extends credit terms of n/30 to all of its customers. At the end of May, Dazzle's inventory consists of 240 books purchased at $6 each. During the month of June, the following merchandise transactions occurred:

June 1 Purchased 130 books on account for $5 each from Reader's World Publishers, FOB shipping point, terms n/30. The appropriate party also made a cash payment of $50 for the freight on this date.
   3 Sold 140 books on account to the Book Nook for $10 each. The cost of each book was $6.
   6 Received $50 credit for 10 books returned to Reader's World Publishers.
   9 Paid Reader's World Publishers in full.
   15 Received payment in full from the Book Nook.
   17 Sold 120 books on account to Read-A-Lot Bookstore for $10 each. The cost of the books sold was $682.
   20 Puchased 120 books on account for $5 each from Read More Publishers, FOB destination, terms n/30. The appropriate party also made a cash payment of $50 for the freight on this date.
   24 Received payment in full from Read-A-Lot Bookstore.
   26 Paid Read More Publishers in full.
   28 Sold 110 books on account to Readers Bookstore for $10 each. The total cost of the books sold was $609.
   30 Granted Readers Bookstore $150 credit for 15 books returned costing $75. These books were restored to inventory.

Dazzle Book Warehouse's chart of accounts includes the following: No. 101 Cash; No. 112 Accounts Receivable; No. 120 Merchandise Inventory; No. 201 Accounts Payable; No. 401 Sales; No. 412 Sales Returns and Allowances; No. 505 Cost of Goods Sold.

Instructions

Journalize the transactions for the month of June for Dazzle Book Warehouse.

P5–3B Eagle Hardware Store completed the following merchandising transactions in the month of May. At the beginning of May, Eagle's ledger showed Cash $5,000 and S. Eagle, Capital $5,000.

Journalize and post transactions, and prepare partial income statement and balance sheet.
(SO 2, 3, 5) AP

May 1 Purchased merchandise on account from Depot Wholesale Supply $5,000, FOB destination, terms n/30.

2 Sold merchandise on account for $4,000, FOB destination, terms n/30. The cost of the merchandise sold was $3,000.

5 Received credit from Depot Wholesale Supply for merchandise returned, $200.

7 Paid $200 freight on May 2 sales.

11 Purchased supplies for cash, $900.

12 Purchased merchandise for cash, $2,400.

15 Received refund for poor-quality merchandise from supplier on cash purchase, $230.

17 Purchased merchandise from Harlow Distributors for $1,900, FOB shipping point, terms n/30.

19 Paid freight on May 17 purchase, $250.

24 Sold merchandise for cash, $6,200. The merchandise sold had a cost of $4,340.

25 Purchased merchandise from Horicon Inc. for $1,000, FOB destination, terms n/30.

27 Received collections in full from customers billed on May 2.

29 Made cash refunds to customers for returned merchandise, $100. The returned merchandise had a cost of $70 and was restored to inventory.

30 Paid Depot Wholesale Supply in full.

31 Sold merchandise on account for $1,600, FOB shipping point, terms n/30. The cost of the merchandise sold was $1,000.

Eagle Hardware's chart of accounts includes the following: No. 101 Cash; No. 112 Accounts Receivable; No. 120 Merchandise Inventory; No. 126 Supplies; No. 201 Accounts Payable; No. 301 S. Eagle, Capital; No. 401 Sales; No. 412 Sales Returns and Allowances; No. 505 Cost of Goods Sold; and No. 644 Freight Out.

Instructions

(a) Journalize the transactions.

(b) Enter the beginning cash and capital balances, and post the transactions.

(c) Prepare a partial income statement, up to gross profit, for the month of May 2003.

(d) Prepare the current assets section of the balance sheet at May 31, 2003.

P5–4B The unadjusted trial balance of Global Enterprises for the year ending December 31, 2002, is shown below:

Prepare financial statements and closing entries.
(SO 4, 5) AP

GLOBAL ENTERPRISES
Trial Balance
December 31, 2002

	Debit	Credit
Cash	$ 13,000	
Accounts Receivable	31,700	
Merchandise Inventory	28,100	
Prepaid Insurance	1,900	
Land	30,000	
Building	150,000	
Accumulated Amortization—Building		$ 18,750
Store Equipment	45,000	
Accumulated Amortization—Store Equipment		9,100
Accounts Payable		34,700
Sales Taxes Payable		4,000
Mortgage Payable		161,250
T. Brown, Capital		50,000
Sales		243,700
Sales Returns and Allowances	4,800	
Cost of Goods Sold	180,300	
Salaries Expense	31,600	
Utilities Expense	5,100	
Totals	$521,500	$521,500

Other data:

1. Merchandise inventory actually on hand at December 31, $28,000.

2. Insurance expired, $900.

3. Amortization expense, $6,850; $4,000 for the building and $2,850 for the store equipment.
4. Accrued property tax, $6,000.
5. A mortgage payment of $5,000 is currently due.

Instructions

(a) Prepared a multiple-step income statement, statement of owner's equity, and balance sheet.
(b) Prepare the closing entries.

Prepare financial statements, adjusting entries, and closing entries.
(SO 4, 5) AP

P5–5B   The Veitch Department Store is located near the Village Shopping Mall. At the end of the company's fiscal year on December 31, 2002, the following accounts appeared in two of its trial balances:

	Trial Balances	
	Unadjusted	Adjusted
Accounts Payable	$ 89,300	$ 89,300
Accounts Receivable	50,300	50,300
Accumulated Amortization—Building	42,100	52,500
Accumulated Amortization—Equipment	29,600	42,900
Amortization Expense—Building		10,400
Amortization Expense—Equipment		13,300
Building	190,000	190,000
S. Veitch, Capital	226,600	226,600
Cash	23,000	23,000
Cost of Goods Sold	424,700	427,200
S. Veitch, Drawings	28,000	28,000
Equipment	110,000	110,000
Insurance Expense		7,200
Interest Expense	3,000	11,000
Interest Payable		8,000
Interest Revenue	4,000	4,000
Land	50,000	50,000
Merchandise Inventory	75,000	72,500
Mortgage Payable	80,000	80,000
Office Salaries Expense	32,000	32,000
Prepaid Insurance	9,600	2,400
Property Taxes Expense		4,800
Property Taxes Payable		4,800
Sales	624,000	624,000
Sales Commissions Expense	11,000	15,500
Sales Commissions Payable		4,500
Sales Returns and Allowances	8,000	8,000
Sales Salaries Expense	76,000	76,000
Sales Taxes Payable	6,000	6,000
Utilities Expense	11,000	11,000

Analysis reveals the following additional data:
1. Insurance expense and utilities expense are 60% selling and 40% administrative.
2. Of the mortgage payable, $20,000 is due for payment next year.
3. Amortization on the building and property tax expense are administrative expenses. Amortization on the equipment is a selling expense.

Instructions

(a) Prepare a multiple-step income statement, a statement of owner's equity, and a classified balance sheet.
(b) Journalize the adjusting entries that were made.
(c) Journalize the closing entries that are necessary.

Classify the accounts of a merchandising company.
(SO 5) K

P5–6B   The following list of accounts has been selected from the financial statements of **Alcan Aluminium Limited**. Alcan, headquartered in Montreal, is involved in most aspects of the aluminum industry in more than 30 countries around the world.

Accumulated Depreciation	Cash and Time Deposits
Cost of Sales	Depreciation Expense
Income Tax Expense	Interest Expense

Inventories—Aluminum	Inventories—Other Supplies
Inventories—Raw Materials	Operating Income
Other Expenses	Payables
Property, Plant, and Equipment	Receivables
Sales	Selling, Administrative, and General Expenses

Instructions

For each account listed above, indicate whether the account was reported on Alcan's balance sheet or multiple-step income statement. Specify where the account was most likely classified. For example, depreciation (amortization) expense is classified under Operating Expenses (Administrative) on the income statement.

P5-7B A part-time bookkeeper prepared the following income statement for the Tao Company for the year ending December 31, 2002:

Prepare correct multiple-step and single-step income statements.
(SO 5) AP

TAO COMPANY
Income Statement
December 31, 2002

Revenues		
Sales		$702,000
Less: Freight out	$ 17,200	
Less: Returns and allowances	4,100	21,300
Net sales		680,700
Other revenues (net)		1,300
Total revenues		682,000
Expenses		
Cost of goods sold	$470,000	
Selling expenses	100,000	
Administrative expenses	50,000	
L. Tao, Drawings	12,000	
Total expenses		632,000
Net income		$ 50,000

As an experienced accountant, you review the statement and determine the following facts:
1. Sales includes $10,000 of deposits from customers for future sales orders.
2. "Other revenues" contains two items: interest expense $4,000 and interest revenue $5,300.
3. Selling expenses consist of sales salaries $76,000, advertising $10,000, amortization on store equipment $7,500, and sales commissions expense $6,500. The commissions figure includes only the amount paid for 2002 sales. At December 31, additional commissions of $1,000 have been earned by salespersons but not yet recorded or paid by the company.
4. Administrative expenses consist of office salaries $19,000, utilities expense $8,000, rent expense $16,000, and insurance expense $7,000. The rent figure includes $1,250 of prepayments for the first part of next year. The insurance includes $1,200 for the year 2003.

Instructions
(a) Prepare a correct, detailed multiple-step income statement.
(b) Prepare a correct, condensed single-step income statement.

P5-8B **SAMsports.com Inc.** is a software company, located throughout Western Canada, marketing high-quality sports education multimedia to help coaches and athletes improve performance. This information is available for SAM for the eight months ended December 31, 1999, and the year ended April 30, 1999. April 30, 1999, was the end of SAM's first full year of operations.

Calculate inventory ratios and comment.
(SO 6, 7) AN

	December 31, 1999	April 30, 1999
Merchandise inventory	$ 8,330	$ 4,966
Current assets	1,973,457	298,499
Current liabilities	1,390,850	259,851
Sales	74,314	1,472
Cost of goods sold	10,931	631

Instructions

Calculate the gross profit margin, inventory turnover, days sales in inventory, and current ratio for SAM as at December 31, 1999, and April 30, 1999. Comment on SAM's liquidity and inventory management.

Journalize inventory transactions, with sales taxes.
(SO 2, 3, 8) AP

*P5–9B   Presented below are selected transactions for the Leeland Company during October of the current year:

Oct. 1 Purchased merchandise on account from Gregory Company at a cost of $75,000 plus GST of $5,250; terms FOB shipping point, n/30.

3 Paid freight charges of $1,800 on the merchandise purchased from Gregory Company on Oct. 1.

5 Returned damaged goods costing $6,000 purchased from Gregory Company. Received a credit for this, plus the applicable 7% GST.

8 Sold merchandise costing $16,000 to Himmel Company on account for $22,000 plus GST of $1,540 and PST of $1,100; terms FOB shipping point, n/30.

12 Made cash purchase of supplies costing $5,000 plus GST of $350 and PST of $250.

15 Made cash purchases of merchandise for $5,000 plus GST of $350.

18 Sold on account to Romeo Company $30,000 of merchandise plus 7% GST and 5% PST; terms FOB shipping point, n/30. The merchandise originally cost $23,000.

20 Purchased delivery equipment on account for $44,000, FOB destination, plus 7% GST and 5% PST.

25 Paid Gregory Company the balance due the October 1 transaction.

27 Received the balance due from Himmel Company.

Instructions

Journalize the October transactions.

Journalize and post transactions, and prepare trial balance and partial income statement, with sales taxes.
(SO 2, 3, 5, 8) AP

*P5–10B   Jana Nejedly, a former professional tennis star, operates Jana's Tennis Shop at Little Lake Resort. At the beginning of the current season, the ledger of Jana's Tennis Shop showed Cash $3,000, Merchandise Inventory $1,850, and J. Nejedly, Capital, $4,850. The following transactions were completed during May 2003:

May 4 Purchased racquets and balls from Jones Co. for $700 on account, plus GST of $49; terms FOB shipping point, n/30.

6 Paid freight charges of $55 on the Jones Co. purchase.

8 Sold merchandise on account to members for $800 plus GST of $56 and PST of $80; terms n/30. The merchandise had a cost of $600.

9 Received credit of $45 plus the applicable GST from Jones Co. for a damaged racquet that was returned.

14 Purchased tennis shoes from Nikko Sports for $400 cash plus GST of $28.

16 Purchased tennis shirts and shorts from Lindsay's Sportswear for $600 plus GST of $42; terms FOB shipping point, n/60.

18 Paid freight charges of $75 on the Lindsay's Sportswear purchase.

21 Received a cash refund of $55 plus GST of $3.85 from Nikko Sports for damaged merchandise that was returned.

23 Made cash sales to members for $900 plus GST of $63 and PST of $90. The merchandise had a cost of $675.

25 Received $400 in cash from members in settlement of their accounts.

27 Granted a credit of $35 plus GST of $2.45 and PST of $3.50 to a member for tennis clothing that did not fit. The cost of the returned clothing was $25.

29 Paid Jones Co. the full amount due.

30 Sold merchandise to members for $1,500 plus GST of $105 and PST of $150; terms n/30. The merchandise had a cost of $1,125.

31 Received cash payments on account from members, $800.

The chart of accounts for the tennis shop includes the following: No. 101 Cash; No. 112 Accounts Receivable; No. 114 GST Recoverable; No. 120 Merchandise Inventory; No. 201 Accounts Payable; No. 214 GST Payable; No. 215 PST Payable; No. 301 J. Nejedly, Capital; No. 401 Sales; No. 412 Sales Returns and Allowances; No. 505 Cost of Goods Sold.

Instructions

(a) Journalize the May transactions.
(b) Enter the beginning balances in the ledger accounts and post the May transactions.
(c) Prepare a trial balance at May 31, 2003.
(d) Prepare a partial income statement, up to gross profit.

Complete work sheet, financial statements, adjusting and closing entries, and post-closing trial balance.
(SO 4, 5, 9) AP

*P5–11B   The trial balance of Brennan Fashion Centre contained the following accounts at November 30, the end of the company's fiscal year:

BRENNAN FASHION CENTRE
Trial Balance
November 30, 2003

	Debit	Credit
Cash	$ 16,700	
Accounts Receivable	40,700	
Merchandise Inventory	48,000	
Store Supplies	5,500	
Land	60,000	
Building	85,000	
Accumulated Amortization—Building		$ 17,000
Delivery Equipment	48,000	
Accumulated Amortization—Delivery Equipment		16,000
Mortgage Payable		51,000
Accounts Payable		48,500
Sales Taxes Payable		7,000
L. Brennan, Capital		161,000
L. Brennan, Drawings	12,000	
Sales		750,300
Sales Returns and Allowances	4,200	
Cost of Goods Sold	497,500	
Salaries Expense	140,000	
Advertising Expense	26,400	
Utilities Expense	14,000	
Repair Expense	12,100	
Delivery Expense	16,700	
Rent Expense	24,000	
Totals	$1,050,800	$1,050,800

Adjustment data:
1. Store supplies on hand totalled $3,500.
2. Amortization is $4,250 on the building and $8,000 on the delivery equipment.
3. Interest of $4,000 is accrued on the mortgage payable at November 30.
4. Merchandise inventory actually on hand at November 30, 2003, is $45,000.
5. Accrued property tax is $5,000.

Other data:
1. Salaries expense is 70% selling and 30% administrative.
2. Rent expense and utilities expense are 80% selling and 20% administrative.
3. Next year, $30,000 of the mortgage payable is due for payment.
4. Repair expense and property tax expense are 100% administrative.

Instructions

(a) Enter the trial balance on a work sheet and complete the work sheet.
(b) Prepare a multiple-step income statement and a statement of owner's equity for the year, and a classified balance sheet as at November 30, 2003.
(c) Journalize the adjusting entries.
(d) Journalize the closing entries.
(e) Prepare a post-closing trial balance.

Broadening Your Perspective

FINANCIAL REPORTING AND ANALYSIS

Financial Reporting Problem

BYP5–1 The 2000 Annual Report for **The Second Cup Ltd.** is reproduced in Appendix A at the end of this text.

Instructions

Answer the following questions regarding The Second Cup:

(a) Is The Second Cup a service company or a merchandising company?

(b) Refer to the upper portion of The Second Cup's statement of operations (i.e., its income statement). Notice that there is a very large difference between the amount of "Systemwide Sales" reported and the amount of "Revenue" reported. What do you think is meant by Systemwide Sales, as opposed to Total Revenue?

(c) Note 15 to the consolidated financial statements presents a breakdown of the company's operations by geographic area. What percentage of The Second Cup's revenue in 2000 was generated in Canada?

(d) How much information does The Second Cup disclose regarding its cost of goods sold and gross profit?

(e) Why do you think the format of The Second Cup's statement of operations differs so much from the format of the income statements shown in this chapter?

Interpreting Financial Statements

Additional Cases

BYP5–2 Mark's Work Wearhouse (L'Équipeur in Quebec) is Canada's largest specialty apparel and footwear store. It carries 4,000 items in stock for sale in 140 stores across Canada. Mark's quantifies its corporate financial goals and carefully monitors its progress in order to assess its success. Some of the goals for fiscal 2000 and 1999 include the following. The goals range from conservative to optimistic.

	Fiscal 2000	Fiscal 1999
Gross profit margin	41.1%–41.2%	40.6%–40.7%
Inventory turnover	2.3–2.4	2.1–2.2
Sales (in thousands)	$328,529–$341,999	$288,616–$297,871
Gross margin (in thousands)	$132,008–$137,979	$117,180–$121,113
Net earnings (in thousands)	$7,814–$9,427	$7,805–$9,450

Mark's Work Wearhouse's statements of earnings (income statements) for the years ended January 29, 2000, and January 30, 1999, are condensed and reproduced here:

Mark's Work Wearhouse

MARK'S WORK WEARHOUSE LTD.
Statements of Earnings
Year ended
(in thousands)

	January 29, 2000		January 30, 1999	
Corporate operations				
Sales		$314,547		$283,401
Cost of sales		186,723		169,163
Gross profit margin		127,824		114,238
Front-line expenses	$89,567		$78,086	
Back-line expenses	25,572		21,879	
Other	375	115,514	3,277	103,242
Earnings before income taxes		12,310		10,996
Income taxes		5,923		5,244
Net earnings		$ 6,387		$ 5,752

Additional information:

1. The statement of earnings is shown in summary form. This means that each account title listed is a summary of several other accounts. For example, the Front-Line Expenses account includes such things as staff and occupancy expenses. The Back-Line Expenses include computer services and maintenance expenses and long-term interest, among other accounts.
2. Merchandise inventories were $60,108,000 as at January 31, 1998; $76,982,000 as at January 30, 1999; and $81,468,000 as at January 29, 2000.

Instructions

(a) In which summary account from the statement of earnings would these merchandising accounts be located:
   1. Sales returns and allowances?
   2. Freight out?
(b) Calculate Mark's Work Wearhouse's gross profit margin, inventory turnover, and days sales in inventory ratios for 2000 and 1999. Compare its actual results to its forecasted goals.

BYP5–3 **Carrefour** is the world's second largest retailer, second only to **Wal-Mart**. Carrefour operates hypermarkets—huge department store and supermarket combinations that sell food, clothing, electronics, and household appliances, among other things. Carrefour has more than 9,000 stores in 27 countries.

Although Wal-Mart is still the world's #1 retailer, its international sales are far lower than those of Carrefour. This is a serious concern for Wal-Mart, since its primary opportunity for future growth lies outside of North America.

Below are selected financial data for Carrefour (in euros) and Wal-Mart (in U.S. dollars). Even though the results are presented in different currencies, by using ratios, we can make some basic comparisons.

	Carrefour (in billions of euros)	Wal-Mart (in billions of US$)
Sales	€51.9	$165.0
Cost of goods sold	40.8	129.7
Average merchandise inventories	4.6	18.4
Current assets	12.3	24.4
Current liabilities	10.1	25.8

Instructions

Compare the two companies by answering the following:

(a) Calculate the gross profit margin, inventory turnover, and days sales in inventory for each company. Compare their ability to control inventory.
(b) Calculate the current ratio. Compare the liquidity of each company.
(c) What concerns might you have about these comparisons?

Accounting on the Web

BYP5–4 Much information about specific companies is available on the internet. This case searches for financial information about the **Hudson's Bay Company** and its competitors.

Instructions

Specific requirements of this Internet case are available on the Weygandt website.

CRITICAL THINKING

Collaborative Learning Activity

BYP5–5   Three years ago, Kathy Webb and her brother-in-law John Utley opened FedCo Department Store. For the first two years, business was good, but the following condensed income results for 2002 were disappointing:

FEDCO DEPARTMENT STORE
Income Statement
For the Year Ended December 31, 2002

Net sales		$700,000
Cost of goods sold		546,000
Gross profit		154,000
Operating expenses		
Selling expenses	$100,000	
Administrative expenses	25,000	125,000
Net income		$ 29,000

Kathy believes the problem lies in the relatively low gross profit margin of 22%. John believes the problem is that operating expenses are too high.

    Kathy thinks the gross profit margin can be improved by making the following changes:
1. Increase average selling prices by 17%. This increase is expected to lower the sales volume so that total sales will increase only 6%.
2. Buy merchandise in larger quantities to get trade discounts.

These changes are expected to increase the gross profit margin by 3%. Kathy does not anticipate that these changes will have any effect on operating expenses.

    John thinks expenses can be cut by making the following changes:
1. Cut 2002 sales salaries of $60,000 in half and give sales personnel a commission of 2% of net sales.
2. Reduce store deliveries to one day per week rather than twice a week. This change will reduce 2002 delivery expenses of $30,000 by 40%.

John feels that these changes will not have any effect on net sales.

    Kathy and John come to you for help in deciding on the best way to improve net income.

Instructions

With the class divided into groups, answer the following:
  (a) Prepare (1) a condensed income statement for 2003 assuming only Kathy's changes are implemented, and (2) another one for 2003 assuming only John's ideas are adopted.
  (b) What is your recommendation to Kathy and John, based upon the results in part (a)?
  (c) Prepare a condensed income statement for 2003 assuming *both* sets of proposed changes are made.

Communication Activity

BYP5–6   Consider the following events, which are listed in chronological order:
1. Dexter Maersk decides to buy a custom-made snowboard and calls The Great Canadian Snowboard Company to inquire about their products.
2. Dexter asks The Great Canadian Snowboard Company to manufacture a custom board for him.
3. The company sends Dexter a purchase order to fill out, which he immediately completes, signs, and sends back.
4. The Great Canadian Snowboard Company receives Dexter's purchase order and begins working on the board.
5. The Great Canadian Snowboard Company has its fiscal year end. At this time, Dexter's board is 75% completed.
6. The company completes the snowboard for Dexter and notifies him that he can take delivery.
7. Dexter picks up his snowboard from the company and carefully takes it home.
8. Dexter tries the snowboard out and likes it so much that he carves his initials on it.
9. The Great Canadian Snowboard Company bills Dexter for the cost of the snowboard.
10. The company receives partial payment from Dexter.
11. The company receives payment of the balance due from Dexter.

Instructions

In a memo to the president of The Great Canadian Snowboard Company, answer these questions:
  (a) When should The Great Canadian Snowboard Company record the revenue related to the snowboard? Refer to the revenue recognition principle in your answer.
  (b) Suppose that, with his purchase order, Dexter was required to make a down payment. Would that change your answer to part (a)?

Ethics Case

BYP5–7 Rita Pelzer was just hired as the Assistant Controller of Yorkshire Stores. The company is a specialty chain store with nine retail stores concentrated in one metropolitan area. Among other things, the payment of all invoices is centralized in one of the departments Rita will manage. Her primary responsibility is to maintain the company's high credit rating by paying all bills when due.

Jamie Caterino, the former Assistant Controller, who has been promoted to Controller, is training Rita in her new duties. He instructs Rita to continue the practice of preparing all cheques and dating the cheques the last day of the credit period. "But," Jamie continues, "we always hold the cheques at least four days beyond the due date before mailing them. That way we get another four days of interest on our money. Most of our creditors need our business and don't complain. And, if they scream about our payment being late, we blame it on the mail room or the post office. I think everybody does it. By the way, welcome to our team!"

Instructions

  (a) What are the ethical considerations in this case?
  (b) Who are the stakeholders that are harmed or benefited in this situation?
  (c) Should Rita continue the practice started by Jamie? Does she have any choice?

Answers to Self-Study Questions

1. c   2. a   3. c   4. a   5. a   6. a   7. d   8. c   9. b   10. b   *11. c *12. b

Answer to Second Cup Review It Question 3

The Second Cup reports Inventories among its current assets: $107,000 in 2000 and $103,000 in 1999. The Second Cup does not disclose its cost of goods sold separately on its statement of operations.

Remember to go back to the Navigator box on the chapter-opening page to check off your completed work.

THE
NAVIGATOR

No Coffee, Just Great Service at University Bookstore

MONTREAL, Que.—There's no coffee bar at the Concordia University Bookstore. What there is, in addition to stationery supplies, stuffed animals, school sweatshirts, and other student-life necessities, is about $6,000,000 worth of textbooks in the course of any given year. As director of the bookstore, it's Lina Lipscombe's job to keep the shelves of both campus bookstores stocked with every textbook Concordia students need.

How many books is that? About 3,000 different titles a term—more in the busy fall term. Determining the number of copies needed for each of these titles is a complex matter. "We have good links with the registrar's office," explains Ms. Lipscombe, "so we know the capacity of the class and the registration numbers for this and past years. We also have our own historical information—if we've never sold more than 50 copies of a book even though there are 100 students in the class,

we'll order low. Then there's the age of the book—for a new edition, we'll order high. A book that's been out a few years will have some used sales, both here at the store and at the student union."

Ms. Lipscombe and her staff use a perpetual inventory system to track the quantities of books on hand. However, they use a periodic inventory system to determine the cost of goods sold and the cost of the ending inventory at the end of the period. "Currently, we do have a computerized 'backroom system' that can track orders and receipts, generate course

lists, etc., but it isn't integrated with the cash registers."

Concordia's students get some of the best bookstore service in Canada. "Ultimately," says Ms. Lipscombe, "I think students find helpful service—and a commitment to work very hard to have all the books they need in stock when they need them—a lot more important in a bookstore than coffee."

THE
NAVIGATOR

relish.concordia.ca/bookstore

THE NAVIGATOR

✔

■ Understand *Concepts for Review* ☐

■ Read *Feature Story* ☐

■ Scan *Study Objectives* ☐

■ Read *Preview* ☐

■ Read text and answer *Before You Go On*
p. 267 ☐ p. 270 ☐ p. 275 ☐ p. 284 ☐
p. 287 ☐ p. 289 ☐ p. 294 ☐ p. 298 ☐

■ Work *Demonstration Problems* ☐

■ Review *Summary of Study Objectives* ☐

■ Answer *Self-Study Questions* ☐

■ Complete assignments ☐

CHAPTER · **6**

INVENTORY COSTING

► STUDY OBJECTIVES ◄

After studying this chapter, you should be able to:

1. *Describe the steps in determining inventory quantities.*
2. *Prepare the entries for purchases and sales of inventory under a periodic inventory system.*
3. *Determine cost of goods sold under a periodic inventory system.*
4. *Identify the unique features of the income statement for a merchandising company using a periodic inventory system.*
5. *Explain the basis of accounting for inventories and use the inventory cost flow methods.*
6. *Demonstrate the effects on the financial statements of each of the inventory cost flow methods.*
7. *Determine the effects of inventory errors on the financial statements.*
8. *Explain and use the lower of cost and market basis of accounting for inventories.*
9. *Apply the inventory cost flow methods to perpetual inventory records (Appendix 6A).*
10. *Use the two methods of estimating inventories (Appendix 6B).*

Accounting for thousands of inventory items, by companies such as the Concordia University Bookstore, can be time-consuming and complex. In this chapter, we explain the procedures for determining inventory quantities. We discuss the differences in perpetual and periodic inventory systems for determining the cost of inventory on hand and the cost of goods sold. We also discuss the effects of inventory errors on a company's financial statements. The chapter is organized as follows:

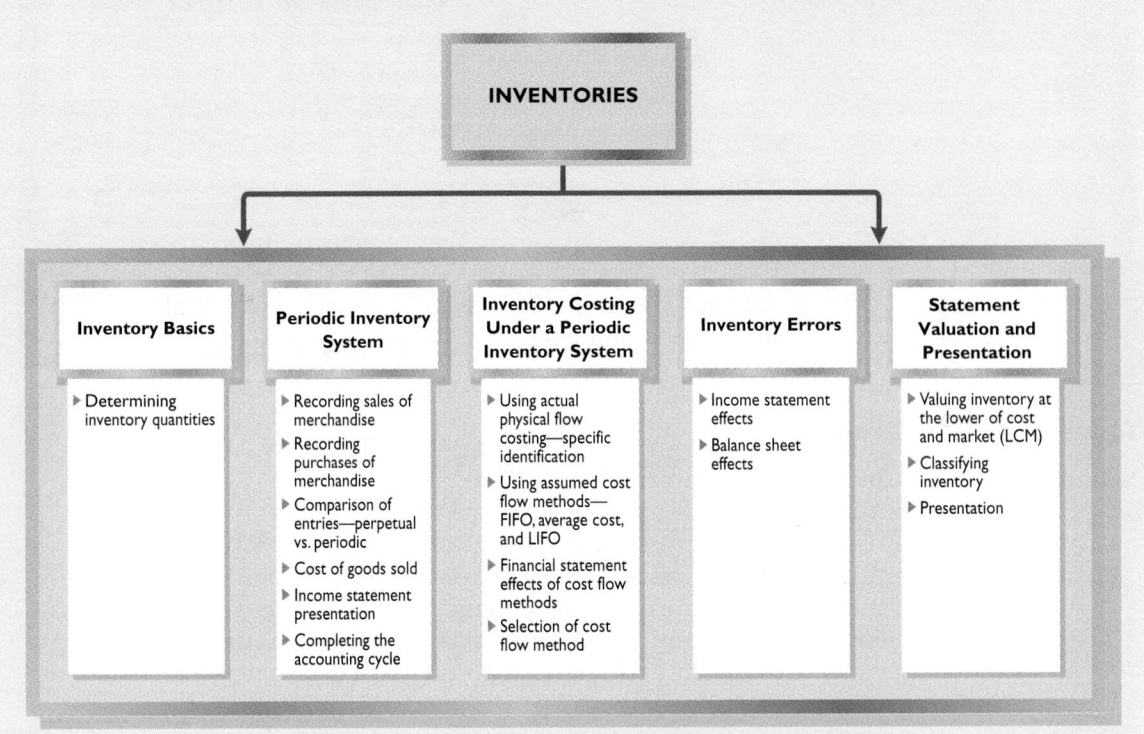

INVENTORIES

Inventory Basics	Periodic Inventory System	Inventory Costing Under a Periodic Inventory System	Inventory Errors	Statement Valuation and Presentation
► Determining inventory quantities	► Recording sales of merchandise ► Recording purchases of merchandise ► Comparison of entries—perpetual vs. periodic ► Cost of goods sold ► Income statement presentation ► Completing the accounting cycle	► Using actual physical flow costing—specific identification ► Using assumed cost flow methods—FIFO, average cost, and LIFO ► Financial statement effects of cost flow methods ► Selection of cost flow method	► Income statement effects ► Balance sheet effects	► Valuing inventory at the lower of cost and market (LCM) ► Classifying inventory ► Presentation

THE NAVIGATOR

▼ Inventory Basics

In our economy, inventories are an important barometer of business activity. The amount of inventories and the time required to sell the goods are two closely watched indicators. During downturns in the economy, there can be an initial buildup of inventories, as it takes longer to sell existing quantities. Inventories generally decrease with an upturn in business activity. A delicate balance must be maintained between too little inventory and too much. A company with too little inventory to meet demand will have dissatisfied customers and sales personnel. One with too much inventory will incur unnecessary costs.

► Accounting in Action ► *Business Insight*

What happens when you have too many size 42 Tall suits and not enough size 42 Tall customers? At Harry Rosen Inc., in Toronto, its In-Store Retail Information System database is used to maintain a listing of customer clothing purchases and preferences. The company believes that this system has increased return customer visits by 58% and produced savings in excess of $700,000 through lower costs and other efficiencies.

Source: Piali Roy, "Information At Their Fingertips," *Canadian Business*, Technology, Winter 1996, 80.

Inventory affects both the balance sheet (through the current asset Merchandise Inventory account) and the income statement (through the Cost of Goods Sold expense account). In the **balance sheet** of merchandising companies, inventory is frequently the most significant current asset. Of course, its amount and relative importance can vary, even for companies in the same industry. For example, Sears reported inventory of $640 million, representing 32% of total current assets. For the same period, Hudson's Bay reported $1.4 billion of inventory, representing 60% of total current assets. In the **income statement**, cost of goods sold is vital in determining the results of operations for a particular period. Also, gross profit (Net sales – Cost of goods sold) is closely watched by management, owners, and other interested parties, as explained in Chapter 5.

Determining Inventory Quantities

To prepare financial statements, we must know the number of units of inventory owned by the company at the statement date before we can assign a cost to these units. Determining inventory quantities requires two steps: (1) taking a physical inventory of goods on hand, and (2) determining the ownership of goods.

> **STUDY OBJECTIVE**
> ············**1**············
> *Describe the steps in determining inventory quantities.*

Taking a Physical Inventory

You will recall from Chapter 5 that merchandisers account for their inventory transactions by using either a perpetual or a periodic inventory system. In a **perpetual inventory system**, the accounting records continuously—perpetually—show the quantity of inventory that should be on hand. A physical count is done at some point in the year to verify the accuracy of the accounting records.

In a **periodic inventory system**, inventory quantities are not maintained on a continuous basis, but are determined at the end of each reporting period by a physical count. Whether inventory quantities are maintained by the perpetual or the periodic inventory method, a physical inventory count is necessary to determine the goods on hand or to confirm their accuracy.

Taking a physical inventory involves actually counting, weighing, or measuring each kind of inventory on hand. Taking an inventory can be a formidable task for many companies, especially if they have thousands of inventory items, like the Concordia University Bookstore. An inventory count is generally more accurate when goods are not being sold or received during the counting. Companies often count their inventory when the business is closed or when business is slow.

To minimize errors in taking the inventory, a company should adhere to internal control. **Internal control** consists of policies and procedures to optimize resources, prevent and detect errors, safeguards assets, and enhance the accuracy and reliability of accounting records. Some internal control procedures for counting inventory include the following:

1. The counting should be done by employees who do not have custodial or record-keeping responsibility for the inventory.
2. Each counter should establish the authenticity of each inventory item. For example, does each box contain a television set? Does each storage tank contain gasoline?
3. There should be a second count by another employee or auditor. Counting should take place in teams of two.
4. Prenumbered inventory tags should be used. All inventory tags should be accounted for.
5. At the end of the count, a designated supervisor should check that all inventory items are tagged and that no items have more than one tag.

We will learn more about these and other internal controls in Chapter 8.

Helpful hint   Many retailers, like Hudson's Bay, take a physical inventory at January 31 when post-holiday-season buying is in a lull and holiday returns have been made.

►Accounting in Action ► *Business Insight*

Failure to observe internal control procedures contributed to the Great Salad Oil Swindle. In this case, management intentionally overstated its salad oil inventory, which was stored in large holding tanks. Three procedures contributed to overstating the oil inventory: (1) Water added to the bottom of the holding tanks caused the oil to float to the top, so that crews who took inventory by viewing the holding tanks from the top observed only salad oil. In fact, as much as 11 out of 12 metres of many of the holding tanks contained water. (2) The company's inventory records listed more holding tanks than it actually had. The company repainted numbers on the tanks after inventory crews had examined them, so the crews counted the same tanks twice. (3) Underground pipes pumped oil from one holding tank to another while inventory was being taken. Therefore, the same salad oil was counted more than once. Although the salad oil swindle was unusual, it demonstrates the complexities involved in ensuring that inventory is properly counted.

After the physical inventory is taken, the quantity of each kind of inventory is listed on inventory summary sheets. To ensure accuracy, the listing should be verified by a second employee, or auditor.

Unit costs are then applied to the quantities in order to determine the total cost of the inventory—this will be explained later in the chapter. To estimate the cost of inventory when a physical count cannot be taken (if the inventory is destroyed, for example) or when it is inconvenient (during interim periods), estimating methods are applied. These methods (gross profit and retail inventory methods) are discussed in Appendix 6B.

Determining Ownership of Goods

Before we can begin to calculate the cost of inventory, we need to consider the ownership of goods. Specifically, we need to be sure that we have not included in the inventory quantities any goods that do not belong to the company, or forgotten any that do.

Goods in Transit.   Goods are considered **in transit** when they are in the hands of a public carrier such as a railway, airline, trucking, or shipping company at the statement date. Goods in transit should be included in the inventory of the party that has legal title to the goods. Legal title is determined by the terms of sale described below, as we learned in Chapter 5.
1. **FOB (free on board) shipping point.** Ownership of the goods passes to the buyer when the public carrier accepts the goods from the seller.
2. **FOB destination.** Ownership of the goods remains with the seller until the goods reach the buyer.

Inventory quantities may be seriously miscounted if goods in transit at the statement date are ignored. Assume that Hill Company, located in Vancouver, has 20,000 units of inventory on hand on December 31. It has the following goods in transit: (1) **sales** of 1,500 units shipped December 31, FOB destination, and (2) **purchases** of 2,500 units shipped FOB shipping point by the seller on December 31. Hill has legal title to both the units sold and the units purchased. If units in transit are ignored, inventory quantities would be understated by 4,000 units (1,500 + 2,500).

►Accounting in Action ► *@ -Business Insight*

Many companies have invested large amounts of time and money in automated shipping systems. One such system is Air Canada's waybill database system. Air Canada drowned in a sea of paper as it tried to maintain waybill slips on file *for seven years*, for every piece of cargo it shipped throughout the world. It was often difficult for Air Canada employees to find a particular slip—a difficulty that was not appreciated by customers trying to track a missing shipment. Now, waybills are scanned into a database and indexed. Customers can check the company's website or call a 1-800 number to find the location of their shipment at any time of the day or night.

Consigned Goods. In some lines of business, it is customary to acquire merchandise on consignment. Under a consignment arrangement, the holder of the goods (called the *consignee*) does not own the goods. Ownership remains with the shipper of the goods (called the *consignor*) until the goods are actually sold to a customer. Because consigned goods are not owned by the consignee, they should not be included in the consignee's physical inventory count. Conversely, the consignor should include merchandise held by the consignee as part of its inventory.

Other Situations. Sometimes goods are not physically on the premises because they have been taken home *on approval* by a customer. Goods on approval should be added to the physical inventory count because they still belong to the seller. The customer will either return the item or decide to buy it.

In other cases, goods are sold but the seller is holding them for alteration, or until they are picked up or delivered to the customer. These goods should not be included in the physical count, because legal title to ownership has passed to the customer. Damaged or unsaleable goods should be segregated from the physical count and any loss recorded. We will discuss the issue of losses in the value of inventories later in the chapter.

Before You Go On . . .

►*Review It*

1. What steps are involved in determining inventory quantities?
2. How is ownership determined for goods in transit at the balance sheet date?
3. Who has title to consigned goods?

►*Do It*

Hasbeen Company, located in Ottawa, completed its inventory count. It arrived at a total inventory value of $200,000, counting everything currently on hand in its warehouse. You have been given the information listed below. Discuss how this information affects the reported cost of inventory.

1. Goods costing $15,000 held on consignment for the Ottawa Senators hockey team were included in the inventory.
2. Purchased goods of $10,000 that were in transit (terms FOB shipping point) were not included in the count.
3. Inventory with a cost of $12,000 that was sold and in transit by rail to a Halifax customer (terms FOB shipping point) was not included in the count.

Action Plan

- Apply the rules of ownership to goods held on consignment.
- Apply the rules of ownership to goods in transit.
- FOB shipping point: Goods sold or purchased, and shipped FOB shipping point belong to the purchaser.

- FOB destination: Goods sold or purchased, and shipped FOB destination belong to the seller until they reach their destination.

Solution

The $15,000 of goods held on consignment should be deducted from Hasbeen's inventory count. They belong to the Ottawa Senators and should not be included in Hasbeen's inventory. The goods worth $10,000 that were purchased FOB shipping point should be added to Hasbeen's inventory count. The sold goods of $12,000 that were in transit FOB shipping point were correctly excluded from Hasbeen's ending inventory, since title passed when the goods were handed over to the railway company in Ottawa. Inventory totals $195,000 ($200,000 − $15,000 + $10,000).

Related exercise material: BE6–1, BE6–2, and E6–1.

THE NAVIGATOR

Periodic Inventory System

STUDY OBJECTIVE

2

Prepare the entries for purchases and sales of inventory under a periodic inventory system.

As we previously learned, one of two basic systems of accounting for inventories may be used: (1) the **perpetual inventory system**, or (2) the **periodic inventory system**. Chapter 5 presented the perpetual inventory system. This chapter presents the periodic inventory system.

In a periodic inventory system, revenues from the sale of merchandise are recorded when sales are made, in the same way as in a perpetual inventory system, but no attempt is made on the date of sale to record the cost of the merchandise sold. Instead, a physical inventory count is taken at or near the end of the period. This count determines the cost of the merchandise on hand. We will use this information, and other information, to determine the cost of the goods sold during the period.

There are other differences between the perpetual and periodic inventory systems. Under a periodic inventory system, purchases of merchandise are recorded in the Purchases expense account, rather than the Merchandise Inventory asset account. Also, under a periodic system, it is customary to record Purchase Returns and Allowances and Freight In in separate accounts. That way, accumulated amounts are known for each.

To illustrate the recording of merchandise transactions under a periodic inventory system, we will use the purchase and sale transactions between Highpoint Electronic and Chelsea Video discussed in Chapter 5.

Recording Sales of Merchandise

The sale of $3,800 of merchandise to Chelsea Video on May 4 shown in the sales invoice in Illustration 5-4 is recorded by the seller, Highpoint Electronic, as follows:

A = L + OE			
+3,800	+3,800		

May 4	Accounts Receivable	3,800	
	Sales		3,800
	To record credit sale per invoice #731 to Chelsea Video.		

Sales Returns and Allowances

The $300 return of goods on May 8 is recorded by Highpoint Electronic as follows:

A = L + OE			
−300	−300		

May 8	Sales Returns and Allowances	300	
	Accounts Receivable		300
	To record return of inoperable goods from Chelsea Video.		

These two sales entries are exactly the same as those illustrated in Chapter 5, with one exception. In a perpetual inventory system, two journal entries are made for each transaction. The first entry records the accounts receivable and sales revenue (or return), as illustrated above. The second journal entry records the cost of the sale by transferring the inventory to the cost of goods sold account (or the opposite in the case of a return). In a periodic inventory system, there is only one journal entry made at the time of the sale to record the sales revenue. The cost of the sale is not recorded. Instead, the cost of goods sold is determined by calculation at the end of the period.

Recording Purchases of Merchandise

On the basis of the sales invoice (Illustration 5-4) and receipt of the merchandise ordered from Highpoint Electronic, Chelsea Video records the $3,800 purchase as follows:

May 4	Purchases	3,800	
	Accounts Payable		3,800
	To record goods purchased on account, terms n/30.		

A = L + OE
+3,800 −3,800

Purchases is a temporary expense account reported on the income statement, whose normal balance is a debit.

Helpful hint Be careful not to fall into the trap of debiting equipment or supplies to Purchases.

Purchase Returns and Allowances

Since some of the merchandise received from Highpoint Electronic is inoperable, Chelsea

May 8	Accounts Payable	300	
	Purchase Returns and Allowances		300
	To record return of inoperable goods purchased from Highpoint Electronics.		

A = L + OE
−300 +300

Video returns $300 worth of goods. The following entry recognizes the purchase return: Purchase Returns and Allowances is a temporary account whose normal balance is a credit. It is a contra account, deducted from Purchases. Purchases less Purchase Returns and Allowances results in net purchases.

Freight Costs

When the purchaser pays for the freight costs, the account Freight In is debited. For example, upon delivery of the goods, Chelsea pays Acme Freight Company $150 for freight charges on its purchase from Highpoint Electronic. The entry on Chelsea's books is as follows:

May 4	Freight In	150	
	Cash		150
	To record payment of freight, terms FOB shipping point.		

A = L + OE
−150 −150

Like Purchases, Freight In is a temporary expense account whose normal balance is a debit. Just as freight was a part of the cost of the merchandise inventory in a perpetual inventory system, **freight in is part of the cost of goods purchased** in a periodic inventory system. Freight in is added to net purchases to determine the cost of goods purchased. In accordance with the cost principle, the cost of goods purchased should include any freight charges necessary to bring the goods to the purchaser.

Comparison of Entries—Perpetual vs. Periodic

Illustration 6-1

Comparison of journal entries under perpetual and periodic inventory systems

The periodic inventory system entries are shown in Illustration 6-1 next to the perpetual inventory system entries that were illustrated in Chapter 5. Having these entries side by side should help you compare the differences. The entries that are different in the two inventory systems are highlighted.

ENTRIES ON CHELSEA VIDEO'S BOOKS (PURCHASER)

Transaction	Perpetual Inventory System		Periodic Inventory System	

May 4 Purchase of merchandise on credit.	Merchandise Inventory 3,800
	   Accounts Payable
		3,800	Purchases 3,800
			   Accounts Payable
				3,800

May 4 Freight cost on purchases.	Merchandise Inventory 150
	   Cash
		150	Freight In 150
			   Cash
				150

May 8 Purchase returns and allowances.	Accounts Payable 300
	   Merchandise Inventory
		300	Accounts Payable 300
			   Purchase Returns
			    and Allowances
				300

ENTRIES ON HIGHPOINT ELECTRONIC'S BOOKS (SELLER)

Transaction	Perpetual Inventory System		Periodic Inventory System	

May 4 Sale of merchandise on credit.	Accounts Receivable 3,800
	   Sales
		3,800	Accounts Receivable 3,800
			   Sales
				3,800

	Cost of Goods Sold 2,400 Merchandise Inventory	2,400	No entry	

May 8 Return of merchandise sold.	Sales Returns and
	Allowances 300
	   Accounts Receivable
		300	Sales Returns and
			Allowances 300
			   Accounts Receivable
				300

	Merchandise Inventory 140 Cost of Goods Sold	140	No entry	

Before You Go On . . .

▶Review It

1. Compare the recording of purchases and sales in periodic and perpetual inventory systems.

Related exercise material: BE6–3 and E6–2.

Cost of Goods Sold

STUDY OBJECTIVE

3

Determine cost of goods sold under a periodic inventory system.

In a periodic inventory system, as we've seen in the entries above, temporary accounts are used to accumulate the increases and decreases in purchases and sales throughout the period. A running account of the changes in inventory is not recorded when purchase or sales transactions occur. The daily amount of merchandise on hand is not known, and neither is the cost of goods sold.

To determine the cost of goods sold in a periodic inventory system, three steps are required: (1) Record purchases of merchandise. (2) Determine the cost of goods purchased. (3) Determine the cost of goods on hand at the beginning and end of the accounting period. We will discuss each of these steps in the following sections.

Determining Cost of Goods Purchased

Earlier in this chapter, we used three accounts to record the purchase of inventory under a periodic inventory system. These accounts and their use are as follows:

Transaction	Periodic Account Title	Normal Balance	Effects on Cost of Goods Purchased
Purchase of merchandise	Purchases	Debit	Increase
Purchase returns and allowances granted by seller	Purchase Returns and Allowances	Credit	Decrease
Freight charges paid by purchaser	Freight In	Debit	Increase

Illustration 6-2

Purchase accounts

The procedure for determining the cost of goods purchased is as follows:

1. The account with a credit balance (Purchase Returns and Allowances) is subtracted from Purchases. The result is **net purchases**.
2. Freight In is added to net purchases. The result is **cost of goods purchased**.

To illustrate, assume that Highpoint Electronic shows the following balances for the accounts above: Purchases, $325,000; Purchase Returns and Allowances, $17,200; and Freight In, $12,200. Net purchases is $307,800, and cost of goods purchased is $320,000, as calculated below:

	Purchases	$325,000
(1)	Less: Purchase returns and allowances	17,200
	Net purchases	**307,800**
(2)	Add: Freight in	12,200
	Cost of goods purchased	**$320,000**

Determining Cost of Goods on Hand

To determine the cost of the inventory on hand, Highpoint Electronic must **take a physical inventory**. As described earlier in this chapter, we use these steps to take a physical inventory:

1. Count the units on hand for each item of inventory.
2. Apply unit costs to the total units on hand for each item of inventory.
3. Total the costs for each item of inventory, to determine the total cost of goods on hand.

The total cost of goods on hand is known as the ending inventory. Highpoint's physical inventory count on December 31, 2002, determines that the cost of its goods on hand, or ending inventory, is $40,000. This ending inventory amount will be used to calculate the cost of goods sold (as shown in the next section) and will be recorded as part of the closing process in the Merchandise Inventory account.

As we will learn later in this chapter, at the end of the year, closing entries are made to eliminate beginning inventory and to record ending inventory in the Merchandise Inventory account. During the year, no entries are made to the Merchandise Inventory account since the temporary Purchases account is used. So the balance in the Merchandise Inventory account through the period is the *beginning inventory*. For Highpoint Electronic, the January 1, 2002, beginning balance in the Merchandise Inventory account is $36,000. We will use both the beginning and ending inventory amounts to calculate cost of goods sold in the next section.

Calculating Cost of Goods Sold

We have now reached the point where we can calculate cost of goods sold. Doing so involves two steps:

1. Add the cost of goods purchased to the cost of goods on hand at the beginning of the period (beginning inventory). The result is the cost of goods available for sale.
2. Subtract the cost of goods on hand at the end of the period (ending inventory) from the cost of goods available for sale. The result is the cost of goods sold.

For Highpoint Electronic, the cost of goods available for sale is $356,000 and the cost of goods sold is $316,000, as shown below:

Illustration 6-3

Calculations of cost of goods available for sale and cost of goods sold

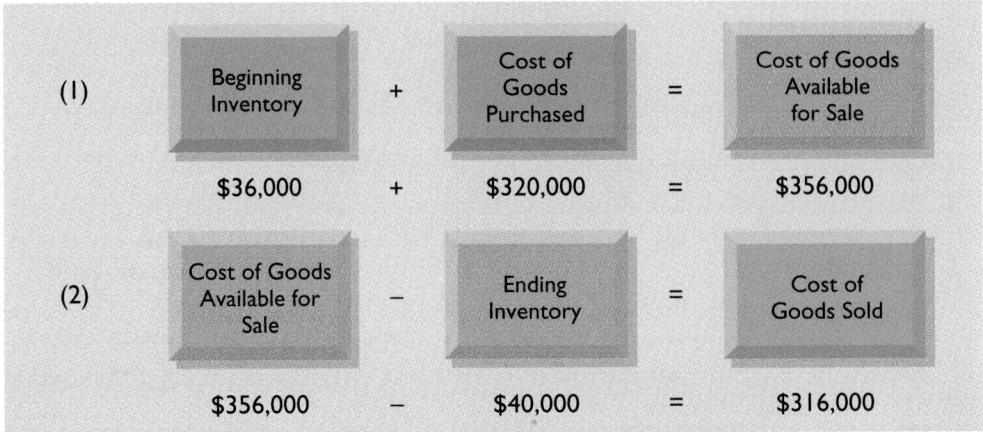

Gross profit, operating expenses, and net income are calculated and reported in a periodic inventory system in the same manner as under a perpetual inventory system.

Income Statement Presentation

STUDY OBJECTIVE
•••••••••• 4 ••••••••••

Identify the unique features of the income statement for a merchandising company using a periodic inventory system.

The adjusted trial balance for Highpoint Electronic has been reproduced in the following illustration. This is the same adjusted trial balance presented in Illustration 5-7 with two exceptions: (1) The Merchandise Inventory account is the beginning inventory amount, not the ending inventory amount. It has not yet been updated. (2) There is no Cost of Goods Sold account. The new accounts for a periodic inventory system are highlighted in red.

Illustration 6-4

Adjusted trial balance

HIGHPOINT ELECTRONICS Adjusted Trial Balance December 31, 2002		
	Debit	Credit
Cash	$ 9,500	
Accounts Receivable	16,100	
Merchandise Inventory	36,000	
Prepaid Insurance	1,800	
Store Equipment	80,000	
Accumulated Amortization		$ 24,000
Accounts Payable		20,400
Salaries Payable		5,000
R. A. Lamb, Capital		83,000
R. A. Lamb, Drawings	15,000	
Sales		480,000
Sales Returns and Allowances	20,000	
Purchases	325,000	
Purchase Returns and Allowances		17,200
Freight In	12,200	
Salaries Expense	45,000	
Rent Expense	19,000	
Utilities Expense	17,000	
Advertising Expense	16,000	
Amortization Expense	8,000	
Freight Out	7,000	
Insurance Expense	2,000	
Totals	$629,600	$629,600

From the adjusted trial balance in Illustration 6-4, we can prepare a multiple-step income statement for Highpoint Electronic. A multiple-step income statement for a merchandising company using a periodic inventory system has the same features as in the case of a perpetual inventory system with one exception: the cost of goods sold section contains more detail. The income statement for Highpoint Electronic is shown in Illustration 6-5.

HIGHPOINT ELECTRONICS Income Statement For the Year Ended December 31, 2002			
Sales revenues			
Sales			$480,000
Less: Sales returns and allowances			20,000
Net sales			460,000
Cost of goods sold			
Inventory, January 1		$ 36,000	
Purchases	$325,000		
Less: Purchase returns and allowances	17,200		
Net purchases	307,800		
Add: Freight in	12,200		
Cost of goods purchased		320,000	
Cost of goods available for sale		356,000	
Inventory, December 31		40,000	
Cost of goods sold			316,000
Gross profit			144,000
Operating expenses			
Salaries expense		$ 45,000	
Rent expense		19,000	
Utilities expense		17,000	
Advertising expense		16,000	
Amortization expense—store equipment		8,000	
Freight out		7,000	
Insurance expense		2,000	
Total operating expenses			114,000
Net income			$ 30,000

Illustration 6-5

Income statement for a merchandising company using a periodic inventory system

Helpful hint The far right column identifies the major subdivisions of the income statement. The next column identifies the main items making up the cost of goods sold of $316,000 and operating expenses of $114,000. The third column explains cost of goods purchased of $320,000.

Completing the Accounting Cycle

After preparing the financial statements, closing entries and a post-closing trial balance complete the accounting cycle. It is now time to consider these two remaining steps.

For a merchandising company, as for a service enterprise, all accounts that affect the determination of net income are closed to the owner's capital account, whether a perpetual or periodic inventory system is used. Data for the preparation of closing entries may be obtained from the adjusted trial balance presented in Illustration 6-4, or from the income statement presented in Illustration 6-5.

In a periodic inventory system, the closing entries are the same as those we previously learned about, with one exception: the treatment of Merchandise Inventory. In the adjusted trial balance, the balance reported for inventory is its beginning balance, not the ending balance reported in a perpetual inventory system. As explained earlier, during the year (or period in question), **no entries are made to the Merchandise Inventory account** since the temporary Purchases account is used. The beginning inventory remains in the account unchanged all year. At year end, entries must be made to eliminate the beginning inventory ($36,000 at January 1, 2002, for Highpoint) and to record this year's new ending inventory ($40,000 at December 31, 2002, for Highpoint).

Two journal entries close the Merchandise Inventory account in a periodic inventory system:

1. The beginning inventory balance is debited to the owner's capital account and credited to Merchandise Inventory to bring the account balance to zero.
2. The ending inventory balance is debited to Merchandise Inventory and credited to the owner's capital account to record the current end of period balance in the account.

The two entries for Highpoint Electronic are as follows:

A	=	L	+	OE
−36,000				−36,000

Dec. 31	R. A. Lamb, Capital		36,000	
	Merchandise Inventory			36,000
	To close beginning inventory.			

A	=	L	+	OE
+40,000				+40,000

Dec. 31	Merchandise Inventory		40,000	
	R. A. Lamb, Capital			40,000
	To close ending inventory.			

After the closing entries are posted, the Merchandise Inventory account will show the following:

Merchandise Inventory

1/1 Bal.	36,000	**12/31 Close**	36,000
12/31 Close	**40,000**		
12/31 Bal.	40,000		

Merchandise Inventory, a balance sheet account, is not actually closed through this process, as temporary accounts are. Instead, the closing process updates the inventory account for the change in beginning and ending inventory during the period. This is similar to the effect the closing process has on the owner's capital account. The ending inventory and capital balances must be updated to agree with the balance sheet at the end of the period. It is these ending balances that are reported on the balance sheet, not the opening balances found in the adjusted trial balance.

The remaining closing entries are as we saw in prior chapters, and are not illustrated here. To summarize:

1. The Merchandise Inventory account is credited for its beginning inventory balance, and debited to the owner's capital account.
2. The Merchandise Inventory account is debited for its ending inventory balance, and credited to the owner's capital account.
3. Temporary accounts with credit balances (the Sales account and the Purchase Returns and Allowances account) are debited for their individual account balance and the total credited to the owner's capital account.
4. Temporary accounts with debit balances (Sales Returns and Allowances, Purchases, Purchase Returns and Allowances, Freight In, Salaries Expense, etc.) are credited for their individual account balances and the total debited to the owner's capital account.
5. The drawings account is credited and its balances is debited to owner's capital.

Closing entries for accounts with credit balances (items 2 and 3), and accounts with debit balances (items 1 and 4) are often combined for convenience. After the closing entries are posted, a post-closing trial balance is prepared. Note that in the post-closing trial balance, the current asset account Merchandise Inventory's balance after closing equals ending inventory. **This amount now becomes the beginning inventory of the new period.**

Preparation of a post-closing trial balance does not differ from that described in earlier chapters and is not illustrated again here.

Before You Go On . . .

▶Review It

1. What accounts are used in determining the cost of goods purchased?
2. Discuss how cost of goods sold is determined in a periodic inventory system.
3. Explain how closing entries in a periodic inventory system differ from those in a perpetual system.

▶Do It

Aerosmith Company's accounting records show the following at year end: freight in $6,100; sales $240,000; purchases $162,500; beginning inventory $18,000; ending inventory $20,000; sales returns $10,000; purchase returns $8,600; operating expenses $57,000. Calculate the following amounts for Aerosmith Company:

(a) Net sales	(d) Gross profit
(b) Cost of goods purchased	(e) Net income
(c) Cost of goods sold	

Action Plan

- Understand the relationships of the cost items in measuring net income for a merchandising company.
- Calculate net sales (sales − sales returns and allowances).
- Calculate cost of goods purchased (Purchases − Purchase returns and allowances = Net purchases + Freight in).
- Calculate cost of goods sold (Beginning inventory + Cost of goods purchased = Cost of goods available for sale − Ending inventory).
- Calculate gross profit (sales − cost of goods sold).
- Calculate net income (Gross profit − Operating expenses).

Solution

(a) Net sales:
   Sales − Sales returns
   $240,000 − $10,000 = $230,000
(b) Cost of goods purchased:
   Purchases − Purchase returns = Net purchases + Freight in
   $162,500 − $8,600 = $153,900 + $6,100 = $160,000
(c) Cost of goods sold:
   Beginning inventory + Cost of goods purchased = Cost of goods available for sale − Ending inventory
   $18,000 + $160,000 = $178,000 − $20,000 = $158,000
(d) Gross profit:
   Net sales − Cost of goods sold
   $230,000 − $158,000 = $72,000
(e) Net income:
   Gross profit − Operating expenses
   $72,000 − $57,000 = $15,000

Related exercise material: BE6–4, BE6–5, BE6–6, E6–3, E6–4, and E6–5.

THE
NAVIGATOR

Inventory Costing Under a Periodic Inventory System

STUDY OBJECTIVE

5

Explain the basis of accounting for inventories, and use the inventory cost flow methods.

In the preceding section, the total dollar amount for the ending inventory was given to you. In reality, this amount must be determined. You will recall that one of the steps during the physical inventory is to apply unit costs to the quantities on hand. When all inventory items have been purchased at the same unit cost, this determination is simple. However, when items have been purchased at different costs during the period, it is difficult to decide which particular item at which unit cost remains in inventory and which particular item at which unit cost has been sold.

For example, assume that Fraser Valley Electronics purchases 1,000 Astro Condenser units for resale throughout the period at different prices. Some Astro Condensers cost $10 when originally purchased. Other units cost $11 in April, $12 in August, and $13 in November. Now suppose Fraser Valley Electronics has 450 Astro Condensers remaining in inventory at the end of the period. Should these inventory items be assigned a cost of $10, $11, $12, $13, or some combination of all four? To determine the cost of ending inventory as well as the cost of goods sold, we must have some means of allocating the purchase cost to each item in inventory and each item that has been sold.

The cost of goods available for sale (beginning inventory plus cost of goods purchased) gives us our starting point. It is these costs that must be allocated between ending inventory and cost of goods sold as shown in Illustration 6-6:

Illustration 6-6

Allocation of cost of goods available for sale

The cost of items must be allocated in a consistent and rational way. The cost and matching principles of accounting help by guiding the determination, and allocation, of the cost of the goods available for sale.

1. Following the **cost principle**, cost is the primary basis of accounting for inventories. This includes all expenditures needed to acquire goods and to make them ready for sale.
2. Following the **matching principle**, in accounting for inventories, the major objective is the matching of appropriate costs with sales revenue.

Under a perpetual method, this allocation is made as each item is sold. Under a periodic method, the allocation is made at the end of the period. We will continue using the periodic inventory system to illustrate the costing methods for allocating cost of goods available for sale, since that is the inventory system we have focused on in this chapter.

Additionally, while many companies use the perpetual inventory system to track their inventory quantities, they may also use the periodic inventory system to track their inventory costs, as does the Concordia University Bookstore in our feature story. These companies take advantage of point-of-sale computer systems to maintain a perpetual inventory of *quantities* on hand, so that reorders are made automatically when inventories fall to certain levels.

Grocery stores, for example, use optical scanning devices to scan the bar codes of goods sold into their computerized cash registers. But these systems, unless highly advanced, seldom maintain a perpetual inventory of *costs*. When the bar code from a bag of McCain Foods french fries is scanned into the cash register, most inventory systems are unable to identify when that particular bag of fries was purchased by the store and at what cost. If you've had experience working in a grocery store, you probably know that goods are unpacked directly from boxes after shipment, and prices and codes are not scanned into the computer *for each individual* good before shelving.

Periodic inventory costing methods include specific identification, FIFO, average cost, and LIFO. These are discussed in the following sections. Perpetual inventory costing methods are illustrated in Appendix 6A.

Using Actual Physical Flow Costing—Specific Identification

The specific identification method tracks the **actual physical flow** of the goods. **Each item of inventory is marked, tagged, or coded with its specific unit cost.** Items still in inventory at the end of the year are specifically costed to determine the total cost of the ending inventory. Assume, for example, that Fraser Valley Electronics purchases three digital CD players at costs of $700, $750, and $800. During the year, two are sold at a selling price of $1,200 each. At December 31, the company determines that the $750 CD player is still on hand. The ending inventory is $750 and the cost of goods sold is $1,500 ($700 + $800).

Illustration 6-7

Specific identification

Helpful hint Remember that inventory cost is the purchase price, not the selling price, of the goods.

Specific identification is possible when a company sells a limited number of high-unit-cost items that can be clearly identified from purchase through to sale. Examples are automobile dealerships and furniture stores.

When possible, specific identification is the ideal method of allocating cost of goods available for sale. This method reports ending inventory at actual cost and matches the actual cost of goods sold against sales revenue. However, specific identification may enable management to manipulate net income. To see how, assume that Fraser Valley Electronics wishes to maximize its net income just before year end. When selling one of the three digital CD players referred to earlier, management could select the player with the lowest cost ($700) to match against revenues ($1,200). Or, it could minimize net income by selecting the highest-cost ($800) CD player.

Ordinarily, however, the identity of goods purchased at a specific cost is lost between the date of purchase and the date of sale. For example, grocery and hardware stores sell thousands of relatively low-unit-cost items of inventory. These are often indistinguishable from one another. It may be impossible or impractical to track each item's cost. In that case, as the next section will show, we must make assumptions about which units were sold.

Using Assumed Cost Flow Methods—FIFO, Average Cost, and LIFO

Because specific identification is often impractical, other cost flow methods are allowed. These assume flows of costs that may be unrelated to the physical flow of goods. For this reason, we call them **assumed cost flow methods** or **cost flow assumptions**. They are as follows:

1. First-in, first-out (FIFO)
2. Average cost
3. Last-in, first-out (LIFO)

To illustrate these three inventory cost flow methods, we will assume that Fraser Valley Electronics uses a periodic inventory system. The information shown in Illustration 6-8 relates to its Z202 Astro Condensers:

Illustration 6-8

Cost of goods available for sale

Helpful hint   Throughout this section, the cost of goods available for sale, $12,000, will remain unchanged regardless of which inventory cost flow method is used. The pool of costs doesn't change with the choice of costing method—just the allocation of these costs between cost of goods sold and ending inventory.

	FRASER VALLEY ELECTRONICS Z202 Astro Condensers			
Date	Explanation	Units	Unit Cost	Total Cost
1/1	Beginning inventory	100	$10	$ 1,000
4/15	Purchase	200	11	2,200
8/24	Purchase	300	12	3,600
11/27	Purchase	400	13	5,200
	Total	1,000		$12,000

During the year, 550 units were sold. At December 31, 450 units (1,000 available for sale less 550 sold) are on hand.

First-In, First-Out (FIFO)

The **FIFO method** assumes that the **earliest goods** purchased are the first to be sold. FIFO often matches the actual physical flow of merchandise, because it generally is good business practice to sell the oldest units first.

Under the FIFO method, the **cost** of the earliest goods purchased is the first to be recognized as the cost of goods sold. This does not necessarily mean that the oldest units *are* sold first, but that the cost of the oldest units is recognized first.

In the periodic inventory system, we ignore the timing of the dates of each of the sales. Instead, we make the allocation **at the end of a period** and assume that the entire pool of costs is available for allocation at that time. The allocation of the cost of goods available for sale at Fraser Valley Electronics under periodic FIFO is shown in Illustration 6-9:

Illustration 6-9

Periodic system—FIFO

	Pool of Costs Cost of Goods Available for Sale			
Date	Explanation	Units	Unit Cost	Total Cost
1/1	Beginning inventory	100	$10	$ 1,000
4/15	Purchase	200	11	2,200
8/24	Purchase	300	12	3,600
11/27	Purchase	400	13	5,200
	Total	1,000		$12,000

Cost of Goods Sold				Ending Inventory			
Date	Units	Unit Cost	Total Cost	Date	Units	Unit Cost	Total Cost
1/1	100	$10	$1,000	11/27	400	$13	$5,200
4/15	200	11	2,200	8/24	50	12	600
8/24	250	12	3,000	Total	450		$5,800
Total	550		$6,200				

The cost flow assumption—FIFO, in this case—is always specified in the order of selling. That is, the order in which the goods are assumed to be sold is first-in, first-out. To determine the cost of goods sold, simply start at the first (beginning inventory) and count forward until the total number of units sold (550) is reached.

If the order of selling is first-in, first-out, then what remains in inventory is the opposite (last-in, still-here!). The ending inventory is based on the latest units purchased. That is, **the cost of the ending inventory is obtained by taking the unit cost of the most recent purchase and working backward until all units of inventory have been costed.**

Another way of determining the ending inventory is to calculate the cost of goods sold and turn around the income statement formula to determine the missing amount:

Cost of goods available for sale	$12,000
Less: Cost of goods sold	6,200
Ending inventory	$ 5,800

Because of the potential for calculation errors, we recommend that both the cost of goods sold and the ending inventory amounts be calculated separately. The cost of goods sold and ending inventory total can then be compared to the cost of goods available for sale amount (e.g., $6,200 + $5,800 = $12,000) to check the accuracy of the reported results.

Average Cost

The average cost method assumes that the goods available for sale are identical or nondistinguishable. Under this method, the allocation of the cost of goods available for sale is on the basis of the **weighted average unit cost**. This average cost is *not* calculated by taking a simple average ([$10 + $11 + $12 + $13] ÷ 4 = $11.50 per unit), but rather by weighting the quantities purchased at each unit cost. The formula and calculation of weighted average unit cost are as follows:

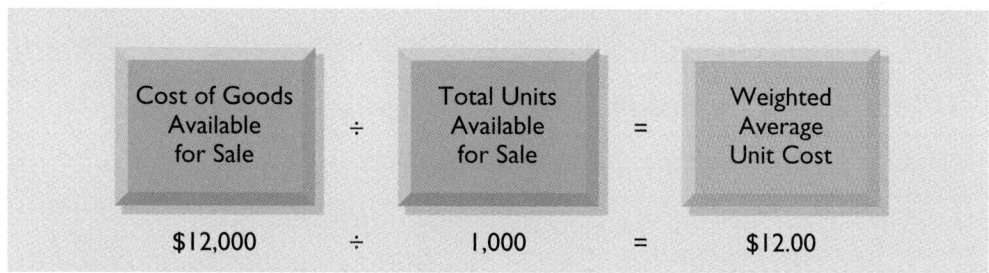

Illustration 6-10

Formula for weighted average unit cost

The weighted average unit cost is then applied to the units on hand to determine the cost of the ending inventory. When the weighted average unit cost is applied to the units sold, the cost of goods sold is determined. The allocation of the cost of goods available for sale at Fraser Valley Electronics using weighted average cost is shown in Illustration 6-11:

Illustration 6-11

Periodic system—weighted average cost

	Pool of Costs Cost of Goods Available for Sale				
Date	Explanation	Units	Unit Cost	Total Cost
1/1	Beginning inventory	100	$10	$ 1,000
4/15	Purchase	200	11	2,200
8/24	Purchase	300	12	3,600
11/27	Purchase	400	13	5,200
	Total	1,000		$12,000

Cost of Goods Sold			Ending Inventory		
$12,000 ÷ 1,000 = $12.00			$12,000 ÷ 1,000 = $12.00		
Units	Unit Cost	Total Cost	Units	Unit Cost	Total Cost
550 × $12.00 = $6,600			450 × $12.00 = $5,400		

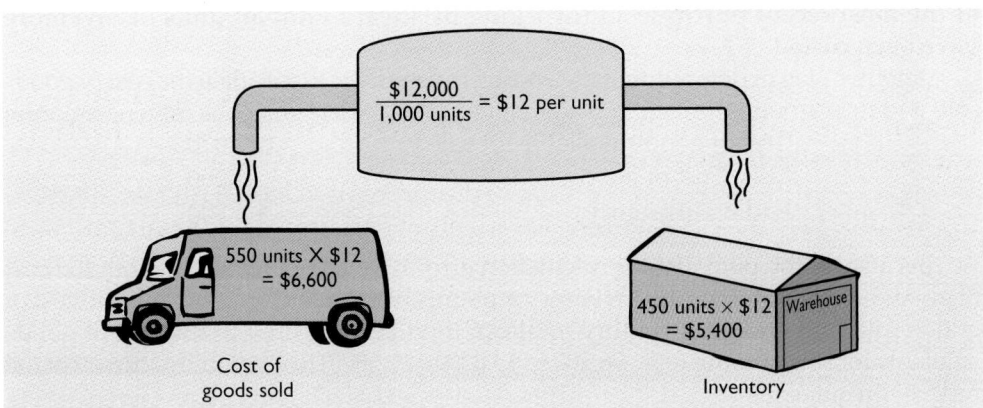

Last-In, First-Out (LIFO)

The **LIFO method** assumes that the **latest goods** purchased are the first to be sold. For the majority of companies, LIFO seldom coincides with the actual physical flow of inventory. Only for goods in piles, such as sand, hay, produce in the grocery store, or products in bins at a store like the Bulk Barn, would LIFO match the physical flow of inventory. But, as explained earlier, this does not mean that the LIFO method cannot be used in these cases. It is the flow of costs that is important, not the physical flow of goods. The allocation of the cost of goods available for sale at Fraser Valley Electronics under LIFO is shown in Illustration 6-12.

Illustration 6-12

Allocation of costs—LIFO method

	Pool of Costs Cost of Goods Available for Sale				
Date	Explanation	Units	Unit Cost	Total Cost
1/1	Beginning inventory	100	$10	$ 1,000
4/15	Purchase	200	11	2,200
8/24	Purchase	300	12	3,600
11/27	Purchase	400	13	5,200
	Total	1,000		$12,000

Cost of Goods Sold				Ending Inventory			
Date	Units	Unit Cost	Total Cost	Date	Units	Unit Cost	Total Cost
11/27	400	$13	$5,200	1/1	100	$10	$1,000
8/24	150	12	1,800	4/15	200	11	2,200
Total	550		$7,000	8/24	150	12	1,800
				Total	450		$5,000

►*Ethics note*

Because goods purchased late in a period are assumed to be available for the first sale, income could be manipulated by a purchase of inventory in December.

Under a periodic inventory system, remember that **all goods purchased during the period are assumed to be available for the first sale, regardless of the date of purchase**. Under the LIFO method, the cost of the **last** goods in is the **first** to be assigned to cost of goods sold. **The cost of the ending inventory is obtained by taking the unit cost of the oldest goods available for sale and working forward until all units of inventory are costed.** As a result, the first costs assigned to ending inventory are the costs of the beginning inventory (first-in, still-here!).

Financial Statement Effects of Cost Flow Methods

Each of the four cost flow methods is acceptable. For example, Ault Foods, Canadian Tire, and Sobeys use the FIFO method. Abitibi Consolidated, Andrés Wines, and Mountain Equipment Co-op use the average cost method. Alberta Natural Gas, Cominco, and Suncor use LIFO. A company may also use more than one cost flow method at the same time. Finning Tractor uses specific identification to account for its equipment inventory, FIFO to account for about 70% of its inventory of parts and supplies, and average cost to account for the remaining 30%. Illustration 6-13 shows the use of cost flow methods in public companies in Canada.

Although each of the cost flow methods is acceptable, it is obvious that very few companies in Canada use LIFO. The Canadian companies that do use LIFO tend to use it to harmonize their reporting practices to the U.S., where use of the LIFO method is more significant.

►**Accounting in Action** ► *International Insight*

Very few companies worldwide use LIFO, except in the U.S. Of companies that use LIFO to value their inventory, 82% are located in the U.S., 1.5% are located in Canada, and the rest are located elsewhere. LIFO is not permitted for use by companies in the UK. Other countries (e.g., Australia, France, Hong Kong, Japan, and Germany) permit only foreign subsidiaries to use LIFO.

STUDY OBJECTIVE
•••••••••• ▼ ••••••••••
6

Demonstrate the effects on the financial statements of each of the inventory cost flow methods.

Illustration 6-13

Use of cost flow methods in Canadian public companies

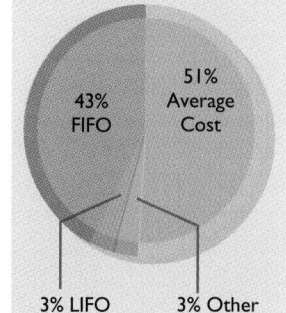

51% Average Cost
43% FIFO
3% LIFO
3% Other

Although the FIFO and average cost methods are more commonly used in Canada, to understand global financial reporting, students need to have some understanding of the impact of the LIFO method of inventory valuation. The reasons companies have for adopting different inventory cost flow methods are varied, but they usually involve one of the following factors:

1. Income statement effects
2. Balance sheet effects

Income Statement Effects

Illustration 6-14

Comparative effects of cost flow methods

To understand why companies might choose a particular cost flow method, let's compare each method's effects on the financial statements of Fraser Valley Electronics. The condensed income statements in Illustration 6-14 assume that Fraser Valley sold its 550 units for $11,500. Its operating expenses were $2,000.

FRASER VALLEY ELECTRONICS Condensed Income Statements					
	FIFO		Average Cost		LIFO
Sales		$11,500		$11,500		$11,500
Beginning inventory	$ 1,000		$ 1,000		$ 1,000	
Purchases	11,000		11,000		11,000	
Cost of goods available for sale	12,000		12,000		12,000	
Ending inventory	5,800		5,400		5,000	
Cost of goods sold		6,200		6,600		7,000
Gross profit		5,300		4,900		4,500
Operating expenses		2,000		2,000		2,000
Net income		$ 3,300		$ 2,900		$ 2,500

The cost of goods available for sale ($12,000) is the same under each of the three inventory cost flow methods. But both the ending inventories and the cost of goods sold are different. This difference is because of the unit costs that are allocated to cost of goods sold and to ending inventory. Each dollar of difference in ending inventory results in a corresponding dollar difference in cost of goods sold and net income. For Fraser Valley, there is an $800 difference between FIFO and LIFO.

In a period of rising prices, FIFO produces a higher income. This happens because the expenses matched against revenues are the lower unit costs of the first units purchased. In a period of rising prices (as is the case here), FIFO reports the highest income ($3,300) and LIFO the lowest ($2,500). Average cost falls somewhere in the middle ($2,900). To management, higher net income is an advantage. It causes external users to view the company more favourably. Also, if management bonuses are based on net income, FIFO will provide the basis for higher bonuses.

If prices are falling, the results from the use of FIFO and LIFO are reversed. FIFO will report the lowest income and LIFO the highest. If prices are stable, all three methods will report the same results.

LIFO provides the best income statement valuation. It matches current costs with current revenues. This is because, under LIFO, the cost of goods sold is assumed to be the cost of the goods most recently acquired. Even though LIFO may produce the best match of revenues and expenses, it is seldom used in Canada. The method can be manipulated, depending on the timing of purchases. The use of LIFO is also not permitted for income tax purposes, and most firms do not wish to maintain two sets of inventory records—one for accounting purposes and another for tax purposes.

Balance Sheet Effects

FIFO produces the best balance sheet valuation. A major advantage of FIFO is that in a period of rising prices, the costs allocated to ending inventory will approximate their current, or replacement, cost. For example, for Fraser Valley, 400 of the 450 units in the ending inventory are costed at the November 27 unit cost of $13. Since management's intention is to replace inventory once sold, a valuation that approximates replacement cost is relevant to decision-making.

A major shortcoming of LIFO is evident during periods of rising prices, because the costs allocated to ending inventory may be understated in terms of current costs. The understatement becomes even more pronounced if the inventory includes goods purchased in one or more prior accounting periods. This is true for Fraser Valley. The cost of the ending inventory includes the $10 unit cost of the beginning inventory.

We have seen that both inventory on the balance sheet and net income on the income statement are higher when FIFO is used in a period of rising prices. Do not confuse this with cash flow. All three methods produce exactly the same cash flow. Revenues and purchases are not affected by the choice of cost flow assumption. The only thing affected is the allocation between ending inventory and cost of goods sold, which does not involve cash.

It is also worth remembering that all three cost flow assumptions will give exactly the same results over the life cycle of the business or its product. That is, the allocation between cost of goods sold and ending inventory may vary within a period, but over time will yield the same cumulative results. Although much has been written about the impact of the choice of inventory cost flow method on a variety of performance measures, in reality there is little real economic distinction among the methods *over time*.

Summary of Effects

The following illustration summarizes the key differences that result from the different cost flow assumptions during a period of rising prices. The effects will be the opposite of those in the illustration if prices are falling. There is no distinction between methods if prices are constant.

	FIFO	Average	LIFO
Cost of goods sold	Lowest	Results will fall in between FIFO and LIFO	Highest
Gross profit/Net income	Highest	Results will fall in between FIFO and LIFO	Lowest
Cash flow (pretax)	Same	Same	Same
Ending inventory	Highest	Results will fall in between FIFO and LIFO	Lowest

Illustration 6-15

Financial statement effects of cost flow methods during a period of rising prices

Selection of Cost Flow Method

Accounting should provide information that is useful to decision-makers. We have learned that the choice of cost flow method can lead to substantially different financial statement effects, depending on the direction of prices. Is the useful information financial reporting objective achieved if managers can select a method depending on its desired influence on their financial results? The answer to this is "No."

While the accounting profession does permit a choice among acceptable methods, the reason is to **accommodate differences in the circumstances of the company and the industry**. It is not to permit managers to manipulate the company's financial position at will. The CICA recommends that in those cases "where the choice of method of inventory valuation is an important factor in determining income, the most suitable method for determining cost is that which results in charging against operations costs which **most fairly match** the sales revenue for the period."

Using Inventory Cost Flow Methods Consistently

Helpful hint As you will learn in Chapter 12, consistency is one of the most important characteristics of accounting information.

Whichever cost flow method is selected by a company, it should be used consistently from one period to the next. Consistent application makes financial statements comparable over successive time periods. Using the FIFO method in one year and the average cost method in the next year would make it difficult to compare the net incomes for the two years.

Although consistent application is preferred, a company may change its method of inventory costing. Such a change and its effects on net income should be disclosed in the financial statements. This conforms with the full disclosure principle, which requires all relevant information to be disclosed. The full disclosure principle is discussed further in Chapter 12.

Before You Go On . . .

►Review It

1. How do the cost, matching, and full disclosure principles apply to inventory costs?
2. How are the three assumed cost flow methods applied in allocating cost of goods available for sale?
3. Which inventory cost flow method produces the highest net income in a period of rising prices? The highest balance sheet valuation? The highest cash flow?
4. What factors should be considered by management in selecting an inventory cost flow method?
5. What amount is reported by The Second Cup Ltd. in its 2000 financial statements as inventories? Which inventory cost flow assumption does The Second Cup use? The answer to these questions is provided at the end of this chapter.

►Do It

The accounting records of Shumway Ag show the following data:

Beginning inventory	4,000 units at $3
Purchases	6,000 units at $4
Sales	5,000 units at $6

Determine the cost of goods sold during the period under a periodic inventory system using (a) FIFO, (b) weighted average, and (c) LIFO.

Action Plan

*   Understand the periodic inventory system.
*   Calculate the cost of goods sold under the periodic inventory system using the FIFO cost flow assumption. Allocate the earliest costs to the goods sold.
*   Calculate the cost of goods sold under the periodic inventory system using the weighted average cost flow assumption. Apply the weighted average unit cost (goods available for sale in $ ÷ goods available for sale units) to the goods sold.
*   Calculate the cost of goods sold under the periodic inventory system using the LIFO cost flow assumption. Allocate the latest costs to the goods sold.

Solution

(a) FIFO: (4,000 @ $3) + (1,000 @ $4) = $16,000
(b) Weighted average: (4,000 @ $3) + (6,000 @ $4) = $36,000 ÷ 10,000 = $3.60; 5,000 @ $3.60 = $18,000
(c) LIFO: 5,000 @ $4 = $20,000

Related exercise material: BE6–7, BE6–8, E6–6, E6–7, E6–8, E6–9, and E6-10.

Inventory Errors

Unfortunately, errors occasionally occur in taking or costing inventory. Some errors are caused by counting or pricing the inventory incorrectly. Other errors occur because of improper recognition of the transfer of legal title for goods in transit. When errors occur, they affect both the income statement and the balance sheet.

STUDY OBJECTIVE
•••••••••• 7 ••••••••••
Determine the effects of inventory errors on the financial statements.

Income Statement Effects

The cost of goods available for sale (beginning inventory plus cost of goods purchased) is allocated between cost of goods sold and ending inventory. Therefore, an error in any one of these components will affect both the income statement (through cost of goods sold and net income) and the balance sheet (ending inventory and owner's capital).

The dollar effects on cost of goods sold and net income can be determined by entering the incorrect data in the income statement formula, and then substituting the correct data.

Illustration 6-16

Income formula

The overall effects of inventory errors on the current year's income statement are summarized in Illustration 6-17. U stands for understatement, O for overstatement and NE for no effect.

Illustration 6–17

Effects of inventory errors on current year's income statement

Nature of Error	Beginning Inventory	+	Cost of Goods Purchased	=	Cost of Goods Available for Sale	−	Ending Inventory	=	Cost of Goods Sold	Sales	−	Cost of Goods Sold	=	Gross Profit/ Net Income
Understate beginning inventory	U	+	NE	=	U	−	NE	=	U	NE	−	U	=	O
Overstate beginning inventory	O	+	NE	=	O	−	NE	=	O	NE	−	O	=	U
Understate cost of goods purchased	NE	+	U	=	U	−	NE	=	U	NE	−	U	=	O
Overstate cost of goods purchased	NE	+	O	=	O	−	NE	=	O	NE	−	O	=	U
Understate ending inventory	NE	+	NE	=	NE	−	U	=	O	NE	−	O	=	U
Overstate ending inventory	NE	+	NE	=	NE	−	O	=	U	NE	−	U	=	O

If **beginning inventory** is understated, cost of goods sold will be understated. If **purchases** are understated, cost of goods sold will also be understated. On the other hand, an understatement of **ending inventory** will overstate cost of goods sold, because ending inventory must be deducted to determine cost of goods sold.

Cost of goods sold is deducted from sales to determine gross profit, and ultimately

▶*Ethics note*

Inventory fraud increases during recessions. Such fraud includes pricing inventory at higher amounts than its actual value, or claiming to have inventory when no inventory exists. Inventory fraud is usually done to over-state ending inventory, thereby understating cost of goods sold, which results in higher income.

net income. An understatement in cost of goods sold will produce an overstatement in net income. An overstatement in cost of goods sold will produce an understatement in net income.

Since the ending inventory of one period becomes the beginning inventory of the next period, **an error in ending inventory of the current period will have a reverse effect on net income of the next period**. This is shown in Illustration 6-18. Note that the $3,000 understatement of ending inventory in 2002 will result in an understatement of beginning inventory in 2003 and an overstatement of net income in 2003 of the same amount.

Condensed Income Statements

| | 2002 | | | 2003 | | |
	Incorrect		Correct	Incorrect		Correct
Sales		$80,000	$80,000		$90,000	$90,000
Beginning inventory	$20,000		$20,000	$12,000		$15,000
Cost of goods purchased	40,000		40,000	68,000		68,000
Cost of goods available for sale	60,000		60,000	80,000		83,000
Ending inventory	12,000		15,000	23,000		23,000
Cost of goods sold		48,000	45,000		57,000	60,000
Gross profit		32,000	35,000		33,000	30,000
Operating expenses		10,000	10,000		20,000	20,000
Net income		$22,000	$25,000		$13,000	$10,000

($3,000)
Net income
understated

$3,000
Net income
overstated

The combined net income for two years is correct because the errors cancel each other out.

Illustration 6-18

Effects of inventory errors on income statements of two successive years

Over the two years, total net income is correct. The errors offset one another. Notice that total income using incorrect data is $35,000 ($22,000 + $13,000). This is the same as the total income of $35,000 ($25,000 + $10,000) using correct data. Nevertheless, the distortion of the year-by-year results can have a serious impact on financial analysis and management decisions.

Note that an error in the beginning inventory does not result in a corresponding error in the ending inventory. The correctness of the ending inventory depends entirely on the accuracy of taking and costing the inventory at the balance sheet date.

Balance Sheet Effects

The effect of errors on the balance sheet can be determined by using the basic accounting equation: **Assets = Liabilities + Owner's Equity**. In the following illustration, U is for understatement, O is for overstatement, and NE is for no effect.

Illustration 6-19

Effects of inventory errors on a balance sheet

Nature of Error	Assets	=	Liabilities	+	Owner's Equity
Understate ending inventory	U	=	NE	+	U
Overstate ending inventory	O	=	NE	+	O

Errors in beginning inventory have no impact on the balance sheet, if ending inventory is correctly calculated in the current period. Understating ending inventory, however, will understate net income, as we saw in Illustration 6-17. If net income is understated, then owner's equity will be understated (because net income is part of owner's equity).

The effect of an error in ending inventory on the next period was shown in Illustration 6-18. If the error is not corrected, total net income for the two periods would be correct. Thus, total owner's equity reported on the balance sheet at the end of 2003 will also be correct.

Regardless of the nature of the error (and there are many combinations of errors possible), using the income statement and balance sheet equation will help ensure that you don't miss the total effect of pervasive inventory errors.

Before You Go On . . .

▶Review It

1. How do inventory errors affect financial statements?

▶Do It

On December 31, 2003, Silas Company counted and recorded $600,000 of inventory. This count did not include by $90,000 of goods in transit, shipped FOB shipping point. Determine the correct December 31, 2003, inventory. If Silas reports ending inventory of $600,000 on its balance sheet, identify any financial statement accounts that may be in error, and the amount and direction of the error.

Action Plan

- Use income statement relationships to determine impact of error on income statement.
- Use accounting equation to determine impact of error on balance sheet.

Solution

The correct inventory count is $690,000 ($600,000 + $90,000). Purchases and Accounts Payable are understated by $90,000 (assuming the purchase has not yet been recorded, since the goods have not yet arrived). Ending inventory is also understated by $90,000. For the year 2004, beginning inventory will also be understated by $90,000 and net income overstated by $90,000, unless the error is caught before the upcoming year begins. Missing this amount does not have significant economic consequences for Silas's overall financial position, since the errors offset each other.

BI	NE		Sales	NE		A	=	L	+	OE
+CGP	$90,000 U		−CGS	NE		$90,000 U	=	$90,000 U	+	NE
CGAS	90,000 O		NI	NE						
−EI	90,000 U									
CGS	NE									

Related exercise material: BE6–9, BE6–10, E6–11, and E6–12.

THE NAVIGATOR

Statement Valuation and Presentation

Valuing Inventory at the Lower of Cost and Market (LCM)

Inventory values sometimes fall due to changes in technology or style. When the value of inventory is lower than its cost, the inventory is written down to its market value. This is done by valuing the inventory at the lower of cost and market (LCM) in the period in which the decline occurs. LCM is an example of the accounting concept of conservatism. **Conservatism** means that when choosing among alternatives, the best choice is the method that is least likely to overstate assets and net income.

The term *market* in the lower of cost and market phrase is not specifically defined in Canada. It may include replacement cost or net realizable value, among other definitions. The majority of Canadian companies use net realizable value to define market

STUDY OBJECTIVE
••••••••••**8**••••••••••
Explain and use the lower of cost and market basis of accounting for inventories.

► *International note*

Almost every country in the world applies the LCM rule; however, the definition of *market* can vary. The International Accounting Standards Committee defines market as net realizable value, as do the UK, France, and Germany. The U.S., Italy, and Japan define market as replacement cost.

for LCM. For a merchandising company, **net realizable value is the selling price less any costs required to make the goods ready for sale**.

LCM is applied to the items in inventory after one of the costing methods (specific identification, FIFO, average, or LIFO) has been applied to determine the cost.

Assume that Wacky World has the following lines of merchandise with costs and market values as indicated. LCM produces the following results:

	Cost	Market	Lower of Cost and Market
Television sets			
Consoles	$ 60,000	$ 55,000	
Portables	45,000	52,000	
Total	105,000	107,000	
Video equipment			
Recorders	48,000	45,000	
Movies	15,000	14,000	
Total	63,000	59,000	
Total inventory	$168,000	$166,000	$166,000

Illustration 6-20

Calculations of lower of cost and market

LCM can be applied separately to each individual item, to categories of items (e.g., television sets and video equipment) or to total inventory. However, it is common practice to use total inventory rather than individual items or major categories in determining the LCM valuation. This approach, although the least conservative, still yields conservative results and allows increases in value (e.g., television sets) to offset decreases (e.g., video equipment), in part or in full. It is also the method that must be used for income tax purposes.

Using total inventory, the journal entry to record the loss for Wacky World would be the following:

A	=	L	+	OE
−2,000				−2,000

Loss Due to Decline in Net Realizable Value of Inventory	2,000	
Merchandise Inventory		2,000
To record decline in inventory value, from original cost of $168,000 to current NRV of $166,000.		

The loss would be reported as Other Expenses on the income statement. LCM should be applied consistently from period to period.

►Accounting in Action ► *Business Insight*

Some industries, such as the computer chip industry, have taken the application of the lower of cost and market rule into their own hands. A practice known as "ship and debit" is quite common in the volatile market of computer chip pricing. Ship and debit—or ship from stock and debit—refers to an accounting and sales practice. Distributors purchase parts from suppliers and then receive rebates from the suppliers when the market price of the product declines below the purchase cost.

While this practice is legal, it also opens the door for unscrupulous distributors to lie to manufacturers about the price received for the chips. Future Electronics Inc. in Montreal is alleged by the FBI to have systematically altered its sales records on a massive scale, in order to take advantage of this ship and debit practice. The National Electronics Dealers Association says that the complicated computer chip industry sales practice known as "ship and debit" should be eliminated. It is extremely difficult to regulate and "we'd do away with it completely if we could," said Robin Gray, President of the Association.

Source: Michael Lewis, "Future, FBI Clash Over Sales Practices," *Financial Post*, November 11, 1999, C1.

Classifying Inventory

How a company classifies its inventory depends on whether the firm is a merchandiser or a manufacturer. A merchandiser *purchases* its inventory. A manufacturer *produces* its inventory. In a **merchandising company**, inventory consists of many different items. Canned goods, dairy products, meats, and produce, for example, are just a few of the inventory items on hand in a grocery store. These items have two common characteristics: (1) they are owned by the company, and (2) they are in a form ready for sale to customers. Only one inventory classification, **merchandise inventory**, is needed to describe the many different items that make up the total inventory.

In a **manufacturing company**, some goods may not yet be ready for sale. As a result, inventory is usually classified into three categories: raw materials, work in process, and finished goods. For example, Bombardier classifies the steel, fibreglass, upholstery material, and other components that are on hand waiting to be used in production as **raw materials**. Motorized consumer products such as Ski-Doos and Sea-Doos that are on the assembly line in various stages of production are classified as **work in process**. Ski-Doos and Sea-Doos that are completed and ready for sale are identified as **finished goods**.

The accounting principles and concepts discussed in this chapter apply to the inventory classifications of both merchandising and manufacturing companies.

> **Helpful hint** Regardless of the classification, all inventories are reported as current assets on the balance sheet.

Presentation

In the balance sheet, inventory is classified as a current asset. It usually follows receivables. In the income statement, inventory affects the cost of goods sold, which is subtracted from sales. There should be disclosure of (1) the major inventory classifications, (2) the basis of accounting (cost or lower of cost and market), and (3) the cost flow method (specific identification, FIFO, average, or LIFO).

Danier Leather, a leading leather fashion manufacturer and retailer headquartered in Toronto, reported inventories of $22,659,000 under current assets in a recent balance sheet. It reported cost of goods sold of $56,313,000 on its income statement. The accompanying notes to the financial statements, shown in Illustration 6-21, disclosed the following additional information:

DANIER LEATHER INC.
Notes to the Financial Statements
June 24, 2000

Note 1: Significant Accounting Policies
(d) Inventories are valued at the lower of cost or market. Cost is determined on a first-in, first-out basis. For finished goods and work in process, market is defined as net realizable value; for raw materials, market is defined as replacement cost.

Illustration 6-21

Inventory disclosures

Before You Go On . . .

►Review It

1. Why is it appropriate to report inventory at the lower of cost and market?
2. What inventory information should be disclosed in the financial statements?

Related exercise material: BE6–11 and E6–13.

THE NAVIGATOR

▶A Look Back at Our Feature Story

Refer back to the feature story concerning the Concordia University Bookstore and answer the following questions:
1. Why does the Concordia University Bookstore use the perpetual inventory method to track inventory quantities and the periodic inventory system to track costs?
2. What inventory cost flow assumption do you think the bookstore likely uses?

Solution

1. The bookstore needs to know how many textbooks it has on hand at any point in time. If there are too few copies, more have to be rushed in, which is expensive. If there are too many, sometimes they can be kept for sale in the next term. Sometimes they have to be returned to the publisher. These returns are costly since the bookstore has to pay the freight both ways.

    While it uses a perpetual inventory system to track quantities, it is much more difficult to track costs in this manner. The bookstore would require an integrated point-of-sale system, which is quite costly. In addition, when books and supplies are received, the bookstore would have to record the cost of each item separately. Imagine being able to identify and record the cost of each of these textbooks! When the text is later sold in a perpetual inventory system, the bookstore must have the information required to record both the sales revenue and the cost of the sale for that specific item.
2. The bookstore most likely uses the FIFO cost flow assumption. As it receives new texts at higher costs, it likely adjusts their selling price to reflect price increases. FIFO would best enable the bookstore to match its costs to these revenues.

DEMONSTRATION PROBLEM

Additional Demonstration Problem

Englehart Company has the following inventory, purchases, and sales data for the month of March:

Inventory, March 1	200 units @ $4.00	$800
Purchases		
March 10	500 units @ $4.50	$2,250
March 20	400 units @ $4.75	1,900
March 30	300 units @ $5.00	1,500
Sales		
March 15	500 units @ $8.00	$4,000
March 25	400 units @ $9.00	3,600

Englehart Company uses a periodic inventory system. The physical inventory count on March 31 shows 500 units on hand.

Instructions

Determine the cost of goods sold for March and the cost of ending inventory at March 31, under (a) the first-in, first-out (FIFO) method, (b) the weighted average cost method, and (c) the last-in, first-out (LIFO) method.

Solution to Demonstration Problem

The cost of goods available for sale is $6,450, calculated as follows:

Inventory	200 units @ $4.00	$ 800
Purchases		
March 10	500 units @ $4.50	2,250
March 20	400 units @ $4.75	1,900
March 30	300 units @ $5.00	1,500
Total cost of goods available for sale	1,400	$6,450

The ending inventory consists of 500 units (1,400 units available for sale − 900 units sold).

(a)   FIFO Method

Cost of goods sold:

Date	Units	Unit Cost	Total Cost
BI	200	$4.00	$ 800
March 10	500	4.50	2,250
March 20	200	4.75	950
	900		$4,000

Ending inventory:

Date	Units	Unit Cost	Total Cost
March 30	300	$5.00	$1,500
March 20	200	4.75	950
	500		$2,450

Check: CGS + EI = GAS
$4,000 + $2,450 = $6,450

(b)   Weighted Average Cost Method

Weighted average unit cost:	$6,450 / 1,400 units = $4.607 per unit	
Ending inventory:	500 units × $4.607 =	$2,304
Cost of goods sold:	900 units × $4.607 =	4,146
Cost of goods available for sale		$6,450

(c)   LIFO Method

Cost of goods sold:

Date	Units	Unit Cost	Total Cost
March 30	300	$5.00	$1,500
March 20	400	4.75	1,900
March 10	200	4.50	900
	900		$4,300

Ending inventory:

Date	Units	Unit Cost	Total Cost
March 1	200	$4.00	$ 800
March 10	300	4.50	1,350
	500		$2,150

Check: CGS + EI = GAS
$4,300 + $2,150 = $6,450

Action Plan
- Ignore the timing of the sale dates in a periodic inventory system. Assume everything happens at the end of the period.
- Calculate the cost of goods sold under the periodic FIFO method by allocating the **earliest costs** to the units sold.
- Calculate the cost of goods sold under the periodic weighted average method by allocating the **weighted average cost** to the units sold.
- Calculate the cost of goods sold under the periodic LIFO method by allocating the **latest costs** to the units sold.

THE NAVIGATOR

*A*PPENDIX 6A ▸ *Inventory Cost Flow Methods in Perpetual Inventory Systems*

Each of the inventory cost flow methods described in the chapter for a periodic inventory system can be used in a perpetual inventory system. To illustrate the application of the three assumed cost flow methods (FIFO, average cost, and LIFO), we will use the data shown on the following page and earlier in this chapter for Fraser Valley Electronics' Astro Condensers.

STUDY OBJECTIVE
· · · · · · · · · 9 · · · · · · · · · ·

Apply the inventory cost flow methods to perpetual inventory records.

Illustration 6A-1

Inventoriable costs and units

	Fraser Valley Electronics Z202 Astro Condensers				
Date	Explanation	Units	Unit Cost	Total Cost	Balance in Units
Jan. 1	Beginning inventory	100	$10	$1,000	100
Apr. 15	Purchases	200	11	2,200	300
Aug. 24	Purchases	300	12	3,600	600
Sept. 10	Sale	550			50
Nov. 27	Purchases	400	13	5,200	450
				$12,000	

First-In, First-Out (FIFO)

Under FIFO, the cost of the earliest goods on hand **prior to each sale** is charged to cost of goods sold. The cost of goods sold on September 10 consists of all the units on hand on January 1, all the units purchased on April 15, and 250 (the number needed to equal the 550 units sold) of the units purchased on August 24. The inventory on a FIFO method perpetual system is shown in Illustration 6A-2.

Illustration 6A-2

Perpetual system—FIFO

Date	Purchases		Sales		Balance	
Jan. 1					(100 @ $10)	$1,000
Apr. 15	(200 @ $11)	$2,200			(100 @ $10) (200 @ $11)	$3,200
Aug. 24	(300 @ $12)	$3,600			(100 @ $10) (200 @ $11) (300 @ $12)	$6,800
Sept. 10			(100 @ $10) (200 @ $11) (250 @ $12)	$6,200	(50 @ $12)	$ 600
Nov. 27	(400 @ $13)	$5,200			(50 @ $12) (400 @ $13)	$5,800

The ending inventory in this situation is $5,800. The cost of goods sold is $6,200.

The results under FIFO in a perpetual system are the **same as in a periodic system** (see Illustration 6-9 where, similarly, the ending inventory is $5,800 and cost of goods sold is $6,200). Regardless of the system, the first costs in are the ones assigned to cost of goods sold.

Average Cost

The average cost method in a perpetual inventory system is called the **moving average cost method**. The average cost is calculated in the same manner as we calculated the weighted average unit cost: by dividing the cost of goods available for sale by the units available for sale. The difference is that under this method a new average is calculated **after each purchase**. The average cost is then applied to (1) the units sold, to determine the cost of goods sold, and (2) the remaining units on hand, to determine the ending inventory amount. The application of the average cost method by Fraser

Valley Electronics is shown in Illustration 6A-3.

Date	Purchases		Sales	Balance	
Jan. 1				(100 @ $10.000)	$1,000
Apr. 15	(200 @ $11)	$2,200		(300 @ $10.667)	$3,200
Aug. 24	(300 @ $12)	$3,600		(600 @ $11.333)	$6,800
Sept. 10			(550 @ $11.333)	(50 @ $11.333)	$ 567
			$6,233		
Nov. 27	(400 @ $13)	$5,200		(450 @ $12.816)	$5,767

Illustration 6A-3

Perpetual system—moving average cost

As indicated, **a new average is calculated each time a purchase (or purchase return) is made**. On April 15, after 200 units are purchased for $2,200, a total of 300 units costing $3,200 ($1,000 + $2,200) are on hand. The average unit cost is $10.667 ($3,200 ÷ 300).

On August 24, after 300 units are purchased for $3,600, a total of 600 units costing $6,800 ($1,000 + $2,200 + $3,600) are on hand at an average cost per unit of $11.333 ($6,800 ÷ 600).

The unit cost of $11.333 is used in costing sales until another purchase is made, when a new unit cost is calculated. Accordingly, the unit cost of the 550 units sold on September 10 is $11.333, and the total cost of goods sold is $6,233.

On November 27, following the purchase of 400 units for $5,200, there 450 units on hand costing $5,767 ($567 + $5,200) with a new average cost of $12.816 ($5,767 ÷ 450).

Compare the moving average cost under the perpetual inventory system to Illustration 6-11 (shown earlier in the chapter) which shows the weighted average cost method under a periodic inventory system.

Last-In, First-Out (LIFO)

Under the LIFO method using a perpetual system, the cost of the most recent purchase prior to sale is allocated to the units sold. Therefore, the cost of the goods sold on September 10 consists of all the units from the August 24 and April 15 purchases and 50 of the units in the beginning inventory. The ending inventory with LIFO is calculated in Illustration 6A-4.

Date	Purchases		Sales	Balance	
Jan. 1				(100 @ $10)	$1,000
Apr. 15	(200 @ $11)	$2,200		(100 @ $10) (200 @ $11)	$3,200
Aug. 24	(300 @ $12)	$3,600		(100 @ $10) (200 @ $11) (300 @ $12)	$6,800
Sept. 10			(300 @ $12) (200 @ $11) (50 @ $10)	(50 @ $10)	$ 500
			$6,300		
Nov. 27	(400 @ $13)	$5,200		(50 @ $10) (400 @ $13)	$5,700

Illustration 6A-4

Perpetual system—LIFO

The use of LIFO in a perpetual system will usually produce cost allocations that differ from using LIFO in a periodic system. In a perpetual system, the latest units purchased before each sale are allocated to cost of goods sold. In a periodic system, the latest units bought during the period are allocated to cost of goods sold. When a purchase is made after the last sale, the LIFO periodic system will apply this purchase to the previous sale. See Illustration 6-12, where the 400 units at $13 purchased on November 27 are applied to the sale of 550 units on September 10. As shown under the LIFO perpetual system, the 400 units at $13 purchased on November 27 are all applied to the ending inventory.

The ending inventory in this LIFO perpetual illustration is $5,700 and cost of goods sold is $6,300, as compared to the LIFO periodic example in Illustration 6-12, where the ending inventory is $5,000 and cost of goods sold is $7,000.

If we compare the cost of goods sold and ending inventory figures for each of these perpetual cost flow assumptions, we find the same proportionate outcomes that we saw with periodic cost flow assumptions. That is, in a period of rising prices (prices rose in this problem), FIFO will always yield the highest ending inventory valuation and LIFO the lowest. LIFO will always result in the highest cost of goods sold figure (and lowest net income) and FIFO the lowest cost of goods sold (and highest net income). Of course, if prices are falling, the reverse situation will result. Finally, remember that the sum of cost of goods sold and ending inventory always equals the cost of goods available for sale, which is the same regardless of the choice of cost flow assumption.

Illustration 6A-5

Comparison of cost flow methods

	FIFO	Average	LIFO
Cost of goods sold	$ 6,200	$ 6,233	$ 6,300
Ending inventory	5,800	5,767	5,700
Cost of goods available for sale	$12,000	$12,000	$12,000

Before You Go On . . .

▶Review It

1. What inventory cost flow assumptions can be used with a perpetual inventory system? A periodic inventory system?
2. What inventory cost flow assumption gives you the same results whether it is applied in a periodic or perpetual inventory system?

THE
NAVIGATOR

Related exercise material: *BE6–12, *BE6–13, and *E6–14.

DEMONSTRATION PROBLEM

**Additional
Demonstration Problem**

The Demonstration Problem on page 290 shows cost of goods sold and ending inventory calculations under a periodic inventory system. Here, we assume that Englehart Company uses a perpetual inventory system and has the same inventory, purchases, and sales data for the month of March as shown there:

Inventory, March 1	200 units @ $4.00	$800
Purchases		
March 10	500 units @ $4.50	$2,250
March 20	400 units @ $4.75	1,900
March 30	300 units @ $5.00	1,500
Sales		
March 15	500 units @ $8.00	$4,000
March 25	400 units @ $9.00	3,600

Instructions

Under a perpetual inventory system, determine the cost of inventory on hand at March 31 and the cost of goods sold for March under (a) the first-in, first-out (FIFO) method, (b) the moving average cost method, and (c) the last-in, first-out (LIFO) method.

Solution to Demonstration Problem

Action Plan

- The timing of each purchase and sale is important in a perpetual inventory system.
- Calculate the cost of goods sold under the perpetual FIFO method by allocating the **earliest cost** to the units sold.
- Calculate the cost of goods sold under the perpetual moving average cost method by allocating a **moving weighted average cost** to each unit sold.
- Calculate the cost of goods sold under the perpetual LIFO method by allocating the **latest cost** to the units sold.

(a)

FIFO Method

Date	Purchases		Sales	Balance	
Mar. 1				(200 @ $4.00)	$ 800
Mar. 10	(500 @ $4.50)	$2,250		(200 @ $4.00) (500 @ $4.50) }	$3,050
Mar. 15			(200 @ $4.00) (300 @ $4.50) $2,150	(200 @ $4.50)	$ 900
Mar. 20	(400 @ $4.75)	$1,900		(200 @ $4.50) (400 @ $4.75) }	$2,800
Mar. 25			(200 @ $4.50) (200 @ $4.75) $1,850	(200 @ $4.75)	$ 950
Mar. 30	(300 @ $5.00)	$1,500		(200 @ $4.75) (300 @ $5.00) }	$2,450

Ending inventory: $2,450. Cost of goods sold: $2,150 + $1,850 = $4,000

Check: CGS + EI = GAS

$4,000 + $2,450 = $6,450

(b)

Moving Average Cost Method

Date	Purchases		Sales	Balance	
Mar. 1				(200 @ $4.000)	$ 800
Mar. 10	(500 @ $4.50)	$2,250		(700 @ $4.357)	$3,050
Mar. 15			(500 @ $4.357)	(200 @ $4.357)	$ 871
Mar. 20	(400 @ $4.75)	$1,900		(600 @ $4.618)	$2,771
Mar. 25			(400 @ $4.618)	(200 @ $4.618)	$ 924
Mar. 30	(300 @ $5.00)	$1,500		(500 @ $4.848)	$2,424

Ending inventory: $2,424. Cost of goods sold: $2,179 + $1,847 = $4,026

Check: CGS + EI = GAS

$4,026 + $2,424 = $6,450

(c)

LIFO Method

Date	Purchases		Sales	Balance	
Mar. 1				(200 @ $4.00)	$ 800
Mar. 10	(500 @ $4.50)	$2,250		(200 @ $4.00) (500 @ $4.50) }	$3,050
Mar. 15			(500 @ $4.50) $2,250	(200 @ $4.00)	$ 800
Mar. 20	(400 @ $4.75)	$1,900		(200 @ $4.00) (400 @ $4.75) }	$2,700
Mar. 25			(400 @ $4.75) $1,900	(200 @ $4.00)	$ 800
Mar. 30	(300 @ $5.00)	$1,500		(200 @ $4.00) (300 @ $5.00) }	$2,300

Ending inventory: $2,300. Cost of goods sold: $2,250 + $1,900 = $4,150

Check: CGS + EI = GAS

$4,150 + $2,300 = $6,450

THE
NAVIGATOR

APPENDIX 6B ▸ *Estimating Inventories*

We assumed in the chapter that a company would be able to physically count its inventory. But what if it cannot? What if the inventory were destroyed by fire? In that case, we would use an estimate.

Two circumstances explain why inventories are sometimes estimated. First, management that uses a periodic inventory system may want monthly or quarterly financial statements, without the time and expense of monthly or quarterly physical inventory counts. Second, a casualty such as fire or flood may make it impossible to take a physical inventory. The need to estimate inventories is associated primarily with a periodic inventory system because of the absence of detailed inventory records.

Helpful hint   Here are two more examples of estimates in the accounting process.

There are two widely used methods of estimating inventories: (1) the gross profit method, and (2) the retail inventory method.

Gross Profit Method

The **gross profit method** estimates the cost of ending inventory by applying a gross profit rate to net sales. It is commonly used to prepare interim (e.g., monthly) financial statements in a periodic inventory system. This method is relatively simple but effective.

To use this method, a company needs to know its net sales, cost of goods available for sale, and gross profit margin. With the gross profit margin, the company estimates its gross profit for the period. The formulas for using the gross profit method are given in Illustration 6B-1.

Illustration 6B-1

Gross profit method formulas

To illustrate, assume that Lalonde Company wishes to prepare an income statement for the month of January. Its records show net sales of $200,000, beginning inventory of $40,000, and cost of goods purchased of $120,000. In the preceding year, the company had a 30% gross profit margin. It expects to earn the same rate this year. Given these facts and assumptions, the estimated cost of the ending inventory at January 31 under the gross profit method is $20,000, calculated as follows:

Step 1:

Net sales	$200,000
Less: Estimated gross profit (30% x $200,000)	60,000
Estimated cost of goods sold	$140,000 ┐

Step 2:

Beginning inventory	$ 40,000
Cost of goods purchased	120,000
Cost of goods available for sale	160,000
Less: Estimated cost of goods sold	140,000 ◂┘
Estimated cost of ending inventory	**$ 20,000**

The gross profit method is based on the assumption that the gross profit margin will remain constant from one year to the next. It may not remain constant, though, because of a change in merchandising policies or in market conditions. In such cases, the margin should be adjusted to reflect current operating conditions. In some cases, a more accurate estimate can be obtained by applying this method on a department or product-line basis.

The gross profit method should not be used in preparing a company's financial statements at the end of the year. These statements should be based on a physical inventory count. Accountants and managers frequently use the gross profit method to test the reasonableness of the ending inventory amount, however.

Retail Inventory Method

A retail store such as Canadian Tire or Zellers has thousands of types of merchandise at low unit costs. In such cases, the application of unit costs to inventory quantities is difficult and time-consuming. An alternative is to use the **retail inventory method** to estimate the cost of inventory. In most retail concerns, a relationship between cost and sales price can be established. The cost to retail percentage is then applied to the ending inventory at retail prices to determine the cost of the inventory.

To use the retail inventory method, a company's records must show both the cost and the retail value of the goods available for sale. The formulas for using the retail inventory method are presented in Illustration 6B-2.

Helpful hint In determining inventory at retail, selling prices on the units are used. Tracing actual units costs to invoices is unnecessary.

Illustration 6B-2

Retail inventory method formulas

Helpful hint
Cost to retail ratio:

$$\frac{\text{GAS at cost}}{\text{GAS at retail}}$$

The logic of the retail method can be demonstrated by using unit cost data. Assume that 10 units purchased at $7 each ($70 in total) are priced to sell for $10 per unit ($100 in total). The cost to retail ratio is 70% ($70 ÷ $100). If four units remain unsold, their retail value is $40 and their cost is $28 ($40 × 70%). This amount agrees with the total cost of goods on hand on a per-unit basis (4 × $7).

The application of the retail method for Zboyovsky Co., using assumed data, is shown in Illustration 6B-3.

Illustration 6B-3

Example of retail inventory method

	At Cost	At Retail
Beginning inventory	$14,000	$ 21,500
Goods purchased	61,000	78,500
Goods available for sale	$75,000	100,000
Net sales		70,000
(1) Ending inventory at retail		$ 30,000
(2) Cost to retail ratio = ($75,000 4 $100,000) = 75%		
(3) Estimated cost of ending inventory = ($30,000 x 75%)	$22,500	

The retail inventory method also facilitates taking a physical inventory at the end of the year. The goods on hand can be valued at the prices marked on the merchandise. The cost to retail ratio is then applied to the goods on hand at retail to determine the ending inventory at cost.

The major disadvantage of the retail method is that it is an averaging technique. It may produce an incorrect inventory valuation if the mix of the ending inventory is not representative of the mix in the goods available for sale. Assume, for example, that the cost to retail ratio of 75% in the Zboyovsky Co. illustration consists of equal proportions of inventory items that have cost to retail ratios of 70%, 75%, and 80%, respectively. If the ending inventory contains only items with a 70% ratio, an incorrect inventory cost will result. This problem can be minimized by applying the retail method on a department or product-line basis.

Before You Go On . . .
▶ Review It

1. How is ending inventory estimated under the gross profit method?
2. How is ending inventory estimated under the retail inventory method?

Related exercise material: *BE6–14, *BE6–15, *E6–15, and *E6–16.

Summary of Study Objectives

1. Describe the steps in determining inventory quantities. The steps in determining inventory quantities are (1) taking a physical inventory of goods on hand and (2) determining the ownership of goods in transit, on consignment, and in like situations.

2. Prepare the entries for purchases and sales of inventory under a periodic inventory system. In recording purchases, entries are required for (1) cash and credit purchases, (2) purchase returns and allowances, and (3) freight costs. Separate temporary accounts are used in a periodic inventory system for purchases, purchase returns and allowances, and freight costs. In recording sales, entries are required for (1) cash and credit sales, and (2) sales returns and allowances. Cost of goods sold is not recorded throughout the period in a periodic inventory system. Instead it is determined at the end of the period.

3. Determine cost of goods sold under a periodic inventory system. The steps in determining cost of goods sold (CGS) are (1) recording the purchase of merchandise, (2) determining the cost of goods purchased (CGP), and (3) determining the cost of goods on hand at the beginning (BI) and end (EI) of the accounting period. $CGS = BI + CGP - EI$.

4. Identify the unique features of the income statement for a merchandising company using a periodic inventory system. The income statement for a merchandising company contains three sections: sales revenue, cost of goods sold, and operating expenses. The cost of goods sold section under a periodic inventory system generally shows more detail than one for a perpetual inventory system by reporting beginning and ending inventory, the cost of goods purchased, and the total goods available for sale.

5. Explain the basis of accounting for inventories and use the inventory cost flow methods. The primary basis of accounting for inventories is cost. Cost includes all expenditures necessary to acquire goods and put them in a condition ready for sale. Cost of goods available for sale includes (1) the cost of beginning inventory and (2) the cost of goods purchased.

The inventory cost flow methods are specific identification, FIFO, average cost, and LIFO. Specific identification allocates the exact cost of each merchandise item to cost of goods sold and ending inventory. FIFO assumes a first-in, first-out cost flow for sales. This method allocates the cost of the earliest goods purchased to cost of goods sold, and the cost of the most recent goods purchased to ending inventory. Average cost assumes an average cost flow for both cost of goods sold and ending inventory. This method uses goods available for sale in dollars and units to determine the weighted average cost. LIFO assumes a last-in, first-out cost flow for sales. This method allocates the cost of the most recent goods purchased to cost of goods sold, and the cost of the earliest goods purchased to ending inventory.

6. Demonstrate the effects on the financial statements of each of the inventory cost flow methods. The cost of goods available for sale may be allocated to cost of goods sold and ending inventory by specific identification or by a method based on an assumed cost flow (FIFO, average, or LIFO). These methods have different effects on financial statements during periods of changing prices. When prices are rising, FIFO results in lower cost of goods sold and higher net income than the average and LIFO methods. The reverse is true when prices are falling. LIFO produces the best income statement valuation. It results in a cost of goods sold that best matches current costs with current revenues. FIFO produces the best balance sheet valuation. It results in an ending inventory that is closest to current value or replacement cost. FIFO and average are the most commonly used methods. LIFO can produce undesirable income effects in certain circumstances and is not permitted for income tax purposes.

7. Determine the effects of inventory errors on the financial statements. In the income statement of the current year, an error in beginning inventory will have a reverse effect on net income (overstatement of beginning inventory results in overstatement of cost of goods sold and understatement of net income). An error in the cost of goods purchased will have a reverse effect on net income (overstatement of purchases results in overstatement of cost of goods sold and understatement of net income). An error in ending inventory will have a similar effect on net income (overstatement of ending inventory results in understatement of cost of goods sold and overstatement of net income). If ending inventory errors are not corrected in the following period, their effect on net income for the second period is reversed. Total net income for the two years will be correct.

8. Explain and use the lower of cost and market basis of accounting for inventories. The lower of cost and market basis (LCM) may be used when the net realizable value (market) is less than cost. Under LCM, the loss is recognized in the period in which the price decline occurs.

9. Apply the inventory cost flow methods to perpetual inventory records (Appendix 6A). Under FIFO, the cost of the earliest goods on hand is charged to cost of goods sold. Under average, a new average (moving average) cost is calculated after each purchase. Under LIFO, the cost of the most recent purchase is charged to cost of goods sold. Each of these methods is applied in the same cost flow order as in a periodic inventory system. The main difference is that in a perpetual inventory system, the cost flow assumption is applied at the date of each sale to determine cost of goods sold. In a periodic inventory system, the cost flow assumption is applied at the end of the period.

10. Use the two methods of estimating inventories (Appendix 6B). The two methods of estimating inventories are the gross profit method and the retail inventory method. Under the gross profit method, the gross profit margin is applied to net sales to determine estimated cost of goods sold. Estimated cost of goods sold is subtracted from cost of goods available for sale to determine the estimated cost of the ending inventory. Under the retail inventory method, a cost to retail ratio is calculated by dividing the cost of goods available for sale by the retail value of the goods available for sale. This ratio is then applied to the ending inventory at retail to determine the estimated cost of the ending inventory.

THE
NAVIGATOR

GLOSSARY

 Key Term Matching Activity

Average cost method   Inventory costing method that assumes that the goods available for sale are identical or nondistinguishable. They have the same average cost per unit. (p. 279)

Consigned goods   Goods shipped by a consignor, who retains ownership, to another party called the consignee. (p. 267)

Cost of goods available for sale   The sum of the beginning merchandise inventory plus the cost of goods purchased. (p. 271)

Cost of goods purchased   The sum of net purchases plus freight in. (p. 271)

Cost of goods sold   The total cost of merchandise sold during the period, determined by subtracting ending inventory from the cost of goods available for sale. (p. 271)

First-in, first-out (FIFO) method   Inventory costing method that assumes that the costs of the earliest goods acquired are the first to be recognized as cost of goods sold. The costs of the latest goods acquired are assumed to remain in ending inventory. (p. 278)

Full disclosure principle   The requirement that all information relevant for decision-making be disclosed. (p. 284)

Gross profit method   A method for estimating the cost of the ending inventory by applying the gross profit margin to net sales. (p. 296)

Last-in, first-out (LIFO) method   Inventory costing method that assumes that the costs of the latest units pur-

chased are the first to be allocated to cost of goods sold. The costs of the earliest units purchased are allocated to ending inventory. (p. 280)

Lower of cost and market (LCM)   A basis for stating inventory at the lower of the original cost and the current market value (usually defined as net realizable value). (p. 287)

Net purchases   Purchases less purchase returns and allowances. (p. 271)

Net realizable value   The estimated amount for which an asset can be sold, less any costs necessary to make it saleable. (p. 287).

Periodic inventory system   An inventory system in which cost of goods available for sale is allocated to ending inventory and cost of goods sold at the end of the period. Cost of goods sold is calculated at the end of the period by subtracting the ending inventory (costs are assigned based on a physical count of items on hand) from the cost of goods available for sale. (p. 268)

Replacement cost   The cost of replacing an asset. (p. 287)

Retail inventory method   A method used to estimate the cost of the ending inventory by applying a cost to retail ratio to the ending inventory at retail prices. (p. 297)

Specific identification method   An actual physical flow inventory costing method in which items are specifically costed to arrive at the cost of goods sold and the cost of the ending inventory. (p. 277).

Note: All **asterisked** Questions, Exercises, and Problems below relate to material contained in the appendices to the chapter.

SELF-STUDY QUESTIONS

 Chapter 6 Self-Test

Answers are at the end of the chapter.

(SO 1) K   1. Which of the following should not be included in the physical inventory of a company?
   a.   Goods held on consignment from another company
   b.   Goods shipped on consignment to another company
   c.   Goods in transit purchased from a manufacturer and shipped FOB shipping point
   d.   None of the above

(SO 2) K   2. When goods are purchased for resale by a company using a periodic inventory system:
   a.   purchases are debited to Merchandise Inventory.
   b.   purchases are debited to Purchases.
   c.   purchase returns are debited to Purchase Returns and Allowances.
   d.   freight costs are debited to Purchases.

(SO 3) K   3. In determining the cost of goods purchased:
   a.   beginning inventory is added to net purchases.
   b.   freight out is added to net purchases.
   c.   purchase returns and allowances are deducted from net purchases.
   d.   freight in is added to net purchases.

4. If beginning inventory is $60,000, cost of goods pur-   (SO 3) AP
chased is $380,000, and ending inventory is $50,000, what is the cost of goods sold?
   a. $330,000
   b. $370,000
   c. $390,000
   d. $420,000

5. A multiple-step income statement in a periodic inven-   (SO 4) K
tory system differs from that in a perpetual inventory system because it has:
   a.   a detailed cost of goods sold section.
   b.   net sales.
   c.   gross profit.
   d.   operating expenses.

6. Kam Company uses a periodic inventory system and   (SO 5) AP
has the following:

	Units	Unit Cost
Inventory, Jan. 1	8,000	$11
Purchase, June 19	13,000	12
Purchase, Nov. 8	5,000	13

If 9,000 units are on hand at December 31, the cost of

the ending inventory under FIFO is:
a. $99,000.
b. $100,000.
c. $113,000.
d. $117,000.

(SO 5, 6) AP   7. Using the data in (6) above, the cost of the ending inventory under LIFO is:
a. $99,000.
b. $100,000.
c. $113,000.
d. $117,000.

(SO 6) C   8. In periods of rising prices, LIFO will produce:
a. higher net income than FIFO.
b. the same net income as FIFO.
c. lower net income than FIFO.
d. higher net income than average costing.

(SO 7) C   9. In Fran Company, ending inventory is understated by $4,000. The effects of this error on the current year's cost of goods sold and net income, respectively, are:
a. understated, overstated.
b. overstated, understated.
c. overstated, overstated.
d. understated, understated.

10. The lower of cost and market basis is usually applied to: (SO 8) K
a. categories of inventory.
b. individual items of inventory.
c. total inventory.
d. all of the above.

*11. In a perpetual inventory system, (SO 9) C
a. LIFO cost of goods sold will be the same as in a periodic inventory system.
b. average costs are based entirely on unit cost averages.
c. average cost of goods sold will be the same as in a periodic inventory system.
d. FIFO cost of goods sold will be the same as in a periodic inventory system.

*12. Somers Company has sales of $150,000 and cost of goods available for sale of $135,000. If the gross profit margin is 30%, the estimated cost of the ending inventory under the gross profit method is: (SO 10) AP
a. $15,000.
b. $30,000.
c. $45,000.
d. $75,000.

THE NAVIGATOR

QUESTIONS

(SO 1) C   1. "The key to successful business operations is effective inventory management." Do you agree? Explain.

(SO 1) K   2. An item must possess two characteristics to be classified as inventory. What are these two characteristics?

(SO 1) C   3. Your friend Tom Wetzel has been hired to help take the physical inventory in Kikujiro's Hardware Store. Explain to Tom what this job will involve.

(SO 1) C   4. (a) Janine Company ships merchandise to Laura Corporation on December 30. The merchandise reaches the buyer on January 5. Indicate the terms of sale that will result in the goods being included in (1) Janine's December 31 inventory, and (2) Laura's December 31 inventory.
(b) Under what circumstances should Janine Company include consigned goods in its inventory?

(SO 3) C   5. Identify the accounts that are added to, or deducted from, purchases to determine the cost of goods purchased. For each account, indicate (a) whether it is added or deducted, and (b) its normal balance.

(SO 2) C   6. Explain why recording sales transactions requires two journal entries in a perpetual inventory system but only one in a periodic inventory system.

(SO 3) K   7. In the following separate situations, using a periodic inventory system, identify each missing item designated by the numbers (1) to (4):
(a) Purchases − (1) = Net purchases.
(b) Cost of goods purchased − Net purchases = (2).
(c) Beginning inventory + (3) = Cost of goods available for sale.

(d) Cost of goods available for sale − Cost of goods sold = (4)

8. Explain when cost of goods sold is determined in a periodic inventory system. In a perpetual inventory system. (SO 2, 3) C

9. Identify the distinguishing features of a multiple-step income statement in a periodic inventory system. (SO 4) C

10. Dave Wier believes that the allocation of goods available for sale should be based on the actual physical flow of the goods. Explain to Dave why this may be both impractical and inappropriate. (SO 5) C

11. Name an advantage and a disadvantage of the specific identification method of inventory costing. (SO 5) K

12. Which assumed inventory cost flow method: (SO 5) K
(a) usually parallels the actual physical flow of merchandise?
(b) assumes that the first units purchased are the first to be sold?
(c) assumes that the goods available for sale are identical?

13. In a period of rising prices, the inventory reported in Plato Company's balance sheet is close to the replacement cost of the inventory. York Company's inventory is considerably below its current cost. Identify the inventory cost flow method being used by each company. Which company has probably been reporting the higher gross profit? (SO 6) C

(SO 6) C   14. "The selection of an inventory cost flow method is a decision made by accountants." Do you agree? Explain. Once a method has been selected, what accounting requirement applies?

(SO 7) C   15. Mila Company discovers in 2002 that its ending inventory at December 31, 2002, was understated by $5,000. What effect will this error have on (a) 2002 net income, (b) 2003 net income, and (c) the combined net income for the two years?

(SO 8) C   16. Lucy Ritter is studying for the next accounting mid-term examination. What should Lucy know about (a) departing from the cost basis of accounting for inventories, and (b) the meaning of "market" in the lower of cost and market method?

(SO 8) AP   17. Rock Music Centre has five CD players on hand at the balance sheet date. Each cost $400. The estimated net realizable value is $320 per unit. Under the lower of cost and market basis of accounting for inventories, what value should be reported for the CD players on the balance sheet? Why?

18. Maureen & Nathan Company's balance sheet shows Inventories $162,800. What additional disclosures should be made?   (SO 8) K

*19. How does the average cost method of inventory costing differ between a perpetual inventory system and a periodic inventory system?   (SO 9) K

*20. When is it necessary to estimate inventories?   (SO 10) K

*21. Pat Voga Company has net sales of $400,000 and cost of goods available for sale of $300,000. If the gross profit margin is 30%, what is the estimated cost of the ending inventory?   (SO 10) AP

*22. Miller Shoe Shop had goods available for sale in 2002 with a retail price of $120,000. The cost of these goods was $84,000. If sales during the period were $100,000, what is the ending inventory, at cost, using the retail inventory method?   (SO 10) AP

BRIEF EXERCISES

....

Identify items to be included in taking a physical inventory.
(SO 1) K

BE6–1   Helgeson Company has identified the following items for possible inclusion when taking a physical inventory. Indicate whether each item should be included or excluded from the inventory.
1. Goods shipped on consignment by Helgeson to another company
2. Goods in transit from a supplier, shipped FOB destination
3. Goods sold but being held for customer pickup
4. Goods held on consignment from another company
5. Goods in transit to a customer, shipped FOB destination

Calculate inventory cost.
(SO 1) AP

BE6–2   Mary Ann's Hat Shop recently purchased a shipment of hats from a wholesaler. The cost of the hats was $3,000. Mary Ann's was also required to pay freight charges of $70. In addition, Mary Ann's paid $100 to cover the travel expenses of an employee who negotiated the purchase of the hats. Calculate the cost of this inventory for financial reporting purposes. Briefly explain your reasoning.

Journalize purchase and sale transactions in a periodic inventory system.
(SO 2) AP

BE6–3   Prepare the journal entries to record the following transactions on (1) Buyer Company's books, and (2) Seller Company's books. Both use a periodic inventory system.
(a) On March 2, Buyer Company purchased $900,000 of merchandise from Seller Company, terms n/30.
(b) On March 6, Buyer Company returned $130,000 of the merchandise purchased on March 2.
(c) On March 29, Buyer Company paid the balance due to Seller Company.

Calculate net purchases and cost of goods purchased.
(SO 3) AP

BE6–4   Bassing Company uses a periodic inventory system and has these account balances: Purchases, $400,000; Purchase Returns and Allowances, $11,000; and Freight In, $16,000. Determine net purchases and cost of goods purchased.

Calculate cost of goods sold and gross profit.
(SO 3, 4) AP

BE6–5   In addition to the information given in BE6–4, Bassing Company has beginning inventory of $60,000, ending inventory of $90,000, and net sales of $630,000. Determine the amounts to report for cost of goods sold and gross profit.

Prepare closing entries.
(SO 4) AP

BE6–6   Prepare the closing journal entries for the accounts listed in BE6–4 and BE6–5 for Bassing Company at its year end, December 31.

BE6–7 In its first month of operations, Quilt Company made three purchases of merchandise in the following sequence: 300 units at $6, 400 units at $7, and 300 units at $8. There are 400 units on hand at the end of the period. Quilt uses a periodic inventory system. Calculate the cost to be allocated to cost of goods sold and ending inventory under (a) the FIFO method, (b) the weighted average cost method, and (c) the LIFO method.

Calculate cost of goods sold and ending inventory using three periodic cost flow methods. (SO 5) AP

BE6–8 Interactive.com just started business and is trying to decide which inventory cost flow assumption to use. Assuming prices are falling, as they often do in the information technology business, answer the following questions for Interactive.com:
(a) Which cost flow assumption gives the highest ending inventory? Why?
(b) Which cost flow assumption gives the highest cost of goods sold? Why?
(c) What factors are important to Interactive.com in its selection of the most appropriate cost flow assumption?

Compare financial effects of inventory cost flow assumptions. (SO 6) AN

BE6–9 Creole Company reports net income of $90,000 in 2002. Ending inventory was understated by $7,000. What is the correct net income for 2002? What effect, if any, will this error have on total assets and owner's equity reported in the balance sheet at December 31, 2002?

Determine effects of inventory error. (SO 7) AP

BE6–10 Johal Company counted and recorded its ending inventory as at December 31, 2002, incorrectly, understating its correct value by $25,000. Assuming that this misstatement was not discovered and corrected, what is the impact of this error on assets, liabilities, and owner's equity at the end of 2002? At the end of 2003?

Determine effect of ending inventory error on balance sheet for two years. (SO 7) AP

BE6–11 Svenska Appliance Centre accumulates the following cost and market data at December 31:

Determine LCM valuation. (SO 8) AP

Inventory Categories	Cost	Market
Cameras	$12,000	$11,200
Camcorders	9,000	9,500
VCRs	14,000	12,800

Calculate the lower of cost and market valuation, applying LCM to total inventory.

*BE6–12 Transactions for Buyer and Seller companies are presented in BE6–3. Prepare the journal entries to record these transactions on (1) Buyer Company's books, and (2) Seller Company's books. Both companies use a perpetual inventory system. Assume that Seller Company marks its merchandise up 45%.

Journalize purchase and sale transactions in perpetual inventory system. (SO 9) AP

*BE6–13 Poirier Department Store uses a perpetual inventory system. Data for a product include the following purchases:

Apply perpetual inventory cost flow methods. (SO 9) AP

Date	Number of Units	Unit
May 5	50	$10
July 29	25	12

On June 1, Poirier sold 30 units. On August 27, Poirier sold 35 more units. What is the cost of goods sold and ending inventory under (a) FIFO, (b) moving average, and (c) LIFO?

*BE6–14 At May 31, Jansen Company has net sales of $350,000 and cost of goods available for sale of $310,000. Calculate the estimated cost of the ending inventory, assuming the gross profit margin is 40%.

Apply gross profit method. (SO 10) AP

*BE6–15 On June 30, Fabricville has the following data related to the retail inventory method: Goods available for sale at cost $35,000, at retail $50,000; net sales $40,000; and ending inventory at retail $20,000. Calculate the estimated cost of the ending inventory, using the retail inventory method.

Apply retail inventory method. (SO 10) AP

EXERCISES

E6–1   First Bank is considering giving Novotna Company a loan. Before doing so, it decides that further discussions with Novotna's accountant may be desirable. One area of particular concern is the inventory account. A physical inventory count revealed a year-end balance of $297,000. Discussions with the accountant reveal the following:

1.   Novotna sold goods that cost $35,000 to Moghul Company, FOB shipping point, on December 28. The goods are not expected to arrive at their destination, in India, until January 12. The goods were not included in the physical inventory because they were not in the warehouse.
2.   The physical count of the inventory did not include goods that cost $95,000 that were shipped to Novotna, FOB destination, on December 27 and were still in transit at year end.
3.   Novotna received goods that cost $25,000 on January 2. The goods were shipped on December 26 by Cellar Co., FOB shipping point. The goods were not included in the physical count.
4.   Novotna sold goods that cost $40,000 to Sterling of Canada, FOB destination, on December 30. The goods were received by Sterling on January 8. They were not included in Novotna's physical inventory.
5.   Novotna received goods that cost $44,000 on January 2 that were shipped, FOB destination, on December 29. The shipment was a rush order that was supposed to arrive December 31. This purchase was not included in the ending inventory of $297,000.

Instructions

Determine the correct inventory amount at December 31.

E6–2   Presented below is information from Olaf Company's books related to DeVito Company:
1.   On April 5, purchased merchandise on account from DeVito Company for $18,000, n/30, FOB shipping point.
2.   On April 6, paid freight costs of $900 on merchandise purchased from DeVito Company.
3.   On April 7, purchased equipment on account for $26,000.
4.   On April 8, returned damaged merchandise to DeVito Company and was granted a $3,000 credit on account.
5.   On April 30, paid the amount due to DeVito Company in full.

Instructions

Prepare the journal entries to record the relevant transactions on the books of (1) Olaf Company, and (2) DeVito Company, using a periodic inventory system.

E6–3   The trial balance of LeBlanc Company at the end of its fiscal year, August 31, 2003, includes the following accounts: Freight In, $4,000; Freight Out, $1,000; Merchandise Inventory, $17,200; Purchases, $142,400; Purchase Returns and Allowances, $2,000; Sales, $190,000; and Sales Returns and Allowances, $3,000. The ending merchandise inventory is $26,000.

Instructions

Prepare a cost of goods sold section for the year ending August 31, 2003.

E6–4   Below is a series of cost of goods sold sections for four companies:

	Co. 1	Co. 2	Co. 3	Co. 4
Beginning inventory	250	120	1,000	(j)
Purchases	1,500	1,080	(g)	44,590
Purchase returns and allowances	40	(d)	290	(k)
Net purchases	(a)	1,020	7,210	44,330
Freight in	110	(e)	(h)	2,240
Cost of goods purchased	(b)	1,230	7,940	(l)
Cost of goods available for sale	1,820	1,350	(i)	49,530
Ending inventory	310	(f)	1,450	6,230
Cost of goods sold	(c)	1,250	7,490	43,300

Instructions

Fill in the lettered blanks to complete the cost of goods sold sections.

E6–5 The following selected information is presented for Okanagan Company for the year ended January 31, 2003:

Prepare multiple-step income statement and closing entries.
(SO 4) AP

Freight in	$ 10,000
Freight out	7,000
Insurance expense	12,000
Merchandise inventory, beginning	42,000
Merchandise inventory, ending	63,000
Purchases	200,000
Purchase returns and allowances	6,000
Rent expense	20,000
Salary expense	61,000
Sales	312,000
Sales returns and allowances	13,000

Instructions

(a) Prepare a multiple-step income statement. Operating expenses need not be divided into selling and administrative expenses. Okanagan uses the periodic inventory system.

(b) Prepare the closing entries.

E6–6 On December 1, Discount Electronics has three DVD players left in stock. All are identical and priced to sell at $750. Of the three DVD players left in stock, one with serial #1012 was purchased on June 1 at a cost of $500, another with serial #1045 was purchased on November 1 for $450. The last player, serial #1056, was purchased on November 30 for $400.

Calculate cost of goods sold using specific identification and periodic FIFO.
(SO 5) AN

Instructions

(a) Calculate the cost of goods sold using the FIFO periodic inventory method, assuming that two of the three players were sold by the end of December, Discount Electronics' year end.

(b) If Discount Electronics used the specific identification method instead of the FIFO method, how might it alter its income by "selectively choosing" which particular players to sell to the two customers? What would Discount's cost of goods sold be if the company wished to maximize income? What would Discount's cost of goods sold be if the company wished to minimize income?

(c) Which inventory method do you recommend that Discount use? Explain why.

E6–7 Mawmey Inc. uses a periodic inventory system. Its records show the following for the month of May, in which 70 units were sold:

Calculate inventory and cost of goods sold using periodic FIFO and weighted average cost.
(SO 5) AP

		Units	Unit Cost	Total Cost
May 1	Inventory	30	$ 8	$240
15	Purchases	25	10	250
24	Purchases	35	12	420
	Totals	90		$910

Instructions

Calculate the cost of goods sold and ending inventory at May 31 using the FIFO and weighted average cost methods.

E6–8 Dene Company reports the following for the month of June:

Calculate inventory and cost of goods sold using periodic FIFO and LIFO. Answer questions about results.
(SO 5, 6) AP

		Units	Unit Cost	Total Cost
June 1	Inventory	200	$ 5	$1,000
12	Purchases	300	6	1,800
23	Purchases	500	7	3,500
30	Inventory	180		

Instructions

(a) Calculate the cost of the ending inventory and the cost of goods sold using a periodic inventory system under (1) FIFO, and (2) LIFO.

(b) Which costing method gives the higher ending inventory? Why?

(c) Which method results in the higher cost of goods sold? Why?

Calculate inventory and cost of goods sold using weighted average cost. Answer questions about results.
(SO 5, 6) AP

E6–9   Inventory data for Dene Company are presented in E6–8.

Instructions

(a) Calculate the cost of the ending inventory and the cost of goods sold using the weighted average cost method.

(b) Will the results in (a) be higher or lower than the results under (1) FIFO, and (2) LIFO?

(c) Why is the average unit cost not $6?

Journalize purchase and sale transactions under periodic and perpetual inventory systems. Identify inventory costing method.
(SO 2, 6) AN

E6–10   Lake Company began its business on January 30, 2003. Before the treasurer made his preference known, the accountant asked him whether the company should use the periodic or the perpetual inventory system. The treasurer asked the accountant to prepare illustrative entries assuming the purchase on account of 100 units @ $10 per unit and the sale on account of 70 units @ $15 per unit.

Instructions

(a) Prepare comparative journal entries using the above data, under the periodic and perpetual inventory methods.

(b) Identify the inventory costing method most closely related to the following statements, assuming a period of rising prices:

1. Results in a balance sheet inventory closest to replacement cost.
2. Matches recent costs against revenue.
3. Is best because each product has unique features that affect cost.
4. Understates current value of inventory on balance sheet.

Source: Adapted from Certified General Accountants' Association of Canada, *Financial Accounting 1 Examination,* June 1998, Question 5.

Determine effects of inventory errors.
(SO 7) AP

E6–11   Seles Hardware reported cost of goods sold as follows:

	2002	2003
Beginning inventory	$ 20,000	$ 30,000
Cost of goods purchased	150,000	175,000
Cost of goods available for sale	170,000	205,000
Ending inventory	30,000	35,000
Cost of goods sold	$140,000	$170,000

Seles made two errors: (1) 2002 ending inventory was overstated by $5,000, and (2) 2003 ending inventory was understated by $4,000.

Instructions

Calculate the correct cost of goods sold for each year.

Prepare correct income statements and comment.
(SO 7) S

E6–12   Brascan Company reported the following income statement data for a two-year period:

	2002	2003
Sales	$210,000	$250,000
Cost of goods sold		
Beginning inventory	32,000	40,000
Cost of goods purchased	173,000	202,000
Cost of goods available for sale	205,000	242,000
Ending inventory	40,000	52,000
Cost of goods sold	165,000	190,000
Gross profit	$ 45,000	$ 60,000

Brascan uses a periodic inventory system. The inventories at January 1, 2002, and December 31, 2003, are correct. However, the ending inventory at December 31, 2002, was overstated by $3,000.

Instructions

(a) Prepare correct income statement data for the two years.

(b) What is the cumulative effect of the inventory error on total gross profit for the two years?

(c) Explain in a letter to the president of Brascan Company what has happened—i.e., the nature of the error and its effect on the financial statements.

E6–13 Cody Camera Shop uses the lower of cost and market basis for its inventory. The following data are available at December 31:

	Units	Unit Cost	Market
Cameras:			
Minolta	5	$175	$160
Canon	7	150	152
Light Meters:			
Vivitar	12	125	119
Kodak	10	115	135

Instructions

Determine the amount of the ending inventory by applying the lower of cost and market rule to the total inventory.

*E6–14 Stracka Appliance uses a perpetual inventory system. For its flat-screen television sets, the January 1 inventory was four sets at $600 each. On Jan. 10, six units were purchased at $700 each. That month, the company had the following sales: Jan. 8, two units at $1,300 each, and Jan. 15, four units at $1,400 each.

Instructions

Calculate the cost of goods sold and ending inventory under (1) FIFO, and (2) moving average cost.

*E6–15 The inventory of Farhad Company was destroyed by fire on March 1. From an examination of the accounting records, the following data for the first two months of the year are obtained: Sales $51,000, Sales Returns and Allowances $1,000, Purchases $28,200, Freight In $1,200, and Purchase Returns and Allowances $1,400.

Instructions

Determine the merchandise lost by fire, assuming a beginning inventory of $25,000 and a gross profit margin of 30% on net sales.

*E6–16 Sharp Shoe Store uses the retail inventory method for its two departments: Women's Shoes and Men's Shoes. The following information is obtained for each department:

Item	Women's Department	Men's Department
Beginning inventory at cost	$ 32,000	$ 46,450
Goods purchased at cost	148,000	137,300
Net sales	185,000	195,000
Beginning inventory at retail	45,000	60,000
Goods purchased at retail	180,000	185,000

Instructions

Calculate the estimated cost of the ending inventory for each department under the retail inventory method.

PROBLEMS: SET A

P6–1A Kananaskis Country Company is trying to determine the value of its ending inventory as at February 28, 2003, the company's year end. The following transactions occurred, and the accountant asked for your help in determining whether these transactions should be recorded or not:

1. On February 26, Kananaskis shipped goods costing $800 to a customer and charged the customer $1,000. The goods were shipped with terms FOB destination and the receiving report indicates that the customer received the goods on March 2.
2. On February 26, Seller Inc. shipped goods to Kananaskis with terms FOB shipping point. The invoice price was $350 plus $25 for freight. The receiving report indicates that the goods were received by Kananaskis on March 2.
3. Kananaskis had $500 of inventory isolated in the warehouse. The inventory is designated for a customer who has requested that the goods be shipped on March 10.
4. Also in Kananaskis' warehouse is $400 of inventory that Craft Producers shipped to Kananaskis on consignment.

5. On February 26, Kananaskis issued a purchase order to acquire goods costing $750. The goods were shipped with terms FOB destination. The receiving report indicates that Kananaskis received the goods on March 2.
6. On February 26, Kananaskis shipped goods to a customer with terms FOB shipping point. The invoice price was $350 plus $25 for freight. The cost of the items was $280. The receiving report indicates that the goods were received by the customer on March 2.

Instructions

For each of the above transactions, specify whether the item in question should be included in ending inventory, and if so, at what amount. Explain your reasoning.

Journalize and post transactions, and prepare trial balance and partial income statement.
(SO 2, 3, 4) AP

P6–2A Joanie Kane, a former professional golfer, operates Kane's Pro Shop at Crowbush Golf Course. At the beginning of the current season on April 1, the ledger of Kane's Pro Shop showed Cash $2,500; Merchandise Inventory $3,500; and Kane, Capital $6,000. The following transactions occurred during April 2003:

Apr. 5 Purchased golf bags, clubs, and balls on account from Balata Co. for $1,600, FOB shipping point, terms n/60.
   7 Paid freight on Balata Co. purchases, $80.
   9 Received credit from Balata Co. for merchandise returned, $100.
   10 Sold merchandise on account to members $900, terms n/30.
   12 Purchased golf shoes, sweaters, and other accessories on account from Arrow Sportswear, $660, terms n/30.
   14 Paid Balata Co. in full.
   17 Received $60 credit from Arrow Sportswear for merchandise returned.
   20 Made sales on account to members, $700, terms n/30.
   21 Paid Arrow Sportswear in full.
   27 Granted credit to members for clothing that did not fit, $30.
   30 Made cash sales, $600.
   30 Received payments on accounts from members, $1,100.

Instructions

(a) Journalize the April transactions for Kane's Pro Shop using a periodic inventory system.
(b) Enter the beginning balances in the ledger accounts and post the April transactions.
(c) Prepare a trial balance as at April 30, 2003.
(d) Prepare a multiple-step income statement up to gross profit, assuming merchandise inventory on hand at April 30 is $4,200.

Prepare multiple-step income statement and closing entries.
(SO 4) AP

P6–3A Metro Department Store is located in midtown Metropolis. Over the past several years, net income has been declining because of competition from suburban shopping centres. At the end of the company's fiscal year on November 30, 2003, the following accounts appeared in alphabetical order in its adjusted trial balance:

Accounts Payable	$ 35,310
Accounts Receivable	13,770
Accumulated Amortization—Building	41,800
Accumulated Amortization—Delivery Equipment	19,680
Amortization Expense—Building	9,500
Amortization Expense—Delivery Equipment	4,000
Building	175,000
Hachey, Capital, December 1, 2002	220,200
Cash	8,000
Delivery Equipment	57,000
Delivery Expense	8,200
Hachey, Drawings	12,000
Freight In	5,060
Insurance Expense	9,000
Land	45,000
Merchandise Inventory	34,360
Mortgage Payable	146,000
Prepaid Insurance	4,500
Property Tax Expense	3,500
Property Tax Payable	3,500
Purchases	630,000

Purchase Returns and Allowances	3,000
Salaries Expense	140,000
Sales	848,000
Sales Commissions Expense	12,000
Sales Commissions Payable	8,000
Sales Returns and Allowances	10,000
Store Equipment	125,000
Utilities Expense	19,600

Additional facts:

1. Merchandise inventory at November 30, 2003, is $36,200.
2. Metro Department Store uses a periodic system.
3. Metro Department Store does not segregate its operating expenses into selling and administrative categories.

Instructions

(a) Prepare a multiple-step income statement for the year ended November 30, 2003.
(b) Prepare the closing journal entries.

P6–4A Choi Company had a beginning inventory on January 1 of 100 units of Product SXL at a cost of $20 per unit. During the year, the following purchases were made:

Mar. 15	300 units at $24
July 20	200 units at $25
Sept. 4	300 units at $28
Dec. 2	100 units at $30

Determine cost of goods sold and ending inventory, using periodic FIFO, weighted average, and LIFO. Answer questions about financial statement effects.
(SO 5, 6) AN

By year end, 750 units were sold. Choi Company uses a periodic inventory system.

Instructions

(a) Determine the cost of goods available for sale.
(b) Determine (1) the cost of the ending inventory, and (2) the cost of goods sold under each of the three assumed cost flow methods (FIFO, weighted average, and LIFO).
(c) During a period of rising prices (as is illustrated in this situation), which cost flow method results in (1) the highest inventory amount for the balance sheet, and (2) the highest cost of goods sold for the income statement?
(d) Which method would have the most favourable impact on the company's cash flows?

P6–5A The management of Réal Novelty is re-evaluating the appropriateness of its present inventory cost flow method, weighted average cost. It requests your help in determining the results of operations for the year ended December 31, 2003, if the FIFO method had been used. For 2003, the accounting records show the following data:

Calculate ending inventory using FIFO and weighted average periodic inventory methods, prepare income statements, and answer questions.
(SO 5, 6) AN

Inventories		Purchases and Sales	
Beginning (15,000 units)	$34,000	Total net sales (225,000 units)	$865,000
Ending (20,000 units)	?	Total cost of goods purchased (230,000 units)	591,500

Purchases were made quarterly, as follows:

Quarter	Units	Unit Cost	Total Cost
1	60,000	$2.40	$144,000
2	50,000	2.50	125,000
3	50,000	2.60	130,000
4	70,000	2.75	192,500
	230,000		$591,500

Operating expenses were $147,000. The periodic inventory system is used.

Instructions

(a) Prepare comparative condensed income statements for 2003 under periodic FIFO and weighted average cost.
(b) Answer the following questions for management in the form of a business letter.
  1. Will gross profit under the weighted average cost method be higher or lower than under FIFO?
  2. How much additional cash will be available for management under weighted average cost than under FIFO? Why?
  3. What factors should management consider in selecting its inventory cost flow assumption?

*Indicate effect of errors and iden-
tify cost flow assumptions.*
(SO 6, 7) AN

P6–6A   JL Company maintains its inventory records on a periodic basis. At the end of 2001, the inventory was properly stated. But, in taking a physical inventory at the end of 2002, a batch of inventory was not included in the count. The inventory was properly stated at the end of 2003.

Instructions

(a) Indicate the effect of the error (overstatement, understatement, or no effect) on the following:
1. Cost of goods sold for 2002
2. Cost of goods sold for 2003
3. Net income for 2002
4. Net income for 2003
5. Combined income for the two years, 2002 and 2003

(b) Identify the inventory costing method most closely related to each of the following statements assuming a period of falling prices:
1. Overstates current value on a balance sheet.
2. Matches recent costs against revenue.
3. Results in a balance sheet inventory value closest to replacement cost.
4. Smooths out the effect of price fluctuations.

Source: Adapted from Certified General Accountants' Association of Canada, *Financial Accounting 1 Examination*, March 1998, Question 5.

*Illustrate impact of inventory
error.*
(SO 7) AN

P6–7A   The records of Alyssa Company show the following data:

Account	2002	2003
Sales	$300,000	$320,000
Beginning inventory	30,000	22,000
Cost of goods purchased	200,000	240,000
Ending inventory	22,000	31,000
Operating expenses	60,000	64,000

Subsequent to its July 31, 2003, year end, Alyssa discovers that its inventory at the end of 2002 was actually $27,000, not $22,000.

Instructions

(a) Prepare both incorrect and corrected income statements for Alyssa for the years ended July 31, 2002, and 2003.
(b) What is the impact of this error on the owner's equity at July 31, 2003?

*Prepare journal entries for pur-
chaser and seller using weighted
average cost. Apply lower of cost
and market.*
(SO 2, 5, 8) AP

P6–8A   You are provided with the following information for Amelia Company. Amelia purchases all its high-tech items from Karina Company and makes sales to a variety of customers. All transactions are settled in cash. Returns are usually not damaged and are restored immediately to inventory for resale. Both Amelia and Karina use the periodic inventory method and the weighted average cost flow assumption. Increased competition has reduced the price of the product.

AMELIA COMPANY

Date	Transaction	Quantity	Unit Dollar Amount
July 1	Beginning inventory	25	$10.00
5	Purchase	60	9.00
8	Sale	45	11.00
10	Sale return	10	11.00
15	Purchase	25	8.00
16	Purchase return	5	8.00
20	Sale	60	9.00
25	Purchase	10	6.50

Instructions

(a) Prepare the required journal entries for the month of July for Amelia Company, the purchaser.
(b) Prepare the required journal entries for the month of July for Karina Company, the seller, to record the purchases made by Amelia.
(c) Determine the ending inventory amount using the weighted average cost flow assumption for Amelia Company.
(d) By July 31, Amelia Company learns that the product has a net realizable value of $7 per unit. What amount should ending inventory be valued at on the July 31 balance sheet?

*P6–9A Powder! sells a snowboard, Xpert, that is popular with snowboard enthusiasts. Below is information relating to Powder!'s purchases and sales of Xpert snowboards during September:

Calculate and journalize FIFO transactions in perpetual and periodic inventory systems.
(SO 2, 5, 9) AP

Date	Transaction	Units	Unit Dollar Amount	Total Sale Price	Total Purchase Cost
Sept. 1	Beginning inventory	26	$ 97		$ 2,522
5	Sale	(12)	199	$2,388	
12	Purchase	45	102		4,590
16	Sale	(50)	199	9,950	
19	Purchase	28	104		2,912
22	Sale	(32)	209	6,688	
26	Purchase	40	105		4,200
	Totals	45		$19,026	$14,224

Instructions

(a) Calculate the ending inventory and cost of goods sold using FIFO, assuming that a perpetual inventory system is utilized by Powder!.

(b) What would the ending inventory and cost of goods sold be if Powder! used FIFO in a periodic inventory system?

(c) Prepare journal entries to record the purchases and sales for Powder! in a perpetual inventory system. Assume all purchases and sales are for cash.

(d) Prepare journal entries to record the purchases and sales for Powder! in a periodic inventory system. Assume all purchases and sales are for cash.

*P6–10A The Reliable Appliance Mart began operations on May 1 and uses a perpetual inventory system. During May, the company had the following purchases and sales for its Model 25 Sureshot camera:

Calculate cost of goods sold and inventory using perpetual inventory system with FIFO and moving average cost. Answer questions about financial statement effects.
(SO 6, 9) AP

Date	Purchases Units	Purchases Unit Cost	Sales Units	Sales Unit Price
May 1	7	$150		
4			5	$250
8	8	170		
12			5	280
15	5	180		
20			4	300
25			2	300

Instructions

(a) Determine the cost of goods sold and ending inventory under a perpetual inventory system using (1) FIFO, and (2) moving average cost.

(b) Which costing method produces (1) the higher ending inventory valuation, and (2) the higher net income?

*P6–11A Chang Company lost all of its inventory in a fire on December 28, 2003. The accounting records showed the following gross profit data for November and December:

Estimate inventory loss using gross profit method.
(SO 10) AP

	November	December (to 12/28)
Net sales	$500,000	$400,000
Beginning inventory	22,100	31,100
Purchases	314,975	236,000
Purchase returns and allowances	11,800	4,000
Freight in	4,402	3,700
Ending inventory	31,100	?

Chang is fully insured for fire losses but must prepare a report for the insurance company.

Instructions

(a) Calculate the gross profit margin for November.

(b) Using the gross profit margin for November, determine the estimated cost of the inventory lost in the fire.

Calculate ending inventory using retail method.
(SO 10) AP

*P6–12A   Varocher's Book Store uses the retail inventory method to estimate its monthly ending inventories. The following information is available at October 31, 2002:

	Cost	Retail
Beginning inventory	$ 260,000	$ 400,000
Purchases	1,180,000	1,800,000
Freight in	5,000	
Sales		1,820,000
Sales returns and allowances		15,000

At December 31, Varocher's Book Store takes a physical inventory at retail. The actual retail value of the inventory is $400,000 at year end.

Instructions

(a) Determine the estimated cost of the ending inventory at October 31, 2002, using the retail inventory method.

(b) Calculate the ending inventory at cost at December 31, assuming the cost to retail ratio for the year remains constant.

PROBLEMS: SET B

Determine items and amounts to be recorded in inventory.
(SO 1) AN

P6–1B   Banff Company is trying to determine the value of its ending inventory as at February 28, 2003, the company's year end. The accountant counted everything that was in the warehouse, as at February 28, which resulted in an ending inventory valuation of $48,000. However, she didn't know how to treat the following transactions, so she didn't record them:

1. On February 26, Banff shipped goods costing $800 to a customer. The goods were shipped FOB shipping point. The receiving report indicates that the customer received the goods on March 2.
2. On February 26, Seller Inc. shipped goods to Banff, FOB destination. The invoice price was $350 plus $25 for freight. The receiving report indicates that the goods were received by Banff on March 2.
3. Banff had $500 of inventory at a customer's warehouse "on approval." The customer was going to let Banff know whether it wanted the merchandise by the end of the week, March 7.
4. Banff also had $400 of inventory on consignment at a Jasper craft shop.
5. On February 26, Banff ordered goods costing $750. The goods were shipped FOB shipping point on February 27. The receiving report indicates that Banff received the goods on March 1.
6. On February 28, Banff packaged goods and had them ready for shipping to a customer, FOB destination. The invoice price was $350 plus $25 for freight. The cost of the items was $280. The receiving report indicates that the goods were received by the customer on March 2.
7. Banff had damaged goods set aside in the warehouse because they were not saleable. These goods originally cost $400. Banff initially expected to sell these items for $600.

Instructions

(a) For each of the above transactions, specify whether the item in question should be included in ending inventory, and if so, at what amount. Explain your reasoning.

(b) How much is the revised ending inventory valuation?

Journalize and post transactions, and prepare trial balance and partial income statement.
(SO 2, 3, 4) AP

P6–2B   At the beginning of the current season, the ledger of Kicked-Back Tennis Shop included Cash $2,500; Merchandise Inventory $1,700; and J. Noya, Capital, $4,200. The following transactions were completed during April 2003:

Apr. 4 Purchased racquets and balls from Robert Co., $640, FOB shipping point, terms n/30.
     6 Paid freight on Robert Co. purchase, $40.
     8 Sold merchandise to members, $900, terms n/30.
    10 Received credit of $40 from Robert Co. for a damaged racquet that was returned.
    11 Purchased tennis shoes from Niki Sports for cash, $300.
    13 Paid Robert Co. in full.
    14 Purchased tennis shirts and shorts from Martina's Sportswear, $700, FOB shipping point, terms n/60.
    15 Received cash refund of $50 from Niki Sports for damaged merchandise that was returned.
    17 Paid freight on Martina's Sportswear purchase, $30.
    18 Sold merchandise to members, $800, terms n/30.

20 Received $500 in cash from members in settlement of their accounts.
21 Paid Martina's Sportswear in full.
27 Granted credit of $30 to members for tennis clothing that did not fit.
30 Sold merchandise to members, $900, terms n/30.
30 Received cash payments on account from members, $500.

Instructions

(a) Journalize the April transactions for the Kicked-Back Tennis Shop using a periodic inventory system.
(b) Enter the beginning balances in the general ledger accounts and post the April transactions.
(c) Prepare a trial balance as at April 30, 2003.
(d) Prepare a multiple-step income statement up to gross profit, assuming merchandise inventory on hand at April 30 is $1,800.

P6–3B The N-Mart Department Store is located near the Village Shopping Mall. At the end of the company's fiscal year on December 31, 2003, the following accounts appeared in alphabetical order in its adjusted trial balance:

Prepare multiple-step income statement and closing entries. (SO 4) AP

Accounts Payable	$ 89,300
Accounts Receivable	50,300
Accumulated Amortization—Building	52,500
Accumulated Amortization—Equipment	42,900
Amortization Expense—Building	10,400
Amortization Expense—Equipment	13,300
Building	190,000
S. Koo, Capital	178,600
Cash	23,000
S. Koo, Drawings	28,000
Equipment	110,000
Freight In	5,600
Insurance Expense	7,200
Merchandise Inventory	40,500
Mortgage Payable	80,000
Office Salaries Expense	32,000
Prepaid Insurance	2,400
Property Tax Expense	4,800
Property Tax Payable	4,800
Purchases	442,000
Purchase Returns and Allowances	6,400
Sales	618,000
Sales Commissions Expense	14,500
Sales Commissions Payable	3,500
Sales Returns and Allowances	8,000
Sales Salaries Expense	76,000
Utilities Expense	18,000

Additional facts:
1. Merchandise inventory on December 31, 2003 is $75,000.
2. N-Mart Department Store uses a periodic system.
3. N-Mart Department Store separates its operating expenses into selling and administrative categories. Sales commissions and sales salaries are selling expenses. All other expenses are classified as administrative expenses.

Instructions

(a) Prepare a multiple-step income statement for the year ended December 31, 2003.
(b) Prepare the closing journal entries.
(c) What is the ending balance reported in the Merchandise Inventory and S. Koo, Capital, accounts after closing entries are prepared and posted?

P6–4B Anil Company had a beginning inventory of 400 units of Product E2-D2 at a cost of $8 per unit. During the year, purchases were as follows:

Determine cost of goods sold and ending inventory, using periodic FIFO, weighted average, and LIFO. Answer questions about financial statement effects. (SO 5, 6) AN

Feb. 20	700 units @ $9	Aug. 12	300 units @ $11
May 5	500 units @ $10	Dec. 8	100 units @ $12

Anil uses a periodic inventory system. Sales totalled 1,500 units.

Instructions

(a) Determine the cost of goods available for sale.

(b) Determine the (1) cost of goods sold and (2) ending inventory under each of the three assumed cost flow methods (FIFO, weighted average, and LIFO).

(c) Which cost flow method results in (1) the lowest inventory amount for the balance sheet, and (2) the lowest cost of goods sold for the income statement?

Calculate ending inventory using FIFO and LIFO periodic inventory methods, prepare income statements, and answer questions.
(SO 5, 6) AN

P6–5B   The management of Audas Company asks for your help in determining the comparative effects of the FIFO and LIFO periodic inventory cost flow assumptions. For 2003, the accounting records show the following data:

Inventory, January 1 (10,000 units)	$ 35,000
Cost of 110,000 units purchased	478,000
Selling price of 95,000 units sold	665,000
Operating expenses	120,000

Units purchased consisted of 40,000 units at $4.20 on May 10; 50,000 units at $4.40 on August 15; and 20,000 units at $4.50 on November 20.

Instructions

(a) Prepare comparative condensed income statements for 2003 under FIFO and LIFO.

(b) Answer the following questions for management, in the form of a business letter:
   1. Which inventory cost flow assumption produces the more meaningful inventory amount for the balance sheet? Why?
   2. Which inventory cost flow assumption produces the more meaningful net income? Why?
   3. Which inventory cost flow assumption is most likely to approximate the actual physical flow of the goods? Why?
   4. How much more cash would be available to management under LIFO than under FIFO? Why?

Indicate effect of errors and identify cost flow assumptions.
(SO 6, 7) AN

P6–6B   Chandra Company maintains its inventory records on a periodic basis. At the end of 2002, the ending inventory was overstated by $25,000 by including inventory that had been sold but not yet shipped. The inventory was properly stated at the end of 2003.

Instructions

(a) Indicate the effect of the error (overstatement, understatement, or no effect) on the following:
   1. Cost of goods sold for 2002
   2. Cost of goods sold for 2003
   3. Net income for 2002
   4. Net income for 2003
   5. 2002 and 2003 combined income
   6. Assets for 2002
   7. Assets for 2003
   8. Owner's equity for 2002
   9. Owner's equity for 2003

(b) Identify the inventory costing method most closely related to each of the following statements, assuming a period of rising prices:
   1. Understates current value on a balance sheet.
   2. Matches recent costs against revenue.
   3. Results in a balance sheet inventory value closest to replacement cost.
   4. Smooths out the effect of price fluctuations.

Illustrate impact of inventory error.
(SO 7) AN

P6–7B   The records of Pelletier Company show the following data:

Account	2002	2003
Sales	$300,000	$320,000
Beginning inventory	30,000	22,000
Cost of goods purchased	200,000	240,000
Ending inventory	22,000	31,000
Operating expenses	60,000	64,000

Subsequent to its July 31, 2003, year end, Pelletier Company discovers two errors. Its ending inventory was understated by $3,000 in 2002. Its purchases were understated by $25,000 in 2003.

Instructions

(a) Prepare both incorrect and corrected income statements for 2002 and 2003.

(b) What is the combined effect of the errors at July 31, 2003, before correction?

Prepare journal entries for purchaser and seller using FIFO periodic method. Apply lower of cost and market.
(SO 2, 5, 8) AP

P6–8B   You are provided with the following information concerning the transactions for Schwinghamer Co. Schwinghamer purchases all items from Pataki Co. and makes sales to a variety of customers. All transactions are settled in cash. Returns are normally not damaged and are restored immediately to inventory for resale. Both companies use the periodic inventory method and the FIFO cost flow assumption.

SCHWINGHAMER CO.

Date	Transaction	Quantity	Unit Dollar Amount
Oct. 1	Beginning inventory	25	$ 7.00
5	Purchase	60	8.00
8	Sale	45	15.00
10	Sale return	10	15.00
15	Purchase	25	9.00
16	Purchase return	5	9.00
20	Sale	60	16.00
25	Purchase	10	10.00

Instructions

(a) Prepare the required journal entries for the month of October for Schwinghamer Co., the purchaser.
(b) Prepare the required journal entries for the month of October for Pataki Co., the seller, to record the purchases made by Schwinghamer.
(c) Determine the ending inventory amount for Schwinghamer, using the FIFO cost flow assumption.
(d) By October 31, Schwinghamer Co. learns that the product has a net realizable value of $11 per unit. What amount should ending inventory be valued at on the October 31 balance sheet?

*P6–9B INL.com sells in-line skates. Below is information relating to INL.com's purchases and sales of one of their top brands of in-line skates during April.

Calculate and journalize average cost transactions in perpetual and periodic inventory systems. (SO 2, 5, 9) AP

Date	Transaction	Units	Unit Dollar Amount	Total Sale Price	Total Purchase Cost
Apr. 1	Beginning inventory	26	$197		$ 5,122
5	Sale	(12)	299	$ 3,588	
12	Purchase	65	202		13,130
16	Sale	(50)	299	14,950	
19	Purchase	38	204		7,752
22	Sale	(62)	309	19,158	
26	Purchase	40	205		8,200
	Totals	45		$37,696	$34,204

Instructions

(a) Calculate the ending inventory and cost of goods sold using moving average, assuming that a perpetual inventory system is used by INL.com. Round averages to the nearest dollar.
(b) What would the ending inventory and cost of goods sold be if INL.com used weighted average in a periodic inventory system?
(c) Prepare journal entries to record the purchases and sales for INL.com in a perpetual inventory system. Assume all purchases and sales are made on account.
(d) Prepare journal entries to record the purchases and sales for INL.com in a periodic inventory system. Assume all purchases and sales are made on account.

*P6–10B The following information comes from Jolie Wholesalers' inventory records for Model 573 SuperSure Barbecue Starters, and represents all the activity for that item of inventory for the month of October:

Calculate ending inventory and gross profit using perpetual system with FIFO costing. (SO 9) AP

	Units	Unit Cost	Unit Selling Price
Inventory, September 30	60	$13	
Purchase, October 9	120	14	
Sale, October 11	100		$35
Purchase, October 17	70	15	
Sale, October 22	80		38
Purchase, October 25	50	16	
Sale, October 28	50		40

Instructions

Using the perpetual inventory system and the FIFO method of costing, calculate the following:
(a) The cost of the inventory on hand at the end of October.
(b) The gross profit on sales during the month of October.

Estimate inventory loss using gross profit method.
(SO 10) AP

*P6–11B   Thierry Company lost 80% of its inventory in a fire on March 23, 2003. The accounting records showed the following gross profit data for February and March:

	February	March (to 3/23)
Net sales	$300,000	$260,000
Net purchases	200,800	191,000
Freight in	2,900	3,500
Beginning inventory	16,500	25,200
Ending inventory	25,200	?

Thierry Company is fully insured for fire losses but must prepare a report for the insurance company.

Instructions

Using the gross profit margin for February, determine both the estimated total inventory and the inventory lost in the March fire.

Estimate ending inventory using retail method.
(SO 10) AP

*P6–12B   Landry Department Store uses the retail inventory method to estimate its monthly ending inventories. The following information is available for two of its departments at August 31, 2003:

	Sporting Goods		Jewellery and Cosmetics	
	Cost	Retail	Cost	Retail
Net sales		$1,120,000		$1,160,000
Purchases	$670,000	1,166,000	$731,000	1,158,000
Purchase returns	26,000	40,000	12,000	20,000
Freight in	6,000		8,000	
Beginning inventory	47,360	74,000	38,000	62,000

At December 31, Landry Department Store takes a physical inventory at retail. The actual retail values of the inventories in each department at the end of the year are as follows: Sporting Goods $85,000 and Jewellery and Cosmetics $54,000.

Instructions

(a) Determine the estimated cost of the ending inventory for each department on August 31, 2003, using the retail inventory method.
(b) Calculate the ending inventory at cost for each department at December 31, assuming the cost to retail ratios are 60% for Sporting Goods and 65% for Jewellery and Cosmetics.

*B*roadening Your Perspective

FINANCIAL REPORTING AND ANALYSIS

Financial Reporting Problem

BYP6–1   The notes that accompany a company's financial statements provide informative details that would clutter the amounts and descriptions presented in the body of the financial statements. Refer to the financial statements and the Notes to Consolidated Financial Statements of **The Second Cup Ltd.** in Appendix A.

Instructions

(a) What categories of inventories does The Second Cup have?
(b) Calculate inventories as a percentage of (1) current assets and (2) total revenues, for 2000 and 1999 (pro forma). Comment on the results.
(c) How does The Second Cup value its inventories? Which inventory cost flow method does it use? Do you think that using a different cost flow assumption would materially affect The Second Cup's results?
(d) What information does The Second Cup disclose regarding its cost of goods sold?

Interpreting Financial Statements

BYP6–2 Specialty coffee shops have been hit with major coffee price increases over the past few years. Since 1997, the cost of green beans has risen by more than 40%. Why are prices increasing? First, Colombia's Coffee Growers' Federation is holding back exports in order to increase prices. Other countries are expected to impose export quotas in an attempt to drive up prices further. Also, drought followed by heavy rains in Brazil affected 25% of the world's supply. Colombia's supply is threatened by strikes at its docks. These combined forces are leading most analysts to predict that coffee prices will most likely remain high.

Additional Cases

An international chain of coffee shops, began accounting for its coffee bean purchases using the moving average cost flow assumption. Analysts hypothesized that this move could help the chain better maintain its net income than use of the LIFO cost flow assumption would.

Instructions

(a) Why do you think the chain uses a perpetual inventory system (moving average) rather than a periodic inventory system (weighted average)?

(b) Explain why the chain moved to the average cost flow assumption. How can this assumption help it to "better maintain its net income"?

BYP6–3 **General Motors** is the largest producer of automobiles in the world, as well as the world's biggest industrial enterprise. After stumbling in the early 1990s, GM has taken numerous cost-cutting measures, including downsizing and renegotiating contracts with suppliers. In addition, it has shifted more of its resources to the hot-selling truck market.

The annual report of General Motors Corporation disclosed the following information about its accounting for inventories:

GENERAL MOTORS CORPORATION
Notes to the Financial Statements
December 31, 2000

Note 6. Inventories
Major Classes of Inventories (U.S. dollars in millions)

Productive material, work in process, and supplies	$ 5,555
Finished product, service parts, etc.	7,319
Total inventories at FIFO	$12,874
Total inventories at last-in, first-out (LIFO)	$10,945

Inventories are stated generally at cost, which is not in excess of market. The cost of substantially all U.S. inventories other than the inventories of Saturn Corporation (Saturn) and Hughes is determined by the last-in, first-out (LIFO) method. The cost of non-U.S., Saturn, and Hughes inventories is determined by either the first-in, first-out (FIFO) or average cost methods.

Instructions

(a) What is meant by "inventories are stated generally at cost, which is not in excess of market"?

(b) GM reports its inventories in its balance sheet using the LIFO cost flow assumption at $10,945 million. It reports this same inventory in its notes using both the FIFO and LIFO cost flow assumptions. Why do you suppose it does this?

(c) GM reports that its inventory at LIFO is $10,945 million. The same inventory at FIFO is $12,874 million. Are prices rising or falling for GM, given the difference in these two cost flow assumptions?

(d) General Motors uses different inventory methods for different types of inventory. Why might it do this?

(e) GM also uses different costing methods for its inventories in the U.S. versus those in other countries. Why might it do this?

Accounting on the Web

BYP6–4 This problem uses an annual report to identify the inventory costing and valuation methods used, and to analyse the effects on the income statement and balance sheet.

Instructions

Specific requirements of this Internet case are available on the Weygandt website.

CRITICAL THINKING

•••

Collaborative Learning Activities

BYP6–5 On April 10, 2003, fire damaged the office and warehouse of Gibson Company. Most of the accounting records were destroyed, but the following account balances were determined as at March 31, 2003: Merchandise Inventory, January 1, 2003, $80,000; Sales (January 1–March 31, 2003), $180,000; Purchases (January 1–March 31, 2003), $94,000. The company's fiscal year ends on December 31. It uses a periodic inventory system.

From an analysis of the April bank statement, you discover cancelled cheques of $4,200 for cash purchases between April 1 and April 10. Deposits during the same period totalled $18,500. Of that amount, 60% represented collections on accounts receivable and the balance was cash sales.

Correspondence with the company's principal suppliers revealed $12,400 of purchases on account from April 1 to April 10. Of that amount, $1,800 was for merchandise in transit on April 10 that was shipped FOB destination.

Correspondence with the company's principal customers produced acknowledgements of credit sales totalling $28,000 from April 1 to April 10. It was estimated that $4,600 of credit sales will never be acknowledged or recovered from customers.

Gibson Company reached an agreement with the insurance company that its fire-loss claim should be based on the average of the gross profit margins for the preceding two years. The financial statements for 2002 and 2001 showed the following data:

	2002	2001
Net sales	$600,000	$480,000
Cost of goods purchased	416,000	356,000
Beginning inventory	60,000	40,000
Ending inventory	80,000	60,000

Inventory with a cost of $19,000 was salvaged from the fire.

Instructions

With the class divided into groups, answer the following:
(a) Determine the balances in (1) Sales, and (2) Purchases at April 10.
(b) Determine the average gross profit margin for the years 2002 and 2001. (*Hint*: Find the gross profit margin for each year, and then divide the sum by two.)
(c) Determine the inventory at the time of the fire, using the gross profit method.
(d) How much should be claimed from the insurance company to cover the inventory loss from the fire?

BYP6–6 Consider the case of a large company which reported inventories of $800 million at December 31, 2003, and $900 million at December 31, 2002. The ending inventory for 2002 had been overstated by $40 million, as a result of errors in the physical counting process. This error was not discovered until after the financial statements for 2003 had been issued.

Instructions

With the class divided into groups, complete the table which follows. Indicate which items in the financial statements would be incorrect, and by how much. For each item, indicate whether it would be overstated(O), understated(U), or not affected (NA). Also, indicate the amount of the error (if any).

	Effect On Fiscal Year	
	2003	2002
Beginning inventory		
Ending inventory		
Cost of goods sold		
Gross profit		
Net income		
Total assets		
Owners' equity		

Communication Activity

BYP6–7 You are the controller of Small Toys. Mutahir Kazmi, the president, recently mentioned to you that he found an error in the 2002 financial statements that he believes has now corrected itself.

In discussions with the Purchasing Department, Mutahir determined that 2002 ending inventory was overstated by $1 million. However, the 2003 ending inventory is correct. Mutahir assumes that 2003 income is correct and comments to you, "What happened has happened—there's no point in worrying about it now."

Instructions

You conclude that Mutahir is incorrect. Write a brief, tactful memo to him, clarifying the situation.

Ethics Case

BYP6–8 Quality Diamonds carries only one brand and size of diamonds—all are identical. Each batch of diamonds purchased is carefully coded and marked with its purchase cost. The following data are available:

Mar. 1 Opening inventory, 150 diamonds at a cost of $300 per diamond.
    3 Purchased 200 diamonds at a cost of $350 each.
    5 Sold 180 diamonds for $600 each.
  10 Purchased 350 diamonds at a cost of $375 each.
  25 Sold 500 diamonds for $650 each.

Instructions

(a) Assume that Quality Diamonds uses the specific identification cost flow method.
  1. Demonstrate how Quality Diamonds could maximize its gross profit for the month by selecting which diamonds to sell on March 5 and March 25.
  2. Demonstrate how Quality Diamonds could minimize its gross profit for the month by selecting which diamonds to sell on March 5 and March 25.

(b) Assume that Quality Diamonds uses the weighted average cost flow assumption and a periodic inventory method. How much gross profit would Quality Diamonds report under this cost flow assumption?

(c) Who are the stakeholders in this situation? Is there anything unethical in choosing which diamonds to sell in a month?

(d) Which cost flow method should Quality Diamonds select? Explain.

Answers to Self-Study Questions
1. a   2. b   3. d   4. c   5. a   6. b   7. c   8. c   9. b   10. c   *11. d   *12. b

Answer to Second Cup Review It Question 5
Second Cup reports $107,000 of total inventories in the current assets section of its balance sheet. It uses the FIFO cost flow assumption.

Remember to go back to the Navigator box on the chapter-opening page to check off your completed work.

Concepts for Review

Before studying this chapter, you should understand or, if necessary, review:

a. *How to perform each of the steps in the accounting cycle. (Ch. 4, p. 164)*

b. *How to record transactions for a merchandising company. (Ch. 5, p. 222, and Ch. 6, pp. 273-274)*

c. *How to prepare financial statements for a merchandising company. (Ch. 5, pp. 223–228, and Ch. 6, p. 273)*

THE NAVIGATOR

Helping the Helpers: Accounting Systems Are for Everyone

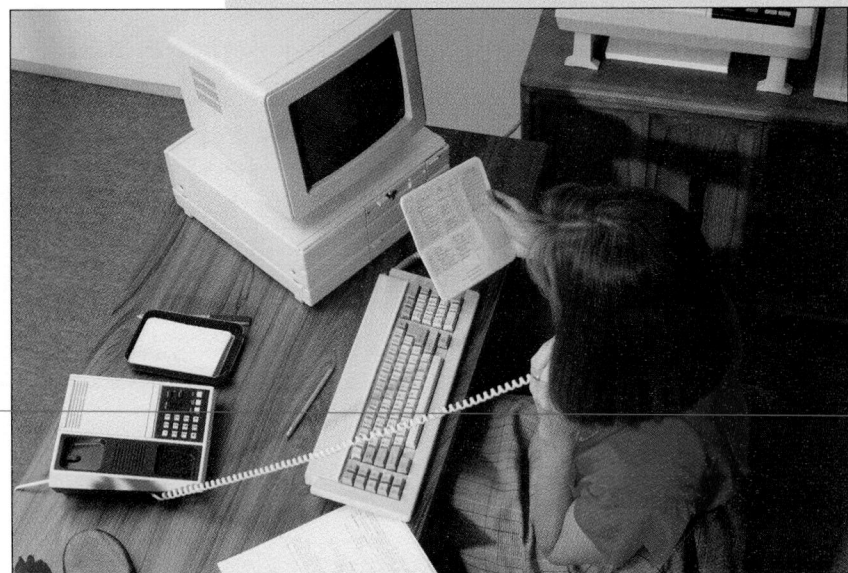

HALIFAX, N.S.—Say the words "accounting system" and most people think of a big corporation keeping track of its profits. But accounting for the money that flows through it is equally crucial to an organization like Bryony House, a Halifax women's shelter.

"We have a budget of about $700,000 a year and 20 employees," says the shelter's administrator, Cathy Love. "We really need our computerized system to track our accounts in detail." For example, once the bookkeeper has posted an expense such as paper towels to the system, the amount is added to total household expenditures for the month, and deducted from the remaining budget at the same time.

"And if something seems odd on the monthly financial statements we prepare for the board of directors— say, the furniture account is suddenly very high—then we can easily find out that it's because we bought a whole bunch of dressers that month."

The shelter uses the popular *Simply Accounting* small business electronic accounting package. In addition, the shelter's fundraising activities are tracked in detail using custom donation management software that was created by a volunteer programmer. This database is useful both for accounting and for organizing and targeting future fundraising.

Like many non-profit organizations, Bryony House could benefit from an upgrade in both hardware and soft-

ware. The cost and time needed to upgrade the system has to be weighed against the advantages, of course.

"We'd need to get funding for an upgrade," says Ms. Love. The bottom line is that the more easily and quickly the shelter's staff can get the information it needs, the more time the staff has to do its main job of working with the women who come for help.

THE NAVIGATOR

bryonyhouse.ca

THE NAVIGATOR

- Understand *Concepts for Review* ☐
- Read *Feature Story* ☐
- Scan *Study Objectives* ☐
- Read *Preview* ☐
- Read text and answer *Before You Go On*
  p. 327 ☐ p. 341 ☐ p. 344 ☐ p. 346 ☐
- Work *Demonstration Problem* ☐
- Review *Summary of Study Objectives* ☐
- Answer *Self-Study Questions* ☐
- Complete assignments ☐

CHAPTER · 7

ACCOUNTING INFORMATION SYSTEMS

▶ STUDY OBJECTIVES ◀

After studying this chapter, you should be able to:

1. *Identify and explain the basic principles of accounting information systems.*
2. *Explain the major phases in the development of an accounting system.*
3. *Describe the nature and purpose of a subsidiary ledger, and determine ledger balances.*
4. *Illustrate how special journals are used in a perpetual inventory system.*
5. *Demonstrate how a multi-column journal is posted.*
6. *Demonstrate how special journals are used in a periodic inventory system (Appendix 7A).*
7. *Describe and demonstrate how sales tax transactions are recorded in special journals (Appendix 7B).*

THE NAVIGATOR

As you can see from the feature story, the majority of businesses today use computerized accounting systems. Many, however, still use manual systems to process all, or part of, their accounting. Whether you use your pen or your computer to maintain accounting records, certain principles and procedures apply. The purpose of this chapter is to explain and illustrate these features. The chapter is organized as follows:

THE
NAVIGATOR

Basic Concepts of Accounting Information Systems

The system that collects and processes transaction data and provides financial information to interested individuals is known as the accounting information system. It includes each of the steps in the accounting cycle that you have studied in earlier chapters. It also includes the documents that provide evidence of the transactions and events, and the accounting records, trial balances, and financial statements that result. An accounting information system may be either manual or electronic (computerized).

Principles of Accounting Information Systems

STUDY OBJECTIVE

1

Identify and explain the basic principles of accounting information systems.

Efficient and effective accounting information systems are based on certain basic principles. These principles are (1) cost-effectiveness, (2) usefulness, and (3) flexibility.

1. **Cost-effectiveness.** The system must be cost-effective. The benefits obtained from the accounting information must outweigh the cost of providing it. For example, the value of each accounting report should be at least equal to the cost of producing it. That is why Bryony House, in our feature story, has to weigh the cost of an upgraded computer system against the benefits it will provide.

2. **Usefulness.** To be useful, information must be understandable, relevant, reliable, timely, and accurate. Designers of accounting systems must consider the needs and knowledge of various users so that the output of the system (reports and statements) will be useful to them. For example, sales managers may need weekly reports of sales, and factory supervisors may need daily reports of

production. Others with differing responsibilities may need such reports only monthly or quarterly.

3. **Flexibility.** The accounting system should be able to accommodate a variety of users and changing information needs. The business environment changes as a result of technological advances, organizational resizing, increased competition, government regulation, and changes in accounting principles. When the environment changes, the accounting system should be sufficiently flexible to meet the resulting changes in the needs of its users.

If the accounting system is cost-effective, provides useful information, and has the flexibility to meet future needs, it can contribute to both individual and organizational goals. Illustration 7-1 illustrates the principles of an efficient and effective accounting information system.

Illustration 7-1

Principles of an efficient and effective accounting information system

Developing an Accounting System

Good accounting systems do not just happen. They are carefully planned, designed, installed, managed, and refined. Generally, an accounting system is developed in the following four phases:

1. **Analysis.** The starting point is to determine the information needs of internal and external users. The system analyst then identifies the sources of needed information, and the records and procedures required to collect and report the data. If an existing system is being analysed, its strengths and weaknesses must be identified.

2. **Design.** A new system must be built from the ground up: forms and documents designed, methods and procedures selected, job descriptions prepared, controls integrated, reports formatted, and equipment selected. Redesigning an existing system may involve only minor changes, or a complete overhaul.

3. **Implementation.** Implementation of new or revised systems requires that documents, procedures, and processing equipment be installed and made operational. Personnel must be trained and closely supervised through a start-up period.

4. **Follow-up.** After the system is up and running, it must be monitored for weaknesses or breakdowns. Also, its effectiveness must be measured based on design and organizational objectives. Changes in design or in implementation may be necessary.

Illustration 7-2 highlights the relationship of these four phases in the life cycle of the accounting system.

STUDY OBJECTIVE
▼ 2

Explain the major phases involved in the development of an accounting system.

Illustration 7-2

Phases in the development of an accounting system

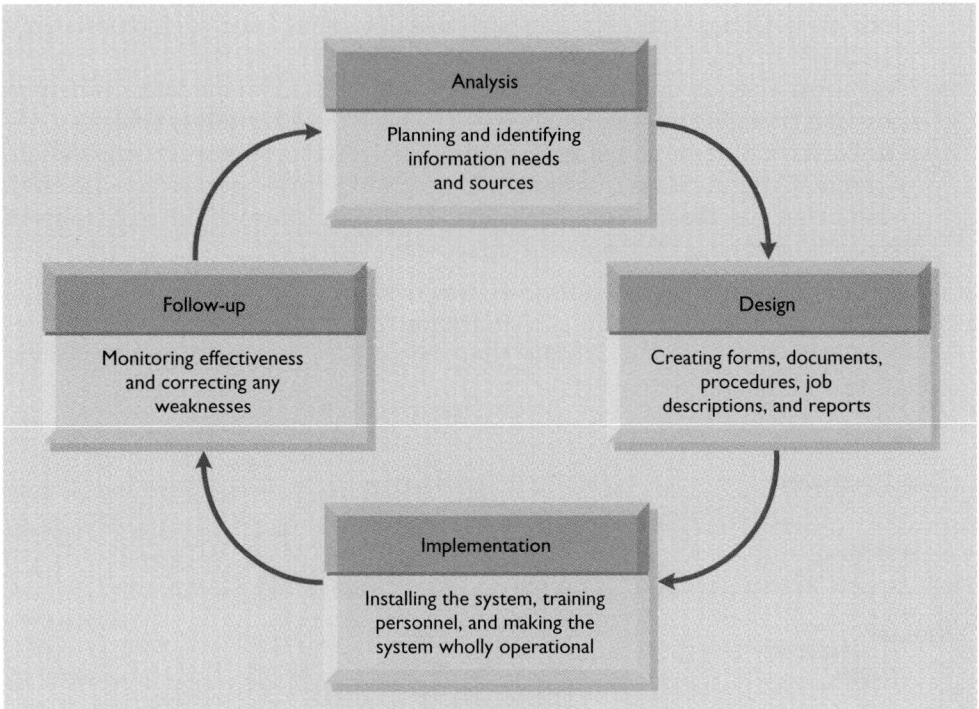

These phases represent the life cycle of an accounting system. They suggest that few systems remain the same forever. As experience and knowledge are acquired, and as technological and organizational changes occur, the accounting system may also have to change.

The accounting system illustrated in the first six chapters is satisfactory in a company where the volume of transactions is low. In most companies, it is necessary to use additional journals and ledgers in the accounting system to record transaction data efficiently.

Manual vs. Computerized Systems

In a **manual accounting system**, each of the steps in the accounting cycle is performed by hand. For example, each accounting transaction is entered manually in the journal. Each is posted manually to the ledger. Other manual calculations must be made to obtain ledger account balances and to prepare a trial balance and financial statements.

In a computerized accounting system, programs perform the steps in the accounting cycle, such as journalizing, posting, and preparing a trial balance. In addition, there is software for business functions such as billing customers, inventory management, preparing the payroll, and budgeting.

Leading financial accounting software packages include Computer Associates' *Simply Accounting*, *ACCPAC for Windows*, and *BPI Accounting*; Intuit's *QuickBooks*; and MYOB's *MYOB Accounting*. These packages offer integrated accounting applications for accounts receivable, accounts payable, inventory, order processing, and general ledgers. Some packages also include foreign currency accounting, intercompany accounting, general ledger structure for segmented company/division reporting, and multiple languages, among other features.

You might be wondering, "Why cover manual accounting systems if the majority of the real world uses computerized systems?" To understand what computerized accounting systems do, you need to understand how manual accounting systems work. The basic principles we describe in the following sections apply to both manual and computerized accounting systems.

Accounting in Action ► @ -*Business Insight*

Accounting software companies have recognized the tremendous opportunities that result from making the accounting system an integral part of a comprehensive e-business package. For example ACCPAC's eTransact™ software integrates closely and easily with ACCPAC's accounting solutions. This package provides businesses with powerful business-to-business (B2B) and business-to-customer (B2C) e-commerce capabilities in a single, robust, and easy to use business-to-everyone (B2E) solution. Forrester Research Inc. predicts that on-line B2B trade in Canada alone will reach $272 billion in 2005.

Subsidiary Ledgers

Imagine a business that has several thousand customers who purchase merchandise from it on account. It records the transactions with these customers in only one general ledger account—Accounts Receivable. It would be virtually impossible to determine the balance owed by an individual customer at any specific time. Similarly, the amount payable to one creditor would be difficult to locate quickly from a single Accounts Payable account in the general ledger.

Instead, companies use subsidiary ledgers to keep track of individual balances. A **subsidiary ledger** is a group of accounts that share a common characteristic (for example, all accounts receivable). The subsidiary ledger frees the general ledger from the details of individual balances. A subsidiary ledger is an addition to, and an expansion of, the general ledger.

Two common subsidiary ledgers are:

1. The **accounts receivable** (or customers') **ledger**, which collects transaction data with individual customers.
2. The **accounts payable** (or creditors') **ledger**, which collects transaction data for individual creditors.

Other subsidiary ledgers include an inventory ledger, which collects transaction data for each inventory item purchased and sold. Some companies also use a payroll ledger, detailing individual employee pay records. We will learn more about payroll in Chapter 11. In each of these subsidiary ledgers, individual accounts are arranged in alphabetical, numerical, or alphanumerical order.

The detailed data from a subsidiary ledger are summarized in a general ledger account. For example, the detailed data from the accounts receivable subsidiary ledger are summarized in Accounts Receivable in the general ledger. The general ledger account that summarizes subsidiary ledger data is called a **control account**.

An overview of the relationship of the accounts receivable and payable subsidiary ledgers to the general ledger is shown in Illustration 7-3. The general ledger control accounts and subsidiary ledger accounts are shown in green. Note that Cash and Owner's Capital in this illustration are not control accounts because there are no subsidiary ledgers related to these accounts.

> **STUDY OBJECTIVE**
> **3**
> *Describe the nature and purpose of a subsidiary ledger, and determine ledger balances.*

Illustration 7-3

Relationship of general ledger and subsidiary ledgers

Each general ledger control account balance must equal the total balance of the individual accounts in the related subsidiary ledger. For example, the balance in Accounts Payable in Illustration 7-3 must equal the total of the subsidiary account balances of creditors X + Y + Z. This is an important internal control function. Internal control will be discussed more fully in the next chapter.

Example

An example of an accounts receivable control account and subsidiary ledger is shown in Illustration 7-4 for Mercier Enterprises.

Illustration 7-4

Accounts receivable subsidiary ledger and general ledger control account

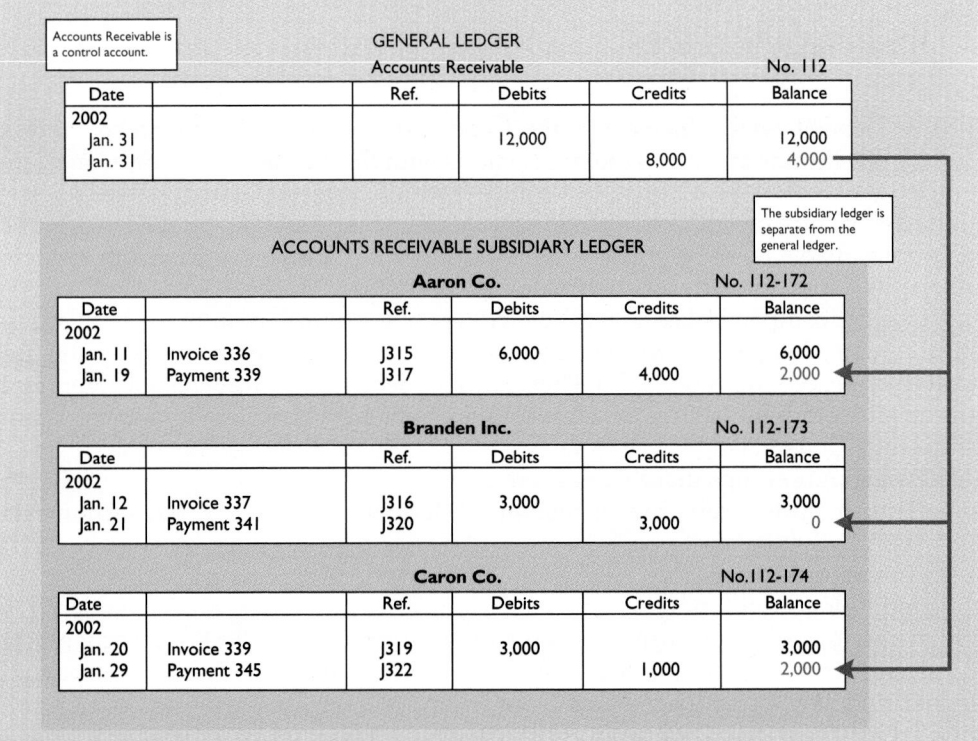

The example is based on the following transactions:

	Credit Sales				Collections on Account	
Jan.	11	Aaron Co.	$ 6,000	Jan.	19	Aaron Co.	$4,000
	12	Branden Inc.	3,000		21	Branden Inc.	3,000
	20	Caron Co.	3,000		29	Caron Co.	1,000
			$12,000				$8,000

The total debits ($12,000) and credits ($8,000) in Accounts Receivable in the general ledger match the detailed debits and credits in the subsidiary accounts. The balance of $4,000 in the control account agrees with the total of the balances in the individual accounts receivable accounts (Aaron $2,000 + Branden $0 + Caron $2,000) in the subsidiary ledger.

Rather than relying on customer or creditor names in a subsidiary ledger, a computer system expands the account number of the control account. For example, if the Accounts Receivable general ledger control account was numbered 112, the first customer account in the accounts receivable subsidiary ledger might be numbered 112-001, the second 112-002, and so on. Most systems allow inquiries about specific customer accounts in the subsidiary ledger (by account number) or about the control account.

As shown, postings are made monthly to the control account in the general ledger. This practice allows monthly trial balances (and interim financial statements, if desired) to be prepared. Postings to the individual accounts in the subsidiary ledger are made daily. The rationale for posting daily is to ensure that account information is current. This enables Mercier Enterprises to monitor credit limits, send statements to customers, and answer inquiries from customers about their account balances. In a computerized accounting system, transactions are simultaneously recorded in journals and posted to both the general and subsidiary ledgers.

Advantages of Subsidiary Ledgers

Subsidiary ledgers have several advantages. They:
1. **Show transactions that affect one customer or one creditor in a single account.** They provide up-to-date information on specific account balances.
2. **Free the general ledger of excessive details.** A trial balance of the general ledger does not contain vast numbers of individual customer account balances.
3. **Help locate errors in individual accounts.** The potential for errors is minimized by reducing the number of accounts in one ledger and by using control accounts.
4. **Make possible a division of labour in posting.** One employee can post to the general ledger while different employees post to the subsidiary ledgers. This strengthens internal control, since one employee verifies the work of the other.

In a computerized accounting system, the last two advantages are not applicable. Computerized accounting systems do not make errors such as calculation errors and posting errors. Other errors, such as entry errors, can and do still occur. Internal control must be done using different means in computerized systems since account transactions are posted automatically.

Before You Go On . . .
▶*Review It*

1. What basic principles are followed in designing and developing an effective accounting information system?
2. What are the major phases in the development of an accounting information system?
3. What is a subsidiary ledger, and what purpose does it serve?

▶*Do It*

Information for the first month of operations of Fu Company is presented below. Determine the balances that appear in the accounts payable subsidiary ledger. What accounts payable control account balance appears in the general ledger at the end of January? You may find it helpful to use T accounts to organize the following information:

Credit Purchases				Cash Paid		
Jan.	5	Ng Co.	$11,000	Jan.	9	Ng Co.	$7,000
Jan.	11	Wong Co.	7,000	Jan.	14	Wong Co.	2,000
Jan.	22	Wu Co.	14,000	Jan.	27	Wu Co.	9,000
			$32,000				$18,000

Action Plan

- Subtract cash paid from credit purchases to determine the balances in the accounts payable subsidiary ledger.
- Sum the individual balances to prove that the Accounts Payable control account balances to the subsidiary ledger.

Solution

Accounts payable subsidiary ledger accounts: General ledger Accounts Payable control account:

	Ng Co.			
Jan. 9	7,000	Jan. 5		11,000
		Jan. 31	Bal.	4,000

	Accounts Payable			
Jan. 31	18,000	Jan. 31		32,000
		Jan. 31	Bal.	14,000

	Wong Co.			
Jan. 14	2,000	Jan. 11		7,000
		Jan. 31	Bal.	5,000

	Wu Co.			
Jan. 27	9,000	Jan. 22		14,000
		Jan. 31	Bal.	5,000

THE
NAVIGATOR

Proof that the subsidiary ledger account balances agree with the general ledger control account balance: Ng $4,000 + Wong $5,000 + Wu $5,000 = $14,000 Accounts Payable.

Related exercise material: BE7–1, BE7–2, BE7–3, and BE7–4.

◤Special Journals

STUDY OBJECTIVE

4

Illustrate how special journals are used in a perpetual inventory system.

So far, you have learned to journalize transactions in a two-column (debit and credit) general journal, and to post each entry to the general ledger. This procedure is satisfactory only when there are few transactions.

To save time when journalizing and posting, one option is to use a one-write system. The one-write system is a method of recording accounting information that is popular with some microbusinesses because it accelerates the recording process. This system uses a board and carbon accounting forms. The board aligns the forms on pegs so that when information is written on them, it transfers to the forms beneath. The first form may be a cheque, invoice, receipt, or other relevant business form. The second form is usually a multi-column journal. As a cheque is written, the information is simultaneously transferred to the journal. Another form could be included to update the general ledger account at the same time. The one-write system is easy to use, minimizes transposition errors, and saves time.

While a one-write system is an efficient method to organize a small number of transactions, it is inadequate for businesses with many recurring transactions. To facilitate the journalizing and posting of these transactions, **most companies use special journals in addition to the general journal**.

A special journal is used to record similar types of transactions. Examples would be all sales of merchandise on account, or all cash receipts. The types of special journals used depend largely on the types of transactions that occur frequently. While the form, type, and number of special journals used will vary among organizations, many merchandising companies use the journals shown in Illustration 7-5 to record transactions daily. The letters that appear in parentheses following the journal name represent the posting reference used for each journal.

Illustration 7-5

Use of special journals and the general journal

If a transaction cannot be recorded in a special journal, it is recorded in the general journal. For example, if you only have four special journals as listed in Illustration 7-5, sales returns and allowances are recorded in the general journal. Similarly, **correcting, adjusting, and closing entries are recorded in the general journal**. Other types of special journals may sometimes be used in certain situations. For example, when sales returns and allowances are frequent, a special journal may be used to record these transactions. A payroll journal is another example of a special journal. It organizes and summarizes payroll details for companies with many employees.

The use of special journals **reduces the time needed for the recording and posting process**. In addition, special journals **permit greater division of labour** because different employees can record entries in different journals. For example, one employee may journalize all cash receipts. Another may journalize credit sales. The division of responsibilities ensures that one person does not have control over all aspects of a transaction. In this instance, recording the sale has been separated from recording the collection of cash from that sale. This may reduce the opportunity for intentional or unintentional error, and is one aspect of a good internal control system, as we will learn in Chapter 8.

For a merchandising company, the same special journals are used whether a company uses the periodic or perpetual system to account for its inventory. The only distinction is the number of, and title for, the columns each journal uses. We will use Karns Wholesale Supply to illustrate the use of special journals in the following sections. Karns uses a perpetual inventory system. The variations between the periodic and perpetual inventory systems are highlighted in **helpful hints** for your information. In addition, special journals under a periodic inventory system are more fully illustrated in Appendix 7A to this chapter.

Sales Journal

The **sales journal** is used to record sales of merchandise on account. Cash sales of merchandise are entered in the cash receipts journal. Credit sales of assets other than merchandise are entered in the general journal.

Journalizing Credit Sales

Under the perpetual inventory system, each entry in the sales journal results in one entry **at selling price and another entry at cost**. The entry at selling price is a debit to Accounts Receivable (a control account supported by a subsidiary ledger) and a credit of an equal amount to Sales. The entry at cost is a debit to Cost of Goods Sold and a credit of an equal amount to Merchandise Inventory. Some companies also set up Merchandise Inventory as a control account supported by a subsidiary ledger.

A sales journal with two amount columns can show a sales transaction recognized at both selling price and cost on only one line. The two-column sales journal of Karns Wholesale Supply is shown in Illustration 7-6, using assumed credit sales transactions.

Illustration 7-6

Journalizing the sales journal—perpetual inventory system

Helpful hint In a periodic inventory system, the sales journal would have only one column to record the sale at selling price (Accts. Receivable Dr., Sales Cr.). The cost of goods sold is not recorded. It is determined by calculation at the end of the period.

				KARNS WHOLESALE SUPPLY Sales Journal	S1
Date	Account Debited	Invoice No.	Ref.	Accts. Receivable Dr. Sales Cr.	Cost of Goods Sold Dr. Merchandise Inventory Cr.
2002					
May 3	Abbot Sisters	101		10,600	6,360
7	Babson Co.	102		11,350	7,370
14	Carson Bros.	103		7,800	5,070
19	Deli Co.	104		9,300	6,510
21	Abbot Sisters	105		15,400	10,780
24	Deli Co.	106		21,210	15,900
27	Babson Co.	107		14,570	10,200
				90,230	62,190

The reference (Ref.) column is not used in journalizing. It is used in **posting** the sales journal, as is explained in the next section. Also, note that, unlike in the general journal, an explanation is not required for each entry in a special journal. Finally, note that each invoice is prenumbered to ensure that all invoices are journalized.

If management wishes to record its sales by department, additional columns may be provided in the sales journal. For example, a department store may have columns for home furnishings, sporting goods, shoes, etc. In addition, the federal government, and practically all provinces, require that sales taxes be charged on items sold. If sales taxes are collected, it is necessary to add additional credit columns to the sales journal for GST Payable and PST Payable. The sales journal, and other special journals that incorporate sales taxes, are illustrated in Appendix 7B to this chapter.

Posting the Sales Journal

STUDY OBJECTIVE
•••••••••• **5** ••••••••••

Demonstrate how a multi-column journal is posted.

Postings from the sales journal are made **daily to the individual accounts receivable accounts** in the subsidiary ledger. Posting **to the general ledger is done monthly**. Illustration 7-7 (facing page) shows both the daily postings to the accounts receivable subsidiary ledger and the monthly postings to the general ledger accounts. We have assumed that Karns Wholesale Supply does not maintain an inventory subsidiary ledger. However, if it did, the procedure is similar to that illustrated for the accounts receivable subsidiary ledger.

A check mark ($\sqrt{}$) is inserted in the reference posting column to indicate that the daily posting to the customer's account has been made. A check mark is used when the subsidiary ledger accounts are not individually numbered. If the subsidiary ledger accounts are numbered, the account number is used instead of the check mark in the reference posting column. At the end of the month, the column totals of the sales journal are posted to the general ledger. Here, the column totals are posted as a debit of $90,230 to Accounts Receivable (account no. 112), a credit of $90,230 to Sales (account no. 401), a debit of $62,190 to Cost of Goods Sold (account no. 505), and a credit of $62,190 to Merchandise Inventory (account no. 120). The insertion of the respective account numbers below the column totals indicates that the postings have been made. In both the general ledger and subsidiary ledger accounts, the reference S1 indicates that the posting came from page 1 of the sales journal.

Illustration 7-7

Sales journal—perpetual inventory system

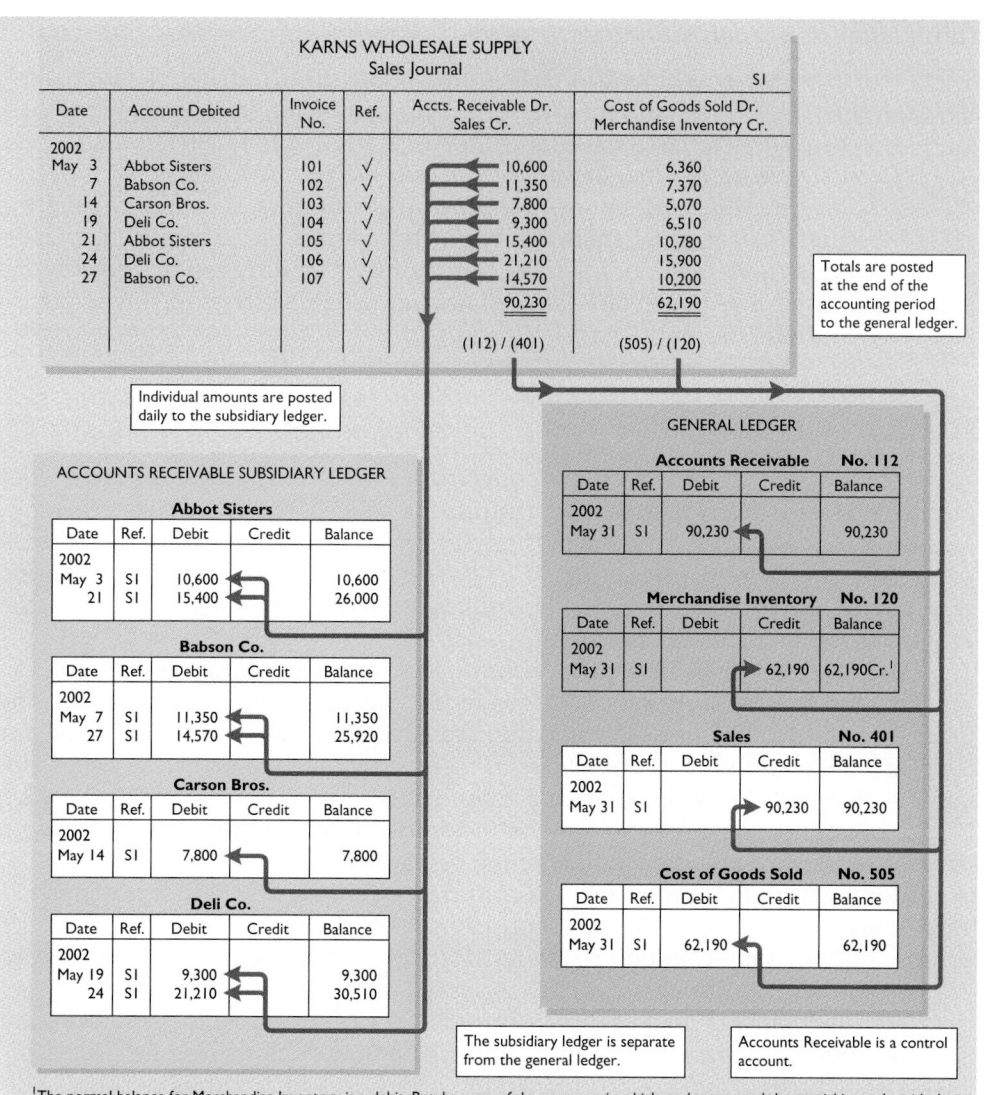

Totals are posted at the end of the accounting period to the general ledger.

Individual amounts are posted daily to the subsidiary ledger.

Helpful hint Postings to subsidiary ledger accounts are done daily, because it is often necessary to know a current balance for the subsidiary accounts.

The subsidiary ledger is separate from the general ledger.

Accounts Receivable is a control account.

¹The normal balance for Merchandise Inventory is a debit. But, because of the sequence in which we have posted the special journals, with the sales journal first, the credits to Merchandise Inventory are posted before the debits. This posting sequence explains the credit balance in Merchandise Inventory, which exists only until the other journals are posted.

Proving the Ledgers

The next step is to "prove" the ledgers. To do so, we must determine two things: (1) The total of the general ledger debit balances must equal the total of the general ledger credit balances. (2) The sum of the subsidiary ledger balances must equal the balance in the control account. The proof of the postings from the sales journal to the general and subsidiary ledgers is shown in Illustration 7-8.

Illustration 7-8

Proving the ledgers

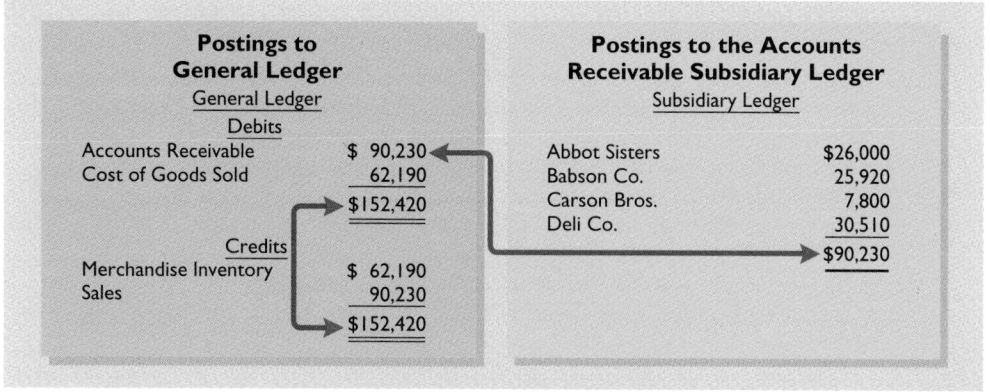

Advantages of the Sales Journal

The use of a special journal to record sales on account has a number of advantages. First, the one-line/two-column entry for each sales transaction **saves time**. In the sales journal, it is not necessary to write out the four account titles for the two transactions. Second, only totals, rather than individual entries, are posted to the general ledger. This **saves posting time and reduces the possibility of errors in posting**. Third, the prenumbering of sales invoices helps to ensure that all sales are recorded and that no sale is recorded more than once. Finally, **a division of labour results**, because one individual can take responsibility for the sales journal alone. These last two advantages facilitate internal control.

Cash Receipts Journal

All receipts of cash are recorded in the cash receipts journal. The most common types of cash receipts are cash sales of merchandise and collections of accounts receivable. Many other possibilities exist, such as receipt of money from bank loans and cash proceeds from disposals of equipment. A one- or two-column cash receipts journal would not have enough space for all possible cash receipt transactions. Therefore, a multiple-column cash receipts journal is used.

Generally, a cash receipts journal includes the following columns: a debit column for cash, and credit columns for accounts receivable, sales, and other accounts. The Other Accounts column is used when the cash receipt does not involve a cash sale or a collection of accounts receivable. Under a perpetual inventory system, each sales entry is accompanied by another entry that debits Cost of Goods Sold and credits Merchandise Inventory. A separate column is added for this purpose. A five-column cash receipt journal is shown in Illustration 7-9 (facing page).

Helpful hint   Another example of an organization that requires special columns in a cash receipts journal is a university, which would have Unearned Tuition Deposits.

Additional credit columns may be used if they significantly reduce postings to a specific account. For example, cash receipts normally include the collection of sales taxes, which are later remitted to the federal and provincial governments. A cash receipts journal with credit columns for sales tax collections is illustrated in Appendix 7B to this chapter. Other examples include the cash receipts of a loan company, such as Household Financial Centre, which include thousands of collections from customers. These collections are credited to Loans Receivable and Interest Revenue. A significant saving in posting time would result from using separate credit columns for Loans Receivable and Interest Revenue, rather than using the Other Accounts credit column. In contrast, a retailer that has only one interest collection a month would not find it useful to have a separate column for Interest Revenue.

Journalizing Cash Receipts Transactions

To illustrate the journalizing of cash receipts transactions, we will continue with the May transactions of Karns Wholesale Supply. Collections from customers relate to the entries recorded in the sales journal in Illustration 7-6. The entries in the cash receipts journal are based on the following cash receipts:

May 1 D. A. Karns makes an investment of $5,000 in the business.
   7 Cash receipts for merchandise sales total $1,900. The cost of goods sold is $1,240.
  10 A cheque for $10,600 is received from Abbot Sisters in full payment of invoice No. 101.
  12 Cash receipts for merchandise sales total $2,600.The cost of goods sold is $1,690.
  17 A cheque for $11,350 is received from Babson Co. in full payment of invoice No. 102.
  22 Cash is received by signing a 4% note for $6,000, payable September 18 to the National Bank.
  23 A cheque for $7,800 is received from Carson Bros. in full payment of invoice No. 103.
  28 A cheque for $9,300 is received from Deli Co. in full payment of invoice No. 104.

Illustration 7-9

Cash receipts journal—per-petual inventory system

KARNS WHOLESALE SUPPLY
Cash Receipts Journal
CR1

Date	Account Credited	Ref.	Cash Dr.	Accounts Receivable Cr.	Sales Cr.	Cost of Goods Sold Dr. Mdse. Inv. Cr.	Other Accounts Cr.
2002							
May 1	D. A. Karns, Capital	301	5,000				5,000
7			1,900		1,900	1,240	
10	Abbot Sisters	√	10,600	10,600			
12			2,600		2,600	1,690	
17	Babson Co.	√	11,350	11,350			
22	Notes Payable	200	6,000				6,000
23	Carson Bros.	√	7,800	7,800			
28	Deli Co.	√	9,300	9,300			
			54,550	39,050	4,500	2,930	11,000
			(101)	(112)	(401)	(505)/(120)	(X)

Individual amounts are posted daily to the subsidiary ledger.

Totals are posted at the end of the accounting period to the general ledger.

ACCOUNTS RECEIVABLE SUBSIDIARY LEDGER

Abbot Sisters

Date	Ref.	Debit	Credit	Balance
2002				
May 3	S1	10,600		10,600
10	CR1		10,600	0
21	S1	15,400		15,400

Babson Co.

Date	Ref.	Debit	Credit	Balance
2002				
May 7	S1	11,350		11,350
17	CR1		11,350	0
27	S1	14,570		14,570

Carson Bros.

Date	Ref.	Debit	Credit	Balance
2002				
May 14	S1	7,800		7,800
23	CR1		7,800	0

Deli Co.

Date	Ref.	Debit	Credit	Balance
2002				
May 19	S1	9,300		9,300
24	S1	21,210		30,510
28	CR1		9,300	21,210

Accounts Receivable is a control account.

The subsidiary ledger is separate from the general ledger.

GENERAL LEDGER

Cash No. 101

Date	Ref.	Debit	Credit	Balance
2002				
May 31	CR1	54,550		54,550

Accounts Receivable No. 112

Date	Ref.	Debit	Credit	Balance
2002				
May 31	S1	90,230		90,230
31	CR1		39,050	51,180

Merchandise Inventory No. 120

Date	Ref.	Debit	Credit	Balance
2002				
May 31	S1		62,190	62,190Cr.
31	CR1		2,930	65,120Cr.

Notes Payable No. 200

Date	Ref.	Debit	Credit	Balance
2002				
May 22	CR1		6,000	6,000

D. A. Karns, Capital No. 301

Date	Ref.	Debit	Credit	Balance
2002				
May 1	CR1		5,000	5,000

Sales No. 401

Date	Ref.	Debit	Credit	Balance
2002				
May 31	S1		90,230	90,230
31	CR1		4,500	94,730

Cost of Goods Sold No. 505

Date	Ref.	Debit	Credit	Balance
2002				
May 31	S1	62,190		62,190
31	CR1	2,930		65,120

Further information about the columns in the cash receipts journal follows:

Debit Columns:

1. **Cash.** The amount of cash actually received in each transaction is entered in this column. The column total indicates the total cash receipts for the month. The total of this column is posted to the Cash account in the general ledger.

2. **Cost of Goods Sold.** The Cost of Goods Sold Dr./Merchandise Inventory Cr. column is used to record the cost of the merchandise sold. Other columns (e.g., Cash and Sales) record the selling price of the merchandise. This column is similar to the one found in the sales journal. The amount debited to Cost of Goods Sold is the same amount credited to Merchandise Inventory. One column total is posted to both accounts at the end of the month.

Credit Columns:

3. **Accounts Receivable.** The Accounts Receivable column is used to record cash collections on account. The amount entered here is the amount to be credited to the individual customer's account.

4. **Sales.** The Sales column is used to record all cash sales of merchandise. Cash sales of other assets (capital assets, for example) are not reported in this column. The total of this column is posted to the Sales account.

5. **Merchandise Inventory.** As noted above, the Cost of Goods Sold Dr./Merchandise Inventory Cr. column is used to record the reduction in the merchandise available for future sale. The amount credited to Merchandise Inventory is the same amount debited to Cost of Goods Sold. One column total is posted to both accounts at the end of the month.

6. **Other Accounts.** The Other Accounts column is used whenever the credit is not to Accounts Receivable, Sales, or Merchandise Inventory. For example, in the first entry, $5,000 is entered as a credit to D. A. Karns, Capital. This column is often referred to as the sundry accounts column.

> **Helpful hint** When is an account title entered in the Account Credited column of the cash receipts journal? A subsidiary ledger title is entered there whenever the entry involves a collection of accounts receivable. A general ledger account title is entered there whenever the entry involves an amount entered in the Other Accounts column. No account title is entered if neither of the above conditions exists.

In a multi-column journal, only one line is generally needed for each entry. In some cases, it is useful to add explanatory information, such as the details of the note payable, or to reference supporting documentation, such as invoice numbers if cash sales are invoiced. Note also that the Account Credited column is used to identify both general ledger and subsidiary ledger account titles. The former is illustrated in the May 1 entry for Karns's investment. The latter is illustrated in the May 10 entry for the collection from Abbot Sisters.

Debit and credit amounts for each line must be equal. When the journalizing has been completed, the amount columns are totalled. The totals are then compared to prove the equality of debits and credits in the cash receipts journal. Don't forget that the Cost of Goods Sold Dr./Merchandise Inventory Cr. column total represents both a debit and a credit amount. Totalling the columns of a journal and proving the equality of the totals is called **footing** (adding down) and **cross-footing** (adding across) a journal.

The proof of the equality of Karns's cash receipts journal is as follows:

Illustration 7-10

Proving the accuracy of the cash receipts journal

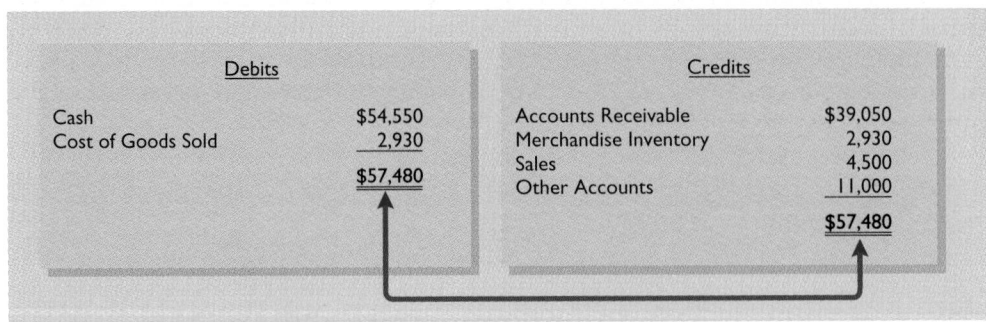

Debits		Credits	
Cash	$54,550	Accounts Receivable	$39,050
Cost of Goods Sold	2,930	Merchandise Inventory	2,930
	$57,480	Sales	4,500
		Other Accounts	11,000
			$57,480

Posting the Cash Receipts Journal

Posting a multi-column journal involves the following steps:
1. **All column totals**, except for the Other Accounts total, **are posted once at the end of the month** to the account title specified in the column heading, such as Cash, Accounts Receivable, Sales, Cost of Goods Sold, and Merchandise Inventory. Account numbers are entered below the column totals to show that they have been posted.
2. **The total of the Other Accounts column is not posted. Individual amounts that make up the Other Accounts total are posted separately** to the general ledger accounts specified in the Account Credited column. See, for example, the credit posting to D. A. Karns, Capital. The symbol X is inserted below the total to this column to indicate that the amount has not been posted.
3. **The individual amounts in a column** (Accounts Receivable, in this case) **are posted daily to the subsidiary ledger** account name specified in the Account Credited column. See, for example, the credit posting of $10,600 to Abbot Sisters.

The symbol CR is used in both the subsidiary and general ledgers to identify postings from the cash receipts journal.

Proving the Ledgers

After the posting of the cash receipts journal is completed, it is necessary to prove the ledgers. As shown in Illustration 7-11, the general ledger totals are in agreement. The sum of the subsidiary ledger account balances also equals the control account balance:

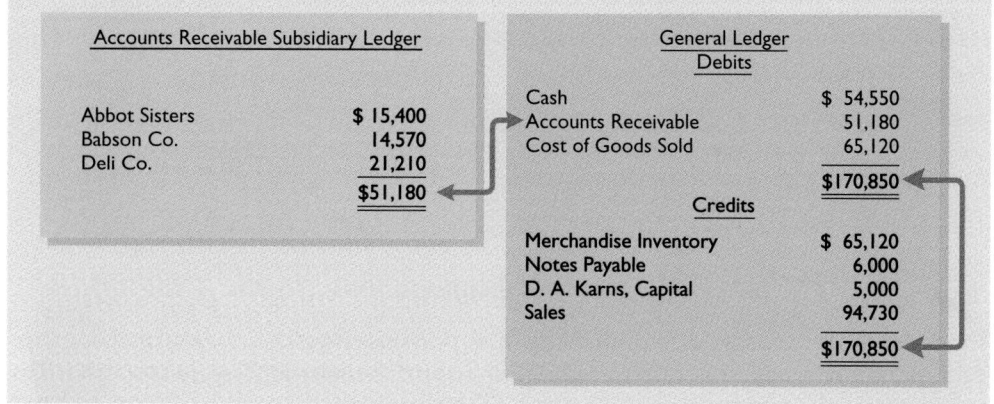

Illustration 7-11

Proving the ledgers

Purchases Journal

All purchases of merchandise on account are recorded in the purchases journal. Each entry in this journal results in a debit to Merchandise Inventory and a credit to Accounts Payable. When a one-column purchases journal is used, other types of purchases on account and cash purchases cannot be journalized in it. For example, credit purchases of equipment or supplies must be recorded in the general journal. Likewise, all cash purchases are entered in the cash payments journal. Where credit purchases for items other than merchandise are numerous, the purchases journal can be expanded to a multi-column format.

The purchases journal for Karns Wholesale Supply is shown in Illustration 7-12, with assumed credit purchases.

Illustration 7-12

Purchases journal—perpetual inventory system

Helpful hint   When a periodic inventory system is used, this journal is still known as a Purchases Journal. The debit to the Merchandise account is replaced by a debit to the Purchases account.

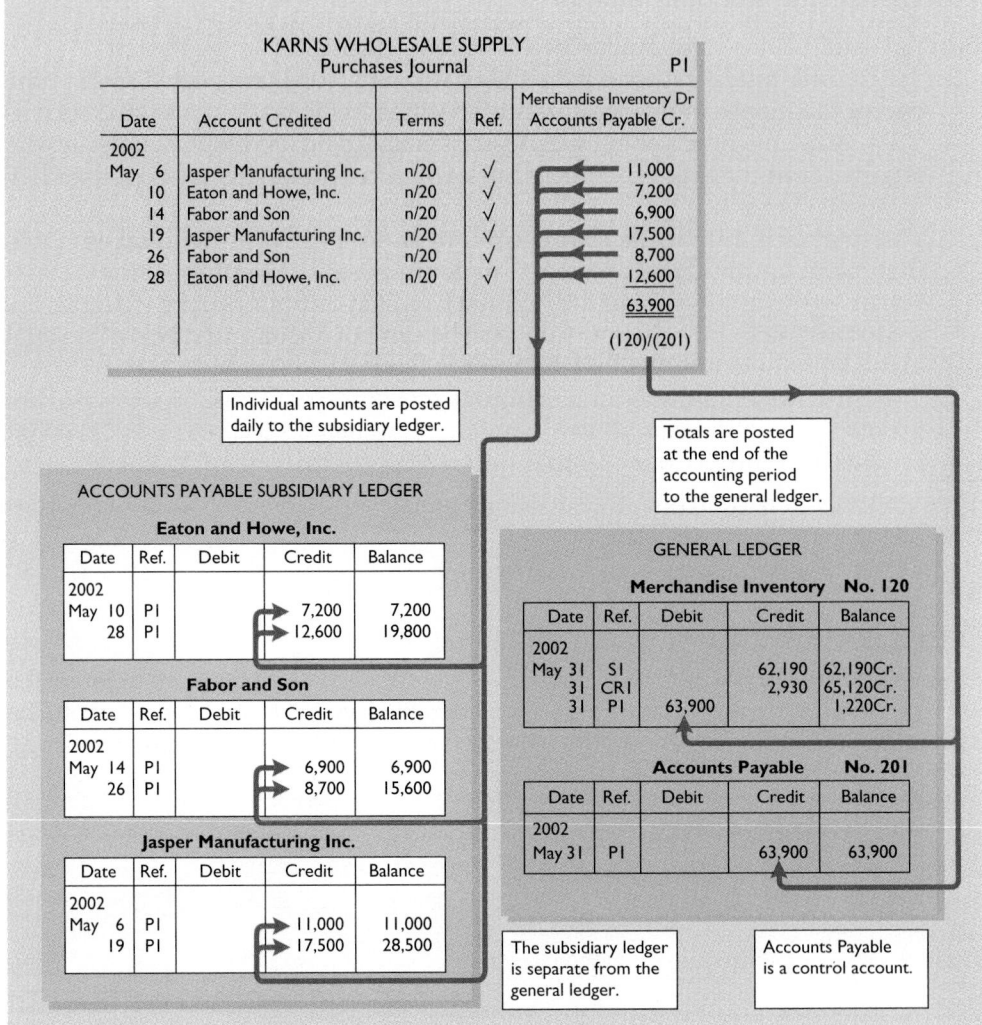

Journalizing Credit Purchases of Merchandise

Entries in the purchases journal are made from purchase invoices. The journalizing procedure for the purchases journal is similar to that for the sales journal. In contrast to the sales journal, the purchases journal may not have an invoice number column, because invoices received from different suppliers would not be in numerical sequence.

Posting the Purchases Journal

The procedures for posting the purchases journal are similar to those for the sales journal. In this case, postings are made **daily** to the accounts payable **subsidiary ledger** accounts and **monthly** to the Merchandise Inventory and Accounts Payable accounts in the **general ledger**. In both ledgers, P1 is used in the reference column to show that the postings are from page 1 of the purchases journal.

Proof of the equality of the postings from the purchases journal to both ledgers is shown by the following:

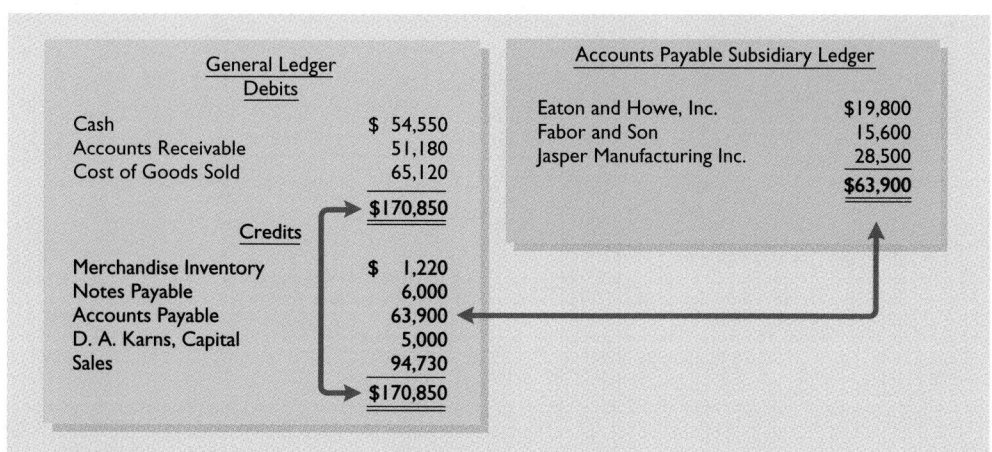

Illustration 7-13

Proving the ledgers

Note that not all the general ledger accounts listed in illustration 7-13 have been included in Illustration 7-12. You will have to refer to Illustration 7-9 to determine the balances for the Cash, Accounts Receivable, Cost of Goods Sold, Notes Payable, Capital, and Sales accounts.

Expanding the Purchases Journal

As mentioned earlier, some companies expand the purchases journal to include all types of purchases on account. Instead of one column for merchandise inventory and accounts payable, they use a multiple-column format. The multi-column format usually includes a credit column for accounts payable and debit columns for purchases of merchandise, office supplies, store supplies, and other accounts. Illustration 7-14 is an example of a multi-column purchases journal for Hanover Co. The posting procedures are similar to those illustrated earlier for posting the cash receipts journal.

Illustration 7-14

Multi-column purchases journal

			Accounts Payable Cr.	Merchandise Inventory Dr.	Office Supplies Dr.	Store Supplies Dr.	Other Accounts Dr.		
Date	Account Credited	Ref.					Account	Ref.	Amount
2002									
June 1	Signe Audio	√	2,000		2,000				
3	Wright Co.	√	1,500	1,500					
5	Apple Tree Co.	√	2,600				Equipment	157	2,600
30	Sue's Business Forms	√	800			800			
			56,600	43,000	7,500	1,200			4,900

HANOVER CO. Purchases Journal — P1

Cash Payments Journal

All disbursements of cash are entered in a cash payments journal. Entries are made from prenumbered cheques. Because cash payments are made for various purposes, the cash payments journal has multiple columns. A four-column journal is shown in Illustration 7-15.

Alternative terminology
The cash payments journal is also called the *cash disbursements journal*.

Illustration 7-15

*Cash payments journal—
perpetual inventory system*

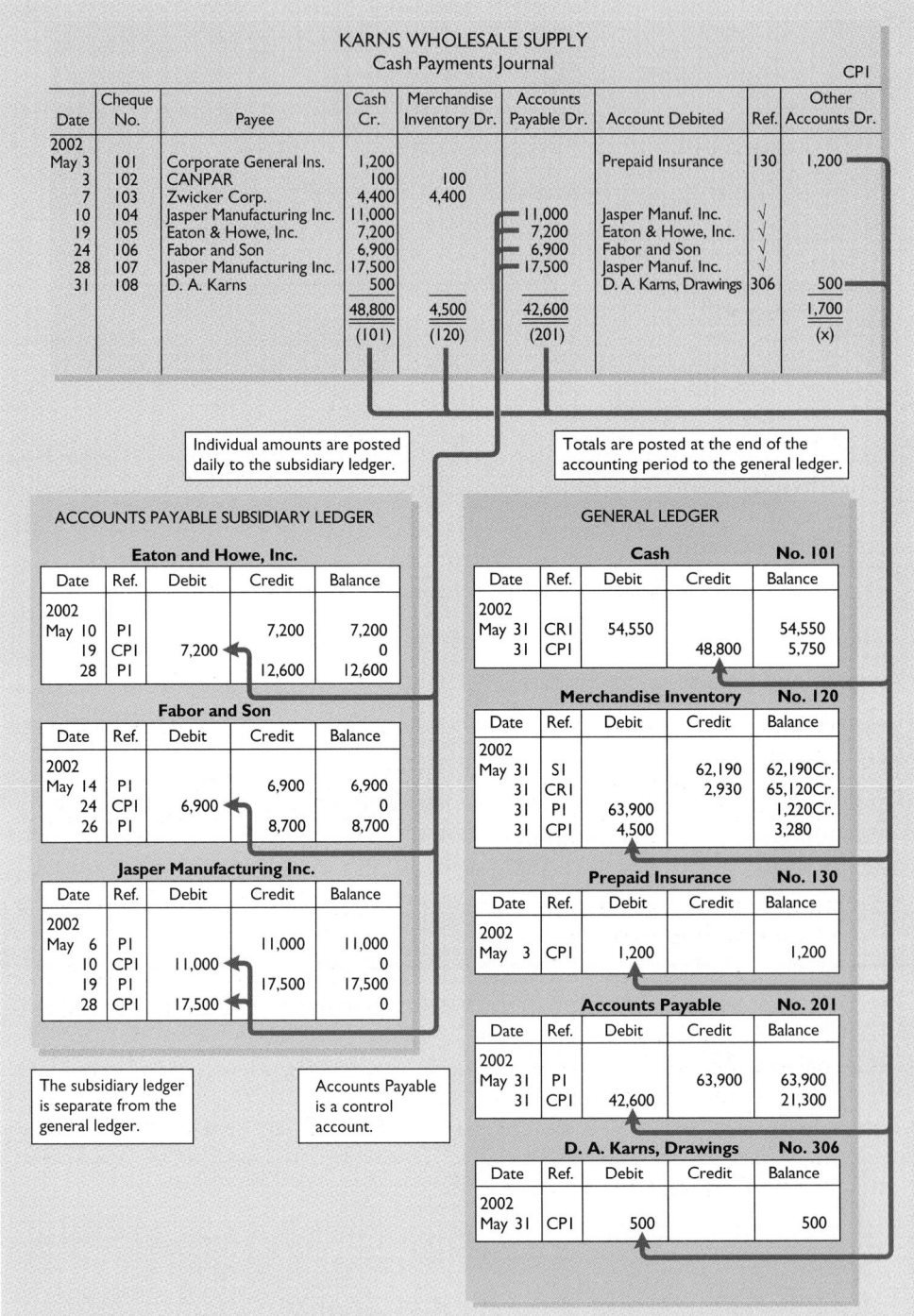

Helpful hint   In a periodic inventory system, the debits to Merchandise Inventory would be recorded to the Purchases and Freight In accounts.

Journalizing Cash Payments Transactions

The procedures for journalizing transactions in this journal are similar to those described earlier for the cash receipts journal. Each transaction is entered on one line, and for each line there must be equal debit and credit amounts. It is common practice in the cash payments journal to record the name of the company or individual receiving the cheque (the payee), so that later reference to the cheque is possible by name in addition to cheque number. The entries in the cash payments journal shown in Illustration 7-15 are based on the following transactions for Karns Wholesale Supply:

May 3 Cheque No. 101 for $1,200 issued for the annual premium on a fire insurance policy issued by Corporate General Insurance.

3 Cheque No. 102 for $100 issued to CANPAR in payment of freight charges on goods purchased.

7 Cheque No. 103 for $4,400 issued for the cash purchase of merchandise from Zwicker Corp.

10 Cheque No. 104 for $11,000 sent to Jasper Manufacturing Inc. in full payment of the May 6 invoice.

19 Cheque No. 105 for $7,200 mailed to Eaton and Howe, Inc., in full payment of the May 10 invoice.

24 Cheque No. 106 for $6,900 sent to Fabor and Son in full payment of the May 14 invoice.

28 Cheque No. 107 for $17,500 sent to Jasper Manufacturing Inc. in full payment of the May 19 invoice.

31 Cheque No. 108 for $500 issued to D. A. Karns as a cash withdrawal for personal use.

Note that whenever an amount is entered in the Other Accounts column, a specific general ledger account must be identified in the Account Debited column. The entries for cheque numbers 101 and 108 illustrate this situation. Similarly, a subsidiary account must be identified in the Account Debited column whenever an amount is entered in the Accounts Payable column (as, for example, the entry for cheque no. 104).

After the cash payments journal has been journalized, the columns are totalled. The totals are then balanced to prove the equality of debits and credits. Debits ($4,500 + $42,600 + $1,700 = $48,800) do equal credits ($48,800) in this case.

Posting the Cash Payments Journal

The procedures for posting the cash payments journal are similar to those for the cash receipts journal:

1. Cash and Merchandise Inventory are posted only as a total at the end of the month.
2. The amounts recorded in the Accounts Payable column are posted **individually to the subsidiary ledger and in total to the general ledger control account**.
3. Transactions in the Other Accounts column are posted individually to the appropriate account(s) noted in the Account Debited column. **No totals are posted for the Other Accounts column.**

The posting of the cash payments journal is shown in Illustration 7-15. Note that the symbol CP is used as the posting reference. After postings are completed, the equality of the debit and credit balances in the general ledger should be determined. The control account balance should also agree with the subsidiary ledger total balance. The agreement of these balances is shown in Illustration 7-16. Note that not all the general ledger accounts have been included in Illustration 7-15. You will also have to refer to Illustration 7-9 to determine the balances for the Accounts Receivable, Cost of Goods Sold, Notes Payable, Capital, and Sales accounts.

Helpful hint If a company has a subsidiary ledger for merchandise inventory, amounts in the merchandise inventory column would be posted daily in the cash payments journal, as well as in the sales, cash receipts, and purchases journals.

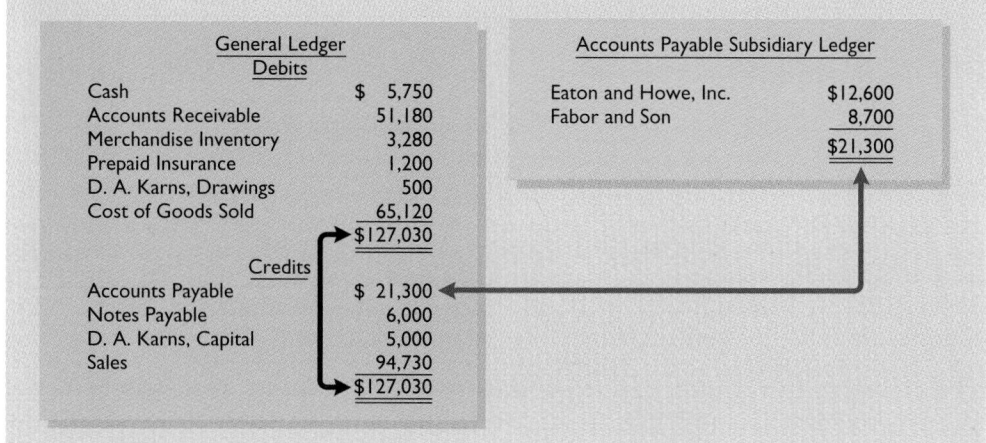

Illustration 7-16

Proving the ledgers

Effects of Special Journals on General Journal

Special journals for sales, purchases, and cash greatly reduce the number of entries that are made in the general journal. **Only transactions that cannot be entered in a special journal are recorded in the general journal.** For example, the general journal may be used to record a transaction granting credit to a customer for a sales return or allowance. It may also be used to record the receipt of a credit from a supplier for purchases returned, the acceptance of a note receivable from a customer, and the purchase of equipment by issuing a note payable. Also, correcting, adjusting, and closing entries are made in the general journal.

When control and subsidiary accounts are not used, the procedures for journalizing and posting transactions in the general journal are the same as those described in earlier chapters. When control and subsidiary accounts are used, two modifications of earlier procedures are required:

1. In **journalizing,** both the control and the subsidiary account must be identified.
2. In **posting,** there must be a **dual posting:** once to the control account and once to the subsidiary account.

To illustrate, assume that on May 31 Karns Wholesale Supply returns $500 of merchandise for credit to Fabor and Son. The entry in the general journal and the posting of the entry are shown in Illustration 7-17. Note that if cash had been received instead of the credit granted on this return, then the transaction would have been recorded in the cash receipts journal.

Illustration 7-17

Journalizing and posting the general journal

Helpful hint   In a periodic inventory system, the credit would be to the Purchase Returns and Allowances account rather than to the Merchandise Inventory account.

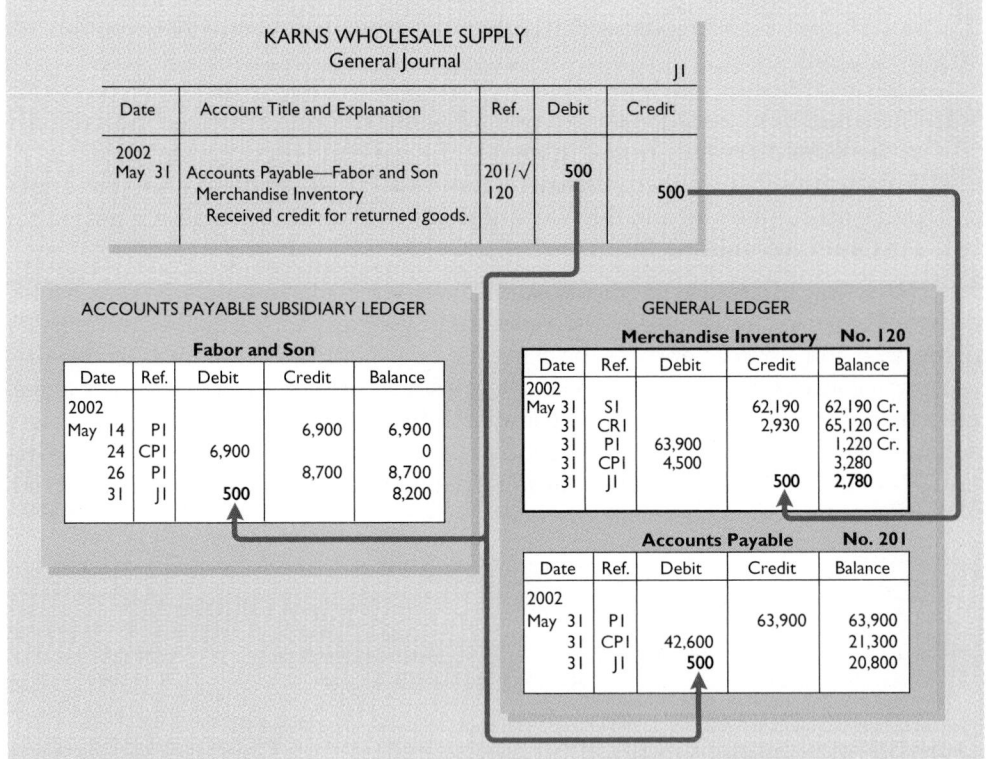

Notice that in the general journal two accounts are indicated for the debit (the Accounts Payable control account and the Fabor and Son subsidiary account). Two postings (201/√) are indicated in the reference column. One amount is posted to the control account in the general ledger (no. 201) and the other to the creditor's account in the subsidiary ledger (Fabor and Son).

Before You Go On . . .

▶Review It

1. What types of special journals are frequently used to record transactions? Why are special journals used?
2. Explain how transactions recorded in the sales journal and the cash receipts journal are posted.
3. Indicate the types of transactions that are recorded in the general journal when special journals are used.

▶Do It

The Mitsui Company has the following selected transactions: (1) purchase of equipment for cash, (2) cash sale, (3) sales return, (4) withdrawal of cash for the proprietor's personal use, and (5) sale of merchandise on account. Identify the journals in which each transaction should be entered.

Action Plan

• Know content of each special journal: Sales journal—sales on account; cash receipts journal—cash receipts; purchases journal—purchases of merchandise on account; cash payments journal—cash payments; and general journal—all other transactions.

Solution

(1) Purchase of equipment for cash—cash payments journal. (2) Cash sale—cash receipts journal. (3) Sales return—general journal. (4) Withdrawal of cash for the proprietor's personal use—cash payments journal. (5) Sale of merchandise on account—sales journal.

Related exercise material: BE7–5, BE7–6, BE7–7, BE7–8, BE7–9, E7–1, E7–2, E7–3, E7–4, E7–5, E7–6, E7–7, E7–8, E7-9, E7-10, and E7-11.

THE NAVIGATOR

▶A Look Back at Our Feature Story

Refer to the feature story about Bryony House at the beginning of the chapter, and answer the following questions:
1. What subsidiary ledgers does Bryony House likely use? Why do companies use subsidiary ledgers?
2. Why do many businesses use computerized accounting systems?
3. Is it likely that in the future some enterprises will continue to use manual systems?
4. What are some of the (a) costs, and (b) benefits of an upgrade in the accounting system for Bryony House?

Solution

1. Bryony House uses a subsidiary ledger to organize its receipts from fundraising. It likely is not large enough to benefit from the use of other subsidiary ledgers. Advantages of a subsidiary ledger for a company like Bryony House are as follows: (1) It shows transactions for one donor in a single account. (2) It frees the general ledger of excessive detail. (3) It helps locate errors in individual accounts. (4) In manual accounting systems, it provides a division of labour.
2. Many businesses use computerized accounting systems because computers can often produce cheaper, faster, and more reliable information than manual accounting systems. Software is inexpensive for small businesses and user-friendly. Having continuous access to financial information is essential for not-for-profit organizations like Bryony House, where resources are limited and must be monitored carefully.
3. While the percentage of enterprises that use manual systems is declining, it will probably always make sense for certain companies to use manual systems. For many start-up businesses, or organizations with few transactions, the advantages of installing a computerized system do not outweigh the costs.
4. (a) The costs of upgrading for an entity such as Bryony House include the cash outlay that is required to upgrade both the hardware and the software and to provide for any required training. Because this cash is also needed elsewhere (e.g., to improve the shelter's services to women), these alternative uses of limited resources must be carefully assessed by not-for-profit organizations.

THE NAVIGATOR

(b) The advantages of upgrading could include improved speed, accuracy, and availability of financial information that would facilitate control and monitoring of the budget, financial position, funding needs, etc. As mentioned in the opening story, an upgrade may also free up staff to perform other essential duties.

DEMONSTRATION PROBLEM

Additional Demonstration Problem

Emelia Company uses a five-column cash receipts journal with the following columns: Cash (Dr.), Accounts Receivable (Cr.), Sales (Cr.), Cost of Goods Sold (Dr.)/Merchandise Inventory (Cr.), and Other Accounts (Cr.). Cash receipts transactions for the month of July 2003 are as follows:

July 3 An amount of $5,800 is borrowed from the Bank of Nova Scotia, signing a short-term note payable.

5 A cheque for $6,370 is received from the Jeltz Company in payment of an invoice dated June 6.

9 An additional investment of $5,000 in cash is made in the business by Betty Emelia, the proprietor.

10 Cash sales totalling $12,519 are recorded. The cost of these sales was $7,511.

12 A cheque for $7,275 is received from R. Eliot & Co. in payment of an invoice dated June 13.

15 A customer advance of $700 cash is received for future sales.

20 Cash sales totalling $15,472 are recorded. The cost of these sales was $9,283.

22 A cheque for $6,000 is received from Beck Company in payment of an invoice dated July 3.

29 Cash sales totalling $17,660 are recorded. The cost of these sales was $10,596.

31 Cash of $200 is received for interest earned during July.

Instructions

(a) Journalize the transactions in the cash receipts journal.

(b) Contrast the posting of the Accounts Receivable and Other Accounts columns.

Solution to Demonstration Problem

Action Plan

- Record all cash receipts in the Cash Receipts Journal.
- Use the Account Credited column for any item which must be posted individually, to either the general ledger or a subsidiary ledger.
- Total debits must equal total credits. The column totals should be added across to ensure that the debits and credits are equal, before any postings are made.

(a)

EMELIA COMPANY
Cash Receipts Journal

CR1

Date	Account Credited	Ref.	Cash Dr.	Accounts Receivable Cr.	Sales Cr.	Cost of Goods Sold Dr. Merchandise Inventory Cr.	Other Accounts Cr.
2003							
July 3	Notes Payable		5,800				5,800
5	Jeltz Company		6,370	6,370			
9	Betty Emelia, Capital		5,000				5,000
10			12,519		12,519	7,511	
12	R. Eliot & Co.		7,275	7,275			
15	Unearned Revenues		700				700
20			15,472		15,472	9,283	
22	Beck Company		6,000	6,000			
29			17,660		17,660	10,596	
31	Interest Revenue		200				200
			76,996	19,645	45,651	27,390	11,700

(b) The Accounts Receivable column total is posted as a credit to the Accounts Receivable control account in the general ledger. The individual amounts are credited to the customers' accounts identified in the Account Credited column. These are maintained in the accounts receivable subsidiary ledger.

The amounts in the Other Accounts column are posted only individually. They are credited to the account titles identified in the Account Credited column.

THE NAVIGATOR

APPENDIX 7A ► *Special Journals in a Periodic Inventory System*

Recording transactions in special journals is essentially the same whether a perpetual or a periodic inventory system is used. Two differences result. The first difference relates to the Merchandise Inventory and Cost of Goods Sold accounts found in a perpetual inventory system. In this system, an additional column is required to record the cost of each sale in the sales and cash receipts journals which is not required in a periodic inventory system. The second difference concerns the account titles used. In a perpetual inventory system, the Merchandise Inventory and Cost of Goods Sold accounts are used to record purchases and the cost of the merchandise sold. In a periodic inventory system, the Purchases and Freight In accounts accumulate the cost of the merchandise purchased until the end of the period. No cost of goods sold is recorded during the period. Cost of goods sold is determined by calculation at the end of the period in a periodic inventory system.

Each of the special journals illustrated in the chapter is shown again in this appendix. Using the same transactions, we assume that Karns Wholesale Supply uses a periodic inventory system instead of a perpetual inventory system.

STUDY OBJECTIVE
6

Demonstrate how special journals are used in a periodic inventory system.

KARNS WHOLESALE SUPPLY
Sales Journal
S1

Date	Account Debited	Invoice No.	Ref.	Accts. Receivable Dr. Sales Cr.
2002				
May 3	Abbot Sisters	101	√	10,600
7	Babson Co.	102	√	11,350
14	Carson Bros.	103	√	7,800
19	Deli Co.	104	√	9,300
21	Abbot Sisters	105	√	15,400
24	Deli Co.	106	√	21,210
27	Babson Co.	107	√	14,570
				90,230

Illustration 7A-1

Sales journal—periodic inventory system

Helpful hint Compare this sales journal to the one presented in Illustration 7-7.

KARNS WHOLESALE SUPPLY
Cash Receipts Journal
CR1

Date	Account Credited	Ref.	Cash Dr.	Accounts Receivable Cr.	Sales Cr.	Other Accounts Cr.
2002						
May 1	D. A. Karns, Capital	301	5,000			5,000
7			1,900		1,900	
10	Abbot Sisters	√	10,600	10,600		
12			2,600		2,600	
17	Babson Co.	√	11,350	11,350		
22	Notes Payable	200	6,000			6,000
23	Carson Bros.	√	7,800	7,800		
28	Deli Co.	√	9,300	9,300		
			54,550	39,050	4,500	11,000

Illustration 7A-2

Cash receipts journal—periodic inventory system

Helpful hint Compare this cash receipts journal to the one presented in Illustration 7-9.

Illustration 7A-3

Purchases journal—periodic inventory system

Helpful hint   Compare this purchases journal to the one presented in Illustration 7-12.

	KARNS WHOLESALE SUPPLY				
	Purchases Journal				P1
Date	Account Credited	Terms	Ref.	Purchases Dr. Accounts Payable Cr.	
2002					
May 6	Jasper Manufacturing Inc.	n/20	√	11,000	
10	Eaton and Howe, Inc.	n/20	√	7,200	
14	Fabor and Son	n/20	√	6,900	
19	Jasper Manufacturing Inc.	n/20	√	17,500	
26	Fabor and Son	n/20	√	8,700	
28	Eaton and Howe, Inc.	n/20	√	12,600	
				63,900	

Illustration 7A-4

Cash payments journal—periodic inventory system

Helpful hint   Compare this cash payments journal to the one presented in Illustration 7-15.

		KARNS WHOLESALE SUPPLY						
		Cash Payments Journal						CP1
Date	Cheque No.	Payee	Cash Cr.	Accounts Payable Dr.	Account Debited	Ref.	Other Accounts Dr.	
2002								
May 3	101	Corporate General Ins.	1,200		Prepaid Insurance	130	1,200	
3	102	CANPAR	100		Freight In	516	100	
7	103	Zwicker Corp.	4,400		Purchases	510	4,400	
10	104	Jasper Manufacturing Inc.	11,000	11,000	Jasper Manuf. Inc.	√		
19	105	Eaton & Howe, Inc.	7,200	7,200	Eaton & Howe, Inc.	√		
24	106	Fabor and Son	6,900	6,900	Fabor and Son	√		
28	107	Jasper Manufacturing Inc.	17,500	17,500	Jasper Manuf. Inc.	√		
31	108	D. A. Karns	500		D. A. Karns, Drawings	306	500	
			48,800	42,600			6,200	

Before You Go On . . .

▸Review It

THE NAVIGATOR

1. Explain how special journals differ when a periodic inventory system is used, rather than a perpetual one.

Related exercise material: *BE7–10, *E7–12, and *E7–13.

*A*PPENDIX 7B ▸ *Sales Taxes*

We learned in Chapter 5 that accounting for sales taxes can be complicated. At this point in your studies, however, you simply need to know that if PST and GST (or HST) columns are required in a special journal, they are easily added to multi-column journals.

Adding Sales Tax Columns to Special Journals

We will continue to use the transactions for Karns Wholesale Supply presented earlier in the chapter. We will assume here that Karns is using a perpetual inventory system. If Karns uses a periodic inventory system, as described in Appendix 7A, sales tax would be recorded in the same manner. The only difference is in the account titles and columns used to record merchandise inventory.

If 7% GST and 8% PST had been added to the taxable transactions described earlier in the chapter, selected extracts from the sales, cash receipts, purchases, and cash payments journals would show the information presented in Illustration 7B-1.

KARNS WHOLESALE SUPPLY
Sales Journal SI

Date	Account Debited	Invoice No.	Ref.	Accounts Receivable Dr.	Sales Cr.	GST Payable Cr.	PST Payable Cr.	Cost of Goods Sold Dr. Merchandise Inventory Cr.
2002 May 3	Abbot Sisters	101	√	12,190	10,600	742	848	6,360

KARNS WHOLESALE SUPPLY
Cash Receipts Journal CR1

Date	Account Credited	Ref.	Cash Dr.	Accounts Receivable Cr.	Sales Cr.	GST Payable Cr.	PST Payable Cr.	Cost of Goods Sold Dr. Merchandise Inventory Cr.	Other Accts. Cr.
2002 May 1	D.A. Karns, Capital	301	5,000						5,000
7			2,185		1,900	133	152	1,240	
10	Abbot Sisters	√	12,190	12,910					

KARNS WHOLESALE SUPPLY
Purchases Journal PI

Date	Account Credited	Terms	Ref.	Merchandise Inventory Dr.	GST Recoverable Dr.	Accounts Payable Cr.
2002 May 6	Jasper Manufacturing Inc.	n/20	√	11,000	770	11,770

KARNS WHOLESALE SUPPLY
Cash Payments Journal CP1

Date	Chq. No.	Payee	Cash Cr.	Merchandise Inventory Dr.	Accounts Payable Dr.	GST Recoverable Dr.	Account Debited	Ref.	Other Accts. Dr.
2002 May 3	101	Corporate General Ins.	1,200				Prepaid Insurance	130	1,200
3	102	CANPAR	115	108		7			
7	103	Zwicker Corp.	4,708	4,400		308			
10	104	Jasper Manufacturing Inc.	11,770		11,770		Jasper Manufacturing Inc.	√	

You might find it helpful to compare these journals with sales taxes to their counterparts in Illustrations 7-7, 7-9, 7-12, and 7-15, which do not include sales taxes.

Sales Journal

Most companies have a GST Payable column in their sales journals to record GST due on credit sales. In accordance with the accrual basis of accounting, GST is recorded at the point of sale, not at the later collection of the receivable. A PST Payable column is also normally added to record the PST due on credit sales. Note that separate columns are required for Accounts Receivable and Sales since the amounts are different because of the sales taxes.

Cash Receipts Journal

The cash receipts journal also uses GST and PST Payable columns. GST and PST collected on cash sales (see May 7 entry) are each recorded in their respective column: GST Payable or PST Payable. Note that GST and PST are not recorded again on later collections of accounts receivable, such as the collection from Abbot Sisters on May 10. The receipt of the $12,190 on May 10 includes the collection of both the sales amount owing ($10,600) and the sales taxes ($742 + $848) that were recorded at the point of sale, on May 3.

Purchases Journal

The purchases journal normally includes a GST Recoverable column. GST is charged at each stage of a business transaction. As discussed in the appendix to Chapter 5, when merchandise is purchased, **the GST paid by a business is not part of the inventory cost**. The GST paid is recoverable as an input tax credit. Therefore, GST paid on taxable purchases is debited to an account called GST Recoverable.

In contrast, PST is only charged to the final consumer, so retail businesses do not pay provincial sales taxes on purchases for resale. Therefore, no PST column is required.

Cash Payments Journal

The cash payments journal includes a column for GST Recoverable on any GST paid on merchandise purchases. The GST Recoverable account is offset against the GST Payable account at the end of each period. The net difference is paid to, or recovered from, the federal government.

No PST column appears in this journal. Recall that no PST is due on purchases. Therefore, the May 7 purchase from Zwicker Corp. includes only GST. PST paid on operating expenses is not recoverable. It becomes part of the cost and is absorbed into the expense account. Note that the May 3 freight charge of $100 results in a $108 ($100 + $8 PST) charge to Merchandise Inventory.

The posting procedures for the special journals remain unchanged. Individual amounts in control account columns (e.g., Accounts Receivable, Accounts Payable) are posted daily to their respective subsidiary ledger. At the end of the month, all column totals are posted to their respective general ledger accounts with the exception of the Other Accounts column. Individual amounts in this column are posted daily to their respective general ledger account.

Before You Go On . . .

▸*Review It*

THE
NAVIGATOR

1. Explain how PST and GST are added to each of the sales, cash receipts, purchases, and cash payments journals.

Related exercise material: *BE7–11, *E7–14, and *E7–15.

Summary of Study Objectives

1. *Identify and explain the basic principles of accounting information systems.* The basic principles in developing an accounting information system are cost-effectiveness, usefulness, and flexibility.

2. *Explain the major phases involved in the development of an accounting system.* The major phases in the development of an accounting system are analysis, design, implementation, and follow-up.

3. *Describe the nature and purpose of a subsidiary ledger, and determine ledger balances.* A subsidiary ledger is a group of accounts that share a common characteristic. It facilitates the recording process by freeing the general ledger from details of individual balances.

4. *Illustrate how special journals are used in a perpetual inventory system.* A special journal is used to group similar types of transactions. In a special journal, only one line is used to record a complete transaction.

5. *Demonstrate how a multi-column journal is posted.* In posting a multi-column journal:
(a) All column totals are posted once at the end of the month to the account title specified in the column heading.
(b) If an Other Accounts column is present, its total is not posted. Instead, the individual amounts that make up the total are posted separately to the general ledger

accounts specified in the Accounts column.
(c) The individual amounts in a column are posted in total to a control account and are posted daily to the subsidiary ledger accounts specified in the Account Debited or Credited column.

6. *Demonstrate how special journals are used in a periodic inventory system (Appendix 7A).* Journalizing in special journals is similar in perpetual and periodic inventory systems. The difference relates to the number of columns required in each journal, and the merchandise inventory accounts used. Sales and cash receipts journals in a perpetual inventory system require an additional column to record cost of goods sold and the reduction in merchandise inventory. These columns are not required in a periodic inventory system. Debits are made to Purchases (and Freight In) rather than to Merchandise Inventory in the purchases and cash payments journals in a periodic inventory system.

7. *Describe and demonstrate how sales tax transactions are recorded in special journals (Appendix 7B).* One additional column (or more) is added to the sales and cash receipts journals as necessary to account for GST Payable and PST Payable (or HST Payable). This column is also added to the purchases and cash payment journals to account for GST (or HST) Recoverable.

THE NAVIGATOR

GLOSSARY

 Key Term Matching Activity

Accounting information system A system that involves collecting and processing transaction data, and providing financial information to interested parties. (p. 322)

Accounts payable ledger A subsidiary ledger that contains accounts for each individual creditor. (p. 325)

Accounts receivable ledger A subsidiary ledger that contains individual customer accounts. (p. 325)

Cash payments journal A special journal used to record all cash paid. (p. 337)

Cash receipts journal A special journal used to record all cash received. (p. 332)

Control account An account in the general ledger that summarizes the detail for a subsidiary ledger and controls it. (p. 325)

Manual accounting system A system in which each of the steps in the accounting cycle is performed by hand. (p. 324)

Purchases journal A special journal used to record all purchases of merchandise on account. (p. 335)

Sales journal A special journal used to record all sales of merchandise on account. (p. 329)

Special journal A journal that is used to record similar types of transactions such as all credit sales. (p. 328)

Subsidiary ledger A group of accounts that provides details of a control account in the general ledger. (p. 325)

Note: All **asterisked** Questions, Exercises, and Problems below relate to material contained in the appendices to the chapter.

SELF-STUDY QUESTIONS

Chapter 7 Self-Test

Answers are at the end of the chapter.

(SO 1) K   1. The basic principles of an accounting information system include all of the following except:
    a. cost-effectiveness.
    b. flexibility.
    c. usefulness of output.
    d. periodicity.

(SO 2) K   2. Which of the following is not a major phase in the development of an accounting information system?
    a. Design
    b. Response
    c. Implementation
    d. Follow-up

(SO 3) K   3. Which of the following is *incorrect* concerning subsidiary ledgers?
    a. The purchases ledger is a common subsidiary ledger for creditor accounts.
    b. The accounts receivable ledger is a subsidiary ledger.
    c. A subsidiary ledger is a group of accounts with a common characteristic.
    d. An advantage of the subsidiary ledger is that it permits a division of labour in posting.

(SO 4) K   4. A sales journal will be used for:

	Credit sales	Cash sales	Sales returns and allowances
a.	no	yes	yes
b.	yes	no	yes
c.	yes	no	no
d.	yes	yes	no

(SO 4) K   5. Which of the following statements is correct?
    a. A Sales Cr. column is included in the cash receipts journal.
    b. The purchases journal records all purchases of merchandise, whether for cash or on account.
    c. The cash receipts journal records sales on account.
    d. Merchandise returned by the buyer is recorded by the seller in the purchases journal.

(SO 4) K   6. When special journals are used:
    a. all purchase transactions, whether for cash or on account, are recorded in the purchases journal.
    b. all cash received, except from cash sales, is recorded in the cash receipts journal.
    c. all cheques issued are recorded in the cash payments journal.
    d. a general journal is not necessary.

(SO 4) K   7. If a customer returns goods for credit, an entry is normally made in the:
    a. cash payments journal.
    b. sales journal.
    c. general journal.
    d. cash receipts journal.

8. Which of the following is *incorrect* concerning the   (SO 5) K
posting of the cash receipts journal?
    a. The total of the Other Accounts column is not posted.
    b. All column totals except the total for the Other Accounts column are posted once, at the end of the month, to the account title specified in the column heading.
    c. The totals of all columns are posted daily to the accounts specified in the column heading.
    d. The individual amounts in a column that are posted in total to a control account are posted daily to the subsidiary ledger account specified in the Account Credited column.

9. Postings from the purchases journal to the subsidiary   (SO 5) K
ledger are generally made:
    a. yearly.
    b. monthly.
    c. weekly.
    d. daily.

10. Which statement is *incorrect* regarding the general   (SO 4, 5) K
journal?
    a. Only transactions that cannot be entered in a special journal are recorded in the general journal.
    b. Dual postings are always required in the general journal.
    c. The general journal may be used to record acceptance of a note receivable in payment of an account receivable.
    d. Correcting, adjusting, and closing entries are made in the general journal.

*11. In a periodic inventory system, the sales journal: (SO 6) K
    a. is the same as in the perpetual inventory system.
    b. has one additional column to record the debit to Cost of Goods Sold and credit to Merchandise Inventory.
    c. has one additional column to record the freight.
    d. has only one column to record the debit to Accounts Receivable and credit to Sales.

*12. When GST and PST are recorded in special journals   (SO 7) K
in a perpetual inventory system, the sales journal:
    a. is a one-column journal, with one column for Accounts Receivable and Sales.
    b. is a two-column journal, with one column for Accounts Receivable/Sales and the second for Cost of Goods Sold/Merchandise Inventory.
    c. is a three-column journal, with columns for Accounts Receivable, Sales, and Sales Taxes Payable.
    d. is a five-column journal, with columns for Accounts Receivable, Sales, GST Payable, PST Payable, and Cost of Goods Sold/Merchandise Inventory.

QUESTIONS

(SO 1) K 1. What is an accounting information system?

(SO 1) C 2. Certain principles should be followed in the development of an accounting information system. Identify and explain each of the principles.

(SO 1) C 3. Khelil Company is thinking about changing its accounting system for accounts receivable billing. At present, the procedure is performed manually by three clerks. A consultant has recommended that a new computer and related software be purchased for $1,000,000. What basic principle of designing and developing an effective accounting system might be violated by this proposal?

(SO 2) C 4. There are four phases in the development of an accounting system. Identify and briefly explain each phase.

(SO 3) K 5. What are the advantages of using subsidiary ledgers?

(SO 3) C 6. (a) When are postings normally made to: (1) the subsidiary accounts, and (2) the general ledger control accounts?

(b) Describe the relationship between a control account and a subsidiary ledger.

(SO 4) C 7. Identify and explain the four special journals discussed in the chapter. List an advantage of using each of these journals, rather than using only a general journal.

(SO 4) C 8. Mega Company uses special journals. A sale made on account to K. Askanas for $435 was recorded in a sales journal. A few days later, Askanas returned $70 worth of merchandise for credit. The returned goods had an original cost of $45. Where should Mega Company record the sales return? Why?

(SO 4) C 9. Why would special journals used in different businesses not be identical in format? Can you think of a business that would maintain a cash receipts journal but not include a column for accounts receivable?

(SO 4) K 10. In what journal would the following transactions be recorded?
(a) Recording amortization expense for the year
(b) Issuing a credit memo to a customer for merchandise purchased on credit and returned
(c) Sales of merchandise for cash
(d) Sales of merchandise on account
(e) Collection of cash on account from a customer
(f) Purchase of merchandise for cash

(SO 4) K 11. In what journal would the following transactions be recorded?
(a) Cash received from signing a note payable
(b) Investment of cash by the owner of the business
(c) Closing of the accounts at the end of the year
(d) Purchase of merchandise on account
(e) Credit received for merchandise purchased and returned to a supplier
(f) Payment of cash on account due a supplier

(SO 4) K 12. What transactions might be included in a multi-column purchases journal that would not be included in a single-column purchases journal?

(SO 4) C 13. Give some examples of general journal transactions for an organization using special journals.

(SO 5) C 14. A $400 purchase of merchandise on account from McKay Company was properly recorded in the purchases journal. When posted, however, the amount recorded in the accounts payable subsidiary ledger was $40. How might this error be discovered?

(SO 5) C 15. The cash and accounts receivable columns in the cash receipts journal were mistakenly overadded by $4,000 at the end of the month. (a) Will the customers' subsidiary ledger agree with the Accounts Receivable control account? (b) Assuming no other errors, will the trial balance totals be equal?

(SO 5) C 16. Give an example of a transaction in the general journal that causes an entry to be posted twice (i.e., to two accounts), once in the general ledger, and once in the subsidiary ledger. Does this affect the debit/credit equality of the general ledger?

(SO 5) K 17. One-column totals are posted at month end to two general ledger accounts in some special journals. To which general ledger accounts is the same month-end total posted and from which special journals?

(SO 6) C *18. Explain the differences in the multi-column format of special journals used in a perpetual inventory system and a periodic inventory system.

(SO 7) C *19. Explain how recording sales taxes affects the format of special journals.

BRIEF EXERCISES

BE7–1 Indicate whether each of the following statements is true or false:
1. When designing an accounting system, we need to think about the needs and knowledge of both management and various other users.
2. When the environment changes as a result of technological advances, increased competition, or government regulation, an accounting system does not have to be flexible to meet the changes.
3. In developing an accounting system, cost is relevant. The system must be cost-effective. That is, the benefits obtained from the information that is produced must outweigh the cost of providing it.

Identify basic principles of accounting information system development.
(SO 1) K

Identify major phases in accounting system development.
(SO 2) K

BE7–2 The development of an accounting system involves four phases: analysis, design, implementation, and follow-up. Identify the phase that each statement best describes.
1. Determining internal and external information needs, identifying information sources and the need for controls, and studying alternatives.
2. Evaluation and monitoring of effectiveness and efficiency, and correction of weaknesses.
3. Creation of forms and documents, selection of procedures, and preparation of job descriptions.
4. Introducing new or revised documents, procedures, reports, and processing equipment. Hiring and training personnel through a start-up or transition period.

Calculate subsidiary ledger and control account balances.
(SO 3) AP

BE7–3 Information related to Bryan Company is presented below for its first month of operations. Calculate (a) the balances that appear in the accounts receivable subsidiary ledger for each customer, and (b) the accounts receivable balance that appears in the general ledger at the end of January.

Credit Sales			Cash Collections		
Jan. 7	Avon Co.	$8,000	Jan. 17	Avon Co.	$7,000
15	Barto Inc.	6,000	24	Barto Inc.	5,000
23	Cecil Co.	9,000	29	Cecil Co.	9,000

Identify general and subsidiary ledger accounts.
(SO 3) K

BE7–4 Identify in what ledger (general or subsidiary) each of the following accounts is shown:
1. Rent Expense
2. Accounts Receivable—O'Malley
3. Notes Payable
4. Accounts Payable—Kerns
5. Merchandise Inventory
6. Sales

Identify special journals.
(SO 4) K

BE7–5 Identify the journal in which each of the following transactions is recorded:
1. Cash sales
2. Owner withdrawal of cash
3. Cash purchase of land
4. Credit sales
5. Purchase of merchandise on account
6. Receipt of cash for services performed

Identify entries to cash receipts journal.
(SO 4) K

BE7–6 Indicate whether each of the following debits and credits is included in the cash receipts journal. Assume a perpetual inventory system is used. (Use "Yes" or "No" to answer this question.)
1. Debit to Sales
2. Debit to Cost of Goods Sold and credit to Merchandise Inventory
3. Credit to Accounts Receivable
4. Debit to Accounts Payable

Identify special journals.
(SO 4) K

BE7–7 Chiasson Co. uses special journals and a general journal. Identify the journal in which each of the following transactions is recorded:
1. Disbursed cash for equipment purchased on account.
2. Purchased merchandise on credit.
3. Paid utility expense in cash.
4. Sold merchandise on account.
5. Granted cash refund for a sales return.
6. Received a credit on account for a purchase return.

Identify special journals.
(SO 4) K

BE7–8 Identify the special journal(s) in which the following column headings appear. Assume a perpetual inventory system is used.
1. Accounts Receivable Cr.
2. Cash Dr.
3. Sales Cr.
4. Merchandise Inventory Dr./ Accounts Payable Cr.
5. Cost of Goods Sold Dr./ Merchandise Inventory Cr.
6. Cash Cr.
7. Accounts Payable Dr.
8. Merchandise Inventory Dr.

Indicate postings for cash receipts journal.
(SO 5) K

BE7–9 Khalil Computer Components uses a multi-column cash receipts journal. For each column below, indicate whether it is posted only in total, only daily, or both in total and daily:
1. Cash
2. Accounts Receivable
3. Sales
4. Cost of Goods Sold/Merchandise Inventory
5. Other Accounts

Identify special journals in a periodic inventory system.
(SO 6) K

***BE7–10** Identify the journal and the specific column title(s) in which each of the following transactions is recorded. Assume the company uses a periodic inventory system.
1. Cash sales
2. Credit sales

3. Sales return on account
4. Cash purchase of merchandise
5. Credit purchase of merchandise
6. Payment of freight on merchandise purchased from a supplier
7. Return of merchandise purchased for cash refund
8. Payment of freight on merchandise delivered to a customer

BE7–11 Identify the special journal and the specific column title(s) in which each of the following transactions is recorded. Assume the company uses a perpetual inventory system.

1. Cash sale, plus GST and PST
2. Credit sale, plus GST and PST
3. Cash purchase of merchandise, plus GST
4. Cash payment for office supplies, plus GST and PST
5. Collection of rent revenue, plus GST
6. Purchase of a piece of office equipment, plus GST

Identify special journals, with sales taxes.
(SO 7) K

EXERCISES

E7–1 Selected accounts from the ledgers of Tasi Company at July 31 showed the following. Tasi uses a perpetual inventory system.

Prepare purchases and general journals.
(SO 3, 4) AP

GENERAL LEDGER

Merchandise Inventory — No. 120

Date	Explanation	Ref.	Debit	Credit	Balance
July 15		J1	400		400
18		J1		100	300
25		J1		200	100
31		P1	8,700		8,800

Accounts Payable — No. 201

Date	Explanation	Ref.	Debit	Credit	Balance
July 1		J1		3,900	3,900
15		J1		400	4,300
18		J1	100		4,200
25		J1	200		4,000
31		P1		8,700	12,700

Store Equipment — No. 153

Date	Explanation	Ref.	Debit	Credit	Balance
July 1		J1	3,900		3,900

ACCOUNTS PAYABLE LEDGER

Andrew Equipment Co.

Date	Explanation	Ref.	Debit	Credit	Balance
July 1		J1		3,900	3,900

Bradley Co.

Date	Explanation	Ref.	Debit	Credit	Balance
July 3		P1		2,000	2,000
20		P1		700	2,700

David Co.

Date	Explanation	Ref.	Debit	Credit	Balance
July 14		P1		1,100	1,100
25		J1	200		900

Erick Co.

Date	Explanation	Ref.	Debit	Credit	Balance
July 12		P1		500	500
21		P1		600	1,100

Craig Materials

Date	Explanation	Ref.	Debit	Credit	Balance
July 17		P1		1,400	1,400
18		J1	100		1,300
21		P1		2,400	3,700

Transit Co.

Date	Explanation	Ref.	Debit	Credit	Balance
July 15		J1		400	400

Instructions

From the data, prepare (a) the purchases journal for July and (b) the general journal entries for July.

Indicate journalizing in special journals.
(SO 4) K

E7–2   Below are some typical transactions for Dartmouth Company:
  1. Payment of creditors on account
  2. Return of merchandise sold for credit
  3. Collection on account from customers
  4. Sale of land for cash
  5. Sale of merchandise on account
  6. Sale of merchandise for cash
  7. Received credit for merchandise returned to a supplier
  8. Payment of employee wages
  9. Revenues and expenses closed to owner's capital
  10. Amortization on building
  11. Purchase of office supplies for cash
  12. Purchase of merchandise on account

Instructions

For each transaction, indicate whether it would normally be recorded in a cash receipts journal, cash payments journal, sales journal, purchases journal, or general journal.

Indicate journalizing in special journals.
(SO 4) K

E7–3   Swirsky Company uses the columnar cash receipts and cash payments journals illustrated in this chapter for a perpetual inventory system. In April, the following selected cash transactions occurred:
  1. Made a refund to a customer for the return of damaged goods.
  2. Received payment from a customer.
  3. Purchased merchandise for cash.
  4. Paid a creditor.
  5. Paid freight on merchandise purchased.
  6. Paid cash for office equipment.
  7. Received cash refund from a supplier for merchandise returned.
  8. Withdrew cash for personal use of owner.
  9. Made cash sales.

Instructions

Indicate (a) the journal, and (b) the columns in the journal that should be used in recording each transaction.

Record transactions in sales and purchases journals.
(SO 4) AP

E7–4   Pitblado Company uses special journals and a general journal. The company uses a perpetual inventory system and had the following transactions:

Sept. 2 Sold merchandise on account to H. Bansal, $600, invoice #101, terms n/30. The cost of the merchandise sold was $360.
   10 Purchased merchandise on account from Miramichi Company, $700, FOB shipping point, terms n/30. Paid freight of $50 to Apex Shippers.
   11 Returned unsatisfactory merchandise to Miramichi Company, $200, for credit on account.
   12 Purchased office equipment on account from Wells Company, $8,000.
   16 Sold merchandise for cash to L. Maillette, for $800. The cost of the merchandise sold was $480.
   18 Purchased merchandise for cash from Miramichi Company, $450, FOB destination.
   20 Accepted returned merchandise from customer L. Maillette, $800 (see Sept. 16 transaction). Gave full cash refund. Restored the merchandise to inventory.

Instructions

(a) Draw a sales journal and a purchases journal (see Illustrations 7-6 and 7-12). Use page 1 for each journal.
(b) Record the transaction(s) for September that should be journalized in the sales journal.
(c) Record the transaction(s) for September that should be journalized in the purchases journal.

Record transactions in cash receipts, cash payments, and general journals.
(SO 4) AP

E7–5   Refer to the information provided for Pitblado Company in E7–4.

Instructions

(a) Draw cash receipts and cash payments journals (see Illustrations 7-9 and 7-15) and a general journal. Use page 1 for each journal.
(b) Record the transaction(s) provided in E7–4 that should be journalized in the cash receipts journal.
(c) Record the transaction(s) provided in E7–4 that should be journalized in the cash payments journal.
(d) Record the transaction(s) provided in E7–4 that should be journalized in the general journal.

E7–6 Yu Company has the following selected transactions during March:

Journalize transactions in general journal, and explain posting.
(SO 3, 4, 5) S

Mar. 2 Purchased equipment on account, costing $6,000, from Lifetime Company.

5 Received credit memorandum for $300 from Lynch Company for merchandise returned that had been damaged in shipment to Yu.

7 Issued a credit memorandum for $400 to Marco Presti for merchandise the customer returned. The returned merchandise has a cost of $260 and was restored to inventory.

Yu Company uses a purchases journal, a sales journal, two cash (receipts and payments) journals, and a general journal. Yu also uses a perpetual inventory system.

Instructions

(a) Journalize the appropriate transactions in the general journal.

(b) In a brief memo to the president of Yu Company, explain the postings to the control and subsidiary accounts.

E7–7 Yan Company uses both special journals and a general journal. On June 30, after all monthly postings had been completed, the Accounts Receivable controlling account in the general ledger had a debit balance of $320,000, and the Accounts Payable controlling account had a credit balance of $97,000.

Determine control account balances and explain posting of special journals.
(SO 3, 5) AP

The July transactions recorded in the special journals are summarized below. Yan Company maintains a perpetual inventory system. No entries that affected accounts receivable and accounts payable were recorded in the general journal for July.

Sales journal: total sales, $161,400; cost of goods sold, $112,800
Purchases journal: total purchases, $54,360
Cash receipts journal: accounts receivable column total, $141,000
Cash payments journal: accounts payable column total, $47,500

Instructions

(a) What is the balance of the Accounts Receivable control account after the monthly postings on July 31?

(b) What is the balance of the Accounts Payable control account after the monthly postings on July 31?

(c) To what accounts are the column totals for total sales of $161,400 and cost of goods sold of $112,800 in the sales journal posted?

(d) To what account(s) is the accounts receivable column total of $141,000 in the cash receipts journal posted?

E7–8 On September 1, 2003, the balance of the Accounts Receivable controlling account in the general ledger of Pirie Company was $10,960. The customers' subsidiary ledger contained account balances as follows: Bannister, $1,440; Crowley, $2,640; Dotson, $2,060; Seaver, $4,820. At the end of September, the various journals contained the following information:

Post various journals to control and subsidiary accounts.
(SO 3, 5) AP

Sales journal: Sales to Seaver, $1,800; to Bannister, $1,350; to DeLeon, $1,030; to Dotson, $1,100. The cost of each sale, respectively, was $1,080, $810, $620, and $660.

Cash receipts journal: Cash received from Dotson, $1,310; from Seaver, $2,300; from DeLeon, $410; from Crowley, $1,800; from Bannister, $1,240.

General journal: A sales allowance is granted to Seaver, $120, on September 30.

Instructions

(a) Set up control and subsidiary accounts, and enter the beginning balances.

(b) Post the various journals to the control and subsidiary accounts. Post the items as individual items or as totals, whichever would be the appropriate procedure. Use page 1 for each journal.

(c) Prepare a list of customers and prove the agreement of the controlling account with the subsidiary ledger at September 30, 2003.

E7–9 The general ledger of the Abekah Company contained the following Accounts Payable control account (in T account form). Also shown is the related subsidiary ledger.

Explain posting to control account and subsidiary ledger.
(SO 3, 5) AN

GENERAL LEDGER

Accounts Payable

Feb. 15	J3	1,200	Feb. 1	Balance	26,025
28	?	?	5	J2	265
			11	J3	550
			28	P5	13,900
			Feb. 28	Balance	9,840

Accounts Payable Subsidiary Ledger

Patee		Wagner	
	Feb. 28 Bal. 4,600		Feb. 28 Bal. ?

Gruber	
	Feb. 28 Bal. 3,000

Instructions

(a) Indicate (1) the missing posting reference and amount in the Accounts Payable control account, and (2) the missing ending balance for the Wagner account in the subsidiary ledger.

(b) Indicate the amounts in the control account that were dual-posted (i.e., posted to the control account and the subsidiary accounts).

Determine correct posting amount to control account.
(SO 3, 5) AP

E7–10   Kai Products uses both special journals and a general journal. Kai also posts customers' accounts in the accounts receivable subsidiary ledger. The postings for the most recent month are included in the subsidiary T accounts below:

Nokuoru			Roemer		
Bal.	340	250	Bal.	150	150
	200			190	

Schulz			Park		
Bal.	0	145	Bal.	120	120
	145			190	
				170	

Instructions

(a) Determine the correct amount for the end-of-month posting from the sales journal to the Accounts Receivable control account.

(b) Determine the correct amount for the end-of-month posting from the cash receipts journal to the Accounts Receivable control account.

Explain postings in subsidiary ledger.
(SO 5) S

E7–11   René Vermette's subsidiary accounts receivable account is presented below:

Date	Ref.	Debit	Credit	Balance
2003				
Sept. 2	S31	61,000		61,000
9	J4		12,000	49,000
27	CR8		49,000	0

Instructions

Write a brief memo that explains each transaction.

Record transactions in sales and purchases journals, in a periodic inventory system.
(SO 6) AP

*E7–12   Refer to the information provided for Pitblado Company in E7–4. Complete instructions (a), (b), and (c), assuming that the company uses a periodic inventory system instead of a perpetual inventory system.

Record transactions in cash receipts, cash payments, and general journals, in a periodic inventory system.
(SO 6) AP

*E7–13   Refer to the information provided for Pitblado Company in E7–5. Complete instructions (a)–(d), assuming that the company uses a periodic inventory system instead of a perpetual inventory system.

Record transactions (including sales taxes) in sales and purchases journals.
(SO 4, 7) AP

*E7–14   Rouse Company uses special journals and a general journal. The following transactions occurred during September. Rouse uses a perpetual inventory system.

Sept. 2   Sold merchandise on account to B. Vell, invoice no. 101, $600, terms n/30. The cost of the sale was $400.

10   Purchased merchandise on account from Cosgrove Company, $700, n/30.

12   Purchased office equipment on account from Wells Suppliers, $6,500.

21   Sold merchandise on account to L. Scott, invoice no. 102, for $800, n/30. The cost of the sale was $500.

25   Purchased merchandise on account from Lewis Crafters, $900, terms n/30.

27   Sold merchandise to R. Cowan for $700 cash. The cost of the sale was $450.

GST of 7% and PST of 7% are to be added to all sales and purchases, except purchases of merchandise for resale—which are exempt from PST.

Instructions

(a) Draw a sales journal and a purchases journal (see Illustration 7B-1). Use page 1 for each journal.

(b) Record the transaction(s) for September that should be journalized in the sales journal.

(c) Record the transaction(s) for September that should be journalized in the purchases journal.

*E7–15 Leahy Enterprises uses special journals and a general journal. The following transactions occurred during May. Leahy uses a perpetual inventory system.

> May 1 L. Leahy invested $72,000 additional cash in the business.
>
> 2 Sold merchandise to L. Bean for $6,000 cash, plus GST of $420 and PST of $480. The cost of the sale was $5,000.
>
> 3 Purchased merchandise for $8,000, plus GST of $560, from Sanchez Solids using cheque No. 101.
>
> 14 Paid salary of $700 to F. Sparks by issuing cheque no. 102.
>
> 16 Sold merchandise on account to B. Ready for $900, plus GST of $63 and PST of $72, terms n/30. The cost of the sale was $700.
>
> 22 A cheque of $9,000 is received from C. Moody in full payment for invoice 709, an April sale.

Record transactions (including sales taxes) in cash receipts and cash payments journals.
(SO 4, 7) AP

Instructions

(a) Draw a cash receipts journal and a cash payments journal (see Illustration 7B-1). Use page 1 for each journal.

(b) Record the transaction(s) for May that should be journalized in the cash receipts journal.

(c) Record the transaction(s) for May that should be journalized in the cash payments journal.

PROBLEMS: SET A

P7–1A Panos Company's chart of accounts includes the following selected accounts:

101	Cash		301	F. Panos, Capital
112	Accounts Receivable		401	Sales
120	Merchandise Inventory		505	Cost of Goods Sold

Journalize transactions in cash receipts journal; post to control account and subsidiary ledger.
(SO 3, 4, 5) AP

On April 1, the accounts receivable subsidiary ledger of Panos Company showed the following balances: Harris, $1,550; Kerl, $1,200; Northeast Co., $2,900; and Smith, $1,600. Panos uses a perpetual inventory system. The April transactions involving the receipt of cash were as follows:

> Apr. 1 The owner, F. Panos, invested additional cash in the business, $6,000.
>
> 4 Received cheque for payment of account from Smith.
>
> 5 Received cheque for $620 in payment of invoice no. 307 from Northeast Co.
>
> 8 Made cash sales of merchandise totalling $7,245. The cost of the merchandise sold was $4,090.
>
> 10 Received cheque from Harris in payment of invoice no. 309 for $900.
>
> 11 Received cash refund from a supplier for damaged merchandise, $550.
>
> 23 Received cheque for $1,600 in payment of invoice no. 310 from Northeast Co.
>
> 29 Received cheque for payment of account from Kerl.

Instructions

(a) Journalize the transactions above in a five-column cash receipts journal with columns for Cash, Dr.; Accounts Receivable, Cr.; Sales, Cr.; Cost of Goods Sold Dr./Merchandise Inventory Cr.; and Other Accounts, Cr. Foot and cross-foot the journal.

(b) Insert the beginning balances in the Accounts Receivable control and subsidiary accounts. Post the April transactions to these accounts.

(c) Prove the agreement of the control account and subsidiary account balances.

P7–2A The chart of accounts of Lai Company includes the following selected accounts:

112	Accounts Receivable		401	Sales
120	Merchandise Inventory		412	Sales Returns and Allowances
126	Supplies		505	Cost of Goods Sold
157	Equipment		610	Advertising Expense
201	Accounts Payable			

Journalize transactions in the sales, purchases, and general journals. Post to general and subsidiary ledgers.
(SO 3, 4, 5) AP

In May, the following selected transactions were completed. The company uses a perpetual inventory system. All purchases and sales were on account. The cost of all merchandise sold was 70% of the sales price.

May 2 Purchased merchandise from Vons Company, $8,000.
   3 Received freight bill from Acme Freight on Vons purchase, $400.
   5 Sales were made to Penner Company, $2,600; Hendrix Bros., $2,700; and Nelles Company, $1,500.
   8 Purchased merchandise from Golden Company, $8,000, and Dorn Company, $8,700.
   10 Received credit on merchandise returned to Dorn Company, $500.
   15 Purchased supplies from Engle Supply, $900.
   16 Purchased merchandise from Vons Company, $4,500, and Golden Company, $6,000.
   17 Returned supplies to Engle Supply, receiving credit for $100.
   18 Received freight bills on May 16 purchases from Acme Freight, $500.
   20 Returned merchandise to Vons Company, receiving credit for $300.
   23 Made sales to Hendrix Bros., $2,400, and Nelles Company, $2,200.
   25 Received bill for advertising from Ball Advertising, $900.
   26 Granted credit to Nelles Company for returned merchandise, $200. The merchandise was restored to inventory.
   28 Purchased equipment from Engle Supply, $250.

Instructions

(a) Journalize the transactions above in a sales journal, a purchases journal, and a general journal.
(b) Post to both the general and subsidiary ledger accounts. (Assume that all accounts have zero beginning balances.)
(c) Prove the agreement of the control and subsidiary accounts.

Journalize transactions in special and general journals.
(SO 3, 4, 5) AP

P7–3A Selected accounts from the chart of accounts of Just-for-You Company are shown below:

101	Cash	201	Accounts Payable
112	Accounts Receivable	401	Sales
120	Merchandise Inventory	412	Sales Returns and Allowances
126	Supplies	505	Cost of Goods Sold
157	Equipment	726	Salaries Expense

The company uses a perpetual inventory system. The cost of all merchandise sold is 60% of the sales price. During January, Just-for-You completed the following transactions:

Jan. 3 Purchased merchandise on account from Bell Co., $18,900.
   4 Purchased supplies for cash, $80.
   4 Sold merchandise on account to Gilbert, $7,550, invoice no. 371.
   5 Issued a debit memorandum to Bell Co. and returned $300 worth of damaged goods.
   6 Made cash sales for the week totalling $3,150.
   8 Purchased merchandise on account from Law Co., $4,500.
   9 Sold merchandise on account to Mays Corp., $5,600, invoice no. 372.
   11 Purchased merchandise on account from Hatch Co., $3,700.
   13 Paid Bell Co. account in full.
   13 Made cash sales for the week totalling $5,340.
   15 Received payment from Mays Corp. for invoice no. 372.
   15 Paid semi-monthly salaries of $14,300 to employees.
   17 Received payment from Gilbert for invoice no. 371.
   17 Sold merchandise on account to Amber Co., $1,200, invoice no. 373.
   19 Purchased equipment on account from Johnson Corp., $5,500.
   20 Cash sales for the week totalled $3,200.
   20 Paid Law Co. account in full.
   23 Purchased merchandise on account from Bell Co., $7,800.
   24 Purchased merchandise on account from Levine Corp., $4,690.
   27 Made cash sales for the week totalling $3,730.
   30 Received payment from Amber Co. for invoice no. 373.
   31 Paid semi-monthly salaries of $13,200 to employees.
   31 Sold merchandise on account to Gilbert, $9,330, invoice no. 374.

Just-for-You Company uses a sales journal, a purchases journal, a cash receipts journal, a cash payments journal, and a general journal.

Instructions

(a) Record, in the appropriate journal, the January transactions.
(b) Foot and cross-foot all special journals.
(c) Show how postings would be made by placing ledger account numbers and check marks as needed in the journals. (Actual posting to ledger accounts is not required.)

P7–4A The purchases and cash payments journal for Saint-Onge Company are presented below for its first month of operations, July 2003:

Journalize in sales, cash receipts, and general journals. Post, prepare trial balance, and prove control account to subsidiary ledger. Prepare adjusting entries and adjusted trial balance.
(SO 3, 4, 5) AP

PURCHASES JOURNAL   P1

Date	Account Credited	Ref.	Merchandise Inventory Dr. Accounts Payable Cr.
July 4	Dixon Co.		6,800
5	W. Engel		7,500
11	Gamble Co.		3,920
13	M. Hill		15,300
20	Jacob Jewels		7,800
			41,320

CASH PAYMENTS JOURNAL   CP1

Date	Account Debited	Ref.	Cash Cr.	Merchandise Inventory Dr.	Accounts Payable Dr.	Other Accounts Dr.
July 4	Store Supplies		600			600
10	W. Engel		7,500		7,500	
11	Prepaid Rent		6,000			6,000
15	Dixon Co.		6,800		6,800	
19	Saint-Onge, Drawings		2,500			2,500
21	M. Hill		15,300		15,300	
			38,700		29,600	9,100

In addition, the following transactions have not been journalized for July. Saint-Onge uses a perpetual inventory system. The cost of all merchandise sold is 55% of the sales price.

July 1 The founder, A. Saint-Onge, invests $80,000 in cash.
6 Sold merchandise on account to Hardy Co., $6,400.
7 Made cash sales totalling $4,000.
8 Sold merchandise on account to D. Washburn, $3,600.
10 Sold merchandise on account to L. Lemansky, $4,900.
13 Received payment from D. Washburn in settlement of account.
16 Received payment from L. Lemansky in settlement of account.
20 Received payment in full from Hardy Co.
21 Sold merchandise on account to S. Kane, $3,000.
25 Issued credit memo to S. Kane as an allowance for damaged merchandise, $100.
29 Returned damaged goods to Dixon Co. and received a cash refund of $450.

Instructions

(a) Open the following accounts in the general ledger:

101	Cash	306	Saint-Onge, Drawings
112	Accounts Receivable	401	Sales
120	Merchandise Inventory	412	Sales Returns and Allowances
127	Store Supplies	505	Cost of Goods Sold
131	Prepaid Rent	631	Supplies Expense
201	Accounts Payable	729	Rent Expense
301	Saint-Onge, Capital		

(b) Journalize the transactions that have not been journalized. Use a sales journal, cash receipts journal, and general journal to record these transactions.
(c) Post the transactions from all five journals to the accounts receivable and accounts payable subsidiary ledgers.
(d) Post the individual entries and totals to the general ledger.
(e) Prepare a trial balance at July 31, 2003.
(f) Determine whether the subsidiary ledgers agree with the control accounts in the general ledger.
(g) The following adjustments at the end of July are necessary:
1. A count of supplies indicates that $140 is still on hand.
2. Rent expense for July, $500, must be recognized.
Prepare the necessary entries in the general journal. Post the entries to the general ledger.
(h) Prepare an adjusted trial balance at July 31, 2003.

Record transactions in special
and general journals; post; prove
that subsidiary ledgers agree
with control accounts.
(SO 3, 4, 5) AP

P7–5A   The post-closing trial balance for Kelly Tire Co. is as follows:

KELLY TIRE CO.
Post-Closing Trial Balance
December 31, 2002

	Debit	Credit
Cash	$ 49,500	
Accounts Receivable	15,000	
Notes Receivable	45,000	
Merchandise Inventory	23,000	
Land	25,000	
Building	75,000	
Accumulated Amortization—Building		$ 18,000
Equipment	6,450	
Accumulated Amortization—Equipment		1,500
Accounts Payable		43,000
Mortgage Payable		82,000
S. Kelly, Capital		94,450
	$238,950	$238,950

Kelly Tire uses a perpetual inventory system. The transactions for January 2003 are as follows:

Jan. 3 Sold merchandise to B. Senton, $2,000. The cost of goods sold was $800.
    5 Purchased merchandise from Warren Parts Co., $2,200.
    7 Received a cheque from S. Devine, $3,500, in partial payment of its account.
   11 Paid freight on merchandise purchased, $300.
   13 Received payment of account in full from B. Senton.
   14 Issued a credit memo to acknowledge receipt of damaged merchandise of $700 returned by R. Barton. The cost of the returned merchandise was $300. (*Hint*: Debit Loss—Damaged Inventory instead of Merchandise Inventory.)
   15 Sent D. Harms a cheque in full payment of account.
   17 Purchased merchandise from Lapeska Co., $1,600.
   18 Pay sales salaries of $2,800 and office salaries of $1,500.
   20 Gave R. Gilson a 60-day note for $18,000 in full payment of account payable.
   23 Total cash sales amounted to $8,600. The cost of goods sold was $3,400.
   24 Sold merchandise on account to B. Cole, $7,700. The cost of goods sold was $3,500.
   27 Sent Warren Parts Co. a cheque for $950 in partial payment of the account.
   29 Received payment on a note of $40,000 from S. Lava.
   30 Returned merchandise costing $500 to Lapeska Co. for credit.

Instructions

(a) Open general and subsidiary ledger accounts for the following:

101	Cash	200	Notes Payable
112	Accounts Receivable	201	Accounts Payable
115	Notes Receivable	275	Mortgage Payable
120	Merchandise Inventory	301	S. Kelly, Capital
140	Land	401	Sales
145	Building	412	Sales Returns and Allowances
146	Accumulated Amortization	505	Cost of Goods Sold
	—Building	726	Sales Salaries Expense
157	Equipment	727	Office Salaries Expense
158	Accumulated Amortization	916	Loss—Damaged Inventory
	—Equipment		

The subsidiary ledgers contain the following information:
   1. Accounts Receivable—R. Barton $2,500; B. Cole $7,500; S. Devine $5,000.
   2. Accounts Payable—S. Field $10,000; R. Gilson $18,000; D. Harms $15,000.

(b) Record the January transactions in a sales journal, a purchases journal, a cash receipts journal, a cash payments journal, and a general journal, as illustrated in this chapter.

(c) Post the appropriate amounts to the subsidiary and general ledger accounts.

(d) Prepare a trial balance at January 31, 2003.

(e) Determine whether the subsidiary ledgers agree with control accounts in the general ledger.

Journalize transactions in special and general journals in periodic inventory system.
(SO 3, 5, 6) AP

*P7–6A   Selected accounts from the chart of accounts on Wider Company are shown below:

101	Cash	401	Sales
112	Accounts Receivable	412	Sales Returns and Allowances
126	Supplies	510	Purchases
157	Equipment	512	Purchase Returns and Allowances
201	Accounts Payable	726	Salaries Expense

During February, Wider completed the following transactions:

Feb. 3 Purchased merchandise on account from Zell Co., $8,500.

  4 Purchased supplies for cash, $70.

  4 Sold merchandise on account to Gilles Co., $7,220, invoice no. 371.

  5 Issued a debit memorandum to Zell Co. and returned $400 worth of goods.

  6 Made cash sales for the week totalling $3,720.

  8 Purchased merchandise on account from Top Co., $4,900,

  9 Sold merchandise on account to Moore Corp., $6,100, invoice no. 372.

  11 Purchased merchandise on account from Thatcher Co., $3,400.

  13 Paid Zell Co. account in full.

  13 Made cash sales for the week totalling $4,600.

  15 Received payment from Moore Corp. for invoice no. 372.

  15 Paid semi-monthly salaries of $15,100 to employees.

  17 Received payment from Gilles for invoice no. 371.

  17 Sold merchandise on account to Lumber Co., $1,400, invoice no. 373.

  19 Purchased equipment on account from Brandon Corp., $5,100.

  20 Cash sales for the week totalled $4,100.

  20 Paid Top Co. account in full.

  23 Purchased merchandise on account from Zell Co., $8,800.

  24 Purchased merchandise on account from Lewis Co., $5,310.

  27 Made cash sales for the week totalling $3,650.

  28 Received payment from Lumber Co. for invoice no. 373.

  28 Paid semi-monthly salaries of $15,400 to employees.

  28 Sold merchandise on account to Gilles, $9,180, invoice no. 374.

Wider Company uses a sales journal, a purchases journal, a cash receipts journal, a cash payments journal, and a general journal. Wider uses a periodic inventory system.

Instructions

(a) Record, in the appropriate journal, the February transactions.

(b) Foot and cross-foot all special journals.

(c) Show how postings would be made by placing ledger account numbers and check marks as needed in the journals. (Actual posting to ledger accounts is not required.)

Record transactions (including GST and PST) in special and general journals; post; prove that subsidiary ledgers agree with control accounts.
(SO 3, 4, 5, 7) AP

*P7–7A   The post-closing trial balance for Marek Co. is as follows:

MAREK CO.
Post-Closing Trial Balance
December 31, 2002

	Debit	Credit
Cash	$ 39,500	
Accounts Receivable	15,000	
GST Recoverable	2,800	
Notes Receivable	42,200	
Merchandise Inventory	23,000	
Equipment	6,450	
Accumulated Amortization—Equipment		$ 1,500
Accounts Payable		43,000
GST Payable		980
PST Payable		1,120
Marek, Capital		82,350
	$128,950	$128,950

Marek uses a perpetual inventory system. The transactions for January 2003 are as follows:

Jan. 3 Sold merchandise to Senton Co., $2,000, plus GST of $140 and PST of $160. The cost of the merchandise sold was $1,200.
　　5 Purchased merchandise from Warren Wares, $2,200, plus GST of $154.
　　7 Received a cheque from S. Devine, $3,500, in partial payment of account.
　　11 Paid freight on merchandise purchased, $300, plus GST of $21 and PST of $24.
　　12 Paid rent of $1,000 for January.
　　13 Received payment in full from Senton Co.
　　14 Issued a credit memo to acknowledge receipt of damaged merchandise of $700, plus GST of $49 and PST of $56, returned by R. Barton.
　　15 Sent Harms Hats a cheque in full payment of account.
　　17 Purchased merchandise from Lapeska Co., $1,600, plus $112 GST.
　　18 Paid sales salaries of $2,800 and office salaries of $1,500.
　　20 Gave Gilson Co. a two-month, 8% note for $18,000 in full payment of account payable.
　　23 Total cash sales amounted to $8,600, plus GST of $602 and PST of $688. The cost of the merchandise sold was $5,000.
　　24 Sold merchandise on account to B. Cole, $7,700, plus $539 GST and $616 PST. The cost of the merchandise sold was $4,600.
　　27 Sent Warren Wares a cheque for $950 in partial payment of account.
　　29 Received payment on a note of $40,000 from S. Lava.
　　30 Returned merchandise costing $500, plus GST of $35, to Lapeska Co. for credit.

Instructions

(a) Open general and subsidiary ledger accounts for the following:

101	Cash	213	GST Payable
112	Accounts Receivable	215	PST Payable
114	GST Recoverable	301	Marek, Capital
115	Notes Receivable	401	Sales
120	Merchandise Inventory	412	Sales Returns and Allowances
157	Equipment	505	Cost of Goods Sold
158	Accumulated Amortization —Equipment	726	Sales Salaries Expense
		727	Office Salaries Expense
200	Notes Payable	729	Rent Expense
201	Accounts Payable		

The subsidiary ledgers contain the following information: (1) accounts receivable—R. Barton $2,500; B. Cole $7,500; S. Devine $5,000; and (2) accounts payable—Field Co. $10,000; Gilson Co. $18,000; Harms Hats $15,000.

(b) Record the January transactions in a sales journal, a purchases journal, a cash receipts journal, a cash payments journal, and a general journal (as illustrated in Appendix 7B).

(c) Post the appropriate amounts to the subsidiary and general ledger accounts.

(d) Prepare a trial balance at January 31, 2003.

(e) Determine whether the subsidiary ledgers agree with the control accounts in the general ledger.

PROBLEMS: SET B

Journalize transactions in cash receipts journal; post to control account and subsidiary ledger. (SO 3, 4, 5) AP

P7–1B Koslo Company's chart of accounts includes the following selected accounts:

101	Cash	301	T. Koslo, Capital
112	Accounts Receivable	401	Sales
120	Merchandise Inventory	505	Cost of Goods Sold

On June 1, the accounts receivable subsidiary ledger of Koslo Company showed the following balances: Bell & Son, $2,500; Ellis Co., $1,900; Gant Bros., $1,600; and Mejia Co., $1,000. The company uses a perpetual inventory system. The June transactions involving the receipt of cash were as follows:

June 1 The owner, T. Koslo, invested additional cash in the business, $9,000.
　　3 Received cheque from Mejia Co. in full payment of its account.
　　6 Received cheque from Ellis Co. in full payment of its account.
　　7 Made cash sales of merchandise totalling $6,135. The cost of the merchandise sold was $4,090.

9 Received cheque from Bell & Son in full payment of its account.

11 Received cash refund from a supplier for returned merchandise, $200.

15 Made cash sales of merchandise totalling $5,250. The cost of the merchandise sold was $3,500.

20 Received cheque from Gant Bros., $1,000, in partial payment of its account.

Instructions

(a) Journalize the above transactions in a cash receipts journal.

(b) Insert the beginning balances in the Accounts Receivable control and subsidiary accounts. Post the June transactions to these accounts.

(c) Prove the agreement of the control account and subsidiary account balances at the end of June.

P7–2B The chart of accounts of Kei Company includes the following selected accounts:

112	Accounts Receivable	401	Sales
120	Merchandise Inventory	412	Sales Returns and Allowances
126	Supplies	505	Cost of Goods Sold
157	Equipment	610	Advertising Expense
201	Accounts Payable		

Journalize transactions in the sales, purchases, and general journals. Post to general and subsidiary ledgers. (SO 3, 4, 5) AP

In July, the following selected transactions were completed. All purchases and sales were on account. The company uses a perpetual inventory system. The cost of all merchandise sold was 40% of the sales price.

July 1 Purchased merchandise from DeVito Company, $7,000, FOB shipping point.

2 Received freight bill from Carlin Shipping on DeVito purchase, $400.

3 Made sales to Laird Company, $1,300, and Flood Bros., $1,900.

5 Purchased merchandise from Granger Company, $3,200, FOB destination.

8 Received credit on merchandise returned to Granger Company, $300.

13 Purchased store supplies from Beyer Supply, $720.

15 Purchased merchandise from DeVito Company, $3,600, and from Reeble Company, $2,800, both FOB destination.

16 Made sales to Marquez Company, $3,450, and to Flood Bros., $1,570.

18 Received bill for advertising from Meyer's Advertisements, $600.

21 Sales were made to Laird Company, $310, and Resch Company, $2,200.

22 Granted allowance to Laird Company for merchandise returned, $40.

24 Purchased merchandise from Granger Company, $3,000, FOB shipping point.

26 Purchased equipment from Beyer Supply, $600.

28 Received freight bill from Carlin Shipping on Granger purchase of July 24, $380.

30 Sales were made to Marquez Company, $4,900.

Instructions

(a) Journalize the transactions above in a sales journal, a purchases journal, and a general journal.

(b) Post to both the general and subsidiary ledger accounts. All accounts have zero beginning balances.

(c) Prove the agreement of the control and subsidiary accounts.

P7–3B Selected accounts from the chart of accounts of Tigau Company are shown below:

101	Cash	145	Buildings
112	Accounts Receivable	201	Accounts Payable
120	Merchandise Inventory	401	Sales
126	Supplies	505	Cost of Goods Sold
140	Land	610	Advertising Expense

Journalize transactions in special and general journals. (SO 3, 4, 5) AP

The company uses a perpetual inventory system. The cost of all merchandise sold was 70% of the sales price. During October, Tigau Company completed the following transactions:

Oct. 2 Purchased merchandise on account from Mason Company, $18,500.

4 Sold merchandise on account to Parker Co., $8,100, invoice no. 204.

5 Purchased supplies for cash, $80.

7 Made cash sales for the week that totalled $9,160.

9 Paid the Mason Company account in full.

10 Purchased merchandise on account from Quinn Corp., $4,200.

12 Received payment from Parker Co. for invoice no. 204.

13 Issued a debit memorandum to Quinn Corp. and returned $250 worth of damaged goods.

14 Made cash sales for the week that totalled $8,180.

16 Sold a parcel of land for $27,000 cash, the land's book value.

17 Sold merchandise on account to Boyton & Co., $5,350, invoice no. 205.

18 Purchased merchandise for cash, $2,125.

21 Made cash sales for the week that totalled $8,465.

23 Paid in full the Quinn Corp. account for the goods kept.

25 Purchased supplies on account from Frey Co., $260.

25 Sold merchandise on account to Green Corp., $5,220, invoice no. 206.

25 Received payment from Boyton & Co. for invoice no. 205.

26 Purchased for cash a small parcel of land and a building on the land to use as a storage facility. The total cost of $35,000 was allocated $21,000 to the land and $14,000 to the building.

27 Purchased merchandise on account from Schmid Co., $8,500.

28 Made cash sales for the week that totalled $8,540.

30 Purchased merchandise on account from Mason Company, $14,000.

30 Paid advertising bill for the month from *The Gazette*, $400.

30 Sold merchandise on account to Boyton & Co., $4,600, invoice no. 207.

Tigau Company uses journals of the type illustrated in this chapter.

Instructions

(a) Record, in the appropriate journals, the October transactions.

(b) Foot and cross-foot all special journals.

(c) Show how postings would be made, by placing ledger account numbers and check marks as needed in the journals. (Actual posting to ledger accounts is not required.)

Journalize in purchase and cash payment journals. Post, prepare trial balance, and prove control account to subsidiary ledger. Prepare adjusting entries and adjusted trial balance.
(SO 3, 4, 5) AP

P7–4B   Presented below are the sales and cash receipts journals for Taco Co. for its first month of operations. The company uses a perpetual inventory system.

	SALES JOURNAL			S1
Date	Account Debited	Ref.	Accounts Receivable Dr. Sales Cr.	Cost of Goods Sold Dr. Mdse. Inventory Cr.
Feb. 3	H. Adams		5,000	3,000
9	R. Babcock		6,500	3,900
12	B. Chambers		7,000	4,200
26	L. Dawson		6,000	3,600
			24,500	14,700

	CASH RECEIPTS JOURNAL						CR1
Date	Account Credited	Ref.	Cash Dr.	Cost of Goods Sold Dr. Merchandise Inventory Cr.	Accounts Receivable Cr.	Sales Cr.	Other Accounts Cr.
Feb. 1	B. Taco, Capital		30,000				30,000
2			6,500	3,900		6,500	
13	H. Adams		5,000		5,000		
18	Merchandise Inventory		150				150
26	B. Babcock		6,500		6,500		
			48,150	3,900	11,500	6,500	30,150

In addition, the following transactions have not been journalized for February 2003:

Feb. 2 Purchased merchandise on account from Healy Co. for $2,000, n/30.

7 Purchased merchandise on account from Held Company for $30,000, n/30.

9 Paid cash of $1,000 for supplies.

12 Paid Healy Co. invoice.

15 Purchased equipment for $8,000 cash.

16 Purchased merchandise on account from Landly & Sons, $2,400, n/30.

17 Paid Held Company invoice.

20 Withdrew cash of $1,100 from business for personal use.

21 Purchased merchandise on account from Able Arms Co. for $6,500, n/30.

28 Paid Landly & Sons invoice.

Instructions

(a) Open the following accounts in the general ledger:

101	Cash	201	Accounts Payable
112	Accounts Receivable	301	B. Taco, Capital
120	Merchandise Inventory	306	B. Taco, Drawings
126	Supplies	401	Sales
157	Equipment	505	Cost of Goods Sold
158	Accumulated Amortization	631	Supplies Expense
	—Equipment	711	Amortization Expense

(b)   Journalize the transactions that have not been journalized. Use a purchases journal and cash payments journal to record these transactions.

(c) Post the transactions from all four journals to the accounts receivable and accounts payable subsidiary ledgers.

(d) Post the individual entries and totals to the general ledger.

(e) Prepare a trial balance at February 28, 2003.

(f) Determine that the subsidiary ledgers agree with the control accounts in the general ledger.

(g) The following adjustments at the end of February are necessary:
1. A count of supplies indicates that $300 is still on hand.
2. Amortization on equipment for February is $200.

Prepare the adjusting entries and then post the adjusting entries to the general ledger.

(h) Prepare an adjusted trial balance at February 28, 2003.

P7–5B   The post-closing trial balance for Jarvis Co. is as follows:

Record transactions in special and general journals; post; prove that subsidiary ledgers agree with control accounts.
(SO 3, 4, 5) AP

JARVIS CO.
Post-Closing Trial Balance
April 30, 2003

	Debit	Credit
Cash	$ 38,900	
Accounts Receivable	15,500	
Notes Receivable—Cole Company	48,000	
Merchandise inventory	22,000	
Equipment	6,900	
Accumulated Amortization—Equipment		$ 1,800
Accounts Payable		45,500
L. Jarvis, Capital		84,000
	$131,300	$131,300

Jarvis uses a perpetual inventory system. The transactions for May 2003 are as follows:

May 3 Sold merchandise to B. Simone, $2,200. The cost of the goods sold was $1,000.

5 Purchased merchandise from Werner Widgits, $2,400, on account.

7 Received a cheque from G. Darvin, $3,700, in partial payment of account.

11 Paid freight on merchandise purchased, $310.

12 Paid rent of $1,200 for May.

13 Received payment in full from B. Simone.

14 Issued a credit memo to acknowledge merchandise of $720 returned by W. Burton. The merchandise (original cost, $300) was restored to inventory.

15 Sent Barnes Co. a cheque in full payment of account.

17 Purchased merchandise from Lancio Lions Co., $1,700, on account.

18 Paid sales salaries of $2,900 and office salaries of $1,600.

20 Gave Gibson Co. a two-month, 10% note for $16,000 in full payment of account payable.

23 Total cash sales amounted to $9,000. The cost of goods sold was $4,250.

27 Sent Werner Widgits a cheque for $1,000, in partial payment of account.

29 Received payment on a note of $42,000 from Cole Company.

30 Returned merchandise costing $550 to Lancio Lions for credit.

Instructions

(a) Open general and subsidiary ledger accounts for the following:

101	Cash	201	Accounts Payable
112	Accounts Receivable	301	L. Jarvis, Capital
115	Notes Receivable	401	Sales
120	Merchandise Inventory	412	Sales Returns and Allowances
157	Equipment	505	Cost of Goods Sold
158	Accumulated Amortization	726	Sales Salaries Expense
	—Equipment	727	Office Salaries Expense
200	Notes Payable	729	Rent Expense

The subsidiary ledgers contain the following information:

1. Accounts Receivable—W. Burton, $2,750; L. Kohl, $7,200; G. Darvin, $5,550.
2. Accounts Payable—Fields Co., $11,000; Gibson Co., $20,000; Barnes Co., $14,500.

(b) Record the May transactions in a sales journal, a purchases journal, a cash receipts journal, a cash payments journal, and a general journal, as illustrated in this chapter.
(c) Post the appropriate amounts to the subsidiary and general ledger accounts.
(d) Prepare a trial balance at May 31, 2003.
(e) Determine whether the subsidiary ledgers agree with the control accounts in the general ledger.

Journalize transactions in special and general journals in periodic inventory system.
(SO 3, 5, 6) AP

*P7–6B   Selected accounts from the chart of accounts of Town Company are shown below:

101	Cash	401	Sales
112	Accounts Receivable	510	Purchases
126	Supplies	512	Purchase Returns and Allowances
140	Land	610	Advertising Expense
201	Accounts Payable	813	Gain on Sale of Land

Town Company uses a periodic inventory system. During September, Town Company completed the following transactions:

Sept. 2 Purchased merchandise on account from Morgan Company, $15,800.
 4 Sold merchandise on account to Peter Co., $8,900, invoice no. 204.
 5 Purchased supplies for cash, $100.
 7 Made cash sales for the week that totalled $8,990.
 9 Paid the Morgan Company account in full.
 10 Purchased merchandise on account from Twin Corp., $5,100.
 12 Received payment from Peter Co. for invoice no. 204.
 13 Issued a debit memorandum to Twin Corp. and returned $100 worth of goods.
 14 Made cash sales for the week that totalled $7,910.
 16 Sold a parcel of land for $30,000 cash. The land's original cost was $20,000.
 17 Sold merchandise on account to Christie & Co., $5,725, invoice no. 205.
 18 Purchased merchandise for cash, $2,315.
 21 Made cash sales for the week that totalled $8,315.
 23 Paid in full the Twin Corp. account for the goods kept.
 25 Purchased supplies on account from Grey Co., $275.
 25 Sold merchandise on account to Black Corp., $5,730, invoice no. 206.
 25 Received payment from Christie & Co. for invoice no. 205.
 27 Purchased merchandise on account from Schmitt Co., $9,000.
 28 Made cash sales for the week that totalled $8,050.
 30 Purchased merchandise on account from Morgan Company, $14,500.
 30 Paid advertising bill for the month from *The Spectator*, $550.
 30 Sold merchandise on account to Christie & Co., $4,700, invoice no. 207.

Town Company uses journals of the type illustrated in Appendix 7A.

Instructions

(a) Record, in the appropriate journals, the September transactions.
(b) Foot and cross-foot all special journals.
(c) Show how postings would be made, by placing ledger account numbers and check marks as needed in the journals. (Actual posting to ledger accounts is not required.)

*P7–7B The sales and cash receipts journals for Tak Co. are presented below for its first month of operations, February 2003. Tak uses a perpetual inventory system. The company operates in Alberta where there is no Provincial Sales Tax.

Journalize in purchases and cash payments journals (including sales taxes). Post. Prove control to subsidiary.
(SO 3, 4, 5, 7) AP

SALES JOURNAL   S1

Date	Account Debited	Ref.	Accounts Receivable Dr.	Sales Cr.	GST Payable Cr.	Cost of Goods Sold Dr. Merchandise Inventory Cr.
Feb. 3	H. Adams		5,350	5,000	350	3,300
9	R. Babcock		6,955	6,500	455	4,290
12	B. Chambers		7,490	7,000	490	5,280
26	L. Dawson		6,420	6,000	420	3,960
			26,215	24,500	1,715	16,830

CASH RECEIPTS JOURNAL   CR1

Date	Account Credited	Ref.	Cash Dr.	Accounts Receivable Cr.	Sales Cr.	Cost of Goods Sold Dr. Merchandise Inventory Cr.	Other Accounts Cr.
Feb. 1	B. Tak, Capital	301	30,000				30,000
2	GST Payable	214	5,885		5,500	4,290	385
13	H. Adams	√	5,350	5,350			
18	Merchandise Inv.	120	214				200
	GST Recoverable	114					14
26	R. Babcock	√	6,955	6,955			
			48,404	12,305	5,500	4,290	30,599

In addition, the following transactions have not been journalized for February 2003:

Feb. 2 Purchased merchandise on account from Healy Bros. for $2,243, plus GST of $157.
  7 Purchased merchandise on account from Held Supply Co. for $30,000, plus GST of $2,100.
  9 Paid cash of $1,000, plus GST of $70, for purchase of supplies.
  12 Paid Healy Bros. for Feb. 2 invoice.
  15 Purchased equipment for $8,000 cash, plus GST of $560.
  16 Purchased merchandise on account from Landly Technology, $2,400, plus GST of $168.
  17 Paid Held Supply for the Feb. 7 invoice.
  20 Withdrew cash of $1,100 from business for personal use.
  21 Purchased merchandise on account from Able Co-op for $6,500, plus GST of $455.
  28 Paid Landly for the Feb. 16 invoice.

Instructions

(a) Open the following accounts in the general ledger:

101	Cash		201	Accounts Payable
112	Accounts Receivable		214	GST Payable
114	GST Recoverable		301	B. Tak, Capital
120	Merchandise Inventory		306	B. Tak, Drawings
126	Supplies		401	Sales
157	Equipment		505	Cost of Goods Sold

(b) Journalize the transactions that have not been journalized. Use a purchases journal and cash payments journal to record these transactions.
(c) Post the transactions from all four journals to the accounts receivable and accounts payable subsidiary ledgers.
(d) Post the individual entries and totals to the general ledger.
(e) Prove that the subsidiary ledgers agree with the control accounts in the general ledger.

CUMULATIVE COVERAGE—CHAPTERS 2 TO 7

Huong Company has the following opening account balances in its general and subsidiary ledgers on January 1. All accounts have normal debit and credit balances. Huong uses a perpetual inventory system. The cost of all merchandise sold was 40% of the sales price.

GENERAL LEDGER

Account Number	Account Title	January 1 Opening Balance
101	Cash	$37,050
112	Accounts Receivable	13,000
115	Notes Receivable	39,000
120	Merchandise Inventory	18,000
125	Office Supplies	1,000
130	Prepaid Insurance	2,000
140	Land	50,000
145	Building	100,000
146	Accumulated Amortization—Building	25,000
157	Equipment	6,450
158	Accumulated Amortization	1,500
201	Accounts Payable	35,000
275	Mortgage Payable	125,000
301	S. Huong, Capital	80,000

ACCOUNTS RECEIVABLE SUBSIDIARY LEDGER		ACCOUNTS PAYABLE SUBSIDIARY LEDGER	
Customer	January 1 Opening Balance	Creditor	January 1 Opening Balance
R. Dansig	$1,500	Lee Co.	$ 9,000
B. Jaggar	7,500	Mannon Bros.	15,000
S. Lowell	4,000	Nordin & Son	11,000

Jan. 3 Sold merchandise on credit to B. Sargent $3,100, invoice No. 510, and J. Eaton $2,800, invoice No. 511.

5 Purchased merchandise from Walden Wares $3,000 and Landell Supplies $5,200.

7 Received cheques for $4,000 from S. Lowell and $2,500 from B. Jaggar on accounts.

8 Paid freight on merchandise purchased $200.

9 Sent cheques to Lee Co. for $9,000 and Nordin & Son for $11,000 in full payment of accounts.

9 Issued credit memo for $300 to J. Eaton for merchandise returned. The merchandise was restored to inventory.

10 Summary cash sales totalled $15,500.

11 Sold merchandise on credit to R. Dansig for $1,300, invoice no. 512, and to S. Lowell $1,900, invoice no. 513.

15 Withdrew $1,800 cash by S. Huong for personal use.

16 Purchased merchandise from Nordin & Son for $15,000, from Lee Co. for $14,200, and from Walden Wares for $1,500.

17 Paid $100 cash for office supplies.

18 Returned $200 of merchandise to Lee and received credit.

20 Summary cash sales totalled $17,500.

21 Issued $15,000 note to Mannon Bros. in payment of balance due. The note bears an interest rate of 10% and is due in three months.

21 Received payment in full from S. Lowell.

22 Sold merchandise on credit to B. Sargent for $1,700, invoice no. 514, and to R. Dansig for $800, invoice no. 515.

23 Sent cheques to Nordin & Son and Lee in full payment of accounts.

25 Sold merchandise on credit to B. Jaggar for $3,500, invoice no. 516, and to J. Eaton for $6,100, invoice no. 517.

27 Purchased merchandise from Nordin & Son for $14,500, from Landell Supplies for $1,200, and from Walden Wares for $2,800.

    28 Paid $800 cash for office supplies.
    31 Summary cash sales totalled $21,300.
    31 Paid sales salaries of $4,300 and office salaries of $2,600.
    31 Received payment in full from B. Sargent and J. Eaton on account.

Instructions

(a) Record the January transactions in the appropriate journal—sales, purchases, cash receipts, cash payments, and general.

(b) Post the journals to the general and subsidiary ledgers. New accounts should be added and numbered in an orderly fashion as needed.

(c) Prepare an unadjusted trial balance at January 31, 2003. Determine whether the subsidiary ledgers agree with the control accounts in the general ledger.

(d) Prepare adjusting journal entries. Prepare an adjusted trial balance, using the following additional information:

    1. Office supplies at January 31 total $500.
    2. Insurance coverage expires on October 31, 2003.
    3. Annual amortization on the building is $6,000 and on the equipment is $1,500.
    4. Interest of $40 has accrued on the note payable.
    5. A physical count of merchandise inventory has found $44,770 worth of goods on hand.

(e) Prepare a multiple-step income statement and a statement of owner's equity for January, and a classified balance sheet at the end of January.

(f) Prepare and post the closing entries.

(g) Prepare a post-closing trial balance.

*B*roadening Your Perspective

FINANCIAL REPORTING AND ANALYSIS

Financial Reporting Problem

BYP7–1   The 2000 annual report for The Second Cup Ltd. is reproduced in Appendix A at the end of this text. If you have not already done so, you should read the sections of the report which describe the company's operations.

Instructions

Consider the nature of the company's operations and answer the following question: What types of (a) special journals, and (b) subsidiary ledgers and control accounts, would you expect a company like The Second Cup to use?

Accounting on the Web

BYP7–2   This problem identifies and compares the features of leading financial accounting software packages.

Instructions

Specific requirements of this Internet case are available on the Weygandt website.

CRITICAL THINKING
....

Collaborative Learning Activity

BYP7–3 Smith & Eng Company is a wholesaler of small appliances and parts. Smith & Eng is operated by two owners, Paul Smith and Dinah Eng. The company has one employee, a repair specialist, who is on a fixed salary. Revenues are earned through the sale of appliances to retailers (approximately 75% of total revenues) and appliance parts to do-it-yourselfers (10%). Revenues are also earned through the repair of appliances brought to the store (15%). Appliance sales are made on both a credit and a cash basis. Customers are billed on prenumbered sales invoices. Credit terms are always net 30 days. All parts sales and repair work are conducted on a cash-only basis.

Merchandise is purchased on account from the manufacturers of both the appliances and the parts. Cash payments are made by cheque. Cheques are most frequently issued to suppliers, to trucking companies for freight on merchandise purchases, and to newspapers and radio and TV stations for advertising. All advertising bills are paid as received. Paul and Dinah each make a monthly drawing in cash for personal living expenses. The salaried repairperson is paid twice monthly.

Smith & Eng uses a perpetual inventory accounting system.

Instructions

With the class divided into groups, answer the following questions:
- (a) Identify the special journals that Smith & Eng should have in its accounting system. List the column headings that would be appropriate for each of the special journals.
- (b) What control and subsidiary accounts should be included in Smith & Eng's accounting system? Why?

Communication Activity

BYP7–4 Demi Morris, a classmate, has a part-time bookkeeping job. She discusses her job with you, and tells you that she is concerned about the inefficiencies in journalizing and posting transactions.

Rami Ali is the owner of the company where Demi works. In response to numerous complaints from Demi and others, Rami hired two additional bookkeepers a month ago. However, the inefficiencies have continued at an even higher rate. The accounting information system for the company has only a general journal and a general ledger. Rami refuses to install an electronic accounting system.

Since Demi is not an expert in manual accounting information systems, she asks you to help her to write a letter to Rami Ali that explains (1) why the additional personnel did not help, and (2) what changes should be made to improve the efficiency of the accounting department.

Instructions

Write the letter that you think Demi should send.

Ethics Case

BYP7–5 Triport Products Company operates three divisions, each with its own manufacturing plant and marketing/sales force. The corporate headquarters and central accounting office are in Triport with the plants in Homeport, Lockeport, and Bayport, all within 50 miles of Triport. Corporate management treats each division as an independent profit centre and encourages competition among them. They each have similar but different product lines. As a competitive incentive, bonuses are awarded each year to the employees of the fastest growing and most profitable division.

Ron Hermann is the manager of Triport's centralized computer accounting operation, which keys the sales transactions into the computer and maintains the accounts receivable for all three divisions. Ron came up through the accounting ranks from the Bayport division where his wife, several relatives, and many friends still work.

As sales documents are keyed into the computer, the originating division is identified by code. Most sales documents are coded, but 5% are not coded or are coded incorrectly. As the manager, Ron has instructed the keyboard operators to assign the Bayport code to all uncoded and incorrectly coded sales documents. This is done, he says, "in order to expedite processing and to keep the computer files current, since they are updated daily." All receivables and cash collections for all three divisions are handled by Triport in one subsidiary accounts receivable ledger.

Instructions

(a) Who are the stakeholders in this situation?
(b) What are the ethical issues in this case?
(c) How might the system be improved to prevent this situation?

Answers to Self-Study Questions

1. d 2. b 3. a 4. c 5. a 6. c 7. c 8. c 9. d 10. b *11. d *12. d

Remember to go back to the Navigator box on the chapter-opening page to check off your completed work.

THE
NAVIGATOR

Minding the Money in Moose Jaw

MOOSE JAW, Sask.—If you're ever looking for a cappuccino in Moose Jaw, Saskatchewan, stop by Stephanie's Gourmet Coffee and More. The staff there serves, on average, 646 cups of coffee a day, not to mention soups, Italian sandwiches, and cheesecakes.

"We've got students who come here," says owner/manager Stephanie Mintenko, who has run the place since opening it in 1995. "We have customers who are retired, and others who are working people and have only 30 minutes for lunch. We have to be pretty quick."

That means that the cashiers have to be efficient. Like most businesses where purchases are low-cost and high-volume, cash control has to be simple.

"We have an electronic cash register, but it's not the fancy kind where you just punch in the item," explains Ms. Mintenko. "You have to punch in the prices." The machine does keep track of sales in several categories. Cashiers punch a button to indicate whether each item is a beverage, a meal, or a charge for the café's Internet connections. All transactions are recorded on an internal tape in the machine; the customer receives a receipt only upon request.

There is only one cash register at Stephanie's, and, unlike in many establishments, the staff members don't have separate floats or passcodes. "We're a small place," says Ms. Mintenko. "No more than three of us operate the cash on any given shift, including myself. I've never had a problem," she adds about sharing control of the cash this way.

She and her staff do two "cashouts" each day—one with the shift change at 5:00 p.m., and one when the shop closes at 10:00 p.m. "The machine gives the total for the shift, and we count what's left in the float, and hopefully they match!" If there's a discrepancy, they do another count. Then, if necessary, "we go through the whole tape to find the mistake," she explains. "It usually turns out to be someone who punched in $18 instead of $1.80, or something like that."

Ms. Mintenko sends all the cash tapes and float (the amount remaining in the cash register) totals to a bookkeeper, who double-checks everything and provides regular reports. "We try to keep the accounting simple, so we can concentrate on making great coffee and food."

THE
NAVIGATOR

THE NAVIGATOR

- Understand *Concepts for Review*
- Read *Feature Story*
- Scan *Study Objectives*
- Read *Preview*
- Read text and answer *Before You Go On*
  p. 378 ☐ p. 385 ☐ p. 394 ☐ p. 396 ☐
- Work *Demonstration Problem*
- Review *Summary of Study Objectives*
- Answer *Self-Study Questions*
- Complete assignments

CHAPTER • 8

INTERNAL CONTROL AND CASH

▶ **STUDY OBJECTIVES** ◀

After studying this chapter, you should be able to:

1. Describe internal control.
2. Explain the principles of internal control and be able to identify weaknesses and suggest improvements in their application.
3. Explain and critique the application of internal control principles to cash receipts.
4. Explain and critique the application of internal control principles to cash disbursements.
5. Demonstrate the operation of a petty cash fund.
6. Describe the control features of a bank account.
7. Prepare a bank reconciliation.
8. Explain the reporting of cash.

THE NAVIGATOR

As the story about Stephanie's Gourmet Coffee and More indicates, control of cash does not need to be complicated, but it is important. Similarly, controls are needed to safeguard other types of assets. For example, Stephanie's undoubtedly has controls to prevent the theft of food, computer equipment, dishes, and supplies.

In this chapter, we explain the essential features of an internal control system and then describe how these controls apply to cash. The applications include some controls you may already be familiar with. Then we describe the use of a bank and explain how cash is reported on the balance sheet. The chapter is organized as follows:

THE
NAVIGATOR

Internal Control

Could there be dishonest employees where you work? Unfortunately, the answer sometimes is "yes." The following real-life occurrences aptly illustrate this point:

- The general accountant of a Canadian charity embezzled $2 million over a four-year period by diverting contributions into her personal bank account.
- The controller of a Canadian manufacturing company paid himself $2 million above his normal pay level by writing unauthorized cheques on the company's payroll account. He got rid of the cancelled cheques when they were returned from the bank, and altered the books.
- An accounting clerk defrauded the Quebec Securities Commission of $600,000 over a four-year period. She intercepted cheques and deposited them in her own bank account.
- A general manager of a golf and country club in Ontario was charged with fraud for issuing $93,000 of cheques in payment of phony advertising invoices.

These situations emphasize the need for a good system of internal control.

Internal control consists of the policies and procedures within an organization that help achieve the following objectives:

1. **Optimize the use of resources** to reduce inefficiencies and waste.
2. **Prevent and detect errors and irregularities** in the accounting process.
3. **Safeguard assets** from theft, robbery, and unauthorized use.
4. **Maintain reliable control systems** to enhance the accuracy and reliability of accounting records.

Helpful hint Errors are unintentional mistakes. Irregularities are intentional mistakes and misrepresentations.

The importance of internal control to the efficient and effective operation of a business organization cannot be underestimated. All federally incorporated companies are required, under the *Canada Business Corporations Act*, to maintain an adequate system of internal control. The CICA's Risk Management and Governance Board stresses that this internal control should address not only external financial reporting, but also the reliability of internal reporting.

Principles of Internal Control

To optimize resources, prevent and detect errors and irregularities, safeguard assets, and maintain reliable control systems, a company follows specific control principles. Of course, internal control measures vary with the size and nature of the business, and with management's control philosophy. The principles listed in Illustration 8-1 apply to most enterprises:

STUDY OBJECTIVE

· · · · · · · · · · 2 · · · · · · · · · ·

Explain the principles of internal control and be able to identify weaknesses and suggest improvements in their application.

Illustration 8-1

Principles of internal control

These principles are explained in the following sections.

Authorization of Transactions and Activities

Transactions and activities must be undertaken, and approved, by the appropriate individuals or departments. For example, the vice-president of sales should have the authority to establish policies for making credit sales. Ordinarily, the policies require that credit sales receive written credit department approval.

An essential characteristic of this internal control principle is the assignment of responsibility to specific employees. **Control is most effective when only one person is responsible for a task.** To illustrate, assume that the cash on hand at the end of the day in a Loblaws supermarket is $50 less than the cash recorded on the cash register. If only one person has operated the register, that person is likely responsible for the shortage. If two or more individuals have worked the register, as is the case in Stephanie's Gourmet Coffee and More, it may be impossible to determine who is

It's your shift now. I'm turning in my cash drawer and heading home.

Transfer of cash drawers

responsible for the error unless each person has a separate cash drawer. To identify any shortages quickly at Stephanie's, two cash-outs are performed each day.

Segregation of Duties

Segregation of duties is essential in a system of internal control. There are two common applications of this principle:

1. Related activities should be assigned to different individuals.
2. Establishing the accountability (keeping the records) for an asset should be separate from the physical custody of that asset.

The rationale for segregation of duties is this: The work of one employee should, without a duplication of effort, provide a reliable basis for monitoring the work of another employee.

Related Activities.   Related activities that should be assigned to different individuals arise in both purchasing and selling. **When one individual is responsible for all of the related activities, the potential for errors and irregularities is increased.** Related purchasing activities include ordering merchandise, receiving the goods, and paying (or authorizing payment) for the merchandise. In purchasing, for example, orders could be placed with friends or with suppliers who give kickbacks. Or, only a cursory count and inspection could be made upon receiving the goods, which could lead to errors and/or acceptance of poor-quality merchandise. Payment might be authorized without a careful review of the invoice. Even worse, fictitious invoices might be approved for payment. When the responsibility for ordering, receiving, and paying is assigned to different individuals, there is less risk of such abuses.

Similarly, related sales activities should be assigned to different individuals. Related selling activities include making a sale, shipping (or delivering) the goods to the customer, and billing the customer. When one person handles related sales transactions, a salesperson could make sales at unauthorized prices to increase sales commissions, a shipping clerk could ship goods to himself or herself, or a billing clerk could understate the amount billed for sales made to friends and relatives. These abuses are reduced by dividing the sales tasks: salespersons make the sale, shipping department employees ship the goods on the basis of the sales order, and billing department employees prepare the sales invoice after comparing the sales order with the report of goods shipped.

Accountability for Assets.   To provide a valid basis of accountability for an asset, the accountant should not have physical custody of the asset or access to it. Similarly, the custodian of the asset should not maintain or have access to the accounting records. **When one employee (the accountant) keeps the records of an asset, and a different employee (the custodian) keeps the asset itself, the employee who keeps the asset is unlikely to use it dishonestly.** The separation of accounting responsibility from the custody of assets is especially important for cash and inventories, because these assets are vulnerable to unauthorized use or theft.

Documentation Procedures

Documents provide evidence that transactions and events have occurred. In Stephanie's Gourmet Coffee and More, the cash register tape is the café's documentation for the sale and the amount of cash received. Similarly, a shipping document indicates that the goods have been shipped. A sales invoice indicates that the customer has been billed for the goods. Adding signatures (or initials) to the document(s) means that the individual(s) responsible for the transaction or event can be identified. Documentation of transactions should be done when the transaction occurs. Documentation of events, such as those leading to adjusting or correcting entries,

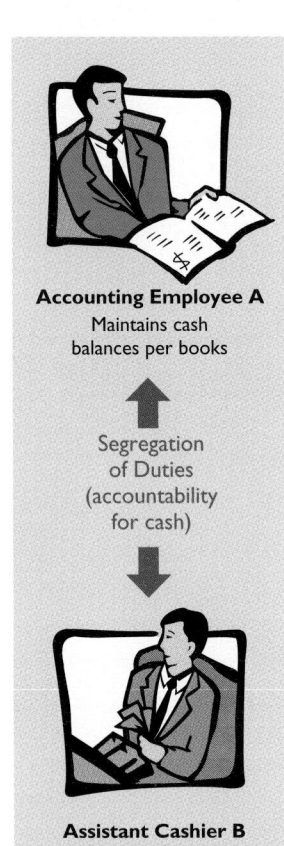

Accounting Employee A
Maintains cash balances per books

Segregation of Duties (accountability for cash)

Assistant Cashier B
Maintains custody of cash on hand

generally occurs when these entries are made.

Several procedures should be established for documents. First, whenever possible, **documents should be prenumbered and all documents should be accounted for**. Prenumbering helps to prevent a transaction from being recorded more than once. It also helps to prevent the transaction from not being recorded. Second, documents that are **source documents (the original receipts, etc.) for accounting entries should be promptly forwarded to the accounting department. This control measure helps to ensure timely recording of the transaction.** This control measure contributes directly to the accuracy and reliability of the accounting records.

In an electronic accounting system, recording usually takes place automatically when an event occurs. In these systems, special program controls are necessary to ensure the accuracy and reliability of data.

Prenumbered invoices

Safeguarding Assets and Records

Physical, mechanical, and electronic controls are needed to adequately control access to, and use of, assets and records. Physical controls are primarily for the safeguarding of assets. Mechanical and electronic controls also safeguard assets, and some enhance the accuracy and reliability of the accounting records. Examples of these controls are shown in Illustration 8-2.

Illustration 8-2

Physical, mechanical, and electronic controls

Program controls are built into computer systems to prevent intentional and unintentional errors and unauthorized access. To prevent unauthorized access, the computer system may require passwords to be entered, and random personal questions to be correctly answered, before system access is allowed. Once access has been allowed, other program controls validate calculations (math checks), detect an improper processing order (sequence checks), and identify data with, for example, a value higher or lower than a predetermined amount (limit checks).

A crucial step when programming computerized systems is to build in controls that limit unauthorized or unintentional tampering. Books and movies have been produced that focus on computer system tampering as a major theme. Most programmers would agree that tamper-proofing and debugging programs are the most difficult and time-consuming phases of their jobs.

▲ **Accounting in Action** ▶ *Ethics Insight*

The Retail Council of Canada reported that retailers lost $4.5 million a day in 1999, due to theft, fraud, and error. About 40% was attributable to shoplifters, 31% to employee theft, and the remainder to administrative error and supplier fraud.

More retailers are now using physical, mechanical, and electronic controls to stem their losses. About 90% now have loss prevention departments. Other measures include attaching security labels to tapes or disks, preventing unauthorized access to computer equipment and data, using alarms, drop safes, and mystery shoppers, and having more employee awareness programs.

Source: "Today, Canadian Retailers Will Lose $4.5M, As They Do Every Day, Because of Theft." *Financial Post*, March 28, 2000, C4.

Independent Verification

Most internal control systems include independent internal and/or external verification of performance and records. This element involves the review, comparison, and reconciliation of data. To obtain maximum benefit from independent verification:

1. The verification should be done periodically or on a surprise basis.
2. The verification should be done by someone who is independent of the employee responsible for the information.
3. Discrepancies and exceptions should be reported to a management level that can take corrective action.

Internal Verification.   Independent internal verification is especially useful when comparing the accounting records with existing assets. In the feature story, the reconciliation of the cash register tape with the cash in the register by Stephanie Mintenko and the bookkeeper is an example of this internal control principle. Another common example is the reconciliation by an independent person of the cash balance according to the books with the cash balance per bank. We will learn about bank reconciliations later in this chapter.

The relationship between this principle and the segregation of duties principle is shown below:

Illustration 8-3

Relationships between segregation of duties and internal verification

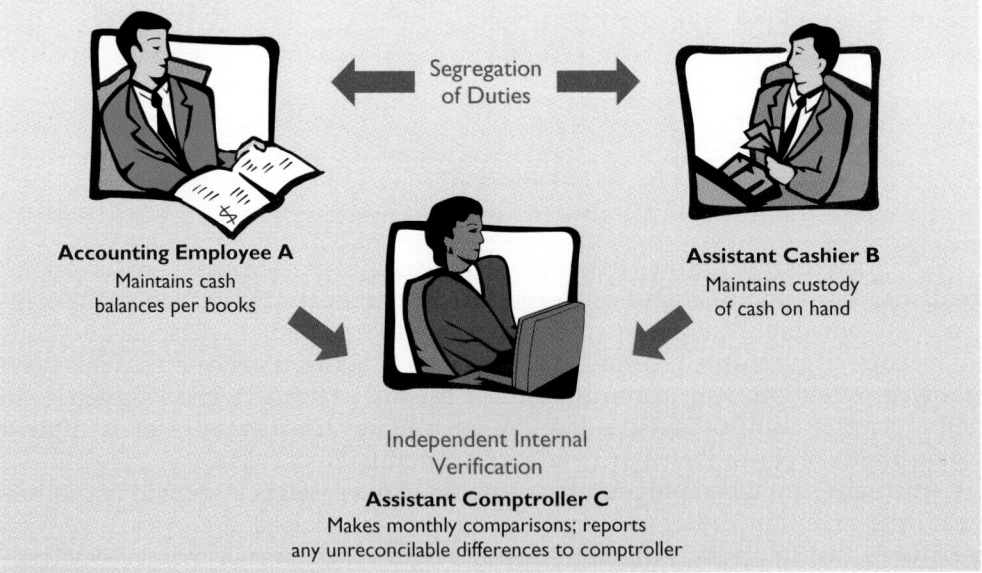

In large companies, independent internal verification is often monitored by internal auditors. **Internal auditors** are company employees who continuously evaluate the effectiveness of the company's system of internal control. They periodically review the activities of departments and individuals to determine whether prescribed internal controls are being followed. They also recommend improvements.

In smaller companies that lack an internal audit division, segregated functions are more important to ensure that the company's internal objectives are still achieved. If the company is very small, such segregation may not be possible at all, or only possible to a limited extent. In such cases, the owner usually assumes responsibility for, or oversees, incompatible functions such as authorization and access to assets.

External Verification.   It is useful to contrast independent *internal* verification with independent external verification. External auditors, in contrast to internal auditors, are **independent** of the company. They are professional accountants and are hired by a company to report on whether or not the company's financial statements fairly present its financial position and results of operations. As part of the evaluation, they also examine internal control.

Other Controls

Other control measures include the following:

1. **Bonding of employees who handle cash.** Bonding involves obtaining insurance protection against misappropriation of assets by dishonest employees. This measure contributes to the safguarding of cash in two ways: First, the insurance company carefully screens all individuals before adding them to the policy and may reject risky applicants. Second, bonded employees know that the insurance company will vigorously prosecute all offenders.
2. **Rotating employees' duties and requiring employees to take vacations.** These measures are designed to deter employees from attempting any thefts since they will not be able to permanently conceal their improper actions. Many bank embezzlements, for example, have been discovered when the perpetrator was on vacation or assigned to a new position.

Limitations of Internal Control

A company's system of internal control is generally designed to provide reasonable assurance that resources are optimized, errors and irregularities are detected, assets are properly safeguarded, and accounting records are reliable. **The concept of reasonable assurance is based on the belief that the costs of establishing control procedures should not exceed their expected benefit.** To illustrate, consider shoplifting losses in retail stores. Such losses could be eliminated by having a security guard stop and search customers as they leave the store. Store managers have concluded, however, that the negative effects of adopting such a procedure cannot be justified. Instead, stores have attempted to control shoplifting losses by less extreme procedures such as (1) posting signs that state "We reserve the right to inspect all packages" and "All shoplifters will be prosecuted," (2) using hidden TV cameras and store detectives to monitor customer activity, and (3) using sensoring equipment at exits.

The **human element** is an important factor in every system of internal control. A good system can become ineffective as a result of employee fatigue, carelessness, or indifference. For example, a receiving clerk may not bother to count goods received, or may just "fudge" the counts.

Occasionally, two or more individuals may work together to get around controls. Such **collusion** reduces the effectiveness of a system because it eliminates the protection offered by segregation of duties. If a supervisor and a cashier collaborate to understate cash receipts, the system of internal control may be beaten (at least in the short run).

The size of the business may also impose limitations on internal control. As mentioned earlier, in small companies it may be difficult to segregate duties or to provide independent internal verification. In these cases, independent external verification is even more important, to provide the necessary assurance.

Computer systems provide unique internal control problems. In many instances, computerization has shifted the responsibility for internal control to programmers and end-users from other people. For example, in point-of-sale systems, accountants are not required to record daily transactions. The computer automatically records the transaction when the cashier or clerk makes the sale. It is especially important to maintain effective control over authorization, documentation, and access in computerized systems.

►Accounting in Action ► *Business Insight*

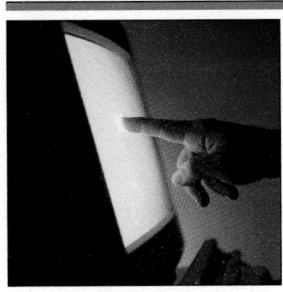

Unfortunately, computer-related frauds are a major concern. The average computer crime loss is nearly $1 million, compared with an average loss of only $30,000 resulting from other types of white-collar crime.

Computer fraud can be perpetrated almost invisibly and done with electronic speed. Psychologically, stealing using an impersonal computer seems far less criminal to some people. Therefore, the moral threshold to commit computer fraud is lower than for fraud involving a person-to-person interaction. Nonetheless, computer crime is still illegal and the *Criminal Code of Canada* and the *Copyright Act* contain provisions to deal with computer crimes.

Before You Go On . . .
►Review It

1. What are the four primary objectives of internal control?
2. Identify and describe the principles of internal control.
3. What are the limitations of internal control?

►Do It

Li Song owns a small retail store. Li wants to establish good internal control procedures but is confused about the difference between segregation of duties and independent internal verification. Explain the differences to Li.

Action Plan

• Understand and explain the differences between (1) segregation of duties and (2) independent internal verification.

Solution

Segregation of duties involves assigning responsibility so that the work of one employee checks the work of another employee. Segregation of duties occurs daily in executing and recording transactions. In contrast, independent internal verification in a small retail store would likely require Li Song to take an active role in reviewing, comparing, and reconciling data prepared by one or several employees. Independent internal verification occurs after the fact, as in the case of reconciling cash register totals at the end of the day with cash on hand.

THE
NAVIGATOR

Related exercise material: BE8–1 and BE8–2.

Cash Controls

Just as cash is the beginning of a company's operating cycle, it is also usually the starting point for a company's system of internal control. Cash is easily concealed and transported, lacks owner identification, and is highly desirable. Because of these characteristics, cash is prone to theft or misuse. In addition, because of the large volume of cash transactions, numerous errors may occur when executing and recording them. To safeguard cash and ensure the accuracy of the accounting records, effective internal control over cash is essential.

Accounting in Action ▸ *ⓔ -Business Insight*

Virtual money is used more often than paper money today. We use debit cards and credit cards to pay for the majority of our purchases. However, debit cards are only usable at specified locations and credit cards are cumbersome for small transactions. They are no good for transferring cash between individuals or to small companies that don't want to pay credit card fees. E-payments are the next on-line wave to try to solve these problems.

Canada's major banks, in conjunction with CertaPay Inc., recently launched an electronic cash system that allows customers to beam money over the Internet into an individual's e-mail inbox. When the e-mail is sent, the payment is charged to the sender's bank account. The recipient can choose to have the money credited to a bank account, or can retrieve the money using other options. Canada is the first country to introduce this system. One million Canadians are expected to e-mail $2.2 billion within the first 12 months of availability.

Source: Karen Howlett, "Banks to Launch E-Mail System to Send Money." *The Globe and Mail*, February 8, 2001, B1.

Cash consists of coins, currency (paper or virtual money), cheques, money orders, travellers' cheques, and money on deposit in a bank or similar depository. The general rule is that if the bank will accept it for deposit, it is cash. Postdated (payable in the future) cheques, and NSF (not sufficient funds) cheques are not cash; they are accounts receivable. Debit card transactions and bank credit card slips, such as Visa and MasterCard, are cash but nonbank (e.g., Diner's Club) credit card slips are not. We will learn more about accounting for debit and credit card transactions in Chapter 9. In the following sections, we explain the application of internal control principles to cash receipts and cash disbursements.

Internal Control over Cash Receipts

Cash receipts come from a variety of sources: cash sales; collections on account from customers; the receipt of interest, dividends, and rents; investments by owners; bank loans; and proceeds for the sale of capital assets. Illustration 8-4 shows how the internal control principles explained earlier apply to cash receipt transactions.

STUDY OBJECTIVE

3

Explain and critique the application of internal control principles to cash receipts.

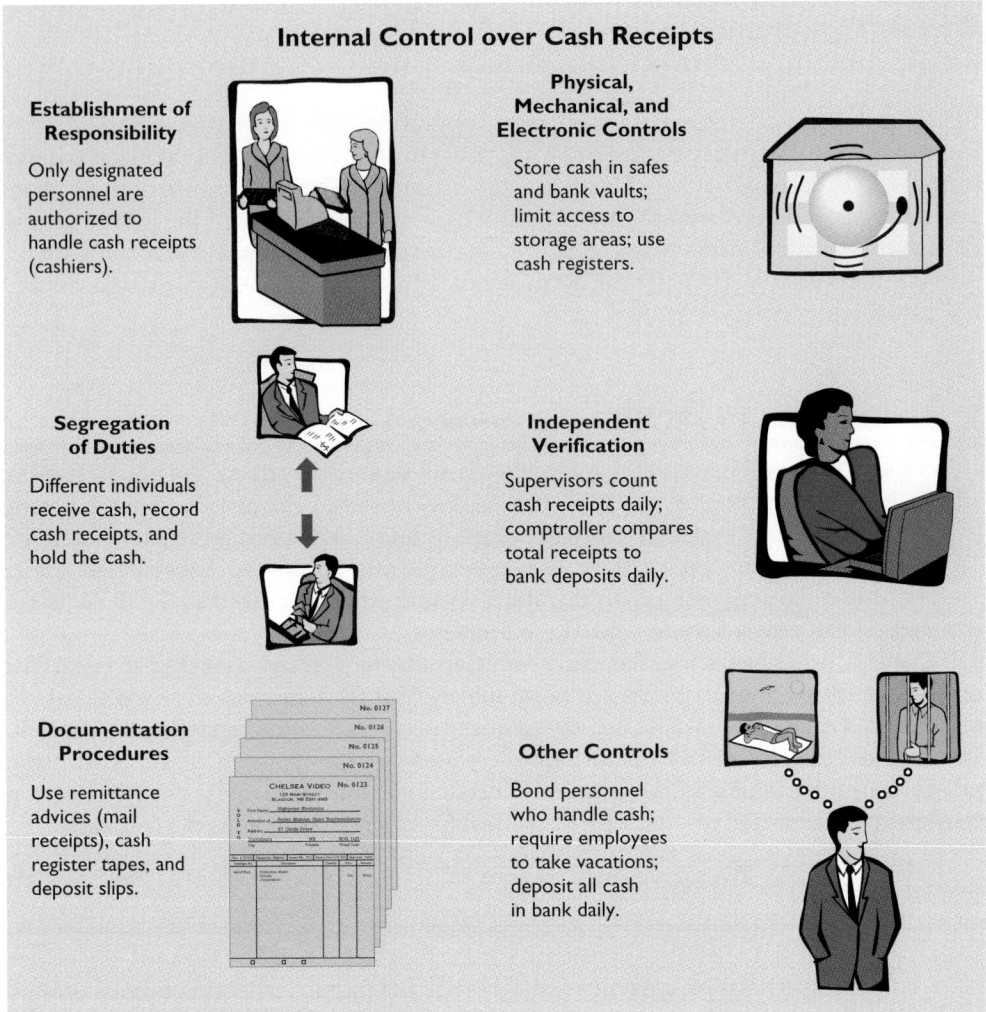

As might be expected, companies vary considerably in how they apply these principles. To illustrate internal control over cash receipts, we will examine manual control measures for a large retail store with both over-the-counter and mail receipts. These same control measures can be adapted for smaller retail stores. However, as noted previously, the owner/manager must take a more active role because there are fewer people among whom the responsibilities can be divided.

Over-the-Counter Receipts

Control of over-the-counter receipts in retail businesses is centred on cash registers that are visible to customers. In supermarkets such as Loblaws, cash registers are placed in check-out lines near the exit. In Sears, each department has its own cash register. A cash sale is "rung up" on a cash register **with the amount clearly visible to the customer**. This measure prevents the cashier from entering a lower amount and pocketing the difference. The customer receives an itemized cash register receipt and is expected to count the change received.

A cash register tape is locked into the register until removed by a supervisor or manager. This tape accumulates the daily transactions and totals. At the end of the day (or shift, if applicable), the tape total is compared to the amount of cash in the register. The findings are reported on a cash count sheet that is signed by both the cashier and the supervisor or manager. The tape should show all registered receipts

Helpful hint The cashier enters a cash sale manually by pushing the appropriate keys on the register, or electronically by using optical scanning equipment.

accounted for. The supervisor's cash count sheet used by the Anthony Food Mart is shown in Illustration 8-5.

Register No. __8__	Date March 8, 2002
1. Opening cash balance	$ 50.00
2. Cash sales per tape	6,956.20
3. Total cash to be accounted for	7,006.20
4. Cash on hand (see list)	6,996.10
5. Cash (short) or over	$ (10.10)
6. Ending cash balance	$ 50.00
7. Cash for deposit (Line 4—Line 6)	$6,946.10
Cashier *J. Cruse*	Supervisor *M. Braun*

Illustration 8–5

Cash count sheet

The count sheets, register tapes, and cash are then given to the head cashier. This individual prepares a daily cash summary that shows the total cash received and the amount from each source, such as cash sales and collections on account. The head cashier sends one copy of the summary to the accounting department for entry into the cash receipts journal. The other copy goes to the comptroller's office for later comparison with the daily bank deposit. Next, the head cashier prepares a deposit slip and makes the bank deposit. The total amount deposited should be equal to the total receipts on the daily cash summary. This will ensure that all receipts have been placed in the custody of the bank. A fundamental control over cash receipts occurs when **all cash receipts are deposited daily, intact, into the bank account.**

Although some bank deposits are made by deposits to ABMs or through electronic funds transfer (discussed later in this chapter), a significant number are still deposited personally by an authorized employee. When the bank accepts a face-to-face bank deposit, it stamps (authenticates) the duplicate deposit slip. This deposit slip is returned to the company comptroller or an appointed designate, who then makes the comparison with the daily cash summary.

Mail Receipts

As an individual customer, you may be more familiar with over-the-counter receipts than with mail receipts. However, mail receipts that result from billings and credit sales are by far the most common way cash is received by businesses. Think, for example, of the number of cheques received through the mail daily by a national retailer such as Sears.

All mail receipts should be opened in the presence of two mail clerks. These receipts are generally in the form of cheques. They are frequently accompanied by a remittance advice that states the purpose of the cheque (sometimes attached to the cheque, but often a part of the bill that the customer tears off and returns). Each cheque should be promptly endorsed "For Deposit Only" using a company stamp. This **restrictive endorsement** reduces the likelihood that the cheque will be diverted to personal use. With this type of endorsement, banks will not give cash to an individual.

A list of the cheques received each day should be prepared in duplicate. This list shows the name of the issuer of the cheque, the purpose of the payment, and the amount of the cheque. Each mail clerk should sign the list to establish responsibility for the data. The original copy of the list, along with the cheques and remittance advices, are then sent to the cashier's department. There, they are added to over-the-counter receipts (if any) when the daily cash summary and the daily bank deposit are

Helpful hint In billing customers, many companies state "Pay by cheque; do not send cash." This is designed to reduce the risk that cash receipts will be misappropriated when received.

prepared. In addition, a copy of the list is sent to the accounting department for comparison with the total mail receipts shown on the daily cash summary. This copy ensures that all mail receipts have been included. The accounting department will record a journal entry to debit Cash and credit Accounts Receivable or Sales, as required.

Internal Control over Cash Disbursements

STUDY OBJECTIVE
· · · · · · · · · · ▼ 4 · · · · · · · · · ·

Explain and critique the application of internal control principles to cash disbursements.

Cash may be disbursed for a variety of reasons, such as to pay expenses and liabilities, or to purchase assets. **Generally, internal control over cash disbursements is more effective when payments are made by cheque, rather than by cash.** Payment by cheque should occur only after specified control procedures have been followed. The paid cheque provides proof of payment. Illustration 8-6 shows how the principles of internal control apply to cash disbursements.

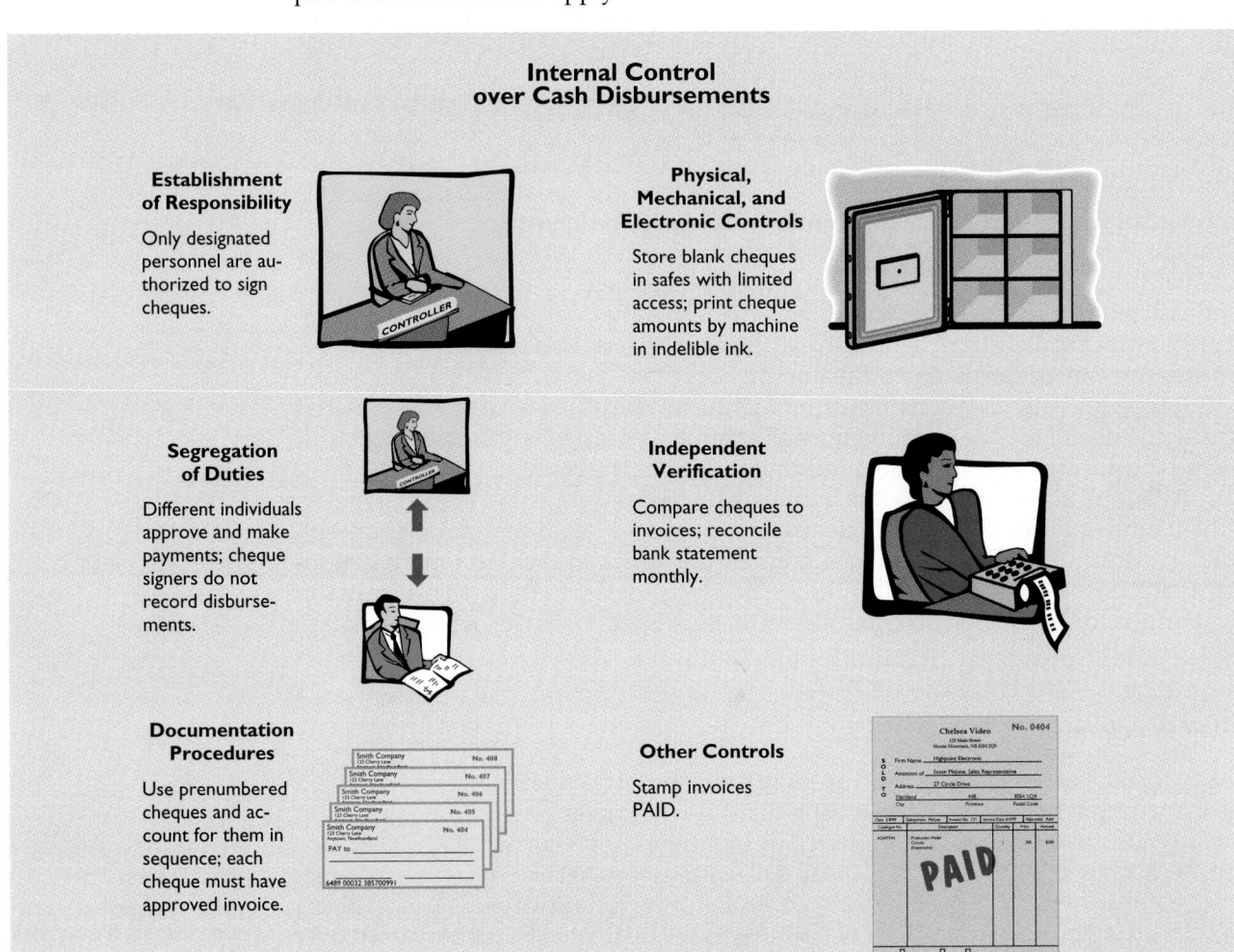

Internal Control over Cash Disbursements

Establishment of Responsibility

Only designated personnel are authorized to sign cheques.

Physical, Mechanical, and Electronic Controls

Store blank cheques in safes with limited access; print cheque amounts by machine in indelible ink.

Segregation of Duties

Different individuals approve and make payments; cheque signers do not record disbursements.

Independent Verification

Compare cheques to invoices; reconcile bank statement monthly.

Documentation Procedures

Use prenumbered cheques and account for them in sequence; each cheque must have approved invoice.

Other Controls

Stamp invoices PAID.

Illustration 8-6

Application of internal control principles to cash disbursements

Petty Cash Fund

As you just learned, better internal control over cash disbursements is possible when payments are made by cheque. However, using cheques to pay for small amounts is both impractical and a nuisance. For example, a company would not want to write cheques to pay for postage, couriers, or taxis. A common way to handle such payments, while maintaining satisfactory control, is to use a petty cash fund. A **petty cash fund** is a cash fund that is used to pay relatively small amounts, while still maintaining satisfactory control. The petty cash fund is usually operated on an **imprest** system. The word *imprest* means an advance of a specified sum of money for a designated purpose. To account for an imprest petty cash fund, you must understand three steps: (1) how the fund is established, (2) how payments are made from the fund, and (3) how the fund is replenished.

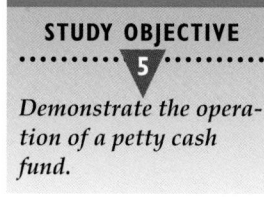

STUDY OBJECTIVE

5

Demonstrate the operation of a petty cash fund.

Establishing the Fund.   Two essential steps are required to establish a petty cash fund: (1) appoint a petty cash custodian to be responsible for the fund, and (2) determine the size of the fund. Ordinarily, the amount is expected to cover anticipated disbursements for a three- to four-week period. To establish the fund, a cheque payable to the petty cash custodian is issued for the determined amount. If the Lee Company decides to establish a $100 petty cash fund on March 1, the entry recorded in the general journal is as follows:

March 1	Petty Cash	100	
	Cash		100
	To establish a petty cash fund.		

A	=	L	+	OE
+100				
−100				

The custodian cashes the cheque and places the proceeds in a locked petty cash box or drawer. No additional entries are made to the Petty Cash account unless management changes the stipulated amount of the fund. For example, if Lee Company decides on July 2 to increase the size of the fund to $250, it will debit Petty Cash $150 and credit Cash $150.

Making Payments from the Fund.   The custodian of the petty cash fund has the authority to make payments from the fund that conform to prescribed management policies. Usually, management limits the size of expenditures that may be made. Likewise, it may not permit use of the fund for certain types of transactions (such as making short-term loans to employees). Each payment from the fund must be documented on a prenumbered petty cash receipt, as shown in Illustration 8-7. Note that the signatures of both the custodian and the person who receives payment are required on the receipt. If other supporting documents such as a freight bill or invoice are available, they should be attached to the petty cash receipt.

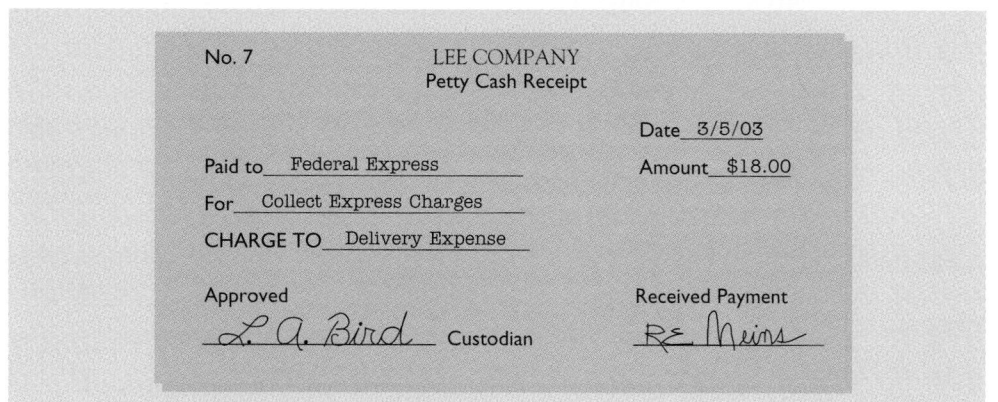

Illustration 8-7

Petty cash receipt

Helpful hint   From the standpoint of internal control, the receipt satisfies two principles: (1) authorization (signature of custodian), and (2) documentation.

The receipts are kept in the petty cash box until the fund runs low and needs to be replenished. The sum of the petty cash receipts and money in the fund should equal the established total at all times. Surprise counts can be made by an independent person, such as a supervisor or internal auditor, to determine whether the fund is being used properly.

No accounting entry is made to record a payment at the time it is made from petty cash. It is considered both inefficient and unnecessary to do so. Instead, the accounting effects of each payment are recognized when the fund is replenished.

Helpful hint Replenishing involves three internal control procedures: segregation of duties, documentation, and independent verification.

Replenishing the Fund. When the money in the petty cash fund reaches a minimum level, the fund is replenished. The request for reimbursement is made by the petty cash custodian. This individual prepares a schedule (or summary) of the payments that have been made and sends the schedule, supported by petty cash receipts and other documentation, to the comptroller's office. The receipts and supporting documents are examined in the comptroller's office to verify that they were proper payments from the fund. The request is approved and a cheque is prepared to restore the fund to its established amount. At the same time, all supporting documentation is stamped "Paid" so that it cannot be submitted again for payment.

To illustrate, assume that on March 15 the petty cash custodian requests a cheque for $87. The fund contains $13 cash and petty cash receipts for postage $44, freight $38 (assume perpetual inventory system), and miscellaneous expenses $5. The entry to record the cheque is as follows:

A	=	L	+	OE
+38				−44
−87				−5

March 15	Postage Expense	44	
	Merchandise Inventory	38	
	Miscellaneous Expense	5	
	Cash		87
	To replenish petty cash.		

Note that the Petty Cash account is not affected by the reimbursement entry. Replenishment changes the composition of the fund by replacing the petty cash receipts with cash. It does not change the balance in the fund.

It may be necessary, in replenishing a petty cash fund, to recognize a cash shortage or overage. This results when the cash plus receipts in the petty cash box do not equal the established amount of the petty cash fund. To illustrate, assume in the example above that the custodian had only $12 in cash in the fund, plus the receipts as listed. The request for reimbursement would, therefore, have been for $88. The following entry would be made:

A	=	L	+	OE
+38				−44
−88				−5
				−1

March 15	Postage Expense	44	
	Merchandise Inventory	38	
	Miscellaneous Expense	5	
	Cash Over and Short	1	
	Cash		88
	To replenish petty cash.		

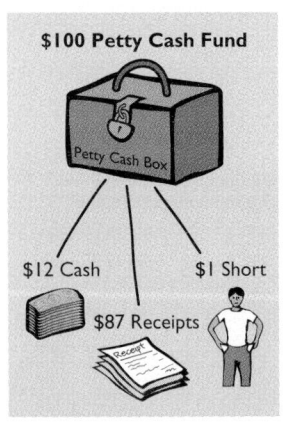

$100 Petty Cash Fund

Petty Cash Box

$12 Cash $1 Short

$87 Receipts

Conversely, if the custodian had $14 in cash, the reimbursement request would have been for $86 and Cash Over and Short would have been credited for $1. A debit balance in Cash Over and Short is reported in the income statement as miscellaneous expense. A credit balance in the account is reported as miscellaneous revenue.

A petty cash fund should be replenished at the end of the accounting period regardless of the cash in the fund. Replenishment at this time is necessary in order to recognize the effects of the petty cash payments on the financial statements.

Internal control over a petty cash fund is strengthened by (1) having a supervisor make surprise counts of the fund to ascertain whether the paid receipts and fund cash equal the imprest amount, and (2) cancelling the paid receipts so they cannot be resubmitted for reimbursement.

Before You Go On . . .

►Review It

1. How do the principles of internal control apply to cash receipts?
2. How do the principles of internal control apply to cash disbursements?
3. When are entries required in a petty cash system?

►Do It

A. Rahim is concerned about the control over cash receipts in his fast food restaurant, Big Cheese. The restaurant has two cash registers. There are never more than two employees who take customer orders and ring up sales. Work shifts for employees range from four to eight hours. Rahim asks for your help to install a good system of internal control over cash receipts.

Action Plan

- Differentiate among the internal control principles of (1) establishing responsibility, (2) using electronic controls, and (3) independent internal verification.
- Design an effective system of internal control over cash receipts.

Solution

Rahim should assign a cash register to each employee at the start of each work shift, with register totals set at zero. Each employee should be instructed to use only the assigned register and to ring up all sales. At the end of each work shift, Rahim or a supervisor/manager should total the register and make a cash count to see whether all cash is accounted for at the end of each shift.

Related exercise material: BE8–3, BE8–4, BE8–5, E8–1, E8–2, E8–3, E8–4, and E8–5.

THE NAVIGATOR

Use of a Bank

The use of a bank contributes significantly to good internal control over cash. A company can safeguard its cash by using a bank as a depository and as a clearing house for cheques received and cheques written. Use of a bank minimizes the amount of currency that must be kept on hand. In addition, the use of a bank facilitates the control of cash, because it creates a double record of all bank transactions—one by the business and the other by the bank. The asset account, Cash, maintained by the depositor, is the opposite of the bank's liability account for each depositor. It should be possible to **reconcile (balance) these accounts** at any time.

STUDY OBJECTIVE
····· **6** ·····
Describe the control features of a bank account.

►Accounting in Action ► *@-Business Insight*

A growing number of people are doing their banking over the Internet. By 2003, 50% of Canadians are expected to bank on-line. In banking, as well as other areas of e-commerce, customers continue to use their neighbourhood bank's electronic banking services, rather than pure dot.com institutions. A friendly face remains important to Canadians, even though they want the convenience of banking on-line 24/7. Forrester Research analyst Brook Newcomb says "a vast majority of consumers prefer to have access to some sort of physical presence. They may not use it, but they want someone to be there if there's a problem."

In Canada, there are only two electronic chartered banks: ING DIRECT and Citizens Bank of Canada. While both have many loyal customers—ING DIRECT claims to have 450,000—neither has come close to denting the market share of the big banks.

Source: Rob Lever, "Virtual Banks Fail to Click With Consumers?" *The Globe and Mail,* July 20, 2000, T3.

ING DIRECT

Opening a bank chequing account is a relatively simple procedure. Typically, the bank runs a credit check on the new customer and the depositor is required to sign a **signature card**. The card contains the signature of each person authorized to sign cheques on the account. The signature card is used by bank employees to validate the signature on the cheques. Many companies require two authorized signatures on each cheque to act as a check and balance on each other.

The bank provides the depositor with a book of serially numbered cheques and deposit slips imprinted with the depositor's name and address. Each cheque and deposit slip is imprinted with both a bank and a depositor identification number. This number, printed in magnetic ink, permits computer processing of the transaction.

Many companies have more than one bank account. For efficiency of operations and better control, national retailers like Sears may have local bank accounts. Similarly, the company may have a payroll bank account, as well as one or more general bank accounts. A company may also maintain accounts with different banks in order to have more than one source for short-term loans when needed.

Making Bank Deposits

Bank deposits should be made by an authorized employee, such as the head cashier. Each deposit must be documented by a deposit slip, as shown in Illustration 8-8 on the next page.

Deposit slips are normally prepared in duplicate. The original is kept by the bank. The duplicate is stamped by the bank to establish its authenticity, then kept by the depositor. Deposits are also made by direct deposit, through ABMs, or through electronic funds transfers from other accounts. In these cases, supporting documentation usually arrives at month end with the bank statement.

Electronic Funds Transfer

To manually control and account for cash is an expensive and time-consuming process. It was estimated recently that the cost for a teller to process a transaction through a bank system is $1.00. It only costs 35 cents if the customer uses a telephone, and one cent if the transaction is done through a computer. It is not surprising, therefore, that funds are most often transferred among parties without the use of paper (deposits, cheques, etc.) as an **electronic funds transfer (EFT)**. Use of EFT is quite common. For example, the authors of this textbook do not receive paycheques from their universities. Instead, our employers electronically deposit our pay to our respective banks. Personal bills, such as those for a house, car, or utilities, are frequently made by EFT. In fact, 85% of banking transactions are done electronically in Canada.

Writing Cheques

A **cheque** is a written order signed by the depositor that directs the bank to pay a specified sum of money to a designated recipient. There are three parties to a cheque: (1) the **maker** (or drawer) who issues the cheque, (2) the **bank** (or payer) on which the cheque is drawn, and (3) the **payee** to whom the cheque is payable. A cheque is a negotiable instrument that can be transferred to another party by endorsement.

Each cheque should clearly explain its purpose. For many businesses, the purpose of the cheque is detailed on the cheque stub, as shown in Illustration 8-9. The purpose of the cheque should also be apparent to the payee, either by referencing the invoice directly on the cheque—see the reference to invoice #27622 on the RE: (for) line of the cheque—or by attaching a copy of the invoice to the cheque.

Most business bank accounts do not allow ABM withdrawals because internal control is strengthened by making all payments by cheque. Other disbursements may include pre-arranged payments, such as for utilities, or EFTs.

For both individuals and businesses, it is important to know the balance in the

MADE IN CANADA NCR BUSINESS FORMS S130979

222678221

Bank of Montreal

PRESS FIRMLY FOR CLEAR COPIES

Br. Tr.	Date
0123	April 25, 2003

Account No.
1050-1800

Account Name
Lee Company

LIST CHEQUES

Particulars (Opt.)	Amount	
74-331/724	175	40
61-157/220	292	60
19-401/710	337	55
22-815/666	165	72
15-360/011	145	53

TOTAL CHEQUES	1116	80

Prod. 1045171 - Form. 638 BK (11/93) Litho. CANADA - 510389

Br. Tr.	Date
0123	April 25, 2003

Account No.
1050-1800

Account Name
Lee Company

Deposited by
S. Gunn

CASH

No.	$	Amount	
	X 2		
20	X 5	100	00
5	X 10	50	00
7	X 20	140	00
2	X 50	100	00
	X 100		

COIN

Rolls of $1

2	X25	50	00
Other		22	10

U.S. $

Cash

Cheques

Exchange

Total Cash	462	10

MasterCard

Total Cheques	1116	80
Sub-Total (M/C & Cheques)	1116	80
Total Deposit (Cash & Sub-Total)	1578	90

Illustration 8-9

Cheque (reproduced with permission of the Bank of Montreal)

0442

April 7, 03

BALANCE FORWARD	12867	19

TO Watkins Wholesale Supply

RE: Invoice #27662

GST	315	65	2420
GST	105134688		

DEPOSITS

DEPOSITS

BALANCE	10447	19

Lee Company ← **Maker**   **Payee**
500 Queen Street
Fredericton, NB E3b 5C2

0442

April 7, 03

PAY TO THE ORDER OF Watkins Wholesale Supply $2420.00

Two Thousand Four hundred & Twenty ——XX/100 DOLLARS

FOR Invoice #27662

Bank Bank of Montreal ← **Bank**
FREDERICTON MAIN OFFICE
505 KING STREET
FREDERICTON, N. B. E3B 1E7

PER MS Lee
PER W. F. Raine

⑈000044⑈ ⑆01234⑈001⑈ 1050⑈800⑈

chequing account at all times. This is easily done in a computerized accounting system, where deposits and cheques are recorded as soon as they are received or issued. In smaller businesses, to keep the balance current, each deposit and cheque must be entered on the cheque stub contained in the cheque book, as shown in Illustration 8-9.

Bank Statements

Each month, the depositor receives a bank statement from the bank. A **bank statement** shows the depositor's bank transactions and balance. A typical statement is presented in Illustration 8-10. It shows (1) cheques paid and other debits that reduce the balance in the depositor's account, (2) deposits and other credits that increase the balance in the depositor's account, and (3) the account balance after each day's transactions.

Illustration 8-10

Bank statement (reproduced with permission of the Bank of Montreal)

Helpful hint Every deposit received by the bank is *credited* to the customer's account. The reverse occurs when the bank "pays" a cheque issued by a company on its chequing account balance: payment reduces the bank's liability. Thus it is *debited* to the customer's account with the bank.

Bank of Montreal ▲ Banque de Montréal

Statement of Account
Relevé de compte

505 King Street
Fredericton, NB
E3B 1E7

Transit No de dom	Date D/J M/M Y/A	Account Title Désignation de compte	Account Type Type de compte	Account No. No de compte	Page
0123	30 04 03	Operating Account	FBOA	1050-800	58

Lee Company
500 Queen Street
Fredericton, NB   E3B 5C2

BALANCE FORWARD SOLDE REPORTÉ   Date 03 31   13,256.90

TRANSACTION CODES *
*CODES DE TRANSACTION *

CODE	Description/Message justificatif	Debits/Débits	Credits/Crédits	Day Mo. Jour	Balance/Solde
CK	NO. 435	644.95		04 02	
CD			4,276.85	04 02	16,888.80
DD			2,137.50	04 03	
CK	NO. 438	776.65		04 03	18,249.65
CK	NO. 437	1,185.79		04 04	17,063.86
CK	NO. 436	3,260.00		04 04	
CD			1,350.47	04 04	15,154.33
CD			982.46	04 07	
CK	NO. 440	1,487.90		04 07	14,648.89
CK	NO. 439	1,781.70		04 08	
CK	NO. 442	2,420.00		04 08	
CD			1,320.28	04 08	11,767.47
CM			1,035.00	04 09	12,802.47
CK	NO. 441	1,585.60		04 11	
CD			2,720.00	04 11	13,936.87
CK	NO. 443	1,226.00		04 11	
CD			757.41	04 14	13,468.28
CD			1,218.56	04 14	14,686.84
CD			715.42	04 14	15,402.26
RC		425.60		04 18	14,976.66
CK	NO. 444	3,477.11		04 23	11,499.55
CD			1,578.90	04 25	13,078.45
CD			1,350.55	04 28	14,429.00
DM		30.00		04 30	
CD			2,128.60	04 30	
CK	NO. 447	620.15		04 30	15,907.45

Transaction codes legend (left column):
AD Adjustment / Rectification
CB By Branch / Chèque ématif par la succ.
CC Certified Cheque / Chèque certifié
CD Customer Deposit / Dépôt
CK CKCheque / Chèque
CM Credit Memo / Avis de débit
CW Telephone Banking / Service bancaires par téléphone
DC Other Charge / Autres frais
DD Direct Deposit/ Pre-authorized Debit / Dépôt ou débit direct
DM Debit Memo / Avis de débit
DN Not Service Chargeable / Sans frais de gestion
DP Overdraft / Découvert
DS Service Chargeable / Avec frais de gestion
EC Error Correction / Correction d'erreur
FX Foreign Exchange / Change
GS Tax / Taxe
IB Instabank / Instabanque
IN Interest / Intérêt
IJ Loan Interest / Intérêt sur prêt
LN Loan Payment / Versement sur prêt
LA Loan Advance / Avance sur prêt
LT Large Volume Account List Total / Liste de chèque - compte supervolô
MB Multi-Branch Banking / Inter-Service
NR Non-Resident Tax / Impôt de non-résident
NS Cheque returned NSF / Chèque retourné - provision insuffisante
NT Nesbitt Burns Entry / Transaction de Nesbitt Burns
OM Other Machine / Autre machine
PR Purchase at Merchant / Achat chez le commerçant
RC NSF Charge / Frais pour provision insuffisante
RN Merchandise Return / Retour de marchandise
RT Returned Item / Article retourné
RV Merchant Reversal / Correction - Commerçant
SC Service Charge / Frais de gestion
SO Standing Order / Ordre de virement
ST Merchant Deposit / Dépôt du commerçant
TF Transfer of Funds / Virement
TX Tax / Taxe
WD Withdrawal / Retrait

Please see the reverse side for the Account Types.
Les types de compte figurent au verso.

Prompt notification of any change of address would be appreciated./Prière de signaler à la Banque tout changement d'adresse.

Please check this statement and report any errors or omissions within 30 days of its delivery.
Prière de vérifier ce relevé de compte et de signaler toute erreur ou omission dans les 30 jours suivant sa réception.

All paid cheques are listed on the bank statement, along with the date the cheque was paid and its amount. A paid cheque is sometimes referred to as a **cancelled** cheque. Most banks offer depositors the option of receiving paid cheques with their bank statements. For those who decline, the bank keeps an electronic record of each cheque. The bank also includes bank statement memoranda that explain other debits and credits made by the bank to the depositor's account.

At first glance, it may appear that the debits and credits reported on the bank statement are backward. How can a cheque be a debit? And how can a deposit be a credit? Debits and credits are not really backward. To the company, cash is an asset account. Assets are increased by debits (e.g., for cash receipts) and decreased by credits (e.g., for cash payments). To the bank, the cash in your bank account is a liability—an amount it must repay to you upon request. Liabilities are increased by credits and decreased by debits. When you deposit money in your bank account, the bank's liability to you increases. That is why the bank shows deposits as credits. When you write a cheque on your account, the bank pays out this amount and decreases (debits) its liability to you.

►Accounting in Action ► *ⓔ-Business Insight*

On-line banking is quickly making cheque writing a thing of the past. On-line banking has a number of advantages over telephone banking or automated banking machines—not the least of which is that it is cheaper. The Royal Bank has on-line banking packages that cost about 20 cents per transaction, compared to 50 cents for ABMs and 60 cents for cheques.

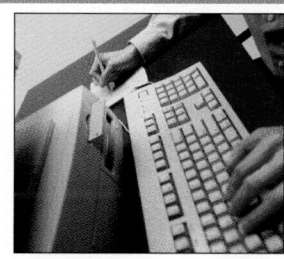

Debit Memorandum

Banks charge a monthly fee for the use of their services, called a **bank service charge**. A debit memorandum that explains the charge is usually included with the bank statement and noted on the statement. The symbol DM (debit memo) is often used for such charges. Separate debit memoranda may also be issued for other bank services such as the cost of printing cheques, issuing traveller's cheques, certifying cheques, and transferring funds to other locations.

A debit memorandum is also used by the bank when a deposited cheque from a customer bounces because of insufficient funds. In such a case, the cheque is marked NSF (not sufficient funds) or RC (returned cheque) by the customer's bank, and is returned to the depositor's bank. The bank then debits the depositor's account, as shown by the symbol RC on the bank statement in Illustration 8-10. The bank sends the NSF cheque and debit memorandum to the depositor as notification of the charge. The company (depositor) will then advise the customer who wrote the NSF cheque that the payment was ineffective and that a payment is still owed on the account. The company also usually passes the bank charges on to the customer by adding them to the customer's account balance. In summary, the overall effect of an NSF cheque to the depositor is to create an account receivable, and to reduce cash in the bank account.

Credit Memorandum

A depositor may ask the bank to collect its notes receivable. In such a case, the bank credits the depositor's account for the cash proceeds of the note. This is illustrated on Lee Company's bank statement by the symbol CM (credit memo). The bank issues a credit memorandum, which is sent with the statement to explain the entry. Some banks also offer interest on chequing accounts. The interest earned may be indicated on the bank statement by the symbol CM or IN (interest).

Reconciling the Bank Account

STUDY OBJECTIVE

7

Prepare a bank reconciliation.

The bank and the depositor maintain independent records of the depositor's chequing account. If you've never had a chequing account, you might assume that the respective balances will always agree. In fact, the two balances are seldom the same at any given time. It is necessary to make the balance per books (the balance recorded in the general ledger cash account) agree with the balance per bank (the balance recorded on the bank statement)—a process called **reconciling the bank account**.

The lack of agreement between the two balances is due to:

1. Time lags that prevent one of the parties from recording the transaction in the same period as the other.
2. Errors by either party in recording transactions.

Except in electronic banking applications, time lags occur frequently. For example, several days pass between the time a cheque is mailed to a payee and the date the cheque is presented to, and paid by, the bank. Similarly, when the depositor uses the bank's night depository to make deposits, there will be a difference between the time the receipts are recorded by the depositor and the time they are recorded by the bank. A time lag also occurs whenever the bank mails a debit or credit memorandum to the depositor.

Errors also occur. The incidence of errors depends on the effectiveness of the internal controls of the depositor and the bank. Bank errors are rare. However, either party could inadvertently record a $450 cheque as $45 or $540. In addition, the bank might mistakenly charge a cheque to the wrong account if the code is missing or if the cheque cannot be scanned.

▶ **Accounting in Action** ▶ *Ethics Insight*

Bank errors may be infrequent, but they can involve a story more suitable for *Ripley's Believe It or Not* than an accounting textbook. The Bank of Nova Scotia's discount brokerage arm accidentally put $17.1 million of somebody else's money into a Toronto doctor's Scotiabank account. It took four months to find and correct the error. Stories about banks misplacing customers' funds are a dime a dozen. But they usually involve misplaced debits, and rarely amounts as high as this.

Source: John Partridge, "Bank Error in Your Favour: Collect $17-Million." *The Globe and Mail*, April 11, 2000, A1.

Reconciliation Procedure

Helpful hint For maximum internal control, the bank statement should be sent by the bank directly to the reconciler to prevent tampering with the contents of the bank statement by the cashier.

To obtain maximum benefit from a bank reconciliation, the reconciliation should be prepared by an employee who has no other responsibilities that relate to cash. If the internal control principles of segregation of duties and internal verification are not followed when the reconciliation is prepared, cash embezzlements may go unnoticed. For example, a cashier who prepares the reconciliation can embezzle cash and conceal the embezzlement by misstating the reconciliation. Thus, the bank accounts would reconcile and the embezzlement would not be detected.

In reconciling the bank account, it is customary to reconcile the balance per books (found in the cash account in the general ledger) and balance per bank (found on the bank statement provided by the bank) to their adjusted (correct) cash balances. The reconciliation schedule is divided into two sections—one for the bank and one for the books (company). The starting point when preparing the reconciliation is to enter the balance per bank statement and balance per books on the schedule. Adjustments are then made to each section, as shown in Illustration 8-11. The following steps should reveal all the reconciling items that cause the difference between the two balances:

1. **Deposits in transit.** Compare the individual deposits on the bank statement with (1) deposits in transit from the preceding bank reconciliation and (2) the deposits according to company records or duplicate deposit slips. Deposits recorded by the depositor that have not been recorded by the bank are deposits in transit. They are added to the balance per bank.

2. **Outstanding cheques.** Compare the paid cheques shown on the bank statement or returned with the bank statement to (1) cheques outstanding from the preceding bank reconciliation, and (2) cheques issued by the company as recorded in the cash payments journal. Issued cheques recorded by the company that have not yet been paid by the bank are outstanding cheques. They are deducted from the balance per bank.

3. **Errors.** Note any **errors** discovered in the previous steps. List them in the appropriate section of the reconciliation schedule. For example, if a paid cheque correctly written by the company for $1,226 was mistakenly recorded by the company for $1,262, the error of $36 is added to the balance per books. All errors made by the depositor are reconciling items in determining the adjusted cash balance per books. In contrast, all errors made by the bank are reconciling items in determining the adjusted cash balance per bank.

4. **Bank memoranda.** Trace **bank memoranda** to the depositor's records. Any unrecorded memoranda should be listed in the appropriate section of the reconciliation schedule. For example, a debit memorandum for bank service charges is deducted from the balance per books. A credit memorandum for interest earned on notes receivable collected by the bank is added to the balance per books.

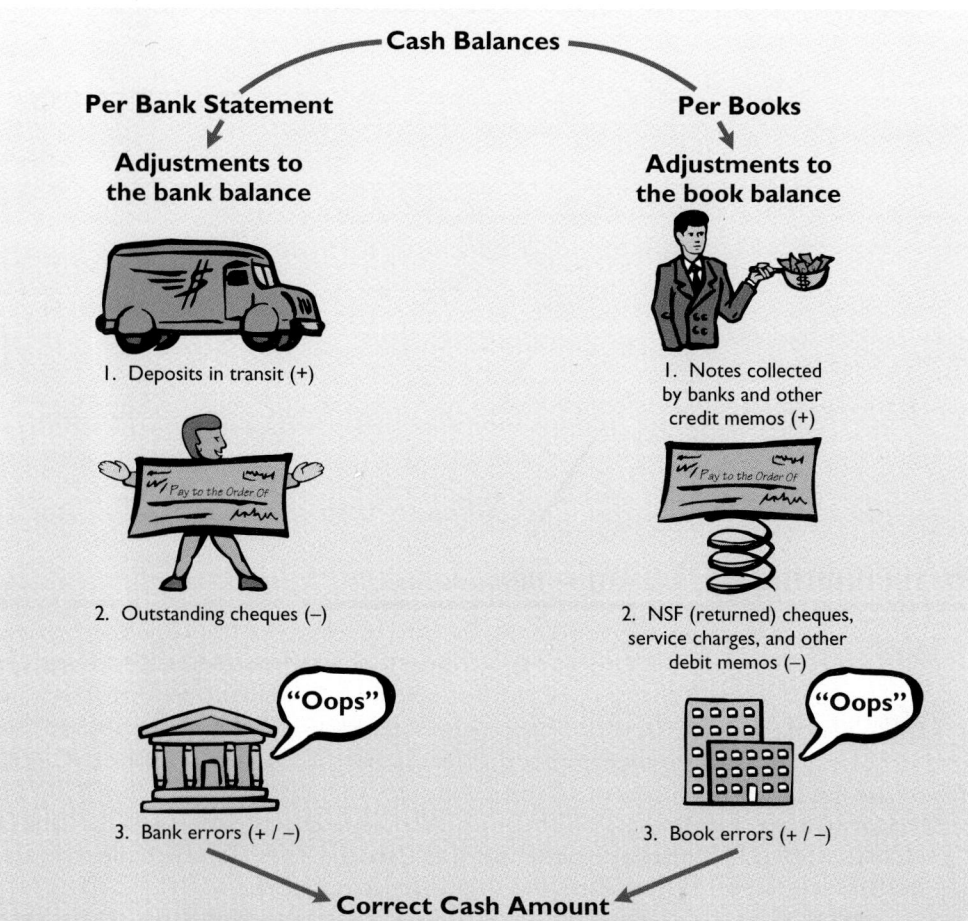

Illustration 8-11

Bank reconciliation procedures

Bank Reconciliation Illustrated

The bank statement for Lee Company was shown in Illustration 8-10. It shows a balance per bank of $15,907.45 on April 30, 2003. On this date, the balance of cash per books is $11,589.45. Using the foregoing steps, the following reconciling items are determined:

1. **Deposits in transit:** April 30 deposit (recorded by bank on May 1). $2,201.40
2. **Outstanding cheques:** No. 445, $3,000.00; No. 446, $1,401.30;
   No. 448, $1,502.70.   5,904.00
3. **Errors:** Cheque No. 443 was correctly written by Lee for $1,226.00
   and was correctly paid by the bank. However, it was recorded as
   $1,262.00 by Lee Company.   36.00
4. **Bank memoranda:**
   (a) Debit—NSF cheque from J. R. Baron for $425.60   425.60
   (b) Debit—Cheque printing charge, $30.00   30.00
   (c) Credit—Collection of note receivable for $1,000.00 plus
        interest earned $50.00, less bank collection fee $15.00   1,035.00

The bank reconciliation is as follows:

Illustration 8-12

Bank reconciliation

LEE COMPANY Bank Reconciliation April 30, 2003		
Cash balance per bank statement		$15,907.45
Add: Deposit in transit		2,201.40
		18,108.85
Less: Outstanding cheques		
No. 445	$3,000.00	
No. 446	1,401.30	
No. 448	1,502.70	5,904.00
Adjusted cash balance per bank		**$12,204.85** ◄
Cash balance per books		$11,589.45
Add: Collection of note receivable $1,000, plus		
interest earned $50, less collection fee $15	$1,035.00	
Error in recording cheque No. 443	36.00	1,071.00
		12,660.45
Less: NSF cheque	$ 425.60	
Bank service charge	30.00	455.60
Adjusted cash balance per books		**$12,204.85** ◄

Alternative terminology
The terms *adjusted, true,* and *correct cash balance* may be used interchangeably.

►Accounting in Action ► *Business Insight*

Bank of Canada

It would be very easy to reconcile the bank statement for Mary Jane Lee, formerly of College Street, Toronto. Her account, with a balance of $25,026.45, was last touched in 1938! Mary Jane's inactive account is far from the only one. There are more than 748,000 unclaimed accounts at the Bank of Canada, worth $165 million.

Financial institutions must transfer dormant accounts to the Bank of Canada if they have not been used in the last 10 years. Accounts with balances of less than $500 are retained for 10 more years by the Bank of Canada. All other accounts remain with the Bank of Canada indefinitely until someone comes forward to claim the funds. To search the database, visit the Bank of Canada's website <ucbswww.bank-banque-canada.ca>.

Entries from Bank Reconciliation

Each reconciling item in determining the **adjusted cash balance per books** should be recorded by the depositor. If these items are not journalized and posted, the Cash account will not show the correct balance. The entries for Lee Company on April 30 are as follows:

Collection of Note Receivable. This entry involves four accounts. Assuming that the interest of $50 has not been accrued and the collection fee is charged to Bank Charges, the entry to record the credit memorandum (CM) is the following:

April 30	Cash	1,035.00	
	Bank Charges Expense	15.00	
	Notes Receivable		1,000.00
	Interest Revenue		50.00
	To record collection of note receivable by bank.		

A	=	L	+	OE
+1,035				−15
−1,000				+50

Book Error. The cash payments journal shows that cheque No. 443 was a payment on account to Asia Company, a supplier. The correcting entry is as follows:

April 30	Cash	36.00	
	Accounts Payable—Asia Co.		36.00
	To correct error in recording cheque No. 443.		

A	=	L	+	OE
+36		+36		

NSF Cheque. As indicated earlier, an NSF cheque (RC) becomes an account receivable to the depositor. The entry follows:

April 30	Accounts Receivable—J. R. Baron	425.60	
	Cash		425.60
	To record NSF cheque.		

A	=	L	+	OE
+425.60				
−425.60				

Bank Service Charges. Cheque printing charges and other bank service charges (DM) are debited to Bank Charges Expense. Some companies use the account Interest Expense; others use Miscellaneous Expense because the charges are often nominal in amount. The entry is as follows:

April 30	Bank Charges Expense	30.00	
	Cash		30.00
	To record charge for printing company cheques.		

A	=	L	+	OE
−30				−30

The four entries above could also be combined into one compound entry.

After the entries above are posted, the Cash account will show the following:

		Cash			
Apr. 30	Bal.	11,589.45	Apr. 30		425.60
30		1,035.00	30		30.00
30		36.00			
Apr. 30	Bal.	**12,204.85**			

The adjusted cash balance in the general ledger should agree with the adjusted cash balance per books in the bank reconciliation shown in Illustration 8-12.

What entries does the bank make? **The bank cannot correct your errors on its books, and you cannot correct the bank's errors on your books.** If any bank errors are discovered in preparing the reconciliation, the bank should be notified. It then can make the necessary corrections on its records. The bank does not make any entries for deposits in transit or outstanding cheques. The bank will record these items when they reach it.

Before You Go On . . .

▶Review It

1. Why is it necessary to reconcile a bank account?
2. What steps are involved in the reconciliation procedure?
3. What information is included in a bank reconciliation?

▶Do It

Samuel Saint-Onge owns Linen Fabrics. Samuel asks you to explain how the following reconciling items should be treated in reconciling the bank account: (1) a debit memorandum for a returned cheque, (2) a credit memorandum for a note collected by the bank, (3) an outstanding cheque from the current period, (4) outstanding cheques from the prior period, and (5) a deposit in transit.

Action Plan

- Understand the purpose of a bank reconciliation.
- Identify time lags and explain how they cause reconciling items.

Solution

In reconciling the bank account, the reconciling items are treated as follows:

Returned cheque: Deducted from balance per books.

Collection of note: Added to balance per books.

Outstanding cheques from the current period: Deducted from balance per bank.

Outstanding cheques from the prior period: Deducted from balance per bank. Note that an outstanding cheque from a prior period means that the cheque was deducted from the books in the prior period, but not yet paid by the bank. If the cheque has been paid by the bank in the current month, both sides (books and bank) are now reconciled, the cheque is no longer outstanding, and no further reconciliation of this item is required. If the cheque continues to be outstanding, then it is still a reconciling item (deduction) for the bank section since the bank has not yet recorded the transaction.

Deposit in transit: Added to balance per bank.

Related exercise material: BE8–6, BE8–7, BE8–8, BE8–9, BE8–10, BE8–11, E8–6, E8–7, E8–8, E8–9, E8–10, and E8–11.

Reporting Cash

STUDY OBJECTIVE
8
Explain the reporting of cash.

Cash on hand, cash in banks, and petty cash are normally combined and reported simply as **Cash** in the balance sheet. Because it is the most liquid asset owned by a company, cash is listed first in the current asset section of the balance sheet. **Many companies combine cash with cash equivalents.** Cash equivalents are highly liquid investments that can be converted into a specified amount of cash. They typically have maturities of three months or less when purchased. These investments include short-term deposits, short-term investments such as treasury bills and money market funds, and short-term notes.

More than 70% of Canadian public companies present cash in this manner. The Second Cup combines its cash with cash equivalents on its balance sheet, as shown on page A12 of Appendix A.

Some companies may be in a cash deficit position at year end. This can happen when the company is in an overdraft position at the bank. A bank overdraft occurs when a cheque is written for more than the amount in the bank account. This, in effect, is a short-term loan from the bank, assuming that the bank does not reject or return the cheque. Most companies have overdraft protection up to a certain amount with their banks. In an overdraft situation, the Cash account shows a credit balance in the general ledger and is reported as a current liability, as shown in a recent extract from Andrés Wines' balance sheet in Illustration 8-13.

Illustration 8-13

Presentation of a cash credit balance

ANDRÉS WINES LTD. Balance Sheet (partial) March 31, 2001 (in thousands of dollars)	
LIABILITIES	
Current Liabilities	
Bank indebtedness	$27,511

A company may have cash that is restricted for a special purpose. An example is funds held on deposit until completion of an offer to purchase real estate. Another example would be a plant expansion fund for financing new construction. If the restricted cash is expected to be used **within the next year**, the amount should be reported as a **current asset**. When restricted funds will not be used in that time, they should be reported as a noncurrent asset.

In making loans to depositors, banks commonly require borrowers to maintain minimum cash balances. These minimum balances, called compensating balances, provide the bank with support for the loans. They are a form of restriction on the use of cash. Compensating balances should be reported as a noncurrent asset and be disclosed in the financial statements.

Using the Information in the Financial Statements

Management must perform a difficult balancing act to properly manage cash. On one hand, it is critical to ensure that enough cash is on hand to pay bills as they come due, to purchase goods, and to take advantage of opportunities as they present themselves. On the other hand, cash itself is an unproductive asset unless invested in other assets (e.g., investments, inventory, capital assets). Too much cash on hand may indicate that management is not maximizing its return on assets.

►**A**ccounting in **A**ction ► *Business Insight*

Is there such a thing as too much cash? Some Canadian companies have upset shareholders by not spending their excess cash. Unused cash hurts a company in a number of ways. Primarily, it is a lost opportunity—all that money sitting around is not producing the best return for shareholders. One Vancouver-based fund manager estimated that 70% of Canadian companies are sitting on excess cash. Companies argue that cash is needed to help them weather cyclical downturns or to be ready for strategic acquisitions. What do you think?

The cash flow statement and the management report are two useful pieces of information. They help readers assess management's effectiveness in managing and controlling cash. The cash flow statement, which will be discussed in Chapter 18, provides information about where cash came from and what it was used for.

A management report is included in all publicly distributed financial statements. The purpose of this report is to acknowledge management's responsibility for—among other items—the development of internal controls over the financial reporting process. On page A9 in Appendix A at the end of this textbook, The Second Cup attaches a statement of Management's Responsibility for Financial Reporting. This report includes the following statements to assure the reader that management takes its responsibility to produce reliable information seriously: "The management of Second Cup Ltd. is responsible for the integrity of the financial statements and all other information...contained within this annual report... The Company maintains systems of internal control which have been designed to provide reasonable assurance that accounting records are reliable and assets are safeguarded."

Before You Go On . . .

▶*Review It*

1. What is included as cash on a company's balance sheet?
2. What is meant by cash equivalents and compensating balances?
3. At what amount does The Second Cup report its cash and cash equivalents on its 2000 consolidated balance sheet? The answer to this question is provided at the end of the chapter.
4. How should a company report its responsibilities for internal control?

Related exercise material: BE8–12 and E8–12.

▶*A Look Back at Our Feature Story*

Refer to the feature story about Stephanie's Gourmet Coffee and More café at the beginning of the chapter, and answer the following questions:
1. Does Stephanie Mintenko have a valid basis for establishing responsibility for cash overages or shortages? Why or why not?
2. What internal control principles are applicable to reconciling the cash register tape and the amount of cash in the cash drawer at the end of each shift?
3. What internal control principle is violated by not printing a receipt for each customer who purchases beverages or a meal, or uses the café's computer?
4. Do you think cashiers are, or should be, bonded (insured against misappropriation of assets)?
5. What entry would the bookkeeper likely make to record a cash shortage of $5?

Solution

1. Establishing responsibility for cash overages or shortages occurs twice a day: at the end of the 5:00 p.m. shift, and at closing. This procedure provides a valid basis for evaluation if only one person worked an assigned register since the last reconciliation. Since up to three people work a single register during a shift, there is no valid basis for establishing who is responsible for any overage or shortage.
2. The following are relevant internal control principles: (a) Authorization—not applicable since cashiers are not assigned to a specific cash register for their shift. (b) Segregation of duties—cashiers (other than the owner/manager, Ms. Mintenko) are not involved in performing the reconciliation. (c) Documentation—the cash register tape provides the documentation for total receipts for the shift. (d) Safeguard assets—an electronic cash register is used with an internal tape that presumably has restricted access. (e) Independent verification—a bookkeeper, in addition to Stephanie Mintenko, performs the reconciliation regularly.
3. The principle of documentation procedures is involved. If a customer making a purchase sees that a sale isn't rung up or if the customer doesn't request a receipt, there is a possibility that the transaction has not been recorded. But the internal control does not reside in the receipt itself. The control is forcing the cashier to ring up each sale so that a receipt is produced. Each receipt is recorded on an internal cash register tape. At the end of the day, the tape is used to determine overages or shortages and to record the cash receipts.
4. It is doubtful that Stephanie's café would bond part-time employees. From the employer's standpoint, bonding is protection against major embezzlements by dishonest employees. The risk of this occurring in a small café which benefits from the active participation of the owner/manager is relatively low.
5. Cash Over and Short (miscellaneous expense account) 5
       Cash 5

THE NAVIGATOR

DEMONSTRATION PROBLEM

Trillo Company's bank statement for May 2003 shows the following data:

Balance May 31	$14,208

Debit memorandum:		Credit memorandum:	
NSF cheque	$175	Collection of note receivable	$505

The cash balance per books at May 31 is $13,319. Your review of the data reveals the following:
1. The NSF cheque was from Hup Co., a customer.
2. The note collected by the bank was a $500, three-month, 12% note. The bank charged a $10 collection fee. No interest has been accrued.
3. Outstanding cheques at May 31 total $2,410.
4. Deposits in transit at May 31 total $1,752.
5. A Trillo Company cheque for $352 dated May 10 cleared the bank on May 15. This cheque, which was a payment to Kwon Company on account, was journalized for $325.
6. The bank made an error in recording one of the company's deposits. The correct amount was $880, but it was processed as $808.

Instructions

(a) Prepare a bank reconciliation at May 31.
(b) Journalize the entries required by the reconciliation.

Additional Demonstration Problem

Solution to Demonstration Problem

(a)

TRILLO COMPANY
Bank Reconciliation
May 31, 2003

Cash balance per bank statement		$14,208
Add: Deposits in transit		1,752
Error in recording deposit ($880 – $808)		72
		16,032
Less: Outstanding cheques		2,410
Adjusted cash balance per bank		$13,622
Cash balance per books		$13,319
Add: Collection of note receivable, $500,		
plus $15 ($500 × 12% × 3/12) interest, less		
$10 collection fee		505
		13,824
Less: NSF cheque	$175	
Error in recording cheque ($352 – $325)	27	202
Adjusted cash balance per books		$13,622

(b)

May 31	Cash		505	
	Bank Charges Expense		10	
	Notes Receivable			500
	Interest Revenue			15
	To record collection of note by bank.			
31	Accounts Receivable—Hup Co.		175	
	Cash			175
	To record NSF cheque from Hup Co.			
31	Accounts Payable—Kwon Company		27	
	Cash			27
	To correct error in recording cheque.			

Action Plan
- Follow the four steps in the reconciliation procedures described in this chapter.
- Be especially careful when you deal with any errors which have been made. Item 5 involves a cheque written by the company for which the company deducted too little from its cash balance. Item 6 involves a deposit made by the company for which the bank added too little to the company's account.
- All the journal entries should be based on the reconciling items per books.
- Make sure the cash ledger account balance, after posting the reconciling items, agrees with the adjusted cash balance per books.

THE NAVIGATOR

Summary of Study Objectives

1. Describe internal control. Internal control consists of the policies and procedures within an organization to optimize its resources, prevent and detect errors and irregularities, safeguard its assets, and maintain reliable control systems.

2. Explain the principles of internal control and be able to identify weaknesses and suggest improvements in their application. The principles of internal control are authorization, segregation of duties, documentation, safeguarding of assets and records, independent verification, and other controls.

3. Explain and critique the application of internal control principles to cash receipts. Internal controls over cash receipts include (a) designating only personnel such as cashiers to handle cash, (b) assigning the duties of receiving cash, recording cash, and maintaining custody of cash to different individuals, (c) obtaining remittance advices for mail receipts, cash register tapes for over-the-counter receipts, and deposit slips for bank deposits, (d) using company safes and bank vaults to store cash with access limited to authorized personnel, and using cash registers to issue over-the-counter receipts, (e) depositing all cash intact daily, (f) making independent daily counts of register receipts and daily comparisons of total receipts with total deposits, and (g) bonding personnel that handle cash.

4. Explain and critique the application of internal control principles to cash disbursements. Internal controls over cash disbursements include (a) authorizing only specified individuals such as the comptroller to sign cheques, (b) assigning the duties of approving items for payment, paying for the items, and recording the payment to different individuals, (c) using prenumbered cheques and accounting for all cheques, with each cheque supported by an approved invoice, (d) storing blank cheques in a safe or vault, with access restricted to authorized per-

THE NAVIGATOR

sonnel, and using a cheque writer to imprint amounts on cheques, (e) comparing each cheque to the approved invoice before issuing the cheque, and making monthly reconciliations of bank and book balances, and (f) after payment, stamping each approved invoice as a "Paid".

5. Demonstrate the operation of a petty cash fund. In operating a petty cash fund, it is necessary to establish the fund, make payments from the fund, and replenish the fund. Journal entries are made only when the fund is established and replenished.

6. Describe the control features of a bank account. A bank account contributes to good internal control by providing physical controls for the storage of cash, minimizing the amount of currency that must be kept on hand, and creating a double record of a depositor's bank transactions.

7. Prepare a bank reconciliation. In reconciling the bank account, it is customary to reconcile the balance per books and balance per bank to their adjusted balances. The steps in determining the reconciling items are to identify each of the following: deposits in transit, outstanding cheques, errors by the depositor or the bank, and unrecorded bank memoranda. Correcting entries must be made for any errors made by the depositor (the company). Entries are also required to update unrecorded bank memoranda (e.g., interest).

8. Explain the reporting of cash. Cash is listed first in the current assets section of the balance sheet. In many cases, cash is reported together with temporary investments (cash equivalents). Cash restricted for a special purpose is reported separately as a current asset or as a noncurrent asset, depending on when the cash is expected to be used. The cash flow statement and the management report on the financial statements are useful tools to assess management's effectiveness in managing and controlling cash.

Glossary

Bank overdraft   Excess of withdrawals over the amount available in the bank account. (p. 394)

Bank service charge   A fee charged by a bank for the use of its services. (p. 389)

Bank statement   A statement received monthly from the bank that shows the depositor's bank transactions and balances. (p. 388)

Cash   Resources such as coins, currency, cheques, and money orders that are acceptable at face value on deposit in a bank or similar depository. (p. 379)

Cash equivalents   Highly liquid investments, with maturities of three months or less when purchased, that can be converted to a specific amount of cash. (p. 394)

Compensating balances   Minimum cash balances required by a bank in support of bank loans. (p. 395)

 Key Term Matching Activity

Deposits in transit   Deposits recorded by the depositor that have not been recorded by the bank. (p. 391)

Electronic funds transfer (EFT)   A disbursement system that uses telephone, computer, or wireless means to transfer cash from one location to another. (p. 386)

External auditors   Auditors who are independent of the organization and attest to the reasonableness of financial statements or other financial information. (p. 377)

Internal auditors   Company employees who evaluate on a continuous basis the effectiveness of the company's system of internal control. (p. 376)

Internal control   The policies and procedures adopted within a business to optimize resources, prevent and detect errors and irregularities, safeguard assets, and maintain reliable control systems. (p. 372)

Outstanding cheques Cheques issued and recorded by a company that have not been paid by the bank. (p. 391).

Petty cash fund A cash fund used to pay relatively small amounts. (p. 383)

SELF-STUDY QESTIONS

Chapter 8 Self-Test

Answers are at the end of the chapter.

(SO 1) K 1. Which of the following is *not* an objective of internal control?
   a. Optimize resources
   b. Eliminate errors
   c. Safeguard assets
   d. Maintain reliable control systems

(SO 2) K 2. The principles of internal control do *not* include:
   a. authorization.
   b. documentation procedures.
   c. cost-benefit.
   d. independent verification.

(SO 2) K 3. Physical controls do *not* include:
   a. safes and vaults to store cash.
   b. bank reconciliations.
   c. locked warehouses for inventories.
   d. bank safety deposit boxes for important papers.

(SO 3) K 4. Which of the following items in a cash drawer at November 30 is not cash?
   a. Debit card slips arising from sales to customers
   b. Bank credit card slips arising from sales to customers
   c. A customer cheque dated December 1
   d. A customer cheque dated November 28

(SO 3) C 5. Permitting only designated personnel to handle cash receipts is an application of the principle of:
   a. segregation of duties.
   b. authorization.
   c. independent verification.
   d. other controls.

(SO 4) C 6. The use of prenumbered cheques in disbursing cash is an application of the principle of:
   a. authorization.
   b. segregation of duties.
   c. physical, mechanical, and electronic controls.
   d. documentation procedures.

(SO 5) AP 7. A cheque is written to replenish a $100 petty cash fund when the fund contains receipts of $94 and $3 in cash. In recording the cheque:
   a. Cash Over and Short should be debited for $3.
   b. Petty Cash should be debited for $94.
   c. Cash should be credited for $94.
   d. Petty Cash should be credited for $3.

(SO 6) C 8. The control features of a bank account do *not* include:
   a. having bank auditors verify the correctness of the bank balance per books.
   b. minimizing the amount of cash that must be kept on hand.
   c. providing a double record of all bank transactions.
   d. safeguarding cash by using a bank as a depository.

(SO 7) C 9. In a bank reconciliation, deposits in transit are:
   a. deducted from the book balance.
   b. added to the book balance.
   c. added to the bank balance.
   d. deducted from the bank balance.

(SO 7) C 10. One reconciling item in a bank reconciliation that will result in an entry by the depositor is:
   a. outstanding cheques.
   b. a deposit in transit.
   c. a bank error.
   d. bank service charges.

(SO 8) K 11. The statement that correctly describes the reporting of cash is:
   a. Cash cannot be combined with cash equivalents.
   b. Restricted cash funds may be combined with Cash.
   c. Cash and cash equivalents are listed first in the current asset section.
   d. Restricted cash funds are always reported as a current asset.

THE NAVIGATOR

QUESTIONS

(SO 2) C 1. "Internal control is concerned only with enhancing the accuracy of the accounting records." Do you agree? Explain.

(SO 2) K 2. What principles of internal control apply to most business enterprises?

(SO 2) C 3. J. Duma is reviewing the principle of segregation of duties. What are two common applications of this principle?

(SO 2) C 4. How do documentation procedures contribute to good internal control?

(SO 2) K 5. What internal control objectives are met by physical, mechanical, and electronic controls?

(SO 2) C 6. (a) Explain the control principle of independent verification. (b) What practices are important in applying this principle?

(SO 2) C   7. The management of Ly Company asks you, as the company accountant, to explain: (a) the concept of reasonable assurance in internal control, and (b) the importance of the human factor in internal control.

(SO 2) AP   8. Sirois Company owns the following assets at the balance sheet date:

Cash in bank—savings account	$ 6,000
Cash on hand	850
Cash refund due from the	
Canada Customs and Revenue Agency	1,000
Cash in bank—chequing account	12,000
Postdated cheques	500

What amount should be reported as cash in the balance sheet?

(SO 3) AN   9. At the corner grocery store, all sales clerks make change out of one cash register drawer using the same password. Is this a violation of internal control? Explain.

(SO 3) AN   10. What principles of internal control are involved in making daily cash counts of over-the-counter receipts?

(SO 3) C   11. Creaghan's Department Stores has just installed electronic cash registers in its stores. How do cash registers improve internal control over cash receipts?

(SO 3) C   12. At Vink Wholesale Company, two mail clerks open all mail receipts. How does this strengthen internal control?

(SO 4) C   13. "To have maximum effective internal control over cash disbursements, all payments should be made by cheque." Is this true? Explain.

(SO 4) C   14. Ouellette Company's internal controls over cash disbursements require the controller to sign cheques imprinted by a computer after comparing the cheque with the approved invoice. Identify the internal control principles that are present in these procedures.

(SO 4) C   15. How do physical, mechanical, electronic, and other controls apply to cash disbursements? Give examples.

(SO 5) C   16. (a) Identify the three activities that pertain to a petty cash fund, and indicate an internal control principle that is applicable to each activity. (b) When are journal entries required in the operation of a petty cash fund?

(SO 6) K   17. What is the essential feature of an electronic funds transfer?

(SO 6) C   18. "The use of a bank contributes significantly to good internal control over cash." Is this true? Explain.

(SO 7) C   19. Paul Reimer is confused about the lack of agreement between the cash balance per books and the balance per bank. Explain the causes for the lack of agreement to Paul, and give an example of each cause.

(SO 7) K   20. What are the four steps involved in finding differences between the balance per books and the balance per bank?

(SO 7) C   21. Omar Basabe asks for your help concerning an NSF cheque. Explain to Omar (a) what an NSF cheque is, (b) how it is treated in a bank reconciliation, and (c) whether it will require an adjusting entry.

(SO 8) C   22. (a) "Cash equivalents are the same as cash." Do you agree? Explain. (b) How should restricted cash funds be reported on the balance sheet?

BRIEF EXERCISES

··

Explain the importance of internal control.
(SO 1) C

BE8–1   Natalie McPhail is the new owner of Liberty Parking—a parking garage. She has heard about internal control but is not clear about its importance for her business. Explain to Natalie the purposes of internal control, and give her one application of each purpose for Liberty Parking.

Identify internal control principles.
(SO 2) K

BE8–2   The internal control procedures in Vanderlinde Company include the following:
1. Employees who have physical custody of assets do not have access to the accounting records.
2. Each month the assets on hand are compared to the accounting records by an internal auditor.
3. A prenumbered shipping document is prepared for each shipment of goods to customers.

Identify the principles of internal control that are being followed.

Identify internal control principles applicable to cash receipts.
(SO 3) K

BE8–3   The Miramichi Company has the following internal control procedures over cash receipts. Identify the internal control principle that is applicable to each procedure.
1. All over-the-counter receipts are recorded on cash registers.
2. All cashiers are bonded.
3. Daily cash counts are made by cashier department supervisors.
4. The duties of receiving cash, recording cash, and maintaining custody of cash are assigned to different individuals.
5. Only cashiers may operate cash registers.
6. All cash is deposited intact in the bank account daily.

Identify internal control principles applicable to cash disbursements.
(SO 4) K

BE8–4   Bujold Company has the following internal control procedures over cash disbursements. Identify the internal control principle that is applicable to each procedure.
1. Company cheques are prenumbered.
2. The bank statement is reconciled monthly by an internal auditor.

3. Blank cheques are stored in a safe in the controller's office.
4. Only the controller or assistant controller may sign cheques.
5. Cheque signers are not allowed to record cash disbursement transactions.
6. All payments, except for petty cash transactions, are made by cheque.

BE8–5   On March 20, Pugh's petty cash fund of $100 is replenished when the fund contains $11 in cash and receipts for postage $52, freight out $26, and travel expense $10. Prepare the journal entry to record the replenishment of the petty cash fund.

Prepare a journal entry to replenish petty cash fund.
(SO 5) AP

BE8–6   Explain the control features of a bank account, including the control benefits of (a) signature cards, (b) cheques, and (c) bank statements.

Identify internal control features of a bank account.
(SO 6) C

BE8–7   The following reconciling items are applicable to the bank reconciliation for Savoie Company: (1) outstanding cheques from the current month, (2) outstanding cheques from prior months that are still outstanding, (3) outstanding cheques from prior months that have cleared the bank and are no longer outstanding, (4) a bank debit memorandum for a service charge, (5) a bank credit memorandum for collecting a note for the depositor, and (6) a deposit in transit. Indicate how each item should be shown on a bank reconciliation. If the item is not included on a bank reconciliation, say so.

Indicate location of items in a bank reconciliation.
(SO 7) K

BE8–8   Referring to BE8–7, indicate (a) the items that will result in an adjustment to the depositor's records, and (b) why the other items do not require adjustment.

Identify reconciling items that require journal entries.
(SO 7) C

BE8–9   In the month of November, Jayasinghe Company wrote and recorded cheques in the amount of $9,250. In December, it wrote and recorded cheques in the amount of $12,716. Of these cheques, $8,578 were presented to the bank for payment in November, $10,889 in December. What is the amount of outstanding cheques at the end of November? At the end of December?

Analyse outstanding cheques.
(SO 7) AP

BE8–10   At July 31, Hubert Company has the following bank information: cash balance per bank $7,920, outstanding cheques $762, deposits in transit $1,700, and bank service charge $20. Determine the adjusted cash balance per bank at July 31.

Prepare partial bank reconciliation.
(SO 7) AP

BE8–11   At August 31, Kahn Company has a cash balance per books of $9,100 and the following additional data from the bank statement: charge for printing Kahn Company cheques $35, interest earned on chequing account balance $25, and outstanding cheques $800. Determine the adjusted cash balance per books at August 31.

Prepare partial bank reconciliation.
(SO 7) AP

BE8–12   Dupré Company has the following cash balances: Cash in Bank $15,742; Payroll Bank Account $6,000; and Plant Expansion Fund Cash $25,000. Dupré maintains a $3,000 compensating bank balance in a separate account. Explain how each balance should be reported on the balance sheet.

Explain statement presentation of various cash balances.
(SO 8) C

EXERCISES

• •

E8–1   Per Paasche is the owner of Luna's Pizza. Luna's is operated strictly on a carry-out basis. Customers pick up their orders at a counter where a clerk exchanges the pizza for cash. While at the counter, the customer can see other employees making the pizzas and the large ovens in which the pizzas are baked.

Identify the principles of internal control.
(SO 2, 3) C

Instructions

Identify the principles of internal control and give an example of each principle that you might observe when picking up your pizza. (*Note*: It may not be possible to observe all of the principles in action.)

E8–2   The following control procedures are used in the Sheridan Company for over-the-counter cash receipts:

1. Cashiers are experienced, so they are not bonded.
2. All over-the-counter receipts are registered by three clerks who use a cash register with a single cash drawer.
3. To minimize the risk of robbery, cash in excess of $100 is stored in a briefcase in the stock room until it is deposited in the bank.
4. At the end of each day, the total receipts are counted by the cashier on duty and reconciled to the cash register total.

Identify weaknesses in internal control over cash receipts, and suggest improvements.
(SO 2, 3) AN

5. The company accountant makes the bank deposit and then records the day's receipts.

Instructions

(a) For each procedure, explain the weakness in internal control and identify the control principle that is violated.

(b) For each weakness, suggest a change in procedure that will result in better internal control.

Identify weaknesses in internal control over cash disbursements, and suggest improvements. (SO 2, 4) AN

E8–3   The following control procedures are used for cash disbursements in Kailyn's Boutique Shoppe:

1. Each week, Kailyn leaves 100 company cheques in an unmarked envelope on a shelf behind the cash register.
2. The store manager personally approves all payments before signing and issuing cheques.
3. When the store manager has to go away for extended periods of time, she presigns some cheques to be used in her absence.
4. The company cheques are not numbered.
5. After payment, bills are filed in a paid invoice folder.
6. The company accountant prepares the bank reconciliation and reports any discrepancies to the owner.

Instructions

(a) For each procedure, explain the weakness in internal control and identify the internal control principle that is violated.

(b) For each weakness, suggest a change in procedure that will result in better internal control.

List weaknesses in internal control over cash disbursements, and suggest improvements. (SO 2, 4) S

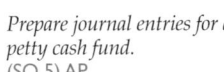

E8–4   In the Abekah Company, cheques are not prenumbered. Both the purchasing agent and the controller are authorized to issue cheques. Each signer has access to unissued cheques kept in an unlocked file cabinet. The purchasing agent pays all bills that pertain to goods purchased for resale. Prior to payment, the purchasing agent determines that the goods have been received and verifies the mathematical accuracy of the vendor's invoice. After payment, the invoice is filed by vendor, and the purchasing agent records the payment in the cash payments journal. The controller pays all other bills after receiving approval from authorized employees. After payment, the controller stamps all bills PAID, files them by payment date, and records the cheques in the cash payments journal. Abekah Company maintains one chequing account that is reconciled by the controller.

Instructions

(a) List the weaknesses in internal control over cash disbursements.

(b) Write a memo to the company controller in which you recommend improvements.

Prepare journal entries for a petty cash fund. (SO 5) AP

E8–5   Auld Company uses an imprest petty cash system. The fund was established on March 1 with a balance of $100. During March, the following petty cash receipts were found in the petty cash box:

Date	Receipt No.	For	Amount
Mar. 5	1	Postage Stamps	$38
7	2	Freight In (assume perpetual inventory system)	19
9	3	Miscellaneous Expense	12
11	4	Travel Expense	24
14	5	Miscellaneous Expense	5

There was $4 in the cash box when the fund was replenished on March 15. On March 20, the amount in the fund was increased to $150.

Instructions

Journalize the entries in March for the operation of the petty cash fund.

Identify bank reconciling items and journalize petty cash reimbursement. (SO 5, 7) AP

E8–6   Part 1: The following items were found on the company's bank reconciliation

1. An outstanding deposit
2. A credit memo, for collection of notes receivable and related interest
3. Outstanding cheques
4. A debit memo for bank service charges
5. An NSF cheque
6. A credit memo for interest on average monthly balance

Part 2: A check of the petty cash fund on May 31 indicated the following:

The petty cash fund was established at $100 on May 1. At the end of the month, the fund contained $18 and had the following receipts:

Transportation charges (on outgoing freight)	$15
Postage	8
Printing	27
Entertainment	24

Instructions

(a) Identify whether each of the items listed in Part 1 affects the bank or book side of a bank reconciliation. Indicate whether the amount would represent an addition or a subtraction.
(b) Which of the items in Part 1 require a journal entry?
(c) Prepare the journal entry for the reimbursement of the petty cash fund in Part 2 on May 31.

Source: Adapted from Certified General Accountants Association of Canada, *Financial Accounting 1 Examination*, March 1998, Question 3.

E8–7 Harvir Bansal is unable to reconcile the Bansal Company's bank balance at January 31. Harvir's reconciliation is as follows:

Prepare a bank reconciliation and related entries. (SO 7) AP

Cash balance per bank	$3,660.20
Add: NSF cheque	630.00
Less: Bank service charge	25.00
Adjusted balance per bank	$4,265.20
Cash balance per books	$3,875.20
Less: Deposits in transit	490.00
Add: Outstanding cheques	930.00
Adjusted balance per books	$4,315.20

Instructions

(a) Prepare a correct bank reconciliation.
(b) Journalize the entries required by the reconciliation.

E8–8 On April 30, the bank reconciliation of Hickley Company shows three outstanding cheques: No. 254 for $650; No. 255 for $820; and No. 257 for $410. The May bank statement and the May cash payments journal show the following:

Determine the outstanding cheques for bank reconciliation. (SO 7) AP

Bank Statement Cheques Paid			Cash Payments Journal Cheques Issued		
Date	Cheque No.	Amount	Date	Cheque No.	Amount
5/2	254	$650	5/2	258	$159
5/4	257	410	5/5	259	275
5/12	258	159	5/10	260	925
5/17	259	275	5/15	261	500
5/20	261	500	5/22	262	750
5/29	263	480	5/24	263	480
5/30	262	750	5/29	264	560

Instructions

List the outstanding cheques at May 31.

E8–9 The following information is for Alaa Company:

Prepare bank reconciliation and related entries. (SO 7) AP

1. Cash balance per bank, July 31, $7,263
2. July bank service charge not recorded by the depositor, $15
3. Cash balance per books, July 31, $7,190
4. Deposits in transit, July 31, $1,500
5. Note for $800 collected for Alaa in July by the bank, plus interest $36, less fee $20. The collection has not been recorded by Alaa, and no interest has been accrued on the note.
6. Outstanding cheques, July 31, $772

Instructions

(a) Prepare a bank reconciliation at July 31.
(b) Journalize the correcting entries at July 31 on the books of Alaa Company.

Prepare bank reconciliation and related entries.
(SO 7) AP

E8–10   The information below relates to the Cash account in the ledger of Sharaf Company:

Balance September 1—$17,150; Cash deposited—$64,000; Cheques written—$63,746; Balance September 30—$17,404

The September bank statement shows a balance of $16,422 on September 30 and the following memorandum:

Credits		Debits	
Collection of $1,800 note plus interest $30	$1,830	NSF cheque: J. Hower	$410
Interest earned on chequing account	45	Safety deposit box rent	30

At September 30, deposits in transit were $4,800 and outstanding cheques totalled $2,383. No errors were made by the bank or the company.

Instructions

(a) Show how the September 30 unadjusted balance of $17,404 in the Cash account was calculated.
(b) Prepare the bank reconciliation at September 30.
(c) Prepare the required entries at September 30, assuming (1) the NSF cheque was from a customer on account, and (2) no interest had been previously accrued on the note.

Calculate the deposits in transit and outstanding cheques for two months.
(SO 7) AP

E8–11   The cash records of Nishijima Company show the following:

1. The June 30 bank reconciliation indicated that deposits in transit totalled $950. During July, the general ledger account Cash showed deposits of $15,750, but the bank statement indicated that only $15,600 of deposits was received during the month.
2. The June 30 bank reconciliation also reported outstanding cheques of $920. During the month of July, Nishijima Company books showed that cheques worth $17,200 were issued, yet the bank statement showed that only $16,400 of cheques cleared the bank in July.
3. In September, deposits per bank statement totalled $26,700, deposits per books totalled $25,400, and deposits in transit at September 30 totalled $2,600.
4. In September, cash disbursements per books were $23,700, cheques clearing the bank were $25,000, and outstanding cheques at September 30 were $2,100.

There were no bank debit or credit memoranda. No errors were made by either the bank or Nishijima Company.

Instructions

Answer the following questions:

(a) In number 1, what were the deposits in transit at July 31?
(b) In number 2, what were the outstanding cheques at July 31?
(c) In number 3, what were the deposits in transit at August 31?
(d) In number 4, what were the outstanding cheques at August 31?

Identify the reporting of cash and cash equivalents and other items.
(SO 8) AP

E8–12   A new accountant at La Maison is trying to identify which of the following amounts should be reported as the current asset "Cash and Cash Equivalents" in the year-end balance sheet, as at April 30, 2003:

1. Currency and coin totalling $57 in a locked box used for petty cash transactions
2. A $10,000 guaranteed investment certificate, due May 31, 2003
3. April-dated cheques worth $300 that La Maison has received from customers but not yet deposited
4. An $85 cheque received from a customer in payment of her April account, but postdated May 1
5. A balance of $2,500 in the Royal Bank chequing account
6. A balance of $4,000 in the Royal Bank savings account
7. Prepaid postage of $75 in the postage meter
8. A $100 IOU from the company receptionist

Instructions

(a) What amount should La Maison report as its "Cash and Cash Equivalents" balance at April 30, 2003?
(b) In which financial statement and in which account should the items not included as "Cash and Cash Equivalents" be reported?

PROBLEMS: SET A

P8–1A Red River Theatre is located in the Red River Mall. A cashier's booth is located near the entrance to the theatre. Two cashiers are employed. One works from 1:00 to 5:00 p.m., the other from 5:00 to 9:00 p.m. Each cashier is bonded. The cashiers receive cash from customers and operate a machine that ejects serially numbered tickets. The rolls of tickets are inserted and locked into the machine by the theatre manager at the beginning of each cashier's shift.

After purchasing a ticket, which may be at different prices depending on the day or age group, the customer takes the ticket to an usher stationed at the entrance of the theatre lobby, about 10 metres from the cashier's booth. The usher tears the ticket in half, admits the customer, and returns the ticket stub to the customer. The other half of the ticket is dropped into a locked box by the usher.

At the end of each cashier's shift, the theatre manager removes the ticket rolls from the machine and makes a cash count. The cash count sheet is initialled by the cashier. At the end of the day, the manager deposits the receipts in total in a bank night deposit vault located in the mall. The manager also sends copies of the deposit slip and the initialled cash count sheets to the theatre company controller for verification, and to the company's accounting department. Receipts from the first shift are stored in a safe located in the manager's office.

Identify internal control weaknesses over cash receipts.
(SO 2, 3) AN

Instructions

(a) Identify the internal control principles and their application to the cash receipts transactions of the Red River Theatre.

(b) If the usher and the cashier decide to collaborate to misappropriate cash, what actions might they take?

P8–2A Cedar Grove Middle School wants to raise money for a new sound system for its auditorium. The primary fundraising event is a dance at which the famous disc jockey Obnoxious Al will play classic and not-so-classic dance tunes. Roger DeMaster, the music and theatre instructor, has been given the responsibility for coordinating the fundraising efforts. This is Roger's first experience with fundraising. He asks the Student Representative Council (SRC) to help him with the event.

Roger had 500 unnumbered tickets printed for the dance. He left the tickets in a box on his desk and told the SRC students to take as many tickets as they thought they could sell for $5 each. In order to ensure that no extra tickets would be floating around, he told them to dispose of any unsold tickets. When the students received payment for the tickets, they were to bring the cash back to Roger. He then put it in a locked box in his desk drawer.

Some of the students were responsible for decorating the gymnasium for the dance. Roger gave each of them a key to the money box. He told them that if they took money out to purchase materials, they should put a note in the box saying how much they took and what it was used for. After two weeks, the money box appeared to be getting full, so Roger asked Freda Stevens to count the money, prepare a deposit slip, and deposit the money in a bank account Roger had opened.

The day of the dance, Roger wrote a cheque from the account to pay Obnoxious Al. Al said that he accepted only cash and did not give receipts. So Roger took $200 out of the cash box and gave it to Al. At the dance, Roger had Sara Billings working at the entrance to the gymnasium. She collected tickets from students and sold tickets to those who had not prepurchased them. Roger estimated 400 students attended the dance.

The following day Roger closed out the bank account, which had $250 in it. He gave that amount plus the $180 in the cash box to Principal Skinner. Principal Skinner seemed surprised that, after generating roughly $2,000 in sales, the dance netted only $430 in cash. Roger did not know how to respond.

Identify internal control weaknesses over cash receipts and cash disbursements.
(SO 2, 3, 4) AN

Instructions

Identify as many internal control weaknesses as you can in this scenario. Suggest how each could be addressed.

P8–3A MTR Company maintains a petty cash fund for small expenditures. The following transactions occurred over a two-month period:

July 1 Established a petty cash fund by writing a cheque on its bank account for $200.

    15 Replenished the petty cash fund by writing a cheque for $196.30. On this date the fund consisted of $3.70 in cash and the following petty cash receipts: Freight out $94.00, postage expense $42.40, entertainment expense $46.60, and miscellaneous expense $10.70.

    31 Replenished the petty cash fund by writing a cheque for $192.00. At this date, the fund consisted of $8.00 in cash and the following petty cash receipts: freight out $82.10,

Journalize and post petty cash fund transactions and identify internal control features.
(SO 2, 5) AP

charitable contributions expense $30.00, postage expense $47.80, and miscellaneous expense $32.10.

Aug. 15 Replenished the petty cash fund by writing a cheque for $188.00. On this date, the fund consisted of $12.00 in cash and the following petty cash receipts: freight out $74.40, entertainment expense $43.00, postage expense $33.00, and supplies expense $38.00.

   16 Increased the amount of the petty cash fund to $300 by writing a cheque for $100.

   31 Replenished the petty cash fund by writing a cheque for $283.00. On this date, the fund consisted of $17 in cash and the following petty cash receipts: postage expense $145.00, entertainment expense $90.60, and freight out $45.40.

Instructions

(a) Journalize the petty cash transactions.
(b) Post to the Petty Cash account.
(c) What internal control features exist in a petty cash fund?

Prepare bank reconciliation and related entries.
(SO 7) AP

P8–4A   On May 31, 2003, Lisik Company had a cash balance per books of $6,781.50. The bank statement on that date showed a balance of $7,804.60. A comparison of the statement with the Cash account revealed the following facts:

1. The statement included a debit memo of $40 for the printing of additional company cheques.
2. Cash sales of $836.15 on May 12 were deposited in the bank. The cash receipts journal entry and the deposit slip were incorrectly made out for $846.15. The bank detected the error on the deposit slip and credited Lisik Company for the correct amount.
3. Outstanding cheques at May 31 totalled $1,276.25, and deposits in transit totalled $936.15.
4. On May 18, the company issued cheque No. 1181 for $685 to M. Helms, on account. The cheque, which cleared the bank in May, was incorrectly journalized and posted by Lisik Company for $658.
5. A $2,000 note receivable plus $80 interest was collected by the bank for Lisik Company on May 31. The bank charged a collection fee of $20. No interest has been accrued on the note.
6. Included with the cancelled cheques was a cheque issued by *Lasik* Company for $600 that was incorrectly charged to Lisik Company by the bank.
7. On May 31, the bank statement showed an NSF charge of $700 for a cheque issued by W. Hoad, a customer, to Lisik Company on account.

Instructions

(a) Prepare the bank reconciliation at May 31, 2003.
(b) Prepare the necessary correcting entries for Lisik Company at May 31, 2003.

Prepare bank reconciliation and related entries.
(SO 7) AP

P8–5A   The bank portion of the bank reconciliation for McIsaac Company at October 31, 2003, was as follows:

McISAAC COMPANY
Bank Reconciliation
October 31, 2003

Cash balance per bank		$12,367.90
Add: Deposits in transit		1,530.20
		13,898.10
Less: Outstanding cheques		

Cheque Number	Cheque Amount	
2451	$1,260.40	
2470	720.10	
2471	844.50	
2472	426.80	
2474	1,050.00	4,301.80
Adjusted cash balance per bank		$ 9,596.30

The adjusted cash balance per bank agreed with the cash balance per books at October 31. The November bank statement showed the following:

McISAAC COMPANY
Bank Statement
November 30, 2003

Date	Deposits Amount	Cheques and Other Debits Number	Amount	Balance
10-31				$12,367.90
11-1	$1,530.20	2470	$ 720.10	13,178.00
11-2		2471	844.50	12,333.50
11-4	1,211.60	2475	1,640.70	11,904.40
11-5		2474	1,050.00	10,854.40
11-8	990.10	2476	2,830.00	9,014.50
11-10		2477	600.00	8,414.50
11-13	2,575.00			10,989.50
11-15		2479	1,750.00	9,239.50
11-18	1,472.70	2480	1,330.00	9,382.20
11-21	2,945.00			12,327.20
11-25	2,567.30	DM	50.00	14,844.50
11-27		2481	695.40	14,149.10
11-28	1,650.00			15,799.10
11-29	CM 2,105.00	2486	900.00	17,004.10
11-30	1,186.00	2483	575.50	17,614.60

The bank statement contained two memoranda:

1. A credit of $2,105 for the collection of a $2,000 note for McIsaac Company, plus interest of $120 and less a collection fee of $15. McIsaac Company had not accrued any interest on the note.
2. A debit for the printing of additional company cheques, $50.

The bank did not make any errors.

The cash records per books for November showed the following:
Two errors were made by McIsaac Company.

	Cash Payments Journal						Cash Receipts Journal	
Date	Number	Amount	Date	Number	Amount	Date	Amount	
11-1	2475	$1,640.70	11-20	2483	$ 575.50	11-3	$ 1,211.60	
11-2	2476	2,830.00	11-22	2484	829.50	11-7	990.10	
11-2	2477	600.00	11-23	2485	974.80	11-12	2,575.00	
11-4	2478	538.20	11-24	2486	900.00	11-17	1,472.70	
11-8	2479	1,570.00	11-29	2487	398.00	11-20	2,954.00	
11-10	2480	1,330.00	11-30	2488	1,200.00	11-24	2,567.30	
11-15	2481	695.40	Total		$14,694.10	11-27	1,650.00	
11-18	2482	612.00				11-29	1,186.00	
						11-30	1,225.00	
						Total	$15,831.70	

Instructions

(a) Determine the unadjusted cash balance per books as at November 30, 2003, prior to reconciliation.
(b) Prepare a bank reconciliation at November 30.
(c) Prepare the required entries based on the reconciliation. (*Note*: The correction of any errors in the recording of cheques should be made to Accounts Payable. The correction of any errors in the recording of cash receipts should be made to Accounts Receivable.)

*Prepare bank reconciliation and
related entries.*
(SO 7) AP

P8–6A   Videosoft Company maintains a chequing account at the Western Bank. At July 31, 2003, selected data from the ledger balance and the bank statement are as follows:

	Cash in Bank	
	Per Books	Per Bank
Balance, July 1	$17,600	$19,200
July receipts	82,000	
July credits		80,470
July disbursements	76,900	
July debits		74,740
Balance, July 31	$22,700	$24,930

An analysis of the bank data reveals that the credits consist of $79,000 of July deposits and a credit memorandum of $1,470 for the collection of a $1,400 note plus interest of $70. The July debits per bank consist of cheques cleared, $74,700, and a debit memorandum of $40 for printing additional company cheques.

You also discover the following errors involving July cheques: (1) A cheque for $230 to a creditor on account that cleared the bank in July was journalized and posted by Videosoft as $320. (2) A salary cheque to an employee for $255 was recorded by the bank for $155.

The June 30 bank reconciliation contained only two reconciling items: deposits in transit of $5,000 and outstanding cheques of $6,600.

Instructions

(a) Prepare a bank reconciliation at July 31.

(b) Journalize the correcting entries to be made by Videosoft Company at July 31, 2003. Assume that the interest on the note has been accrued.

*Prepare bank reconciliation and
related entries.*
(SO 7) AP

P8–7A   The March bank statement showed the following for Yap Co.:

			YAP CO.		
			Bank Statement		
			March 31, 2003		
	Deposits	Cheques and Other Debits			
Date	Amount	Number	Amount	Balance	
2-28				$14,368	
3-1	$2,530	3451	$2,260	14,638	
3-2		3471	845	13,793	
3-5	1,212			15,005	
3-7		3472	1,427	13,578	
3-10		NSF—Jordan	550	13,028	
3-15		3473	1,641	11,387	
3-22		3474	2,130	9,257	
3-27	2,567			11,824	
3-31		SC	49	11,775	

Additional information:

1. The bank statement contained two debit memoranda:
   (a) An NSF cheque in the amount of $550 that had been previously deposited by Yap was returned due to insufficient funds in the maker's bank account. This cheque was originally given to Yap by Mr. Jordan, a customer, in payment of his account. Yap believes it will be able to recollect this amount from Mr. Jordan.
   (b) A service charge (SC) of $49 for bank services provided throughout the month.
2. No errors were made by the bank.

Yap's cash receipts and cash payments journals showed the following for the month of March:

Cash Receipts		Cash Payments		
Date	Amount	Date	Cheque Number	Amount
3-4	$1,221	3-7	2472	$1,427
3-26	2,567	3-15	3473	1,641
3-20	1,025	3-22	3474	2,130
	$4,813	3-29	3475	600
				$5,798

The bank portion of last month's bank reconciliation for Yap Co., at February 28, 2003, was as follows:

YAP CO.
Bank Reconciliation
February 28, 2003

Cash balance per bank		$14,368
Add: Deposits in transit		2,530
		16,898
Less: Outstanding cheques		
Cheque Number	Cheque Amount	
3451	$2,260	
3470	720	
3471	845	3,825
Adjusted cash balance per bank		$13,073

Instructions

(a) Determine Yap Co.'s unadjusted cash balance in its general ledger, on March 31.
(b) What is the amount of the deposits in transit, if any, at March 31?
(c) What is the amount of the outstanding cheques, if any, at March 31?
(d) Prepare a bank reconciliation for Yap Co. for the month of March 2003.
(e) Prepare the required journal entries for Yap Co. on March 31, 2003.

P8–8A Aura Whole Foods is a very profitable small business. It has not, however, given much consideration to internal control. For example, in an attempt to keep clerical and office expenses to a minimum, the company has combined the jobs of cashier and bookkeeper. As a result, Jake Stickyfingers handles all cash receipts, keeps the accounting records, and prepares the monthly bank reconciliations.

Prepare bank reconciliation, and identify internal control deficiencies.
(SO 2, 3, 4, 7) AN

The balance per bank statement on October 31, 2003, was $22,075.51. Outstanding cheques were No. 62 for $326.75, No. 183 for $150, No. 284 for $253.25, No. 862 for $190.71, No. 863 for $226.80, and No. 864 for $165.28. Included with the statement was a credit memorandum for $300 that indicated the collection of a note receivable for Aura Whole Foods by the bank on October 25. This memorandum has not been recorded by Aura Whole Foods.

The company's ledger showed one Cash account, with a balance of $21,892.72. The balance included undeposited cash on hand of $1,430. Because of the lack of internal controls, Stickyfingers took for personal use all of the undeposited receipts. He then prepared the following bank reconciliation in an effort to conceal his theft of cash:

Cash balance per books, October 31		$21,892.72
Add: Outstanding cheques		
No. 862	$ 190.71	
No. 863	226.80	
No. 864	165.28	482.79
		22,375.51
Less: Undeposited receipts	$3,795.51	
Bank credit memorandum	300.00	4,095.51
Cash balance per bank statement, October 31		$18,280.00

Instructions

(a) Prepare a correct bank reconciliation. (*Hint*: Deduct the amount of the theft from the adjusted balance per books.)

(b) Indicate the ways that Stickyfingers attempted to conceal the theft and the dollar amount pertaining to each method.
(c) What principles of internal control were violated in this case?

Calculate cash balance.
(SO 8) AP

P8–9A   A first year co-op student is trying to determine the amount of cash that should be reported on a company's balance sheet. The following information was provided to the student at year end:
1. Cash on hand in the cash registers totals $5,000.
2. The petty cash fund is $500.
3. The balance in the commercial bank savings account is $100,000 and in the commercial bank chequing account, $25,000. The company also has $45,000 Canadian dollars in a U.S. bank account.
4. A special bank account holds cash in the amount of $150,000 that is restricted for capital asset replacement.
5. A line of credit in the amount of $50,000 is available at the bank on demand.
6. The amount due from employees (travel advances) totals $12,000.
7. Temporary investments held by the company include $32,000 in a money market fund, $25,000 in shares of Nortel Networks, and $75,000 in bonds of BCE Inc.
8. The company has a supply of unused postage stamps totalling $150.
9. The company has NSF cheques that were returned by the bank totalling $2,500.
10. The company has cash deposits (advances) paid by customers in the amount of $7,500 held in a special account.

Instructions

(a) Calculate the Cash balance that should be reported on the year end balance sheet as a current asset.
(b) Would your answer for (a) change if the company combines its Cash and Cash Equivalents?
(c) Identify where any items that were not reported in the Cash balance in (a) should be reported.

Problems: Set B

Identify internal control weaknesses over cash receipts.
(SO 2, 3) AN

P8–1B   The board of trustees of a local church is concerned about the internal accounting controls of its offering collections made at weekly services. Its members ask you to serve on a three-person audit team including yourself, the internal auditor of the university, and a CA who has just joined the church. At a meeting of the audit team and the board of trustees, you learn the following:
1. The church's board of trustees has delegated responsibility for the financial management and audit of the financial records to the finance committee. This group prepares the annual budget and approves major disbursements but is not involved in collections or record keeping. No audit has been done in recent years, because the same trusted employee has kept church records and served as financial secretary for 15 years. The church does not carry any fidelity insurance.
2. The collection at the weekly service is taken by a team of ushers who volunteer to serve for one month. The ushers take the collection plates to a basement office at the rear of the church. They hand their plates to the head usher and return to the church service. After all plates have been turned in, the head usher counts the cash received. The head usher then places the cash in the church safe along with a notation of the amount counted. The head usher volunteers to serve for three months.
3. The next morning, the financial secretary opens the safe and recounts the collection. The secretary withholds from $150 to $200 in cash, depending on the cash expenditures expected for the week, and deposits the remainder of the collections in the bank. To facilitate the deposit, church members who contribute by cheque are asked to make their cheques payable to Cash.
4. Each month the financial secretary reconciles the bank statement and submits a copy of the reconciliation to the board of trustees. The reconciliations have rarely contained any bank errors and have never shown any errors per books.

Instructions

(a) Indicate the weaknesses in internal control in the handling of collections.
(b) List the improvements in internal control procedures that you plan to recommend at the next meeting of the audit team for (1) the ushers, (2) the head usher, (3) the financial secretary, and (4) the finance committee.
(c) What church policies should be changed to improve internal control?

P8–2B   Vernette Office Supply Company recently changed its system of internal control over cash disbursements. The system includes the following features:

Identify internal control weaknesses over cash disbursements.
(SO 2, 4) AN

1. Instead of being unnumbered and manually prepared, all cheques are now prenumbered and written by an electronic cheque-writer purchased by the company. Before a cheque can be issued, each invoice must have the approval of Cindy Moonti, the purchasing agent, and Ian Methven, the receiving department supervisor. Cheques must be signed by either Frank Kepros, the controller, or Mary Arno, the assistant controller. Before signing a cheque, the signer is expected to compare the amount of the cheque with the amount on the invoice.
2. After signing a cheque, the signer stamps the invoice PAID and writes, within the stamp, the date, cheque number, and amount of the cheque. The paid invoice is then sent to the accounting department for recording.
3. Blank cheques are stored in a safe in the controller's office. The combination to the safe is known only by the controller and the assistant controller. Each month, the bank statement is reconciled by the assistant chief accountant.

Instructions

Identify the internal control principles and their application to the cash disbursements of Vernette Office Supply Company.

P8–3B   Vickers Company maintains a petty cash fund for small expenditures. The following transactions occurred over a two-month period:

Journalize and post petty cash fund transactions and identify internal control features.
(SO 2, 5) AP

Jan. 1   Established petty cash fund by writing a cheque on First Bank for $250.00.
     15   Replenished the petty cash fund by writing a cheque for $195.00. On this date, the fund consisted of $55.00 in cash and the following petty cash receipts: freight out $94.00, postage expense $42.40, office supplies expense $46.60, and miscellaneous expense $11.90.
     31   Replenished the petty cash fund by writing a cheque for $192.00. At this date, the fund consisted of $58.00 in cash and the following petty cash receipts: freight out $82.10, charitable contributions expense $40.00, postage expense $27.80, and miscellaneous expense $42.10.
Feb. 15   Replenished the petty cash fund by writing a cheque for $247.00. On this date, the fund consisted of $3.00 in cash and the following petty cash receipts: freight out $74.60, entertainment expense $43.00, postage expense $33.00, freight in $60.00 (assume perpetual inventory system), and miscellaneous expense $37.00.
     16   Increased the amount of the petty cash fund to $400.
     28   Replenished the petty cash fund by writing a cheque for $337.00. On this date, the fund consisted of $63 in cash and the following petty cash receipts: postage expense $140.00, travel expense $95.60, freight out $46.40, and office supplies expense, $55.00.

Instructions

(a) Journalize the petty cash transactions.
(b) Post to the Petty Cash account.
(c) It was stated in the chapter that "better internal control over cash disbursements is possible when payments are made by cheque." Why, then, are some cash payments made from petty cash rather than by cheque? Does this mean that there is no internal control over payments from petty cash? Explain.

P8–4B   Agricultural Genetics Company of Saskatoon spreads herbicides and applies liquid fertilizer for local farmers. On May 31, 2003, the company's cash account per general ledger showed the following balance:

Prepare bank reconciliation and related entries.
(SO 7) AP

Cash					No. 101
Date	Explanation	Ref.	Debit	Credit	Balance
May 31	Balance				7,393.50

The bank statement from the Western Bank on that date showed the following:

Cheques and Debits	Deposits and Credits	Daily Balance	
XXX	XXX	5-31	8,161.50

A comparison of the details in the bank statement to the details in the cash account revealed the following facts:

1. The statement included a debit memo of $50 for bank service charges.
2. Cash sales of $638 on May 12 were deposited in the bank. The cash receipts journal entry and the deposit slip were correctly made for $638. The bank credited Agricultural Genetics Company for $836.
3. Outstanding cheques at May 31 totalled $276, and deposits in transit totalled $936.

4. On May 18, the company issued cheque No. 1181 for $585 to L. Kingston, on account. The cheque, which cleared the bank in May, was incorrectly journalized and posted by Agricultural Genetics Company for $505.

5. A $2,000 note receivable was collected by the bank for Agricultural Genetics Company on May 31, plus interest. The note had an 8% interest rate and had been outstanding for six months. The bank charged a collection fee of $20. No interest has been accrued on the note.

6. On May 31, the bank statement showed an NSF charge of $700 for a cheque issued by Pete Dell, a customer, to Agricultural Genetics Company on account.

Instructions

(a) Prepare the bank reconciliation at May 31, 2003.

(b) Prepare the necessary entries for Agricultural Genetics Company at May 31, 2003.

Prepare bank reconciliation and related entries.
(SO 7) AP

P8–5B   The bank portion of the bank reconciliation for Hilo Company at November 30, 2003, was as follows:

HILO COMPANY
Bank Reconciliation
November 30, 2003

Cash balance per bank		$14,367.90
Add: Deposits in transit		2,530.20
		16,898.10
Less: Outstanding cheques		

Cheque Number	Cheque Amount	
3451	$2,260.40	
3470	720.10	
3471	844.50	
3472	1,426.80	
3474	1,050.00	6,301.80
Adjusted cash balance per bank		$10,596.30

The adjusted cash balance per bank agreed with the cash balance per books at November 30. The December bank statement showed the following:

HILO COMPANY
Bank Statement
December 31, 2003

	Deposits	Cheques and Other Debits		
Date	Amount	Number	Amount	Balance
11-30				$14,367.90
12-1	$2,530.20	3451	$2,260.40	14,637.70
12-2		3471	844.50	13,793.20
12-4	1,211.60	3475	1,640.70	13,364.10
12-7		3472	1,426.80	11,937.30
12-8	2,365.10	3476	1,300.00	13,002.40
12-10		3477	2,130.00	10,872.40
12-15	2,145.00	3479	3,080.00	9,937.40
12-16	2,672.70			12,610.10
12-21	2,945.00			15,555.10
12-26	2,567.30	DM	550.00	17,572.40
12-27		3480	600.00	16,972.40
12-29	2,836.00	3483	1,140.00	18,668.40
12-30	1,025.00	3482	475.50	19,217.90
12-31		3485	540.80	18,677.10
12-31		DM	45.00	18,632.10

The bank statement contained three memoranda:

1. A credit of $2,145 for the collection of a $2,000 note for Hilo Company, plus interest of $160 and less a collection fee of $15. Hilo Company had not accrued any interest on the note.

2. A debit of $550 for an NSF cheque written by A. Shoaib, a customer. At December 31, the account had still not been paid.

3. A debit of $45 for service charges for the month.

The bank did not make any errors, but errors were made by Hilo Company.
The cash records per the company's books for December showed the following:

	Cash Payments Journal					Cash Receipts Journal	
Date	Number	Amount	Date	Number	Amount	Date	Amount
12-1	3475	$1,640.70	12-20	3482	$ 475.50	12-3	$1,211.60
12-2	3476	1,300.00	12-22	3483	1,140.00	12-7	2,365.10
12-2	3477	2,130.00	12-23	3484	832.00	12-15	2,672.70
12-4	3478	538.20	12-24	3485	450.80	12-20	2,954.00
12-8	3479	3,080.00	12-30	3486	1,389.50	12-25	2,567.30
12-10	3480	600.00	Total		$14,384.10	12-28	2,836.00
12-17	3481	807.40				12-30	1,025.00
						12-31	1,190.40
						Total	$16,822.10

Instructions

(a) Determine the unadjusted cash balance per books as at December 31, prior to reconciliation.
(b) Prepare a bank reconciliation at December 31.
(c) Prepare the correcting entries based on the reconciliation. (*Note*: The correction of any errors in the recording of cheques should be made to Accounts Payable. The correction of any errors in the recording of cash receipts should be made to Accounts Receivable.)

P8–6B Betterdorf Company's bank statement from the National Bank at August 31, 2003, shows the following information:

Prepare bank reconciliation and related entries.
(SO 7) AP

Balance, August 1	$17,400
August deposits	72,000
Cheques cleared in August	69,660
Bank credit memorandum:	
Collection of note receivable, $5,000	
plus $90 interest	5,090
Other interest earned	45
Bank debit memorandum:	
Safety deposit box rent	25
Balance, August 31	24,850

A summary of the Cash account in the ledger for August shows the following: Balance, August 1, $16,900; cash receipts $77,000; cash disbursements $73,570. An analysis reveals that the only reconciling items on the July 31 bank reconciliation were a deposit in transit for $4,000 and outstanding cheques of $4,500. The deposit in transit was the first deposit recorded by the bank in August. In addition, you determine that there were two errors involving company cheques drawn in August: (1) A cheque for $400 to a creditor on account that cleared the bank in August was journalized and posted for $40. (2) A salary cheque for $275 to an employee was recorded by the bank for $572.

Instructions

(a) Determine the unadjusted Cash balance at August 31.
(b) Prepare a bank reconciliation at August 31.
(c) Journalize the correcting entries to be made by Betterdorf Company at August 31. Assume the interest on the note has been accrued by the company.

P8–7B You are provided with the following information for Exploits River Adventures.

Prepare bank reconciliation and related entries.
(SO 7) AP

EXPLOITS RIVER ADVENTURES
Bank Reconciliation
April 30, 2003

Cash balance per bank	$8,008.53
Add: Deposits in transit	846.33
	8,854.86

Less: Outstanding cheques

Cheque Number	Cheque Amount	
526	$1,357.99 ✓	
533	89.78	
541	363.44 ✓	
555	78.82	1,890.03
Adjusted cash balance per bank		$6,964.83

The adjusted cash balance per bank agreed with the cash balance per books at April 30, 2003. The May bank statement showed the following:

EXPLOITS RIVER ADVENTURES
Bank Statement
May 31, 2003

Date	Deposits Amount	Cheques and Other Debits Number	Amount	Balance
4-30				$8,008.53
5-3	$ 846.33 ✓	526	$ 1,357.99 ✓	7,496.87
5-4		541	363.44 ✓	7,133.43
5-6		556	223.46 ✓	6,909.97
5-6	1,250.00 ✓	557	1,800.00 ✓	6,359.97
5-10	980.00 ✓			7,339.97
5-10		559	1,650.00 ✓	5,689.97
5-13	426.00 ✓			6,115.97
5-13	CM[1] 1,650.00			7,765.97
5-14		561	799.00 ✓	6,966.97
5-18		562	2,045.00 ✓	4,921.97
5-18	222.00 ✓			5,143.97
5-19		563	2,487.00 ✓	2,656.97
5-21		564	603.00 ✓	2,053.97
5-25		565	1,033.00 ✓	1,020.97
5-26	980.00 ✓			2,000.97
5-28	1,771.00 ✓			3,771.97
5-31		DM[2]	25.00	3,746.97
	$8,125.33		$12,386.89	

Note:
1. The CM is for proceeds of a $1,500 note plus interest.
2. The DM is for service charges.

The company's cash payments and cash receipts journals showed the following:

Cash Payments Journal			
Date	Number	Amount	
5-4	556	$ 223.46	✓
5-5	557	1,800.00	✓
5-7	558	943.00	✓
5-7	559	1,650.00	✓
5-8	560	890.00	✓
5-10	561	799.00	✓
5-15	562	2,045.00	✓
5-18	563	2,487.00	✓
5-20	564	603.00	✓
5-25	565	1,033.00	✓
5-31	566	750.00	
		$13,223.46	

Cash Receipts Journal		
Date	Amount	
5-5	$1,250.00	✓
5-8	980.00	✓
5-12	426.00	✓
5-18	222.00	✓
5-25	980.00	✓
5-28	1,771.00	✓
5-31	1,086.00	
Total	$6,715.00	

Instructions

(a) Calculate the unadjusted Cash balance at May 31, 2003, according to Exploits River Adventures' general ledger.

(b) Prepare a bank reconciliation and the necessary journal entries for Exploits River Adventures as at May 31, 2003. The company has not accrued interest on the note.

P8–8B Your newly hired assistant prepared the following bank reconciliation:

Prepare bank reconciliation, and identify internal control features. (SO 2, 3, 4, 7) AP

CAREFREE COMPANY
Bank Reconciliation
March 31, 2003

Book balance		$1,405		Bank balance			$5,630
Add: Deposit in transit	$ 750			Add: Error re: cheque No. 173			45 [3]
Collection of note	2,500						5,675
Interest on note	150	3,400		Deduct: Pre-authorized payments [4]			
		4,805		Hydro		$ 120	
Deduct: Error re:				Telephone		85	
Careless Company's deposit to our account	$1,100 [1]			NSF cheque		220	
Bank service charge	45 [2]	1,145		Outstanding cheques		1,650	2,075
Adjusted book balance		$3,660 [5]		Adjusted bank balance			$3,600 [5]

Notes:

1. The bank credited Carefree's account for a deposit made by Careless Company. Carefree and Careless are unrelated parties.
2. Of the bank service charge, $20 was due to the NSF cheque.
3. Carefree's cheque No. 173 was made for the proper amount of $249 in payment of an account payable; however, it was entered in the cash payments journal as $294.
4. Carefree authorized the bank to automatically pay its hydro and telephone bills, as directly submitted to the bank by the hydro and telephone companies. These amounts have not yet been recorded by Carefree.
5. A difference of $60 is undetermined.

Instructions

(a) Prepare a correct bank reconciliation.

(b) Prepare the required journal entries resulting from the corrected bank reconciliation. Assume no interest has previously been accrued.

(c) Identify the internal control features added by the bank reconciliation process.

Source: Adapted from Certified General Accountants Association of Canada, *Financial Accounting 1 Examination*, December 1997, Question 3.

P8–9B A new CA student has been asked to determine the balance that should be reported as Cash and Cash Equivalents as at December 31, 2003 for one of the firm's clients. The following information is available:

Calculate cash balance. (SO 8) AP

1. Cash on hand in the cash registers on December 31 totals $1,600. Of this amount, $500 is kept on hand as a cash float.
2. The petty cash fund has an imprest amount of $200. Actual petty cash on hand at December 31 is $43. Paid-out receipts total $155. Of these receipts, $100 is in IOUs from company employees.
3. The balance in the bank chequing account at December 31 is $4,900.
4. Temporary investments include $5,000 in a BMO money market fund and an investment of $2,500 in a six-month term deposit.
5. The company sold $250 of merchandise to a customer late in the day on December 31. The customer had forgotten her wallet and promised to pay the amount on January 1.
6. The company has debit card slips totalling $890.
7. At December 31, the company has Diner's Club credit card slips totalling $500 that have not yet been submitted to Diner's Club for payment.
8. The company received $500 of cash on December 31 as an advance deposit in trust on a property sale.
9. In order to hook up utilities, the company is required to deposit $1,000 in trust with Ontario Hydro. This amount must remain on deposit until a satisfactory credit history has been established. The company anticipates having this deposit back within the year.

Instructions

(a) Calculate the Cash and Cash Equivalents balance that should be reported on the year end balance sheet as a current asset.

(b) Identify where any items that were not reported in the Cash and Cash Equivalents balance in (a) should be reported.

*B*roadening Your Perspective

FINANCIAL REPORTING AND ANALYSIS

Financial Reporting Problem

BYP8–1   The Second Cup Ltd.'s annual report is presented in Appendix A of this textbook.

Instructions

Using the financial statements and other sections of the annual report, answer the following questions about The Second Cup's internal controls and cash:

(a) What comments concerning the company's system of internal control are included in the report?

(b) What references are made to the Audit Committee in the annual report?

(c) What types of information about cash and cash equivalents are included in the balance sheet and summary of significant accounting policies?

(d) The Second Cup combines cash and cash equivalents for reporting purposes. How liquid are these cash equivalents?

(e) By how much did cash and cash equivalents increase during the 2000 fiscal year?

(f) How large was the balance of cash and cash equivalents at the end of the 2000 fiscal year? Express it: (1) in dollars, (2) as a percentage of total assets, (3) as a percentage of current assets, and (4) as a percentage of current liabilities.

Interpreting Financial Statements

BYP8–2   **Corel Corporation** is an internationally recognized developer of graphics applications and business tools. To continue to be successful, Corel must generate new products. Generating new products requires significant amounts of cash. Shown below is the current assets section of Corel's 2000 balance sheet. Following the Corel data is the current assets section of **Microsoft, Inc.**, Corel's primary competitor.

Additional Cases

COREL CORPORATION
Balance Sheet (partial)
November 30
(in thousands of U.S. dollars)

	2000	1999
Current assets		
Cash and cash equivalents	$127,430	$18,021
Restricted cash	1,136	
Accounts receivable	29,393	58,724
Inventory	3,117	13,567
Income taxes recoverable	479	6,777
Prepaid expenses	1,050	2,042
Total current assets	$162,605	$99,131
Total current liabilities	$ 55,943	$79,350

MICROSOFT, INC.
Balance Sheet (partial)
June 30
(in millions of U.S. dollars)

	2000	1999
Current assets		
Cash	$ 4,846	$17,236
Accounts receivable	3,250	2,245
Other	22,212	752
Total current assets	$30,308	$20,233
Total current liabilities	$ 9,755	$ 8,718

Instructions

(a) What is the definition of a cash equivalent? Give some examples of cash equivalents that Corel might be referring to in its balance sheet. How do cash equivalents differ from other types of temporary investments?

(b) Comment on Corel's presentation of restricted cash in its balance sheet.

(c) Determine Corel's and Microsoft's liquidity, using the current ratio.

(d) Is it possible to have too many liquid assets?

BYP8–3 TELUS Corporation is Canada's second largest telecommunications company (after BCE). It's 1999 Management's Report, included in its financial statements, follows:

MANAGEMENT'S REPORT

Management is responsible to the Board of Directors for the preparation of the consolidated financial statements of the Company and its subsidiaries. These statements have been prepared in accordance with generally accepted accounting principles and necessarily include some amounts based on estimates and judgements. Financial information presented elsewhere in this Annual Report is consistent with that in the consolidated financial statements.

The Company maintains a system of internal control which provides management with reasonable assurance that assets are safeguarded and that reliable financial records are maintained. This system includes written policies and procedures, an organizational structure that segragates duties and a comprehensive program of periodic audits by the internal auditors. The Company has also instituted policies and guidelines which require employees to maintain the highest ethical standards.

The external auditors of the Company, Arthur Andersen LLP, have been appointed by the shareholders to express an opinion as to whether these consolidated financial statements present fairly the Company's consolidated financial position and operating results in accordance with generally accepted accounting principles. Their report follows.

The Board of Directors has reviewed and approved these consolidated financial statements. To assist the Board in meeting its responsibility, it has appointed an Audit Committee which is composed entirely of outside directors. The committee meets periodically with management, the internal auditors and the external auditors to review internal controls, audit results and accounting principles and practices. The committee's terms of reference are available, on request, to shareholders.

Barry A. Baptie
Executive Vice-President
and Chief Financial Officer

Instructions

Identify the internal control features outlined in management's report. Explain how each of these features strengthens internal control within TELUS.

Accounting on the Web

BYP8–4   Internal control and governance are tightly linked. The management of a company, including the board of directors, must ensure that effective control exists in the organization. This problem reviews the annual report of a well-known Canadian retailer that demonstrates good corporate governance and control practices.

Instructions

Specific requirements of this Internet case are available on the Weygandt website.

CRITICAL THINKING

Collaborative Learning Activity

BYP8–5   From your employment or personal experiences, identify situations in which cash was received and disbursed.

Instructions

In groups of five or six students, do the following:
- (a) Identify the internal control principles used for cash receipts in the situations you have selected.
- (b) Identify the internal control principles used for cash disbursements in the situations you have selected.
- (c) Identify any weaknesses in internal control related to these cash receipts and disbursements.

Communication Activity

BYP8–6   As a new auditor for the public accounting firm of Rawls, Keoto, and Landry, you have been assigned to review the internal controls over the mail cash receipts of Avalon Company. Your review reveals the following: cheques are promptly endorsed "For Deposit Only" but no list of the cheques is prepared by the person opening the mail. The mail is opened either by the cashier or by the employee who maintains the accounts receivable records, depending upon who is less busy. Mail receipts are deposited in the bank weekly by the cashier.

Instructions

Write a letter to L. S. Osman, owner of the Avalon Company, explaining the weaknesses in internal control and your recommendations for improving the system.

Ethics Case

BYP8–7   Banks charge fees of up to $25 for "bounced" cheques—that is, cheques that exceed the balance in the account. It has been estimated that processing bounced cheques costs a bank roughly $1.50 per cheque. Thus, the profit margin on a bounced cheque is very high. Recognizing this, some banks have started to process cheques from largest to smallest. By doing this, they maximize the number of cheques that bounce if a customer overdraws an account. One bank projected a $14-million increase in fee revenue as a result of processing the largest cheques first. In response to criticism, banks have responded that their customers prefer to have large cheques processed first, because those tend to be the most important. At the other extreme, some banks will cover their customers' bounced cheques, effectively extending them an interest-free loan while their account is overdrawn.

Instructions

Answer each of the following questions:

(a) Antonio Freeman had a balance of $1,500 in his chequing account on a day when the bank received the following five cheques for processing against his account:

Cheque Number	Amount	Cheque Number	Amount
3150	$ 35	3165	$ 550
3158	1,510	3169	180
3162	400		

Assuming a $25 fee is assessed by the bank, how much fee revenue would the bank generate if it processed cheques (1) from largest to smallest, (2) from smallest to largest, and (3) in the order of the cheque numbers?

(b) Do you think that processing cheques from largest to smallest is an ethical business practice?

(c) Besides ethical issues, what other considerations must a bank make in deciding whether to process cheques from largest to smallest?

(d) If you were managing a bank, what policy would you adopt on bounced cheques?

Answers to Self-Study Questions

1. b 2. c 3. b 4. c 5. b 6. d 7. a 8. a 9. c 10. d 11. c

Answer to The Second Cup Review It Question 3

The Second Cup's cash and cash equivalents were $1,446,000 as at June 24, 2000.

Remember to go back to the Navigator box on the chapter-opening page to check off your completed work.

Concepts for Review

Before studying this chapter, you should understand or, if necessary, review:

a. *How to record revenue. (Ch. 3, p. 103 and Ch. 5, pp. 216–218)*
b. *Why adjusting entries are made. (Ch. 3, p. 106)*
c. *How to calculate interest. (Ch. 3, pp. 113–114)*

THE NAVIGATOR

How Long Should the Cheque Be in the Mail?

TORONTO, Ont.—The office of *The Independent Weekly*, an alternative community newspaper for the University of Toronto, is upstairs in a historic, almost spooky-looking, gothic building in the heart of Toronto. Because it is not officially sanctioned by the administration, *The Independent Weekly* receives no funding from the University and depends on advertising for almost 100% of its annual revenues—about $100,000 a year, explains Glenn Oldford, co-editor of the newspaper.

Some of the ads are local, either from the University or from neighbourhood businesses. Others are brokered through Campus Net, a national multi-market advertising service. There is also a small amount of revenue from the free newspaper stands, which have additional literature pockets that are rented through a marketing firm.

When advertisers place an ad, they sign a contract that promises payment within 30 days. Most customers do pay by the due date, and some local merchants even pay up front. But if payments are late, the paper still has to meet its expenses.

Customers with accounts past due are sent—usually by fax—a second copy of the invoice along with a reminder letter. They are also charged 2% a month interest, although Mr. Oldford will waive this fee for some local advertisers in the interest of good client relations. If necessary, a firm personal letter is the next step. "I'll say 'You still haven't paid—please call us to discuss terms,'" Mr. Oldford explains. "After that it gets difficult."

"We do have a contract on file," points out Mr. Oldford. For really stubborn cases, the paper does have recourse to a lawyer. "That's an expensive route, however," says Mr. Oldford, "so hopefully it doesn't come to that." At each stage, the cost—monetary and administrative—of pursuing the matter has to be weighed against the amount outstanding.

THE NAVIGATOR

www.independentweekly.net

THE NAVIGATOR

✔

- Understand *Concepts for Review* ☐
- Read *Feature Story* ☐
- Scan *Study Objectives* ☐
- Read *Preview* ☐
- Read text and answer *Before You Go On*
  p. 430 ☐ p. 434 ☐ p. 437 ☐ p. 440 ☐
- Work *Demonstration Problem* ☐
- Review *Summary of Study Objectives* ☐
- Answer *Self-Study Questions* ☐
- Complete assignments ☐

CHAPTER • **9**

ACCOUNTING FOR RECEIVABLES

▶ STUDY OBJECTIVES ◀

After studying this chapter, you should be able to:

1. *Identify and distinguish between the different types of receivables.*
2. *Show how accounts receivable are recognized in the accounts.*
3. *Describe and use the methods and bases used to value accounts receivable.*
4. *Determine the entries to record the disposition of accounts receivable.*
5. *Determine the interest on notes receivable.*
6. *Show how notes receivable are recognized in the accounts.*
7. *Demonstrate how notes receivable are valued.*
8. *Determine the entries to record the disposition of notes receivable.*
9. *Illustrate the statement presentation of receivables.*
10. *Evaluate short-term liquidity.*

THE NAVIGATOR

As you read this chapter, you will learn what journal entries *The Independent Weekly* makes when it sells its ad space on account, when it collects the cash for those sales, and when it writes off an uncollectible account. The types of entries *The Independent Weekly* at the University of Toronto makes are typical of most businesses. Our economy depends heavily on the use of credit, which takes the form of accounts and notes receivable.

The chapter is organized as follows:

THE
NAVIGATOR

▼Types of Receivables

STUDY OBJECTIVE
•••••••• **1** ••••••••

Identify and distinguish between the different types of receivables.

The term receivables refers to amounts due from individuals and other companies. They are claims that are expected to be collected in cash. Receivables are frequently classified as (1) accounts, (2) notes, and (3) other.

Accounts receivable are amounts owed by customers on account. They result from the sale of goods and services. These receivables generally are expected to be collected within 30 days or so, and are classified as current assets. They are usually the most significant type of claim held by a company.

Notes receivable are claims for which formal instruments of credit are issued as proof of the debt. A note normally requires the debtor to pay interest and extends for time periods of 30 to 90 days or longer. Notes receivable may be either current assets or long-term assets, depending on their due dates. Notes and accounts receivable that result from sales transactions are often called trade receivables.

Other receivables include nontrade receivables. Examples are accruals (e.g., interest receivable), recoverable GST, loans to company officers, advances to employees, and recoverable income taxes. Accruals and other receivables due within one year or the operating cycle of the business are classified as current assets. Loans and advances are unusual. They are generally classified and reported as separate items in the current or noncurrent sections of the balance sheet, according to their due dates.

Accounts Receivable

Three primary accounting issues are associated with accounts receivable.
1. **Recognizing** accounts receivable
2. **Valuing** accounts receivable
3. **Disposing** of accounts receivable

Recognizing Accounts Receivable

Recognizing accounts receivable is relatively straightforward. In Chapter 5, we saw how accounts receivable are affected by the sale of merchandise. To illustrate, assume that Adorable Junior Garment sells merchandise on account to Zellers on July 1, 2003, for $1,000. On July 5, Zellers returns merchandise worth $100 to Adorable Junior Garment. On July 31, Adorable Junior Garment receives payment from Zellers for the balance due. The journal entries to record these transactions on the books of Adorable Junior Garment are as follows:

STUDY OBJECTIVE
2
Show how accounts receivable are recognized in the accounts.

July 1	Accounts Receivable	1,000	
	Sales		1,000
	To record sale on account.		

A	=	L	+	OE
+1,000				+1,000

5	Sales Returns and Allowances	100	
	Accounts Receivable		100
	To record merchandise returned.		

A	=	L	+	OE
–100				–100

31	Cash ($1,000 – $100)	900	
	Accounts Receivable		900
	To record collection of accounts receivable.		

A	=	L	+	OE
+900				
–900				

If Adorable Junior Garment used a perpetual inventory system, a second journal entry to record the cost of the goods sold (and the cost of the goods returned) would be required in the July 1 and July 5 transactions.

The retailer sends the customer a monthly statement of transactions that have occurred during the month. If the customer does not pay in full within a specified period (usually 30 days), most retailers add an interest (financing) charge to the balance due. Interest rates vary from company to company, but a common rate for retailers is 18% per year.

When financing charges are added, the seller recognizes interest revenue. If Zellers still owes $900 at the end of the month, and Adorable Junior Garment charges 18% on the balance due, the entry that Adorable Junior Garment will make to record interest revenue of $13.50 ($900 x 18% x 1/12) is the following:

July 31	Accounts Receivable	13.50	
	Interest Revenue		13.50
	To record interest on amount due.		

A	=	L	+	OE
+13.50				+13.50

The Independent Weekly, in our opening story, charges 24% (2% per month) on its overdue accounts. Interest revenue is often substantial for many retailers.

Valuing Accounts Receivable

STUDY OBJECTIVE
••••••••••
3
••••••••••
Describe and use the methods and bases used to value accounts receivable.

Once receivables are recorded in the accounts, the next question is how these receivables should be reported on the balance sheet. They are reported on the balance sheet as a current asset. But, determining the **amount** to report as an asset is sometimes difficult, because some receivables will be uncollectible.

Even if each customer must satisfy the credit requirements of the seller before the credit sale is approved, inevitably, some accounts receivable become uncollectible. For example, one of your customers may not be able to pay because he has been laid off from his job or is faced with unexpected bills.

Credit losses are debited to Bad Debts Expense. Such losses are considered a normal and necessary risk of doing business on a credit basis. From a management point of view, a reasonable number of uncollectible accounts can be evidence of a sound credit policy. When bad debts are abnormally low, the company may be losing profitable business by following a credit policy that is too strict. Of course, abnormally high bad debts can indicate a credit policy that may be too lenient.

Two methods are used in accounting for uncollectible accounts: (1) the direct write-off method, and (2) the allowance method. These methods are explained in the following sections.

Direct Write-Off Method for Uncollectible Accounts

Under the direct write-off method, when an account is determined to be uncollectible, the loss is charged to Bad Debts Expense. Assume, for example, that the Pereira Company sells merchandise on account on March 1, 2003, to E. Schaefer. After unsuccessful attempts to collect this receivable, Pereira writes off the $200 balance as uncollectible on January 12, 2004. The entry is as follows:

A	=	L	+	OE
−200				−200

Jan. 12	Bad Debts Expense	200	
	Accounts Receivable—E. Schaefer		200
	To write off E. Schaefer account.		

When this method is used, bad debts expense will show only **actual losses** from uncollectibles. Accounts receivable will be reported at their gross amount.

Although this method is simple, its use can reduce the usefulness of both the income statement and balance sheet. Consider the following example. Assume that in 2002, Quick Buck Computer Company decides it could increase its revenues by offering computers to students without requiring any money down, and with no credit approval process. On campuses across the country, it distributes one million computers with a selling price of $1,200 each. This increases Quick Buck's revenues and receivables by $1.2 billion. The promotion is a huge success! The 2002 balance sheet and income statement look great. Unfortunately, during 2003, nearly 40% of the student customers default on their accounts. This makes the year 2003 income statement and balance sheet look terrible. Illustration 9-1 shows that the promotion in 2002 was not such a great success after all.

Illustration 9-1

Effects of mismatching bad debts

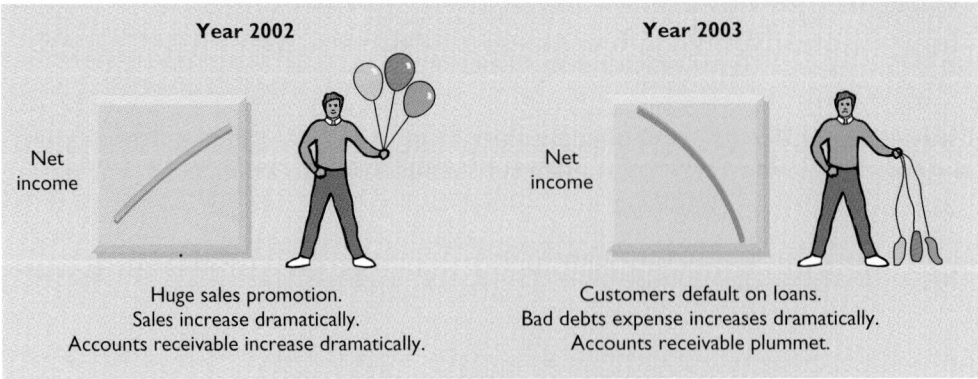

Year 2002

Net income

Huge sales promotion.
Sales increase dramatically.
Accounts receivable increase dramatically.

Year 2003

Net income

Customers default on loans.
Bad debts expense increases dramatically.
Accounts receivable plummet.

Under the direct write-off method, bad debts expense is often recorded in a period other than the period in which the revenue was recorded. No attempt is made to match bad debts expense to sales revenues in the income statement. Also, the direct write-off method does not show accounts receivable in the balance sheet at the amount actually expected to be received. Consequently, unless bad debt losses are insignificant, **the direct write-off method is not acceptable for financial reporting purposes**.

Allowance Method for Uncollectible Accounts

The allowance method of accounting for bad debts involves estimating uncollectible accounts at the end of each period. This provides better matching on the income statement and ensures that receivables are stated at their net (cash) realizable value on the balance sheet. Net realizable value is the amount expected to be received in cash. It excludes the amounts that the company estimates it will not collect. With this method, receivables are reduced by estimated uncollectible receivables on the balance sheet.

The allowance method is required for financial reporting purposes when bad debts are material or significant in amount. Its essential features are as follows:

1. Uncollectible accounts receivable are **estimated**. This estimate is treated as an expense and is **matched** against sales in the accounting period in which the sales occurred.
2. Estimated uncollectibles are debited to Bad Debts Expense and credited to Allowance for Doubtful Accounts (a contra asset account) through an adjusting entry at the end of each period.
3. When a specific account is written off, the actual uncollectible amount is debited to Allowance for Doubtful Accounts and credited to Accounts Receivable.

Recording Estimated Uncollectibles. To illustrate the allowance method, assume that Adorable Junior Garment has total credit sales of $1,200,000 in 2002. Of this amount, $200,000 remains uncollected at December 31. The credit manager estimates that $24,000 of these receivables will be uncollectible. The adjusting entry to record the estimated uncollectible accounts follows:

Dec. 31	Bad Debts Expense	24,000	
	Allowance for Doubtful Accounts		24,000
	To record estimate of uncollectible accounts.		

A	=	L	+	OE
−24,000				−24,000

Bad Debts Expense is reported in the income statement as an operating expense (usually as a selling expense). Thus, the estimated uncollectibles are **matched** with sales in 2002. The expense is recorded in the year the sales are made.

Allowance for Doubtful Accounts is a contra asset account that shows the receivables that are expected to become uncollectible in the future. This contra account is used instead of a direct credit to Accounts Receivable for two reasons. First, we do not know which individual customers will not pay. Therefore, we are unable to credit specific accounts in the accounts receivable subsidiary ledger. It is important that the subsidiary ledger accounts balance with the Accounts Receivable control account. This would not happen if the control account were credited and the subsidiary ledger accounts were not. Second, the estimate for uncollectibles is just an estimate. A contra account helps to separate estimates from actual amounts, such as those found in the Accounts Receivable account.

The credit balance in the Allowance for Doubtful Accounts account will absorb the specific write-offs when they occur. It is deducted from Accounts Receivable in the current assets section of the balance sheet, as follows:

Alternative terminology
Bad debts expense is also called *uncollectible* or *doubtful accounts expense.*

Alternative terminology
Allowance for doubtful accounts is also called *allowance* or *provision for uncollectibles,* or *allowance for bad debts.*

Illustration 9-2

Presentation of allowance for doubtful accounts

ADORABLE JUNIOR GARMENT
Balance Sheet (partial)
December 31, 2002

Current assets		
Cash		$ 14,800
Accounts receivable	$200,000	
Less: Allowance for doubtful accounts	24,000	176,000
Merchandise inventory		310,000
Prepaid expenses		25,000
Total current assets		$525,800

The amount of $176,000 represents the expected **net realizable value** of the accounts receivable at the statement date.

Recording the Write-Off of an Uncollectible Account.   Companies use various methods of collecting past-due accounts, including a sequence of letters, calls, and legal actions. In the opening story, the staff of *The Independent Weekly* used faxes and personal letters, and then threatened to involve a lawyer. When all means of collecting a past-due account have been exhausted and collection appears impossible, the account should be written off. To prevent premature write-offs, each write-off should be approved in writing by management. To maintain good internal control, authorization to write off accounts should not be given to someone who also has responsibilities related to cash or receivables.

To illustrate a receivables write-off, assume that the vice-president of finance of Adorable Junior Garment authorizes the write-off of a $500 balance owed by a delinquent customer, Nadeau Clothing, on March 1, 2003. The entry to record the write-off is as follows:

A	=	L	+	OE
+500				
−500				

Mar. 1	Allowance for Doubtful Accounts	500	
	Accounts Receivable—Nadeau Clothing		500
	Write-off of Nadeau account.		

Bad Debts Expense is not increased (debited) when the write-off occurs. **Under the allowance method, every account write-off is debited to the allowance account rather than to Bad Debts Expense.** A debit to Bad Debts Expense would be incorrect. The expense was already recognized when the adjusting entry was made for estimated bad debts in the year in which the sale was made.

Instead, the entry to record the write-off of an uncollectible account reduces both Accounts Receivable and the Allowance for Doubtful Accounts. After posting, the general ledger accounts will appear as follows:

Accounts Receivable				Allowance for Doubtful Accounts			
Jan. 1 Bal.	200,000	Mar. 1	500	Mar. 1	500	Jan. 1 Bal.	24,000
Mar. 1 Bal.	199,500					Mar. 1 Bal.	23,500

A write-off affects only balance sheet accounts. The write-off of the account reduces both the Accounts Receivable and the Allowance for Doubtful Accounts. Net realizable value in the balance sheet remains the same, as illustrated below:

Illustration 9-3

Net realizable value comparison

	Before Write-Off	After Write-Off
Accounts receivable	$200,000	$199,500
Less: Allowance for doubtful accounts	24,000	23,500
Net realizable value	$176,000	$176,000

►Accounting in Action ► *Business Insight*

In February 1997, when the venerable T. Eaton Co. Ltd. admitted that it was insolvent after 127 years of operations, it left behind a multitude of uncollectible receivables that totalled nearly $170 million. Eaton's unfortunate trade creditors covered all sectors of the Canadian economy, including clothing and accessories, cosmetics, electronics, furniture, shopping centres, utilities, newspapers, and municipalities. Cosmetics supplier Estée Lauder was left with the largest outstanding trade receivable, $4.2 million. Tommy Hilfiger Canada was on the hook for nearly $3 million, and Sony of Canada for $1.8 million. These companies had to provide for any unrecoverable amounts as bad debts.

Source: John Heinzl and Marina Strauss, "Eaton's Leaves 4,000 Creditors Short." *Globe and Mail*, March 26, 1997, B1.

Recovery of an Uncollectible Account. Occasionally, a company collects from a customer after the account has been written off. This was the case when Eaton's announced a financial restructuring plan, in October 1997, that resulted in the full recovery of the previously determined uncollectible accounts receivable by its creditors.

Two entries are required to record the recovery of a bad debt: (1) The entry made in writing off the account is reversed to reinstate the customer's account. (2) The collection is journalized in the usual manner.

To illustrate, assume that on July 1, 2003, Nadeau Clothing pays the $500 amount that had been written off on March 1. The entries are as follows:

	(1)			A = L + OE
July 1	Accounts Receivable—Nadeau Clothing	500		+500
	Allowance for Doubtful Accounts		500	−500
	To reverse the write-off of Nadeau Clothing account.			

	(2)			A = L + OE
1	Cash	500		+500
	Accounts Receivable—Nadeau Clothing		500	−500
	To record collection from Nadeau Clothing.			

Note that the recovery of a bad debt, like the write-off of a bad debt, affects only balance sheet accounts. The net effect of the two entries is a debit to Cash and a credit to Allowance for Doubtful Accounts for $500. Accounts Receivable is debited and later credited, for two reasons. First, the company must reverse the write-off. Second, Nadeau Clothing did pay, and therefore the Accounts Receivable account in the general ledger and Nadeau's account in the subsidiary ledger should show this collection for possible future credit purposes.

Bases Used for Allowance Method. To simplify the preceding explanation, we assumed we knew the amount of the expected uncollectibles. In real life, companies must estimate that amount if they use the allowance method. Two bases are used to determine this amount: (1) **percentage of sales**, and (2) **percentage of receivables**.

Both bases are generally accepted. The choice is a management decision. It depends on the emphasis that management wishes to give to expenses and revenues on the one hand, or to net realizable value of the accounts receivable on the other.

One basis emphasizes income statement relationships; the other emphasizes balance sheet relationships. Illustration 9-4 compares the two bases.

► *International note*

In France, Germany, and Japan, doubtful accounts are calculated by reviewing individual accounts rather than through estimates based on a percentage of sales or receivables. These specific accounts are not written off, as in the direct write-off method, but are viewed as doubtful until actually determined to be uncollectible (or not).

Illustration 9-4

*Comparison of bases of
estimating uncollectibles*

The percentage of sales basis results in a better matching of expenses with revenues—an income statement viewpoint. The percentage of receivables basis produces the better estimate of net realizable value—a balance sheet viewpoint. Under both bases, it is necessary to determine the company's past experience with bad debt losses.

Percentage of Sales Basis.   In the percentage of sales basis, management indicates what percentage of credit sales will be uncollectible. This percentage is based on past experience and anticipated credit policy.

The percentage is applied to either total credit sales or net credit sales of the current year. To illustrate, assume that the Pereira Company decides to use the percentage of sales basis. It concludes that 1% of net credit sales will become uncollectible. If net credit sales for the calendar year 2002 are $170,000, the estimated bad debts expense is $1,700 (1% × $170,000). The adjusting entry follows:

A	=	L	+	OE
−1,700				−1,700

Dec. 31	Bad Debts Expense		1,700	
	Allowance for Doubtful Accounts			1,700
	To record estimated bad debts for year.			

After the adjusting entry is posted, assuming the allowance account has an opening credit balance of $1,793, the accounts will show the following:

Bad Debts Expense			Allowance for Doubtful Accounts		
Dec. 31 Adj.	1,700			Jan. 1 Bal	1,793
				Dec. 31 Adj.	1,700
				Dec. 31 Bal.	3,493

This basis of estimating uncollectibles emphasizes the matching of expenses with revenues. As a result, Bad Debts Expense will show a direct percentage relationship to the sales amount on which it is calculated. **When the adjusting entry is made, the existing balance in Allowance for Doubtful Accounts is disregarded.** The adjusted balance in this account should be a reasonable approximation of the realizable value of the receivables. If actual write-offs differ significantly from the amount estimated, the percentage for future years should be modified.

Percentage of Receivables Basis.   Under the percentage of receivables basis, management estimates what percentage of receivables will result in losses from uncollectible accounts. This percentage can be assigned to receivables in total, or stratified by age of receivable. Stratifying the percentage classifies customer balances by the length of time they have been unpaid, which can improve the reliability of the estimate. Because of its emphasis on time, this is called ageing the accounts receivable.

An ageing schedule is an example of output that can be obtained from a computerized accounts receivable system. Preparing this schedule by hand is an onerous and time-consuming task. The schedule can be done in minutes on a computer.

►Accounting in Action ► *e-Business Insight*

Companies that provide services and bill on an hourly basis spend considerable time tracking their hours and preparing detailed bills. OpenAir.com created the first on-line service delivery product to simplify time management and billing. It can be accessed anywhere there's an Internet connection—your office, your client's office, or your hotel room, for example. This "virtual office" provides a Web-based invoicing, time, and expense tracking service that manages and records data.

To use the service, you create an electronic record that lists the type of project, customer name, product dates, and billing rate. By clicking on the "timer" function, you can automatically track time spent on a particular project as the work is being performed. OpenAir.com will either mail or e-mail invoices to customers. It also keeps track of collections and provides an ageing schedule. Its services allow companies to concentrate on generating revenue through their core businesses by cutting down on time-consuming administrative tasks.

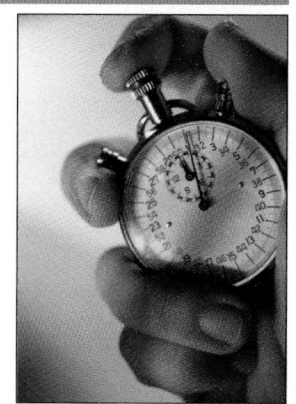

After the accounts are aged, the expected bad debt losses are determined. This is done by applying percentages based on past experience to the totals in each category. The longer a receivable is past due, the less likely it is to be collected. So, the estimated percentage of uncollectible debts increases with the number of days past due. An ageing schedule for the Pereira Company is shown in Illustration 9-5.

| Customer | Total | Number of Days Outstanding | | | | |
		0–30	31–60	61–90	91–120	Over 120
E. Bansal	$ 600		$ 300		$ 200	$ 100
C. Bortz	300	$ 300				
A. Rashad	450		200	$ 250		
L. Su	700	500			200	
O. Woznow	600			300		300
Others	36,950	26,200	5,200	2,450	1,600	1,500
	$39,600	$27,000	$5,700	$3,000	$2,000	$1,900
Estimated Percentage Uncollectible		2%	4%	10%	50%	75%
Estimated Bad Debts	$ 3,493	$ 540	$ 228	$ 300	$1,000	$1,425

Illustration 9-5

Ageing schedule

Note the increasing percentages from 2% to 75%.

Total estimated bad debts for the Pereira Company ($3,493) represent the amount of existing receivables expected to become uncollectible in the future. This amount represents the **required balance** in the Allowance for Doubtful Accounts at the balance sheet date. **The amount of the bad debt adjusting entry is the difference between the required balance and the existing balance in the allowance account.** If the trial balance shows the Allowance for Doubtful Accounts with a credit balance of $1,793, an adjusting entry for $1,700 ($3,493 − $1,793) is necessary, as shown below:

Helpful hint Because of the emphasis on net realizable value, under the percentage of receivables approach, the existing balance in the allowance account must be considered in making the adjusting entry.

Dec. 31	Bad Debts Expense	1,700	
	Allowance for Doubtful Accounts		1,700
	To adjust allowance account to total		
	estimated uncollectibles.		

A	=	L	+	OE
−1,700				−1,700

After the adjusting entry is posted, the accounts of the Pereira Company will show the following:

Bad Debts Expense	
Dec. 31 Adj.	1,700

Allowance for Doubtful Accounts	
Jan. 1 Bal.	1,793
Dec. 31 Adj.	1,700
Dec. 31 Bal.	3,493

Occasionally, the allowance account will have a **debit balance** prior to adjustment. This occurs when write-offs during the year exceed previous estimates for bad debts. In such a case, **the debit balance is added to the required balance** when the adjusting entry is made. If there had been a $500 debit balance in the Pereira Company allowance account before adjustment, the adjusting entry would have been for $3,993 to arrive at a credit balance in the allowance account of $3,493.

The percentage of receivables method will normally result in the better approximation of net realizable value. But it will not result in the better matching of expenses with revenues if some customers' accounts are more than one year past due. In such a case, bad debts expense for the current period includes amounts related to the sales of a prior period.

Before You Go On . . .

▶Review It

1. What types of receivables does The Second Cup report on its balance sheet? The answer to this question is at the end of the chapter.
2. What is the primary criticism of the direct write-off method?
3. What are the essential features of the allowance method?
4. Explain the difference between the percentage of sales and the percentage of receivables bases.

▶Do It

The unadjusted trial balance for Woo Wholesalers Co. reveals the following selected information:

	Debit	Credit
Accounts receivable	$120,000	
Allowance for doubtful accounts		$ 2,000
Net credit sales		820,000

Prepare the journal entry to record bad debts expense for each of the following *independent* situations:
1. Using the percentage of sales approach, Woo estimates uncollectible accounts to be 1% of net credit sales.
2. Using the percentage of receivables approach, Woo estimates uncollectible accounts to be 8% of total accounts receivable.

Action Plan

*   Report receivables at their net realizable value.
*   Estimate the amount the company does not expect it will collect.
*   Do not consider the existing balance in the allowance acount to determine the required adjusting entry when the percentage of sales basis is used. Consider the existing balance in the allowance account to determine the required adjusting entry when the percentage of receivables basis is used.

Solution

		Debit	Credit
1.	Bad Debts Expense ($820,000 × 1%)	8,200	
	Allowance for Doubtful Accounts		8,200
	To record estimate of uncollectible accounts.		
2.	Bad Debts Expense ($120,000 × 8% = $9,600 − $2,000)	7,600	
	Allowance for Doubtful Accounts		7,600
	To record estimate of uncollectible accounts.		

THE NAVIGATOR

Related exercise material: BE9–1, BE9–2, BE9–3, BE9–4, BE9–5, BE9–6, E9–1, E9–2, E9–3, and E9–4.

Disposing of Accounts Receivable

In the normal course of events, accounts receivable are collected in cash and removed from the books. However, as credit sales and receivables grow in significance, the normal course of events changes. Companies frequently sell their receivables to another company for cash, thereby shortening the cash-to-cash operating cycle.

Receivables are sold for two major reasons. **First, receivables may be sold because they are the only reasonable source of cash.** When money is tight, companies may not be able to borrow money in the usual credit markets. Even if credit is available, the cost of borrowing may be too high.

A second reason for selling receivables is that billing and collection are often time-consuming and costly. It is often easier for a retailer to sell its receivables to another party with expertise in billing and collection matters. Credit card companies, such as Visa and MasterCard, specialize in billing and collecting accounts receivable.

STUDY OBJECTIVE
·········· ▼ ··········
4
Determine the entries to record the disposition of accounts receivable.

Factored Receivables

A common kind of sale of receivables is to a factor. A *factor* buys receivables from businesses, and then collects the payments directly from the customers. Factoring is a million-dollar business. For example, Bell Canada recently sold its accounts receivable for $650 million.

Factoring arrangements vary widely, but, typically, the factor (purchaser of the receivables) will advance up to 90% of the net realizable value of approved invoices, less the factor's fee. Fees are negotiable and can range from 16% to 36% of the amount of receivables purchased.

Accounting for factored receivables becomes quite complex, as the receivables can be sold with, or without, **recourse** (risk). Further discussion of factored receivables is left for a future accounting course.

►Accounting in Action ► *Business Insight*

TCE Capital is one of a growing number of companies that help companies in a cash crunch by purchasing outstanding receivables at a discount. It doesn't call itself a factor; it prefers to be called an invoice discounter and transaction financier. "It seems that almost everyone takes at least 30 days to pay, and many companies are edging up through 60 days to 90 days," says Jim Shoniker, TCE's vice-president of business development. "By discounting invoices, businesses get the money today, when it's needed. That makes it possible for them to take on orders or projects they simply couldn't have done otherwise because of a lack of financing." In 1999, TCE provided Canadian businesses with short-term financing of $100 million, earning a base rate of $1 per $1,000 per day. That works out to 3% for 30 days, or about 36% per year.

Source: Terrence Belford, "Sell Your Invoices." *CAmagazine,* May 1999, 25.

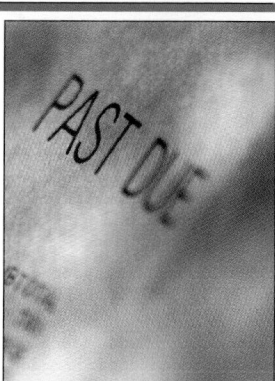

Credit Card Sales

Approximately 54 million credit cards were recently estimated to be in use in Canada more than 2.3 credit cards for every adult over 18 years of age. Of these, about 70% are bank cards, such as Visa or MasterCard. The other 30% are cards issued by large department stores, gasoline companies, and other issuers such as American Express and Diners Club/enRoute.

Three parties are involved when credit cards are used in making retail sales: (1) the credit card issuer, who is independent of the retailer, (2) the retailer, and (3) the customer. A retailer's acceptance of a credit card is another form of selling (factoring) a receivable.

The major advantages of these credit cards to the retailer are shown in Illustration 9-6.

Illustration 9-6

Advantages of credit cards to the retailer

▸*Ethics note*

On-line credit card fraud occurs three times as often as regular credit card fraud. Visa recently instituted new security rules for transactions over the Internet to combat on-line fraud and boost consumer confidence in electronic commerce.

In exchange for these advantages, the retailer pays the credit card issuer a fee (a percentage of the invoice price) for its services.

Cash Sales: Bank Credit Cards.   Sales that result from the use of credit cards issued by banks, such as Visa and MasterCard, are considered cash sales by the retailer. When a credit card sale is transacted, the bank immediately adds the amount to the seller's bank balance, less a service fee. Banks generally charge a fee of about 3.5% of the credit card sales slip, or a transaction fee, for this service.

To illustrate, Anita Ferreri purchases $1,000 of compact discs for her restaurant from Kerr Music Co., using her RBC Financial Group Visa card. The service fee that RBC charges Kerr for credit card sales is 3.5%. The entry made to record this transaction by Kerr Music is as follows:

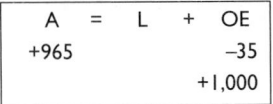

A	=	L	+	OE
+965				–35
				+1,000

Cash	965	
Credit Card Expense ($1,000 × 3.5%)	35	
Sales		1,000
To record Visa credit card sale.		

Credit Sales: Nonbank Credit Cards.   Sales that involve nonbank cards such as American Express, Diners Club/enRoute, and Petro-Canada Card, are **reported as credit sales, not cash sales**. Conversion into cash does not occur until these companies remit the net amount to the seller.

To illustrate, assume that Kerr Music accepts an American Express card for a $500 bill. The entry for the sale by Kerr (assuming a 5% service fee) follows:

Accounts Receivable—American Express	475		
Credit Card Expense ($500 × 5%)	25		
Sales		500	
To record American Express credit card sales.			

A	=	L	+	OE
+475				−25
				+500

American Express will subsequently pay Kerr $475. The music store will record this collection as follows:

Cash	475		
Accounts Receivable—American Express		475	
To record redemption of credit card billing.			

A	=	L	+	OE
+475				
−475				

Credit Card Expense is reported as a selling expense in the income statement.

▸Accounting in Action ▸ *e-Business Insight*

A Canadian company, EcomCard Inc., is targeting teens with a prepaid e-commerce card it hopes will surpass traditional credit cards as the main method of purchasing on-line goods. "This finally gives the teenage market a way to pay for the MP3 music over the Internet," says Juergen Weber, EcomCard's president. EcomCards can be purchased at any participating store or bank and programmed with the maximum spendable amount. The card is anonymous and, when the desired sum is spent, it is disposable. The EcomCard is expected to allay fears some consumers have about credit card security on the Internet.

Source: Daniel McHardie, "EcomCard After Teens with New E-Card." *The Globe and Mail*, August 7, 2000, B1.

Debit Card Sales

Canadians are the world's most frequent users of debit cards, second only to the inhabitants of the Netherlands. In 2000, Canadians initiated nearly two billion debit card transactions to purchase goods and services, according to Interac, Canada's debit network. What's the difference between a debit card and a credit card? Debit cards allow customers to spend only what is in their bank account. Credit cards allow access to money made available to a customer by a bank or other financial institution, like a loan. Credit cards are issued with the understanding that the amount charged will be repaid, plus interest, if the account is not paid in full each month.

When a debit card sale is transacted, the bank deducts the cost of the purchase immediately from the customer's bank account. This amount is electronically transferred into the retailer's bank account, less a service fee. Banks usually charge a transaction fee for this service. The entries to record a debit card sale are identical to those illustrated earlier for bank credit card sales except that the expense account used is Debit Card Expense, not Credit Card Expense.

Loans Secured by Receivables

Rather than selling receivables, a common way to speed up cashflow from accounts receivable is to go to a bank and borrow money using accounts receivable as collateral. While this does have a cost (interest has to be paid to the bank on the loan), the company gets the use of its cash sooner. The loan can be repaid as the receivables are collected. Generally, banks are willing to provide financing of up to 75% of receivables that are less than 90 days old. Quite often, these arrangements occur through an **operating line of credit**, which is discussed in a later chapter.

Before You Go On . . .

▸Review It

THE
NAVIGATOR

1. Why do companies sell their receivables?
2. What is the journal entry made to record bank credit card sales? Nonbank credit card sales? Debit card sales?

Related exercise material: BE9–7, E9–5, and E9–6.

Notes Receivable

Credit may also be granted in exchange for a promissory note. A **promissory note** is a written promise to pay a specified amount of money on demand or at a definite time. Promissory notes may be used (1) when individuals and companies lend or borrow money, (2) when the amount of the transaction and the credit period exceed normal limits, or (3) in settlement of accounts receivable.

In a promissory note, the party making the promise to pay is called the maker. The party to whom payment is to be made is called the payee. The payee may be specifically identified by name, or may be designated simply as the bearer of the note. In the note shown in Illustration 9-7, Brent Company is the maker and Wilma Company is the payee. To Wilma Company, the promissory note is a note receivable. To Brent Company, it is a note payable.

Illustration 9-7

Promissory note

Helpful hint Note the similarities and differences between a note receivable and an account receivable.

Similarities: Both are credit instruments. Both are valued at their net realizable values. Both can be sold to another party.

Differences: An account receivable is an informal promise to pay. A note receivable is secured by a formal, written promise to pay. An account receivable results from a credit sale. A note receivable arises from financing a purchase, lending money, or extending an account receivable beyond normal amounts or due dates. An account receivable is usually due within a short period of time (e.g., 30 days), while a note can extend for longer periods of time (e.g., 30 days to a number of years). An account receivable does not incur interest, unless the account is overdue. A note usually bears interest for the entire period.

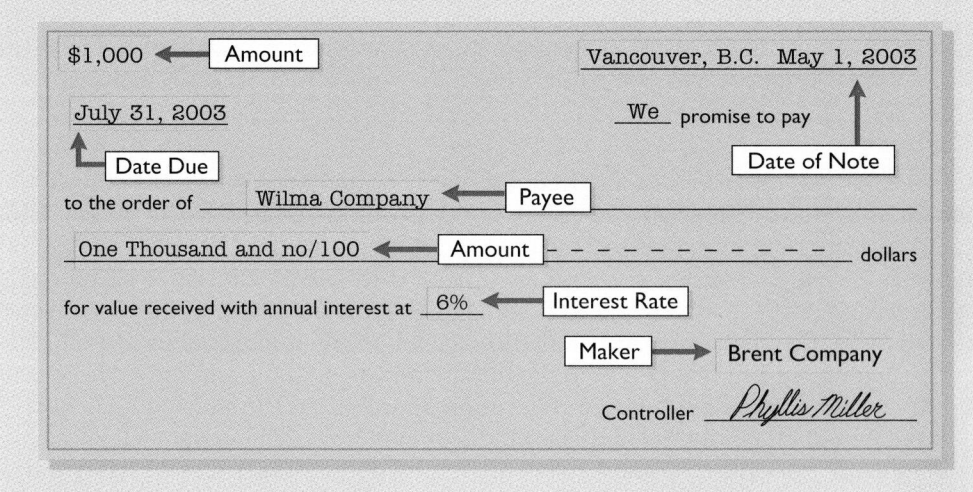

Notes receivable give the payee a stronger legal claim to assets than accounts receivable. Like accounts receivable, notes receivable can be readily sold to another party. Promissory notes are negotiable instruments (as are cheques). This means that they can be transferred to another party by endorsement (signature of the payee).

Notes receivable are frequently accepted from customers who need to extend the payment of an account receivable. They are often required from high-risk customers. In some industries (such as the heavy equipment industry), all credit sales are supported by notes. The majority of notes originate from loans.

The basic issues in accounting for notes receivable are the same as those for accounts receivable, as follows:

1. **Recognizing** notes receivable
2. **Valuing** notes receivable
3. **Disposing** of notes receivable

On the following pages, we will look at these issues. Before we do, we need to consider an issue that does not normally apply to accounts receivable if paid when due—the calculation of interest.

Calculating Interest

As we learned in Chapter 3, the basic formula for calculating interest on an interest-bearing note is the following:

Principal Value of Note	×	Annual Interest Rate	×	Time in Terms of One Year	=	Interest
$1,000	×	6%	×	3/12	=	$15

STUDY OBJECTIVE
5
Determine the interest on notes receivable

Illustration 9-8
Formula for calculating interest

The interest rate specified in a note is an **annual** rate of interest. The time factor in the above formula expresses the fraction of a year the note is outstanding. The calculation of interest revenue for Wilma Company and interest expense for Brent Company is also shown in Illustration 9-8. As we did in Chapter 3, we will assume that interest is calculated in months, rather than days, for simplicity.

Some notes are due on demand, rather than at a specified date. For these notes, interest is calculated for the length of time from the issue date until the note is called in for repayment. If it is necessary to accrue interest for an interim period, interest is calculated for the period that the note has been outstanding.

Interest on notes receivable is sometimes due monthly. Often, especially for short-term notes, interest is collected along with the principal when the note matures.

Recognizing Notes Receivable

To illustrate the basic entry for notes receivable, we will use the $1,000, 6% promissory note due on July 31 illustrated on the previous page. Assuming that the note was written to settle an open account, the entry for the receipt of the note by Wilma Company follows:

STUDY OBJECTIVE
6
Show how notes receivable are recognized in the accounts.

May 1	Notes Receivable—Brent Company	1,000	
	Accounts Receivable—Brent Company		1,000
	To record acceptance of Brent Company note.		

A	=	L	+	OE
+1,000				
−1,000				

The note receivable is recorded at its **principal** or **face value**, which is the value shown on the face of the note. No interest revenue is reported when the note is accepted. The revenue recognition principle does not recognize revenue until it is earned. Interest is earned (accrued) as time passes.

If a note is exchanged for cash instead of an account receivable, the entry is a debit to Notes Receivable and a credit to Cash for the amount of the loan.

Valuing Notes Receivable

Valuing short-term notes receivable is the same as valuing accounts receivable. Like accounts receivable, short-term notes receivable are reported at their **net realizable value**. The notes receivable allowance account is called Allowance for Doubtful Notes. The estimations involved in determining net realizable value and in recording the bad debts expense and related allowance are similar.

STUDY OBJECTIVE
7
Demonstrate how notes receivable are valued.

▶Accounting in Action ▸ *Business Insight*

Long-term notes receivable pose additional estimation problems. As an example, we need only look at the problems a number of large banks are having in collecting their receivables. Loans to less developed countries are particularly worrisome. Developing countries need loans for development but often find repayment difficult. Recently, outstanding loans to some of the 48 countries designated as less developed totalled more than $3 billion for Scotiabank. Determining the proper allowance is understandably difficult for these types of long-term receivables.

Disposing of Notes Receivable

STUDY OBJECTIVE

▼8

Determine the entries to record the disposition of notes receivable.

Notes may be held to their maturity date, at which time the principal plus any unpaid interest is due. Sometimes, the maker of the note defaults and an appropriate adjustment to the accounts must be made. At other times, the holder of the note speeds up the conversion to cash by selling the note. The entries for honouring (paying) and dishonouring (not paying) notes are illustrated on the following pages.

Honouring of Notes Receivable

A note is **honoured** when it is paid in full at its maturity date. For an interest-bearing note, the amount due at maturity is the principal of the note plus interest for the length of time the note is outstanding (assuming interest is due at maturity rather than monthly).

Helpful hint Wolder's entry on June 1 is as follows:

Dr. Notes Receivable 10,000
  Cr. Cash   10,000

To illustrate, assume that Wolder Co. lends Higly Inc. $10,000 on June 1, accepting a note due on September 30 (four months hence) at 4.5% interest. Total interest is $150 ($10,000 × 4.5% × 4/12). The amount due, the maturity value, is $10,150 ($10,000 + $150). To obtain payment, Wolder (the payee) must present the note either to Higly Inc. (the maker) or to the maker's agent, such as a bank. Assuming that Wolder presents the note to Higly Inc. on the maturity date, the entry by Wolder to record the collection is as follows:

A	=	L	+	OE
+10,150				+150
−10,000				

Sept. 30	Cash	10,150	
	Notes Receivable—Higly		10,000
	Interest Revenue		150
	To record collection of Higly note.		

Dishonouring of Notes Receivable

A **dishonoured note** is a note that is not paid in full at maturity. A dishonoured note receivable is no longer negotiable. However, the payee still has a claim against the maker of the note. Therefore, the Notes Receivable account is usually transferred to an Accounts Receivable account.

To illustrate, assume that on September 30, Higly Inc. says that it cannot pay at the present time. The entry to record the dishonouring of the note depends on whether eventual collection is expected. If Wolder Co. expects eventual collection, the amount due (principal and interest) on the note is debited to Accounts Receivable. Wolder Co. would make the following entry at the time the note is dishonoured (assuming no previous accrual of interest):

A	=	L	+	OE
+10,150				+150
−10,000				

Sept. 30	Accounts Receivable—Higly	10,150	
	Notes Receivable—Higly		10,000
	Interest Revenue		150
	To record the dishonouring of the Higly note.		

If there is no hope of collection, the principal of the note would be written off by debiting the Allowance for Doubtful Notes account. No interest revenue would be recorded, because collection will not occur. Any interest which had previously been accrued must also be written off.

Sale of Notes Receivable

Notes receivable may be sold to a third party prior to the maturity date in order to immediately receive cash on the note. The proceeds that a company receives for discounting the note are equal to the maturity value of the note less the third party's discount fee. Since these notes are purchased at a discount, the sale of notes receivable is widely called **discounting** notes receivable. The accounting entries for the sale of notes receivable are left for a more advanced course.

Before You Go On . . .

►Review It

1. What is the basic formula for calculating interest?
2. At what value are notes receivable reported on the balance sheet?
3. Explain the difference between honouring and dishonouring a note receivable.

►Do It

On May 10, Gambit Stores accepts from J. Nyznyk a $3,400, three-month, 6% note in settlement of Nyznyk's overdue account. Interest is due at maturity. What are the entries made by Gambit on May 10 and on August 10, the maturity date, assuming Nyznyk pays the note and interest in full at that time?

Action Plan

- Determine the length of time the note has been outstanding.
- Determine whether interest has been accrued. The entry here assumes that no interest has been accrued on this note.

Solution

May 10	Notes Receivable—J. Nyznyk	3,400	
	Accounts Receivable—J. Nyznyk		3,400
	To replace account receivable with a 6% note		
	receivable, due August 10.		

The interest payable at the maturity date is $51, calculated as follows:

$$\text{Principal} \times \text{Rate} \times \text{Time} = \text{Interest}$$
$$\$3,400 \times 6\% \times 3/12 = \$51$$

Aug. 10	Cash	3,451	
	Notes Receivable—J. Nyznyk		3,400
	Interest Revenue		51
	To record collection of Nyznyk note.		

Related exercise material: BE9–8, BE9–9, BE9–10, E9–7, E9–8, and E9–9.

THE NAVIGATOR

Statement Presentation of Receivables

Each of the major types of receivables should be identified in the balance sheet or in the notes to the financial statements. Short-term receivables are reported in the current assets section of the balance sheet, below cash and temporary investments (or cash and cash equivalents). Both the gross amount of receivables and the allowance for doubtful accounts should be reported. Illustration 9-9 shows the presentation of receivables for Mark's Work Wearhouse.

Illustration 9-9

Balance sheet presentation of receivables

MARK'S WORK WEARHOUSE LTD.	
Balance Sheet (partial)	
January 29, 2000	
(in thousands)	
Assets	
Current assets	
Cash and cash equivalents	$ 1,774
Accounts receivable	15,010
Merchandise inventories	81,468
Other current assets	3,223
	$101,475

In a note to the financial statements, Mark's discloses that gross receivables are $16,809,000. The allowance for doubtful accounts of $1,799,000 is related primarily to receivables from franchise stores. Accounts receivable also include the current portion of notes receivable from Mark's franchises.

In the income statement, Bad Debts Expense, Credit Card Expense, and Debit Card Expense are reported as selling expenses in the operating expenses section. Interest Revenue is shown under other revenues and gains in the non-operating section of the income statement.

Using the Information in the Financial Statements

Collection of trade receivables has a significant effect upon a company's cash position. Consequently, control and evaluation of short-term liquidity require an assessment of the efficiency of collection of receivables. Four ratios assist in evaluating short-term liquidity: the current ratio, the acid test ratio, the receivables turnover, and the collection period.

The **current ratio** (current assets ÷ current liabilities) was introduced in Chapter 4. The acid test ratio (frequently called the **quick ratio**) tightens the current ratio. It measures a company's ability to satisfy its short-term debts immediately; that is, it uses only current assets that can be quickly converted into cash (e.g., temporary investments and accounts receivable). Note that The Second Cup's cash and temporary investments have been combined into one figure for reporting purposes on its balance sheet.

Illustration 9-10

Calculation of acid test ratio

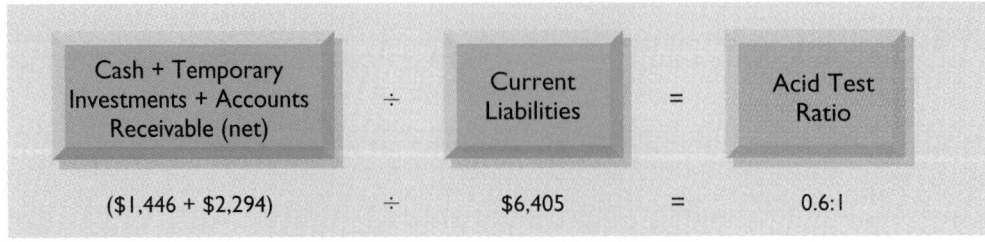

Cash + Temporary Investments + Accounts Receivable (net)	÷	Current Liabilities	=	Acid Test Ratio
($1,446 + $2,294)	÷	$6,405	=	0.6:1

The Second Cup's acid test ratio, shown in Illustration 9-10, means that $0.60 of assets are available to be quickly converted into cash to cover every $1 of current liabilities. Whether this is a strong or weak ratio depends on many factors, including the industry average. In this particular case, The Second Cup's acid test ratio is exactly equal to the industry average of 0.6:1.

A high acid test ratio is not necessarily indicative of a strong liquidity position either. The acid test ratio might be artificially high if there are many slow-paying customers for whom an adequate allowance for doubtful accounts has not been provided.

The **receivables turnover** is a useful measure for assessing a company's efficiency in converting its credit sales into cash. Often, the amount of credit sales is not available to the general public. In such instances, total sales can be used as a substitute for comparison. Total sales was used to calculate the receivables turnover for The Second Cup in Illustration 9-11. In this calculation, we used The Second Cup's total revenue, not system-wide sales. System-wide sales are the sales reported by all Second Cup franchise operations. These franchise operations are owned by individuals, not The Second Cup. Total revenues is the amount that has been earned specifically by the corporate entity The Second Cup Ltd.

Whenever a ratio compares a balance sheet figure (e.g., accounts receivable) to an income statement figure (e.g., sales), the balance sheet figure must be averaged. Average balance sheet figures are determined by adding beginning and ending balances together and dividing by 2. The rationale for using averages is to ensure that the balance sheet figures (which represent the end-of-period amounts) cover the same period of time as the income statement figures (which represent amounts for the entire period).

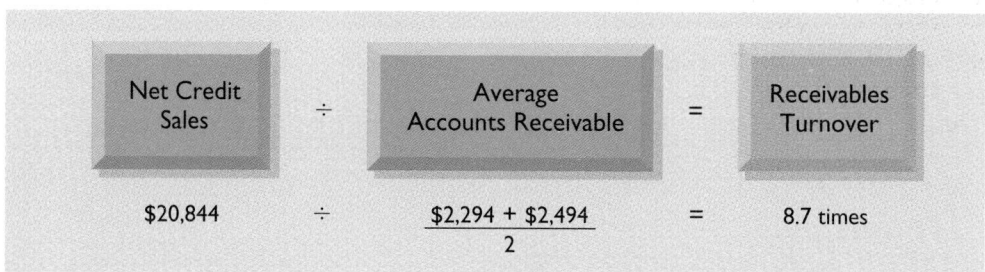

Illustration 9-11

Calculation of receivables turnover

The result indicates an accounts receivable turnover ratio of 8.7 times per year for The Second Cup. The higher the turnover ratio is, the more liquid the company's receivables are.

It is informative to convert the receivables turnover ratio into the number of days it takes the company to collect its receivables. This ratio, called the **collection period**, is calculated by dividing 365 days by the receivables turnover ratio, as illustrated for The Second Cup below.

Illustration 9-12

Collection period

This means that The Second Cup collects its receivables, on average, in approximately 42 days. The collection period is frequently used to assess the effectiveness of a company's credit and collection policies. The general rule is that the collection period should not greatly exceed the credit term period (i.e., the time allowed for payment).

Before You Go On . . .

▶ Review It

1. Explain where accounts and notes receivable are reported on the balance sheet.
2. Where are bad debts expense, credit card expense, debit card expense, and interest revenue reported on the income statement?
3. How does a company evaluate its short-term liquidity with respect to receivables?

Related exercise material: BE9–11, BE9–12, E9–10, E9–11, and E9–12.

▶ *A Look Back at Our Feature Story*

Refer back to the feature story about the *The Independent Weekly* at the beginning of the chapter. Answer the following questions:

1. If you had sold advertising space to a slow-paying client, how would you persuade the client to pay?
2. At what point would you recommend that *The Independent Weekly* write off uncollectible receivables?
3. Indicate the accounts to be debited and credited for each of the following transactions of *The Independent Weekly*: (a) ad space is sold on account and published, (b) ad space is sold and prepaid but will not be published until the next issue, (c) cash is collected on account, (d) the ad is run for the advertiser who prepaid, (e) an uncollectible account is written off.

Solution

1. The collection process used by *The Independent Weekly* appears to be suitably persuasive: a reminder letter sent by fax, interest added to overdue accounts, a personal letter, and finally, the threat of legal action if efforts to collect are still unsuccessful.
2. An unpaid receivable should be written off when it is determined that it is uncollectible. Past experience with small unpaid ad bills will usually indicate when to consider bills as uncollectible. With the limited information given in this case, the write-off would seem proper at the conclusion of an unsuccessful court claim.
3. (a) Debit Accounts Receivable, credit Advertising Revenue.
   (b) Debit Cash, credit Unearned Advertising Revenue.
   (c) Debit Cash, credit Accounts Receivable.
   (d) Debit Unearned Advertising Revenue, credit Advertising Revenue.
   (e) Debit Allowance for Doubtful Accounts, credit Accounts Receivable.

DEMONSTRATION PROBLEM

Selected transactions for Dylan Co. are presented below:

Mar. 1 Sold $20,000 of merchandise to Potter Company.

    1 Accepted Juno Company's $16,500, six-month, 6% note for the balance due on account.

    11 Potter Company returned $600 worth of goods and paid the remaining balance due in full.

    13 Made Dylan Co. credit card sales for $13,200.

    15 Made MasterCard credit sales that totalled $6,700. A 3% service fee is charged by MasterCard.

Apr. 13 Received collections of $8,200 on Dylan Co. credit card sales. Added interest charges of 18% to the remaining balance.

May 10 Wrote off as uncollectible $16,000 of accounts receivable.

June 30 Dylan uses the percentage of sales basis to estimate bad debts. Credit sales for the first six months total $2,000,000. The estimated bad debt percentage is 1%. At June 30, the balance in the allowance account is $3,500.

    30 Recorded the interest accrued on the Juno Company note.

July 16 One of the accounts receivable written off in May pays the amount due, $4,000, in full.

Instructions

Prepare the journal entries for the transactions.

Solution to Demonstration Problem

Date	Account	Debit	Credit
Mar. 1	Accounts Receivable—Potter	20,000	
	Sales		20,000
	To record sale on account.		
1	Notes Receivable—Juno	16,500	
	Accounts Receivable—Juno		16,500
	To record acceptance of Juno Company note.		
11	Cash	19,400	
	Sales Returns and Allowances	600	
	Accounts Receivable—Potter		20,000
	To record return of goods and collection of accounts receivable.		
13	Accounts Receivable	13,200	
	Sales		13,200
	To record company credit card sales.		
15	Cash	6,499	
	Credit Card Expense (3% × $6,700)	201	
	Sales		6,700
	To record bank credit card sales.		
Apr. 13	Cash	8,200	
	Accounts Receivable		8,200
	To record collection of accounts receivable.		
13	Accounts Receivable [($13,200 − $8,200) × 18% × $\frac{1}{12}$]	75	
	Interest Revenue		75
	To record interest on amount due.		
May 10	Allowance for Doubtful Accounts	16,000	
	Accounts Receivable		16,000
	To record write-off of accounts receivable.		
June 30	Bad Debts Expense ($2,000,000 × 1%)	20,000	
	Allowance for Doubtful Accounts		20,000
	To record estimate of uncollectible accounts.		
30	Interest Receivable ($16,500 × 6% × $\frac{4}{12}$)	330	
	Interest Revenue		330
	To record interest earned.		
July 16	Accounts Receivable	4,000	
	Allowance for Doubtful Accounts		4,000
	To reverse write-off of accounts receivable.		
16	Cash	4,000	
	Accounts Receivable		4,000
	To record collection of accounts receivable.		

Action Plan
- Accounts receivable are recorded at invoice price.
- Sales returns and allowances reduce the amount received on accounts receivable.
- Bad debts expense is an adjusting entry.
- Percentage of sales basis ignores any balance in the allowance account. Percentage of receivables basis does not ignore this balance.
- Write-offs of accounts receivable affect only balance sheet accounts.

Summary of Study Objectives

1. *Identify and distinguish between the different types of receivables.* Receivables are frequently classified as (1) accounts, (2) notes, and (3) other. Accounts receivable are amounts owed by customers on account. Notes receivable are formal instruments of credit. Other receivables include non-trade receivables such as accruals, GST recoverable, loans to company officers, advances to employees, and income taxes recoverable.

2. *Show how accounts receivable are recognized in the accounts.* Accounts receivable are recorded at invoice price. They are reduced by Sales Returns and Allowances. When interest is charged on a past-due receivable, this interest is added to the accounts receivable balance and is recognized as interest revenue.

3. *Describe and use the methods and bases used to value accounts receivable.* There are two methods of accounting for uncollectible accounts: (1) the direct write-off method, and (2) the allowance method. The allowance method is the preferred method. Either the percentage of sales or the percentage of receivables basis may be used to estimate uncollectible accounts when using the allowance method. The percentage of sales basis emphasizes the matching principle. The percentage of receivables basis emphasizes the net realizable value of the accounts receivable. An ageing schedule is usually used with this basis.

4. *Determine the entries to record the disposition of accounts receivable.* When an account receivable is collected, or written off, Accounts Receivable is credited. Accounts receivable can also be sold to a factor in advance of collection, for a reduced value. Credit and debit card sales and using receivables as security for a loan help speed up collection.

5. *Determine the interest on notes receivable.* The formula for calculating interest is the following: Principal × Annual Interest Rate × Fraction of Year Outstanding.

6. *Show how notes receivable are recognized in the accounts.* Notes receivable are recorded at their principal, or face, value. In some cases, it is necessary to accrue interest prior to maturity. In these cases, Interest Receivable is debited and Interest Revenue is credited.

7. *Demonstrate how notes receivable are valued.* Like accounts receivable, notes receivable are reported at their

net realizable value. The notes receivable allowance account is called Allowance for Doubtful Notes. The calculations and estimates involved in valuing notes receivable at net realizable value, and in recording the proper amount of bad debts expense and related allowance, are similar to those required for accounts receivable.

8. *Determine the entries to record the disposition of notes receivable.* Notes are normally held to maturity. At that time, the principal plus any unpaid interest is due and the note is removed from the accounts. If a note is not paid at maturity, it is said to be dishonoured. If ultimate collection is still anticipated, an account receivable replaces the note receivable and any unpaid interest. Otherwise, the note must be written off.

9. *Illustrate the statement presentation of receivables.* Each major type of receivable should be identified in the balance sheet or in the notes to the financial statements. Short-term receivables are current assets. The gross amount of receivables and the allowance for doubtful accounts/ notes should be reported. Bad debts and credit and debit card expenses are reported in the income statement as operating (selling) expenses. Interest expense is shown as other expenses and losses, and interest revenue is shown as other revenues and gains in the non-operating section of the statement.

10. *Evaluate short-term liquidity.* Four ratios are commonly used to assess the short-term liquidity of a company. The current ratio (discussed in Chapter 4) divides current assets by current liabilities. This ratio measures the ability of a company to meet its obligations. The acid test ratio divides the sum of cash, temporary investments, and net accounts receivable by current liabilities. It measures a company's ability to realize cash quickly. The receivables turnover is calculated by dividing net credit sales by average net accounts receivable. This ratio measures how well the company is converting its receivables into sales. The collection period converts the receivables turnover into days, dividing 365 days by the receivables turnover ratio. It shows the number of days, on average, it takes a company to collect its accounts receivable.

Glossary

 Key Term Matching Activity

Acid test (quick) ratio   A measure of the company's immediate short-term liquidity, calculated by dividing the sum of cash, temporary investments, and net receivables by current liabilities. (p. 438)

Ageing the accounts receivable   Analysing customer balances by the length of time they have been unpaid. (p. 428)

Allowance method   A method of accounting for bad debts that involves estimating uncollectible accounts at

the end of each period. (p. 425)

Bad debts expense   An expense account to record uncollectible receivables. (p. 424)

Collection period   The result of 365 days divided by the receivables turnover. Determines the average number of days that receivables are outstanding. (p. 439)

Direct write-off method A method of accounting for bad debts that involves expensing amounts at the time they are determined to be uncollectible. (p. 424).

Dishonoured note A note that is not paid in full at maturity. (p. 436).

Factor A finance company or bank that buys receivables from businesses and then collects the payments directly from the customers. (p. 431).

Net realizable value Gross receivables less allowance for doubtful accounts. The net amount of receivables expected to be received in cash. (p. 425).

Percentage of receivables basis Management establishes a percentage relationship between the amount of receivables and the expected losses from uncollectible accounts. (p. 428).

Percentage of sales basis Management establishes a percentage relationship between the amount of credit sales and the expected losses from uncollectible accounts. (p. 428).

Promissory note A written promise to pay a specified amount of money on demand or at a definite time. (p. 434).

Receivables turnover A measure of the liquidity of receivables. Calculated by dividing net credit sales by average net receivables. (p. 439).

Trade receivables Notes and accounts receivable that result from sales transactions. (p. 422).

SELF-STUDY QUESTIONS

 Chapter 9 Self-Test

Answers are at the end of the chapter.

(SO 2) AP 1. On June 15, Patel Company sells merchandise on account to Bullock Co. for $1,000, terms n/30. On June 20, Bullock returns merchandise worth $300 to Patel. On July 14, payment is received from Bullock for the balance due. What is the amount of the receivable reported at the end of June?
   a. $0 c. $1,300
   b. $700 d. None of the above

(SO 3) AP 2. Sanderson Company has a credit balance of $5,000 in its Allowance for Doubtful Accounts before any adjustments are made. Based upon a review and ageing of its accounts receivable at the end of the period, the company estimates that $60,000 of its receivables are uncollectible. The amount of Bad Debts Expense which should be reported for this accounting period is:
   a. $5,000. c. $60,000.
   b. $55,000. d. $65,000.

(SO 3) AP 3. Assume Sanderson Company has a debit balance of $5,000 in Allowance for Doubtful Accounts before any adjustments are made. Based upon a review and ageing of its accounts receivable at the end of the period, the company estimates that $60,000 of its receivables are uncollectible. The amount of Bad Debts Expense which should be reported for this accounting period is:
   a. $5,000. c. $60,000.
   b. $55,000. d. $65,000.

(SO 3) AP 4. Net sales for the month are $800,000 and bad debts are expected to be 1.5% of net sales. The company uses the percentage of sales basis. If the Allowance for Doubtful Accounts has a credit balance of $15,000 before adjustment, what is the balance in the Allowance account after adjustment?
   a. $15,000 c. $27,000
   b. $23,000 d. $31,000

(SO 3) AP 5. In 2003, Lawrence Company had net credit sales of $750,000. On January 1, 2003, Allowance for Doubtful Accounts had a credit balance of $18,000. During 2003, $30,000 of uncollectible accounts receivable were writ- ten off. Past experience indicates that 3% of net credit sales become uncollectible. What should the adjusted balance of Allowance for Doubtful Accounts be at December 31, 2003?
   a. $9,600 c. $22,500
   b. $10,500 d. $40,500

6. Which of the following statements about Visa credit (SO 4) K card sales is incorrect?
   a. The credit card issuer does the credit investigation of the customer.
   b. The retailer is not involved in the collection process.
   c. Two parties are involved.
   d. The retailer receives cash more quickly than it would from individual credit customers.

7. Morgan Retailers accepted $50,000 of TD Bank Visa (SO 4) K credit card charges for merchandise sold on July 1. TD Bank charges 4% for its credit card use. The entry to record this transaction by Morgan Retailers will include a credit to sales of $50,000 and debit(s) to:
   a. Cash $48,000, and Credit Card Expense $2,000.
   b. Accounts Receivable $48,000, and Credit Card Expense $2,000.
   c. Cash $50,000.
   d. Accounts Receivable $50,000.

8. Sorenson Co. accepts a $1,000, three-month, 8% (SO 6) K promissory note in settlement of an account with Parton Co. The entry to record this transaction is as follows:

a.	Notes Receivable	1,020	
	Accounts Receivable		1,020
b.	Notes Receivable	1,000	
	Accounts Receivable		1,000
c.	Notes Receivable	1,000	
	Sales		1,000
d.	Notes Receivable	1,080	
	Accounts Receivable		1,080

(SO 5, 8) K   9. Schlicht Co. holds Osgrove Inc.'s $10,000, four-month, 9% note. If no interest has been accrued when the note is collected, the entry made by Schlicht Co. is:

a. Cash   10,300
    Notes Receivable   10,300
b. Cash   10,900
    Interest Revenue   900
    Notes Receivable   10,000
c. Accounts Receivable   10,300
    Notes Receivable   10,000
    Interest Revenue   300

d. Cash   10,300
    Notes Receivable   10,000
    Interest Revenue   300

(SO 10) AP   10. Moore Company had net credit sales during the year of $800,000 and a cost of goods sold of $500,000. The balance in receivables at the beginning of the year was $100,000 and at the end of the year was $150,000. What was the receivables turnover ratio?

a. 4.0   c. 6.4
b. 5.3   d. 8.0

QUESTIONS

(SO 1) C   1. Identify the three major types of receivables. Where is each type of receivable generally classified on a balance sheet?

(SO 1) K   2. What are some common types of receivables other than accounts receivable and notes receivable?

(SO 2) C   3. Assume that Petro-Canada charges you $50 interest on an unpaid balance. Prepare the journal entry that Petro-Canada makes to record this interest.

(SO 3) C   4. How are bad debts accounted for under the direct write-off method? What are the disadvantages of this method?

(SO 3) K   5. What are the essential features of the allowance method of accounting for bad debts?

(SO 3) C   6. Soo Eng cannot understand why net realizable value does not decrease when an uncollectible account is written off under the allowance method. Clarify this point for Soo Eng.

(SO 3) C   7. Distinguish between the two bases that may be used in estimating uncollectible accounts under the allowance method.

(SO 3) AP   8. Kyoto Company has a credit balance of $3,500 in Allowance for Doubtful Accounts. The estimated uncollectible amount under the percentage of sales basis is $4,100. The total estimated uncollectible amount under the percentage of receivables basis is $5,800. Prepare the adjusting entry under each basis.

(SO 4) C   9. When an account receivable that was previously written off is subsequently collected, two journal entries are usually made. Explain why.

(SO 4) K   10. Why do companies sometimes sell their receivables?

(SO 4) C   11. Sears accepts debit cards, bank credit cards, and its own nonbank Sears credit card. What are the advantages of accepting each type of card? Explain how the accounting for sales differs for each type of card.

(SO 5) AP   12. Calculate the missing amounts for each of the following notes:

	Principal	Interest Rate	Time	Total Interest
(a)	?	9%	4 months	$ 360
(b)	$30,000	6%	3 years	?
(c)	$60,000	?	6 months	$2,500
(d)	$50,000	7%	?	$ 875

(SO 6) C   13. Compare the characteristics of a note receivable with those of an account receivable.

(SO 8) C   14. May Company dishonours a note at maturity. Assuming eventual payment is intended, what entries should the payee and the maker (May Company) of the note make on their respective books?

(SO 9) C   15. Paul Company has accounts receivable, notes receivable, allowance for doubtful accounts, and allowance for doubtful notes. How should the receivables be reported on the balance sheet?

(SO 10) C   16. The President proudly announces her company's improved liquidity. Its current ratio increased substantially this year. Does an increase in the current ratio always indicate improved liquidity? What other ratio(s) might you review to determine whether or not the increase in the current ratio is an improvement in financial health?

(SO 10) AP   17. If **Clearly Canadian Beverage Corporation**'s receivables turnover ratio was 8.0583 times in 1999 and average accounts receivable during the period was $4,542,500, what was the amount of net credit sales for the period? Round your answer to the nearest thousand.

BRIEF EXERCISES

BE9–1 Presented below are three receivables transactions. Indicate whether these receivables are reported as accounts receivable, notes receivable, or other receivables on a balance sheet.
(a) Advanced $10,000 to an employee.
(b) Received a promissory note of $57,000 for services performed.
(c) Sold merchandise on account to a customer for $60,000.

Identify types of receivables. (SO 1) K

BE9–2 Record the following transactions on the books of Essex Co.:
(a) On July 1, Essex Co. sold merchandise on account to Cambridge Inc. for $14,000, terms n/30.
(b) On July 8, Cambridge Inc. returned merchandise worth $3,800 to Essex Co.
(c) On July 31, Cambridge Inc. paid for the merchandise.

Record accounts receivable transactions. (SO 2) AP

BE9–3 St. Pierre Co. uses the percentage of sales basis to record bad debts expense. It estimates that 2% of net credit sales will become uncollectible. Sales are $800,000 for the year ended April 30, 2003, sales returns and allowances are $50,000, and the allowance for doubtful accounts has a credit balance of $12,000. Prepare the adjusting entry to record bad debts expense in 2003.

Prepare adjusting entry using percentage of sales basis. (SO 3) AP

BE9–4 Groleskey Co. uses the percentage of receivables basis to record bad debts expense. It estimates that 1% of total accounts receivable will become uncollectible. Accounts receivable are $400,000 at the end of the year. The allowance for doubtful accounts has a credit balance of $3,000.
(a) Prepare the adjusting journal entry to record bad debts expense for the year ended December 31.
(b) If the allowance for doubtful accounts had a debit balance of $800 instead of a credit balance of $3,000, determine the amount to be reported for bad debts expense.

Prepare adjusting entry using percentage of receivables basis. (SO 3) AP

BE9–5 At the end of 2002, Searcy Co. has accounts receivable of $700,000 and an allowance for doubtful accounts of $54,000. On January 24, 2003, it is learned that the company's receivable from Hutley Inc. is not collectible. Management authorizes a write-off of $7,000.
(a) Prepare the journal entry to record the write-off.
(b) What is the net realizable value of the accounts receivable (1) before the write-off, and (2) after the write-off?

Prepare entry for write-off; determine net realizable value. (SO 3) AP

BE9–6 Assume the same information as in BE9–5. Hutley's financial difficulties are reversed. On March 4, 2003, Searcy Co. receives $7,000, payment in full, from Hutley Inc. Prepare the journal entries to record this transaction.

Prepare entry for subsequent collection of write-off. (SO 3) AP

BE9–7 St. Pierre Restaurant accepted a Visa card in payment of a $75 lunch bill on July 27. The bank charges a 3.5% fee. What entry should St. Pierre make? How would this entry change if (a) the payment had been made with a debit card instead of a Visa card, or (b) the payment had been made with an American Express card instead of a Visa card?

Prepare entries to record credit and debit card transactions. (SO 4) AP

BE9–8 Presented below are data on three promissory notes. Determine the missing amounts.

Calculate interest on notes receivable. (SO 5) AN

	Date of Note	Terms	Principal	Interest Rate	Total Interest
(a)	April 1	2 months	$900,000	10%	?
(b)	July 2	1 month	79,000	?	$526.67
(c)	March 7	6 months	?	6%	$1,680.00

BE9–9 On January 10, 2003, Raja Co. sold merchandise on account to Opal Co. for $9,000, n/30. On February 9, Opal gave Raja a 10% promissory note in settlement of this account. Prepare the journal entries to record the sale and the settlement of the account receivable.

Prepare entry for note receivable exchanged for account receivable. (SO 6) AP

BE9–10 Lee Company accepts a $10,000, 7%, three-month note receivable in settlement of an account receivable on April 1, 2003.
(a) Prepare the journal entries required to record the issue of the note on April 1, and the settlement of the note on July 1, assuming the note is honoured. No interest has previously been accrued.
(b) Repeat part (a) assuming that the note is dishonoured, but eventual collection is expected.
(c) Repeat part (a) assuming that the note is dishonoured, and eventual collection is not expected.

Record acceptance, honouring, and dishonouring of note. (SO 5, 6, 8) AP

Prepare entries for allowance method, balance sheet presentation.
(SO 3, 9) AP

BE9–11   During its first year of operations, Wendy Company had credit sales of $3,000,000. At year end, February 28, 2003, $600,000 remained uncollected. The credit manager estimates that $36,000 of these receivables will become uncollectible.

(a) Prepare the journal entry to record the estimated uncollectibles.

(b) Prepare the current assets section of the balance sheet for Wendy Company, assuming that in addition to the receivables, it has cash of $90,000, merchandise inventory of $130,000, and prepaid expenses of $13,000.

Calculate ratios to analyse receivables.
(SO 10) AP

BE9–12   The financial statements of **Sobeys Inc.** report sales of $11,006 million for the year ended May 6, 2000. Accounts receivable are $420 million at the end of fiscal 2000, and $380 million at the end of fiscal 1999. Calculate Sobey's receivables turnover and collection period.

EXERCISES

Journalize entries for accounts receivable.
(SO 2) AP

E9–1   Presented below are two independent situations:

1. On January 6, Ni Co. sells merchandise on account to Watson Inc. for $5,000, terms n/30. On February 5, Watson pays the amount due. Prepare the entries on Ni's books to record the sale and related collection.

2. On January 10, Margaret Giger uses her Canadian Tire credit card to purchase merchandise from Canadian Tire for $11,000. On February 10, Giger is billed by Canadian Tire for the amount due of $11,000. On February 12, Giger pays $6,000 on the balance due. On March 10, Giger is billed for the amount due, including interest at 2% per month on the unpaid balance as of February 12. Prepare the entries on Canadian Tire's books related to the transactions that occurred on January 10, February 12, and March 10.

Journalize entries to record allowance for doubtful accounts using two bases.
(SO 3) AP

E9–2   The ledger of the Ott Company at the end of the current year shows Accounts Receivable $110,000, Sales $840,000, and Sales Returns and Allowances $40,000.

Instructions

(a) If Allowance for Doubtful Accounts has a credit balance of $2,500 in the trial balance, journalize the adjusting entry at December 31, assuming bad debts are estimated to be (1) 1% of net sales, and (2) 10% of accounts receivable.

(b) If Allowance for Doubtful Accounts has a debit balance of $500 in the trial balance, journalize the adjusting entry at December 31, assuming bad debts are estimated to be (1) 0.5% of net sales, and (2) 5% of accounts receivable.

Determine bad debts expense and prepare adjusting entry.
(SO 3) AP

E9–3   Roy Company has accounts receivable of $97,500 at March 31. An analysis of the accounts shows the following:

Month of Sale	Balance, March 31
March	$65,000
February	17,600
December and January	8,500
November and October	6,400
	$97,500

Credit terms are n/30. At March 31, Allowance for Doubtful Accounts has a credit balance of $1,800, prior to adjustment. The company uses the percentage of receivables basis to estimate uncollectible accounts. The company's percentage estimates of bad debts are as follows:

Age of Accounts	Estimated Percentage Uncollectible
0–30 days outstanding	2%
31–60 days outstanding	10%
61–90 days outstanding	30%
Over 90 days outstanding	50%

Instructions

(a) Determine the total estimated uncollectibles.

(b) Prepare the adjusting entry at March 31 to record bad debts expense.

E9–4   On December 31, 2002, Ceja Co. estimated that 2% of its net sales of $400,000 will become uncollectible. On May 11, 2003, Ceja Co. determined that Robert Worthy's account was uncollectible and wrote off $1,100. On June 12, 2003, Worthy paid the amount previously written off.

Prepare journal entries for percentage of sales basis, write-off, and recovery.
(SO 3) AP

Instructions

Prepare the journal entries on December 31, 2002, May 11, 2003, and June 12, 2003.

E9–5   Presented below are two independent situations:

(a) On December 15, Guy Benicoeur uses his Visa Desjardins bank credit card to purchase artwork for $250 from the Galerie d'art Bégin located in the Marché Bonsecours. Le Mouvement Desjardins charges the gallery a 3% credit card transaction fee. Prepare the entries on the Galerie d'art Bégin's books to record this sale on December 15.

(b) On April 2, P. Zachos uses her Bay credit card to purchase merchandise from a Hudson's Bay store for $1,300. On May 1, Zachos is billed for the $1,300 amount due. Zachos pays $700 on the balance due on May 3. On June 1, Zachos receives a bill for the amount due, including interest of 28.8% on the unpaid balance for the month. Prepare the entries on The Bay's books related to the transactions that occurred on April 2, May 3, and June 1.

Journalize entries for credit card sales.
(SO 4) AP

E9–6   The annual report of **The Canadian National Railway Company (CN)**'s notes that CN entered into an agreement to sell eligible freight trade receivables. It sold $219 million of these receivables in 1998, $205 million in 1999, and 208 million in 2000.

Identify reason for sale of receivables.
(SO 4) C

Instructions

Explain why CN, a financially stable company, might choose to sell its receivables.

E9–7   Mazerolle Supply Co. has the following transactions related to notes receivable during the last two months of the year:

Nov. 1 Loaned $18,000 cash to A. Morgan on a one-year, 10% note.
Dec. 1 Sold goods to Wright, Inc. receiving a $3,600, three-month, 6% note.
   15 Received a $4,000, six-month, 8% note on account from Barnes Company.
   31 Accrued interest revenue on all notes receivable. Interest is due at maturity.

Journalize entries for notes receivable transactions.
(SO 5, 6) AP

Instructions

Journalize the transactions for Mazerolle Supply Co. Round your answers to the nearest dollar.

E9–8   Record the following transactions for the Appleby Co. in the general journal:

2002

May 1 Received a $10,500, one-year, 10% note on account from Jones Bros.
Dec. 31 Accrued interest on the Jones note.

2003

May 1 Received principal plus interest on the Jones note. (No interest has been accrued in 2003.)

Journalize entries for notes receivable.
(SO 5, 6) AP

E9–9   On May 2, Chang Company lends $4,000 to Fein Inc., issuing a six-month, 10% note. At the maturity date, November 1, Fein indicates that it cannot pay.

Journalize entries for dishonouring of notes receivable.
(SO 5, 8) AP

Instructions

(a) Prepare the entry to record the dishonouring of the note, assuming that Chang Company expects that collection in full will occur in the future.

(b) Prepare the entry to record the dishonouring of the note, assuming that Chang Company does not expect any collection for this note.

E9–10   Kasko Stores accepts both its own and national credit cards, in addition to debit cards. During the year, the following selected summary transactions occurred:

Jan. 15 Made Kasko credit card sales totalling $15,000.
   20 Made Visa credit card sales (service charge fee, 5%) totalling $4,500.
   30 Made debit card sales (service charge fee, 3%) totalling $1,000.
Feb. 10 Collected $12,000 on Kasko credit card sales.
   15 Added finance charges of 18% to Kasko credit card balances.

Journalize credit and debit card sales and indicate statement presentation of related charges.
(SO 4, 9) AP

Instructions

(a) Journalize the transactions for Kasko Stores.

(b) Indicate the statement presentation of the financing charges and the credit card and debit card expense for Kasko Stores.

Prepare balance sheet presentations of receivables.
(SO 9) AP

E9–11   Drost Company reports the following balances in its receivables accounts at October 31, 2003, (in millions): Accounts Receivable, $2,907; Advances to Employees, $5; Allowance for Doubtful Accounts, $31; Notes Receivable, $228; and HST Recoverable, $25.

Instructions

Prepare the balance sheet presentation of Drost Company's receivables as at October 31, 2003.

Calculate and interpret ratios.
(SO 10) AN

E9–12   Presented here is basic financial information (in millions) for **Nike** and **Reebok** for a recent fiscal year.

	Nike	Reebok
Sales	$8,995.1	$2,899.9
Average accounts receivable, net	1,569.4	417.4

The receivables turnover ratio for the industry was 6.8 times.

Instructions

Calculate the receivables turnover and collection period for both companies. Comment on the difference in their collection experiences, compared to each other and compared to the industry.

PROBLEMS: SET A

Prepare journal entries related to bad debts expense.
(SO 2, 3) AP

P9–1A   At December 31, 2002, Cellular Ten Co. reported the following information on its balance sheet:

Accounts receivable	$960,000
Less: Allowance for doubtful accounts	70,000

During the first quarter of 2003, the company had the following transactions related to receivables:

1.	Sales on account	$3,300,000
2.	Sales returns and allowances	50,000
3.	Collections of accounts receivable	2,800,000
4.	Write-offs of accounts receivable deemed uncollectible	90,000
5.	Recovery of accounts previously written off as uncollectible	25,000

Instructions

(a) Prepare the summary journal entries to record each of these five transactions.

(b) Enter the January 1, 2003, balances in the Accounts Receivable and Allowance for Doubtful Accounts general ledger accounts. Post the entries to the two accounts and determine the balances.

(c) Prepare the journal entry to record bad debts expense for the first quarter of 2003. An ageing of accounts receivable indicates that expected bad debts are $125,000.

Calculate bad debts using various methods.
(SO 3) AP

P9–2A   Information related to Hohenberger Company for 2003 is summarized below:

Total credit sales	$2,100,000
Accounts receivable at December 31	840,000
Bad debts written off	38,000

Instructions

(a) What amount of bad debts expense will Hohenberger Company report if it uses the direct write-off method of accounting for bad debts?

(b) Assume that Hohenberger Company estimates its bad debts expense at 3% of credit sales. What amount of bad debts expense will Hohenberger Company record if it has an Allowance for Doubtful Accounts credit balance of $4,000?

(c) Assume that Hohenberger Company estimates its bad debts expense based on 6% of total accounts receivable. What amount of bad debts expense will Hohenberger Company record if it has an Allowance for Doubtful Accounts credit balance of $3,000?

(d) Assume the same facts as in (c), except that there is a $3,000 debit balance in Allowance for Doubtful Accounts. What amount of bad debts expense will Hohenberger record?

(e) What are the primary weaknesses of the direct write-off method of reporting bad debts expense?

Journalize transactions related to bad debts using ageing schedule.
(SO 3) AP

P9–3A Presented below is an ageing schedule for Hinton Company for the year ended December 31, 2002:

Customer	Total	Number of Days Outstanding			
		0–30	31–60	61–90	Over 90
Aber	$ 20,000		$ 9,000	$11,000	
Bohr	30,000	$ 30,000	.		
Case	50,000	15,000	5,000		$30,000
Datz	38,000				38,000
Others	120,000	92,000	15,000	13,000	
	$258,000	$137,000	$29,000	$24,000	$68,000
Estimated Percentage Uncollectible		3%	6%	12%	24%
Estimated Bad Debts	$ 25,050	$ 4,110	$ 1,740	$ 2,880	$16,320

At December 31, 2002, the unadjusted balance in Allowance for Doubtful Accounts is a credit of $9,000.

Instructions

(a) Journalize and post the adjusting entry for bad debts at December 31, 2002.

(b) Journalize and post the following events and transactions for 2003 to the allowance account:
1. March 1, a $1,000 customer balance originating in 2002 is judged uncollectible.
2. May 1, a cheque for $1,000 is received from the customer whose account was written off as uncollectible on March 1.

(c) Journalize the adjusting entry for bad debts on December 31, 2003, assuming that the unadjusted balance in Allowance for Doubtful Accounts is $25,050 (credit) and the 2003 ageing schedule indicates that total estimated bad debts will be $37,100.

Calculate bad debts and journalize transactions using ageing schedule.
(SO 3) AP

P9–4A The following represents selected information taken from a company's ageing schedule to estimate uncollectible accounts receivable at year end:

	Total	Number of Days Outstanding			
		0–30	31–60	61–90	Over 90
Accounts receivable	$ 240,000	$100,000	$60,000	$50,000	$30,000
Percentage uncollectible		1%	5%	10%	25%
Estimated bad debts					

Instructions

(a) Calculate the total estimated bad debts based on the above information.

(b) Prepare the year-end adjusting journal entry to record the bad debts using the allowance method and the aged uncollectible accounts receivable determined in (a). Assume the opening balance in the Allowance for Doubtful Accounts account is a $10,000 credit.

(c) Of the above accounts, $2,000 is determined to be uncollectible. Prepare the journal entry to write off the uncollectible accounts.

(d) The company collects $1,000 on an account that had been determined to be uncollectible in (c). Prepare the journal entry (or entries) necessary to restore the account and record the cash collection.

(e) Explain how establishing an allowance satisfies the matching principle.

Journalize transactions related to bad debts using percentage of sales.
(SO 3) AP

P9–5A Huang Co. uses 3% of net sales to determine its bad debts expense for the period. At the beginning of the current period, Huang had an Allowance for Doubtful Accounts of $9,000 (credit). During the period, it had net credit sales of $1,000,000 and wrote off accounts receivable of $37,000 as uncollectible. One of the accounts written off as uncollectible in the amount of $5,000 was recovered before the end of the current period.

Instructions

(a) Prepare the entry to record bad debts expense for the current period.

(b) Prepare the entry to record the write-off of uncollectible accounts during the current period.

(c) Prepare the entries to record the recovery of the uncollectible account during the current period.

(d) Determine the ending balance in Allowance for Doubtful Accounts.

(e) How does the recovery of an account previously written off affect the bad debts expense for the current period?

Analyse accounts and prepare journal entries for receivables and bad debts.
(SO 2, 3) AN

P9–6A The balance sheets of Wilton Corporation on December 31, Year 1 and Year 2, showed gross accounts receivable of $8,300,000 and $9,500,000, respectively. The balances in the Allowance for Doubtful Accounts at the end of Year 1 and Year 2—after adjusting entries—were $750,000 and $930,000, respectively.

The income statements for Year 1 and Year 2 showed bad debts expense of $249,000 and $285,000, respectively, which was equal to 1% of sales. All sales were on account.

Instructions

Prepare summary journal entries for Year 2 to record the bad debts expense, sales, write-offs, and collections. (*Hint:* You may find the use of T accounts helpful in determining the amounts involved.)

Determine missing amounts related to sales and accounts receivable.
(SO 2, 9) AN

P9–7A The following information is for Moosa Merchandising Company:

Merchandise inventory at beginning of year	$36,000
Merchandise inventory at end of year	32,000
Purchases made during year	60,000
Gross profit on sales	27,000
Cash sales made during year	15,000
Accounts receivable at beginning of year	24,000
Accounts receivable written off during year	1,000
Accounts receivable collected during year	61,000

Moosa uses a periodic inventory system.

Instructions

(a) Calculate the amount of credit sales made during the year. (*Hint:* You will need to use the income statement relationships introduced in Chapter 6 in order to determine this.)

(b) Calculate the balance of Accounts Receivable at the end of the year.

Prepare entries for various receivables transactions.
(SO 2, 4, 5, 6, 7, 8) AP

P9–8A On January 1, 2003, Bleumortier Company had Accounts Receivable of $54,200 and Allowance for Doubtful Accounts of $4,700. Bleumortier Company prepares financial statements annually for the calendar year. During the year, the following selected transactions occurred:

Jan. 5 Sold $7,000 of merchandise to Brooks Company, terms n/30.

Feb. 2 Accepted a $7,000, four-month, 8% promissory note from Brooks Company for balance due.

 12 Sold $7,800 of merchandise to Gage Company and accepted Gage's $7,800, two-month, 10% note for the balance due.

 26 Sold $4,000 of merchandise to Mathias Co., terms n/10.

Apr. 5 Accepted a $4,000, three-month, 8% note from Mathias Co. for balance due.

 12 Collected Gage Company note in full.

June 2 Collected Brooks Company note in full.

July 4 Mathias Co. dishonours its note of April 5. It is expected that Mathias will eventually pay the amount owed.

 15 Sold $5,000 of merchandise to Tritt Inc. and accepted Tritt's $5,000, three-month, 8% note for the amount due.

Oct. 13 The Tritt Inc. note was dishonoured. Tritt Inc. is bankrupt and there is no hope of future settlement.

Dec. 31 Accrued interest is recorded on any outstanding notes.

Instructions

Journalize the transactions. Round your answers to the nearest dollar.

Prepare entries for various notes receivable transactions. Show balance sheet presentation.
(SO 4, 5, 6, 7, 8, 9) AP

P9–9A Tardif Company closes its books monthly. On September 30, 2003, selected ledger account balances are as follows:

Notes Receivable	$28,000
Interest Receivable	160

Notes Receivable include the following:

Date	Maker	Principal	Interest	Term
Aug. 1	Foran Inc.	$ 8,000	6%	2 months
Aug. 31	Drexler Co.	8,000	12%	2 months
Sept. 30	MGH Corp.	12,000	9%	6 months

Interest is due at maturity. During October, the following transactions were completed:

Oct. 1 Received payment in full from Foran Inc. on the amount due.
    7 Made sales of $6,900 on Tardif credit cards.
  12 Made sales of $750 on Visa credit cards. The credit card service charge is 3.5%.
  15 Added $485 to Tardif charge-customer balances for finance charges on unpaid balances.
  31 Received notice that Drexler note had been dishonoured. (Assume that Drexler is expected to pay in the future.)

Instructions

(a) Journalize the October transactions and the October 31 adjusting entry for accrued interest receivable.
(b) Enter the balances at October 1 in the receivable accounts, and post the entries to all of the receivable accounts.
(c) Show the balance sheet presentation of the receivable accounts at October 31.
(d) How would the journal entry on October 31 differ if Drexler were not expected to pay in the future?

P9–10A The following information was taken from the financial statements of **CN**:

Calculate ratios to evaluate short-term liquidity.
(SO 10) AN

CANADIAN NATIONAL RAILWAY COMPANY
Selected Financial Information
(in millions)

	December 31		
	2000	1999	1998
Cash and equivalents	$ 19	$ 307	$ 263
Accounts receivable, gross	$800	$849	$445
Allowance for doubtful accounts	63	46	41
Accounts receivable, net	737	803	404
Materials and supplies	110	116	132
Other current assets	259	301	251
Total current assets	1,125	1,527	1,050
Total current liabilities	1,903	1,777	1,392
Revenues	5,446	5,261	4,101

Instructions

(a) Calculate the current and acid test ratios for 2000 and 1999.
(b) Calculate the receivables turnover and collection period for 2000 and 1999.
(c) Comment on any improvement or deterioration in CN's short-term liquidity.

PROBLEMS: SET B

•••

P9–1B At December 31, 2002, Muslow Imports reported the following information on its balance sheet:

Prepare journal entries related to bad debts expense.
(SO 2, 3) AP

Accounts receivable	$1,000,000
Less: Allowance for doubtful accounts	60,000
Net realizable value	$ 940,000

During 2003, the company had the following transactions related to receivables:

1. Sales on account	$2,600,000
2. Sales returns and allowances	40,000
3. Collections of accounts receivable	2,300,000
4. Write-offs of accounts deemed uncollectible	65,000
5. Recovery of bad debts previously written off as uncollectible	25,000

Instructions

(a) Prepare the summary journal entries to record each of these five transactions.
(b) Prepare the journal entry to record bad debts expense for 2003. Bad debts are estimated at 2% of net credit sales.
(c) Enter the January 1, 2003 balances in the Accounts Receivable and Allowance for Doubtful Accounts general ledger accounts. Post the entries to the two accounts and determine the balances at December 31, 2003.

Calculate bad debts using various methods.
(SO 3) AP

P9–2B   Information related to Tisipai Company for 2003 is summarized below:

Total credit sales	$1,500,000
Accounts receivable at December 31	600,000
Accounts receivable written off	24,000
Accounts receivable subsequently recovered	4,000

Instructions

(a) What amount of bad debts expense will Tisipai Company report if it uses the direct write-off method of accounting for bad debts?
(b) Assume that Tisipai Company estimates its bad debts expense to be 3% of credit sales. What amount of bad debts expense will the company record if Allowance for Doubtful Accounts has a credit balance of $3,000?
(c) Assume that Tisipai Company estimates its bad debts expense to be 5% of total accounts receivable. What amount of bad debts expense will the company record if Allowance for Doubtful Accounts has a credit balance of $3,000?
(d) Assume the same facts as in (c), except that there is a $2,000 debit balance in Allowance for Doubtful Accounts. What amount of bad debts expense will the company record?
(e) Explain why the direct write-off method is not in accordance with generally accepted accounting principles.
(f) Which of the two bases for estimating bad debts under the allowance method—percentage of sales and percentage of receivables—do you prefer? Explain why.

Journalize transactions related to bad debts using ageing schedule.
(SO 3) AP

P9–3B   Presented below is an ageing schedule for Hake Company for the year ended December 31, 2002:

Customer	Total	Number of Days Outstanding			
		0–30	31–60	61–90	Over 90
Benson	$ 22,000		$ 10,000	$12,000	
Ripper	40,000	$ 40,000			
Bilck	57,000	16,000	6,000		$35,000
Freeland	34,000				34,000
Others	126,000	96,000	16,000	14,000	
	$279,000	$152,000	$32,000	$26,000	$69,000
Estimated Percentage Uncollectible		4%	7%	13%	25%
Estimated Bad Debts	$28,950	$6,080	$2,240	$3,380	$17,250

At December 31, the unadjusted balance in Allowance for Doubtful Accounts is a credit of $10,000.

Instructions

(a) Journalize and post the adjusting entry for bad debts at December 31, 2002.
(b) Journalize and post the following transactions in the year 2003 to the allowance account:
  1. On March 31, an $800 customer balance originating in 2002 is judged uncollectible.
  2. On May 31, a cheque for $800 is received from the customer whose account was written off as uncollectible on March 31.
(c) Journalize the adjusting entry for bad debts on December 31, 2003. Assume that the unadjusted balance in Allowance for Doubtful Accounts is a credit balance of $37,030. The 2003 ageing schedule indicates that total estimated bad debts in 2003 will be $40,000.

P9–4B Image.com uses the allowance method to estimate uncollectible accounts receivable. The computer produced the following ageing of the accounts receivable at year end:

	Total	Number of Days Outstanding			
		0–30	31–60	61–90	Over 90
Accounts receivable	$ 375,000	$220,000	$90,000	$40,000	$25,000
Percentage uncollectible		1%	4%	5%	10%
Estimated bad debts					

Instructions

(a) Calculate the total estimated bad debts based on the above information.

(b) Prepare the year-end adjusting journal entry to record the bad debts using the aged uncollectible accounts receivable determined in (a). Assume the opening balance in the Allowance for Doubtful Accounts is a $10,000 debit.

(c) Of the above accounts, $5,000 is determined to be uncollectible. Prepare the journal entry to write off the uncollectible accounts.

(d) The company collects $5,000 on an account that had been determined to be uncollectible in (c). Prepare the journal entry (or entries) necessary to restore the account and record the cash collection.

(e) Comment on how your answers to parts (a) to (d) would change if Image.com used a percentage of total accounts receivable of 3%, rather than ageing the accounts receivable.

(f) What are the advantages for the company of ageing the accounts receivable rather than applying a percentage to total accounts receivable?

P9–5B Hong Co. uses 12% of total accounts receivable to determine its bad debts expense for the period. At the beginning of the current period, Hong had Accounts Receivable of $150,000 and an Allowance for Doubtful Accounts of $10,000 (credit). During the period, it had credit sales of $1,300,000 and collections of $1,225,000. It wrote off as uncollectible accounts receivable of $41,000. One of the accounts written off as uncollectible in the amount of $5,200 was recovered before the end of the current period.

Instructions

(a) Prepare the entry to record credit sales for the current period.

(b) Prepare the entry to record the write-off of uncollectible accounts during the current period.

(c) Prepare the entries to record the recovery of the uncollectible account during the current period.

(d) Determine the unadjusted ending balance in Accounts Receivable and Allowance for Doubtful Accounts.

(e) Prepare the entry to record bad debts expense for the period.

(f) Determine the ending balance in Accounts Receivable and Allowance for Doubtful Accounts.

P9–6B The balance sheets of Beancounter Corporation on December 31, Year 1 and Year 2, showed gross accounts receivable of $4,100,000 and $4,800,000, respectively. The credit balances in the Allowance for Doubtful Accounts at the end of Year 1 and Year 2—after adjusting entries—were $350,000 and $425,000, respectively. Accounts receivable written off amounted to $125,000 during Year 1 and $150,000 during Year 2.

All sales were made on account. Bad debts expense for each year was estimated as 1% of sales.

Instructions

Show (in summary form) all the journal entries made during Year 2 that had an effect on Accounts Receivable or the Allowance for Doubtful Accounts. (*Hint*: You may find T accounts helpful in analysing this problem.)

P9-7B The following information is for the Mercury Merchandising Company:

Cost of goods sold during year	$66,000
Gross profit on sales during year	31,000
Accounts receivable at beginning of year	27,000
Cash sales made during year	18,000
Accounts receivable written off during year	1,500
Accounts receivable collected during year	80,000

Instructions

(a) Calculate the amount of credit sales made during the year. (*Hint*: You will need to use the income statement relationships introduced in Chapter 5 in order to determine this.)

(b) Calculate the balance of Accounts Receivable at the end of the year.

Prepare entries for various receivables transactions.
(SO 2, 4, 5, 6, 7, 8) AP

P9–8B On January 1, 2003, Dot.com Company had Accounts Receivable of $146,000, Note Receivable of $15,000, and Allowance for Doubtful Accounts of $13,200. The note receivable is from the Annabelle Company. It is a four-month, 8% note dated December 31, 2002. Dot.com Company prepares financial statements annually for the year ended December 31. During the year, the following selected transactions occurred:

Jan. 5 Sold $18,000 of merchandise to George Company, terms n/15.

20 Accepted George Company's $18,000, three-month, 9% note for balance due.

Feb. 18 Sold $8,000 of merchandise to Swaim Company and accepted Swaim's $8,000, six-month, 10% note for the amount due.

Apr. 20 Collected George Company note in full.

30 Received payment in full from Annabelle Company of the amount due.

May 25 Accepted Avery Inc.'s $6,000, three-month, 8% note in settlement of a past-due balance on account.

Aug. 18 Received payment in full from Swaim Company of the note due.

23 The Avery Inc. note was dishonoured. Avery Inc. is bankrupt. Future payment is not expected.

Sept. 1 Sold $12,000 of merchandise to Young Company and accepted a $12,000, six-month, 10% note for the amount due.

Nov. 22 News reports indicate that several key officers of Young Company have been arrested on charges of fraud and embezzlement, and that the company's operations have been shut down indefinitely.

Dec. 31 Accrued interest is recorded on any outstanding notes at year end.

Instructions

(a) Journalize the transactions.

(b) If there have been no further reports on the situation regarding Young Company, do you think the note should be written off? If not, do you think interest should be accrued on the note receivable at year end?

Prepare entries for various notes receivable transactions. Show balance sheet presentation.
(SO 4, 5, 6, 7, 8, 9) AP

P9–9B Ouellette Co. closes its books monthly. On June 30, 2003, selected ledger account balances are as follows:

Notes Receivable	$20,800
Interest Receivable	???

Notes Receivable include the following:

Date	Maker	Principal	Term	Interest
May 1	Don Co.	$ 6,000	2 months	12%
May 31	Jean Co.	4,800	2 months	11%
June 30	MJH Corp.	10,000	6 months	9%

Interest is due at maturity. During July, the following transactions were completed:

July 1 Received payment in full from Don Co. on the amount due.

5 Made sales of $6,200 on Ouellette credit cards.

14 Made sales of $700 on MasterCard credit cards. The credit card service charge is 3%.

16 Added $415 to Ouellette credit card customer balances for finance charges on unpaid balances.

31 Received notice that the Jean Co. note has been dishonoured. Assume that Jean Co. is expected to pay in the future.

Instructions

(a) Calculate the interest receivable at June 30.

(b) Journalize the July transactions and the July 31 adjusting entry for accrued interest receivable.

(c) Enter the balances at July 1 in the receivable accounts. Post the entries to all the receivable accounts.

(d) Show the balance sheet presentation of the receivable accounts at July 31, 2003.

(e) How would the journal entry on July 31 differ if Jean Co. were not expected to pay in the future?

P9–10B The following information was taken from the financial statements of the **Becker Milk Company Limited**:

BECKER MILK COMPANY LIMITED
Selected Financial Information
April 30

	2000	1999	1998
Cash	$ 22,376	$ 0	$ 0
Accounts receivable, net of allowance for doubtful accounts	245,301	273,084	250,581
Prepaid expenses and deposits	92,266	85,627	94,592
Current portion of long-term receivables	422,935	775,195	52,552
Total current assets	782,878	1,133,906	397,725
Total current liabilities (from recurring operations)	899,684	1,874,643	3,820,040
Revenue	4,210,313	4,160,167	4,554,824

Instructions

(a) Calculate the current and acid test ratios for 2000 and 1999.
(b) Calculate the receivables turnover and collection period for 2000 and 1999.
(c) Comment on any improvement or deterioration in Becker's short-term liquidity.

*B*roadening *Your Perspective*

FINANCIAL REPORTING AND ANALYSIS

Financial Reporting Problem

BYP9–1   The acid test ratio, receivables turnover, and collection period for **The Second Cup Ltd.** were calculated in this chapter, based upon its financial statements for the 2000 fiscal year. These financial statements are presented (along with the 1999 financial statements, for comparative purposes) in Appendix A.

Instructions

(a) Calculate The Second Cup's acid test ratio, receivables turnover, and collection period for the 1999 fiscal year (use pro forma results). Note: The company's Accounts Receivable at the end of its 1998 fiscal year amounted to $7,196,000.
(b) Comment upon any significant differences which you observe between the ratios for 2000 (as calculated in the chapter) and 1999 (as calculated in part a).

Interpreting Financial Statements

BYP9–2   High Liner Foods processes and markets quality seafood products. It is one of the largest Canadian deep sea fishing companies, harvesting over 24 million pounds of seafood annually from Georges Bank to Northern Labrador.
   The following selected information is available:

Additional Cases

HIGH LINER FOODS INCORPORATED
(in thousands)

	January 1, 2000	January 2, 1999
Cash	$ 7,474	$ 359
Accounts receivable, gross	30,634	31,432
Allowance for doubtful accounts	679	656
Accounts receivable, net	29,955	30,776
Inventories	54,415	79,855
Prepaid expenses	1,836	1,234
Other current assets	2,066	1,573

Total current assets	95,746	113,797
Total current liabilities	56,862	71,817
Sales (assume all are credit)	302,392	291,655

Additional detail about High Liner's receivables (in thousands) includes the following table and the excerpt which follows:

Accounts Receivable	January 1, 2000	January 2, 1999
Canada Trade	$13,793	$10,353
U.S. Trade	14,360	17,026
Japan Trade	672	483
Affiliates	73	47
Other	1,057	2,867
	$29,955	$30,776

"Terms range from 7 to 30 days, with most accounts being collected in 35 days. No one customer represents more than 7% of outstanding amounts. The Company has experienced a bad debt expense of less than 0.1% of sales over the past five years."

Instructions

(a) Calculate the current and acid test ratios for fiscal 1999 (January 1, 2000) and 1998 (January 2, 1999).
(b) Calculate the receivables turnover and collection period for fiscal 1999 and 1998. High Liner's opening accounts receivable balance at the beginning of fiscal 1998 was $23,379,000.
(c) Comment on High Liner Foods' short-term liquidity and management of its receivables.
(d) High Liner provides the same allowance for doubtful accounts of 2% of trade receivables, regardless of their location. Is this a reasonable policy? Explain

Accounting on the Web

BYP9–3 This problem examines the use of factoring, or discounting of receivables, in Canada. We will research two websites to obtain information on what factoring is and its advantages and disadvantages.

Instructions

Specific requirements of this Internet case are available on-line on the Weygandt website.

CRITICAL THINKING

Collaborative Learning Activity

BYP9–4 Johanna and Jake Berkvom own Campus Fashions. Since its beginning, Campus Fashions has sold merchandise either for cash or on account. No credit cards have been accepted. During the past several months, the Berkvoms have begun to question their sales policies. First, they have lost some sales because of their refusal to accept credit cards. Second, representatives of two banks have been persuasive, almost convincing them to accept their credit cards. One of these, the National Bank, has stated that its credit card fee is 3%.

The Berkvoms decide that they should determine the cost of issuing their own credit card. From the accounting records of the past three years, they accumulate the following data:

	2003	2002	2001
Net credit sales	$500,000	$600,000	$400,000
Collection agency fees, for slow-paying customers	2,450	2,500	2,400
Salary of part-time accounts receivable clerk	3,800	3,800	3,800

Credit and collection expenses as a percentage of net credit sales are as follows: uncollectible accounts, 1.6%; billing and mailing costs, 0.5%; and credit investigation fees on new customers, 0.15%.

Johanna and Jake also determine that the average accounts receivable balance outstanding during the year is 5% of net credit sales. The Berkvoms estimate that they could earn an average of 8% annually on cash invested in other business opportunities.

annually on cash invested in other business opportunities.

Instructions

With the class divided into groups, answer the following:
(a) Prepare a table showing total credit and collection expenses in dollars and as a percentage of net credit sales, for each year.
(b) Determine the net credit and collection expenses, in dollars and as a percentage of sales, after considering the revenue not earned from other investment opportunities.
(c) Discuss both the financial and non-financial factors that are relevant to the decision.

Communication Activity

BYP9–5 Lois, a friend of yours, overheard a discussion at work about changes her employer wants to make in accounting for uncollectible accounts. Lois knows little about accounting. She asks you to help make sense of what she heard. Specifically, she asks you to explain the differences between the direct write-off and allowance methods for uncollectible accounts. She also wonders what "percentage of sales" and "percentage of receivables" mean. Are these other methods of accounting for uncollectible accounts?

Instructions

In a letter, explain to Lois the methods of accounting for uncollectibles. Be sure to discuss the differences among these methods.

Ethics Case

BYP9–6 Shirt Co. is a subsidiary of Clothes Corp. The controller of Shirt Co. believes that the yearly allowance for doubtful accounts should be 2% of net credit sales. The president of Shirt Co., nervous that the shareholders might expect the company to sustain its current 10% growth rate, suggests that the controller increase the allowance for doubtful accounts to 4% of net credit sales. The president thinks that the lower net income (because of the increased bad debts expense) will be more sustainable for Shirt Co.

Instructions

(a) Who are the stakeholders in this case?
(b) Does the president's request pose an ethical dilemma for the controller?
(c) Should the controller be concerned with Shirt Co.'s growth rate in estimating the allowance? Explain your answer.

Answers to Self-Study Questions
1. b   2. b   3. d   4. c   5. b   6. c   7. a   8. b   9. d   10. c

Answer to Second Cup Review It Question 1
The only receivables The Second Cup reports are accounts receivable of $2,294,000 in its current assets section of the balance sheet.

Remember to go back to the Navigator box on the chapter-opening page to check off your completed work.

Before studying this chapter, you should understand or, if necessary, review:

a. *The time period assumption. (Ch. 3, p. 103)*
b. *The cost principle (Ch. 1, p. 11) and the matching principle. (Ch. 3, p. 104)*
c. *What amortization is. (Ch. 3, p. 116)*
d. *How to make adjustments for amortization. (Ch. 3, pp. 116–117)*

THE
NAVIGATOR

On the Books, Your Classroom May Be Worthless

CALGARY, Alta.—For a college or university, the buildings where its classes and other activities take place are some of its most important assets. Look around the campus of your own school. Where did the money for these buildings come from? Who pays to maintain them? And how much are they worth?

For the Southern Alberta Institute of Technology (SAIT) in Calgary, the first of these questions is easy. "The provincial government originally financed the buildings, and gave them to SAIT," explains Karen Keebler, supervisor of corporate reporting for the college.

The second question is a little more complex. "Maintenance comes from several sources," says Ms. Keebler. "We get government funding, some of it specially earmarked to keep up the buildings. We get donations, often for specific maintenance projects. And we pay for the day-to-day upkeep with general college revenue, which comes in part from tuition."

How much the buildings are worth is the trickiest question. For SAIT, the cost of a building is amortized over 40 years, based on its cost at the time SAIT acquired it. SAIT uses the straight-line method of amortization. In addition, the school's policy is to amortize major renovations over 25 years. In many organizations, renovations are amortized over the remaining useful life of the asset. But SAIT finds the fixed 25-year policy easier to capitalize and administer. It also avoids the problem of trying to combine original cost and renovation costs in the same account if the buildings have a remaining useful life of less than 25 years.

A few older buildings, such as Heritage Hall, where Ms. Keebler's office is located, have now been completely amortized. This means that, on the books, this handsome historic building, which dates from 1926, has no net book value. Of course, says Ms. Keebler, "this is not reflective of its fair market value!"

www.sait.ab.ca

THE
NAVIGATOR

THE NAVIGATOR

✔

- Understand *Concepts for Review*
- Read *Feature Story*
- Scan *Study Objectives*
- Read *Preview*
- Read text and answer *Before You Go On*
  - p. 464 p. 474 p. 478
  - p. 481 p. 486 p. 488
- Work *Demonstration Problems*
- Review *Summary of Study Objectives*
- Answer *Self-Study Questions*
- Complete assignments

CHAPTER · 10

CAPITAL ASSETS

► STUDY OBJECTIVES ◄

After studying this chapter, you should be able to:

1. Distinguish between tangible and intangible capital assets.
2. Demonstrate the application of the cost principle to property, plant, and equipment specifically, and to capital assets in general.
3. Explain the concept of, and be able to calculate, amortization.
4. Calculate periodic amortization using different methods.
5. Describe and demonstrate the procedure for revising periodic amortization.
6. Distinguish between operating and capital expenditures, and prepare the entries for these expenditures.
7. Explain and demonstrate how to account for the disposal of property, plant, and equipment.
8. Calculate the periodic amortization of natural resources.
9. Contrast the accounting for intangible assets with the accounting for tangible assets.
10. Illustrate how capital assets are reported on the balance sheet.
11. Demonstrate how to assess the profitability of total assets.

The accounting for campus buildings at the Southern Alberta Institute of Technology has important implications for the school's reported results. In this chapter, we explain the application of the cost principle of accounting to capital assets such as property, plant, and equipment, natural resources, and intangible assets. We describe the methods that may be used to allocate the cost of an asset over its useful life. In addition, we discuss the accounting for expenditures which occur during the useful life of assets, such as the cost of renovations incurred by SAIT. We also discuss the disposition of these assets during and at the end of their useful lives.

The chapter is organized as follows:

THE NAVIGATOR

▼Capital Assets

STUDY OBJECTIVE
·········▼·········
1

Distinguish between tangible and intangible capital assets.

Capital assets are long-lived assets acquired for use in the operation of a business. They are not for sale to customers. Contrary to current assets, which are used or consumed in the current accounting period, capital assets provide benefits over many accounting periods. These assets are held by the company to support the production and sale of goods or services to consumers.

Capital assets can be tangible (with physical substance) or intangible (without physical substance). **Tangible capital assets** include (1) property, plant, and equipment, and (2) natural resources. **Intangible capital assets** provide benefits through the special rights and privileges they give, rather than through any physical characteristics.

TANGIBLE CAPITAL ASSETS

As explained on the previous page, tangible capital assets can be subdivided into two categories: property, plant, and equipment, and natural resources. A key distinction between property, plant, and equipment and natural resources is that natural resources physically lose substance, or **deplete**, as they are used. For example, there is less of a tract of timberland (a natural resource), as the timber is cut and sold. When we use equipment, its physical substance remains the same regardless of the product it produces. We discuss each category of tangible capital assets in the next two sections of the chapter.

Property, Plant, and Equipment

Property, plant, and equipment are tangible resources that are used in the operation of a business. While these assets are not for sale to customers, their products or services are.

Many companies have a substantial investment in property, plant, and equipment. In public utility and telecommunications companies, for example, property, plant, and equipment can represent more than 75% of total assets. Recently, net property, plant, and equipment (property, plant, and equipment less accumulated amortization) amounted to more than 88% of the assets of Canadian Utilities Limited.

Illustration 10-1 shows the percentages of net property, plant, and equipment in relation to total assets in some other companies.

Alternative terminology
Property, plant, and equipment are also commonly known as *fixed assets; land, building, and equipment;* or *plant assets.*

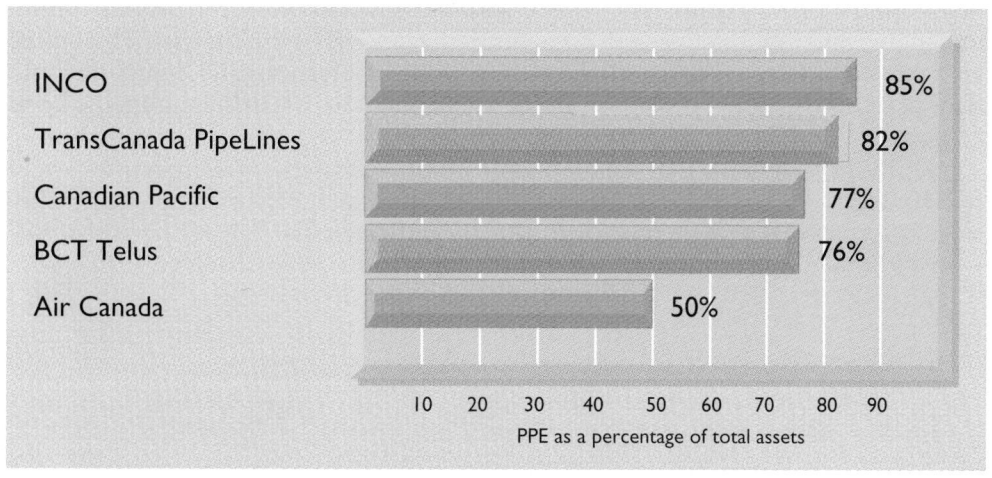

INCO — 85%
TransCanada PipeLines — 82%
Canadian Pacific — 77%
BCT Telus — 76%
Air Canada — 50%

10 20 30 40 50 60 70 80 90
PPE as a percentage of total assets

Illustration 10-1

Percentage of net property, plant, and equipment (PPE) to total assets

Determining the Cost of Property, Plant, and Equipment

Property, plant, and equipment (in addition to other capital assets) are recorded **at historical cost**, in accordance with the **cost principle** of accounting. The buildings at the Southern Alberta Institute of Technology are recorded at cost. Cost consists of all expenditures made to acquire the asset and **make it ready for its intended use**. For example, the cost of factory machinery includes the purchase price, freight costs paid by the purchaser, and any installation costs. All of these costs are **capitalized** (recorded as a capital asset), rather than expensed, because they will provide benefits over future periods.

Cost is measured either by the cash paid in a cash transaction or by the **cash equivalent price** paid when non-cash assets are used in payment. **The cash equiva-**

STUDY OBJECTIVE
▼ **2**

Demonstrate the application of the cost principle to property, plant, and equipment specifically, and to capital assets in general.

lent price is the fair market value of the asset given up. Or, if that value is not clearly determinable, the cash equivalent price is the fair market value of the asset received. Once cost is established, it becomes the basis of accounting for the asset over its useful life. Current market or replacement values are not used after an asset is aquired unless the values decline below net book value (cost less accumulated amortization). If an asset's fair market value falls below its net book value, an impairment loss should be recorded. An impairment loss recognizes the decline in value, reducing the asset's net book value to its fair market value. If the fair market value subsequently increases, the book value is **not** subsequently adjusted for any recovery in value.

Property, plant, and equipment is often subdivided into four classes:
1. **Land**, such as a building site
2. **Land improvements**, such as driveways, parking lots, fences, and underground sprinkler systems
3. **Buildings**, such as stores, offices, factories, and warehouses
4. **Equipment**, such as store checkout counters, cash registers, coolers, office furniture, factory machinery, and delivery equipment

The application of the cost principle to each of the major classes of property, plant, and equipment is explained in the following sections.

Land

The cost of land includes the purchase price and other related costs. These costs might include closing costs such as survey and legal fees, and accrued property tax to be paid by the purchaser. Once the land is ready for its intended use, recurring costs such as property tax are expensed against the revenues the land helps to generate.

All the costs which come from preparing land for its intended use are also debited from the Land account. For vacant land, these include costs for clearing, draining, filling, and grading the land. Sometimes the land has a building on it that must be removed before construction of a new building. In this case, all demolition and removal costs (less any proceeds from salvaged materials) are debited from the Land account.

To illustrate, assume that the Budovitch Manufacturing Company acquires land for $100,000 cash. An old warehouse on the property is removed at a net cost of $6,000 ($7,500 in costs less $1,500 proceeds from salvaged materials). The legal fee of $3,000 is an additional expenditure. The cost of the land is $109,000, calculated as follows:

Illustration 10-2

Calculation of cost of land

Land	
Cash price of property	$100,000
Net removal cost of warehouse	6,000
Legal fee	3,000
Cost of land	$109,000

In recording the acquisition, Land is debited for $109,000, and Cash is credited for $109,000.

Land Improvements

Land is a unique capital asset. Its cost is not amortized—allocated over its useful life—because land has an unlimited useful life. However, there are costs incurred to improve the land that do have limited useful lives. The costs of such things as paving, fencing, signs, lighting, and landscaping are recorded separately from Land as Land Improvements and are amortized over their useful lives.

Buildings

All costs related to the purchase or construction of a building are debited from the Buildings account. When a building is purchased, such costs include the purchase price and closing costs (e.g., legal fees). Costs to make the building ready for its intended use include expenditures for remodeling, and for replacing or repairing the roof, floors, electrical wiring, and plumbing.

When a new building is constructed, at your school, for example, cost consists of the contract price for construction of the building plus payments for architects' fees, building permits, and excavation costs. Interest costs incurred to finance the project are also included in the cost of the asset when a significant period of time passes before the building is ready for use. These interest costs are considered to be as necessary as materials and labour. Only the interest costs which occur during the construction period are included. After construction is finished, future interest payments on funds borrowed to finance the construction are debited from Interest Expense.

Equipment

The cost of equipment consists of the cash purchase price and other related costs. These costs include freight charges and insurance during transit if they are paid by the purchaser. They also include costs to assemble, install, and test the unit. Motor vehicle licences and insurance on company trucks and cars are not capital costs. They are annual recurring expenditures that do not benefit future periods.

To illustrate, assume that O'Reilly Company purchases a used delivery truck on August 1 at a cash price of $22,000. Related expenditures consist of painting and lettering, $500; motor vehicle licence, $80; and an insurance policy, $1,600. The cost of the delivery truck is $22,500, calculated as follows:

Helpful hint Two criteria apply in determining cost here: (1) the frequency of the cost—one-time or recurring—and (2) the benefit period—life of asset or one year.

Delivery Truck	
Cash price	$22,000
Painting and lettering	500
Cost of delivery truck	$22,500

Illustration 10-3
Calculation of cost of delivery truck

The motor vehicle licence is expensed when its cost is incurred and the insurance policy is a prepaid asset. The entry to record the purchase of the truck and related expenditures is as follows:

Aug. 1	Delivery Truck	22,500	
	Licence Expense	80	
	Prepaid Insurance	1,600	
	Cash		24,180
	To record purchase of delivery truck and related expenditures.		

A	=	L	+	OE
+22,500				–80
+1,600				
–24,180				

Basket Purchase

Capital assets are often purchased as a group for a single price. This is known as a **basket purchase**. We need to know the cost of each individual asset in order to journalize the purchase, and to calculate amortization. When a basket purchase occurs, we determine individual costs by allocating the total price paid for the group of capital assets to each individual asset based on their **relative fair market values**.

To illustrate, assume Sega Company paid $150,000 cash to acquire a building and a parcel of land. The land was recently appraised at $60,000. The building was appraised at $100,000. The $150,000 cost should be allocated on the basis of fair market (appraised) values as shown in Illustration 10-4.

Alternative terminology A basket purchase is also known as a *lump-sum purchase*.

Illustration 10-4

Allocating cost in a basket purchase

	Fair Market Value	Allocated Percentage	Allocated Cost
Land	$ 60,000	37.5% ($60,000 ÷ $160,000)	$ 56,250 ($150,000 × 37.5%)
Building	100,000	62.5% ($100,000 ÷ $160,000)	93,750 ($150,000 × 62.5%)
Totals	$160,000	100.0%	$150,000

Before You Go On . . .

▶Review It

1. What are capital assets? What are the major classes of capital assets?
2. What are property, plant, and equipment? How is the cost principle applied to accounting for property, plant, and equipment?
3. What is a basket purchase?
4. What types and amounts of capital assets does The Second Cup Ltd. report in Note 6 to its balance sheet? The answer to this question is at the end of the chapter.

▶Do It

Assume that factory machinery is purchased on November 6 for $50,000 cash. Related expenditures include insurance during shipping, $500; and installation and testing, $1,000. Prepare the journal entry to record these expenditures.

Action Plan

- Identify which expenditures are made to get the machinery ready for its intended use.
- Expense the operating costs that benefit only the current period, or which are recurring costs.

Solution

Factory Machinery	
Cash price	$50,000
Insurance during shipping	500
Installation and testing	1,000
Cost of machinery	$51,500

The entry to record the purchase and related expenditures follows:

Nov. 6	Factory Machinery	51,500	
	Cash		51,500
	To record purchase of factory machinery.		

Related exercise material: BE10–1, BE10–2, BE10–3, BE10–4, E10–1, and E10–2.

Amortization

STUDY OBJECTIVE
··········▼··········
3
Explain the concept of, and be able to calculate, amortization.

As explained in Chapter 3, amortization **is the allocation of the cost of a capital asset (such as property, plant, and equipment) to expense over its useful (service) life in a rational and systematic manner**. The allocation of cost matches expenses with revenues, in accordance with the matching principle.

Illustration 10-5

Amortization as an allocation concept

As you know from Chapter 3, the journal entry to record periodic amortization is a debit to Amortization Expense and a credit to Accumulated Amortization. Amortization Expense is an income statement account. Accumulated Amortization appears on the balance sheet as a contra account to the related capital asset account. This contra asset account is similar in purpose to the one used in Chapter 9 for the allowance for doubtful accounts. Both contra accounts reduce assets to their respective carrying values (*net realizable value* for accounts receivable and *net book value* for capital assets).

Amortization is a process of cost allocation, not a process of asset valuation. Accountants do not measure the change in an asset's market value during ownership, because the property, plant, and equipment are not for resale. Current market values are not relevant. So, the **net book value** of property, plant, or equipment (cost less accumulated amortization) may differ significantly from its market value. This is why Heritage Hall, in our feature story, can have a zero book value and still have a substantial market value.

Amortization applies to three classes of property, plant, and equipment: land improvements, buildings, and equipment. Each of these classes is considered an **amortizable asset**. Why? Because the usefulness to the company and the revenue-producing ability of each class declines over the asset's useful life. Amortization does not apply to land, because its usefulness and revenue-producing ability generally remain the same over time. In fact, in many cases, the usefulness of land increases because of the scarcity of good land sites. Thus, **land is not an amortizable asset**.

During an amortizable asset's useful life, its revenue-producing ability declines because of **physical factors** such as wear and tear. A delivery truck that has been driven 100,000 kilometres is less useful to a company than one driven only 1,000 kilometres. Revenue-producing ability may also decline because of **economic factors** such as obsolescence. Obsolescence means being out of date before the asset physically wears out. For example, the rapid pace of technological change forces frequent computer and other electronic upgrades long before the useful life of the current equipment ends. It is important to understand that amortization only approximates the decline in revenue-producing ability. It does not exactly measure the true effects of physical or economic factors.

Also, **amortization does not result in the accumulation of cash for replacement of the asset.** The balance in the Accumulated Amortization account only represents the total cost that has been charged to expense. There is no cash involved when amortization is recorded.

Factors in Calculating Amortization

Three factors affect the calculation of amortization:
1. **Cost.** The issues that affect the cost of an amortizable asset were explained earlier in this chapter. Recall that property, plant, and equipment are recorded at cost, in accordance with the cost principle.
2. **Useful life.** Useful life is an estimate of the expected productive life, also called the *service life*, of the asset. Useful life may be expressed in terms of time, units of activity (such as machine hours), or units of output. Useful life is an estimate. In making the estimate, management considers factors such as the intended use of the asset, its expected need for repair and maintenance, and its vulnerability to obsolescence. Past experience with similar assets is often helpful in estimating expected useful life.
3. **Residual value.** Residual value is an estimate of the asset's value at the end of its useful life. This value may be based on the asset's worth as scrap or on its expected trade-in value. Residual value is not amortized, since the amount is

Alternative terminology Amortization is also commonly known as *depreciation*.

Helpful hint Land is not amortized, because it does not wear out.

Alternative terminology Another term sometimes used for residual value is *salvage value*.

expected to be recovered at the end of the asset's useful life. Like useful life, residual value is an estimate. In making the estimate, management considers how it plans to dispose of the asset and its experience with similar assets.

Illustration 10-6 summarizes these three factors.

Illustration 10-6

Three factors in calculating amortization

Cost: all expenditures necessary to acquire the asset and make it ready for its intended use

Useful life: estimate of the expected life based on need for repair, service life, and vulnerability to obsolescence

Residual value: estimate of the asset's value at the end of its useful life

▶Accounting in Action ▸ *Business Insight*

Not all companies use the same useful life for assets, even when the assets are similar. Compare the useful lives assumed by the North American auto makers known as The Big Three, for example. At one time, General Motors amortized its machinery over 10 years, Ford used 12 years, and Chrysler used 11 years. GM amortized its buildings over 28 years, while Ford used 30 years and Chrysler 26 years. GM amortized the dies and equipment used to manufacture car bodies about twice as fast as Ford and three times as fast as Chrysler. Then, GM changed and aligned itself with its principal competitors. By applying more liberal amortization policies, GM increased its annual income. Should companies in the same industry use the same useful life for the same type of assets?

Amortization Methods

STUDY OBJECTIVE
••••••••• **4** •••••••••

Calculate periodic amortization using different methods.

Amortization is generally calculated using one of the following methods:
1. Straight-line
2. Declining-balance
3. Units-of-activity

Each method is acceptable under generally accepted accounting principles. Management selects the method it believes to be appropriate in the circumstances. The objective is to select the amortization method that best measures an asset's contribution to revenue over its useful life. Once a method is chosen, it should be applied consistently over the useful life of the asset. Consistency makes the comparison of financial statements easier.

We will compare the three amortization methods, using the following data for a small delivery truck purchased by Kim's Florists on January 1, 2002:

Cost	$25,000
Expected residual value	$2,000
Estimated useful life (in years)	5
Estimated useful life (in kilometres)	200,000

Straight-Line. Under the straight-line method, amortization is the same for each year of the asset's useful life. It is measured solely by the passage of time.

In order to calculate amortization expense, we must first determine the amortizable cost. Amortizable cost is the cost of the asset less its residual value. It is the total amount that can be amortized. Amortizable cost is divided by the asset's useful life to determine the annual amortization expense. The calculation of amortization expense in the first year for Kim's Florists' delivery truck is shown in Illustration 10-7.

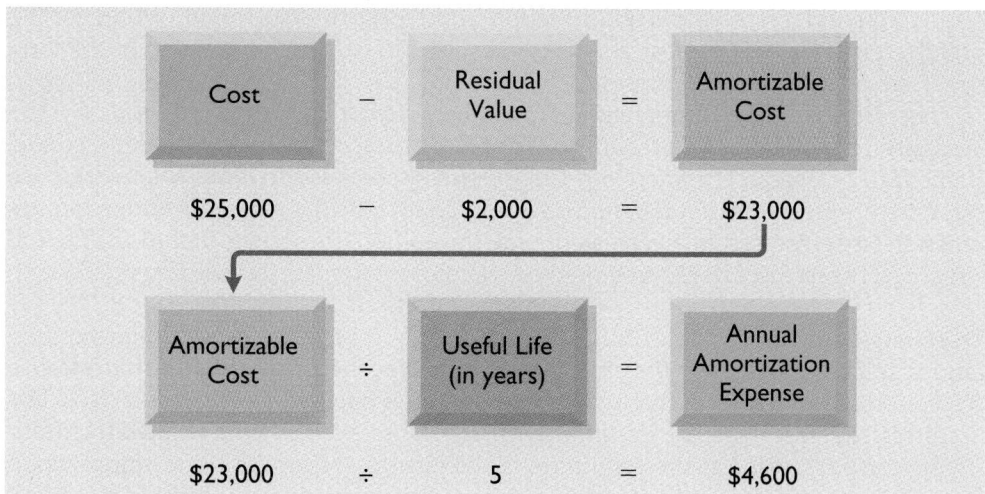

Alternatively, we can calculate an annual rate of amortization.

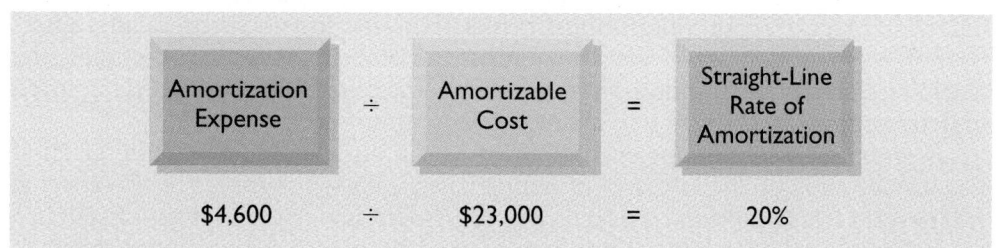

A faster way to find the straight-line rate of amortization is to divide the estimated useful life into 100%. For Kim's Florists, this would be as follows: 100% ÷ 5 (years) = 20% per year. When an annual rate is used, the straight-line percentage rate is applied to the **amortizable cost** of the asset. The use of an annual rate is shown in the following **amortization schedule**:

	KIM'S FLORISTS				
Year	Amortizable Cost	× Amortization Rate	= Amortization Expense	Accumulated Amortization	Net Book Value
					$25,000
2002	$23,000	20%	$ 4,600	$ 4,600	20,400
2003	23,000	20%	4,600	9,200	15,800
2004	23,000	20%	4,600	13,800	11,200
2005	23,000	20%	4,600	18,400	6,600
2006	23,000	20%	4,600	23,000	**2,000**
			$23,000		

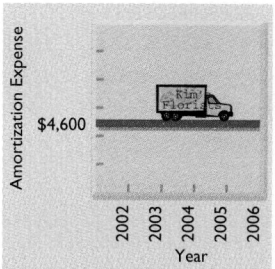

Note that the amortization expense of $4,600 is the same each year. The column's total is the amortizable cost of the asset over its accounting life. The book value at the end of the useful life is equal to the estimated $2,000 residual value.

What happens when an asset is purchased **during** the year, rather than on January

1 as in our example? Most companies **prorate the annual amortization** for the time used. If Kim's Florists had purchased the delivery truck on April 1, 2002, the amortization for 2002 would be $3,450 ($23,000 × 20% × $^9/_{12}$ of a year). Other companies may choose to charge a full year's amortization in the year of acquisition and none in the year of disposal. Others may charge a half year's amortization in the year of acquisition and a half year's amortization in the year of disposition. Whatever the policy chosen for partial-year acquisitions, the impact is not significant in the long run if the policy is applied consistently.

Nearly 92% of the companies surveyed by *Financial Reporting in Canada* use the straight-line method of amortization. Many large companies, including Bell Canada, Bombardier, Canadian Pacific, Coca-Cola, Domtar, Loblaw, and Nortel Networks, use the straight-line method. It is simple to apply, and it matches expenses with revenues when the asset is used in a consistent way throughout its service life. In the feature story, SAIT uses the straight-line method of amortization for its buildings.

Declining-Balance.   The declining-balance method produces a decreasing annual amortization expense over the asset's useful life. The method has this name because the periodic amortization is based on a **declining net book value** of the asset (cost less accumulated amortization). The annual amortization expense is calculated by multiplying the book value at the beginning of the year by the straight-line amortization rate. **The amortization rate remains constant from year to year, but the net book value to which the rate is applied declines each year.**

Net book value for the first year is the cost of the asset. This is because the balance in accumulated amortization at the beginning of the asset's useful life is zero. In the following years, the book value is the difference between cost and accumulated amortization at the beginning of the year. Unlike the other amortization methods, the declining-balance method does not use amortizable cost. **Residual value is ignored in determining the amount to which the rate of amortization is applied.**

Residual value does, however, limit the total amortization that can be taken. If you use the straight-line rate on a declining-balance basis, the asset's net book value will never reach its expected residual value. A straight-line rate will always result in a final value which is higher than the estimated residual value. Amortization stops when the asset's net book value equals its expected residual value.

Varying rates of amortization may be used, depending on how fast the company wishes to accelerate amortization. You will find rates such as 1 time (single), 1.5 times, 2 times (double), and even 3 times (triple) the straight-line rate of amortization. An amortization rate that is often used is double the straight-line rate. This method is referred to as the **double declining-balance method**. If Kim's Florists uses the double declining-balance method, the amortization rate is 40% (2 × the straight-line rate of 20%). The calculation of amortization for the first year on the delivery truck follows:

Illustration 10-10

Formula for double declining-balance method

Net Book Value at Beginning of Year	×	Straight-Line Rate × 2	=	Annual Amortization Expense
$25,000	×	40%	=	$10,000

The amortization schedule under this method is as follows:

	Net Book Value Beginning of	× Amortization =	Amortization	Accumulated	Net Book
Year	Year	Rate	Expense	Amortization	Value
					$25,000
2002	$25,000	40%	$10,000	$10,000	15,000
2003	15,000	40%	6,000	16,000	9,000
2004	9,000	40%	3,600	19,600	5,400
2005	5,400	40%	2,160	21,760	3,240
2006	3,240	40%	1,240*	23,000	**2,000**
			$23,000		

KIM'S FLORISTS

*Calculation of $1,296 ($3,240 x 40%) is adjusted to $1,240 in order for net book value to equal residual value.

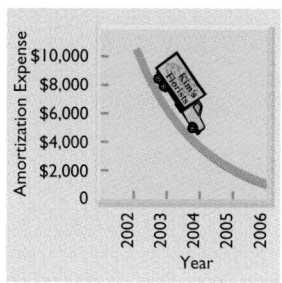

Illustration 10-11

Double declining-balance amortization schedule

You can see that the delivery truck is 70% amortized ($16,000 ÷ $23,000) at the end of the second year. Under the straight-line method it would be amortized 40% ($9,200 ÷ $23,000) at that time. Because the declining-balance method produces a higher amortization expense in the early years than the later years, it is considered an **accelerated amortization method**.

The declining-balance method respects the matching principle. The higher amortization expense in early years is matched with the higher benefits received in these years. A lower amortization expense is recognized in later years when the asset's contribution to revenue is less. Also, some assets lose their usefulness rapidly because of obsolescence. In these cases, the declining-balance method provides a more appropriate amortization amount.

When an asset is purchased during the year, the first year's declining-balance amortization must be prorated. For example, if Kim's Florists had purchased the delivery truck on April 1, 2002, the amortization for the partial year would be $7,500 ($25,000 × 40% × $^9/_{12}$). The net book value for calculating amortization in 2003 would then become $17,500 ($25,000 − $7,500). The amortization for 2003 would be $7,000 ($17,500 × 40%). Future calculations would follow from these amounts until the net book value equalled the residual value.

While the declining-balance method is not as popular as the straight-line method, it is still used by many companies, including Canadian Tire, Cara Operations, Le Château, and Maclean Hunter. In some cases, this method is chosen because it provides the best match of cost and benefit. In other cases, declining-balance is chosen because it must be used for income tax purposes (discussed later in this chapter), and it is simpler to use the same method for both accounting and tax purposes.

Units-of-Activity. Under the units-of-activity method, useful life is expressed as the total units of activity or production expected from the asset, rather than as a time period. The units-of-activity method is ideally suited to factory machinery where production is measured in units of output or machine hours. This method can also be used for assets such as delivery equipment (kilometres driven) and airplanes (hours in use). The units-of-activity method is generally not suitable for buildings or furniture, because amortization for these assets is more a function of time than of use.

In this method, the total units of activity for the entire useful life are estimated. This amount is divided into the amortizable cost to determine the amortization cost per unit. The amortization cost per unit is then applied to the units of activity during the year to determine the annual amortization expense.

Alternative terminology
The units-of-activity method is often called the *units-of-production* method.

To illustrate, assume that the delivery truck of Kim's Florists is driven 30,000 kilometres in the first year. The calculation of amortization expense in the first year follows:

Illustration 10-12

Formula for units-of-activity method

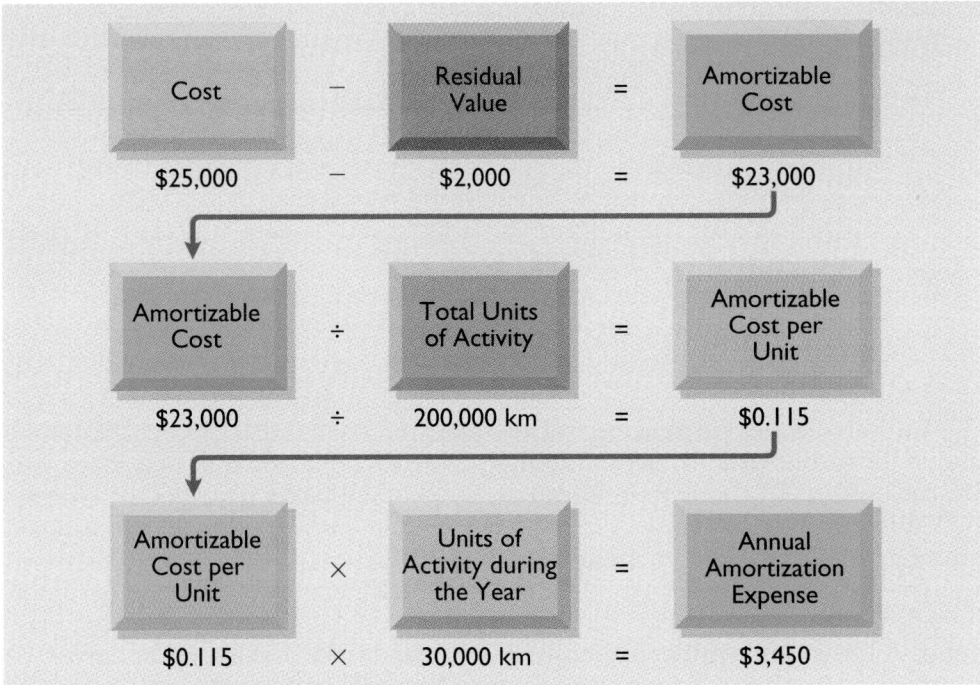

The units-of-activity amortization schedule, using assumed kilometres, is as follows:

Illustration 10-13

Units-of-activity amortization schedule

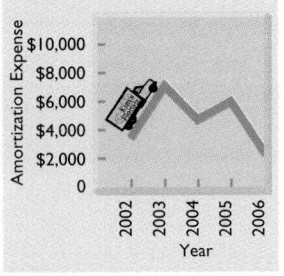

	KIM'S FLORISTS				
Year	Units of Activity	× Amortizable Cost/Unit	= Amortization Expense	Accumulated Amortization	Net Book Value
					$25,000
2002	30,000	$0.115	$3,450	$ 3,450	21,550
2003	60,000	$0.115	6,900	10,350	14,650
2004	40,000	$0.115	4,600	14,950	10,050
2005	50,000	$0.115	5,750	20,700	4,300
2006	20,000	$0.115	2,300	23,000	**2,000**
	200,000		$23,000		

This method is easy to apply when assets are purchased during the year. In such a case, the productivity of the asset for the partial year is used in calculating the amortization. The units of activity, therefore, are not adjusted for partial periods as they already reflect how much the asset was used during the specific period.

The units-of-activity method is not nearly as popular as the other methods, mostly because it is often difficult to make a reasonable estimate of total activity. However, this method is used by some very large companies such as Boise Cascade, Imperial Metals, Imperial Oil, and Pan-Canadian. When the productivity of the asset varies significantly from one period to another, the units-of-activity method results in the best matching of expenses with revenues.

▶Accounting in Action ▸ *Business Insight*

Why does Gingiss Formalwear have 70 amortization accounts and use the units-of-activity method for its tuxedos? The reason is that Gingiss wants to track wear and tear on each of its 16,000 tuxedos individually. Each tuxedo has a bar code, like a box of cereal at the grocery store. When a tux is rented, a clerk runs its code across an electronic scanner. At year end, the computer adds up the total rentals for each of the tuxedos, then divides by expected total use to calculate the rate. For instance, on one dolphin-grey tux, Gingiss expects a life of 30 rentals. In one year, the tux was rented 13 times. The amortization rate for that period was 43% (13 ÷ 30) of the amortizable cost.

Comparison of Amortization Methods

A comparison of annual and total amortization expense under each of the three methods is shown for Kim's Florists in Illustration 10-14.

Year	Straight-Line	Double Declining-Balance	Units-of-Activity
2002	$ 4,600	$10,000	$ 3,450
2003	4,600	6,000	6,900
2004	4,600	3,600	4,600
2005	4,600	2,160	5,750
2006	4,600	1,240	2,300
	$23,000	$23,000	$23,000

Illustration 10-14

Comparison of amortization expense

The amortization expense pattern under each method is presented in Illustration 10-15.

Illustration 10-15

Patterns of amortization expense

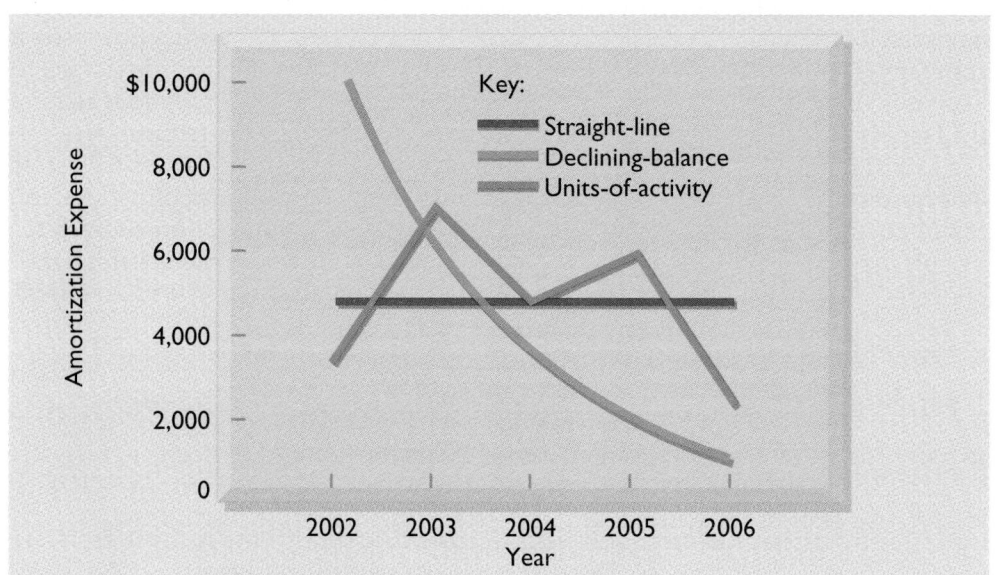

The choice of amortization method affects the income statement through amortization expense. Assume that net income, before deducting amortization expense, is $50,000 for each of the five years. We can clearly see the impact each method has on net income after amortization has been deducted in the schedule on the following page.

Straight-line amortization results in a constant amount of amortization expense and net income, each year. Declining-balance results in a higher amortization expense

Illustration 10-16

Comparison of net income

Year	Straight-Line	Double Declining-Balance	Units-of-Activity
2002	$ 45,400	$ 40,000	$ 46,550
2003	45,400	44,000	43,100
2004	45,400	46,400	45,400
2005	45,400	47,840	44,250
2006	45,400	48,760	47,700
	$227,000	$227,000	$227,000

in early years, and lower income. This method results in a lower amortization expense in later years, with higher income. Results with the units-of-activity method vary depending on actual usage each year. For each year, the annual amortization expense and net income vary considerably among the methods. However, *total* amortization expense and *total* net income is the same over the five-year period.

Each method is acceptable because each recognizes the decline in service potential of the asset in a rational and systematic manner.

Which method is preferable? There is no easy answer to this question. GAAP requires businesses to match the cost of a capital asset to the revenue produced by that asset. Since the pattern of revenue production is different for each type of asset, each amortization method should be chosen based on the revenue pattern of the asset in question. For a capital asset that generates revenues fairly consistently over time, the straight-line method is appropriate. The declining-balance method best fits assets that are more productive—generating greater revenues—in the earlier years of their life. The units-of-activity method applies well to assets whose usage varies substantially over time.

▸ *Ethics note*

Often practical considerations, rather than theoretical ones, influence a manager's choice of amortization method—ease of use, convenience, tradition.

Amortization and Income Tax

The Canada Customs and Revenue Agency (CCRA) allows taxpayers to deduct amortization expense when calculating taxable income. For accounting purposes, a company should choose the amortization method that best matches revenues to expenses. Tax regulations have different objectives. Income tax regulations require the taxpayer to use the single declining-balance method on the tax return.

In addition, the CCRA does not permit taxpayers to estimate the useful lives, or amortization rates, of assets. It groups assets into various classes and provides maximum amortization rates for each class of capital assets. Amortization allowed for income tax purposes is calculated on a class (group) basis, and is called **capital cost allowance (CCA)**. Selected asset classes and CCA rates are shown in Illustration 10-17.

▸ *International note*

In Germany, income tax laws have a strong influence on financial accounting. The amortization expense required by the tax code must also be used for preparing financial statements.

Illustration 10-17

Selected capital cost allowance rates

Class	Capital Asset Group	CCA Rate
Class 1	Buildings	4%
Class 8	Office equipment	20%
Class 10	Automobiles	30%
Class 10	Computers	30%
Class 12	Computer software	100%
Class 43	Manufacturing and processing equipment	30%

Helpful hint Guideline useful lives (amortization rates) for specific types of assets are provided by the CCRA for income tax purposes. However, the useful life chosen for accounting purposes must be based on management's own expectations.

As part of its policy to minimize alternative treatments, the CCRA also sets partial-year amortization rules. Only one-half of the CCA is allowed in the year of acquisition. Capital cost allowance is an optional deduction from taxable income. While businesses must deduct amortization for accounting purposes (required to fulfill the matching principle), they may choose to deduct varying amounts of CCA for tax purposes, ranging from none to the maximum specified amount for the class.

Software packages to account for capital assets exist for both large and small companies. Although these packages vary in complexity, even the least sophisticated can maintain a control and subsidiary ledger for each capital asset. They can also make the necessary amortization calculations and adjusting entries. Many packages also maintain separate amortization schedules for both financial statement and income tax needs, and they make reconciliations for any differences.

Revising Periodic Amortization

Amortization is one example of the use of estimates in the accounting process. Amortization calculations should be reviewed periodically by management. If physical or economic factors indicate that the estimates are inadequate or excessive, a change should be made.

> **STUDY OBJECTIVE**
> ....**5**..........
> *Describe and demonstrate the procedure for revising periodic amortization.*

When a change in an estimate is required, the change is made for current and future years. **It is not made retroactively for prior periods.** In other words, there is no correction of previously recorded amortization expense. Instead, amortization expense for current and future years is revised. The rationale is that the estimate made in the past was based on the best information available at that time. Estimates are necessary in the accounting process. Continually restating prior periods because of changes in estimates could also adversely affect the reader's confidence in financial statements.

To determine the new annual amortization expense, we first calculate the asset's net book value at the time of the change in estimate. We deduct any revised residual value to determine the amortizable cost at the time of the revision. The revised amortizable cost is then divided by the **remaining** useful life.

> **Helpful hint** Use a step-by-step approach: (1) determine new amortizable cost (net book value less revised residual value), and (2) divide by remaining useful life.

To illustrate, assume that Kim's Florists decides on January 1, 2005, to extend the useful life of the truck an additional year (to December 31, 2007) because of its good condition. The estimated residual value is expected to decline from its original estimate of $2,000 to $700. The company has used the straight-line method to amortize the asset to date. The book value at January 1, 2005, is $11,200 (refer to Illustration 10-9 and the net book value at December 31, 2004). The new annual amortization is $3,500, calculated as follows:

Net book value, Jan. 1, 2005	$11,200	
Less: Revised residual value	700	
Revised amortizable cost	10,500	
Remaining useful life	÷ 3 years	(2005–2007)
Revised annual amortization	$ 3,500	

Illustration 10-18

Revised amortization calculation

Kim's Florists makes no entry for the change in estimate. On December 31 of 2005, 2006, and 2007, during the preparation of adjusting entries, it records an amortization expense of $3,500. Significant changes in estimates must be described in the financial statements.

►Accounting in Action ► *Business Insight*

Willamette Industries owns more than 100 pulp, paper, and other wood-product manufacturing plants in France, Ireland, Mexico, and the U.S. In March 1999, it changed its accounting estimates for the amortization of certain assets due to advances in technology that increased the service life of its equipment by five years. The accounting changes increased Willamette's 1999 annual earnings by about $57 million, or $0.52 per share. Its 1998 earnings were $89 million, or $0.80 per share. Imagine a 56% improvement in earnings from a mere change in the estimated life of equipment!

Before You Go On . . .

▸*Review It*

1. What is the relationship, if any, of amortization to (a) cost allocation, (b) asset valuation, and (c) cash accumulation?
2. What are the formulas for calculating annual amortization under each of the amortization methods—straight-line, declining-balance, and units-of-activity?
3. How do the effects of the methods on annual amortization and net income differ over the useful life of the asset?
4. Are revisions of periodic amortization made to prior periods or future periods? Explain.

▸*Do It*

On January 1, 2002, Iron Mountain Ski Company purchased a new snow grooming machine for $50,000. The machine is estimated to have a five-year life with a $2,000 residual value. It is also expected to have a total useful life of 6,000 hours. It was used 1,000 hours during 2002 and 1,200 hours during 2003. How much amortization expense would Iron Mountain Ski record in each of 2002 and 2003 using each of the following methods of amortization: (a) straight-line, (b) double declining-balance, and (c) units-of-activity?

Action Plan

- Amortization is an allocation concept.
- Under straight-line amortization, an equal amount of the amortizable cost (cost less residual value) is allocated to each period.
- Under declining-balance amortization, more amortization is allocated in the early years than in the later years. Apply double the straight-line rate of amortization to the net book value. Residual values are ignored in this method.
- Under units-of-activity amortization, determine an amortizable cost per unit. Multiply this amount by the actual usage in each period to determine amortization expense.

Solution

	2002	2003
Straight-line	$ 9,600	$ 9,600
Double declining-balance	20,000	12,000
Units-of-activity	8,000	9,600

(a) Straight-line: ($50,000 − $2,000) ÷ 5 years = $9,600
(b) Double declining-balance: 100 ÷ 5 years = 20% straight-line rate
     2002: $50,000 × 20% × 2 = $20,000
     2003: ($50,000 − $20,000) × 20% × 2 = $12,000
(c) Units-of-activity: ($50,000 − $2,000) ÷ 6,000 hours = $8.00 per hour
     2002: 1,000 × $8.00 = $8,000
     2003: 1,200 × $8.00 = $9,600

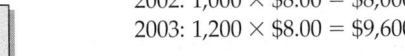

Related exercise material: BE10–5, BE10–6, BE10–7, BE10–8, E10–3, E10–4, E10–5, and E10–6.

Expenditures During Useful Life

During the useful life of a capital asset, a company may incur costs for ordinary repairs, additions, or improvements. Ordinary repairs are costs to *maintain* the operating efficiency and expected life of the unit. They are usually fairly small amounts that occur frequently. Motor tune-ups and oil changes, painting of buildings, and replacement of worn-out gears on machinery are examples. Such repairs are debited to Repair (or Maintenance) Expense as they occur. Because they are immediately charged as an expense against revenues, these costs are referred to as operating expenditures.

Additions and improvements are costs incurred to *increase* the operating efficiency, productive capacity, or expected useful life of a capital asset. They are usually substantial and occur less often. Additions and improvements increase the company's investment in productive facilities and are generally debited to the appropriate property, plant, or equipment asset account affected. They are called capital expenditures. They are amortized over the remaining life of the original structure or the useful life of the addition, if it is not dependent on the original asset. SAIT amortizes its building renovations over 25 years, regardless of the remaining life of the building. Using a fixed life like this does not always provide the best match of expenses to revenues. SAIT argues that this practice is simpler and that any mismatch is likely not material.

STUDY OBJECTIVE

·········· **7** ··········

Explain and demonstrate how to account for the disposal of property, plant, and equipment.

Disposals of Property, Plant, and Equipment

Property, plant, and equipment may be disposed of in one of three ways—retirement, sale, or exchange—as shown in Illustration 10-19.

Retirement
Equipment is scrapped or discarded.

Sale
Equipment is sold to another party.

Exchange
Existing equipment is traded for new equipment.

Illustration 10-19

Methods of property, plant, and equipment disposal

At the time of disposal, it is necessary to determine the net book value of the property, plant, or equipment. As noted earlier, the net book value is the difference between the cost of the asset and the accumulated amortization to date. At the time of disposal, amortization for the fraction of the year to the date of disposal must also be recorded. The net book value is then eliminated by debiting (decreasing) Accumulated Amortization for the total amortization to date and crediting (decreasing) the asset account for the cost of the asset. Any proceeds and gain or loss (which results when proceeds differ from the net book value) must also be recorded.

In this section, we will examine the accounting for each of the three methods of capital asset disposal.

Retirement of Property, Plant, and Equipment

To illustrate the retirement of a piece of property, plant, and equipment, assume that Basayev Enterprises retires its computer printers, which cost $32,000, on August 8. The accumulated amortization on these printers is also $32,000. The equipment is fully amortized (zero book value). The entry to record this retirement is as follows:

Aug. 8	Accumulated Amortization—Printing Equipment	32,000	
	Printing Equipment		32,000
	To record retirement of fully amortized printing equipment.		

A	=	L	+	OE
+32,000				
–32,000				

What happens if a fully amortized asset is still useful to the company? In this case, the asset and its accumulated amortization continue to be reported on the balance sheet without further amortization, until the asset is retired. Reporting the asset and related amortization on the balance sheet informs the reader of the financial statements that the asset is still being used by the company. Once an asset is fully amortized, even if it is still being used, no additional amortization should be taken. The accumulated amortization on a piece of property, plant, and equipment can never exceed its cost.

Helpful hint When a capital asset is disposed of, all amounts related to the asset must be removed from the accounts. These include the original cost in the asset account and the total amortization to date.

If a piece of property, plant, and equipment is retired before it is fully amortized, and no residual value is received, a loss on disposal occurs. Assume that Basayev Enterprises retires delivery equipment on September 24 that cost $28,000 and has accumulated amortization of $24,000. The loss on disposal is calculated by subtracting the net book value of the asset from the proceeds received. In this case, there are no proceeds and the net book value is $4,000 (Cost of $28,000 − Accumulated amortization of $24,000), resulting in a loss of $4,000.

Illustration 10-20

Calculation of loss on disposal; no proceeds received

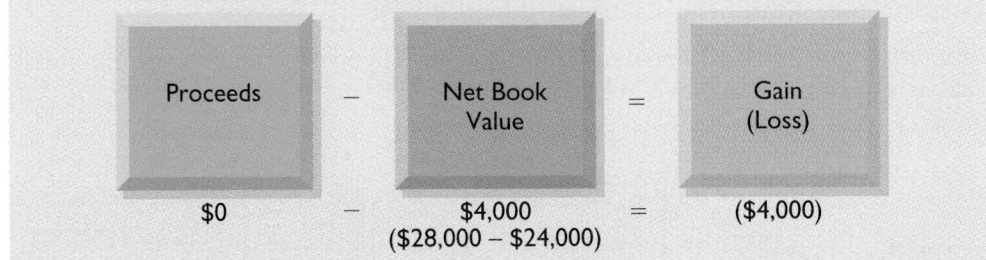

The entry to record the retirement of equipment and loss on disposal is as follows:

A	=	L	+	OE
+24,000				−4,000
−28,000				

Sept. 24	Accumulated Amortization—Delivery Equipment	24,000	
	Loss on Disposal	4,000	
	Delivery Equipment		28,000
	To record retirement of delivery equipment at a loss.		

This loss is reported in the other expenses section of the income statement. The loss represents a necessary catch-up amount or correction because previously recorded amortization was understated.

Sale of Property, Plant, and Equipment

In a disposal by sale, the net book value of the asset is also compared with the proceeds received from the sale. If the proceeds of the sale exceed the net book value of the piece of property, plant, and equipment, a **gain on disposal** occurs. If the proceeds of the sale are less than the book value of the asset sold, a **loss on disposal** occurs.

Only by coincidence will the net book value and the fair market value of the asset be the same when the asset is sold. Gains and losses on sales of capital assets are quite common. For example, Canadian Pacific reported a $37 million loss on the sale of its CP Trucks. Loblaw Companies reported a $900,000 gain on the sale of fixed assets.

Gain on Disposal. To illustrate a gain, assume that on July 1, 2003, Basayev Enterprises sells office furniture for $16,000 cash. The office furniture originally cost $60,000. As at January 1, 2003, it had accumulated amortization of $41,000. Amortization for the first six months of 2003 is $8,000.

The first step is to update any unrecorded amortization. The entry to record amortization expense and update accumulated amortization for the first six months of 2003 is as follows:

A	=	L	+	OE
−8,000				−8,000

July 1	Amortization Expense	8,000	
	Accumulated Amortization—Office Furniture		8,000
	To record amortization expense for the first six months of 2003.		

After the accumulated amortization balance is updated to $49,000 ($41,000 + $8,000), a gain on disposal of $5,000 is calculated as follows:

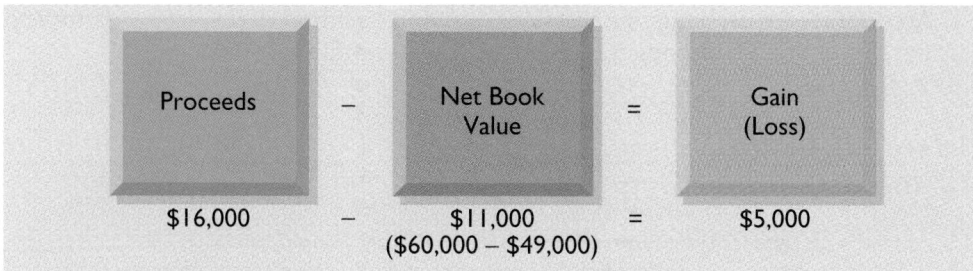

Illustration 10-21

Calculation of gain on disposal

The entry to record the sale and gain on disposal is as follows:

July 1	Cash	16,000		
	Accumulated Amortization—Office Furniture	49,000		
	Office Furniture		60,000	
	Gain on Disposal		5,000	
	To record sale of office furniture at a gain.			

```
A    =  L  +  OE
+16,000         +5,000
+49,000
–60,000
```

The gain on disposal is reported in the other revenues section of a multiple-step income statement. This gain does not represent a direct source of income; instead, it corrects previously recorded amortization that was overstated.

Loss on Disposal.   Assume that instead of selling the office furniture for $16,000, Basayev sells it for $9,000. In this case, a loss of $2,000 is calculated as follows:

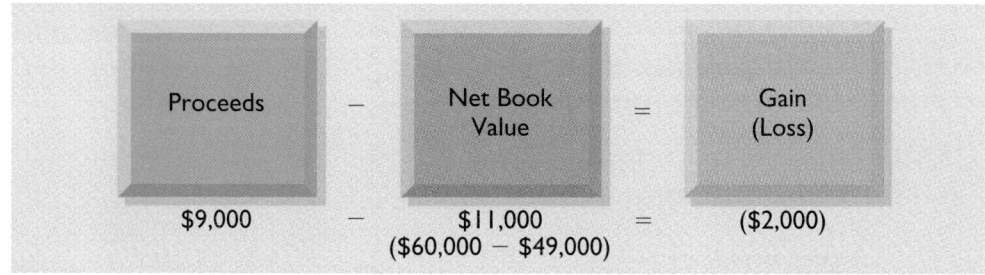

Illustration 10-22

Calculation of loss on disposal

The entry to record the sale and loss on disposal is as follows:

July 1	Cash	9,000		
	Accumulated Amortization—Office Furniture	49,000		
	Loss on Disposal	2,000		
	Office Furniture		60,000	
	To record sale of office furniture at a loss.			

```
A    =  L  +  OE
+9,000          –2,000
+49,000
–60,000
```

As noted earlier in the chapter, the loss on disposal is reported in the other expenses section of the income statement.

Exchanges of Property, Plant, and Equipment

Many capital assets are sold for cash when they are no longer needed. Others are commonly exchanged for new assets. In an exchange of assets, a new asset is typically purchased by trading in an old asset, on which a **trade-in allowance** is given toward the purchase price of the new asset. Cash may also be involved. It is usually a payment for the difference between the trade-in allowance and the purchase price of the new asset.

Accounting for exchange transactions, the third method of disposal, is complex. Further discussion of exchanges is left for future accounting courses.

Before You Go On . . .

► Review It

1. How does a capital expenditure differ from an operating expenditure?
2. What is the proper accounting for the retirement and sale of a piece of property, plant, and equipment?
3. What is the formula to calculate a gain or loss on disposal?

► Do It

Overland Trucking has an old truck that originally cost $75,000. It has accumulated amortization of $70,000. Assume each of the following three independent situations: (1) Overland Trucking retires the truck. (2) Overland sells the truck for $6,500 cash. (3) Overland sells the truck for $4,500 cash. Prepare the journal entries to record each of these situations.

Action Plan

- Update any unrecorded amortization for partial-year dispositions.
- Compare the proceeds with the asset's net book value to determine whether any gain or loss has occurred.
- Record any proceeds received and any gain or loss. Remove both the asset and any related accumulated amortization from the accounts.

Solution

(1)	Retirement of truck:		
	Loss on Disposal [($0 − ($75,000 − $70,000)]	5,000	
	Accumulated Amortization	70,000	
	Truck		75,000
	To record retirement of truck.		
(2)	Sale of truck for $6,500:		
	Cash	6,500	
	Accumulated Amortization	70,000	
	Truck		75,000
	Gain on Disposal [($6,500 − ($75,000 − $70,000)]		1,500
	To record sale of truck at a gain.		
(3)	Sale of truck for $4,500:		
	Cash	4,500	
	Loss on Disposal [($4,500 − ($75,000 − $70,000)]	500	
	Accumulated Amortization	70,000	
	Truck		75,000
	To record sale of truck at a loss.		

Related exercise material: BE10–9, BE10–10, BE10–11, E10–7, E10–8, and E10–9.

◢ Natural Resources
· ·

Natural resources consist of standing timber and underground deposits of oil, gas, and minerals. Canada is rich in natural resources, ranging from the towering rainforests in coastal British Columbia to the world's largest nickel deposits in Voisey's Bay, Labrador. These long-lived productive assets have two distinguishing characteristics: (1) They are physically extracted in operations such as mining, cutting, or pumping. (2) They are replaceable only by an act of nature. Because of these characteristics, natural resources are frequently called **wasting assets**.

The acquisition cost of a natural resource is the cash or cash equivalent price of acquiring the resource and preparing it for its intended use. For an already-discovered resource, such as an existing coal mine, cost is the price paid for the property.

Amortization

Amortization for natural resources is calculated in the same manner as for property, plant, and equipment, with one additional consideration. The amortizable cost of the natural resource is affected not only by any residual value, but also by any future removal or site restoration costs.

STUDY OBJECTIVE
▼
8

Calculate the periodic amortization of natural resources.

Future Removal and Site Restoration Costs

With natural resources, issues such as site restoration, reforestation, and environmental cleanup are significant. Environmental legislation requires companies to protect the natural resource, especially at the completion of its use. To return the resource as closely as possible to its natural state at the end of its use, restoration and removal costs are usually required.

The matching principle suggests that restoration and removal costs should be estimated in advance and allocated over the useful life of the natural resource. They should not be recorded simply in the year of closure of the resource.

Units-of-Activity Method

The units-of-activity method (learned earlier in the chapter) is generally used to calculate the amortization of wasting assets. It is used because natural resource amortization is, most often, a function of the units extracted during the year. Under the units-of-activity method, the total cost of the natural resource minus residual value and plus any restoration costs is divided by the number of units estimated to be in the resource. The result is an amortizable cost per unit of product. The amortizable cost per unit is then multiplied by the number of units extracted and sold, to determine the annual amortization expense.

To illustrate, assume that the Lane Coal Company invests $5 million in a mine estimated to yield 10 million tonnes of coal. It has a $200,000 residual value. To restore the site after the coal has been extracted, $500,000 will be required. In the first year, 800,000 tonnes of coal are extracted and sold. Using the formulas on the following page, the calculations are as follows:

Illustration 10-23

Formula to calculate amortization expense for natural resources

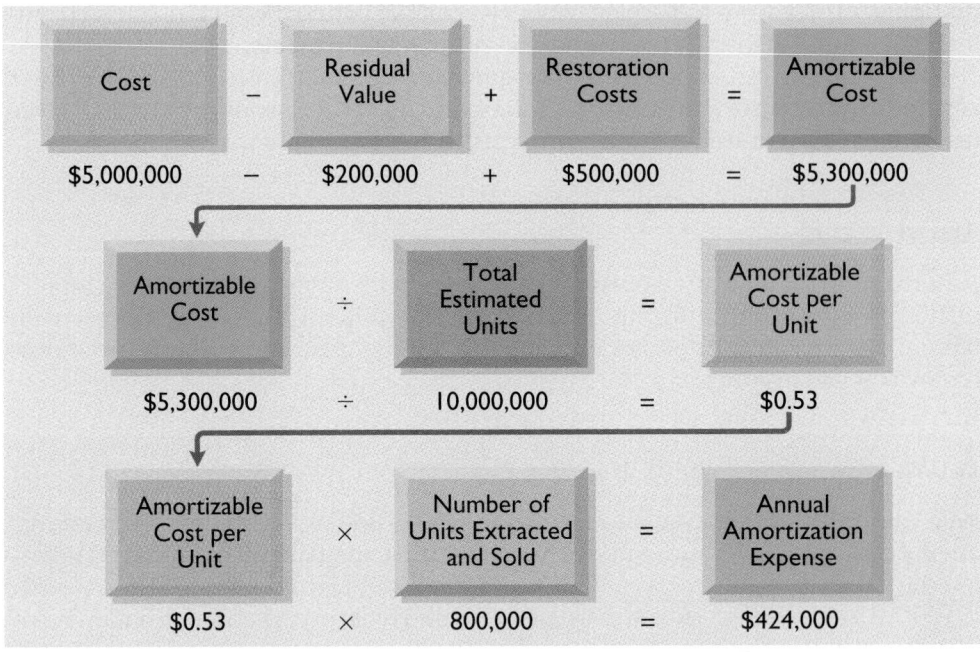

The entry to record amortization expense for the first year of operation, ended December 31, 2003, is as follows:

A	=	L	+	OE
–384,000		+40,000		–424,000

Dec. 31	Amortization Expense	424,000	
	Accumulated Amortization—Coal Mine		384,000
	Liability for Restoration		40,000
	($500,000 ÷ 10,000,000 × 800,000)		
	To record amortization expense on coal deposits.		

The account Amortization Expense is reported on the income statement as part of the cost of producing the product. Accumulated Amortization, a contra asset account, is deducted from the cost of the natural resource in the balance sheet, as follows:

Illustration 10-24

Statement presentation of accumulated amortization for natural resources

LANE COAL COMPANY
Balance Sheet (partial)
December 31, 2003

Assets

Capital assets		
Coal mine		$5,000,000
Less: Accumulated amortization		384,000
Net book value		4,616,000

In some companies, an Accumulated Amortization account is not used. In such cases, the amount of amortization is credited directly to the natural resource account.

Restoration and removal costs are included in the debit from amortization expense. They are not, however, credited to Accumulated Amortization. Instead, **they are recorded separately as a long-term liability (Liability for Restoration) on the balance sheet**. If the costs cannot be reasonably estimated, a contingent liability should be disclosed in the notes to the financial statements. We will learn more about contingent liabilities in the next chapter.

Sometimes, natural resources extracted in one accounting period will not be sold until a later period. In this case, amortization is not expensed until the resource is sold. The amount not sold is reported in the current asset section as inventory.

Other capital assets, such as property, plant, and equipment, are frequently acquired for use in the development and production of the natural resource. If these assets are not expected to have any productive use after the natural resource is fully extracted, their estimated useful lives are limited to the years of expected productive capacity of the natural resource.

Before You Go On . . .

►*Review It*

1. Why do restoration costs affect amortization expense for natural resources?
2. How is amortization expense calculated for natural resources?

►*Do It*

Calculate annual amortization for the High Timber Company. Assume that High Timber invests $12 million in a tract of timber land. It is estimated to have 10 million cunits (1 cunit = 100 cubic feet) of timber, a $500,000 residual value, and $2,000,000 of site restoration costs. In the first year, 40,000 cunits of timber are cut, of which 30,000 cunits are sold.

Action Plan

- Determine the amortizable cost in total and per unit.
- Allocate the amortization between expense (units sold) and inventory (units on hand).

Solution

Under the units-of-activity method, an amortizable cost per unit is determined by dividing total cost minus residual value plus restoration costs by the total estimated units. The calculation is as follows:

($12,000,000 − $500,000 + $2,000,000) ÷ 10,000,000 cunits = $1.35 amortizable cost per cunit

The cost per unit is then multiplied by the number of units cut and sold, to determine the amortization expense. Amortization expense for High Timber is $40,500 ($1.35 × 30,000) in the first year. The cost related to the remaining 10,000 cunits that have been cut, but not yet sold, will be allocated to inventory in the amount of $13,500 ($1.35 × 10,000).

Related exercise material: BE10–12 and E10–10.

THE
NAVIGATOR

Intangible Capital Assets

Both tangible and intangible capital assets benefit future periods and are used to produce products or provide services over these periods. Intangible capital assets are different from tangible capital assets because of their lack of physical existence. Intangible assets are rights, privileges, and competitive advantages that result from the ownership of these long-lived assets. Intangibles may arise from:

1. Government grants such as patents, copyrights, and trademarks.
2. The acquisition of another business in which the purchase price includes a payment for the company's favourable goodwill.
3. Private monopolistic arrangements arising from contractual agreements such as franchises and leases.

Some widely known intangibles are Alexander Graham Bell's patent on the telephone, the franchises of The Second Cup, and the CBC trademark of the Canadian Broadcasting Corporation.

Accounting for intangible assets parallels the accounting for tangible assets. That is, **intangible assets are recorded at cost**, and this cost is **amortized over the useful life of the intangible asset in a rational and systematic manner**. As with tangible assets, cost includes all costs of acquisition and other costs necessary to make the intangible asset ready for its intended use—including legal fees and similar charges.

STUDY OBJECTIVE
··········**9**··········
Contrast the accounting for intangible assets with the accounting for tangible assets.

There are several differences between accounting for intangible capital assets and accounting for other capital assets. To record amortization of an intangible asset, many companies do not credit an accumulated amortization account, as is common in the amortization of property, plant, and equipment, and natural resources. Instead, the specific intangible asset account is credited directly.

As time is usually the most relevant factor for the pattern of use of intangible assets, these assets are typically amortized on a straight-line basis. The widespread use of this method adds comparability in accounting for intangible assets. The life of most intangible assets is limited by law. The amortizable cost for these assets (cost less residual value, which is usually negligible for intangible assets) is allocated over the shorter of (1) the useful life of the intangible, and (2) the legal life of the intangible.

Similar to tangible capital assets that are amortized, intangible assets that are amortized must be reviewed when events or circumstances indicate that there may be a permanent impairment (decline) in value. In such cases, the difference between the asset's fair market value and net book value is recorded as an impairment loss. If the fair market value later increases, the net book value of the asset is **not** adjusted for any recovery in value.

When an intangible asset has no legally determined life and its useful life appears to be indefinite, **it is not amortized**. However, its cost is reviewed and tested for impairment annually, or more often if circumstances dictate.

At disposal, just as with other capital assets, the net book value of the intangible asset is eliminated, and a gain or loss, if any, is recorded.

Patents

A patent is an exclusive right issued by the Canadian Intellectual Property Office of Industry Canada that enables the recipient to manufacture, sell, or otherwise control an invention for a period of 20 years from the date of the application. A patent is non-renewable. The legal life of a patent may be extended if the recipient obtains new patents for improvements or other changes in the basic design.

Helpful hint The cost of a patent generally includes two items: the price paid (if any), and the legal fees to defend the patent.

The initial cost of a patent is the cash or cash equivalent price paid to acquire it. The saying "A patent is only as good as the money you're prepared to spend defending it" is very true. Many patents are subject to some type of litigation. Polaroid won a patent infringement suit against Eastman Kodak in protecting its patent on instant cameras. Legal costs to successfully defend the patent in an infringement suit are considered necessary to prove the validity of the patent. They are added to the patent account and amortized over the remaining life of the patent.

The cost of a patent should be amortized over its 20-year legal life or its useful life, whichever is shorter. In determining useful life, obsolescence, demand, competition, and other economic factors should be considered. These may cause a patent to become economically ineffective before the end of its legal life.

To illustrate the calculation of amortization expense, assume that National Labs purchases a patent at a cost of $60,000. If the useful life of the patent is eight years, the annual amortization expense is $7,500 ($60,000 ÷ 8). The entry to record the annual amortization for the calendar year is as follows:

A	=	L	+	OE	
–7,500				–7,500	

Dec. 31	Amortization Expense	7,500	
	Patents		7,500
	To record patent amortization.		

As mentioned earlier in the chapter, the credit is normally recorded directly to the intangible asset account rather than to an accumulated amortization account.

Copyrights

Copyrights, granted by the Canadian Intellectual Property Office, give the owner an exclusive right to reproduce and sell an artistic or published work. Copyrights extend for the life of the creator plus 50 years. Generally, the useful life of a copyright is significantly shorter than its legal life.

The cost of a copyright consists of the **cost of acquiring and defending it**. The cost may only be the fee paid to register the copyright. Or, it may amount to a great deal more if a copyright infringement suit is involved.

> **Helpful hint** The first Canadian copyright was issued in 1841 to protect *Canada's Spelling Book*.

▶Accounting in Action ▶ *@-Business Insight*

On-line music company MP3.com recently paid US$53.4 million to Universal Music Group, the world's largest record company, to settle a copyright infringement lawsuit. A judge had previously ruled that MP3.com wilfully violated copyrights of music companies when it copied their songs from CDs and made them available free on its website. MP3.com has also reached settlements with the four other major music companies—Warner Music Group, BMG, EMI, and Sony Music Entertainment—and has arranged licensing deals with each of them. The overall amount of the settlements has not been disclosed, but is believed to be in the US$170 million range.

The MP3.com decision comes as lawyers, Internet entrepreneurs, and the global entertainment industry are embroiled in a war over copyright and compensation. Forrester Research estimates that record labels lose $3.1 billion annually in music sales to piracy and other methods of digital distribution.

Source: Steven Chase, "Web Music Scofflaws Take Hard Hit." *The Globe and Mail*, September 7, 2000, A1.

Trademarks and Trade Names

A **trademark** or **trade name** is a word, phrase, jingle, or symbol that identifies a particular enterprise or product. Trade names like President's Choice, Benetton, KFC, Nike, Nissan, Sony, Sunkist, Kleenex, Coke, Big Mac, the Blue Jays, and TSN create immediate product identification. They also enhance the sale of the product. The creator may obtain exclusive legal right to the trademark or trade name by registering it with the Canadian Intellectual Property Office. This registration provides continuous protection. It may be renewed every 15 years, as long as the trademark or trade name is in use.

In most cases, companies continuously renew their trademarks or trade names. In such cases, as long as the trademark or trade name continues to be marketable, it will have an indefinite useful life. **Intangible assets with indefinite useful lives are not amortized.** Instead, their values are tested annually for impairment, as explained earlier in this chapter.

If the trademark or trade name is **purchased**, its cost is the purchase price. If the trademark or trade name is developed internally rather than purchased, the cost includes legal fees, registration fees, design costs, successful legal defence costs, and other expenditures directly related to securing it.

> ▶ *International note*
> A panel of international judges recently ranked the world's top 50 corporate logos. The Michelin man ranked first as "a fabulous piece of corporate iconography, and probably the first example of a liquid identity." Nike's swoosh symbol was ranked 4th, Coca-Cola's symbol 9th.

▶Accounting in Action ▶ *@-Business Insight*

Domain names are a good example of a trade name. Buying domain names is a hot market these days. Canada's domain name system has strict regulations to ensure that dot.ca web addresses are granted to legitimate organizations and holders of registered trademarks. While the cost of registration is negligible, if a company has to purchase its name from a cybersquatter—people who register names in the hopes of reselling them for a profit—the cost can rise quickly.

When eBay Inc., the world's largest on-line auction house, tried to register <www.ebay.ca>, it discovered that the name had been registered previously by a Dartmouth, N.S., entrepreneur. eBay now has two options to consider. Since eBay is a registered trademark around the world, the company could take legal action. Or, eBay could negotiate to buy the name from the current registrant. In the meantime, eBay is using the domain name <www.ebaycanada.ca>, which also had been previously registered by a self-described "Internet entrepreneur." This Kelowna, B.C., entrepreneur said he hoped to make some quick money when he registered <www.ebay-canada.ca> last year. He eventually gave up the name without a fight to avoid going to court and facing huge legal bills.

Franchises and Licences

When you drive down the street in your Protegé purchased from a Mazda dealer, fill up your gas tank at the corner Petro-Canada station, buy coffee from The Second Cup, eat lunch at Wendy's, live in a home purchased through a Royal LePage real estate broker, or vacation at a Delta Hotel, you are dealing with franchises. A franchise is a contractual arrangement between a franchisor and a franchisee. The franchisor gives the franchisee permission to sell certain products, offer specific services, or use certain trademarks or trade names.

Another type of franchise is a contract between a government body (often a municipality) and a company. This franchise permits the company to use public property in performing its services. Examples are the use of city streets for a bus line or taxi service, the use of public land for telephone and electric lines, and the use of airwaves for radio or TV broadcasting. Such operating rights are referred to as licences.

When costs can be identified with the acquisition of the franchise or licence, an intangible asset should be recognized. Franchises and licences may be granted for a definite period of time, an indefinite period, or in perpetuity. The cost of a franchise or licence should be amortized over the useful life. If the life is indefinite or in perpetuity, the cost should not be amortized. It should, however, be tested annually for impairment and written down, if required.

Annual payments, proportionate with sales, are sometimes required under a franchise agreement. These are called royalties and are recorded as **operating expenses** in the period in which they are incurred.

Goodwill

Usually, the largest intangible asset that appears on a company's balance sheet is goodwill. Goodwill is the value of favourable attributes that relate to a business enterprise. These include exceptional management, a desirable location, good customer relations, skilled employees, high-quality products, and harmonious relations with labour unions. Some view goodwill as expected earnings in excess of normal earnings. Unlike other assets, such as investments and capital assets, that can be sold individually in the marketplace, goodwill cannot be sold individually as it is part of the business as a whole.

Helpful hint Goodwill is recorded only when it has been purchased along with the tangible and identifiable intangible assets of a business.

If goodwill can be identified only with the business as a whole, how can it be determined? One could try to put a dollar value on the factors above (exceptional management, a desirable location, and so on), but the results would be very subjective. Subjective valuations would not contribute to the reliability of financial statements. Therefore, **goodwill is recorded only when there is a purchase of an entire business**. In that case, **goodwill is the excess of cost over the fair market value of the net assets (assets less liabilities) acquired**.

In recording the purchase of a business, the net assets are recorded (debited) at their fair market values. Cash is credited for the purchase price and goodwill is debited for the difference. Because goodwill has an indefinite life, just as the company has an indefinite life, **goodwill is not amortized**. Since goodwill is measured using the market value of a company—a subjective valuation which can easily be overvalued—it must be tested regularly for impairment. Write-downs of goodwill are common and can be substantial. For example, the Canadian technology company JDS Uniphase reported a recent net loss of US $50.56 billion—the largest loss on record in Canada and the United States. Of this loss, $44.88 billion was due to a write-down of goodwill.

Accounting for goodwill is challenging. Further details about it are left to advanced accounting cources.

Research and Development Costs

Research and development costs are not intangible assets. But because they may lead to patents and copyrights, we discuss them in this section. Many companies spend considerable sums of money on research and development (R&D). For example, in a recent year, Nortel Networks spent nearly $3 billion on R&D. That's as much as some provincial governments have in their total expenditure budgets!

Research and development costs present two accounting problems: (1) It is sometimes difficult to determine the costs for specific projects. (2) It is also hard to know the extent and timing of future benefits. As a result, accounting distinguishes between research costs and development costs.

Research is planned investigation undertaken to gain new knowledge and understanding. **All research costs should be expensed when incurred.**

Development is the use of research findings and knowledge for a plan or design. **Certain development costs with reasonably assured future benefits can be capitalized.** Otherwise, they must also be expensed. In other words, development costs can be capitalized if they relate to a clearly defined product or process that is technically feasible. Management must intend to produce and market the product or process, a future market must be defined, and adequate resources must exist to complete the project.

To illustrate, assume that Laser Scanner Company spent $3 million on research and $2 million on development. These costs resulted in the development of two highly successful patents. The $3 million research costs are expensed. The development costs of $2 million are capitalized and included in the cost of the patent, since the development was successful.

Many disagree with this accounting approach. They argue that to expense research and some development costs leads to understated assets and net income. Others argue that capitalizing these costs will lead only to highly speculative assets on the balance sheet. Who is right? There is no easy answer. The controversy shows how difficult it is to establish proper guidelines for financial reporting.

▶ *International note*

Accounting for R&D differs dramatically across nations. U.S. GAAP and German GAAP do not allow any R&D expenses to be capitalized. Other nations, such as Canada, Great Britain, Japan, and Korea, permit limited capitalization of some development costs. Still other countries, such as Italy, Sweden, and Brazil, have much more liberal R&D policies, allowing full capitalization.

Other Intangible Assets

Other intangible assets sometimes found in corporate balance sheets include items such as customer lists, noncompetition agreements, sports contracts, startup costs, and rearrangement costs. As with other examples of intangibles that we have discussed, these assets are amortized over the shorter of their useful lives or legal lives. In reality, these types of costs usually have a very short useful life over which they provide benefit to the company. Some companies use the term **Deferred Charges** to classify these items. Others use the term **Other Assets**. The trend has been toward listing these items separately, as neither term—Deferred Charges or Other Assets—has much value as information.

As noted throughout this section on intangible assets, amortizable intangible assets have varying useful lives and legal lives. These assets are amortized over the shorter of the two. Similar to tangible assets, intangible assets are tested for impairment if circumstances change and net book value declines below fair market value.

Unamortizable intangible assets have indefinite useful lives and are not amortized. Instead, their values are tested annually (or more often, if required) for impairment. The following illustration summarizes the varying lives for intangible assets.

Illustration 10-25

Summary of amortization requirements

Intangible Asset	Legal Life	Amortization Period
Amortized		
Patents	20 years	Shorter of EUL* or legal life
Copyrights	Life of creator plus 50 years	Shorter of EUL or legal life
Franchises/Licences	Contract term	Shorter of EUL or contract term
Other	Contract term	Shorter of EUL or legal life
Unamortized		
Trademarks/Trade names	15 years, renewable	Not amortized
Franchises/Licences	Indefinite	Not amortized
Goodwill	Indefinite	Not amortized
Other		
Research		Recorded as Research Expense
Development		Capitalized (if criteria met) as specific intangible asset

*EUL—Estimated Useful Life

Before You Go On . . .

▶Review It

1. What are the main differences between accounting for intangible and tangible assets?
2. Identify the major types of intangibles and the proper accounting for them.
3. Give some examples of company or product trademarks or trade names (that have not been mentioned in this textbook).
4. Explain the accounting for research and development costs.

Related exercise material: BE10–13, E10–11 and E10–12.

THE NAVIGATOR

Statement Presentation of Capital Assets

STUDY OBJECTIVE

10

Illustrate how capital assets are reported on the balance sheet.

Property, plant, and equipment, natural resources, and intangible assets may be listed separately under the heading Capital Assets or disclosed under each individual group heading. Natural resources are commonly grouped under the label Property, Plant, and Equipment. For assets subject to amortization, the balances and accumulated amortization should be disclosed in the balance sheet or notes. In addition, the amortization methods used should be described. The amount of amortization expense for the period should also be disclosed. For assets that are not amortized, the carrying value of each major type of capital asset should be disclosed in the balance sheet or notes. Goodwill should be presented separately in the balance sheet, and other intangibles can be grouped as a one line item on the balance sheet. Impairment losses, if any, should be shown as separate line item on the income statement, with their details disclosed in a note.

Illustration 10-26 is an excerpt from the annual report for Andrés Wines Ltd. Capital assets are summarized in the balance sheet and detailed in Note 2. The note to the financial statements reports that amortization is calculated on the straight-line basis using the following rates and useful lives: Buildings, 2.5% per year; manufacturing machinery and equipment, 7.5% per year; other equipment, 10%–20% per year; and goodwill, 15 years. Note that goodwill has been amortized by Andrés Wines. This presentation was prepared prior to the changes in accounting for goodwill recommended by the CICA late in 2000.

Illustration 10-26

Presentation of capital assets

Andrés Wines Ltd.
Notes to the Financial Statements
March 31, 2000
(in thousands)

3. CAPITAL ASSETS

	Cost	Accumulated Amortization	Net
Land	$ 2,349		$ 2,349
Vineyards	5,937		5,937
Buildings	17,181	$ 4,971	12,210
Machinery and equipment	38,914	21,744	17,170
Goodwill	25,000	2,906	22,094
	$89,381	$29,621	$59,760

Using the Information in the Financial Statements

Typically, capital assets are a substantial portion of a company's total assets. Asset turnover and return on assets are two commonly used ratios to assess the profitability of *total* assets. The asset turnover ratio, determined by dividing net sales by average total assets, shows how efficiently a company uses its assets to generate sales revenue. The asset turnover ratio for The Second Cup is calculated below:

STUDY OBJECTIVE
·········▼·········

Demonstrate how to assess the profitability of total assets.

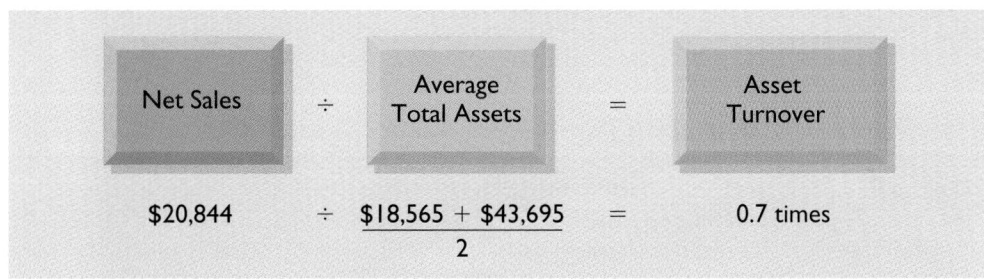

Net Sales	÷	Average Total Assets	=	Asset Turnover
$20,844	÷	$\dfrac{\$18{,}565 + \$43{,}695}{2}$	=	0.7 times

Illustration 10-27

Asset turnover

The asset turnover ratio shows the dollars of sales produced for each dollar invested in assets. Each dollar invested in assets produced $0.70 in sales for The Second Cup. If a company is using its assets efficiently, each dollar of assets will create a high amount of sales. This ratio varies greatly among different industries—from those that are asset-intensive (e.g., utility companies) to those that are not (e.g., service companies).

The return on assets, calculated by dividing net income by average total assets, shows the profitability of assets used in the earnings process. The return on assets for The Second Cup follows:

Illustration 10-28

Return on assets

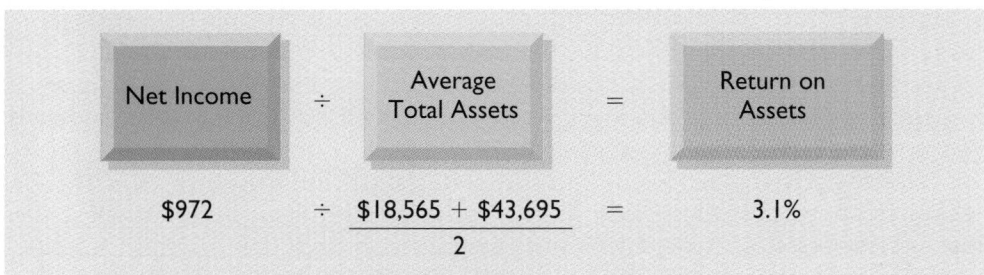

Net Income	÷	Average Total Assets	=	Return on Assets
$972	÷	$\dfrac{\$18{,}565 + \$43{,}695}{2}$	=	3.1%

The asset turnover ratio shows the amount of sales generated by each dollar invested in assets. The return on assets ratio focuses instead on net income, showing the amount of net income generated by each dollar invested in assets. The Second Cup's return on assets was 3.1%. A high return on assets indicates a profitable company.

Before You Go On . . .

▸*Review It*

THE
NAVIGATOR

1. What is the purpose of the asset turnover and return on assets ratios?

Related exercise material: BE10–14, BE10–15, E10–13, and E10–14.

▸*A Look Back at Our Feature Story*

Refer back to the opening story about SAIT and answer the following questions:
1. Why should SAIT amortize its buildings?
2. How can SAIT have a building with a zero book value yet a substantial market value?
3. Give some examples of intangibles that you might find on your campus.

Solution

1. SAIT should amortize its buildings because amortization is necessary in order to allocate (match) the cost of the buildings to the periods in which they are used (produce benefits).
2. A building can have a zero book value if it has no residual value and is fully amortized. Because amortization is used to allocate cost rather than to reflect actual value, it is not unusual for a building to have a low or zero book value and a positive market value.
3. Examples of other intangibles that might be found on campus are franchises of a food company such as Harvey's or The Second Cup, a licence to operate a radio station, a trade name used by an athletic team, patents developed by professors, and a permit to operate a bus service.

DEMONSTRATION PROBLEM 1

DuPage Company purchases a factory machine at a cost of $18,000 on January 1, 2002. The machine is expected to have a residual value of $2,000 at the end of its four-year useful life.

During its useful life, the machine is expected to be used for 16,000 hours. Actual annual use was as follows: in 2002, 4,500 hours; in 2003, 4,000 hours; in 2004, 3,500 hours; and in 2005, 4,000 hours.

Instructions

Prepare amortization schedules for the following methods: (a) straight-line, (b) units-of-activity, and (c) declining-balance using double the straight-line rate.

Action Plan

- Deduct the residual value in the straight-line and units-of-activity methods, but not in the declining-balance method.
- In the declining-balance method, the amortization rate is applied to the net book value (cost − accumulated amortization).
- Amortization should never reduce the net book value of the asset below its expected residual value.

Solution to Demonstration Problem 1

(a)   **Straight-Line Method**

Year	Amortizable Cost	×	Amortization Rate	=	Amortization Expense	Accumulated Amortization	Net Book Value
							$18,000
2002	$16,000*		25%		$4,000	$ 4,000	14,000
2003	16,000		25%		4,000	8,000	10,000
2004	16,000		25%		4,000	12,000	6,000
2005	16,000		25%		4,000	16,000	2,000

*$18,000 − $2,000 = $16,000

(b)   **Units-of-Activity Method**

| | | | | | End of Year | |
Year	Unit of Activity	×	Cost per Unit	= Amortization Expense	Accumulated Amortization	Net Book Value
						$18,000
2002	4,500		$1*	$4,500	$ 4,500	13,500
2003	4,000		1	4,000	8,500	9,500
2004	3,500		1	3,500	12,000	6,000
2005	4,000		1	4,000	16,000	2,000

*$18,000 − $2,000 = $16,000 amortizable cost ÷ 16,000 total units = $1

(c)   **Double Declining-Balance Method**

| | Net Book Value Beginning of Year | × | Amortization Rate (25%×2) | = Amortization Expense | End of Year | |
Year					Accumulated Amortization	Net Book Value
						$18,000
2002	$18,000		50%	$9,000	$ 9,000	9,000
2003	9,000		50%	4,500	13,500	4,500
2004	4,500		50%	2,250	15,750	2,250
2005	2,250		50%	250*	16,000	2,000

*Adjusted to $250 because ending book value should not be less than expected residual value.

DEMONSTRATION PROBLEM 2

On January 1, 2002, Skyline Limousine Co. purchased a limo for $78,000. The vehicle is being amortized by the straight-line method using a four-year service life and a $4,000 residual value. The company's fiscal year ends on December 31.

Instructions

Prepare the journal entry or entries to record the disposal of the limo, assuming that it is:
(a) Retired with no residual value on January 1, 2006.
(b) Sold for $5,000 on July 1, 2005.

Solution to Demonstration Problem 2

$$\frac{\$78,000 - \$4,000}{4 \text{ years}} = \$18,500 \text{ annual amortization expense}$$

(a)

Jan. 1, 2006	Accumulated Amortization ($18,500 × 4)	74,000	
	Loss on Disposal	4,000	
	Limo		78,000
	To record retirement of limo.		

(b)

July 1, 2005	Amortization Expense ($18,500 × $^6/_{12}$)	9,250	
	Accumulated Amortization		9,250
	To record amortization.		
	Cash	5,000	
	Accumulated Amortization ($18,500 × 3.5)	64,750	
	Loss on Disposal	8,250	
	Limo		78,000
	To record sale of limo.		

Action Plan
• Update the amortization to the date of the disposal for any partial period.
• Determine the book value of the asset at the time of disposal.
• Calculate any gain or loss by comparing proceeds to book value.
• Remove the book value of the asset from the records, by debiting accumulated amortization (for the total amortization to the date of disposal) and crediting the asset account for the cost of the asset. Record proceeds and any gain or loss.

THE NAVIGATOR

Summary of Study Objectives

1. Distinguish between tangible and intangible capital assets. Both tangible and intangible capital assets are long-lived assets that benefit future periods. They are used to produce products or to provide services over these periods. Tangible capital assets have physical substance. Intangible capital assets do not.

2. Demonstrate the application of the cost principle to property, plant, and equipment specifically, and to capital assets in general. The cost of all capital assets—whether property, plant, and equipment, natural resources, or intangible assets—includes all costs necessary to acquire the asset and make it ready for its intended use. Cost is measured by the cash or cash equivalent price paid. In a basket purchase situation, cost is allocated to each individual asset using relative fair market values.

3. Explain the concept of, and be able to calculate, amortization. Amortization is the allocation of the cost of a capital asset to expense over its useful (service) life in a rational and systematic manner. Amortization is not a process of valuation. Nor is it a process that results in an accumulation of cash.

4. Calculate periodic amortization using different methods. There are three commonly used amortization methods:

Method	Effect on Annual Amortization	Calculation
Straight-line	Constant amount	(Cost − Residual value) ÷ Estimated useful life (in years)
Declining-balance	Decreasing amount	Net book value at beginning of year × Straight-line amortization rate × Declining-balance multiplier
Units-of-activity	Varying amount	(Cost − Residual value) ÷ Estimated useful life (in units of activity) × Actual activity during year

5. Describe and demonstrate the procedure for revising periodic amortization. Revisions of periodic amortization are made in present and future periods, not retroactively. The new annual amortization is found by dividing the net book value less the revised (if applicable) residual value at the time of the revision by the remaining useful life.

6. Distinguish between operating and capital expenditures, and prepare the entries for these expenditures. Operating expenditures are incurred to maintain the operating efficiency and expected productive life of the asset. These costs are debited from Repair Expense as incurred. Capital costs increase the operating efficiency, productive capacity, or expected useful life of the asset. These expenditures are debited from the property, plant, or equipment account affected. They are subsequently amortized over an appropriate period of time, usually the remaining life of the asset.

7. Explain how to account for the disposal of property, plant, and equipment. The accounting for the disposal of piece of property, plant, and equipment through retirement or sale is as follows:
(a) Update any unrecorded amortization.
(b) Eliminate the asset and accumulated amortization accounts at the date of disposal.
(c) Record the cash proceeds or payment, if any.
(d) Account for the difference between the cash proceeds and the net book value as a gain (proceeds less net book value) or loss (net book value less proceeds) on disposal.

8. Calculate the periodic amortization of natural resources. Natural resources generally use the units-of-activity method of amortization. Cost less residual value plus any restoration costs equals the amortizable cost. Calculate amortizable cost per unit by dividing the total amortizable cost by the number of units estimated to be in the resource. Then multiply the amortizable cost per unit by the number of units extracted and sold.

9. Contrast the accounting for intangible assets with the accounting for tangible assets. The accounting for intangible assets and the accounting for tangible assets are much the same. The straight-line method is normally used for amortizing intangible assets with useful lives. The accumulated amortization is usually credited directly to the relevant intangible asset account. Intangible assets are normally amortized over the shorter of their useful lives or their legal lives. When an intangible asset has an indefinite life, it is not amortized but is tested annually for impairment. Other amortizable capital assets are also tested for impairment, but only when circumstances or events require.

10. Illustrate how capital assets are reported on the balance sheet. All classes of assets are usually listed in detail under the heading Capital Assets. It is also common for property, plant, and equipment, and natural resources to be combined under the heading Property, Plant, and Equipment. In this case, intangibles are shown separately under Intangible Assets. The balances of the major classes of assets and accumulated amortization (if the asset is amortizable) should be disclosed either within the balance sheet or in the notes. The amortization methods used should be described. The amount of amortization expense for the period should be disclosed.

11. Demonstrate how to assess the profitability of total assets. The asset turnover ratio (Net sales ÷ Average total assets) is one measure used by companies to show how efficiently assets are used to generate sales revenue. A second ratio, return on assets (Net income ÷ Average total assets), calculates how profitably assets are used to generate net income.

THE NAVIGATOR

GLOSSARY

Additions and improvements Costs incurred to increase the operating efficiency, productive capacity, or expected useful life of property, plant, or equipment. (p. 474)

Amortizable cost The cost of a capital asset less its residual value. (p. 466)

Amortization The allocation of the cost of a capital asset to expense in a rational and systematic manner over the useful life of the asset. (p. 464)

Asset turnover A measure of how efficiently a company uses its total assets to generate sales. (p. 487)

Basket purchase The acquisition of a group of assets for a total price. Individual asset costs are determined by allocating relative fair market values. (p. 463)

Capital assets Tangible (property, plant, and equipment, and natural resources) and intangible long-lived resources that are used in the operations of a business. They are not intended for sale to customers. (p. 460)

Capital cost allowance (CCA) The concept used in the *Income Tax Act* to amortize capital assets for income tax purposes. Most capital assets use the declining-balance method with maximum rates specified for each class of assets. (p. 472)

Capital expenditures Expenditures that increase the company's investment in productive facilities. (p. 475)

Copyright An exclusive right granted by the federal government allowing the owner to reproduce and sell an artistic or published work. (p. 483)

Declining-balance method An amortization method that applies a constant rate to the declining net book value of the asset. It produces a decreasing annual amortization expense over the useful life of the asset. (p. 468)

Franchise A contractual arrangement under which the franchisor grants the franchisee the right to sell certain products, offer specific services, or use certain trademarks or trade names, usually within a designated geographical area. (p. 484)

Goodwill The value of the business in excess of the net identifiable assets. (p. 484)

Impairment loss An impairment loss results when the fair market value of an asset declines below its net book value. (p. 462)

Intangible assets Rights, privileges, and competitive advantages that result from the ownership of long-lived assets that do not possess physical substance. (p. 481)

Licences Operating rights to use property. (p. 484)

Natural resources Long-lived assets that consist of standing timber and underground deposits of oil, gas, and minerals. Also called wasting assets. (p. 478)

Net book value The result of deducting accumulated amortization from the cost of a capital asset. This value is based on historical cost and is not intended to approximate fair market value. (p. 465)

Operating expenditures Expenditures that are immediately charged against revenues as expenses. (p. 474)

Ordinary repairs Expenditures to maintain the operating efficiency and productive life of the unit. (p. 474)

Patent An exclusive right issued by the federal government enabling the recipient to manufacture, sell, or otherwise control an invention for a period of 20 years from the date of the application. (p. 482)

Property, plant, and equipment Tangible long-lived capital assets that are used in the operation of the business and are not intended for sale to customers. (p. 461)

Research and development costs Expenditures that may lead to patents, copyrights, new processes, and new products. (p. 485)

Residual value An estimate of the asset's value at the end of its useful life. (p. 465)

Return on assets An overall measure of the profitability of total assets. (p. 487)

Royalties Recurring amounts owed in payment for services provided (e.g., advertising, purchasing). These amounts are usually calculated as a percentage of sales. They are found in intercompany relationships such as franchises. (p. 484)

Straight-line method A method in which periodic amortization is the same for each year of the asset's useful life. (p. 466)

Trademark (trade name) A word, phrase, jingle, or symbol that distinguishes or identifies a particular enterprise or product. (p. 483)

Units-of-activity method An amortization method in which useful life is expressed in terms of the total units of production or use expected from the asset. (p. 469)

Useful life An estimate of the expected productive life of an asset. It is also called the service life. (p. 465)

SELF-STUDY QUESTIONS

Answers are at the end of the chapter.

(SO 2) AP   1. Corrieten Company purchased equipment, incurring the following costs:

Cash price	$24,000
Insurance during transit	200
Installation and testing	400
Total costs	$24,600

What amount should be recorded as the cost of the equipment?
a. $24,000
b. $24,200
c. $24,600
d.   None of the above

(SO 2) AP   2. Asura Company purchased land and a building for $200,000. The fair market value of the land at the time of acquisition was $100,000. The fair market value of the building was $120,000. What costs should be debited from the Land and Building accounts, respectively?
a. $90,909 and $109,091
b. $100,000 and $120,000
c. $109,091 and $90,909
d. $200,000

(SO 3) K   3. Amortization is a process of:
a.   valuation.
b.   cost allocation.
c.   cash accumulation.
d.   appraisal.

(SO 4) AP   4. Cuso Company purchased equipment on January 1, 2001, at a total cost of $40,000. The equipment has an estimated residual value of $10,000 and an estimated useful life of five years. The amount of accumulated amortization at December 31, 2003, if the straight-line method of amortization is used, is:
a. $6,000.
b. $12,000.
c. $18,000.
d. $24,000.

(SO 4) AP   5. Kant Enterprises purchased a truck for $21,000 on January 1, 2002. The truck will have an estimated residual value of $1,000 at the end of five years. Using the units-of-activity method, the amortization expense for 2002 can be calculated by the following formula:
a.   ($21,000 ÷ Total estimated activity) × Units of activity for 2002.
b.   ($20,000 ÷ Total estimated activity) × Units of activity for 2002.
c. $21,000 ÷ 5 years.
d. $20,000 ÷ 5 years.

(SO 4) K   6. A company can minimize its net income in the first year of owning an asset, if it uses the:
a.   straight-line method.
b.   declining-balance method.
c.   units-of-activity method.
d.   None of the above

(SO 5) K   7. When there is a change in estimated amortization:
a.   previous amortization should be corrected.
b.   current and future years' amortization should be revised.
c.   only future years' amortization should be revised.
d.   None of the above

(SO 6) K   8. Additions are:
a.   capital expenditures.
b.   debited from a Repair Expense account.
c.   debited from a Purchases account.
d.   operating expenditures.

(SO 7) AP   9. Oviatt Company sold equipment on June 1, 2004, for $10,000. At that time, the equipment had a cost of $45,000 and accumulated amortization of $30,000. At disposition, Oviatt should record:
a.   a $5,000 loss on disposal.
b.   a $5,000 gain on disposal.
c.   a $15,000 loss on disposal.
d.   a $15,000 gain on disposal.

(SO 8) AP   10. Averroes Company expects to extract 20 million tonnes of coal from a mine that cost $12 million. If no residual value or restoration costs are expected, and 2 million tonnes are mined and sold in the first year, the entry to record amortization will include a:
a.   credit to Amortization Expense of $1,200,000.
b.   debit from Amortization Expense of $1,200,000.
c.   debit from Accumulated Amortization of $2,000,000.
d.   credit to Accumulated Amortization of $2,000,000.

(SO 9) AP   11. Pierce Company incurred $150,000 of research costs in its laboratory to develop a patent granted on January 2, 2002. On July 31, 2002, Pierce paid $35,000 for legal fees in a successful defence of the patent. The total amount debited from Patents through July 31, 2002, should be:
a. $35,000.
b. $150,000.
c. $185,000.
d.   some other amount.

(SO 10) K   12. Indicate which of the following statements is true:
a.   Since intangible assets lack physical substance, they should only be disclosed in the notes to the financial statements.
b.   Goodwill should be reported as part of the Owner's Equity section.
c.   Totals of the major classes of assets can be shown in the balance sheet, with the asset details disclosed in the notes to the financial statements.
d.   Intangible assets are typically listed with the prepaid expenses on the balance sheet.

(SO 11) K   13. Which of the following measures provides an indication of how efficiently a company is using its assets?
a.   Current ratio
b.   Inventory turnover ratio
c.   Asset turnover ratio
d.   Return on assets ratio

QUESTIONS

(SO 1) C 1. Identify the similarities and differences between tangible and intangible capital assets.

(SO 2) C 2. Susan Day is uncertain about the applicability of the cost principle to capital assets. Explain the principle to Susan.

(SO 2) C 3. How is cost for a capital asset measured in (a) a cash transaction, and (b) a noncash transaction?

(SO 2) C 4. Market values of capital assets are more relevant than historical cost for decisions made by users, such as creditors, investors, and managers. Why do you suppose that the cost principle has survived, despite its apparent lack of usefulness?

(SO 2) C 5. Jacques asks why it is necessary to allocate the total cost to individual assets in a basket purchase situation. For example, if we purchase land and a building for $250,000, why can't we just debit an account called Land and Building for $250,000?

(SO 2) AP 6. Fitworks purchases a fitness centre from Health Styles Company for a bargain price of $500,000 for the entire establishment. The building was appraised at $350,000 and the equipment at $400,000. What cost amounts would be allocated to the building and to the equipment in the accounting records?

(SO 3) C 7. In a recent newspaper release, the president of Lawton Company asserted that something has to be done about amortization. The president said, "Amortization does not come close to accumulating the cash needed to replace the asset at the end of its useful life." What is your response to the president's statement?

(SO 3) K 8. Cecile is studying for the next accounting examination. She asks for your help on two questions: (a) What is residual value? (b) Is residual value used in determining amortizable cost under each amortization method? Answer each question for her.

(SO 4) K 9. Contrast the straight-line, declining-balance, and units-of-activity methods in terms of (a) useful life, and (b) the pattern of periodic amortization over useful life.

(SO 4) C 10. Contrast the effects of the three amortization methods on the balance sheet (net book value of an asset) and income statement (amortization expense and net income).

(SO 5) C 11. In the fourth year of an asset's five-year useful life, the company decides that the asset will have a six-year service life. How should the revision of amortization be recorded? Why?

(SO 6) C 12. Distinguish between operating expenditures and capital expenditures during useful life.

(SO 7) K 13. How is a gain or loss on the sale of a capital asset calculated?

(SO 7) C 14. Ewing Corporation owns a machine that is fully amortized but is still being used. How should Ewing account for this asset and report it in the financial statements?

(SO 8) C 15. Explain why restoration costs are allocated as part of amortization expense over the life of a natural resource and not expensed when incurred.

(SO 8) C 16. Explain how annual amortization expense is calculated for natural resources.

(SO 9) C 17. Heflin Company hires an accounting student who says that intangible assets should always be amortized over their legal lives. Is the student correct? Explain.

(SO 9) C 18. Goodwill is related to the favourable attributes of a business enterprise. What types of attributes could result in goodwill?

(SO 9) C 19. Bob Leno, a business student, is working on a case problem for one of his classes. In this case problem, the company needs to raise cash to market a new product it has developed. Saul Cain, an engineering student, takes one look at the company's balance sheet and says, "This company has an awful lot of goodwill. Why don't you recommend that they sell some of it to raise cash?" How should Bob respond to Saul's suggestion?

(SO 9) C 20. Often, research and development costs provide companies with benefits that last a number of years. (For example, these costs can lead to the development of a patent that will increase the company's income for many years.) However, generally accepted accounting principles require that most of these costs be recorded as an expense when incurred. Why?

(SO 10) K 21. What information related to capital assets should be disclosed in the notes to the financial statements?

(SO 11) AP 22. **Salter Street Films** of Halifax, Nova Scotia, is an integrated entertainment company that develops, produces, and distributes original film and television programming, including the top-rated comedy series "This Hour Has 22 Minutes". It reported average total assets of $78,811,768 and production and distribution revenues (assume equal to net sales) of $48,766,938 for the year ended October 31, 2000. What is Salter Street's asset turnover ratio?

BRIEF EXERCISES

••

Classify capital assets.
(SO 1) K

BE10–1 Indicate whether each of the following assets is property, plant, and equipment (PPE), a natural resource (NR), or an intangible asset (I). If the asset doesn't fit one of these categories, insert NA (not applicable) in the space provided.

_____ (a) Patent   _____ (i) Cut and processed timber
_____ (b) Land   _____ (j) Trademark
_____ (c) Building   _____ (k) Franchise
_____ (d) Cash   _____ (l) Investment in common shares
_____ (e) Licence right   _____ (m) Oil well
_____ (f) Machinery   _____ (n) Coal mine
_____ (g) Inventory   _____ (o) Natural gas deposit
_____ (h) Timber tract   _____ (p) Goodwill

Determine cost of land.
(SO 2) AP

BE10–2 The following costs were incurred by Plourde Company in purchasing land: cash price, $54,000; accrued property tax, $3,000; legal fees, $2,500; and clearing and grading, $3,500. What is the cost of the land?

Determine cost of a truck.
(SO 2) AP

BE10–3 Basler Company incurs the following costs in purchasing a truck: cash price, $25,000; painting and lettering, $400; motor vehicle licence, $100; and accident insurance, $2,000. What is the cost of the truck?

Record basket purchase.
(SO 2) AP

BE10–4 Olympic Company purchased land and a building on January 1, 2002, for $280,000. The company paid $80,000 cash and signed a mortgage note payable for the remainder. Management's best estimate of the value of the land was $100,000 and of the building, $200,000. Prepare the journal entry to record the acquisition of the land and building.

Calculate straight-line amortization.
(SO 4) AP

BE10–5 Mabasa Company acquires a delivery truck at a cost of $32,000. The truck is expected to have a residual value of $2,000 at the end of its four-year useful life. Calculate annual amortization expense for the first and second years using the straight-line method.

Calculate declining-balance amortization.
(SO 4) AP

BE10–6 Amortization information for Mabasa Company is given in BE10–5. Assuming the declining-balance amortization rate is double the straight-line rate, calculate the annual amortization expense for the first and second years under the declining-balance method.

Calculate amortization using the units-of-activity method.
(SO 4) AP

BE10–7 Speedy Taxi Service uses the units-of-activity method in calculating amortization on its taxicabs. Each cab is expected to be driven 100,000 kilometres. Taxi No. 10 cost $36,500 and is expected to have a residual value of $500. Taxi No. 10 is driven 30,000 kilometres in Year 1 and 20,000 kilometres in Year 2. Calculate the amortization expense for each year.

Calculate revised amortization.
(SO 5) AP

BE10–8 On January 1, 2002, the Asler Company ledger shows Equipment $32,000 and Accumulated Amortization $12,000. The amortization resulted from using the straight-line method with a useful life of five years and a residual value of $2,000. On this date, the company concludes that the equipment has a remaining useful life of only two years with the same residual value. Calculate the revised annual amortization.

Identify operating or capital expenditures.
(SO 6) K

BE10–9 Indicate whether each of the following items is an operating expenditure (O) or a capital expenditure (C). If the expenditure is neither, insert NA (not applicable) in the space provided.

_____ (a) Repaired building roof, $500   _____ (f) Purchased oil and gas for truck, $75
_____ (b) Replaced building roof, $7,500   _____ (g) Replaced tires on truck, $500
_____ (c) Purchased building, $80,000   _____ (h) Rebuilt engine on truck, $5,000
_____ (d) Purchased supplies, $350   _____ (i) Added a new wing to building, $250,000
_____ (e) Purchased truck, $35,000   _____ (j) Painted interior of building, $1,500

Record disposal by retirement.
(SO 7) AP

BE10–10 Prepare journal entries to record the following on August 2:
 (a) Mohapatra Company retires its delivery equipment which cost $41,000. Accumulated amortization on the delivery equipment is also $41,000. No residual value is received.
 (b) Assume the same information as (a) except that accumulated amortization for Mohapatra's delivery equipment is $39,000 instead of $41,000.

BE10–11   Wiley Company sells office equipment on September 30, 2002, for $26,000 cash. The office equipment originally cost $72,000 and, as at December 31, 2001, had accumulated amortization of $42,000. Amortization for the first nine months of 2002 is $6,000. Prepare the journal entries to (a) update amortization to September 30, 2002, and (b) record the sale of the equipment.

Record disposal by sale.
(SO 7) AP

BE10–12   Cuono Mining Co. purchased for $7 million a mine that is estimated to have 28 million tonnes of ore, a residual value of $500,000, and estimated restoration costs at the end of its useful life of $1 million. In the first year, 6 million tonnes of ore are extracted and sold.
(a) Prepare the journal entry to record the amortization expense for the first year ended August 31, 2003.
(b) Show how this mine is reported on the balance sheet at the end of the first year.

Record amortization and show balance sheet presentation for natural resources.
(SO 8) AP

BE10–13   Surkis Company purchases a patent for $160,000 cash on January 2, 2002. Its legal life is 20 years and its estimated useful life is 10 years.
(a) Prepare the journal entry to record the purchase of the patent on January 2, 2002.
(b) Prepare the journal entry to record the amortization expense for the first year ended December 31, 2002.
(c) Show how this patent is reported on the balance sheet at the end of the first year.

Record acquisition and amortization, and show balance sheet presentation for patent.
(SO 9) AP

BE10–14   Information related to property, plant, and equipment, natural resources, and intangibles at December 31, 2002 for Joker Company is as follows: buildings, $800,000; accumulated amortization—buildings, $650,000; goodwill, $410,000; coal mine, $200,000; and accumulated amortization—coal mine, $108,000. Prepare a partial balance sheet for Joker Company for these items.

Prepare capital assets section of balance sheet.
(SO 10) AP

BE10–15   **The Gap**'s most recent financial statements report beginning total assets of US$3,963.9 million; ending total assets of US$5,188.8 million; net sales of US$11,635.4 million; and net income of US$1,127.1 million. Calculate The Gap's asset turnover and return on assets ratios.

Calculate profitability ratios.
(SO 11) AP

EXERCISES

E10–1   The following expenditures related to assets were made by Kosinski Company during the first two months of 2003:
1. Paid $250 to have the company name and advertising slogan painted on a new delivery truck.
2. Paid a $75 motor vehicle licence fee for the new truck.
3. Paid $17,500 for paving the parking lots and driveways on a new plant site.
4. Paid $5,000 of accrued property tax at the time the plant site was acquired.
5. Paid $8,000 for the installation of new factory machinery.
6. Paid $900 for a one-year accident insurance policy on the new delivery truck.
7. Paid $200 for insurance to cover a possible accident to the new factory machinery while the machinery was in transit.

Comment on, and classify, expenditures.
(SO 2) S

Instructions
(a) Write a business letter that explains the application of the cost principle in determining the acquisition cost of capital assets.
(b) List the numbers of the foregoing transactions, and opposite each number indicate the account title from which the expenditure should be debited.

E10–2   On March 1, 2003, Chowdhury Company acquired land for which it paid $90,000 cash. It planned to construct a small office building. An old warehouse on the property was torn down at a cost of $6,600. The residual materials were sold for $1,700. Additional costs before construction began included a $1,100 legal fee for work concerning the land purchase, a $7,800 architect's fee, and $14,000 to put in driveways and a parking lot.

Determine acquisition cost of land.
(SO 2) AP

Instructions
(a) Determine the amount to be reported as the cost of the land.
(b) For each cost not used in part (a), indicate the account to be debited.

Calculate amortization under units-of-activity method.
(SO 4) AP

E10–3   Interprovincial Bus Lines uses the units-of-activity method to amortize its buses. One bus was purchased on January 1, 2002, at a cost of $128,000. Over its four-year useful life, the bus is expected to be driven 100,000 kilometres. Residual value is expected to be $8,000.

Instructions

(a) Calculate the amortizable cost per unit.
(b) Prepare an amortization schedule assuming that the actual distance driven was: 28,000 kilometres in 2002, 30,000 in 2003, 25,000 in 2004, and 17,000 in 2005.

Determine amortization using three methods, and answer questions about impact of each method.
(SO 4) AP

E10–4   Stojko Company purchased a new machine on January 1, 2002, at a cost of $89,000. The company estimated that the machine will have a residual value of $12,000. The machine is expected to be used for 10,000 working hours during its six-year life. Stojko Company uses a calendar year end.

Instructions

(a) Calculate the amortization expense under the following methods for each of the years ended December 31, 2002 and 2003: (1) straight-line, (2) units-of-activity, assuming machine usage was 1,700 hours for 2002 and 1,500 hours for 2003, and (3) declining-balance using double the straight-line rate.
(b) Which method results in the highest income for the first two years?
(c) Which method results in the highest cash flow for the first two years?

Calculate and record revised amortization.
(SO 5) AP

E10–5   I-Chun Ting, the new controller of Waterloo Company, has reviewed the expected useful lives and residual values of selected amortizable assets at the beginning of 2002. Her findings are as follows:

Type of Asset	Date Acquired	Cost	Accumulated Amortization Jan. 1, 2002	Useful Life in Years Old	Proposed	Residual Value Old	Proposed
Building	Jan. 1, 1996	$800,000	$114,000	40	45	$40,000	$70,000
Warehouse	July 1, 1999	100,000	9,500	25	20	5,000	3,600

After discussion, management agrees to accept I-Chun's proposed changes. All assets are amortized by the straight-line method. Waterloo Company uses a calendar year in preparing annual financial statements.

Instructions

(a) Calculate the revised annual amortization on each asset in 2002.
(b) Prepare the entry (or entries) to record amortization on the building and the warehouse in 2002.

Discuss implications of amortization period.
(SO 5, 9) S

E10–6   Alliance Atlantis Communications changed its accounting policy to amortize broadcast rights for programs over the contracted exhibition period effective January 1, 1999. The exhibition period is based on the estimated useful life of the program. Previously, the company amortized broadcast rights over the lesser of two years or the contracted exhibition period.

Instructions

Write a short memo explaining the implications this has for the analysis of Alliance Atlantis's results. Also, discuss whether this change in amortization period appears reasonable.

Journalize asset addition and amortization.
(SO 2, 4, 5, 6) AP

E10–7   Mactaquac Company purchased a piece of high-tech equipment on July 1, 2001 for $25,000 cash. The equipment was expected to last four years, and has a residual value of $2,500. Mactaquac uses the straight-line method of amortization. The company's fiscal year end is June 30.

On July 1, 2002, Mactaquac purchased and installed a new part for the equipment that is expected to substantially improve its productivity. Mactaquac paid $5,000 cash for the part. It paid an additional $500 for the installation and testing of this part. The equipment is expected to last five years in total now and has a revised residual value of $5,000.

Instructions

(a) Prepare the journal entry to record the purchase of the equipment on July 1, 2001.
(b) Prepare the journal entry to record the amortization of the equipment on June 30, 2002.
(c) Prepare the journal entry to record the purchase of the part, and its installation and testing, on July 1, 2002.
(d) Prepare the journal entry to record the amortization of the equipment on June 30, 2003.

E10–8   Presented below are selected transactions of Leger Company for 2002:

Jan. 1 Retired a piece of machinery that was purchased on January 1, 1992. The machinery cost $62,000 on that date. It had a useful life of 10 years with no residual value.

June 30 Sold a computer that was purchased on January 1, 2000. The computer cost $5,000. It had a useful life of three years with no residual value. The computer was sold for $500.

Dec. 31 Discarded a delivery truck that was purchased on January 1, 1998. The truck cost $30,000. It was amortized based on a six-year useful life with a $3,000 residual value.

Journalize entries for disposal of capital assets.
(SO 7) AP

Instructions

Journalize all entries required on the above dates. Include entries to update amortization for partial periods, where applicable, on the disposal of assets. Leger Company uses straight-line amortization.

E10–9   The Rahim Corporation purchased a computer for $10,000. The company planned to keep it for four years, after which it hoped to sell it for $1,000.

Determine effect of amortization method over life of asset.
(SO 4, 7) AN

Instructions

(a) Calculate the amortization expense for each of the four years under (1) the straight-line method and (2) the double declining-balance method.

(b) Assume Rahim sold the computer for $1,500 at the end of the *third* year. Calculate the loss on disposal under each amortization method.

(c) Determine the impact of each method on net income (total amortization expense plus loss on disposal) related to use of the computer over the three-year period.

E10–10   On July 1, 2002, Phillips Inc. invested $480,000 in a mine estimated to have 800,000 tonnes of ore. At the end of production at the mine, the company estimates it will have to spend $150,000 to restore the site to an environmentally acceptable condition. The property will then be sold for $90,000. During the last six months of 2002, 100,000 tonnes of ore were mined and sold.

Journalize natural resource amortization.
(SO 8) AP

Instructions

(a) Prepare the journal entry to record the amortization expense.

(b) Assume that 100,000 tonnes of ore were mined but only 80,000 were sold. How much amortization expense is recorded in 2002? How are the costs applied to the 20,000 unsold tonnes?

E10–11   The following are selected transactions of Arseneault Corporation during 2002:

Jan. 1 Paid $150,000 to develop a trademark. The trademark has an estimated useful life of five years.

May 1 Purchased a patent with an estimated useful life of five years and a legal life of 20 years for $45,000.

Journalize intangible asset amortization.
(SO 4, 9) AP

Instructions

Prepare all adjusting entries at December 31 to record the amortization required by the events above.

E10–12   Doucette Company, established in 2002, has the following transactions related to intangible assets:

Jan. 2 Purchased a patent (7-year life) for $420,000.

Apr. 1 Goodwill purchased (indefinite life) for $360,000.

July 1 A 10-year franchise which expires on July 1, 2012 is purchased for $450,000.

Sept. 1 Research costs of $185,000 are incurred.

30 Development costs of $50,000 are incurred. (No marketable products have yet been identified.)

Record acquisition and amortization of intangible assets.
(SO 4, 9) AP

Instructions

(a) Prepare the necessary entries to record these intangibles. All costs incurred were for cash.

(b) Make the entries as at December 31, 2002, recording any necessary amortization. There was no impairment of goodwill.

Classify accounts and prepare capital assets section of balance sheet.
(SO 10) AP

E10–13   Northwest Sports Enterprises, owner of the Vancouver Canucks National Hockey League team, reported the following selected information as at June 30, 2000:

Accumulated amortization—leasehold improvements	$ 230,697
Accumulated amortization—equipment	860,074
Accumulated amortization—hockey franchise and rights to players	1,693,850
Amortization expense	220,171
Equipment	1,081,364
Investments	13,700,434
Hockey franchise and rights to players	7,528,235
Leasehold improvements	1,124,248

Instructions

(a) Identify which financial statement (i.e., balance sheet or income statement) and which section (e.g., current assets, capital assets, etc.) each of the above items should be reported in.

(b) Prepare the capital assets section of the balance sheet, as at June 30, 2000.

Calculate asset turnover and return on assets ratios.
(SO 11) AN

E10–14   Imax Corporation of Mississauga makes and leases projection and sound systems for 210 giant-screen IMAX theatres in 26 countries. During a recent year, it reported total revenue (assume equal to net sales) of US$208,569,000, net income of US$23,219,000, and average total assets of US$525,710,500.

Instructions

(a) Calculate the asset turnover and return on assets ratios for Imax Corporation.

(b) The asset turnover for Imax's industry is 0.5 times. The return on assets for the industry is 5.7%. Comment on how Imax's management of its assets compares to that of its industry.

PROBLEMS: SET A

Determine acquisition costs of land and building.
(SO 2) AP

P10–1A   Kadlec Company was established on January 1. During the first year of operations, the following capital asset expenditures and receipts were recorded:

Debits

1. Cost of real estate purchased as a plant site (land fair market value $100,000 and building fair market value $60,000)	$145,000
2. Accrued property tax paid at time of purchase of real estate	2,000
3. Property tax on land paid for the current year	5,000
4. Cost of demolishing building to make land suitable for construction of new building	13,000
5. Excavation costs for new building	20,000
6. Cost of filling and grading the land	4,000
7. Architect's fees for building plans	10,000
8. Full payment to building contractor	600,000
9. Cost of fences around the property	3,000
10. Paving of the parking lots and driveways	15,000
	$817,000

Credits

11. Proceeds for residual materials of demolished building	$ 2,500

Instructions

Analyse the above transactions using the following column headings. Insert the number of each transaction in the Item space. Insert the amounts in the appropriate columns. For amounts entered in the Other Accounts column, indicate the account titles.

Item	Land	Building	Other Accounts (specify title)

P10–2A In recent years, Flakeboard Company purchased three machines. Various amortization methods were selected. Information concerning the machines is summarized below:

Machine	Acquired	Cost	Residual Value	Useful Life in Years	Amortization Method
1	Jan. 1/99	$96,000	$ 6,000	10	Straight-line
2	Jan. 1/00	60,000	10,000	8	Declining-balance
3	Nov. 1/01	66,000	6,000	6	Units-of-activity

For the declining-balance method, the company uses double the straight-line rate. For the units-of-activity method, total machine hours are expected to be 24,000. Actual hours of use in the first two years were 1,000 in 2001 and 4,500 in 2002.

Instructions

(a) Calculate the amount of accumulated amortization on each machine at December 31, 2002. Round your answers to the nearest dollar.
(b) If Machine 2 had been purchased on April 1 instead of January 1, what would the amortization expense be for this machine in (1) 2000, (2) 2001, and (3) 2002?

P10–3A Whitley Corporation purchased machinery on January 1, 2002, at a cost of $100,000. The estimated useful life of the machinery is three years, with an estimated residual value at the end of that period of $10,000. The company is considering different amortization methods that could be used for financial reporting purposes.

Instructions

(a) Prepare separate amortization schedules for the machinery for its three-year life using the straight-line method and the declining-balance method using double the straight-line rate. Round your answers to the nearest dollar.
(b) Which method would result in the higher reported net income in 2002? In the higher total net income over the three-year period?
(c) Which method would result in the higher cash flow from operations in 2002? In the higher total cash flow over the three-year period?

P10–4A At the beginning of 2000, Bérubé Company acquired equipment costing $40,000. It was estimated that this equipment would have a useful life of five years and a residual value of $4,000. The straight-line method of amortization was considered the most appropriate to use with this type of equipment, and amortization is to be recorded at the end of each year.

At the beginning of 2002 (the third year of the equipment's life), the company's engineers reconsidered their expectations, and estimated that the equipment's useful life would probably be six years (in total) instead of five years. The estimated residual value was not changed.

Three years later, at the beginning of 2005, the estimated residual value was reduced to $2,500.

Instructions

Indicate how much amortization expense should be recorded for this equipment each year, by completing the following table:

Year	Amortization Expense	Accumulated Amortization
2000		
2001		
2002		
2003		
2004		
2005		

P10–5A The transactions below involve expenditures related to capital assets:

1. Operator controls on equipment were replaced for $7,000, because the control devices that came with it were not adequate.
2. The amount of $4,600 was spent for decorative landscaping (planting flowers and shrubs, etc.).
3. A new air-conditioning system for the factory offices was bought for $36,000.
4. Windows broken in a labour dispute (not covered by insurance) were replaced for $2,400.
5. An amount of $1,500 was paid for adjusting and testing new machinery prior to its use.
6. Machinery damaged by a fork-lift truck was repaired for $5,000.

Instructions

For each of the transactions listed above, indicate the title of the account that you think should be debited in recording the transaction. Briefly explain your reasoning.

Record operating and capital expenditures. Calculate revision to amortization expense.
(SO 4, 5, 6) AP

P10–6A   Cuylits Company owned processing equipment that had a cost of $100,000. It had an expected useful life of five years, and an expected residual value of $10,000. Amortization was recorded each December 31. The straight-line method of amortization is used.

During its third year of service, the following cash expenditures were made on this equipment:

Jan. 7   Completed an overhaul of the equipment at a cost of $14,000. The work included the installation of new computer controls to replace the original controls, which were technologically obsolete. As a result of this work, the estimated useful life of the equipment was increased to a total of seven years. The estimated residual value was increased to $12,000.

Feb. 7   Lubricated and adjusted the equipment to maintain optimum performance, at a cost of $1,000.

Mar. 19   Replaced a number of belts, hoses, etc., which were showing signs of wear, at a cost of $2,500.

Instructions

(a)   Prepare journal entries to record each of the transactions listed above.

(b)   Calculate the amortization expense that should be recorded for this equipment in (1) the second year of its life, (2) the third year of its life (the year in which the above transactions took place), and (3) the fourth year of its life.

Calculate amortization under straight-line and declining-balance methods. Calculate gain or loss on disposal and total expense over life of asset and comment.
(SO 4, 7) AN

P10–7A   Forristal Farmers purchased a piece of equipment at a cost of $21,000. The equipment has an estimated useful life of four years with an estimated residual value at the end of the four years of $1,000. The president is debating the merits of using the single (not double) declining-balance method of amortization as opposed to the straight-line method of amortization. The president feels that the straight-line method will have a more favourable impact on the income statement.

Instructions

(a)   Prepare a schedule comparing the amortization expense and net book values for each of the four years, and in total for the four years, under (1) the straight-line method, and (2) the declining-balance method.

(b)   Assume that the equipment is sold at the end of year 3 for $7,000.

1.   Calculate the gain or loss on the sale of the equipment, under:
   i.   the straight-line method, and
   ii. the declining-balance method.

2.   Prepare a schedule to show the overall impact of the total amortization expense combined with the gain or loss on sale for the three -year period under each method of amortization (consider the total effect on net income over the three -year period). Comment on your results.

Journalize alternatives related to disposals of capital assets.
(SO 4, 7) AP

P10–8A   Express Co. has delivery equipment that cost $45,000 when it was purchased on July 1, 2000. The delivery equipment has a useful life of five years, with an expected residual value of $5,000. The equipment was sold on June 30, 2003. Express Co. uses the straight-line method of amortization.

Instructions

Record the disposal under the following assumptions:

(a)   It was scrapped as having no value.

(b)   It was sold for $25,000.

(c)   It was sold for $18,000.

Classify operating and capital expenditures.
(SO 2, 6, 9) AP

P10–9A   Cumby Company incurred the following expenditures in a recent year:

Account Title	Expenditure
_____	Architect fees
_____	Cost to demolish an old building that is on a piece of land where Cumby intends to construct a new building
_____	Lawyer's fees associated with a successful patent application
_____	Lawyer's fees associated with an unsuccessful patent application
_____	Cost of a grease and oil change on the company's truck
_____	Cost of installing a new roof on the company's building
_____	Cost of painting the president's office
_____	Cost of CDs and toner for the office computer and printer

_____ Payment to a celebrity for endorsement of a product. The celebrity's endorsement is featured in television advertisements which have been airing for the past three months and will continue to be televised for another six months after year end.

_____ Cost of four new tires for the company delivery van

_____ Cost to rebuild the engine on the company delivery van

_____ Cost to pave the company parking lot

_____ Cost of painting the corporate logo on the sides of the company delivery van

Instructions

For each of the above expenditures, indicate the account title under which the expenditure should be recorded (debited).

P10–10A Due to rapid turnover in the accounting department, a number of transactions involving intangible assets were improperly recorded by Riley Corporation in the year ended December 31, 2002:

Prepare entries to correct errors made in recording and amortizing intangible assets.
(SO 9) AN

1. Riley developed a new patented manufacturing process early in the year, incurring research and development costs of $120,000. Of this amount, 40% was considered to be development costs that could be capitalized. Riley recorded the entire $120,000 in the Patents account and amortized it using a 20-year estimated useful life.
2. The company purchased a patent for $45,000. In early January, Riley capitalized $139,400 as the cost of the patent as that's how much Riley believed it was worth. Riley credited a Gain on Patent Appreciation account for the difference, $94,400. Patent amortization expense of $6,970 was recorded, based on a 20-year estimated useful life.
3. On July 1, 2002, Riley purchased a small company and, as a result, acquired goodwill of $60,000. Riley recorded a half-year's amortization in 2002, $1,500. There was no impairment of goodwill and it is expected to benefit the company indefinitely.
4. The company made a $5,000 charitable donation at year end, which it debited from goodwill.

Instructions

Prepare all journal entries needed to correct any errors made during the year 2002.

P10–11A The intangible assets reported by Tar Company at December 31, 2002, are presented below:

Record transactions related to acquisition and amortization of intangibles. Prepare capital assets section of balance sheet.
(SO 9, 10) AP

Patent ($70,000 cost less $7,000 amortization)	$63,000
Copyright ($48,000 cost less $19,200 amortization)	28,800
Total	$91,800

The patent was acquired in January 2002 and has an estimated useful life of 10 years. The copyright was acquired in January 1999 and also has an estimated useful life of 10 years. The following cash transactions may have affected intangible assets during the year 2003:

Jan. 2 Paid $12,000 of legal costs to successfully defend the patent against infringement by another company.

June 30 Developed a new product, incurring $125,000 in development costs, which were paid in cash. A patent was granted for the product on July 1. Its expected useful life is equal to its legal life.

Sept. 1 Paid $80,000 to an Olympic gold medalist to appear in commercials advertising the company's products. The commercials will air in September and October.

Oct. 1 Acquired a copyright for $120,000 cash. The copyright has an expected useful life of 6 years.

Instructions

(a) Prepare journal entries to record the above transactions.
(b) Prepare journal entries to record the 2003 amortization expense for intangible assets. Round your answers to the nearest dollar.
(c) Prepare the capital assets section of the balance sheet at December 31, 2003.

Journalize a series of equipment transactions related to purchase, sale, retirement, and amortization. Prepare capital assets section of balance sheet.
(SO 4, 7, 10) AP

P10–12A At December 31, 2002, Dufour Company reported the following as capital assets:

DUFOUR COMPANY
Balance Sheet (partial)
December 31, 2002

Land		$ 4,000,000
Buildings	$28,500,000	
Less: Accumulated amortization—buildings	12,100,000	16,400,000
Equipment	$48,000,000	
Less: Accumulated amortization—equipment	5,000,000	43,000,000
Total capital assets		63,400,000

During 2003, the following selected cash transactions occurred:

Apr. 1 Purchased land for $2,630,000.

May 1 Sold equipment that cost $570,000 when purchased on January 1, 1999. The equipment was sold for $350,000.

June 1 Sold land for $1,800,000. The land cost $200,000 when purchased on June 1, 1993.

July 1 Purchased equipment for $2,000,000.

Dec. 31 Retired equipment that cost $500,000 when purchased on December 31, 1993. It had no residual value.

Instructions

(a) Journalize the above transactions. The company uses straight-line amortization for buildings and equipment. The buildings are estimated to have a 30-year life and no residual value. The equipment is estimated to have a 10-year useful life and no residual value. Update the amortization on the disposed assets, at the time of their sale or retirement.

(b) Record adjusting entries for amortization for 2003.

(c) Prepare the capital assets section of Dufour's balance sheet at December 31, 2003.

Calculate and comment on asset turnover and return on assets ratios.
(SO 11) AN

P10–13A Andrew Company and Michael Company, two companies of roughly the same size, both manufacture in-line skates. Each company amortizes its capital assets using the straight-line method. An investigation of their financial statements reveals the following information:

	Andrew Company	Michael Company
Sales	$1,400,000	$1,300,000
Net income	700,000	1,000,000
Average total assets	2,500,000	2,000,000

Instructions

(a) For each company, calculate the asset turnover and return on assets ratios.

(b) Based on your results in part (a), comment on the relative effectiveness of the two companies in using their assets to generate sales and produce net income.

PROBLEMS: SET B

Record acquisition costs of land and building.
(SO 2) AN

P10–1B Vienneau Company was organized on January 1. During the first year of operations, capital asset expenditures were recorded by the accountant in a T account called Land and Building:

Land and Building	
145,000 (1)	
4,000 (2)	
2,000 (3)	
5,000 (4)	
10,000 (5)	
3,000 (6)	
Balance 169,000	

Explanations of the T account amounts follow:

1. Cost of real estate purchased. Fair market value of land was $100,000. Fair market value of building was $50,000.

2. Installation cost of fences around property

3. Accrued property taxes on land and building paid at time of purchase of real estate
4. Property taxes on land and building for current year
5. Landscaping costs
6. Interior and exterior painting

Instructions

Prepare any entries necessary to correct the recording of the above transactions. Round your answers to the nearest dollar.

P10–2B SR Company purchased a machine on account on December 2, 2000, at an invoice price of $45,000. On December 2, 2000, SR paid $800 for delivery of the machine. On December 31, 2000, SR paid its account with the supplier of the machine. On December 31, 2000, SR paid $3,100 for installation and testing of the machine. The machine was ready for use on January 1, 2001. It was estimated that the machine would have a useful life of five years, and a residual value of $8,000. Engineering estimates indicated that the useful life in productive units was 200,000. Units actually produced during the first two years were 30,000 in 2001 and 48,000 in 2002.

Record capital asset acquisition. Calculate amortization under different methods.
(SO 2, 4) AP

Instructions

(a) Prepare the journal entries for each of the December 2000 dates.
(b) Prepare the journal entries for December 31, 2001, and December 31, 2002, to record the amortization expense using the following methods:
   1. Straight-line
   2. Units-of-activity
   3. Declining-balance at double the straight-line rate

Adapted from Certified General Accountants Association of Canada, *Financial Accounting 1 Examination*, March 1998, Question 6.

P10–3B On January 1, 2002, the Grind Company purchased a machine for use in its production process. The cash price of the machine was $35,000. Related expenditures included shipping costs, $175; insurance during shipping, $75; installation and testing costs, $50; and $90 of oil and lubricants to be used on the machinery during its first year of operations.

Grind estimates that the useful life of the machine is four years with a $5,000 residual value remaining at the end of that period. In terms of activity, it estimates the useful life of the machine to be 25,000 units. Actual usage is as follows: for 2002, 6,500 units; for 2003, 7,500 units; for 2004, 6,000 units; and for 2005, 5,000 units.

Determine acquisition cost. Calculate amortization under different methods, and consider effects.
(SO 2, 4) AN

Instructions

(a) Determine the cost of the machine on January 1, 2002.
(b) Calculate the amount of amortization expense that Grind should record during each year of the machine's four-year useful life under the following assumptions:
   1. Grind uses the straight-line method of amortization.
   2. Grind uses the declining-balance method. The rate used is twice the straight-line rate.
   3. Grind uses the units-of-activity method.
(c) Which amortization method reports the lowest amount of amortization expense in 2002? The lowest amount in 2005? The lowest total amount for the four-year period?
(d) Which amortization method reports the lowest net income in 2002? In 2005? Over the four-year period?
(e) Which amortization method reports the lowest cash flow in 2002? In 2005? Over the four-year period?

P10–4B On January 1, 2000, Harrington Company acquired equipment costing $50,000. It was estimated at that time that this equipment would have a useful life of six years and a residual value of $2,000. The straight-line method of amortization is used by Harrington for its equipment. Its fiscal year end is December 31.

At the beginning of 2002 (the beginning of the third year of the equipment's life), the company's engineers reconsidered their expectations. They estimated that the equipment's useful life would more likely be five years in total, instead of the previously estimated six years. The estimated residual value was also reduced to $1,400.

Calculate revisions to amortization expense.
(SO 5) AP

Instructions

(a) Indicate how much amortization expense should be recorded each year for the equipment by completing the following table:

Year	Amortization Expense	Accumulated Amortization
2000		
2001		
2002		
2003		
2004		

(b) What is the net book value of the asset at the end of its useful life, on December 31, 2004? What should the net book value equal at the end of its useful life?

Account for various operating and capital expenditures.
(SO 6) AP

P10–5B   The transactions below involve expenditures for a forklift:
1. Rebuild the diesel engine that has over 20,000 hours, $10,000
2. New tires, $6,000
3. New safety cab, $5,000
4. Replacement of a windshield (not covered by insurance), $1,200
5. Training the operator, $1,600
6. New paint job, after the company changed its logo and colours, $2,000

Instructions

For each of the transactions listed above, indicate the title of the account that you think should be debited in recording the transaction. Briefly explain your reasoning.

Record operating and capital expenditures. Calculate revision to amortization expense.
(SO 4, 5, 6) AP

P10–6B   Copps Co. owns woodworking equipment that had a cost of $112,000. When new, it had an expected useful life of five years and an expected residual value of $12,000. Amortization is recorded each December 31. The straight-line method is used.

During its fourth year of service, the following expenditures were made for this equipment:
Jan. 18 Painted the equipment to make it look new, at a cost of $1,500.
Mar. 5 Replaced a number of bearings and guides which were showing signs of wear, at a cost of $2,400.
Dec. 31 Completed an overhaul of the equipment at a cost of $35,000. The work included the installation of new optimizer controls to replace the original controls, which were obsolete. As a result of this work, the total estimated useful life of the equipment was expected to be increased by four years to nine years. The estimated residual value was reduced to $5,000.

Instructions

(a) Prepare journal entries to record each of the transactions listed above.
(b) Calculate the amortization expense that should be recorded for this equipment in (1) the third year of its life, (2) the fourth year of its life (the year in which the above transactions took place), and (3) the fifth year of its life.

Calculate gain or loss on disposal and total expense over life of asset and comment.
(SO 7) AN

P10–7B   Refer to Demonstration Problem 1 presented in this chapter. Assume that rather than keep the machine until the end of its useful life, DuPage Company sells it at the end of 2004 for $4,400. Note that since the disposal occurs at the end of the year, the full amount of amortization is charged for 2004.

Instructions

(a) Calculate the gain or loss on the sale of the machine under each of the three methods of amortization used in the Demonstration Problem (straight-line, units-of-activity, and declining-balance).
(b) Comment on the results obtained in part (a). Can you say which of the amortization methods was the "best" in this particular situation?
(c) For each of the three methods of amortization, calculate the overall impact of the amortization expense combined with the gain or loss on the sale of the machine. Consider the total effect on net income over the three-year period.
(d) Comment on the results obtained in part (c). What do they tell you about the relationship between the amount of amortization expense that is recorded during the asset's life and the gain or loss that is recorded on its disposal?

Journalize alternatives related to disposals of capital assets.
(SO 4, 7) AP

P10–8B   Hemmingsen Co. has office furniture that cost $75,000 when purchased on January 1, 1998. At that time, it was expected to have a useful life of five years and a $1,000 residual value. Hemmingsen Co. uses the straight-line method of amortization and has a calendar year end.

Instructions

Update amortization and record the disposal of this furniture four and one-half years later, on July 1, 2002, under the following assumptions:
- (a) It was scrapped as having no value.
- (b) It was sold for its residual value of $1,000.
- (c) It was sold for $8,000.
- (d) It was sold for $8,500.

P10–9B The following expenditures were made for Cohlmeyer Company, as it commenced its first year of operations. Its year end is May 31, 2003.

Jan. 10 Land was purchased for $65,000.

Jan. 15 The land was surveyed at a cost of $3,000.

Feb. 1 An existing building on the land was removed at a cost of $5,500 to provide room for the new structure.

    10 A security fence was built around the land for $2,500.

    23 An architectural firm was paid $15,000 for plans for the new building.

Mar. 15 In preparation for construction of the new building, $3,500 was spent to remove trees and level the land.

    17 A building permit was acquired for $1,000.

Apr. 10 Legal and application costs of $5,000 were paid for a patent on a newly developed product that will be sold by Cohlmeyer.

May 1 An amount of $460,000 was spent to construct the building.

    15 An amount of $4,000 was spent on landscaping.

    20 A parking lot was constructed for $8,000.

    25 The company's domain name, <www.cohlmeyer.com>, was registered for $150.

    28 A lawyer was paid $4,000 for organizing the new company.

    31 The building was occupied and business commenced.

Classify operating and capital expenditures. Prepare capital assets section of balance sheet. (SO 2, 6, 9, 10) AP

Instructions

- (a) For each of the above expenditures, indicate the account under which the expenditure should be recorded (debited).
- (b) Prepare the capital assets section of the balance sheet for Cohlmeyer Company on May 31.

P10–10B Due to rapid turnover in the accounting department, a number of transactions that involved intangible assets were improperly recorded by the Hahn Company in the year ended August 31, 2002.

1. Hahn developed a newly shaped Z-cleat for running shoes. It incurred research costs of $50,000 and development costs of $25,000. It debited these costs from the Patent account.
2. The company registered the patent for the Z-cleat. Legal fees and registration costs totalled $20,000. The company debited these costs from Legal Fees Expense.
3. The company fought a competitor successfully in court, defending its patent. It incurred $40,000 of legal fees. These were debited from Legal Fees Expense.
4. The company sold the rights to manufacture and distribute these cleats to Fleet Foot Inc. for an annual fee of $50,000. Hahn recorded the receipt of this fee as a credit to the Patent account.
5. The company recorded amortization of the patent of $5,000 [($50,000 + $25,000 − $50,000) ÷ 5 years] over its expected useful life of five years.

Prepare entries to correct errors made in recording and amortizing intangible assets. (SO 9) AN

Instructions

Prepare all journal entries needed to correct any errors made during 2002.

P10–11B CAM Software Company (CAM) is an established computer software company. In 2002, the firm incurred the following costs in the process of designing, developing, and producing new software using Java technology to access the Internet:

Designing and planning	$500,000
Code development	600,000
Testing	160,000
Production of product master	400,000

The costs of designing and planning, code development, and testing were all incurred before the technological feasibility of the product was established. In 2003, CAM incurred $100,000 in costs to produce the software for sale. CAM began marketing the software later that year. It earned revenues from these sales of $800,000 in 2003. It estimates that total revenues over the four-year life of the product will be $8,000,000. Development costs are amortized on the basis of expected sales.

At the end of 2003, CAM was offered $3,000,000 for the rights to distribute the software.

Record transactions related to acquisition and amortization of intangibles. Prepare capital assets section of balance sheet. (SO 9, 10) AN

Instructions

(a) How much of the cost should be expensed in 2002 and 2003? Include costs expensed when incurred and costs expensed indirectly through amortization expense.

(b) How, if at all, should the offer of $3,000,000 for the rights to the software be recognized or disclosed in the financial statements for 2003? Explain the rationale for your answer.

Adapted from Certified General Accountants' Association of Canada, *Financial Accounting 2 Examination*, March 1998, Question 6.

Journalize a series of equipment transactions related to purchase, sale, retirement, and amortization. Prepare capital assets section of balance sheet.
(SO 4, 7, 10) AP

P10–12B   At December 31, 2002, Bowman Company reported the following as capital assets:

BOWMAN COMPANY
Balance Sheet (partial)
December 31, 2002

Land		$ 3,000,000
Buildings	$26,500,000	
Less: Accumulated amortization—buildings	12,100,000	14,400,000
Equipment	$40,000,000	
Less: Accumulated amortization—equipment	5,000,000	35,000,000
Total capital assets		52,400,000

During 2003, the following selected cash transactions occurred:

Apr. 1 Purchased land for $2,200,000.

May 1 Sold equipment that cost $600,000 when purchased on January 1, 1999. The equipment was sold for $360,000.

June 1 Sold land purchased on January 1, 1993, for $1,800,000. The land cost $500,000.

July 1 Purchased equipment for $1,400,000.

Dec. 31 Retired equipment that cost $500,000 when purchased on December 31, 1993.

Instructions

(a) Journalize the above transactions. Bowman uses straight-line amortization for buildings and equipment. The buildings are estimated to have a 40-year useful life and no residual value. The equipment is estimated to have a 10-year useful life and no residual value. Update the amortization on the disposed assets at the time of their sale or retirement.

(b) Record adjusting entries for the amortization for 2003.

(c) Prepare the capital assets section of Bowman's balance sheet at December 31, 2003.

Calculate and comment on asset turnover and return on assets ratios.
(SO 11) AN

P10–13B   St. Amand Company and St. Helene Company, two companies of roughly the same size, both manufacture sea kayaks. Each company amortizes its capital assets using the straight-line method. An investigation of their financial statements reveals the following information:

	St. Amand Company	St. Helene Company
Sales	$1,600,000	$1,350,000
Net income	400,000	600,000
Average total assets	2,000,000	800,000

Instructions

(a) For each company, calculate the asset turnover and return on assets ratios.

(b) Based on your results in part (a), comment on the relative effectiveness of the two companies in using their assets to generate sales and produce net income.

CUMULATIVE COVERAGE—CHAPTERS 3 TO 10

The unadjusted trial balance of LeBrun Company at its year end, July 31, 2003, is as follows:

LEBRUN COMPANY
Trial Balance
July 31, 2003

Account No.	Account Title	Debit	Credit
101	Cash	$ 18,000	
105	Petty Cash	200	
112	Accounts Receivable	25,000	
113	Allowance for Doubtful Accounts		$ 2,000
115	Notes Receivable (due December 31, 2003)	10,000	
120	Merchandise Inventory	58,000	
133	Prepaid Expenses	16,000	
140	Land	50,000	
145	Building	105,000	
146	Accumulated Amortization—Building		10,800
151	Equipment	25,000	
152	Accumulated Amortization—Equipment		12,200
177	Patent (net of $11,250 accumulated amortization)	63,750	
201	Accounts Payable		81,000
275	Mortgage Payable (due August 1, 2025)		121,190
301	LeBrun, Capital		119,937
306	LeBrun, Drawings	15,000	
401	Sales		750,000
505	Cost of Goods Sold	600,000	
645	Operating Expenses	100,000	
905	Interest Expense	11,177	
	Totals	$1,097,127	$1,097,127

Additional accounts will be required: No. 118 Interest Receivable; No. 230 Interest Payable; No. 612 Bad Debt Expense; No. 711 Amortization Expense; and No. 820 Interest Revenue.

Adjustment Data:

1. The July 31 bank statement included a debit memo for interest of $15 and an NSF cheque received from a customer on account of $75.
2. Estimated uncollectible accounts receivable at July 31 are $2,500.
3. The 8% note receivable was issued on January 1, 2003. Interest has not previously been received or accrued.
4. A physical count of inventory determined that $57,000 of inventory was actually on hand.
5. Prepaid expenses of $2,000 expired during the year (use Operating Expenses summary account).
6. Amortization is calculated on the capital assets using the following methods and useful lives:

    Building, straight-line, 25 years, $15,000 residual value
    Equipment, single declining-balance, 5 years, $2,000 residual value
    Patent, straight-line, 20 years, no residual value

7. The 10% mortgage payable was issued on August 1, 2000. Interest is paid monthly, at the beginning of each month for the previous month's interest. Of the mortgage principal, $1,596 is currently due.
8. Accrued liabilities at July 31 are $1,400 (use the Accounts Payable account).

Instructions

(a) Prepare the adjusting journal entries required at July 31, 2003. Round your calculations to the nearest dollar.
(b) Prepare an adjusted trial balance at July 31, 2003.
(c) Prepare a multiple-step income statement and statement of owner's equity for the year ended July 31, and a classified balance sheet as at July 31, 2003.

Broadening Your Perspective

FINANCIAL REPORTING AND ANALYSIS

Financial Reporting Problem

BYP10–1   Refer to the financial statements and the Notes to Consolidated Financial Statements for **The Second Cup Ltd.**, which are reproduced in Appendix A. Notice that The Second Cup uses the term "depreciation," rather than amortization, for its tangible capital assets.

Instructions

Answer the following questions:
(a) What were the following amounts for the company's capital assets at June 24, 2000: (1) the cost, (2) the accumulated depreciation, and (3) the net book value?
(b) What was the amount of capital assets that was purchased during the 2000 fiscal year?
(c) What was the amount received from the disposal of capital assets in 2000? What was the net book value of the capital assets that were disposed of during 2000?
(d) What method of depreciation and amortization is used by The Second Cup for financial reporting purposes?
(e) What expected useful life was used for calculating the depreciation on the equipment, furniture, fixtures, and other?
(f) Identify the primary source of the goodwill that is reported by The Second Cup Ltd.

Interpreting Financial Statements

Additional Cases

BYP10–2   **Maple Leaf Foods** is Canada's largest food processor. The company produces fresh and processed pork, poultry, and seafood for retailers and wholesalers, along with pet and livestock feeds. Its bakery groups produce fresh and frozen baked goods, fresh pasta, and pasta sauces. Maple Leaf Foods also has operations in the U.S., Asia, and Europe.

Early in the 1990s, labour disputes occurred at three of Maple Leaf's meat products plants—one of which was a fresh pork facility. Prior to the labour dispute, the fresh pork facility in Burlington, Ontario, processed about 32,000 hogs per week on a single shift. After the dispute was over, the facility processed only about 18,000 hogs per week at first. The hog supply was gradually increased over the rest of the year until 44,000 hogs per week were processed on each shift.

This dispute had a negative impact on Maple Leaf's financial results. Maple Leaf paid $37 million of labour dispute costs and payments to employees when the strike at the Burlington fresh pork facility was settled.

On a more positive note, Maple Leaf announced a $40-million investment that would be made over the next few years to add a second shift capacity to the facility. When this is complete, Maple Leaf anticipates that it will be able to process 85,000 hogs per week on a double shift.

Instructions

(a) Identify and discuss the advantages and disadvantages of each amortization method for Maple Leaf Foods' pork facilities. Which method would you recommend that Maple Leaf use to amortize the capital assets associated with its Burlington plant? Explain why you chose the method you did.
(b) How should Maple Leaf account for the $37 million of labour dispute costs? Determine which financial statement this amount should be reported on and where it should appear in the statement.
(c) How should Maple Leaf account for the $40 million investment it will make to create a world-class prepared meats facility? Discuss whether these costs should be treated as operating expenditures or capital expenditures.

Accounting on the Web

BYP10–3   This problem uses a corporate annual report to identify a company's capital assets and amortization method. The profitability of capital assets is also calculated.

Instructions

Specific requirements of this Internet case are available on the Weygandt website.

CRITICAL THINKING
••

Collaborative Learning Activity

BYP10–4 Lévesque Company and Ferris Company are two proprietorships that are similar in many respects. One difference is that Lévesque Company uses the straight-line method of amortization and Ferris Company uses the declining-balance method at double the straight-line rate. On January 2, 2000, both companies acquired the following amortizable assets:

Asset	Cost	Residual Value	Useful Life
Building	$320,000	$20,000	50 years
Equipment	110,000	10,000	10 years

Including the appropriate amortization expense, annual net income for the companies in the years 2000, 2001, and 2002, and total income for the three years were as follows:

	2000	2001	2002	Total
Lévesque Company	$84,000	$88,400	$90,000	$262,400
Ferris Company	68,000	76,000	85,000	229,000

At December 31, 2002, the balance sheets of the two companies are similar, but Ferris Company has fewer assets and less owner's equity than Lévesque Company.

Steven Yajchuk is interested in buying one of the companies, and he comes to you for advice.

Instructions

With the class divided into groups, answer the following:
  (a) Determine the annual and total amortization recorded by each company during the three years. Round your answers to the nearest dollar.
  (b) Assuming that Ferris Company also used the straight-line method of amortization instead of the declining-balance method as in (a), prepare comparative income data for the three years.
  (c) Which company should Mr. Yajchuk buy? Why?

Communication Activity

BYP10–5 The chapter presented some concerns regarding the current accounting standards for research and development. Assume that you are the president of a company that is dependent on ongoing research and development. Or, take the opposing stance, and assume that you are the CICA member defending the current standards regarding research and development.

Consider the following questions:
  1. If research costs must be expensed, do you think companies will spend less on R&D? Why or why not? What are the possible implications for the competitiveness of Canadian companies?
  2. If a company makes a commitment to spend money for R&D, it must believe that the R&D has future benefits. Shouldn't all these costs be capitalized? After all, the purchase of other long-lived assets with future benefits is capitalized.

Instructions

Write a memo complaining about, or defending, the current R&D accounting standards, depending on the role you assume.

Ethics Case

BYP10–6 Finney Container Company has declining sales of its principal product, non-biodegradable plastic cartons. The president, Philip Shapiro, instructs his controller to lengthen the estimated asset lives in order to reduce the amortization expense and increase net income.

A processing line of automated plastic extruding equipment, purchased for $2.7 million in January 2002, was originally estimated to have a useful life of five years and a residual value of

$300,000. Amortization has been recorded for two years on that basis. The president wants its estimated useful life changed to eight years (total), and continued use of the straight-line method. The controller is hesitant to make the change, believing it is unethical to increase net income in this manner. The president says, "Hey, the useful life is only an estimate. Besides, I've heard that our competition uses an eight-year estimated life on its production equipment."

Instructions

(a) Who are the stakeholders in this situation?

(b) Is the suggested change in asset life unethical, or simply a shrewd business practice by an astute president?

(c) What is the effect of the president's proposed change on net income, in the year of the change?

Answers to Self-Study Questions

1. c 2. a 3. b 4. c 5. b 6. b 7. b 8. a 9. a 10. b 11. a 12. c 13. c

Answer to Second Cup Review It Question 4

The Second Cup reports leasehold improvements of $1,157,000, equipment, furniture, fixtures, and other of $1,099,000; computer software and hardware of $757,000; and accumulated depreciation of $1,245,000, for a capital asset net book value of $1,768,000.

Remember to go back to the Navigator box on the chapter-opening page to check off your completed work.

Before studying this chapter, you should understand or, if necessary, review:

a. *How to make adjusting entries related to unearned revenue (Ch. 3, p. 110) and accrued expenses. (Ch. 3, pp. 113–115)*

b. *The importance of liquidity in evaluating the financial position of a company. (Ch. 4, pp. 171–172)*

c. *The principles of internal control. (Ch. 8, p. 373)*

d. *Accounting for notes receivable. (Ch. 9, pp. 434–435)*

THE
NAVIGATOR

Does Size Matter?

EDMONTON, Alta.–Sometimes the word "big" just isn't enough.

Consider the West Edmonton Mall, which is not only the largest shopping mall in the world, but boasts ten entries in the *Guinness Book of World Records*. These entries include the largest parking lot (over 20,000 cars) and largest indoor theme park (with its triple-loop "Mindbender" roll coaster).

In addition to the theme park, the indoor lake, the Fantasyland Hotel, and the NHL-sized arena (second home of the Edmonton Oilers), the mall in the west end of the City of Edmonton has over 800 places to shop. Each of these businesses is a tenant, renting space from West Edmonton Mall Property Inc. This company is privately held and family owned.

Needless to say, for a place of this size, the bills are also, well, big. Paul Balchen, West Edmonton Mall Controller, estimates that current liabilities usually total between $9 million and $12 million.

Still, it's "much like any other business," Mr. Balchen says, glancing at the mall's balance sheet for July 31, 2000. "We've got payables of about $2 million on here," he says. "And sales taxes—

GST only, of course, since this is Alberta —of about $450,000." The next line, accrued liabilities, is another $2 million. That includes notes payable and "probably our three-quarter-of-a-million-dollar power bill," explains Mr. Balchen, "which would be accrued for July but not due until August." Clearly, a mall that covers 48 city blocks uses a lot of air conditioning!

Then, of course, there is the accrued interest on the long-term obligation for the property itself, which amounts to about $1 million a month. There's another $1 million in property taxes.

The final line on this section of the balance sheet, says Mr. Balchen, is unearned revenue. "That's another million dollars or so," he explains. "Mostly payments from the tenant businesses for the coming month, or things like advance payments from hockey leagues for use of the ice rink."

"Basically, we've got the same balance sheet as anyone," Mr. Balchen explains. Large or small, every business needs to keep careful track of its liabilities, pay them in a timely fashion, and plan for the future.

THE
NAVIGATOR

www.westedmontonmall.com

THE NAVIGATOR ✔

■ Understand *Concepts for Review* ☐
■ Read *Feature Story* ☐
■ Scan *Study Objectives* ☐
■ Read *Preview* ☐
■ Read text and answer *Before You Go On*
    p. 521 ☐   p. 524 ☐   p. 526 ☐
    p. 527 ☐   p. 538 ☐
■ Work *Demonstration Problem* ☐
■ Review *Summary of Study Objectives* ☐
■ Answer *Self-Study Questions* ☐
■ Complete assignments ☐

CHAPTER • 11

CURRENT LIABILITIES

▶ **STUDY OBJECTIVES** ◀

....

After studying this chapter, you should be able to:

1. *Explain a current liability and distinguish between the major types of current liabilities.*
2. *Explain the accounting, and prepare the journal entries, for definitely determinable liabilities.*
3. *Explain the accounting, and prepare the journal entries, for estimated liabilities.*
4. *Describe the accounting and disclosure requirements for contingent liabilities and prepare the necessary journal entries.*
5. *Explain and illustrate the financial statement presentation of current liabilities.*
6. *Discuss the objectives of internal control for payroll, and be able to identify weaknesses and suggest improvements in their application (Appendix 11A).*
7. *Calculate the payroll for a pay period (Appendix 11A).*

THE NAVIGATOR

Whether it is a huge company such as the West Edmonton Mall, or a small company such as your local convenience store, every company has current liabilities. In Chapter 4, we defined liabilities as creditors' claims on total assets. These claims (debts) must be paid some time in the future by the transfer of assets or services. This future payment date is the reason for the two basic classifications of liabilities: (1) current liabilities and (2) long-term liabilities. We will explain current liabilities in this chapter. We will explain long-term liabilities in Chapter 16.

The chapter is organized as follows:

THE
NAVIGATOR

Accounting for Current Liabilities

STUDY OBJECTIVE
· · · · · · · · · · 1 · · · · · · · · · ·

Explain a current liability and distinguish between the major types of current liabilities.

As explained in Chapter 4, a **current liability** is a debt with two key features: (1) It is likely to be paid within one year (or the operating cycle, if longer). (2) It will be paid from existing current assets (e.g., cash) or through the creation of other current liabilities. Most companies pay current liabilities out of current assets, rather than by creating other liabilities (e.g. paying an account payable by issuing a note payable). Debts that do not meet **both criteria** are classified as long-term liabilities.

Liabilities may be described as **definitely determinable**, **estimable**, or **contingent**. With a definitely determinable liability, we know who we owe, when we owe, and how much we owe. There is no uncertainty as to existence, amount, or timing. Examples of definitely determinable current liabilities include operating lines of credit, notes payable, accounts payable, unearned revenues, and current maturities of long-term debt. This category also includes accrued liabilities such as sales taxes, payroll and employee benefits, and interest payable.

For some other liabilities, we may know that we owe someone, but must estimate the amount or timing. In most cases, we can estimate these types of liabilities and match expenses with associated revenues in the appropriate period. Examples of estimable current liabilities include property taxes and product warranties.

Contingent liabilities are potential liabilities that depend on a future event confirming their existence, amount, or timing. A typical example of a contingent liability is a pending lawsuit.

We will discuss each type of current liability in the following sections.

Definitely Determinable Liabilities

As mentioned earlier, a definitely determinable liability is one with a known amount, payee, and due date. Most current liabilities fall into this category. The entries for many of these liabilities have been explained in previous chapters, including the entries for accounts payable. We will discuss the accounting for other types of current liabilities in this section, including operating lines of credit, notes payable, sales taxes payable, payroll and employee benefits payable, unearned revenues, and current maturities of long-term debt.

STUDY OBJECTIVE

2

Explain the accounting, and prepare the journal entries, for definitely determinable liabilities.

►Accounting in Action ► *Business Insight*

Procurement cards have cut administrative workloads significantly and sped up the payment of current liabilities. These cards work much the way credit cards do. They allow low-value goods and services to be purchased and paid for quickly. With fewer purchase orders and subsequent cheque payments, transaction volume drops. Less than one day passes between when a purchase is made and when it is paid for. After introducing Visa and MasterCard procurement cards, Siemens Canada Limited, a worldwide leader in electronics and technology, was able to reduce the number of its vendors from 3,000 to 500. It also reduced its accounts payable clerks from four to one.

Operating Line of Credit

Current assets (such as accounts receivable) do not always turn into cash at the exact time that current liabilities (such as accounts payable) must be paid. Consequently, most companies have an operating line of credit at their bank to help them manage temporary cash shortfalls. This means that the company has been pre-authorized by the bank to borrow money, up to a preset limit, when it is needed.

Air Canada, for example, has a $560-million line of credit. As an Air Canada spokesperson said, "It's good policy to have additional cash available if we need it." Security, called collateral, is usually required by the bank as protection in the event of a default on the loan. Collateral normally includes some, or all, of the company's current assets (e.g., accounts receivable or inventories) or capital assets.

Line of credit borrowings are normally on a short-term basis, repayable immediately upon request—that is, on demand—by the bank. In reality, repayment is seldom demanded without notice. A line of credit makes it very easy for a company to borrow money. It doesn't have to make a call or visit its bank to actually arrange the transaction. The bank simply covers any cheques written in excess of the bank account balance, up to the approved credit limit.

A number of companies show a negative, or overdrawn, cash balance at year end as a result of using their line of credit. This amount is usually termed **bank indebtedness**, **bank overdraft**, or **bank advances**. No special entry is required to record the overdrawn amount. The normal credits to cash will simply accumulate and be reported as a current liability with a suitable note disclosure. Interest is usually charged on the overdrawn amount at a floating rate, such as prime plus.[1] Such interest is normally payable monthly.

An extract from a recent annual report of Andrés Wines shows how bank indebtedness is reported. Andrés Wines does not report any current asset cash balance. Instead, it presents a current liability related to cash:

Illustration 11-1

Disclosure of bank indebtedness

Andrés Wines Ltd. Balance Sheet (partial) March 31, 2000 (in thousands)	
Current liabilities	
Bank indebtedness (Note 4)	$21,024

Note 4 adds that Andrés has a $38-million operating line of credit, which incurs interest at the Royal Bank prime rate[1]. Accounts receivable, inventories, and capital assets serve as collateral for this demand loan.

Notes Payable

Helpful hint Notes payable are the inverse of notes receivable, and the accounting is similar.

The line of credit described above is similar to a note payable. Notes payable are obligations in the form of written promissory notes. Notes payable are often used instead of accounts payable. This gives the lender proof of the obligation in case legal action is needed to collect the debt. Notes payable are also frequently issued to meet short-term financing needs. The West Edmonton Mall's $1.25 million of notes payable mentioned in our feature story are likely used for this purpose.

Notes are issued for varying periods. **Those due for payment within one year of the balance sheet date are classified as current liabilities.** Most notes are interest-bearing.

To illustrate the accounting for notes payable, assume that the Caisse Populaire agrees to lend $100,000 on March 1, 2003, to Kok Co. through a $100,000, 6%, four-month note payable. Interest is payable at the maturity date of the note. Kok Co. will receive $100,000 cash and make the following journal entry:

A = L + OE
+100,000 +100,000

Mar. 1	Cash	100,000	
	Note Payable		100,000
	To record issue of 6%, 4-month note to the Caisse Populaire.		

Interest is due at maturity. However, interest accrues over the life of the note, and must be recorded periodically. If Kok Co. prepares financial statements quarterly during a calendar year, an adjusting entry is required to recognize interest expense and interest payable of $500 ($100,000 × 6% × $1/12$) at March 31. The adjusting entry is as follows:

A = L + OE
+500 −500

Mar. 31	Interest Expense	500	
	Interest Payable		500
	To accrue interest for one month on Caisse Populaire note.		

---

[1] The prime rate is the interest rate that banks charge their best customers. This rate is usually increased by a specified percentage that reflects the risk profile of the company.

In the March 31 interim financial statements, the current liabilities section of the balance sheet will show notes payable of $100,000 and interest payable of $500. In addition, interest expense of $500 will be reported in the income statement.

Helpful hint The formula to calculate interest is as follows:
Face Value of Note ×
Annual Interest Rate ×
Time in Terms of One Year =
Interest

At maturity (July 1, 2003), Kok Co. must pay the face value of the note ($100,000) plus $2,000 interest ($100,000 × 6% × $^4/_{12}$). But first, the interest must be brought up to date for the preceding three months ($1,500 = $100,000 × 6% × $^3/_{12}$), since interest was last recorded on March 31. The entries to record the accrual of interest and payment of the note and accrued interest follow:

July 1	Interest Expense	1,500	
	Interest Payable		1,500
	To accrue interest for April, May, and June.		

A	=	L	+	OE
		+1,500		−1,500

1	Note Payable	100,000	
	Interest Payable ($500 + $1,500)	2,000	
	Cash ($100,000 + $2,000)		102,000
	To record payment of Caisse Populaire note and accrued interest.		

A	=	L	+	OE
−102,000		−100,000		
		−2,000		

Sales Taxes Payable

As a consumer, you are well aware that many of the products you purchase at retail stores are subject to sales taxes. The taxes are expressed as a stated percentage of the sales price. As discussed in Chapter 5, sales taxes usually take the form of **Goods and Services Tax (GST) and Provincial Sales Tax (PST)**. Federal GST is assessed at 7% across Canada. Provincial sales tax rates vary as shown in Illustration 11-2 and are subject to change:

Province/Territory	Provincial Sales Tax Rate
Alberta	0.0%
British Columbia	7.0%
Manitoba	7.0%
Northwest Territories	0.0%
Nunavut	0.0%
Ontario	8.0%
Prince Edward Island	10.0%
Quebec	7.5%
Saskatchewan	6.0%
Yukon	0.0%

Illustration 11-2
Provincial sales tax rates

As Paul Balchen notes in our feature story about the West Edmonton Mall, the mall owes no provincial sales tax (Alberta has a 0% provincial sales tax rate) but does owe $450,000 of GST. In Newfoundland and Labrador, Nova Scotia, and New Brunswick, the PST and GST have been combined into one 15% **harmonized sales tax (HST)**.

Whether GST, PST, or HST, the retailer collects the tax from the customer when the sale occurs. Periodically (normally monthly), the retailer remits (sends) the GST (or HST) collected to the Receiver General of Canada and PST collections to the provincial Minister of Finance or Treasurer, as the case may be. In the case of GST (or HST), collections may be offset against payments. In such cases, only the net amount owing (recoverable) must be paid (refunded).

The amount of the sale and the amount of the sales tax collected are usually rung up separately on the cash register. The cash register readings are then used to credit sales or services and the respective sales taxes payable accounts. For example, if the March 25 cash register reading for Comeau Company shows sales of $10,000, goods and services tax of $700 (7% GST rate), and provincial sales tax of $800 (8% PST rate), the entry is as follows:

A	=	L	+	OE
+11,500		+700		+10,000
		+800		

Mar. 25	Cash	11,500	
	Sales		10,000
	GST Payable		700
	PST Payable		800
	To record daily sales and sales taxes.		

When the taxes are remitted to the Receiver General and Minister of Finance/Treasurer, the GST Payable and PST Payable (or HST Payable) accounts are debited and Cash is credited. The company does not report sales taxes as an expense. It simply forwards to the government the amount paid by the customer. Comeau Company serves only as a **collection agent** for the government.

Some businesses account for their sales on a tax-inclusive basis. They do not separate sales taxes from the price of the goods purchased. When this occurs, sales taxes must still be recorded separately from sales revenues. To extract the sales amount, divide total receipts by 100% plus the sales tax percentage. To illustrate, assume that Comeau Company has total receipts of $11,500. The receipts from the sale are equal to 100% of the sales price plus 15% (7% + 8%) of sales, or 1.15 times the sales total. We can calculate the sales amount as follows:

$$\$11,500 \div 1.15 = \$10,000$$

The sales tax amounts of $700 and $800 can be found by multiplying sales by the respective sales tax rates ($10,000 × 7% = $700, and $10,000 × 8% = $800).

Helpful hint   In Quebec the PST is called QST.

In some provinces, PST is charged on the total purchase price plus GST. For example, in Quebec a $100 sale includes $7 GST (7%) and $8.02 QST [($100 + $7) × 7.5%]. The escalated sales tax rate is 15% [($7 + $8.02) ÷ $100] rather than 14.5% (7% GST + 7.5% QST). Prince Edward Island also charges 10% PST on the purchase price plus GST. It is important to be careful when extracting sales tax amounts from total receipts, because of the varying rate combinations that may be in use.

▶Accounting in Action ▶ *Business Insight*

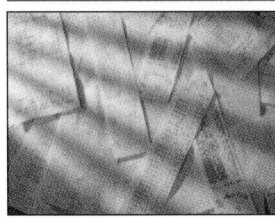

Sales taxes do not apply only to retail companies. They also apply to other types of businesses, such as manufacturing companies, service companies, and public utilities. The extent and complexity of the taxes have increased so much that Canada has the dubious distinction of having one of the world's most complicated sales tax systems. Some movement was made to embrace the principles of a single rate with the institution of the HST in several Atlantic provinces in 1997. However, much more work needs to be done across the country. Catherine McCutcheon, Tax Partner and Head of Arthur Andersen's Commodity Tax Practice, comments: "We have a patchwork of complex sales tax systems in Canada. What we need is consistency across the country. Only with uniformity and simplicity will we be able to realize the projected cost savings of $100 million for provincial governments and between $400 and $700 million for business."

Payroll and Employee Benefits

Every employer incurs liabilities related to employees' salaries or wages. One is the amount of salary or wages owed to employees—**Salaries** or **Wages Payable**. Managerial, administrative, and sales personnel are generally paid salaries. Salaries are often expressed as a specified amount per month or per year. Part-time employees, store clerks, factory employees, and manual labourers are normally paid wages.

Wages are based on a rate per hour or on piecework (an amount per unit of product). The terms salaries and wages are frequently used interchangeably.

Another liability is the amount required by law to be withheld from employees' gross or total pay. These **withholdings** include federal and provincial income taxes, Canada Pension Plan (CPP) contributions, and employment insurance (EI) premiums. Employees may also voluntarily authorize withholdings for charitable, retirement, medical, and other purposes. Until these withholdings are remitted to government taxing authorities or other bodies, they are recorded as increases (credits) to the appropriate liability accounts. Illustration 11-3 summarizes the types of payroll deductions that normally occur.

Illustration 11-3
Payroll deductions

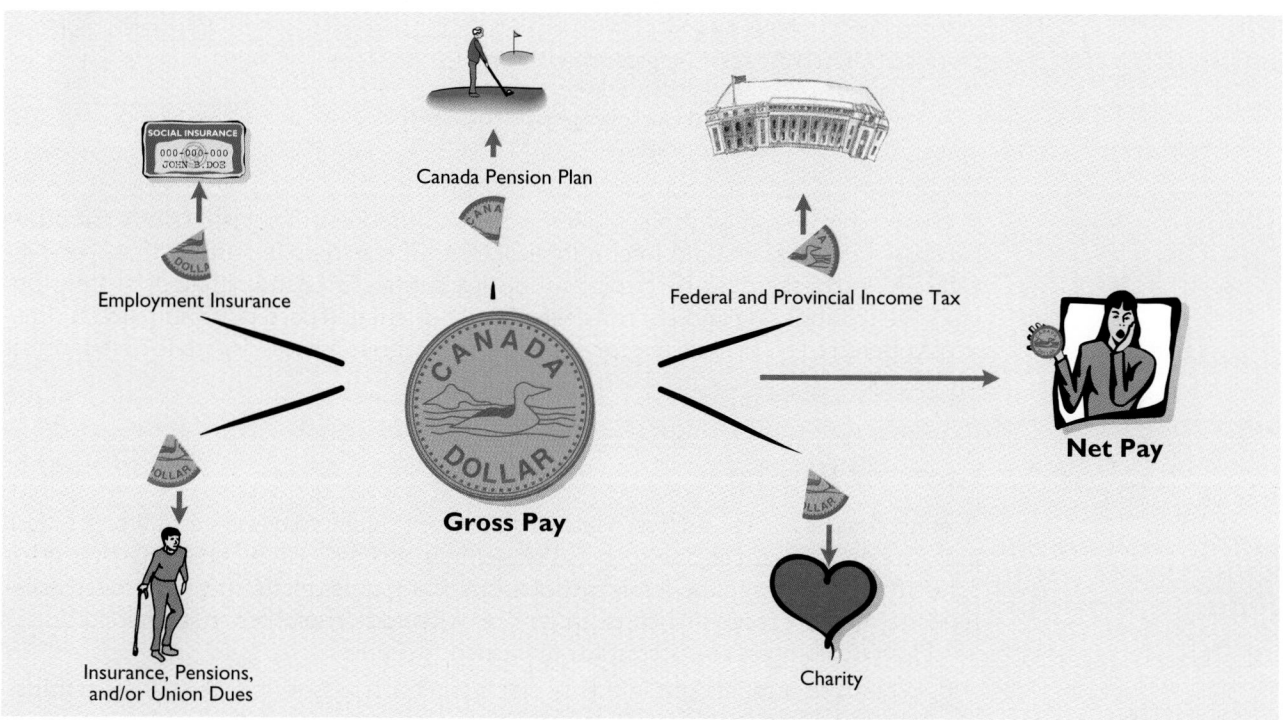

The following entry illustrates the accrual and payment of a $100,000 payroll on which a corporation withholds assumed deductions from its employees' wages and salaries:

				A = L + OE
Mar. 7	Salaries and Wages Expense	100,000		
	CPP Payable		3,870	+3,870 −100,000
	EI Payable		2,250	+2,250
	Income Taxes Payable		30,000	+30,000
	United Way Payable		2,445	+2,445
	Union Dues Payable		1,435	+1,435
	Salaries and Wages Payable		60,000	+60,000
	To record payroll and withholdings for the week ending March 7.			
7	Salaries and Wages Payable	60,000		A = L + OE
	Cash		60,000	−60,000 −60,000
	To record payment of the March payroll.			

The amount recorded in the Salaries and Wages Expense account is called gross earnings. The amount recorded in the Salaries and Wages Payable account is known as net pay. Net pay is calculated by deducting the employee payroll deductions from gross earnings.

While **employee** payroll deductions do not create an expense for employers, **employer** payroll contributions do. With every payroll, the employer incurs liabilities to pay various **payroll costs**. These include costs such as the employer's share of CPP and EI that are levied upon the company. In addition, the provincial governments require employer funding of a Workplace Health, Safety and Compensation Plan. Some provinces also levy an education or health tax on the employer. Each of these contributions, plus items such as paid vacations and employer-sponsored pensions, are collectively referred to as employee benefits.

Based on the $100,000 payroll in our example, the following entry would be made to record the employer's expense and liability for these payroll costs:

A	=	L	+	OE
+3,870		−12,011		
+3,150				
+998				
+3,993				

Mar. 7	Employee Benefits Expense		12,011	
	CPP Payable			3,870
	EI Payable			3,150
	Workers' Compensation Payable			998
	Vacation Pay Payable			3,993
	To record employer payroll costs on the March 7 payroll.			

The payroll and payroll liability accounts are classified as current liabilities because they must be paid to employees, or remitted to taxing authorities, periodically, and in the short term. Taxing authorities impose fines and penalties on employers if the withholding and payroll costs are not calculated correctly and paid on time.

Appendix 11A to this chapter explains more about how to calculate and account for payrolls.

Unearned Revenues

A magazine publisher such as Macleans receives a customer's cheque when magazines are ordered. An airline such as WestJet may receive cash when it sells tickets for future flights. Through these transactions, both companies incur unearned revenues—revenues that are received before goods are delivered or services are provided.

How do companies account for unearned revenues?

1. When the advance payment is received, Cash is debited. A current liability account identifying the source of the unearned revenue is credited.
2. When the revenue is earned, the unearned revenue account is debited. An earned revenue account is credited.

To illustrate, assume that Superior University sells 1,000 season hockey tickets at $200 each for its 25-game home schedule. The entry for the sale of season tickets on September 6 follows:

A	=	L	+	OE
+200,000		+200,000		

Sept. 6	Cash		200,000	
	Unearned Hockey Ticket Revenue			200,000
	To record sale of 1,000 season tickets.			

The balance in the Unearned Hockey Ticket Revenue account is reported as a current liability on the balance sheet. As revenue is earned, a transfer from unearned revenue to earned revenue occurs. As each game is completed, Superior makes the following entry to recognize 1/25 of the revenue ($200,000 × $1/_{25}$ = $8,000):

A	=	L	+	OE
		−8,000		+8,000

Sept. 25	Unearned Hockey Ticket Revenue		8,000	
	Hockey Ticket Revenue			8,000
	To record hockey ticket revenue earned.			

Unearned revenue is significant for some companies. The West Edmonton Mall has $1 million of unearned revenue from advance rent payments from tenants and hockey leagues.

Current Maturities of Long-Term Debt

Companies often have a portion of long-term debt that will be due in the current year. That amount is considered a current liability. Assume that Wynneck Construction issues a five-year, $25,000 note payable on January 1, 2002. Each January 1, starting January 1, 2003, $5,000 of the note is due to be paid. When financial statements are prepared on December 31, 2002, $5,000 should be reported as a current liability. The remaining $20,000 of the note should be reported as a long-term liability on the December 31, 2002, balance sheet.

It is not necessary to prepare an adjusting entry to recognize the current maturity of long-term debt. The proper statement classification of each liability account is recognized when the balance sheet is prepared.

Before You Go On . . .

►*Review It*

1. What are the two criteria for classifying a debt as a current liability?
2. What are some examples of current liabilities?
3. What are three items generally withheld from employees' wages or salaries?
4. Identify three examples of unearned revenues.

►*Do It*

Prepare the journal entries to record the following transactions:
1. Accrue interest on December 31 (year end) for a $10,000, 8%, three-month note payable issued November 1.
2. The cash register total for a four-day craft sale was $256,000. This total included sales taxes. The GST tax rate is 7% and the PST is 8%. Record the sales and sales taxes.
3. A company's gross wages amount to $10,000. Amounts deducted from the employees' wages are CPP of $387, EI of $225, income tax of $3,965, and health insurance of $950. The employer's portion of CPP is $387 and of EI, $315. The wages have been paid to the employees, but the withholdings have not been remitted as yet. Record weekly payroll.

Action Plan

- The formula for interest is as follows: face value × annual interest rate × time.
- Separate sales tax from sales before recording any amounts. Divide the total proceeds by 100% plus the sales tax rates.
- Record both the employees' portion of the payroll and the benefits paid by the employer. Employee deductions are not an expense to the employer.

Solution

1.	Interest Expense ($10,000 × 8% × $2/_{12}$)	133	
	Interest Payable		133
	To accrue interest on note payable.		
2.	Cash	256,000	
	Sales ($256,000 ÷ 115%)		222,608
	GST Payable ($222,608 × 7%)		15,583
	PST Payable ($222,608 × 8%)		17,809
	To record sales and sales taxes.		

3.	Wages Expense	10,000	
	CPP Payable		387
	EI Payable		225
	Income Tax Payable		3,965
	Health Insurance Payable		950
	Cash		4,473
	To record payment of wages.		
	Employee Benefits Expense	702	
	CPP Payable		387
	EI Payable		315
	To record employee benefits.		

THE
NAVIGATOR

Related exercise material: BE11–1, BE11–2, BE11–3, BE11–4, BE11–5, E11–1, E11–2, E11–3, and E11–4.

▼Estimated Liabilities

STUDY OBJECTIVE

••••••••• 3 •••••••••

Explain the accounting, and prepare the journal entries, for estimated liabilities.

An **estimated liability** is an obligation that exists but whose amount and timing are uncertain. However, the uncertainty is not so great that the company cannot reasonably estimate the liability. Commonly estimated liabilities include property taxes payable and warranty liabilities. We discuss these two examples in the following sections. Other examples include employee benefits such as vacation pay and pensions, income tax payable for corporate organizations, employee bonuses, and promotional activities including frequent flyer points for airlines.

►Accounting in Action ► *Business Insight*

The world's first frequent flyer program was launched by American Airlines 20 years ago. Its power as a marketing tool to develop customer loyalty was immediately apparent and the AAdvantage program was copied by airlines around the world.

Airlines have billions of frequent flyer points outstanding, but the liability associated with them is estimated to be much less. This is because not all of these points will be redeemed. In addition, tickets purchased through frequent flyer points are generally considered to be seats that would otherwise go unsold. In Air Canada's case, its frequent flyer liability is estimated to fall between $300 million and $500 million.

Source: Keith McArthur, "Air Canada Cautious With Spinoff." *The Globe and Mail*, May 21, 2001, B1.

Property Taxes

Businesses pay property taxes annually. These taxes are charged by the municipal and provincial governments, and are calculated at a specified rate for every $100 of the assessed value of the property (i.e., land and building). It is difficult to determine the property tax expense as the amount due for the current year is unknown until the bill is received, usually sometime in the spring of each year. Until that time, property taxes must be estimated and accrued. Once the bill is received, the annual expense must be adjusted for the portion already accrued.

To illustrate, assume that Tantramar Management owns land and a building in the city of Regina. Tantramar's year-end is December 31. It receives its property tax bill of $6,000 on March 1, and it is due to be paid on May 31.

For the months of January and February, Tantramar accrues the monthly property tax expense based on last year's property tax bill of $5,520 as follows:

				A	=	L	+	OE
Jan. 31	Property Tax Expense ($5,520 ÷ 12)	460				+460		−460
	Property Tax Payable		460					
	To accrue estimated property tax.							

Tantramar would repeat this entry on February 28. In March, when Tantramar receives the property tax bill, it adjusts its monthly expense for the remaining ten months (March–December) as follows:

Total property tax expense for the year	$6,000
Less: Amount accrued to date ($460 × 2 months)	920
Property tax expense to accrue over remainder of year	5,080
	÷ 10 months
Monthly expense, March to December	$ 508

You will recall from previous chapters that changes in estimates are accounted for in future periods, rather than retroactively.

In March and April, Tantramar accrues monthly property tax expense as follows:

				A	=	L	+	OE
Month End	Property Tax Expense	508				+508		−508
	Property Tax Payable		508					
	To accrue property tax.							

Tantramar repeats this entry on April 30. In May, when Tantramar pays the property tax bill, it (1) satisfies the payable recorded for the last four months (January–April), (2) records the expense for the current month of May, (3) records the property tax now prepaid for the remaining seven months of the year (June–December), and (4) records the payment of the annual property tax. The entry follows:

				A	=	L	+	OE
May 31	Property Tax Payable ($460 + $460 + $508 + $508)	1,936		+3,556		−1,936		−508
	Property Tax Expense	508		−6,000				
	Prepaid Property Tax ($508 × 7 months)	3,556						
	Cash		6,000					
	To pay property tax.							

For the remainder of the year, Tantramar adjusts the prepaid expense for the portion that expires each month as follows:

				A	=	L	+	OE
Month end	Property Tax Expense	508		−508				−508
	Prepaid Property Tax		508					
	To record property tax expense.							

Some companies make annual adjustments rather than monthly adjustments. Either is appropriate.

Product Warranties

Product warranties are another example of a liability that must be estimated in the accounts. Warranty contracts may lead to future costs for replacement or repair of defective units. Generally, a manufacturer such as Black & Decker knows that some warranty costs will be incurred. From prior experience with the product, the company usually can reasonably estimate the anticipated cost of servicing (honouring) the warranty.

The accounting for warranty costs is based on the **matching principle. The estimated cost of honouring product warranty contracts should be recognized as an**

expense in the period in which the sale occurs. To illustrate, assume that in 2002 Hermann Manufacturing Company sells 10,000 washers and dryers at an average price of $600. The selling price includes a one-year warranty on parts. Based on past experience, it is expected that 500 units (5%) will be defective, and that warranty repair costs will average $100 per unit. In 2002, warranty contracts are honoured on 300 units at a total cost of $30,000.

At December 31, it is necessary to accrue the estimated warranty costs on the 2002 sales. The calculation is as follows:

Number of units sold	10,000
Estimated rate of defective units	× 5%
Total estimated defective units	500
Average warranty repair cost	× $100
Estimated product warranty liability	$50,000

The adjusting entry, therefore, is as follows:

A	=	L	+	OE
		+50,000		−50,000

Dec. 31	Warranty Expense	50,000	
	Warranty Liability		50,000
	To accrue estimated warranty costs.		

The entry to record the repair costs incurred in 2002 to honour warranty contracts on sales is shown below:

A	=	L	+	OE
−30,000		−30,000		

Dec. 31	Warranty Liability	30,000	
	Repair Parts Inventory (and/or Wages Payable)		30,000
	To record honouring of 300 warranty contracts		
	on 2002 sales.		

A warranty expense of $50,000 is reported under selling expenses in the income statement. The estimated warranty liability of $20,000 ($50,000 − $30,000) is classified as a current liability on the balance sheet.

In the following year, all expenses incurred to honour warranty contracts on 2002 sales should be debited to the Warranty Liability account. To illustrate, assume that 20 defective units are replaced in January 2003, at an average cost of $100 in parts and labour. The summary entry for the month of January 2003 follows:

A	=	L	+	OE
−2,000		−2,000		

Jan. 31	Warranty Liability	2,000	
	Repair Parts Inventory (and/or Wages Payable)		2,000
	To record honouring of 20 warranty contracts		
	on 2002 sales.		

Before You Go On...

▸*Review It*

THE
NAVIGATOR

1. Distinguish between definitely determinable and estimated liabilities.
2. How do estimated liabilities fulfill the matching principle?

Related exercise material: BE11–6, BE11–7, E11–5, and E11–6.

Contingent Liabilities

The current liabilities in the preceding sections were either **definitely determinable** or **estimable**. There is no uncertainty about their existence. We knew how much was owed and when it was due, or we were able to reasonably estimate this. But suppose your company is currently involved in a dispute with the Canada Customs and Revenue Agency over the amount of the company's income tax liability. Should you report the disputed amount as a liability on the balance sheet? Or suppose your company is involved in a lawsuit, which, if you lose, might result in bankruptcy. Liabilities such as these depend upon the occurrence or non-occurrence of a future event. This event will confirm either the existence of the liability, the amount payable, the payee, and/or the date payable. These are called contingent liabilities.

A contingency exists when there is uncertainty about the outcome. Although contingent receivables exist, contingent liabilities are far more common. *Financial Reporting in Canada* reports that 65% of the 200 public companies surveyed disclosed contingent liabilities. No company reported any contingent receivables.

STUDY OBJECTIVE

⋯⋯⋯⋯ ▼ ⋯⋯⋯⋯
4

Describe the accounting and disclosure requirements for contingent liabilities and prepare the necessary journal entries.

Recording Contingent Liabilities

Recording contingent liabilities is difficult, because these losses and liabilities are dependent—contingent—upon some future event. The principle of conservatism requires that these contingencies be accrued by a debit to an expense (loss) account and a credit to a liability account if **both of the following conditions are met**:

1. The contingency is likely (the chance of occurrence is high); and
2. The amount of the contingency can be reasonably estimated.

Some people find it difficult to distinguish between a contingent liability and an estimated liability. However, remember that estimated liabilities are known to exist; it is only the amount or timing that is unknown. For example, a product warranty liability is dependent on the future failure of a product and that will definitely happen for some of the products sold. Estimates do not constitute the type of uncertainty which characterizes a contingency. Contingent liabilities are for unusual situations and not for ongoing and recurring activities such as product warranties.

► *International note*

International accounting standards use criteria similar to those used in Canada to account for contingencies.

Accounting in Action ► *Business Insight*

Contingencies abound in the real world. Imperial Tobacco Canada's note on contingencies in its financial statements takes up more than an entire page listing all the lawsuits against the company. Environmental contingencies are frequently reported. Companies with underground storage tanks or toxic waste sites can end up with cleanup costs that may reach as high as $500 million depending on the type of contamination or waste.

Disclosure of Contingent Liabilities

When a contingent liability is **likely but cannot be reasonably estimated**, or if it is not determinable—neither likely nor unlikely—only disclosure of the contingency is required. Examples of contingencies that may require disclosure are pending or threatened lawsuits, threat of expropriation of capital assets, and loan guarantees. If a contingency is **unlikely**—the chance of occurrence is slight—it should still be disclosed if the event could have a substantial negative effect on the company's financial position. Otherwise, it need not be disclosed.

The disclosure should identify the nature of the item and the expected outcome of the event. Illustration 11-4 illustrates the disclosure of a contingent liability by Cominco Ltd., a natural resource company headquartered in Vancouver.

Illustration 11-4

Disclosure of contingent liability

COMINCO LTD. **December 31, 1999** **Notes to the Financial Statements**
Note 11 (d) Provisions for Site Restoration and Reclamation Cominco's operations are affected by federal, provincial, state, and local laws and regulations concerning environmental protection. Under current regulations, the company is required to meet performance standards to minimize environmental impact from operations and to perform site restoration and other closure activities. Cominco's provisions for future reclamation and site restoration are based on known requirements. It is not currently possible to estimate the impact on operating results, if any, of future legislative or regulatory developments.

Illustration 11-5 summarizes the treatment of contingent liabilities:

Illustration 11-5

Accounting treatment of contingent liabilities

	Contingent Liability	
Probability of Occurrence	Accrue	Disclose
Likely and reasonably estimable	X	
Likely but not estimable		X
Neither likely nor unlikely (not determinable)		X
Unlikely (but substantial negative effect possible)		X

Before You Go On . . .

▶ *Review It*

1. What are the accounting guidelines for contingent liabilities?
2. Distinguish between estimated liabilities and contingent liabilities.
3. When should a contingent liability be recorded? Disclosed?

Related exercise material: BE11–8 and E11–7.

◥ Financial Statement Presentation

STUDY OBJECTIVE
5

Explain and illustrate the financial statement presentation of current liabilities.

As indicated in Chapter 4, current liabilities are the first category under liabilities on the balance sheet. Each of the principal types of current liabilities is listed separately. In addition, the terms of operating lines of credit, notes payable, and other information concerning the individual items are disclosed in the notes to the financial statements.

Current liabilities are usually listed in **order of liquidity**, by maturity date. Sometimes, it is difficult to determine which specific obligations should be listed in which order. A more common method of presenting current liabilities is to list them by **order of magnitude**, with the largest ones first. Many companies, as a matter of custom, show bank loans, notes payable, and accounts payable first, regardless of amount. The following excerpt from a recent balance sheet of Cominco illustrates this practice:

Illustration 11-6

Balance sheet presentation of current liabilities

COMINCO LTD. Balance Sheet (partial) December 31, 2000 (in millions)	
Current liabilities	
Bank loans and notes payable	$ 5
Accounts payable and accrued liabilities	230
Income and resource taxes	36
Current portion of long-term debt payable	30
	301

Companies must carefully monitor the relationship of current liabilities to current assets. This relationship is critical in evaluating a company's short-term debt-paying ability. A company that has more current liabilities than current assets is usually the subject of some concern, because it may not be able to make its payments when they become due.

Before You Go On

►Review It

1. How does The Second Cup order its current liabilities in its balance sheet? The answer to this question is at the end of the chapter.
2. Describe the disclosure requirements for current liabilities.

Related exercise material: BE11–9, E11–8, E11–9, and E11–10.

THE NAVIGATOR

►A Look Back at Our Feature Story

Refer back to the story about the West Edmonton Mall at the beginning of the chapter. Answer the following questions:

1. What kind of transactions likely gave rise to the West Edmonton Mall's accounts payable of $2 million?
2. Other than those mentioned in the feature story, what additional current liabilities might you expect the West Edmonton Mall to report?
3. Although current assets weren't mentioned in the feature story, do you believe the West Edmonton Mall likely has a positive or negative working capital? Why?

Solution

1. The West Edmonton Mall might incur accounts payable from purchases of supplies (e.g., office and cleaning supplies) on account. It might also owe subcontractors for repairs and maintenance.
2. The West Edmonton Mall might have an operating line of credit that would result in a current liability (demand loan payable) when used. It might also report the current portion of long-term debt.
3. The mall most likely has negative working capital (current liabilities that exceed current assets). Relative to the current liabilities, the company's current assets are likely fairly small. Current assets probably include few accounts receivable (as most tenants pay in advance or at the beginning of the month), some prepaids, and little else. It doesn't report any inventory, since it doesn't sell a product. The current liabilities, on the other hand, are quite large.

DEMONSTRATION PROBLEM

Cornerbrook Company had the following selected transactions:

Feb. 1 Signs a $50,000, six-month, 9% note payable to the CIBC, receiving $50,000 in cash. Interest is payable at maturity.

10 Cash register receipts total $43,200, which includes GST of $2,630 and PST of $3,005.

28 The payroll for the month consists of Sales Salaries of $32,000 and Office Salaries of $18,000. CPP and EI contributions are $2,000 and $1,125, respectively. A total of $15,000 in income taxes is withheld. The salaries are paid on March 1.

28 The following adjustment data are noted:

1. Interest expense has been incurred on the note.
2. Employer payroll costs include CPP of $2,000 and EI of $1,575. The company also pays for a dental plan for its employees, at a monthly cost of $500.
3. Some sales were made under warranty. Of the units sold under warranty this month, 350 are expected to become defective. Repair costs are estimated to be $40 per unit.

Instructions

(a) Journalize the February transactions.

(b) Journalize the adjusting entries at February 28.

Solution to Demonstration Problem

Action Plan

- Employee deductions for CPP, EI, and income tax reduce the Salaries Payable.
- Employer contributions to CPP, EI, and the dental plan create an additional expense.
- Expense warranty costs in the period in which the sale occurs.

(a)	Feb. 1	Cash	50,000	
		Notes Payable		50,000
		Issued 6-month, 9% note to the CIBC.		
	10	Cash	43,200	
		Sales		37,565
		GST Payable		2,630
		PST Payable		3,005
		To record sales and sales taxes payable.		
	28	Sales Salaries Expense	32,000	
		Office Salaries Expense	18,000	
		CPP Payable		2,000
		EI Payable		1,125
		Income Taxes Payable		15,000
		Salaries Payable		31,875
		To record February salaries.		
(b)	Feb. 28	Interest Expense ($50,000 × 9% × $^1/_{12}$)	375	
		Interest Payable		375
		To record accrued interest for February.		
	28	Employee Benefits Expense	4,075	
		CPP Payable		2,000
		EI Payable		1,575
		Dental Plan Payable		500
		To record employee benefit costs for February.		
	28	Warranty Expense (350 × $40)	14,000	
		Warranty Liability		14,000
		To record estimated product warranty liability.		

APPENDIX 11A ► *Payroll Accounting*

Payroll and related fringe benefits make up a large percentage of current liabilities. Employee compensation is often the most significant expense that a company incurs. For example, Air Canada recently reported total employees of 23,000 and labour costs of $1.7 billion, which is 28% of total operating expenses.

Payroll accounting involves more than paying employees' wages. Companies are required by law to maintain payroll records for each employee, to report and remit payroll deductions, and to respect provincial and federal laws related to employee compensation.

The term "payroll" covers all salaries and wages paid to employees. It does not include payments made for services of professionals such as accountants, lawyers, and architects. Such professionals are independent contractors rather than salaried employees. Payments to them are called **fees**, rather than salaries or wages. This distinction is important, because government regulations for the payment and reporting of payroll apply only to employees.

Internal Control

Internal control was introduced in Chapter 8. As applied to payroll, the objectives of internal control are (1) to safeguard company assets against unauthorized payment of payroll, and (2) to ensure the accuracy and reliability of the accounting records for payroll.

Irregularities can result if internal control is lax. Overstating hours, using unauthorized pay rates, adding fictitious employees to the payroll, keeping terminated employees on the payroll, and distributing duplicate payroll cheques are all methods of stealing from a company. Inaccurate records result in incorrect amounts in paycheques, financial statements, and payroll reports.

Payroll activities involve four functions: hiring employees, timekeeping, preparing the payroll, and paying the payroll. For effective internal control, these four functions should be assigned to different departments or individuals. To illustrate these functions, we will examine the case of Academy Company and one of its employees, Mark Jordan.

> **STUDY OBJECTIVE**
> **6**
> *Discuss the objectives of internal control for payroll, and be able to identify weaknesses and suggest improvements in their application.*

Hiring Employees

The human resources department is responsible for posting job openings, screening and interviewing applicants, and hiring employees. From a control perspective, this department provides important documentation and authorization. When Mark Jordan is hired by Academy Company, the human resources department prepares an authorization form detailing the terms of the position (Shipping Clerk), the approved pay rate ($10 per hour), and other relevant information (e.g., starting date).

The authorization form is then sent to the payroll department, where it is used to place the new employee on the payroll. The human resources department must ensure the accuracy of this form, since one of the most common types of payroll fraud is the addition of fictitious employees to the payroll.

Hiring Employees

Human resources department documents and authorizes employment.

▸Accounting in Action ▸ *Business Insight*

Padding the payroll is not a new idea. In 1930, Abitibi's Sturgeon Falls, Ontario, plant closed. The mill was the town's only source of employment. By 1932 the town of Sturgeon Falls was destitute. At that time, employment insurance did not exist but federal and provincial governments paid 85% of welfare relief costs. Civic officials, desperate for relief for their town, padded the welfare payroll with horses. "Owners couldn't buy feed for their horses, so the horses were given jobs by the town," explained one witness to the enquiry commission. One retailer noted, "The town had to have money [to avoid starvation], and there did not appear to be any other way to get it."

Source: Report of the Royal Commission into Unemployment and Relief at Sturgeon Falls, March 1933.

The human resources department is also responsible for changes in employment status. Specifically, it must authorize (1) changes in pay rates, and (2) terminations of employment. Every authorization should be in writing, and a copy of the change in status should be sent to the payroll department.

Timekeeping

Timekeeping

Supervisors monitor hours worked through time cards and time reports.

Another area in which internal control is important is timekeeping. Hourly employees are usually required to record time worked by "punching" a time clock. The time of arrival and departure are automatically recorded by the employee by inserting a time card into the clock.

In large companies, time-clock procedures are often monitored to make sure an employee punches only one card. At the end of the pay period, the employee's supervisor approves the hours shown by signing the time card. When overtime hours are involved, approval by a supervisor is usually mandatory. This guards against unauthorized overtime. The approved time cards are then sent to the payroll department. For salaried employees, a weekly or monthly time report kept by a supervisor may be used to record time worked.

Preparing the Payroll

Preparing the Payroll

Two (or more) employees verify payroll amounts; a supervisor approves.

The payroll is prepared in the payroll department using two inputs: (1) human resources department authorizations, and (2) approved time cards. Numerous calculations are involved in determining gross wages and payroll deductions. A second payroll department employee, working independently, verifies all calculated amounts. A payroll department supervisor approves the payroll. The payroll department is also responsible for preparing (but not signing) payroll cheques, maintaining payroll records, and preparing payroll reports.

Paying the Payroll

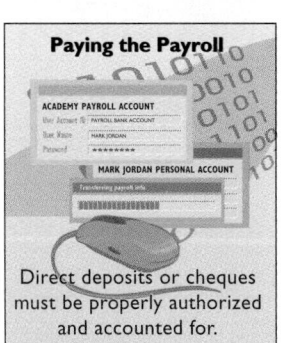

Paying the Payroll

Direct deposits or cheques must be properly authorized and accounted for.

The payroll is the responsibility of the controller's department, or an independent payroll service bureau. Wages and salaries are often transferred electronically by means of direct deposit to each employee's bank account. The controller (or payroll service bureau) provides the bank with a list of individual payroll amounts to be posted to each employee's account. The bank withdraws (debits) the total payroll amount from the company's bank account and deposits (credits) the pay in each employee's personal bank account. **Payment by direct deposit minimizes the risk of errors in cheque preparation.** It is also cost-effective and efficient.

If payroll cheques are used, they should be prenumbered and accounted for to maintain good internal control. Cheques must be signed by the controller (or a designated agent). Their distribution to employees should be controlled by the accounting department. Cheques may be distributed by the controller or a designated paymaster.

Occasionally, the payroll is paid in currency. In such cases, it is customary to have a second person count the cash in each pay envelope. The paymaster should also obtain a signed receipt from the employee upon payment. If alleged discrepancies arise, adequate safeguards then exist to protect each party involved.

►Accounting in Action ► *Business Insight*

Payroll processing is considered by many business owners to be a tedious and painful chore fraught with legal and tax headaches. As a result, service bureaus that process payrolls are very popular. One such example is Ceridian Canada Ltd., a leading provider of payroll services. It accounts for 42,000 payrolls in Canada, paying 16% of the Canadian workforce.

Companies appreciate the advantages that service bureaus such as Ceridian offer—relatively low cost, simplicity, confidentiality, accuracy, fast turnaround, and up-to-date information on changes in payroll deduction rates and regulations.

CERIDIAN

▼Payroll Costs

Payroll costs take two forms—employee costs and employer costs. The first, employee costs, involves both amounts paid to employees (earnings) and amounts paid by employees (payroll deductions). The second, employer costs, involves amounts paid by the employer on behalf of the employee (employee benefits). We will explore employee and employer payroll costs in the following sections.

Determining Employee Payroll Costs

Determining the payroll costs for employees involves calculating (1) gross earnings, (2) payroll deductions, and (3) net pay.

Gross Earnings

Gross earnings is the total compensation earned by an employee. It consists of wages or salaries, plus any bonuses and commissions.

Total **wages** for an employee are determined by multiplying the hours worked by the hourly rate of pay. In addition to the hourly pay rate, most companies are required by law to pay hourly workers at least one and one-half times the minimum hourly wage for overtime work.

Assume that Mark Jordan's authorized pay rate is $10 per hour. The calculation of Mark's gross earnings (total wages) for the 48 hours shown on his time card for the weekly pay period ending June 15 is as follows:

Type of Pay	Hours	×	Rate	=	Gross Earnings
Regular	44	×	$10	=	$440
Overtime	4	×	15	=	60
Total wages					$500

This calculation assumes that Jordan receives one and one-half times his regular hourly rate ($10 × 1.5) for any hours worked in excess of 44 hours per week (overtime). Over-

Helpful hint The average Canadian work week is 42 hours. Employees in 28 other countries, led by Korea, work longer hours.

Illustration 11A-1
Calculation of total wages

time rates can be as much as twice the regular rates.

The **salary** for an employee is generally based on a monthly or yearly rate. These rates are then prorated to the payroll periods used by the company. Most executive and administrative positions are salaried and without overtime pay.

Many companies have bonus agreements for management and other employees. Bonus arrangements may be based on such factors as increased sales or net income. Bonuses may be paid in cash and/or by granting executives and employees the opportunity to acquire shares in the company at favourable prices (called stock option plans).

►Accounting in Action ► *Business Insight*

Jim Shaw, CEO of Shaw Communications, led the 1999 Canadian salary stakes, with more than $30 million in executive compensation. Of this amount, $26 million was in the form of a bonus. Compare this to the average pay earned by CEOs in 1999 in Canada, $444,000; the U.S., $900,000; Japan, $324,000; and the UK, $445,000.

Source: "50 Best Paid Executives." *Report on Business Magazine,* July 2000, 135.

Payroll Deductions

As anyone who has received a paycheque knows, gross earnings are usually very different from the amount actually received. The difference is due to payroll deductions. **Such deductions do not result in an expense to the employer.** The employer is merely a collection agent. It subsequently transfers the deductions to the government or other agency (such as a union, an insurance company, or the United Way). The designated collection agency for the federal government is known as the **Receiver General**, a division of the Canada Customs and Revenue Agency (CCRA).

Payroll deductions may be mandatory or voluntary. Mandatory deductions are required by law and include Canada Pension Plan contributions, employment insurance premiums, and personal income tax. Voluntary deductions are at the option of the employee.

Canada Pension Plan.   All employees between the ages of 18 and 70, except those employed in the Province of Quebec, must contribute to the Canada Pension Plan (CPP). Quebec administers its own similar program, the **Quebec Pension Plan (QPP)**. These plans provide supplemental disability, retirement, and death benefits to qualifying Canadians.

Contribution rates are set by the federal government and are adjusted every January if there are increases in the cost of living. At the time of writing, employee contributions under the *Canada Pension Plan Act* were 4.3% of pensionable earnings. Pensionable earnings are gross earnings less a basic yearly exemption (currently $3,500). A maximum ceiling (currently $38,300) is imposed on pensionable earnings. The exemption and ceiling are prorated to the relevant pay period.

Mark Jordan's CPP contribution for the weekly pay period ending June 15 is $18.61, calculated as follows:

> Salary: $500
> Basic yearly CPP exemption: $3,500
> Prorate basic exemption per week: $3,500 ÷ 52 = $67.31
> Weekly deduction: $500 − $67.31 = $432.69 × 4.3% = $18.61

In addition to withholding employee deductions for remittance to the Receiver General, companies must contribute on behalf of their employees. We will discuss the employer's contributions later in this appendix.

Employment Insurance.   The Canada Pension Plan applies to all employees, whether self-employed or employed by others. Employment insurance is paid only by those employees who are not self-employed. **Employment Insurance (EI)** is designed to provide income protection for a limited period of time to employees who are temporarily laid off, who are on parental leave, or who lose their jobs.

Under the provisions of the *Employee Insurance Act*, an employee is currently required to pay a premium of 2.25% on insured earnings, to a maximum earnings ceiling of $39,000. In most cases, insured earnings are gross earnings plus any taxable benefits. There is no specified yearly exemption. The employment insurance premium for Mark Jordan for the June 15 payroll is $11.25 ($500 × 2.25%).

Personal Income Tax. In accordance with the *Income Tax Act*, employers are required to withhold income tax from employees for each pay period. The amount to be withheld is determined by three variables: (1) the employee's gross earnings, (2) the number of credits claimed by the employee, and (3) the length of the pay period. To indicate to the CCRA the number of credits claimed, the employee must complete a Personal Tax Credits Return (TD1). There is no limit on the amount of gross earnings subject to income tax withholdings. The higher the earnings, the higher the amount of taxes withheld.

The calculation of personal income tax withholdings is complicated. The best way to determine how much should be withheld from an employee's wages for federal and provincial income taxes is to use payroll deductions tables supplied by the CCRA.

Payroll Deductions Tables. Payroll deductions tables indicate the amount of income tax that should be withheld from gross wages based on the number of credits claimed. Separate tables are provided for weekly, biweekly, semimonthly, and monthly pay periods. Income tax deductions vary by province. CPP and EI also vary, but by wage level. The easiest way to determine all of these payroll deductions is to use tables, rather than to try to calculate the deductions. Tables can be requested from your local CCRA office or downloaded in PDF format from the CCRA's website <www.ccra-adrc.gc.ca/tax/business/tod>. Simply download the "Tables on Diskette for Windows." This program, which can also be used directly on the CCRA's website, performs the lookup function and accurately calculates payroll information. Through this site, information returns can also be transmitted electronically.

Illustration 11A-2 shows the results of our inputting payroll information for Mark Jordan. For a weekly salary of $500, with an assumed TD1 claim code of 4, the federal and Ontario provincial income taxes to be withheld total $55.30. CPP and EI contributions are $18.61 and $11.25, respectively.

> **Helpful hint** Combined federal and provincial personal income tax rates range approximately from 23% to 48% depending on the province of residence.

Illustration 11A-2

Payroll deductions

Payroll Deductions for Regular Salary			⊠
Employee's name (optional)	Mark Jordan		
Pay period ending date (optional)	2001-06-15		
Gross salary (or pension income) for the pay period			500.00
EI insurable earnings for the pay period			500.00
Taxable income for the pay period			500.00
Canada Pension Plan (CPP) deductions		18.61	
Employment Insurance (EI) deductions		11.25	
Deductions for federal tax	39.75		
Deductions for provincial tax	15.55		
Total Tax	55.30	55.30	
Requested additional tax deduction		0.00	
Total Deductions		85.16	85.16
Net pay amount			414.84
Federal claim code from the TD1(E)	Claim code 4		
Provincial claim code from the TD1(E)	Claim code 4		
Employer's pay period	Weekly payments (52)		
Province of employment	Ontario		
Print Screen	Cancel		OK

These are the same amounts calculated earlier manually. Whether you calculate employee payroll deductions manually or by using the tables, be careful to use the appropriate guide, as rates, exemptions, and other regulations can and do change often.

Voluntary Deductions.   Employees may voluntarily authorize withholdings for charitable, retirement, and other purposes. All voluntary deductions from gross earnings should be authorized in writing by the employee. The authorization may be made individually or as part of a group plan. Deductions for charitable organizations such as the United Way, or for financial arrangements such as Canada Savings Bonds and repayment of loans from company credit unions, are made individually. In contrast, deductions for union dues, extended health insurance, life insurance, and pension plans are often made on a group basis. For the illustration, we will assume that Jordan has voluntary deductions of $10 for the United Way and $5 for union dues.

Net Pay

Alternative terminology
Net pay is also called *take-home pay.*

Illustration 11A-3

Calculation of net pay

Net pay is determined by subtracting payroll deductions from gross earnings. For Mark Jordan, net pay for the weekly pay period ending June 15 is $399.84, calculated as follows:

Gross earnings		$500.00
Payroll deductions:		
CPP	$18.61	
EI	11.25	
Income tax	55.30	
United Way	10.00	
Union dues	5.00	100.16
Net pay		$399.84

Before we learn how to journalize employee payroll costs and deductions, we will turn our attention to specific *employer* payroll costs. After this discussion, we will record the total employee and employer payroll costs for Academy Company.

Determining Employer Payroll Costs

Employee payroll deductions do not create an expense for the employer. Employer payroll contributions do. Payroll costs for businesses and institutions, like the West Edmonton Mall, result from costs levied on employers by the federal and provincial governments. The federal government requires CPP and EI employer contributions. The provincial governments require employer funding of a Workplace Health, Safety and Compensation Plan. Some provinces also levy an education or health tax on employers. These contributions, plus such items as paid vacations and pensions, are collectively referred to as employee benefits.

Canada Pension Plan

We have seen that each employee must contribute to the Canada Pension Plan. The employer must **match** each employee's CPP contribution. The matching contribution results in an **employee benefits expense** to the employer. The employer's contributions are subject to the same rate and maximum earnings that apply to the employee. The account, CPP Payable, is used for both the employee's and the employer's CPP contributions.

Employment Insurance

Employers are required to contribute 1.4 times an employee's EI deductions during a calendar year. The account EI Payable is used to recognize this liability.

Workplace Health, Safety and Compensation

The Workplace Health, Safety and Compensation Plan provides supplemental benefits for workers who are injured or disabled on the job. The cost of this program is paid entirely by the employer; the employee is not required to make contributions to this plan. Employers are assessed a rate—usually between 1% and 10% of their gross payroll—based on the risk of injury to employees and past experience.

Helpful hint CPP and EI premiums are paid by both the employer and the employee. Workers' compensation is paid entirely by the employer.

Additional Employee Benefits

In addition to the three payroll contributions described above, employers have other employee benefit costs. Two of the most important are paid absences and post-employment benefits. In addition to these, some provinces impose other payroll costs on businesses of certain sizes. For example, Ontario and Quebec have a health tax. Manitoba and Newfoundland have both a health and a post-secondary education tax.

Paid Absences. Employees are given rights to receive compensation for absences when certain conditions of employment are met. The compensation may be for paid vacations, sick pay benefits, and paid holidays. A liability should be estimated and accrued for future paid absences. When the amount cannot be estimated, the potential liability should be disclosed. Ordinarily, vacation pay is the only paid absence that is accrued. Other types of paid absences are only disclosed in notes to the statements.

Helpful hint Paid absences and post-employment benefits are other examples of an estimated liability.

Post-Employment Benefits. Post-employment benefits are payments by employers to retired or terminated employees. These payments are for (1) supplemental health care, dental care, and life insurance, and (2) pensions.

Employers must use the **accrual basis** in accounting for post-employment benefits. It is important to **match** the cost of these benefits with the periods in which the employer benefits from the services of the employee.

Recording the Payroll

Recording the payroll involves maintaining payroll department records, recognizing payroll expenses and liabilities, paying the payroll, and filing and remitting payroll deductions.

Maintaining Payroll Department Records

Employers must provide each employee with a Statement of Remuneration Paid (Form T4), following the end of each calendar year, to file with their personal income tax return. This statement shows employment income, CPP contributions, EI premiums, and income tax deducted for the year, in addition to other voluntary deductions. The record that provides this information and other essential data is the **employee earnings record**. Mark Jordan's employee earnings record for the month of June is shown in Illustration 11A-4. This record includes the pay details calculated in Illustration 11A-2 for the week ending June 15.

ACADEMY COMPANY
Employee Earnings Record
For the Year 2001

Name	Mark Jordan	Address	162 Bowood Avenue
Social Insurance Number	113-114-468		Toronto
Date of Birth	December 24, 1962		Ontario, M4N 1Y6
Date Employed	September 1, 1998	Telephone	416-486-0669
Date Employment Ended		E-mail	jordan@sympatico.ca
Job Title	Shipping Clerk	Claim Code	4

2001 Period Ending	Total Hours	Gross Earnings				Deductions						Payment	
		Regular	Overtime	Total	Cumulative	CPP	EI	Income Tax	United Way	Union Dues	Total	Net Amount	Cheque #
06/01	46	440.00	30.00	470.00	10,470.00	17.32	10.58	66.50	10.00	5.00	109.40	360.60	974
06/08	47	440.00	45.00	485.00	10,955.00	17.96	10.91	69.60	10.00	5.00	113.47	371.53	1028
06/15	48	440.00	60.00	500.00	11,455.00	18.61	11.25	55.30	10.00	5.00	100.16	399.84	1077
06/22	46	440.00	30.00	470.00	11,925.00	17.32	10.58	66.50	10.00	5.00	109.40	360.60	1133
06/29	44	440.00		440.00	12,365.00	16.03	9.90	60.25	10.00	5.00	101.18	338.82	1188
June Total		11,440.00	925.00	12,365.00		528.80	278.21	1,755.50	260.00	130.00	2,952.51	9,412.49	

Illustration 11A-4

Employee earnings record

A separate earnings record is kept for each employee and updated after each pay period. The cumulative payroll data on the earnings record are used by the employer to (1) determine when an employee has reached the maximum earnings subject to CPP and EI premiums, (2) file information returns with the CCRA (as explained later in this section), and (3) provide each employee with a statement of gross earnings and withholdings for the year on the T4 form.

In addition to employee earnings records, many companies find it useful to prepare a payroll register. It accumulates the gross earnings, deductions, and net pay per employee for each pay period and provides the documentation for preparing a paycheque for each employee.

In some companies, the payroll register is a special journal. Postings are made directly to ledger accounts. In other companies, the payroll register is a supplementary record that provides the data for a general journal entry and later posting to the ledger accounts.

In a computerized accounting system, the payroll register is automatically updated from inputted information on the employees' earnings records. The register also supports electronic funds transfers between the company's bank account and those of its employees. Alternatively, the register is used to generate electronically printed payroll cheques. Automatic outputs from a computerized payroll system also include monthly reports for the CCRA and annual T4 slips.

Recognizing Payroll Expenses and Liabilities

Payroll costs are incurred only for the employees' salaries and wages and employer's contributions. Employee payroll deductions are not an expense to the company, since they have been collected for the government or other third party. They remain a current liability to the company until remitted.

Employee Payroll Costs. A journal entry is made to record the employee portion of the payroll. For the week ending June 15, the entry for Academy Company using assumed total amounts from the company's payroll register for the period, is as follows:

June 15	Salaries Expense	5,200.00	
	Wages Expense	12,010.00	
	CPP Payable		654.03
	EI Payable		387.23
	Income Tax Payable		5,646.90
	United Way Payable		421.50
	Union Dues Payable		215.00
	Salaries and Wages Payable		9,885.34
	To record payroll for the week ending June 15.		

```
A    =    L     +   OE
        +654.03    −5,200.00
        +387.23    −12,010.00
      +5,646.90
        +421.50
        +215.00
      +9,885.34
```

Specific liability accounts are credited for the mandatory and voluntary deductions made during the pay period. Separate expense accounts are used for gross earnings, because office workers are on a salary and other employees are paid an hourly rate. The amount credited to Salaries and Wages Payable is the sum of the individual cheques the employees will receive.

Employer Payroll Costs. Employer payroll costs are usually recorded when the payroll is journalized. The entire amount of gross pay is subject to each of the three employer payroll costs mentioned earlier: CPP, EI, and Workers' Compensation. For the June 15 payroll, Academy Company's CPP is $654.03 ($654.03 × 1). Its EI premium is $542.12 ($387.23 × 1.4).

Assume that Academy Company is also assessed workers' compensation at a rate of 1%. It compensation expense for the week would therefore be $172.10 [($5,200 + $12,010) × 1%]. For vacation pay, assume that Academy Company employees accrue vacation days at an average rate of 4% of the gross payroll (equivalent to two weeks of vacation). The accrual for vacation benefits in one pay period—one week—is $688.40 [($5,200 + $12,010) × 4%]. Academy Company is exempt from Ontario's health tax.

Accordingly, the entry to record the payroll costs or employee benefits associated with the June 15 payroll is as follows:

June 15	Employee Benefits Expense	2,056.65	
	CPP Payable		654.03
	EI Payable		542.12
	Workers' Compensation Payable		172.10
	Vacation Pay Payable		688.40
	To record employer payroll costs on June 15 payroll.		

```
A    =    L     +   OE
        +654.03    −2,056.65
        +542.12
        +172.10
        +688.40
```

The liability accounts are classified as current liabilities, since they will be paid within the next year. Employee Benefits Expense is often combined with Salaries and Wages Expense on the income statement, and classified as an operating expense.

Recording Payment of the Payroll

Payment by cheque or electronic funds transfer is made from either the employer's regular bank account or a payroll bank account. Each paycheque or EFT is usually accompanied by a **statement of earnings** document. This shows the employee's gross earnings, payroll deductions, and net pay for the period and for the year to date.

Following payment of the payroll, the cheque numbers are entered in the payroll register. The entry to record payment of the payroll for Academy Company follows:

June 15	Salaries and Wages Payable	9,885.34	
	Cash		9,885.34
	To record payment of payroll.		

```
A      =    L       +   OE
−9,885.34   −9,885.34
```

Many companies use a separate bank account for payroll. Only the total amount of each period's payroll is transferred, or deposited, into that account prior to distribution. This helps the company determine if there are any unclaimed amounts. This is another example of an imprest fund, first introduced with petty cash in Chapter 8.

Filing and Remitting Payroll Deductions

Preparation of information returns is the responsibility of the payroll department. Payment of the deductions is made by the controller's department. Much of the information for the returns is obtained from employee earnings records.

For the purposes of reporting and remitting, companies combine withholdings of CPP, EI, and income tax. **The withholdings must be reported and remitted monthly** on a Statement of Account for Current Source Deductions (Form PD7A), no later than the 15th day of the month following the month's pay period. There are allowable variations from the pattern of monthly remittances. For example, large employers must remit more often, and smaller companies with perfect payroll deduction remittance records can remit quarterly. Workplace Health, Safety and Compensation is remitted quarterly to the Workplace Health, Safety and Compensation Commission. Remittances can be made by mail or through deposits at any Canadian financial institution. When payroll deductions are remitted, payroll liability accounts are debited and cash is credited.

The entry to record the remittance of payroll deductions by Academy Company, in the following month, is as follows:

Alternative terminology
The commission is known as the *Workers' Compensation Board* (or similar) in some provinces.

A	=	L	+	OE
−9,381.31		−1,308.06		
		−929.35		
		−5,646.90		
		−421.50		
		−215.00		
		−172.10		
		−688.40		

July 13	CPP Payable ($654.03 + $654.03)	1,308.06	
	EI Payable ($387.23 + $542.12)	929.35	
	Income Tax Payable	5,646.90	
	United Way Payable	421.50	
	Union Dues Payable	215.00	
	Workers' Compensation Payable	172.10	
	Vacation Pay Payable	688.40	
	Cash		9,381.31
	To record payment of payroll deductions for		
	June 15 payroll.		

Other information returns must be filed by the last day of February each year. In addition, as noted previously, employers must provide employees with a Statement of Remuneration Paid (T4) by the same date.

Before You Go On . . .

▶Review It

1. Identify two internal control procedures that are applicable to each payroll function.
2. What payroll deductions are (a) mandatory, and (b) voluntary?
3. What payroll costs result in an expense for the employer?

▶Do It

On February 15, the payroll supervisor determines that the biweekly gross earnings in the Rebagliati Company are $70,000. Employee deductions include $2,795 of CPP, $1,575 of EI, $21,000 of personal income tax, and $1,000 of dental insurance. You are asked to record the employee and employer payroll costs for this period, and the payment of all payroll liabilities on March 15. For the employer's payroll contributions, there is no Workplace Health, Safety and Compensation Plan, pension plan, or vacation pay to record at this point.

Action Plan

- Gross payroll forms the Salaries and Wages Expense. Gross payroll less employee deductions equals net pay.
- Employee deductions are current liabilities until remitted.
- Employer deductions are also current liabilities. They also form Employee Benefits Expense. The employer must match CPP and pay 1.4 times the employee's EI premiums.

Solution

The entry to record the employees' payroll costs is:

Feb. 15	Salaries and Wages Expense	70,000	
	CPP Payable		2,795
	EI Payable		1,575
	Income Tax Payable		21,000
	Dental Insurance Payable		1,000
	Salaries and Wages Payable		43,630
	To record payroll for the biweekly period ending Feb. 15.		

The entry to record the employer's payroll costs is:

Feb. 15	Employee Benefits Expense	5,000	
	CPP Payable ($2,795 × 1)		2,795
	EI Payable ($1,575 × 1.4)		2,205
	To record employer's payroll costs on Feb. 15 payroll.		

The entry to pay the liabilities is:

Mar. 15	Salaries and Wages Payable	43,630	
	CPP Payable ($2,795 + $2,795))	5,590	
	EI Payable ($1,575 + $2,205)	3,780	
	Income Tax Payable	21,000	
	Dental Insurance Payable	1,000	
	Cash		75,000
	To record payment of payroll and related liabilities for the biweekly period ending Feb. 15.		

*Related exercise material: *BE11–10, *BE11–11, *BE11–12, *BE11–13, *BE11–14, *E11–11, *E11–12, *E11–13, *E11–14, and *E11–15.*

THE NAVIGATOR

Summary of Study Objectives

1. Explain a current liability and distinguish between the major types of current liabilities. A current liability is a debt that is likely to be paid as follows: (1) within one year or the operating cycle, whichever is longer, and (2) from existing current assets or through the creation of other current liabilities. There are three major types of liabilities. Definitely determinable liabilities are those with no uncertainty as to existence, amount, or timing. Estimated liabilities exist, but their amount or timing is uncertain. Contingent liabilities depend on a future event to confirm their existence (and possibly the amount and timing).

2. Explain the accounting, and prepare the journal entries, for definitely determinable current liabilities. Operating lines of credit help companies cover temporary bank overdrafts, and are repayable upon demand. Interest is normally paid and recorded monthly on these demand loans.

When an interest-bearing promissory note payable is issued, interest expense is accrued over the life of the note.

At maturity, the amount paid is equal to the face value of the note plus any accrued interest.

Sales taxes payable are recorded at the time the related sales occur. The company serves as a collection agent for the taxing authority. Sales taxes are not an expense to the company.

In recording payroll, wage or salary expense is debited for the gross payroll. Employee deductions are credited to current liability accounts until remitted. The employer's share of the withholdings are debited from Employee Benefits Expense and credited to current liability accounts until remitted.

Unearned revenues are initially recorded in an unearned revenue account. As the revenue is earned, a transfer from unearned revenue to earned revenue occurs.

The current maturities of long-term debt should be reported as a current liability in the balance sheet.

3. *Explain the accounting, and prepare the journal entries, for estimated liabilities.* Property taxes are estimated and accrued until the actual property tax amount becomes known. At that time, the property tax expense and payable accounts for the remainder of the year are adjusted for the portion already accrued. Product warranties are estimated and recorded as an expense and a liability in the period in which the sales occur. This liability is reduced as repairs under warranty occur and is adjusted annually for outstanding or expired warranties.

4. *Describe the accounting and disclosure requirements for contingent liabilities and prepare the necessary journal entries.* If it is probable that the contingency will happen (if it is likely to occur) and the amount is reasonably estimable, the liability should be recorded in the accounts. However, if the contingency is probable but the amount is not estimable, or if the likelihood is not determinable, then the contingency should be disclosed in the notes to the statements.

5. *Explain and illustrate the financial statement presentation of current liabilities.* The nature and amount of

each current liability and contingency should be reported in the balance sheet or in the notes accompanying the financial statement.

6. *Discuss the objectives of internal control for payroll, and be able to identify weaknesses and suggest improvements in their application.* The objectives of internal control for payroll are (1) to safeguard company assets against unauthorized payroll payments, and (2) to ensure the accuracy and reliability of the accounting records for payrolls (Appendix 11A).

7. *Calculate the payroll for a pay period.* In recording employee payroll costs, salaries (or wages) expense is debited for gross earnings, individual tax and other liability accounts are credited for payroll deductions, and salaries (wages) payable is credited for net pay. In recording employer payroll costs, Employee Benefits Expense is debited for the employer's share of CPP, EI, workers' compensation, vacation pay, and any other benefits provided. Each benefit is credited to its respective current liability account (Appendix 11A).

GLOSSARY

Bonus Compensation to management and other employees, based on factors such as increased sales or net income. (p. 532)

Canada Pension Plan (CPP) Contributions designed to provide workers with supplemental retirement, disability, and death benefits. (p. 532)

Collateral Property pledged as security for a loan. (p. 515)

Contingent liability A potential liability that may become an actual liability in the future. (p. 525)

Definitely determinable liability A liability with no uncertainty as to existence, amount, or timing. (p. 515)

Employee benefits Payments made by an employer, in addition to wages and salaries, to provide pension, insurance, medical, or other benefits for its employees. (p. 520)

Employment insurance (EI) Premiums that provide benefits and assistance for a limited time period, to employees who are no longer employed. (p. 533)

Estimated liability An existing liability whose amount or timing is uncertain and must be estimated. (p. 522)

 Key Term Matching Activity

Gross earnings Total compensation earned by an employee. Also known as gross pay. (p. 519)

Net pay Gross earnings less payroll deductions. (p. 519)

Notes payable Obligations in the form of written promissory notes. (p. 516)

Operating line of credit Pre-authorized approval to borrow money at a bank, up to a preset limit, when required. (p. 515)

Payroll deductions Deductions from gross earnings to determine the amount of a paycheque. (p. 532)

Payroll register A payroll record that accumulates the gross earnings, deductions, and net pay by employee for each pay period. (p. 536)

Salaries Specified amounts per month or per year paid to executive and administrative personnel. (p. 518)

Wages Amounts paid to employees based on a rate per hour or on piecework. (p. 518)

Note: All **asterisked** Questions, Exercises, and Problems below relate to material contained in the appendix to the chapter.

SELF-STUDY QUESTIONS

Chapter 11 Self-Test

Answers are at the end of the chapter.

(SO 1) K   1. The time period for classifying a liability as current is one year or the operating cycle, whichever is:
    a. longer.   c. probable.
    b. shorter.   d. possible.

(SO 1) K   2. To be classified as a current liability, a debt must be expected to be paid:
    a. out of existing current assets.
    b. by creating other current liabilities.
    c. within two years.
    d. either (a) or (b)

(SO 2) AP   3. Gilbert Company borrows $88,500 on September 1, 2002, from the Bank of Nova Scotia by signing an $88,500, 6% note due September 1, 2003. Interest is payable at maturity. What is the accrued interest at December 31, 2002?
    a. $1,327.50   c. $1,770.00
    b. $1,760.00   d. $5,310.00

(SO 2) AP   4. Reeves Company has total proceeds from sales of $4,515. If the proceeds include GST of 7% and PST of 8%, the amount (rounded to the nearest dollar) to be credited to Sales is:
    a. $3,838.   c. $4,000.
    b. $3,926.   d. $5,192.

(SO 2) K   5. Employer payroll costs do not include:
    a. employment insurance.
    b. Canada Pension Plan.
    c. income tax deducted from employees' earnings.
    d. workers' compensation.

(SO 2) K   6. The account Unearned Subscription Revenue:
    a. is a revenue account.
    b. has a normal debit balance.
    c. is a contra account to Subscription Revenue.
    d. is a current liability.

(SO 3) K   7. Harmonized Sales Tax (HST) collected by a retailer is recorded by:
    a. crediting Sales Revenue.
    b. crediting HST Payable.
    c. debiting HST Recoverable.
    d. The retailer does not record HST. The customer pays this amount directly to the government on April 30 of each year.

(SO 3) AP   8. On January 1, 2003, Swift Current Company estimates that its property tax for the current year will be $12,000. On March 1, Swift Current receives its prop- erty tax assessment of $14,000 for 2003. The property tax bill is due May 1. If Swift Current prepares quarterly financial statements, how much property tax expense should the company report for the quarter ended March 31, 2003?
    a. $3,000   c. $3,500
    b. $3,200   d. $14,000

9. Recording estimated warranty expense in the year of the sale best follows which accounting principle? (SO 3) K
    a. Consistency
    b. Full disclosure
    c. Matching
    d. Materiality

10. If a contingent liability is reasonably estimable and it is likely that the contingency will occur, the contingent liability: (SO 4) K
    a. should be accrued in the accounts.
    b. should be disclosed in the notes accompanying the financial statements.
    c. should not be recorded or disclosed until the contingency actually happens.
    d. must be paid immediately.

11. Current liabilities are listed in the balance sheet in order of: (SO 5) K
    a. liquidity (due date).
    b. magnitude.
    c. In no particular order
    d. All of the above

*12. The department that should pay the payroll is the: (SO 6) K
    a. timekeeping department.
    b. human resources department.
    c. purchasing department.
    d. controller's department.

*13. Rebecca works for the Blue Company at a salary of $550 per week. Canada Pension Plan contributions are $20.76 for the employee and the same for the employer. Income taxes are $88.75. Employment Insurance premiums are $12.38 for the employee, and $17.33 for the employer. Rebecca's weekly net (take-home) pay is: (SO 7) AP
    a. $390.02.   c. $461.25.
    b. $428.11.   d. $550.00.

THE NAVIGATOR

QUESTIONS

(SO 1) K 1. Li Feng believes a current liability is a debt that is likely to be paid in one year. Is Li correct? Explain.

(SO 2) C 2. (a) Your roommate says, "Sales taxes are reported as expenses in the income statement." Do you agree? Explain. (b) Hard Walk Café has cash proceeds from sales of $10,700. This amount includes $700 in GST. Give the entry to record the proceeds.

(SO 2) AP 3. Gridiron University sold 1,000 season football tickets at $90 each for its five-game home schedule. What entries should be made (a) when the tickets are sold, and (b) after each game?

(SO 2) C 4. Is the income tax withheld from an employee paycheque an expense for the employer? Explain your answer.

(SO 2) C 5. Distinguish between the types of payroll deductions, and give examples of each.

(SO 2) K 6. Identify the main types of employer payroll costs.

(SO 2) C 7. Anwar Company incurred a long-term liability of $100,000 on January 1, 2003. Of this debt, $25,000 must be repaid annually, each January 1. Explain how Anwar should classify this liability on its December 31, 2003, balance sheet.

(SO 3) C 8. The accountant for Amiable Appliances feels that warranty expense should not be recorded unless an appliance is returned for repair. Otherwise, how do you know if the appliance will be returned, and if so, how much it will cost to fix? Do you agree? Explain.

(SO 3) C 9. Explain how recording property taxes can result in both a liability (property tax payable) and an asset (prepaid property tax) in the same year.

10. How are estimated and contingent liabilities alike? (SO 3, 4) K How do they differ?

11. What is a contingent liability? Give an example of a (SO 4) C contingent liability that is likely but not estimable, and an example of a contingency that is not determinable.

12. Under what circumstances is a contingent liability (SO 4) C recorded in the accounts? Under what circumstances is a contingent liability disclosed only in the notes to the financial statements?

13. St. Lawrence Company obtains $25,000 in cash on July (SO 5) C 1 by signing a 9%, six-month, $25,000 note payable to the National Bank. St. Lawrence's fiscal year ends on September 30. What information should be reported for the note payable in the annual financial statements?

14. In what order should current liabilities be listed on the (SO 5) K balance sheet?

*15. You are a newly hired accountant with Steeples Com- (SO 6) C pany. On your first day, the controller asks you to identify the main internal control objectives related to payroll accounting. How do you respond?

*16. What are the primary uses of the employee earnings (SO 6) K record?

*17. Identify two types of employee benefits commonly (SO 6) K associated with employee compensation.

*18. What is the difference between gross pay and net pay? (SO 7) C Which amount (gross or net) should a company record as wages or salaries expense?

*19. What are paid absences? How are they accounted for? (SO 7) K

BRIEF EXERCISES

Identify current liabilities.
(SO 1) K

BE11–1 Passera Company has the following obligations at December 31: (a) a note payable for $100,000 due in two years, (b) a 10-year mortgage payable of $300,000, payable in ten $30,000 annual payments, (c) interest payable of $24,000 on the mortgage, and (d) accounts payable of $60,000. For each obligation, indicate what portion (if any) should be classified as a current liability.

Identify current liabilities.
(SO 1) K

BE11–2 Identify which of the following transactions would be classified as a current liability. For those that are not current liabilities, identify where they should be classified.
1. A product warranty on an IBM Thinkpad
2. A demand loan
3. Cash received in advance by WestJet Airlines for airline tickets
4. PST collected on sales
5. GST collected on sales
6. Cash receipts from sales
7. Interest owing on an overdue account payable
8. Interest due on an overdue account receivable
9. A lawsuit pending against the company
10. Amounts withheld from the employees' weekly pay
11. Property tax payable

BE11–3   Bourque Company borrows $60,000 from the bank on July 1, 2002, by signing a $60,000, 10% note payable. Interest and principal are due on July 1, 2003.
  (a) Prepare the journal entries to record the receipt of the proceeds of the note.
  (b) Prepare the journal entry to record accrued interest at December 31, 2002, assuming adjusting entries are made only at the end of the year.

Prepare entries for note payable. (SO 2) AP

BE11–4   Auto Supply Company does not segregate sales and sales taxes at the time of sale. The register total for March 16 is $6,900. All sales are subject to 7% GST and 8% PST. Calculate the sales taxes payable, and make the entry to record the sales and the sales taxes payable.

Calculate and record sales taxes payable. (SO 2) AP

BE11–5   Centennial College sells 2,000 season basketball tickets at $90 each for its 12-game home schedule. Give the entry to record (a) the sale of the season tickets, and (b) the revenue earned by playing the first home game.

Prepare entries for unearned revenues. (SO 2) AP

BE11–6   Pierce Co. has a June 30 fiscal year end. It estimated its annual property taxes to be $24,000, based on last year's property tax bill, and had accrued $2,000 of property tax each month to March 31. Its actual property tax assessment, received on April 30, is $25,200 for the calendar year. The property tax bill is payable on July 15. How much property tax expense will Pierce report on its June 30 income statement? How much property tax payable and/or prepaid property tax will Pierce report at June 30 on its balance sheet?

Determine amounts reported for property tax. (SO 3) AP

BE11–7   On December 1, Ng Company introduces a new product that includes a one-year warranty on parts. In December, 1,000 units are sold. Management believes that 5% of the units will be defective and that the average warranty cost will be $75 per unit. Prepare the adjusting entry at December 31 to accrue the estimated warranty cost.

Prepare adjusting entry for warranty costs. (SO 3) AP

BE11–8   Athabasca Toil & Oil Company is a defendant in a lawsuit for improper discharge of pollutants and waste into the Athabasca River. Athabasca's lawyers have advised that the company will likely lose this lawsuit and that it could settle out of court for $50,000. How should Athabasca journalize this current liability? What are the arguments for and against recording this contingent liability?

Record contingent liability. (SO 4) AP

BE11–9   **MGI Software** reports the following selected liabilities (in thousands) at January 31, 2000. The liabilities are listed in alphabetical order.

Accounts payable and accrued liabilities	$10,632
Current portion of long-term debt	167
Long-term debt	165
Unearned revenue	1,013

Prepare the current liabilities section of MGI's balance sheet, in good format, at January 31, 2000.

Prepare current liabilities section of balance sheet. (SO 5) AP

BE11–10   Gutierrez Company has the following payroll procedures:
  1. Supervisor approves overtime work.
  2. Human resources department prepares hiring authorization forms for new employees.
  3. A second payroll department employee verifies payroll calculations.
  4. Controller's department pays the employees.

Identify the main payroll function for each procedure.

Identify payroll functions. (SO 6) K

BE11–11   Becky Sherrick's regular hourly wage rate is $15, and she receives an hourly rate of $22.50 for work in excess of 40 hours. During a January pay period, Becky works 43 hours. Becky's income tax withholding is $120.20. CPP deductions total $25.81. EI deductions total $15.02. Calculate Becky's gross earnings and net pay for the pay period.

Calculate gross earnings and net pay. (SO 7) AP

BE11–12   Data for Becky Sherrick are presented in BE11–11. Prepare the journal entries to record (a) Becky's pay for the period, and (b) the payment of Becky's wages. Use January 15 for the end of the pay period and the payment date.

Record payroll and payment of wages. (SO 7) AP

BE11–13   In January, gross earnings in the Bri Company totalled $70,000, from which $2,730 was deducted for the Canada Pension Plan, $1,575 for Employment Insurance, and $15,300 for income tax. Prepare the entries to record the January payroll, including the employee benefit costs.

Record employer payroll costs. (SO 7) AP

BE11–14   At Sublette.Com, employees are entitled to one day's vacation for each month worked. In January, 50 employees worked the full month. Record the vacation pay liability for January, assuming the average daily pay for each employee is $150.

Record vacation pay benefits. (SO 7) AP

EXERCISES

Journalize note payable.
(SO 2) AP

E11–1   On May 31, Microchip Company borrows $50,000 and issues a six-month, 9% note, due on November 30. Interest is payable at maturity.

Instructions

(a) Prepare the entry on May 31.
(b) Prepare the adjusting entry on June 30, Microchip's year end.
(c) Prepare the entry at maturity, assuming monthly adjusting entries have not been made since June 30.
(d) What is the total financing cost (interest expense)?

Journalize note receivable and note payable.
(SO 2) AP

E11–2   Briffet Construction borrows $250,000 from the TD Bank on October 1, 2003. It signs a two-year, 10% note payable. Interest is payable monthly.

Instructions

(a) Prepare the journal entries to record the transactions on October 1, 2003, and the first interest payment on November 1 for Briffet Construction. Round your answers to the nearest dollar.
(b) Prepare the journal entries to record the transactions on October 1, 2003, and the first interest receipt on November 1 for the TD Bank. (*Hint*: You might find it helpful to review accounting for notes receivable in Chapter 9.)

Journalize sales and sales taxes.
(SO 2) AP

E11–3   In providing accounting services to small businesses, you encounter the following situations:

1. Sainsbury Company rings up sales and sales taxes separately on its cash register. On April 10, the register totals are sales $25,000, GST $1,750, and PST $2,006.
2. Hockenstein Company does not segregate sales and sales taxes. Its register total for April 15 is $18,240, which includes 7% GST and 7% PST.

Instructions

Prepare the entry to record the sales transactions and related taxes for each client.

Journalize unearned subscription revenue.
(SO 2) AP

E11–4   Westwood Company publishes a monthly extreme sports magazine, *Adventure Time*. Subscriptions to the magazine cost $36 per year. During November 2002, Westwood sells 6,000 subscriptions which begin with the December issue. Westwood prepares financial statements quarterly and recognizes subscription revenue earned at the end of each quarter. Westwood's year end is December 31.

Instructions

(a) Prepare the entry in November for the receipt of the subscriptions.
(b) Prepare the adjusting entry at December 31, 2002, to record subscription revenue earned in December.
(c) Prepare the adjusting entry at March 31, 2003, to record subscription revenue earned in the first quarter of 2003.

Journalize warranty costs.
(SO 3) AP

E11–5   Sinclair Company sells automatic can openers under a 90-day warranty for defective merchandise. Based on past experience, Sinclair estimates that 4% of the units sold will become defective during the warranty period. Management estimates that the average cost of replacing or repairing a defective unit is $10. The units sold and units defective during the last two months of 2002 are as follows:

Month	Units Sold	Units Defective
November	30,000	700
December	32,000	500

Instructions

(a) Determine the estimated warranty liability at December 31 for the units sold in November and December.
(b) Prepare the journal entries to record (1) the estimated liability for warranties, and (2) the costs (assume actual costs of $12,000) incurred in honouring the 1,200 warranty claims as of December 31.
(c) Give the entry to record the honouring of 550 warranty claims in January, at an average cost of $10 per claim.

E11–6   Seaboard Co. receives its property tax bill for the calendar year for $26,400 on May 1, payable July 1. Prior to receiving this bill, it had estimated that its property taxes would be $24,000. Seaboard accrues property taxes monthly and has a September 30 year end.

Journalize property tax.
(SO 3) AP

Instructions

(a) Prepare the journal entry necessary to record the accrual of the property tax expense for each of the months from October through April.

(b) Prepare the journal entry to record the property tax expense for the months of May and June.

(c) Prepare the journal entry to record the payment of the property tax bill on July 1.

(d) Prepare the journal entry to record the property tax expense for the months of August and September.

E11–7   The Sleep-a-Bye Baby Company is the defendant in a lawsuit alleging that its portable baby cribs are unsafe. The company has offered to replace the crib free of charge for any concerned parent. Nonetheless, it has been sued for damages and distress amounting to $500,000. The company plans to vigorously defend its product safety record in court.

Analyse contingent liability.
(SO 4) AP

Instructions

What should the company record or report in its financial statements for this situation? Explain why.

E11–8   **Bombardier** reports the following liabilities (in millions) on its January 31, 2001, balance sheet and notes to the financial statements:

Identify current liabilities. Prepare current liabilities section of balance sheet.
(SO 1, 5) AP

Accounts payable	$2,142.3
Accrued benefit liability	494.4
Accrued liabilities	1,534.9
Advances on long-term contracts	2,362.8
Current portion of long-term debt	974.6
Deferred income taxes	944.4
Income taxes payable	91.3
Long-term debt	5,156.6
Payroll-related liabilities	359.4
Short-term borrowings	2,531.2
Unused operating line of credit	4,123.7

Instructions

(a) Identify which of the above liabilities are likely current liabilities and which are long-term liabilities. Say if an item fits in neither category. Explain the reasoning for your selection.

(b) Prepare the current liabilities section of Bombardier's balance sheet as at January 31, 2001.

E11–9   Atkinson On-line has the following liability accounts at August 31, 2003, after posting adjusting entries: Accounts Payable $66,000, Unearned Revenue $24,000, Property Tax Payable $8,000, Warranty Liability $18,000, Interest Payable $8,000, Mortgage Payable $120,000, Notes Payable $80,000, and Provincial Sales Tax Payable $10,000. Assume warranty costs are expected to be incurred within one year. Of the mortgage, $10,000 is due each year. The notes mature in three years.

Prepare current liabilities section of balance sheet. Calculate current ratio.
(SO 5) AP

Instructions

(a) Prepare the current liabilities section of the balance sheet.

(b) Calculate Atkinson's current ratio, assuming total current assets are $300,000.

E11–10   **Loew's Cineplex Entertainment Corporation** has theatres in Canada, the U.S., Austria, Hungary, Spain, Turkey, and Italy. Its February 28, 2001, financial statements contained the following selected data (in thousands of U.S. dollars):

Prepare current liabilities section of balance sheet. Calculate liquidity ratios.
(SO 5) AP

Accounts payable and accrued expenses	$ 88,059
Accounts receivable	11,453
Cash and cash equivalents	47,200
Current maturities of long-term debt and other obligations	739,665
Inventories	4,056
Prepaid expenses and other current assets	7,340
Unearned revenue	22,423

Instructions

(a) Prepare the current liabilities section of Loew's balance sheet at February 28, 2001.
(b) Calculate these values:
   1. Total current assets for Loew's
   2. Working capital
   3. Current ratio

Identify internal control for payroll.
(SO 6) AN

*E11–11   The **Ottawa International Hostel** has 18 employees on its payroll. Four of the employees are full-time. Their salaries are determined by contracts approved by the hostel's board of directors. The remaining employees are hired through verbal agreements. They are paid by the hour. Their time worked is tracked by having them sign in and out of a log book. A payroll service bureau, Comcheq, calculates the payroll deductions and pays the payroll through direct deposit. Employees and the hostel receive detailed and summary reports every pay period.

Instructions

(a) Identify the internal controls used by the hostel in its payroll procedures.
(b) Identify any weaknesses in internal controls in the payroll procedures used by the hostel.

Calculate payroll amounts and record payment to employee.
(SO 7) AP

*E11–12   Donna Grace's regular hourly wage rate is $12, and she receives a wage of 1.5 times the regular hourly rate for work in excess of 40 hours. During a September weekly pay period, Donna worked 42 hours. Donna lives in Alberta and has a claim code of 1 for tax deductions.

After this information is inputted, the following information is generated:

Payroll Deductions for Regular Salary			✕
Employee's name (optional)	**Donna Grace**		
Pay period ending date (optional)	**2001-09-13**		
Gross salary (or pension income) for the pay period			516.00
EI insurable earnings for the pay period			516.00
Taxable income for the pay period			516.00
Canada Pension Plan (CPP) deductions		19.29	
Employment Insurance (EI) deductions		11.61	
Deductions for federal tax	54.80		
Deductions for provincial tax	24.90		
Total Tax	79.70	79.70	
Requested additional tax deduction		0.00	
Total Deductions		110.60	110.60
Net pay amount			405.40
Federal claim code from the TD1(E)	Claim code 1		
Provincial claim code from the TD1(E)	Claim code 1		
Employer's pay period	Weekly payments (52)		
Province of employment	Alberta		
Print Screen	Cancel		OK

Instructions

Record the payment of Donna's pay on September 13.

Journalize payroll and employee benefits expense.
(SO 7) AP

*E11–13   Ahmad Company has the following data for the weekly payroll ending January 31:

Employee	Hours Worked M Tu W Th F S	Hourly Rate	Income Tax Withholding	Health Insurance
A. Hope	8 8 9 8 10 0	$10	$ 74	$10
B. Innes	8 8 8 8 8 2	12	87	15
C. Stone	9 10 8 8 9 0	13	118	15

Employees are paid 1.5 times the regular hourly rate for all hours worked in excess of 40 hours per week. CPP is deducted at a rate of 4.3% on earnings less the $67.31 weekly exemption, EI at a rate of 2.25% of gross earnings. Ahmad Company must make payments to the Workers' Compensation Plan equal to 2% of the gross payroll. In addition, Ahmad matches the employees' health insurance contributions.

Instructions

(a) Calculate the total weekly payroll.

(b) Prepare the journal entry to record the payroll and Ahmad's employee benefits.

*E11–14 Selected data from the February payroll register for Yue Company are presented below, with some amounts intentionally omitted:

Calculate missing payroll amounts. Journalize the payroll and its payment.
(SO 7) AN

Gross earnings:	
Regular	(1)
Overtime	$1,050
Total	(2)
Deductions:	
Canada Pension Plan	(3)
Employment Insurance	294
Income tax	3,262
Union dues	139
United Way	300
Total deductions	(4)
Net pay	(5)
Accounts debited:	
Warehouse wages	4,900
Store wages	(6)

Pensionable earnings are $11,800. CPP premiums are 4.3% of pensionable earnings, and EI premiums are 2.25% of gross earnings.

Instructions

(a) Fill in the missing amounts. Round all answers to the nearest dollar.

(b) Calculate the company's contributions for the Canada Pension Plan (1 time) and Employment Insurance (1.4 times).

(c) Journalize all aspects of the February 28 payroll and its payment.

*E11–15 Yackness Company has two benefit plans for its employees:

Journalize employee benefits.
(SO 7) AP

1. It grants employees two days of vacation for each month worked. Eight employees worked the entire month of March at an average daily wage of $100 per employee.

2. The company provides supplementary medical-care insurance for its eight employees. The cost is $50 per employee per month and is paid on the 15th of the following month.

Instructions

Prepare the adjusting entries at March 31.

PROBLEMS: SET A

P11–1A The following transactions occurred in Wendell Company. Wendell's fiscal year end is December 31.

Identify liabilities.
(SO 1, 3, 4, 5) AP

1. Wendell purchased goods for $150,000 on December 23, terms n/30.

2. The Wendell chief executive is to be paid a bonus of $35,000 six months after year end.

3. Weekly salaries of $5,000 are paid every Friday for a five-day (Monday to Friday) work week. This year, December 31 is a Wednesday. Payroll deductions include CPP of 4.3% and EI of 2.25% of gross salaries, and income tax withholdings of $1,800.

4. Property taxes of $40,000 were assessed on October 1 for the upcoming calendar year. They are payable by March 1.

5. Wendell is the defendant in a negligence suit. Wendell's legal counsel estimates that Wendell may suffer a $40,000 loss if it loses the suit. In legal counsel's opinion, the likelihood of success in the case is not determinable at this time.

6. Wendell entered into a $500,000, 10% note payable on July 1. The note requires payment of the principal in instalments of $100,000, each June 30, for the next five years. Interest is due monthly, on the first of each month.

Instructions

(a) Identify which of the above transactions should be presented in the current liabilities section, and which should be recorded in the long-term liabilities section, of Wendell's balance sheet on December 31. Identify the account title(s) and amount(s) for each reported liability.

(b) Indicate any information that should be disclosed in the notes to Wendell's financial statements.

Journalize and post note transactions. Show balance sheet presentation.
(SO 2, 5) AP

P11–2A The following are selected transactions of Learnstream Company. Learnstream prepares financial statements quarterly and uses a perpetual inventory system.

Jan. 12 Purchased merchandise on account from McCoy Company for $18,000, terms n/30.

Feb. 1 Issued a two-month, 10%, $18,000 note to McCoy Company in payment of account. Interest is payable at maturity.

Mar. 31 Accrued interest on the McCoy note.

Apr. 1 Paid the face value and interest on the McCoy note.

July 1 Purchased equipment from Scottie Equipment by paying $11,000 in cash and signing a 10%, three-month note for $25,000. Interest is payable at maturity.

Sept. 30 Accrued interest on the Scottie note.

Oct. 1 Paid the face value and interest on the Scottie note.

Dec. 1 Borrowed $20,000 from the Toronto-Dominion Bank by issuing a 9%, three-month note. Interest is payable monthly, on the first of each month.

Dec. 31 Recognized interest expense on the Toronto-Dominion Bank note.

Instructions

(a) Prepare journal entries for the above transactions and events.

(b) Post to the accounts Notes Payable, Interest Payable, and Interest Expense.

(c) Show the balance sheet presentation of Notes Payable and Interest Payable at December 31, 2003.

(d) What is the total interest expense for the year?

Prepare current liability entries, adjusting entries, and current liabilities section of the balance sheet.
(SO 2, 3, 5) AP

P11–3A On January 1, 2003, the ledger of Molega Software Company contains the following liability accounts:

Accounts Payable	$42,500
Goods and Services Tax Payable	5,800
Provincial Sales Tax Payable	5,800
Unearned Service Revenue	15,000

During January the following selected transactions occurred:

Jan. 1 Borrowed $15,000 in cash on a four-month, 10%, $15,000 note. Interest is payable at maturity.

5 Sold merchandise for cash totalling $7,752, which included 7% GST and 7% PST. The cost of this sale was $4,600. Molega Software uses a perpetual inventory system.

12 Provided services for customers who had made advance payments of $8,000.

14 Paid the Receiver General and Provincial Treasurer for sales taxes collected in December of 2002, $11,600 ($5,800 + $5,800).

20 Sold 500 units of a new product on credit at $52 per unit, plus 7% GST and 7% PST. This new product is subject to a one-year warranty. The cost of this sale was $20 per unit.

25 Sold merchandise for cash totalling $14,820, which included sales taxes (7% GST and 7% PST). The cost of this sale was $9,000.

Instructions

(a) Journalize the January transactions.

(b) Journalize the adjusting entries at January 31 for (1) interest on the outstanding note payable, and (2) estimated warranty liability, assuming warranty costs are expected to equal 8% of sales of the new product.

(c) Prepare the current liabilities section of the balance sheet at January 31, 2003. Assume no change in Accounts Payable.

Record warranty.
(SO 3) AP

P11–4A On January 1, 2002, Hopewell Company began a three-year warranty program designed to stimulate sales. The warranty costs are estimated at 3% of sales in 2002 and 5% of sales in 2003. The sales and warranty figures for the years ended December 31, 2002 and 2003, are as follows:

Year	Sales	Warranty Expenditures
2002	$660,000	$16,000
2003	840,000	35,000

Instructions

Prepare journal entries to record the warranty expense liability and warranty expenditures (all cash) for 2002 and 2003.

P11–5A Fury's Fireworks' explosive product division is uninsurable because of the high risk of injury to employees and losses due to fire and explosion. The year 2002 is considered to be one of the safest (luckiest) in the division's history because no accidents occurred. Having suffered an average of four accidents a year during the past five years (with costs ranging from $200,000 to $2,000,000), management is afraid that next year the company will not be so fortunate.

Discuss contingency reporting.
(SO 4) C

Instructions

What should the company record or disclose in its financial statements relative to this situation? Explain why.

*P11–6A The payroll procedures used by three different companies are described below:

1. In EComm Company, department managers interview applicants and, on the basis of the interview, either hire or reject the applicants. When an applicant is hired, the applicant fills out a TD1 form (for income tax deduction purposes). One copy of the form is sent to the human resources department and one copy is sent to the payroll department, as notice that the individual has been hired. On the copy of the TD1 sent to payroll, the managers manually indicate the hourly pay rate for the new employee.
2. In Yerxa Computer Company, each employee is required to mark the hours worked on a time card. At the end of each pay period, the employee must have this time card approved by the department manager. The approved card is then given to the payroll department by the employee. Subsequently, the controller's department pays the employee by cheque.
3. In Crescent Company, time-clock cards are used. At the end of each pay period, the department manager initials the cards, indicates the rates of pay, and sends them to payroll. Earnings records are prepared from the cards by the payroll department. Cash equal to the total net pay in each department is given to the department manager, who then pays the employees in cash.

Identify internal control weaknesses and recommend improvements.
(SO 6) AN

Instructions

(a) Indicate the weakness(es) in internal control in each company.
(b) For each weakness, describe the control procedure(s) that will provide effective internal control. Use the following format for your answer:

      Weaknesses   Recommended Procedures

*P11–7A Sure Value Hardware has four employees who are paid on an hourly basis plus time-and-a-half for all hours worked in excess of 40 hours a week. Payroll data for the week ended March 15, 2003, are presented below:

Calculate payroll. Prepare payroll entries.
(SO 7) AP

Employee	Hours Worked	Hourly Rate	CPP	EI	Income Tax Withholdings	United Way
A. Pima	40	$13.00	$19.47	$11.70	$ 89.65	$5.00
C. Zuni	42	13.00	21.14	12.58	99.65	5.00
E. Hopi	44	13.00	22.82	13.46	110.50	8.00
G. Mohav	46	13.00	24.50	14.33	123.65	5.00

The first three employees are sales clerks (store wages expense) and the other employee performs administrative duties (office wages expense).

Instructions

(a) Calculate the weekly payroll.
(b) Journalize the payroll on March 15, 2003, and the accrual of employee benefits expense.
(c) Journalize the payment of the payroll on March 16, 2003.
(d) Journalize the payment on April 15, 2003, of the amounts payable to the Receiver General and the United Way.

Journalize payroll transactions.
(SO 7) AP

*P11–8A   The following payroll liability accounts are included in the ledger of Costa Company on January 1, 2003:

Canada Pension Plan Payable	$ 2,978
Employment Insurance Payable	1,811
Income Tax Payable	16,400
Workers' Compensation Payable	5,634
Union Dues Payable	1,250
Canada Savings Bonds Payable	2,500
Vacation Pay Payable	3,220

In January, the following transactions occurred:

Jan. 10 Sent a cheque for $1,250 to the union treasurer for union dues.

12 Issued a cheque for $21,189 to the Receiver General for CPP, EI, and income tax.

15 Purchased Canada Savings Bonds for employees by writing a cheque for $2,500.

20 Paid the amount due to the Workers' Compensation Plan.

31 Completed the monthly payroll register, which shows office salaries $24,600, store wages $37,400, CPP withheld $2,294, EI withheld $1,395, income tax withheld $12,400, union dues withheld $800, United Way contributions $300, and net pay $44,811.

31 Prepared payroll cheques for the net pay and distributed the cheques to the employees.

At January 31, the company also makes the following accruals for employee compensation:

1. CPP in an amount equal to the employees' contributions, and EI in an amount equal to 1.4 times the employees' contributions

2. Workers' Compensation Plan at 7% of the gross payroll

3. Vacation pay at 4% of gross earnings

Instructions

Journalize the January transactions and adjustments.

Prepare entries for payroll, including employee benefit costs.
(SO 7) AP

*P11–9A   For the year ended December 31, 2002, Western Electric Company reports the following summary payroll data:

Gross earnings:	
Administrative salaries	$180,000
Electricians' wages	370,000
Total	$550,000

Deductions:	
CPP contributions	$ 21,450
Income tax	123,000
EI contributions	12,375
United Way contributions	5,000
Dental insurance premiums	2,400
Long-term disability insurance	1,500
Total	$165,725

Western Electric Company's payroll costs include CPP, EI, and Workers' Compensation. The workers' compensation amounts to $11,000 for the current year.

In addition, the company matches the employees' contributions to the long-term disability insurance plan, and pays the entire cost of a medical insurance plan. The latter amounts to $24,400 for the current year.

Instructions

(a) Prepare a summary journal entry, at December 31, for the full year's payroll.

(b) Journalize the entry at December 31 to record the employee benefit expense for the year.

(c) Calculate the company's total payroll-related expense for the year.

PROBLEMS: SET B

Identify liabilities.
(SO 1, 3, 4, 5) AP

P11–1B   The following transactions occurred in Iqaluit Company. Iqaluit's fiscal year end is April 30.

1. Iqaluit purchased goods for $10,000 on April 29, terms n/30, FOB destination. The goods arrived on May 3.

2. The company chief executive officer is to be paid a bonus equal to 6% of net income, six months after year end. Net income is estimated to be $600,000.

3. Weekly salaries of $10,000 are paid every Friday for a five-day (Monday to Friday) work week. This year, April 30 is a Thursday. Payroll deductions include CPP of 4.3% and EI of 2.25% of gross salaries, and income tax withholdings of $3,000.

4. Iqaluit received $25,000 from customers on April 27 for services to be performed in May.

5. Iqaluit was named in a lawsuit alleging negligence for oil spillage that leaked into the neighbouring company's water system. Iqaluit's legal counsel estimates that the company will likely lose the suit. Restoration costs are anticipated to total $250,000.

6. The company purchased equipment for $25,000 on April 1. It issued an 8%, six-month note in payment. Interest is payable monthly, on the first of each month.

Instructions

(a) Identify which of the above transactions should be presented in the current liabilities section, and which should be recorded in the long-term liabilities section, of Iqaluit's balance sheet on April 30. Identify the account title(s) and amount(s) for each reported liability.

(b) Indicate any information that should be disclosed in the notes to Iqaluit's financial statements.

P11–2B MileHi Mountain Bikes markets mountain-bike tours to clients vacationing in various locations in the mountains of British Columbia. In preparation for the upcoming summer biking season, MileHi entered into the following transactions related to notes payable:

Journalize and post note transactions. Show balance sheet presentation.
(SO 2, 5) AP

Mar. 2 Purchased Mongoose bikes for use as rentals by issuing an $8,000, 9% note payable that is due in three months. Interest is due at maturity.

31 Recorded accrued interest for the Mongoose note.

Apr. 1 Issued a $20,000 note to Mountain Real Estate for the purchase of mountain property on which to build bike trails. The note bears 12% interest and is due in nine months. Interest on this note is payable the first of each month.

30 Recorded accrued interest for the Mongoose and Mountain Real Estate notes.

May 1 Paid interest on Mountain Real Estate note.

2 Issued a note to Western Bank for $15,000 at 6%. The funds will be used for working capital for the beginning of the season. The note and the interest are due in four months.

31 Recorded accrued interest for all three notes.

June 1 Paid principal and interest on the Mongoose note.

1 Paid interest on Mountain Real Estate note.

30 Recorded accrued interest for the Mountain Real Estate note and the Western Bank note.

Instructions

(a) Prepare journal entries for the above transactions.

(b) Post the above entries to the Notes Payable, Interest Payable, and Interest Expense accounts.

(c) Assuming that MileHi's year end is June 30, 2003, show the balance sheet presentation of notes payable and interest payable at that date.

(d) How much interest expense relating to notes payable did MileHi incur during the year?

P11–3B On January 1, 2003, the ledger of Burlington Company contained these liability accounts:

Prepare current liability entries, adjusting entries, and current liabilities section of the balance sheet.
(SO 2, 5) AP

Accounts Payable	$52,000
GST Payable	7,500
PST Payable	8,570
Unearned Service Revenue	16,000

During January, the following selected transactions occurred. Burlington uses a periodic inventory system.

Jan. 5 Sold merchandise for cash totalling $16,632, which includes 7% GST and 8% PST.

12 Provided services for customers who had made advance payments of $9,000.

14 Paid Receiver General and Minister of Finance for sales taxes collected in December 2002 ($7,500 and $8,570, respectively).

20 Sold 500 units of a new product on credit at $50 per unit, plus 7% GST and 8% PST.

21 Borrowed $18,000 from HSBC Bank on a three-month, 10%, $18,000 note. Interest is payable monthly, on the 21st of each month.

25 Sold merchandise for cash totalling $11,340, which includes 7% GST and 8% PST.

Instructions

(a) Journalize the January transactions. Round all amounts to the nearest dollar.
(b) Journalize the adjusting entry at January 31 for the interest on the outstanding note payable. Use one-third of a month for the period January 21–31.
(c) Prepare the current liabilities section of the balance sheet at January 31, 2003.

Record warranty.
(SO 3) AP

P11–4B On January 1, 2002, Logue Company began a one-year warranty program designed to stimulate sales. The warranty costs are estimated at 4% of sales in 2002 and 2003. The sales and warranty figures for the years ended December 31, 2002 and 2003, are as follows:

Year	Sales	Warranty Expenditures
2002	$50,000	$1,600
2003	85,000	3,500

Instructions

Prepare journal entries to record the warranty expense liability and warranty expenditures (credit the Repair Parts Inventory account) for 2002 and 2003.

Discuss contingency reporting.
(SO 4) C

P11–5B On October 9, 2000, **Bridgestone/Firestone Inc.** recalled 14.4 million defective Firestone tires. Firestone tires had been linked to numerous deaths, injuries, and incidents of tire separation and blowouts. Bridgestone/Firestone offered to provide free tire inspections and replace suspect tires through its dealership network. When a dealer replaces the recalled tires with a Firestone brand, the company reimburses the dealer for the wholesale price of the tires, plus $20 per tire to cover mounting and balancing and the extra paperwork involved. When non-Firestone brands are used to replace the recalled tire, Firestone reimburses the dealer up to $100 per tire, which gives the dealer the usual profit margin.

Instructions

What should the company record or disclose in its December 31, 2000, financial statements for this situation? Explain why.

Identify internal control weaknesses and recommend improvements.
(SO 6) AN

*P11–6B Selected payroll procedures of Wee Company are described below:

1. Employees are required to record hours worked on cards by punching a time clock. At the end of each pay period, the cards are collected by the department manager. The manager prepares a payroll register in duplicate and forwards the original to payroll. In payroll, the summaries are checked for mathematical accuracy and a payroll supervisor pays each employee by cheque.
2. Two clerks in the payroll department divide the payroll alphabetically. One clerk has employees A to L and the other has employees M to Z. Each clerk calculates the gross earnings, deductions, and net pay for the relevant employees and posts the data to the employee earning records.
3. The payroll cheques are manually signed by the chief accountant and given to the department managers for distribution to employees in each department. The managers are responsible for ensuring that absent employees receive their cheques.

Instructions

(a) Indicate the weaknesses in internal control.
(b) For each weakness, describe the control procedures that will provide effective internal control. Use the following format for your answer:

Weaknesses	Recommended Procedures

Prepare payroll entries.
(SO 7) AP

*P11–7B Scoot Scooters has four employees who are paid on an hourly basis. Payroll data for the week ended February 15, 2003, are presented below:

Employee	Hours Worked	Hourly Rate	Gross Pay	CPP	EI	Income Tax	United Way	Net Pay
L. Scott	39	$8.00	$ 312.00	$10.52	$ 7.02	$ 33.70	$ 0.00	$ 260.76
S. Stahl	32	8.00	256.00	8.11	5.76	22.10	5.00	215.03
M. Rashid	34	9.00	306.00	10.26	6.89	32.45	7.50	248.90
L. Quick	36	9.50	342.00	11.81	7.70	39.95	5.00	277.54
Totals			$1,216.00	$40.70	$27.37	$128.20	$17.50	$1,002.23

Instructions

(a) Journalize the payroll on February 15, 2003, and the accrual of employee benefits expense.
(b) Journalize the payment of the payroll on February 15, 2003.
(c) Journalize the payment of the employee benefits on March 14, 2003.

P11–8B The following payroll liability accounts are included in the ledger of Amora Company on January 1, 2003:

Journalize and post payroll transactions. Calculate liability balances.
(SO 7) AP

Canada Pension Plan Payable	$ 3,508
Income Tax Withholdings Payable	28,400
Employment Insurance Payable	2,133
Workers' Compensation Payable	5,689
Union Dues Payable	1,200
Canada Savings Bonds Payable	1,210
Vacation Pay Payable	3,793
United Way Donations Payable	750
Salaries and Wages Payable	0

In January, the following transactions occurred:

Jan. 10 Sent a cheque to the union treasurer for union dues.
  12 Issued a cheque to the Receiver General for the amounts due.
  17 Issued a cheque to the United Way.
  20 Paid the Workers' Compensation Plan.
  31 Completed the monthly payroll register, which showed office salaries $44,600, store wages $48,400, CPP withheld $3,441, EI withheld $2,092, income tax withheld $27,900, union dues withheld $1,200, United Way contributions $750, and Canada Savings Bonds deductions $1,210.
  31 Prepared payroll cheques for the net pay and distributed them to employees.

At January 31, the company also made the following adjustments pertaining to employee compensation:

1. CPP and EI; Workers' Compensation in an amount equal to 6% of the gross payroll
2. Vacation pay at 4% of gross earnings

Instructions

(a) Enter the beginning balances in T accounts.
(b) Journalize and post the January transactions and adjustments.
(c) Calculate the balances in the payroll liability accounts, as at January 31.

P11–9B Selected data from a payroll register for Czech Company are presented below in alphabetical order, with some amounts intentionally omitted:

Calculate missing payroll amounts. Prepare all related journal entries.
(SO 7) AN

Store wages expense	$ (1)
Warehouse wages expense	9,800
CPP deductions	975
EI deductions	(2)
Group insurance plan	400
Union dues	230
United Way	600
Income tax	(3)
Net pay	11,195
Overtime earnings	1,500
Regular earnings	21,900
Total gross earnings	(4)

EI premiums are 2.25% of the gross payroll.

Instructions

(a) Fill in the missing amounts.
(b) Journalize the payroll, including the employer's portion of CPP and EI, for the week ended June 30.
(c) Journalize the payment of the payroll to the employees on June 30, and the remittance of the amounts due to the Receiver General on July 15.

CUMULATIVE COVERAGE—CHAPTERS 9 TO 11

Johan Company and Nordlund Company are competing businesses. Both began operations six years ago and they are quite similar in most respects. The current balance sheet data for the two companies are as follows:

	Johan Company	Nordlund Company
Cash	$ 50,300	$ 48,400
Accounts receivable	309,700	312,500
Allowance for doubtful accounts	(13,600)	0
Merchandise inventory	463,900	520,200
Capital assets	245,300	257,300
Accumulated amortization, capital assets	(107,650)	(189,850)
Total assets	$947,950	$948,550
Current liabilities	$440,200	$436,500
Long-term liabilities	78,000	80,000
Total liabilities	518,200	516,500
Owner's equity	429,750	432,050
Total liabilities and owner's equity	$947,950	$948,550

You have been engaged as a consultant to conduct a review of the two companies. Your goal is to determine which of them is in a stronger financial position. Your review of their financial statements quickly reveals that the two companies have not followed the same accounting practices. The differences, and your conclusions regarding them, are summarized below:

1. Johan Company has used the allowance method of accounting for bad debts. A review shows that the amount of its write-offs each year has been quite close to the allowances that have been provided. It seems reasonable to have confidence in its current estimate of bad debts.

   Nordlund Company has used the direct write-off method for bad debts. It has been somewhat slow to write off its uncollectible accounts. Based on an ageing analysis and review of its accounts receivable, it is estimated that $14,000 of its existing accounts will become uncollectible.

2. Johan Company has determined the cost of its merchandise inventory on a LIFO basis. The result is that its inventory appears on the balance sheet at an amount that is below its current replacement cost. Based on a detailed physical examination of its merchandise on hand, the current replacement cost of its inventory is estimated at $500,000.

   Nordlund Company has used the FIFO method of valuing its merchandise inventory. The result is that its ending inventory appears on the balance sheet at an amount that quite closely approximates its current replacement cost.

3. Johan Company estimated a useful life of 12 years and a residual value of $30,000 for its capital assets, and has been amortizing them on a straight-line basis.

   Nordlund Company has the same type of capital assets. However, it estimated a useful life of 10 years and a residual value of $10,000. It has been amortizing its capital assets using the double declining-balance method.

   Based on engineering studies of these types of capital assets, you conclude that Nordlund's estimates and method for calculating amortization are the more appropriate.

4. Among its current liabilities, Johan has included the portions of long-term liabilities that become due within the next year. Nordlund has not done so.

   You find that $30,000 of Nordlund's $80,000 of long-term liabilities are due to be repaid in the current year.

Instructions

(a) Using similar accounting principles, revise the balance sheets presented above so that the data are comparable and reflect the current financial position of each of the companies.

(b) State your conclusions in a brief report to your client.

*B*roadening Your Perspective

FINANCIAL REPORTING AND ANALYSIS

••

Financial Reporting Problem

BYP11–1 Refer to the financial statements of **The Second Cup Ltd.** and the Notes to Consolidated Financial Statements in Appendix A.

Instructions

Answer the following questions about the company's current and contingent liabilities:

  (a) What were The Second Cup's total current liabilities at June 24, 2000? What was the increase/decrease in total current liabilities from the pro forma 1999 figures?
  (b) What were the components of total current liabilities on June 24, 2000?
  (c) Explain why "Deposits" would be considered liabilities.
  (d) Does The Second Cup report any contingent liabilities? If so, where are they disclosed? Explain the nature, amount, and significance of The Second Cup's contingent liabilities, if any.

Interpreting Financial Statements

BYP11–2 Listed in alphabetical order below, **La Senza Corporation** (formerly known as **Suzy Shier**) and **Reitmans (Canada) Limited** report the following current assets and current liabilities, in thousands of dollars, at February 3, 2001.

	La Senza	Reitmans
Accounts payable and accrued liabilities	$27,290	$35,187
Accounts receivable	4,728	2,556
Cash and short-term investments	33,018	20,008
Current maturity of long-term debt	14,892	
Income tax payable	2,043	5,124
Inventory	41,418	38,481
Marketable securities	20,746	
Prepaid expenses	2,607	8,816

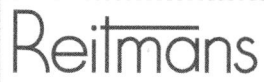

Instructions

  (a) Determine the total current assets and total current liabilities for each company.
  (b) Calculate working capital and the current ratio for each company.
  (c) The industry current ratio is 2:1. Compare the liquidity of La Senza and Reitmans to that of the industry.

Additional Cases

BYP11–3 **Cott Corporation** is the world's leading producer of store-brand soft drinks, operating in Canada, the UK, and the U.S. The company reports the following information about contingencies in the notes to its January 1, 2000, financial statements:

COTT CORPORATION
Notes to the Financial Statements
January 1, 2000

Note 25: Contingencies

(c) The Company is subject to environmental legislation in jurisdictions in which it carries on business. The Company anticipates that environmental legislation may become more restrictive but at this time is not in a position to assess the impact of future potential legislation. The Company, along with other industry participants, is not in compliance with the *Environmental Protection Act (Ontario)*. The requirements under the Act are not presently being enforced, and the Company has made no provision for any possible assessments thereon. The Company continues to work with industry groups and the Ministry of the Environment to seek alternative means to meet the requirements for a minimum percentage of sales in refillable containers.

> (d) The Company is subject to various claims and legal proceedings with respect to matters such as governmental regulations, income taxes and other actions arising out of the normal course of business. Management believes that the resolution of these matters will not have a material adverse effect on the Company's financial position or results from operations.

Instructions

(a) In note (c), Cott states that it is not in compliance with the *Environmental Protection Act*. Yet, it has not made any provisions for future costs under this legislation. Do you agree with Cott's treatment of this issue? Comment. If you suggest an alternative method of treatment, describe how it should be reported in the financial statements.

(b) Identify the contingent liability described in note (d). Is it likely? Reasonably estimable? Do you agree with Cott's reporting of this contingent liability? Explain your reasoning.

Accounting on the Web

BYP11–4   Payroll deductions for CPP contributions, EI premiums, and income tax withheld are remitted periodically to the Canada Customs and Revenue Agency. This case explores the Canada Customs and Revenue Agency website, viewing payroll deduction guides and forms.

Instructions

Specific requirements for this Internet case are available on the Weygandt website.

CRITICAL THINKING
....

Collaborative Learning Activities

BYP11–5   Until the fall of 2001 when it was taken over by Crossair, **SAirGroup** (formerly Swissair) operated a diversified airline, aviation service, air cargo and catering company. On September 2, 1998, Swissair flight 111 en route to Geneva, Switzerland, plunged into the Atlantic Ocean near Peggy's Cove, Nova Scotia, while trying to make an emergency landing at the Halifax airport after the pilots reported smoke in the cockpit. There were no survivors.

Lawsuits against Swissair and its co-defendants totalled $24 billion. Analysts said that this figure was unrealistic and inflated on purpose to keep the plaintiffs' options open. SAirGroup offered compensatory damages to the families of the 229 people who died in the crash, totalling $8 million. SAirGroup was well insured and a company spokesperson stated that the accident, while tragic, was unlikely to have financial repercussions for the company.

Instructions

With the class divided into groups, answer the following questions:

(a) Do you think that a contingent loss such as the compensatory damages estimated above was relevant to users of SAirGroup's financial statements?

(b) How reliable do you think the estimate of the loss was? What information should the company have used to estimate the loss?

(c) SAirGroup recorded an estimated loss and liability (less anticipated insurance recoveries) related to this lawsuit. Where in its financial statements would you have expected to find these two amounts—that is, in what part of the income statement should the loss have been presented and in what part of the balance sheet should the liability have been presented? What type of note disclosure would you have expected for this event?

BYP11–6   Datis Processing Company provides word-processing services for clients and students in a university community. The work for clients is fairly steady throughout the year, but the work for students peaks significantly in November and March as a result of term papers, research project reports, and dissertations.

Two years ago, the company attempted to meet the peak demand by hiring part-time help. This led to numerous errors and considerable customer dissatisfaction. A year ago, the company hired four experienced employees on a permanent basis, instead of using part-time help. This proved to be much better in terms of productivity and customer satisfaction. However, it has caused an increase in annual payroll costs and a significant decline in annual net income.

Recently, Sue Fields, a sales representative for Advanced Temp Services (ATS), made a proposal to the company. Under the plan, ATS would provide up to four experienced workers at a daily rate of $100 per person for an eight-hour workday. (ATS workers are not available on an hourly basis.) Datis Processing would have to pay only the daily rate for the workers used.

The owner of Datis Processing, Denise Diab, asks you, as the company's accountant, to prepare a report on the expenses that are pertinent to the decision. If the ATS plan is adopted, Denise will terminate the employment of two permanent employees who are each earning an average annual salary of $32,000. The remaining permanent employees also each earn an annual income of $32,000. Datis Processing pays Canada Pension Plan contributions and Employment Insurance premiums, as specified in the chapter, and Workers' Compensation Plan payments equal to 1.5% of the gross payroll. In addition, Datis Processing pays $40 per month for each employee for medical and dental insurance.

Denise indicates that if the ATS plan is accepted, her needs for workers will be as follows:

Months	Number of Workers	Working Days per Month (for each worker)
January to March	3	20
April and May	2	25
June to October	2	18
November and December	3	23

Instructions

With the class divided into groups, do the following:
(a) Prepare a report showing the total costs associated with keeping four permanent workers versus the payroll costs associated with adopting the ATS plan.
(b) What other factors should Denise consider before taking her decision?

Communication Activity

BYP11–7 Consider the case of a movie theatre which sells thousands of gift certificates per year. Similar to warranties, the certificates can be redeemed at any time—they have no expiry date. Some of them are never redeemed (because they are lost or forgotten, for example).

The owner of the theatre understands warranties. However, he has raised a number of questions with respect to the accounting for these gift certificates.

Instructions

Prepare a memorandum to answer the following questions asked by the owner. Relate the accounting for the gift certificates to what you know about accounting for warranties.
(a) Why is a liability recorded when these certificates are sold? After all, they bring customers into the theatre where they spend money on snacks and drinks, etc. Why should something which helps generate additional revenue be treated as a liability?
(b) How should the gift certificates which are never redeemed be treated? At some point in the future, can the liability related to them be eliminated? If so, what type of journal entry would be made?

Ethics Case

BYP11–8 The July 10, 1998, issue of *Inc.* magazine includes an article by Jeffrey L. Seglin entitled "Would You Lie to Save Your Company?" It recounts the following true situation:

A Chief Executive Officer (CEO) of a $20-million company that repairs aircraft engines received notice from a number of customers that engines that had recently been repaired had failed, and that the company's parts were to blame. The CEO had not yet determined whether the parts were, in fact, the cause of the problem. The Federal Aviation Administration (FAA), responsible for air transportation and safety in the U.S., had been notified and was investigating the matter.

What complicated the situation was that the company was in the midst of its year-end audit. As part of the audit, the CEO was required to sign a letter saying that he was not aware of any significant outstanding circumstances that could negatively impact the company—in accounting terms, any contingent liabilities. The auditor was not aware of the problem.

The company relied heavily on short-term loans from a number of banks. The CEO feared that if these lenders learned of the situation, they would pull their loans. The loss of these loans would force the company into bankruptcy, leaving hundreds of people without jobs. Prior to this problem, the company had a stellar performance record.

Instructions

(a) Who are the stakeholders in this situation?

(b) What are the CEO's possible courses of action? What are the potential results of each course of action? (Take into account the two alternatives: (1) the FAA determines the company was not at fault, and (2) the FAA determines the company was at fault.)

(c) What would you do and why?

(d) Suppose that the CEO decides to conceal the situation and during the next year the company is found to be at fault and is forced into bankruptcy. What losses are incurred by the stakeholders in this situation? Do you think the CEO should suffer the legal consequences if he decides to conceal the situation?

Answers to Self-Study Questions

1. a   2. d   3. c   4. b   5. c   6. d   7. b   8. b   9. c   10. a   11. d   *12. d *13. b

Answer to Second Cup Review It Question 1

The Second Cup reports accounts payable and accrued liabilities first, followed by the current portion of long-term debt. Other liabilities, deposits, and income taxes payable follow in the listing. Current liabilities are not listed in order of magnitude. They may be listed in order of maturity.

Remember to go back to the Navigator box on the chapter-opening page to check off your completed work.

Concepts for Review

Before studying this chapter, you should understand or, if necessary, review:

a. *The organization primarily responsible for setting accounting standards in Canada. (Ch. 1, p. 10)*

b. *The going concern assumption, the monetary unit assumption, the economic entity assumption, and the time period assumption. (Ch. 1, pp. 12–14 and Ch. 3, p. 103)*

c. *The cost principle, the revenue recognition principle, and the matching principle. (Ch. 1, p. 11 and Ch. 3, pp. 103–104)*

THE NAVIGATOR

The Big Question

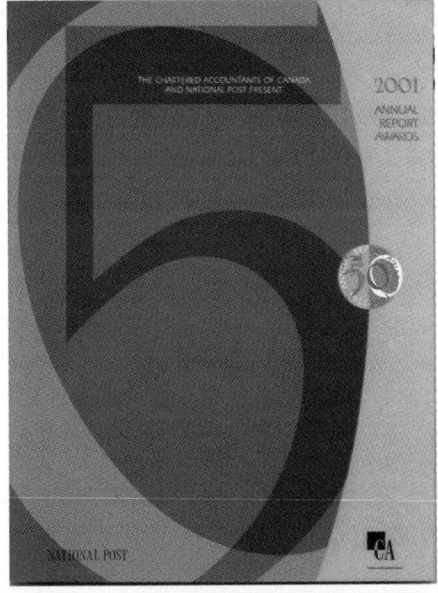

TORONTO, Ont.—Accountants and others who work with financial statements spend a lot of time answering "what," "when," and, of course, "how much." But, as with any task, it's important to step back from time to time and look at larger questions. What's the purpose of reporting financial information? Who will actually use it? And who will notice if it's done well?

There are several responses to the first two of these questions. The third could well be answered "The CICA, that's who." Since 1951, the Canadian Institute of Chartered Accountants (CICA) has played a lead role in the annual report awards—first as judges and since the mid-1980s, as organizer and host with media sponsor *National Post* (formerly *Financial Post*). The purpose of the awards program is to recognize the best reporting models in Canada and to strengthen corporate reporting in this country.

Contestants are drawn from the National Post's FP500 and related lists. Eligible contestants must be incorporated in Canada and have securities that are publicly traded.

The 50th anniversary of the awards in 2001 showcased gold, silver and bronze winners in each of the 13 industry categories of the Annual Report Awards, with one Overall Award of Excellence. Gold, silver and bronze awards were also presented for Environ-

mental and Sustainability Reporting, Electronic Disclosure, and Design. An Award of Excellence for Corporate Governance Disclosure was also presented. Top winners are featured in the Judges' Comments Book (shown above).

Judges include chartered accountants, financial analysts and investor relations professionals. This provides a good overview of the points of view of various users of financial reports.

While the judges consider all the elements of the reports, including the profile and overview of the company, business operations, supplementary disclosures, general readability and design, the most important element is the financial information. This should be timely, include all required information and

meet generally accepted accounting principles (GAAP).

But a truly excellent report integrates the financial statements with the body of the report. Although financial statements must have complete and thorough Notes, the quality and effectiveness of the MD&A (Management's Discussion and Analysis) is crucial.

Financial information is about communication. Investors should be able to pick up an annual report and get a clear picture of the company – where it's going and where it has been. Good corporate reporting is about sending a clear, accurate message.

www.cica.ca

THE NAVIGATOR

THE NAVIGATOR ✔

- Understand *Concepts for Review* ☐
- Read *Feature Story* ☐
- Scan *Study Objectives* ☐
- Read *Preview* ☐
- Read text and answer *Before You Go On*
  p. 567 ☐ p. 569 ☐ p. 576 ☐ p. 579 ☐
- Work *Demonstration Problem* ☐
- Review *Summary of Study Objectives* ☐
- Answer *Self-Study Questions* ☐
- Complete assignments ☐

CHAPTER · 12

ACCOUNTING PRINCIPLES

▶ STUDY OBJECTIVES ◀

After studying this chapter, you should be able to:

1. *Explain the meaning of generally accepted accounting principles and identify the key items of the conceptual framework.*
2. *Describe the basic objective of financial reporting.*
3. *Describe the qualitative characteristics of accounting information and apply them to the elements of financial statements.*
4. *Identify and apply the basic assumptions used by accountants.*
5. *Identify and apply the basic principles of accounting.*
6. *Identify and apply the constraints in accounting.*
7. *Explain the purpose of international accounting standards.*

THE NAVIGATOR

What you have learned up to this point in your accounting principles course is a process that leads to the preparation of a company's financial reports. As indicated in the feature story, these reports must effectively communicate financial information to users. In order to do so, generally accepted accounting principles must be adhered to. Otherwise, we would have to be familiar with every company's particular accounting and reporting practices in order to understand its financial statements. It would be difficult, if not impossible, to compare the financial results of different companies.

This chapter explores the conceptual framework used to develop generally accepted accounting principles. The chapter is organized as follows:

THE NAVIGATOR

The Conceptual Framework of Accounting

STUDY OBJECTIVE

••••••••••• 1 •••••••••••

Explain the meaning of generally accepted accounting principles and identify the key items of the conceptual framework.

The accounting profession has established a set of standards and rules that are recognized as a general guide for financial reporting. This recognized set of standards is called generally accepted accounting principles (GAAP). "Generally accepted" means that these principles have authoritative support.

Provincial securities commissions and federal and provincial incorporating acts have given the Canadian Institute of Chartered Accountants the primary responsibility for the development of generally accepted accounting principles in Canada. GAAP is established by the CICA's Accounting Standards Board (AcSB). The Accounting Standards Oversight Council (AcSOC) oversees the activities of the AcSB and provides input. The AcSOC is composed of senior members from business, finance, government, universities, the accounting and legal professions, regulators, and the financial analyst community. These members have a broad perspective on the issues facing standard setters.

A complete conceptual framework is published in the *CICA Handbook*, which outlines accounting and auditing recommendations and guidelines. Section 1000 of the

Handbook, "Financial Statements Concepts," presents the concepts that underlie the development and use of accounting principles. These concepts guide the choice of what to present in financial reports, decisions about alternative ways of reporting economic events, and the selection of appropriate ways of communicating such information. This increases the usefulness of financial statements. It also provides an understanding of the limitations of accounting.

Helpful hint Accounting principles are affected by economic and political conditions, which change over time. As a result, accounting principles are not carved in stone like the periodic table in chemistry or a formula in math.

The conceptual framework is designed to:

1. Ensure that existing standards and practices are coherent and consistent
2. Provide a structure to permit a quick response to new issues
3. Increase the understandability, relevance, reliability, and comparability of financial reporting results

It is impossible to create accounting principles for all existing and future situations. Thus, the conceptual framework is especially important in situations where standards do not exist. It helps professionals determine which accounting alternatives fall outside of the framework and are therefore unacceptable. The conceptual framework also guides the development of new accounting principles.

►Accounting in Action ► *International Insight*

You should recognize that different religious, political, and cultural influences affect the accounting that occurs in many countries. For example, in some Islamic countries, religious tenets—such as the prohibition of interest charges—have been introduced into accounting practice. In Sweden, accounting is considered an instrument that shapes fiscal policy. In Europe, more emphasis is given to social reporting (information on employment statistics, the health of workers, and so on) than in Canada.

The CICA's **conceptual framework** consists of four major sections:

1. Objective of financial reporting
2. Qualitative characteristics of accounting information
3. Elements of financial statements
4. Recognition and measurement criteria (assumptions, principles, and constraints)

We will discuss these sections on the following pages.

The Objective of Financial Reporting

Determining the objective of financial reporting requires answers to such basic questions as these: Who uses financial statements? Why? What information do they need? How knowledgeable about business and accounting are financial statement users? How should financial information be reported so that it is best understood?

STUDY OBJECTIVE
•••••••••**2**•••••••••
Describe the basic objective of financial reporting.

The primary objective of financial reporting is to provide useful information for decision-making. More specifically, the conceptual framework states that the objective of financial statements is to communicate information that is useful to investors, creditors, and other users in making investment and lending decisions and in assessing management's performance. Consequently, financial statements provide information about the following:

1. Economic resources (assets), obligations (liabilities), and equity
2. Changes in economic resources, obligations, and equity
3. Economic performance

The conceptual work also describes the characteristics that make accounting information useful.

Qualitative Characteristics of Accounting Information

STUDY OBJECTIVE
·········· ▼ 3 ··········
Describe the qualitative characteristics of accounting information and apply them to the elements of financial statements.

How does a company like The Second Cup decide how much financial information to disclose? In what format should its financial information be presented? How should assets, liabilities, revenues, and expenses be measured? The primary criterion for judging such accounting choices is **decision usefulness**. The accounting practice selected should be the one that generates the most useful financial information for making a decision. To be useful, information should possess the following qualitative characteristics: understandability, relevance, reliability, and comparability.

Understandability

In order for the information provided in financial statements to be useful, it must be **understandable** to the users. Financial statements cannot realistically satisfy the varied needs of all users. Consequently, the objective of financial statements focuses primarily on the information needs of investors and creditors. Even within these two groups, users may vary widely in the types of decisions they make and in their level of interest in the information. At one extreme is a sophisticated creditor who carefully scrutinizes all aspects of the financial information. At the other extreme is an unsophisticated shareholder who may only scan the text and not study the numbers.

It is therefore necessary to establish a base level of understandability to assist both the preparer of financial information and its user. **The average user is assumed to have a reasonable understanding of accounting concepts and procedures, as well as of general business and economic conditions.** If this level of understanding does not exist, the user is expected to rely upon professionals with an appropriate level of expertise. With your study of this course, you are well on your way to becoming an average user!

Relevance

Accounting information has relevance if it makes a difference in a decision. Relevant information has predictive or feedback value, or both. **Predictive value** helps users forecast future events. For example, when The Second Cup issues financial statements, the information in them is considered relevant because it provides a basis for predicting future earnings. **Feedback value** confirms or corrects prior expectations. When The Second Cup issues financial statements, it also confirms or corrects expectations about the financial health of the company.

In addition, accounting information has relevance if it is **timely**. It must be available to decision-makers before it loses its ability to influence decisions. Many people believe that by the time annual financial statements are issued—sometimes up to six months after year end—the information has limited usefulness for decision-making. Timely *interim* financial reporting is essential to relevant decision-making.

Reliability

Reliability of information means that the information is free of error and bias. In short, it can be depended on. To be reliable, accounting information must be **verifiable**: we must be able to prove that it is free of error and bias. It also must also be a faithful representation of the economic substance, not just the form, of the transaction. If The Second Cup reports a financial instrument as a liability rather than as equity, then the statement is not a **faithful representation**. To ensure reliability, external professional accountants audit financial statements. Accounting information must also be **neutral.** It cannot be selected, prepared, or presented to favour one set of interested users over another. These three characteristics—verifiability, faithful representation, and neutrality—are often combined and called objectivity. Objectivity means that two individuals, each working independently, can review the same information and reach the same results or similar conclusions. Objectivity is affected by the use of **conservatism** in situations of uncertainty. Conservatism in accounting means that, when preparing financial statements, a company should choose the method that will be least likely to overstate assets and income. It does **not** mean, however, deliberately understating assets or income.

Comparability

Accounting information about a company is most useful when it can be compared with accounting information about other enterprises. Comparability results when different companies use the same accounting principles.

At one level, accounting principles are fairly comparable because they are based on generally accepted accounting principles. These principles, however, do allow for some variation on methods. For example, there are a variety of ways to report inventory. Often, these different methods result in different amounts of net income. As we will learn later in this chapter, the **full disclosure principle** makes comparisons of companies easier, as each company must disclose the accounting methods used. From the disclosures, the external user can determine whether the financial information is comparable.

Comparability is easier when accounting policies are used consistently. Consistency means that a company uses the same accounting principles and methods from year to year. If a company selects FIFO as the inventory costing method in the first year of operations, it is expected to use FIFO in succeeding years. When financial information has been reported on a consistent basis, the financial statements permit meaningful analysis of trends within a company.

A company *can* change to a new method of accounting. To do so, management must justify the claim that the new method results in more meaningful financial information. In the year in which the change occurs, the change (and its impact) must be disclosed in the notes to the financial statements. This disclosure makes users of the financial statements aware of the lack of consistency. In addition, the past years of corporate performance must be presented as if the new method had been used.

►Accounting in Action ► *Business Insight*

Many people mistakenly believe that because companies prepare financial statements in accordance with generally accepted accounting principles, it isn't necessary to scrutinize the numbers because they are relevant, reliable, and comparable. Remember, though, that GAAP means generally accepted, not guaranteed accurate. The principles permit many different ways of accounting for the same economic transaction. The principles incorporate many estimates, with only management's professional judgement to rely on. The principles themselves change over time as the economic environment and the views of regulators and standard setters change. And the principles vary across countries. Canadian GAAP is not always the same as U.S. GAAP or UK GAAP.

Given GAAP's flexibility, a reader must understand both the strengths and the limitations of the characteristics of accounting information and be cautious when making definitive comparisons.

Source: Robin Schwill, "Full Disclosure." *Canadian Business*, May 28, 2001, 35.

The qualitative characteristics of accounting information are summarized in Illustration 12-1.

Understandability
1. Of accounting concepts and procedures
2. Of general business and economic conditions

Relevance
1. Provides a basis for forecasts
2. Confirms or corrects prior expectations
3. Is timely

Reliability
1. Is verifiable
2. Is a faithful representation
3. Is neutral
4. Is conservative

Comparability
1. Different companies use similar accounting principles.
2. A company uses the same accounting principles consistently from year to year.

Illustration 12-1

Qualitative characteristics of accounting information

Trade-Offs Between Qualitative Characteristics

Many accounting choices require trade-offs between qualitative characteristics. For example, there is often a trade-off between relevance and reliability. That is, there may be a trade-off between ensuring that financial information is produced on a timely basis and verifying the accuracy of the information included. In order to produce financial statements annually, estimates are required. These estimates reduce the accuracy of the information provided. If we were to wait until estimates were no longer necessary for things like uncollectible accounts, useful lives of capital assets, and warranty recalls, however, the financial information would no longer be relevant. The conceptual framework does not always provide obvious solutions to accounting issues such as these. Rather, it enables professionals to judge the appropriate balance between these characteristics in a particular situation.

Elements of Financial Statements

An important part of the conceptual framework is a set of definitions that describe the basic terms used in accounting. This set of definitions is referred to as the **elements of financial statements**. They include such terms as assets, liabilities, equity, revenues, and expenses.

Because these elements are so important, they must be precisely defined and universally applied. Finding the appropriate definition for many of these elements is not easy. For example, should the value of a company's employees be reported as an asset on a balance sheet? Should the death of the company's president be reported as a loss? A good set of definitions should provide answers to these types of questions. Because you have already encountered most of these definitions in earlier chapters, they are not repeated here.

Recognition and Measurement Criteria

The objective of financial reporting, the qualitative characteristics of accounting information, and the elements of financial statements are very broad. Because accountants must solve practical problems, more detailed criteria are needed. **Recognition criteria help determine when items should be included or recognized in the financial statements. Measurement criteria outline how to measure or assign an amount to those items.** We classify these criteria as assumptions, principles, and constraints.

Assumptions provide a foundation for the accounting process. **Principles** indicate how economic events should be reported in the accounting process. **Constraints** allow a relaxation of the principles under certain circumstances. Illustration 12-2 outlines these recognition and measurement criteria (some of which you know from earlier chapters). They are discussed in more detail in the following sections.

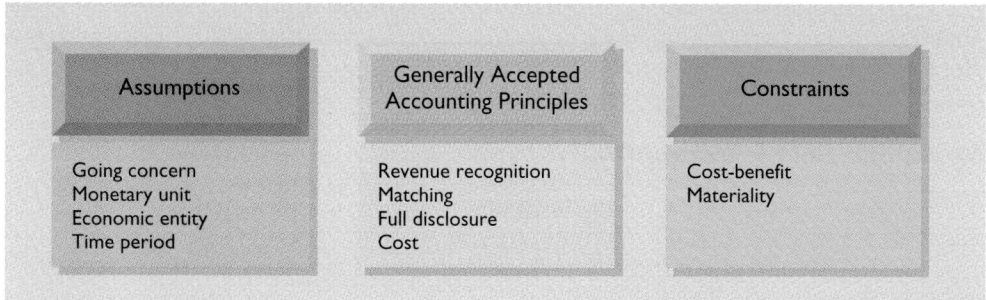

Illustration 12-2

Recognition and measurement criteria

Assumptions	Generally Accepted Accounting Principles	Constraints
Going concern	Revenue recognition	Cost-benefit
Monetary unit	Matching	Materiality
Economic entity	Full disclosure	
Time period	Cost	

Before You Go On . . .

►Review It

1. What are generally accepted accounting principles?
2. What is stated about generally accepted accounting principles in the Auditors' Report to the shareholders of The Second Cup? The answer to this question is at the end of the chapter.
3. What is the basic objective of financial information?
4. What are the qualitative characteristics that make accounting information useful? Give an example of a trade-off between qualitative characteristics.

Related exercise material: BE12–1, BE12–2, BE12–3, BE12–4, BE12–5, and BE12–6.

THE
NAVIGATOR

Assumptions

Assumptions provide a foundation for the accounting process. You already know the major assumptions from preceeding chapters—the going concern, monetary unit, economic entity, and time period assumptions. We will review them here briefly.

STUDY OBJECTIVE
••••••••••4••••••••••

Identify and apply the basic assumptions used by accountants.

Going Concern Assumption

The going concern assumption assumes that the company will continue operating for the foreseeable future—that is, long enough to carry out its existing objectives. In spite of business failures, most companies have a fairly high continuance rate. The accounting implications of this assumption are critical. If a going concern assumption is not used, then capital assets should be stated at their liquidation value (selling price less cost of disposal)—not at their historical cost. Amortization of these assets would not be needed. In each period, these assets would simply be reported at their anticipated liquidation value. Also, without this assumption, the current/long-term classification of assets and liabilities would not matter. Labelling anything as long-term would be difficult to justify.

Acceptance of the going concern assumption gives credibility to the cost principle. The going concern assumption is only inapplicable when liquidation appears likely. In that case, assets would be better stated at liquidation value than at cost.

Monetary Unit Assumption

The monetary unit assumption states that only transaction data that can be expressed in terms of money should be included in the accounting records. For example, the value of a company president would not be reported in a company's financial records because it cannot be expressed in dollars.

An important counterpart to the monetary unit assumption is the assumption that the unit of measure remains stable over time. That is, any inflationary (or deflationary) effects are assumed to be minimal and are ignored.

Economic Entity Assumption

The economic entity assumption states that the activities of the entity must be kept separate and distinct from the activities of the owner and of all other economic entities. For example, it is assumed that the activities of Diedrich Coffee can be distinguished from those of The Second Cup.

Time Period Assumption

Illustration 12-3

Assumptions used in accounting

The time period assumption states that the economic life of a business can be divided into artificial time periods. Thus, it is assumed that the activities of business enterprises, such as The Second Cup, can be subdivided into months, quarters, or years for meaningful financial reporting purposes.

Going Concern

Now   Future

The business will continue operating for the foreseeable future.

Monetary Unit

Accounting Records
Salaries expense 2,500
Cash 2,500

Measure of employee satisfaction | Salaries paid
Total number of employees | Percent of international employees

Only those things that can be expressed in terms of money should be included in the accounting records.

Economic Entity

Ford
Chrysler
GM

Every economic entity can be separately identified and accounted for.

Time Period

1998   2008
2000 2002 2004 2006

Start of business   End of business

QTR 1 QTR 2 QTR 3 QTR 4
F M A M J J A S O N D

The economic life of a business can be divided into artificial time periods.

As discussed in Chapter 3, time periods of less than one year are called **interim** periods. Periods of one year are known as **fiscal** years or, if extending from January through December, **calendar** years. Public companies are required to present both quarterly (interim) and annual financial statements.

These basic accounting assumptions are shown in Illustration 12-3.

Before You Go On . . .

▶Review It

1. What are the going concern assumption, the monetary unit assumption, the economic entity assumption, and the time period assumption?

Related exercise material: E12–1.

THE
NAVIGATOR

Principles

From these fundamental assumptions of accounting, the accounting profession has developed principles that dictate how economic events should be recorded and reported. In earlier chapters, we discussed the cost principle (Chapter 1) and the revenue recognition and matching principles (Chapter 3). Here we now examine a number of reporting issues related to these principles. In addition, another principle, the full disclosure principle, is discussed.

STUDY OBJECTIVE
············· 5 ·············
Identify and apply the basic principles of accounting.

Revenue Recognition Principle

The revenue recognition principle says that revenue should be recognized in the accounting period in which it is earned. Applying this general principle can be difficult. In Chapter 3, for example, we noted how difficult it was for Twentieth Century Fox to estimate its Star Wars revenues and match these revenues with expenses.

Another example is apparent in long-term construction projects. For example, Strait Crossing built the Confederation Bridge, linking the provinces of Prince Edward Island and New Brunswick. Construction started in 1992 and was completed in June 1997 when the bridge opened, and Strait Crossing started earning toll revenue immediately. Thus expenses were incurred starting in 1992, but no revenue was received until 1997. In situations such as this, when should revenues be recorded and how should they be matched to expenses?

Revenue recognition guidelines help accountants determine when to recognize revenue. More specifically, revenue should be recognized when all of the guidelines below are met:

1. The production and/or sales effort is substantially complete
2. Revenues can be objectively measured
3. Collection is reasonably assured (an estimate can be made of amounts anticipated to be uncollectible)
4. Material expenses can be determined and matched

Ontario

►Accounting in Action ► *Business Insight*

The Ontario Securities Commission (OSC) recently reviewed the revenue recognition practices of 70 TSE-listed technology companies. It found many areas where revenue recording or disclosure was inadequate. For example, the OSC says that stating "Revenue is recognized when earned" in the notes to a company's statements is not an adequate explanation of a company's revenue recognition policies. The OSC also says the practice of recognizing revenue when goods are shipped is often inadequate, especially when those goods have only been shipped to a distributor. Then there is the issue of returns. Some companies recognized revenue on software even when there was the potential for significant amounts of it to be returned by retailers.

In addition, the OSC criticized those companies that recorded revenue before all sales obligations were met. One company recognized revenue even though there was substantial installation required for its product. Others recorded revenue before doing an extensive customization of software products that was required.

The OSC found much to be concerned with and detailed a number of reporting standards where guidelines were not specific enough. It will also begin reviewing the revenue reporting of all TSE-listed companies at least once every four years.

Source: Janet McFarland, "Companies Must Be Compelled to Report Meaningful Revenue Figures." *The Globe and Mail*, March 17, 2001, B9.

Depending on the circumstances, the four criteria for revenue recognition can be satisfied at various points in time. These points range from at point of sale to the later collection of cash. The most common points of revenue recognition are as follows:

1. At point of sale
2. During production
3. At completion of production
4. Upon collection of cash

Point of Sale

Helpful hint   Revenue should be recognized in the accounting period in which it is earned. This may not be the period in which the related cash is received. In a retail establishment, the point of sale is usually the critical point in the process of earning revenue.

When a sale is involved, revenue is usually recognized at the point of sale. Consider a sale by The Second Cup. At the point of sale, the customer pays the cash and takes (and drinks!) the merchandise. The company records the sale by debiting Cash and crediting Sales Revenue. If the sale were on account rather than for cash (assuming the company accepts credit sales, and the customer has a good credit rating), the company would record the sale by debiting Accounts Receivable and crediting Sales Revenue. This is the most common point of revenue recognition for goods and services. The product is complete and delivered, revenue can be objectively measured, collection has occurred or is reasonably assured, and expenses can be matched to the revenue.

During Production

In long-term construction contracts, revenue recognition is usually possible (and desirable) before the contract is completed. For example, assume that Warrior Construction Co. has a contract to build a dam for the Province of British Columbia for $400 million. Construction is estimated to take three years (starting early in 2002) at a cost of $360 million. If Warrior recognizes revenue only at the point of sale, it will report no revenues and no profit in the first two years. When completion and sale take place, in 2004, Warrior will report $400 million in revenues, costs of $360 million, and the entire profit of $40 million. Did Warrior really produce no revenues and earn no profit in 2002 and 2003? Obviously not. The earnings process is considered substantially completed at various stages. Therefore, revenue should be recognized as construction progresses during production.

The percentage-of-completion method recognizes revenue on a long-term project on the basis of reasonable estimates of the progress toward completion. Progress toward completion is measured by comparing the costs incurred in a period to the total estimated costs for the entire project. That percentage is multiplied by the total revenue for the project. The result is then recognized as revenue for the period. The formulas for this method are presented in Illustration 12-4.

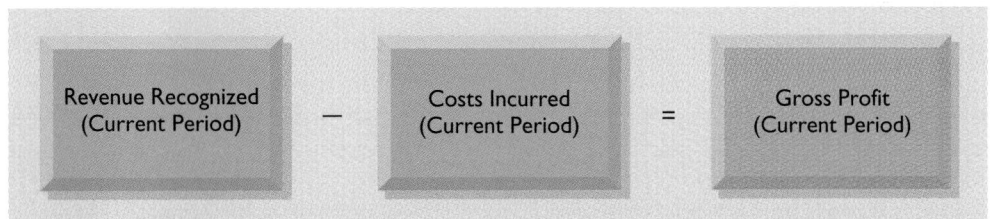

Illustration 12-4

Formula to recognize revenue in the percentage-of-completion method

The costs incurred in the current period are then subtracted from the revenue recognized during the current period to arrive at the gross profit. This formula is shown in Illustration 12-5.

Illustration 12-5

Formula to calculate gross profit

Let's look at an illustration of the percentage-of-completion method. Assume that Warrior Construction Co. has costs of $54 million in 2002, $180 million in 2003, and $126 million in 2004 on the dam project. The portion of the $400 million of revenue recognized in each of the three years is shown in Illustration 12-6:

Illustration 12-6

Revenue recognized—percentage-of-completion method

Year	Costs Incurred	÷	Total Estimated Cost	=	Percent Complete	×	Total Revenue	=	Revenue Recognized
2002	$ 54,000,000		$360,000,000		15%		$400,000,000		$ 60,000,000
2003	180,000,000		360,000,000		50%		400,000,000		200,000,000
2004	126,000,000				Balance required to complete the contract				140,000,000
Totals	$360,000,000								$400,000,000

No estimate is made of the percentage of work completed during the final period. Instead, all remaining revenue is now recognized. In this example, the company's cost estimates were totally accurate. The costs incurred in the third year brought the total cost to $360,000,000—exactly what had been estimated. In reality, this does not always happen. Revisions of remaining estimates may be necessary as additional information becomes available.

The gross profit recognized each period is as follows:

Illustration 12-7

Gross profit recognized— percentage-of-completion method

Year	Revenue Recognized	−	Actual Cost Incurred	=	Gross Profit Recognized
2002	$ 60,000,000		$ 54,000,000		$ 6,000,000
2003	200,000,000		180,000,000		20,000,000
2004	140,000,000		126,000,000		14,000,000
Totals	$400,000,000		$360,000,000		$40,000,000

Use of the percentage-of-completion method involves some subjectivity. Error is possible in determining the amount of revenue to be recognized and gross profit to be reported. But to wait until completion would seriously distort each period's financial statements. Naturally, **if it is not possible to obtain dependable estimates of costs and progress, then the revenue should be recognized at the completion of production** and not by the percentage-of-completion method.

Completion of Production

Helpful hint The completed-contract method is not applicable to ordinary manufacturing situations.

If Warrior Construction Co. were not able to estimate its costs with any degree of reliability, it would wait until the completion of production to recognize revenue. This is known as the **completed-contract method**. Revenue of $400 million, costs of $360 million, and a gross profit of $40 million would be reported at the completion of production in the year 2004. It is not until production is complete, in this case, that revenue, expenses, and gross profit can be reasonably determined.

Collection of Cash

Another basis for revenue recognition is the receipt of cash. The **cash basis** is generally used only when it is very difficult to determine the revenue amount at the time of a credit sale because collection is uncertain. The cash basis is also commonly used to account for instalment sales. Because of this, this revenue recognition approach is known as the **instalment method**.

Many consumer products are sold on an instalment basis, where customers make payments over an extended period of time. Cars, computers, home appliances and furnishings are often sold on an instalment payment plan. If the company meets the revenue recognition guidelines (in particular, if it has a reasonable basis for estimating uncollectible accounts), it recognizes revenue from instalment sales at the point of sale.

Often, however, down payments are relatively small (or non-existent) and ultimate collection of the sales price is not reasonably estimable. For example, Leon's Furniture advertises a promotional payment plan with no money down and no payments for the first year. In cases such as these, companies use the instalment method, recognizing revenue when the cash is collected rather than at the point of sale.

Under the instalment method, each cash collection from a customer consists of (1) a partial recovery of the cost of the goods sold, and (2) partial gross profit from the sale. For example, if the gross profit margin on the sale is 40%, each subsequent receipt of cash consists of 60% recovery of the cost of goods sold and 40% gross profit.

The formula to recognize gross profit is as follows:

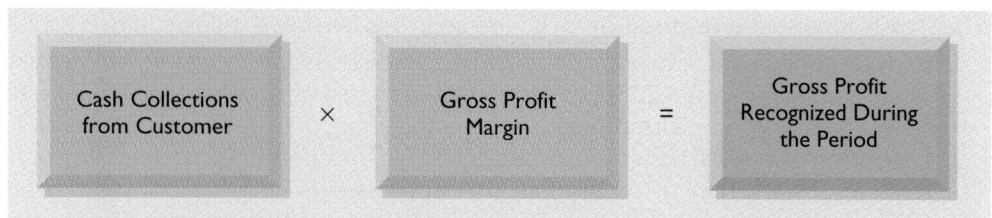

Illustration 12-8

Gross profit formula—instalment method

To illustrate, assume that in its first year of operations, a Saskatchewan farm machinery dealer had instalment sales of $600,000. Its cost of goods sold on these instalment sales was $420,000. Total gross profit is $180,000 ($600,000 − $420,000). The gross profit margin is 30% ($180,000 ÷ $600,000). The collections on the instalment sales were as follows: first year, $280,000 (down payment plus monthly payments); second year, $200,000; and third year, $120,000. The gross profit recognized is shown in Illustration 12-9 (interest charges are ignored in this illustration):

Helpful hint The gross profit margin or percentage is calculated by dividing gross profit by sales revenue.

Year	Cash Collections from Customers		Gross Profit Margin		Gross Profit Recognized
2002	$280,000	×	30%	=	$ 84,000
2003	200,000		30%		60,000
2004	120,000		30%		36,000
Totals	$600,000				$180,000

Illustration 12-9

Gross profit recognized—instalment method

Under the instalment method of accounting, gross profit is recognized in the period in which the cash is collected. As indicated earlier, the instalment method is used when there is a risk of not collecting an account receivable. In that case, the sale itself is not sufficient evidence for revenue to be recognized.

Matching Principle (Expense Recognition)

The expression "Let the expense follow the revenue," shows that expense recognition is traditionally tied to revenue recognition. As you learned in Chapter 3, this practice is referred to as the matching principle. It says that expenses must be matched with revenues in the period in which efforts are made to generate revenues. Expenses are not necessarily recognized when cash is paid, or when the work is performed, or when the product is produced. They are recognized when the labour (service) or the product actually makes its contribution to revenue.

It is sometimes difficult to determine the accounting period in which the expense contributed to revenues. Several approaches have been developed for matching expenses and revenues on the income statement.

To understand these approaches, you need to understand the nature of costs. Costs that will only generate revenues in the current accounting period are expensed immediately. However, it is sometimes difficult to specifically associate costs with revenue generation. For example, it is virtually impossible to match administrative salaries or interest costs with the revenue they help earn. These costs are expensed immediately during the period in which they are incurred. They are reported as operating expenses in the income statement and are called **expired costs**.

►*Ethics note*
Many appear to do it, but few like to discuss it. It's earnings management. It's a clear violation of the revenue recognition and matching principles. Companies may time the sale of investments, or the expensing of bad debts to accomplish earnings objectives. Prominent companies have been accused of matching one-time gains with one-time write-offs so that current-period earnings are not so high that they can't be surpassed next period.

Costs that will generate revenues in future accounting periods are recognized as assets. Examples include merchandise inventory, prepaid expenses, and capital assets. These costs represent **unexpired costs**. Unexpired costs become expenses in two ways:

1. **Cost of goods sold.** Costs carried as merchandise inventory become expenses when the inventory is sold. They are expensed as cost of goods sold in the period when the sale occurs. Thus, there is a direct matching of expenses with revenues.
2. **Operating expenses.** Other unexpired costs become operating expenses through use or consumption (as in the case of capital assets and store supplies), or through the passage of time (as in the case of prepaid insurance). Operating expenses contribute to the revenues of the period, but their association with revenues is less direct than that of cost of goods sold.

These points about expense recognition are shown in Illustration 12-10.

Illustration 12-10

Expense recognition pattern

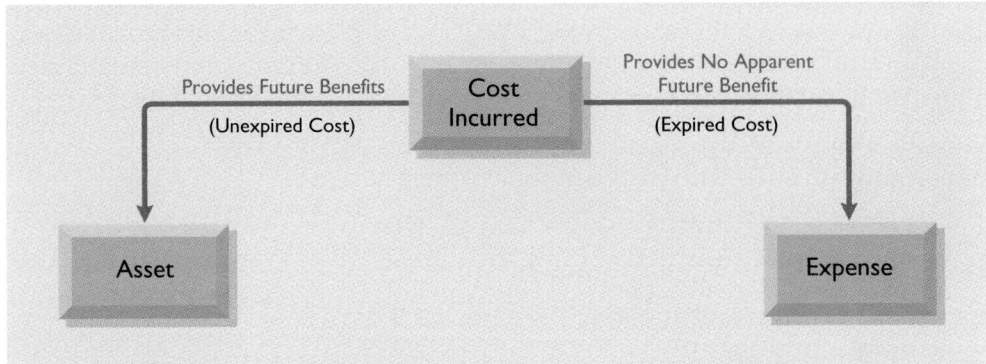

▸Accounting in Action ▸ *Business Insight*

Implementing expense recognition guidelines can be difficult. Consider, for example, the Casino Windsor, a gambling establishment located in Windsor, Ontario. How should the Casino report expenses that are related to the payoff of its progressive slot machines? Progressive slot machines, which generally have no ceiling on their jackpots, provide a lucky winner with all the money that many losers previously put in. Payoffs tend to be huge but infrequent. The basic accounting question is this: when it determines net income, should the Casino Windsor deduct (as an expense) the thousands of dollars sitting in its progressive slot machines from the revenue recognized during the accounting period? One might argue that no, you cannot deduct the money until it is won. However, a winning handle pull might not occur for many months, or even years. Although an estimate would have to be used, the better answer is to match these costs with the revenue recognized, assuming that an average payout period can be documented. And the revenue amounts can be significant. The Casino Windsor grosses nearly $750 million annually! It can be difficult to apply the matching principle in practice.

Full Disclosure Principle

The full disclosure principle requires disclosure of circumstances and events which make a difference to financial statement users. For example, most accountants would agree that Lafarge Canada Inc. should disclose lawsuits (totalling more than $65 million) arising from alleged defective building materials so that interested parties are made aware of this potential liability.

The full disclosure principle is respected through two elements in the financial statements: the data they contain and the accompanying notes. The first note in most cases is a **summary of significant accounting policies**. The summary includes the methods used by the company when a choice is made between acceptable accounting policies. It includes, among others, the methods used for inventory costing and the amortization of capital assets. For example, The Second Cup Ltd.'s first note in Appendix A at the end of this textbook discloses that the company has chosen the FIFO method of inventory costing and the straight-line method of amortizing its capital assets.

The information that is disclosed in the notes to the financial statements generally falls into three additional categories. These categories:

1. Provide supplementary detail or explanation (for example, a schedule of capital assets)
2. Explain unrecorded transactions (for example, contingencies, commitments, subsequent events)
3. Supply new information (for example, information about related party transactions)

Deciding how much disclosure is enough can be difficult. Accountants could disclose every financial event that occurs and every contingency that exists. But the benefits of providing this additional information may be less than the costs of doing so. Many companies complain of an accounting standards overload. They also object to requirements that force them to disclose confidential information. Determining where to draw the line on disclosure is not easy.

►Accounting in Action ► *Business Insight*

New financial reporting rules have been issued by the Ontario Securities Commission and the CICA to beef up public companies' quarterly financial statement disclosure. In the past, only income and cash flow statements for the quarter were required. Now, all items normally required for annual financial statements (including the balance sheet, statement of retained earnings, and notes) are also required for the current quarter and year to date. John Hughes, manager of the OSC's continuous disclosure team, said, "In today's marketplace, quarterly reporting plays an increasingly important role in providing the public with timely information for purposes of making investment decisions." These requirements bring Canadian interim financial reporting standards in line with international and U.S. standards.

Cost Principle

As you know, the cost principle requires assets to be recorded at cost. Cost is used because it is both relevant and reliable. Cost is **relevant** because it represents the price paid, the assets sacrificed, or the commitment made at the date of acquisition. Cost is **reliable** because it is objectively measurable, factual, and verifiable. It is the result of an exchange transaction. Cost is also the basis used in preparing financial statements.

The cost principle, however, has been criticized. One criticism is that it is irrelevant. After acquisition, the argument goes, cost is not equivalent to market value or current value. Consider the classic story about the person who went to sleep and woke up 100 years later. She called her stockbroker and asked what her formerly modest investment portfolio was worth. She was told that she was a multimillionaire—her HSBC Bank shares were worth $5 million and her Nortel shares were up to $10 million. Elated, she was about to inquire about her other holdings when the telephone operator cut in with, "Your time is up. Please deposit $100,000 for the next three minutes."

Despite the inevitability of changing prices due to inflation (or deflation), the accounting profession still follows the **monetary unit assumption** (referred to earlier

Illustration 12-11

Basic principles used in accounting

in this chapter) in preparing financial statements. While admitting that some changes in prices do occur, the profession believes the unit of measure—the dollar—has remained sufficiently constant over time to provide meaningful financial information.

The basic principles of accounting are summarized in Illustration 12-11.

Revenue Recognition

During production

At completion of production

At point of sale

At time cash received

Revenue should be recognized in the accounting period in which it is earned (generally at point of sale).

Matching

Costs   Match   Sales Revenue

Materials

Labour

Delivery

AD

Advertising   Utilities

Operating Expenses

Expenses should be matched with revenues.

Cost

Assets should be recorded at cost.

Full Disclosure

✓ Financial Statements
✓ Balance Sheet
✓ Income Statement
  Statement of Retained Earnings
✓ Cash Flow Statement

Circumstances and events that make a difference to financial statement users should be disclosed.

Before You Go On . . .

► *Review It*

1. What are the revenue recognition principle, the matching principle, the full disclosure principle, and the cost principle?
2. Identify the four points of revenue recognition. Provide an example of a company or product that would use each different point of revenue recognition.

Related exercise material: BE12–7, BE12–8, BE12–9, E12–2, E12–3, E12–4 and E12–5.

Constraints in Accounting

STUDY OBJECTIVE

6

Identify and apply constraints in accounting

Constraints permit a company to modify generally accepted accounting principles without reducing the usefulness of the reported information. The constraints are cost-benefit and materiality.

Cost-Benefit Constraint

The cost-benefit constraint ensures that the value of the information exceeds the cost of providing it. As we discussed earlier in this chapter, accountants could, in applying the full disclosure principle, disclose every financial event that occurs and every contingency that exists. However, providing additional information increases costs. The benefits of providing this information may be less than the costs in some cases.

Some believe that the benefit of applying GAAP to small businesses is not worth the cost. This has led to what is called the Big GAAP–Little GAAP controversy. Should there be one set of GAAP to which all businesses adhere, or should there be a different set for small businesses? The CICA is currently reviewing this matter, recognizing that the cost-benefit constraint often overrides the principle of one standard for all.

Materiality Constraint

Materiality relates to an item's impact on a firm's overall financial condition and operations. An item is material when it is likely to influence the decision of a reasonably careful investor or creditor. It is immaterial if its inclusion or omission has no impact on a decision-maker. In short, if the item does not make a difference in decision-making, GAAP does not have to be followed. To determine the materiality of an amount, the accountant usually compares it to such items as total assets, total liabilities, gross revenues, and cash and/or net income.

To illustrate how the materiality constraint is applied, assume that Yanik Co. purchases a number of low-cost capital assets, such as wastepaper baskets. Although the proper accounting would appear to be to amortize these wastepaper baskets over their useful lives, they are usually expensed immediately. This practice is justified because these costs are immaterial. Establishing amortization schedules for these assets is costly and time-consuming. It will not make a material difference in total assets and net income. Other applications of the materiality constraint are the nondisclosure of minor contingencies, or the expensing of any capital assets under a certain dollar amount.

The two constraints in accounting are shown in illustration 12-12.

Illustration 12-12

Accounting constraints

Summary of Conceptual Framework

As we have seen, the conceptual framework for developing sound reporting practices starts with the objective for financial reporting. It contines with the description of qualities that make information useful. Elements of financial statements are then defined. Finally, more detailed recognition and measurement criteria are provided.

These criteria take the form of assumptions, principles, and constraints. The conceptual framework is shown in Illustration 12-13.

Illustration 12-13

Conceptual framework

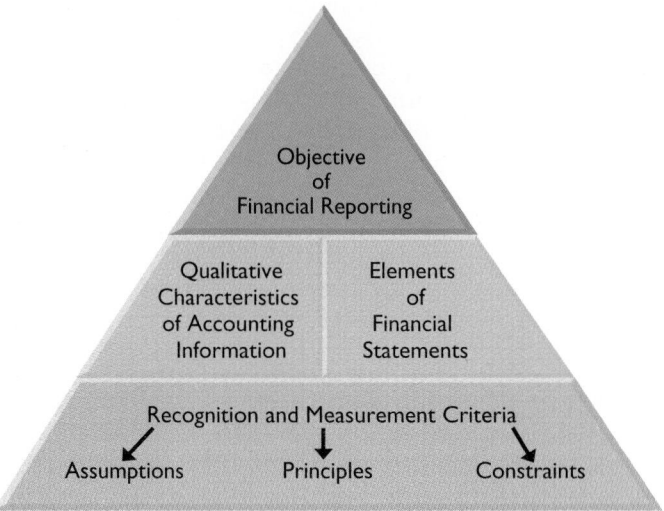

International Accounting Standards

STUDY OBJECTIVE
············ **7** ············
Explain the purpose of international accounting standards.

Foreigners buy Canadian grain, drink Canadian water, heat with Canadian fuels, celebrate with Canadian Christmas trees, eat Canadian potatoes, fly in Canadian planes, defend their countries with Canadian ships, listen to CBC radio, and guzzle Canadian beer. Canadians, in turn, drive Japanese and U.S. cars (often built with Canadian auto parts), wear Italian shoes and Scottish woollens, drink Brazilian coffee and Indian tea, eat Swiss chocolate bars, smoke Cuban cigars, watch U.S. television, sit on Danish furniture, and use Arabian oil. The variety and volume of exported and imported goods indicates the extensive involvement of Canadian business in international trade. Almost 40% of all Canadian-made goods and services are sold as exports. For many Canadian companies, the world is their market.

Canadian companies are expanding foreign operations, selling to foreign interests, and merging with companies located in other countries in record numbers in order to compete in the global marketplace more effectively. Firms that conduct operations in more than one country through subsidiaries, divisions, or branches in foreign countries are referred to as **multinational corporations**. The accounting for these corporations is complicated, because differing accounting standards and foreign currencies are involved.

Differences in Standards

In the global economy, many investment and credit decisions require the analysis of foreign financial statements. For example, one of The Second Cup's competitors is U.S.-based Starbucks. Investors interested in investing in one of these two companies find comparing their financial statements challenging.

Unfortunately, accounting standards differ from country to country. This lack of uniformity results from differences in legal systems, processes for developing accounting standards, government requirements, and economic environments. With no universally accepted set of international accounting standards, companies have responded with a variety of strategies, including preparing different sets of statements that report results in different languages, currencies, and accounting principles.

►Accounting in Action ► *International Insight*

Pity the Canadian investor. Public companies are required by law to prepare their financial statements in accordance with generally accepted accounting principles. However, investors face a dilemma because companies can report in Canadian GAAP, U.S. GAAP, or both. Canadian GAAP allows for considerable judgement. U.S. GAAP tends to allow less flexibility. The differences in GAAP from country to country can be large, as the following comparison of Canadian versus U.S. net income (loss), in millions, for fiscal 2000 illustrates:

Company	Canadian GAAP	U.S. GAAP	Difference
Fairfax Financial	$137.4	($84.3)	$221.7
Intrawest	$52.0	$46.7	$5.3
Nortel Networks	($2,957.0)	($3,470.0)	$513.0

Source: Al Rosen, "Mind the GAAP." *Canadian Business,* May 14, 2001, 39.

Uniformity in Standards

Much effort has been made to obtain uniformity in international accounting practices. The International Accounting Standards Board (IASB) includes more than 150 accounting organizations from over 110 countries. These countries have joined together to participate in the development of international accounting standards.

To date, over 40 International Accounting Standards have been issued for IASB members to introduce to their respective countries. But the IASB has no enforcement powers, so these standards are by no means universally applied. Countries weigh the benefits of uniformity in international financial reporting against the social and economic costs of changing local—and often legitimate—reporting practices.

In Canada, the President and Chief Executive Officer of the Toronto Stock Exchange said, "It is therefore desirable, not only that Canadian companies disclose the fact that they have followed accounting principles generally accepted in Canada in preparing their financial statements, but also that they disclose conformity with, or identify deviations from, International Accounting Standards." Many public Canadian companies do so.

Other large multinational companies have found benefits in adhering to the international accounting standards. Nearly 500 companies from around the world issue financial statements which conform to IASB standards. Considerable progress has been made toward greater uniformity in international accounting.

As a critical step to internationally harmonizing accounting standards, uniformity is also sought between Canada and the U.S. Since the U.S. is a major economic partner, the harmonization of accounting practices is critical to serve the needs of the marketplace. The Financial Accounting Standards Board in the U.S. and the CICA are working closely with each other to harmonize new accounting standards and to review the differences between existing ones.

Before You Go On . . .

►*Review It*

1. What are the cost-benefit constraint and the materiality constraint?
2. What is the purpose of the International Accounting Standards Board?

Related exercise material: BE12–10, E12–6, E12–7, E12–8, and E12–9.

THE
NAVIGATOR

►*A Look Back at Our Feature Story*

Refer back to the feature story at the beginning of the chapter, and answer the following question:

1. How does rewarding annual reporting benefit the objective of financial reporting?

Solution

1. The objective of financial reporting is to communicate information that is useful to investors, creditors, and other users in making decisions. A company's ability to communicate both financial and non-financial information clearly and understandably is the key to meeting its users' needs. By recognizing the best corporate reporting models in Canada, the annual report awards program encourages companies to meet the objective of financial reporting, and identifies leaders in the areas of corporate reporting, governance, and design.

THE
NAVIGATOR

DEMONSTRATION PROBLEM 1

**Additional
Demonstration Problem**

Wu Construction Company is under contract to build a condominium building at a contract price of $2,000,000. The building will take 18 months to complete, at an estimated cost of $1,400,000. Construction began in November 2002 and will be finished in April 2004. Actual construction costs incurred in each year were as follows: in 2002, $140,000; in 2003, $910,000; and in 2004, $350,000.

Instructions

Calculate the gross profit to be recognized in each year using the percentage-of-completion method.

Action Plan

- Percentage-of-completion method recognizes revenue as construction occurs. It is viewed as a series of sales.
- Percent complete is determined by dividing costs incurred by total estimated costs.
- Percent complete is multiplied by contract price to find revenue to be recognized in the current period.
- Gross profit equals revenue recognized less actual costs incurred.

Solution to Demonstration Problem 1

Year	Costs Incurred	÷	Total Estimated Cost	=	Percent Complete	×	Total Revenue	=	Revenue Recognized
2002	$ 140,000		$1,400,000		10%		$2,000,000		$ 200,000
2003	910,000		1,400,000		65%		2,000,000		1,300,000
2004	350,000			Balance required to complete contract					500,000
	$1,400,000								$2,000,000

Year	Revenue Recognized	–	Actual Cost Incurred	=	Gross Profit Recognized
2002	$ 200,000		$ 140,000		$ 60,000
2003	1,300,000		910,000		390,000
2004	500,000		350,000		150,000
	$2,000,000		$1,400,000		$600,000

DEMONSTRATION PROBLEM 2

Wacky Web Company uses the instalment method to account for its sales. In 2002, its first year of operations, it had instalment sales of $900,000 and a cost of goods sold on its instalment sales of $600,000. The collections on instalment sales were as follows: in 2002, $330,000; in 2003, $420,000; and in 2004, $150,000.

Instructions

Calculate the amount of gross profit to be recognized each year using the instalment method.

Solution to Demonstration Problem 2

Year	Cash Collected	×	Gross Profit Margin	=	Gross Profit Recognized
2002	$330,000		33⅓%*		$110,000
2003	420,000		33⅓%		140,000
2004	150,000		33⅓%		50,000
	$900,000				$300,000

* $900,000 − $600,000 = $300,000 ÷ $900,000 = 33⅓%

Action Plan
- Use the instalment method when cash collection is uncertain.
- Calculate the gross profit margin: gross profit ÷ net sales.
- Gross profit recognized each period equals cash collected × gross profit margin.

THE NAVIGATOR

Summary of Study Objectives

1. Explain the meaning of generally accepted accounting principles and identify the key items of the conceptual framework. Generally accepted accounting principles are a set of rules and practices that are recognized as a general guide for financial reporting purposes. The key items of the conceptual framework are (1) the objective of financial reporting, (2) the qualitative characteristics of accounting information, (3) the elements of financial statements, and (4) recognition and measurement criteria (assumptions, principles, and constraints).

2. Describe the basic objective of financial reporting. The basic objective of financial reporting is to communicate information that is useful to investors, creditors, and other users in making investment and lending decisions and in assessing management's performance.

3. Describe the qualitative characteristics of accounting information and apply them to the elements of financial statements. To be judged useful, information should pos-
sess the following qualitative characteristics: understandability, relevance, reliability, and comparability. The elements of financial statements are a set of definitions that can be used to describe the basic terms used in accounting.

4. Identify and apply the basic assumptions used by accountants. The major assumptions are going concern, monetary unit, economic entity, and time period.

5. Identify and apply the basic principles of accounting. The major principles are revenue recognition, matching, full disclosure, and cost.

6. Identify and apply the constraints in accounting. The major constraints are cost-benefit and materiality.

7. Explain the purpose of international accounting standards. The International Accounting Standards Board attempts to achieve uniformity in international accounting practices to simplify trade in world markets.

THE NAVIGATOR

GLOSSARY

 Key Term Matching Activity

Comparability Ability to compare accounting information of different companies because they use the same accounting principles. (p. 565)

Completed-contract method When revenues or costs cannot be reliably estimated, revenue, expenses, and profit are recognized at the completion of production. (p. 572)

Conceptual framework A coherent system of interrelated objectives, qualitative characteristics of accounting information, elements of financial statements, and recognition and measurement criteria that guides the development and application of accounting principles. (p. 563)

Conservatism Choosing an accounting method, when in doubt, that is least likely to overstate assets and net income. Modifies the reliability characteristic of accounting information. (p. 565)

Consistency Use of the same accounting principles and methods from year to year. Part of comparability characteristic of accounting information. (p. 565)

Cost-benefit The constraint that the costs of obtaining and providing information should not exceed the benefits gained. (p. 577).

Cost principle Accounting principle that requires assets to be recorded at their historical cost. (p. 575)

Economic entity assumption Accounting assumption that requires the activities of an economic entity to be kept separate from the activities of the owner and of all other entities. (p. 568)

Full disclosure principle Accounting principle that requires circumstances and events which make a difference to financial statement users to be disclosed. (p. 574)

Generally accepted accounting principles (GAAP)   A set of rules and practices, having substantial authoritative support, that are recognized as a general guide for financial reporting purposes. (p. 562)

Going concern assumption   Accounting assumption that the enterprise will continue operating for the foreseeable future. (p. 567)

Instalment method   A method of recognizing revenue using the cash basis. Each cash collection consists of a partial recovery of cost of goods sold and partial gross profit from the sale. (p. 572)

Matching principle   Accounting principle that says expenses should be matched with revenues in the period when efforts are made to generate revenues. (p. 573)

Materiality   The constraint of determining if an item is important enough to influence the decision of a reasonably careful investor or creditor. (p. 577)

Monetary unit assumption   Accounting assumption that only transaction data expressed in monetary terms should be included in accounting records. Also assumes that the monetary unit (e.g. dollar) is stable. (p. 568)

Objectivity   Two individuals, each working independently, would review the same information and reach the same results or similar conclusions. (p. 565)

Percentage-of-completion method   A method of recognizing revenue on a long-term construction project. When costs can be reliably estimated, a portion of the total revenue can be recognized in each period by applying a percentage of completion. This percentage is determined by dividing the actual costs incurred during the period by the estimated costs for the entire project. (p. 571)

Point of sale   The most common basis of revenue recognition, where revenue is recognized when sold. Alternatives to this method are the percentage-of-completion, completed-contract, and instalment methods. (p. 570)

Relevance   The quality of information that indicates that the information makes a difference in a decision. (p. 564)

Reliability   The quality of information that gives assurance that the information is free of error and bias. (p. 564)

Revenue recognition principle   Accounting principle that says revenue should be recognized in the accounting period in which it is earned (generally at the point of sale). (p. 569)

Time period assumption   Accounting assumption that says the economic life of a business can be divided into artificial time periods. (p. 568)

Understandability   A quality obtained if information provided in the financial statements is understandable to its users. (p. 564)

SELF-STUDY QUESTIONS

 Chapter 12 Self-Test

Answers are at the end of the chapter.

(SO 1) K   1. Generally accepted accounting principles are:
 a. a set of standards and rules that are recognized as a general guide for financial reporting.
 b. established by the Canada Customs and Revenue Agency.
 c. the guidelines used to resolve ethical dilemmas.
 d. fundamental truths that can be derived from the laws of nature.

(SO 2) K   2. Which of the following is not an objective of financial reporting?
 a. Provide information that is useful in investment and lending decisions.
 b. Provide information about economic resources, claims on those resources, and changes in them.
 c. Provide information that is useful in assessing management's performance.
 d. Provide information about the market value of a business.

(SO 3) K   3. The primary criterion by which accounting information can be judged is:
 a. consistency.
 b. objectivity.
 c. usefulness for decisions.
 d. comparability.

4. Verifiability is an ingredient of: (SO 3) K

	Reliability	Relevance
a.	Yes	Yes
b.	No	No
c.	Yes	No
d.	No	Yes

5. Valuing assets at their market value, rather than at their cost, is inconsistent with the: (SO 4, 5, 6) K
 a. time period assumption.
 b. matching principle.
 c. going concern assumption.
 d. materiality constraint.

6. Rioux Construction Company began a long-term construction contract on January 1, 2003. The contract is expected to be completed in 2004 at a total cost of $20,000,000. Rioux's revenue for the project is $24,000,000. Rioux incurred contract costs of $4,000,000 in 2003. What gross profit should be recognized in 2003?   (SO 5) AP
 a. $800,000
 b. $1,000,000
 c. $2,000,000
 d. $4,000,000

(SO 5) AP 7. Glackin Company had instalment sales of $1,000,000 in its first year of operations. The cost of goods sold on these instalment sales was $650,000. Glackin collected a total of $500,000 cash on the instalment sales. Using the instalment method, how much gross profit should be recognized in the first year?
    a. $140,000
    b. $175,000
    c. $350,000
    d. $500,000

(SO 5) K 8. The full disclosure principle says that:
    a. financial statements should disclose all assets at their cost.
    b. financial statements should disclose only those events that can be measured in dollars.
    c. financial statements should disclose all events and circumstances that would matter to users of financial statements.
    d. financial statements should not be relied on unless an auditor has expressed an unqualified opinion on them.

9. The accounting term that refers to the tendency of accountants to favour understating assets and revenues in situations of uncertainty is known as: (SO 4, 5, 6) K
    a. the matching principle.
    b. materiality.
    c. conservatism.
    d. the monetary unit assumption.

10. The organization that issues international accounting standards is the: (SO 7) K
    a. Canadian Institute of Chartered Accountants.
    b. International Accounting Standards Board.
    c. Global Standards Agency.
    d. None of the above

THE NAVIGATOR

QUESTIONS

(SO 1) K   1. (a) What are generally accepted accounting principles (GAAP)?
      (b) What organization provides authoritative support for GAAP in Canada?

(SO 2) K   2. What is the basic objective of financial reporting?

(SO 3) K   3. What elements form the CICA's conceptual framework?

(SO 3) K   4. Identify the essential qualitative characteristics of accounting information.

(SO 3) C   5. Raynard Company substantially increased its net income in 2003 while keeping its inventory relatively the same. The president is very pleased with this. The chief accountant cautions him, however. She points out that since Raynard changed from the Average Cost to the FIFO method of inventory valuation this year, there is a comparability problem. It will be difficult to determine whether the company's performance is better. Do you agree? Explain.

(SO 3) C   6. How is the concept of consistency related to the qualitative characteristic of comparability?

(SO 3) C   7. The type and amount of information included in financial reports results from a series of judgemental trade-offs. What are the objectives of these trade-offs?

(SO 3) C   8. How is the concept of objectivity related to the qualitative characteristic of reliability?

(SO 4) C   9. Why does it matter whether accountants assume an economic entity will remain a going concern?

(SO 5) C   10. When should revenue be recognized? Why is the point of sale usually chosen as the date at which to recognize revenue?

(SO 5) AP   11. Ryder Construction Company has a $200-million contract to build a bridge. Its total estimated cost for the project is $170 million. Costs incurred in the first year of the project were $34 million. Appropriately, Ryder uses the percentage-of-completion method. How much revenue and gross profit should Ryder recognize in the first year of the project?

12. Merchandise with a cost of $80,000 was sold during the year for $100,000. Cash collected for the year amounted to $40,000. How much gross profit should be recognized during the year, if the company uses the instalment method?   (SO 5) AP

13. Distinguish between expired costs and unexpired costs.   (SO 5) C

14. Where does the accountant disclose information about an entity's financial position, operations, and cash flows?   (SO 5) C

15. Sue Leonard is the president of Better Books. She has no accounting background and cannot understand why market value is not used as the basis for accounting measurement and reporting. Explain what basis is used and why.   (SO 5) C

16. Describe the two constraints in the presentation of accounting information.   (SO 6) C

17. The controller rounded all dollar figures in the company's financial statements to the nearest thousand dollars. "It's not important for our users to know how many pennies we spend," she said. Do you believe rounded financial figures can provide useful information for decision-making? Explain why or why not.   (SO 6) C

18. Your roommate believes that accounting standards are uniform throughout the world. Is your roommate correct? Explain.   (SO 7) C

19. Do multinational companies have to use international accounting standards? Explain why or why not.   (SO 7) C

BRIEF EXERCISES

Identify generally accepted accounting principles.
(SO 1) K

BE12–1   Indicate whether each of the following statements is true or false.
(a) GAAP is a set of rules and practices established by the accounting profession to serve as a general guide for financial reporting purposes.
(b) Authoritative support for GAAP usually comes from two standard-setting bodies: the CICA and the Canada Customs and Revenue Agency.
(c) "Generally accepted" means that these principles must have "authoritative support."
(d) There are two different sets of GAAP—one for big companies and one for small companies.

Identify items included in the conceptual framework.
(SO 1) K

BE12–2   Indicate which of the following items are included in the CICA's conceptual framework. (Write "Yes" or "No" beside each item in the list below.)
(a) Analysis of financial statement ratios
(b) Objective of financial reporting
(c) Qualitative characteristics of accounting information
(d) Elements of financial statements

Identify objective of financial reporting.
(SO 2) K

BE12–3   According to the CICA's conceptual framework, which of the following is an objective of financial reporting? (Write "Yes" or "No" beside each item in the list below.)
(a) To provide information that is helpful in maximizing share prices
(b) To provide information that is useful to those making investment and lending decisions
(c) To provide information that identifies the economic resources (assets), the claims on those resources (liabilities), and the changes in those resources and claims

Identify qualitative characteristics of accounting information.
(SO 3) K

BE12–4   Presented below is a chart showing the qualitative characteristics of accounting information. Fill in the blanks from (a) to (f).

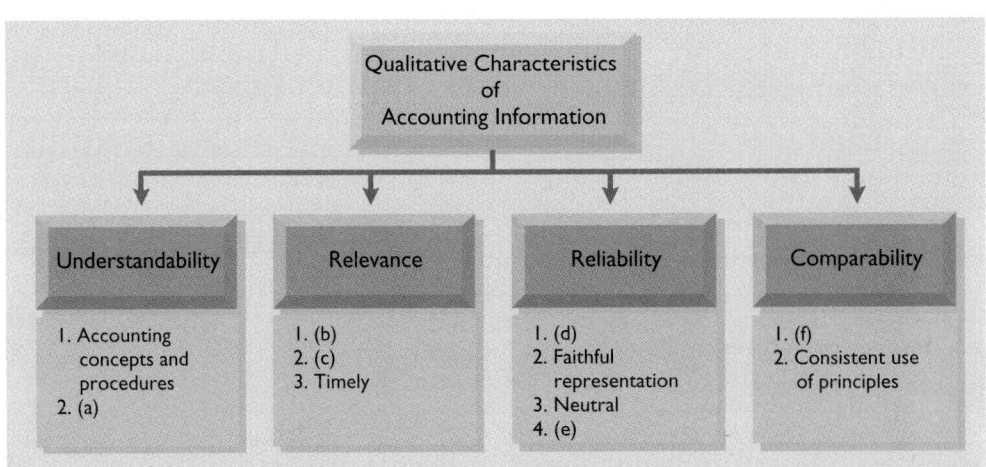

Identify qualitative characteristics of accounting information.
(SO 3) K

BE12–5   Using the qualitative characteristics of accounting established by the conceptual framework, complete each of the following statements:
(a) For information to be _____, it should have predictive or feedback value, and it must be presented on a timely basis.
(b) _____ is the quality of information that ensures that it is free of error and bias; it can be depended upon.
(c) _____ means using the same accounting principles and methods from year to year within a company.
(d) _____ means that two individuals, each working independently, can review the same information and reach the same results or similar conclusions.

Identify qualitative characteristics of accounting information.
(SO 3) K

BE12–6   Presented below is a set of qualitative characteristics of accounting information:
1. Predictive value
2. Neutrality
3. Verifiability
4. Timeliness

Match these qualitative characteristics to the following statements, using numbers 1–4.

(a) ____ Accounting information must be available to decision-makers before it loses its capacity to influence their decisions.

(b) ____ Accounting information cannot be selected, prepared, or presented to favour one set of interested users over another.

(c) ____ Accounting information must be free of error and bias.

(d) ____ Accounting information should help users make predictions about the outcome of past, present, and future events.

BE12–7 Presented below are four concepts discussed in this chapter:
1. Time period assumption
2. Cost principle
3. Full disclosure principle
4. Conservatism

Identify recognition and measurement criteria.
(SO 3, 4, 5) K

Match these concepts to the following accounting practices:

(a) ____ Recording inventory at its purchase price.

(b) ____ Using notes and supplementary schedules in the financial statements.

(c) ____ Preparing financial statements on an interim and annual basis.

(d) ____ Using the lower of cost and market method for inventory valuation.

BE12–8 Hard Hat Construction Company is under contract to build a commercial building at a price of $3,800,000. Construction begins in January 2002 and finishes in December 2004. Total estimated construction costs are $2,800,000. Actual construction costs incurred in each year are as follows: in 2002, $560,000; in 2003, $1,820,000; in 2004, $420,000. Calculate the revenue and gross profit to be recognized in each year, using the percentage-of-completion method.

Calculate revenue and gross profit—percentage-of-completion method.
(SO 5) AP

BE12–9 Brassard Co. uses the instalment method to determine its net income. In 2002, its first year of operations, it had instalment sales of $800,000 and a cost of goods sold of $560,000. The collections on instalment sales were as follows: in 2002, $360,000; and in 2003, $440,000. Determine the gross profit recognized for 2002 and 2003.

Calculate gross profit—instalment method.
(SO 5) AP

BE12–10 The Yoon Company uses the following accounting practices:
(a) Inventory is reported at cost when market value is lower.
(b) Revenue on instalment sales is recognized at the time of sale.
(c) Small tools are recorded as capital assets and amortized.
(d) Paper clips expense appears on the income statement, for $10.
(e) Yoon currently records its accounting transactions and prepares its financial reports manually. The cost of implementing a new computerized accounting system to do these tasks is estimated to be $25,000. Annual savings are anticipated to be $10,000.

Identify violation of accounting principle or constraint.
(SO 5, 6) C

Indicate the accounting principle or constraint, if any, that has been violated by each practice.

EXERCISES

- -

E12–1 Skate Stop is owned by Marc Bélanger. It sells in-line skates and accessories. It shares space with another company, called Ride Snowboards. Ride Snowboards is owned by Marc's wife, Lise Ert-Bélanger, who was an Olympic bronze medallist in snowboarding. Ride Snowboards sells snowboards and related accessories. The following transactions occurred during a recent year:
(a) In January, Lise purchased fire and theft insurance for the year to cover the rented space and inventory. She paid for all the insurance since she had more cash than Marc.
(b) Marc paid the rent for the month of July since he had more cash that month than Lise.
(c) Marc recorded skate sales for the month of September.
(d) Lise purchased and paid for her winter inventory of snowboards in September.
(e) Marc and Lise had such a successful year that they went out to a fancy restaurant to celebrate. They charged the bill to Lise's company.
(f) Lise paid her annual membership fee to the local ski hill from company funds.
(g) Marc paid his annual membership fee to the curling club from company funds.

Apply economic entity assumption.
(SO 4) AP

Instructions

Identify which of the above transactions should be recorded by Skate Stop (SS), and which should be recorded by Ride Snowboards (RS). State if the cost is a personal one, or relates to both companies and should be allocated to each of them.

Determine amount of revenue to be recognized.
(SO 5) AP

E12–2   Consider the following transactions of Kokomo Company for 2002:
  (a) Leased office space to Excel Supplies for a one-year period begininning September 1. The rent of $18,000 was paid in advance.
  (b) Received a sales order for merchandise that cost $9,000. It was sold for $12,000 on December 28, 2002, to Warfield Company. The goods were shipped FOB destination on December 31. Warfield received them on January 3, 2003.
  (c) Signed a long-term contract to construct a building at a total price of $1,300,000. The total estimated cost of construction is $1,200,000. During 2002, the company incurred $300,000 of costs and collected $330,000 in cash. The percentage-of-completion method is used to recognize revenue.
  (d) Had merchandise inventory on hand at year end that amounted to $160,000. Kokomo expects to sell the inventory in 2003 for $180,000.
  (e) Issued a $5,000, six-month, 8% note receivable on September 1.

Instructions

For each item above, indicate the amount of revenue Kokomo should recognize for the year ended December 31, 2002. Explain.

Identify point of revenue recognition.
(SO 5) C

E12–3   The following independent situations require professional judgement for determining when to recognize revenue from the transactions.
  (a) **Air Canada** sells you an advance purchase airline ticket in September for your flight home at Christmas.
  (b) **Leon's Furniture** sells you a home theatre on a "no money down, no interest, and no payments for one year" promotional deal.
  (c) The **Toronto Blue Jays** sell season tickets to games in the Skydome on-line. Fans can purchase the tickets at any time, although the season doesn't officially begin until April. It runs from April through October.
  (d) You borrow money in August from the **RBC Financial Group**. The loan and the interest are repayable in full in November.
  (e) In September, **Centennial College** collects tuition revenue for the term from new and returning students. The term runs from September through December.
  (f) In August, you order a sweater from **Sears** using its on-line catalogue. It arrives in September and you charge it to your Sears credit card. You receive and pay the Sears bill in October.

Instructions

Identify when revenue should be recognized in each of the above situations.

Determine gross profit for a construction project.
(SO 5) AP

E12–4   Shen Construction Company currently has one long-term construction project. The project has a contract price of $125 million with total estimated costs of $100 million. Shen uses the percentage-of-completion method. After two years of construction, the following costs have been accumulated:

Actual cost incurred, 2002	$30 million
Total estimated cost remaining after 2002	70 million
Actual cost incurred, 2003	50 million
Total estimated cost remaining after 2003	20 million

Instructions

Determine the gross profit that should be recognized for each of the first two years of the construction contract, 2002 and 2003.

Determine gross profit using the instalment and point-of-sale bases of revenue recognition.
(SO 5) AP

E12–5   Churchill Company sold equipment for $300,000 in 2002. Collections on the sale were as follows: in 2002, $70,000; in 2003, $190,000; and in 2004, $40,000. Churchill's cost of goods sold is typically 60% of sales.

Instructions

  (a) Determine Churchill's gross profit for 2002, 2003, and 2004, assuming that Churchill recognizes revenue under the instalment method.
  (b) Determine Churchill's gross profit for 2002, 2003, and 2004, assuming that Churchill recognizes revenue using the point-of-sale basis.

E12–6 A number of reporting situations are described below:

Identify assumption, principle, or constraint violated.
(SO 4, 5, 6) C

- (a) Tercek Company recognizes revenue during the production cycle. The price of the product, as well as the amount that can be sold, is not certain.
- (b) In preparing its financial statements, Seco Company omitted information concerning its cost flow assumption for inventories.
- (c) Shea Company uses the direct write-off method of accounting for uncollectible accounts.
- (d) Ravine Hospital Supply Corporation reports only current assets and current liabilities on its balance sheet. Capital assets are reported as current assets. Notes payable are reported as current liabilities. Liquidation of the company is unlikely.
- (e) Barton Company reports its inventory on the balance sheet at its current market value of $100,000. Inventory has an original cost of $110,000.
- (f) Bonilla Company is in its fifth year of operation and has yet to issue financial statements.
- (g) Watts Company has inventory on hand that cost $400,000. Watts reports inventory on its balance sheet at its current market value of $425,000.
- (h) Steph Wolfson, president of the Download Music Company, bought a computer for her personal use. She paid for the computer by using company funds and debited the Computers account.

Instructions

For each of the above, list the assumption, principle, or constraint that has been violated, if any. List only one violation for each case.

E12–7 Presented below are some business transactions that occurred during 2002 for Brooks Co.:

Identify assumption, principle, or constraint violated. Prepare correct entries.
(SO 4, 5, 6) AN

1. Equipment worth $90,000 was acquired at a cost of $64,000 from a company that had water damage in a flood. The following entry is made:

Equipment	90,000	
Cash		64,000
Gain		26,000

2. The president of Brooks Co., Jan Brooks, purchased a truck for personal use and charged it to her expense account. The following entry is made:

Travel Expense	28,000	
Cash		28,000

3. An account receivable has become a bad debt. The following entry is made:

Bad Debts Expense	17,000	
Accounts Receivable		17,000

4. Merchandise inventory with a cost of $208,000 is reported at its market value of $260,000. The following entry is made:

Merchandise Inventory	52,000	
Gain		52,000

5. An electric pencil sharpener costing $135 is being amortized over five years. The following entry is made:

Amortization Expense	27	
Accumulated Amortization—Pencil Sharpener		27

Instructions

In each of the situations above, identify the assumption, principle, or constraint that has been violated, if any. Discuss the appropriateness of the journal entries and give the correct journal entry, if one is needed.

E12–8 Presented below are accounting assumptions, principles, and constraints discussed in this chapter:

Identify assumption, principle, or constraint related to various situations.
(SO 4, 5, 6) C

1. Economic entity assumption
2. Going concern assumption
3. Monetary unit assumption
4. Time period assumption
5. Cost principle

6. Matching principle
7. Full disclosure principle
8. Revenue recognition principle
9. Materiality
10. Cost-benefit

Instructions

Identify by number the accounting assumption, principle, or constraint that describes each situation below. Do not use a number more than once.

(a) _____ Is the rationale for why capital assets are not reported at liquidation value. (Do not use the cost principle.)

(b) _____ Indicates that personal and business record-keeping should be separately maintained.

(c) _____ Ensures that all relevant financial information is reported.

(d) _____ Assumes that the dollar is the "measuring stick" for reporting financial performance.

(e) _____ Requires that GAAP be followed for all significant items.

(f) _____ Separates financial information into time periods for reporting purposes.

(g) _____ Requires recognition of expenses in the same period as related revenues.

(h) _____ Indicates that market value changes after a purchase are not recorded in the accounts.

Discuss comparison of international companies.
(SO 7) C

E12–9   Mark's Work Wearhouse's closest competitor is **The Gap**. Mark's Work Wearhouse, headquartered in Canada, has 299 stores, all located in Canada. The Gap, headquartered in the U.S., has 3,300 stores in Canada, the UK, the U.S., France, Germany, and Japan.

Instructions

Discuss the difficulties a potential investor would have in comparing the financial statements of Mark's and The Gap.

Problems: Set A

* *

Consider nature of conservatism and impact of conservative accounting policies.
(SO 3) C

P12–1A   Some companies adopt a policy of writing off items such as computers over a very short period of time. They defend this as a "conservative" accounting practice.

Instructions

Comment on this policy. Consider (1) the intent of conservatism and (2) the effects of such a policy on net income during the period over which the asset is written off and in subsequent periods.

Comment on objective and qualitative characteristics of accounting information.
(SO 3) C

P12–2A   Net Nanny Software International Inc., headquartered in Vancouver, specializes in Internet safety and computer security products for both the home and enterprise markets. Its balance sheet, as at June 30, 2000, reported a deficit (negative retained earnings) of US$8.6 million. It has reported only net losses since its inception, June 30, 1996. In spite of these losses, Net Nanny's common shares have traded anywhere from a high of $3.70 to a low of $0.32.

Until a few years ago, Net Nanny's financial statements had been prepared in Canadian dollars. As at June 30, 1998, the company adopted the U.S. dollar as its reporting currency.

Instructions

(a) What is the objective of financial reporting? How does this objective meet or not meet Net Nanny's investors' needs?

(b) Why would investors want to buy Net Nanny's shares if the company has consistently reported losses over the last few years? Include in your answer an assessment of the relevance and reliability of the information reported on Net Nanny's financial statements.

(c) Comment on how the change in reporting information from Canadian dollars to U.S. dollars likely affected the readers of Net Nanny's financial statements. Include in your answer an assessment of the comparability of the information.

Analyse transactions to identify principle or assumption violated. Prepare correct entries.
(SO 4, 5) AN

P12–3A   Jeter and Yu are accountants for Kwick Kopy Printers. They are having disagreements concerning the following transactions that occurred during the year ended December 31, 2002:

1. Kwick Kopy bought equipment for $40,000, including installation costs. The equipment has a useful life of five years. Kwick Kopy amortizes equipment using the straight-line method. "Since the equipment as installed into our system cannot be removed without considerable damage, it will have no resale value. It should not be amortized but, instead, expensed immediately," argues Jeter.

2. Amortization for the year was $26,000. Since net income is expected to be low this year, Jeter suggests deferring amortization to a year when there is more net income.

3. Kwick Kopy purchased equipment at a fire sale for $20,000. The equipment would normally have cost $26,000. Jeter believes that the following entry should be made:

Equipment	26,000	
Cash		20,000
Gain on Purchase of Equipment		6,000

4. Jeter says that Kwick Kopy should carry its furnishings on the balance sheet at their liquidation value, which is $20,000 less than cost.
5. Kwick Kopy rented office space for one year, starting October 1, 2002. The total rent of $20,000 was paid in advance. Jeter believes that the following entry should be made on October 1:

| Rent Expense | 20,000 | |
| Cash | | 20,000 |

The company's fiscal year ends on December 31.

6. Land that cost $41,000 was appraised at $49,000. Jeter suggests the following journal entry:

| Land | 8,000 | |
| Gain on Appreciation of Land | | 8,000 |

Yu disagrees with Jeter on each of the situations above.

Instructions

For each transaction, indicate why Yu disagrees. Identify the accounting principle or assumption that Jeter would be violating if his suggestions were used. Prepare the correct journal entry for each transaction, if any.

P12–4A Presented below are a number of business transactions that occurred during the current year for D'Artagnon Company:

Determine appropriateness of journal entries, in terms of generally accepted accounting principles or assumptions.
(SO 4, 5) AN

1. An order for $70,000 was received from a customer for products on hand. This order is to be shipped on January 9 next year. The following entry was made:

| Accounts Receivable | 60,000 | |
| Sales | | 60,000 |

2. Because of a "flood sale," equipment worth $300,000 was acquired at a cost of $240,000. The following entry was made:

Equipment	300,000	
Cash		240,000
Gain on Purchase of Equipment		60,000

3. Because the general level of prices increased during the current year, D'Artagnon determined that there was a $40,000 understatement of amortization expense on its equipment. The company decided to record the understatement in its accounts. The following entry was made:

| Amortization Expense | 40,000 | |
| Accumulated Amortization | | 40,000 |

4. The president of D'Artagnon used his expense account to purchase a pre-owned Mercedes-Benz SL500 solely for personal use. The following entry was made:

| Automobiles | 68,000 | |
| Cash | | 68,000 |

5. Land was purchased on April 30 for $200,000. This amount was recorded in the Land account. On December 31, the land would have cost $230,000, so the following entry was made:

| Land | 30,000 | |
| Gain on Land | | 30,000 |

Instructions

In each of the situations above, discuss the appropriateness of the journal entry in terms of generally accepted accounting principles.

Discuss various alternatives regarding revenue recognition.
(SO 5) C

P12–5A   Santa's Christmas Tree Farm grows pine, fir, and spruce trees. The company cuts and sells the trees for cash during the Christmas season. The majority of the trees are exported to the U.S. The remaining trees are sold to local tree lot operators.

It normally takes about 12 years for a tree to grow to a suitable size. The average selling price for a mature tree is $24. The owner of Santa's Christmas Tree Farm believes that the company should recognize revenue at the rate of $2 ($24 ÷ 12 years) a year for each tree that it cuts. The biggest cost of this business is the cost of fertilizing, pruning, and maintaining the trees over the twelve-year period. These costs average $22 a tree and the owner believes they should also be spread over the twelve-year period.

Instructions

(a) Do you agree with the proposed revenue recognition policy for Santa's Christmas Tree Farms? Explain why or why not. Use the criteria for revenue recognition to explain when you believe revenue should be recognized for this tree farming business.
(b) When should the annual cost of fertilizing, pruning, and maintaining the trees be recognized? Explain.

Recognize gross profit using percentage-of-completion method.
(SO 5) AP

P12–6A   Beaver Construction Company is involved in a long-term construction contract to build an office building. The estimated cost is $30 million and the contract price is $40 million. Additional information follows:

Year	Cash Collections	Actual Costs Incurred
2001	$ 7,000,000	$ 4,500,000
2002	9,000,000	6,000,000
2003	14,500,000	12,000,000
2004	9,500,000	7,500,000

The project is completed in 2004.

Instructions

Prepare a schedule to determine the gross profit in each year of the contract, using the percentage-of-completion method.

Recognize gross profit using percentage-of-completion method, with complexities.
(SO 5) AP

P12–7A   Karim Construction Company has a contract for the construction of a new health and fitness centre. It is accounting for this project using the percentage-of-completion method. The contract amount is $2,500,000 and the cost of construction is initially expected to total $1,500,000. The actual costs incurred each year, the estimated remaining costs to complete the contract, and the expected total cost of the construction are shown below for the three-year life of the project:

Year	Actual Cost Incurred During the Year	Remaining Cost to Be Incurred	Expected Total Cost
2002	$500,000	$1,000,000	$1,500,000
2003	500,000	500,000	1,500,000
2004	400,000	Contract completed	1,400,000 (actual)

Instructions

(a) Calculate the amount of gross profit to be recognized in each of 2002 and 2003.
(b) Calculate the amount of gross profit (if any) to be recognized in 2004. (*Hint*: Note that the overall gross profit earned on the project is different from previously expected. You should begin by calculating the overall gross profit actually realized on the contract, and then compare it to the cumulative amount that has already been recognized, in 2002 and 2003.)
(c) Comment on the above results.

Recognize gross profit using instalment method.
(SO 5) AP

P12–8A   Zaur Construction sold apartments it had constructed to Mattson Management Company for $2.5 million. Zaur's cost to construct the apartments was $1.5 million. Appropriately, Zaur uses the instalment method. Additional information follows:

Year	Cash Collected
2002	$ 800,000
2003	1,200,000
2004	500,000

Instructions

(a) Determine the gross profit for each year using the instalment method.
(b) Repeat (a) assuming the construction cost was $1.6 million.

P12–9A Crazy Carl's Deep Discount Furniture Store makes many of its sales on long-term instalment contracts. It accounts for these using the instalment method. During 2000, Crazy Carl's had $840,000 of instalment sales. The related cost of goods sold was $504,000. The instalment contracts called for the customers' payments to be made as follows:

Recognize gross profit using the instalment method, with complexities.
(SO 5) AP

Year	Payment
2000	$160,000
2001	200,000
2002	200,000
2003	200,000
2004	80,000

The company collected the payments for 2000 through 2002 exactly as scheduled above. However, in 2003 and 2004 things were quite different:

1. Collections in 2003 were only $180,000. Nevertheless, the company was hopeful that the amounts in arrears would soon be collected.
2. Collections in 2004 were only $50,000, and the company conceded that none of the amounts in arrears (neither the $20,000 from 2003 nor the $30,000 from 2004) would ever be collected.

Instructions

(a) Calculate the amount of gross profit to be recognized in the years 2000 through 2002.
(b) Calculate the amount of gross profit to be recognized in 2003. (*Hint*: Note that the overall gross profit expected to be earned on these instalment sales has not been changed by the year's events. You can follow the usual instalment method procedures in this situation.)
(c) Calculate the amount of gross profit (if any) to be recognized in 2004. (*Hint*: Note that the overall gross profit earned on these instalment sales has been changed by this year's developments. You should begin by calculating the overall gross profit actually realized on these sales, and then compare it to the cumulative amount already recognized, in the years 2000 through 2003.)
(d) Comment on the above results.

P12–10A Presented below are accounting assumptions, principles, and constraints discussed in this chapter:

Identify accounting assumptions, principles, and constraints.
(SO 4, 5, 6) C

1. Economic entity assumption
2. Going concern assumption
3. Monetary unit assumption
4. Time period assumption
5. Full disclosure principle
6. Revenue recognition principle
7. Matching principle
8. Cost principle
9. Materiality
10. Cost-benefit

Instructions

Identify by number the accounting assumption, principle, or constraint that describes each situation below. Do not use a number more than once.

(a) _____ Assets are not stated at their liquidation value.
(b) _____ The death of the president is not recorded in the accounts.
(c) _____ Repair tools are expensed when purchased.
(d) _____ An allowance for doubtful accounts is established.
(e) _____ Market value changes after purchase are not recorded in the accounts.
(f) _____ Reporting must be done at defined intervals.
(g) _____ Revenue is recorded at the point of sale.
(h) _____ Small businesses do not have to comply with everything in GAAP when preparing financial statements.
(i) _____ All important information is presented in the notes or in the financial statements.
(j) _____ This indicates that personal and business record keeping should be separate.

P12–11A A friend of yours, Ryan Konotopsky, has come to you looking for some answers about financial statements. Ryan tells you that he is thinking about opening a movie theatre in his home town. Before doing so, he wants to find out how much sales he could expect to make from food concessions as opposed to ticket sales. He wants to know what portion of ticket sales he could expect for children, youth, and seniors, who pay less, versus adults, who pay the highest admission rate. He also wants to know how much profit he would make on ticket sales versus sales at the concession stands, and the average wage per employee.

Comment on accounting constraints.
(SO 6) C

Ryan knows that Empire Theatres operates in many cities and towns in Atlantic Canada. He downloaded the financial statements of Empire Company Limited from the Internet. He noticed that the company's income statement reported revenues for the year ended April 30, 2000, of $11.2 billion and cost of sales, selling, and administrative expenses of $10.7 billion. He read through Empire Company Limited's annual report and learned that Empire Theatres is just one part of the investments division of the company. There are food distribution and real estate divisions as well.

Ryan is disillusioned when he cannot find many details about Empire Theatres in the annual report. He has come to you looking for explanations.

Instructions

What are two constraints in accounting? What impact have these constraints had on the financial reporting by Empire Theatres?

PROBLEMS: SET B

Consider trade-off between relevance and reliability.
(SO 3) C

P12–1B   Many high-tech companies report continued losses, yet their share prices skyrocketed for several years. Take, for example, **JDS Uniphase**, which makes fibre-optic equipment in Nepean, Ontario. Its share price went from a low of $16 to a high of $210, an increase of 1,312%! Yet JDS reported no dividend payments and a loss per share of $2.14 during this period.

Instructions

Explain why investors are willing to pay high prices to purchase the shares of companies that are losing money. Include a discussion of the trade-off between relevance and reliability in your answer.

Comment on objective and qualitative characteristics of financial reporting.
(SO 3) C

P12–2B   A friend of yours, Emily Collis, recently completed an undergraduate degree in science and has just started working with a Canadian biotechnology company. Emily tells you that the owners of the business are trying to secure new sources of financing which are needed for the company to proceed with development of a new healthcare product. Emily said that her boss told her the company must put together a report to present to potential investors.

Emily thought that the company's report should include the detailed scientific findings related to the Phase I clinical trials for this product. "I know that the biotech industry sometimes has only a 10% success rate with new products," she said to you, "but if we report all the scientific findings, everyone will see what a sure success this is going to be!

"The president was talking about the importance of following some set of accounting principles. Why do we need to look at some accounting rules? What they need to realize is that we have scientific results that are quite encouraging, some of the most talented employees around, and the start of some really great customer relationships. We haven't made any sales yet, but we will. We just need the funds to get through all the clinical testing and get government approval for our product. Then these investors will be quite happy that they bought into our company early!"

Instructions

(a) What is the objective of financial reporting? Explain to Emily how her proposal meets or does not meet this objective.
(b) Comment on how Emily's suggestions for what to report to prospective investors conform to the qualitative characteristics of accounting information. Do you think that the things that Emily wants to include in the information for investors will conform to generally accepted accounting principles?

Analyse transactions to identify principle or assumption violated. Prepare correct entries.
(SO 4, 5) AN

P12–3B   Ghosh and Gupta are accountants for Desktop Computers. They disagree over the following transactions that occurred during the calendar year 2002:

1. Desktop purchased equipment for $35,000 at a going-out-of-business sale. The equipment was worth $45,000. Ghosh believes that the following entry should be made:

Equipment	45,000	
Cash		35,000
Gain on Acquisition of Equipment		10,000

2. Land costing $60,000 was appraised at $90,000. Ghosh suggests the following journal entry.

Land	30,000	
Gain on Appreciation of Land		30,000

3. Amortization for the year was $18,000. Since net income is expected to be lower this year, Ghosh suggests deferring amortization to a year when there is more net income.

4. Desktop bought a custom-made piece of equipment for $24,000. This equipment has a use-ful life of six years. Desktop amortizes equipment using the double declining-balance method. "Since the equipment is custom-made, it will have no resale value. It shouldn't be amortized but instead should be expensed immediately," argues Ghosh. "Besides, it provides for lower net income." Ghosh suggests the following entry:

Equipment Expense	24,000	
Cash		24,000

5. Ghosh suggests that their building should be reported on the balance sheet at the lower of cost and market value. Market value is $15,000 less than its cost.

Gupta disagrees with Ghosh on each of the above situations.

Instructions

For each transaction, indicate why Gupta disagrees. Identify the accounting principle or assumption that Ghosh would be violating if his suggestions were used. Prepare the correct journal entry for each transaction, if any.

P12–4B Presented below are a number of business transactions that occurred during the current year for GIS Company:

1. Materials were purchased on March 31 for $65,000. This amount was entered in the Materials Inventory account. On December 31, the materials would have cost $85,000, so the following entry was made:

Materials Inventory	20,000	
Gain on Inventory		20,000

2. An order for $30,000 has been received from a customer for products on hand. This order is to be shipped on January 9 next year. The following entry was made:

Accounts Receivable	30,000	
Sales		30,000

3. The president of GIS used her expense account to purchase a new Saab 9000 solely for personal use. The following entry was made:

Miscellaneous Expense	34,000	
Cash		34,000

4. Because of a "fire sale," equipment worth $230,000 was acquired at a cost of $150,000. It had soot and smoke damage, but was otherwise in good order. The following entry was made:

Equipment	230,000	
Cash		150,000
Gain on Purchase of Equipment		80,000

5. Because the general level of prices decreased during the current year, GIS determined that its equipment and amortization were overstated by $25,000. The following entry was made.

Accumulated Amortization	25,000	
Equipment		25,000

Instructions

In each situation, discuss the appropriateness of the journal entries in terms of generally accepted accounting principles.

P12–5B Cal-Ed develops and sells home-study courses to improve a user's math skills. Each course consists of 10 lessons on CD-ROM with an accompanying manual. The manual and first les-son CD are mailed to a student upon registration for the course. Thereafter, one lesson CD is shipped to a student every two weeks over a period of approximately five months, unless the student informs Cal-Ed that he or she wishes to withdraw from the course. Once a lesson is shipped, the stu-dent is responsible for paying for it. After completing the program, the student takes an examina-tion and, if successful, is awarded a certificate.

In 2002, the company developed the course at a cost of $180,000. The development costs were capitalized as development cost. They are amortized on a units-of-activity (lesson) basis.

The cost of duplicating the manual is $15 per unit. The cost of copying a CD and shipping it to the customer is $4 per unit ($30 for the set of 10). These costs are incurred as the materials are needed. The cost of administering the examination is $30 per course. The total cost per course, excluding development costs, is $75.

Determine appropriateness of journal entries, in terms of gen-erally accepted accounting prin-ciples or assumptions.
(SO 4, 5) AN

Discuss various alternatives regarding revenue recognition.
(SO 5) AN

The course fee is $500, receivable from the student as follows:
- $100 when the student registers for the course and receives the manual and first lesson
- $270 ($30 every two weeks) as the student receives the remaining nine lessons
- $130 when the student writes the examination

The company expected that it would sell 1,000 manuals and 9,000 lessons in total. It expects that 800 of the 1,000 students will complete the course and write the final examination.

In 2003, Cal-Ed sold 200 courses and shipped 200 manuals. It also shipped 200 lesson 1 CDs and 800 additional lesson CDs. It administered 100 examinations.

Cal-Ed is undecided about the proper basis for revenue recognition.

Instructions

(a) Assume that all revenue expected to be received from a course is recognized when a student registers for the course. Calculate the amount of income (revenue minus expenses) to be recorded for 2003.

(b) Assume, alternatively, that the company recognizes 10% of the course fee each time it ships a lesson for the course. Calculate the amount of income (revenue minus expenses) to be recorded for 2003.

(c) When do you think revenue should be recognized? Use the criteria for revenue recognition to support your position. You can recommend one of the two methods described in (a) and (b), or recommend another method.

Source: Adapted from Certified General Accountants Association of Canada. *Financial Accounting 2 Examination,* June 1998, Question 2.

Recognize revenue, expense, and gross profit using percentage-of-completion and completed-contract methods.
(SO 5) AP

P12–6B   Brisson Construction Company is involved in a long-term construction contract to build a shopping centre. The centre has a total estimated cost of $20 million, and a contract price of $28 million. Additional information follows:

Year	Cash Collections	Actual Costs Incurred
2001	$ 4,500,000	$ 3,000,000
2002	10,000,000	9,000,000
2003	7,000,000	5,000,000
2004	6,500,000	3,000,000
	$28,000,000	$20,000,000

The shopping centre is completed in 2004 as scheduled. All cash collections related to the contract are received.

Instructions

(a) Prepare a schedule to determine the revenue, expense, and gross profit for each year of the long-term construction contract, using the percentage-of-completion method.

(b) How would your answer in (a) change if Brisson used the completed-contract method rather than the percentage-of-completion method?

Calculate revenue, expense, and gross profit using percentage-of-completion method, with complexities.
(SO 5) AN

P12–7B   Harvey Construction Company has a contract for the construction of a new recreation centre. It accounts for this project using the percentage-of-completion method. The contract amount is $2,800,000 and the cost of construction is initially expected to total $2,100,000.

The actual costs incurred each year, the estimated remaining costs to complete the contract, and the expected total cost of the construction are shown below for the three-year life of the project:

Year	Actual Cost Incurred During the Year	Remaining Cost to Be Incurred	Expected Total Cost
2002	$ 500,000	$1,600,000	$2,100,000
2003	1,000,000	600,000	2,100,000
2004	500,000	Contract completed	2,000,000 (actual)
	$2,000,000		

Instructions

(a) Calculate the amount of revenue, expense, and gross profit to be recognized in each of 2002 and 2003.

(b) Calculate the amount of gross profit (if any) to be recognized in 2004. (*Hint*: Note that the overall gross profit earned on the project is different from previously expected. You should begin by calculating the overall gross profit actually realized on the contract, and then com-

pare it to the cumulative amount that has already been recognized in 2002 and 2003.)
(c) Comment on the above results.

P12–8B The Scotia Trawler Shipyard builds custom trawlers. During its first year of operations, it signed a two-year contract to build a 42-foot trawler for Ken Anthony. The sale price was $600,000. Scotia's cost to construct the boat was estimated to be $390,000. Additional information follows:

Recognize gross profit, using percentage-of-completion and instalment methods.
(SO 5) AN

Year	Cash Collections	Actual Costs Incurred
2002	$250,000	$175,000
2003	350,000	215,000
	$600,000	$390,000

Instructions

(a) Prepare a schedule to determine the gross profit for each year, using the percentage-of-completion method.
(b) Prepare a schedule to determine the gross profit for each year, using the instalment method.
(c) Which method is more appropriate for the Scotia Trawler Shipyard to use? Explain your reasoning.

P12–9B Furniture Warehouse makes many of its sales on long-term instalment contracts. It accounts for these using the instalment method. During 2001, Furniture Warehouse had $960,000 of instalment sales. The related cost of goods sold was $576,000. The instalment contracts called for the customers' payments to be made as follows:

Recognize gross profit using instalment method, with complexities.
(SO 5) AN

Year	Anticipated	Actual
2001	$144,000	$144,000
2002	192,000	192,000
2003	192,000	192,000
2004	192,000	175,000
2005	240,000	40,000
Total	$960,000	$743,000

The company collected the payments for 2001 through 2003 exactly as scheduled above. However, in 2004 and 2005 things were quite different, as follows:

1. Collections in 2004 were only $175,000. Nevertheless, the company was hopeful that the amounts in arrears would soon be collected.
2. Collections in 2005 were only $40,000, and the company conceded that none of the amounts in arrears (neither the $17,000 from 2004 nor the $200,000 from 2005) would ever be collected.

Instructions

(a) Calculate the amount of gross profit to be recognized in the years 2001 though 2003.
(b) Calculate the amount of gross profit to be recognized in 2004. (*Hint*: Note that the overall gross profit expected to be earned on these instalment sales has not been changed by the year's events. You can follow the usual instalment method procedures in this situation.)
(c) Calculate the amount of gross profit (if any) to be recognized in 2005. (*Hint*: Note that the overall gross profit earned on these instalment sales has been changed by this year's developments. You should begin by calculating the overall gross profit actually realized on these sales, and then compare it to the cumulative amount recognized already in the years 2001 through 2003.)
(d) Comment on the above results.

*Identify accounting
assumptions, principles, and
constraints.*
(SO 4, 5, 6) C

P12–10B   Presented below are the assumptions, principles, and constraints discussed in this chapter:

1. Economic entity assumption
2. Going concern assumption
3. Monetary unit assumption
4. Time period assumption
5. Full disclosure principle

6. Revenue recognition
7. Matching principle
8. Cost principle
9. Materiality
10. Cost-benefit

Instructions

Identify by number the accounting assumption, principle, or constraint that describes each situation below. Do not use a number more than once.

(a) ____ Barb Denton runs her accounting practice out of her home. She separates her accounting practice records from her household accounts.

(b) ____ Companies prepare quarterly reports.

(c) ____ Revenue is sometimes recognized at various points of production.

(d) ____ The cost should not exceed the benefits.

(e) ____ Significant accounting policies are reported in the notes to the financial statements.

(f) ____ Companies have indefinite lives.

(g) ____ The effect of inflation for the current year is ignored in determining net income.

(h) ____ Dollar amounts on financial statements are often rounded to the nearest thousand.

(i) ____ Bad debt expense is recorded using the allowance method of accounting.

(j) ____ Land is recorded at its cost of $100,000 rather than at its market value of $150,000.

*Comment on accounting con-
straints.*
(SO 6) AN

P12–11B   No separate disclosure is required on the income statement for the cost of goods sold (the cost of merchandise sold to customers). Because this disclosure is not specifically required, less than half of reporting companies disclose their cost of goods sold separately on their income statement. Most companies include it with other expenses, as **Sears Canada Inc.** did in its income statement for the year ended December 31, 2001:

Cost of merchandise sold, operating, administrative and selling expenses	$5.8 billion

Instructions

(a) Why do you think Sears does not report its cost of merchandise sold separately on its income statement? Comment on how this disclosure meets the objective of financial reporting.

(b) What are the two constraints in accounting? Does either of these constraints likely have an impact on Sears' reporting policy for cost of merchandise sold? Give an example of how each constraint might affect Sears' reporting of its financial information.

Broadening Your Perspective

FINANCIAL REPORTING AND ANALYSIS

Financial Reporting Problem

BYP12–1   Refer to the Notes to Consolidated Financial Statements for **The Second Cup Ltd.**, in Appendix A.

Instructions

Answer the following questions:

(a) Note 1, Basis of Presentation of Pro Forma Financial Information (Unaudited), describes why the 1999 results have been restated and included in the 2000 financial statements. Do you think this additional disclosure was necessary? Explain why or why not, referring to the appropriate generally accepted accounting principles in your answer.

(b) One of the subsections of Note 2, Summary of Significant Accounting Practices, describes The Second Cup's accounting policy regarding Store Pre-opening Costs. Explain how the company's treatment of these costs relates to (1) the matching principle, and (2) the going concern assumption.

(c) Note 3, Acquisition and Divestiture, refers to the company's sale of Coffee People. What accounting principles and constraints are reflected in this disclosure?

(d) Note 13 provides information about transactions with companies that are related (in terms of ownership) to The Second Cup. Why might it be important for readers of the financial statements to be aware of these transactions?

Interpreting Financial Statements

BYP12–2   Today, companies must compete in a global economy. For example, Canada's oldest candy company, **Ganong Bros., Limited**, which has been making chocolates since 1873, must compete with **Nestlé S.A.**, among others. Nestlé, a Swiss company, although best known for its chocolates and confections, is also the largest food company in the world. Comparing companies such as Ganong and Nestlé can pose some challenges. Consider the following excerpts from the notes to Nestlé's financial statements:

Additional Cases

NESTLÉ GROUP
Notes to the Financial Statements (partial)
December 31, 2000

Accounting policies
Accounting convention and accounting standards

   The Consolidated accounts comply with International Accounting Standards (IAS) issued by the International Accounting Standards Committee (IASC) and with the Standing Interpretations issued by the Standing Interpretation Committee of the IASC (SIC).

   The accounts have been prepared under the historical cost convention and on an accrual basis. All significant consolidated companies have a 31st December accounting year end. All disclosures required by the 4th and 7th European Union company law directives are provided.

Instructions

Discuss the implications of each of these items in terms of the effect it might have (positive or negative) on your ability to compare Nestlé to Ganong. (*Hint:* In your answer, include a discussion of relevant principles and assumptions in financial reporting.)

Accounting on the Web

BYP12–3   Annual reports cannot be effective unless the proper information is presented to the reader. This case reviews required and optional report elements.

Instructions

Specific requirements of this Internet case are available on the Weygandt website.

BYP12–4   Revenue recognition is an area that the Ontario Securities Commission has been reviewing and in which it has found many companies to be lacking. This case reviews three Canadian companies to ascertain how they disclose their method(s) of revenue recognition.

Instructions

Specific requirements of this Internet case are available on the Weygandt website.

CRITICAL THINKING
• •

Collaborative Learning Activities

BYP12–5   Hague Industries has two operating divisions—Devany Construction Division and Security Equipment Division. Both divisions maintain their own accounting systems and methods of revenue recognition.

Devany Construction Division

During the fiscal year ending November 30, 2003, Devany Construction Division has one construction project in progress. A $30,000,000 contract for construction of a civic centre was granted on June 19, 2003. Construction begins on August 1, 2003. Estimated costs of completion at the contract date are $26,000,000 over a two-year period. By November 30, 2003, construction costs of $8,000,000 have been incurred.

   The construction costs to complete the remainder of the project are reviewed on November 30, 2003. They are estimated to amount to only $16,000,000 because of an expected decline in raw materials costs.

   Revenue recognition is based upon the percentage-of-completion method.

Security Equipment Division

Security Equipment Division works through manufacturers' agents in various cities. Orders for alarm systems, and down payments, are forwarded from the agents. The division ships the goods FOB destination directly to customers (usually police departments and security-guard companies). Customers are billed directly for the balance due.

   The firm receives orders for $6,000,000 of goods during the fiscal year ending November 30, 2003. Down payments of $600,000 are received, and goods with a selling price of $5,500,000 are billed and shipped. Commissions of 10% of the product price are paid to the agents, after the goods are shipped to the customers. Such goods are covered under warranty for 90 days after shipment. Warranty returns have been about 1% of sales.

   Revenue is recognized at the point of sale by this division.

Instructions

With the class divided into groups, answer the following:
  (a) There are various methods of revenue recognition. Define and describe each of the following methods of revenue recognition. Indicate the circumstances under which each of them follows generally accepted accounting principles.
     1. Point of sale
     2. Percentage-of-completion
     3. Completed-contract
     4. Instalment
  (b) Calculate the amount of revenue to be recognized in the fiscal year 2003 for each operating division of Hague Industries, in accordance with generally accepted accounting principles.

BYP12–6 Nadeau Company reported the following capital assets in its financial statements at the end of the years 2001, 2002, and 2003:

	2001	2002	2003
Land, at cost	$200,000	$200,000	$200,000
Buildings, at cost	900,000	900,000	900,000
Less: Accumulated amortization	100,000	150,000	200,000
Net book value	800,000	750,000	700,000
Equipment, at cost	100,000	100,000	100,000
Less: Accumulated amortization	30,000	40,000	50,000
Net book value	70,000	60,000	50,000

The estimated current market values of these assets (after taking "wear and tear," age, etc., into consideration) were as follows:

	2001	2002	2003
Land	$300,000	$325,000	$350,000
Buildings	850,000	875,000	900,000
Equipment	75,000	70,000	65,000

Instructions

With the class divided into groups, answer the following questions:

(a) Notice that the net book values of the capital assets shown on the financial statements are consistently below their current market values, and that the gap is generally widening each year. Discuss this situation, criticizing or defending it in light of (1) generally accepted accounting principles, and (2) the likely implications (if any) for the users of the financial statements.

(b) The amount shown for the land in the financial statements indicates that the cost of this asset is the same in 2003 as it was in 2001. Comment on the extent to which this is, or is not, a reasonable representation. (*Hint:* Consider whether the owners of the business are "better off" in 2003 than in 2001 as a result of the increase in the current market value of the land.)

(c) The amounts shown for equipment and buildings in the financial statements indicate that the net book value of these assets is considerably less in 2003 than it was in 2001. Comment on how reasonable this presentation is, or is not, in light of the information about the current market values of the equipment and buildings. (*Hint:* You should consider—among other things—whether the increase in market values is likely to be temporary or permanent.)

Communication Activity

BYP12–7 The Southern Alberta Institute of Technology (SAIT) is a post-secondary technical institution with nearly 70,000 students. About 50% of its revenues come from its provincial government grants. About 15% come from tuition fees, and the remaining 35% from donations and internally generated revenue.

One of the difficulties in receiving these grants is to match expenses against revenues in the right fiscal year. For example, SAIT receives funding from the federal government, which allows it to offer classes to students for work preparation. The government specifies the grant periods, for instance, from July 1 to June 30. SAIT therefore has to ensure that all transactions for that project are completed within the fiscal year.

By year end, the goal is to break even. Excess funds, if any, may have to be returned or they will affect next year's budget allocations. SAIT doesn't want a deficit either, however because any overspending will come from the Institute's general fund and reduce next year's budget allocation!

Instructions

Write a letter to your instructor covering the following points:

(a) Why is the matching principle important in accounting for government grants?

(b) Give some examples of a grant or special program to which the matching principle might be applied at your college or university.

(c) What are some examples of costs that SAIT might properly charge to its work preparation programs?

Ethics Case

BYP12–8   When the CICA issues new accounting recommendations, the required implementation date is usually 12 months or more after the date of issuance. Early implementation is encouraged.

Carol DesChenes, an accountant at Grocery Online.com, discusses with her financial vice-president the need for early implementation of a recently issued recommendation. She says it will result in a much fairer presentation of the company's financial position. When the financial vice-president determines that early implementation would adversely affect reported net income for the year, he strongly discourages Carol from implementing the recommendation until it is required.

Instructions
(a) Who are the stakeholders in this situation?
(b) What, if any, are the ethical considerations in this situation?
(c) What could Carol gain by supporting early implementation? Who might be affected by the decision against early implementation?

Answers to Self-Study Questions
1. a 2. d 3. c 4. c 5. c 6. a 7. b 8. c 9. c 10. b

Answer to Second Cup Review It Question 2
PricewaterhouseCoopers, the auditors, state that the financial statements are presented fairly in accordance with generally accepted accounting principles.

Remember to go back to the Navigator box on the chapter-opening page to check off your completed work.

THE
NAVIGATOR

Concepts for Review

Before studying this chapter, you should understand or, if necessary, review:

a. *The cost principle of accounting. (Ch. 1, p. 11)*
b. *The statement of owner's equity. (Ch. 1, p. 26)*
c. *How to make closing entries and prepare the post-closing trial balance. (Ch. 4, pp. 158–159 and p. 163)*
d. *The steps in the accounting cycle. (Ch. 4, p. 164)*
e. *The format of a classified balance sheet. (Ch. 4, pp. 170–171)*

Partners Come and Go, But the Beat Goes On

HALIFAX, N.S.—Cinnamon Toast Records may not be a household name, but the alternative pop bands such as Plumtree and Sloan that have appeared under its label are popular on campus and community radio stations across the country. Several have been nominated for East Coast Music Awards.

In 1992, Cinnamon Toast was founded as a partnership by four young music lovers in Halifax. "We weren't exactly very formal about it," says Walter Forsyth, one of the founding partners, "but we did draw up a partnership agreement—though I don't think we even typed it. The agreement set out the mandate of the company and what the partners should expect to put into the business and get out of it. We agreed we would figure out what it was worth and split the assets equally."

Typed or not, the agreement's basic principles have become important over the years as the structure of Cinnamon Toast's ownership has changed. For example, one partner left after about a year. The departing partner's interest was bought out by the partnership, in accordance with the withdrawal clause in the agreement. Fortunately for the remaining partners, although the label had produced one album, it hadn't realized a profit yet. Therefore, the value of the partnership assets hadn't changed very much.

Another time, a new partner joined by investing assets in the partnership, which brought an infusion of capital at a time when it was greatly needed. On another occasion, a departing partner paid a bonus to the remaining ones. He recovered less than his original investment because the fair market value of the partnership assets was low.

Cinnamon Toast has found this flexibility to be only one advantage of the partnership structure. Another advantage is the pooling of skills that has been facilitated. At one time, one of the partners was a graphic designer who was able to contribute to marketing material and album covers.

Today, the company is owned by three partners: Walter Forsyth, Colin MacKenzie, and Shawn Duggan. Their current catalogue lists five CDs and cassettes, plus a dozen seven-inch singles in good old-fashioned vinyl, which the bands use "like business cards." None of the partners expects to get rich from Cinnamon Toast—all have other sources of income—but they are serious players in the East Coast independent music scene.

Their advice to anyone thinking of forming a partnership? "Communication is essential. When money gets involved, things can get difficult. Strive for fairness."

THE
NAVIGATOR

THE NAVIGATOR

■ Understand *Concepts for Review* ☐
■ Read *Feature Story* ☐
■ Scan *Study Objectives* ☐
■ Read *Preview* ☐
■ Read text and answer *Before You Go On*
    p. 609 ☐   p. 615 ☐   p. 623 ☐   p. 628 ☐
■ Work *Demonstration Problems* ☐
■ Review *Summary of Study Objectives* ☐
■ Answer *Self-Study Questions* ☐
■ Complete assignments ☐

CHAPTER · 13

ACCOUNTING FOR PARTNERSHIPS

▶ STUDY OBJECTIVES ◀

After studying this chapter, you should be able to:

1. *Describe the characteristics of the partnership form of business organization.*
2. *Describe and generate the accounting entries for the formation of a partnership.*
3. *Apply various bases to divide net income or net loss.*
4. *Describe and illustrate the form and content of partnership financial statements.*
5. *Prepare and explain the effects of the entries when a new partner is admitted.*
6. *Prepare and explain the effects of the entries when a partner withdraws from the firm.*
7. *Prepare the entries to record the liquidation of a partnership.*

THE
NAVIGATOR

It is not surprising that the four music lovers who founded Cinnamon Toast Records decided to use the partnership form of organization. They saw the need for hands-on control of their product and its promotion. In this chapter, we will discuss why the partnership form of organization is often selected. We will also explain the major issues in accounting for partnerships.

The chapter is organized as follows:

THE NAVIGATOR

▼Partnership Form of Organization

All provinces in Canada have a *Partnership Act* which provides the basic rules for the formation and operation of partnerships. These acts define a partnership as two or more people who do business with the intention of making a profit. This does not necessarily mean that you must make a profit—just that profit is your objective. Partnerships are common among small retail and manufacturing companies. Similarly, if you enter a profession such as accounting, advertising, law, or medicine, you may find it desirable to form a partnership with other professionals in your field. Professional partnerships can vary in size from two partners to thousands.

There are different forms of partnership organizations. The most common is the general partnership. Unless otherwise indicated, our discussion in this chapter focuses on this type of partnership organization.

Characteristics of Partnerships

STUDY OBJECTIVE
•••••••••**1**•••••••••

Describe the characteristics of the partnership form of business organization.

Partnerships are fairly easy to form, as indicated in the feature story. They can be formed simply by a verbal agreement, or more formally by putting in writing the rights and obligations of the partners. Partners who have not put their agreement in writing have found that the absence of a written agreement can sometimes lead to later difficulties.

Illustration 13-1
Partnership characteristics

The principal characteristics of the partnership form of business organization are shown in Illustration 13-1, and are explained in the following sections.

Association of Individuals

The voluntary association of two or more individuals in a partnership may be based on an act as simple as a handshake. It is preferable, however, to state the agreement in writing.

A partnership is a legal entity for certain purposes. For instance, property (land, buildings, equipment) can be owned in the name of the partnership. The firm can sue or be sued. **A partnership is also an accounting entity for financial reporting purposes.** Thus, the personal assets, liabilities, and transactions of the partners are excluded from the accounting records of the partnership, just as they are in a proprietorship.

Division of Income

The partners specify how the partnership net income (loss) will be divided when they form the partnership. If the division isn't specified, net income (loss) is assumed to be shared equally. We will learn more about dividing partnership income in a later section of this chapter.

The net income of a partnership is not taxed as a separate entity. Instead, each partner's share is personally taxable. This share of income is recorded on the partner's personal income tax return and taxed at his or her personal tax rate regardless of the amount withdrawn from the partnership during the year.

Mutual Agency

Mutual agency means that each partner acts for the partnership when doing partnership business. The action of any partner is binding on all other partners. This is true even when partners exceed their authority, so long as the act appears appropriate for the partnership. For example, a partner of a grocery store who purchases a delivery truck creates a binding contract in the name of the partnership, even if the

Helpful hint Because of mutual agency, an individual should be extremely cautious in selecting partners.

partnership agreement denies this authority. On the other hand, if a partner in a law firm were to purchase a snowmobile for the partnership, the act would not be binding on the partnership, because the purchase is unrelated to the business.

Co-Ownership of Property

Partnership assets are owned jointly by the partners. If the partnership is dissolved, the assets do not legally return to the original contributor. Each partner has a claim on total assets equal to the balance in his or her respective capital account. This claim does not give a right to specific assets that an individual partner contributed to the firm. Similarly, if a partner invests a building in the partnership that is valued at $100,000 and the building is later sold at a gain of $20,000, that partner does not receive the entire gain.

Partnership net income (or net loss) is also co-owned. As mentioned in the Division of Income section, **all net income or net loss is shared equally by the partners if the partnership contract does not specify to the contrary**. As you will see later, partners may agree to unequal sharing of net income or net loss.

Limited Life

A partnership does not have an unlimited life. Any change in ownership dissolves the partnership. Partnership dissolution occurs whenever a partner withdraws (whether voluntarily or involuntarily through death, incapacitation, or mandatory retirement) or a new partner is admitted. Dissolution of a partnership does not necessarily mean that the business ends. If the continuing partners agree, operations can continue without interruption through the formation of a new partnership.

Unlimited Liability

Each partner is **jointly and severally (individually) liable** for all partnership liabilities. If one partner incurs a liability, the other partners are also held responsible. Creditors' claims are first on partnership assets. If these are insufficient, the claims then attach to the personal resources of any partner, regardless of that partner's equity in the partnership. Because each partner is responsible for all the debts of the partnership, each partner is said to have **unlimited liability**.

▶Accounting in Action ▸ *Business Insight*

Until recently, auditors faced a liability crisis brought on for the most part by the application of joint and several liability. That is, "deep-pocketed" auditors were often held responsible for financial losses because the audit firms (or at least their insurers) were pretty well the only people around left with any money when a client collapsed.

Recent changes to federal legislation have replaced joint and several liability with modified proportionate liability for certain professionals. The new amendments make liability proportional to the degree of fault for claims involving financial information. In other words, defendants in such cases will be held responsible only for their fair share of financial loss as determined by the courts.

Organizations with Partnership Characteristics

Most partnerships are general partnerships, in which the partners have unlimited liability. Special forms of business organizations have been created that include many partnership characteristics but that modify the characteristic of unlimited liability. These special forms include limited partnerships and limited liability partnerships. Multidisciplinary practices are another form of organization with modified partnership characteristics. These three forms of organizations are discussed in the following paragraphs.

Limited Partnerships

In a limited partnership, one or more of the partners have unlimited liability. This type of partner is called a **general partner**. And one or more partners have limited liability for the debts of the partnership. This type of partner is called a **limited partner**. A limited partner's liability for the debts of the partnership is limited to the amount of capital contributed by him or her. For the privilege of limited liability, a limited partner usually accepts less compensation than a general partner and has less influence on the partnership business. Limited partnerships are normally used as an income tax shelter or investment. For example, more than 4,000 limited partners have invested in Journey's End hotels and motels across Canada. This type of organization is identified in its name with the words "Limited Partnership," "Ltd.," or "LP."

Limited Liability Partnerships

Many provinces do not allow professionals such as lawyers, doctors, and accountants to incorporate and limit their liability. They are, however, permitted to form a limited liability partnership or "LLP." The LLP is designed to protect innocent partners from negligence claims resulting from the acts of another partner. Of course, partners are always responsible for their own negligence.

▶ Accounting in Action ▸ *Business Insight*

PricewaterhouseCoopers is the largest LLP in the world. This accounting and professional services practice has fees of more than $17 billion. It has 850 offices in 150 countries with 170,000 employees. Of these, more than 8,500 are partners.

PRICEWATERHOUSECOOPERS 🖎

Multidisciplinary Practices

Multidisciplinary practices, or MDPs, are professional services organizations in which lawyers become partners with accountants or other professionals. For example, the partnership of Donahue Ernst & Young is a multidisciplinary accounting, business advisory, and law practice. The firm's promotional literature says, "We deliver greater value by seamlessly integrating the capabilities of both an innovative law firm and a leading professional services firm." There is much controversy because of fear of conflict of interest and confidentiality in multidisciplinary practices. The confidentiality concern is heightened because accountants have public disclosure obligations, whereas lawyers are bound by solicitor-client privilege. MDPs are not yet allowed in most provinces. In Ontario, MDPs are controlled by lawyers and the main business must be the practice of law.

Advantages and Disadvantages of Partnerships

Why do people choose partnerships? Often, it is to combine the **skills and resources of two or more individuals**. For example, the partners of Cinnamon Toast Records are able to share their knowledge of the music scene. They can also divide operating responsibilities such as the acquisition of new bands, promotion and marketing, and financing and accounting.

A partnership is **easily formed and is relatively free from government regulations and restrictions**. Also, decisions can be made quickly on important matters that affect the firm. There is no board of directors that must be consulted.

On the other hand, partnerships also have some major disadvantages: **mutual agency, limited life, and unlimited liability** in general partnerships. Unlimited liability is particularly troublesome. Many individuals fear they may lose not only their initial investment, but also their personal assets if those assets are needed to pay partnership creditors. As a result, partnerships often find it difficult to obtain large amounts of investment capital. That is one reason why the largest business enterprises in Canada are corporations, not partnerships.

The advantages and disadvantages of the general partnership form of business organization are summarized in Illustration 13-2:

Illustration 13-2

Advantages and disadvantages of a general partnership

Advantages	Disadvantages
Combines skills and resources of two or more individuals	Mutual agency
Easily formed	Limited life
Relatively free of government regulations and restrictions	Unlimited liability
Ease of decision-making	

Partnership Agreement

►*Ethics note*

A well-developed partnership agreement reduces ethical conflict among partners. It specifies, in clear language, the process for solving ethical and legal problems. This is especially important when the partnership experiences financial distress.

Ideally, the agreement of two or more individuals to form a partnership should be in the form of a written contract, known as the partnership agreement. The partnership agreement contains such basic information as the name and principal location of the firm, the purpose of the business, and the date of inception. In addition, relationships among the partners must be specified, such as:

1. The names and capital contributions of partners
2. The rights and duties of partners
3. The basis for sharing net income or net loss
4. Provisions for withdrawal of assets
5. Procedures for submitting disputes to arbitration
6. Procedures for the withdrawal, or addition, of a partner
7. The rights and duties of surviving partners in the event of a partner's death

We cannot overemphasize the importance of a written contract—even a handwritten contract like that of Cinnamon Toast. If a partnership agreement does not exist, the provisions of the *Partnership Act* will apply, which may not be what the partners want. The partnership agreement should be written with care to anticipate all possible situations, contingencies, and disagreements.

►Accounting in Action ► *Business Insight*

A partnership may be created unintentionally. For example, the Partnership Act for British Columbia states that if you receive a share of income from a business, you will be considered a partner in the business unless evidence exists to the contrary. In B.C., then, it would be wise to have a formal agreement that specifies the partners of a firm. Without one, you may be part of a partnership without knowing it!

Before You Go On . . .

►*Review It*

1. What are the distinguishing characteristics of a partnership?
2. How can partners limit their liability?
3. What are the principal advantages and disadvantages of a partnership?
4. What are the major items in a partnership agreement?
5. Why do you suppose The Second Cup was formed as a corporation, and not a partnership? The answer to this question is at the end of the chapter.

THE NAVIGATOR

Related exercise material: BE13–1 and E13–1.

▼Basic Partnership Accounting

We now turn to the basic accounting for partnerships. The major accounting issues relate to forming the partnership, dividing income or loss, and preparing financial statements.

Forming a Partnership

Each partner's initial investment in a partnership is entered in the partnership records. These investments should be recorded at the **fair market value of the assets at the date of their transfer to the partnership**. The values given must be agreed to by all of the partners.

> To illustrate, assume that M. Gan and K. Sin combine their proprietorships on January 2 to start a partnership named Interactive Software. The firm will specialize in developing financial-modelling software packages. Gan and Sin have the following assets prior to the formation of the partnership:

> **STUDY OBJECTIVE**
> ········· ▼ **2** ·········
>
> *Describe and generate the accounting entries for the formation of a partnership.*

	Book Value		Market Value	
	Gan	Sin	Gan	Sin
Cash	$ 8,000	$ 9,000	$ 8,000	$ 9,000
Office equipment	5,000		4,000	
Accumulated amortization	(2,000)			
Accounts receivable		4,000		4,000
Allowance for doubtful accounts		(700)		(1,000)
	$11,000	$12,300	$12,000	$12,000

Illustration 13-3

Book and market value of assets invested

The entries to record the investments are:

Investment of M. Gan

A	=	L	+	PE
+8,000				+12,000
+4,000				

Jan. 2	Cash	8,000	
	Office Equipment	4,000	
	M. Gan, Capital		12,000
	To record investment of Gan.		

Investment of K. Sin

A	=	L	+	PE
+9,000				+12,000
+4,000				
−1,000				

2	Cash	9,000	
	Accounts Receivable	4,000	
	Allowance for Doubtful Accounts		1,000
	K. Sin, Capital		12,000
	To record investment of Sin.		

Helpful hint   The cost principle applies. Cash and the fair market value of noncash assets are recorded at the date of acquisition. The fair market value is what the assets would have cost if they had been purchased at that time.

Note that neither the original cost of the office equipment ($5,000) nor its book value ($5,000 − $2,000) is recorded by the partnership. Instead, the equipment is recorded at its fair market value of $4,000. Because the equipment has not yet been used by the partnership, there is no accumulated amortization.

In contrast, the gross claims on customers ($4,000) are carried forward to the partnership. The allowance for doubtful accounts is adjusted to $1,000 to arrive at a net realizable value of $3,000. A partnership may start with an allowance for doubtful accounts, because it will continue to collect existing accounts receivable, some of which are expected to be uncollectible. In addition, this practice maintains the relationship between the accounts receivable control account in the general ledger and the accounts receivable subsidiary ledger.

After the partnership has been formed, the accounting for transactions is similar to the accounting for any other type of business organization. For example, all transactions with outside parties, such as the purchase or sale of merchandise inventory, the performance of services, and the payment or receipt of cash, should be recorded in the same way for a partnership as for a proprietorship.

Accounting Cycle Tutorial

The steps in the accounting cycle that are described in Chapter 4 for a proprietorship also apply to a partnership. However, there are minor differences in journalizing and posting closing entries and in preparing financial statements, as explained in the following sections. The differences occur because there is more than one owner.

Dividing Net Income or Net Loss

Partnership net income or net loss is shared equally unless the partnership agreement indicates a different division. The same basis of division usually applies to both net income and net loss. It is customary to refer to this basis as the **income ratio**. It is also known as the income and loss ratio, or the profit and loss ratio. A partner's share of net income or net loss is recognized in the accounts through closing entries.

Closing Entries

Four entries are required in preparing closing entries for a partnership, as follows:

1. Debit each revenue account for its balance and credit Income Summary for total revenues.
2. Debit Income Summary for total expenses and credit each expense account for its balance.

3. Debit Income Summary for its balance (which should equal the net income amount) and credit each partner's capital account for his or her share of net income. Conversely, credit Income Summary and debit each partner's capital account for his or her share of net loss.

4. Debit each partner's capital account for the balance in that partner's drawings account, and credit each partner's drawings account for the same amount.

Compared to a proprietorship, there is one more account and entry. You will recall that we closed revenues and expenses directly to the owner's capital account in a proprietorship. Because it is necessary to divide net income (or net loss) among the partners' numerous capital accounts, it is easiest to first close revenues and expenses to a new account called Income Summary. Income Summary is used specifically for this purpose—to summarize net income or net loss before allocating it to each partner. Income Summary is a temporary account, used only during the closing process.

To illustrate closing entries, we will assume, for simplicity, that Interactive Software has one revenue and one expense account. Sales Revenue totalled $100,000 and Operating Expenses totalled $68,000 for the year ended December 31, 2003. The partners, M. Gan and K. Sin, share net income and net loss equally. Drawings for the year were Gan, $8,000, and Sin, $6,000. The closing entries are as follows:

Dec. 31	Sales Revenue	100,000		
	Income Summary		100,000	
	To close revenue to income summary.			

A	=	L	+	PE
				−100,000
				+100,000

31	Income Summary	68,000		
	Operating Expenses		68,000	
	To close expenses to income summary.			

A	=	L	+	PE
				−68,000
				+68,000

31	Income Summary ($100,000 − $68,000)	32,000		
	M. Gan, Capital ($32,000 × 50%)		16,000	
	K. Sin, Capital ($32,000 × 50%)		16,000	
	To close net income to capital accounts.			

A	=	L	+	PE
				−32,000
				+16,000
				+16,000

31	M. Gan, Capital	8,000		
	K. Sin, Capital	6,000		
	M. Gan, Drawings		8,000	
	K. Sin, Drawings		6,000	
	To close drawings accounts to capital accounts.			

A	=	L	+	PE
				−8,000
				−6,000
				+8,000
				+6,000

As in a proprietorship, the partners' capital accounts are permanent accounts. Revenue, expense, income summary, and the partners' drawings accounts are temporary accounts.

Income Ratios

As noted earlier, the partnership agreement should specify the basis for sharing net income or net loss. The following are typical income ratios:

1. A fixed ratio, expressed as a proportion (2:1), a percentage (67% and 33%), or a fraction (⅔ and ⅓).
2. A ratio based either on capital balances at the beginning or end of the year, or on average capital balances during the year.
3. Salaries to partners and the remainder in a fixed ratio.
4. Interest on partners' capital balances and the remainder in a fixed ratio.
5. Salaries to partners, as well as interest on partners' capital balances, and the remainder in a fixed ratio.

STUDY OBJECTIVE
••••••••••• 3 •••••••••••

Apply various bases to divide net income or net loss.

The objective is to agree to a basis that will equitably reflect the partners' capital investment and service to the partnership.

A fixed ratio is easy to apply, and it may be an equitable basis in some circumstances. Assume, for example, that Hughes and Lane are partners. Each contributes the same amount of capital, but Hughes expects to work full-time in the partnership, while Lane expects to work only half-time. Accordingly, the partners agree to a fixed ratio of ⅔ to Hughes and ⅓ to Lane.

A ratio based on capital balances may be appropriate when the funds invested in the partnership are considered the critical factor. Capital balances may also be fair when a manager is hired to run the business and the partners do not plan to take an active role in daily operations.

The three remaining income ratios (items 3, 4, and 5 in the list on the previous page) give specific recognition to differences among partners. These ratios provide salary allowances for time worked and interest allowances for capital invested. Any remaining net income or net loss is allocated using a fixed ratio.

Caution needs to be used in working with these types of income ratios. **These ratios are only for the calculations that divide net income or net loss.** Salaries to partners and interest on partners' capital balances are used only to allocate income or loss among partners. They are not expenses of the partnership. For a partnership, as with other entities, salaries expense is for the cost of services performed by employees. Likewise, interest expense relates to the cost of borrowing from creditors. As owners, partners are not considered either **employees** or **creditors**. Some partnership agreements permit partners to make monthly withdrawals of cash based on their salary allowance. These may or may not be the same as the salary allowance specified in the income ratio. In such cases, the withdrawals are debited to the partner's drawings account. They are *not* debited to salaries expense.

▶ Accounting in Action ▸ *Business Insight*

Partners in large public accounting firms can make substantial incomes. A few senior partners may earn as much as $1,000,000 a year. However, the average earnings of partners are more likely to be in the $300,000 range. The compensation of partners in most large partnerships differs in both form and substance from the compensation of a corporate executive. Partners are not guaranteed an annual salary, nor are they granted stock options. Compensation depends entirely on each year's operating results, which could be negative (net loss) as well as positive (net income). Also, substantial investment is required of each partner. This capital is at risk for the partner's entire career—often 25 to 30 years—without an established return. Upon leaving, it is repayable to the partner without an adjustment for inflation or appreciation in value.

Salaries, Interest, and Remainder in a Fixed Ratio

Under one income ratio (item 5 in the list on the previous page), **salaries and interest must be allocated before the remainder is divided according to the specified fixed ratio**. This is true even if the salary and interest provisions exceed net income. It is also true even if the partnership has suffered a net loss for the year.

To illustrate this income ratio, assume that Sara King and Ray Lee are partners in the Kingslee Company. The partnership agreement provides for (1) salary allowances of $8,400 to King and $6,000 to Lee, (2) interest allowances of 10% on capital balances at the beginning of the year, and (3) the remainder to be distributed equally. Capital balances on January 1 were King $28,000 and Lee $24,000. For the year ended

December 31, 2003, partnership net income is $22,000. The division of net income for the year ended December 31, 2003 is as follows:

KINGSLEE COMPANY
Division of Net Income
For the Year Ended December 31, 2003

	Sara King	Ray Lee	Total
Salary allowance	$ 8,400	$ 6,000	$14,400
Interest allowance			
King ($28,000 × 10%)	2,800		
Lee ($24,000 × 10%)		2,400	5,200
			19,600
Remaining income			
$22,000 − $19,600 = $2,400			
King ($2,400 × 50%)	1,200		
Lee ($2,400 × 50%)		1,200	2,400
Division of net income	$12,400	$9,600	$22,000

Illustration 13-4

Division of net income

The entry to record the division of net income follows:

Dec. 31	Income Summary	22,000	
	Sara King, Capital		12,400
	Ray Lee, Capital		9,600
	To close net income to partners' capital accounts.		

A	=	L	+	PE
				−22,000
				+12,400
				+9,600

Now let's look at a situation in which the salary and interest allowances exceed net income or there is a loss. Assume that Kingslee Company reports a net loss of $18,000. In this case, the salary and interest allowances create a deficiency of $37,600 ($18,000 + $19,600). This deficiency is divided equally among the partners as shown below:

KINGSLEE COMPANY
Division of Net Loss
For the Year Ended December 31, 2003

	Sara King	Ray Lee	Total
Salary allowance	$ 8,400	$ 6,000	$14,400
Interest allowance			
King ($28,000 × 10%)	2,800		
Lee ($24,000 × 10%)		2,400	5,200
			19,600
Remaining deficiency			
($18,000) − $19,600 = $37,600			
King ($37,600 × 50%)	(18,800)		
Lee ($37,600 × 50%)		(18,800)	(37,600)
Division of net loss	($ 7,600)	($10,400)	($18,000)

Illustration 13-5

Division of net loss

The salary and interest allowances are calculated first, as in the preceding example, regardless of whether the partnership reports a net income or a net loss. Any remaining excess or deficiency is then allocated to the partners.

The journal entry to record the division of the net loss would be as follows:

A	=	L	+	PE
				−7,600
				−10,400
				+18,000

Dec. 31	Sara King, Capital	7,600	
	Ray Lee, Capital	10,400	
	Income Summary		18,000
	To close net loss to partners' capital accounts.		

Partnership Financial Statements

STUDY OBJECTIVE
········· **4** ·········
Describe and illustrate the form and content of partnership financial statements.

The financial statements of a partnership are similar to those of a proprietorship. The differences are due to the number of owners involved.

The income statement for a partnership is identical to the income statement for a proprietorship. The allocation (division) of the partnership net income or loss is often disclosed as a separate schedule or note to the statement.

The statement of equity for a partnership is called the statement of partners' capital. Its function is to explain the changes in each partner's capital account and in total partnership capital during the year. As in a proprietorship, changes in capital may result from three causes: additional capital investments, drawings, and each partner's share of the net income or net loss.

The statement of partners' capital for Kingslee Company is shown in Illustration 13-6. It is based on the division of $22,000 of net income in Illustration 13-4. The statement includes assumed data for the investments and drawings.

Illustration 13-6

Statement of partners' capital

KINGSLEE COMPANY
Statement of Partners' Capital
For the Year Ended December 31, 2003

	Sara King	Ray Lee	Total
Capital, January 1	$28,000	$24,000	$52,000
Add: Investments	2,000	0	2,000
Net income	12,400	9,600	22,000
	42,400	33,600	76,000
Less: Drawings	7,000	5,000	12,000
Capital, December 31	$35,400	$28,600	$64,000

The statement of partners' capital is prepared from the income statement and the partners' capital and drawings accounts.

The balance sheet for a partnership is the same as for a proprietorship, except for the equity section. In a proprietorship, the equity section of the balance sheet is called **owner's equity**. A one-line capital account is reported for the owner. In a partnership, the capital balances of each partner are shown in the balance sheet, in a section called **partners' equity**. The partners' equity section in Kingslee Company's balance sheet shows the following:

Illustration 13-7

Partners' equity section of a partnership balance sheet

KINGSLEE COMPANY
Balance Sheet (partial)
December 31, 2003

Total liabilities (assumed amount)		$115,000
Partners' equity		
Sara King, Capital	$35,400	
Ray Lee, Capital	28,600	64,000
Total liabilities and partners' equity		$179,000

It is impractical for large partnerships, such as those found in international accounting firms, to report each individual partner's equity separately. For reporting purposes, these amounts are usually aggregated in the balance sheet.

Before You Go On . . .

►Review It

1. How should a partner's initial investment of assets be valued?
2. What are the closing entries for a partnership?
3. What types of income ratios may be used in a partnership?
4. How do partnership financial statements differ from proprietorship financial statements?

►Do It

LeMay Company reports net income of $44,000 for the year ended May 31. The partnership agreement provides for a salary allowance of $30,000 to L. Lee and $24,000 to R. May. The remainder is to be shared on a 60:40 basis, (60% to Lee, 40% to May). L. Lee asks for your help to divide the net income between the two partners and prepare the closing entry.

Action Plan

• Allocate the salary allowance first, followed by the interest allowance, if any.
• Apply the partners' income ratios to the remaining net income or deficiency.
• Prepare the closing entry distributing net income or loss among the partners' capital accounts.

Solution

The division of net income is as follows:

	L. Lee	R. May	Total
Salary allowance	$30,000	$24,000	54,000
Remaining deficiency			
$44,000 − $54,000 = ($10,000)			
Lee (60% × $10,000)	(6,000)		
May (40% × $10,000)		(4,000)	(10,000)
Division of net income	$24,000	$20,000	$44,000

The closing entry for net income is therefore as follows:

May 31	Income Summary	44,000	
	L. Lee, Capital		24,000
	R. May, Capital		20,000
	To close net income to partners' capital accounts.		

Related exercise material: BE13–2, BE13–3, BE13–4, BE13–5, BE13–6, BE13–7, E13–2, E13–3, and E13–4.

Admission and Withdrawal of Partners

We have seen how the basic accounting for a partnership works. We now look at how to account for a common occurrence in partnerships—the addition or withdrawal of a partner.

Admission of a Partner

STUDY OBJECTIVE
·········· **5** ··········

Prepare and explain the effects of the entries when a new partner is admitted.

The admission of a new partner results in the **legal dissolution of the existing partnership and the beginning of a new one**. From an economic standpoint, the admission of a new partner (or partners) may be of minor significance to the continuity of the business. For example, in large public accounting or law firms, partners are admitted without any change in operating policies. **To recognize the economic effects, it is only necessary to open a capital account for each new partner.** In most cases, the accounting records of the predecessor partnership will continue to be used by the new partnership.

A new partner may be admitted by either (1) purchasing the interest of an existing partner, or (2) investing assets in the partnership, as shown in Illustration 13-8. The former involves only a transfer of capital among the partners who are involved in the transaction: the total capital of the partnership is not affected. The latter (an investment of assets) increases both net assets (total assets less total liabilities) and total capital of the partnership.

Illustration 13-8

Ways of adding partners

How Partners Can Be Admitted

1. Purchase of a Partner's Interest

2. Investment of Assets in the Partnership

Purchase of a Partner's Interest

Helpful hint In a purchase of an interest, the partnership is *not* a participant in the transaction. No cash is contributed to the partnership.

The admission by purchase of an interest is a personal transaction between one or more existing partners and the new partner. Each party acts as an individual, separate from the partnership entity. The price paid is negotiated by the individuals involved. It may be equal to or different from the partner's capital in the accounting records of the partnership. The purchase price passes directly from the new partner to the partner who is giving up part or all of his or her ownership claims. Any money or other consideration exchanged is the personal property of the participants and **not** the property of the partnership.

Accounting for the purchase of an interest is straightforward. In the partnership, only the transfer of a partner's capital is recorded. **The old partner's capital account is debited for the ownership claims that have been relinquished. The new partner's capital account is credited with the ownership interest purchased.** Total assets, total liabilities, and total capital remain unchanged, as do all individual asset and liability accounts.

To illustrate, assume that, on July 1, L. Carson agrees to pay $10,000 each to two partners, D. Arbour and D. Baker, for one-third of their interest in the Arbour-Baker partnership. At the time of the admission of Carson, each partner has a $30,000 capital balance. Both partners, therefore, give up $10,000 (⅓ × $30,000) of their capital. The entry to record the admission of Carson is as follows:

July 1	D. Arbour, Capital	10,000	
	D. Baker, Capital	10,000	
	L. Carson, Capital		20,000
	To record admission of Carson by purchase.		

A	=	L	+	PE
				−10,000
				−10,000
				+20,000

The effect of this transaction on the partners' capital accounts is shown below:

D. Arbour, Capital		D. Baker, Capital		L. Carson, Capital	
10,000	Bal. 30,000	10,000	Bal. 30,000		20,000
	Bal. 20,000		Bal. 20,000		Bal. 20,000

Each partner now has a $20,000 ending capital balance. Net assets and total capital remain unchanged at $60,000 (Net assets = Partners' equity; $60,000 = $20,000 + $20,000 + $20,000). Arbour and Baker continue as partners in the firm, but the capital interest of each has changed from $30,000 to $20,000. The cash paid by Carson goes directly to the individual partners and not to the partnership.

Regardless of the amount paid by Carson for the one-third interest, the entry above would be exactly the same. If Carson pays $12,000 each to Arbour and Baker for one-third of their interest in the partnership, the above entry is still made.

Investment of Assets in a Partnership

The admission of a partner by an investment of assets is a transaction between the new partner and the partnership. It is often referred to simply as admission by investment. This transaction **increases both the net assets and the total capital of the partnership**. In the feature story, Cinnamon Toast admitted a partner by investment, which increased both assets and capital.

To illustrate, assume that instead of purchasing a partner's interest as illustrated in the previous section, Carson invests $30,000 in cash in the Arbour-Baker partnership for a one-third capital interest. In such a case, the entry is as follows:

July 1	Cash	30,000	
	L. Carson, Capital		30,000
	To record admission of Carson by investment.		

A	=	L	+	PE
+30,000				+30,000

Both net assets and total capital increase by $30,000. The effect of this transaction on the partners' capital accounts is shown below:

D. Arbour, Capital		D. Baker, Capital		L. Carson, Capital	
	Bal. 30,000		Bal. 30,000		30,000
	Bal. 30,000		Bal. 30,000		Bal. 30,000

Remember that Carson's one-third capital interest might not result in a one-third income ratio. Carson's income ratio should be specified in the new partnership agreement. It may or may not be equal to the one-third capital interest.

The different effects of an admission by purchase of an interest or by investment are shown in the comparison of the net assets and capital balances in Illustration 13-9.

Illustration 13-9

Comparison of admission by purchase of an interest and by investment

Admission by Purchase of an Interest		Admission by Investment	
Net Assets	$60,000	Net Assets	$90,000
Capital		Capital	
D. Arbour	$20,000	D. Arbour	$30,000
D. Baker	20,000	D. Baker	30,000
L. Carson	20,000	L. Carson	30,000
Total Capital	$60,000	Total Capital	$90,000

When an interest is purchased, the total net assets and the total capital of the partnership do not change. In contrast, when a partner is admitted by investment, both the total net assets and the total capital change.

In the case of admission by investment, complications occur when the new partner's investment differs from the capital equity acquired. When those amounts are not the same, the difference is considered a bonus either (1) to the existing (old) partners or (2) to the new partner.

Bonus to Old Partners.   The existing partners may be unwilling to admit a new partner without receiving a bonus. In an established firm, existing partners may insist on a bonus as compensation for the work they have put into the partnership over the years.

Two accounting factors explain why a bonus may be wanted. First, total partners' capital equals the **net book value** of the recorded net assets of the partnership. When the new partner is admitted, the fair market values of assets such as land and buildings may be higher than their book values. The bonus will help make up the difference between fair market value and net book value. Second, when the partnership has been profitable, goodwill may exist. But the goodwill is not recorded among the assets or reflected in total partners' capital. In such cases, the new partner is usually willing to pay the bonus to become a partner.

A bonus to old partners results when the new partner's investment in the partnership is **greater** than the capital credit on the date of admittance. The bonus results in **an increase in the capital balances of the old partners. It is allocated to them on the basis of their income ratios before the admission of the new partner.**

To illustrate, assume that the Bart-Simpson partnership, owned by Sam Bart and Hal Simpson, has total capital of $120,000. Lisa Trent acquires a 25% ownership (capital) interest in the partnership by making a cash investment of $80,000 on November 1. The procedure for determining Trent's capital credit and the bonus to the old partners is as follows:

1. **Determine the total capital of the new partnership:** Add the new partner's investment to the total capital of the old partnership. In this case, the total capital of the new firm is $200,000, calculated as follows:

Total capital of existing partnership	$120,000
Investment by new partner, Trent	80,000
Total capital of new partnership	$200,000

2. **Determine the new partner's capital credit:** Multiply the total capital of the new partnership by the new partner's ownership interest. Trent's capital credit is $50,000 ($200,000 × 25%).

3. **Determine the amount of the bonus:** Subtract the new partner's capital credit from the new partner's investment. The bonus in this case is $30,000 ($80,000 − $50,000).

4. **Allocate the bonus to the old partners on the basis of their income ratios**: Assuming the ratios are Bart 60% and Simpson 40%, the allocation is $18,000 to Bart ($30,000 × 60%) and $12,000 to Simpson ($30,000 × 40%).

The entry to record the admission of Trent on November 1 follows:

Nov. 1	Cash	80,000	
	Sam Bart, Capital		18,000
	Hal Simpson, Capital		12,000
	Lisa Trent, Capital		50,000
	To record admission of Trent and bonuses to old partners.		

A	=	L	+	PE
+80,000				+18,000
				+12,000
				+50,000

Bonus to New Partner.   A bonus to a new partner results when the new partner's investment in the partnership is **less** than his or her capital credit. This may occur when the new partner possesses resources or special attributes that are desired by the partnership. For example, the new partner may be able to supply cash that is urgently needed for expansion or to meet maturing debts. Or the new partner may be a recognized expert or authority in a relevant field. Thus, an engineering firm may be willing to give a renowned engineer a bonus to join the firm. The partners of a restaurant may offer a bonus to a sports celebrity in order to add the athlete's name to the partnership. A bonus to a new partner may also result when recorded net book values on the partnership books are higher than their market value.

A bonus to a new partner results in a **decrease in the capital balances of the old partners. The amount of the decrease for each partner is based on the income ratios before the admission of the new partner.** To illustrate, assume that Lisa Trent invests $20,000 in cash for a 25% ownership interest in the Bart-Simpson partnership on November 1. Using the four procedures described in the preceding section, the calculations for Trent's capital credit and bonus are:

1. **Determine the total capital of the new partnership:**

Total capital of Bart-Simpson partnership	$120,000
Investment by new partner, Trent	20,000
Total capital of new partnership	$140,000

2. **Determine the new partner's capital credit:** Multiply the total capital of the new partnership by the new partner's ownership interest.

Trent's capital credit ($140,000 × 25%)	$ 35,000

3. **Determine the amount of the bonus:** Subtract the new partner's capital credit from the new partner's investment. In the Bonus to Old Partners section above, this difference was a positive amount and the bonus was allocated to the old partners. Here, the difference is a negative amount, so the bonus is allocated to the new partner from the existing partners' capital accounts.

Bonus ($20,000 − $35,000)	($ 15,000)

4. **Allocate the bonus to the old partners on the basis of their income ratios:**

Allocation of bonus to new partner:		
From Bart ($15,000 × 60%)	$9,000	
From Simpson ($15,000 × 40%)	6,000	$ 15,000

The entry to record the admission of Trent on November 1 follows:

A	=	L	+	PE
+20,000				−9,000
				−6,000
				+35,000

Nov. 1	Cash	20,000	
	Sam Bart, Capital	9,000	
	Hal Simpson, Capital	6,000	
	Lisa Trent, Capital		35,000
	To record Trent's admission and bonus.		

Withdrawal of a Partner

STUDY OBJECTIVE

••••••••▼••••••••
6

Prepare and explain the effects of the entries when a partner withdraws from the firm.

Now let's look at the opposite situation—the withdrawal of a partner. A partner may withdraw from a partnership **voluntarily**, by selling his or her equity in the firm. He or she may withdraw **involuntarily**, by reaching mandatory retirement age, by expulsion, or by dying. The withdrawal of a partner, like the admission of a partner, legally dissolves the partnership. The legal effects may be recognized by dissolving the firm. However, it is customary to record only the economic effects of the partner's withdrawal, while the partnership reorganizes itself and continues to operate.

As indicated earlier, the partnership agreement should specify the terms of withdrawal. The withdrawal of a partner may be accomplished by payment from partners' personal assets or payment from partnership assets, as shown in Illustration 13-10. The former affects only the partners' capital accounts. The latter decreases the total net assets and total capital of the partnership.

Illustration 13-10

Partnership withdrawals

How Partners Can Withdraw

1. Payment from Partners' Personal Assets

Bye

Bye

2. Payment from Partnership Assets

Payment from Partners' Personal Assets

Withdrawal by payment from partners' personal assets is a personal transaction between the partners. It is **the direct opposite of admitting a new partner who purchases a partner's interest**. Payment to the departing partner is made directly from the remaining partners' personal assets. **Partnership assets are not involved in any way, and total capital does not change.** The effect on the partnership is limited to a transfer of the partners' capital balances.

To illustrate, assume that Javad Dargahi, Dong Kim, and Robert Viau have capital balances of $25,000, $15,000, and $10,000, respectively. The partnership equity totals $50,000. Dargahi and Kim agree to buy out Viau's interest. Each agrees to pay Viau $8,000 in exchange for one-half of Viau's total interest of $10,000 on February 1. The entry to record the withdrawal is as follows:

Feb. 1	Robert Viau, Capital		10,000	
	Javad Dargahi, Capital			5,000
	Dong Kim, Capital			5,000
	To record purchase of Viau's interest.			

A	=	L	+	PE
				−10,000
				+5,000
				+5,000

The effect of this transaction on the partners' capital accounts is shown below:

Javad Dargahi, Capital		Dong Kim, Capital		Robert Viau, Capital
	Bal. 25,000		Bal. 15,000		Bal. 10,000
	5,000		5,000	10,000	
	Bal. 30,000		Bal. 20,000		Bal. 0

Net assets and total capital remain the same at $50,000 (Dargahi, Capital, $30,000 + Kim, Capital, $20,000). All that has happened is a reallocation of capital amounts. Note also that the $16,000 paid to Viau personally is not recorded. Viau's capital is debited for only $10,000, not the $16,000 cash that he received. Similarly, both Dargahi and Kim credit their capital accounts for only $5,000, not the $8,000 they each paid.

After Viau's withdrawal, Dargahi and Kim will share net income or net loss equally unless they specifically indicate another income ratio in the partnership agreement.

Payment from Partnership Assets

Withdrawal by payment from partnership assets is a transaction that involves the partnership. **Both partnership net assets and total capital are decreased.** Using partnership assets to pay for a withdrawing partner's interest is the **reverse of admitting a partner through the investment of assets in the partnership**.

Many partnership agreements state that the amount paid should be based on the fair market value of the assets at the time of the partner's withdrawal. When this basis is used, some accountants believe that any differences between recorded asset balances and their fair market values should be (1) recorded by an adjusting entry, and (2) allocated to all partners on the basis of their income ratios.

This view, however, has serious flaws. Recording the revaluations violates the cost principle, which requires assets to be stated at original cost. It is also a departure from the going concern assumption, which assumes that the entity will continue indefinitely. The terms of the partnership contract should not dictate the accounting for this event.

In accounting for a withdrawal by payment from partnership assets, asset revaluations should not be recorded. Any difference between the amount paid and the withdrawing partner's capital balance should be considered a bonus to the departing partner or a bonus to the remaining partners.

Bonus to Departing Partner.   A bonus may be paid to a departing partner when:

1. The fair market value of partnership assets is more than their net book value,
2. There is unrecorded goodwill resulting from the partnership's superior earnings record, or
3. The remaining partners are anxious to remove the partner from the firm.

The bonus is deducted from the remaining partners' capital balances on the basis of their income ratios at the time of the withdrawal.

To illustrate, assume that the following capital balances exist in the RST partnership: Fred Roman, $50,000; Dee Sand, $30,000; and Betty Terk, $20,000. The partners share income in the ratio of 3:2:1, respectively. Terk retires from the partnership on March 1 and receives a cash payment of $25,000 from the firm. The procedure for determining the bonus to the departing partner and the allocation of the bonus to the remaining partners is as follows:

1. **Determine the amount of the bonus:** Subtract the departing partner's capital balance from the cash paid by the partnership. The bonus in this case is $5,000 ($25,000 – $20,000).
2. **Allocate the bonus to the remaining partners on the basis of their income ratios:** The ratios of Roman and Sand are 3:2. Thus, the allocation of the $5,000 bonus is: $3,000 to Roman ($5,000 × ⅗) and $2,000 to Sand ($5,000 × ⅖).

The entry to record the withdrawal of Terk on March 1 is as follows:

A	=	L	+	PE					
–25,000				–20,000	March 1	Betty Terk, Capital		20,000	
				–3,000		Fred Roman, Capital		3,000	
				–2,000		Dee Sand, Capital		2,000	
						Cash			25,000
						To record withdrawal of, and bonus to, Terk.			

The remaining partners, Roman and Sand, will recover the bonus given to Terk as the undervalued assets are used or sold.

Bonus to Remaining Partners.   As in the Cinnamon Toast Records partnership, the departing partner may give a bonus to the remaining partners if:

1. Recorded assets are overvalued,
2. The partnership has a poor earnings record, or
3. The partner is anxious to leave the partnership.

In such cases, the cash paid to the departing partner will be less than the departing partner's capital balance. **The bonus is allocated (credited) to the capital accounts of the remaining partners on the basis of their income ratios**.

To illustrate, assume, instead of the example above, that Terk is paid only $16,000 for her $20,000 equity when she withdraws from the partnership on March 1. In that case, the calculations are as follows:

1. The bonus to remaining partners is $4,000 ($16,000 – $20,000).
2. The allocation of the $4,000 bonus is $2,400 to Roman ($4,000 × ⅗) and $1,600 to Sand ($4,000 × ⅖).

The entry to record the withdrawal on March 1 follows:

A	=	L	+	PE					
–16,000				–20,000	March 1	Betty Terk, Capital		20,000	
				+2,400		Fred Roman, Capital			2,400
				+1,600		Dee Sand, Capital			1,600
						Cash			16,000
						To record withdrawal of Terk and bonus to remaining partners.			

Note that if Sand withdrew from the partnership, any bonus would be divided between Roman and Terk on the basis of their income ratio, which is 3:1 (¾ and ¼).

Before You Go On . . .

►Review It

1. How does the accounting for admission in a partnership by purchase of an interest differ from the accounting for admission by an investment of assets?
2. Contrast the accounting for withdrawal of a partner by payment from (a) personal assets, and (b) partnership assets.

►Do It

Chandler, Phoebe, and Ross have a partnership. There is a $40,000 balance in each capital account. Record the journal entries on September 1 for each of the independent events listed below:

1. Chandler, Phoebe, and Ross agree to admit Rachel as a new one-quarter interest partner. Rachel pays $10,000 in cash directly to each partner.
2. Chandler, Phoebe, and Ross agree to admit Rachel as a new one-quarter interest partner. Rachel contributes $40,000 to the partnership.
3. Phoebe withdraws from the partnership and receives $30,000 of partnership cash. Chandler and Ross share income and losses equally.
4. Chandler and Ross agree to let Phoebe withdraw from the partnership. They each pay Phoebe $25,000 out of their personal assets.

Action Plan

- Recognize that the admission by purchase (or withdrawal by sale) of a partnership interest is a personal transaction between one or more existing partners and the new (or withdrawing) partner.
- Recognize that the admission by investment (or withdrawal by distribution) of partnership assets is a transaction between the new (or withdrawing) partner and the partnership.

Solution

1. Sept. 1	Chandler, Capital	10,000	
	Phoebe, Capital	10,000	
	Ross, Capital	10,000	
	Rachel, Capital		30,000
	To record admission of Rachel by purchase.		
2. Sept. 1	Cash	40,000	
	Rachel, Capital		40,000
	To record admission of Rachel by investment.		
3. Sept. 1	Phoebe, Capital	40,000	
	Cash		30,000
	Chandler, Capital		5,000
	Ross, Capital		5,000
	To record withdrawal of Phoebe and bonus to remaining partners.		
4. Sept. 1	Phoebe, Capital	40,000	
	Chandler, Capital		20,000
	Ross, Capital		20,000
	To record purchase of Phoebe's interest.		

THE NAVIGATOR

Related exercise material: BE13–8, BE13–9, BE13–10, BE13–11, E13–5, E13–6, E13–7, and E13–8.

Liquidation of a Partnership

STUDY OBJECTIVE

7

Prepare the entries to record the liquidation of a partnership.

The liquidation of a partnership terminates the business. It involves selling the assets of the firm, paying liabilities, and distributing any remaining assets to the partners. Liquidation may result from the sale of the business by mutual agreement of the partners, from the death of a partner, or from bankruptcy. In contrast to the dissolution of a partnership, a partnership liquidation ends both the legal and economic life of the entity.

Before the liquidation process begins, the accounting cycle for the partnership must be completed for the final operating period. This includes the preparation of adjusting entries, a trial balance, financial statements, closing entries, and a post-closing trial balance. Only balance sheet accounts should be open as the liquidation process begins.

In liquidation, the sale of noncash assets for cash is called **realization**. Any difference between the net book value and the cash proceeds is called the **gain or loss on realization**. To liquidate a partnership, it is necessary to follow these steps:

1. Sell noncash assets for cash and recognize any gain or loss on realization.
2. Allocate any gain or loss on realization to the partners, based on their income ratios.
3. Pay partnership liabilities in cash.
4. Distribute the remaining cash to partners, based on their **capital balances**.

Each of the steps must be performed in sequence, and **creditors must be paid before partners receive any cash distributions**. Each step must also be recorded by an accounting entry.

When a partnership is liquidated, all partners may happen to have credit balances in their capital accounts. This situation is called no capital deficiency. Alternatively, one or more of the partners' capital accounts may have a debit balance. This situation is called a capital deficiency. To illustrate each of these conditions, assume that the Ace Company is liquidated on April 15, 2003, when its ledger shows the assets, liabilities, and partners' equity accounts in Illustration 13-11 below.

Illustration 13-11

Account balances prior to liquidation

ACE COMPANY Balance Sheet April 15, 2003			
Assets		**Liabilities and Partners' Equity**	
Cash	$ 5,000	Notes payable	$15,000
Accounts receivable	15,000	Accounts payable	16,000
Inventory	18,000	R. Aube, Capital	15,000
Equipment	35,000	P. Chordia, Capital	17,800
Accumulated amortization—		W. Elliott, Capital	1,200
equipment	(8,000)		
	$65,000		$65,000

No Capital Deficiency

The partners of Ace Company agree to liquidate the partnership on the following terms: (1) the noncash assets of the partnership will be sold to Moriyama Enterprises for $75,000 cash, and (2) the partnership will pay its partnership liabilities. The income ratios of the partners are 3:2:1 for Aube, Chordia, and Elliott. The steps in the liquidation process are as follows:

1. The noncash assets (accounts receivable, inventory, and equipment) are sold on April 18 for $75,000. The net book value of these assets is $60,000 ($15,000 +

$18,000 + $35,000 − $8,000). Thus, a gain of $15,000 is realized on the sale, and the following entry is made:

(1)

April 18	Cash	75,000	
	Accumulated Amortization—Equipment	8,000	
	Accounts Receivable		15,000
	Inventory		18,000
	Equipment		35,000
	Gain on Realization		15,000
	To record realization of noncash assets.		

A	=	L	+	PE
+75,000				+15,000
+8,000				
−15,000				
−18,000				
−35,000				

2. The gain on realization of $15,000 is allocated to the partners based on their income ratios, which are 3:2:1 (or ⅜ , ⅔ , and ⅙). The entry is as follows:

(2)

April 18	Gain on Realization	15,000	
	R. Aube, Capital ($15,000 × ³⁄₆)		7,500
	P. Chordia, Capital ($15,000 × ²⁄₆)		5,000
	W. Elliott, Capital ($15,000 × ⅙)		2,500
	To allocate gain to partners' capital accounts.		

A	=	L	+	PE
				−15,000
				+7,500
				+5,000
				+2,500

3. Partnership liabilities consist of Notes Payable, $15,000, and Accounts Payable, $16,000. Creditors are paid in full on April 23 by a cash payment of $31,000. The entry follows:

(3)

April 23	Notes Payable	15,000	
	Accounts Payable	16,000	
	Cash		31,000
	To record payment of partnership liabilities.		

A	=	L	+	PE
−31,000		−15,000		
		−16,000		

4. The remaining cash is distributed to the partners on April 25 based on their **capital balances**. After the entries in the first three steps are posted, all partnership accounts will have zero balances except for four accounts: Cash, $49,000; R. Aube, Capital, $22,500; P. Chordia, Capital, $22,800; and W. Elliott, Capital, $3,700, as shown below:

Cash				R. Aube, Capital			P. Chordia, Capital			W. Elliott, Capital	
Bal.	5,000				Bal.	15,000		Bal.	17,800		Bal.	1,200
(1)	75,000	(3)	31,000		(2)	7,500		(2)	5,000		(2)	2,500
Bal.	**49,000**				Bal.	**22,500**		Bal.	**22,800**		Bal.	**3,700**

The entry to record the distribution of cash on April 25 is as follows:

(4)

April 25	R. Aube, Capital	22,500	
	P. Chordia, Capital	22,800	
	W. Elliott, Capital	3,700	
	Cash		49,000
	To record distribution of cash to partners.		

A	=	L	+	PE
−49,000				−22,500
				−22,800
				−3,700

After this entry is posted, all partnership general ledger accounts will have zero balances.

A word of caution: **Cash should not be distributed to partners on the basis of their income-sharing ratios.** On this basis, Aube would receive ³⁄₆, or $24,500. This would produce an incorrect debit balance of $2,000. While the income ratio is the proper basis for allocating net income or loss and any gains or losses on the realization of assets, it is not a proper basis for making the final distribution of cash to the partners.

Helpful hint   Zero balances after posting is a quick proof of the accuracy of the cash-distribution entry.

Capital Deficiency

Helpful hint These entries are the same as those in the No Capital Deficiency section except for the loss on realization.

A capital deficiency may be caused by recurring net losses, excessive drawings, or losses from the realization during liquidation. To illustrate, assume that Ace Company is almost bankrupt. The partners decide to liquidate by having a going-out-of-business sale on April 18. Merchandise is sold at substantial discounts, and the equipment is sold at auction. Cash proceeds from these sales and collections from customers total only $42,000. The loss from liquidation is $18,000 ($60,000 in net book value − $42,000 in proceeds). The steps in the liquidation process are as follows:

1. The entry for the realization of noncash assets is recorded on April 18:

(1)

A	=	L	+	PE
+42,000				−18,000
+8,000				
−15,000				
−18,000				
−35,000				

April 18	Cash	42,000	
	Accumulated Amortization—Equipment	8,000	
	Loss on Realization	18,000	
	Accounts Receivable		15,000
	Inventory		18,000
	Equipment		35,000
	To record realization of noncash assets.		

2. The loss on realization is allocated to the partners on the basis of their income ratios and recorded as follows:

(2)

A	=	L	+	PE
				−9,000
				−6,000
				−3,000
				+18,000

April 18	R. Aube, Capital ($18,000 × $\frac{3}{6}$)	9,000	
	P. Chordia, Capital ($18,000 × $\frac{2}{6}$)	6,000	
	W. Elliott, Capital ($18,000 × $\frac{1}{6}$)	3,000	
	Loss on Realization		18,000
	To allocate loss on realization to partners.		

3. Partnership liabilities are paid on April 23 and recorded:

(3)

A	=	L	+	PE
−31,000		−15,000		
		−16,000		

April 23	Notes Payable	15,000	
	Accounts Payable	16,000	
	Cash		31,000
	To record payment of partnership liabilities.		

4. After posting of the three entries, two accounts will have debit balances: Cash, $16,000 and W. Elliott, Capital, $1,800. Two accounts will have credit balances: R. Aube, Capital, $6,000, and P. Chordia, Capital, $11,800. All four accounts are shown below:

Cash			
Bal.	5,000		
(1)	42,000	(3)	31,000
Bal.	16,000		

R. Aube, Capital			
(2)	9,000	Bal.	15,000
		Bal.	6,000

P. Chordia, Capital			
(2)	6,000	Bal.	17,800
		Bal.	11,800

W. Elliott, Capital			
(2)	3,000	Bal.	1,200
Bal.	1,800		

Elliott has a capital deficiency of $1,800. He therefore owes the partnership $1,800. Aube and Chordia have a legally enforceable claim for that amount against Elliott's personal assets. The distribution of cash is still made on the basis of capital balances. But the amount will vary depending on how Elliott's deficiency is settled. Two alternatives for settling are presented next:

Payment of Deficiency

If the partner with the capital deficiency pays the amount owed to the partnership, the deficiency is eliminated. To illustrate, assume that Elliott pays $1,800 to the partnership on April 24. The entry and account balances are as follows:

(4)

April 24	Cash	1,800	
	W. Elliott, Capital		1,800
	To record payment of capital deficiency by Elliott.		

A	=	L	+	PE
+1,800				+1,800

Cash				R. Aube, Capital				P. Chordia, Capital				W. Elliott, Capital		
Bal.	5,000			(2)	9,000	Bal.	15,000	(2)	6,000	Bal.	17,800			Bal.	1,200
(1)	42,000	(3)	31,000			Bal.	6,000			Bal.	11,800	(2) 3,000	(4) 1,800
(4)	1,800													Bal.	0
Bal.	17,800														

The cash balance of $17,800 is now equal to the credit balances in the capital accounts (Aube $6,000 + Chordia $11,800). Cash is distributed on the basis of these balances on April 25, and the following entry is made:

April 25	R. Aube, Capital	6,000	
	P. Chordia, Capital	11,800	
	Cash		17,800
	To record distribution of cash to partners.		

A	=	L	+	PE
−17,800				−6,000
				−11,800

After this entry is posted, all accounts will have zero balances.

Nonpayment of Deficiency

If a partner with a capital deficiency is unable to pay the amount owed to the partnership, the partners with credit balances must absorb the loss. The loss is allocated on the basis of the income ratios that exist between the partners with credit balances.

For example, the income ratios of Aube and Chordia are 3:2 (or ⅗ and ⅖), respectively. The following entry would be made to remove Elliott's capital deficiency on April 25:

(4)

April 25	R. Aube, Capital ($1,800 × ⅗)	1,080	
	P. Chordia, Capital ($1,800 × ⅖)	720	
	W. Elliott, Capital		1,800
	To record write-off of capital deficiency.		

A	=	L	+	PE
				−1,080
				−720
				+1,800

The cash balance of $16,000 now equals the sum of the credit balances in the capital accounts (Aube $4,920 + Chordia $11,080). The entry to record the distribution of cash follows:

Cash				R. Aube, Capital				P. Chordia, Capital				W. Elliott, Capital		
Bal.	5,000			(2)	9,000	Bal.	15,000	(2)	6,000	Bal.	17,800			Bal.	1,200
(1)	42,000	(3)	31,000	(4)	1,080			(4)	720			(2) 3,000	(4) 1,800
Bal.	16,000					Bal.	4,920			Bal.	11,080			Bal.	0

April 25	R. Aube, Capital	4,920	
	P. Chordia, Capital	11,080	
	Cash		16,000
	To record distribution of cash to partners.		

A	=	L	+	PE
−16,000				−4,920
				−11,080

After this entry is posted, all accounts will have zero balances.

Before You Go On . . .

▶*Review It*

1. What are the steps in liquidating a partnership?
2. What basis is used in making the final distribution of cash to the partners?

Related exercise material: BE13–12, E13–9, E13–10, and E13–11.

▶*A Look Back at Our Feature Story*

Refer back to the feature story about Cinnamon Toast Records at the begining of the chapter. Answer the following questions:
1. Why might the four founders have selected the partnership form of organization for their business, Cinnamon Toast Records?
2. What are some of the major items that should probably be written into the partnership agreement for Cinnamon Toast Records?
3. Explain the impact on the financial position of the partnership when one of the partners joined by investment. What about when one of the partners departed and paid a bonus to the remaining partners?

Solution

1. The founders may have chosen to form a partnership, rather than a corporation, for a number of reasons. First, the partnership can be formed (and reformed) quickly and easily, with little of the red tape a corporation faces. Second, the partnership form allows skills and talents to be combined, which is a distinct advantage over a proprietorship. Third, since the partners work closely together, their concerns about the risk of unlimited liability that might be incurred by the other partners are reduced.
2. The partnership agreement of Cinnamon Toast Records should specify the capital contributed by each partner, and the basis for sharing income and losses and for withdrawing funds. In addition, it should specify a mechanism to resolve disputes, add or remove a partner, and deal with the death of one of the partners. A well-written partnership agreement can significantly reduce conflicts as the firm changes size.
3. Admission by investment will give the partnership an increase in net assets (normally cash) and capital (an added capital account for the new partner). Purchase of a departing partner's interest reduces the partnership's capital (the departing partner's account is eliminated) and net assets (normally cash). In addition, the capital accounts of the remaining partners are increased, proportionately, by the amount of the bonus (the amount paid in excess of the departing partner's capital balance).

DEMONSTRATION PROBLEM

Additional Demonstration Problem

On January 1, 2002, the capital balances in Hollingsworth Company are Lois Holly, $26,000, and Jim Worth, $24,000. For the year ended December 31, 2002, the partnership reports net income of $30,000. The income ratio provides for salary allowances of $12,000 for Holly and $10,000 for Worth. The remainder is distributed equally. Neither partner had any drawings in 2002.

In 2003, assume that the following independent transactions occur on January 1:

1. Donna Reichenbacher purchases one-half of Holly's capital interest for $25,000.
2. Marsha Mears is admitted with a 25% capital interest by a cash investment of $40,000.
3. Stan Wells is admitted with a 35% capital interest by a cash investment of $40,000.

Instructions

(a) Prepare a schedule showing the distribution of net income in 2002.
(b) Journalize the division of 2002 net income and its distribution to the partners.
(c) Journalize each of the independent transactions that occurred on January 1, 2003.

Solution to Demonstration Problem

(a)

Division of Net Income

	Lois Holly	Jim Worth	Total
Salary allowance	$12,000	$10,000	$22,000
Remaining income			
$30,000 − $22,000 = $8,000			
Lois Holly ($8,000 × 50%)	4,000		
Jim Worth ($8,000 × 50%)		4,000	8,000
Division of net income	$16,000	$14,000	$30,000

(b)

Dec. 31	Income Summary	30,000	
	Lois Holly, Capital		16,000
	Jim Worth, Capital		14,000
	To close net income to partners' capital accounts.		

(c)

1.	Jan. 1	Lois Holly, Capital ($26,000 + $16,000) × 50%	21,000	
		Donna Reichenbacher, Capital		21,000
		To record purchase of one-half of Holly's interest.		

2.	Jan. 1	Cash	40,000	
		Lois Holly, Capital		5,000
		Jim Worth, Capital		5,000
		Marsha Mears, Capital		30,000
		To record admission of Mears and bonus to old partners.		

Total capital after investment: $120,000
(Holly, $42,000; Worth $38,000;
Mears investment, $40,000)

Mears's capital credit (25% × $120,000)			$30,000
Bonus to old partners ($40,000 − $30,000)			$10,000

Allocation of bonus:

Holly ($10,000 × 50%)	$ 5,000	
Worth ($10,000 × 50%)	5,000	$10,000

3.	Jan. 1	Cash	40,000	
		Lois Holly, Capital	1,000	
		Jim Worth, Capital	1,000	
		Stan Wells, Capital		42,000
		To record Wells's admission and bonus.		

Wells's capital credit (35% × $120,000)			$42,000
Bonus to Wells ($40,000 − $42,000)			($ 2,000)

Allocation of bonus:

Holly ($2,000 × 50%)	$ 1,000	
Worth ($2,000 × 50%)	1,000	$ 2,000

Action Plan

• Allocate the partners' salaries (and interest, if any) to their capital accounts.

• Divide the remaining net income among the partners, based on the income ratio.

• Journalize the division of net income in a closing entry, using the Income Summary account.

• Recognize the admission by purchase of a partnership interest as a personal transaction between an existing partner and the new partner.

• Recognize the admission by investment of partnership assets as a transaction between the new partner and the partnership.

THE NAVIGATOR

Summary of Study Objectives

1. *Describe the characteristics of the partnership form of business organization.* The principal characteristics of a partnership are (a) the association of individuals, (b) mutual agency, (c) co-ownership of property, (d) limited life, and (e) unlimited liability.

2. *Describe and generate the accounting entries for the formation of a partnership.* When a partnership is formed, each partner's initial investment should be recorded at the fair market value of the assets at the date of their transfer to the partnership.

3. *Apply various bases for dividing net income or net loss.* Net income or net loss is divided on the basis of the income ratio, which may be any of the following: (a) a fixed ratio, (b) a ratio based on beginning, ending, or average capital balances, (c) salaries allocated to partners and the remainder in a fixed ratio, (d) interest on partners' capital balances and the remainder in a fixed ratio, and (e) salaries allocated to partners, interest on partners' capital balances, and the remainder in a fixed ratio.

4. **Describe and illustrate the form and content of partnership financial statements.** The financial statements of a partnership are similar to those of a proprietorship. The principal differences are that (a) the statement of owners' equity is called the statement of partners' equity, and (b) each partner's capital is usually reported on the balance sheet.

5. **Prepare and explain the effects of the entries when a new partner is admitted.** The entry to record the admission of a new partner by purchase of a partner's interest affects only partners' capital accounts. The entries to record the admission by investment of assets in the partnership (a) increase both net assets and total capital, and (b) may result in the recognition of a bonus to either the old partners or the new partner.

6. *Prepare and explain the effects of the entries when a partner withdraws from the firm.* The entry to record a withdrawal from the firm when payment is made from partners' personal assets affects only partners' capital accounts. The entry to record a withdrawal when payment is made from partnership assets (a) decreases net assets and total capital, and (b) may result in recognizing a bonus to either the departing partner or the remaining partners.

7. *Prepare the entries to record the liquidation of a partnership.* When a partnership is liquidated, it is necessary to record (a) the sale of noncash assets, (b) the allocation of the gain or loss on realization, (c) the payment of partnership liabilities, and (d) the distribution of cash to the partners, on the basis of their capital balances.

GLOSSARY

 Key Term Matching Activity

Admission by investment Admission of a partner by an investment of assets in the partnership. Both partnership net assets and total capital increase. (p. 617)

Admission by purchase of an interest Admission of a partner by means of a personal transaction between one or more existing partners and the new partner. It does not change total partnership assets or total capital. (p. 616)

Capital deficiency A debit balance in a partner's capital account after the allocation of a gain or loss in a liquidation of a partnership. Capital deficiencies can be repaid, or allocated among the remaining partners. (p. 624)

Income ratio The basis for dividing both net income and net loss in a partnership. (p. 610)

Limited liability partnership (LLP) A partnership in which partners are given limited liability for the obligations of the partnership. (p. 607)

Limited partnership (LP) A partnership in which one or more general partners have unlimited liability, and one or more partners have limited liability for the obligations of the partnership. (p. 607)

Multidisciplinary practices (MDP) Professional services organizations in which lawyers are partners with accountants or other professionals. (p. 607)

No capital deficiency All partners have credit balances after the allocation of a gain or a loss in liquidation of a partnership. (p. 624)

Partnership An association of two or more individuals to carry on as co-owners of a business for profit. (p. 604)

Partnership agreement A written contract that expresses the voluntary agreement of two or more individuals in a partnership. (p. 608)

Partnership dissolution A change in the number of partners that does not necessarily terminate the business. (p. 606)

Partnership liquidation An event that ends both the legal and economic life of a partnership. (p. 624)

Statement of partners' capital The equity statement for a partnership that shows the changes in each partner's capital balance, and in total partnership capital, during the year. (p. 614)

Withdrawal by payment from partners' personal assets Withdrawal of a partner by a personal transaction between partners. It does not change total partnership assets or total capital. (p. 620)

Withdrawal by payment from partnership assets Withdrawal of a partner by a transaction that decreases both partnership net assets and total capital. (p. 621)

SELF-STUDY QUESTIONS

www.wiley.com/canada/we...indiz **Chapter 13 Self-Test**

Answers are at the end of the chapter.

(SO 1) K   1. Which of the following is not a characteristic of a partnership?
  a. Taxable entity
  b. Co-ownership of property
  c. Mutual agency
  d. Limited life

(SO 1) K   2. The advantages of a general partnership do not include:
  a. ease of formation.
  b. unlimited liability.
  c. little government regulation.
  d. ease of decision-making.

(SO 2) K   3. Upon formation of a partnership, each partner's initial investment of assets should be recorded at its:
  a. net book value.
  b. original cost.
  c. fair market value.
  d. liquidation value.

(SO 3) AP   4. The ABC Company reports net income of $60,000. If partners A, B, and C have an income ratio of 50%, 30%, and 20%, respectively, C's share of the net income is:
  a. $12,000.
  b. $18,000.
  c. $30,000.
  d. No correct answer is given.

(SO 3) AP   5. Using the data in (4), what is B's share of net income if the percentages are used after each partner receives a $10,000 salary allowance?
  a. $12,000
  b. $19,000
  c. $20,000
  d. $21,000

(SO 4) K   6. Which of the following statements about partnership financial statements is true?
  a. Details of the distribution of net income are shown in the cash flow statement.
  b. The distribution of net income is shown on the balance sheet.
  c. Partner capital balances are usually shown in the income statement.

  d. The statement of owners' equity is called the statement of partners' capital.

(SO 5) AP   7. R. Ranken purchases 50% of L. Lars's capital interest in the Kim & Lars partnership for $22,000. The capital balances of Kim and Lars are $40,000 and $30,000, respectively. Ranken's capital balance after the purchase is:
  a. $15,000.
  b. $20,000.
  c. $22,000.
  d. $35,000.

(SO 5) AP   8. Capital balances in the DEA partnership are D, Capital, $60,000; E, Capital, $50,000; and A, Capital, $40,000. Income ratios are 5:3:2, respectively. The DEAR partnership is formed by admitting R to the firm with a cash investment of $60,000 for a 25% capital interest. The bonus to be credited to A, Capital, in admitting R is:
  a. $1,500.
  b. $3,750.
  c. $7,500.
  d. $10,000.

(SO 6) AP   9. Capital balances in the TERM partnership are T, Capital, $50,000; E, Capital, $40,000; R, Capital, $30,000; and M, Capital, $20,000. Income ratios are 4:3:2:1, respectively. M withdraws from the firm after receiving $29,000 in cash from the partnership. E's capital balance after recording the withdrawal of M is:
  a. $36,000.
  b. $37,000.
  c. $38,000.
  d. $40,000.

(SO 7) K   10. In the liquidation of a partnership, it is necessary to (1) distribute cash to the partners, (2) sell noncash assets, (3) allocate any gain or loss on realization to the partners, and (4) pay liabilities. These steps should be performed in the following order:
  a. (2), (3), (4), (1).
  b. (2), (3), (1), (4).
  c. (3), (2), (1), (4).
  d. (3), (2), (4), (1).

THE NAVIGATOR

QUESTIONS

(SO 1) C   1. The characteristics of a partnership include the following: (a) association of individuals, (b) limited life, and (c) co-ownership of property. Explain each of these terms.

(SO 1) C   2. Carla Cardosa is confused about the partnership characteristics of (a) mutual agency, and (b) unlimited liability. Explain these two characteristics to Carla.

(SO 1) C   3. K. Nasser and T. Yoko are considering a business venture. They ask you to explain the advantages and disadvantages of the partnership form of organization.

(SO 1) K   4. Identify two other types of business organization having partnership characteristics.

(SO 2) AP   5. S. Brown and D. Barclay form a partnership. Brown contributes land and a building with a net book value of $50,000 and $40,000 and a fair market value of

$75,000 and $50,000, respectively. He also contributes equipment with a net book value of $52,000 and a fair market value of $57,000. The partnership assumes a $20,000 mortgage on the building. What should the balance in Brown's capital account be once the partnership is formed?

(SO 3) C 6. R. Hay, S. Innis, and L. Joyce have a partnership called Express Wings. There is a dispute among the partners. Hay has invested twice as much as the other two partners. She believes net income and net losses should be shared in accordance with the capital contributions. The partnership agreement does not specify the division of profits and losses. How will net income and net loss be divided?

(SO 3) C 7. S. Hark and R. Green are discussing how income and losses should be divided in a partnership they plan to form. What factors should be considered in determining the division of net income or net loss?

(SO 3) C 8. H. Astro and S. Sund share partnership net income and net loss equally. (a) Which accounts are debited and credited to record the division of net income between the partners? (b) If H. Astro withdraws $30,000 in cash for personal use, which accounts are debited and credited?

(SO 3) AP 9. Partners R. Rowe and B. Zander are provided with salary allowances of $30,000 and $25,000, respectively. They divide the remainder of the partnership income in a ratio of 60:40. If partnership net income is $60,000, how much is allocated to each partner? How does your answer change if the partnership net income is $50,000 rather than $60,000?

(SO 4) C 10. Are the financial statements of a partnership similar to those of a proprietorship? Discuss.

(SO 5) C 11. Holly Canter decides to pay $50,000 for a one-third interest in a partnership. What effect does this transaction have on the partnership net assets?

(SO 5) AP 12. R. Minoa decides to invest $25,000 in a partnership for a one-sixth capital interest. How much do the partnership's net assets increase? Does Minoa also acquire a one-sixth income ratio through this investment?

13. Laurie Leger purchases, for $72,000 cash, Robert Robichaud's interest in the Big R Ranch partnership. Robert has a $63,000 capital balance in the partnership. What journal entry is made by the partnership to record this transaction? (SO 5) AP

14. Won Jang has a $37,000 capital balance in a partnership. She sells her interest to Karen Crest for $45,000 cash. What entry is made by the partnership for this transaction? (SO 6) AP

15. Rorey Rolf retires from the partnership of Suarez, Tanks, and Rolf. She receives $89,000 of partnership assets for her capital balance of $77,000. If the income-sharing ratios are 5:3:2, respectively, how much of Rolf's bonus is debited to Tanks' capital account? (SO 6) AP

16. Your roommate argues that partnership assets should be revalued when a new partner is admitted. Why is this generally not done? (SO 6) C

17. How does the liquidation of a partnership differ from the dissolution of a partnership? (SO 7) C

18. Joe and Jean are discussing the liquidation of a partnership. Joe maintains that all cash should be distributed to partners on the basis of their income ratios. Is he correct? Explain. (SO 7) C

19. In continuing their discussion, Jean says that even in the case of a capital deficiency, all cash should be distributed on the basis of capital balances. Is Jean correct? Explain. (SO 7) C

20. Mike, Larry, and Joan have income ratios of 5:3:2, respectively. They also have capital balances of $34,000, $31,000, and $28,000, respectively. Noncash assets are sold at a gain. After creditors are paid, $119,000 of cash is available for distribution to the partners. How much cash should be paid to Mike? (SO 7) AP

21. Before the final distribution of cash, account balances are as follows: Cash, $25,000; R. Katz, Capital, $19,000 (Cr.); M. Moss, Capital, $12,000 (Cr.); and T. Zaret, Capital, $6,000 (Dr.). Zaret is unable to pay any of the capital deficiency. If the income-sharing ratios are 5:3:2, respectively, how much cash should be paid to Katz? (SO 7) AP

BRIEF EXERCISES

Identify partnership terminology.
(SO 1) K

BE13–1 The following terms were introduced in this chapter.

1. Admission by investment
2. Salary allowance
3. Capital deficiency
4. Limited liability partnership
5. General partnership
6. Partnership liquidation
7. Withdrawal by payment from partners' personal assets
8. Income ratio

Match the above terms with the following descriptions:

(a) _____ Partners have limited liability.
(b) _____ Partners have unlimited liability.
(c) _____ Is the basis for dividing net income and loss.
(d) _____ Partnership assets and capital increase with the change in partners.
(e) _____ Partnership assets and capital stay the same with the change in partners.

(f) ____ Is a compensation for differences in personal effort put into the partnership.
(g) ____ Is a debit balance in a partner's capital account.
(h) ____ Is the termination of the partnership.

BE13–2 R. Alfredo and B. Panos decide to organize the All-Star partnership. Alfredo invests $15,000 cash. Panos contributes $10,000 cash and equipment having a book value of $3,500. The equipment has a fair market value of $6,000. Prepare the entry to record each partner's investment in the partnership on July 10, 2003.

Journalize entry for formation of partnership.
(SO 2) AP

BE13–3 C. Held and G. Kamp decide to merge their proprietorships into a partnership called HeldKamp Company. Immediately before the merger, the balance sheet of Kamp Co. shows the following:

Prepare partial opening balance sheet for partnership.
(SO 2) AP

Accounts Receivable	$16,000	
Less: Allowance for Doubtful Accounts	1,200	$14,800
Equipment	$20,000	
Less: Accumulated Amortization	8,000	12,000

The partners agree that the net realizable value of the receivables is $12,500. The fair market value of the equipment is $10,000. Indicate how these items should appear in the opening balance sheet of the partnership, on December 31, 2003.

BE13–4 Brung & Rohls Co. reports net income of $70,000 for the year ended March 31, 2003. The income ratios are Brung 60% and Rohls 40%. Indicate the division of net income to each partner. Prepare the entry to distribute the net income.

Calculate and journalize division of net income.
(SO 3) AP

BE13–5 MET Co. reports net income of $60,000. Partner salary allowances are Moses $10,000, Eaton $5,000, and Talty $5,000. Indicate the division of net income to each partner. The income ratios are 5:3:2, respectively.

Calculate division of net income, with salary allowances.
(SO 3) AP

BE13–6 S&T Co. reports net income of $24,000. Interest allowances for the partners are Siebrasse $6,000 and Tong $5,000. Salary allowances are Siebrasse $15,000 and Tong $10,000. The remainder is shared equally. Show the distribution of income.

Show division of net income when allowances exceed income.
(SO 3) AP

BE13–7 The medical practice of Drs. Jarratt and Bramstrup had the following general ledger account balances at April 30, 2003, its fiscal year end: Cash, $10,000; Equipment, $50,000; Accumulated Amortization—Equipment, $15,000; Note Payable, due 2004, $20,000; Dr. Jarratt, Capital, $10,000; Dr. Jarratt, Drawings, $5,000; Dr. Bramstrup, Capital, $15,000; Dr. Bramstrup, Drawings, $5,000; Fees Earned, $60,000; and Operating Expenses, $50,000. Prepare the year-end partnership financial statements, assuming the doctors share income or loss equally.

Prepare partnership financial statements.
(SO 4) AP

BE13–8 In ABC Co., the capital balances of the partners are Ali, $30,000; Babson, $25,000; and Carter, $20,000. The partners share income equally. Dutton is admitted to the firm by purchasing one-half of Carter's interest for $15,000 on June 9, 2003. Journalize the admission of Dutton to the partnership.

Journalize admission by purchase of interest.
(SO 5) AP

BE13–9 In the EZ Co., the capital balances of the partners are Edie, $40,000; and Zane, $30,000. The partners share income equally. Kerns is admitted to the firm on October 1, 2003, with a 45% interest by a cash investment of $42,000. Journalize the admission of Kerns.

Journalize admission by investment.
(SO 5) AP

BE13–10 The capital balances of the partners in DEB Co. are Ditka, $40,000; Embs, $30,000; and Boyd, $25,000. The partners share income equally. Ditka and Embs each agree to pay Boyd $12,000 from their personal assets to receive 50% each of Boyd's equity. Journalize the withdrawal of Boyd on December 31, 2002.

Journalize withdrawal paid by personal assets.
(SO 6) AP

BE13–11 Data pertaining to DEB Co. are presented in BE13–10. Instead of a payment from personal assets, assume that Boyd receives $32,000 from partnership assets in withdrawing from the firm. Journalize the withdrawal of Boyd on December 31, 2002.

Journalize withdrawal paid by partnership assets.
(SO 6) AP

BE13–12 After liquidating noncash assets and paying creditors, account balances in the Greenscape Partnership are Cash, $19,000; Dupuis, Capital, $9,000 (Cr.); Dueck, Capital, $7,000 (Cr.); and Veitch, Capital, $3,000 (Cr.). The partners share income equally. Journalize the final distribution of cash to the partners on November 15, 2003.

Journalize cash distribution in a liquidation.
(SO 7) AP

EXERCISES

Determine form of organization.
(SO 1) AN

E13–1   Presented below are three independent situations:

1. Angelique Gloss and Esther Deutsch, students looking for summer employment, open a home meal replacement business. Each day, they prepare nutritious, ready-to-bake meals, which they sell to people on their way home from work.
2. Joe Daigle and Cathy Goodfellow own a ski repair business and a ski shop. They have decided to combine their businesses. They expect that within the coming year, they will need significant funds to expand their operations.
3. Three business professors have formed a business to offer income tax services to the community. They expect to hire students during the busy season.

Instructions

In each of the above situations, explain whether the partnership form of organization is the most appropriate one for the business. Explain your reasoning.

Journalize entry for formation of partnership.
(SO 2) AP

E13–2   Ted Karl has owned and operated a proprietorship for several years. On January 1, he decides to terminate this business and become a partner in the firm of Kurl and Karl. Karl's investment in the partnership consists of $15,000 in cash and the following assets of the proprietorship: Accounts Receivable of $14,000 less an Allowance for Doubtful Accounts of $2,000, and Equipment of $20,000 less Accumulated Amortization of $4,000. It is agreed that the Allowance for Doubtful Accounts should be $4,000 for the partnership. The fair market value of the equipment is $17,000.

Instructions

Journalize Karl's admission to the firm of Kurl and Karl.

Calculate and journalize division of income.
(SO 3) AP

E13–3   R. Huma and W. How have capital balances on July 1, 2002 of $50,000 and $40,000, respectively. The partnership income-sharing agreement provides for (1) salary allowances of $20,000 for Huma and $12,000 for How, (2) interest at 10% on beginning capital balances, and (3) remaining income or loss to be shared 70% by Huma and 30% by How.

Instructions

(a) Prepare a schedule showing the division of net income for the year ended June 30, 2003, assuming net income is (1) $55,000, and (2) $30,000.
(b) Journalize the allocation of net income in each of the situations above.

Prepare statement of partners' capital and partial balance sheet.
(SO 4) AP

E13–4   In Schott Co., beginning capital balances of the partners on January 1, 2003, are M. Salz, $20,000, and C. Toni, $18,000. During the year, drawings were Salz, $8,000, and Toni, $3,000. Net income was $30,000. The partners share income equally.

Instructions

(a) Prepare the statement of partners' capital for the year.
(b) Prepare the partners' equity section of the balance sheet at December 31, 2003.

Journalize admission of partner by purchase of interest.
(SO 5) AP

E13–5   T. Halo, K. Rose, and J. Lamp share income on a 5:3:2 basis, respectively. They have capital balances of $30,000, $26,000, and $18,000, respectively, when R. Zahn is admitted to the partnership on July 1 of the current year.

Instructions

Prepare the journal entry to record the admission of Zahn under each of the following assumptions:
(a) Zahn purchases 50% of Halo's equity for $19,000.
(b) Zahn purchases 50% of Rose's equity for $10,000.
(c) Zahn purchases 33⅓% of Lamp's equity for $9,000.

Journalize admission of partner by investment.
(SO 5) AP

E13–6   Joe Keho and Mike McLain share income on a 6:4 basis, respectively. They have capital balances of $90,000 and $70,000, respectively, when Ed Kehler is admitted to the partnership on January 1, 2003.

Instructions

Prepare the journal entry to record the admission of Ed Kehler on January 1 under each of the following assumptions:
(a) Kehler invests $100,000 cash for a 25% ownership interest, with bonuses to the existing partners.
(b) Kehler invests $36,000 cash for a 25% ownership interest, with a bonus to the new partner.

E13–7 Mary Lane, Vera Miles, and Debra Noll have capital balances of $50,000, $30,000, and $22,000, respectively. Their income ratios are 5:3:2, respectively. Noll withdraws from the partnership on December 31 of the current year under each of the following conditions:

1. Lane and Miles agree to purchase Noll's equity by paying $15,000 each from their personal assets. Each purchaser receives 50% of Noll's equity.
2. Miles agrees to purchase all of Noll's equity by paying $20,000 cash from her personal assets.
3. Lane agrees to purchase all of Noll's equity by paying $23,000 cash from her personal assets.

Journalize withdrawal of partner, with payment from partners' personal assets.
(SO 6) AP

Instructions

Journalize the withdrawal of Noll under each of the above assumptions.

E13–8 Dale Nagel, Keith White, and Dan Neal have capital balances of $95,000, $75,000, and $60,000, respectively. They share income or loss on a 5:3:2 basis, respectively. White withdraws from the partnership on September 30, 2003, under each of the following conditions:

1. White is paid $82,000 in cash from partnership assets, and he receives a bonus.
2. White is paid $68,000 in cash from partnership assets, and the remaining partners receive bonuses.

Journalize withdrawal of partner, with payment from partnership's assets.
(SO 6) AP

Instructions

Journalize the withdrawal of White under each of the above assumptions.

E13–9 At December 31, Baylee Company, has cash of $15,000, noncash assets of $100,000, liabilities of $55,000, and the following partners' capital balances: Bayer, $40,000, and Leech, $20,000. The firm is liquidated on December 31, 2002. Cash of $120,000 is received for the noncash assets. Bayer and Leech have income ratios of 55% and 45%, respectively.

Calculate amounts paid to partners on liquidation of partnership.
(SO 7) AP

Instructions

Calculate how much will be paid to each of the partners when the firm is liquidated on December 31, 2002.

E13–10 Data for the Baylee Company partnership are presented in E13–9.

Journalize transactions in partnership liquidation.
(SO 7) AP

Instructions

Prepare the entries to record (a) the sale of noncash assets, (b) the allocation to the partners of the gain or loss on liquidation, (c) the payment of creditors, and (d) the distribution of cash to the partners.

E13–11 Prior to the distribution of cash to the partners on September 30, 2003, the accounts in the MEL Company are as follows: Cash, $31,000; McDonald, Capital, $18,000 (Cr.); El Bayouni, Capital, $16,000 (Cr.); and Lodge, Capital, $3,000 (Dr.). The income ratios are 5:3:2, respectively.

Journalize transactions in partnership liquidation with capital deficiency.
(SO 7) AP

Instructions

(a) Prepare the entry on September 30 to record (1) Lodge's payment of $3,000 in cash to the partnership, and (2) the distribution of cash to the partners.
(b) Prepare the entry on September 30 to record (1) the absorption of Lodge's capital deficiency by the other partners, and (2) the distribution of cash to the partners.

PROBLEMS: SET A

P13–1A **The Calgary Flames Limited Partnership** was formed by nine partners, led by Harley Hotchkiss. Hotchkiss is also the Chair of the National Hockey League's Board of Governors. The team faced off against the Montreal Canadiens twice for the Stanley Cup in the 1980s, winning the title in 1989. In addition to operating the Calgary Flames hockey franchise, the partnership also operates the Pengrowth Saddledome, a 17,104-seat arena that is the home of the Flames. The partnership had 155 employees and reported sales of more than $40 million in 2000.

Discuss partnership characteristics.
(SO 1) AN

Instructions

Discuss why you think the nine owners of the Calgary Flames chose to organize as a partnership. Do you think this form of organization will serve the Flames well in the future?

Prepare entries for formation of partnership and balance sheet.
(SO 2, 4) AP

P13–2A   The post-closing trial balances of two proprietorships on January 1, 2003, follow:

	Hamp Company		Vong Company	
	Dr.	Cr.	Dr.	Cr.
Cash	$ 14,000		$13,000	
Accounts receivable	17,500		26,000	
Allowance for doubtful accounts		$ 3,000		$ 4,400
Merchandise inventory	26,500		18,400	
Equipment	45,000		28,000	
Accumulated amortization—equipment		24,000		12,000
Notes payable		20,000		15,000
Accounts payable		20,000		31,000
L. Hamp, Capital		36,000		
P. Vong, Capital				23,000
	$103,000	$103,000	$85,400	$85,400

Hamp and Vong decide to form a partnership on January 1 with the following agreed-upon valuations for the noncash assets contributed by each:

	Hamp Company	Vong Company
Accounts receivable	$17,500	$26,000
Allowance for doubtful accounts	4,500	4,000
Merchandise inventory	30,000	20,000
Equipment	25,000	18,000

All cash will be transferred to the partnership. The partnership will also assume all the liabilities of the two proprietorships. Further, it is agreed that Hamp will invest $30,000 in cash and Vong will invest $18,000 in cash.

Instructions

(a) Prepare separate journal entries to record the transfer of each proprietorship's assets and liabilities to the partnership on January 1, 2003.
(b) Journalize the additional cash investment by each partner.
(c) Prepare a balance sheet for the partnership at January 1, 2003.

Prepare opening balance sheet.
(SO 2, 4) AP

P13–3A   On June 30, 2003, two separate proprietorships—Playstation and 3D Gaming—which develop computer games agree to combine their operations and form a partnership. The new partnership will be known as Interplay@. Playstation doesn't have any assets worth transferring into the new partnership. The owner, G. LeBlanc, agrees to invest $1,000 in cash. 3D Gaming transfers the following assets and liabilities into the partnership at fair market values:

	Net Book Value	Fair Market Value
Cash	$ 9,000	$ 9,000
Accounts receivable	20,000	18,000
Allowance for doubtful accounts	1,000	1,500
Computer hardware and software	50,000	15,000
Accumulated amortization— computer hardware and software	30,000	
Accounts payable	15,000	15,000
Notes payable	25,000	25,000

Instructions

Prepare a balance sheet for the Interplay@ partnership at June 30, 2003.

Journalize division of net income under various assumptions. Prepare statement of partners' capital.
(SO 3, 4) AP

P13–4A   At the end of its first year of operations, on December 31, 2003, the LMN Company's accounts show the following:

Partner	Drawings	Capital
Lois Lang	$12,000	$33,000
Mary Mio	9,000	20,000
Sue Norton	6,000	10,000

The capital balance represents each partner's initial capital investment. Net income or net loss for 2003 has not been closed to the partners' capital accounts.

Instructions

(a) Prepare a schedule showing the division of net income for 2003 under each of the following assumptions:
   1. Net income is $28,000. Income is shared 5:3:2 (Lang, Mio, Norton).
   2. Net income is $30,000. Lang and Mio are given salary allowances of $10,000 and $8,000, respecively. The remainder is shared equally.
   3. Net income is $25,200. Each partner is allowed interest of 10% on beginning capital balances. Lang is given a $15,000 salary allowance. The remainder is shared equally.

(b) Prepare the entry to record the division of net income calculated in (a) for each of the three assumptions.

(c) Prepare a statement of partners' capital for the year under assumption 3 in (a) above.

P13–5A **Metfin Properties Limited Partnership** has the following accounts, at December 31, 2000, its year end:

Prepare partnership financial statements.
(SO 4) AP

METFIN PROPERTIES LIMITED PARTNERSHIP
Alphabetical List of Accounts
December 31, 2000

Accounts payable and accrued liabilities	$ 46,237
Capital account—general partner, beginning of year (debit balance)	(92)
Capital accounts—limited partners, beginning of year	1,257,839
Cash	1,292,192
Distributions (drawings)—general partner	0
Distributions (drawings)—limited partners	57,360
General and administrative expenses	532
Interest revenue	60,900
Partnership management fee expense	6,000
Professional fees expense	8,800

Instructions

Prepare an income statement, statement of partners' capital, and balance sheet for Metfin Properties Limited Partnership. Assume any net income or loss earned by the partnership is distributed as follows: General partner's share, 5%; Limited partners' share, 95%.

P13–6A At April 30, partners' capital balances in the ELM Company are as follows: V. Easi, $49,000; K. Lester, $24,000; and W. Matt, $17,000. The income-sharing ratios are 3:2:1, respectively. On May 1, the ELMO Company is formed by admitting N. Ortiz to the firm as a partner.

Journalize admission of partner under various assumptions.
(SO 5) AP

Instructions

(a) Journalize the admission of Ortiz under each of the following assumptions:

   1. Ortiz purchases 50% of Matt's ownership interest by paying Matt $9,000 in cash.
   2. Ortiz purchases 50% of Lester's ownership interest by paying Lester $16,000 in cash.
   3. Ortiz invests $35,000 cash in the partnership for a 40% ownership interest that includes a bonus to the new partner.
   4. Ortiz invests $30,000 in the partnership for a 15% ownership interest. Bonuses are given to the old partners.

(b) Matt's capital balance is $18,000 after admitting Ortiz to the partnership by investment. If Matt's ownership interest is 15% of total partnership capital after the admission of Ortiz, what were (1) Ortiz's cash investment, and (2) the total bonuses to the old partners?

P13–7A On December 31, the capital balances and income ratios in the ART Company are as follows:

Journalize withdrawal of partner under various assumptions.
(SO 6) AP

Partner	Capital Balance	Income Ratio
E. Atlas	$70,000	60%
P. Ross	30,000	30%
L. Tower	21,500	10%

Instructions

(a) Journalize the withdrawal of Tower under each of the following assumptions:
   1. Each of the remaining partners agrees to pay $12,000 in cash from personal funds to purchase Tower's ownership equity. Each receives 50% of Tower's equity.
   2. Ross agrees to purchase Tower's ownership interest for $18,000 in cash.
   3. From partnership assets, Tower is paid $29,000, which includes a bonus to him.

4. Tower is paid $17,000 from partnership assets, and bonuses to the remaining partners are recognized.

(b) If Ross's capital balance after Tower's withdrawal is $33,000, what were (1) the total bonuses to the remaining partners, and (2) the cash paid by the partnership to Tower?

Prepare and post entries for liquidation of partnership—no capital deficiency.
(SO 7) AP

P13–8A   The partners in Inland Lakes Company decide to liquidate the firm when the balance sheet shows the following:

INLAND LAKES COMPANY
Balance Sheet
April 30, 2003

Assets		Liabilities and Partners' Equity	
Cash	$24,000	Notes payable	$14,000
Accounts receivable	14,000	Accounts payable	24,000
Allowance for doubtful accounts	(1,000)	Wages payable	2,000
Merchandise inventory	30,000	T. E. Huron, Capital	25,000
Equipment	22,000	P. A. Erie, Capital	12,800
Accumulated amortization—equipment	(8,000)	C. R. Lake, Capital	3,200
	$81,000		$81,000

The partners share income and loss 5:3:2 (Huron, Erie, Lake). During the process of liquidation, the transactions below were completed in the sequence shown:

1. A total of $48,000 was received from converting noncash assets into cash on May 2, 2003.
2. Liabilities were paid in full on May 6, 2003.
3. Cash was paid to the partners on May 9, 2003.

Instructions

(a) Prepare the entries to record the transactions. (Hint: Remember to distribute any gain or loss on realization to the partners' capital accounts.)

(b) Open T accounts and post to the cash and capital accounts.

Prepare entries for liquidation of partnership under various assumptions.
(SO 7) AP

P13–9A   On June 1, 2003, the musical partnership of A.J., Nick, Howie, Brian, and Kevin decides to separate and liquidate the partnership. The partners have capital balances of $1,000,000 each except for Kevin, whose capital balance is $600,000. Cash, noncash assets, and liabilities total $1,900,000, $5,800,000, and $3,100,000, respectively. The five partners share income and loss equally.

Instructions

Journalize the liquidation of the partnership under each of the following independent assumptions:

(a) The noncash assets are sold for $3,000,000 cash, the liabilities are paid, and the remaining cash is paid to the partners.

(b) The noncash assets are sold for $2,000,000 cash and the liabilities are paid. The partner with the debit capital balance pays the amount owed to the partnership and the remaining cash is paid to the partners.

(c) The noncash assets are sold for $2,000,000 cash and the liabilities are paid. The partner with the debit capital balance is unable to pay the amount owed to the partnership. The cash is paid to the four other partners.

PROBLEMS: SET B

Discuss partnership characteristics.
(SO 1) AN

P13–1B   **The Boston Celtics Limited Partnership** owns about 48% of the National Basketball Association's (NBA's) Boston Celtics. The partnership, formed in 1983, generates revenue through ticket sales, licensing of television and radio rights, and promotions.

The luck of the Irish hasn't been enough to help the Celtics' fortunes during the past few years. Though the team has 16 NBA championships to its credit, its last one came in 1986. The Celtics haven't appeared in the NBA playoffs since the 1994–1995 season, which also happened to be the team's last season in Boston Garden. It now plays in the 19,300-seat FleetCenter.

The partnership has 47 employees. In 2000, it reported sales of US$4.4 million and a net loss of US$1 million.

Instructions

Discuss why you think the owners of the Boston Celtics Limited Partnership chose to organize as a partnership. Do you think this form of organization will serve them well in the future?

P13–2B The post-closing trial balances of two proprietorships on January 1, 2003, are presented below:

Prepare entries for formation of partnership, and balance sheet. (SO 2, 4) AP

	Valsangkar Company		Vahtra Company	
	Debit	Credit	Debit	Credit
Cash	$ 6,500		$ 8,000	
Accounts receivable	15,000		23,000	
Allowance for doubtful accounts		$ 2,500		$ 4,000
Merchandise inventory	28,000		17,000	
Equipment	52,000		30,000	
Accumulated amortization—equipment		24,000		13,000
Notes payable		20,000		
Accounts payable		25,000		37,000
Valsangkar, Capital		30,000		
Vahtra, Capital				24,000
	$101,500	$101,500	$78,000	$78,000

Valsangkar and Vahtra decide to form the Valhalla Company partnership, with the following agreed-upon valuations for the noncash assets contributed by each :

	Valsangkar Company	Vahtra Company
Accounts receivable	$15,000	$23,000
Allowance for doubtful accounts	3,000	5,000
Merchandise inventory	30,000	20,000
Equipment	35,000	25,000

All cash will be transferred to the partnership on January 1. The partnership will also assume all the liabilities of the two proprietorships. Further, it is agreed that Valsangkar will invest $15,000 in cash. Vahtra will invest $5,000 in cash.

Instructions

(a) Prepare separate journal entries to record the transfer of each proprietorship's assets and liabilities to the partnership on January 1, 2003.
(b) Journalize the additional cash investment by each partner.
(c) Prepare a balance sheet for the partnership at January 1, 2003.

P13–3B The post-closing trial balances of two proprietorships on January 1, 2003, are presented below:

Prepare opening balance sheet. (SO 2, 4) AP

	Kreal Company		Donal Company	
	Dr.	Cr.	Dr.	Cr.
Cash	$ 9,000		$ 8,000	
Accounts receivable	15,000		23,000	
Allowance for doubtful accounts		$ 2,500		$ 5,000
Merchandise inventory	28,000		20,000	
Equipment	50,000		25,000	
Accumulated amortization—equipment		24,000		13,000
Notes payable		20,000		
Accounts payable		25,000		37,000
T. Kreal, Capital		30,500		
C. Donal, Capital				21,000
	$102,000	$102,000	$76,000	$76,000

Kreal and Donal decide to form the Donal Kreal Company with the following agreed-upon valuations for the noncash assets contributed by each:

	Kreal Company	Donal Company
Accounts receivable	$15,000	$23,000
Allowance for doubtful accounts	3,500	6,000
Merchandise inventory	30,000	21,000
Equipment	31,000	18,000

All cash will be transferred to the partnership, and the partnership will assume all the liabilities of the two proprietorships.

Instructions

Prepare a balance sheet for the partnership at January 1, 2003.

Journalize division of net income under various assumptions. Prepare statement of partners' capital.
(SO 3, 4) AP

P13–4B   At the end of its first year of operations, on December 31, 2003, HRZ Company's accounts show the following:

Partner	Drawings	Capital
Sue Horton	$23,000	$48,000
Tracey Rugen	14,000	30,000
Eileen Zak	10,000	25,000

The capital balance represents each partner's initial capital investment. Net income or net loss for 2003 has not been closed to the partners' capital accounts.

Instructions

(a) Journalize the entry to record the division of net income for the year 2003 under each of the following assumptions:
   1. Net income is $34,000. Horton and Rugen are given salary allowances of $15,000 and $10,000, respectively. The remainder is shared equally.
   2. Net income is $22,000. Each partner is allowed interest of 10% on beginning capital balances. Horton is given a $15,000 salary allowance. The remainder is shared equally.
(b) Prepare a schedule showing the division of net income under assumption 2 in (a) above.
(c) Prepare a statement of partners' capital for the year under assumption 2 in (a) above.

Prepare partnership financial statements.
(SO 4) AP

P13–5B   Marina Limited Partnership owns about 345 acres of real estate. Most of it has been developed into subdivisions with waterfront views. It also operates a marina on two artificail lakes, as well as Marina Village, a retail and office development. The partnership reported the following at December 31, 2000, its year end:

MARINA LIMITED PARTNERSHIP
Alphabetical List of Accounts
December 31, 2000
(U.S. dollars)

Accounts payable	$ 705,514
Accrued bonuses payable	133,023
Cash and cash equivalents	7,719,350
Cost of homes and homesites sold	3,075,020
Distributions (drawings) to partner—general	1,418,736
Distributions (drawings) to partners—limited	2,291,933
General and administrative expenses	1,234,431
General partner's equity, January 1, 2000	8,511,679
Home and homesite sales revenue	4,551,986
Limited partners' equity, January 1, 2000	13,709,785
Marina operations expenses	3,829,346
Marina operations revenue	4,919,091
Other investments	3,275,370
Other revenues	2,674,445
Properties held for sale	5,219,518
Property and equipment, net	5,004,323
Receivables	2,390,043
Unearned revenue	252,547

Instructions

Prepare an income statement, statement of partners' capital, and balance sheet for Marina Limited Partnership. Any income or loss of the partnership is distributed 38% to the general partner, 62% to the limited partners.

P13–6B At September 30, partners' capital balances in NSW Company are A. Nolan, $62,000; D. Spoda, $36,000; and T. Wuhan, $12,000. The income-sharing ratios are 5:4:1, respectively. On May 1, the NSWO Company is formed by admitting M. Otton to the firm as a partner.

Journalize admission of partner under various assumptions.
(SO 5) AP

Instructions

(a) Journalize the admission of Otton under each of the following assumptions:
1. Otton purchases 50% of Wuhan's ownership interest by paying Wuhan $16,000 in cash.
2. Otton purchases 33⅓% of Spoda's ownership interest by paying Spoda $15,000 in cash.
3. Otton invests $70,000 for a 30% ownership interest. Bonuses are given to the old partners.
4. Otton invests $40,000 for a 35% ownership interest. A bonus is given to the new partner.

(b) Assume that Spoda's capital balance is $30,000 after Otton is admitted to the partnership by investment. If Spoda's ownership interest is 20% of total partnership capital, what were (1) Otton's cash investment, and (2) the bonus to the new partner?

P13–7B On December 31, the capital balances and income ratios in the BAG Company are as follows:

Journalize withdrawal of partner under various assumptions.
(SO 6) AP

Partner	Capital Balance	Income Ratio
R. Beano	$60,000	50%
D. Alman	40,000	30%
P. Garth	34,000	20%

Instructions

(a) Journalize the withdrawal of Garth under each of the following assumptions:
1. Each of the continuing partners agrees to pay $18,000 in cash from personal funds to purchase Garth's ownership equity. Each receives 50% of Garth's equity.
2. Alman agrees to purchase Garth's ownership interest for $30,000 cash.
3. Garth is paid $38,000 from partnership assets, which includes a bonus to him.
4. Garth is paid $28,000 from partnership assets. Bonuses to the remaining partners are recognized.

(b) If Alman's capital balance after Garth's withdrawal is $43,000, what were (1) the total bonus to the remaining partners, and (2) the cash paid by the partnership to Garth?

P13–8B The partners in the Wilkowski Company decide to liquidate the firm when the balance sheet shows the following:

Prepare and post entries for partnership liquidation—capital deficiency.
(SO 7) AP

WILKOWSKI COMPANY
Balance Sheet
May 31, 2003

Assets		Liabilities and Partners' Equity	
Cash	$24,000	Notes payable	$14,000
Accounts receivable	25,000	Accounts payable	27,000
Allowance for doubtful accounts	(1,000)	Wages payable	3,800
Merchandise inventory	34,500	S. Wilkowski, Capital	32,000
Equipment	21,000	K. Richards, Capital	20,000
Accumulated amortization—equipment	(5,500)	R. Simka, Capital	1,200
Total	$98,000	Total	$98,000

The partners share income and loss 5:3:2 (Wilkowski, Richards, Simka). During the process of liquidation, the following transactions were completed in the sequence shown:

1. A total of $53,000 was received from converting noncash assets into cash.
2. Liabilities were paid in full.
3. Simka paid her capital deficiency.
4. Cash was paid to the partners with credit balances.

Instructions

(a) Prepare the entries to record the transactions.

(b) Open T accounts and post to the cash and capital accounts.

(c) Assume that Simka is unable to pay the capital deficiency. (1) Prepare the entry to allocate Simka's debit balance to Wilkowski and Richards. (2) Prepare the entry to record the final distribution of cash.

Prepare entries for liquidation of partnership under various assumptions.
(SO 7) AP

P13–9B   On September 1, 2003, the CGA accounting partnership of A. Choquette and G. Legere separated and liquidated the partnership. The partners Choquette and Legere share income and loss in a 1:3 ratio, respectively. Immediately prior to the liquidation, the partnership balance sheet showed the following:

CHOQUETTE AND LEGERE
Balance Sheet
September 1, 2003

Assets		Liabilities and Partners' Equity	
Cash	$ 90,000	Accounts payable	$ 50,000
Office equipment	75,000	Choquette, Capital	50,000
Accumulated amortization	(50,000)	Legere, Capital	15,000
	$115,000		$115,000

Instructions

Journalize the liquidation of the partnership under each of the following independent assumptions:

(a) The equipment is sold for $30,000 cash, the accounts payable are paid, and the remaining cash is paid to the two partners.

(b) The equipment is scrapped and the accounts payable are paid. Legere pays his capital deficiency and the remaining cash is distributed to the partners.

(c) The equipment is sold for $2,500 cash and the accounts payable are paid. Legere does not pay his capital deficiency. The remaining cash is distributed to Choquette.

*B*roadening *Your Perspective*

FINANCIAL REPORTING AND ANALYSIS
....

Financial Reporting Problem

PRICEWATERHOUSE COOPERS ⬚

BYP13–1   The global merger of accounting and management consulting firms Coopers & Lybrand and Price Waterhouse resulted in the largest accounting and professional services partnership in the world, **PricewaterhouseCoopers**. In Canada, this merger brought together 6,000 employees, generating almost $1 billion in revenues. Worldwide, the combined firm employs more than 170,000 people—including more than 8,500 partners—in over 150 countries, with revenues of over $17 billion.

Instructions

(a) Explain how the assets and equities of the old partnerships would be transferred to the new partnership. At what values would the assets be recorded? How would the partners agree the values are fair?

(b) Describe the types of entries that would be necessary to record the formation of the new partnership.

(c) When mergers such as this occur, some partners of the old firms usually "retire." On what basis should cash payments to the withdrawing partners (in settlement of their partnership interests) be made?

Accounting on the Web

BYP13–2 This case reviews the increasingly popular practice of mergers and alliances of public accounting firms.

Instructions

Specific requirements of this Internet case are available on the Weygandt website.

CRITICAL THINKING

Collaborative Learning Activities

BYP13–3 Bart Holmar and Sally Izod, two professionals in the finance area, have worked for Advanced Leasing for a number of years. Advanced Leasing is a company that leases high-tech medical equipment to hospitals. Bart and Sally have decided that, with their financial expertise, they might start their own company to provide consulting services to individuals interested in leasing equipment. One form of organization they are considering is a partnership.

If they start a partnership, each individual plans to contribute $50,000 in cash. In addition, Bart has a used computer that originally cost $5,000, which he intends to invest in the partnership. The computer has a current market value of $1,500.

Although both Bart and Sally are financial wizards, they do not know a great deal about how a partnership operates. As a result, they have come to you for advice.

Instructions

With the class divided into groups, answer the following questions:

(a) What are the major disadvantages of operating a business as a partnership?

(b) What type of document is needed for a partnership? What should this document contain?

(c) Both Bart and Sally plan to work full-time in the new partnership. They believe that net income or net loss should be shared equally. However, they are wondering how they can provide compensation to Bart for his additional investment of the computer. What would you tell them?

(d) Bart and Sally have worked together for a number of years. Bart's skills complement Sally's and vice versa. If one of them dies, it will be very difficult for the other to maintain the business, not to mention pay the deceased partner's estate for his or her partnership interest. What concerns would you have if you were either Bart or Sally?

BYP13–4 In groups of five or six students, form a partnership. Decide as a group what you will be selling or providing as a service.

Instructions

With the class divided into groups, do the following:

(a) Discuss what each member will contribute to the partnership, and what income-sharing ratio would be appropriate.

(b) Assume that one member of your group wishes to provide one-half of the total assets of the partnership but does not otherwise wish to participate in the partnership. Discuss how this would affect your partnership's income-sharing ratio.

Communication Activity

BYP13–5 You are an expert in the field of forming partnerships. Doug Stahl and Enid Hall want to establish a partnership to start "Enid's Pasta Shop." They are going to meet with you to discuss their plans. Prior to the meeting, you will send them a memo discussing the issues they need to consider before their visit.

Instructions

Write a memo, in good form, to be sent to Doug and Enid. In it, provide an overview of the various aspects of a partnership agreement and the issues that need to be addressed in order for the agreement to be a well-thought-out document.

Ethics Case

BYP13–6   Susan and Erin operate a beauty salon as partners who share profits and losses equally. The success of their business has exceeded their expectations and it is operating quite profitably. Erin is anxious to maximize profits. She schedules appointments from 8 a.m. to 6 p.m. daily—even sacrificing some lunch hours to accommodate regular customers. Susan schedules her appointments from 9 a.m. to 5 p.m. and takes long lunch hours. Susan regularly makes significantly larger withdrawals of cash than Erin does, but she says, "Erin, you needn't worry; I never make a withdrawal without you knowing about it, so it is properly recorded in my drawings account and charged against my capital at the end of the year." Susan's withdrawals to date are double Erin's.

Instructions

(a) Who are the stakeholders in this situation?
(b) Identify the problems with Susan's actions, and discuss the ethical considerations of her actions.
(c) How might the partnership agreement be designed to accommodate the differences in Susan's and Erin's work and withdrawal habits?

Answers to Self-Study Questions

1. a   2. b   3. c   4. a   5. b   6. d   7. a   8. a   9. b   10. a

Answer to Second Cup Review It Question 5

Mutual agency, limited life, unlimited liability, and co-ownership of property are major characteristics of a partnership. As a company like The Second Cup becomes very large, it is difficult for it to remain a partnership because of these factors. The corporate form of organization separates ownership and management and makes it easier to raise capital. The unlimited liability of a partnership hinders raising capital because owners may lose not only their initial investment but also their personal assets, if those assets are needed to pay partnership creditors.

Remember to go back to the Navigator box on the chapter-opening page to check off your completed work.

Before studying this chapter, you should understand or, if necessary, review:

a. *The differences between the three forms of business organization. (Ch. 1, pp. 13–14 and pp. 16–17)*

b. *The content of the equity section of the balance sheet for a proprietorship (Ch. 1, pp. 15–16) and for a partnership. (Ch. 13, pp. 614–615)*

c. *How to prepare closing entries for a proprietorship (Ch. 4, pp. 158–159) and for a partnership (Ch. 13, pp. 610–611)*

THE
NAVIGATOR

Student Savvy Pays Off for Research In Motion

WATERLOO, Ont.—In 1984, University of Waterloo co-op engineering student Mike Lazaridis incorporated Research In Motion (RIM) with partner Douglas Fregin.

The company sold its first wireless e-mail system in 1987—a large, clunky system with a very small market. But Lazaridis knew the potential of the technology was great. "Wireless data was something I believed in," he explains. Through the late 1980s and early 1990s, RIM designed and built products such as interactive pagers, wireless modems, and tiny radios that they marketed to other manufacturers to incorporate into various products.

In 1996, the company was poised for a major expansion. RIM's 1997 initial public offering (IPO) raised more than $100 million from the sale of 13.8 million common shares, issued at $7.25 on the Toronto Stock Exchange (TSE).

The financing was used to build, and then expand, a new production facility outside of Waterloo. It also helped fund sales and marketing and, especially, expand research and development activities. That R&D focus paid off when, in 1999, RIM launched what has become its signature product, the wildly success-

ful BlackBerry wireless handheld device.

This sleek "e-mail on steroids" quickly became a must-have item not only for techno-wizards but for stock-brokers and others whose business depends on time-sensitive information.

In 1999, RIM's revenues soared to $70 million and its income to $9.5 million. Its share price went on a roller-coaster ride, trading as high as $260 and as low as $50 on the TSE during the year. The same year also saw RIM get a listing on the NASDAQ market, the big kids' playground for high-tech firms.

RIM's 2000 annual report lists share-holders' equity of $311 million, including $293 million of share capital and $18 million of retained earnings. (In 2000, RIM switched its reporting currency to U.S. dollars, since so many of its customers are American.) The company

continues to grow, fuelled by significant R&D grants from the federal government and a new public share offering in October of 2000.

But in an industry characterized by hype, RIM, and Lazaridis himself, retain a certain Canadian modesty. Lazaridis is known to still drop by former professor Mohamed Elmasry's office at the University of Waterloo for advice. This low-key approach is reflected in RIM's focus on devices that help customers use the computers and e-mail accounts they already have. Says Lazaridis simply, "We don't want to become the centre of your life."

THE
NAVIGATOR

www.rim.net

THE NAVIGATOR

■ Understand *Concepts for Review*

■ Read *Feature Story*

■ Scan *Study Objectives*

■ Read *Preview*

■ Read text and answer *Before You Go On*
  p. 658 ☐ p. 662 ☐ p. 666 ☐ p. 669 ☐

■ Work *Demonstration Problem*

■ Review *Summary of Study Objectives*

■ Answer *Self-Study Questions*

■ Complete assignments

CHAPTER · **14**

CORPORATIONS: ORGANIZATION AND SHARE CAPITAL TRANSACTIONS

▶ STUDY OBJECTIVES ◀

After studying this chapter, you should be able to:

1. *Identify and discuss the major characteristics of a corporation.*
2. *Differentiate between contributed capital and retained earnings.*
3. *Record the issue of common shares.*
4. *Differentiate and journalize preferred and common share transactions.*
5. *Prepare the shareholders' equity section of the balance sheet.*
6. *Calculate return on equity and book value per share.*

THE NAVIGATOR

Incorporated companies can start out small and grow large, as Research In Motion has. It should not be surprising, then, that the corporation is the dominant form of business organization. In this chapter, we will explain the essential features of a corporation and the accounting for a corporation's share capital transactions. In Chapter 15, we will look at other issues related to accounting for corporations.

The chapter is organized as follows:

THE
NAVIGATOR

The Corporate Form of Organization

Helpful hint In Canada, you can tell whether a company is incorporated by looking at its name. The words "Limited" (Ltd.), "Incorporated" (Inc.), or "Corporation" (Corp.) follow the name of an incorporated company.

A corporation is a **legal entity that is separate and distinct from its owners**. As a legal entity, a corporation has most of the rights and privileges of a person. The major exceptions are privileges that only a living person can exercise, such as the right to vote, to hold public office, or to marry. A corporation has the same duties and responsibilities as a person. It must respect laws and it must pay income tax.

Corporations may be classified in a variety of ways. Two common bases are by purpose and by ownership. A corporation may be organized for the purpose of making a **profit**, or it may be **not-for-profit** (also known as nonprofit). Corporations for profit include well-known companies such as Cineplex Odeon Corp., Corel Corp., Maple Leaf Foods Inc., Rocky Mountain Bicycle Co. Ltd., and The Second Cup Ltd. Not-for-profit corporations are organized for cultural, social, charitable, medical, educational, and religious purposes. Examples are Big Brothers/Big Sisters, the Canadian National Institute for the Blind, the Canadian Chamber of Commerce, the Red Cross, and the Society for the Prevention of Cruelty to Animals.

Classification by **ownership** distinguishes between publicly held and privately held corporations. A publicly held corporation may have thousands of shareholders. Its shares are usually traded in an organized securities market, such as the Toronto Stock Exchange. Most of the largest Canadian corporations are publicly held. Examples of publicly held corporations are BCE Inc., Canadian Pacific Ltd., Sears Canada Inc. and The Second Cup Ltd. In contrast, a privately held corporation, often called a closely held corporation, usually has only a few shareholders. It does not offer its shares for sale to the general public. Privately held companies are generally much smaller than publicly held companies, although there are notable exceptions such as the Jim Pattison and Irving groups of companies. Research In Motion in our feature story was a privately held corporation before it offered its shares for sale to the public in 1997 and became a publicly held corporation. A Crown corporation is similar to a privately held company except that it is owned by the government. Atlantic Lotteries, Canada Post, Ontario Hydro, and BC Ferries are examples of Crown corporations.

Characteristics of a Corporation

Many characteristics distinguish corporations from proprietorships and partnerships. The most important of these characteristics are explained below.

Separate Legal Existence

As an entity separate and distinct from its owners, the corporation acts under its own name rather than in the name of its shareholders. A corporation may buy, own, and sell property. It may borrow money, and enter into legally binding contracts in its own name. It may also sue or be sued, and it pays its own income tax.

Remember that in a partnership, the acts of the owners (partners) bind the partnership. In contrast, the acts of its owners (shareholders) do not bind a corporation unless these owners are also duly appointed agents of the corporation. For example, if you owned shares of Sleeman Breweries Ltd., you would not have the right to purchase a brewery for the company unless you were appointed an agent of the corporation.

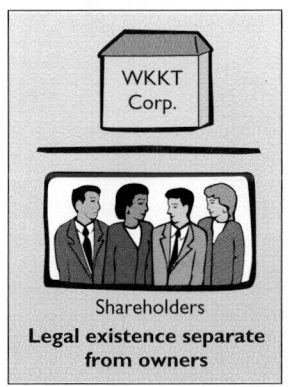

Legal existence separate from owners

Limited Liability of Shareholders

Since a corporation is a separate legal entity, creditors only have access to corporate assets to have their claims repaid to them. The liability of shareholders is normally limited to their investment in the corporation. Creditors have no legal claim on the personal assets of the owners unless fraud has occurred. Even in bankruptcy, shareholders' losses are generally limited to their capital investment in the corporation.

Limited liability of shareholders

Transferable Ownership Rights

Ownership of a corporation is held in capital shares. These are transferable units. Shareholders may dispose of part or all of their interest (ownership) in a corporation simply by selling their shares. Remember that the transfer of an ownership interest in a partnership, in contrast, requires the consent of each owner or partner. In a corporation, the transfer of shares is entirely decided by the shareholder. It does not require the approval of either the corporation or other shareholders.

The transfer of ownership rights between shareholders normally has no effect on the operating activities of the corporation. Nor does it affect the corporation's assets, liabilities, and total equity. The transfer of these ownership rights is a transaction between individual owners. The company does not participate in such transfers after it has initially issued the share capital.

Transferable ownership rights

Ability to Acquire Capital

It is relatively easy for a large corporation to obtain capital by issuing shares. Buying shares in a corporation is often attractive to an investor because a shareholder has limited liability and shares are easily transferable. Also, many individuals can become shareholders by investing small amounts of money. For these reasons, a successful corporation's ability to obtain capital is virtually unlimited.

Continuous Life

Most corporations have an unlimited life. Since a corporation is a separate legal entity, its continuance as a going concern is not affected by the withdrawal, death, or incapacity of a shareholder, employee, or officer. As a result, a successful enterprise can have a continuous and indefinite life. For example, the Hudson's Bay Co., Canada's oldest corporation, was founded in 1670 and is still going strong.

Corporation Management

Shareholders legally own the corporation. But they manage the corporation indirectly through a board of directors they elect. The board, in turn, formulates the operating policies for the company, and selects officers—such as a president and one or more vice-presidents—to execute policy and to perform daily management functions.

The organizational structure of corporations enables a company to hire professional managers to run the business. On the other hand, the separation of ownership and management prevents owners from having an active role in managing the company, which is difficult for some owners to accept.

▶Accounting in Action ▶ *@-Business Insight*

When investors are unhappy with a company's performance, they sometimes try to elect new members to the board of directors at the company's shareholdes' meeting. This is referred to as a proxy fight. These efforts usually fail because it is expensive to contact all of the company's shareholders to convince them to vote for a specific nominee.

But the Internet has changed that, says James Heard, chief executive officer of Proxy Monitor, Inc. Proxy Monitor, based in the U.S., advises institutional shareholders on how to vote on global corporate governance issues. "Increasingly, the Internet is being used as a tool of communication among shareholders to pressure managements," says Mr. Heard. One recent case involved an effort by a shareholder at Luby's, Inc. to get four new people elected to the cafeteria restaurant chain's board of directors. He attracted considerable support from other Luby's shareholders by posting messages on a Yahoo! message board.

Source: Aaron Elstein, "Online Griping Over Luby's Leading to Proxy Call." *The Wall Street Journal*, October 25, 2000. <WSJ.com>.

Government Regulations

Canadian companies may be incorporated federally, under the terms of the *Canada Business Corporations Act,* or provincially, under the terms of a provincial business corporations or company act. A federally incorporated corporation can do business in every province and territory. A provincially incorporated corporation, however, must obtain a licence to do business in other jurisdictions.

Federal and provincial laws specify the requirements for issuing shares, the permitted distributions of earnings to shareholders, and the effects of retiring shares. Securities laws govern the sale of share capital and the disclosure of financial information to the general public. When corporate shares are traded on organized securities exchanges, the corporation must also comply with the reporting requirements of these exchanges. Respecting federal, provincial, and securities regulations increases costs and complexity for corporations.

These regulations are designed to protect the owners of the corporation. Such protection is needed because most shareholders do not participate in the day-to-day management of the company.

► Accounting in Action ► *Ethics Insight*

 The collapse of the Calgary-based Bre-X company in 1997 represents the world's biggest mining hoax and shareholder disaster. It has raised questions that remain unanswered about the integrity of the world's stock markets and financial regulatory agencies. On top of that, the story has all the makings of a soap opera, including suicide, murder, adultery, greed, and conspiracy plots.

Bre-X collapsed after an independent audit found that its Indonesian gold discovery, proclaimed to be the world's largest, contained almost no gold. At the peak of their trading, Bre-X shares were worth $6 billion. The shares are now worthless. The share price moved like a yo-yo in response to information leaks on the Internet. Regulators halted trading, but unofficial markets outside the stock exchanges sprang up.

While many fingers were pointed in all directions to assign blame for this debacle, Canadian regulatory authorities and investors learned an important lesson. "No one in Canada is protected from cyber sellers who post insider information or lies on the Internet."

Source: Diane Francis, "The Bre-X Fiasco and Important Trading Laws." *Maclean's,* June 2, 1997, 61.

Entity Income Tax

Neither proprietorships nor partnerships pay entity income tax. Each owner's share of income from these organizations is reported on his or her personal income tax return. Income tax is then paid by the individual on this amount. Corporations, on the other hand, must pay federal and provincial income taxes as separate legal entities. These taxes can be substantial. They can amount to as much as 50% of taxable income.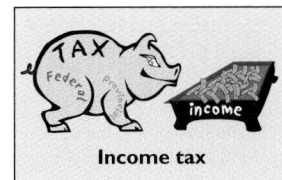

Income tax

There are tax deductions available to some corporations. Deductions such as the manufacturing and processing profits deduction and the small business deduction can reduce the tax rate to between 20% and 25%. With eligible deductions, or other corporate tax incentives, a corporation's tax rate may be reduced to 20% to 25%. This tax rate is likely much lower than the tax rate for the same amount of income earned by an individual.

In some circumstances, an advantage of incorporation is the deferral of personal income tax. The shareholders of a corporation do not pay tax on the corporate earnings until they are distributed to them. Shareholders pay tax on cash dividends, which are pro rata distributions of net income. Many people argue that corporate income is taxed twice (double taxation)—at the corporate level and again at the individual level. This is not exactly true, however, as individuals receive a dividend tax credit to reduce some of the tax burden.

To determine whether incorporating will result in more or less income tax than a proprietorship or partnership, it is wise to seek expert advice. Income tax laws are complex, and care in tax planning is essential for any business venture.

Based on the foregoing, Illustration 14-1 shows the advantages and disadvantages of a corporation compared to a proprietorship or partnership.

Illustration 14-1

Advantages and disadvantages of a corporation

Advantages	Disadvantages
• Corporation management—professional managers • Separate legal existence • Limited liability of shareholders • Potential for deferred or reduced income tax • Transferable ownership rights • Ability to acquire capital • Continuous life	• Corporation management—ownership separated from management • Increased costs and complexity to follow government regulations • Potential for additional income tax

It is worth noting that many of these advantages and disadvantages depend on the size of the entity. For example, in a small, private (closely held) corporation, such as the Diab Corner Grocery Store Ltd., it is just as hard to sell shares of ownership, or to acquire capital, as it is for an unincorporated business. The limited liability feature also makes it harder for a small corporation to obtain loans. Lenders often require officers to personally guarantee the loans, which eliminates the limited liability advantage.

Forming a Corporation

▸ *International note*

As noted previously, corporations in Canada are identified by *Ltd., Inc.,* or *Corp.* In Brazil and France, the letters used are *SA* (Sôciedade Anonima, Société Anonyme); in Japan, *KK* (Kabushiki Kaisha); in the Netherlands, *NV* (Naamloze Vennootschap); in Italy, *SpA* (Società per Azioni); in Sweden, *AB* (Aktiebolag); and in the U.S., *Inc.*

In the UK, public corporations are identified by *Plc* (Public limited company), while private corporations are denoted by *Ltd.* The parallel designations in Germany are *AG* (Aktiengesellschaft) for public corporations and *GmbH* (Gesellschaftmit beschränkter Haftung) for private corporations.

As previously mentioned, a company can incorporate federally or provincially. The federal government and the majority of provinces file **articles of incorporation** to incorporate a company, although other methods also exist.

The initial step for forming a corporation is to file an application as required by the corporations or company act. The application contains information such as (1) the name and purpose of the proposed corporation, (2) the amounts and kinds of share capital to be authorized and the number of shares, (3) the names and addresses of the incorporators, and (4) the location of the corporation's head office. Anyone can apply to incorporate a company, as long as he or she is over the age of 18, of sound mind, and not bankrupt.

The costs of forming a corporation are called organization costs. These costs include legal fees, accounting fees, and registration costs. It may be argued that organization costs should be capitalized as they have an asset life equal to the life of the corporation. However, most companies expense organization costs in the year they occur. Determining the amount and timing of future benefits is so difficult that the **conservative** approach of expensing these costs immediately is more justifiable.

Ownership Rights of Shareholders

When chartered, the corporation may begin selling ownership rights in the form of shares. The shares of the company are divided into different classes, such as Class A, Class B, and so on. The rights and privileges assigned to each class of shares are stated in the articles of incorporation. The different classes are usually identified by the generic terms **common shares** and **preferred shares**. When a corporation has only one class of shares, it has the rights and privileges of **common shares**. Each common share gives the shareholder the ownership rights shown in Illustration 14-2 on the next page.

A form known as a **share certificate proves that a shareholder owns shares**. The face of the certificate shows the name of the corporation, the shareholder's name, the class and special features of the shares, the number of shares owned, and the signatures of duly authorized corporate officials. Certificates should be prenumbered to

Illustration 14-2

Ownership rights of shareholders

Shareholders have the right to:

1. Vote in the election of the board of directors at an annual meeting. Vote on actions that require shareholder approval.

2. Share the corporate income by receiving dividends.

3. Keep the same percentage ownership when new shares are issued (called the **pre-emptive right**).

4. Share in the assets upon liquidation, in proportion to their holdings. (This is called a **residual claim** because owners are paid with assets remaining after all claims have been paid.)

Helpful hint A number of companies have eliminated the pre-emptive right, because they believe it makes an unnecessary and cumbersome demand on management.

facilitate accountability. They may be issued for any quantity of shares. Most share certificates are preprinted with the relevant information. Some, especially in smaller corporations, provide space for the certificate details to be inserted as shown in Illustration 14-3.

Illustration 14-3

Share certificate

▲Accounting in Action ▸ *International Insight*

 In Japan, shareholders are considered to be far less important to a corporation than employees, customers, and suppliers. There, shareholders are rarely asked to vote on an issue. The notion of bending corporate policy to favour shareholders borders on heresy. The attitude towards shareholders appears to be slowly changing, however. Influential Japanese are encouraging companies to listen to investors, to raise the extremely low dividends paid by Japanese corporations, and to improve their disclosure of financial information.

Share Issue Considerations

Alternative terminology
The word issued also means *sold*.

When considering the issue of shares, a corporation must answer some basic questions. How many shares should be authorized for sale? How should the shares be issued? At what price should the shares be issued? What value should be assigned to the shares? These questions are answered in the following sections.

Authorized Share Capital

The amount of shares that a corporation is **authorized** to sell is indicated in its articles of incorporation. It may be specified as an unlimited amount or a certain number (e.g., 500,000 shares authorized). More than three-quarters of public companies with share capital in Canada have an unlimited amount of authorized shares. If a number is specified, the amount of authorized shares normally anticipates a company's initial and later capital needs. If a corporation has sold all of its authorized shares, it must obtain legislative approval to amend its articles of incorporation before it can issue additional shares.

To determine the number of unissued shares that can be issued without amending the articles of incorporation, the total shares issued are subtracted from the total authorized. For example, if Advanced Micro Corp. is authorized to sell 100,000 common shares but has issued only 80,000 shares, 20,000 shares remain unissued. If Advanced Micro had an unlimited amount of common shares authorized, an unlimited number of shares would remain unissued.

The authorization of share capital does not result in a formal accounting entry, since the event has no immediate effect on either corporate assets or shareholders' equity. However, disclosure of the authorized and issued shares is required in the shareholders' equity section of the balance sheet.

Issue of Shares

A corporation can issue common shares either directly to investors or indirectly through an investment dealer (brokerage house) that specializes in bringing securities to the attention of potential investors. ScotiaMcleod and RBC Dominion Securities are two examples of such investment firms. Direct issue is typical in closely held companies. Indirect issue is customary for a publicly held corporation, such as Research In Motion in our feature story.

The first time a corporation's shares are offered to the public, the offer is called an initial public offering (IPO). The company receives the cash (less any issuance fees) from the sale of the IPO shares whether done by a direct or indirect issue. The company's assets (cash) increase, and its shareholders' equity (share capital) also increases.

Once these shares have been initially issued, they continue trading on the **secondary market**. That is, investors buy and sell shares from each other, rather than from the company. In these cases, there is no impact on the company's financial position. It receives no additional assets, and issues no additional shares. The only change in the company records is the name of the shareholder, not the number of shares issued.

In Canada, shares are offered for sale to the public (whether through an IPO or through the secondary market) using organized securities exchanges, such as the Toronto Stock Exchange (TSE) or the Montreal Exchange (ME). Shares may also be traded on the "over-the-counter" market, the Canadian Dealing Network (CDN), which is managed by the TSE.

How does a corporation like Research In Motion in our opening story set the price for its initial issue of shares? Among the factors to be considered are (1) the company's anticipated future earnings, (2) its expected dividend rate per share, (3) its current financial position, (4) the current state of the economy, and (5) the current state of the securities market. The subject can be complex and is usually taught in a finance course.

Market Value of Shares

After the initial issue of new shares, the subsequent market price per share is established by the interaction between buyers and sellers. In general, the price follows the trend of a company's earnings and dividends. Research In Motion's share price climbed from its initial offering price of $7.25 to a high of $260. Factors beyond a company's control (such as an embargo on oil, changes in interest rates, the outcome of an election, and terrorist attacks) can also influence market prices.

The volume of trading on national and international exchanges is heavy. More than 150 million shares are often traded daily on the Toronto Stock Exchange alone. For each listed security, the financial press reports the highs and lows of the shares for the year, the annual dividend rate, the dividend yield, and the price-earnings ratio. The total volume of shares traded on a particular day, the high and low prices for the day, and the closing market price with the net change for the day are also reported. A recent listing published in *FP Investing* for The Second Cup Ltd. is shown below:

Illustration 14-4

Market price information for The Second Cup

52w high	52w low	Stock	Ticker	Div	Yield %	P/E	Vol 00s	High	Low	Close	Net chg
17.00	6.00	Second Cup	SKL	p2.00	25.0	80.0	8	8.00	8.00	8.00	

These numbers indicate that the high and low market prices for the last 52 weeks were $17.00 and $6.00. Ticker is the basic trading symbol for the company used by the exchange. The Second Cup paid a $2.00 per share special dividend in the past year. The symbol "p" means that it is not a regular dividend. The dividend yield (the dividend divided by the closing share price) is 25% ($2.00 ÷ $8.00). The price-earnings (P/E) ratio for The Second Cup Ltd. was 80.0, indicating that the market price ($8.00) is 80 times The Second Cup's earnings per share. The dividend yield and price-earnings ratios will be discussed further in the next chapter. The trading volume was 800 shares. The high, low, and closing prices for that date were $8.00 each. There was no net change in the share price for the day over the previous day. That is, The Second Cup's shares closed at $8.00 per share the previous day, as well.

► **International note**

The United States has the world's largest market capitalization. Nearly half of all companies in the world list their shares on U.S. stock market exchanges. Europe has 24%, Japan and the UK each 10%, and Canada and the rest of the Pacific less than 3% each of the world's market capitalization.

▶**Accounting in Action** ▸ *@-Business Insight*

Investment dealer TD Evergreen is the target of the first ever inquiry into stock market manipulation by a Canadian stockbroker who used an Internet bulletin board. Internet bulletin boards are popular with small investors and day traders who can read information on-line about the shares.

Using a popular French-language financial forum called Webfin.com, a TD Evergreen staff member encouraged people to buy shares of DelSecur Corp. DelSecur is a small company traded over the counter on the OTCBB, an electronic bulletin-board exchange in the U.S. Based on these comments, the share price climbed from US$2 to more than US$18. A spokesperson said, "All TD Evergreen employees are governed by rigorous compliance rules about information they impart in their capacity as an employee....We take these matters very seriously."

Source: Suzanne Craig, "Chat Room Stock Promotion Scrutinized." *The Globe and Mail*, August 3, 2000, A1.

Par, No Par, and Stated Value Shares

A **par value share** is share capital that has a specific value stated in the corporate charter. The par value may be any amount selected by the corporation. Generally, the par value is quite low, because filing fees may vary with the amount of legal capital. Par values are also set low to try to avoid the possibility of market prices falling below par values.

Par value does not indicate the worth or the market value of the shares. **Par value has legal significance.** It represents the **legal capital** per share that must be kept in the business for the protection of corporate creditors. That amount cannot be withdrawn by shareholders. Thus, corporations are required to sell shares only at par or above.

Par value shares have two significant drawbacks. As market prices increase further above par values, creditors may have an inadequate cushion of protection if the company only retains assets equal to its minimum legal capital. On the other hand, if market prices fall below par value, corporations cannot use the equity markets to raise capital, because they are not allowed to sell their shares for less than par. Because of these difficulties, many jurisdictions, such as the Province of Ontario and the federal government, have abolished par value shares in favour of no par value shares.

A **no par value share** is share capital that has not been assigned a value in the corporate charter. If shares have no par value, the questionable practice of using par value as a basis for legal capital never arises. No par value shares are the most common form of shares today. More than 90% of Canadian public companies now issue no par value shares.

In many provinces, the board of directors is permitted to assign a **stated value** to the no par value shares. This value becomes the legal capital per share. The stated value may be changed at any time by the directors. Stated value, like par value, does not indicate the market value of the shares. When there is no assigned stated value, all proceeds received from the share issue are considered legal capital. Only a few companies in Canada use stated values. Sears Canada is one that does.

The relationship of par, no par, and stated value to legal capital is shown in Illustration 14-5 below:

Illustration 14-5

Relationship of par, no par, and stated value shares to legal capital

Shares	Legal Capital per Share
Par value	Par value
No par value	Entire proceeds
Stated value	Stated value

As will be explained later, each time shares are issued, a common (or preferred) shares account is credited for the legal capital per share.

Corporate Capital

Equity in a corporation is identified as **shareholders' equity**. The shareholders' equity section of a corporation's balance sheet consists of (1) contributed capital, and (2) retained earnings (earned capital). The distinction between contributed capital and retained earnings is important from both a legal and a financial point of view. Legally, dividends (distributions of earnings) can be paid out of retained earnings. In most jurisdictions, dividends cannot be paid out of contributed capital.

> **STUDY OBJECTIVE**
> ··········**2**··········
> *Differentiate between contributed capital and retained earnings.*

Contributed Capital

Contributed capital are the total amount of cash and other assets paid or contributed to the corporation by shareholders in exchange for share capital. Share capital consists of different classes of shares. As noted earlier in this chapter, if a company has only one class of shares, it is **common shares**. The company may also issue another class of shares—preferred shares—as we will learn later.

In a complex capital structure, other transactions may also affect contributed capital. A discussion of complex capital structures is left to an intermediate accounting course.

Retained Earnings

Retained earnings are the cumulative net income (loss) that has been retained (i.e., not distributed to shareholders) in a corporation. Retained earnings are distributed to shareholders through dividends, which are discussed later in this chapter and in Chapter 15.

Net income is recorded in Retained Earnings by closing entries in which revenue accounts are debited and expense accounts are credited. The Dividends account, similar to Drawings in a proprietorship, is also credited in the closing process. Instead of crediting and debiting the owner's capital account, as is the case in a proprietorship, the Retained Earnings account is used.

> **Helpful hint** Chapter 4 has a full explanation of closing entries for a proprietorship, Chapter 13 for a partnership.

For example, assume for simplicity that Delta Robotics Ltd. has three temporary accounts at its June 30, 2003, year end: Service Revenue, $500,000; Operating Expenses, $290,000; and Dividends, $80,000. The closing entries follow:

Date	Account	Debit	Credit				
June 30	Service Revenue	500,000		A	= L	+	SE
	Retained Earnings		500,000				−500,000
	To close revenue to retained earnings.						+500,000
30	Retained Earnings	290,000		A	= L	+	SE
	Operating Expenses		290,000				−290,000
	To close expenses to retained earnings.						+290,000
30	Retained Earnings	80,000		A	= L	+	SE
	Dividends		80,000				−80,000
	To close dividends to retained earnings.						+80,000

Presentation

To illustrate the presentation of contributed capital and retained earnings in a corporate balance sheet, assume Delta Robotics has an unlimited number of authorized no par value common shares, with 50,000 issued for a total of $800,000. Delta Robotics reported $210,000 ($500,000 − $290,000) of net income in its first year of operations and $80,000 of dividends paid. Because there is no opening balance of retained earnings, ending retained earnings is net income ($210,000) less dividends ($80,000), which equals $130,000. The company's shareholders' equity section is as follows:

Illustration 14-6

Shareholders' equity section

DELTA ROBOTICS LTD. Balance Sheet (partial) June 30, 2003	
Shareholders' equity	
Contributed capital	
Common shares, unlimited number of no par value shares authorized, 50,000 issued	$800,000
Retained earnings	130,000
Total shareholders' equity	$930,000

The following illustration compares the permanent equity accounts for a proprietorship, a partnership, and a corporation:

Illustration 14-7

Comparison of equity accounts

Before You Go On . . .

▶Review It

1. What are the advantages and disadvantages of a corporation compared to a proprietorship or partnership?
2. What rights are inherent in owning a common share in a corporation?
3. How many authorized common shares did The Second Cup have at June 24, 2000? Issued? The answers to these questions are at the end of this chapter.
4. Distinguish between par value, no par value, stated value, and market value.

▶Do It

At the end of its first year of operations, October 31, 2003, Dai-ichi Corporation has $750,000 from an issue of 25,000 no par value common shares (unlimited number of shares authorized) and a net income of $122,000. No dividends were paid. Prepare the shareholders' equity section of the balance sheet at year end.

Action Plan

• In the shareholders' equity section, show (1) contributed capital, and (2) retained earnings.

Solution

DAI-ICHI CORPORATION
Balance Sheet (partial)
October 31, 2003

Shareholders' equity		
Contributed capital		
Common shares		
Authorized: Unlimited		
Issued: 25,000 no par value shares	$750,000	
Retained earnings	122,000	
Total shareholders' equity	$872,000	

Related exercise material: BE14–1, BE14–2, and E14–1.

THE NAVIGATOR

Accounting for Common Share Issues

•••

Let's now look at how to account for common share issues. The primary objectives in accounting for the issue of common shares are to (1) identify the specific sources of contributed capital, and (2) maintain the distinction between contributed capital and retained earnings. **The issue of common shares affects only contributed capital accounts.**

STUDY OBJECTIVE
••••••••• **3** •••••••••
Record the issue of common shares.

Issuing No Par Value Shares for Cash

Shares are most commonly issued in exchange for cash. As discussed earlier, when no par value common shares are issued, the entire proceeds from the issue become legal capital. To illustrate the issue of no par value common shares, assume that Hydro-Slide, Inc. is authorized to issue 10,000 no par value common shares. It issues 1,000 of these shares for $1 per share on January 12, 2003. The entry to record this transaction is as follows:

Jan. 12	Cash	1,000	
	Common Shares		1,000
	To record issue of 1,000 no par value		
	common shares.		

A	=	L	+	SE
+1,000				+1,000

Note that the remaining 9,000 authorized but unissued shares are not recorded until sold.

If the share price climbs and Hydro-Slide issues an additional 1,000 of the no par value common shares for $5 per share on March 18, the entry is as follows:

Mar. 18	Cash	5,000	
	Common Shares		5,000
	To record issue of 1,000 no par value		
	common shares.		

A	=	L	+	SE
+5,000				+5,000

In each case, the entire proceeds are credited to the Common Shares account. The total amount of legal capital for Hydro-Slide after these two transactions is $6,000 ($1,000 + $5,000).

Issuing Stated Value Shares for Cash

Helpful hint Contributed Capital in Excess of Stated Value is not reported in the income statement, because it is not a gain.

As discussed earlier, stated value does not indicate a share's market value. The cash proceeds from issuing stated value shares may be equal to or greater than stated value. The proceeds cannot be less than stated value, since it is prohibited to issue shares at less than stated value. When the issue of common shares for cash is recorded, the stated value of the shares is credited to the Common Shares account. The portion that is above stated value is recorded in a separate contributed capital account.

This contributed capital account is called by many names. We call it Contributed Capital in Excess of Stated Value. It is also sometimes recorded as Premium, Contributed Surplus, Paid-In Capital, Additional Paid-In Capital, or Capital Surplus.

To illustrate the issue of common shares with a stated value, assume that Hydro-Slide, Inc. is authorized to issue 10,000 $1 stated value common shares. It issues 1,000 of these shares at their stated value of $1 on January 12 for cash. The entry to record this transaction follows:

A	=	L	+	SE
+1,000				+1,000

Jan. 12	Cash	1,000	
	Common Shares		1,000
	To record issue of 1,000 common shares at stated value.		

Note that the remaining authorized shares are not recorded until sold.

If Hydro-Slide issues an additional 1,000 of the $1 stated value common shares on March 18 for cash of $5 per share, the entry is as follows:

A	=	L	+	SE
+5,000				+1,000
				+4,000

Mar. 18	Cash	5,000	
	Common Shares (1,000 × $1 value)		1,000
	Contributed Capital in Excess of Stated Value		
	[1,000 × ($5 − $1)]		4,000
	To record issue of 1,000 common shares.		

The total contributed capital from these two transactions is $6,000 ($1,000 + $5,000). The legal capital is $2,000 ($1,000 + $1,000). If Hydro-Slide has retained earnings of $27,000, the shareholders' equity section at March 31, 2003, is as in Illustration 14-8:

Illustration 14-8

Shareholders' equity— contributed capital in excess of stated value

HYDRO-SLIDE INC. Balance Sheet (partial) March 31, 2003	
Shareholders' equity	
Contributed capital	
Common shares, 10,000 shares of $1 stated value	
authorized, 2,000 shares issued	$ 2,000
Contributed capital in excess of stated value	4,000
Total contributed capital	6,000
Retained earnings	27,000
Total shareholders' equity	$33,000

Issuing Par Value Shares for Cash

The entries for par value shares are similar to those illustrated for stated value shares. The par value represents legal capital, and the number of shares issued multiplied by the par value is credited to the Common Shares account. When the selling price of par value shares exceeds their par value, the excess is credited to the Contributed Capital in Excess of Par Value account. Contributed Capital in Excess of Par Value is reported as part of contributed capital in the shareholders' equity section. Because of the limited use of par value shares in Canada, this text will emphasize the accounting for no par and stated value shares.

Issuing Shares for Services or Noncash Assets

Shares may also be issued for services (compensation to lawyers or consultants) or for noncash assets (land, buildings, and equipment). In such cases, what cost should be recognized in the exchange transaction? To comply with the **cost principle** in a noncash transaction, **cost is the cash equivalent price**. The cash equivalent price is the **fair market value of the consideration given up**. If this amount cannot be determined, we look to the **fair market value of the consideration received** to determine the cash equivalent price, and thus the cost.

To illustrate, assume that lawyers have helped the Panjer Corporation incorporate. They have billed the company $5,000 for their services. On September 18, they agree to accept 4,000 no par value common shares in payment of their bill. At the time of the exchange, there is no established market price for the shares. In this case, the market value of the consideration received, $5,000, is the best (only) measure of the asset. Accordingly, the entry is as follows:

Sept. 18	Legal Fees Expense	5,000	
	Common Shares		5,000
	To record issue of 4,000 no par value shares		
	to lawyer.		

A	=	L	+	SE
				−5,000
				+5,000

In contrast, assume that Schafer Research Inc. is a publicly held corporation. Its no par value shares are actively traded at $8 per share. The company issues 10,000 shares on October 1 to acquire land recently advertised for sale at $90,000. The best value is the market price of the consideration given, $80,000 (10,000 × $8). The transaction is recorded as follows:

Oct. 1	Land	80,000	
	Common Shares		80,000
	To record issue of 10,000 no par value shares		
	for land.		

A	=	L	+	SE
+80,000				+80,000

If, instead of a no par value, these shares had a stated value of $5 per share, the land would not be recorded at the stated value of the shares issued, $50,000. It would still be recorded at their fair market value of $80,000. The difference of $30,000 would be recorded as contributed capital in excess of stated value. **The stated value of the shares is never a factor in determining the cost of the assets received, because it does not represent economic value.**

Reacquisition of Shares

Companies can purchase their own shares on the open market. A corporation may acquire shares to meet any of the following objectives:
1. To increase trading of the company's shares in the securities market in the hopes of enhancing its market value.
2. To reduce the number of shares issued and thereby increase earnings per share.
3. To have additional shares available to reissue to officers and employees under bonus and stock compensation plans.
4. To have additional shares available for use in the acquisition of other companies.
5. To comply with percentage share ownership requirements (i.e., limit foreign ownership).

Another infrequent reason for purchasing one's own shares is that management may want to eliminate hostile shareholders by buying them out. Canadian Occidental Petroleum Ltd. (CanOxy) repurchased nearly half of its shares in 2000 to stop the

Los Angeles–based Occidental Petroleum Corp. from taking over its huge Syncrude oil sands project in northern Alberta.

When a federally incorporated company reacquires its own shares, the repurchased shares must be retired and cancelled. This effectively restores the shares to the status of authorized but unissued shares. Some provincially incorporated companies are also allowed to hold reacquired shares for future use. Shares for this purpose are called **treasury shares**. Treasury share transactions are rare in Canada and only permitted in restricted circumstances.

If a company has treasury shares, this will result in a difference between the number of shares issued and the number of shares outstanding. Issued shares are those that have been sold. Outstanding shares are those that have been sold and are held outside the company. In most circumstances, issued and outstanding shares are the same.

▶Accounting in Action ▶ *Business Insight*

Late in 1998, CHUM Limited, owner of MuchMusic, was considered by investors to be a "hot" share. One year later, investors were bored and CHUM's Class B nonvoting share price fell to around $38 from a peak of $60. That's why CHUM repurchased 5% of its shares on the Toronto Stock Exchange the next year.

Why do companies buy back their own shares? A share repurchase reduces the number of shares. Fewer shares mean increased earnings per share. Investors are attracted to higher earnings per share, and the company's share price rises with the increased demand for its shares. A recent study confirmed that buyback shares outperform the markets by an average of 7% in each of the three years following their repurchase announcements.

Source: Keith Kalawsky, "They Take It Back." *Canadian Business*, October 8, 1999, 29.

Before You Go On . . .
▶*Review It*

1. Explain the accounting for no par value and stated value common shares that are issued for cash.
2. Explain the accounting for the issue of common shares for services or noncash assets.
3. Why might a company wish to repurchase its own shares on the open market?

▶*Do It*

Victoria Corporation begins operations on March 1 by issuing 100,000 no par value common shares for cash at $12 per share. On March 15, it issues 5,000 common shares to its lawyers in settlement of their bill of $65,000. The shares continue to trade at $12 per share on March 15. Journalize the two share issues.

Action Plan

- Credit the Common Shares account for the entire share issue proceeds when the shares have no par value.
- Use the cash equivalent price when shares are issued for services.
- The cash equivalent price is equal to the fair market value of what is given up. If this amount cannot be determined, use the fair market value of what is received.

Solution

Mar. 1	Cash	1,200,000	
	Common Shares (100,000 × $12)		1,200,000
	To record issue of 100,000 shares at $12 per share.		

Mar. 15	Legal Fees Expense	60,000	
	Common Shares (5,000 × $12)		60,000
	To record issue of 5,000 shares for		
	lawyers' fees.		

THE NAVIGATOR

Related exercise material: BE14–3, BE14–4, BE14–5, BE14–6, E14–2, E14–3, and E14–4.

Preferred Shares

A corporation may issue preferred shares in addition to common shares. **Preferred shares** have contractual provisions that give them a preference, or priority, over common shares in certain areas. Typically, preferred shareholders have priority over (1) dividends (distributions of earnings), and (2) assets in the event of liquidation. They generally do not have voting rights.

STUDY OBJECTIVE

4

Differentiate and journalize preferred and common share transactions.

Accounting in Action ► *Business Insight*

Companies are gradually eliminating having two classes of shares. Agra Inc., Laidlaw Inc., and SNC-Lavalin Group Inc. are examples of companies that have combined voting and nonvoting shares into one class of shares with equal voting rights. James Bullock, CEO of Laidlaw, summed it up: "It was clearly inappropriate to have a situation where 15% of the shareholders had all of the votes." There is, however, at least one downside to this move for nonvoting shareholders: they may gain the right to vote, but their equity decreases as voting shareholders demand an increasingly generous premium to give up their advantage.

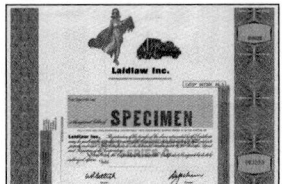

Source: David Thomas, "Class Struggle." *Financial Post,* July 5, 1997, 12.

Like common shares, preferred shares may be issued for cash or for noncash assets. They can also be reacquired. The entries for all these transactions are similar to the entries for common shares. Assume that Staudinger Corporation issues 10,000 no par value preferred shares for $12 cash per share on January 28. The entry to record the issue is as follows:

Jan. 28	Cash	120,000	
	Preferred Shares		120,000
	To record the issue of 10,000 no par value		
	preferred shares.		

A	=	L	+	SE
+120,000				+120,000

The Preferred Shares account is used to record the issue of preferred shares. As with common shares, no par value shares are most commonly issued. If preferred shares have a stated value, any excess proceeds received should be recorded in a separate contributed capital account. For example, a company might have the following accounts: Preferred Shares and Contributed Capital in Excess of Stated Value. In the shareholders' equity section, preferred shares are presented first because of their dividend and liquidation preferences over common shares.

Dividend Preference

I hope there's some money left when it's my turn.

Preferred   Common
Shareholder Shareholder

Dividend preference

As indicated before, corporate income is distributed to **preferred shareholders before it goes to common shareholders**. For example, if the dividend rate on preferred shares is $5 per share, common shareholders will not receive any dividends in the current year until preferred shareholders have received $5 per share. The first claim to dividends does not, however, guarantee the payment of dividends. Dividends depend on many factors, such as adequate retained earnings and the availability of cash.

The per share dividend amount is usually given as an **annual** amount, similar to interest rates. It will be stated either as a specified amount or as a percentage of the stated (or par) value of the preferred shares. For example, TransCanada PipeLines Limited has a $2.80 dividend on one of its classes of no par value preferred shares. Sun Ice Limited specifies a 9% dividend on its first preferred shares. If the dividend is expressed as a percentage of the stated value, the annual per share dividend is calculated by multiplying the dividend rate by the stated value amount of the shares.

Cumulative Dividend

Preferred shares often contain a cumulative dividend feature. This means that preferred shareholders must be paid both current year dividends and any unpaid prior year dividends before common shareholders receive dividends. When preferred shares are cumulative, preferred dividends that are not declared in a given period are called **dividends in arrears**. When preferred shares are not cumulative (known as noncumulative), a dividend unpaid in any year is lost forever.

To illustrate the cumulative dividend feature, assume that Staudinger's 10,000 no par value preferred shares have a $3.50 cumulative dividend. The annual dividend is $35,000 (10,000 × $3.50 per share). If dividends are two years in arrears, preferred shareholders are entitled to receive the following dividends:

Dividends in arrears ($35,000 × 2)	$ 70,000
Current year dividends	35,000
Total preferred dividends	$105,000

No distribution can be made to common shareholders until this entire preferred dividend is paid. In other words, dividends cannot be paid on common shares while any preferred shares are in arrears.

Dividends in arrears are not considered a liability. No payment obligation exists until a dividend is declared by the board of directors. However, the amount of dividends in arrears should be disclosed in the notes to the financial statements. This enables investors to assess the potential impact of this future declaration on the corporation's financial position.

Companies that are unable to meet their dividend obligations are not looked upon favourably by the investment community. When discussing one company's failure to pay its cumulative preferred dividend, a financial officer noted, "Not meeting your obligations on something like that is a major black mark on your record." The accounting entries for dividends are explained in Chapter 15.

Convertible Preferred

As an investment, preferred shares are even more attractive when there is a conversion privilege. Convertible preferred shares give shareholders the option of exchanging preferred shares for common shares at a specified ratio.

Convertible preferred shares are purchased by investors who want the greater security of preferred shares but who also want the option of conversion if the market value of the common shares increases significantly.

To illustrate, assume that Ross Industries Inc. issues 1,000 shares of no par value convertible preferred shares at $100 per share. One share of preferred is convertible into 10 shares of no par value common (current market price $9 per share). At this point, holders of the preferred shares would not want to convert, because they would exchange preferred shares worth $100,000 (1,000 × $100) for common shares worth only $90,000 (10,000 × $9). However, if the price of the common shares were to increase above $10 per share, conversion would be advantageous for the preferred shareholders.

To record the conversion, the original amount paid for the preferred shares is transferred to appropriate common share accounts. To illustrate, assume that the 1,000 preferred shares of Ross Industries are converted into 10,000 common shares when the market values of the two classes of shares are $101 and $12 per share, respectively, on June 10. The entry to record the conversion follows:

June 10	Preferred Shares	100,000	
	Common Shares		100,000
	To record conversion of 1,000 preferred shares of no par value into 10,000 common shares of no par value.		

A = L + SE
       −100,000
       +100,000

If Ross Industries' preferred shares had a stated value of $75 instead of no par value, the entry to record the conversion would be as follows:

June 10	Preferred Shares	75,000	
	Contributed Capital in Excess of Stated Value	25,000	
	Common Shares		100,000
	To record conversion of 1,000 preferred shares of $75 stated value into 10,000 common shares of no par value.		

A = L + SE
       −75,000
       −25,000
       +100,000

Regardless of whether the preferred shares have no par value or a stated value, the book value of the preferred shares is used to record the conversion. **The conversion of preferred shares does not result in either a gain or a loss to the corporation. Note that the market values of the shares at the time of the transaction are not considered in recording the transaction.** The reason is that the corporation has not received any assets equal to fair market value.

Helpful hint Only shareholders' equity accounts are involved when conversion occurs. This transaction may be viewed as a realignment of a company's shares.

Redeemable and Retractable Preferred

Many preferred shares are issued with a redemption or call feature. Redeemable (or callable) preferred shares give the issuing corporation the right to purchase the shares from shareholders at specified future dates and prices. The redemption feature enables a corporation to eliminate the preferred shares when it is advantageous to do so.

Often, shares that are redeemable are also convertible. Sometimes, companies will redeem or call their preferred shares to induce investors to convert those preferred shares into common shares.

Retractable preferred shares are similar to redeemable preferred shares except that the shareholders can redeem shares at their option instead of the corporation's. This usually occurs at an arranged price and date.

When preferred shares are redeemable or retractable, the distinction between equity and debt begins to blur. Redeemable and retractable preferred shares are similar in some ways to debt. They both offer a rate of return to the investor, and with the redemption of the shares, they both offer a repayment of the principal investment.

Contractual arrangements of this sort are known as **financial instruments**. The CICA requires companies to present financial instruments in accordance with their economic substance rather than their form. That is, redeemable and retractable preferred shares are usually presented in the *liabilities* section of the balance sheet rather than in the equity section. This is because they often have more of the features of debt

Helpful hint The two features differ in terms of benefit. *Retractable* is at the option of the shareholder. *Redeemable* is at the option of the corporation.

than of equity. Accounting for such financial instruments presents unique challenges to accountants. Further discussion of this topic is left to an intermediate accounting course.

Liquidation Preference

Most preferred shares also have a preference on corporate assets if the corporation fails. This means that assets will be used to pay the preferred shareholders first if the corporation goes bankrupt. This feature provides security for the preferred shareholders. The preference to assets may be for the legal capital of the shares or for a specified liquidating value. The liquidation preference establishes the respective claims of creditors and preferred shareholders.

Before You Go On . . .

▸*Review It*

THE
NAVIGATOR

1. Compare the normal rights and privileges of common and preferred shareholders.
2. Distinguish between cumulative and noncumulative dividends.
3. Distinguish between convertible, redeemable, and retractable preferred shares.

Related exercise material: BE14–7, E14–5, and E14–6.

Statement Presentation of Shareholders' Equity

STUDY OBJECTIVE
5

Prepare the shareholders' equity section of the balance sheet.

In the shareholders' equity section of the balance sheet, contributed capital and retained earnings are reported. The specific sources of contributed capital are identified.
  Within contributed capital, two classifications are recognized:

1. **Share capital**. This category consists of preferred and common shares. Preferred shares are shown before common shares because of the additional rights they give. The legal value (e.g., no par or stated), shares authorized, and shares issued are reported for each class of shares.
2. **Additional contributed capital**. This includes the amounts paid over stated (or par) value. This category will result only if stated (or par) values exist. If the shares are no par value, there will be no additional contributed capital. In this case, it is usual to just use the caption "share capital" rather than "contributed capital."

Presentation

The assumed shareholders' equity section of Zaboschuk Inc., shown in Illustration 14-9, includes most of the accounts discussed in this chapter. Zaboschuk's preferred shares section discloses that the dividend rate is $9 per annum, 10,000 preferred shares of no par value have been authorized, and 6,000 shares are issued. Although we do not know the original issue price of each preferred share, we can calculate the *average* issue price of $128.33 per share ($770,000 ÷ 6,000).

The common shares have a $5 stated value with an unlimited amount of shares authorized. To date, 400,000 shares have been issued. The average issue price of the common shares is $7.15 per share [($2,000,000 + $860,000) ÷ 400,000].

Illustration 14-9

Shareholders' equity section

ZABOSCHUK INC. Balance Sheet (partial) December 31, 2003	
Shareholders' equity	
Contributed capital	
Share capital	
$9 preferred shares, no par value,	
cumulative, 10,000 shares authorized,	
6,000 shares issued	$ 770,000
Common shares, $5 stated value, unlimited	
shares authorized, 400,000 shares issued	2,000,000
Total share capital	2,770,000
Additional contributed capital	
Contributed capital in excess of stated	
value—common shares	860,000
Total contributed capital	3,630,000
Retained earnings	1,058,000
Total shareholders' equity	$4,688,000

Using the Information in the Financial Statements

There are many valuable ratios that can be determined from the shareholders' equity section of the balance sheet. Two of the most important are the return on equity ratio and the book value per share.

STUDY OBJECTIVE
·········▼·········
6

Calculate return on equity and book value per share.

Return on Equity

Return on equity, also known as return on investment, is considered by many to be *the* most important measure of a firm's profitability and efficiency. This ratio is used by management and investors to evaluate how many dollars are earned for each dollar invested by the shareholders. It can be used to compare investment opportunities in the marketplace.

Return on equity is a widely published figure. The highest return on equity among Canada's top 1000 corporations in a recent year was reported by Hollinger Inc., 432%. The lowest was Goran Capital, which reported a negative 400%.

The following illustration calculates the return on equity ratio for The Second Cup:

Illustration 14-10

Return on equity

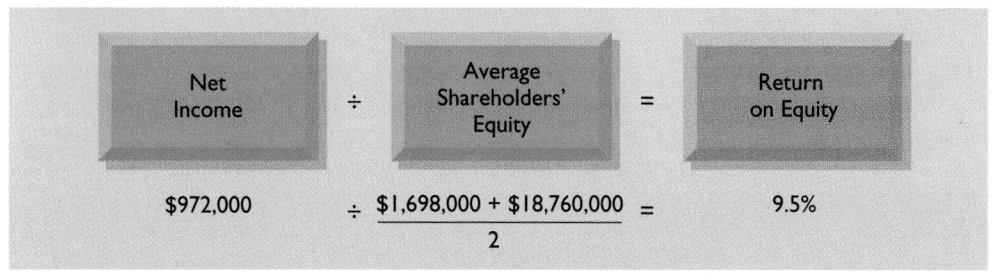

Book Value Per Share

You have learned about several per share amounts in this chapter. Another important per share amount is book value per share. It represents **the equity a common shareholder has in the net assets of the corporation** from owning one share. Remember that the net assets (assets less liabilities) of a corporation equal total shareholders' equity. The formula for calculating book value per share when a company has only one class of shares is illustrated below, using The Second Cup's data:

Illustration 14-11

Book value per share

When a company has both preferred and common shares, the calculation of book value for the common shareholders is more complex. Since preferred shareholders have a prior claim over common shareholders on net assets, their equity must be deducted from total shareholders' equity to determine the shareholders' equity that applies to the common shares. The calculation of book value per common share involves the following steps:

1. **Calculate the preferred shareholders' equity.** This equity is equal to the sum of the legal capital of the preferred shares plus any dividends in arrears.
2. **Determine the common shareholders' equity.** Subtract the preferred shareholders' equity from total shareholders' equity.
3. **Determine book value per common share.** Divide common shareholders' equity by the number of common shares.

Book value is usually calculated only for common shareholders. The book value per preferred share can be calculated by dividing the preferred shareholders' equity (determined in step 1 above) by the number of preferred shares. However, this ratio is seldom included.

Illustration.   To illustrate the calculation, we will use the shareholders' equity section of Zaboschuk Inc., as presented in Illustration 14-9. Zaboschuk's preferred shares are cumulative. Assume that dividends on Zaboschuk's preferred shares are one year in arrears, for a total of $54,000 (6,000 × $9). The calculation of the preferred shareholders' equity is as follows:

Step 1:

Legal capital	$770,000
Dividends in arrears (6,000 shares × $9)	54,000
Preferred shareholders' equity	$824,000

The calculation of book value per common share follows:

Steps 2 and 3:

Total shareholders' equity	$4,688,000
Less: Preferred shareholders' equity	824,000
Common shareholders' equity	$3,864,000
Common shares issued	400,000
Book value per common share ($3,864,000 ÷ 400,000)	$ 9.66

Book Value versus Market Value. Book value per share seldom, if ever, equals market value. Book value is based on recorded historical costs. Market value reflects the subjective judgement of shareholders and potential investors about a company's potential for future earnings and dividends. Market value per share may exceed book value per share, but that does not necessarily mean that the shares are overpriced. Conversely, market value may also be less than book value. The correlation between book value per share and the company's market value per share is often remote, as indicated by the following recent data:

Company	Book Value Per Share	Market Value Per Share
Chapters Inc.	$14.54	$ 8.10
Loblaw Cos. Ltd.	11.55	50.60
Mark's Work Wearhouse Ltd.	1.68	3.10
Nortel Networks Corporation	9.18	12.53

Helpful hint Companies that have real estate, trade names, licences, or other intellectual property worth more than cost are closely watched. The market value of the shares often reflects these hidden values.

Illustration 14-12

Book and market values compared

Book value per share is useful for determining the trend of a shareholder's per share equity in a corporation. It is also significant in many contracts and in court cases, where the rights of individual parties are based on cost information.

Before You Go On . . .

►Review It

1. Distinguish between contributed capital and retained earnings.
2. Explain how to calculate the return on equity.
3. What is the method for calculating book value per share when there is (a) only one class of shares, and (b) both preferred and common shares?

Related exercise material: BE14–8, BE14–9, BE14–10, BE14–11, E14–7, E14–8, E14–9, and E14–10.

THE NAVIGATOR

►A Look Back at Our Feature Story

Refer back to the opening story about Research In Motion and answer the following questions:

1. Why did Research In Motion change its form of organization from a partnership to a corporation?
2. What entry would Research In Motion make to record its first initial public offering of common shares, if the shares were of no par value?
3. In addition to common shares, Research In Motion also has an unlimited number of cumulative redeemable retractable preferred shares. Explain what this means.
4. The market value of Research In Motion's common shares was as high as $200 in 2000. Its book value per share in 2000 was $8. Explain how these two numbers can be so different.

Solution

1. Forming a corporation allowed Research In Motion greater access to financing through share capital, which enabled it to expand more rapidly. In addition, it provided shareholders with limited liability, which is an important feature in high-tech companies. The corporate form of organization may also have provided Research In Motion with income tax advantages, depending on the availability of research tax credits.

2. Cash   100,050,000
   Common Shares   100,050,000
      To record issue of 13.8 million common shares
      at $7.25 per share

3. An unlimited number of authorized shares means that there is no limit on the number of preferred shares Research In Motion can issue. Cumulative means that the preferred shareholders have the right to unpaid dividends before common shareholders receive any. Redeemable means RIM has the right to purchase preferred shares from its shareholders in the future, at the company's option. Retractable means that shareholders also have the right to sell the shares to RIM in the future, at the shareholders' option.

4. Book value per share is based on recorded historical cost. It is not surprising that the book value is low for Research In Motion. A significant number of its assets are likely "knowledge" assets which are not quantified and recorded on the financial statements. The market value also reflects shareholders' expectations for the future of Research In Motion. These two values are seldom, if ever, the same.

THE NAVIGATOR

DEMONSTRATION PROBLEM

Additional Demonstration Problem

The Rolman Corporation is authorized to issue an unlimited number of no par value common shares and 100,000 $50 stated value 6% cumulative preferred shares. In its first year, the company has the following share transactions:

Jan. 10 Issued 400,000 common shares at $8 per share.
July 1 Issued 100,000 common shares in exchange for land. The land had an asking price of $900,000. The shares are currently selling on the Toronto Stock Exchange at $8.25 per share.
Sept. 1 Issued 20,000 preferred shares at stated value.
Dec. 1 Issued 4,000 preferred shares at $60 per share.

Instructions

(a) Journalize the transactions.
(b) Prepare the shareholders' equity section, assuming the company had retained earnings of $900,000 at December 31, 2003.

Solution to Demonstration Problem

Action Plan

- When shares have no par value, credit Common Shares for the full amount of the proceeds.

- When shares have a stated value, credit only the amount of the stated value to the Preferred Shares account. Any excess is credited to an account for contributed capital in excess of stated value.

- Use separate accounts for each type or class of shares.

- Fair market value should be used in a noncash transaction.

(a) Jan. 10	Cash	3,200,000	
	Common Shares		3,200,000
	To record issue of 400,000 no par value shares at $8 each.		
July 1	Land	825,000	
	Common Shares		825,000
	To record issue of 100,000 no par value shares for land.		
Sept. 1	Cash	1,000,000	
	Preferred Shares		1,000,000
	To record issue of 20,000 preferred shares at $50 each.		
Dec. 1	Cash	240,000	
	Preferred Shares		200,000
	Contributed Capital in Excess of Stated Value—Preferred		40,000
	To record issue of 4,000 preferred shares at $60 each.		

(b)

ROLMAN CORPORATION
Balance Sheet (partial)
December 31, 2003

Shareholders' equity
    Contributed capital
        Share capital

Preferred shares, $50 stated value, 6% cumulative, 100,000 authorized, 24,000 issued	$1,200,000
Common shares, no par value, unlimited number of shares authorized, 500,000 issued	4,025,000
Total share capital	5,225,000
Additional contributed capital	
Contributed capital in excess of stated value—preferred shares	40,000
Total contributed capital	5,265,000
Retained earnings	900,000
Total shareholders' equity	$6,165,000

Summary of Study Objectives

1. Identify and discuss the major characteristics of a corporation. The major characteristics of a corporation are as follows: separate legal existence, limited liability of shareholders, transferable ownership rights, ability to acquire capital, continuous life, corporation management, government regulations, and entity income tax.

2. Differentiate between contributed capital and retained earnings. Contributed capital is the total amount paid to acquire share capital. Retained earnings are the cumulative net income retained (not distributed through dividends) in a corporation.

3. Record the issue of common shares. When no par value shares are issued, the entire proceeds from the issue become legal capital and are credited to the Common Shares account. When stated value common shares are issued, the stated value of the shares is credited to the Common Shares account. The portion of the proceeds that is above the stated value is recorded in a separate contributed capital account. When par value common shares are issued, the entries are similar to those for stated value shares.

4. Differentiate and journalize preferred and common share transactions. Preferred shares have contractual provisions that give them priority over common shares in certain areas. Typically, preferred shareholders have priority over (1) dividends, and (2) assets in the event of liquida-

tion. They usually do not have voting rights. In addition, preferred shares may be convertible, redeemable, and/or retractable. Convertible preferred shares allow their holder to convert them into common shares at a specified ratio. The redemption feature gives the issuing corporation the right to purchase the shares from shareholders at specified future dates and prices. Retractable preferred shares give shareholders the option of selling their shares to the corporation, at specified future dates and prices. Redeemable and retractable preferred shares are often more like debt than equity.

5. Prepare the shareholders' equity section of the balance sheet. In the shareholders' equity section, contributed capital and retained earnings are reported. Within contributed capital, two classifications may be shown if applicable: share capital and additional contributed capital.

6. Calculate return on equity and book value per share. Return on equity is calculated by dividing net income by average shareholders' equity. It is an important measure of a firm's profitability and efficiency. Book value per share represents the equity a common shareholder has in the net assets of a corporation from owning one common share.

GLOSSARY

Authorized shares The amount of share capital that a corporation is authorized to sell, as indicated in its charter. This amount may be unlimited or specified. (p. 654)

Book value per share The equity a common shareholder has in the net assets of the corporation from owning one share. (p. 688)

Contributed capital Total amount of cash and other assets contributed or paid into the corporation by shareholders in exchange for share capital. (p. 657)

Convertible preferred shares Preferred shares that the shareholder can convert into common shares at a specified ratio. (p. 664)

Corporation A business organized as a legal entity, separate and distinct from its owners, under corporation law. (p. 648)

Crown corporation A corporation owned by a government. (p. 649)

Cumulative dividend A feature of preferred shares that entitles the shareholder to receive current and unpaid prior year dividends before common shareholders receive any dividends. (p. 664)

Initial public offering (IPO) The initial offering of a corporation's shares to the public. (p. 654)

Issued shares The portion of authorized shares that has been sold. (p. 662)

No par value shares Share capital that has not been assigned a value. All the proceeds from the sale of no par value shares are treated as legal capital. (p. 656)

Organization costs Costs incurred in the formation of a corporation. (p. 652)

 Key Term Matching Activity

Outstanding shares Share capital that has been issued and is being held by shareholders. Treasury shares held by a corporation (a rare occurrence) are subtracted from issued shares to determine outstanding shares. (p. 662)

Par value shares Share capital that has been assigned a value per share. It is the legal capital of the corporation. (p. 656)

Preferred shares Share capital that has contractual preferences over common shares. (p. 663)

Privately held corporation A corporation that has only a few shareholders. Its shares are not available for sale to the general public. (p. 648)

Publicly held corporation A corporation that may have thousands of shareholders. Its shares are usually traded on an organized securities market. (p. 648)

Redeemable (callable) preferred shares Preferred shares that give the issuer the right to purchase the shares from shareholders at specified future dates and prices. (p. 665)

Retained earnings Net income after subtracting net losses and dividends distributed to shareholders since incorporation. If negative (i.e., a debit balance), it is called a deficit. (p. 657)

Retractable preferred shares Preferred shares that give the shareholder the right to sell the shares to the issuer at specified future dates and prices. (p. 665)

Return on equity Net income expressed as a percentage of average shareholders' equity. (p. 667)

Stated value The amount per share assigned by the board of directors to no par value shares. This becomes legal capital per share. (p. 656)

SELF-STUDY QUESTIONS

Chapter 14 Self-Test

Answers are at the end of the chapter.

(SO 1) K 1. Which of the following is not a major advantage of a corporation?
  a. Separate legal existence
  b. Continuous life
  c. Government regulations
  d. Transferable ownership rights

(SO 1) AP 2. Cossette Corporation has 100,000 common shares authorized and 75,000 common shares issued. How many more shares is Cossette allowed to sell?
  a. 0
  b. 25,000
  c. 75,000
  d. 100,000

(SO 2) K 3. Which of the following statements is *false*?
  a. Ownership of common shares gives the owner a voting right.
  b. The shareholders' equity section begins with contributed capital.

  c. The authorization of share capital does not result in a formal accounting entry.
  d. Legal capital per share applies to stated value shares but not to no par value shares.

4. The account Retained Earnings is: (SO 2) K
  a. a subdivision of contributed capital.
  b. net income kept in the corporation.
  c. reported as an expense in the income statement.
  d. closed to share capital.

5 . ABC Corporation issues 1,000 no par value common (SO 3) AP shares at $12 per share. In recording the transaction, a credit is made to:
  a. Gain on Sale of Shares for $12,000.
  b. Common Shares for $12,000.
  c. Contributed Capital for $12,000.
  d. Retained Earnings for $12,000.

6. A company will buy back its own shares: (SO 3) C
  a. to force the share price up.
  b. to force the share price down.

c. to increase the number of shares available for dividends.

d. to save cash.

(SO 4) K 7. Preferred shares may have priority over common shares *except* in:
a. dividends.
b. assets in the event of liquidation.
c. conversion.
d. voting.

(SO 5) K 8. Which of the following is reported under additional contributed capital?
a. Retained earnings
b. Common shares
c. Contributed capital in excess of stated value
d. All of the above

(SO 6) C 9. The ledger of NWT, Inc., shows common shares and preferred shares. For this company, the formula for calculating book value per common share is:
a. Total contributed capital divided by the number of common shares.
b. The balance in the Common Shares account divided by the number of common shares.
c. Total shareholders' equity divided by the number of common shares.
d. Total shareholders' equity less preferred shareholders' equity divided by the number of common shares.

THE NAVIGATOR

QUESTIONS

(SO 1) C 1. Pat Kabza, a student, asks for your help in understanding the following characteristics of a corporation: (a) separate legal existence, (b) limited liability of shareholders, and (c) transferable ownership rights. Explain these characteristics to Pat.

(SO 1) C 2. (a) Your friend R. Cedras cannot understand how income taxation can be both an advantage and a disadvantage for a corporation. Clarify this problem.
(b) Identify and explain two other advantages and disadvantages of a corporation.

(SO 1) C 3. (a) The following terms pertain to the forming of a corporation: (1) articles of incorporation, and (2) organization costs. Explain the terms.
(b) Cary Brant believes a corporation must be incorporated federally if it wishes to operate in more than one province. Is Cary correct? Explain.

(SO 1) K 4. What are the basic ownership rights of common shareholders?

(SO 1) C 5. What factors help determine the market value of shares?

(SO 2) K 6. What are the two principal components of shareholders' equity?

(SO 2) C 7. How do the financial statements for a corporation differ from the statements for a proprietorship?

(SO 3) AP 8. The corporate charter of Letterman Corporation authorizes a maximum of 100,000 common shares. During its first two years of operations, Letterman sold 60,000 shares to shareholders and reacquired 7,000 of these shares. After these transactions, how many shares are authorized and issued?

(SO 3) C 9. Which is the better investment—common shares with a stated value of $5 per share or common shares with no stated value?

(SO 3) C 10. What effect does the issue of shares at no par value have on the issuer's net income? If the issue is at a price above stated value? Explain.

(SO 3) C 11. Explain why the majority of companies in Canada issue no par value shares rather than par or stated value shares.

(SO 3) AP 12. Jean-Guy LeBlanc purchases 100 common shares of Innovate.com for $10 per share from the company's initial public offering. Subsequently, Jean-Guy purchases 200 more Innovate.com common shares for $15 on the Toronto Stock Exchange, using his own Web Broker account. Explain the impact each of these transactions will have on Innovate.com's assets, liabilities, and shareholders' equity.

(SO 3) AP 13. **Chapters Inc.'s** share price fell 62% in the first six months of 2001, from $17.15 to $6.50. Explain the effects of this decline in share price on Chapters' financial statements.

(SO 3) AP 14. Land appraised at $80,000 is purchased by issuing 1,000 no par value common shares. The market price of the shares at the time of the exchange, based on active trading in the securities market, is $90 per share. Should the land be recorded at $80,000 or $90,000? Explain.

(SO 3) C 15. For what reasons might a company repurchase some of its shares?

(SO 3) C 16. Wilmor, Inc., purchases 1,000 of its own previously issued common shares. What effect does this transaction have on (a) total assets, (b) total liabilities, and (c) total shareholders' equity?

(SO 4) C 17. (a) What are the principal differences between common shares and preferred shares?
(b) Preferred shares may be cumulative. Discuss this feature.
(c) How are dividends in arrears presented in the financial statements?

(SO 4) C 18. A preferred shareholder converts her convertible preferred shares into common shares. What effect does this have on the corporation's (a) total assets, (b) total liabilities, and (c) total shareholders' equity?

(SO 5) C   19. Indicate how each of the following accounts should be classified in the shareholders' equity section:
   (a) Common Shares
   (b) Retained Earnings
   (c) Contributed Capital in Excess of Stated Value
   (d) Preferred Shares

20. What is the formula for calculating book value per share when a corporation has only common shares?   (SO 6) K

21. WAT Inc.'s common shares have a book value of $29 and a current market value of $15. Explain why these amounts are different.   (SO 6) C

BRIEF EXERCISES

···

Identify the advantages and disadvantages of a corporation.
(SO 1) C

BE14–1   Zofia Laubitz is studying for her accounting test. Identify for Zofia the advantages and disadvantages of the corporate form of business organization.

Prepare closing entries.
(SO 2) AP

BE14–2   At December 31, Enviro Corporation reports revenues of $2,000,000 and expenses of $1,500,000. Prepare the entries required to close revenues and expenses in summary form.

Identify reasons for repurchase of shares.
(SO 1, 3) C

BE14–3   Ontario-based Open Text Corporation offered to purchase for cancellation up to 1,000,000 (5%) of its issued common shares. The offer allows shareholders to retain the same pre-emptive right or ownership interest in the company that they held before the offer. What are some of the reasons why Open Text may wish to repurchase shares? Explain what the pre-emptive right included in this offer means.

Prepare entries for issue of common shares.
(SO 3) AP

BE14–4   On June 1, Eagle Inc. issues 2,000 no par value common shares at a cash price of $6 per share. Journalize the issue of the shares, assuming (a) the shares have no stated value, and (b) the shares have a stated value of $1 per share.

Prepare entries for issue of shares in noncash transaction.
(SO 3) AP

BE14–5   Spiro Inc.'s no par value common shares are actively traded at a market value of $14 per share. On December 20, Spiro issues 5,000 shares to purchase land advertised for sale at $80,000. Journalize the issue of the shares for acquiring the land.

Analyse noncash share issue.
(SO 3) AP

BE14–6   Intrawest Corporation issued 325,000 no par value common shares to acquire the Raven golf resorts and Alpine Helicopters in 1999. The fair market value of these common shares at the time of acquisition was $9.1 million. If the fair market value of Raven and Alpine was $10 million at the time of acquisition, at what value did Intrawest record these assets and the issue of common shares?

Prepare entries for issue of preferred shares.
(SO 4) AP

BE14–7   First Nations Inc. issues 5,000 no par value preferred shares for cash at $110 per share on January 28. Journalize the issue of the preferred shares.

Prepare shareholders' equity section.
(SO 5) AP

BE14–8   Kaposi Corporation has the following accounts at December 31, 2003: Common Shares, no par value, unlimited number of shares authorized, 5,000 shares issued, $50,000; Contributed Capital in Excess of Stated Value—Preferred Shares, $10,000; Preferred Shares, 8% cumulative, $25 stated value, unlimited number of shares authorized, 800 shares issued, $20,000; and Retained Earnings, $29,000. Prepare the shareholders' equity section of the balance sheet.

Calculate book value per share.
(SO 6) AP

BE14–9   The balance sheet for Paulatak Inc. shows the following: share capital, $600,000; retained earnings, $260,000; common shares issued, 40,000 shares. There are no preferred shares. Calculate the book value per share.

Evaluate factors affecting a company's share price.
(SO 6) C

BE14–10   The share prices of dozens of high-tech companies soared in early to mid-2000. Take, for example, NHC Communications Inc., located in Quebec. NHC provides cross-connection solutions for voice/data networks. Its share price went from a low of $0.08 to a high of $22, an increase of 27,500%! Yet NHC reported a loss of $2,180,000 and a 33% negative return on equity in this same period. Why do you think shareholders were anxious to pay increasing amounts for NHC's shares?

Evaluate impact of share price on financial position.
(SO 6) C

BE14–11   The share prices of technology companies started dropping like stones near the middle of the year 2000. Nortel Networks' share price, for example, dropped from a 52-week high of $124.50 in July 2000 to $18.99 in July 2001. What is the impact of this drop in share price on Nortel's financial position?

EXERCISES

....

E14–1 Presented below is a stock market listing for Research In Motion's common shares. You will recall that Research In Motion (RIM) is the company discussed in our feature story.

Read and interpret stock market listing.
(SO 1) AN

52w high	52w low	Stock	Ticker	Div	Yield %	P/E	Vol 00s	High	Low	Close	Net chg
260.00	35.00	RschMotn	RIM	0	0	1371	5750	164.50	152.15	164.50	+17.25

Instructions

(a) What is the highest price RIM's shares traded for during the last year? The lowest?

(b) How many of RIM's common shares were sold on the trading day in question?

(c) If you had purchased 1,000 common shares at RIM's high price of the day of the above listing, what would be the total cost of your share purchase?

(d) What would be your likely motivation for purchasing these shares—future dividend income or price increase?

(e) What was the closing price of RIM's common shares on the previous day?

E14–2 During its first year of operations, the Algonquin Corporation had the following transactions for its common shares:

Journalize issue of common shares.
(SO 3) AP

Jan. 10 Issued 70,000 shares for cash at $5 per share.
July 1 Issued 40,000 shares for cash at $7 per share.

Instructions

(a) Journalize the transactions assuming that the common shares are no par value.

(b) Journalize the transactions assuming that the common shares are no par value with a stated value of $2 per share.

E14–3 As an auditor for the CGA firm of Bell and Whistle, you encounter the following situations when auditing different clients:

Journalize noncash common share transactions.
(SO 3) AP

1. The Ruth Corporation is a closely held corporation whose shares are not publicly traded. On December 5, the corporation acquired land by issuing 5,000 no par value common shares. The owner's asking price for the land was $120,000. The fair market value of the land was $115,000.

2. The Hache Corporation is a publicly held corporation whose common shares are traded on the Toronto Stock Exchange. On June 1, it acquired land by issuing 20,000 no par value shares. At the time of the exchange, the land was advertised for sale at $250,000. The shares were selling at $11 per share.

Instructions

Prepare the journal entries for each of the situations above.

E14–4 After an unsuccessful takeover attempt by Onex in 1999, **Air Canada** spent $1.1 million to buy back common shares.

Identify reasons for share repurchase.
(SO 3) AP

Instructions

(a) Explain how a buyback of shares affects the number of shares authorized and issued, and the amounts recorded in the Common Shares account.

(b) Why do you think Air Canada repurchased $1.1 million of its shares late in 1999?

E14–5 Moosonee Co. Ltd. had the following transactions during the current period:

Journalize issue of common and preferred shares.
(SO 3, 4) AP

Mar. 2 Issued 1,600 no par value common shares to lawyers as payment for a bill of $25,000 for services rendered in helping the company to incorporate. The shares have a market value of $15 per share.

June 12 Issued 60,000 no par value common shares for used equipment that had originally cost $800,000. It currently has a book value of $300,000 and a market value of $400,000. The shares have a market value of $6 per share.

July 11 Issued 1,000 no par value preferred shares for cash at $105 per share.

Instructions

Journalize the transactions.

Journalize conversion of preferred shares.
(SO 3, 4) AP

E14–6   Kerr Corporation has 10,000 no par value preferred shares, which had been issued at $100 per share. Each share is convertible into five no par value common shares. When the market values of the two classes of shares are $110 and $25, respectively, on November 15, 2,000 preferred shares are converted into common shares.

Instructions
(a) Journalize the conversion of the 2,000 shares.
(b) Repeat (a) assuming that the market values at conversion are $95 and $25, respectively.
(c) Repeat (a) assuming that each share is convertible into eight no par value common shares.

Answer questions about shareholders' equity section.
(SO 3, 4, 5) S

E14–7   The shareholders' equity section of Shumway Corporation at December 31 is as follows:

SHUMWAY CORPORATION
Balance Sheet (partial)
December 31, 2003

Shareholders' equity	
Contributed capital	
Share capital	
Preferred shares, cumulative, no par value,	
10,000 shares authorized, 6,000 shares issued	$ 600,000
Common shares, ? stated value, 750,000	
shares authorized, 600,000 shares issued	1,800,000
	2,400,000
Additional contributed capital	
Contributed capital in excess of stated value—	
common shares	600,000
Total contributed capital	3,000,000
Retained earnings	1,158,000
Total shareholders' equity	$4,158,000

Instructions
From a review of the shareholders' equity section, write a memo to the president of the company answering the following questions:
(a) What is the stated value of the common shares?
(b) What was the average issue price per share of the common shares?
(c) If the annual dividend on preferred shares is $36,000, what is the dividend per share?
(d) If dividends of $72,000 were in arrears on the preferred shares, where would these be reported in Shumway's financial statements?

Classify financial statement accounts.
(SO 5) AP

E14–8   The ledger of Val d'Or Corporation contains the following selected accounts:
1. Cash
2. Common Shares
3. Contributed Capital in Excess of Stated Value—Preferred Shares
4. Gain on Sale of Capital Assets
5. Patents
6. Preferred Shares
7. Retained Earnings
8. Legal Fees Expense

Instructions
Using the following table headings, indicate whether or not each of the above accounts should be reported in the shareholders' equity section of the balance sheet. If so, indicate whether the account should be reported as share capital, additional contributed capital, or retained earnings. If not, indicate in which financial statement (balance sheet or income statement) and in which section the account should be reported. The first account has been done for you as an example.

		Shareholders' Equity			Other	
		Contributed Capital				
Account		Share Capital	Additional Contributed Capital	Retained Earnings	Financial Statement	Classification
1.	Cash				Balance Sheet	Current asset

E14–9 **Future Shop Ltd.** reported the following selected accounts and information, as at April 1, 2000:

FUTURE SHOP LTD.
Selected Financial Data
April 1, 2000
(in thousands)

Common shares, unlimited number of shares authorized, with no par value, 16,189,545 shares issued	$78,783
Preferred shares, unlimited number of shares authorized, with no par value, none issued	
Net income	23,680
Retained earnings, April 1, 2000	1,450
Total shareholders' equity, April 1, 2000	80,233
Total shareholders' equity, April 3, 1999	56,329

Instructions

(a) Prepare the shareholders' equity section of the balance sheet for Future Shop as at April 1, 2000.
(b) Calculate Future Shop's return on equity and book value per common share at April 1, 2000.

E14–10 At December 31, Kilgora Corporation has total shareholders' equity of $4,000,000. Included in this total are Preferred Shares, $500,000, and Contributed Capital in Excess of Stated Value—Preferred Shares, $50,000. There are 10,000 $50 stated value 10% cumulative preferred shares. At year end, there are 250,000 common shares.

Instructions

Calculate the book value per common share, under each of the following assumptions:
(a) There are no preferred dividends in arrears.
(b) Preferred dividends are one year in arrears (that is, the dividends for the current year have not been paid).

PROBLEMS: SET A

P14–1A Presented below are five independent situations:

(a) Three physics professors have formed a business to improve the speed of information transfer over the Internet for stock market transactions. Each has contributed an equal amount of cash and knowledge to the venture. While their approach looks promising, they are concerned about the legal liabilities that their business might confront.
(b) Joseph LeBlanc, a student looking for summer employment, opened a bait shop in a small shed on a local fishing dock.
(c) Robert Steven and Tom Cheng each owned separate shoe manufacturing businesses. They have decided to combine their businesses. They expect that within the coming year, they will need significant funds to expand their operations.
(d) Darcy Becker, Ellen Sweet, and Meg Dwyer recently graduated with marketing degrees. They have been friends since childhood. They have decided to start a consulting business focused on marketing sporting goods over the Internet.
(e) Hervé Gaudet wants to rent portable CD players and CDs in airports across the country. His idea is that customers will be able to rent equipment and CDs at one airport, listen to the CDs on their flight, and return the equipment and CDs at their destination airport. This will require a substantial investment in equipment and CDs, as well as in employees and locations in each airport. Hervé has no savings or personal assets. He wants to maintain control over the business.

Instructions

In each case, explain what form of organization the business is likely to take—proprietorship, partnership, or corporation. Give reasons for your choice.

*Answer questions about
shareholders' equity section.*
(SO 2, 3, 4, 5) AP

P14–2A   The shareholders' equity section of Maple Corporation, after closing on December 31, 2003, presented the following information:

MAPLE CORPORATION
Balance Sheet (partial)
December 31, 2003

Shareholders' equity		
Contributed capital		
Share capital		
8% cumulative preferred shares, $60 stated value,		
25,000 shares authorized, ? shares issued		$1,200,000
Common shares, no par value, 500,000 shares		
authorized,100,000 shares issued		1,000,000
Total share capital		2,200,000
Additional contributed capital		
Contributed capital in excess of stated value—		
preferred shares		200,000
Total contributed capital		2,400,000
Retained earnings		
January 1, 2003	$500,000	
Net income	175,000	675,000
Total shareholders' equity		$3,075,000

Instructions

(a) How many preferred shares were issued at December 31, 2003?
(b) What was the average selling price of the preferred shares, expressed on a per share basis?
(c) What is the annual total preferred share dividend requirement, stated in dollars?
(d) What was the total amount of dividends, if any, declared by Maple Corporation in 2003?
(e) Assuming that there were no dividends in arrears at the beginning of 2003, are there any dividends in arrears at the end of 2003? If so, for what amount?

*Journalize and post share trans-
actions. Prepare contributed capital section.*
(SO 3, 4, 5) AP

P14–3A   The Wetland Corporation was organized on January 1, 2003. It is authorized to issue 10,000 shares of 8% no par value preferred shares and 500,000 shares of no par value common shares with a stated value of $2 per share. The following transactions were completed during the first year:

   Jan. 10 Issued 80,000 common shares for cash at $3 per share.
   Mar. 1 Issued 5,000 preferred shares for cash at $105 per share.
   Apr. 1 Issued 24,000 common shares for land. The asking price of the land was $90,000. The fair market value of the land was $80,000. The market value of the common shares was $3.50 per share on this date.
   June 20 Issued 80,000 common shares for cash at $4 per share.
   Aug. 1 Issued 10,000 common shares to lawyers in payment of their bill of $50,000 for services rendered in helping the company organize. The market value of the common shares was $5 on this date.
   Sept. 1 Issued 10,000 common shares for cash at $5 per share.
   Nov. 1 Issued 1,000 preferred shares for cash at $108 per share.

Instructions

(a) Journalize the transactions.
(b) Open general ledger accounts and post to the shareholders' equity accounts.
(c) Prepare the contributed capital section of the shareholders' equity at December 31, 2003.

*Journalize and post shareholders'
equity transactions. Prepare
shareholders' equity section.*
(SO 3, 4, 5) AP

P14–4A   Remmers Corporation is authorized to issue 10,000 shares of $100 stated value 10% convertible preferred shares and 200,000 no par value common shares. On January 1, 2003, the ledger contained the following shareholders' equity balances:

Preferred Shares (4,000 shares)	$ 400,000
Contributed Capital in Excess of Stated Value—Preferred	60,000
Common Shares (70,000 shares)	1,050,000
Retained Earnings	300,000

During 2003, the following transactions occurred:

Feb. 1 Issued 1,050 preferred shares for land having a fair market value of $125,000. The market value of the shares on this date was $115 per share.

Mar. 1 Issued 1,000 preferred shares for cash at $120 per share.

July 1 Holders of 1,000 preferred shares purchased at $115 per share converted the shares into common shares. Each preferred share was convertible into 10 common shares. The market value of the preferred shares was $125 per share.

Sept. 1 Issued 400 preferred shares for a patent. The asking price of the patent was $60,000. The market value of the preferred shares was $125 per share.

Dec. 1 Holders of 1,000 preferred shares purchased at $120 per share converted the shares into common shares. Each preferred share was convertible into 10 common shares. Market values were preferred shares, $125, and common shares, $16.

Dec. 31 Total revenues and expenses for the year were $400,000 and $250,000, respectively. No dividends were declared.

Instructions

(a) Prior to 2003, what was the average price at which the preferred shares were issued?

(b) Journalize the transactions that occurred during 2003 and the closing entries.

(c) Enter the beginning balances in the accounts and post the journal entries to the shareholders' equity accounts.

(d) Prepare the shareholders equity section of the balance sheet at December 31, 2003.

P14–5A The shareholders' equity accounts of Chung Corporation at January 1, 2003, were as follows:

Journalize and post share transactions, and prepare shareholders' equity section. Calculate return on equity and book value.
(SO 3, 4, 5, 6) AP

Preferred Shares (no par value, $10 noncumulative, 5,000 shares authorized, 3,000 shares issued)	$ 320,000
Common Shares (no par value, unlimited number of shares authorized, 200,000 shares issued)	1,425,000
Retained Earnings	488,000

During 2003, the corporation had the following transactions and events related to its shareholders' equity:

Feb. 1 Issued 4,000 common shares for $25,000.

July 20 Issued 1,000 preferred shares for $107,000.

Sept. 3 Issued 2,000 common shares for a patent valued at $13,000.

Dec. 31 Determined that net income for the year was $240,000.

Instructions

(a) Journalize the transactions.

(b) Prepare summary closing entries, assuming revenues totalled $500,000 and expenses totalled $260,000.

(c) Enter the beginning balances in the accounts and post the journal entries to the shareholders' equity accounts.

(d) Prepare a shareholders' equity section of the balance sheet at December 31, 2003.

(e) Calculate the return on equity at December 31, 2003.

(f) Calculate the book value per common share at December 31, 2003.

P14–6A The following shareholders' equity accounts, arranged alphabetically, are in the ledger of Huy Corporation at December 31, 2003:

Prepare shareholders' equity section and calculate book value.
(SO 5, 6) AP

Common Shares (no par value, unlimited number of shares authorized, 150,000 shares issued)	$2,400,000
Contributed Capital in Excess of Stated Value—Preferred Shares	300,000
Preferred Shares ($6, cumulative, $100 stated value, 100,000 shares authorized, 4,000 shares issued)	400,000
Retained Earnings	1,276,000

Instructions

(a) Prepare a shareholders' equity section at December 31, 2003.

(b) Calculate the book value per common share, assuming the current year's dividend has been paid.

(c) Repeat part (b) assuming the current year's dividend has not been paid and that Retained Earnings are $1,300,000 instead of $1,276,000.

Show impact of transactions on ratios.
(SO 6) AP

P14–7A Branch Inc.'s book value per common share and return on equity were $10 and 10%, respectively, before each of the following independent transactions occurred:

Transaction	Book Value per Share ($10)	Return on Equity (10%)
(a) Branch issued 1,000 no par value common shares for $25 per share.		
(b) The company issued 100 no par value preferred shares for $50 per share.		
(c) The company reported net income of $100,000 for the current year.		

Instructions

Indicate whether the above transactions will increase (I), decrease (D), or have no effect (NE) on each of the ratios presented.

Calculate book values; compare to amounts paid in.
(SO 3, 6) AN

P14–8A The following shareholders' equity accounts, arranged alphabetically, are in the ledger of Hussain Corporation at December 31, 2003:

Common Shares—no par value (500,000 shares issued)	$4,000,000
Preferred Shares—no par value, $4 cumulative (20,000 shares issued)	1,600,000
Retained Earnings	250,000

Instructions

(a) Calculate the book value per common share, assuming the preferred dividends are two years (i.e., the current year and one previous year) in arrears.
(b) Repeat part (a) using five years of dividends in arrears.
(c) How does the book value compare to the average price paid per common share when the shares were issued?

Prepare balance sheet; calculate return on equity and book value.
(SO 5, 6) AP

P14–9A Reitmans has the following selected accounts, listed in alphabetical order, as at February 3, 2001:

REITMANS (CANADA) LIMITED
Selected Accounts
February 3, 2001
(in thousands)

Accounts payable and accrued items	$ 35,187
Accounts receivable	2,556
Accrued pension asset (long-term)	6,903
Accumulated amortization—capital assets	41,136
Capital assets	127,172
Cash and short-term deposits	20,008
Class A nonvoting shares (unlimited authorized; 6,709,582 issued)	8,065
Common shares (unlimited authorized; 1,680,000 issued)	482
Dividends and other deductions from retained earnings	11,498
Future income taxes payable (long-term)	1,381
Income taxes payable	5,124
Investments	81,399
Merchandise inventories	38,481
Net income for the year	20,202
Prepaid expenses	8,816
Retained earnings, January 29, 2000	185,256

Instructions

(a) Prepare Reitmans' classified balance sheet at February 3, 2001.
(b) Calculate Reitmans' return on equity for the year ended February 3, 2001. Reitmans' shareholders' equity at January 29, 2000, was $194,121.
(c) Calculate Reitmans' book value per common share at February 3, 2001. Treat the Class A shares as you would treat preferred shares in the book value calculation.

PROBLEMS: SET B

P14–1B Presented below are five independent situations:

Determine forms of business organization.
(SO 1) AN

(a) Dawn Addington, a student looking for summer employment, opened a vegetable stand along a busy local highway. Each morning, she buys produce from local farmers, then sells it in the afternoon as people return home from work.

(b) Joseph LeBlanc and Sabra Surkis each own separate bike shops. They have decided to combine their businesses and try to expand their operations to include skis and snowboards. They expect that, within the coming year, they will need significant funds to expand their operations.

(c) Three chemistry professors have formed a business to employ bacteria to clean up toxic waste sites. Each has contributed an equal amount of cash and knowledge to the venture. The use of bacteria in this situation is experimental, and legal obligations could result.

(d) Abdur Rahim has run a successful, but small, cooperative health and organic food store for over twenty years. The increased sales of his own store have made him believe that the time is right to open a chain of health and organic food stores across the country. Of course, this will require a substantial investment in inventories and capital assets, as well as employees and other resources. Abdur has no savings or personal assets.

(e) Mary Emery and Richard Goedde recently graduated with advanced degrees in economics. They have decided to start a consulting business focused on teaching the basics of international economics to small business owners interested in international trade.

Instructions

In each case, explain what form of organization the business is likely to take—proprietorship, partnership, or corporation. Give reasons for your choice.

P14–2B The shareholders' equity section of Moreau Corporation, after closing on December 31, 2003, presented the following information:

Answer questions about shareholders' equity section.
(SO 1, 2, 3, 4, 5) AP

MOREAU CORPORATION
Balance Sheet (partial)
December 31, 2003

Shareholders' equity		
Share capital		
$4 cumulative preferred shares, no par value, unlimited		
number of shares authorized, ? shares issued		$3,125,000
Common shares, no par value, unlimited number		
of shares authorized, 250,000 shares issued		1,000,000
Total share capital		4,125,000
Retained earnings		
January 1, 2003	$500,000	
Net income	175,000	
Dividends—preferred	(75,000)	600,000
Total shareholders' equity		$4,725,000

There are no dividends in arrears at the end of 2002 or 2003.

Instructions

(a) How many preferred shares were issued at December 31, 2003?

(b) What was the average selling price of the preferred shares, expressed on a per share basis? The common shares?

(c) In terms of the limited liability characteristic of a corporation, what is the dollar amount of the investment subject to liability (legal capital) for the preferred shareholders? The common shareholders?

Journalize and post share trans-
actions. Prepare contributed
capital section.
(SO 3, 4, 5) AP

P14–3B   The Highland Corporation was organized on January 1, 2003. It is authorized to issue 20,000 shares of no par value preferred shares with a $3 dividend rate, and 500,000 no par value common shares. The following transactions were completed during the first year:

Jan. 10 Issued 100,000 common shares for cash at $3 per share.
Mar. 1   Issued 10,000 preferred shares for cash at $52 per share.
Apr. 1   Issued 25,000 common shares for land. The fair market value of the land was $85,000. The market value of the common shares was $3.50 per share on this date.
May 1   Issued 75,000 common shares for cash at $4 per share.
July 24 Issued 10,000 common shares to lawyers in payment of their bill of $50,000 for services rendered in helping the company organize. The market value of the common shares was $4.50 on this date.
Sept. 1 Issued 5,000 common shares at $6 per share for cash and used equipment. The equipment originally cost $10,000. It now has a net book value of $4,000 and a fair market value of $5,000.
Nov. 1   Issued 2,000 preferred shares for cash at $54 per share.

Instructions

(a) Journalize the transactions.
(b) Open general ledger accounts and post to the shareholders' equity accounts.
(c) Prepare the contributed capital section of shareholders' equity at December 31, 2003.

Journalize and post shareholders'
equity transactions. Prepare
shareholders' equity section. Cal-
culate return on equity.
(SO 3, 4, 5, 6) AP

P14–4B   Denison Corporation is authorized to issue 10,000 no par value $10 convertible preferred shares and 125,000 no par value common shares. On January 1, 2003, the ledger contained the following shareholders' equity balances:

Preferred Shares (5,000 shares)	$ 575,000
Common Shares (70,000 shares)	1,050,000
Retained Earnings	300,000

During 2003, the following transactions occurred:

Feb. 6   Issued 1,000 preferred shares for a building having a fair market value of $125,000. The market value of the shares on this date was $120 per share.
July 15 Holders of 2,000 preferred shares purchased at $110 per share converted the shares into common shares. Each preferred share was convertible into eight common shares. Market values were preferred shares, $122, and common shares, $17.
Sept. 22 Issued 400 preferred shares for land. The asking price of the land was $60,000. The market value of the preferred shares was $130 per share.
Dec. 1   Holders of 1,000 preferred shares purchased at $130 per share converted the shares into common shares. Each preferred share was convertible into eight common shares. Market values were preferred shares, $134, and common shares, $16.
Dec. 31 Total revenues and expenses for the year were $600,000 and $340,000, respectively. No dividends were declared.

Instructions

(a) Journalize the transactions and the closing entries.
(b) Enter the beginning balances in the accounts and post the journal entries to the shareholders' equity accounts.
(c) Prepare a shareholders' equity section of the balance sheet at December 31, 2003.
(d) Calculate the company's return on equity for 2003.

Journalize and post share trans-
actions, and prepare sharehold-
ers' equity section. Calculate the
book value and return on equity.
(SO 3, 4, 5, 6) AP

P14–5B   The shareholders' equity accounts of the Daoust Corporation on January 1, 2003, were as follows:

Preferred Shares (no par value, $6 cumulative, 10,000 shares authorized, 8,000 issued)	$ 500,000
Common shares (no par value, unlimited number of shares authorized, 1,000,000 issued)	2,450,000
Retained Earnings	1,816,000

During 2003, the corporation had the following transactions and events related to its shareholders' equity:

Feb. 1   Issued 28,000 common shares for $100,000.
Sept. 3 Issued 5,000 common shares for equipment valued at $25,000.
Dec. 31 Determined that net income for the year was $402,000.

No dividends were declared during the year and the preferred dividends are one year in arrears.

Instructions

(a) Journalize the transactions.

(b) Prepare summary closing entries, assuming revenue totalled $750,000 and expenses totalled $348,000.

(c) Enter the beginning balances in T accounts and post the journal entries to the shareholders' equity accounts.

(d) Prepare a shareholders' equity section at December 31, 2003, including the disclosure of the preferred dividends in arrears.

(e) Calculate the book value per common share at December 31, 2003. (Round to two decimals.)

(f) Calculate the return on equity for 2003.

P14–6B The following shareholders' equity accounts, arranged alphabetically, are in the ledger of Desserud Corporation at August 31, 2003:

Prepare shareholders' equity section and calculate book value.
(SO 5, 6) AP

Common Shares (no par value, unlimited number of shares authorized, 500,000 shares issued)	$4,000,000
Preferred Shares ($8 noncumulative, no par value, unlimited number of shares authorized, 4,000 shares issued)	800,000
Retained Earnings	1,958,000

Instructions

(a) Prepare the shareholders' equity section of the balance sheet at August 31, 2003.

(b) Calculate the book value per common share.

P14–7B Talty Inc.'s book value per share and return on equity were $10 and 10%, respectively, before each of the following independent transactions.

Show impact of transactions on ratios.
(SO 6) AP

Transaction	Book Value per Share ($10)	Return on Equity (10%)
(a) Talty Inc. issued 10,000 no par value common shares for $25 per share.		
(b) The company reported net income of $200,000 for the current year.		
(c) The company reacquired and cancelled 4,000 no par value common shares for $100,000 cash.		

Instructions

Indicate whether the above transactions will increase (I), decrease (D), or have no effect (NE) on each of the ratios presented.

P14–8B Sears Canada Inc. reported the following selected information:

Calculate return on equity and book value.
(SO 6) AN

SEARS CANADA INC.
December 31
(in millions)

	2000	1999	1998
Net income	$225.8	$199.6	$146.4
Shareholders' equity	$1,549.3	$1,346.3	$1,164.3
Number of common shares	106.5	106.2	106.1

Instructions

(a) Calculate Sears' return on equity for 2000 and 1999. Comment on whether its return on equity has improved or deteriorated.

(b) The return on equity for Sears's industry is 11.3%. Compare Sears' performance to the industry average.

(c) Calculate Sears' book value per share for 2000 and 1999. Sears' share price is around $36. What relationship does Sears' market value have to its book value?

Prepare balance sheet; calculate return on equity and book value.
(SO 5, 6) AP

P14–9B **Leon's Furniture Limited** has the following selected accounts, listed in alphabetical order, as at December 31, 2000:

LEON'S FURNITURE LIMITED
Selected Accounts
December 31, 2000
(in thousands)

Accounts payable and accrued liabilities	$ 68,742
Accounts receivable	14,605
Accumulated amortization—fixed assets	70,754
Cash and cash equivalents	24,802
Common shares (unlimited authorized; 20,228,542 issued)	9,518
Customers' deposits	6,507
Dividends and other deductions from retained earnings	14,782
Dividends payable	2,098
Fixed assets	179,335
Future tax assets (long-term)	4,930
Income taxes payable	885
Inventory	49,171
Marketable securities	78,567
Net income for the year	36,700
Redeemable share liability (long-term)	79
Retained earnings, January 1, 1999	170,909

Instructions

(a) Prepare Leon's classified balance sheet at December 31, 2000.
(b) Calculate Leon's return on equity for the year ended December 31, 2000. Leon's shareholders' equity at December 31, 1999, was $178,313.
(c) Calculate Leon's book value per common share at December 31, 2000.

*B*roadening Your Perspective

FINANCIAL REPORTING AND ANALYSIS
• •

Financial Reporting Problem

BYP14–1 The shareholders' equity section for **The Second Cup Ltd.** is shown in the Consolidated Balance Sheets in Appendix A. You will also find data related to this problem in the notes to the financial statements.

Instructions

Answer the following questions:
(a) Does The Second Cup have preferred shares? If so, how many preferred shares is the company authorized to issue? How many shares were issued at June 24, 2000?
(b) What was the average issue price of the common shares as at June 24, 2000, and June 30, 1999?
(c) Did The Second Cup repurchase any shares in fiscal 2000? Fiscal 1999? If so, identify how many shares and at what amount.
(d) Calculate The Second Cup's return on equity for fiscal 1999, using its pro forma 1999 results. Shareholders' equity at June 27, 1998, was $10,950,000. How does this compare to the 2000 return on equity calculated for The Second Cup in Illustration 14-10 in the chapter?
(e) Calculate the book value per share for fiscal 1999 (use The Second Cup's pro forma 1999 results). How has the book value changed from fiscal 1999 to 2000 (see the 2000 book value calculated for The Second Cup in Illustration 14-11 in the chapter).

Interpreting Financial Statements

BYP14–2 In January 1995, Vancouver-based Net Nanny Software International Inc. introduced the first filtering software product of its kind. Today, Net Nanny develops and sells the world's most recognized Internet filtering and personal computer security products.

Additional Cases

Net Nanny has 100,000,000 no par value common shares authorized. The following information about issued share capital (expressed in U.S. dollars) is provided for Net Nanny for the years ended June 30, 2000, 1999, and 1998.

	2000		1999		1998	
	Shares	Amount	Shares	Amount	Shares	Amount
Balance, beginning of year	12,507,998	$ 6,254,451	11,686,883	$5,975,679	7,819,794	$3,784,760
Issued during year	9,220,750	6,375,355	821,115	278,772	3,867,089	2,190,919
Balance, end of year	21,728,748	$12,629,806	12,507,998	$6,254,451	11,686,883	$5,975,679

The following additional information is also available:

	2000	1999
Net loss	($2,977,729)	($1,089,966)
Average shareholders' equity	2,220,967	979,635
Market price per share	1.52	0.93

Instructions

(a) Calculate the return on equity ratios for 2000 and 1999.

(b) Net Nanny reported a loss in both 2000 and 1999. Yet, its market price per share is positive and increasing. Can you explain why investors might be willing to pay an increasing price for a Net Nanny share despite its apparent poor operating performance?

(c) Speculate as to why Net Nanny is likely financing its operations by issuing additional common shares rather than long-term debt.

Accounting on the Web

BYP14–3 Originally incorporated in 1878, the Toronto Stock Exchange (TSE) is the second-largest stock exchange in North America. It is Canada's largest capital market, accounting for 95% of all equity trading in Canada. This case explores the TSE website to learn more about the exchange, stock market terminology, indices, and processes. We also learn how to use this website to obtain a current share quote for a listed company.

Instructions

Specific requirements of this Internet case are available on the Weygandt website.

CRITICAL THINKING

Collaborative Learning Activities

BYP14–4   The annual meeting for Resolute Corporation has been in progress for some time. The chief financial officer for Resolute is presently reviewing the company's financial statements. She is explaining the items that make up the shareholders' equity section of the balance sheet for the current year. The shareholders' equity section of Resolute Corporation at December 31, 2003, is as follows:

RESOLUTE CORPORATION
Balance Sheet (partial)
December 31, 2003

Shareholders' equity	
Contributed capital	
Share capital	
$8 preferred shares, authorized 1,000,000 shares,	
cumulative, no par value, 6,000 shares issued	$ 600,000
Common shares, authorized 5,000,000 shares,	
$1 stated value, 3,000,000 shares issued	3,000,000
Total share capital	3,600,000
Additional contributed capital	
Contibuted capital in excess of stated value—common shares	25,050,000
Total contributed capital	28,650,000
Retained earnings	900,000
Total shareholders' equity	$29,550,000

The shareholders have raised a number of questions regarding the shareholders' equity section of Resolute Corporation's balance sheet at the meeting.

Instructions

With the class divided into groups, answer the following questions from shareholders as if you were the chief financial officer for Resolute Corporation:

  (a) "What does the cumulative provision related to the preferred shares mean?"
  (b) "I thought the common shares were presently selling at $30, but the company has the shares stated at $1 per share. How can that be?"
  (c) "Why is it necessary to show additional contributed capital? Why not just show common shares at the total amount paid or contributed?"
  (d) "The company repurchased shares during the year. I don't see this reported in the equity section. Where is it reported?"

BYP14–5   You are employed as an auditor for the firm of Honest and Accurate. On the last two engagements, you encountered the following situations:

  1. Beaty Corporation is a closely held corporation whose shares are not publicly traded. The most recent issue of the company's shares was last year, at $20 per share. On May 15, the corporation acquired property (land and building) by issuing 20,000 no par value common shares. The day before the exchange, the property was advertised for sale at $500,000. This listing was based on a qualified independent appraisal, with 25% of the amount attributed to the land and 75% to the building.
  2. Wood Corporation is a publicly held corporation whose common shares are traded on the Toronto Stock Exchange. On September 10, it acquired land by issuing 8,000 no par value common shares. At the date of the exchange, the land was listed with a real estate firm at an advertised selling price of $175,000. It was assessed (for property tax purposes) at a value of $150,000. The shares were selling at $20 a share. The company intended to improve the land, at a cost of $25,000, and then sell it for $210,000.

Instructions

Do the following in groups of five or six people:

  (a) Discuss the approach that should be taken or the basis used when recording the above situations.
  (b) Prepare the journal entry for each situation.

Communication Activity

BYP14–6   Louis Des Champs, your uncle, is an inventor who has decided to incorporate. Uncle Lou knows that you are an accounting major and hopes that you can help him set up his business. In a recent letter to you, he ends with the question, "I'm filling out an incorporation application. Can you tell me the differences in the following terms: (1) authorized shares, (2) issued shares, (3) preferred shares, (4) common shares?"

Instructions

In a brief note, differentiate these different share terms for Uncle Lou. Make the letter friendly yet professional.

Ethics Case

BYP14–7   The R&D division of Simplex Chemical Corp. has just developed a chemical for sterilizing the voracious Asian long-horned beetles that are invading most of North America. The president of Simplex is anxious to get the chemical on the market. Simplex's profits need a boost and his job is in jeopardy because of decreasing sales and profits. Simplex has an opportunity to sell this chemical in several Central American countries, where the laws are much more relaxed than in North America.

  The director of Simplex's R&D division strongly recommends further laboratory testing for side effects of this chemical on other insects, birds, animals, plants, and even humans. He cautions the president, "We could be sued from all sides if the chemical has tragic side effects that we didn't even test for in the labs." The president answers, "We can't wait an additional year for your lab tests. We can avoid losses from such lawsuits by establishing a separate wholly owned corporation to shield Simplex Corp. We can't lose any more than our investment in the new corporation, and we'll invest just the patent covering this chemical. We'll reap the benefits if the chemical works and is safe, and avoid the losses from lawsuits if it's a disaster."

  The following week Simplex creates a new wholly owned corporation called Zoebeetle Inc. It sells the chemical patent to it for $10, and watches the spraying begin.

Instructions

  (a) Who are the stakeholders in this situation?
  (b) Are the president's motives and actions ethical?
  (c) Can Simplex shield itself against losses of Zoebeetle Inc.?

Answers to Self-Study Questions

1. c 2. b 3. d 4. b 5. b 6. a 7. d 8. c 9. d

Answer to Second Cup Review It Question 3

Second Cup has an unlimited number of common shares authorized. It has 9,359,559 common shares issued at June 24, 2000. It had an average of 9,347,389 common shares issued during the year. Note that it is this average share number that is used in the calculation of book value per share in Illustration 14-11.

Remember to go back to the Navigator box on the chapter-opening page to check off your completed work.

Concepts for Review

Before studying this chapter, you should understand or, if necessary, review:

a. *The significance of legal capital in accounting for share capital transactions.* (Ch. 14, pp. 656–657)
b. *The distinction between contributed capital and retained earnings. (Ch. 14, p. 657)*
c. *The rights of preferred shareholders to dividends. (Ch. 14, p. 664)*
d. *The form and content of the shareholders' equity section of the balance sheet.* (Ch. 14, pp. 666–667)

Standing on Guard for High-Tech Business

GUELPH, Ont.—"In the early part of this century, entrepreneurs made fortunes by seeking out valuable resources such as forests or mines," explains Brian Cox, Chief Executive Officer of GUARD, Inc., in Guelph, Ontario. "Today's route to wealth is finding valuable processes."

GUARD, Inc., exemplifies the knowledge- and process-based corporation of the information age. It is a management company that establishes new advanced-technology businesses based on scientific breakthroughs made at the University of Guelph and elsewhere. "The University supplies the good ideas, then leaves it up to us. We do what business does best: exploit those ideas, and run businesses based on them," says Dr. Cox.

GUARD was incorporated in 1994, the brainchild of a group of business people from science-driven industries and, as Dr. Cox calls them, "a few visionary professors" from the University of Guelph.

In 1996, it became a publicly traded company, floating an initial common share offering that yielded nearly $6.6

million in contributed capital. In 1998, a further common share offering raised another $5.4 million. GUARD is traded on the Canadian Venture Exchange (CDNX), a venture capital marketplace owned by the Toronto Stock Exchange.

A corporation like GUARD is a long-term venture. By 2000, it had founded three new companies based on breakthrough technologies in the pharmaceutical, electronic, and biomedical fields, with a fourth—involving livestock breeding technology—in an advanced stage of development. These fields, however, require major capitalization, and profits are not generated instantly. For example, 2000 was the first year GUARD reported any net income.

GUARD's 2000 annual report showed a net income of $3.3 million

($0.49 earnings per share) and total shareholders' equity of just $3.8 million—its $12.5 million in share capital was largely offset by a deficit of $8.7 million. Its shareholders receive no dividends.

Investors in GUARD, says Dr. Cox, "are playing a game of long-term capital gains. A high-tech company can often take twelve to fifteen years to mature. The shareholders' reward will be through rapid capital appreciation" as GUARD's spinoff technologies take off.

Meanwhile, the company creates sophisticated, top-quality jobs in Canada for high-tech professionals and managers who might otherwise go to the United States.

www.guardinc.com

THE NAVIGATOR ✔

- Understand *Concepts for Review* ☐
- Read *Feature Story* ☐
- Scan *Study Objectives* ☐
- Read *Preview* ☐
- Read text and answer *Before You Go On*
  p. 697 ☐ p. 703 ☐ p. 709 ☐ p. 712 ☐
- Work *Demonstration Problems* ☐
- Review *Summary of Study Objectives* ☐
- Answer *Self-Study Questions* ☐
- Complete assignments ☐

CHAPTER • 15

CORPORATIONS: DIVIDENDS, RETAINED EARNINGS, AND INCOME REPORTING

▶ STUDY OBJECTIVES ◀

After studying this chapter, you should be able to:

1. *Prepare the entries for cash dividends, stock dividends, and stock splits, and compare their financial impact.*
2. *Prepare a statement of retained earnings.*
3. *Prepare the shareholders' equity section of a balance sheet.*
4. *Illustrate the proper form and content of corporation income statements.*
5. *Explain the concept of intraperiod tax allocation and illustrate its impact on the financial statements.*
6. *Illustrate the statement presentation of material items not typical of regular operations.*
7. *Calculate earnings and dividend ratios.*

THE
NAVIGATOR

A profitable corporation distributes a portion of its earnings to its shareholders by declaring and paying dividends. A young corporation, like GUARD, Inc. in the feature story, will normally retain all of its earnings until it accumulates enough equity to sustain its operations.

This chapter discusses dividends, retained earnings, corporation income statements, and key earnings and dividend ratios. The chapter is organized as follows:

THE NAVIGATOR

◢ **D**ividends

STUDY OBJECTIVE

1

Prepare the entries for cash dividends, stock dividends, and stock splits, and compare their financial impact.

A dividend **is a pro rata (equal) distribution of a portion of a corporation's earnings to its shareholders**. Potential buyers and sellers of shares are very interested in a company's dividend policies and practices. Cash dividends are the most common. Stock dividends are also declared often. These two forms of dividends will be the focus of this chapter.

Dividends may be expressed in two ways: (1) as a dollar amount per share, or (2) as a percentage of the stated or par value of the shares if shares have been issued with stated or par values. In the financial press, **dividends are generally reported quarterly as a dollar amount per share**. For example, the Bank of Montreal has a quarterly dividend rate of $0.30 per share on one of its classes of preferred shares.

If the shares have a stated or par value, the dividend rate is sometimes expressed as a percentage rather than as a dollar amount. In this case, the percentage must be multiplied by the legal capital value to determine the annual dividend rate. With 8%, $100 stated value, preferred shares, the annual dividend rate would be $8 per share (8% × $100).

Cash Dividends

A **cash dividend** is a pro rata distribution of cash to shareholders. For a corporation to pay a cash dividend, it must have all of the following:

1. **Sufficient retained earnings.** Dividends are normally paid out of retained earnings, which represent the undistributed, cumulative income and losses of the corporation. Although laws governing cash dividends vary by jurisdiction, in general, a deficit cannot be created by the declaration of the dividend. That is why GUARD, in our feature story, cannot currently pay dividends to its shareholders. It has a deficit of $8.7 million and a dividend would create an even larger deficit.

2. **Adequate cash.** Sufficient retained earnings does not necessarily indicate a company's ability to pay a dividend. For example, Sobeys, with a retained earnings balance of $170 million, could legally pay a dividend of $170 million. But Sobeys' cash balance is only $53 million. In order to pay the dividend, Sobeys would need to raise additional cash through the sale of other assets or through additional financing.

   Before declaring a cash dividend, a company's board of directors must carefully consider current and future demands on the company's cash resources. In some cases, current (or planned future) liabilities may make a cash dividend inappropriate.

3. **A declaration of dividends.** A company does not pay dividends unless its board of directors decides to do so, at which point the board "declares" the dividend. The board of directors has full authority to determine the amount of income to be distributed in the form of a dividend and the amount to be retained in the business. Dividends do not accrue like interest on a note payable. **They are not a liability until declared.**

The amount and timing of a dividend are important issues. The payment of a large cash dividend could lead to liquidity problems for the enterprise. On the other hand, a small dividend—or a missed dividend—may cause unhappiness among shareholders. Many of them expect to receive a reasonable cash payment from the company on a periodic basis. Most companies declare and pay cash dividends quarterly.

Helpful hint The board of directors is not obligated to declare dividends.

► *International note*
In some emerging countries, such as Turkey and Brazil, companies are required by law to distribute 50% of their net income annually as dividends.

►Accounting in Action ► *Business Insight*

In order to remain in business, companies must honour their interest payments to creditors, bankers, and bondholders. The payment of dividends to shareholders is another matter. Many companies can survive, even thrive, without such payouts. In fact, the management of some companies considers dividend payments unnecessary, or even harmful to the company. Pay your creditors, by all means. But fork over perfectly good cash to shareholders? "Why give money to those strangers?" is the response of one company president.

Investors must keep an eye on the company's dividend policy and understand what it may signal. For most companies, increased dividends despite irregular earnings can be a warning signal of financial trouble. Companies with high dividends and rising debt may be borrowing money to pay shareholders. Low dividends sometimes indicate an expectation by management of low future earnings. Or they may indicate a policy of retaining earnings for corporate expansion that will result in a higher share price in the future.

Entries for Cash Dividends

Three dates are important for dividends: (1) the declaration date, (2) the record date, and (3) the payment date. Normally, there are two to four weeks between each date and the next one. Accounting entries are required on two of the dates—the declaration date and the payment date.

On the declaration date, the board of directors formally declares (authorizes) the cash dividend and announces it to shareholders. **Declaration of a cash dividend commits the corporation to a legal obligation.** The obligation is binding and cannot be rescinded (reversed). An entry is required to recognize the decrease in retained earnings and the increase in the current liability Dividends Payable.

To illustrate, assume that on December 1, 2003, the directors of Media General declare a $0.50 per share cash dividend on 100,000 common shares. The dividend is $50,000 (100,000 × $0.50). The entry to record the declaration follows:

A	=	L	+	SE
		+50,000		−50,000

Declaration Date

Dec. 1	Cash Dividends—Common	50,000	
	Dividends Payable		50,000
	To record declaration of cash dividend.		

Dividends Payable is a current liability. It will normally be paid within the next month or so.

Instead of debiting the Cash Dividends account, some accountants debit the Retained Earnings account directly, in order to avoid a later closing entry. Use of the Dividends account, however, provides additional information in the ledger. Also, a company may have separate dividend accounts for each class of shares or for each type of dividend. When a dividend account is used, its balance is transferred to Retained Earnings at the end of the year by a closing entry. Whatever account is used for the dividend declaration, the effect is the same: retained earnings are decreased and the current liability is increased.

Helpful hint Between the declaration date and the record date, the number of shares remains the same. The purpose of the record date is to identify the persons or entities that will receive the dividend, not to determine the total amount of the dividend liability.

On the record date, ownership of the shares is determined so that the corporation knows who to pay the dividend to. The records maintained by the corporation supply this information. In the interval between the declaration date and the record date, the corporation updates its share ownership records. Remember that shares trade among investors on organized stock markets after an initial public offering, and not between the company and its investors.

For Media General, assume the record date is December 22. No entry is required on this date because the corporation's liability recognized on the declaration date is unchanged.

On the payment date, dividend cheques are mailed to shareholders and the payment of the dividend is recorded. The entry on January 20, the assumed payment date, is shown below:

A	=	L	+	SE
−50,000		−50,000		

Payment Date

Jan. 20	Dividends Payable	50,000	
	Cash		50,000
	To record payment of cash dividend.		

Note that payment of the dividend reduces both current assets and current liabilities. It has no effect on shareholders' equity. The cumulative effect of the **declaration and payment** of a cash dividend is to **decrease both shareholders' equity and total assets**.

Allocating Cash Dividends between Preferred and Common Shares

As explained in Chapter 14, preferred shares have priority over common shares in regard to dividends. A dividend priority does not guarantee that dividends will be paid. It simply means that if dividends are declared, preferred dividends must be paid before dividends can be paid on common shares.

To illustrate, assume that at December 31, 2003, IBR Inc. has 1,000 $8 cumulative preferred shares. It also has 50,000 common shares. At December 31, 2003, the directors declare a $6,000 cash dividend. The required annual preferred dividend is $8,000 (1,000 × $8). In this case, the entire $6,000 dividend amount goes to preferred shareholders because of their dividend preference. The entry to record the declaration of the dividend is as follows:

Dec. 31	Cash Dividends—Preferred	6,000	
	Dividends Payable		6,000
	To record partial cash dividend to preferred shareholders.		

A	=	L	+	SE
		+6,000		−6,000

Because of the cumulative feature, dividends of $2 per share are in arrears on preferred shares for 2003. These dividends must be paid to preferred shareholders before they receive their current year dividend and before any future dividends can be paid to common shareholders. Dividends in arrears are not recorded as a liability (until declared). They should be disclosed in the financial statements.

At December 31, 2004, IBR declares a $50,000 cash dividend. Illustration 15-1 shows the allocation of the dividend to the two share classes.

Total dividend		$50,000
Allocated to preferred shares		
Dividends in arrears, 2003 (1,000 × $2)	$2,000	
2004 dividend (1,000 × $8)	8,000	10,000
Remainder allocated to common shares		$40,000

Illustration 15-1

Allocating dividends to preferred and common shares

The entry to record the declaration of the dividend follows:

Dec. 31	Cash Dividends—Preferred	10,000	
	—Common	40,000	
	Dividends Payable		50,000
	To record declaration of cash dividends.		

A	=	L	+	SE
		+50,000		−10,000
				−40,000

What if IBR's preferred shares were not cumulative? In that case, preferred shareholders would have received only $8,000 in dividends in 2004. Common shareholders would have received $42,000.

In the majority of cases, a company does not declare a combined dividend amount for both classes of shares, as we have assumed with IBR's declaration of a $50,000 total cash dividend. Rather, it would declare a specified dividend, say $10,000, payable to the preferred shareholders and a specified dividend, say $40,000, payable to the common shareholders. This illustration has been included to reinforce the priority that preferred shareholders have when determining dividend allocations.

Stock Dividends

A stock dividend is a pro rata distribution to shareholders of the corporation's own shares. Whereas a cash dividend is paid in cash, a stock dividend is distributed (paid) in shares. **A stock dividend results in a decrease in retained earnings and an increase in share capital** (contributed capital if the shares have a stated or par value). There is no change in *total* assets, liabilities, or shareholders' equity. Unlike a cash dividend, a stock dividend does not decrease total shareholders' equity or total assets.

To illustrate, assume that you have a 2% ownership interest in IBR Inc. You own 1,000 of its 50,000 common shares. If IBR declares a 10% stock dividend, it would issue 5,000 shares (50,000 × 10%). You would receive 100 shares (2% × 5,000 or 10% × 1,000). Would your ownership interest change? No, it would remain at 2% (1,100 ÷ 55,000).

Helpful hint Dividends were declared by 24% of the companies surveyed by *Financial Reporting in Canada*. Of these, only 4% were stock dividends.

You now own more shares, but your ownership interest has not changed. Illustration 15-2 shows the effect of a stock dividend for shareholders.

Illustration 15-2

Effect of stock dividend for shareholders

From the company's point of view, no cash has been paid, and no liabilities have been assumed. What are the purposes and benefits of a stock dividend? A corporation generally issues stock dividends for one or more of the following reasons:

1. To satisfy shareholders' dividend expectations without spending cash.
2. To increase the marketability of the corporation's shares. When the number of shares increases, the market price per share decreases. Decreasing the market price makes it easier for investors to purchase the shares.
3. To emphasize that a portion of shareholders' equity has been permanently retained in the business and is unavailable for cash dividends.

Helpful hint Because of its effects, declaring a stock dividend is also referred to as capitalizing retained earnings.

The size of the stock dividend and the value to be assigned to each share are determined by the board of directors when the dividend is declared. The *Canada Business Corporations Act* recommends that directors of federally incorporated companies assign the **fair market value per share** for stock dividends. This directive is based on the assumption that a stock dividend will have little effect on the market price of the shares previously issued. While the stock dividend value can be decided by the directors in some provincial jurisdictions, it is widespread practice to use fair market values. This text follows this common practice.

Entries for Stock Dividends

To illustrate the accounting for stock dividends, assume that Medland Corporation has a balance of $300,000 in retained earnings. On June 30, 2003, it declares a 10% stock dividend on its 50,000 no par value common shares. The current fair market value of its shares is $15 per share. The number of shares to be issued is 5,000 (10% × 50,000). The total amount to be debited to the Stock Dividends account is $75,000 (5,000 × $15). The entry to record the declaration of the stock dividend is as follows:

A	=	L	+	SE
				−75,000
				+75,000

June 30	Stock Dividends—Common	75,000	
	Common Stock Dividends Distributable		75,000
	To record declaration of 10% stock dividend.		

Helpful hint Note that the dividend account title is "Distributable," not "Payable."

Medland's common shares have no par value. If the common shares had a stated (or par) value of, say, $10 per share, the account Stock Dividends would be debited for the fair market value of the shares issued (5,000 × $15). Common Stock Dividends Distributable would be credited for the stated (or par) value of the dividend shares (5,000 × $10). The excess over stated (or par) value (5,000 × $5) would be credited to an additional contributed capital account.

Common Stock Dividends Distributable is a **shareholders' equity account**. It is not a liability, because assets will not be used to pay the dividend. Illustration 15-3 shows that if a balance sheet is prepared before the dividend shares are issued, the distributable account is reported under share capital as an addition to common shares issued.

MEDLAND CORPORATION Balance Sheet (partial) June 30, 2003		
Shareholders' equity		
Share capital		
Common shares	$500,000	
Common stock dividends distributable	75,000	$575,000
Retained earnings		225,000
Total shareholders' equity		$800,000

When the dividend shares are issued on August 5, the Common Stock Dividends Distributable account is debited and the Common Shares account is credited, as follows:

Aug. 5	Common Stock Dividends Distributable	75,000	
	Common Shares		75,000
	To record issue of 5,000 shares in a stock dividend.		

A	=	L	+	SE
				−75,000
				+75,000

Effects of Stock Dividends

How do stock dividends affect shareholders' equity? They **change the composition of shareholders' equity**, because a portion of retained earnings is transferred to share capital. However, **total shareholders' equity remains the same**. Stock dividends also have no effect on the legal capital per share. But the number of shares issued increases and the book value per share decreases. These effects are shown in Illustration 15-4 for Medland Corporation.

Illustration 15-4

Stock dividend effects

	Before Stock Dividend	After Stock Dividend
Shareholders' equity		
Common shares	$500,000	$575,000
Retained earnings	300,000	225,000
Total shareholders' equity	$800,000	$800,000
Issued shares	50,000	55,000
Book value per share	$ 16.00	$ 14.55

In this example, total share capital is increased by $75,000 and retained earnings are decreased by the same amount. Total shareholders' equity remains unchanged.

Stock Splits

A stock split, like a stock dividend, involves the issue of additional shares to shareholders according to their percentage ownership. **A stock split causes a reduction in the legal capital per share.** The purpose of a stock split is to increase the marketability of the shares by lowering the market value per share. A lower market value also increases investor interest and makes it easier for the corporation to issue additional shares.

The effect of a split on market value is generally inversely proportional to the size of the split. Sometimes, due to increased investor interest, the share price rises beyond its intended split value.

For example, Future Shop Ltd. split its common shares two for one (one share before the split was exchanged for two shares after the split) in September 2000. The company believed that increasing its number of shares would improve its market value. The lower price per share would make it more attractive for smaller investors to purchase the company's shares and broaden the base of ownership in the common shares. Before the stock split, Future Shop's 16,257,045 shares were trading at nearly $12 a share. After the split, its number of shares doubled to 32,514,090 and its share price dropped to about $9.50. The lower market value and increased number of shares stimulated market activity.

Helpful hint   Some companies with penny shares do a **reverse stock split**, i.e., 1-for-2, to increase the market value per share.

In a stock split, the number of shares is increased in the same proportion that legal capital per share is decreased. For example, in a 2-for-1 split, one no par value share is exchanged for two no par value shares. If the shares have a stated (par) value of $10, then one share of $10 stated (par) value is exchanged for two shares of $5 stated (par) value. **A stock split does not have any effect on total share (contributed) capital, retained earnings, or shareholders' equity.** But the number of shares increases and the book value per share decreases.

These effects are shown in Illustration 15-5 for Medland Corporation. For the illustration, we assume that, instead of a 10% stock dividend, Medland splits its 50,000 no par value common shares on a 2-for-1 basis.

Illustration 15-5

Stock split effects

	Before Stock Split	After Stock Split
Shareholders' equity		
Common shares	$500,000	$500,000
Retained earnings	300,000	300,000
Total shareholders' equity	$800,000	$800,000
Issued shares	50,000	100,000
Book value per share	$ 16.00	$ 8.00

A stock split does not affect the balances in any shareholders' equity accounts. **Therefore, it is not necessary to journalize a stock split.** A memo entry noting the details of the split is sufficient.

Significant differences between stock splits, stock dividends, and cash dividends (after payment) are shown in Illustration 15-6. In the illustration, "NE" means "no effect."

Illustration 15-6

Effects of stock splits, stock dividends, and cash dividends

Item	Stock Split	Stock Dividend	Cash Dividend
Total assets	NE	NE	Decrease
Total liabilities	NE	NE	NE
Total shareholders' equity	NE	NE	Decrease
Total share capital	NE	Increase	NE
Total retained earnings	NE	Decrease	Decrease
Legal capital per share	Decrease	NE	NE
Book value per share	Decrease	Decrease	Decrease
Number of shares	Increase	Increase	NE
% of shareholder ownership	NE	NE	NE

Accounting in Action ► *Business Insight*

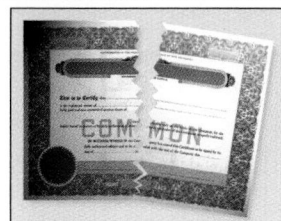

A handful of companies have no intention of keeping their share price trading in a range accessible to mere mortals. These companies never split their shares, no matter how high their share price gets. The world's most expensive publicly traded shares are U.S. investment company Berkshire Hathaway's Class A shares, which trade at a pricey US$75,000 per share!

Before You Go On . . .

►Review It

1. What entries are made for cash dividends on (a) the declaration date, (b) the record date, and (c) the payment date?
2. Contrast the effects of a stock dividend and a 2-for-1 stock split on (a) shareholders' equity, (b) the number of shares, and (c) the book value per share.
3. Did The Second Cup declare any dividends or stock splits in 2000? The answer to this question is at the end of the chapter.

►Do It

Sing CD Corporation has had five years of record earnings. Due to this success, the market price of its 500,000 no par value common shares tripled from $15 to $45 per share. During this period, the Common Shares account remained the same, at $2,000,000. Retained Earnings increased from $1,500,000 to $10,000,000. President Diane Wood is considering either (1) a 10% stock dividend, or (2) a 2-for-1 stock split. She asks you to show the before and after effects of each option on the Common Shares and Retained Earnings accounts, and the book value per share.

Action Plan

• Calculate the stock dividend effect on retained earnings by multiplying the stock dividend percentage by the number of existing shares to determine the number of new shares to be issued. Multiply the number of new shares by the market price of the shares.
• A stock dividend increases the number of shares, and reduces the book value per share.
• A stock split only changes the legal capital per share and the number of shares issued.

Solution

With a 10% stock dividend (option 1), the stock dividend amount is $2,250,000 [(500,000 × 10%) × $45]. The new balance in retained earnings is $7,750,000 ($10,000,000 − $2,250,000).

With a stock split (option 2), the Common Shares and Retained Earnings account balances after the stock split are the same as they were before: $2,000,000 and $10,000,000, respectively. The legal capital per share is $4 before the split ($2,000,000 ÷ 500,000). It is $2 after the split ($2,000,000 ÷ 1,000,000).

The balances and book values are as follows:

	Original Balances	After Stock Dividend	After Stock Split
Common shares	$ 2,000,000	$ 4,250,000	$ 2,000,000
Retained earnings	10,000,000	7,750,000	10,000,000
Total shareholders' equity	$12,000,000	$12,000,000	$12,000,000
Shares issued	500,000	550,000	1,000,000
Book value per share	$ 24.00	$ 21.82	$ 12.00

Related exercise material: BE15–1, BE15–2, BE15–3, BE15–4, E15–1, E15–2, E15–3, and E15–4.

THE NAVIGATOR

Retained Earnings

As you learned in Chapter 14, **retained earnings** comprise the cumulative total since incorporation of net income (less losses) less any declared dividends. In other words, it is the earnings that have been retained or kept in the business. The balance in retained earnings is part of the shareholders' claim on the total assets of the corporation. It does not, though, represent a claim on any specific asset. Nor can the amount of retained earnings be associated with the balance of any individual asset account. For example, a $100,000 balance in retained earnings does not mean that there should be $100,000 in cash. The reason is that the cash resulting from the excess of revenues over expenses and dividends may have been used to purchase buildings, equipment, and other assets, or to pay liabilities. To illustrate the fact that retained earnings and cash may be quite different, Illustration 15-7 shows the relationship of recent amounts of retained earnings and cash (including cash equivalents) in selected companies in a recent year.

Illustration 15-7

Retained earnings and cash balances

	(in millions)	
Company	Retained Earnings	Cash
Air Canada	($676)	$437
Canadian Tire	774	539
Onex	602	1,023
Reitmans	185	53

Recall that retained earnings is a shareholders' equity account whose normal balance is a credit. A debit (negative) balance in retained earnings, such as has been reported by Air Canada, is identified as a deficit. It is reported as a deduction in the shareholders' equity section, as shown in Illustration 15-8.

Illustration 15-8

Shareholders' equity with deficit

AIR CANADA Balance Sheet (partial) December 31, 2000 (in millions)	
Shareholders' equity	
Share capital	$977
Contributed surplus	15
Deficit	(676)
Total shareholders' equity	$316

Retained Earnings Restrictions

Helpful hint *Financial Reporting in Canada* reported in a recent year that 13% of the companies surveyed have restrictions on their retained earnings.

The balance in retained earnings is generally available for dividend declarations. Of course, it would not be prudent for a company to declare a dividend equal to its balance in retained earnings. A company must retain sufficient net assets to sustain its operations. In some cases, there may be specific retained earnings restrictions. These make a portion of the balance unavailable for dividends. Restrictions generally are of one or more of the following types:

1. **Contractual restrictions.** Long-term debt contracts may restrict retained earnings as a condition for the loan. The restriction limits the use of corporate assets for payment of dividends. This increases the likelihood that the corporation will be able to meet required loan payments.
2. **Voluntary restrictions.** The board of directors may voluntarily create retained earnings restrictions for specific purposes. For example, the board may authorize a restriction for future plant expansion. By reducing the amount of retained earnings available for dividends, more cash is available for the planned expansion.

Retained earnings restrictions are generally disclosed in the notes to the financial statements.

Prior Period Adjustments

Suppose that a corporation's books have been closed and the financial statements have been issued. The corporation then discovers that a material error has been made in reporting net income of a prior year. Or suppose that the corporation changes an accounting policy that affects the comparison of prior year figures. How should these situations be recorded in the accounts and reported in the financial statements of prior periods?

An adjustment of financial results for prior periods is only appropriate in two circumstances: (1) when correcting an error related to a prior period, and (2) when changing an accounting principle. When a correction of an error or a change in accounting principle results, the accounting treatment is similar.

1. The corrected amount or new principle should be used in reporting the results of operations of the current year.
2. The cumulative effect of the correction or change should be disclosed net of (after subtracting) applicable income tax, as an adjustment of opening retained earnings.
3. All prior period financial statements should be corrected or restated to make comparison easier.
4. The effects of the change should be detailed and disclosed in a footnote.

Let's now look in more detail at the accounting for corrections of errors and for changes in accounting principle.

Correction of Prior Period Errors

The correction of a prior period error in previously issued financial statements is made directly to Retained Earnings since the effect of the error is now in this account. The revenues and expenses (net income) for the previous period have been recorded in retained earnings through the journalizing and posting of closing entries.

If a correction affects revenues or expenses, then income tax expense will also be in error. Note that income tax expense is an additional expense we did not see in the income statements of proprietorships or partnerships. Corporations pay income tax on revenues less expenses, known as income before income tax.

To illustrate the correction of a prior period error, assume that General Microwave Corp. discovers in 2003 that it overstated its cost of goods sold in 2002 by $30,000 as a result of errors in counting inventory. These errors overstated expenses and understated income before income tax by $30,000. If we assume an income tax rate of 45%, income tax would be understated by $13,500 ($30,000 × 45%). The overall effect on net income is to understate it by $16,500 ($30,000 − $13,500). In other words, net income is understated by the difference after tax [$30,000 × (100% − 45%)].

The following illustration details this effect, using assumed data for revenues and expenses:

	Incorrect (overstated CGS)	Correct	Difference
Revenues	$200,000	$200,000	$ 0
Less: Expenses	125,000	95,000	30,000
Income before income tax	75,000	105,000	30,000
Less: Income tax (45%)	33,750	47,250	13,500
Net income	$ 41,250	$ 57,750	$16,500

On the balance sheet, current assets (Merchandise Inventory) and retained earnings

Helpful hint Normally, any errors made in a given year are discovered and corrected before the financial statements for the year are issued. Thus, corrections of prior period errors seldom happen.

Illustration 15-9

Income effects of overstating cost of goods sold

are also understated. The entry for the correction is as follows:

A = L + SE	Dec. 31	Merchandise Inventory	30,000	
+30,000 +13,500 +16,500		Income Tax Payable		13,500
		Retained Earnings		16,500
		To adjust for overstatement of cost of goods sold in a prior period.		

A credit to an income statement account, Cost of Goods Sold, instead of the Retained Earnings account, would be incorrect because the error is for a prior year.

Prior period corrections are reported in the statement of retained earnings, net of associated income tax. Corrections are added to (or deducted from as the case may be), the beginning retained earnings balance. This results in an adjusted beginning balance. Assuming General Microwave has a beginning balance of $800,000 in retained earnings, the correction is reported as in Illustration 15-10.

Illustration 15-10

Statement presentation of correction of prior period error

GENERAL MICROWAVE CORP. Statement of Retained Earnings (partial) For the Year Ended December 31, 2003	
Balance, January 1, 2003, as previously reported	$800,000
Add: Correction for overstatement of cost of goods sold in 2002, net of income tax expense of $13,500	16,500
Balance, January 1, 2003, as adjusted	816,500

Reporting either the correction or the related income tax amounts in the current year's income statement would be incorrect, because they apply to the prior year's income.

If 2002 financial results are presented with the 2003 financial statements for comparative purposes, 2002 amounts would be restated using the correct cost of goods sold expense and inventory amounts. An appropriately cross-referenced note should show the impact of the correction. It would also note the fact that the prior year's statements have been restated.

Change in Accounting Principle

► *Ethics note*

Changes in accounting principles should result in financial statements that are more informative for statement users. They should not be used to artificially improve the reported performance and financial position of the corporation.

To make comparisons easier, financial statements for the current period should be prepared using the same accounting principles that were used for the preceding period. That is, there is a general presumption that generally accepted accounting principles are consistently applied from period to period. This does not mean that accounting principles can never change. A change in an accounting principle (also known as a change in accounting policy) occurs when the principle used in the current year is different from the one used in the preceding year.

Examples of a change in accounting principle include a change in amortization method (e.g., declining-balance to straight-line) and a change in inventory cost flow assumption (e.g., FIFO to average cost). A change in accounting principle is permitted when the new generally accepted accounting principle results in a more appropriate presentation of events or transactions in the financial statements. Changes in accounting principles are influenced by changes in *CICA Handbook* recommendations.

Accounting in Action ► *Business Insight*

In 1996, the most common change in accounting principle was related to financial instruments, reflecting the addition of a new section to the CICA Handbook. For 1997 and 1998, new sections relating to income tax, segment disclosure, and cash flow statements resulted in changes in accounting principles. In 1999, a change in the accounting for employee future benefits was the most often reported change in accounting principle.

Like the correction of a prior period error, the cumulative effect of a change in accounting principle on net income is reported, net of applicable income tax, as an adjustment to the opening balance of retained earnings. To illustrate, assume that at the beginning of 2003, St. Onge Limited changes from the straight-line method of amortization for equipment to the declining-balance method. The equipment had been purchased on January 1, 1999. The cumulative effect of this change is to increase amortization expense and decrease net capital assets (because of the increase in accumulated amortization) for the years 1999–2002.

Retained earnings is affected by the change in amortization expense and income tax expense, both of which affect net income of the prior periods. Assume that the total increase in amortization expense during the period 1999–2002 amounts to $24,000. This decreases income before income tax by $24,000. If the company had a 30% tax rate, the after-tax effect of the change would be $16,800 [$24,000 × (100% − 30%)]. The entry to record this change in accounting principle follows:

Dec. 31	Income Tax Payable (or Recoverable)	7,200	
	Retained Earnings	16,800	
	Accumulated Amortization		24,000
	To record retroactive effect on capital assets		
	of change in amortization method.		

A	=	L	+	SE
−24,000		−7,200		−16,800

The presentation of this change in the statement of retained earnings is similar to the correction of prior period errors. Assuming that the opening balance of retained earnings is $500,000, the presentation is shown in the following illustration:

ST. ONGE LIMITED
Statement of Retained Earnings (partial)
For the Year Ended December 31, 2003

Balance, January 1, 2003, as previously reported	$500,000
Less: Cumulative effect of change in amortization method,	
net of $7,200 income tax savings	(16,800)
Balance, January 1, 2003, as adjusted	483,200

Illustration 15-11

Statement presentation of change in accounting principle

Any financial statements from prior years which are presented for comparative purposes would be restated using the declining-balance method of amortization. St. Onge's income statement would also show amortization expense for the current year on a declining-balance basis (i.e., using the new method of amortization). Accumulated amortization on the balance sheet would be calculated as though declining-balance had always been used. An appropriately cross-referenced note to the statements should detail the impact of the change and the fact that prior years' statements have been restated.

Statement of Retained Earnings

The statement of retained earnings shows the changes in retained earnings during the year. The statement is prepared from the Retained Earnings account. Transactions and events that affect retained earnings are shown in Illustration 15-12.

Illustration 15-12

Debits and credits to retained earnings

Retained Earnings	
Debits (Decreases)	Credits (Increases)
1. Correction of a prior period error that overstated income 2. Cumulative effect of a change in accounting principle that decreased income 3. Net loss 4. Cash dividends 5. Stock dividends	1. Correction of a prior period error that understated income 2. Cumulative effect of a change in accounting principle that increased income 3. Net income

As indicated, net income increases retained earnings and a net loss decreases retained earnings. Prior period adjustments—a correction of an error or a change in accounting principle—may either increase or decrease retained earnings. Both cash and stock dividends decrease retained earnings. Stock splits do not affect retained earnings, so they do not appear in this list of transactions.

The statement of retained earnings for Graber Inc., based on assumed data, appears in Illustration 15-13.

Illustration 15-13

Statement of retained earnings

GRABER INC.
Statement of Retained Earnings
For the Year Ended December 31, 2003

Balance, January 1, as previously reported		$ 800,000
Add: Correction for understatement of net income due to unrecorded sales in prior period, net of $40,000 income tax expense		60,000
Cumulative effect of a change in accounting principle, completed-contract method to percentage-of-completion method, net of $80,000 income tax expense		120,000
Balance, January 1, as adjusted		980,000
Add: Net income		360,000
		1,340,000
Less: Cash dividends	$100,000	
Stock dividends	200,000	300,000
Balance, December 31		$1,040,000

Some companies combine the statement of retained earnings with their income statement, instead of presenting them separately. For example, The Second Cup does this in its Consolidated Statements of Operations and Deficit. However, the majority of companies present a separate statement of retained earnings.

Reporting Shareholders' Equity

STUDY OBJECTIVE
3

Prepare the shareholders' equity section of a balance sheet.

The shareholders' equity section of the balance sheet of Graber Inc., based on assumed data, is presented in Illustration 15-14.

Illustration 15-14

Shareholders' equity section

GRABER INC.
Balance Sheet (partial)
December 31, 2003

Shareholders' equity
    Contributed capital
        Share capital

$9 preferred shares, no par value, cumulative,		
10,000 shares authorized, 6,000 shares issued		$ 630,000
Common shares, no par value, $5 stated value,		
unlimited number of shares authorized,		
400,000 shares issued	$2,000,000	
Common stock dividends distributable	50,000	2,050,000
Total share capital		2,680,000
Additional contributed capital		
Contributed capital in excess of stated value—common shares		1,050,000
Total contributed capital		3,730,000
Retained earnings		1,040,000
Total shareholders' equity		$4,770,000

▶ *International note*

In Switzerland, there are no specific disclosure requirements for shareholders' equity. But Swiss companies typically disclose separate categories of capital on the balance sheet.

Instead of presenting a detailed shareholders' equity section in the balance sheet, many companies detail the components of the shareholders' equity accounts in the notes to the statements. Refer to The Second Cup's Note 8 in Appendix A for an illustration of this type of presentation.

Before You Go On ...
▶ *Review It*

1. How are retained earnings restrictions reported?
2. Distinguish between a correction of a prior period error and a change in accounting principle.
3. What are the principal sources of debits and credits to the Retained Earnings account?

▶ *Do It*

Vega Corporation has retained earnings of $5,130,000 on January 1, 2003. During the year, the company earns $2,000,000 of net income. It declares and pays a $250,000 cash dividend. In 2003, Vega records an adjustment of $180,000, net of $95,000 applicable income tax, for an overstatement resulting from a mathematical error affecting 2002 ending inventory. Prepare a statement of retained earnings for the year ended December 31, 2003.

Action Plan

- A statement of retained earnings begins with retained earnings as reported at the end of the previous year.
- Add or subtract any prior period adjustments to arrive at the adjusted opening retained earnings.
- Add net income and subtract dividends declared to arrive at the ending balance in retained earnings.

Solution

VEGA CORPORATION
Statement of Retained Earnings
For the Year Ended December 31, 2003

Balance, January 1, as previously reported	$5,130,000
Less: Correction for overstatement of ending inventory, net of $95,000 applicable income tax	(180,000)
Balance, January 1, as adjusted	4,950,000
Add: Net income	2,000,000
	6,950,000
Less: Cash dividend	250,000
Balance, December 31	$6,700,000

Related exercise material: BE15–5, BE15–6, BE15–7, E15–5, E15–6, E15–7, E15–8, and E15–9.

Corporation Income Statements

STUDY OBJECTIVE

4

Illustrate the proper form and content of corporation income statements.

The income statement helps users to evaluate the past performance of managers and to estimate future cash flows. **Income statements for corporations are the same as the statements for proprietorships or partnerships except for one thing: the reporting of income tax.**

Corporate Income Tax

For income tax purposes, a corporation is a separate legal entity. As a result, **income tax expense** is reported in a separate section of the corporation income statement, which is located before net income. The condensed income statement for Leads Inc. in Illustration 15-15 shows a typical presentation. Note that the corporation reports "income before income tax" before "income tax expense."

Illustration 15-15

Income statement with income tax expense

LEADS INC.
Income Statement
For the Year Ended December 31, 2003

Sales	$800,000
Cost of goods sold	600,000
Gross profit	200,000
Operating expenses	50,000
Income from operations	150,000
Other revenues and gains	10,000
Other expenses and losses	4,000
Income before income tax	156,000
Income tax expense	46,800
Net income	$109,200

Helpful hint Corporations may also use the single-step form of income statement discussed in Chapter 5, modified for the separate presentation of income tax.

Income tax is calculated annually on the income of the corporation, but must be estimated and remitted monthly. Therefore, the year-end current liability on the balance sheet is usually much less than the income tax expense reported for the period on the income statement. Most small businesses have three months (two months for larger companies) after year end to remit any balance due without penalty (or to request any refund). They have six months after their fiscal year end to file their completed income tax return, called a T2.

The final determination of income tax expense (or recovery) and liability (or receivable) usually results in an adjusting entry. Assume Leads Inc. had originally estimated its income tax would total $42,000. It remitted monthly instalments to the Canada Customs and Revenue Agency in the amount of $3,500 per month ($42,000 ÷ 12). At year end, Leads actually reports taxable income of $156,000, with a total income tax liability of $46,800. Assuming it has already recorded and remitted $42,000 of income tax, the required adjusting entry will be as follows:

Dec. 31	Income Tax Expense	4,800	
	Income Tax Payable		4,800
	To adjust estimated income tax		
	expense to actual.		

A	=	L	+	SE
		+4,800		−4,800

Leads' income statement reports income before income tax of $156,000 and income tax expense of $46,800. The balance sheet reports a current liability of $4,800, due three months after year end.

Accounting in Action ► *@-Business Insight*

The Canada Customs and Revenue Agency (CCRA) worked with the business community to redesign the corporation tax processing system. This new design has led to a system based on electronic commerce and client service. Corporate EFILE, an electronic filing option using Electronic Data Interchange, has been introduced to provide corporations with a more efficient way to file federal and provincial income tax returns. EFILE is already an accepted method of transmitting personal income tax returns.

Interperiod Tax Allocation

Income taxes are, in reality, far more complicated than the preceding presentation implies. As discussed in earlier chapters, the accounting objectives for revenues and expenses for GAAP purposes differ from the accounting objectives for revenues and expenses for CCRA purposes. Because of this, timing differences often occur. Transactions are sometimes recorded in one period for accounting purposes (in order to determine income tax expense) and in another period for income tax purposes (to determine the amount owed to the CCRA). These timing differences result in **future income taxes**.

Future income taxes are discussed at length in intermediate accounting courses. For now, it should be said that the income tax expense amount presented in many financial statements is usually divided between the amount currently due or receivable and the amount due or receivable in the future. The act of dividing the amounts is called interperiod tax allocation. An illustration of interperiod income tax allocation is presented in the income statement of The Second Cup Ltd. in Appendix A. The Second Cup reports income tax payable as a current liability and future income taxes (receivable) as a long-term asset.

Alternative terminology
Future income taxes are also known as *deferred income taxes.*

Intraperiod Tax Allocation

Intraperiod tax allocation refers to associating income taxes in a specified period with their related item of income. This can be contrasted with **interperiod tax allocation**, in which income taxes are allocated between two or more periods. Under intraperiod tax allocation, the relevant income tax expense or saving is associated with each non-typical item, as discussed in the next section of this chapter.

Earlier in the chapter, intraperiod tax allocation was applied to the adjustments made to opening retained earnings (to corrections of prior period errors, and to

STUDY OBJECTIVE
•••••••• **5** ••••••••

Explain the concept of intraperiod tax allocation and illustrate its impact on the financial statements.

Helpful hint *Intra* means within the current year's income statement; *inter* means between two or more income statements.

changes in accounting principles). Intraperiod tax allocation discloses useful information to statement users about the income tax effects of these adjustments. The general concept is "let the tax follow the income or loss."

Presentation of Non-Typical Items

STUDY OBJECTIVE
··········▼6▼··········
Illustrate the statement presentation of material items not typical of regular operations.

The income statements we have studied so far provide insight into a company's income-related activities. In studying such statements, the user may ask these questions: (1) Are the results typical for this company? (2) Are the results a reasonable indicator of the company's future earnings?

To answer these questions, **material items not typical of regular operations** are reported separately in the income statement. These items are reported immediately before net income. Non-typical items include (1) discontinued operations and (2) extraordinary items. Each item reported in the income statement should be carefully explained in the notes to the financial statements. The income statement should also show the intraperiod tax allocation, reporting the income tax expense or savings applicable to each item. We will now turn our attention to the presentation of discontinued operations and extraordinary items.

Discontinued Operations

Discontinued operations refer to the disposal of a **significant segment** of a business. Examples are the elimination of an entire activity or of a major class of customers. Thus, Shaw Communications Inc.'s decision to transfer its specialty television and radio media business to Corus Entertainment Inc. was reported as discontinued operations on its 2000 financial statements. On the other hand, Shaw's transfer of its cable operations in Southern Ontario and New Brunswick to Rogers Communications is not considered discontinued operations, as Shaw continues to operate in the cable industry in other areas of Canada.

When the disposal of a significant segment occurs, the income statement should report both income from continuing operations and income (or loss) from discontinued operations. **The income (loss) from discontinued operations consists of two parts: the income (loss) from these operations and the gain (loss) on disposal of the segment. Both items are presented net of applicable income tax.**

To illustrate, assume that Hwa Energy Inc. has revenues of $2.5 million and expenses of $1.7 million from continuing operations in 2003. The company, therefore, has income before income tax of $800,000. During 2003, HWA discontinues and sells its unprofitable chemical division. The loss in 2003 from chemical operations is $140,000 ($200,000 less $60,000 income tax, assuming a 30% tax rate). The loss on disposal of the chemical division is $70,000 ($100,000 less $30,000 income tax). The income statement is presented in Illustration 15-16.

Illustration 15-16

Statement presentation of discontinued operations

Helpful hint Observe the dual disclosures: (1) the results of operations of the discontinued division (which must be eliminated from the results of continuing operations), and (2) the disposal of the operation.

HWA ENERGY INC. Income Statement (partial) For the Year Ended December 31, 2003		
Income before income tax		$800,000
Income tax expense		240,000
Income from continuing operations		560,000
Discontinued operations		
Loss from operations of chemical division, net of $60,000 income tax saving	$140,000	
Loss on disposal of chemical division, net of $30,000 income tax saving	70,000	210,000
Net income		$350,000

Note that the caption "Income from continuing operations" is used, and that a section called "Discontinued operations" is added. **In the new section, both the operating loss and the loss on disposal are reported net of applicable income tax.** This presentation clearly indicates the separate effects of continuing operations and discontinued operations on net income. Discontinued operations are relatively common. In a recent year, 28% of the companies surveyed by *Financial Reporting in Canada* reported discontinued operations.

Extraordinary Items

Extraordinary items are events and transactions that meet three conditions. They are:
1. **not expected to occur frequently,**
2. **not typical of normal business activities, and**
3. **not subject to management's discretion.**

To be infrequent, the item should not be expected again in the foreseeable future. To be atypical, the item should be only incidentally related to normal activities. To be outside of management's discretion, the item should not depend on decisions by management or owners.

In reality, extraordinary items are rare. *Financial Reporting in Canada* notes that only one company reported an extraordinary item in a recent year. Illustration 15-17 shows the appropriate classification of extraordinary and ordinary items.

▶ *International note*

Canada, Australia, the U.S., and the UK segregate extraordinary items (they are called exceptional in the UK). Other countries, however, do not distinguish between ordinary and extraordinary items.

Illustration 15-17

Examples of extraordinary and ordinary items

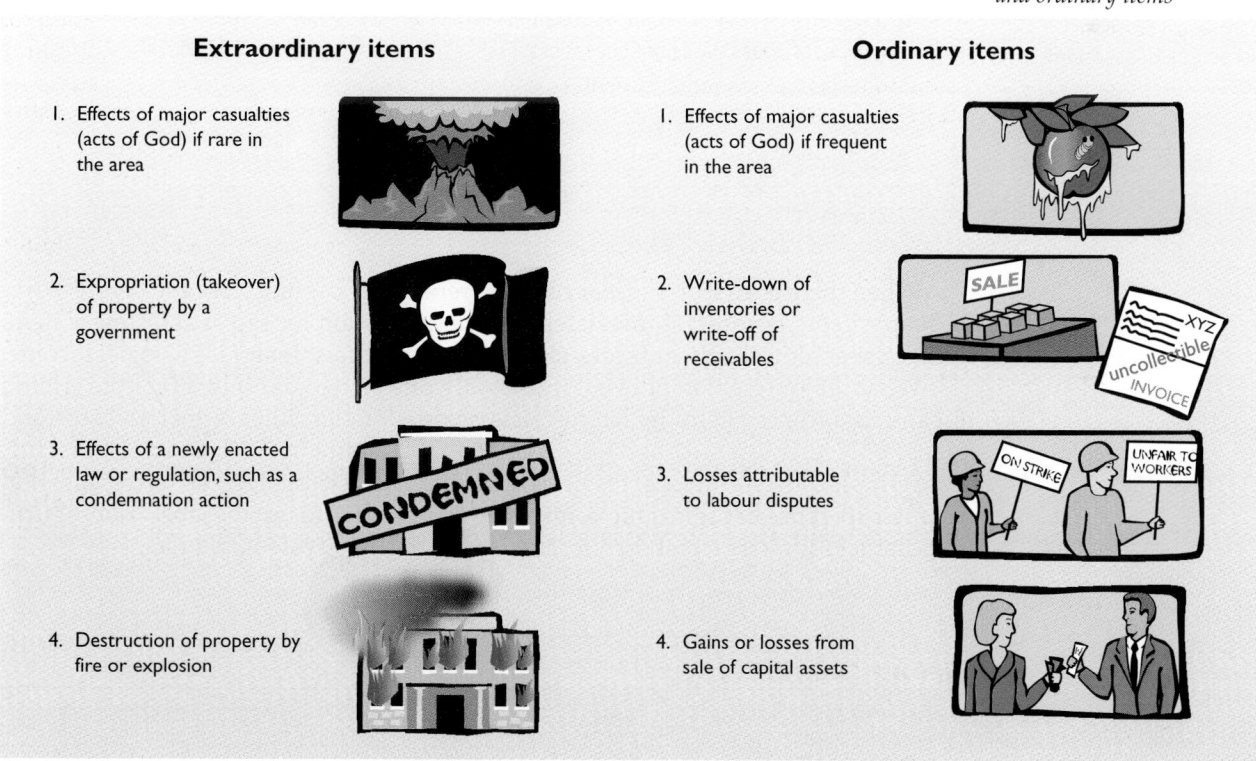

All three criteria must be evaluated in terms of the company's operating environment. Le Groupe Vidéotron Ltée reported $13.7 million in damages from the 1998 ice storm as an extraordinary loss. Although snow and ice are not unusual in Quebec, the extent of the damages from this particular ice storm made them infrequent, atypical, and not determined by management. The ice storm in Quebec and neighbouring provinces was the most costly natural disaster in Canadian history, with losses totalling $2 billion.

In contrast, the costs resulting from the September 11, 2001, terrorist attacks in New York and Washington were *not* reported as extraordinary. While the *events* were certainly extraordinary, the economic effects of the events were so extensive and pervasive that it was impossible to capture them in any one financial statement line item. Additionally, companies had no way to separate costs that were related more to the general economic downturn than to the specific impact of the disaster.

Extraordinary items are reported net of income tax in a separate section of the income statement, immediately below discontinued operations. To illustrate, assume that, for the construction of a highway in 2003, the government expropriates property held by Hwa Energy Inc. If the loss is $70,000 before applicable income tax of $21,000, the income statement will report a deduction of $49,000, as shown in Illustration 15-18.

Illustration 15-18

Statement presentation of extraordinary items

Helpful hint If there are no discontinued operations, the third line of the income statement would be labelled "Income before extraordinary item."

HWA ENERGY INC. Income Statement (partial) For the Year Ended December 31, 2003		
Income before income tax		$800,000
Income tax expense		240,000
Income from continuing operations		560,000
Discontinued operations		
Loss from operations of chemical division, net of $60,000 income tax saving	$140,000	
Loss on disposal of chemical division, net of $30,000 income tax saving	70,000	210,000
Income before extraordinary item		350,000
Extraordinary item		
Expropriation of property, net of $21,000 income tax saving		49,000
Net income		$301,000

When there is an extraordinary item to report, the caption "Income before extraordinary item" is added immediately before the section for the extraordinary item. This presentation clearly indicates the effect of the extraordinary item on net income.

What if a transaction or event meets only one or two (but not all) of the criteria for an extraordinary item? In that case, it is reported under either "Other revenues and gains" or "Other expenses and losses" at its gross amount (not net of tax). This is true, for example, of gains (losses) resulting from the sale of capital assets, as explained in Chapter 10. It has become quite common for companies to use the label "non-returning charges" for losses that do not meet the extraordinary item criteria.

Before You Go On . . .

▶ *Review It*

1. What is the unique feature of a corporation income statement?
2. What is the primary objective of intraperiod tax allocation?
3. What are the similarities and differences in reporting material items not typical of regular operations?

►*Do It*

In its 2003 income statement, Laws Ltd. reported a $75,000 loss incurred from closing 6 of 30 stores, an extraordinary loss from fire of $100,000, income tax (45%) of $135,000, and net income of $165,000. Prepare an income statement, using intraperiod tax allocation, beginning with income before income tax.

Action Plan

• Apply the criteria for discontinued operations to the closure of stores. This closure does not meet the criteria because Laws continues to operate other stores in the same line of business. The loss should be reported as part of continuing income.
• Apply the criteria for an extraordinary item to the fire loss. This loss meets the criteria since it is infrequent, unusual, and not determined by management.
• Allocate income tax between income from continuing operations and income from non-typical (extraordinary) items.
• Report the extraordinary item separately, net of income tax.

Solution

LAWS LTD.
Income Statement (partial)
Year Ended December 31, 2003

Income before income tax	$400,000
Income tax expense (45%)	180,000
Income before extraordinary item	220,000
Extraordinary loss from fire, net of $45,000 income tax saving	55,000
Net income	$165,000

Related exercise material: BE15–8, BE15–9, E15–10, and E15–11.

THE NAVIGATOR

Using the Information in the Financial Statements

Shares are generally purchased by investors for potential capital gains (market price appreciation) or for potential income (dividends). Consequently, investors are interested in both a company's earnings performance and its dividend record.

Earnings Performance

Two ratios related to income are frequently reported in the financial press. They are widely used by shareholders and potential investors in evaluating the profitability of a company. The first ratio—a convenient measure of earnings—is the **earnings per share ratio**. Earnings per share disclosures are required for publicly held companies and recommended for private companies. Investors, and others, link earnings per share to the market price per share. This relationship produces the second ratio—the **price-earnings ratio**.

Earnings Per Share

Earnings per share (EPS) indicates the net income earned by each common share. Thus, **earnings per share is reported only for common shares**. When a company has both preferred and common shares, the current year's dividend declared on preferred shares is subtracted from net income to determine **income available to common**

shareholders. The formula for calculating EPS is as follows:

Illustration 15-19

Earnings per share formula

To illustrate, assume that Rally Inc. reports net income of $211,000 and has 102,500 common shares. During the year, it also declares a $6,000 dividend on its preferred shares. Therefore, Rally has $205,000 ($211,000 − $6,000) available for dividends. Earnings per share is $2 ($205,000 ÷ 102,500). If the preferred shares are cumulative, the dividend for the current year is deducted whether or not it is declared.

Because of the importance of earnings per share, most companies are required to report it directly in their income statement, rather than elsewhere in the statements. Generally, this amount is simply reported below net income on the statement.

▸Accounting in Action ▸ *Business Insight*

Reitmans

When a company publicly announces its latest earnings per share figure, a change in the company's share price will often result. The change in share price may be large if the company's net income figure differs from what investors were expecting. When Reitmans announced earnings per share that exceeded investor expectations, its share price jumped 31% in a single day. When telecommunications giant Nortel announced that its business would likely grow at a rate of 10%, rather than 30% as previously anticipated, its share price plummeted 35% in one day. To avoid "earnings surprises," and the resultant wide swings in share prices, companies continually try to keep analysts informed.

When the income statement includes a non-typical item—discontinued operations or extraordinary items—EPS should be disclosed for each component. Assume that Hwa Energy had 100,000 common shares during the year. The additional EPS disclosures for the income statement shown in Illustration 15-18 would be as follows:

Illustration 15-20

Earnings per share disclosures

HWA ENERGY INC.	
Income Statement (partial)	
For the Year Ended December 31, 2003	
Net income	$301,000
Earnings per share	
Income from continuing operations	$5.60
Loss from discontinued operations	(2.10)
Income before extraordinary item	3.50
Extraordinary loss	(0.49)
Net income	$3.01

These disclosures enable decision-makers to recognize the effects on EPS of income from continuing operations, separate from income or loss from material items not typical of regular operations. **Earnings per share from continuing operations is generally the most useful per share amount.** It represents the results of continuing and ordinary business activity. Thus, it provides the best basis for predicting future operating results.

The calculation of earnings per share is actually much more complicated than we have indicated in this section. The number of shares may change during the year. If so, a weighted average number of common shares needs to be determined. The company may have a complex capital structure—securities that may be converted into common shares. The impact of these potential conversions on common shares is reported as **fully diluted earnings per share**. The details of weighted average and complex earnings per share calculations are left for future accounting courses.

Price-Earnings Ratio

Comparisons of earnings per share across companies are not very meaningful because of the wide variations in the numbers of shares among companies and in the share prices. In order to compare earnings across companies, we calculate the price-earnings (PE) ratio. The price-earnings ratio is a frequently quoted statistic that measures **the ratio of the market price of each common share to its earnings per share**.

To illustrate, we will calculate the price-earnings ratio for The Second Cup Ltd. The Second Cup's earnings per share for the year ended June 24, 2000, was $0.10. Its market price at year end was $6.60. Illustration 15-21 shows The Second Cup's price-earnings ratio:

Illustration 15-21

Calculation of price-earnings ratio

This ratio indicates that The Second Cup shares are trading at 66 times earnings. The PE ratio reflects investors' assessment of a company's future earnings. A high PE ratio, such as The Second Cup's, is one indicator that investors believe the company has future growth potential.

Dividend Record

One way that companies reward investors for their investment is to pay dividends. The **payout ratio** measures the percentage of earnings distributed in the form of cash dividends. Another measure, the **dividend yield**, reports the rate of return an investor earned from dividends during the year.

Payout Ratio

The payout ratio tells you what percentage of earnings the company is distributing to its shareholders. If the number is very high, consider it a red flag—it could mean the company is failing to reinvest enough of its earnings in its operations. A high payout ratio can also mean the company's earnings are falling or that it is trying to attract investors who find little else to get excited about.

The payout ratio is calculated by dividing total cash dividends by net income. This ratio can also be expressed on a per share basis by dividing common dividends per share by earnings per share. The Second Cup's payout ratio is calculated as in Illustration 15-22:

Illustration 15-22

Calculation of payout ratio

Cash Dividends	÷	Net Income	=	Payout Ratio
$18,719,000	÷	$972,000	=	1,926%

The Second Cup's payout ratio is normally zero. A one-time, special dividend of $2 per common share was paid in 2000.

Dividend Yield

The **dividend yield** indicates how much income is generated by each common share. Investors often compare dividend yields to other investment returns, such as those generated by money-market funds, when deciding whether or not to purchase shares for their income potential.

The dividend yield is calculated by dividing cash dividends per share by the share price at the time of purchase. If we assume a market price of $6.60 per common share for The Second Cup Ltd., its dividend yield would be calculated as in Illustration 15-23.

Illustration 15-23

Calculation of dividend yield

Cash Dividends Per Share	÷	Share Price	=	Dividend Yield
$2.00	÷	$6.60	=	30.3%

As mentioned earlier, however, this dividend was a special dividend and shareholders should not expect to sustain this dividend yield.

Like most ratios, the payout ratio and dividend yield vary with the industry. Real estate investment trusts pay out almost all their earnings because of a provision in the law that exempts them from income tax if they do so. Utilities also have high payout ratios. By contrast, companies that have high growth rates generally have low payout ratios and dividend yields because they reinvest most of their net income in the company. Illustration 15-24 lists payout ratios and dividend yields for some well-known companies.

Illustration 15-24

Dividend record

Company	Payout Ratio	Dividend Yield
Aliant	74.8%	3.9%
Bank of Montreal	39.5%	3.8%
BCE	16.3%	2.4%
Corel Corporation	0.0%	0.0%

Before You Go On . . .

▸Review It

1. Explain how to calculate earnings per share when there is only one class of shares.
2. What effect do preferred shares have on the formula for calculating earnings per share?

3. How is the price-earnings ratio calculated?
4. What two ratios provide information about a company's dividend record?

Related exercise material: BE15–10, BE15–11, BE15–12, BE15–13, E15–12, and E15–13.

►*A Look Back at Our Feature Story*

Refer back to the feature story about GUARD at the begining of the chapter, and answer the following questions:
1. Although GUARD has chosen not to pay cash dividends to its shareholders in the past, would it be permitted to pay a cash dividend in the upcoming year if management chose that option?
2. If GUARD is unable to declare a cash dividend, would a stock dividend be a suitable option instead?
3. GUARD's market price per share at the end of 2000 was $0.80. Calculate GUARD'S price-earnings ratio.

Solution

1. In order for GUARD to pay a cash dividend, it must have sufficient retained earnings, adequate cash, and a formal declaration of the dividend by the Board of Directors. All three criteria must be met. GUARD does not have any retained earnings. It is not permitted to create (or increase) a deficit through the payment of dividends. Therefore, no dividend can be declared.
2. As discussed in the answer for question 1, GUARD has insufficient retained earnings to declare or pay any type of dividend—whether cash or stock.
3. GUARD's price-earnings ratio is 1.6. This means that GUARD's shares are trading at 1.6 times their earnings.

Share Price	÷	Earnings per Share	=	Price-Earnings Ratio
$0.80	÷	$0.49	=	1.6 times

DEMONSTRATION PROBLEM

Additional Demonstration Problem

The events and transactions of Dever Corporation for the year ending December 31, 2003, resulted in the following data:

Cost of goods sold	$2,600,000
Net sales	4,400,000
Other expenses and losses	9,600
Other revenues and gains	5,600
Selling and administrative expenses	1,100,000
Cash dividends	40,000
Income from operations of plastics division	70,000
Gain on sale of plastics division	500,000
Retained earnings, January 1, 2003	700,000
Loss from ice storm disaster (extraordinary loss)	600,000
Cumulative effect of changing from straight-line amortization to double declining-balance (increase in amortization expense)	300,000

Analysis reveals the following:

1. All items are before the applicable income tax rate of 30%.
2. There were 100,000 common shares.

Instructions

Prepare (a) an income statement for the year, including the presentation of earnings per share data, and (b) a statement of retained earnings.

Action Plan

- Remember that material items not typical of operations are reported in separate sections, net of income tax.
- Extraordinary losses affect the current period's income statement.
- A change in accounting principle affects the comparability of prior periods, and is reported in the statement of retained earnings.
- Associate income tax with the item that affects the tax.
- Apply the corporate income tax rate to income before income tax and to each non-typical item to determine income tax expense.

Solution to Demonstration Problem

(a)

DEVER CORPORATION
Income Statement
For the Year Ended December 31, 2003

Net sales		$4,400,000
Cost of goods sold		2,600,000
Gross profit		1,800,000
Selling and administrative expenses		1,100,000
Income from operations		700,000
Other revenues and gains	$ 5,600	
Other expenses and losses	9,600	4,000
Income before income tax		696,000
Income tax expense ($696,000 × 30%)		208,800
Income from continuing operations		487,200
Discontinued operations		
Income from operations of plastics division, net of		
$21,000 ($70,000 × 30%) income tax	$ 49,000	
Gain on sale of plastics division, net of $150,000		
($500,000 × 30%) income tax	350,000	399,000
Income before extraordinary item		886,200
Extraordinary item		
Ice storm loss, net of income tax saving of $180,000 ($600,000 × 30%)		420,000
Net income		$ 466,200
Earnings per share		
Income from continuing operations		$4.87
Income from discontinued operations		3.99
Income before extraordinary item		8.86
Extraordinary loss		(4.20)
Net income		$4.66

(b)

DEVER CORPORATION
Statement of Retained Earnings
For the Year Ended December 31, 2003

Retained earnings, January 1, 2003—as previously reported	$700,000
Less: Effect on prior years of change in accounting principle (method of amortization), $300,000, less 30% income tax saving, $90,000	210,000
Retained earnings, January 1, 2003—as adjusted	490,000
Add: Net income for 2003	466,200
	956,200
Less: Cash dividends	40,000
Retained earnings, December 31, 2003	$916,200

Summary of Study Objectives

1. Prepare the entries for cash dividends, stock dividends, and stock splits, and compare their financial impact. Entries for both cash and stock dividends are required at the declaration date and the payment or distribution date. There is no entry for a stock split. Cash dividends reduce assets and shareholders' equity (retained earnings). Stock dividends reduce retained earnings and increase common shares, but have no impact on total shareholders' equity. Stock splits reduce the market price of the shares and the legal capital per share, and increase the number of shares issued. Overall, they have no impact on the financial position of the firm.

2. Prepare a statement of retained earnings. Additions to retained earnings include net income, corrections of understatements of prior years' net income, and increases due to the cumulative effect of a change in accounting principle. Deductions consist of net loss, corrections of overstatements of prior years' net income, decreases due to the cumulative effect of a change in accounting principle, and cash and stock dividends.

3. Prepare the shareholders' equity section of a balance sheet. A shareholders' equity section consists of two subsections: share capital (contributed if stated or par values exist) and retained earnings. It should also include notes to the financial statements that explain adjustments to opening retained earnings, restrictions on retained earnings, and dividends in arrears, if any.

4. Illustrate the proper form and content of corporation income statements. The form and content of corporation income statements are similar to the statements of proprietorships and partnerships with one exception. Income tax expense must be reported in a separate section before net income in the corporation's income statement.

5. Explain the concept of intraperiod tax allocation and illustrate its impact on the financial statements. Intraperiod tax allocation refers to associating income tax with the specific item that directly affects the income tax for the period.

6. Illustrate the statement presentation of material items not typical of regular operations. Material items not typical of regular operations are reported net of income tax on the income statement immediately before net income. These items include (a) discontinued operations, and (b) extraordinary items.

7. Calculate earnings and dividend ratios. Earnings (loss) per share is calculated by dividing net income (loss) available to the common shareholders by the number of common shares. When preferred dividends exist, they must be deducted from net income. The price-earnings ratio is calculated by dividing the share price by the earnings per share. The payout ratio is calculated by dividing cash dividends by net income. The dividend yield is calculated by dividing cash dividends per share by the share price at the time of purchase.

THE NAVIGATOR

GLOSSARY

 Key Term Matching Activity

Cash dividend A pro rata (equal) distribution of cash to shareholders. (p. 691)

Change in accounting principle The use of a generally accepted accounting principle in the current year that is different from the one used in the preceding year. (p. 700)

Correction of a prior period error The correction of an error in previously issued financial statements. (p. 699)

Declaration date The date the board of directors formally declares a dividend and announces it to shareholders. (p. 692)

Deficit A debit (negative) balance in retained earnings. (p. 698)

Discontinued operations. The disposal of a significant segment of a business. (p. 706)

Dividend A distribution of cash or shares by a corporation to its shareholders on a pro rata (equal) basis. (p. 690)

Dividend yield—Indicates how much income is generated by each common share. It is calculated by dividing cash dividends per share by the share price at the time of purchase. (p. 712)

Earnings per share (EPS) The net income (or loss) earned by each common share. (p. 710)

Extraordinary items Events and transactions that are infrequent, atypical, and not at the discretion of management or owners. (p. 707)

Interperiod tax allocation The allocation of income tax expense between two or more periods to record the amount which is currently due and the amount which is due in the future (deferred). (p. 705)

Intraperiod tax allocation The procedure of associating income tax expense with the specific item that directly affects the income tax for the period. (p. 706)

Payment date The date cash dividend cheques are mailed to shareholders. For a stock dividend, the date the shares are distributed to shareholders. (p. 692)

Payout ratio Measures the percentage of earnings distributed in the form of cash dividends. It is calculated by dividing cash dividends by net income. (p. 711)

Price-earnings (PE) ratio The ratio of the price of a common share to earnings per common share. (p. 711)

Record date The date when ownership of shares is determined for dividend purposes. (p. 692)

Retained earnings restrictions Circumstances that make a portion of retained earnings currently unavailable for dividends. (p. 698)

Statement of retained earnings A financial statement that shows the changes in retained earnings during the year. (p. 701)

Stock dividend A pro rata (equal) distribution of the corporation's own shares to shareholders. (p. 693)

Stock split The issue of additional shares to shareholders according to their percentage ownership, accompanied by a reduction in the legal value per share. (p. 695)

SELF-STUDY QUESTIONS

 Chapter 15 Self-Test

Answers are at the end of the chapter.

(SO 1) K 1. Entries for cash dividends are required on the:
   a. declaration date and payment date.
   b. record date and payment date.
   c. declaration date, record date, and payment date.
   d. declaration date and record date.

(SO 1) K 2. Which of the following statements about stock dividends is true?
   a. A stock dividend increases total shareholders' equity.
   b. A stock dividend decreases total shareholders' equity.
   c. Market value per share is usually assigned to the dividend shares.
   d. A stock dividend ordinarily will have no effect on book value per share.

(SO 2) K 3. Which one of the following is not reported in a statement of retained earnings?
   a. Cash and stock dividends
   b. Stock splits
   c. Corrections of errors in income of prior periods
   d. Changes in accounting principles

(SO 2) K 4. A prior period adjustment is:
   a. reported in the income statement as a non-typical item.
   b. reported directly in the shareholders' equity section.
   c. reported in the statement of retained earnings as an adjustment of the opening balance of retained earnings.
   d. reported in the statement of retained earnings as an adjustment of the ending balance of retained earnings.

(SO 3) K 5. In the balance sheet, Stock Dividends Distributable is reported as:
   a. a deduction from shareholders' equity.
   b. an addition to share capital.
   c. a deduction from retained earnings.
   d. a current liability.

(SO 4) K 6. Corporation income statements may be the same as the income statements for unincorporated companies, except for:
   a. gross profit.
   b. income tax expense.
   c. operating income.
   d. net sales.

(SO 5) K 7. Intraperiod tax allocation refers to the:
   a. association of income tax with the items that directly affect the income tax expense for the period.
   b. allocation of income tax to different accounting periods.
   c. payment of income tax by instalments.
   d. reporting of income tax by interim accounting periods.

(SO 6) K 8. In reporting discontinued operations, the income statement should have a special section that shows:
   a. gains and losses from the disposal of the discontinued segment.
   b. gains and losses from operations of the discontinued segment.
   c. Both (a) and (b)
   d. Neither (a) nor (b)

(SO 6) AP 9. The Rand Corporation has income before tax of $400,000, including an extraordinary loss of $100,000. If the income tax rate is 25% on all items, the income statement should show income before extraordinary items and after extraordinary items, respectively, of:
   a. $300,000 and $225,000.
   b. $375,000 and $300,000.
   c. $400,000 and $300,000.
   d. $500,000 and $400,000.

(SO 7) AP 10. The income statement for Nadeen, Inc., shows income before income tax of $700,000, income tax expense of $210,000, and net income of $490,000. If Nadeen has 100,000 common shares, earnings per share is:
   a. $2.10.
   b. $4.90.
   c. $7.00.
   d. No correct answer is given.

(SO 7) C 11. Bernard Dupuis is nearing retirement and would like to invest in shares that will provide a steady income. Bernard should choose shares with a:
   a. high earnings per share.
   b. high price-earnings ratio.
   c. high payout ratio.
   d. high dividend yield.

THE NAVIGATOR

QUESTIONS

(SO 1) C
1. (a) What is a dividend?
   (b) "Dividends must be paid in cash." Do you agree? Explain.

(SO 1) C
2. Robin O'Malley maintains that adequate cash is the only requirement for the declaration of a cash dividend. Is Robin correct? Explain.

(SO 1) C
3. (a) Three dates are important in connection with cash dividends. Identify these dates, and explain their significance to the corporation and its shareholders.
   (b) Identify the journal entries that are made for a cash dividend on each of the above dates.

(SO 1) C
4. Contrast the effects of a cash dividend and a stock dividend on (a) a corporation's balance sheet and (b) an individual shareholder's personal financial position.

(SO 1) C
5. Jill Simmons asks, "Since stock dividends don't change anything, why declare them?" What is your answer to Jill?

(SO 1) AP
6. Pella Corporation has 10,000 common shares when it announces a 2-for-1 split. Before the split, the shares had a market price of $140 per share. After the split, how many shares will be issued? What will be the approximate market price per share?

(SO 1) C
7. The board of directors is considering either a stock split or a stock dividend. It understands that total shareholders' equity will remain the same under either action. However, it is not sure of the different effects of the two types of actions on the components of shareholders' equity. Explain the differences to the directors.

(SO 2) C
8. What is a prior period adjustment? How is it reported in the financial statements?

(SO 2) AP
9. ABC Corporation has a retained earnings balance of $240,000 on January 1. During the year, a correction of a prior period error of $90,000 before income tax of 25% is recorded because of the understatement of amortization in the prior period. Show the presentation of this information in the statement of retained earnings.

(SO 2) C
10. (a) What is the purpose of a retained earnings restriction?
    (b) Identify the possible causes of retained earnings restrictions.

(SO 2) K
11. How are retained earnings restrictions generally reported in the financial statements?

(SO 2) C
12. Identify the events that result in increases (credits) and decreases (debits) to retained earnings.

(SO 2) C
13. When studying for an accounting test, a fellow student says, "Changes in accounting principles are reported in the statement of retained earnings." Is your friend correct, or should he study harder?

(SO 3) C
14. Omar Radhah believes that both the beginning and ending balances in retained earnings are shown in the shareholders' equity section. Is Omar correct? Discuss.

(SO 3) AP
15. Indicate how each of the following accounts should be classified in the shareholders' equity section of the balance sheet.
    (a) Common shares
    (b) Preferred shares
    (c) Stock dividends distributable
    (d) Contributed capital in excess of stated value
    (e) Retained earnings

(SO 4) C
16. Nels Olsen, who owns many investments in common shares, says, "I don't care what a company's net income is. The balance sheet tells me everything I need to know!" How do you respond to Nels?

(SO 4) AP
17. What is the unique feature of a corporation income statement? Illustrate this feature, using assumed data.

(SO 5) C
18. Define the term "intraperiod tax allocation." Why is this type of allocation important?

(SO 6) C
19. Why is it important to report discontinued operations separately from income from continuing operations?

(SO 6) C
20. Indicate which of the following items would be reported as an extraordinary item in Corus Corporation's income statement:
    (a) Loss from damages caused by earthquake tremors
    (b) Loss from sale of short-term investments
    (c) Loss attributable to a labour strike
    (d) Loss caused when manufacture of a product was prohibited by the federal government
    (e) Loss from flood damage (the nearby Black River floods every two to three years)
    (f) Write-down of obsolete inventory
    (g) Expropriation of a factory by a foreign government

(SO 7) C
21. You are considering investing in Track Transportation. The company reports 2003 earnings per share of $6.50 on income before extraordinary items and $4.75 on net income. Which EPS figure would you consider more relevant to your investment decision? Why?

(SO 7) C
22. Holding all other factors constant, indicate whether each of the following is generally considered favourable or unfavourable by a potential investor:
    (a) Increase in earnings per share
    (b) Decrease in the price-earnings ratio
    (c) Increase in the payout ratio
    (d) Decrease in the dividend yield

BRIEF EXERCISES

••

Prepare entries for cash dividend.
(SO 1) AP

BE15–1   The Boudin Corporation has 50,000 common shares. It declares a $2 per share cash dividend on November 1 to shareholders of record on December 1. The dividend is paid on December 31. Prepare the entries on the appropriate dates to record the cash dividend.

Prepare entries for stock dividend.
(SO 1) AP

BE15–2   Patina Corporation has 80,000 no par value common shares. It declares a 10% stock dividend on December 1, when the market value per share is $15. The dividend shares are issued on December 31. Prepare the entries for the declaration and distribution of the stock dividend.

Show before and after effects of stock dividend.
(SO 1) AP

BE15–3   The shareholders' equity section of Mertz Corporation consists of 100,000 no par value common shares worth $1,000,000, and retained earnings of $300,000. A 10% stock dividend is declared when the market value per share is $16. For each of the following, write the amounts before and after declaration to show the effects of the dividend on the (a) common shares, (b) retained earnings, (c) total shareholders' equity, (d) shares issued, and (e) book value per share.

Analyse impact of stock split.
(SO 1) AP

BE15–4   North Vancouver–based **CyPost Corp.** is a hot share with a hot e-mail encryption product. On October 12, CyPost split its shares 3-for-2. Prior to the split, its share price was $12. What would you anticipate its share price to be immediately after the split? Explain why CyPost, a relatively new company, might split its shares.

Prepare statement of retained earnings.
(SO 2) AP

BE15–5   For the year ending December 31, 2003, Cadien Inc. reports net income, $150,000, and dividends, $85,000. Prepare the statement of retained earnings for the year, assuming the balance in retained earnings on January 1, 2003, was $220,000.

Explain how a change in accounting principle is reported.
(SO 2) AP

BE15–6   On January 1, 2003, Ouellet, Inc. changed from the straight-line method of amortization to the declining-balance method. The cumulative effect of the change was to increase prior years' amortization by $70,000 and 2003 amortization by $8,000. Explain how the company should report the effects of this change on (a) prior years, and (b) the current year. The income tax rate is 30%.

Prepare shareholders' equity section.
(SO 3) AP

BE15–7   Ménard Corporation has these accounts at December 31, 2003: Common Shares, no par value, unlimited number authorized, 5,000 issued, $50,000; Stock Dividend Distributable, $15,000; and Retained Earnings, $29,000. Of the retained earnings, $20,000 has been restricted because of loan agreements. Prepare the shareholders' equity section of the balance sheet.

Prepare extraordinary item section of income statement.
(SO 4, 5) AN

BE15–8   An inexperienced accountant for Tec.com Corporation showed the following in the income statement: Income before income tax and extraordinary item, $300,000, and extraordinary loss from flood (before tax), $80,000. The extraordinary loss and taxable income are both subject to a 25% tax rate. Prepare a correct income statement for the year ended November 30, 2003.

Prepare discontinued operations section of income statement.
(SO 5, 6) AP

BE15–9   On June 30, Osbern Corporation discontinued its operations in Mexico. During the year, the operating loss on these operations was $300,000 before income tax. On September 1, Osbern disposed of the Mexico facility at a pre-tax loss of $160,000. The applicable tax rate is 35%. Show the discontinued operations section of the income statement for the year ended December 31, 2003.

Show earnings per share data in income statement.
(SO 7) AP

BE15–10   Richelieu Corporation's income statement shows the following: Income from continuing operations, $580,000, loss from discontinued operations, $200,000, and extraordinary loss, $90,000. Show the earnings per share data that should be presented in the income statement, assuming there are 100,000 common shares.

Calculate earnings per share, with and without preferred shares.
(SO 7) AP

BE15–11   Darlin Corporation reports net income of $370,000 and 200,000 common shares.
  (a) Calculate the earnings per share.
  (b) Assume also that Darlin has cumulative preferred dividends for the current year of $20,000 that were declared and paid. Recalculate the earnings per share.
  (c) Assume that the preferred dividends referred to in part (b) were not declared and paid. What difference would this make in calculating the earnings per share?

Explain effects of stock dividend and stock splits on price-earnings ratio.
(SO 1, 7) AP

BE15–12   Lake Company reports earnings per share of $5.00. Its common shares are currently selling at $52.50 per share. Explain how its price-earnings ratio would be affected by (a) a 2% stock dividend and (b) a 2-for-1 stock split.

Calculate payout ratio and dividend yield.
(SO 7) AP

BE15–13   Madeleine Argonne purchased 100 common shares in Pepin Company for $25 per share. Pepin paid a $1 per share cash dividend to its common shareholders in 2002. For the same year, it reported earnings per share of $3.75. Calculate the payout ratio and dividend yield.

EXERCISES

··

E15–1 The Oshawa Corporation was organized on January 1, 2002. During its first year, the corporation issued 2,000 no par value preferred shares and 100,000 no par value common shares. At December 31 of each year, the company declared the following cash dividends: for 2002, $6,000; for 2003, $12,000; and for 2004, $28,000.

Allocate cash dividends to preferred and common shareholders. (SO 1) AP

Instructions

(a) Show the allocation of dividends to preferred and common shareholders for each year, assuming the preferred share dividend is $4.00 and noncumulative.

(b) Show the allocation of dividends to preferred and common shareholders for each year, assuming the preferred share dividend is $5.00 and cumulative.

(c) Journalize the declaration of the cash dividend for the year 2004, under each of part (a) and (b).

E15–2 On October 31, the shareholders' equity section of Laine Company consists of common shares, $800,000 and retained earnings, $400,000. The company is considering the following two courses of action: (1) declaring a 5% stock dividend on the 80,000 no par value shares, or (2) effecting a 2-for-1 stock split. The current market price is $14 per share.

Compare effects of stock dividend and stock split. (SO 1) AP

Instructions

Prepare a tabular summary of the effects that the alternative actions would have on the shareholders' equity accounts, the number of shares, and the book value per share. Use the following column headings: Before Action, After Stock Dividend, and After Stock Split.

E15–3 On October 1, Valen Corporation's shareholders' equity is as follows:

Calculate book value per share; indicate account balances after stock dividend. (SO 1) AP

VALEN CORPORATION
Balance Sheet (partial)
October 1, 2003

Shareholders' equity	
Common shares, no par value (20,000 shares issued)	$225,000
Retained earnings	175,000
Total shareholders' equity	$400,000

On October 1, Valen declares and distributes a 10% stock dividend when the market value of the shares is $18 per share.

Instructions

(a) Calculate the book value per share (1) before the stock dividend, and (2) after the stock dividend. (Round to two decimals.)

(b) Indicate the balances in the shareholders' equity accounts after the dividend shares have been distributed.

E15–4 Before preparing financial statements for the current year, the chief accountant for Kaufel Ltd. discovered the following errors in the accounts:

Prepare correcting entries for dividends and stock split. (SO 1) AP

1. The declaration and payment of a $30,000 cash dividend was recorded as a debit to Dividends Expense of $30,000 and a credit to Cash of $30,000.

2. A 10% stock dividend (1,000 shares) was declared on the no par value common shares when the market value per share was $10. The only entry made was as follows: (Dr.) Retained Earnings $10,000 and (Cr.) Dividend Payable $10,000. The shares have not been issued.

3. The company declared a 4-for-1 stock split involving the issue of 400,000 $5 stated value preferred shares for 100,000 $20 stated value preferred shares. The split was recorded as a debit to Retained Earnings of $2,000,000 and a credit to Preferred Shares of $2,000,000.

Instructions

Prepare the correcting entries.

E15–5 On January 1, Tashia Corporation had 75,000 no par value common shares. During the year, the following occurred:

Journalize cash dividends and indicate statement presentation. (SO 1, 2) AP

  Apr. 1 Issued 5,000 additional common shares for $17 per share.
 June 15 Declared a cash dividend of $1 per share to shareholders of record on June 30.
 July 10 Paid the $1 cash dividend.
  Dec. 1 Issued 2,000 additional common shares for $19 per share.
      15 Declared a cash dividend of $1.30 per share to shareholders of record on December 31.

Instructions

(a) Prepare the entries required to record the above transactions.

(b) How are dividends and dividends payable reported in the financial statements prepared at December 31, Tashia's year end?

Prepare statement of retained earnings.
(SO 2) AP

E15–6 On January 1, 2003, Windsor Corporation had Retained Earnings of $580,000. During the year, Windsor had the following selected transactions:

1. Declared cash dividends, $120,000.
2. Corrected overstatement of 2002 net income because of amortization error, $20,000 (net of $15,000 income tax).
3. Earned net income, $350,000.
4. Declared stock dividends, $60,000.

Instructions

Prepare a statement of retained earnings for the year ended December 31, 2003.

Indicate various effects on shareholders' equity components.
(SO 1, 2, 3) AP

E15–7 During 2003, Kettle Corporation had the following transactions and events:

1. Declared a cash dividend.
2. Issued no par value common shares for cash.
3. Completed a 3-for-1 stock split.
4. Declared a stock dividend.
5. Made a prior period correction for overstatement of net income.
6. Issued the common shares required by the stock dividend declaration in (4) above.
7. Paid the cash dividend declared in (1) above.
8. Issued stated value preferred shares for cash, at a price above stated value.

Instructions

Indicate the effect(s) of each of the above items on the subdivisions of shareholders' equity. Present your answer in tabular form with the following columns. Use "I" for increase, "D" for decrease, and "NE" for no effect. Item 1 is given as an example.

	Contributed Capital			
Item	Share Capital	Additional	Retained Earnings	Total Shareholders' Equity
1.	NE	NE	D	D

Journalize stock dividend; prepare shareholders' equity section.
(SO 1, 3) AP

E15–8 On January 1, 2003, Knowledge Corporation had an unlimited number of no par value common shares authorized, of which 150,000 had been issued for $1,500,000, and retained earnings of $750,000. The company issued 50,000 common shares at $14 on July 1, and earned net income of $400,000 for the year.

Instructions

(a) Journalize the declaration of a 15% stock dividend on December 10, 2003, when the market value is $16 per share.

(b) Prepare the shareholders' equity section at December 31, 2003, assuming that the stock dividend has not yet been distributed.

Prepare shareholders' equity section.
(SO 3) AP

E15–9 The following accounts appear in the ledger of Byung-Kee Inc. after the books are closed at December 31:

Common Shares, no par value, 400,000 shares authorized,	
300,000 shares issued	$866,000
Common Stock Dividends Distributable	75,000
8% Preferred Shares, $5 stated value, cumulative, 40,000	
shares authorized, 30,000 shares issued	150,000
Retained Earnings	900,000
Contributed Capital in Excess of Stated Value—Preferred Shares	244,000

Instructions

Prepare the shareholders' equity section of the balance sheet at December 31, 2003, assuming $100,000 of retained earnings is restricted for a plant expansion.

E15–10 For its fiscal year ending October 31, 2003, Grometer Corporation reports the following partial data:

Prepare corrected income statement and comment.
(SO 4, 5, 6) S

GROMETER CORPORATION
Income Statement (partial)
For the Year Ended October 31, 2003

Income before income tax	$640,000
Income tax expense (30% × $540,000)	162,000
Income before extraordinary items	478,000
Extraordinary loss from fire	100,000
Net income	$378,000

The fire loss is an extraordinary item. The income tax rate is 30% on all items.

Instructions

(a) Prepare a corrected income statement, beginning with income from continuing operations.
(b) Explain, in memo form, why the original income statement data are misleading.

E15–11 Dasola Corporation has income from continuing operations of $240,000 for the year ended December 31, 2003. It also has the following items (before considering income tax): (1) an extraordinary loss of $80,000, (2) a gain of $50,000 on the discontinuation of a division, (3) a change in an accounting principle that resulted in an increase in prior years' amortization of $35,000, and (4) a correction of an error in last year's financial statements that resulted in a $20,000 understatement of 2002 net income. Assume all items are subject to a 30% income tax rate.

Prepare income statement with non-typical items.
(SO 4, 5, 6) AP

Instructions

(a) Prepare an income statement, beginning with income from continuing operations.
(b) Indicate the statement presentation of any items not included in (a) above.

E15–12 At December 31, 2003, Morse Corporation has 2,000 no par value $8 cumulative preferred shares and 100,000 no par value common shares. Morse's net income for the year is $547,000.

Calculate earnings per share under different dividend assumptions.
(SO 7) AP

Instructions

Calculate the earnings per share for each of the following separate situations. (Round to two decimals.)

(a) The dividend to preferred shareholders was declared.
(b) The dividend to preferred shareholders was not declared.

E15–13 The following financial information is available for the **Bank of Montreal** as at October 31, 2000, 1999, and 1998:

Calculate ratios to evaluate earnings and dividend performance.
(SO 7) AP

	2000	1999	1998
Net income (in millions)	$1,857	$1,382	$1,350
Number of common shares	265,659,000	265,862,000	262,511,000
Dividends per common share	$2.00	$1.88	$1.76
Market price of common shares	$45.88	$32.72	$36.65

Instructions

Calculate the earnings per share, price-earnings ratio, payout ratio, and dividend yield for each of the three years. Comment on the Bank of Montreal's earnings and dividend performance.

PROBLEMS: SET A

Compare impact of cash and stock dividends on company and shareholder.
(SO 1) AN

P15–1A   The condensed balance sheet of Laporte Corporation reports the following amounts:

LAPORTE CORPORATION
Balance Sheet (partial)
June 30, 2003

Total assets	$13,500,000
Liabilities and shareholders' equity	
Total liabilities	$ 1,500,000
Shareholders' equity	
Common shares, 50,000 shares authorized,	
40,000 shares issued, no par value	2,000,000
Retained earnings	10,000,000
Total shareholders' equity	12,000,000
Total liabilities and shareholders' equity	$13,500,000

Laporte wishes to assess the impact of two possible dividend alternatives on the corporation and its shareholders.

1. Payment of a $2 per share cash dividend.
2. Distribution of a 5% stock dividend. The market price of the common shares is currently $40 per share.

Instructions

(a) Determine the impact on assets, liabilities, shareholders' equity (common shares and retained earnings), and the number of shares of each of the two alternatives for Laporte Corporation.
(b) 1. Assess the impact of each alternative from a shareholder's perspective. Which alternative is more beneficial for the shareholder? Assume the shareholder currently owns 1,000 common shares at a cost of $35,000.
   2. How would shareholders record receipt of the cash dividend or stock dividend on their own records?

Prepare statement of retained earnings, reflecting dividends and correction of error.
(SO 1, 2) AP

P15–2A   The shareholders' equity accounts of Tmao, Inc. at 1, 2003, are as follows:

TMAO INC.
Balance Sheet (partial)
January 1, 2003

Shareholders' equity	
Preferred shares, no par value, 100,000 shares authorized,	
4,000 shares issued	$ 400,000
Common shares, no par value, 500,000 shares authorized,	
180,000 shares issued	900,000
Retained earnings	500,000
Total shareholders' equity	$1,800,000

During 2003, the company had the following transactions and events:

July 1 Declared a $0.25 cash dividend to common shareholders.
Aug. 1 Discovered a $72,000 overstatement of 2002 amortization. The income tax effect of this error is $22,000.
Sept. 1 Paid the cash dividend declared on July 1.
Dec. 1 Declared a 10% common stock dividend when the market value of the shares was $15 per share.
   15 Declared a $10 per share cash dividend to preferred shareholders, payable January 31, 2004.
   31 Determined that net income for the year was $350,000.

Instructions

Prepare a statement of retained earnings for the year ended December 31, 2003. There are no preferred dividends in arrears.

P15–3A On January 1, 2003, Cedeno Inc. had the following shareholders' equity balances:

Journalize and post transactions; prepare shareholders' equity section.
(SO 1, 2, 3) AP

CEDENO INC.
Balance Sheet (partial)
January 1, 2003

Shareholders' equity

Common shares, no par value (unlimited number of shares authorized, 500,000 shares issued)	$1,500,000
Stock dividends distributable	200,000
Retained earnings	600,000
Total shareholders' equity	$2,300,000

During 2003, the following transactions and events occurred:

Jan. 20 Issued 50,000 common shares as a result of a 10% stock dividend declared on December 15, 2002.

Feb. 12 Issued 30,000 common shares for cash at $5 per share.

Mar. 31 Corrected an error that had understated the cost of goods sold for 2002 by $70,000. The income tax effect of this error was $20,000.

Dec. 31 Declared and paid a cash dividend of $100,000.

    31 Earned net income of $300,000 (total revenues, $900,000; total expenses, $600,000).

Instructions

(a) Journalize the transactions and summary closing entries for revenues, expenses, and dividends.

(b) Enter the beginning balances, and post the entries in (a) to the shareholders' equity accounts. (*Note*: Open additional shareholders' equity accounts as needed.)

(c) Prepare the shareholders' equity section of the balance sheet at December 31, 2003.

P15–4A On January 1, 2003, LeBlanc Corporation had the following shareholders' equity accounts:

Prepare dividend entries and shareholders' equity section.
(SO 1, 3) AP

LEBLANC CORPORATION
Balance Sheet (partial)
January 1, 2003

Shareholders' equity

Common shares (no par value, unlimited number of shares authorized, 70,000 shares issued)	$ 900,000
Retained earnings	540,000
Total shareholders' equity	$1,440,000

During the year, the following transactions occurred:

Jan. 15 Declared a $1 cash dividend per share to shareholders of record on January 31, payable February 15.

Feb. 15 Paid the dividend declared in January.

Apr. 15 Declared a 10% stock dividend to shareholders of record on April 30, distributable May 15. On April 15, the market price of each share was $13.

May 15 Issued the shares for the stock dividend.

July 1 Announced a 2-for-1 stock split. The market price per share prior to the announcement was $15.

Dec. 1 Declared a $0.50 per share cash dividend to shareholders of record on December 15, payable January 10, 2004.

    31 Determined that net income for the year was $250,000 (total revenues, $1,000,000; total expenses, $750,000).

Instructions

(a) Journalize the transactions and the summary closing entries for revenues, expenses, and dividends.

(b) Enter the beginning balances and post the entries in part (a) to the shareholders' equity accounts. (*Note*: Open additional shareholders' equity accounts as needed.)

(c) Prepare the shareholders' equity section of the balance sheet at December 31, 2003.

Allocate dividend. Prepare state-
ment of retained earnings and
shareholders' equity section,
reflecting various events.
(SO 1, 2, 3) AP

P15–5A   After the books have been closed, the ledger of Jajoo Corporation at December 31, 2003, contains the following shareholders' equity accounts:

Preferred Shares (10,000 shares issued)	$1,200,000
Common Shares (400,000 shares issued)	2,000,000
Contributed Capital in Excess of Stated Value—Common	1,100,000
Common Stock Dividend Distributable	140,000
Retained Earnings	2,590,000

A review of the accounting records reveals the following:

1. Preferred shares are no par value, noncumulative, with a $10 dividend. Since January 1, 2003, 10,000 shares have been issued; 20,000 shares are authorized.
2. Common shares are no par value, with a stated value of $5 per share; 600,000 shares are authorized.
3. The January 1 balance in Retained Earnings was $2,450,000.
4. On October 1, 100,000 common shares were sold for cash at $8 per share.
5. A cash dividend of $600,000 was declared and properly allocated to preferred and common shares on November 1. No dividends were paid to preferred shareholders in 2002.
6. On December 31, a 5% common stock dividend was declared when the market price per share was $7.
7. Net income for the year was $880,000.
8. On December 31, 2003, the directors authorized a $100,000 restriction of retained earnings for a plant expansion.

Instructions

(a) Calculate the allocation of the cash dividend to preferred and common shareholders.
(b) Prepare a statement of retained earnings for the year ended December 31, 2003.
(c) Prepare the shareholders' equity section of the balance sheet at December 31, 2003.

Prepare income statement, with
non-typical items including
earnings per share data.
(SO 4, 5, 6, 7) AP

P15–6A   The ledger of Hyperchip Corporation at November 30, 2003, contains the following summary data:

Net sales	$1,400,000
Cost of goods sold	800,000
Selling expenses	110,000
Administrative expenses	140,000
Other revenues and gains	40,000
Other expenses and losses	30,000

Your analysis reveals the following additional information that is *not included in the above data*:

1. The entire ceramics division was discontinued on August 31. The loss from operations for this division before income tax was $150,000. The ceramics division was sold at a pre-tax gain of $60,000.
2. On July 12, a transport truck crashed into one of the company's plants. This resulted in an extraordinary loss of $90,000 before income tax.
3. During the year, Hyperchip changed its amortization method from straight-line to declining-balance. The cumulative effect of the change on prior years' net income was a decrease of $30,000 before income tax. (Assume that amortization under the new method is correctly included in the ledger data for the current year.)
4. The income tax rate on all items is 30%.

Instructions

(a) Prepare an income statement for the year ended November 30, 2003.
(b) Prepare the earnings per share data that should appear in the income statement, assuming there were 100,000 common shares.

Prepare income statement and
statement of retained earnings,
with non-typical items.
(SO 2, 4, 5) AP

P15–7A   The following is a partial trial balance for Blue Bay Limited for the year ended December 31, 2003:

Amortization expense	$ (363,000)
Change in accounting policy	(166,000)
Common shares (32,500 shares issued)	250,000
Cost of goods sold	(7,220,000)
Dividends	(30,000)
Extraordinary gain	102,000
Income tax expense[1]	(37,000)

Loss from discontinued operations	(245,000)
Operating expenses	(1,219,000)
Retained earnings, January 1, 2003	979,000
Sales	9,214,000

¹ Income tax expense can be allocated to the following items:

Change in accounting policy	$ 40,000
Extraordinary gain	(25,000)
Loss from discontinued operations	63,000
Continuing operations	(115,000)
Total	($37,000)

Instructions

(a) Using the information on Blue Bay, prepare, in proper form, a multiple-step income statement for the year ended December 31, 2003.

(b) Using the information on Blue Bay, prepare, in proper form, a statement of retained earnings for the year ended December 31, 2003.

Source: Adapted from Certified General Accountants Association of Canada, *Financial Accounting 2 Examination*, June 2000, Question 8.

P15–8A The following selected information is available for the **Canadian National Railway Company (CN)** (in millions, except for market price per common share):

Calculate earnings and dividend ratios and comment.
(SO 7) AP

	December 31, 2000	December 31, 1999
Number of common shares	197.9	199.3
Net income	$772	$602
Common cash dividends	$136	$118
Preferred cash dividends	$11	$9
Market price per common share	$44.35	$38.20

Instructions

(a) Calculate the following ratios for CN for 2000 and 1999:
   1. Earnings per share
   2. Price-earnings ratio
   3. Payout ratio (for common shares only)
   4. Dividend yield (for common shares only)

(b) Comment on the above ratios for 2000, in comparison to the prior year, 1999.

PROBLEMS: SET B

• •

P15–1B Gull Lake Enterprises Inc. has 100,000 no par value common shares outstanding at July 1, 2003, the beginning of the current fiscal year. Mark Bradbury is the president and largest shareholder of Gull Lake Enterprises and owns 18% of the common shares. On July 1, the common shares were trading for $25 per share. On July 1, 2003, Gull Lake Enterprises' retained earnings were $120,000 and the Common Shares account had a book value of $2,000,000.

Compare impact of equity transactions on company and on shareholder.
(SO 1, 2, 3) AN

You are provided with the following information about selected events and transactions that occurred during the year:

1. On August 1, Mark issued a press release stating that the company was very close to closing a lucrative deal to supply products to two neighbouring provinces. The company's share price immediately jumped by 6%.

2. On August 31, Gull Lake declared and issued a 4% stock dividend. The shares were trading at $28 per share on that day.

3. On November 1, 2003, Mark issued another press release concerning the imminent deal with the provinces. The company's shares were now trading at $32 per share.

4. On December 1, 2003, the company issued another 20,000 no par value common shares. This issue was needed in order to finance new product development. Mark Bradbury acquired 3,600 of these shares in order to maintain his 18% interest in the shares of the company. The market value was $30 per share.

5. By March 31, 2004, investors were growing weary of waiting for the company to close the deal that Mark had discussed in the press releases. On that date, the company's shares were trading at $26 per share and the company effected a 2-for-1 stock split. After the stock split, each share was trading at $13.
6. By June 30, 2004, the products were still in development. The company's income statement for the year showed considerable expenses related to product development. This contributed to the company's net loss for the fiscal year of $42,000. The share price at the close of business on June 30, 2004, was $10.50.

Instructions

(a) Prepare a schedule illustrating the impact of each transaction on the following:
1. The balance of retained earnings (deficit)
2. The number of shares issued by Gull Lake
3. The number of shares held by Mark Bradbury
4. The market value of Mark Bradbury's portfolio of common shares
(b) Comment on the change in retained earnings and the change in the market value of Mark Bradbury's portfolio during the fiscal year ended June 30, 2004

Journalize dividend transactions; prepare shareholders' equity section.
(SO 1,3) AP

P15–2B   Cash and Kind Corporation's equity appeared as follows on September 20, 2003:

CASH AND KIND CORPORATION
Balance Sheet (partial)
September 20, 2003

Shareholders' equity

Common shares, no par value, 50,000 shares issued	$465,000
Retained earnings	245,000
Total shareholders' equity	$710,000

On September 20, 2003, when the shares were selling at $8, the directors voted in favour of a 20% stock dividend and a $2 per share cash dividend. Both the cash and stock dividends were to be distributed on October 15 to the shareholders of record as at September 27. The market prices of common shares on September 27 and October 15, 2003, were $10 and $11, respectively.

Instructions

(a) Prepare journal entries to record the declaration of the stock and cash dividends on September 20, 2003.
(b) Prepare the shareholders' equity section of the balance sheet after the dividend payments on October 15, 2003. Assume there were no other transactions affecting the shareholders' equity section between September 20 and October 15, 2003.

Source: Adapted from the Certified General Accountants Association of Canada, *Financial Accounting 1 Examination*, December 1999, Question 6.

Journalize and post transactions; prepare shareholders' equity section.
(SO 1, 2, 3) AP

P15–3B   The shareholders' equity accounts of Fryman Company Ltd. at January 1, 2003, are as follows:

FRYMAN COMPANY LTD.
Balance Sheet (partial)
January 1, 2003

Shareholders' equity

Preferred shares, no par value, 100,000 shares authorized, 12,000 shares issued	$ 800,000
Common shares, no par value, 1,000,000 shares authorized, 250,000 shares issued	500,000
Retained earnings	900,000
Total shareholders' equity	$2,200,000

During 2003, the company had the following transactions and events:

July 7   Declared a $0.50 cash dividend on common shares.
Aug. 1   Discovered a $45,000 overstatement of 2002 amortization. The income tax effect of this error was $15,000.
Sept. 1   Paid the cash dividend declared on July 1.
Dec. 1   Declared a 10% stock dividend on common shares when the market value of the shares

was $18 per share.

15 Declared a $4.50 cash dividend on preferred shares, payable January 15, 2004. This was the full regular annual dividend on the preferred shares; there are no dividends in arrears.

31 Determined that net income for the year was $385,000 (total revenues, $900,000; total expenses, $515,000).

31 Recognized a $200,000 restriction of retained earnings for a plant expansion.

Instructions

(a) Journalize the transactions and summary closing entries.

(b) Enter the beginning balances in the accounts and post to the shareholders' equity accounts. (Note: Open additional shareholders' equity accounts as needed.)

(c) Prepare the shareholders' equity section of the balance sheet at December 31, 2003.

P15–4B On January 1, 2003, Asaad Corporation had the following shareholders' equity accounts:

Prepare dividend entries and shareholders' equity section.
(SO 1, 3) AP

ASAAD CORPORATION
Balance Sheet (partial)
January 1, 2003

Shareholders' equity

Common shares (no par value, unlimited number of shares authorized, 65,000 shares issued)	$1,500,000
Retained earnings	600,000
Total shareholders' equity	$2,100,000

During the year, the following transactions occurred:

Feb. 1 Declared a $1 cash dividend per share to shareholders of record on February 15, payable March 1.

Mar. 1 Paid the dividend declared in February.

Apr. 1 Announced a 4-for-1 stock split. Prior to the split, the market price per share was $36.

July 1 Declared a 5% stock dividend to shareholders of record on July 15, distributable July 31. On July 1, the market price of the shares was $13 per share.

31 Issued the shares for the stock dividend.

Dec. 1 Declared a $0.50 per share dividend to shareholders of record on December 15, payable January 5, 2004.

31 Determined that net income for the year was $350,000 (total revenues, $900,000; total expenses, $550,000).

Instructions

(a) Journalize the transactions and summary closing entries for revenues, expenses, and dividends.

(b) Enter the beginning balances, and post the entries in (a) to the shareholders' equity accounts. (*Note*: Open additional shareholders' equity accounts as needed.)

(c) Prepare the shareholders' equity section of the balance sheet at December 31, 2003.

P15–5B The post-closing trial balance of Michaud Corporation at December 31, 2003, contains the following shareholders' equity accounts:

Allocate dividend. Prepare statement of retained earnings and shareholders' equity section; calculate earnings per share and price-earnings ratios.
(SO 1, 2, 3, 7) AP

Preferred Shares (15,000 shares issued)	$1,000,000
Common Shares (250,000 shares issued)	2,900,000
Common Stock Dividends Distributable	320,000
Retained Earnings	1,053,000

A review of the accounting records reveals the following:

1. Preferred shares are no par value, with cumulative dividends of $5 per share.

2. An unlimited number of preferred shares, and 500,000 common shares with no par value are authorized.

3. The January 1 balance in Retained Earnings was $1,170,000.

4. On July 1, 20,000 common shares were sold for cash at $16 per share.

5. On September 1, the company discovered an error of $60,000 that understated amortization expense in 2002. The net-of-tax effect of $42,000 was properly debited to Retained Earnings.

6. A cash dividend of $250,000 was declared and properly allocated to preferred and common shareholders on October 1. No dividends were paid to preferred shareholders in 2002.

7. On December 31, an 8% common stock dividend was declared when the market price per share was $16.
8. Net income for the year was $495,000.
9. On December 31, 2003, the directors authorized the disclosure of a $200,000 restriction of retained earnings for a plant expansion.

Instructions

(a) Calculate the allocation of the cash dividend to preferred and common shareholders.
(b) Prepare a statement of retained earnings for the year.
(c) Prepare the shareholders' equity section of the balance sheet as at December 31, 2003.
(d) Calculate the earnings per share. Use the ending balance of common shares as your denominator.
(e) Calculate the price-earnings ratio as at December 31, 2003.

Prepare income statement including earnings per share data and statement of retained earnings, with non-typical items.
(SO 2, 4, 5, 6, 7) AP

P15–6B   The ledger of Zurich Corporation at December 31, 2003, contains the following summary data:

Net sales	$1,700,000
Cost of goods sold	1,000,000
Selling expenses	120,000
Administrative expenses	130,000
Other revenues and gains	20,000
Other expenses and losses	28,000

Your analysis reveals the following additional information that is *not included in the above data*:

1. The entire Personal Communication Devices division was discontinued on August 31. The gain from operations for this division before income taxes was $50,000. The Personal Communication Devices division was sold at a loss of $70,000 before income tax.
2. On May 15, company property was expropriated for a highway. The settlement resulted in an extraordinary gain of $90,000 before income tax.
3. During the year, Zurich changed its amortization method from double declining-balance to straight-line. The cumulative effect of the change on prior years' net income was an increase of $60,000 before tax. Amortization under the new method is correctly included in the ledger data for the current year.
4. The income tax rate on all items is 30%.
5. The retained earnings balance at the beginning of the year was $340,000.
6. Dividends declared during the year totalled $25,000.
7. There were 100,000 common shares.

Instructions

(a) Prepare an income statement for the year, including earnings per share data.
(b) Prepare a statement of retained earnings for the year ended December 31, 2003.

Prepare income statement with non-typical items; show earnings per share data.
(SO 4, 5, 6, 7) AP

P15–7B   Coquitlam Corporation owns a number of travel agencies and a chain of motels in western Canada. Its condensed operating results for the year ended December 31, 2003, show the following:

COQUITLAM CORPORATION
Income Statement (partial)
For the Year Ended December 31, 2003

Operating revenues	$14,800,000
Operating expenses	10,700,000
Income from operations	$ 4,100,000

An additional analysis of the data indicates that the travel agencies are very profitable but that the motel chain has been unprofitable. During the first nine months of 2003, the motels lost $500,000 from operating revenues of $4,200,000 and operating expenses of $4,700,000. On October 1, the motel operation was discontinued and sold at a loss of $1,200,000 before income tax. The motel operating results are included in income from operations, but the loss on disposal is not included in the operating results shown above.

In November, an expropriation action was taken against the company to obtain property for a new national park. As a result, the corporation suffered an extraordinary loss of $800,000 before income tax. That loss is not included in the operating results.

During the year, Coquitlam had other expenses and losses of $80,000, which are not included in the operating results. The corporation is in a 30% income tax bracket. At December 31, Coquitlam has 400,000 common shares.

Instructions

Prepare an income statement for the year, including the earnings per share presentations.

P15–8B The following selected information is available for the Telus Corporation (in millions, except for market price per common share):

Calculate earnings and dividend ratios and comment.
(SO 7) AP

	December 31, 2000	December 31, 1999
Number of common shares	247	236.6
Net income	$461	$349.7
Common cash dividends	$349.5	$331.4
Preferred cash dividends	$3.5	$3.5
Market price per common share	$41.55	$35.15

Instructions

(a) Calculate the following ratios for Telus for 2000 and 1999:
   1. Earnings per share
   2. Price-earnings ratio
   3. Payout ratio (for common shares only)
   4. Dividend yield (for common shares only)
(b) Comment on the above ratios for 2000, in comparison to the prior year, 1999.

Broadening Your Perspective

FINANCIAL REPORTING AND ANALYSIS
••

Financial Reporting Problem

BYP15–1 Refer to the consolidated financial statements, and accompanying notes, for The Second Cup Ltd., which are reproduced in Appendix A.

Instructions

Answer the following questions:
   (a) How many common shares were issued for cash to employees and directors during the year ended June 24, 2000?
   (b) As at June 24, 2000, what percentage of the company assets was financed by shareholders' equity?
   (c) Did the company report any discontinued operations or extraordinary items during the years ended June 24, 2000, and June 30, 1999?
   (d) How much were the earnings (loss) per share for the years ended June 24, 2000, and June 30, 1999?
   (e) How much (if anything) was paid in dividends during the years ended June 24, 2000, and June 30, 1999?

Interpreting Financial Statements

BYP15–2 Nortel Networks Corporation is a global leader in telephony, data, wireless, and wireline solutions for the Internet. In July 1999, Nortel announced a stock dividend and a 2-for-1 stock split. In January, and again in May 2000, Nortel announced two more 2-for-1 stock splits. Nortel's common shares now number 3 billion.

Additional Cases

From 1999 to 2000, Nortel's revenue grew by 40%. Its share price ranged from $20 to $123. Interestingly, its earnings (loss) per share was only ($0.95) in fiscal 2000 and ($0.15) in fiscal 1999. Its dividend yield is less than 1%.

How the world shares ideas.

Instructions

   (a) Explain the different effects that a stock dividend and stock split would have on Nortel's financial position and number of shares.
   (b) Why do you think Nortel has split its common shares so often over the past few years?

(c) Nortel reported a loss per share in both 1999 and 2000. Yet its market price per share was positive and increasing. Can you explain why investors might be willing to pay an increasing price for a Nortel share despite its poor operating performance and low dividend yield?

BYP15–3 **Intrawest Corporation**, headquartered in Vancouver, is a leading developer and operator of resorts in North America. It reported the following selected accounts and information, as at June 30, 2000 and 1999.

INTRAWEST CORPORATION
Consolidated Statements of Operations (partial)
For the Years Ended June 30, 2000 and 1999
(in thousands of U.S. dollars, except per share amounts)

	2000	1999
Income from continuing operations	$52,091	$38,628
Results of discontinued operations (note 3)	(99)	(4,565)
Net income	$51,992	$34,063
Income per common share:		
Income from continuing operations	$1.20	$0.96
Net income	$1.20	$0.85
Number of common shares (in thousands)	43,362	40,237

INTRAWEST CORPORATION
Consolidated Statements of Retained Earnings
For the Years Ended June 30, 2000 and 1999
(in thousands of U.S. dollars)

	2000	1999
Retained earnings, beginning of year		
As previously reported	$136,288	$106,607
Adjustment to reflect change in accounting for income tax (note 1(n))	(57,457)	
Adjustment to reflect change in accounting for employee future benefits (note 1(t))	(1,743)	
As restated	77,088	106,607
Net income	51,992	34,063
Dividends	(4,715)	(4,382)
Other adjustments	7,588	
Retained earnings, end of year	$131,953	$136,288

Instructions

(a) Note 3 to Intrawest's financial statements details the impact of the discontinued operations on the financial position of the company, on a net-of-tax basis. Explain why these results are disclosed separately from those of continuing operations. Why are discontinued operations reported on a net-of-tax basis?

(b) Why are earnings per share disclosed separately for continuing operations and discontinued operations? What was the impact of the discontinued operations on earnings per share in 2000? In 1999?

(c) Intrawest's shares traded at $28.20 on June 30, 2000, and at $22.60 on June 30, 1999. Calculate its price-earnings ratio for each year, before and after the impact of discontinued items. The price-earnings ratio for the industry was 36.37. Are Intrawest's investors viewing Intrawest as a good future investment or as a poor future investment?

(d) Note 1 discloses the impact of the change in accounting policy, as Intrawest adopted new *CICA Handbook* sections for future income taxes and employee future benefits. Why are these adjustments reported in the statement of retained earnings rather than the income statement (statement of operations)? Do 1999 earnings per share reflect the impact of these changes or not?

Accounting on the Web

BYP15–4 SEDAR (System for Electronic Document Analysis and Retrieval) contains securities filings by Canadian public companies. This includes financial statements, annual reports, prospectuses, press releases, and other public company filings. This case views a selection of public documents available on this website.

Instructions

Specific requirements of this Internet case are available on the Weygandt website.

CRITICAL THINKING

Collaborative Learning Activity

BYP15–5 The Track Corporation is a diversified manufacturer of tires and vinyl products. Selected financial data, in millions of dollars, for a recent two-year period were as follows.

	Current Year	Prior Year
Sales	$2,416.7	$2,023.5
Total operating expenses	2,118.7	1,822.8
Total operating income	298.0	200.7
Income from continuing operations	209.9	83.6
Loss from discontinued operations (net of income tax)	16.9	4.4
Extraordinary gain (net of income tax)	–	25.8
Cumulative effect on prior years' incomes of change in method of accounting for income tax	2.7	–
Preferred dividends	8.8	9.8
Common dividends	43.3	37.0
Retained earnings, end of year	548.9	405.3

The notes to the company's financial statements indicate that the number of common shares was 25,179,000 for the current year and 23,651,000 for the prior year.

Instructions

With the class divided into groups, answer the following questions:
  (a) Explain the difference between total operating income and income from continuing operations.
  (b) Present the earnings per share data for the company for each year.
  (c) Comment on the relative importance of the non-typical items in each year.
  (d) Prepare a statement of retained earnings for the current year.

Communication Activity

BYP15–6 In the past year, Alaa Corporation declared a 10% stock dividend. Butte, Inc., announced a 2-for-1 stock split. Your parents own 100 of each company's common shares. During a recent phone call, your parents ask you, as an accounting student, to explain the difference between the two events.

Instructions

Write a letter to your parents explaining the impact of the two events on shareholders, and the effects of each event on the financial statements of each corporation.

Ethics Case

BYP15–7 Flambeau Corporation has paid 60 consecutive quarterly cash dividends (15 years' worth). The last six months, however, have been a real cash drain on the company, as profit margins have been greatly narrowed by increasing competition. With a cash balance sufficient to meet only day-to-day operating needs, the president, Vince Ramsey, has decided that a stock dividend instead of a cash dividend should be declared. He tells Flambeau's financial vice-president, Janice Rahn, to issue a press release stating that the company is extending its consecutive dividend record with the issue of a 5% stock dividend. "Write the press release to convince the shareholders that the stock dividend is just as good as a cash dividend," he orders. "Just watch our share price rise when we announce the stock dividend. It must be a good thing if that happens."

Instructions

(a) Who are the stakeholders in this situation?

(b) Is there anything unethical about Ramsey's intentions or actions?

(c) Which would you rather receive as a shareholder—a cash dividend or a stock dividend? Why?

Answers to Self-Study Questions

1. a   2. c   3. b   4. c   5. b   6. b   7. a   8. c   9. b   10. b   11. d

Answer to Second Cup Review It Question 3

On April 26, 2000, The Second Cup declared a special dividend of $2.00 per common share to shareholders of record on May 19, 2000, that was paid May 31, 2000. It totalled $18,719,000. The company did not split any shares.

Remember to go back to the Navigator box on the chapter-opening page to check off your completed work.

Concepts for Review

Before studying this chapter, you should understand or, if necessary, review:

a. *What is a current liability? What is a long-term liability? (Ch. 4, p. 169 and Ch. 11, p. 514)*

b. *How to record adjusting entries for interest expense. (Ch. 3, pp. 113–114)*

c. *How to record entries for the issue of notes payable and related interest expense. (Ch. 11, p. 516–517).*

d. *How to calculate the present value of bonds. (Appendix B, pp. B9–B11)*

THE NAVIGATOR

Confederation Bridge Is Attractive to Both Travellers and Bondholders

CAPE JOURIMAIN, N.B.—A link to the mainland was a condition of the deal through which Prince Edward Island joined Confederation in 1873. For nearly 125 years, this provision had been fulfilled through a ferry service subsidized by the federal government. But since the spring of 1997, travellers to the land made famous by Anne of Green Gables can arrive, without risk of seasickness, via the Confederation Bridge.

At 13 kilometres long, the structure is one of the longest bridges in the world. Building it was a complex engineering feat. Raising the capital to build it was equally complex, explains Chad King, the former Liability and Trust Fund Advisor to the New Brunswick Department of Finance.

The bridge was developed and built by Strait Crossing Development Inc., a private company. It now has the right to operate the bridge (and keep any proceeds from tolls) for 35 years. To raise the capital needed up front for this huge project, the Province of New Brunswick created Strait Crossing Financial Inc. This crown corporation, wholly owned by the province, issued bonds for $661,542,612 in October 1993. The bond proceeds were then loaned to Strait Crossing Development, with the same interest rates and repayment terms.

The bonds mature in April 2032, and have a principal value of $661 million, with an interest rate of 4.5%. Annual payments to bondholders of principal, interest, and accrued interest began in May 1997.

"Even though the payments didn't begin for a few years, the bonds were very attractive to investors and sold quickly," explains Mr. King, who also served as secretary-treasurer of Strait Crossing Financial. For one thing, they are indexed, so they won't lose any of their value in case of inflation. Second, they are secured by a legal obligation of the Government of Canada to make annual subsidy payments (essentially, the federal money that formerly went to subsidize the ferry lines now goes toward paying the bondholders). Finally, the bonds were given an Aaa rating by Moody's Investors Service, which signals that they are of the very best investment quality.

At the end of 35 years, about the time the bonds mature, ownership of the bridge reverts to Canada.

THE NAVIGATOR

www.confederationbridge.com

THE NAVIGATOR ✔

- Understand *Concepts for Review* ☐
- Read *Feature Story* ☐
- Scan *Study Objectives* ☐
- Read *Preview* ☐
- Read text and answer *Before You Go On*
  p. 742 ☐ p. 752 ☐ p. 754 ☐ p. 760 ☐
- Work *Demonstration Problems* ☐
- Review *Summary of Study Objectives* ☐
- Answer *Self-Study Questions* ☐
- Complete *assignments* ☐

CHAPTER • 16

LONG-TERM LIABILITIES

▶ **STUDY OBJECTIVES** ◀

After studying this chapter, you should be able to:

1. *Describe the advantages and illustrate the impact of issuing bonds instead of common shares.*
2. *Prepare the entries for the issue of bonds and the recording of interest expense.*
3. *Contrast the effects of the straight-line and effective interest methods of amortizing bond discounts and premiums.*
4. *Prepare the entries when bonds are retired.*
5. *Account for long-term notes payable.*
6. *Contrast the accounting for operating leases and capital leases.*
7. *Explain and illustrate the methods for the financial statement presentation and analysis of long-term liabilities.*

THE NAVIGATOR

As you can see from the feature story, Strait Crossing Financial chose to issue bonds to fund the construction of the Confederation Bridge. When the bond proceeds were lent to Strait Crossing Development, a note payable resulted. The portion of the bonds and note payable not due within the next year are classified as **long-term liabilities**. In this chapter, we will explain the accounting for the major types of long-term liabilities reported on the balance sheet. These liabilities include bonds, long-term notes, and lease obligations. The chapter is organized as follows:

THE
NAVIGATOR

▼Bond Basics

STUDY OBJECTIVE

•••••••••• **1** ••••••••••

Describe the advantages and illustrate the impact of issuing bonds instead of common shares.

Bonds are a form of interest-bearing note payable. They are issued by corporations, governments, and government agencies such as Strait Crossing Financial. Bonds are usually sold in denominations of a thousand dollars (or multiples of a thousand dollars). As a result, bonds attract many investors.

Why Issue Bonds?

A corporation may use long-term financing other than bonds, such as notes payable and leasing. These other forms of financing involve finding an individual, a company, or a financial institution willing to supply the needed funds. Notes payable and leasing rarely provide enough money for a plant expansion or major projects like new buildings. To obtain **large amounts of long-term capital**, corporate management usually must decide whether to issue common shares (equity financing) or bonds (debt financing).

From the standpoint of the corporation seeking long-term financing, bonds offer some advantages over common shares, as shown in Illustration 16-1.

Illustration 16-1

Advantages of bond financing over common shares

Bond Financing	Advantages
	1. **Shareholder control is not affected.** Bondholders do not have voting rights, so shareholders retain full control of the company.
	2. **Tax savings result.** Bond interest is deductible for income tax purposes. Dividends are not.
	3. **Earnings per share may be higher.** Although bond interest expense reduces net income, earnings per share are often higher under bond financing, because no additional common shares are issued.

To illustrate the potential effect on earnings per share, assume that Microsystems, Inc., is considering two plans for financing the construction of a new $5-million plant. Plan A involves the issue of 200,000 common shares at the current market price of $25 per share. Plan B involves the issue of $5 million of 6% bonds at face value. Income before interest and income tax on the new plant will be $1.5 million. Income tax is expected to be 45%. Microsystems currently has 100,000 common shares. The effects on earnings per share for each plan are shown in Illustration 16-2.

Illustration 16-2

Effects on earnings per share—common shares vs. bonds

	Plan A Issue Shares	Plan B Issue Bonds
Income before interest and income tax	$1,500,000	$1,500,000
Interest expense (6% × $5,000,000)	0	300,000
Income before income tax	1,500,000	1,200,000
Income tax expense (45%)	675,000	540,000
Net income	$ 825,000	$ 660,000
Issued shares	300,000	100,000
Earnings per share	$ 2.75	$ 6.60

Note that net income is $165,000 lower with long-term debt financing (bonds). However, earnings per share is higher, because there are 200,000 fewer shares.

The major disadvantages of issuing bonds are the interest that must be paid on a periodic basis and the principal (face value) of the bonds that must be paid at maturity. In contrast, if common shares are issued, a company is not required to pay dividends or repay the shareholders' investment.

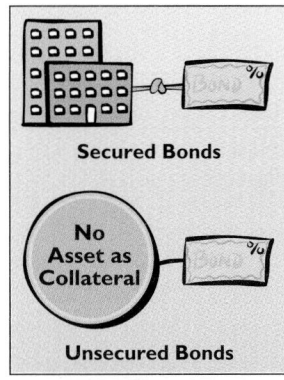

Secured Bonds

Unsecured Bonds

Types of Bonds

Bonds may have many different features. The common types of bonds are described below.

Secured and Unsecured Bonds

Secured bonds have specific assets of the issuer pledged as collateral for the bonds. A bond secured by real estate, for example, is called a mortgage bond. Debenture bonds are issued against the general credit of the borrower. There are no assets used as collateral. These bonds, also called **unsecured bonds**, are used extensively by large corporations with good credit ratings. For example, Bombardier recently reported $550 million of debenture bonds outstanding.

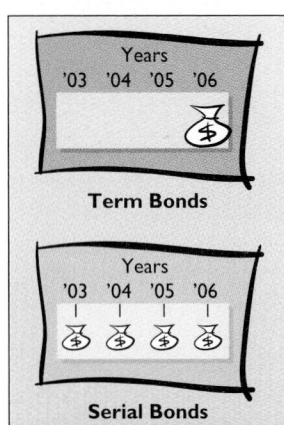

Term Bonds

Serial Bonds

Term and Serial Bonds

Bonds that mature (are due for payment) at a single specified future date are called term bonds. In contrast, bonds that mature in instalments are called serial bonds. The Confederation Bridge bonds referred to in the feature story are serial bonds, since annual payments include both principal and interest. If none of the principal was due to be repaid until April 2032, the bonds would be considered term bonds.

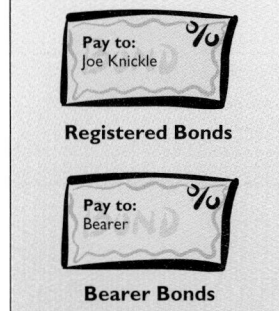

Registered Bonds

Bearer Bonds

Registered and Bearer Bonds

Bonds issued with the name of the owner are called registered bonds. Interest payments on registered bonds are made by cheque or direct deposit to registered bondholders. Canada Savings Bonds, issued by the federal government each fall, are an example of registered bonds. Bonds that are not registered are called bearer (or coupon) bonds. Holders of bearer bonds must send in coupons to receive interest payments. Bearer bonds may be transferred directly to another party. In contrast, the transfer of registered bonds requires the cancellation of the bonds by the institution and the issue of new bonds. Most bonds issued today are registered bonds.

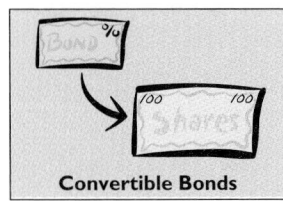

Convertible Bonds

Convertible Bonds

Bonds that can be converted into shares by the bondholder are called convertible bonds. Convertible bonds have features that are attractive to both the bondholder and the issuer. The conversion gives bondholders an opportunity to benefit if the market price of the common shares increases. As well, the bondholder receives interest on the bond until a decision is made to convert it. For the issuer, the bonds sell at a higher price and pay a lower rate of interest than comparable debt securities that do not have a conversion option.

Redeemable/Retractable Bonds

Redeemable/Retractable Bonds

Bonds subject to retirement at a stated dollar amount prior to maturity, at the option of the issuer, are known as redeemable bonds or **callable bonds**. Retractable bonds are bonds which can be redeemed before maturity, at the option of the bondholder.

With some types of bonds, the distinction between debt financing and equity financing is blurred. For example, convertible bonds—especially redeemable or retractable convertible bonds—can be converted into equity at specified periods of time. In many cases, the company will never have to repay the principal amount of the bonds. The CICA requires that these types of securities be separated into their liability and equity components for financial accounting and reporting purposes.

There are many more innovative debt financing options—known as financial instruments. Accounting for financial instruments, including convertible, redeemable, and retractable bonds, is complex and is left to future accounting courses.

▶ Accounting in Action ▶ *Business Insight*

Bonds have many different features, and interesting variations have been created to diversify their level of risk. At the high-risk level is the junk bond, which is unsecured and pays a high rate of interest. Three Canadian banks rank in the top 10 worldwide in the lucrative business of junk bond lending. At the low-risk level is the deep discount or zero interest (also known as stripped) bond, which pays little or no interest.

Canadian bond-rating agencies, such as Moody's Investors Service, Standard and Poor's (formerly the Canadian Bond Rating Service), and Dominion Bond Rating Service, help investors assess the risk level or credit-worthiness of bonds. The highest quality bonds are graded as Aaa (or AAA) bonds; superior quality, Aa (or AA); and good quality, A. The credit scale descends to C, and finally to the D or default category. Generally, bonds rated below Bbb (or its equivalent) are referred to as junk bonds. Junk bonds are considered speculative and have a higher risk of default.

Issuing Procedures

Within a corporation, approval by the board of directors (and sometimes the shareholders) is required before bonds can be issued. **In authorizing the bond issue, the board of directors must state the number of bonds to be authorized, the total face value, and the contractual interest rate.** Similar to issues of share capital, the total bond authorization often exceeds the number of bonds actually issued. This is done intentionally, to help ensure that the corporation will have the flexibility it needs to meet future cash requirements by selling more bonds.

The face value is the amount of principal the issuer must pay at the maturity date. The contractual interest rate is the rate stated on the bond certificate. This rate is used to determine the amount of cash interest the borrower pays and the investor receives. The contractual rate is stated as an annual rate. Interest is generally paid semi-annually.

The terms of the bond issue are stated in a legal document called a bond indenture. In addition to the terms, the indenture summarizes the rights of the bondholders and their trustees, as well as the obligations of the issuing company. The **trustee** (usually a financial institution) keeps records of each bondholder, maintains custody of unissued bonds, and holds conditional title to any pledged property (collateral).

After the bond indenture is prepared, **bond certificates** are printed. The indenture and the certificate are separate documents. Illustration 16-3 shows a bond certificate for one of Bombardier's bond issues. As shown in this illustration, a bond certificate provides information such as the following: name of issuer, face value, contractual interest rate, and maturity date.

Bonds are generally sold through an investment company that specializes in selling debt securities. In some cases, the issue is **underwritten** by the investment company. The issuing company sells the bonds to the investment company. In turn, the investment company sells the bonds to individual investors.

Costs are usually incurred in preparing and marketing a bond issue. **Bond issue costs** can include legal, accounting, underwriting, commission, printing, registration,

Alternative terminology
Face value is also called *par value*, or *maturity value*. The contractual interest rate is commonly known as the *coupon*, or *stated, interest rate*.

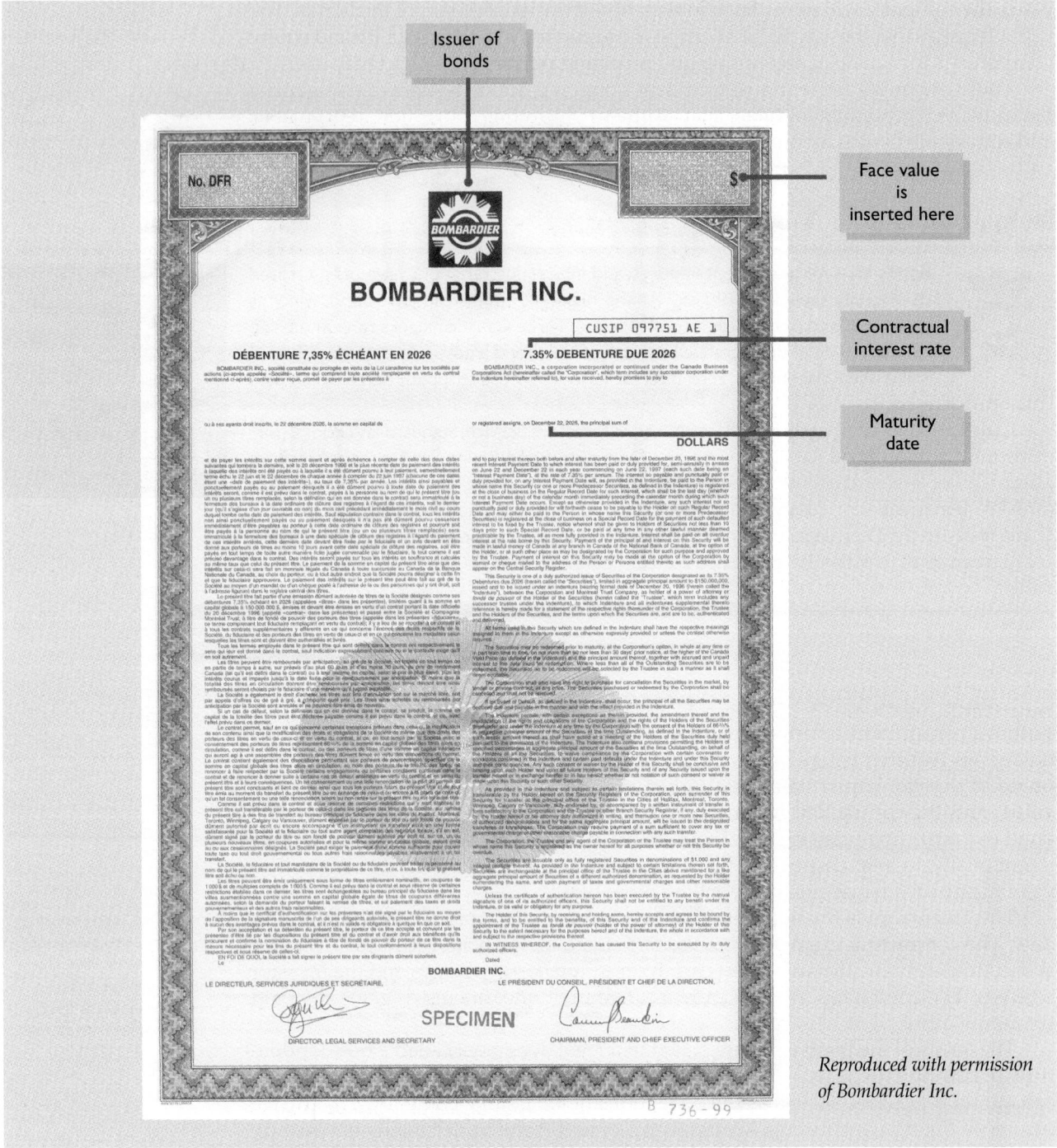

Issuer of bonds

Face value is inserted here

Contractual interest rate

Maturity date

Reproduced with permission of Bombardier Inc.

Illustration 16-3

Bond certificate

and promotion costs. These costs are paid by the issuer and reduce the proceeds from the bond issue. There are several methods used to account for bond issue costs. They are beyond the scope of this text and left for future accounting courses.

Bond Trading

Corporate bonds, like share capital, are traded on organized securities exchanges. Thus, bondholders have the opportunity to convert their bonds into cash at any time by selling the bonds at the current market price. The following illustration shows bond prices and yields, which are published daily in the financial press:

	Coupon	Mat. date	Bid $	Yld %
Bombardier	7.350	Dec 22/26	103.12	6.35

Illustration 16-4

Market information for bonds

Helpful hint The face value of most marketable bonds is $1,000, but it can be any value, such as $100 or $5,000 or $10,000.

This bond listing indicates that Bombardier has 7.35% bonds that mature on December 22, 2026. They yield a 6.35% return on the bid price. **The bid or bond price is quoted as a percentage of the face value of the bond, which is usually $1,000.** A $1,000 bond with a quoted price of 103.12 means that the selling price of the bond is 103.12% of face value, or $1,031.20.

Transactions between a bondholder and other investors **are not journalized by the issuing corporation**. If Vinod Thakkar sells his Bombardier bonds to Julie Tarrel, the issuing corporation, Bombardier, does not journalize the transaction. The issuer (or its trustee) does keep records of the names of bondholders in the case of registered bonds. A corporation makes journal entries **only when it issues or buys back bonds**.

Determining the Market Value of Bonds

If you were an investor wanting to purchase a bond, how would you determine how much to pay? To be more specific, assume that Thibodeau, Inc., issues a zero-interest bond (pays no interest) with a face value of $1,000,000 due in 20 years. For this bond, the only cash you receive is a million dollars at the end of 20 years. Would you pay a million dollars for this bond? We hope not! A million dollars received 20 years from now is not the same as a million dollars received today.

The reason you should not pay a million dollars relates to the **time value of money**. If you had a million dollars today, you could invest it. From that investment, you would earn interest. At the end of 20 years, your investment would be worth much more than a million dollars. If someone were going to pay you a million dollars 20 years from now, you would want to find its equivalent today. In other words, you would want to determine how much must be invested today at current interest rates to have a million dollars in 20 years. That amount—that must be invested today at a given rate of interest over a specified time—is called **present value**.

The present value of a bond is the value at which it should sell in the marketplace. Market value, therefore, is a function of the three factors that determine present value: (1) the dollar amounts to be received, (2) the length of time until the amounts are received, and (3) the market interest rate. The market interest rate is the rate investors demand for lending their money. This rate is also commonly known as the **effective interest rate** or **yield**. The process of finding the present value is called **discounting** the future amounts.

To illustrate, assume that on January 1, 2003, Daoust Company issues $100,000 of 4% bonds, due in five years, with interest payable semi-annually. The purchaser of the bonds would receive two cash inflows: (1) the **principal** of $100,000 to be paid at maturity, and (2) ten $2,000 **interest payments** ($100,000 × 4% × $\frac{6}{12}$ months) over the term of the bonds. The time diagram for both cash flows is shown below:

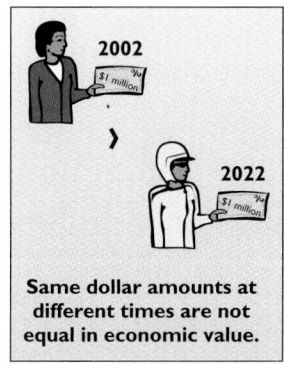

Same dollar amounts at different times are not equal in economic value.

Illustration 16-5

Time diagram depicting cash flows

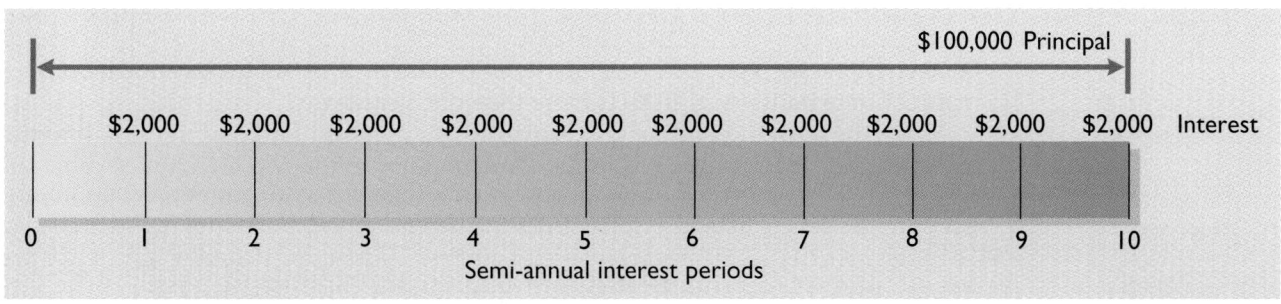

The current market value of a bond is equal to the present value of all the future cash inflows promised by the bond. The present values of these amounts are as shown in Illustration 16-6.

Illustration 16-6

Calculating the present value of bonds

Present value of $100,000 received in 10 periods	
$100,000 × 0.82035 (Table B-1: $n = 10$, $i = 2\%$)	$ 82,035
Present value of $2,000 received annually for 10 periods	
$2,000 × 8.98259 (Table B-2: $n = 10$, $i = 2\%$)	17,965
Present value (market price) of bonds	$100,000

Where n = number of interest periods and i = interest rate

The present value of the bonds always equals the principal when the market interest rate is the same as the contractual interest rate, as it is in this case. The present value tables on pages B4 and B7 in Appendix B can be used to find the present value numbers used, or these values can be determined mathematically.

There is further discussion of time value of money calculations in Appendix B at the end of the book.

Before You Go On...

▸ Review It

1. What are the advantages of bond versus common share financing?
2. What are secured versus unsecured bonds, term versus serial bonds, registered versus bearer bonds, and redeemable versus retractable bonds?
3. Explain the terms "face value," "contractual interest rate," and "market interest rate."
4. Explain why you would prefer to receive $1 million today rather than five years from now.

Related exercise material: BE16–1 and E16–1.

THE NAVIGATOR

Accounting for Bond Issues

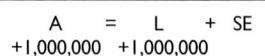
STUDY OBJECTIVE

2

Prepare the entries for the issue of bonds and the recording of interest expense.

Bonds may be issued at face value, below face value (at a discount), or above face value (at a premium). They are also sometimes issued between interest dates.

Issuing Bonds at Face Value

To illustrate the accounting for bonds, assume that Candlestick, Inc. issues one thousand $1,000, five-year, 5% bonds on January 1, 2003, at 100 (100% of face value). The entry to record the sale is as follows:

A	=	L	+	SE
+1,000,000		+1,000,000		

Jan. 1	Cash		1,000,000	
	Bonds Payable			1,000,000
	To record sale of bonds at face value.			

Bonds payable are reported in the long-term liabilities section of the balance sheet. The maturity date (January 1, 2008) is more than one year away.

Over the term (life) of the bonds, entries are required for bond interest. Interest on bonds payable is calculated in the same manner as interest on notes payable, as explained in Chapter 11. Assume that interest is payable semi-annually on January 1 and July 1 on the bonds described above. Interest of $25,000 ($1,000,000 × 5% × ½) must be paid on July 1, 2003. The following is the entry for the payment, assuming no previous accrual of interest:

July 1	Bond Interest Expense	25,000	
	Cash		25,000
	To record payment of bond interest.		

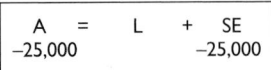

A = L + SE
−25,000   −25,000

At December 31, an adjusting entry is required to recognize the $25,000 of interest expense incurred since July 1. The entry is as follows:

Dec. 31	Bond Interest Expense	25,000	
	Bond Interest Payable		25,000
	To accrue bond interest.		

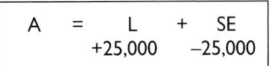

A = L + SE
+25,000   −25,000

Bond interest payable is classified as a current liability, because it is scheduled for payment within the next year (in fact, it is due the next day). When the interest is paid on January 1, 2004, Bond Interest Payable is debited and Cash is credited for $25,000.

Discount or Premium on Bonds

The previous illustrations assumed that the contractual interest rate paid on bonds and the market interest rate of the bond were the same. When the contractual interest rate and the market interest rate are the same, bonds sell at face value, as shown in the preceding section. However, market interest rates change daily. They are influenced by the type of bond issued, the state of the economy, current industry conditions, and the company's performance. The contractual and market interest rates often differ. As a result, bonds sell below or above face value.

To illustrate, suppose that investors have one of two options: (1) purchase bonds that have just been issued with a market interest rate of 6%, or (2) purchase bonds issued at an earlier date with a lower contractual interest rate of 5%. If the bonds are of equal risk, investors will select the 6% investment. To make the investments equal, investors will demand a rate of interest higher than the 5% contractual interest rate. But investors cannot change the contractual interest rate. What they can do is pay less than the face value for the bonds. By paying less for the bonds, investors can effectively obtain the market interest rate of 6%. In these cases, **bonds sell at a** discount.

On the other hand, the market interest rate may be **lower** than the contractual interest rate. In that case, investors will have to pay more than face value for the bonds. That is, if the market interest rate is 4% and the contractual interest rate is 5%, the issuer will require more funds from the investors. In these cases, **bonds sell at a** premium. The Confederation Bridge bonds were issued at a premium.

These relationships are shown in Illustration 16-7.

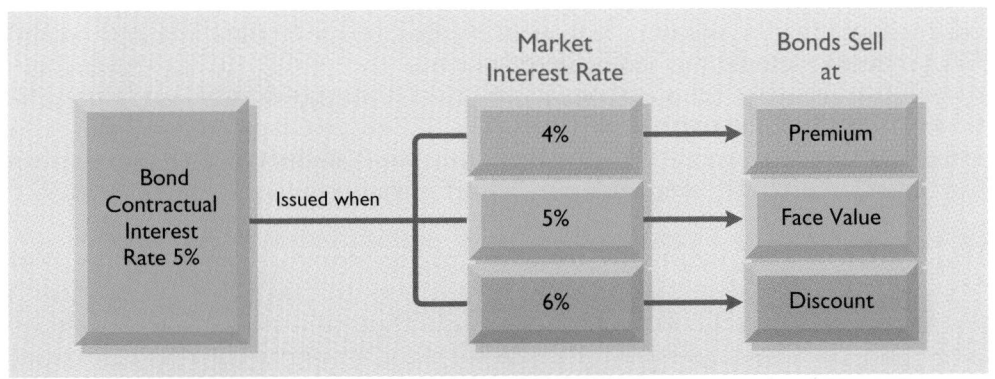

Illustration 16-7

Interest rates and bond prices

Issuing bonds at an amount different from face value is quite common. By the time a company prints the bond certificates and markets the bonds, it will be a coincidence if the market rate and the contractual rate are the same. Thus, the sale of bonds at a discount does not mean that the issuer's financial strength is suspect. Nor does the sale of bonds at a premium indicate exceptional financial strength.

Issuing Bonds at a Discount

To illustrate the issue of bonds at a discount, assume that on January 1, 2003, Candlestick, Inc. sells $1,000,000 of five-year 5% bonds at 95.7345 (95.7345% of face value). Interest is payable on July 1 and January 1. The entry to record the issue is as follows:

A	=	L	+	SE
+957,345		–42,655		
		+1,000,000		

Jan. 1	Cash	957,345	
	Discount on Bonds Payable	42,655	
	Bonds Payable		1,000,000
	To record sale of bonds at a discount.		

Although Discount on Bonds Payable has a debit balance, it is not an asset. Rather, it is a **contra liability account**. This account is **deducted from bonds payable** on the balance sheet, as shown in Illustration 16-8.

Illustration 16-8

Statement presentation of discount on bonds payable

CANDLESTICK, INC.		
Balance Sheet (partial)		
January 1, 2003		
Long-term liabilities		
Bonds payable	$1,000,000	
Less: Discount on bonds payable	42,655	$957,345

Alternative terminology
The balance in the Discount on Bonds Payable account is often referred to as *Unamortized Discount on Bonds Payable.*

The $957,345 represents the **carrying (or book) value** of the bonds. On the date of issue, this amount equals the market price of the bonds.

The issue of bonds at a discount (below face value) makes the total cost of borrowing higher than the bond interest paid. That is, the issuing corporation must pay not only the contractual interest rate over the term of the bonds, but also the face value (rather than the issue price) at maturity. Therefore, the difference between the issue price ($957,345) and the face value ($1,000,000) of the bonds—the discount ($42,655)—is an **additional cost of borrowing**. This additional cost should be recorded as bond interest expense over the life of the bonds.

Amortizing Bond Discount

Helpful hint Amortization of the bond discount is charged to Interest Expense, not to Amortization Expense.

To comply with the **matching principle**, the bond discount must be allocated to each accounting period that benefits from the use of the cash proceeds. There are two methods for allocating this discount to interest expense: (1) the straight-line method and (2) the effective interest method of amortization.

Straight-Line Method of Amortization. The straight-line method of amortization is the simpler of the two methods. It allocates the same amount to interest expense in each interest period. The amount is determined as shown in Illustration 16-9.

Illustration 16-9

Formula for straight-line method of bond discount amortization

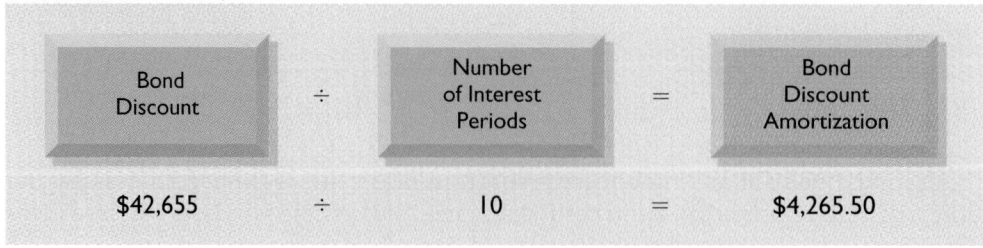

In this example, the bond discount amortization is $4,265.50 ($42,655 ÷ 10 six-month periods). The entry to record the payment of bond interest and the amortization of bond discount on the first interest date (July 1, 2003) is as follows:

July 1	Bond Interest Expense	29,265.50	
	Discount on Bonds Payable		4,265.50
	Cash		25,000.00
	To record payment of bond interest and amortization of bond discount.		

A	=	L	+	SE
−25,000.00		+4,265.50		−29,265.50

Note that it is the *interest payment*, and not the *interest expense*, that is calculated by applying the contractual interest rate for the period (5% × ½) to the face value ($1,000,000) of the bonds. The interest expense includes both the interest payment ($25,000) and the bond discount amortization ($4,265.50).

At December 31, the adjusting entry is recorded as follows:

Dec. 31	Bond Interest Expense	29,265.50	
	Discount on Bonds Payable		4,265.50
	Bond Interest Payable		25,000.00
	To record accrued bond interest and amortization of bond discount.		

A	=	L	+	SE
		+4,265.50		−29,265.50
		+25,000.00		

Over the term of the bonds, the balance in Discount on Bonds Payable will decrease annually by the same amount until it reaches zero at maturity. The carrying value of the bonds at maturity will be equal to the face value.

A bond discount amortization schedule, as shown in Illustration 16-10, is a useful tool to organize and summarize this information. The schedule shows the interest payment, interest expense, discount amortization, and carrying value of the bond for each interest period. Note that the carrying value of the bond increases by $4,265.50 each period until it reaches its face value of $1,000,000 at the end of period 10 (January 1, 2008).

Illustration 16-10

Bond discount amortization schedule—straight-line method

CANDLESTICK, INC.
Bond Discount Amortization Schedule
Straight-Line Method

Semi-annual Interest Period	(A) Interest Payment (5% × ½ × $1,000,000)	(B) Interest Expense (A + C)	(C) Discount Amortization ($42,655 ÷ 10)	(D) Unamortized Discount (D − C)	(E) Bond Carrying Value ($1,000,000 − D)
Issue date				$42,655.00	$ 957,345.00
1	$ 25,000	$ 29,265.50	$ 4,265.50	38,389.50	961,610.50
2	25,000	29,265.50	4,265.50	34,124.00	965,876.00
3	25,000	29,265.50	4,265.50	29,858.50	970,141.50
4	25,000	29,265.50	4,265.50	25,593.00	974,407.00
5	25,000	29,265.50	4,265.50	21,327.50	978,672.50
6	25,000	29,265.50	4,265.50	17,062.00	982,938.00
7	25,000	29,265.50	4,265.50	12,796.50	987,203.50
8	25,000	29,265.50	4,265.50	8,531.00	991,469.00
9	25,000	29,265.50	4,265.50	4,265.50	995,734.50
10	25,000	29,265.50	4,265.50	0.00	1,000,000.00
	$250,000	$292,655.00	$42,655.00		

Column (A) remains constant because the face value of the bonds ($1,000,000) is multiplied by the semi-annual contractual interest rate each period.
Column (B) is calculated as the interest paid (Column A) plus the discount amortization (Column C).
Column (C) indicates the discount amortization each period.
Column (D) decreases each period by the same amount until it reaches zero at maturity.
Column (E) increases each period by the same amount of discount amortization until it equals the face value at maturity.

We have highlighted columns (A), (B), and (C) in the amortization schedule to emphasize their importance. These three columns provide the numbers for each year's journal entries. They are the primary reason for preparing the schedule. Column (A) provides the amount of the credit to Cash (or Interest Payable). Column (B) shows the debit to Bond Interest Expense. And column (C) is the credit to Discount on Bonds Payable.

Effective Interest Method of Amortization.   The straight-line method of amortization has a conceptual weakness. It does not completely satisfy the matching principle. With the straight-line method, interest expense as a percentage of the carrying value of the bond for the preceding period varies each interest period. Illustration 16-11 shows this by using data from the first three interest periods of the bond amortization schedule shown in Illustration 16-10.

Illustration 16-11

Interest percentage rates under straight-line method

			CANDLESTICK, INC. **Bond Interest Expense Percentage** **Straight-Line Method**		

Semi-annual Interest Period	Interest Expense (B)	Bond Carrying Value (E)	Interest Expense as a Percentage of Carrying Value (B ÷ E)
1	$29,265.50	$957,345.00	3.06%
2	29,265.50	961,610.50	3.04%
3	29,265.50	965,876.00	3.03%
10	29,265.50	995,734.50	2.94%

Note that interest expense as a percentage of carrying value decreases in each interest period. To comply with the matching principle, interest expense as a percentage of carrying value should not change over the life of the bonds. This percentage, referred to as the market or **effective interest rate**, is established when the bonds are issued. It remains constant in each interest period.

Helpful hint   The straight-line method results in constant amounts of amortization and interest expense each period but varying percentage rates.

Under the effective interest method of amortization, the amortization of bond discount (or bond premium as we will see in the next section) results in a periodic interest expense which is equal to a constant percentage of the carrying value of the bonds. The effective interest method results in varying amounts of amortization and interest expense per period but a **constant percentage rate**.

The effective interest method requires the following three steps:

1. **Calculate the bond interest expense:** Multiply the carrying value of the bonds at the beginning of the interest period (or end of the preceding period) by the market (effective) interest rate.
2. **Calculate the bond interest paid (or accrued):** Multiply the face value of the bonds by the contractual interest rate.
3. **Calculate the amortization amount:** Determine the difference between the amounts calculated in steps (1) and (2).

These steps are shown in Illustration 16-12.

Illustration 16-12

Calculation of amortization—effective interest method

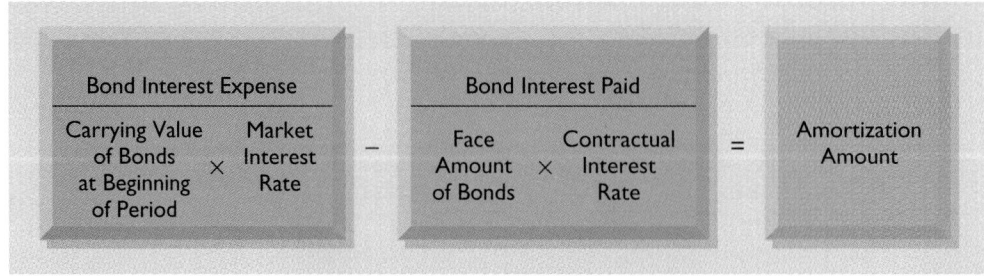

To illustrate the effective interest method of bond discount amortization, we will continue to use Candlestick, Inc., as an example. As you recall, Candlestick issued $1,000,000 of five-year 5%. Interest is payable semi-annually on July 1 and January 1.

The bonds are issued to yield a market interest rate of 6% (the effective interest rate). The bonds will sell for $957,345 (95.7345% of face value), which results in a bond discount of $42,655 ($1,000,000 − $957,345). (Note that the $957,345 selling price can be proven by using the time value of money techniques shown in Appendix B at the end of this book.)

Illustration 16-13

Bond discount amortization schedule—effective interest method

A bond discount amortization schedule, as shown in Illustration 16-13, makes it easier to record the interest expense and the discount amortization. For simplicity, amounts have been rounded to the nearest dollar in this schedule.

CANDLESTICK, INC.					
Bond Discount Amortization Schedule					
Straight-Line Method					
Semi-annual Interest Period	(A) Interest Payment (5% × %₁₂ × $1,000,000)	(B) Interest Expense (6% × %₁₂ × preceding bond carrying value)	(C) Discount Amortization (B − A)	(D) Unamortized Discount (D − C)	(E) Bond Carrying Value ($1,000,000 − D)
Issue date				$42,655	$ 957,345
1	$ 25,000	$ 28,720	$ 3,720	38,935	961,065
2	25,000	28,832	3,832	35,103	964,897
3	25,000	28,947	3,947	31,156	968,844
4	25,000	29,065	4,065	27,091	972,909
5	25,000	29,187	4,187	22,904	977,096
6	25,000	29,313	4,313	18,591	981,409
7	25,000	29,442	4,442	14,149	985,851
8	25,000	29,576	4,576	9,573	990,427
9	25,000	29,713	4,713	4,860	995,140
10	25,000	29,860*	4,860	0	1,000,000
	$250,000	$292,655	$42,655		

Column (A) remains constant because the face value of the bonds ($1,000,000) is multiplied by the semi-annual contractual interest rate (5% × %₁₂ = 2.5%) each period.
Column (B) is the bond carrying value at the end of the preceding period multiplied by the semi-annual market interest rate.
Column (C) indicates the discount amortization each period.
Column (D) decreases each period by the amortization amount until it reaches zero at maturity.
Column (E) increases each period by the amortization amount until it equals the face value at maturity.
* $6 difference due to rounding.

As stated for Illustration 16-10, columns (A), (B), and (C) provide information for the required journal entries.

For the first interest period, the entry to record the payment of interest and amortization of bond discount by Candlestick is as follows:

July 1	Bond Interest Expense ($957,345 × 6% × %₁₂)	28,720	
	Discount on Bonds Payable		3,720
	Cash ($1,000,000 × 5% × %₁₂)		25,000
	To record payment of bond interest and amortization of bond discount.		

A	=	L	+	SE
−25,000		+3,720		−28,720

For the second interest period, the following adjusting entry is made:

Dec. 31	Bond Interest Expense ($961,065 × 6% × %₁₂)	28,832	
	Discount on Bonds Payable		3,832
	Bond Interest Payable ($1,000,000 × 5% × %₁₂)		25,000
	To record accrued bond interest and amortization of bond discount.		

A	=	L	+	SE
		+3,832		−28,832
		+25,000		

Note that interest expense as a percentage of carrying value remains constant at 3% using the effective interest method. Illustration 16-13 may be compared with Illustration 16-10 to see the differences between the straight-line and effective interest methods over the life of the bonds. Note that the total interest expense over the life of the bond, $292,655, is the same in both methods.

Issuing Bonds at a Premium

The issue of bonds at a premium can be illustrated by assuming the Candlestick bonds are sold at 104.4915 (104.4915% of face value) rather than at 95.7345.

The entry to record the sale would be as follows:

A	=	L	+	SE
+1,044,915		+1,000,000		
				+44,915

Jan. 1	Cash		1,044,915	
	Bonds Payable			1,000,000
	Premium on Bonds Payable			44,915
	To record sale of bonds at a premium.			

Premium on bonds payable is **added to bonds payable** on the balance sheet, as shown in Illustration 16-14.

Illustration 16-14

Statement presentation of bond premium

Helpful hint Both discount and premium accounts are valuation accounts. A discount account is a contra-type valuation account (its balance is deducted from Bonds Payable). A premium account is an adjunct-type valuation account (its balance is added to the balance of Bonds Payable).

CANDLESTICK, INC.
Balance Sheet (partial)
January 1, 2003

Long-term liabilities		
Bonds payable	$1,000,000	
Add: Premium on bonds payable	44,915	$1,044,915

The sale of bonds above face value causes the total cost of borrowing to be **less than the bond interest paid**. The bond premium is considered to be **a reduction in the cost of borrowing**. It should be credited to Bond Interest Expense over the life of the bonds, not to Amortization Expense or a revenue account.

Amortizing Bond Premium

The same two methods—straight-line and effective interest—used to amortize a bond discount are also used to amortize a bond premium and calculate interest expense.

Straight-Line Method of Amortization. The formula for determining bond premium amortization under the straight-line method is to divide the bond premium by the number of interest periods.

Illustration 16-15

Formula for straight-line method of bond premium amortization

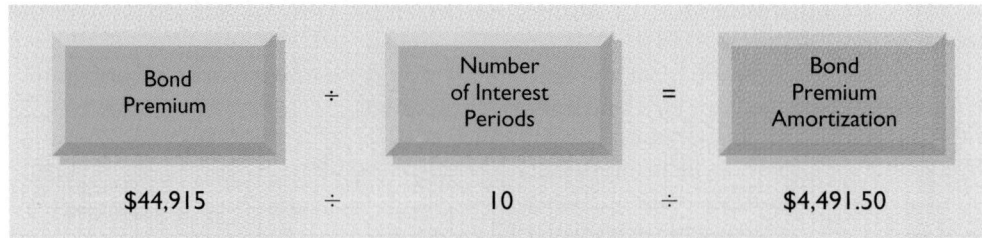

Bond Premium	÷	Number of Interest Periods	=	Bond Premium Amortization
$44,915	÷	10	÷	$4,491.50

The premium amortization for each interest period is $4,491.50 ($44,915 ÷ 10). The entry to record the first payment of interest on July 1 follows:

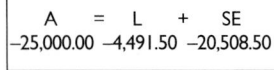

A	=	L	+	SE
−25,000.00		−4,491.50		−20,508.50

July 1	Bond Interest Expense		20,508.50	
	Premium on Bonds Payable		4,491.50	
	Cash			25,000.00
	To record payment of bond interest			
	and amortization of bond premium.			

At December 31, the adjusting entry is as below:

Dec. 31	Bond Interest Expense	20,508.50	
	Premium on Bonds Payable	4,491.50	
	Bond Interest Payable		25,000.00
	To record accrued bond interest		
	and amortization of bond premium.		

A	=	L	+	SE
		−4,491.50		−20,508.50
		+25,000.00		

Over the term of the bonds, the balance in Premium on Bonds Payable will decrease semi-annually by the same amount until it reaches zero at maturity.

A bond premium amortization schedule, as shown in Illustration 16-16, shows interest expense, premium amortization, and the carrying value of the bond. The interest expense recorded each period for the Candlestick bond is $20,508.50 under the straight-line method. This is the amount of the interest payment ($25,000) reduced by the premium amortization ($4,491.50). Note also that the carrying value of the bonds decreases by $4,491.50 each period until it reaches the face value of $1,000,000 at the end of period 10.

Helpful hint Carrying values *increase* to maturity value with a bond discount and *decrease* to maturity value with a bond premium.

Illustration 16-16

Bond premium amortization schedule—straight-line method

CANDLESTICK, INC.
Bond Discount Amortization Schedule
Straight-Line Method

Semi-annual Interest Period	(A) Interest Payment (5% × %₁₂ × $1,000,000)	(B) Interest Expense (A − C)	(C) Discount Amortization ($42,915 ÷ 10)	(D) Unamortized Discount (D − C)	(E) Bond Carrying Value ($1,000,000 + D)
Issue date				$44,915.00	$1,044,915.00
1	$ 25,000	$ 20,508.50	$ 4,491.50	40,423.50	1,040,423.50
2	25,000	20,508.50	4,491.50	35,932.00	1,035,932.00
3	25,000	20,508.50	4,491.50	31,440.50	1,031,440.50
4	25,000	20,508.50	4,491.50	26,949.00	1,026,949.00
5	25,000	20,508.50	4,491.50	22,457.50	1,022,457.50
6	25,000	20,508.50	4,491.50	17,966.00	1,017,966.00
7	25,000	20,508.50	4,491.50	13,474.50	1,013,474.50
8	25,000	20,508.50	4,491.50	8,983.00	1,008,983.00
9	25,000	20,508.50	4,491.50	4,491.50	1,004,491.50
10	25,000	20,508.50	4,491.50	0.00	1,000,000.00
	$250,000	$205,085.00	$44,915.00		

Column (A) remains constant because the face value of the bonds ($1,000,000) is multiplied by the semi-annual contractual interest rate each period.
Column (B) is calculated as the interest paid (Column A) less the premium amortization (Column C).
Column (C) indicates the premium amortization each period.
Column (D) decreases each period by the same amount until it reaches zero at maturity.
Column (E) decreases each period by the same amount of premium amortization until it equals the face value at maturity.

Effective Interest Method of Amortization. The amortization of bond premium by the effective interest method is similar to the procedures described for bond discount. Illustration 16-17 presents the formula shown earlier in this chapter (Illustration 16-12) to determine amortization.

Illustration 16-17

Calculation of amortization—effective interest method

Using our previous example, assume that Candlestick, Inc., issues its $1,000,000 of five-year 5% bonds on January 1, 2003, with interest payable on July 1 and January 1. In this case, the bonds are issued to yield a market (effective) interest rate of 4%. Using the time value of money techniques illustrated in Appendix B, we can determine that the bonds will sell for $1,044,915. This sale price results in a premium of $44,915.

Illustration 16-18

Bond premium amortization schedule—effective interest method

The bond premium amortization schedule is shown in Illustration 16-18. Figures have been rounded to the nearest dollar for simplicity.

CANDLESTICK, INC.
Bond Premium Amortization Schedule
Effective Interest Method

Semi-annual Interest Period	(A) Interest Payment (5% × ½ × $1,000,000)	(B) Interest Expense (4% × ½ × preceding bond carrying value)	(C) Premium Amortization (A − B)	(D) Unamortized Premium (D − C)	(E) Bond Carrying Value ($1,000,000 + D)
Issue date				$44,915	$1,044,915
1	$ 25,000	$ 20,898	$ 4,102	40,813	1,040,813
2	25,000	20,816	4,184	36,629	1,036,629
3	25,000	20,733	4,267	32,362	1,032,362
4	25,000	20,647	4,353	28,009	1,028,009
5	25,000	20,560	4,440	23,569	1,023,569
6	25,000	20,471	4,529	19,040	1,019,040
7	25,000	20,381	4,619	14,421	1,014,421
8	25,000	20,288	4,712	9,709	1,009,709
9	25,000	20,194	4,806	4,903	1,004,903
10	25,000	20,097*	4,903	0	1,000,000
	$250,000	$205,085	$44,915		

Column (A) remains constant because the face value of the bonds ($1,000,000) is multiplied by the semi-annual contractual interest rate each period.
Column (B) is the bond carrying value at the end of the preceding period multiplied by the semi-annual market interest rate.
Column (C) indicates the premium amortization each period.
Column (D) decreases each period by the amoritzation amount until it reaches zero at maturity.
Column (E) decreases each period by the amoritzation amount until it equals the face value at maturity.
* $1 difference due to rounding.

The entry on the first interest date is as follows:

A	=	L	+	SE
−25,000		−4,102		−20,898

July 1	Bond Interest Expense ($1,044,915 × 4% × ½)		20,898	
	Premium on Bonds Payable		4,102	
	Cash ($1,000,000 × 5% × ½)			25,000
	To record payment of bond interest and amortization of bond premium.			

For the second interest period, interest expense will be $20,816 and the premium amortization will be $4,184. While the interest expense and amortization amounts vary, the cash payment is a constant $25,000 every interest period. Illustration 16-18 may be compared with Illustration 16-16 to see the difference between the straight-line and the effective interest amortization methods on a bond premium.

Comparing the Straight-Line and Effective Interest Methods of Amortization. There are two methods used to amortize a bond discount or a bond premium—the straight-line and effective interest methods. The straight-line method is the simpler of the two. It allocates the *same dollar amount* to interest expense each interest period. The effective interest method allocates a *varying dollar amount* to interest expense each interest period. The interest expense is, however, the *same percentage (the market or effective interest rate) of the carrying value* for each period. Both methods of amortization result in the *same total amount* of interest expense over the life of the bonds.

Illustration 16-19 summarizes some of the differences between these two methods.

> **STUDY OBJECTIVE**
> ·········▼·········
> **3**
>
> *Contrast the effects of the straight-line and effective interest methods of amortizing bond discounts and premiums.*

Interest Expense	Straight-Line Method	Effective Interest Method
Dollar amount per period	Constant amount	Changing amount: Increases (discount); Decreases (premium)
Percentage of carrying value	Changing amount: Increases (premium); Decreases (discount)	Constant %
Total dollar amount over bond term	Same as effective interest total	Same as straight-line total

Illustration 16-19

Comparison of straight-line and effective interest methods of amortization

So which method of bond amortization should be used? In practice, the straight-line method of amortizing a bond discount or bond premium is the most widely used method in Canada. However, the effective interest method is better in theory than the straight-line method, because it matches the cost of borrowing to each period when the borrowed money was used. The effective interest method is also widely used for other types of liabilities, such as mortgage notes payable, leases, and pensions.

Issuing Bonds Between Interest Dates

Bonds are often issued between interest payment dates. **When this occurs, the investor must pay the market price for the bonds plus accrued interest since the last interest date.** At the next interest date, the corporation will return the accrued interest to the investor by paying the full amount of interest due since the last interest payment date.

To illustrate, assume that Candlestick sells its $1,000,000 of five-year 5% bonds at face value plus accrued interest on March 1. Interest is payable semi-annually on July 1 and January 1. The accrued interest is $8,333 ($1,000,000 × 5% × 2/12). The total proceeds on the sale of the bonds, therefore, are $1,008,333 ($1,000,000 + $8,333). The entry to record the sale is as follows:

Mar. 1	Cash	1,008,333	
	Bonds Payable		1,000,000
	Bond Interest Payable		8,333
	To record sale of bonds at face value plus accrued interest.		

A	=	L	+	SE
+1,008,333		+1,000,000		
		+8,333		

At the first interest date, it is necessary to do two things with regard to bond interest: (1) Eliminate the bond interest payable balance. (2) Recognize interest expense for the four months (March 1–June 30) that the bonds have been outstanding. Interest expense for the four-month period in this example is $16,667 ($1,000,000 × 5% × 4/12). The entry on July 1 for the $25,000 interest payment follows:

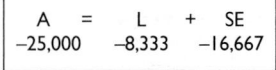

A	=	L	+	SE
−25,000		−8,333		−16,667

July 1	Bond Interest Payable	8,333	
	Bond Interest Expense	16,667	
	Cash		25,000
	To record payment of bond interest.		

Why does the issuer, Candlestick, Inc., collect interest at the time of issue, then return it at the time of payment? Collection of accrued interest at the issue date allows the company to pay a full period's (six months' worth) interest to all bondholders at the next interest payment date. Candlestick, as the issuer, does not have to determine the individual amount of interest due to each holder based on the time each bond has been held by the investor.

If bonds were not sold "plus accrued interest," the issuer would have to keep track of the purchaser and the date of purchase to ensure that each bondholder received the correct amount of interest. It is both simpler and less expensive for the issuer to sell the bonds "plus accrued interest."

If bonds are issued above or below face value, it is necessary to amortize any premium or discount over the period that the bonds have been outstanding. That is, the total amortization period must be reduced by the accrued interest period. For example, assume Desjardins Corporation sells its $1,000,000 of 7% bonds at 104 plus accrued interest on March 1. The premium amortization recorded on the first interest payment date, July 1, would be spread over the remaining 56 months—five years less four months—rather than 60 months (five years).

In the opening story, the Confederation Bridge bonds also had accrued interest at the first interest payment date, May 1997. However, this interest did not result from selling the bonds between interest dates. It resulted because interest had not been paid for the period from the date of issue, October 1993, until the first payment date, May 1997.

Before You Go On . . .

▶*Review It*

1. What journal entry is made to record the issue of bonds payable of $1 million at 100? At 96? At 102?
2. Why do bonds sell at a discount? At a premium? At face value?
3. Distinguish between the straight-line and effective interest methods of amortization.
4. Explain the accounting for bonds sold between interest dates.

▶*Do It*

A bond amortization table shows (a) interest to be paid, $50,000, (b) interest expense to be recorded, $52,000, and (c) amortization, $2,000. Answer the following questions: (1) Were the bonds sold at a premium or at a discount? (2) After recording the interest expense, will the bond carrying value increase or decrease?

Action Plan

- Understand the effects that the amortization of a bond discount or bond premium has on bond interest expense and on the carrying value of the bond.
- Remember that bond discount amortization increases both bond interest expense and the carrying value of the bond.
- Remember that bond premium amortization decreases both bond interest expense and the carrying value of the bond.

Solution

The bond amortization table indicates that interest expense is $2,000 greater than the interest paid. This difference is equal to the amortization amount. (1) The bonds were sold at a discount. (2) The interest entry will decrease Discount on Bonds Payable and increase the carrying value of the bonds.

Related exercise material: BE16–2, BE16–3, BE16–4, BE16–5, BE16–6, BE16–7, BE16–8, E16–2, E16–3, E16–4, E16–5, and E16–6.

Accounting for Bond Retirements

Bonds may be retired either when they mature or when they are redeemed (purchased on the open market) by the issuing corporation before they mature. These transactions are explained in the following sections.

STUDY OBJECTIVE
•••••••••4•••••••••
Prepare the entries when bonds are retired.

Redeeming Bonds at Maturity

Regardless of the issue price of bonds, the book value of the bonds at maturity will equal their face value. This can be seen in Illustrations 16-10, 16-13, 16-16, and 16-18. The carrying value of the bonds in these illustrations at the end of their five-year life ($1 million) is equal to the face value of the bonds.

Assuming that the interest for the last interest period has been paid and recorded, the entry to record the redemption of the Candlestick bonds at maturity, January 1, 2008, is as folows:

Jan. 1	Bonds Payable	1,000,000	
	Cash		1,000,000
	To record redemption of bonds at maturity.		

A	=	L	+	SE
−1,000,000		−1,000,000		

Redeeming Bonds Before Maturity

A company may decide to retire bonds before maturity to reduce interest cost or to remove debt from its balance sheet. A company should retire its bonds early only if it has sufficient cash reserves.

When bonds are retired before maturity, it is necessary to (1) update any unrecorded interest if the bonds are sold between interest periods, (2) eliminate the carrying value of the bonds at the redemption date, (3) record the cash paid, and (4) recognize the gain or loss on redemption. The carrying value of the bonds is the face value of the bonds less the unamortized bond discount, or plus the unamortized bond premium, at the redemption date.

To illustrate, assume that Candlestick sells its bonds at a premium and uses the effective interest method of amortization as shown in Illustration 16-18. It retires its bonds at 103 at the end of the eighth period, after paying the semi-annual interest. The carrying value of the bonds at the redemption date, as shown in the bond premium amortization schedule, is $1,009,709. The following is the entry to record the redemption at the end of the eighth interest period (January 1, 2007):

Jan. 1	Bonds Payable	1,000,000	
	Premium on Bonds Payable	9,709	
	Loss on Bond Redemption	20,291	
	Cash ($1,000,000 × 103%)		1,030,000
	To record redemption of bonds at 103.		

A	=	L	+	SE
−1,030,000		−1,000,000		−20,291
		−9,709		

The loss of $20,291 is the difference between the cash paid of $1,030,000 and the carrying value of the bonds of $1,009,709. This is very similar to the calculation of a loss or gain on the sale of capital assets. In both cases, cash is compared to carrying value. However, the determination of whether a loss or a gain results naturally differs, depending on whether you are selling capital assets (assets) or purchasing bonds (liabilities). For example, when you sell an asset, you gain when the cash received is **greater than** the carrying value. When you retire a liability, you gain when the cash paid is **less than** the carrying value.

Illustration 16-20

Comparison of asset and liability gain and loss

Capital Assets	Bonds Payable
Sale price (proceeds)	Purchase price
– Carrying value	– Carrying value
Gain (loss)	Loss (gain)

Losses (gains) on bond redemption are reported separately in the income statement.

Before You Go On . . .

▸Review It

1. Explain the accounting for the redemption of bonds at maturity, and before maturity, by a payment in cash.
2. Distinguish between gains (losses) from the sale of capital assets and the redemption of bonds.

▸Do It

R & B Inc. issues $500,000 of 10-year bonds at a premium. Prior to maturity, on June 30 when the carrying value of the bonds is $508,000, the company redeems the bonds at 101. Prepare the entry to record the redemption of the bonds.

Action Plan

- Update any partial period interest expense, amortization, and interest payable.
- Determine and eliminate the carrying value of the bonds.
- Record the cash paid.
- Calculate and record the gain or loss (the difference between the cash paid and the carrying value).

Solution

There is a $3,000 gain on redemption. The cash paid, $505,000, is lower than the carrying value of $508,000 ($500,000 + $8,000). The entry is as follows:

June 30	Bonds Payable	500,000	
	Premium on Bonds Payable	8,000	
	Gain on Bond Redemption		3,000
	Cash ($500,000 × 101%)		505,000
	To record redemption of bonds at 101.		

Related exercise material: BE16–9, E16–7, E16–8, and E16–9.

Accounting for Other Long-Term Liabilities

Other common types of long-term obligations are notes payable and capital lease liabilities. The accounting for these liabilities is explained in the following sections.

Long-Term Notes Payable

The use of notes payable in debt financing is common. Long-term notes payable are similar to short-term notes payable except that the terms of the notes exceed one year. In periods of unstable interest rates, the interest rate on long-term notes may be tied to changes in the market rate. An example of this is The Second Cup's long-term borrowing rate, which may be based on any of the following interest rates plus an appropriate interest spread: prime, bankers' acceptances, or the London InterBank Offering Rate (LIBOR).

A long-term note may be unsecured or secured. The Strait Crossing Development note payable referred to in the feature story is unsecured. A secured note pledges title to specific assets as security for the loan. Secured notes are commonly known as mortgages. A mortgage note payable is widely used by individuals to purchase homes. It is also used by many companies to acquire capital assets.

►Accounting in Action ► *@-Business Insight*

 Mortgage.com Inc., a pioneer in one of the Internet's more promising ideas, exited the on-line home lending business. A study of Internet consumers showed that only 4% had applied on-line for a mortgage. Fewer than 1% closed a loan. "The fact is, there is still a lot about getting a mortgage that can't be done on-line," says Diane Glossman, an analyst. Although technology allows you to send your signature electronically, "in most cases, you still need to sign paper documents, someone to visit the property and appraise it, and these loans usually need to be closed in person."

Source: Aaron Elstein, "Mortgage.com Plans to Quit Web Business." *The Wall Street Journal*, November 1, 2000, C20.

While short-term notes are normally repayable in full at maturity, most long-term notes are repayable in a series of periodic payments. These payments are known as **instalments** and are paid monthly, quarterly, semi-annually, or at another defined period. Each payment consists of (1) interest on the unpaid balance of the loan, and (2) a reduction of loan principal. Payments generally take one of two forms: (1) fixed principal payments plus interest, or (2) blended principal and interest payments. Let's look at each of these payment patterns in more detail.

Fixed Principal Payments

Instalment notes with fixed principal payments are repayable in **equal periodic amounts, plus interest**. Interest may be either **fixed** or **floating**. A fixed interest rate will be constant over the term of the note. A floating (or variable) interest rate will change with fluctuating market rates. Generally, floating rates are tied to changes in the **prime rate**. Prime is the rate that banks use to loan money to their most credit-worthy customers. It is usually set slightly above the Bank of Canada rate, the lending rate at which financial institutions borrow.

To illustrate, assume that, on January 1, 2003, Belanger Ltée issues a $120,000, 7%, five-year note payable to obtain financing for a new research laboratory. The terms

Illustration 16-21

Instalment payment schedule—fixed principal payment

provide for equal monthly instalment payments of $2,000 ($120,000 ÷ 60 periods) on the first of each month, plus interest of 7% on the outstanding principal balance. The instalment payment schedule for the first few months for Belanger Ltée, rounded to the nearest dollar, is shown in Illustration 16-21:

	(A) Cash Payment (B + C)	(B) Interest Expense (D × 7% × $\frac{1}{12}$)	(C) Reduction of Principle ($120,000 ÷ 60)	(D) Principal Balance (D − C)
BELANGER LTÉE				
Instalment Payment Schedule—Fixed Principal Payment				
Interest Period				
Issue date				$120,000
1	$2,700	$700	$2,000	118,000
2	2,688	688	2,000	116,000
3	2,677	677	2,000	114,000

With fixed principal payments, the interest decreases each period (as the principal decreases). The portion applied to the reduction of loan principal stays constant, but because of the decreasing interest, the total payment decreases.

The entries to record the note payable and the first instalment payment one month later are as follows:

A = L + SE	Jan. 1	Cash	120,000	
+120,000 +120,000		Notes Payable		120,000
		To record 5-year 7% note payable.		

A = L + SE	Feb. 1	Interest Expense	700	
−2,700 −2,000 −700		Notes Payable	2,000	
		Cash		2,700
		To record monthly payment on note.		

Blended Principal and Interest Payments

Instalment notes with blended principal and interest payments are repayable in **equal periodic amounts, including interest**. Blended principal and interest payments result in changing amounts of interest and principal applied to the loan. As with fixed principal payments, the interest decreases each period (as the principal decreases). In contrast to fixed principal payments, the portion applied to the loan principal increases each period.

To illustrate, assume that instead of fixed principal payments, Belanger Ltée repays its $120,000 7% note payable in equal monthly instalments of $2,376. Illustration 16-22 shows the instalment payment schedule for the first few months for Belanger Ltée, rounded to the nearest dollar.

	(A) Cash Payment	(B) Interest Expense (D × 7% × $\frac{1}{12}$)	(C) Reduction of Principal (A − B)	(D) Principal Balance (D − C)
BELANGER LTÉE				
Instalment Payment Schedule—Blended Principal and Interest				
Interest Period				
Issue date				$120,000
1	$2,376	$700	$1,676	118,324
2	2,376	690	1,686	116,638
3	2,376	680	1,696	114,942

The entries to record the note payable and the first instalment payment one month later are as follows:

Jan. 1	Cash	120,000			
	Notes Payable		120,000		
	To record 5-year 7% note payable.				

A	=	L	+	SE
+120,000		+120,000		

Feb. 1	Interest Expense	700			
	Notes Payable	1,676			
	Cash		2,376		
	To record monthly payment on note.				

A	=	L	+	SE
–2,376		–1,676		–700

With both types of instalment notes payable, as with any other long-term note payable, **the reduction in principal for the next year must be reported as a current liability. The remaining unpaid principal is classified as a long-term liability.**

Lease Liabilities

As indicated in Chapter 10, a lease is a contractual arrangement between a **lessor** (owner of a property) and a **lessee** (renter of a property). It grants the right to use specific property for a period of time in return for cash payments. The two main types of lease are an operating lease and a capital lease.

STUDY OBJECTIVE
·········· 6 ··········
Contrast the accounting for operating leases and capital leases.

►Accounting in Action ► *Business Insight*

Leasing is big business in Canada. How big? In a recent year, 25% of the machinery and equipment purchased was financed by lease. Nearly half of new vehicles sold in Canada are leased. The reasons often stated for leasing include favourable income tax treatment, increased flexibility, and increased cash flow.

Operating Leases

Rental of an apartment and rental of a car are examples of operating leases. **An operating lease implies temporary use of the property by the lessee.** The lessor continues to own the property. The lease (or rental) payments are recorded as an expense by the lessee and as revenue by the lessor. For example, assume that a sales representative for Western Inc. leases a car from Hertz Car Rental at the airport on July 17. Hertz charges a total of $275. The entry by the lessee, Western Inc., would be as follows:

Helpful hint *Financial Reporting in Canada* notes that 68% of the companies surveyed reported operating leases and 37% reported capital leases.

July 17	Car Rental Expense	275			
	Cash		275		
	To record payment of lease rental charge.				

A	=	L	+	SE
–275				–275

The lessee may have other costs during the lease period. For example, in the case above, the lessee may pay for gas and insurance. These costs are also reported as an expense.

Capital Leases

In some cases, the lease contract transfers all the benefits and risks of ownership to the lessee. Such a lease is, in effect, a purchase of the property. This type of lease is called a capital lease. The name comes from the fact that the present value of the cash payments for the lease are capitalized and recorded as an asset. Illustration 16-23 indicates the major difference between an operating and a capital lease.

Illustration 16-23

Types of leases

Operating lease	Capital lease
Lessor has substantially all of the benefits and risks of ownership	Lessee has substantially all of the benefits and risks of ownership

The lessee must classify the lease as a capital lease and record the purchase **as an asset** if **any one** of the following conditions exists:

1. **The lease transfers ownership of the property to the lessee.** *Rationale:* If, during or at the end of the lease term, the lessee receives ownership of the asset or can purchase the asset at a price substantially below its fair market value, the leased asset should be reported as an asset on the lessee's books.
2. **The lease term is equal to 75% or more of the economic life of the leased property.** *Rationale*: If the lease term is for much of the asset's useful life, the asset has effectively been purchased and should be recorded by the lessee.
3. **The present value of the lease payments equals or exceeds 90% of the fair market value of the leased property.** *Rationale*: If the present value of the lease payments is equal to, or almost equal to, the fair market value of the asset, the lessee has essentially purchased the asset. As a result, the leased asset should be recorded on the books of the lessee.

To illustrate, assume that Fortune Company Ltd. decides to lease new equipment on November 27. The lease period is four years and the economic life of the leased equipment is estimated to be five years. The present value of the lease payments is $190,000 and the fair market value of the equipment is $200,000. There is no transfer of ownership during the lease term.

In this example, Fortune has essentially purchased the equipment. Conditions (2) and (3) have been met. First, the lease term is 80% (≥ 75%) of the economic life of the asset. Second, the present value of cash payments is 95% (≥ 90%) of the equipment's fair market value. The entry to record the transaction is as follows:

A	=	L	+	SE
+190,000		+190,000		

Nov. 27	Leased Asset—Equipment	190,000	
	Lease Liability		190,000
	To record leased asset and lease liability.		

The leased asset is reported on the balance sheet under capital assets. **The portion of the lease liability expected to be paid in the next year is reported as a current lia-**

bility. The remainder is classified as a long-term liability.

Most lessees do not like to report leases on their balance sheets. Why? Because the lease liability increases the company's total liabilities. This, in turn, may make it more difficult for the company to obtain needed funds from lenders. As a result, companies attempt to keep leased assets and lease liabilities off the balance sheet by not meeting any of the three conditions listed above. This practice of keeping liabilities off the balance sheet is called **off balance sheet financing**.

Helpful hint Off balance sheet financing is a major reporting problem. Some other off balance sheet items are guarantees and unfunded pension obligations.

Statement Presentation and Analysis of Long-Term Liabilities

Long-term liabilities are reported in a separate section of the balance sheet, immediately after current liabilities, as shown in Illustration 16-24.

STUDY OBJECTIVE

7

Explain and illustrate the methods for the financial statement presentation and analysis of long-term liabilities.

ANY COMPANY LTD. Balance Sheet (partial)		
Long-term liabilities		
Bonds payable, 10%, due in 2009	$1,000,000	
Less: Discount on bonds payable	80,000	$ 920,000
Mortgage notes payable, 11%, due in 2015 and secured by capital assets		500,000
Lease liability		540,000
Total long-term liabilities		$1,960,000

Illustration 16-24

Balance sheet presentation of long-term liabilities

Summary data are usually presented in the balance sheet and detailed data (interest rates, maturity dates, conversion privileges, and assets pledged as collateral) are shown in a supporting schedule. The current maturities of long-term debt should be reported under current liabilities if they will be paid from current assets.

Using the Information in the Financial Statements

Long-term creditors and shareholders are interested in a company's long-term solvency. Of particular concern is the company's ability to pay interest when it is due and to repay its debt at maturity. The debt to total assets and interest coverage ratios explained below provide information about a company's ability to meet its debt obligations.

Debt to Total Assets

Debt to total assets measures the percentage of the total assets provided by creditors. It is calculated, using The Second Cup data, as shown in the formula below, by dividing total debt (both current and long-term liabilities) by total assets. The higher the percentage of debt to total assets, the greater the risk that the company may be unable to meet its maturing obligations.

Illustration 16-25

Debt to total assets

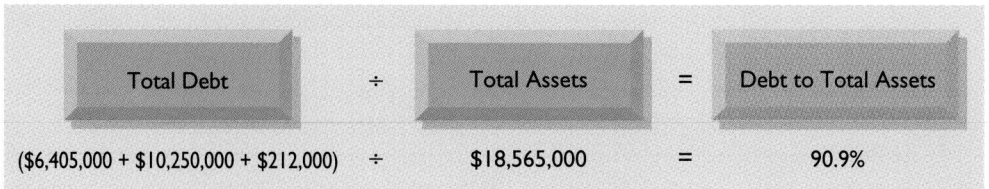

Total Debt	÷	Total Assets	=	Debt to Total Assets
($6,405,000 + $10,250,000 + $212,000)	÷	$18,565,000	=	90.9%

The Second Cup's debt to total assets is very high. Nearly 91% of its assets are financed by debt, rather than equity. This situation has arisen, in part, because of The Second Cup's increasing deficit.

Interest Coverage

Alternative Terminology
The interest coverage ratio is also commonly known as the *times interest earned ratio.*

The interest coverage ratio indicates the company's ability to meet interest payments as they come due. It is calculated by dividing income before interest expense and income tax expense by interest expense. The numerator is often abbreviated and called EBIT, which stands for "earnings before interest expense and income tax expense."

However, interest coverage is an accrual-based measure. It does not necessarily indicate whether the company has cash available to pay the interest. By removing amortization expense from EBIT, we can calculate a *cash-based* interest coverage ratio. The numerator in this ratio is known as EBITDA, which is an abbreviation for "earnings before interest expense, income tax expense, and depreciation and amortization expense." EBITDA is a basic measure of a company's ability to generate cash from operating activities. It is frequently cited in annual reports and in the financial press.

Illustration 16-26

Interest coverage ratios

The cash interest coverage ratio is calculated by dividing EBITDA by interest expense. Illustration 16-26 calculates both interest coverage and cash interest coverage for The Second Cup.

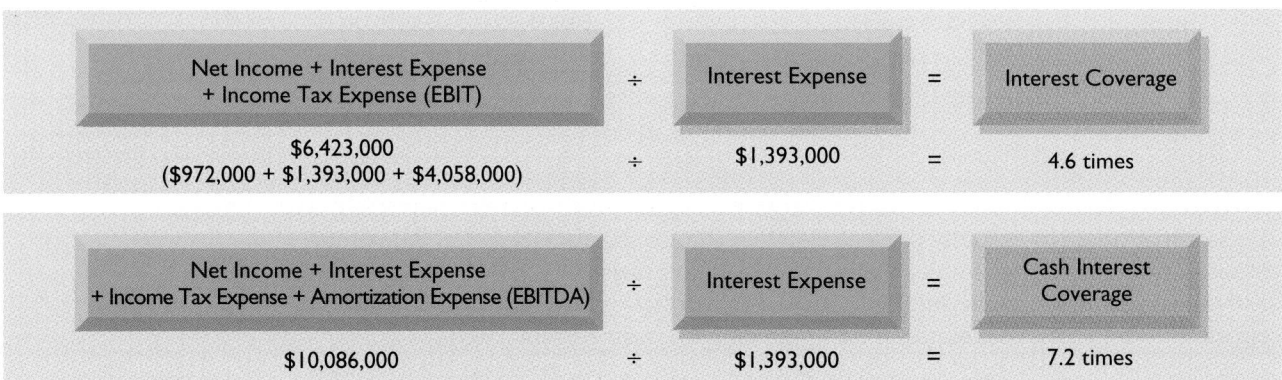

Note that the interest reported on The Second Cup's financial statements is net of investment income so we must look to the detail presented in Note 9 to determine the interest expense. Additionally, note that The Second Cup reports EBITDA directly on its Consolidated Statement of Operations, so it need not be calculated in this case.

Even though The Second Cup has a very high debt to total assets ratio, it is equipped to handle its interest payments in the year 2000. Its EBIT can cover interest charges 4.6 times. On a cash basis, it has a larger interest coverage ratio, at 7.2 times.

Before You Go On . . .

▸Review It

1. Explain the accounting for long-term notes payable.
2. What is the difference in accounting for an operating lease and a capital lease?
3. How would you measure a company's capacity to meet its debt obligations?
4. Does The Second Cup report the figures for EBIT or EBITDA in its financial statements? If so, where? The answers to these questions are at the end of the chapter.

Related exercise material: BE16–10, BE16–11, BE16–12, BE16–13, BE16–14, E16–10, E16–11, E16–12, and E16–13.

► *A Look Back at Our Feature Story*

● ●

Refer back to the feature story about the Confederation Bridge bonds and answer the following questions:

1. The Confederation Bridge bonds, with a principal value of $661 million, were issued for proceeds of $661,542,612. What was the amount of the bond premium or discount? Was the contractual interest rate higher or lower than the market interest rate at the date of issue?
2. Annual payments to bondholders began in 1997 and included accrued interest. Why do you suppose interest payments were deferred until 1997? Would Strait Crossing have made any journal entries to recognize this interest before 1997? If so, provide the entries it would have made.
3. The Strait Crossing Financial Inc. (Confederation Bridge) bonds are rated Aaa by Moody's Investors Service. Why is it important to this Crown corporation that its bonds have a high bond rating?

Solution

1. The bonds were issued at a premium of $542,612 ($661,542,612 − $661,000,000). Bondholders were willing to pay more than the principal value of the bonds, since the contractual interest rate (4.5%) was higher than what could be earned in the marketplace.
2. Interest payments were likely deferred until 1997 in order to coincide with the bridge opening. These payments probably depended on the cash flow from bridge receipts and the federal government subsidy that used to go to the ferry lines. Note that this point relates only to the timing of the cash flows, not to the recognition—or matching—of expenses.

    Because interest payments did not begin until May 1997, interest for the period from October 1993 to May 1997 was accrued. At each interest payment date, Strait Crossing would make the following journal entry:

May 1994 or 1995 or 1996	Interest Expense
	Premium on Bonds Payable
	Interest Payable
	To record accrued interest and premium amortization.

3. Having a high-quality bond rating is as important to a Crown corporation as it is to a business corporation. A high bond rating indicates that the bonds are less risky. They are, therefore, more attractive to purchasers. A lower interest rate also results when bonds have a high rating, so the cost to the issuer of the bonds is less.

THE
NAVIGATOR

DEMONSTRATION PROBLEM 1

Gardner Corporation issues $1,750,000 of 10-year 12% bonds on January 1, 2003, at $1,968,090 to yield a market interest rate of 10%. The bonds pay semi-annual interest on July 1 and January 1. Round your answers to the nearest dollar.

Instructions

1. Using the information provided in Appendix B at the end of this text, show how the selling price of the bonds, $1,968,090, was calculated.
2. Assuming Gardner uses the straight-line method of bond amortization, do the following:
    (a) Prepare the journal entry to record the issue of the bonds.
    (b) Prepare the journal entry to record the payment of interest on July 1, 2003.
    (c) Prepare the adjusting entry required on December 31, 2003.
3. Assuming Gardner uses the effective interest method of bond amortization, do the following:
    (a) Prepare the journal entry to record the issue of the bonds.
    (b) Prepare the journal entry to record the payment of interest on July 1, 2003.
    (c) Prepare the adjusting entry required on December 31, 2003.

Solution to Demonstration Problem 1

1. Present value (PV) of principal to be received at maturity:
   $1,750,000 × 0.37689
   (PV of $1 due in 20 periods at 5% (10% × %₂) from Table B-1) $ 659,558

   Present value of interest to be received periodically over the term of the bonds:
   $1,750,000 × 12% × %₂ = $105,000 × 12.46221
   (PV of $1 due each period for 20 periods at 5% (10% × %₂) from Table B-2)   1,308,532

   Present value of bonds $1,968,090

2. (a)

Jan. 1	Cash	1,968,090	
	Premium on Bonds Payable		218,090
	Bonds Payable		1,750,000
	To record issue of bonds at a premium.		

(b)

July 1	Bond Interest Expense	94,095	
	Premium on Bonds Payable ($218,090 ÷ 20 periods)	10,905	
	Cash ($1,750,000 × 12% × %₂)		105,000
	To record payment of semi-annual interest and amortization of bond premium.		

(c)

Dec. 31	Bond Interest Expense	94,095	
	Premium on Bonds Payable ($218,090 ÷ 20 periods)	10,905	
	Interest Payable ($1,750,000 × 12% × %₂)		105,000
	To record accrual of semi-annual interest and amortization of bond premium.		

3. (a)

Jan. 1	Cash	1,968,090	
	Premium on Bonds Payable		218,090
	Bonds Payable		1,750,000
	To record issue of bonds at a premium.		

(b)

July 1	Bond Interest Expense ($1,968,090 × 10% × %₂)	98,405	
	Premium on Bonds Payable ($105,000 − $98,405)	6,595	
	Cash ($1,750,000 × 12% × %₂)		105,000
	To record payment of semi-annual interest and amortization of bond premium.		

(c)

Dec. 31	Bond Interest Expense		
	($1,750,000 + $218,090 − $6,595) × 10% × %₂)	98,075	
	Premium on Bonds Payable ($105,000 − $98,075)	6,925	
	Interest Payable ($1,750,000 × 12% × %₂)		105,000
	To record accrual of semi-annual interest and amortization of bond premium.		

DEMONSTRATION PROBLEM 2

Snyder Software Inc. successfully developed a new spreadsheet program. To produce and market the program, the company needed $500,000 of additional financing. On December 31, 2003, Snyder issued a $500,000, 12%, 15-year mortgage note payable. The terms provide for semi-annual blended instalment payments of $36,324, principal and interest, on June 30 and December 31. Round your answers to the nearest dollar.

Instructions

(a) Prepare the entry for the issue of the note on December 31, 2003.

(b) Prepare a payment schedule for the first four instalment payments.

(c) Indicate the current and noncurrent amounts for the mortgage note payable at December 31, 2004.

Solution to Demonstration Problem 2

(a)

Dec. 31	Cash	500,000	
	Mortgage Notes Payable		500,000
	To record issue of mortgage note payable.		

(b)

Semi-annual Interest Period	Cash Payment	Interest Expense	Reduction of Principal	Principal Balance
Issue Date				$500,000
1	$36,324	$30,000[1]	$6,324[2]	493,676[3]
2	36,324	29,621	6,703	486,973
3	36,324	29,218	7,106	479,867
4	36,324	28,792	7,532	472,335

[1] $500,000 × 12% × 6/12 = $30,000

[2] $36,324 − $30,000 = $6,324

[3] $500,000 − $6,324 = $493,676

(c) The current liability is $14,638 ($7,106 + $7,532).

The long-term liability is $472,335.

The total liability is $486,973, the balance at the end of the second period, December 31, 2004.

Action Plan

- Determine the interest expense for the mortgage by multiplying the semi-annual interest rate by the principal balance at the beginning of the period. The reduction of principal is the difference between the cash payment and the interest expense amounts.

- Recognize that as the principal amount decreases, so does the interest expense.

- Record mortgage payments, recognizing that each payment consists of (1) interest on the unpaid loan balance, and (2) a reduction of the loan principal.

THE NAVIGATOR

Summary of Study Objectives

1. Describe the advantages and illustrate the impact of issuing bonds instead of common shares. Bonds may be sold to many investors. They offer the following advantages over common shares: (a) shareholder control is not affected, (b) income tax savings result, (c) the borrower may benefit from leverage, and (d) earnings per share may be higher.

2. Prepare the entries for the issue of bonds and the recording of interest expense. When bonds are issued, Cash is debited for the cash proceeds and Bonds Payable is credited for the face value of the bonds. Bond Interest Payable is credited if there is accrued interest. The accounts Premium on Bonds Payable and Discount on Bonds Payable are used to show the bond premium or bond discount. The straight-line method or effective interest method of amortization is used to allocate any bond discount or bond premium to interest expense.

3. Contrast the effects of the straight-line and effective interest methods of amortizing bond discounts and premiums. The straight-line method of amortization results in a constant amount of amortization and interest expense per period but a varying rate of interest. In contrast, the effective interest method results in varying amounts of amortization and interest expense per period but a constant rate of interest. The effective interest method results in a better matching of expenses with revenues.

4. Prepare the entries when bonds are retired. When bonds are redeemed at maturity, Cash is credited and Bonds

Payable is debited for the face value of the bonds. When bonds are redeemed before maturity, it is necessary to (a) update any unrecorded interest, (b) eliminate the carrying value of the bonds at the redemption date, (c) record the cash paid, and (d) recognize the gain or loss on redemption.

5. Account for long-term notes payable. Each payment consists of (1) interest on the unpaid balance of the loan, and (2) a reduction of the loan principal. The interest decreases each period, while the portion applied to the loan principal increases each period.

6. Contrast the accounting for operating leases and capital leases. For an operating lease, lease (or rental) payments are recorded as an expense by the lessee (renter). For a capital lease, the lessee records the asset and related obligation at the present value of the future lease payments.

7. Explain and illustrate the methods for the financial statement presentation and analysis of long-term liabilities. The nature and amount of each long-term debt should be reported in the balance sheet or in the notes accompanying the statements. The long-term solvency of a company may be analysed by calculating three ratios. Debt to total assets indicates the proportion of company assets financed by debt. Interest coverage measures a company's ability to meet its interest payments as they come due. Cash interest coverage measures a company's ability to generate sufficient cash to meet its interest payments as they come due.

THE NAVIGATOR

GLOSSARY

 Key Term Matching Activity

Bearer (coupon) bonds   Bonds that are not registered. (p. 738)

Bond   A form of interest-bearing note payable issued by corporations, governments, and government entities. (p. 736)

Bond certificate   A legal document indicating the name of the issuer, the face value of the bond, and other data such as the contractual interest rate and maturity date of the bond. (p. 739)

Bond indenture   A legal document that states the terms of the bond issue. (p. 739)

Capital lease   A contractual arrangement that transfers all the benefits and risks of ownership to the lessee, so that the lease is, in effect, a purchase of the property. (p. 758)

Cash interest coverage   A measure of a company's ability to pay annual interest obligations. It is calculated by dividing EBITDA by interest expense. (p. 760)

Contractual interest rate   Rate used to determine the amount of interest the borrower pays and the investor receives. (p. 739)

Convertible bonds   Bonds that permit bondholders to convert them into common shares. (p. 738)

Debenture bonds   Bonds issued against the general credit of the borrower. Also called unsecured bonds. (p. 738)

Debt to total assets   The ratio of total liabilities to total assets. Indicates the proportion of assets financed by debt. (p. 759)

Discount (on bonds payable)   The difference that results when the selling price of the bonds is less than the face value of the bonds. This occurs when the market interest rate is greater than the contractual interest rate. (p. 743)

EBIT   Earnings before interest expense and income tax expense. (p. 760)

EBITDA   Earnings before interest expense, income tax expense, and depreciation and amortization expense. (p. 760)

Effective interest method of amortization   A method of amortizing bond discount or bond premium that results in periodic interest expense equal to a constant percentage of the carrying value of the bonds. (p. 746)

Face value   Amount of principal the issuer must pay at the maturity date of the bond. (p. 739)

Interest coverage   A measure of a firm's ability to meet its interest obligations. It is calculated by dividing income before interest expense and income tax expense (EBIT) by interest expense. (p. 760)

Market (effective) interest rate   The rate investors require for lending money to the corporation. (p. 741)

Mortgage bonds   Bonds secured by capital assets. (p. 738)

Mortgage note payable   A long-term note that pledges title to specific capital assets as security for a loan. (p. 755)

Operating lease   A contractual arrangement that gives the lessee temporary use of the property, with continued ownership of the property by the lessor. (p. 757)

Premium (on bonds payable)   The difference that results when the selling price of the bonds is greater than the face value of the bonds. This occurs when the market interest rate is less than the contractual interest rate. (p. 743)

Redeemable bonds   Bonds that the issuer can redeem at a stated dollar amount prior to maturity. Also known as callable bonds. (p. 738)

Registered bonds   Bonds issued in the name of the owner. (p. 738)

Retractable bonds   Bonds that the bondholder can redeem at a stated dollar amount prior to maturity. (p. 738)

Secured bonds   Bonds that have specific assets of the issuer pledged as collateral. (p. 738)

Serial bonds   Bonds that mature in instalments. (p. 738)

Straight-line method of amortization   A method of amortizing bond discount or bond premium that allocates the same amount to interest expense in each interest period. (p. 744)

Term bonds   Bonds that mature at a single specified future date. (p. 738)

SELF-STUDY QUESTIONS

 Chapter 16 Self-Test

Answers are at the end of the chapter.

(SO 1) K 1. The term used for bonds that are unsecured is:
  a. redeemable bonds.
  b. indenture bonds.
  c. debenture bonds.
  d. convertible bonds.

(SO 2) K 2. If bonds are issued at a premium, it indicates that:
  a. the contractual interest rate exceeds the market interest rate.
  b. the market interest rate exceeds the contractual interest rate.
  c. the contractual interest rate and the market interest rate are the same.
  d. no predictable relationship exists between the two rates.

(SO 2) AP 3. On January 1, Hurley Corporation issues $500,000 of five-year 12% bonds at 96 with interest payable on July 1 and January 1. The entry on July 1 to record the payment of bond interest and the amortization of bond discount using the straight-line method will include a:
  a. debit to Interest Expense, $30,000.
  b. debit to Interest Expense, $60,000.
  c. credit to Discount on Bonds Payable, $4,000.
  d. credit to Discount on Bonds Payable, $2,000.

(SO 2) AP 4. For the bonds issued in question 3, above, what is the carrying value of the bonds at the end of the third interest period?
  a. $464,000
  b. $472,000
  c. $486,000
  d. $488,000

(SO 2) AP 5. On January 1, Dias Corporation issued $2,000,000 of five-year 7% bonds with interest payable on July 1 and January 1. The bonds sold for $1,918,880. The market rate of interest for these bonds was 8%. Assuming the effective interest method is used, on the first interest date, the debit entry to Bond Interest Expense (rounded to the nearest dollar) is for:
  a. $67,161.
  b. $70,000.
  c. $76,755.
  d. $80,000.

(SO 2) C 6. When the interest payment dates of a bond are May 1 and November 1, and a bond issue is sold on June 1, the amount of cash received by the issuer will be:
  a. decreased by accrued interest from June 1 to November 1.
  b. decreased by accrued interest from May 1 to June 1.
  c. increased by accrued interest from May 1 to June 1.
  d. increased by accrued interest from June 1 to November 1.

(SO 3) K 7. The effective interest method of amortization results in a:
  a. constant dollar amount of interest expense each period.
  b. varying dollar amount of interest payment each period.
  c. constant rate of interest each period.
  d. constant dollar amount of discount or premium amortization each period.

(SO 4) AP 8. Gester Corporation redeems its $100,000 face value bonds at 105 on January 1, after the payment of semi-annual interest. The carrying value of the bonds at the redemption date is $103,745. The entry to record the redemption will include a:
  a. credit of $3,745 to Premium on Bonds Payable.
  b. debit of $1,255 to Loss on Bond Redemption.
  c. credit of $1,255 to Gain on Bond Redemption.
  d. debit of $5,000 to Premium on Bonds Payable.

(SO 5) AP 9. Andrews Inc. issues a $497,000, 10% three-year instalment note payable on January 1. The note will be paid in three annual blended instalments of $200,000, each payable at the end of the year. What is the amount of interest expense that should be recognized by Andrews Inc. in the second year?
  a. $16,567
  b. $34,670
  c. $49,700
  d. $347,600

(SO 6) C 10. The lease term for Lease A is equal to 90% of the estimated economic life of the leased property. The lease term for Lease B is equal to 60% of the estimated economic life of the leased property. Assuming no other conditions are met, how should the lessee classify these leases?

	Lease A	Lease B
a.	Operating lease	Capital lease
b.	Operating lease	Operating lease
c.	Capital lease	Operating lease
d.	Capital lease	Capital lease

(SO 7) AP 11. In a recent year, Yung Kee Corporation had net income of $150,000, amortization expense of $50,000, interest expense of $30,000, and income tax expense of $20,000. What was Yung Kee's cash interest coverage ratio?
  a. 4.00
  b. 5.00
  c. 6.66
  d. 8.33

THE NAVIGATOR

QUESTIONS

(SO 1) C   1. What are long-term liabilities? Give three examples.

(SO 1) C   2. (a) As a source of long-term financing, what are the major advantages of bonds over common shares?

(b) What are the major disadvantages of using bonds for long-term financing?

(SO 1) C   3. Contrast the following types of bonds: (a) secured and unsecured, (b) term and serial, (c) redeemable and retractable.

(SO 1) C   4. The following terms are important in issuing bonds: (a) face value, (b) contractual interest rate, and (c) market interest rate. Explain each of these terms.

(SO 1) C   5. Describe the two major obligations a company has to pay after it issues bonds.

(SO 1) C   6. What is a convertible bond? Discuss the advantages of a convertible bond from the standpoint of (a) the bondholders, and (b) the issuing corporation.

(SO 2) AP   7. Assume that Stoney Inc. sold bonds with a face value of $100,000 for $98,000. Was the market interest rate equal to, less than, or greater than the bonds' contractual interest rate? Explain.

(SO 2) AP   8. If a 10%, 10-year, $600,000 bond is issued at face value and interest is paid semi-annually, what is the amount of the interest payment at the end of the first semi-annual period? What is the amount of the interest expense using the straight-line method of amortization? Using the effective interest method of amortization?

(SO 2) AP   9. If the Bonds Payable account has a balance of $900,000 and the Discount on Bonds Payable account has a balance of $40,000, what is the carrying value of the bonds?

(SO 2) C   10. Explain the straight-line and effective interest methods of amortizing a discount and a premium on bonds payable.

(SO 2) AP   11. Genji Corporation issues $200,000 of 8% five-year bonds on January 1, 2003, at 104. Assuming that the straight-line method is used to amortize the premium, what is the total amount of interest expense for 2003? For 2004?

(SO 2) AP   12. Summit Corporation issues $400,000 of 9% five-year bonds on January 1, 2003, at 104. If Summit uses the effective interest method to amortize the premium, will the annual interest expense increase or decrease over the life of the bonds? Explain.

(SO 3) AP   13. A $1,000, 8%, five-year bond is sold at 98, plus accrued interest, on November 1. Its semi-annual interest payment dates are January 1 and July 1. How much accrued interest will the investor pay on November 1? What period of time will the amortization of the bond discount be spread over?

(SO 3) C   14. Julia Amant is explaining the advantages of the effective interest method of bond amortization to her accounting staff. What should Julia be saying?

(SO 4) AP   15. Which accounts are debited and which are credited if a bond issue originally sold at a premium is redeemed before maturity at 97?

(SO 5) C   16. Distinguish between instalment notes payable with fixed principal payments and those with blended principal and interest payments.

(SO 5) AP   17. Doug Bareak, a friend of yours, has recently purchased a home for $125,000. He paid $25,000 down and financed the remainder with a 20-year 10.5% mortgage, payable in blended payments of principal and interest at $998.38 per month. At the end of the first month, Doug received a statement from the bank indicating that only $123.38 of the principal was paid during the month. At this rate, he calculated that it will take over 67 years to pay off the mortgage. Explain why this is not the case.

(SO 6) C   18. (a) What is a lease agreement?
(b) What are the two major types of lease?
(c) Distinguish between the two types of lease.

(SO 6) AP   19. Rasch Company entered into an agreement to lease computers from Elgin Electronics Inc. The present value of the lease payments is $186,300. Assuming that this is a capital lease, what entry would Rasch Company make on the date of the lease agreement?

(SO 7) K   20. In general, what are the requirements for the financial statement presentation of long-term liabilities?

(SO 7) C   21. Distinguish between EBIT and EBITDA.

(SO 7) C   22. Why do some investors consider the cash interest coverage ratio to be a better measure of a company's ability to pay interest than the accrual-based interest coverage ratio?

BRIEF EXERCISES

BE16–1 Ouellet Inc. is considering two alternatives to finance its construction of a new $2-million plant:
  (a) Issue of 200,000 common shares at a market price of $10 per share.
  (b) Issue of $2,000,000 of 8% bonds at face value.

Compare financing alternatives—common shares versus bonds. (SO 1) AP

Complete the following table, and indicate which alternative is preferable:

	Issue Shares	Issue Bonds
Income before interest and income tax	$ 1,000,000	$ 1,000,000
Interest expense	_____	_____
Income before income tax		
Income tax expense (30%)	_____	_____
Net income	$_____	$_____
Issued shares	_____	500,000
Earnings per share	_____	_____

BE16–2 Keystone Corporation issued one thousand 9%, five-year, $1,000 bonds dated March 1, 2003, at 100. (a) Prepare the journal entry to record the sale of these bonds on March 1. (b) Prepare the journal entry to record the first interest payment on September 1, 2003, if interest is payable semi-annually. Assume no previous accrual of interest. (c) Prepare the adjusting journal entry on December 31, 2003, Keystone's year end, to record interest expense.

Prepare entries for bonds issued at face value. (SO 2) AP

BE16–3 Repeat the requirements of BE16–2, assuming (a) the bonds were issued at 98, rather than 100, and (b) the bonds were issued at 102, rather than 100. The straight-line method of amortization is used.

Prepare entries for bonds, using straight-line method of amortization. (SO 2) AP

BE16–4 Dominic Company issues $2,000,000 of ten-year 9% bonds at 96, with interest payable on July 1 and January 1. The straight-line method of amortization is used. (a) Prepare the journal entry to record the sale of these bonds on January 1, 2003. (b) Prepare the journal entry to record interest expense and amortization on July 1, 2003. Assume no previous accrual of interest.

Prepare entries for bonds, using straight-line method of amortization. (SO 2) AP

BE16–5 Hebert Inc. issues $3,000,000 of five-year 10% bonds at 103, with interest payable on July 1 and January 1. The straight-line method of amortization is used. (a) Prepare the journal entry to record the sale of these bonds on January 1, 2003. (b) Prepare the journal entry to record interest expense and amortization on July 1, 2003. Assume no previous accrual of interest.

Prepare entries for bonds, using straight-line method of amortization. (SO 2) AP

BE16–6 Niagara Corporation issued $100,000 of 10%, five-year bonds on April 1, 2003, with interest payable on October 1 and April 1. The bonds were issued at $92,639 to yield a market interest rate of 12%. Answer the following questions:
  (a) How much interest expense would Niagara record on each of the first two interest payment dates (October 1, 2003, and April 1, 2004) if it used the straight-line method of bond amortization?
  (b) How much interest expense would Niagara record on each of the first two interest payment dates if it used the effective interest method of bond amortization?

Compare amortization for bonds, using straight-line and effective interest methods of amortization. (SO 2) AP

BE16–7 The partial bond discount amortization schedule for Rushton Corp. is presented below. Rushton uses the effective interest method of amortization.

Prepare entries for bonds and answer questions, using effective interest method of amortization. (SO 2, 3) AP

Semi-annual Interest Period	Interest Payment	Interest Expense	Discount Amortization	Unamortized Discount	Bond Carrying Value
Issue Date				$62,311	$937,689
1	$45,000	$46,884	$1,884	60,427	939,573
2	45,000	46,979	1,979	58,448	941,552

  (a) Prepare the journal entry to record the payment of interest and the discount amortization at the end of period 1.
  (b) What is the contractual interest rate on the bonds? The market interest rate?
  (c) Explain why interest expense is greater than interest paid.
  (d) Explain why interest expense will increase each period.
  (e) Outline the advantages of using the effective interest method rather than the straight-line method of amortization.

Prpare entries for bonds issued between interest dates.
(SO 3) AP

BE16–8   Guidry Inc. has $1,000,000 of 10-year 9% bonds outstanding with interest payable on July 1 and January 1. The bonds were dated January 1, 2003, but were issued on May 1, 2003, at face value plus accrued interest. (a) Prepare the journal entry to record the sale of the bonds on May 1, 2003. (b) Prepare the journal entry to record the first interest payment on July 1, 2003. Guidry uses the straight-line method of bond amortization.

Prepare entry for redemption of bonds.
(SO 4) AP

BE16–9   The balance sheet for Hathaway Corporation reports the following information on July 1, 2003:

HATHAWAY CORPORATION
Balance Sheet (partial)
July 1, 2003

Long-term liabilities		
Bonds payable	$ 1,000,000	
Less: Discount on bonds payable	60,000	$940,000

Hathaway redeems these bonds at 99 on July 1, 2003. Prepare the journal entry to record the redemption.

Prepare entries for long-term notes payable.
(SO 5) AP

BE16–10   Eyre Inc. issues a $300,000, 10%, 10-year mortgage note payable on November 30, 2003, to obtain financing for a new building. The terms provide for monthly payments. Prepare the entries to record the mortgage loan on November 30, 2003, and the first two payments on December 31, 2003 and January 31, 2004 assuming:

(a) the payment is a fixed principal payment of $2,500.
(b) the payment is a blended principal and interest payment of $3,964.52.

Prepare instalment schedule for long-term notes payable.
(SO 5) AP

BE16–11   You qualify for a $10,000 loan from the Canada Student Loans Program to help finance your education. Once you graduate, you start repaying this note payable at an interest rate of 10%. The monthly cash payment is $132.15, principal and interest, for 120 payments (10 years). Prepare an instalment payment schedule for the first three payments.

Prepare entries for operating and capital leases.
(SO 6) AP

BE16–12   Prepare the journal entries that the lessee should make to record the following transactions:

1. The lessee makes a lease payment of $70,000 to the lessor in an operating lease transaction.
2. Chang Company leases a new building from Bracer Construction, Inc. The present value of the lease payments is $600,000. The lease is a capital lease.

Prepare long-term liabilities section of balance sheet.
(SO 7) AP

BE16–13   Long-term liability items are presented below for Waugh Company at December 31, 2003. Prepare the long-term liabilities section of the balance sheet for Waugh Company.

Bonds payable, due 2005	$900,000
Discount on bonds payable	45,000
Lease liability	50,000
Notes payable, due 2007	80,000

Calculate debt ratios.
(SO 7) AP

BE16–14   The **Molson Inc.**'s financial statements contain the following selected data at March 31, 2000 (in millions):

Total assets	$3,111.8
Total liabilities	2,086.1
Amortization expense	100.3
Interest expense	77.8
Income tax expense (recovery)	(4.9)
Net income (loss)	(70.8)

Calculate Molson's (a) debt to total assets, (b) interest coverage, and (c) cash interest coverage.

EXERCISES

••

E16–1   Charter Airlines is considering two alternatives to finance the purchase of a fleet of air-planes. These alternatives are (1) to issue 60,000 common shares at $45 per share, and (2) to issue 10-year 13% bonds at face value for $2,700,000.

It is estimated that the company will earn $500,000 before interest and income tax as a result of this purchase. The company has an income tax rate of 30%. It has 90,000 common shares issued prior to the new financing.

Compare financing alternatives —common shares versus bonds.
(SO 1) AN

Instructions

Compare the effect on net income and earnings per share for these two methods of financing.

E16–2   On January 1, Laramie Company issued $100,000 of 10-year 10% bonds at face value. Inter-est is payable semi-annually, on July 1 and January 1. Laramie uses the straight-line method of amortization.

Prepare entries for bonds, using straight-line method of amortiza-tion.
(SO 2) AP

Instructions

Prepare journal entries to record the following:
  (a) The issue of the bonds on January 1, 2003
  (b) The payment of interest on July 1, assuming interest is not accrued on June 30
  (c) The accrual of interest on December 31

E16–3   Québec Corporation issued $650,000 of 10-year 9% bonds on January 1, 2003, for $609,497. This price resulted in a market (effective) interest rate of 10% on the bonds. Interest is payable semi-annually, on July 1 and January 1. Québec uses the effective interest method to amortize bond pre-mium or discount and has a December 31 year end.

Prepare entries for bonds, using effective interest method of amor-tization.
(SO 2) AP

Instructions

Prepare the journal entries (rounded to the nearest dollar) to record the following:
  (a) The issue of the bonds on January 1, 2003
  (b) The payment of interest and the amortization on July 1, 2003
  (c) The accrual of interest and the amortization on December 31, 2003

E16–4   Tagawa Company issued $600,000 of 10-year 11% bonds on January 1, 2003, for $637,378. This price resulted in an effective interest rate of 10% on the bonds. Interest is payable semi-annu-ally, on July 1 and January 1. Tagawa uses the effective interest method to amortize bond premium or discount and has a December 31 year end.

Prepare entries for bonds, using effective interest method of amor-tization.
(SO 2) AP

Instructions

Prepare the journal entries (rounded to the nearest dollar) to record the following:
  (a) The issue of the bonds on January 1, 2003
  (b) The payment of interest and the amortization on July 1, 2003
  (c) The accrual of interest and the amortization on December 31, 2003

E16–5   On April 1, Varma Company issued $120,000 of 10-year 10% bonds dated January 1 at face value plus accrued interest. Interest is payable semi-annually, on July 1 and January 1. Varma uses the straight-line method of bond amortization.

Prepare entries for bonds issued between interest dates, using straight-line method of amortiza-tion.
(SO 3) AP

Instructions

Present journal entries to record the following:
  (a) The issue of the bonds on April 1.
  (b) The payment of interest on July 1. Interest is not previously accrued.
  (c) Repeat parts (a) and (b) assuming the bonds had been issued at 101, rather than at face value.

E16–6   Villeneuve Inc. issues $1,000,000 of 6% bonds for proceeds of $864,100, at a time when the market rate of interest is 8%. The bonds pay interest semi-annually and mature in 10 years.

Compare straight-line and effec-tive interest methods of amorti-zation.
(SO 3) AN

Instructions

  (a) Prepare the journal entry to record the issue of the bonds.
  (b) Prepare the journal entry to record the payment of interest and discount amortization at period 1 (the first period) and at period 20 (the last period) assuming that Villeneuve uses (1) the straight-line method of amortization, and (2) the effective interest method of amortization. [*Hint*: Use the present value tables in Appendix B to determine the carrying value of the bond at the end of period 19 (beginning of period 20).]

(c) Calculate the market (effective) rate of interest by dividing the interest expense by the carrying value of the bond for each of period 1 and period 20 using (1) the straight-line method of amortization, and (2) the effective interest method of amortization.

(d) Discuss which method of amortization provides the best measure of the effective cost of borrowing.

Prepare entries for bonds, using straight-line method of amortization, and redemption at maturity.
(SO 2, 4) AP

E16–7   Bhog Company issued $400,000 of 20-year 9% bonds on January 1, 2003, at 103. Interest is payable semi-annually, on July 1 and January 1. Bhog uses straight-line amortization.

Instructions

Prepare the journal entries to record the following:
(a) The issue of the bonds on January 1, 2003
(b) The payment of interest and the amortization on July 1, 2003 (the first interest payment), assuming that interest was not previously accrued
(c) The accrual of interest and the amortization on December 31, 2022 (the last interest payment)
(d) The redemption of the bonds at maturity

Prepare entries for bonds, using straight-line method of amortization, and redemption at maturity.
(SO 2, 4) AP

E16–8   Jyoti Company issued $300,000 of 10-year 11% bonds on December 31, 2003, for $280,000. Interest is payable semi-annually, on June 30 and December 31. Jyoti uses the straight-line method to amortize any bond premium or discount.

Instructions

Prepare the journal entries to record the following:
(a) The issue of the bonds on December 31, 2003
(b) The payment of interest and the amortization on June 30, 2004
(c) The payment of interest and the amortization on December 31, 2004
(d) The redemption of the bonds at maturity, assuming interest for the last interest period has been paid and recorded

Prepare entries for redemption of bonds.
(SO 4) AP

E16–9   Two separate situations are presented below:
1. Ernst Corporation retired $120,000 face value 12% bonds on June 30, 2003, at 101. The carrying value of the bonds at the redemption date was $107,500. The bonds pay semi-annual interest on December 31 and June 30. The interest payment due on June 30, 2003, has been made and recorded.
2. Young, Inc., retired $150,000 face value 12.5% bonds on June 30, 2003, at 96. The carrying value of the bonds at the redemption date was $151,000. The bonds pay semi-annual interest on December 31 and June 30. The interest payment due on June 30, 2003, has been made and recorded.

Instructions

For each independent situation above, prepare the appropriate journal entry for the redemption of the bonds.

Prepare entries to record mortgage note payable.
(SO 5) AP

E16–10   Ste. Anne Co. receives $150,000 when it issues a $150,000, 10% mortgage note payable to finance the construction of a building at December 31, 2003. The terms provide for semi-annual instalment payments on June 30 and December 31.

Instructions

Prepare the journal entries to record the mortgage loan and the first two instalment payments assuming:
(a) the payment is a fixed principal payment of $7,500.
(b) the payment is a blended principal and interest payment of $12,036.39.

Prepare entries for operating lease and capital lease.
(SO 6) AP

E16–11   Two separate situations are presented below:
1. Ready Car Rental leased a car to Dumfries Company for one year. Terms of the operating lease agreement call for monthly payments of $500, beginning on May 21.
2. On January 1, 2003, InSynch.com entered into an agreement to lease 60 computers from Hi-Tech Electronics. The terms of the lease agreement require three annual rental payments of $60,000 (including 10% interest) beginning on December 31, 2003. The present value of the three rental payments is $149,211. InSynch.com considers this a capital lease.

Instructions

(a) Prepare the appropriate journal entry to be made by Dumfries Company for the first lease payment.
(b) Prepare the journal entry to record the lease agreement on the books of InSynch.com on January 1, 2003.

E16–12 Sears Canada Inc.'s January 1, 2000, financial statements contain the following selected data (in millions):

Calculate debt ratios.
(SO 6, 7) AN

Total assets	$3,546.2
Total liabilities	2,199.9
Amortization expense	113.5
Interest expense	72.3
Income tax expense	145.0
Net income	199.6

Instructions

(a) Calculate these ratios:
   1. Debt to total assets
   2. Interest coverage
   3. Cash interest coverage

(b) The notes to Sears' financial statements detail that the company has future minimum lease payments for its operating leases, subsequent to the year 2000, of $1,085.2 million. Discuss the implications of these unrecorded obligations for the analysis of Sears's solvency.

E16–13 The adjusted trial balance for Priya Corporation at the end of the current year, July 31, 2004, contained the following accounts:

Prepare long-term liabilities section of balance sheet.
(SO 7) AP

Bond interest payable	$ 9,000
Lease liability	59,500
Bonds payable, due 2010	150,000
Premium on bonds payable	32,000

Of the amount shown as lease liability, $11,000 is due within the next year.

Instructions

(a) Prepare the long-term liabilities section of the balance sheet as at July 31, 2004.
(b) Indicate the proper balance sheet classification for the accounts listed above that do not belong in the long-term liabilities section.

PROBLEMS: SET A

. . . .

P16–1A Ecomdrive.com Corporation sold $2,500,000 of 10-year 8% bonds on January 1, 2003. The bonds were dated January 1, 2003, and pay interest on July 1 and January 1. Ecomdrive.com Corporation uses the straight-line method to amortize any bond premium or discount. Ecomdrive.com's year end is December 31.

Prepare entries for bonds, using straight-line method of amortization. Show balance sheet presentation.
(SO 2, 7) AP

Instructions

(a) Prepare all the necessary journal entries to record the issue of the bonds and bond interest expense for 2003, assuming:
   1. that the bonds sold at 100.
   2. that the bonds sold at 103.
   3. that the bonds sold at 96.
(b) Show the balance sheet presentation for each bond issue assumption at December 31, 2003.

P16–2A Easter Electric sold $4,000,000 of 10-year 10% bonds on January 1, 2003. The bonds were sold at 104. The bonds were dated January 1 and pay interest on July 1 and January 1. Easter Electric uses the straight-line method to amortize any bond premium or discount. Easter Electric's year end is December 31.

Prepare entries for bonds, using straight-line method of amortization. Show balance sheet presentation.
(SO 2, 7) AP

Instructions

(a) Prepare the journal entry to record the issue of the bonds on January 1, 2003.
(b) Prepare a bond amortization schedule for the first four interest periods.
(c) Prepare the journal entries for interest and amortization in 2003 and 2004.
(d) Show the balance sheet presentation of the bond liability at December 31, 2004.

Prepare entries for bonds using effective interest method of amortization.
(SO 2) AP

P16–3A   On July 1, 2003, Global Satellites issued $2,700,000 face value 9%, 10-year bonds at $2,531,760. This price resulted in a market (effective) interest rate of 10% on the bonds. Global uses the effective interest method to amortize any bond premium or discount. The bonds pay semi-annual interest on July 1 and January 1. Global has a December 31 year end.

Instructions

(Round all calculations to the nearest dollar.)
(a) Prepare the journal entry to record the issue of the bonds on July 1, 2003.
(b) Prepare an amortization table for this bond issue through December 31, 2004 (three interest periods).
(c) Prepare the journal entry to record the accrual of interest and the amortization on December 31, 2003.
(d) Prepare the journal entry to record the payment of interest and the amortization on July 1, 2004.
(e) Prepare the journal entry to record the accrual of interest and the amortization on December 31, 2004.

Prepare entries for bonds sold between interest periods.
(SO 3) AP

P16–4A   On December 1, 2003, Veilleux and Steinert Ltd. sold $1,000,000 of 20-year bonds dated October 1, 2003. The bonds pay 12% interest, to be paid semi-annually on March 31 and September 30. The bonds were sold at their face value, plus the interest that had accrued since their original issue date. Its fiscal year end is December 31.

Instructions

(a) Prepare the journal entry to record the sale of the bonds on December 1, 2003.
(b) Prepare the journal entry to accrue the interest expense on December 31, 2003.
(c) Prepare the journal entry to record the payment of interest on March 31, 2004.

Source: Adapted from Certified General Accountants Association of Canada, *Financial Accounting 1 Examination,* June 2000, Question 8.

Prepare entries for bonds, using effective interest method of amortization. Show balance sheet presentation. Answer analytical questions.
(SO 2, 3, 7) AN

P16–5A   On July 1, 2003, Webhancer Corp. issued $5,000,000 face value 12%, 10-year bonds at $5,623,112. This price resulted in a 10% market (effective) interest rate on the bonds. Webhancer uses the effective interest method to amortize any bond premium or discount. The bonds pay semi-annual interest on each July 1 and January 1. Webhancer has a December 31 year end.

Instructions

(a) Prepare the journal entries to record the following transactions:
1. The issue of the bonds on July 1, 2003
2. The accrual of interest and the amortization on December 31, 2003
3. The payment of interest and the amortization on July 1, 2004
4. The accrual of interest and the amortization on December 31, 2004
(b) Show the proper balance sheet presentation for the liability for bonds payable on the December 31, 2004, balance sheet.
(c) Write answers to the following questions in letter form:
1. Would the bond interest expense reported in 2004 be the same, greater, or less if the straight-line method of amortization were used?
2. What is the total cost of borrowing over the life of the bonds?
3. Would the total bond interest expense be greater, the same, or less if the straight-line method of amortization were used?

Prepare entries for bonds, using straight-line method of amortization, and redemption of bonds.
(SO 2, 4) AP

P16–6A   The following is taken from the Bermuda Corp. balance sheet at December 31, 2003:

BERMUDA CORP.
Balance Sheet (partial)
December 31, 2003

Current liabilities		
Bond interest payable (for six months		
from July 1 to December 31)		$ 120,000
Long-term liabilities		
Bonds payable, 10%, due		
January 1, 2014	$2,400,000	
Less: Discount on bonds payable	90,000	2,310,000

Interest is payable semi-annually, on January 1 and July 1. Bermuda uses straight-line amortization for any bond premium or discount. From December 31, 2003, the bonds will be outstanding for an additional 10 years (20 periods).

Instructions

(Round all calculations to the nearest dollar.)
(a) Journalize the payment of bond interest on January 1, 2004.
(b) Prepare the entry to amortize the bond discount and to pay the interest due on July 1, 2004. Assume no interest is accrued on June 30.
(c) Assume that after paying interest on July 1, 2004, Bermuda Corp. redeems bonds that have a face value of $600,000. Record the redemption of the bonds, at a price of 102.
(d) Prepare the adjusting entry at December 31, 2004, to amortize the bond discount and accrue interest on the remaining bonds.

P16–7A Kinyae Electronics issues a $800,000, 10%, 10-year mortgage note on December 31, 2003, to help finance a plant expansion. The terms provide for semi-annual blended instalment payments of $64,194. Payments are due on June 30 and December 31.

Prepare instalment payments schedule and entries for mortgage note payable. Show balance sheet presentation.
(SO 5, 7) AP

Instructions

(a) Prepare an instalment payment schedule for the first two years.
(b) Prepare the entries for (1) the mortgage loan, and (2) the first two instalment payments.
(c) Show how the total mortgage liability should be reported on the balance sheet at December 31, 2004. (Hint: Remember to divide the liability between long-term and current portions.)

P16–8A Three different lease transactions are presented below for Manitoba Enterprises. Assume that all lease transactions start on January 1, 2003. Manitoba does not receive title to the properties leased during, or at the end of, the lease term.

Analyse various lease situations, prepare entries, and discuss financial statement presentation.
(SO 6) AP

	Lessor		
	Lornegren Associates	Potter Co.	Haskins Inc.
Type of property	Bulldozer	Truck	Furniture
Lease term	4 years	6 years	3 years
Estimated economic life	8 years	7 years	5 years
Yearly rental	$13,000	$12,000	$ 4,000
Fair market value of leased asset	$80,000	$58,000	$27,500
Present value of the lease rental payments	$48,000	$50,000	$12,000

Instructions

(a) Are the leases above operating or capital leases? Explain your reasoning for each lease.
(b) How should each of the lease transactions be recorded in 2003?
(c) What would appear on the balance sheet for Manitoba Enterprises for each of the lease contracts?

P16–9A Loblaw Companies Limited reported the following selected comparative information in its 2000 financial statements (in millions):

Calculate and analyse debt ratios.
(SO 7) AN

	2000	1999
Total assets	$7,979	$7,105
Total liabilities	5,075	4,510
Amortization expense	273	183
Interest expense	112	68
Income tax expense	280	199
Net income	376	261

Instructions

(a) Calculate Loblaw's debt to total assets, interest coverage, and cash interest coverage ratios for each year.
(b) What conclusions concerning Loblaw's long-term solvency can be drawn from the ratios calculated in (a)?

PROBLEMS: SET B

Prepare entries for bonds, using straight-line method of amortization. Show balance sheet presentation.
(SO 2, 7) AP

P16–1B   Eatsleepmusic.com Inc. sold $500,000, of 10-year 12% bonds on July 1, 2003. The bonds were dated July 1, and pay interest on January 1 and July 1. Eatsleepmusic.com uses the straight-line method to amortize any bond premium or discount and has a December year end.

Instructions

(a) Prepare all the necessary journal entries to record the issue of the bonds and bond interest expense for 2003, assuming:
  1. that the bonds sold at 100.
  2. that the bonds sold at 104.
  3. that the bonds sold at 98.
(b) Show the balance sheet presentation for each bond issue assumption at December 31, 2003.

Prepare entries for bonds, using straight-line method of amortization. Show balance sheet presentation.
(SO 2, 7) AP

P16–2B   Kyberpass Corp. sold $3,000,000 of 20-year 9% bonds on April 1, 2003. They were sold at 98. The bonds were dated April 1, 2003, and pay interest on October 1 and April 1. Kyberpass uses the straight-line method to amortize any bond premium or discount. Kyberpass's year end is December 31.

Instructions

(a) Prepare the journal entry to record the issue of the bonds on April 1, 2003.
(b) Prepare a bond amortization schedule for the first two interest periods.
(c) Prepare the journal entries:
  1. for payment of interest and amortization of bond premium or discount on October 1, 2003.
  2. for accrual of interest and amortization of bond premium or discount on December 31, 2003.
  3. for payment of interest and amortization of bond premium or discount on April 1, 2004.
(d) Show the balance sheet presentation of the bond liability at December 31, 2003.

Prepare entries for bonds, using effective interest method of amortization.
(SO 2) AP

P16–3B   On July 1, 2002, Clio Corporation issued $1,500,000 face value 12%, 10-year bonds at $1,686,934. This price resulted in a market (effective) interest rate of 10%. Clio uses the effective interest method to amortize any bond premium or discount. The bonds pay semi-annual interest on July 1 and January 1. Clio has a December 31 year end.

Instructions

(Round all calculations to the nearest dollar.)
(a) Prepare the journal entry to record the issuance of the bonds on July 1, 2002.
(b) Prepare an amortization table for this bond issue through December 31, 2003 (three interest periods).
(c) Prepare the journal entry to record the accrual of interest and the amortization on December 31, 2002.
(d) Prepare the journal entry to record the payment of interest and the amortization on July 1, 2003.
(e) Prepare the journal entry to record the accrual of interest and the amortization on December 31, 2003.

Prepare entries for bonds sold between interest periods, using straight-line method of amortization.
(SO 3) AP

P16–4B   On September 1, 2003, Mount Champlain Corporation issued $1,500,000 face value 6%, 10-year bonds. The bonds sold at 102, plus the interest that had accrued since their original issue date. The bonds were dated July 1, 2003 and pay interest semi-annually on January 1 and July 1. Mount Champlain uses the straight-line method of amortization. Its fiscal year end is June 30.

Instructions

(a) Calculate the accrued interest investors must pay to Mount Champlain Corporation on September 1, 2003.
(b) Prepare the journal entry to record the issue of the bonds on September 1.
(c) Prepare the journal entry to record the payment of interest and amortization on January 1, 2004. (Hint: The number of remaining months to spread the amortization over is 118 [(10 years × 12 months) − 2 months from July 1 to September 1].)

P16–5B On July 1, 2003, Waubonsee Company Ltd. issued $2,200,000 face value 10%, 10-year bonds at $1,947,651. This price resulted in a market (effective) interest rate of 12% on the bonds. Waubonsee uses the effective interest method to amortize any bond premium or discount. The bonds pay semi-annual interest on July 1 and January 1. Waubonsee has a December 31 year end.

Prepare entries for bonds, using effective interest method of amortization. Show balance sheet presentation. Answer analytical questions.
(SO 2, 3, 7) AN
◂▭▭▭

Instructions

(a) Prepare the journal entries to record the following transactions:
   1. The issue of the bonds on July 1, 2003
   2. The accrual of interest and amortization on December 31, 2003
   3. The payment of interest and the amortization on July 1, 2004
   4. The accrual of interest and amortization on December 31, 2004

(b) Show the proper balance sheet presentation for the liability for the bonds payable on the December 31, 2004, balance sheet.

(c) Write answers to the following questions in letter form:
   1. What amount of interest expense is reported for 2004?
   2. Would the bond interest expense reported in 2004 be the same as, greater than, or less than the amount that would be reported if the straight-line method of amortization were used? Explain the reason for your answer.
   3. Determine the total cost of borrowing over the life of the bond.
   4. Would the total bond interest expense be greater than, the same as, or less than the total interest expense that would be reported if the straight-line method of amortization were used?
   5. Compare the advantages and disadvantages of the straight-line method to those of the effective interest method.

P16–6B The following is taken from the Western Oil Company balance sheet at December 31, 2003:

Calculate interest rate on bonds; prepare entries for bonds, using straight-line method of amortization, and redemption of bonds.
(SO 2, 4) AP

WESTERN OIL COMPANY
Balance Sheet (partial)
December 31, 2003

Current liabilities		
Bond interest payable (for six months,		
from July 1 to December 31)		$ 90,000
Long-term liabilities		
Bonds payable, due January 1, 2009	$3,000,000	
Add: Premium on bonds payable	200,000	3,200,000

Interest is payable semi-annually, on January 1 and July 1. Western uses straight-line amortization for any bond premium or discount. From December 31, 2003, the bonds will be outstanding for an additional five years (10 periods).

Instructions

(a) Calculate the contractual rate of interest on these bonds.

(b) Prepare the entry to amortize the bond premium and pay interest due on July 1, 2004, assuming no accrual of interest on June 30.

(c) Assume that, after paying interest on July 1, 2004, Western Company redeems bonds having a face value of $1,200,000. The redemption price paid is 99. Record the redemption of the bonds.

(d) Prepare the adjusting entry at December 31, 2004, to amortize the bond premium and to accrue interest on the remaining bonds.

P16–7B Elite Electronics issues a $400,000, 12%, 10-year mortgage note on December 31, 2003. The proceeds from the note will be used to finance a new research laboratory. The terms of the note provide for semi-annual instalment principal payments of $20,000, plus interest. Payments are due on June 30 and December 31.

Prepare instalment payments schedule and entries for mortgage note payable. Show balance sheet presentation.
(SO 5, 7) AP

Instructions

(a) Prepare an instalment payment schedule for the first two years.

(b) Prepare the entries for (1) the mortage loan, and (2) the first two instalment payments.

(c) Show how the mortgage liability should be reported on the balance sheet at December 31, 2004. (*Hint*: Remember to report any current portion separately from the long-term liability.)

Analyse various lease situations, prepare entries, and discuss financial statement presentation.
(SO 6) AP

P16–8B   Presented below are three different lease transactions that occurred for Choi Inc. in 2003. Assume that all lease contracts start on January 1, 2003. Choi does not receive title to any of the properties leased during, or at the end of, the lease term.

	Lessor		
	SameDay Delivery	Duncan Co.	Riverview Auto
Type of property	Computer	Delivery equipment	Automobile
Yearly rental	$6,000	$4,200	$3,700
Lease term	6 years	4 years	2 years
Estimated economic life	7 years	7 years	5 years
Fair market value of lease asset	$33,000	$19,000	$11,000
Present value of the lease rental payments	$31,000	$13,000	$6,400

Instructions

(a) Which of the leases above are operating leases and which are capital leases? Explain.

(b) How should the lease transaction for each of the above companies be recorded in 2003?

(c) Describe how the transaction would be reported on the income statement and balance sheet of each company at the end of 2003.

Calculate and analyse debt ratios.
(SO 7) AN

P16–9B   **Sobeys Inc.** reported the following selected comparative information in its 2000 financial statements (in thousands):

	2000	1999
Total assets	$2,890,999	$2,878,817
Total liabilities	2,073,335	2,128,828
Amortization expense	98,055	72,415
Interest expense	88,875	46,301
Income tax expense (recovery)	77,541	(10,197)
Net income (loss)	80,246	(8,074)

Instructions

(a) Calculate Sobeys' debt to total assets, interest coverage, and cash interest coverage ratios for each year.

(b) What conclusions concerning Sobeys' long-term solvency can be drawn from the ratios calculated in (a)?

*B*roadening Your Perspective

FINANCIAL REPORTING AND ANALYSIS
••

Financial Reporting Problem

BYP16–1   Refer to the consolidated financial statements and notes of **The Second Cup Ltd.** in Appendix A.

(a) What was The Second Cup's long-term debt at June 24, 2000? What was the increase (decrease) in total long-term debt (excluding other deferred liabilities) from the pro forma figures presented for 1999?

(b) Does The Second Cup separate the current portion due from its long-term debt? If so, how much of its long-term debt is currently due?

(c) What kind of long-term debt does The Second Cup have?

(d) Does The Second Cup have any leases? If so, are they capital or operating leases? What are the total minimum lease commitments for The Second Cup in the future?

Interpreting Financial Statements

BYP16–2   **Reitmans (Canada) Limited** and **La Senza Corporation** (formerly known as Suzy Shier) are two specialty women's clothing store merchandisers.

Here are financial data for both companies at their most recent year ends (in thousands):

	Reitmans January 29, 2000	La Senza January 30, 2000
Total assets	$253,849	$222,590
Total liabilities	59,728	108,588
Amortization expense	12,371	15,284
Interest expense	608	486
Income tax expense	20,159	4,855
Net income	51,707	6,070
Total operating lease commitments for next five years and subsequent	189,300	229,145
Total capital lease commitments for next five years and subsequent		41,610

Additional Cases

Instructions

Using the data, perform the following analysis:

(a) Calculate the debt to assets, interest coverage, and cash interest coverage for each company. Discuss their relative solvency.

(b) The notes to the financial statements indicate that in many of the retail stores, furniture and fixture and the like are leased using operating leases. In addition, La Senza has capital leases. Discuss the implications of these leases for each company's solvency.

BYP16–3   Below is a sample of how bond market data are frequently presented in newspapers:

CANADIAN BONDS

Provided by RBC Dominion Securities

Selected quotations, with changes since the previous day, on actively traded bond issues yesterday. Yields are calculated to full maturity. Price is the final bid-side price as of 5 pm yesterday.

Issuer	Coupon	Maturity	Price	Yield	Price $ Chg
GOVERNMENT OF CANADA					
Canada	8.500	Apr 01/02	103.87	5.27	0.03
Canada	10.000	May 01/02	106.01	5.29	0.03
Canada	5.750	Jun 01/02	100.65	5.26	0.04
Canada	5.500	Sep 01/02	100.38	5.25	0.05
Canada	6.000	Dec 01/02	101.40	5.22	0.06
Canada	11.250	Dec 15/02	110.95	5.30	0.05
Canada	11.750	Feb 01/03	112.57	5.32	0.06
Canada	5.750	Jun 01/03	101.17	5.23	0.08
Canada	7.250	Jun 01/03	104.49	5.25	0.07
Canada	5.250	Sep 01/03	100.00	5.25	0.08
Canada	7.500	Dec 01/03	106.00	5.26	0.09
Canada	10.250	Feb 01/04	113.91	5.31	0.07
Canada	6.500	Jun 01/04	103.80	5.27	0.08
Canada	5.000	Sep 01/04	99.11	5.27	0.09
Canada	9.000	Dec 01/04	113.00	5.29	0.09
Canada	6.000	Sep 01/05	103.07	5.25	0.10
Canada	8.750	Dec 01/05	114.82	5.29	0.11
Canada	5.750	Sep 01/06	102.46	5.24	0.11
Canada	14.000	Oct 01/06	142.44	5.33	0.13
Canada	7.000	Dec 01/06	108.62	5.28	0.12
Canada	7.250	Jun 01/07	110.51	5.30	0.12
Canada	6.000	Jun 01/08	104.23	5.30	0.07
Canada	10.000	Jun 01/08	128.29	5.33	0.07
Canada	5.500	Jun 01/09	101.32	5.30	0.05
Canada	10.750	Oct 01/09	136.85	5.41	0.05
Canada	9.500	Jun 01/10	130.43	5.35	0.05
Canada	5.500	Jun 01/10	101.42	5.31	0.05
Canada	9.000	Mar 01/11	127.96	5.39	0.06
Canada	6.000	Jun 01/11	105.46	5.31	0.05
Canada	10.250	Mar 15/14	144.38	5.48	0.08
Canada	11.250	Jun 01/15	156.69	5.50	0.08
Canada	9.750	Jun 01/21	149.03	5.67	0.22
Canada	8.000	Jun 01/23	130.27	5.61	0.21
Canada	9.000	Jun 01/25	143.72	5.67	0.23
Canada	8.000	Jun 01/27	132.76	5.61	0.23
Canada	5.750	Jun 01/29	103.15	5.53	0.20
CMHC	5.000	Jun 01/04	98.78	5.39	0.08
CMHC	5.750	Dec 01/04	101.16	5.42	0.09
CMHC	6.250	Dec 01/05	103.45	5.44	0.10
Exp Dev	5.500	Jun 18/04	100.31	5.40	0.08
PROVINCIAL					
Alberta	6.250	Mar 01/01	100.10	5.55	0.00
Alberta	6.375	Jun 01/04	103.07	5.38	0.06
B C	9.000	Jan 09/02	103.58	5.38	0.03
B C	7.750	Jun 16/03	105.33	5.41	0.07
B C	6.000	Jun 09/08	102.05	5.66	0.04
B C	6.375	Aug 23/10	104.68	5.74	0.01
B C	9.500	Jan 09/12	129.35	5.85	0.01
B C	8.500	Aug 23/13	123.13	5.88	0.02
B C	6.150	Nov 19/27	100.29	6.13	0.11
B C	5.700	Jun 18/29	94.40	6.12	0.11
B C	6.350	Jun 18/31	103.18	6.12	0.12
B C Mun Fin	7.750	Dec 01/05	109.12	5.60	-0.03
B C Mun Fin	5.500	Mar 24/08	98.56	5.74	-0.05
Hydro Quebec	5.500	May 15/03	100.20	5.41	0.10
Hydro Quebec	7.000	Jun 01/04	104.67	5.48	0.08
Hydro Quebec	6.500	Feb 15/11	104.55	5.90	0.05
Hydro Quebec	10.250	Jul 16/12	135.20	5.98	0.05
Hydro Quebec	9.625	Jul 15/22	138.30	6.34	0.30
Hydro Quebec	6.000	Aug 15/31	96.15	6.28	0.20
Manitoba	7.875	Apr 07/03	105.13	5.44	0.07
Manitoba	5.750	Jun 02/08	100.40	5.68	0.04
Manitoba	7.750	Dec 22/25	119.69	6.19	0.12
New Brunswic	8.000	Mar 17/03	105.25	5.45	0.07
New Brunswic	5.700	Jun 02/08	99.89	5.72	0.04
New Brunswic	6.000	Dec 27/17	99.86	6.01	0.02
Newfoundland	6.150	Apr 17/28	97.15	6.37	0.11
Nova Scotia	5.250	Jun 02/03	99.43	5.50	0.08
Nova Scotia	6.600	Jun 01/27	102.84	6.38	0.11
Ontario	10.875	Jan 10/01	100.20	4.50	0.00
Ontario	8.000	Mar 11/03	105.31	5.40	0.07
Ontario	7.750	Dec 08/03	106.29	5.41	0.09
Ontario	4.875	Jun 02/04	98.19	5.46	0.07
Ontario	9.000	Sep 15/04	111.70	5.47	0.07
Ontario	6.250	Mar 08/05	102.89	5.47	0.08
Ontario	7.500	Jan 19/06	108.75	5.49	0.08
Ontario	6.125	Sep 12/07	103.02	5.58	0.09
Ontario	5.700	Dec 01/08	100.39	5.64	0.04
Ontario	6.200	Nov 19/09	103.53	5.69	0.01
Ontario	6.100	Nov 19/10	102.90	5.71	0.01
Ontario	7.600	Jun 02/27	119.77	6.09	0.13
Ontario	6.500	Mar 08/29	105.68	6.08	0.12
Ontario Hyd	8.625	Feb 06/02	103.45	5.36	0.03
Ontario Hyd	9.000	Jun 24/02	105.12	5.37	0.04
Ontario Hyd	5.375	Jun 02/03	100.01	5.37	0.08
Ontario Hyd	7.750	Nov 03/05	109.38	5.52	0.08
Ontario Hyd	5.600	Jun 02/08	99.73	5.64	0.04
Ontario Hyd	8.250	Jun 22/26	127.30	6.12	0.13
Quebec	5.250	Apr 01/02	99.85	5.37	0.05
Quebec	7.500	Dec 01/03	105.44	5.46	0.09
Quebec	6.500	Dec 01/05	103.90	5.58	0.10
Quebec	6.500	Oct 01/07	104.40	5.70	0.10
Quebec	11.000	Apr 01/09	133.05	5.89	0.05
Quebec	5.500	Jun 01/09	97.60	5.86	0.05
Quebec	6.250	Dec 01/10	102.66	5.89	0.05
Quebec	8.500	Apr 01/26	127.45	6.31	0.20
Quebec	6.000	Oct 01/29	96.21	6.29	0.18
Quebec	6.250	Jun 01/32	99.50	6.29	0.20
Saskatchewan	6.125	Oct 10/01	100.36	5.63	0.01
Saskatchewan	5.500	Jun 02/08	98.81	5.70	0.04
Saskatchewan	8.750	May 30/25	132.39	6.17	0.13
Toronto -Met	6.100	Aug 15/07	102.14	5.71	-0.04
Toronto -Met	6.100	Dec 12/17	100.69	6.03	-0.08
CORPORATE					
AGT Limited	8.800	Sep 22/25	101.90	8.61	0.14
Air Canada	6.750	Feb 02/04	96.00	8.24	0.00
Associates	5.400	Sep 04/01	99.72	5.81	0.01
Avco Fin	5.750	Jun 02/03	99.63	5.92	0.00
Bank Of Mont	7.000	Jan 28/10	106.25	6.09	0.05
Bank Of N S	5.400	Apr 01/03	99.57	5.60	0.07
Bank Of N S	6.250	Jul 16/07	101.08	6.05	0.11
Bell Canada	6.500	May 09/05	101.37	6.14	-0.09
Can Cred Tst	5.625	Mar 24/05	99.17	5.85	0.09
Cards Trust	5.510	Jun 21/03	99.65	5.66	0.08
Cdn Pacfc	5.850	Mar 30/09	93.75	6.85	0.04
Clearnet	0.000	May 15/08	82.25	9.65	0.00
Coca-Cola	5.650	Mar 17/04	98.70	6.10	0.08
DlmrCCFin	6.440	Apr 03/02	100.31	6.17	0.10
DlmrCCFin	6.600	Jun 03/03	100.32	6.45	-0.04
Domtar Inc	10.000	Apr 15/11	114.54	7.91	0.05
Ford Credit	5.730	Dec 01/03	98.34	6.36	-0.04
Ford Credit	6.650	Jun 20/05	100.44	6.54	-0.28
Genesis Trus	6.869	Feb 15/05	104.11	5.74	0.10
Grtr TTO Air	5.400	Dec 03/02	99.81	5.50	0.06
Grtr TTO Air	5.950	Dec 03/07	99.74	6.00	0.12
Grtr TTO Air	6.450	Dec 03/27	94.43	6.91	0.16
Grtr TTO Air	6.450	Jul 30/29	95.18	6.84	0.23
Gtc Trans	6.200	Jun 01/07	96.93	6.80	0.11
Gulf Can Res	6.450	Oct 01/07	96.56	7.10	0.11
HydroOne	6.940	Jun 03/05	104.65	5.74	0.10
HydroOne	7.150	Jun 03/10	108.01	6.02	0.05
HydroOne	7.350	Jun 03/30	109.29	6.63	0.19
IADB	5.625	Jun 29/09	98.92	5.79	0.01
Interprv Pip	8.200	Feb 15/24	114.77	6.91	0.17
Legacy	5.930	Nov 15/02	98.97	6.52	0.06
Loblaws Co	6.650	Nov 08/27	93.74	7.18	0.15
MerrilCanFin	6.500	Nov 18/02	101.49	5.65	0.06
Milit - Air	5.750	Jun 30/19	98.70	5.87	-0.26
Morguard Ret	6.700	Oct 09/07	93.78	7.80	0.11
Mstr Cr Trus	5.760	Aug 21/02	100.31	5.56	0.05
Mstr Cr Trus	6.150	Dec 21/04	101.45	5.74	0.09
Nav Canada	7.560	Mar 01/27	114.03	6.44	0.09
Nexen	6.300	Jun 02/08	95.70	7.05	0.07
Oxford	6.860	Jul 21/04	96.46	8.02	0.08
Renaissance	6.850	Feb 06/07	99.33	6.98	0.11
Rogers Cable	8.750	Jul 15/07	98.00	9.16	0.00
Rogers Cant	10.500	Jun 01/06	107.38	8.76	0.00
Royal Bank	5.400	Apr 07/03	99.67	5.55	0.07

Instructions

Based upon these data, answer the following questions:

(a) There are two sets of interest rates given, called "Coupon" and "Yield." Which of these is the contractual rate of interest and which is the market (effective) rate of interest?

(b) Look at the range of interest rates listed under "Coupon" and "Yield." Which column of rates has the widest range? What do you think is the reason for this greater range?

(c) As the term to maturity gets longer, does the yield rate tend to get higher or lower? Explain why this may be logical.

(d) Compare the yields for the Government of Canada bonds, the Provincial bonds, and the Corporate bonds. Determine which category has the lowest yield rates. Explain the reason for this.

(e) Are most of the bonds listed selling at a premium or at a discount?

Accounting on the Web

BYP16–4 Bonds have complex terminology associated with them. In this question, we review the Bonds Online website and explore a glossary of bond terms.

Instructions

Specific requirements of this Internet case are available on the Weygandt website.

BYP16–5 Bond or debt securities pay a contractual rate of interest. This interest rate is dependent on the risk associated with the investment. The Dominion Bond Rating Service Limited provides ratings for companies that issue debt securities. We will now explore this site to learn about bond ratings and relative risk.

Instructions

Specific requirements of this Internet case are available on the Weygandt website.

CRITICAL THINKING

Collaborative Learning Activity

BYP16–6 On January 1, 2002, Landry Corporation issued $1,200,000 of five-year 8% bonds at 97. The bonds pay interest semi-annually on July 1 and January 1. By January 1, 2004, the market rate of interest for bonds of similar risk to those of Landry Corporation had risen. As a result, the market value of the Landry bonds was $1,000,000 on January 1, 2004—which is below their carrying value. Barbara Landry, president of the company, suggests repurchasing all of these bonds in the open market at the $1,000,000 price. To do so, the company will have to issue $1,000,000 (face value) of new ten-year 6% bonds. The president asks you, as the company controller, "What is the feasibility of my proposed repurchase plan?"

Instructions

With the class divided into groups, answer the following:

(a) What is the carrying value of the outstanding Landry Corporation five-year bonds on January 1, 2004? Landry uses straight-line amortization.

(b) Prepare the journal entry to retire the five-year bonds on January 1, 2004. Prepare the journal entry to issue the new ten-year bonds.

(c) Prepare a short memo to the president in response to her request for advice. List the economic factors that you believe should be considered in her repurchase proposal.

Communication Activity

BYP16–7 Finn Berge, president of the Blue Marlin, is thinking of issuing bonds to finance an expansion of his business. He has asked you to (1) discuss the advantages of bonds over common share financing, (2) indicate the type of bonds he might issue, and (3) explain the issuing procedures used in bond transactions.

Instructions

Write a memo to the president, answering his request.

Ethics Case

BYP16–8 Andy Vicks is the president, founder, and majority owner of Custom Medical Corporation, an emerging medical technology products company. Custom is in great need of additional capital to keep operating and to bring several promising products to final development, testing, and production. Andy, as owner of 51% of the share capital, manages the company's operations. He places heavy emphasis on research and development and long-term growth. The other principal shareholder is Jill Caterino, who, as a non-employee investor, owns 40% of the shares. Jill would like to de-emphasize the R&D function and emphasize the marketing function, to maximize short-term sales and profits from existing products. She believes this strategy will raise the value of Custom's shares.

All of Andy's personal capital and borrowing power are tied up in his 51% share ownership. He knows that any offering of additional shares will dilute his controlling interest, because he won't be able to participate in such an issue. Jill, however, has money and would likely buy enough shares to gain control of Custom. She would then dictate the company's future direction, even if it meant replacing Andy as president and CEO.

The company already has considerable debt. Raising additional debt will be costly, will adversely affect Custom's credit rating, and will increase the company's reported losses (due to the growth in interest expense). Jill and the other minority shareholders express opposition to additional debt, fearing the company will be pushed close to bankruptcy.

Wanting to maintain his control and to preserve the direction of "his" company, Andy is doing everything possible to avoid a share capital issue. He is contemplating a large issue of bonds, even if it means the bonds are issued with a high interest rate.

Instructions

(a) Who are the stakeholders in this situation?
(b) What are the ethical issues in this case?
(c) What would you do if you were Andy?

Answers to Self-Study Questions

1. c   2. a   3. d   4. c   5. c   6. c   7. c   8. b   9. b   10. c   11. d

Answer to Second Cup Review It Question 4

The Second Cup does not report EBIT separately on its financial statements. It does report EBITDA of $10,086,000 separately on its consolidated statement of operations and deficit.

Remember to go back to the Navigator box on the chapter-opening page to check off your completed work.

THE NAVIGATOR

Students Learn and Earn

VANCOUVER, B.C.—Joe McInnis and the other five fund managers of the Portfolio Management Foundation (PMF) in Vancouver face the pressures typical of the investment industry. They research and write detailed reports on potential investments. They balance risk and return on the $2.4 million in assets they oversee. And they regularly defend their decisions in high-pressure meetings with a demanding board of trustees.

But they also have to worry about how the 30 hours a week they spend at the office are affecting their grades.

Mr. McInnis and his colleagues are undergraduate commerce students at the University of British Columbia. They are part of a program, begun in 1986, in which students manage a substantial endowment of real money in the real marketplace.

As a teaching tool, the program is a great success. Former PMF participants can be found working in the investment industry from New York to Hong Kong, often with such top names as Merrill Lynch and Goldman Sachs.

But perhaps more surprisingly, the PMF is a success as an investment fund as well. The core of its asset pool was originally about $1 million in donations from alumni and corporations. It has grown to over $2.4 million since then, while covering the program's expenses, which include summer work terms in Vancouver and Toronto for the student managers.

It's no surprise that several other Canadian universities have instituted similar programs in recent years.

These include McGill University, where 12 teams of undergraduate commerce and graduate MBA students manage funds of about $250,000 each, and the University of New Brunswick, where nine students manage a $1.5 million civil-service pension fund for the New Brunswick Investment Management Corp.

THE NAVIGATOR

www.commerce.ubc.ca/pmf

THE NAVIGATOR

- Understand *Concepts for Review*
- Read *Feature Story*
- Scan *Study Objectives*
- Read *Preview*
- Read text and answer *Before You Go On*
  p. 789 ☐ p. 795 ☐ p. 800 ☐
- Work *Demonstration Problems*
- Review *Summary of Study Objectives*
- Answer *Self-Study Questions*
- Complete assignments

CHAPTER · 17

INVESTMENTS

▶ STUDY OBJECTIVES ◀

After studying this chapter, you should be able to:

1. Identify the reasons why corporations invest in debt and equity securities.
2. Distinguish between temporary and long-term investments.
3. Explain and illustrate the accounting for debt investments.
4. Explain and illustrate the accounting for equity investments.
5. Describe the purpose and usefulness of consolidated financial statements.
6. Indicate how debt and equity investments are valued and reported on the financial statements.

THE
NAVIGATOR

▶ *PREVIEW OF CHAPTER 17*

Investments can include debt and equity, and can be made by individuals or corporations. Investments can be purchased for a short or a long period of time. They can be made as either a passive investment, as is the case in our feature story, or to control a company. As you will see in this chapter, the way in which a company accounts for its investments is determined by a number of factors.

The chapter is organized as follows:

THE
NAVIGATOR

Why Corporations Invest

STUDY OBJECTIVE
·········· ▼ ··········

Identify the reasons why corporations invest in debt and equity securities.

Helpful hint Money market instruments include certificates of deposit issued by banks, money market certificates issued by banks and credit institutions, treasury bills issued by governments, and commercial paper issued by corporations.

Illustration 17-1

Temporary investments and the operating cycle

Corporations generally purchase investments in **debt securities** (money market instruments and bonds) and **equity securities** (preferred and common shares) for one of three reasons. First, a corporation may have **excess cash** that it does not immediately need for the purchase of operating assets. For example, many companies experience seasonal fluctuations in sales. A Georgian Bay marina has more sales in spring and summer than in the fall and winter. The reverse is true for a Whistler ski shop.

At the end of an operating cycle, many companies have cash on hand that is idle until the start of another operating cycle. These companies may invest the excess funds to earn a greater return than they would get by just holding the funds in the bank. The role that such temporary investments play in the operating cycle of a merchandising company is shown in Illustration 17-1.

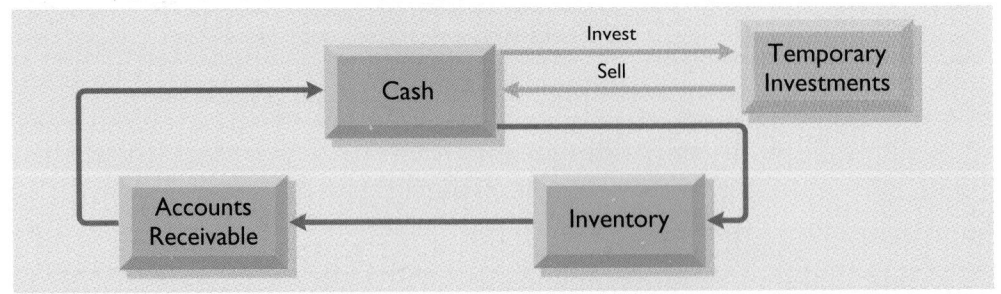

Excess cash may also result from economic cycles. For example, when the economy is booming, Magna International, a manufacturer of automobile systems, generates considerable excess cash. It uses some of this cash to purchase new capital assets. It pays out some of this cash in dividends. It may also invest excess cash in liquid assets to prepare for a future downturn in the economy. It can then liquidate these investments during a recession, when automobile sales slow down and cash is scarce.

When investing excess cash for short periods of time, corporations invest in low-risk, highly liquid securities—most often short-term government securities. It is generally unwise to invest short-term excess cash in common shares, because equity investments can experience rapid price changes. If you did invest your short-term excess cash in shares and the price of the shares declined significantly just before you needed cash again, you would be forced to sell your equity investment at a loss.

A second reason some companies purchase investments is to **generate investment income**. The Portfolio Management Foundation in our feature story invests its funds for this purpose. It generates interest and dividend income by investing in debt and equity securities. Although some common shares pay dividends, most companies purchase preferred shares to generate dividend income. Companies also invest in debt and equity securities hoping that they can sell them at a higher price than they originally paid for them. They speculate that the investment will increase in value and result in a gain when sold.

Companies also invest for **strategic reasons**. A company may purchase a non-controlling interest in another company in a related industry in which it wishes to establish a presence. For example, The Second Cup purchased a noncontrolling interest (5%) in The Great Canadian Bagel in 1996. Coffee and bagels were a logical combination, and in many locations, The Second Cup and The Great Canadian Bagel shared space. In 1999, The Second Cup sold its investment in The Great Canadian Bagel so that it could focus its energies on its coffee business. A company can also exercise some influence over a customer or supplier by purchasing a significant, but noncontrolling, interest in that company. That was the case when Cara Operations purchased 39% of The Second Cup in 1997.

A company may also choose to purchase a controlling interest in another company. This might be done to enter a new industry without the costs and risks associated with starting from scratch. Or a company might purchase another company in the same industry as itself. The purchase of a company that is in the industry, but involved in a different activity, is called a **vertical acquisition**. In a **horizontal acquisition**, the purchased company engages in the same activity as the company buying it. Early in 2002, Cara Operations increased its investment in The Second Cup from 39% to 100%. This horizontal acquisition changed Cara's level of interest from significant to controlling.

►Accounting in Action ► *Business Insight*

The number of strategic investments in the Canadian business community continued at a fast pace in 2000. Giant deals were commonplace as mature companies consolidated operations to achieve the scale and scope necessary to dominate global markets. The top Canadian acquisition in 2000 was Vivendi's $49.5-billion acquisition of Seagram.

Other recent strategic investments include Nortel Network's $11.5-billion acquisition of Alteon WebSystems, Alcatel's $10.4-billion acquisition of Newbridge Networks, and BCE's $6.4-billion acquisition of Teleglobe.

In summary, businesses invest in other companies for the reasons shown in Illustration 17-2.

Illustration 17-2

Why corporations invest

Reason	Typical Investment
To house excess cash until needed	Low-risk, high-liquidity, short-term securities such as government-issued securities
To generate investment income	Debt securities (money market instruments and bonds) and equity securities (preferred and common shares)
To meet strategic goals	Common shares of companies in a related industry or an unrelated industry that the company wishes to enter

▼ Temporary and Long-Term Investments

In addition to being classified as debt or equity investments, investments are also categorized as temporary or long-term investments.

Temporary Investments

Temporary investments are debt or equity securities held by a company, that are (1) **readily marketable**, and (2) **intended to be converted into cash** in the near future. When debt and/or equity securities of several different corporations or institutions are held, the group of securities is called an **investment portfolio**.

Readily Marketable

An investment is readily marketable when it can be sold easily, whenever the need for cash arises. Money market instruments meet this criterion because they can easily be sold to other investors. Shares and bonds that are traded on organized securities exchanges, such as the Toronto Stock Exchange, are readily marketable. They can be bought and sold daily. In contrast, there may be only a limited market for the securities issued by small corporations and no market at all for the securities of a privately held company.

Intent to Convert

"Intent to convert" means that management intends to sell the investment when the need for cash arises. It is the intention to sell that determines whether or not the investment is classified as temporary, not the length of time it is held. For example, an Intrawest ski resort may invest idle cash during the summer months and intend to sell the securities to buy supplies and equipment before the next ski season. This investment is considered temporary even if a lack of snow cancels the next ski season and there is no need to convert the securities into cash as intended.

Long-Term Investments

Long-term investments can also include debt or equity securities, among other items. To determine whether a debt or equity security is short-term or long-term, we test the investment against the short-term investment criteria. Investments that do not meet both investment criteria—readily marketable and intent to convert—are long-term investments. The majority of the Portfolio Management Foundation's investments are long-term. PMF holds less than 3% in money market instruments. The remainder of the fund is invested in debt investments of Canadian and foreign issuers and equity investments in Canada and the United States.

Accounting for Debt Investments

Debt investments are investments in money market instruments, as well as investments in government and corporation bonds. As we just learned, these investments may be classified as temporary or long-term.

STUDY OBJECTIVE

3

Explain and illustrate the accounting for debt investments.

Temporary Debt Investments

In accounting for debt investments, entries are required to record (1) the acquisition, (2) the interest revenue, and (3) the sale. In this section, we will focus our attention on the entries for bonds. However, the entries for money market instruments are similar.

Recording of Bonds

At acquisition, the cost principle applies. Cost includes all expenditures made to acquire these investments, such as the price paid plus brokerage fees (commissions), if any. If bonds are purchased between interest payment dates, as discussed in Chapter 16, the accrued interest that is paid by the purchaser is not included in the Investment account. Accrued interest is recorded separately in a current asset account, Interest Receivable.

Assume that Kuhl Corporation acquires 50 Doan Inc. 8% 10-year, $1,000 bonds on January 1, 2003, for $54,000, including brokerage fees of $1,000. Kuhl Corporation, as the bondholder, is known as the investor. Doan Inc., as the issuer of the bonds, is known as the investee. The bonds pay interest semi-annually, on July 1 and January 1. The entry to record the investment follows:

Jan. 1	Debt Investment—Doan Bonds	54,000	
	Cash		54,000
	To record purchase of 50 Doan Inc. bonds.		

A	=	L	+	SE
+54,000				
−54,000				

Recording Bond Interest

The bonds pay interest of $2,000 (50 × $1,000 = $50,000; $50,000 × 8% × ½) semi-annually on July 1 and January 1. The following entry is for the receipt of interest on July 1:

July 1	Cash	2,000	
	Interest Revenue		2,000
	To record receipt of interest on Doan Inc. bonds.		

If Kuhl Corporation's fiscal year ends on December 31, it is necessary to accrue the interest of $2,000 earned since July 1. The adjusting entry is as follows:

Dec. 31	Interest Receivable	2,000	
	Interest Revenue		2,000
	To accrue interest on Doan Inc. bonds.		

Note that Interest Receivable is reported as a current asset in the balance sheet. Interest Revenue is reported as other revenue in the income statement.

When the interest is received on January 1, the entry is as follows:

Jan. 1	Cash	2,000	
	Interest Receivable		2,000
	To record receipt of accrued interest.		

A credit to Interest Revenue at this time would be incorrect. Why? Because the interest revenue was earned and accrued in the preceding accounting period.

Recording Sale of Bonds

When the bonds are sold, it is necessary to (1) update any unrecorded interest up to the date of sale, and (2) credit the investment account for the cost of the bonds. Any difference between the net proceeds from the sale of the bonds (the sales price less brokerage fees) and their original cost is recorded as a gain or loss.

Assume, for example, that Kuhl Corporation receives net proceeds of $58,000 on the sale of the Doan Inc. bonds on January 1, 2004, after receiving (and recording) the interest due. Since the securities cost $54,000, a gain of $4,000 has been realized. The entry to record the sale follows:

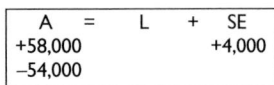

Jan. 1	Cash	58,000	
	Debt Investment—Doan Bonds		54,000
	Gain on Sale of Investment in Doan Bonds		4,000
	To record sale of Doan Inc. bonds.		

The gain on sale of debt investments is reported as other revenue in the income statement.

Long-Term Debt Investments

The accounting for temporary debt investments and for long-term debt investments is similar. The major exception is when bonds are purchased at a premium or discount. As we saw in Chapter 16, this results when a bond is purchased above (premium) or below (discount) its face value.

For temporary investments, the bond premium or discount is not recorded separately from the investment. And no premium or discount is amortized to interest revenue. This is because the bonds are held for a short period of time and any misstatement of interest revenue is not significant.

For long-term investments, any bond premium or discount is amortized to interest revenue over the remaining term of the bonds. Like the issuer of the bonds, the investor uses either the straight-line or the effective interest method of amortization.

Accounting for a long-term investment in bonds is essentially the inverse of accounting for long-term bonds payable, discussed in Chapter 16. Using the Kuhl Corporation example introduced earlier, the following illustration compares the entries for Kuhl to record the acquisition of 50 Doan 8% 10-year $1,000 bonds as a long-term investment and Doan's recording of the bonds as a long-term liability. The entries for the first interest period, using the effective interest method of amortization, are also included. For the purpose of this illustration, it has been assumed that the bonds yield an effective interest rate of 7%.

Helpful hint Note that, for the investor, Premium on Bonds is a **debit** balance account, because the premium represents part of the cost of the investment.

Illustration 17-3

Comparison of long-term bond investment and liability

	Kuhl Corporation (Investor)				Doan Inc. (Investee)		
Jan. 1	Debt Investment—Doan Bonds	50,000			Cash	54,000	
	Premium on Bonds	4,000			Premium on Bonds		4,000
	Cash		54,000		Bonds Payable		50,000
	To record purchase of 50 Doan Bonds.				To record issue of 8% 10-year bonds.		
July 1	Cash ($50,000 × 8% × ½)	2,000			Interest Expense ($54,000 × 7% × ½)	1,890	
	Premium on Bonds		110		Premium on Bonds	110	
	Interest Revenue ($54,000 × 7% × ½)		1,890		Cash ($50,000 × 8% × ½)		2,000
	To record receipt of semi-annual interest and amortization of bond premium.				To record payment of semi-annual interest and amortization of bond premium.		

Before You Go On . . .

►Review It

1. Why might a company make investments in debt or equity securities?
2. What criteria must be met for an investment to be classified as temporary?
3. What entries are required for a temporary investment in bonds?
4. How does the accounting for a temporary debt investment differ from that for a long-term debt investment?

►Do It

The Wang Corporation had the following transactions for temporary debt investments:

Feb. 1 Purchased 30 5% $1,000 Hillary Co. bonds for $29,500, plus accrued interest of $125 and brokerage fees of $900. Interest is payable semi-annually, on July 1 and January 1.
July 1 Received semi-annual interest on Hillary Co. bonds.
July 1 Sold 15 Hillary Co. bonds for $14,650 less $400 of brokerage fees.

(a) Journalize the transactions for Wang Corporation.
(b) Prepare the adjusting entry for the accrual of interest on December 31, Wang's year end.

Action Plan

• Record bond investment at cost, including brokerage fees.
• Interest accruing from the last interest payment date is paid to the seller of the bonds when bonds are purchased between interest dates. This interest will be recovered by the investor at the next semi-annual interest payment date.
• When bonds are sold, credit the investment account for the cost of the bonds.
• Record any difference between the cost and the net proceeds as a gain or loss.

Solution

(a) Feb. 1	Interest Receivable ($30,000 × 5% × ½)	125	
	Debt Investment—Hillary Bonds ($29,500 + $900)	30,400	
	Cash ($29,500 1 $900 1 $125)		30,525
	To record purchase of 30 Hillary Co. bonds.		
July 1	Cash ($30,000 × 5% × ⁶⁄₁₂)	750	
	Interest Receivable		125
	Interest Revenue ($30,000 × 5% × ⁵⁄₁₂)		625
	To record receipt of interest on Hillary Co. bonds.		
July 1	Cash ($14,650 − $400)	14,250	
	Loss on Sale of Investment in Hillary Bonds	950	
	Debt Investment—Hillary Bonds ($30,400 × ¹⁵⁄₃₀)		15,200
	To record sale of 15 Hillary Co. bonds.		
(b) Dec. 31	Interest Receivable	375	
	Interest Revenue ($15,000 × 5% × ⁶⁄₁₂)		375
	To accrue interest on Hillary Co. bonds.		

THE
NAVIGATOR

Related exercise material: BE17–1, BE17–2 and E17–1.

Accounting for Equity Investments

Equity investments are investments in the share capital of other corporations. A company may purchase the shares of another company to (1) earn dividend income, (2) realize gains by selling share investments at a higher price than originally paid (at least one always hopes to realize gains rather than losses), or (3) expand, diversify, or create a profitable operating relationship. As we learned earlier in this chapter, preferred shares usually are held to earn dividend income. Either common or preferred shares are held for share price appreciation. Common shares are held to influence relationships between companies.

The accounting for equity investments is based on how much influence the investor has over the operating and financial affairs of the issuing corporation (the investee). Illustration 17-4 shows the guidelines for three levels of influence.

The presumed influence may be reduced by other circumstances. For example, a company that acquires a 25% interest in a "hostile" takeover may not have significant influence over the investee. Among the questions that should be considered in determining an investor's influence are these: (1) Does the investor have representation on the investee's board of directors? (2) Does the investor participate in the investee's policy-making process? (3) Are there material transactions between the investor and investee? (4) Are the common shares held by other shareholders concentrated or dispersed? In other words, companies are required to use judgement instead of blindly following the guidelines. On the following pages, we will explain and illustrate the application of each guideline.

Illustration 17-4

Accounting guidelines for equity investments

Investor's Ownership Interest in Investee's Common Shares	Presumed Influence on Investee	Accounting Guidelines
Less than 20%	Insignificant	Cost method
Between 20% and 50%	Significant	Equity method
More than 50%	Controlling	Equity method for accounting; consolidated financial statements for financial reporting

Holdings of Less Than 20%

In accounting for equity investments of less than 20%, the cost method is used. Under the cost method, the investment is recorded at cost. Revenue is recognized only when cash dividends are received. UBC's Portfolio Management Foundation, featured in our chapter-opening story, has nearly two-thirds of its assets invested in equities. It would use the cost method to account for its investments. The entries for equity investments under the cost method follow.

Recording Acquisition of Shares

At acquisition, the cost principle applies. Cost includes all expenditures made to acquire these investments, such as the price paid plus brokerage fees (commissions), if any. Assume, for example, that on July 1, 2003, St. Amand Corporation acquires 1,000 common shares (10% ownership) of Beal Corporation at $40 per share plus brokerage fees of $500. The entry for the purchase is as follows:

Helpful hint The entries for investments in common shares also apply to investments in preferred shares.

July 1	Equity Investment—Beal Common Shares	40,500	
	Cash [(1,000 × $40) + $500]		40,500
	To record purchase of 1,000 common shares of Beal Corporation.		

A	=	L	+	SE
+40,500				
−40,500				

While the investor, St. Amand Corporation, must record this acquisition, no entry is required at this time by Beal Corporation. Recall that shares, once issued, are traded among investors. St. Amand Corporation did not purchase these shares directly from Beal Corporation. It purchased these shares from investors on organized stock exchanges, such as the Toronto Stock Exchange.

Recording Dividends

During the time the shares are held, entries are required for any cash dividends received. If a $2 per share dividend is received by St. Amand Corporation on December 1, the entry is as follows:

Dec. 1	Cash (1,000 × $2)	2,000	
	Dividend Revenue		2,000
	To record receipt of a cash dividend.		

A	=	L	+	SE
+2,000				+2,000

Dividend Revenue is reported under other revenues in the income statement. Unlike interest, dividends do not accrue until declared. When dividends are declared in advance of the payment date, Dividend Receivable should be debited and Dividend

Revenue credited. When the dividend is subsequently received, Cash is debited and Dividend Receivable credited. Typically, however, the investor uses the Dividend Receivable account only when financial statements are prepared between the declaration date and the payment date.

Recording Sale of Shares

When shares are sold, the difference between the net proceeds (the sale price less brokerage fees) from the sale and the cost of the shares is recognized as a gain or a loss. Assume that St. Amand Corporation receives net proceeds of $39,500 on the sale of its Beal common shares on February 10, 2004. Because the shares cost $40,500, a loss of $1,000 has been incurred. The entry to record the sale follows:

A	=	L	+	SE
+39,500				−1,000
−40,500				

Feb. 10	Cash	39,500	
	Loss on Sale of Investment in Beal Common Shares	1,000	
	Equity Investment—Beal Common Shares		40,500
	To record sale of Beal common shares.		

The loss is reported under other expenses in the income statement. A gain on sale would be reported as other revenue.

▶Accounting in Action ▸ *@ -Business Insight*

Amazon.com's website receives many "hits" each day. Because of this, Amazon earns significant revenue by allowing other companies to advertise there. Many of them pay with shares, since dot.coms often have very little cash. When Amazon receives the shares, it debits Equity Investment and credits Unearned Revenue for the market value of the shares on the day they are received. It then recognizes revenue over the life of the advertising agreement.

Holdings of Between 20% and 50%

When an investor company owns only a small portion of the shares of another company, the investor cannot exercise control over the investee. But when an investor owns between 20% and 50% of the common shares of a corporation, it is presumed that the investor has significant influence over the financial and operating activities of the investee. The investor probably has a representative on the investee's board of directors. Through that representative, the investor begins to exercise some control over the investee. The investee company, to some extent, becomes part of the investor company.

For example, between 1997 and 2001, Cara Operations owned 39% of The Second Cup's common shares. Because it exercised significant control over the decisions made by The Second Cup, Cara used an approach called the equity method. Under the equity method, **the investor records its share of the net income of the investee in the year in which it is earned**. An alternative might be to delay recognizing the investor's share of net income until a cash dividend is declared. But that approach would ignore the fact that the investor and investee are, in some sense, one company, which means the investor benefits from the investee's net income.

Under the equity method, the investment in common shares is initially recorded at cost. After that, the investment account is adjusted annually to show the investor's equity in the investee. Each year, the investor does the following: (1) It debits the investment account and credits revenue for its share of the investee's net income.[1] (2) The investor also credits the investment account when dividends are received. The investment account is reduced for dividends received, because the net assets of the investee are decreased when a dividend is paid.

Recording Acquisition of Shares

Assume that Milar Corporation acquires 30% of the common shares of Beck Company for $120,000 on January 1, 2003. Milar is assumed to have significant influence over Beck. The following entry records this transaction:

Jan. 1	Equity Investment—Beck Common Shares	120,000	
	Cash		120,000
	To record purchase of Beck common shares.		

A	=	L	+	SE
+120,000				
−120,000				

Recording Revenue and Dividends

For 2003, Beck reports net income of $100,000. It declares and pays a $40,000 cash dividend. Milar is required to record (1) its share of Beck's income, $30,000 (30% × $100,000), and (2) the reduction in the investment account for the dividends received, $12,000 ($40,000 × 30%). The entries are as follows:

(1)

Dec. 31	Equity Investment—Beck Common Shares	30,000	
	Revenue from Investment in Beck Company		30,000
	To record 30% equity in Beck's net income.		

A	=	L	+	SE
+30,000				+30,000

(2)

31	Cash	12,000	
	Equity Investment—Beck Common Shares		12,000
	To record dividends received.		

A	=	L	+	SE
+12,000				
−12,000				

After the transactions for the year have been posted, the investment and revenue accounts will show the following:

Equity Investment—Beck Common Shares					Revenue from Investment in Beck Company		
Jan. 1	120,000					Dec. 31	30,000
Dec. 31	30,000	Dec. 31	12,000				
Dec. 31	Bal. 138,000						

During the year, the investment account has increased by $18,000 ($138,000 − $120,000). This $18,000 is Milar's 30% equity in the $60,000 increase in Beck's retained earnings ($100,000 − $40,000). In addition, Milar will report $30,000 of revenue from its investment, which is 30% of Beck's net income of $100,000.

The difference between income reported under the cost method and reported under the equity method can be significant. For example, if Milar were assumed not to have significant influence, it would report only $12,000 of dividend revenue (30% × $40,000) using the cost method. Illustration 17-5 compares the journal entries used

---

[1] Or the investor debits a loss account and credits the investment account for its share of the investee's net loss.

Illustration 17-5

Comparison of cost and equity method journal entries

to record these investment transactions. First, it is assumed that the cost method (no significant influence) is used by Milar. Then we assume that the equity method (as discussed in this section) is used.

	Cost Method		Equity Method	
Acquisition				
Equity Investment—Beck	120,000		Equity Investment—Beck	120,000	
Cash		120,000	Cash		120,000
Investee reports earnings				
No entry			Equity Investment—Beck	30,000	
			Revenue from Investment		30,000
Investee pays dividends				
Cash	12,000		Cash	12,000	
Dividend Revenue		12,000	Equity Investment—Beck		12,000

Holdings of More Than 50%

STUDY OBJECTIVE
••••••••• **5** •••••••••

Describe the purpose and usefulness of consolidated financial statements.

A company that owns more than 50% of the common shares of another entity is known as the parent company. The entity whose shares are owned by the parent company is called the subsidiary company. Because of its share ownership, the parent company has a controlling interest in the subsidiary company. After Cara Operations doubled its equity investment in The Second Cup's common shares, it had a controlling interest in The Second Cup. Voting control can also occur with share ownership of less than 50%, depending on how widely dispersed share ownership is and other factors mentioned previously.

▶Accounting in Action ▸ *Business Insight*

Hudson's Bay Company owns 100% of the common shares of Zellers Inc. The common shareholders of Hudson's Bay elect its board of directors. The board of directors controls the property owned by the corporation, which includes the common shares of Zellers. Thus, the Hudson's Bay board of directors is in a position to elect the board of directors of Zellers and, in effect, control Zellers' operations.

When a company **controls** the common shares of another company, the equity method is used by the parent company for investment accounting purposes. In addition, **for financial reporting purposes only**, consolidated financial statements are prepared. Consolidated financial statements present the total assets and liabilities controlled by the parent company. Consolidated statements are prepared in addition to the financial statements for the individual parent and subsidiary companies. For example, Cara Operations uses the equity method to account for its investment in The Second Cup in its own individual statements. But, for external reporting, Cara Operations consolidates The Second Cup's results with its own financial statements. Under this approach, the individual assets and liabilities of The Second Cup are included with those of Cara Operations.

Consolidated statements are useful because they indicate the size and range of operations of the companies under common control. Consolidation is a complex topic dealt with in advanced accounting courses.

Before You Go On . . .

►Review It

1. Compare the accounting entries for equity investments for which ownership is (a) less than 20% with no significant influence, and (b) more than 20% with significant influence.
2. What is the purpose of consolidated financial statements?
3. Are The Second Cup's financial statements consolidated? If so, identify its subsidiary(ies). The answer to this question is provided at the end of this chapter.

►Do It

Two separate situations are presented below:

1. CJW Inc. acquired 5% of the 400,000 common shares of Stillwater Corp. at a total cost of $6 per share on May 18, 2003. On August 30, Stillwater declared and paid a $0.10 per share dividend. On December 31, Stillwater reported net income of $244,000 for the year.
2. Dumas, Inc. obtained significant influence over North Sails by buying 40% of North Sails' 60,000 common shares at a cost of $12 per share on January 1, 2003. On April 15, North Sails declared and paid a cash dividend of $0.75 per share. On December 31, North Sails reported net income of $120,000 for the year.

Prepare all necessary journal entries for 2003 for (1) CJW Inc., and (2) Dumas, Inc.

Action Plan

- Use the cost method for ownership of less than 20% of the common shares of another corporation. Little influence is presumed.
- Use the equity method for ownership of more than 20% of the common shares of another corporation. Significant influence is presumed.
- Record the investor's share of the net income of the investee under the equity method. Wait until dividends are declared to recognize income under the cost method.

Solution

(1) CJW Inc.: Cost Method

May 18	Equity Investment—Stillwater Common Shares	120,000	
	(400,000 × 5% = 20,000; 20,000 × $6)		
	Cash		120,000
	To record purchase of 20,000 shares of		
	Stillwater Corp.		
Aug. 30	Cash	2,000	
	Dividend Revenue ($0.10 × 20,000)		2,000
	To record receipt of cash dividend.		
Dec. 31	No entry to record investee's net income.		

(2) Dumas, Inc.: Equity Method

Jan. 1	Equity Investment—North Sails Common Shares	288,000	
	(60,000 × 40% = 24,000; 24,000 × $12)		
	Cash		288,000
	To record purchase of 24,000 shares of		
	North Sails.		
Apr. 15	Cash	18,000	
	Equity Investment —North Sails Common Shares		18,000
	($0.75 × 24,000)		
	To record receipt of cash dividend.		
Dec. 31	Equity Investment—North Sails Common Shares	48,000	
	($120,000 × 40%)		
	Revenue from Investment in North Sails		48,000
	To record 40% equity in North Sails' net income.		

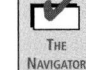

Related exercise material: BE17–3, BE17–4, BE17–5, E17–2, E17–3, E17–4, and E17–5.

THE NAVIGATOR

Valuation and Reporting of Investments

The value of debt and equity investments may change greatly during the time they are held. Bond and share equity prices may jump dramatically with favourable economic events and drop drastically with unfavourable economic developments. For example, in the first full week of trading following the September 11, 2001, terrorist attack on the U.S., the Dow Jones Industrial Average had its biggest drop in nearly 70 years. The Dow Jones is the oldest and most widely known index of the U.S. stock market, measuring the price movements of the 30 large and well-known companies that best represent the American economy.

If prices fluctuate so much, how should investments be valued at the balance sheet date? Valuation could be at cost, at market value, or at the lower of cost and market value. Some argue that market value is the best valuation because it is the expected realizable value. Market value is the amount for which a security can be sold in a normal market. Others say, however, that unless the investment is going to be sold soon, the market value is not relevant because the price will likely change again. **Conservatism** resolves this issue by requiring the application of the lower of cost and market (LCM) rule.

You were introduced to the LCM rule in Chapter 6, for inventories. Just as inventories are reported at the lower of their cost and market values, so too are investments. If the market value of the investments falls below their cost, this potential loss should be recognized when it becomes known, so that decision-makers have access to timely information. Use of the LCM rule varies depending upon whether the investment is temporary or long-term.

Temporary Investments

To illustrate the valuation of temporary debt and equity investments, assume that on December 31, 2003, Plano Corporation's investment portfolio has the following costs and market values:

Illustration 17-6

Valuation of temporary investments

Investments	Cost	Market Value	Gain (Loss)
Bell Canada bonds	$50,000	$48,000	$(2,000)
Nexfor shares	90,000	91,000	1,000
Total	$140,000	$139,000	$(1,000)

The LCM rule is normally applied to the total portfolio and not to individual investments. Applying LCM individually would result in an overly conservative valuation for what is already a conservative rule.

The adjusting entry for Plano Corporation is as follows:

A = L + SE
−1,000   −1,000

Dec. 31	Loss on Decline in Value of Investment	1,000	
	Allowance to Reduce Cost to Market Value		1,000
	To record loss in value of temporary investment.		

The decline in value from cost to market is reported as a loss on the income statement (in the other expenses section).

A valuation allowance account, Allowance to Reduce Cost to Market Value, is used to record the difference between the cost and market value of the securities. By using this **contra asset account**, the company can keep a record of its original investment cost. The actual cost is needed to determine the gain or loss when individual securities are sold. The Allowance account balance is deducted from the cost of the temporary investments to arrive at the lower of cost and market valuation reported on the balance sheet.

The Allowance account is carried forward into future accounting periods, as is the Allowance for Doubtful Accounts to offset Accounts Receivable. No entries are made to the Allowance to Reduce Cost to Market Value account during the period. At the end of each reporting period, the balance in the account is adjusted to the difference between cost and market value (assuming market is lower than cost). If the market value rises above the cost, the Allowance account is adjusted to a zero balance. The valuation allowance should never have a debit balance. This would result in the recognition of a gain. Remember that while conservatism allows losses to be recognized before realization, gains are not recognized until they are realized.

►*Ethics note*
Some managers would like to avoid writing down temporary investments that have experienced losses. They argue that the decline is only due to short-term fluctuations in the market value. Doing this would improve income. Do you think this is ethical?

Long-Term Investments

Because long-term investments have longer maturities than temporary investments, **their carrying values should not be adjusted to reflect temporary fluctuations in market values**. If market value falls substantially below cost and the decline is considered permanent, the investment must be reduced to its market value. This value becomes the investment's new cost base. Any write-down to market value is directly credited to the investment account, as no later recovery in value is expected.

To illustrate, assume that Hébert Corporation purchased 10,000 shares of Bre-X Minerals Ltd. at a cost of $20 per share, as a long-term investment. These shares are now worthless. The adjusting entry for Hébert to record the $200,000 loss is as follows:

Helpful hint Note that while an allowance is used to record declines in market value below cost in the total portfolio of temporary investments, individual long-term investments are directly written down if the decline is permanent.

Dec. 31	Loss on Decline in Value of Investment	200,000	
	Investment in Bre-X Minerals Shares		200,000
	To record loss on long-term investment in Bre-X shares.		

A	=	L	+	SE
−200,000				−200,000

Financial Statement Presentation

In the balance sheet, investments must be classified as temporary or long-term. No distinction is made between debt and equity securities for financial reporting purposes. The securities are combined and reported as one portfolio amount for each of the temporary or long-term classifications in the financial statements.

Temporary Investments

Cash, the most liquid asset, is listed first in the current assets section of the balance sheet. Highly liquid temporary investments of a very short-term duration (typically less than three months) are viewed as a substitute for cash. These temporary investments are commonly combined with cash and reported as a single line item called **"Cash and Cash Equivalents."**

Other temporary investments rank next in order of liquidity. These are presented in the current assets section immediately following cash and cash equivalents.

Temporary investments are reported at the lower of cost and market value. When they are reported at cost, the market value should also be disclosed, usually in parentheses or in the notes to the financial statements. Often there is a statement that says market approximates cost. When temporary investments are reported at market, as was the case in our example earlier in this chapter, one possible presentation is as in Illustration 17-7:

Illustration 17-7

Presentation of temporary investments—at market

PLANO CORPORATION		
Balance Sheet (partial)		
December 31, 2003		
Current assets		
Cash and cash equivalents		$42,000
Temporary investments, at cost	$140,000	
Less: Allowance to reduce cost to market value	1,000	
Temporary investments, at market		139,000

More often, however, the allowance is not reported separately. Temporary investments are simply stated to be at the lower of cost and market and presented in one line, similar to the presentation style indicated in Illustration 17-8 on the following page.

Long-Term Investments

Debt and equity securities held for other than temporary investment purposes are classified as long-term investments. **Long-term investments** are generally reported in a separate section of the balance sheet, immediately below current assets, as shown in Illustration 17-8. Note also how The Second Cup Ltd. presents its investment in Diedrich Coffee, Inc. on its balance sheet, reproduced in Appendix A.

Comprehensive Balance Sheet

Numerous examples of sections of classified balance sheets have been presented in this and preceding chapters. The balance sheet shown in Illustration 17-8 includes key topics from previous chapters in one place: the issue of long-term bonds, the issue of common shares, and restrictions on retained earnings. From this chapter, the statement includes (highlighted in red) temporary and long-term investments (reported at cost and at equity), and informative descriptions within the statement.

Illustration 17-8

Comprehensive balance sheet

ZABOSCHUK CORPORATION
Balance Sheet
December 31, 2003

Assets

Current assets

Cash and cash equivalents		$ 21,000
Temporary investments, at lower of cost and market		
(market $75,000)		60,000
Accounts receivable	$ 84,000	
Less: Allowance for doubtful accounts	4,000	80,000
Merchandise inventory		130,000
Prepaid insurance		23,000
Total current assets		314,000

Investments

Debt investments	$100,000	
Equity investments, at cost	50,000	
Equity investments, at equity	150,000	
Total long-term investments		300,000

Capital assets

Land		$200,000	
Buildings	$800,000		
Less: Accumulated amortization	200,000	600,000	
Equipment	$180,000		
Less: Accumulated amortization	54,000	126,000	
Patents, net of amortization		170,000	
Total capital assets			1,096,000
Total assets			$1,710,000

Liabilities and Shareholders' Equity

Current liabilities

Accounts payable		$ 185,000
Bond interest payable		10,000
Income tax payable		60,000
Total current liabilities		255,000

Long-term liabilities

Bonds payable, 7%, due 2010	$300,000	
Less: Discount on bonds	10,000	
Total long-term liabilities		290,000
Total liabilities		545,000

Shareholders' equity

Common shares, no par value, 200,000 shares authorized		
80,000 shares issued	$900,000	
Retained earnings (of which $100,00 is restricted for		
plant expansion)	265,000	
Total shareholders' equity		1,165,000
Total liabilities and shareholders' equity		$1,710,000

Income Statement

In the income statement, the following items for investment-related accounts are reported in the non-operating section:

Illustration 17-9

Non-operating items related to investments

Other Revenue and Gains	Other Expenses and Losses
Interest Revenue	Loss on Sale of Investment
Dividend Revenue	Loss on Decline in Value
Gain on Sale of Investment	of Investment

Before You Go On . . .

▸ *Review It*

1. Describe the proper valuation and reporting of temporary and long-term investments on a balance sheet.
2. Explain where temporary and long-term investments are reported on a balance sheet.

Related exercise material: BE17–6, BE17–7, BE17–8, BE17–9, BE17–10, E17–6, E17–7, E17–8, E17–9, E17–10, and E17–11.

▶ *A Look Back at Our Feature Story*

Refer back to the feature story about the Portfolio Management Foundation at the beginning of the chapter, and answer the following questions:

1. The Portfolio Management Foundation averaged a 6.5% rate of return in 1999 on its investment in Canadian equities. Is it more likely that this return has been earned from dividends or from appreciation in share value? Why?
2. PMF has about one-third of its money invested in debt securities. Why do you think it would invest in bonds? If it sells one of its investments in bonds, would PMF report a gain or a loss if bond prices have risen since acquisition?
3. Would PMF have to apply the lower of cost and market rule to its portfolio at year end?

Solution

1. Most funds like this earn their money from buying and selling shares. They will hold some shares for dividend income, but the majority of their return is likely from share price appreciation.
2. The investment in debt securities provides a fixed income (interest) for the fund. It also allows for gains (or losses) if bond prices rise (or fall). If PMF sells a bond that it originally purchased at $1,200 for $1,500, it would report a gain on sale.
3. Since the majority of PMF's portfolio is long-term, it would apply the lower of cost and market rule only if the decline of market value of the long-term investment was expected to be permanent.

DEMONSTRATION PROBLEM

In its first year of operations, the DeMarco Company Ltd. had the following selected transactions in temporary equity investments:

June 1 Purchased for cash 600 Sanburg common shares at $24 per share plus $300 of brokerage fees.

July 1 Purchased for cash 800 Cey common shares at $33 per share plus $600 of brokerage fees.

Sept. 1 Received a $1 per share cash dividend from Cey Corporation.

Nov. 1 Sold 200 Sanburg common shares for cash at $27 per share less $150 of brokerage fees.

Dec. 15 Received a $0.50 per share cash dividend on Sanburg common shares.

At December 31, the market values per share were $25 for Sanburg and $30 for Cey.

Instructions

(a) Journalize the transactions, assuming DeMarco uses the cost method to account for these investments.

(b) Prepare the adjusting entry at December 31 to report the total investment portfolio at the lower of cost and market value.

Solution to Demonstration Problem

Action Plan

- Cost includes the price paid plus brokerage fees.
- Record dividend revenue when received (or declared).
- Determine the gain or loss by the difference between the net selling price and the cost of the securities.
- Determine the adjustment to LCM based on the difference between the total cost and total market value of the securities.

(a)

June 1	Equity Investment—Sanburg Common	14,700	
	Cash [(600 × $24) + $300]		14,700
	To record purchase of 600 Sanburg common shares.		
July 1	Equity Investment—Cey Common	27,000	
	Cash [(800 × $33) + $600]		27,000
	To record purchase of 800 Cey common shares.		
Sept. 1	Cash (800 × $1)	800	
	Dividend Revenue		800
	To record receipt of $1 per share cash dividend from Cey Corporation.		
Nov. 1	Cash [(200 × $27) − $150]	5,250	
	Equity Investment—Sanburg Common [(200 ÷ 600) × $14,700)]		4,900
	Gain on Sale of Equity Investments		350
	To record sale of 200 Sanburg common shares.		
Dec. 15	Cash [(600 − 200) × $0.50]	200	
	Dividend Revenue		200
	To record receipt of $0.50 per share dividend from Sanburg.		

(b) The following table shows the relevant values at the end of the fiscal year:

Investment	Cost	Market Value	Gain (Loss)
Sanburg common shares (400)	$ 9,800	$10,000	$ 200
Cey common shares (800)	27,000	24,000	(3,000)
Totals	$36,800	$34,000	$(2,800)

The lower of cost and market valuation is usually applied to the portfolio as a whole. This results in the following adjusting journal entry:

Dec. 31	Loss on Decline in Value of Temporary Investments	2,800	
	Allowance to Reduce Cost to Market Value		2,800
	To record loss on temporary investments.		

THE NAVIGATOR

Summary of Study Objectives

1. *Identify the reasons why corporations invest in debt and equity securities.* Corporations invest for three primary reasons: (a) They have excess cash. (b) They view investments as a revenue source. (c) They have strategic goals such as gaining control of a competitor, promoting strategic alliances, or moving into a new line of business.

2. *Distinguish between temporary and long-term investments.* Temporary investments are securities held by a company that are (a) readily marketable and (b) intended to be exchanged for cash in the near future as the need for cash arises. Investments that do not meet both criteria are classified as long-term investments.

3. *Explain and illustrate the accounting for debt investments.* Entries for investments in debt securities are required when the bonds are purchased, when interest is received or accrued, and when the bonds are sold. The accounting for long-term investments in bonds is the same as for temporary investments in bonds, except that bond premiums and bond discounts must be recorded and amortized.

4. *Explain and illustrate the accounting for equity investments.* Entries for investments in shares are required when the shares are purchased, when dividends are received, and when the shares are sold. When the investor company is not able to exert significant influence (ownership is usually less than 20%) over the operating and financial policies of the investee company, the cost method is used. When significant influence exists (ownership is usually 20% or more), the equity method should be used. When control is exercised (ownership is usually greater than 50%), consolidated financial statements should be prepared for financial reporting purposes.

5. *Describe the purpose and usefulness of consolidated financial statements.* When a company controls the common shares of another company, consolidated financial statements detailing the financial position of the combined entity must be prepared. These statements are useful because they indicate the size and scope of operations of the companies under common control.

6. *Indicate how debt and equity investments are valued and reported on the financial statements.* Temporary investments are reported as current assets on the balance sheet. These investments are valued at the lower of cost and market, with market values separately disclosed. Long-term investments are valued at cost. If market value is expected to be less than cost permanently, the investment should be written down to market, which now becomes its new cost base.

GLOSSARY

Consolidated financial statements   Financial statements that present the assets and liabilities controlled by the parent company, and the total profitability of the combined companies. (p. 794)

Controlling interest   Ownership of more than 50%, or voting control, of the common shares of another entity. (p. 794)

Cost method   An accounting method in which the equity investment in shares is recorded at cost. Investment revenue is recognized only when cash dividends are received. (p. 791)

Debt investments   Investments in money market instruments and government and corporation bonds. (p. 787)

Equity investments   Investments in the share capital of corporations. (p. 790)

Equity method   An accounting method in which the investment in common shares is initially recorded at cost. The investment account is then adjusted annually to show the investor's equity in the investee. (p. 793)

Investee   The corporation that issues the debt or equity securities. (p. 787)

 Key Term Matching Activity

Investor   The corporation that purchases (owns) the debt or equity securities. (p. 787)

Long-term investments   Investments that are not readily marketable or that management does not intend to convert into cash in the near future. (p. 787)

Lower of cost and market (LCM)   A conservative rule that states that investments must be carried at the lower of their cost and market value. (p. 796)

Market value   Amount for which a security could be sold in a normal market. (p. 796)

Parent company   A company that controls, or owns more than 50% of the common shares of, another company. (p. 794)

Subsidiary company   A company whose common shares are controlled by another company (usually more than 50% of its common shares are owned by the other company). (p. 794)

Temporary investments   Investments that are readily marketable and intended to be exchanged for cash in the near future when the need for cash arises. (p. 786)

Self-Study Questions

Answers are at the end of the chapter.

(SO 1) K **1.** Which of the following is not a reason that corporations invest in debt and equity securities?
  a. They have excess cash.
  b. They wish to lose money and generate losses to reduce income.
  c. They wish to generate investment income.
  d. They invest to meet strategic goals.

(SO 2) K **2.** Temporary investments must be readily marketable and be expected to be sold:
  a. within the operating cycle.
  b. within the next year or operating cycle, whichever is shorter.
  c. within the next year or operating cycle, whichever is longer.
  d. whenever the need for cash arises.

(SO 2) K **3.** Long-term investments:
  a. are expected to be held for more than one year.
  b. are expected to be sold within the next year or operating cycle.
  c. are not intended to be sold if a need for cash arises.
  d. consist of debt securities only.

(SO 3) K **4.** Debt investments are initially recorded at:
  a. cost.
  b. cost plus accrued interest.
  c. market value.
  d. lower of cost and market value.

(SO 2) K **5.** Hanes Company has debt investments costing $26,000. They are sold for $28,000 plus accrued interest (which has been recorded). In journalizing the sale, credits are to:
  a. Debt Investments, Loss on Sale of Debt Investments, and Bond Interest Receivable.
  b. Debt Investments, Gain on Sale of Debt Investments, and Bond Interest Receivable.
  c. Debt Investments, Gain on Sale of Debt Investments, and Bond Interest Revenue.
  d. Debt Investments and Bond Interest Receivable.

(SO 3, 4) AP **6.** Pryor Company receives net proceeds of $42,000 on the sale of investments that cost $39,500. This transaction should be reported in the income statement as a:

  a. loss of $2,500 under other expenses.
  b. loss of $2,500 under operating expenses.
  c. gain of $2,500 under other revenues.
  d. gain of $2,500 under operating revenues.

(SO 4) K **7.** The equity method of accounting for long-term investments in common shares should be used when the investor has significant influence over an investee and owns:
  a. between 20% and 50% of the investee's common shares.
  b. 20% or more of the investee's common shares.
  c. more than 50% of the investee's common shares.
  d. less than 20% of the investee's common shares.

(SO 5) K **8.** Which of the following statements is false? Consolidated financial statements are useful to determine the:
  a. profitability of specific subsidiaries.
  b. total profitability of enterprises under common control.
  c. range of a parent company's operations.
  d. full extent of the total obligations of enterprises under common control.

(SO 6) AP **9.** At the end of the first year of operations, the total cost of the temporary investments portfolio is $120,000. Total market value is $115,000. The financial statements should show:
  a. a $5,000 reduction of a long-term asset in the balance sheet and a loss of $5,000 in the income statement.
  b. a $5,000 reduction of a current asset and a loss of $5,000 in the shareholders' equity section.
  c. a $5,000 reduction of a current asset and a loss of $5,000 in the income statement.
  d. no reduction and no loss.

(SO 6) K **10.** A loss on the decline in value of investments is reported as a:
  a. contra asset account.
  b. contra shareholders' equity account.
  c. loss in the income statement.
  d. loss in the statement of retained earnings.

Questions

(SO 1) K **1.** What are the reasons that corporations invest in debt and equity securities?

(SO 2) C **2.** Kirk Wholesale Supply owns common shares in Rogers Wireless Communications Inc., which it intends to hold indefinitely because of some negative tax consequences if the investment is sold. Should the investment in Rogers be classified as a temporary investment? Why?

(SO 3) K **3.** (a) What is the cost of an investment in bonds?
  (b) When is interest on bonds recorded?

(SO 3) C **4.** Ann Adler is confused about gains and losses on the sale of debt investments. Explain to Ann (a) how the gain or loss is calculated, and (b) the statement presentation of the gains and losses.

(SO 3) AP **5.** Clio Company sells an investment in bonds for $45,000. The bonds originally cost $40,000. In recording the sale, Clio records a $5,000 loss. Is this correct? Explain.

(SO 4) C   6. What is the cost of an equity investment in shares?

(SO 4) AP   7. To acquire Mega Corporation common shares, Duran Ltd. pays $65,000 in cash plus $1,500 of broker's fees. Assuming the shares are readily marketable and the company intends to sell them when the need for cash arises, prepare the entry to record this transaction. How should this investment be reported on Duran's balance sheet?

(SO 4) K   8. (a) When should a long-term investment in common shares be accounted for by the cost and equity methods?
           (b) When is revenue recognized under each method?

(SO 4) AP   9. Malon Corporation uses the equity method to account for its ownership of 25% of the common shares of Flynn Packing. During 2003, Flynn reports a net income of $80,000 and declares and pays cash dividends of $10,000. What recognition should Malon Corporation give to these events?

(SO 4) K   10. What constitutes "significant influence"? Is it safe to conclude that significant influence exists when a company owns more than 20% of the common shares of another company?

(SO 5) K   11. What are consolidated financial statements? When must they be prepared?

(SO 6) K   12. What are the valuation guidelines for reporting investments at a balance sheet date?

(SO 6) AP 13. At December 31, G-Products, Inc.'s temporary investments cost $74,000 and have a market value of $68,000. Indicate how G-Products would report these data in the financial statements prepared on December 31.

(SO 6) C   14. Using the data in question 13, how would G-Products report the data if the investments were long-term and the decline were thought to be temporary? Permanent?

(SO 6) C   15. What is the proper statement presentation of the account Loss on Decline in Value of Temporary Investments?

(SO 6) C   16. What is the purpose of reporting the Allowance to Reduce Cost to Market Value as a contra asset in the balance sheet?

(SO 6) AP 17. Rioux Corporation's investment portfolio in securities at November 30, its year end, shows a total cost of $192,000 and a total market value of $150,000. Prepare the adjusting entry to record the investments at the lower of cost and market under three different assumptions.
           (a) Assume the investments are temporary.
           (b) Assume the investments are long-term and the decline is temporary.
           (c) Assume the investments are long-term and the decline is permanent.

(SO 6) C   18. The **Hudson's Bay Company** reported Short-Term Deposits of $86 million and Investments of $46 million on its January 31, 2001, balance sheet. The short-term deposits have maturity dates of less than three months. The investments consist mostly of bonds, held primarily to support long-term funding obligations. Explain where each of these amounts should be classified and presented.

BRIEF EXERCISES

Journalize debt investment transactions.
(SO 3) AP

BE17–1   Phelps Corporation purchased debt investments for $98,000 on January 1, 2003. On July 1, 2003, Phelps received cash interest of $2,450. Journalize the purchase and the receipt of interest. Assume that no interest has been accrued.

Journalize debt investment and issue transactions.
(SO 3) AP

BE17–2   Assume that 10-year 10% bonds are issued at their face value of $50,000 on June 30. Interest is payable semi-annually each June 30 and December 31.

   (a) Prepare the journal entries to record the purchase of the temporary debt investment on June 30 and the receipt of the first interest payment on December 31 on the books of the investor.
   (b) Prepare the journal entries to record the issue of the debt on June 30 and the first interest payment on December 31 on the books of the issuer. You may find it helpful to refer to Chapter 16, where the entries on the books of the issuer were first illustrated.

Journalize equity investment transactions.
(SO 4) AP

BE17–3   On August 1, McLellan Company buys 1,000 Datawave common shares for $36,000 cash plus brokerage fees of $600. On December 1, McLellan sells the shares for $38,000 in cash. Journalize the purchase and sale of the investment in common shares.

Journalize entries under equity method of accounting.
(SO 4) AP

BE17–4   Loop Company owns 25% of Hook Company. For the current year, Hook reports net income of $180,000 and declares and pays a $50,000 cash dividend. Record Loop's equity in Hook's net income and the receipt of dividends from Hook. How much revenue was reported by Loop?

P17–5B McReynolds Mariners has 150,000 common shares and a fiscal year which begins on October 1. On October 1, 2002, LeTourneau Enterprises purchases 30% of the common shares of McReynolds Mariners from another shareholder for $40 per share. LeTourneau intends to hold these shares as a long-term investment. On December 31, 2002, McReynolds Mariners issues a 4% common stock dividend when the shares are trading for $42 per share. On May 31, 2003, McReynolds Mariners pays a cash dividend of $2.00 per share to common shareholders. McReynolds Mariners' net income for the year ended September 30, 2003, is $350,000. The market value of each share of McReynolds Mariners at September 30, 2003, is $50.

Prepare entries under cost and equity methods of accounting; compare statement presentation.
(SO 4, 5, 6) AN

Instructions

(a) Prepare all entries for LeTourneau Enterprises for the year ended September 30, 2003, assuming that it exercises significant influence over McReynolds Mariners.

(b) Prepare all entries for LeTourneau Enterprises for the year ended September 30, 2003, assuming that it does not exercise significant influence over McReynolds Mariners.

(c) Compare the balance sheet and income statement accounts of LeTourneau Enterprises at September 30, 2003, under the two assumptions.

(d) If LeTourneau had purchased 100% of McReynolds' common shares, what method of accounting for this investment would LeTourneau use? What kind of financial statements should it issue? Whose name would be on the financial statements—LeTourneau's, McReynolds', or both names?

P17–6B On December 31, 2002, Karen Associates owns the following securities that are held as long-term investments. The securities are not held for influence or control of the investees.

Journalize equity investment transactions and LCM adjusting entry. Show statement presentation.
(SO 4, 6) AP

Common Shares	Quantity	Cost
Xenos Co.	6,000	$90,000
Yan Co.	5,000	45,000
Zhao Co.	1,500	30,000

In 2003, the following transactions occur:

July 1 Receives $1 per share semi-annual cash dividend on Yan Co. common shares.
July 8 Receives 6,000 Xenos Co. common shares in a 2-for-1 stock split.
Aug. 1 Receives $0.50 per share cash dividend on Xenos Co. common shares.
Sept. 1 Sells 1,000 Yan Co. common shares for cash at $8 per share less brokerage fees of $200.
Oct. 1 Sells 800 Xenos Co. common shares for cash at $9 per share less brokerage fees of $500.
Dec. 15 Receives $0.50 per share cash dividend on Xenos Co. common shares.
Dec. 31 Receives $1 per share semi-annual cash dividend on Yan Co. common shares.

At December 31, the market values per share are as follows: Xenos Co. $7.75, Yan Co. $8, and Zhao Co. $17.

Instructions

(a) Journalize the 2003 transactions and post them to each long-term investment account.

(b) Prepare the adjusting entry at December 31, 2003, to show the securities at the lower of cost and market value. Assume that any declines are not due to temporary market fluctuations.

(c) How would your answer to part (b) differ if the declines *are* considered to be due to temporary market fluctuations?

(d) Show the balance sheet presentation of the investments at December 31, 2003.

P17–7B The following data are in Big Head Todd Corporation's portfolio of temporary investments at December 31, 2002:

Journalize equity investment transactions and show statement presentation.
(SO 4, 6) AP

	Cost
500 shares of Aglar Corporation common shares	$26,000
700 shares of BAL Corporation common shares	42,000
400 shares of Hicks Corporation preferred shares	16,800

Big Head Todd has the following transactions related to the securities during 2003:

Jan. 7 Sells 500 Aglar Corporation common shares at $56 per share less brokerage fees of $700.
Jan. 10 Purchases 200 common shares of Miley Corporation at $78 per share, plus brokerage fees of $240.
Jan. 26 Receives a cash dividend of $1.15 per share on BAL Corporation common shares.
Feb. 2 Receives a cash dividend of $0.40 per share on Hicks Corporation preferred shares.
Feb. 10 Sells all 400 Hicks Corporation preferred shares at $30 per share less brokerage fees of $180.

Sept. 1 Purchases an additional 400 common shares of Miley Corporation at $82 per share, plus brokerage fees of $400.

Dec. 15 Receives a cash dividend of $1.50 per share on Miley Corporation common shares.

At December 31, 2003, the market values of the securities are $64 per share for the BAL Corporation common shares and $72 per share for the Miley Corporation common shares.

Instructions

(a) Prepare journal entries to record the transactions.

(b) Post to the investment accounts.

(c) Prepare the adjusting entry at December 31, 2003, to report the portfolio at the lower of cost and market value.

(d) Show the balance sheet presentation at December 31, 2003.

Determine valuation of debt and equity investments.
(SO 6) AN

P17–8B The following table summarizes information about the temporary and long-term investment portfolios of Daoust Corporation at year end, January 31, 2004:

	Quantity Purchased	Cost/Security	Market Value/Security
Temporary Investments			
T-Bills	10,000	$ 1	$ 1
Nortel Networks	5,000	75	12
Microsoft	5,000	120	105
Laidlaw	1,000	5	1
Long-Term Investments			
Government of Canada bonds	1,000	100	140
CIBC bonds	2,000	98	100

Instructions

(a) Calculate the total cost and total market value of each investment portfolio.

(b) At what value should the temporary investment portfolio be reported at year end?

(c) Prepare any required adjusting entry to apply the lower of cost and market rule at year end.

(d) The president of Daoust Corporation is speculating about holding Nortel Networks, Microsoft, and Laidlaw for the long term, rather than the short term. She doesn't believe there is any point in selling these shares in the near term until their values recover. What impact would it have on Daoust's income statement if the Microsoft and Laidlaw shares were classified as long-term investments?

1. Assume first that the decline in market value of these shares is supposed to be temporary.

2. Then assume that the decline in market value is permanent.

Prepare balance sheet.
(SO 6) AP

P17–9B The following data, presented in alphabetical order, are taken from the records of Scheer Corporation:

Accounts payable	$ 244,000
Accounts receivable	140,000
Accumulated amortization—building	180,000
Accumulated amortization—equipment	52,000
Allowance for doubtful accounts	6,000
Allowance to reduce temporary investments from cost to market value	20,000
Bonds payable (10%, due 2010)	500,000
Building	950,000
Cash	72,000
Common shares (no par value; 500,000 shares authorized; 220,000 issued)	1,500,000
Dividends payable	80,000
Debt investment	200,000
Equipment	275,000
Equity investment—Dion common shares (10% ownership), at cost	278,000
Equity investment—Huston common shares (30% ownership), at equity	230,000
Income tax payable	100,000
Land	500,000
Merchandise inventory, at FIFO cost	170,000
Notes payable (due 2004)	70,000
Patent (net of amortization)	200,000

Premium on bonds payable	40,000
Prepaid insurance	10,000
Retained earnings ($100,000 restricted for expansion)	413,000
Temporary investments, at cost	180,000

Instructions

Prepare a classified balance sheet at December 31, 2003.

CUMULATIVE COVERAGE—CHAPTERS 13 TO 17

Part I

Monique Bergeron and her two colleagues, Jared Nimitz and Rosaline Soileau, are personal trainers at an upscale health spa/resort in Kelowna, B.C. They want to start a health club that specializes in plans for people in the 50+ age group. The growing population in this age group and strong consumer interest in the health benefits of physical activity have convinced them they can profitably operate their own club. In addition to many other decisions, they need to determine what type of business organization they want. Jared believes there are more advantages to the corporate form than a partnership. He hasn't yet convinced Monique and Rosaline. They have come to you, a small business consulting specialist, looking for information and advice about starting a partnership versus a corporation.

Instructions

Prepare a memo that describes the advantages and disadvantages of both partnerships and corporations. Advise Monique, Jared, and Rosaline about the organizational form you believe would be best for them. Include reasons supporting your advice.

Part II

After deciding to incorporate, each of the three receives 20,000 no par value common shares on June 12, 2001, in exchange for their co-owned building ($180,000 market value) and the $120,000 total cash they contributed to the business. Monique, Jared, and Rosaline now need to decide how to obtain financing for renovations and equipment. They understand the difference between equity securities and debt securities, but do not understand the income tax, net income, and earnings per share consequences of equity versus debt financing on the future of their business.

Instructions

Prepare notes for a discussion with the three entrepreneurs in which you will compare the consequences of using equity versus debt financing. As part of your notes, show the differences in interest and income tax expense assuming $1,400,000 is financed. Assume 140,000 shares will be issued at $10 per share in order to raise the required capital. Also assume the interest rate on debt is 9%, the income tax rate is 30%, and income before interest and tax is $160,000.

Part III

During the discussion about financing, Rosaline mentions that one of her clients, Antonio Sandoval, has approached her about buying a significant interest in the new club. Having an interested investor convinces the three to issue equity to provide the financing they need. On July 21, 2001, Mr. Sandoval buys 140,000 shares at a price of $10 per share.

The club, LifePath Fitness, opens on January 12, 2002, and after a slow start, begins to produce the revenue desired by the owners. The owners decide to pay themselves a stock dividend, since cash has been less than abundant since they opened their doors. The 5% stock dividend is declared by the owners on July 27, 2002. The market value of the shares is $1.50 on the declaration date. The date of record is July 31, 2002 (there have been no changes in share ownership since the initial issue), and the issue date is August 15, 2002. By the middle of the fourth quarter of 2002, the cash flow of

LifePath Fitness has improved to the point that the owners feel ready to pay themselves a cash dividend. They declare a $0.10 cash dividend on December 4, 2002. The record date is December 14, 2002, and the payment date is December 24, 2002.

Instructions

Record all of the transactions related to the common shares of LifePath Fitness during the years 2001 and 2002. Also indicate the total number of shares in existence after the stock dividend is issued.

Part IV

Since the club opened, a major concern has been the pool facilities. Although the existing pool is adequate, Monique, Jared, and Rosaline want LifePath to be a cutting-edge facility. Until the end of 2002, financing concerns prevented this improvement. However, because there has been steady growth in clientele, revenue, and income since the fourth quarter of 2002, the owners have explored possible financing options. They are hesitant to issue more shares and change the ownership mix because they have been able to work together as a team with great effectiveness. They have formulated a plan to issue secured term bonds to raise the needed $500,000 for the pool facilities. By the end of April 2003, everything is in place for the bond issue to go ahead. On June 1, 2003, the bonds are issued for $463,200. The bonds pay semi-annual interest of 7% on December 1 and June 1 of each year. The bonds mature in 10 years, and amortization is calculated using the straight-line method.

Instructions

Prepare journal entries to record the following transactions:

  (a) The issue of the bonds on June 1, 2003
  (b) The interest payment made on December 1, 2003
  (c) The adjusting entry required at December 31, 2003
  (d) The interest payment made on June 1, 2004

Part V

Mr. Sandoval's purchase of LifePath Fitness was done through his business. The investment has always been accounted for using the cost method on his firm's books. Early in 2004, however, he decides to take his company public. He is preparing an IPO (initial public offering), and he needs to have the firm's financial statements audited. One of the issues is restating the investment in LifePath Fitness using the equity method, since Mr. Sandoval's ownership percentage is 70%.

Instructions

  (a) Give the entries that would have been made on Sandoval's books if the equity method of accounting for investments had been used since the initial investment. Assume the following data:

	2001	2002	2003
Net income	$19,000	$70,000	$105,000
Total cash dividends	0	21,000	50,000

  (b) Calculate the balance in Sandoval's LifePath Fitness Investment account at the end of 2003.
  (c) What type of financial statements will Sandoval's business issue to properly report its 70% investment in LifePath Fitness?

*B*roadening *Your Perspective*

FINANCIAL REPORTING AND ANALYSIS
....

Financial Reporting Problem

BYP17–1   Refer to the financial statements and accompanying notes for The Second Cup Ltd., which are presented in Appendix A.

Instructions
(a) On the balance sheet, notice that cash equivalents have been combined with cash. What type of investments are these? (Hint: Refer to Note 2 to the consolidated financial statements.)
(b) On the 1999 balance sheet, there is information about the company's investment in Great Canadian Bagel, Ltd.
   1. Was this a debt investment, an equity investment, or both?
   2. Was this investment made to earn investment income or to establish a business relationship? (Refer to management's discussion and analysis of the operating results.)
   3. Was this investment accounted for by the cost method or the equity method?
(c) The Second Cup reports an Investment in Diedrich Coffee, Inc. on its 2000 balance sheet.
   1. Was this a debt investment or an equity investment?
   2. Was this investment made to earn investment income or to establish a business relationship?
   3. Was this investment accounted for by the cost method or by the equity method?
(d) Explain the meaning of the terms "consolidated financial statements" and "subsidiary company."

Interpreting Financial Statements

BYP17–2   Shock waves rippled through nationalistic Canadians when the forestry icon, MacMillan Bloedel, was sold to the world's largest integrated forest products company. Weyerhaeuser paid US$3 billion in November 1999 to purchase 100% of MacMillan Bloedel's shares. Weyerhaeuser is now the world's largest private owner of softwood timber, with about 32 million acres in Canada and 6 million acres in the southern U.S. and the Pacific Northwest.

Weyerhaeuser

Instructions
(a) What method—cost or equity—did Weyerhaeuser use to record its initial investment in MacMillan Bloedel? Explain how this equity investment account will change (increase or decrease) after the acquisition.
(b) How does Weyerhaeuser likely report its investment in MacMillan Bloedel on its consolidated statements?

Additional Cases

BYP17–3   SPS Technologies, Inc. was formed in 1903 as Standard Pressed Steel. The company designs, manufactures, and markets high-strength mechanical fasteners, superalloys, and magnetic materials for the aerospace, automotive, and off-highway industries. The company has facilities in Canada, the United Kingdom, the United States, Ireland, Australia, China, Spain, Brazil, Mexico, and India.

   The following note to the financial statements appeared in a recent SPS annual report:

SPS TECHNOLOGIES, INC.
Notes to the Financial Statements (Partial)
December 31, 1999

Note 5. Investments in Affiliates

At December 31, 1999, the Company's investments in affiliates consist of a 22.05 percent interest in Precision Fasteners Limited (PFL), Bombay, India, and a 55 percent interest in Shanghai SPS Biao Wu Fasteners Co. Ltd. (SSBW), Shanghai, China. ...the Company is not able to exercise effective control over the operations [of SSBW]. The Company received $99,000 of dividends from affiliates in 1997. No dividends were received in 1999 and 1998.

Instructions

(a) Do the investments in these two companies likely represent temporary or long-term investments? Are these equity or debt investments?

(b) The ownership percentages in these companies vary. Based on the information given, which accounting method seems appropriate for each company? What other information would you like to have before deciding how to account for each investment?

(c) What is the most likely method used to account for dividends received from PFL? From SSBW?

Accounting on the Web

BYP17–4 The Investor Learning Centre of Canada is an independent, not-for-profit organization, created by the Canadian Securities Institute. We explore the glossary of this site to learn commonly used investment terms.

Instructions

Specific requirements of this Internet case are available on the Weygandt website.

BYP17–5 Many Canadian corporations make equity investments in shares of other corporations. These investments can be accounted for using either the cost or the equity method. This case will review a Canadian corporation's annual report to examine which methods are used in practice.

Instructions

Specific requirements of this Internet case are available on the Weygandt website.

CRITICAL THINKING

Collaborative Learning Activity

BYP17–6 At the beginning of the question-and-answer portion of the annual shareholders' meeting of Réno-Déco Corporation, shareholder Carol Finstrom asks, "Why did management sell the holdings in AHM Company at a loss when this company was very profitable during the period its shares were held by Réno-Déco?"

Since president Nathalie Clément has just concluded her speech on the recent success and bright future of Réno-Déco, she is taken aback by this question and responds, "I remember we paid $1,100,000 for the shares some years ago, and I am sure we sold those shares at a much higher price. You must be mistaken."

Finstrom retorts, "Well, right here in note number 7 to the financial statements, it shows that 240,000 shares—a 30% interest in AHM—were sold on the last day of the year. Also, it states that AHM earned $550,000 this year and paid out $150,000 in cash dividends. Further, a summary statement indicates that in past years, while Réno-Déco held AHM shares, AHM earned $1,240,000 and paid out $440,000 in dividends. Finally, the income statement for this year shows a loss on the sale of AHM shares of $180,000. So, I doubt that I am mistaken."

Red-faced, president Clément turns to you, the vice-president finance, for answers.

Instructions

With the class divided into groups, help the vice-president finance answer the following:

(a) What dollar amount did Réno-Déco receive when it sold the AHM shares?

(b) Explain why both shareholder Finstrom and president Clément are correct.

Communication Activity

BYP17-7 Chapperal Corporation has purchased two securities for its portfolio. The first is an equity investment in Ray Corporation, one of its suppliers. Chapperal purchased 10% of Ray with the intention of holding it for a number of years. It has no intention of purchasing more shares.

The second investment is a purchase of real-return bonds. Chapperal purchased the debt securities because its analysts believe that changes in market interest rates will cause these securities to increase in value in a short period of time. Chapperal intends to sell the securities as soon as they have increased in value.

Instructions

Write a memo to Jean Talon, the Chief Financial Officer, explaining how to account for each of these investments. Discuss the implications of this accounting treatment on reported income.

Ethics Case

BYP17-8 Kreiter Financial Services Company holds a large portfolio of debt and equity securities as an investment. The total market value of the portfolio at December 31, 2003, is greater than total cost. Some securities have increased in value and others have decreased. Vicki Lemke, the financial vice-president, and Ula Greenwood, the controller, are in the process of classifying the securities in the portfolio for the first time.

Lemke suggests classifying the securities that have increased in value as temporary investments, in order to increase net income for the year. She wants to classify the securities that have decreased in value as long-term investments, and attribute the declines to temporary fluctuations in market values. This way, the decreases in value will not affect 2003 net income.

Greenwood disagrees. She recommends classifying the securities that have decreased in value as temporary investments and those that have increased in value as long-term investments. Greenwood argues that the company is having a good earnings year and that recognizing the losses now will help to smooth income for this year. Moreover, for future years, when the company may not be as profitable, it will have built-in gains "held in reserve."

Instructions

(a) Will classifying the securities as Lemke and Greenwood suggest actually affect income as each says it will?

(b) Is there anything unethical in what Lemke and Greenwood propose?

(c) Who are the stakeholders affected by their proposals?

Answers to Self-Study Questions

1. b 2. d 3. c 4. a 5. b 6. c 7. b* 8. a 9. c 10. c

*Although "a" and "c" are also correct, neither of these choices is as complete as "b".

Answer to Second Cup Review It Question 3

The Second Cup's financial statements are consolidated. It has one subsidiary, Diedrich Coffee.

Remember to go back to the Navigator box on the chapter-opening page to check off your completed work.

Before studying this chapter, you should understand or, if necessary, review:

a. *The difference between the accrual basis and the cash basis of accounting. (Ch. 3, pp. 102–103)*

b. *The major items included in a corporation's income statement. (Ch. 15, pp. 704–706)*

c. *How to calculate EPS. (Ch. 15, pp. 710–711)*

d. *The major items included in a corporation's balance sheet. (Ch. 17, pp. 798–799)*

THE
NAVIGATOR

Looking for the Big Picture in Small Business Loans

HALIFAX, N.S.—If you're a small business owner or manager, what determines whether or not your loan application is approved? What, exactly, is the person on the other side of that desk looking for?

If that person is Shelley LeBrun, Manager of Small Business Banking at TD Canada Trust in Halifax, the answer is, all kinds of things.

The first thing a loan officer usually asks to see, she says, is the balance sheet, "to see how much equity the company has. Then the income statement, to see if it's actually making any money." But the process, she insists, shouldn't stop there.

The rest of the company's financial statements also help clarify the picture, especially the cash flow statement. Sometimes, for example, a company may not look profitable from its income statement, but its cash flow statement will show it actually has significant resources available.

The bottom line, after all, says Ms. LeBrun, is that "we need to know that the company is able to service the debt. The cash flow statement can show us that." If the cash flow statement, together with previous years' statements and a good business plan, shows the bank that the company is financially sound and can meet its loan payments, then the application is likely to be approved.

"At TD Canada Trust, we try to see the big picture," she explains. Factors like a sound business plan, signed contracts for major orders in the near future, and the owner's personal financial situation and relationship with the bank can make all the difference in getting the small business loan needed for the next step.

www.tdcanadatrust.com

THE
NAVIGATOR

CHAPTER • 18

THE CASH FLOW STATEMENT

THE NAVIGATOR ✔

- Understand *Concepts for Review* ☐
- Read *Feature Story* ☐
- Scan *Study Objectives* ☐
- Read *Preview* ☐
- Read text and answer *Before You Go On*
  p. 828 ☐ p. 840 ☐ p. 852 ☐
  p. 857 ☐ p. 864 ☐
- Work *Demonstration Problems* ☐
- Review *Summary of Study Objectives* ☐
- Answer *Self-Study Questions* ☐
- Complete assignments ☐

▶ STUDY OBJECTIVES ◀

After studying this chapter, you should be able to:

1. Describe the primary purpose of the cash flow statement.
2. Distinguish among operating, investing, and financing activities.
3. Prepare a cash flow statement using the indirect method.
4. Prepare a cash flow statement using the direct method.
5. Analyse the cash flow statement.
6. Explain and apply the procedural steps in using a work sheet to prepare the cash flow statement using the indirect method (Appendix 18A).

THE NAVIGATOR

As Shelley LeBrun in our feature story indicates, the cash flow statement provides information for decision-making that is not always available from the balance sheet, income statement, and statement of retained earnings. In fact, looking at the these three financial statements of some well-known companies, a thoughtful reader might have questions like the following: How did Andrés Wines pay cash dividends in a year in which it had no cash, only bank indebtedness? How did the Student Centre of McGill University purchase more than $97,000 of capital assets in a year in which it reported a loss of $114,000? How did Rogers Communications finance its US $112 million purchase of the Toronto Blue Jays baseball team? Answers to these and similar questions can be found in this chapter, which presents the cash flow statement.

The chapter is organized as follows:

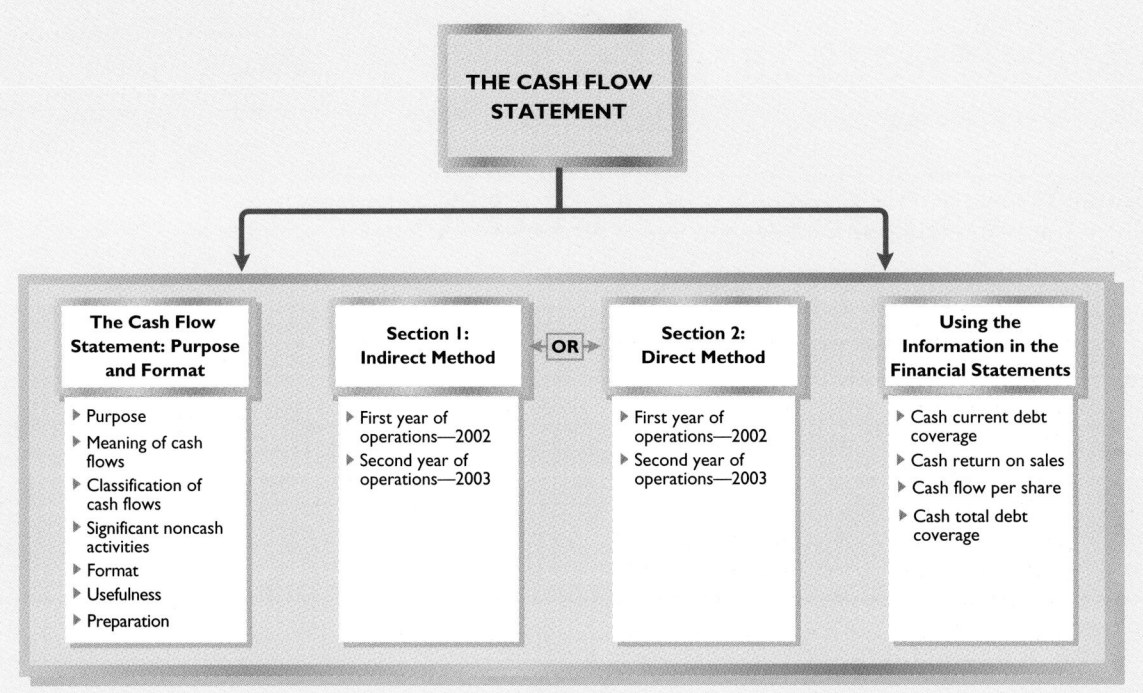

The Cash Flow Statement: Purpose and Format

The three financial statements we've studied so far present only partial information about a company's cash flows (cash receipts and cash payments). For example, comparative balance sheets show the increase in capital assets during the year. But they do not show how the additions were financed or paid for. The income statement shows net income. But it does not indicate the amount of cash generated by operating activities. Similarly, the statement of retained earnings shows cash dividends declared, but not the cash dividends paid during the year. None of these statements presents a detailed summary of the change in cash as a result of operating, investing, and financing activities during the period.

Purpose of the Cash Flow Statement

The primary purpose of the cash flow statement is to provide information about an entity's cash receipts and cash payments during a period. A secondary objective is to provide information about its operating, investing, and financing activities. The cash flow statement reports the cash receipts, cash payments, and net change in cash that result from operating, investing, and financing activities during a period. It does so in a format that reconciles the beginning and ending cash balances.

Reporting the causes of changes in cash helps investors, creditors, and other interested parties understand what is happening to a company's most liquid resource—its cash. As the feature story about small business banking demonstrates, a cash flow statement helps us understand what is happening. It provides answers to the following simple but important questions about an enterprise:

1. Where did the cash come from during the period?
2. What was the cash used for during the period?
3. What was the change in the cash balance during the period?

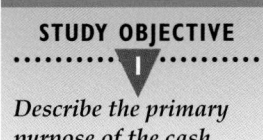

STUDY OBJECTIVE
········· **1** ·········
Describe the primary purpose of the cash flow statement.

Meaning of Cash Flows

The cash flow statement is generally prepared using **cash and cash equivalents** as its basis. You will recall from Chapter 8 that cash equivalents are temporary, highly liquid investments that are both:

1. Readily convertible to known amounts of cash, and
2. So near to their maturity that their market value is relatively unaffected by changes in interest rates.

Generally, only investments with original maturities of three months or less qualify under this definition. Examples of cash equivalents are treasury bills, commercial paper (short-term corporate notes), and money market funds. Cash with restrictions, such as compensating balances, is excluded from cash equivalents. Because of the varying items that can be included in cash equivalents, companies should define cash equivalents when they are combined with cash.

Since cash and cash equivalents are viewed as the same, transfers between cash and cash equivalents are not treated as cash receipts and cash payments. That is, such transfers are not reported in the cash flow statement.

Classification of Cash Flows

The cash flow statement classifies cash receipts and cash payments as operating, investing, and financing activities. Transactions and other events characteristic of each kind of activity are as follows:

1. **Operating activities** include the cash effects of transactions that create revenues and expenses. They affect net income.
2. **Investing activities** include (a) acquiring and disposing of investments and productive long-lived assets, and (b) lending money and collecting the loans. They affect investments that are not cash equivalents and long-term asset accounts.
3. **Financing activities** include (a) obtaining cash from issuing debt and repaying the amounts borrowed, and (b) obtaining cash from shareholders and providing them with a return on their investment. They affect long-term liability and equity accounts.

STUDY OBJECTIVE
········· **2** ·········
Distinguish among operating, investing, and financing activities.

Operating activities is the most important category. It shows the cash that is provided by company operations. This source of cash is generally considered to be the best measure of a company's ability to generate sufficient cash to continue as a going concern.

Illustration 18-1 lists typical cash receipts and cash payments within each of the three classifications.

Illustration 18-1

Typical receipts and payments classified by business activity

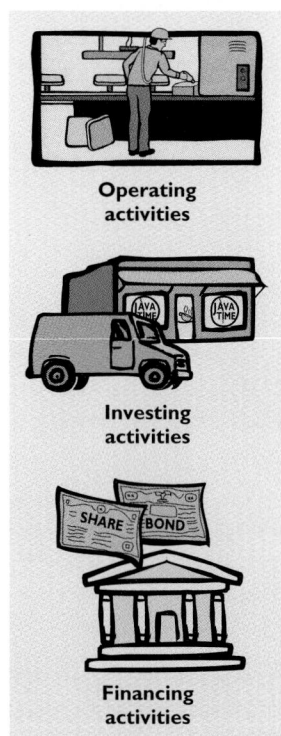

Operating activities

Investing activities

Financing activities

Types of Cash Inflows and Outflows
Operating activities
Cash inflows:
From the sale of goods or services
From returns on debt securities (interest received) and on equity securities (dividends received)
Cash outflows:
To suppliers for inventory
To employees for services
To governments for taxes
To lenders for interest
To others for expenses
Investing activities
Cash inflows:
From the sale of capital assets
From the sale of investments (debt or equity securities of other entities)
From the collection of principal on loans to other entities
Cash outflows:
To purchase capital assets
To purchase investments (debt or equity securities of other entities)
To make loans to other entities
Financing activities
Cash inflows:
From the sale of equity securities (company's own shares)
From the issue of debt securities (bonds and notes)
Cash outflows:
To shareholders as dividends
To redeem long-term debt or reacquire share capital

As you can see, some cash flows related to investing or financing activities are classified as operating activities. For example, receipts of investment revenue (interest and dividends) are classified as operating activities. So are payments of interest to lenders. Why are these considered operating activities? **Because these items are reported in the income statement where results of operations are shown.**

Note the following general guidelines: (1) Operating activities involve income statement items. These items are also affected by noncash working capital (current asset and current liability) accounts. (2) Investing activities involve cash flows resulting from changes in investments and long-term asset items (noncurrent items on the left-hand side of the balance sheet). (3) Financing activities involve cash flows resulting from changes in long-term liability and shareholders' equity items (noncurrent items on the right-hand side of the balance sheet).

Significant Noncash Activities

Not all of a company's significant activities involve cash. The following are examples of significant noncash activities:

1. The issue of common shares to purchase assets
2. The conversion of debt or preferred shares to common shares
3. The issue of debt (including capital leases) to purchase assets
4. Exchanges of capital assets

Significant financing and investing activities that do not affect cash are not reported in the body of the cash flow statement. These noncash activities are reported in a separate note, which satisfies the **full disclosure principle**.

Format of the Cash Flow Statement

The general format of the cash flow statement is organized around the three activities discussed above (operating, investing, and financing). A widely used form of cash flow statement is condensed in Illustration 18-2.

Illustration 18-2

Cash flow statement

COMPANY NAME Cash Flow Statement Period Covered		
Cash flows from operating activities		
(List of individual inflows and outflows)	$ XX	
Net cash provided (used) by operating activities		$ XXX
Cash flows from investing activities		
(List of individual inflows and outflows)	$ XX	
Net cash provided (used) by investing activities		XXX
Cash flows from financing activities		
(List of individual inflows and outflows)	$ XX	
Net cash provided (used) by financing activities		XXX
Net increase (decrease) in cash		XXX
Cash at beginning of period		XXX
Cash at end of period		$ XXX
Note x:		
Noncash investing and financing activities		
(List of significant noncash investing and financing transactions)		$ XXX

The cash flow statement covers the same period of time as the income statement (e.g., for the year ended). The section for cash flows from operating activities always appears first. It is followed by the investing activities and financing activities sections. **Individual inflows and outflows from investing and financing activities are reported separately.** Thus, the cash outflow for the purchase of capital assets is reported separately from the cash inflow from the sale of capital assets. Similarly, the cash inflow from the issue of debt securities is reported separately from the cash outflow for the retirement of debt. If a company did not report the inflows and outflows separately, the investing and financing activities of the enterprise would be unclear. This would make the assessment of future cash flows more difficult.

The reported operating, investing, and financing activities result in net cash being either provided or used by each activity. The amounts of net cash provided or used by each activity are totalled. The result is the net increase (decrease) in cash for the period. This amount is then added to, or subtracted from, the beginning-of-period cash balance. This gives the end-of-period cash balance. Finally, any significant noncash investing and financing activities are reported in a note to the statement.

Usefulness of the Cash Flow Statement

The information in a cash flow statement should help investors, creditors, and others assess the following aspects of the firm's financial position:

1. **The entity's ability to generate future cash flows.** Investors and others examine the relationships between items in the cash flow statement. From these, users can predict the amounts, timing, and uncertainty of future cash flows better than they can from accrual-based data.
2. **The entity's ability to pay dividends and meet obligations.** If a company does not have adequate cash, employees cannot be paid, debts settled, or dividends paid. Employees, creditors, and shareholders are particularly interested in this statement, because it alone shows the flow of cash in a business.

Helpful hint Income from operations and cash flow from operating activities are different. Income from operations is based on accrual accounting. Cash flow from operating activities is prepared on a cash basis.

3. **The reasons for the difference between net income and cash provided (used) by operating activities.** Net income provides information on the success or failure of a business enterprise. However, some people are critical of accrual-based net income because it requires many estimates, allocations, and assumptions. As a result, the reliability of the number is often challenged. Such is not the case with cash. Many readers of the cash flow statement want to know the reasons for the difference between net income and net cash provided by operating activities. They can then assess for themselves the reliability of the income number.

4. **The cash investing and financing transactions during the period.** By examining a company's investing and financing transactions, a financial statement reader can better understand why assets and liabilities changed during the period.

▶Accounting in Action ▸ *Business Insight*

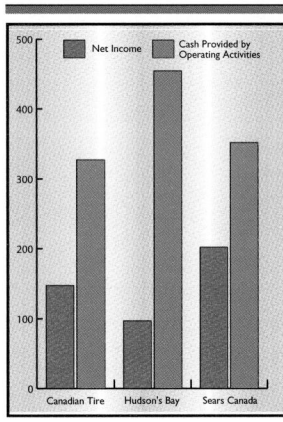

Variations between net income and cash provided by operating activities are illustrated by the following results for three companies. All are engaged in similar types of retail merchandising for the same fiscal year (all data are in millions of dollars).

Company	Net Income	Cash Provided by Operating Activities
Canadian Tire	$145.9	$323.5
Hudson's Bay	96.0	449.6
Sears Canada	199.6	347.9

Preparation of the Cash Flow Statement

The cash flow statement is prepared differently from the three other basic financial statements. First, it is not prepared from an adjusted trial balance. The statement requires detailed information about the changes in account balances that occurred between two periods of time. An adjusted trial balance will not provide the necessary data. Second, the cash flow statement deals with cash receipts and payments. As a result, **the accrual concept is not used in the preparation of a cash flow statement**.

The information to prepare this statement usually comes from three sources:

1. **Comparative balance sheet.** Information in the comparative balance sheet indicates the amount of the changes in assets, liabilities, and shareholders' equity from the beginning to the end of the period.

2. **Current income statement.** Information in this statement helps determine the amount of cash provided, or used, by operating activities during the period.

3. **Additional information.** This includes transaction data that are needed to determine how cash was provided or used during the period.

Preparing the cash flow statement from these data sources involves three major steps, explained in Illustration 18-3.

Step 1: Determine the net increase (decrease) in cash.

 + or −

The difference between the beginning and ending cash balances can easily be calculated from the comparative balance sheet.

Step 2: Determine net cash provided (used) by operating activities.

Buying & selling goods

The current year's income statement is analysed, as well as the comparative balance sheet and selected additional data.

Step 3: Determine net cash provided (used) by investing and financing activities.

Investing   Financing

Comparative balance sheet data and selected additional information are analysed for their effects on cash.

Illustration 18-3

Steps in preparing the cash flow statement

Indirect and Direct Methods

In order to perform step 2, **the operating activities section must be converted from an accrual basis to a cash basis**. This conversion may be done by either of two methods: (1) the indirect method, or (2) the direct method. **Both methods arrive at the same total amount** for "Net cash provided (used) by operating activities." They differ in disclosing the items that make up the total amount.

The indirect method is used extensively in practice. Companies favour the indirect method for two reasons: (1) It is easier to prepare. (2) It focuses on the differences between net income and net cash flow from operating activities.

A minority of companies favour the direct method. This method shows operating cash receipts and payments. It is more consistent with the objective of a cash flow statement. The CICA encourages the use of the direct method of reporting cash provided (used) by operating activities, but allows the use of either method. Despite the CICA's preference for the direct method, its use is rare in Canadian practice. Only two of the two hundred companies surveyed by *Financial Reporting in Canada* used the direct method in 1999. The authors of the publication state: "We continue to be surprised by the failure to use the direct method for presenting this important figure."

▶ *International note*

International accounting requirements are quite similar in most respects for the cash flow statement. Some interesting exceptions: In Australia, the direct method is mandatory. In Japan, operating and investing activities are combined. In Spain, the indirect method is mandatory. Also, in a number of European countries, a cash flow statement is not required at all, although in practice most publicly traded firms provide one.

Before You Go On . . .

▶Review It

1. What is the primary purpose of a cash flow statement?
2. What are the major classifications of cash flows in the cash flow statement?
3. Why is the cash flow statement useful? What key information does it give?
4. What are the three major steps in preparing a cash flow statement?

▶Do It

During its first week of existence, Carrier Molding Company Ltd. had the following transactions:

1. Issued 100,000 common shares for $800,000 cash.
2. Borrowed $200,000 from the National Bank, signing a five-year note at prime plus 1% interest.
3. Purchased two semi-trailer trucks for $170,000 cash.
4. Paid employees $12,000 for salaries and wages.
5. Collected $20,000 cash for services rendered.

Classify each of these transactions by type of cash flow activity. Indicate whether the transaction would be reported as a cash inflow or cash outflow.

Action Plan

- Identify the three types of activities used to report all cash inflows and outflows.
- Report as operating activities the cash effects of transactions that create revenues and expenses and enter into the determination of net income.
- Report as investing activities the transactions that (a) acquire and dispose of investments and productive long-lived assets, and (b) lend money and collect loans.
- Report as financing activities the transactions that (a) obtain cash by issuing debt and repay the amounts borrowed, and (b) obtain cash from shareholders and pay them dividends.

Solution

1. Financing activity; cash inflow
2. Financing activity; cash inflow
3. Investing activity; cash outflow
4. Operating activity; cash outflow
5. Operating activity; cash inflow

THE
NAVIGATOR

Related exercise material: BE18–1, BE18–2, BE18–3, E18–1, and E18–2.

On the following pages, in two separate sections, we describe the use of the two methods. Section 1 illustrates the indirect method. Section 2 illustrates the direct method. These sections are independent of each other. When you have finished the section(s) assigned by your instructor, turn to the next topic, "Using the Information in the Financial Statements," on page 854.

SECTION 1 ▸ Indirect Method

To explain and illustrate the indirect method, we will use the transactions of the Computer Services Corporation for two years, 2002 and 2003, to prepare annual cash flow statements. We will show basic transactions in the first year. Additional transactions will be added in the second year.

STUDY OBJECTIVE
·········· **3** ··········

Prepare a cash flow statement using the indirect method.

First Year of Operations—2002

Computer Services Corporation started operations on January 1, 2002. At that time, it issued 50,000 no par value common shares for $60,000 cash. Throughout the first year, the company rented its office and sales space and sold computers. The comparative balance sheets at the beginning and end of 2002, showing changes in each account, appear in Illustration 18-4.

Illustration 18-4

Comparative balance sheet, 2002

COMPUTER SERVICES CORPORATION Balance Sheet			
Assets	Dec. 31, 2002	Jan. 1, 2002	Change Increase/Decrease
Cash	$34,000	$0	$34,000 Increase
Accounts receivable	30,000	0	30,000 Increase
Inventory	25,000	0	25,000 Increase
Equipment	10,000	0	10,000 Increase
Total	$99,000	$0	
Liabilities and Shareholders' Equity			
Accounts payable	$15,000	$0	$15,000 Increase
Accrued expenses payable	4,000	0	4,000 Increase
Common shares	60,000	0	60,000 Increase
Retained earnings	20,000	0	20,000 Increase
Total	$99,000	$0	

Helpful hint Although each of the balance sheet items increased, their individual effects are not the same. Some of these increases are cash inflows and some are cash outflows.

The income statement and additional information for Computer Services Corporation are shown in Illustration 18-5.

Illustration 18-5

Income statement and additional information, 2002

COMPUTER SERVICES CORPORATION Income Statement For the Year Ended December 31, 2002	
Revenues	$150,000
Cost of goods sold	65,000
Gross profit	85,000
Operating expenses	40,000
Income before income tax	45,000
Income tax expense	10,000
Net income	$ 35,000

Additional information:
1. A dividend of $15,000 was declared and paid during the year.
2. The equipment was purchased at the end of 2002. No amortization was taken in 2002.

Step 1: Determine the Net Increase (Decrease) in Cash

To prepare a cash flow statement, the first step is to **determine the increase or decrease in cash**. This is a simple calculation. For example, Computer Services Corporation had no cash on hand at the beginning of 2002. It had $34,000 on hand at the end of 2002. Thus, the change in cash for 2002 was an increase of $34,000.

Step 2: Determine Net Cash Provided (Used) by Operating Activities

To determine net cash provided (or used) by operating activities under the indirect method, **net income is adjusted for items that did not affect cash**. A useful starting point is to understand **why** net income must be adjusted. Under generally accepted accounting principles, most companies use the accrual basis of accounting. As you have learned, this basis requires that revenue be recorded when earned and that expenses be matched against the revenue they were incurred to generate. Earned revenues may include credit sales that have not been collected in cash. Expenses incurred, such as amortization or cost of goods sold, may not have been paid in cash. Thus, under the accrual basis of accounting, net income does not reflect net cash. Under the indirect method, accrual-based net income must be adjusted to convert certain items to the cash basis.

The indirect method (or reconciliation method) starts with net income and converts it to net cash provided or used by operating activities. In other words, **the indirect method adjusts net income for items that affected reported accrual-based net income but did not affect cash**. That is, noncash expenses and other charges in the income statement are added back to net income. Likewise, noncash revenues and other credits are deducted. The result is net cash provided (used) by operating activities.

Illustration 18-6

Net income versus net cash provided by operating activities

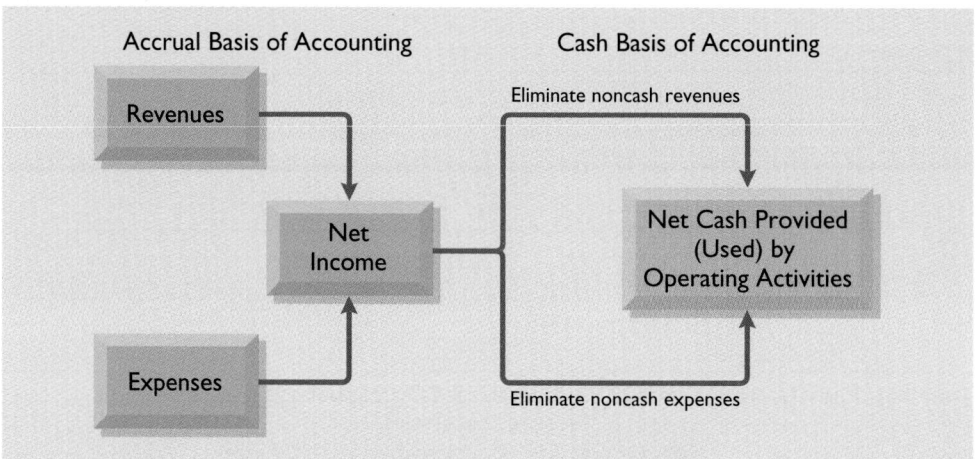

A useful starting point for identifying the adjustments to net income is the current asset and current liability accounts other than cash. Those accounts—receivables, prepayments, inventories, and payables, for example—should be analysed for their effects on cash. We will do this now for the Computer Services accounts.

Increase in Accounts Receivable.   When accounts receivable increase during the year, revenues on an accrual basis are higher than revenues on a cash basis. In other words, operations of the period lead to increased revenues, but **not all of these revenues result in an increase in cash**. Some of the increase in revenues results in an increase in accounts receivable.

The income statement in Illustration 18-5 shows that Computer Services Corporation had $150,000 in revenues. To determine how much cash was collected from sales revenues, it is useful to analyse the Accounts Receivable account.

Accounts Receivable					
1/1/02	Balance	0			
	Revenues	150,000	Receipts from customers	120,000	$30,000 net increase
12/31/02	Balance	30,000			

The ending balance of Accounts Receivable is $30,000 and revenues (assumed to be sales on account) journalized during the period were $150,000 (Dr. Accounts Receivable; Cr. Revenues). Cash receipts from customers (Dr. Cash; Cr. Accounts Receivable) must have been $120,000 ($150,000 − $30,000). Revenues reported on the accrual-based income statement are higher than cash collections. To convert net income to net cash provided by operating activities, the $30,000 increase in accounts receivable must be deducted from net income because $30,000 less cash was collected than reported in the accrual-based revenues section of the income statement.

Increases in all noncash current asset accounts, not just accounts receivable, must be deducted from net income to convert an accrual basis figure to a cash basis figure. **An increase in a noncash current asset is deducted from net income to determine net cash provided (used) by operating activities. Conversely, a decrease in a noncash current asset is added to net income to determine net cash provided (used) by operating activities.**

Increase in Inventory. Assuming a perpetual inventory system is in use, the merchandise inventory account is increased by the cost of goods purchased. It is decreased by the cost of goods sold. When inventory increases during the year, the cost of goods purchased is greater than the cost of goods sold expense recorded in the income statement. Any increase in the Inventory account must be deducted from net income, in a manner similar to the increase in the Accounts Receivable account explained above.

Inventory increased by $25,000 for Computer Services Corporation. Because the Inventory account is increased by the purchase of goods (Dr. Inventory; Cr. Accounts Payable) and is decreased by the cost of goods sold (Dr. Cost of Goods Sold; Cr. Inventory), Computer Services must have purchased $25,000 more inventory than it sold.

Inventory					
1/1/02	Balance	0			
	Purchases	90,000	Cost of goods sold	65,000	$25,000 net increase
12/31/02	Balance	25,000			

Cost of Goods Sold, reported on the income statement, is $65,000. Purchases of merchandise during the year must have been $90,000 ($65,000 + $25,000). To convert net income to net cash provided by operating activities, the $25,000 increase in inventory must be deducted from net income. The increase in Inventory means that the cash-based expense must be increased, which has the effect of reducing net income.

This deduction does not completely convert an accrual-based figure to a cash-based figure. It does not tell us how much cash was paid for the goods purchased. It just converts the cost of goods sold to the cost of goods purchased during the year. The analysis of accounts payable—shown next—completes this analysis by converting the cost of goods purchased from an accrual basis to a cash basis.

Increase in Accounts Payable. In the first year of operations, Computer Services' purchases of merchandise on account were credited to Accounts Payable. The Accounts Payable account is increased by purchases (Dr. Inventory; Cr. Accounts Payable) and decreased by payments to suppliers (Dr. Accounts Payable; Cr. Cash). We determined the amount of purchases made by Computer Services in the Inventory analysis above: $90,000. Using this figure, we can now determine that payments to suppliers must have been $75,000.

Helpful hint Once you understand why, and how, changes in noncash current account balances affect revenues and expenses, you will find it faster to simply look at the difference between ending and beginning balances, and at the direction of the change.

Accounts Payable				
		1/1/02	Balance	0
Payments to suppliers	75,000		Purchases	90,000
		12/31/02	Balance	15,000

$15,000 net increase

Helpful hint Increases in noncash current assets are deducted from net income to increase expenses (or to reduce revenue in some other instances). Increases in noncash current liabilities are added to net income to reduce expenses (or to increase revenue in some other instances).

To convert net income to net cash provided by operating activities, the $15,000 increase in Accounts Payable must be added to net income. The increase in Accounts payable means that less cash was paid for the purchases than that deducted in the accrual-based expenses section of the income statement. Decreasing an expense has the effect of increasing net income. **An increase in a current liability is added to net income to determine net cash provided (used) by operating activities. Conversely, a decrease in a current liability is deducted from net income to determine net cash provided (used) by operating activities.**

Previously, cost of goods sold was converted to cost of goods purchased. The addition of $15,000 completes the adjustment required to convert the cost of goods purchased to the cash paid for these goods. In summary, the conversion of the cost of goods sold on the accrual-based income statement to the cash paid for goods purchased involves two steps. First, the change in the inventory account adjusts the cost of goods sold to the accrual-based figure, cost of goods purchased. Second, the change in the Accounts Payable account adjusts the accrual-based cost of goods purchased to the cash-based payments to creditors.

Cost of goods sold	$65,000
Add: Increase in inventory	25,000
Cost of goods purchased	90,000
Less: Increase in accounts payable	15,000
Cash payments to suppliers	$75,000

Remember that adjustments to accrual-based expense accounts result in an adjustment in the opposite direction to net income. That is, when an expense account such as cost of goods sold is increased because of an increase in inventory, this amount must be *deducted* from net income. This is because expenses reduce net income. Likewise, when cost of goods sold is decreased because of an increase in accounts payable, this amount must be *added* to net income.

If a periodic inventory system was in use, the Purchases and related expense accounts, rather than the Cost of Goods Sold account, would be adjusted in a similar manner for any change in accounts payable. There would be no change in the Inventory account throughout the period in a periodic inventory system.

Increase in Accrued Expenses Payable.   In the first year, operating expenses on account were debited to Operating Expenses and credited to Accrued Expenses Payable.

Accrued Expenses Payable				
Payments for operating expenses	36,000	1/1/02	Balance	0
			Operating expenses	40,000
		12/31/02	Balance	4,000

$4,000 net increase

When accrued expenses payable increase during the year, operating expenses on an accrual basis are higher than they are on a cash basis. For Computer Services Corporation, operating expenses reported in the income statement were $40,000. But, since Accrued Expenses Payable increased by $4,000, only $36,000 of the expenses were paid in cash. To adjust net income to net cash provided by operating activities, the $4,000 increase in accrued expenses payable must be added to net income to reflect the fact that Operating Expenses deducted on the accrual-based income statement did not use as much cash.

For Computer Services, the changes in Accounts Receivable, Accounts Payable, and Accrued Expenses Payable were the only changes in noncash current asset and current liability accounts. This means that any other revenues or expenses reported in the income statement were received or paid in cash. Thus, the income tax expense of $10,000 was paid in cash, and no further adjustment of net income is necessary.

The operating activities section of the cash flow statement for Computer Services Corporation is shown in Illustration 18-7.

COMPUTER SERVICES CORPORATION Cash Flow Statement—Indirect Method (partial) For the Year Ended December 31, 2002		
Cash flows from operating activities		
Net income		$35,000
Adjustments to reconcile net income to		
net cash provided by operating activities:		
Increase in accounts receivable	$(30,000)	
Increase in inventory	(25,000)	
Increase in accounts payable	15,000	
Increase in accrued expenses payable	4,000	(36,000)
Net cash used by operating activities		(1,000)

Illustration 18-7

Net cash provided by operating activities, 2002—indirect method

Helpful hint Whether the indirect or direct method (Section 2) is used, total cash provided or used by operating activities will be the same.

Step 3: Determine Net Cash Provided (Used) by Investing and Financing Activities

The third and final step in preparing the cash flow statement begins with a study of the balance sheet. We look at it to determine changes in noncurrent accounts. The change in each noncurrent account is then analysed to determine what effect the change had on cash, if any.

In Computer Services Corporation, the three noncurrent accounts are Equipment, Common Shares, and Retained Earnings, and all three increased during the year. What caused these increases? No transaction data are given for the increases in Equipment of $10,000 and Common Shares of $60,000. In doing your assignments, you should assume that **any unexplained differences in noncurrent accounts involve cash**. Thus, the increase in Equipment is assumed to be a purchase of equipment for $10,000 cash. This purchase of equipment is reported as a cash outflow in the investing activities section of the cash flow statement. The increase in Common Shares resulted from the issue of common shares for $60,000 cash. The issue of shares is reported as an inflow of cash in the financing activities section of the cash flow statement.

What caused the net increase of $20,000 in the Retained Earnings account? First, net income increased retained earnings by $35,000. Second, the additional information provided in Illustration 18-5 indicates that a cash dividend of $15,000 was declared and paid.

		Retained Earnings			
		1/1/02	Balance	0	
Cash dividend	15,000		Net income	35,000	$20,000 net increase
		12/31/02	Balance	20,000	

The $20,000 increase in Retained Earnings in 2002 is a net change. When a net change in a noncurrent balance sheet account has occurred during the year, the individual items that caused the net change are usually reported separately. Therefore, the $35,000 increase due to net income is reported in the operating activities section. The cash dividend paid is reported in the financing activities section. Note that this is different than our practice with current balance sheet accounts, where we report only the net change.

Cash Flow Statement—2002

We can now prepare the cash flow statement. The statement starts with the operating activities, followed by the investing activities, and is completed with the financing activities. The 2002 cash flow statement for Computer Services is shown in Illustration 18-8.

Illustration 18-8

Cash flow statement, 2002—indirect method

COMPUTER SERVICES CORPORATION
Cash Flow Statement—Indirect Method
For the Year Ended December 31, 2002

Cash flows from operating activities		
Net income		$35,000
Adjustments to reconcile net income to		
net cash provided by operating activities:		
Increase in accounts receivable	$(30,000)	
Increase in inventory	(25,000)	
Increase in accounts payable	15,000	
Increase in accrued expenses payable	4,000	(36,000)
Net cash used by operating activities		(1,000)
Cash flows from investing activities		
Purchase of equipment	$(10,000)	
Net cash used by investing activities		(10,000)
Cash flows from financing activities		
Issue of common shares	$60,000	
Payment of cash dividend	(15,000)	
Net cash provided by financing activities		45,000
Net increase in cash		34,000
Cash, January 1		0
Cash, December 31		$34,000

Helpful hint Note that in the investing and financing activities sections, positive numbers indicate cash inflows (receipts) and negative numbers indicate cash outflows (payments).

Computer Services' cash flow statement for 2002 shows the following: Operating activities **used** $1,000 cash. Investing activities **used** $10,000 cash. Financing activities **provided** $45,000 cash. The $34,000 increase in cash reported in the cash flow statement agrees with the $34,000 increase shown as the change in the cash account in the comparative balance sheet in Illustration 18-4.

Notice how the cash flow statement links the income statement with the beginning and ending balance sheets. Net income from the income statement is the starting point in determining operating activities. The changes in the balance sheet accounts are explained in terms of their impact on cash. These changes lead to the end-of-period cash balances on the balance sheet and on the cash flow statement.

Second Year of Operations—2003

In Illustrations 18-9 and 18-10, there is information related to the second year of operations for Computer Services Corporation.

Illustration 18-9

Comparative balance sheet, 2002 and 2003

			Change
Assets	2003	2002	Increase/Decrease
Cash	$ 56,000	$34,000	$22,000 Increase
Accounts receivable	20,000	30,000	10,000 Decrease
Inventory	75,000	25,000	50,000 Increase
Prepaid expenses	4,000	0	4,000 Increase
Land	130,000	0	130,000 Increase
Building	160,000	0	160,000 Increase
Accumulated amortization—building	(11,000)	0	11,000 Increase
Equipment	27,000	10,000	17,000 Increase
Accumulated amortization—equipment	(3,000)	0	3,000 Increase
Total	$458,000	$99,000	
Liabilities and Shareholders' Equity			
Accounts payable	$115,000	$15,000	$100,000 Increase
Accrued expenses payable	9,000	4,000	5,000 Increase
Bonds payable	130,000	0	130,000 Increase
Common shares	60,000	60,000	0
Retained earnings	144,000	20,000	124,000 Increase
Total	$458,000	$99,000	

COMPUTER SERVICES CORPORATION
Balance Sheet
December 31

Step 1: Determine the Net Increase (Decrease) in Cash

To prepare a cash flow statement from this information, the first step is to **determine the increase or decrease in cash**. As the information presented shows, cash increased by $22,000 ($56,000 − $34,000). Increases and decreases have also been determined for the other balance sheet acccounts. These figures will be needed later for the remaining steps.

Illustration 18-10

Income statement and additional information, 2003

COMPUTER SERVICES CORPORATION
Income Statement
For the Year Ended December 31, 2003

Revenues		$900,000
Cost of goods sold		393,000
Gross profit		507,000
Operating expenses (excluding amortization)	$261,000	
Amortization expense	15,000	
Loss on sale of equipment	3,000	279,000
Income from operations		228,000
Income tax expense		89,000
Net income		$139,000

Additional information:
1. In 2003, the company declared and paid a $15,000 cash dividend.
2. The company obtained land through the issue of $130,000 of long-term bonds.
3. A building costing $160,000 was purchased for cash. Equipment costing $25,000 was also purchased for cash.
4. During 2003, the company sold equipment with a book value of $7,000 (cost of $8,000, less accumulated amortization of $1,000) for $4,000 cash.

Step 2: Determine Net Cash Provided (Used) by Operating Activities

As in step 2 in 2002, net income on an accrual basis must be adjusted to arrive at net cash provided (used) by operating activities. Remember from the previous section that increases in noncash current assets and decreases in current liabilities are deducted from net income. Decreases in noncash current assets and increases in current liabilities are added to net income. Explanations for the adjustments to net income for Computer Services in 2003 follow:

Decrease in Accounts Receivable.   Accounts receivable decrease during the period which means that on an accrual basis, cash receipts are higher than revenues reported. To adjust net income to net cash provided by operating activities, the $10,000 decrease in accounts receivable must be added to net income to determine cash receipts from customers.

Increase in Inventory.   Inventory increases during the period. The cost of goods purchased must be greater than the cost of goods sold. Just as described in the first year of operations, the increase in inventory must be deducted from net income to determine the cost of goods purchased.

Increase in Prepaid Expenses.   Prepaid expenses increase during the period which means that on an accrual basis, cash paid for expenses is higher than expenses reported. In other words, cash payments have been made in the current period, but expenses have been deferred to future periods. To adjust net income to net cash provided by operating activities, the $4,000 increase in prepaid expenses must be deducted from net income to determine the cash paid for expenses.

Increase in Accounts Payable.   Like the increase in 2002, the 2003 increase of $100,000 in accounts payable must be added to net income to determine the cash payments to suppliers.

Increase in Accrued Expenses Payable.   Like the increase in 2002, the $5,000 increase in accrued expenses payable during the year 2003 must be added to net income to adjust to cash paid for operating expenses.

Helpful hint Amortization is similar to any other noncash expense that reduces net income. If it does not involve a current cash outflow, it must be added back to net income to arrive at cash provided by operating activities.

Amortization Expense.   During 2003, Computer Services Corporation reported an amortization expense of $15,000. Of this amount, $11,000 was related to the building and $4,000 to the equipment. These two amounts were determined by analysing the accumulated amortization accounts in the balance sheets.

Increase in Accumulated Amortization—Building.   As shown in Illustration 18-9, accumulated amortization increased by $11,000. This change represents the amortization expense on the building for the year. **Amortization expense is a noncash charge. So it is added back to net income** in order to arrive at net cash provided by operating activities.

It is important to recognize that this amount is not added to operating activities as if it were a source of cash. Amortization does not involve cash. It is added to cancel the deduction created by the amortization expense in the determination of net income.

Increase in Accumulated Amortization—Equipment.   Accumulated Amortization—Equipment increased by $3,000. But this change does not represent the overall amortization expense for the year. The additional information at the bottom of the income statement indicates why not. This account was decreased (debited $1,000) as a result of the sale of some equipment. Thus, amortization expense for 2003 was $4,000 ($3,000 + $1,000). That amount is added to net income to determine net cash provided by operating activities.

The T account that follows provides information about the changes that occurred in this account in 2003:

Accumulated Amortization—Equipment				
Accumulated amortization on equipment sold	1,000	1/1/03	Balance	0
			Amortization expense	4,000
		12/31/03	Balance	3,000

$3,000 net increase

Other charges to expense that do not require the use of cash, such as the amortization of bond discounts, are treated in the same way as the amortization of capital assets. The amortization of bond premiums would be the opposite—deducted from net income—since bond premium amortization reduces interest expense.

Loss on Sale of Equipment. In the income statement, Computer Services Corporation reported a $3,000 loss on the sale of equipment (net book value of $7,000 less cash proceeds of $4,000). Like amortization, **the loss reduced net income but did not reduce cash**. So, the loss is **added to net income** in determining net cash provided by operating activities.

If we did not add back a loss to remove it from net income, we would count the loss twice—once in the operating activities section (as part of net income), and again in the investing activities section (as part of the cash proceeds from the sale). As a result, a loss must be added to net income to calculate net cash provided by operating activities. If there is a gain on sale, the reverse occurs.

As a result of the previous adjustments, net cash provided by operating activities is $218,000, as calculated in Illustration 18-11.

COMPUTER SERVICES CORPORATION Cash Flow Statement—Indirect Method (partial) For the Year Ended December 31, 2003		
Cash flows from operating activities		
Net income		$139,000
Adjustments to reconcile net income to net cash provided by operating activities:		
Amortization expense	$ 15,000	
Loss on sale of equipment	3,000	
Decrease in accounts receivable	10,000	
Increase in inventory	(50,000)	
Increase in prepaid expenses	(4,000)	
Increase in accounts payable	100,000	
Increase in accrued expenses payable	5,000	79,000
Net cash provided by operating activities		218,000

Illustration 18-11

Net cash provided by operating activities, 2003—indirect method

Summary of Conversion to Net Cash Provided by Operating Activities—Indirect Method. The cash flow statement prepared by the indirect method starts with net income. It then adds (or deducts) items not affecting cash to arrive at net cash provided by operating activities. The additions and deductions consist of (1) changes in specific noncash current assets and current liabilities, and (2) noncash items reported in the income statement. A summary of the adjustments for the changes in the account balances of the noncash current assets and current liabilities is provided in Illustration 18-12.

Illustration 18-12

Adjustments for noncash current assets and current liabilities

Helpful hint Decreases in noncash current assets are added to net income. Increases are deducted.

Helpful hint Increases in noncash current liabilities are added to net income. Decreases are deducted.

	Adjustments to Convert Net Income to Net Cash Provided (Used) by Operating Activities	
	Add to Net Income	Deduct from Net Income
Current Assets		
Accounts receivable	Decrease	Increase
Inventory	Decrease	Increase
Prepaid expenses	Decrease	Increase
Other current assets	Decrease	Increase
Current Liabilities		
Accounts payable	Increase	Decrease
Accrued expenses payable	Increase	Decrease
Other current liabilities	Increase	Decrease

Adjustments for the noncash items reported in the income statement are made as shown in Illustration 18-13.

Illustration 18-13

Adjustments for noncash income statement items

Helpful hint Noncash expenses (debits) are added to net income. Noncash revenues (credits) are deducted.

Noncash Items	Adjustments to Convert Net Income to Net Cash Provided (Used) by Operating Activities
Amortization (of capital assets) expense	Add
Amortization of bond discount to interest expense	Add
Amortization of bond premium to interest expense	Deduct
Loss on sale of asset	Add
Gain on sale of asset	Deduct
Income from long-term equity investment	Deduct

Step 3: Determine Net Cash Provided (Used) by Investing and Financing Activities

The next step involves analysing the remaining changes in balance sheet accounts to determine net cash provided (used) by investing and financing activities.

Increase in Land. As indicated from the change in the Land account and the additional information, land of $130,000 was purchased through the issue of long-term bonds. The issue of bonds payable for land has no effect on cash. But it is a significant noncash investing and financing activity that merits disclosure in a note to the statement.

Increase in Building. The additional data indicate that a building was acquired for $160,000 cash. This is a cash outflow reported in the investing section.

Increase in Equipment. The Equipment account increased by $17,000. The additional information explains that this was a net increase resulting from two transactions: (1) the purchase of equipment for $25,000, and (2) the sale of equipment that cost $8,000 for $4,000. The T account on the next page details the changes in this account during the year:

Equipment					
1/1/03	Balance	10,000			
	Purchase of equipment	25,000	Cost of equipment sold	8,000	} $17,000 net increase
12/31/03	Balance	27,000			

The following entries show the details of the equipment transactions:

Equipment	25,000		
Cash		25,000	
To record purchase of equipment.			

A	=	L	+	SE
+25,000				
−25,000				

Cash	4,000		
Accumulated Amortization	1,000		
Loss on Sale of Equipment	3,000		
Equipment		8,000	
To record sale of equipment.			

A	=	L	+	SE
+4,000				−3,000
+1,000				
−8,000				

These transactions are classified as investing activities. Each transaction should be reported separately. Thus the purchase of equipment should be reported as an outflow of cash for $25,000 and the sale should be reported as an inflow of cash for $4,000.

Increase in Bonds Payable. The bonds payable account increased by $130,000. As indicated in the additional information, land was acquired from the issue of these bonds. This noncash transaction is reported in a note to the statement.

Increase in Retained Earnings. Retained earnings increased by $124,000 during the year. This increase can be explained by two factors: (1) Net income of $139,000 increased retained earnings. (2) A dividend of $15,000 decreased retained earnings. Net income is adjusted to net cash provided by operating activities in the operating activities section. Payment of the dividend is a cash outflow that is reported as a financing activity.

Helpful hint When shares or bonds are issued for cash, it is the amount of the issue price (proceeds) that appears on the cash flow statement as a financing inflow, not the legal capital of the shares or the face value of the bonds. Use the amount recorded in the Cash account.

Cash Flow Statement

By combining the previous items, we obtain a cash flow statement for the year 2003 for Computer Services Corporation, as presented in Illustration 18-14.

Illustration 18-14

Cash flow statement, 2003—indirect method

COMPUTER SERVICES CORPORATION Cash Flow Statement—Indirect Method For the Year Ended December 31, 2003		
Cash flows from operating activities		
Net income		$139,000
Adjustments to reconcile net income to net cash		
provided by operating activities:		
Amortization expense	$ 15,000	
Loss on sale of equipment	3,000	
Decrease in accounts receivable	10,000	
Increase in inventory	(50,000)	
Increase in prepaid expenses	(4,000)	
Increase in accounts payable	100,000	
Increase in accrued expenses payable	5,000	79,000
Net cash provided by operating activities		218,000

Cash flows from investing activities		
Purchase of building	$(160,000)	
Purchase of equipment	(25,000)	
Sale of equipment	4,000	
Net cash used by investing activities		(181,000)
Cash flows from financing activities		
Payment of cash dividend	$ (15,000)	
Net cash used by financing activities		(15,000)
Net increase in cash		22,000
Cash, January 1		34,000
Cash, December 31		$ 56,000
Note x: Noncash investing and financing activities		
Issue of bonds payable to purchase land		$130,000

Before You Go On . . .

▸Review It

1. What is the format of the operating activities section of the cash flow statement for the indirect method?
2. Where is amortization expense shown on a cash flow statement using the indirect method?
3. Where are significant noncash investing and financing activities shown in a cash flow statement? Give some examples.
4. Which method of calculating net cash provided by operating activities does The Second Cup use? Does The Second Cup use cash or cash and cash equivalents in its statement? If the latter, what is included in cash equivalents? The answer to these questions is provided at the end of this chapter.

▸Do It

Presented below is information related to Reynolds Company. Use the indirect method to prepare a cash flow statement.

REYNOLDS COMPANY LTD.
Balance Sheet
December 31

Assets	2003	2002	Change Increase/Decrease
Cash	$ 54,000	$ 37,000	$17,000 Increase
Accounts receivable	68,000	26,000	42,000 Increase
Inventories	54,000	0	54,000 Increase
Prepaid expenses	4,000	6,000	2,000 Decrease
Land	45,000	70,000	25,000 Decrease
Buildings	200,000	200,000	0
Accumulated amortization—buildings	(21,000)	(11,000)	10,000 Increase
Equipment	193,000	68,000	125,000 Increase
Accumulated amortization—equipment	(28,000)	(10,000)	18,000 Increase
Totals	$569,000	$386,000	
Liabilities and Shareholders' Equity			
Accounts payable	$ 23,000	$ 40,000	$17,000 Decrease
Accrued expenses payable	10,000	0	10,000 Increase
Bonds payable	110,000	150,000	40,000 Decrease
Common shares	220,000	60,000	160,000 Increase
Retained earnings	206,000	136,000	70,000 Increase
Totals	$569,000	$386,000	

REYNOLDS COMPANY LTD.
Income Statement
For the Year Ended December 31, 2003

Revenues		$890,000
Cost of goods sold	$465,000	
Operating expenses	221,000	
Interest expense	12,000	
Loss on sale of equipment	2,000	700,000
Income from operations		190,000
Income tax expense		65,000
Net income		$125,000

Additional information:
1. Operating expenses include amortization expense of $33,000.
2. $25,000 of land was sold for cash.
3. Cash dividends of $55,000 were declared and paid in 2003.
4. Interest expense of $12,000 was paid in cash.
5. Equipment with a cost of $166,000 was purchased for cash. Equipment with a cost of $41,000 and a net book value of $36,000 was sold for $34,000 cash.
6. Bonds of $40,000 were redeemed at their face value for cash.
7. Common shares of $160,000 were issued for cash.
8. Accounts payable pertain to merchandise suppliers.

Action Plan

- Determine the net increase (decrease) in cash.
- Determine the net cash provided (used) by operating activities. Operating activities generally relate to revenues and expenses, which are affected by changes in noncash current assets and current liabilities and noncash items in the income statement.
- Determine the net cash provided (used) by investing and financing activities. Investing activities generally relate to changes in noncurrent assets. Financing activities generally relate to changes in noncurrent liabilities and shareholders' equity accounts.

Solution

REYNOLDS COMPANY LTD.
Cash Flow Statement—Indirect Method
For the Year Ended December 31, 2003

Cash flows from operating activities		
Net income		$125,000
Adjustments to reconcile net income to net cash		
provided by operating activities:		
Amortization expense	$ 33,000	
Loss on sale of equipment	2,000	
Increase in accounts receivable	(42,000)	
Increase in inventories	(54,000)	
Decrease in prepaid expenses	2,000	
Decrease in accounts payable	(17,000)	
Increase in accrued expenses payable	10,000	(66,000)
Net cash provided by operating activities		59,000
Cash flows from investing activities		
Sale of land	$ 25,000	
Sale of equipment	34,000	
Purchase of equipment	(166,000)	
Net cash used by investing activities		(107,000)

Cash flows from financing activities		
Redemption of bonds	$ (40,000)	
Sale of common shares	160,000	
Payment of dividends	(55,000)	
Net cash provided by financing activities		65,000
Net increase in cash		17,000
Cash, January 1		37,000
Cash, December 31		$ 54,000

THE NAVIGATOR

Related exercise material: BE18–4, BE18–5, BE18–6, E18–3, E18–4, and E18–5.

Note: This concludes Section 1 on the preparation of the cash flow statement using the indirect method. Unless your instructor assigns Section 2, you should turn to the concluding section of the chapter, "Using the Information in the Financial Statements."

SECTION 2 ▸ Direct Method

To illustrate the direct method, we will use the transactions of Computer Services Corporation for two years, 2002 and 2003, to prepare annual cash flow statements. We will show basic transactions in the first year, with additional transactions added in the second year.

First Year of Operations—2002

STUDY OBJECTIVE
••••••••• **4** •••••••••

Prepare a cash flow statement using the direct method.

Illustration 18-15

Comparative balance sheet, 2002

Computer Services Corporation began business on January 1, 2002. At that time, it issued 50,000 no par value common shares for $60,000 cash. Throughout the first year, the company rented its office and sales space and sold computers. The comparative balance sheets at the beginning and end of 2002, and the changes in each account, are shown in Illustration 18-15.

COMPUTER SERVICES CORPORATION Balance Sheet			
Assets	2003	2002	Change Increase/Decrease
Cash	$34,000	$0	$34,000 Increase
Accounts receivable	30,000	0	30,000 Increase
Inventory	25,000	0	25,000 Increase
Equipment	10,000	0	10,000 Increase
Total	$99,000	$0	
Liabilities and Shareholders' Equity			
Accounts payable	$15,000	$0	$15,000 Increase
Accrued expenses payable	4,000	0	4,000 Increase
Common shares	60,000	0	60,000 Increase
Retained earnings	20,000	0	20,000 Increase
Total	$99,000	$0	

The income statement and additional information for Computer Services Corporation are shown in Illustration 18-16.

COMPUTER SERVICES CORPORATION	
Income Statement	
For the Year Ended December 31, 2002	
Revenues	$150,000
Cost of goods sold	65,000
Gross profit	85,000
Operating expenses	40,000
Income before income tax	45,000
Income tax expense	10,000
Net income	$ 35,000

Additional information:
1. A dividend of $15,000 was declared and paid during the year.
2. The equipment was purchased at the end of 2002. No amortization was taken in 2002.

Illustration 18-16

Income statement and additional information, 2002

Step 1: Determine the Net Increase (Decrease) in Cash

The comparative balance sheet for Computer Services Corporation shows a zero cash balance at January 1, 2002, and a cash balance of $34,000 at December 31, 2002. The change in cash for 2002 was a net increase of $34,000.

Step 2: Determine the Net Cash Provided (Used) by Operating Activities

Under the direct method, **cash provided (or used) by operating activities is calculated by adjusting each item in the income statement from the accrual basis to the cash basis.** To simplify and condense the operating activities section, **only major classes of operating cash receipts and cash payments are reported.** The difference between these cash receipts and cash payments for these major classes is the net cash provided by operating activities. These relationships are shown in Illustration 18-17.

Helpful hint You may wish to immediately insert the beginning and ending cash balances, and the increase (decrease) in cash, into the cash flow statement. The net increase (decrease) is the target amount. The net cash flows from the three classes of activities must equal the target amount.

Illustration 18-17

Major classes of cash receipts and payments

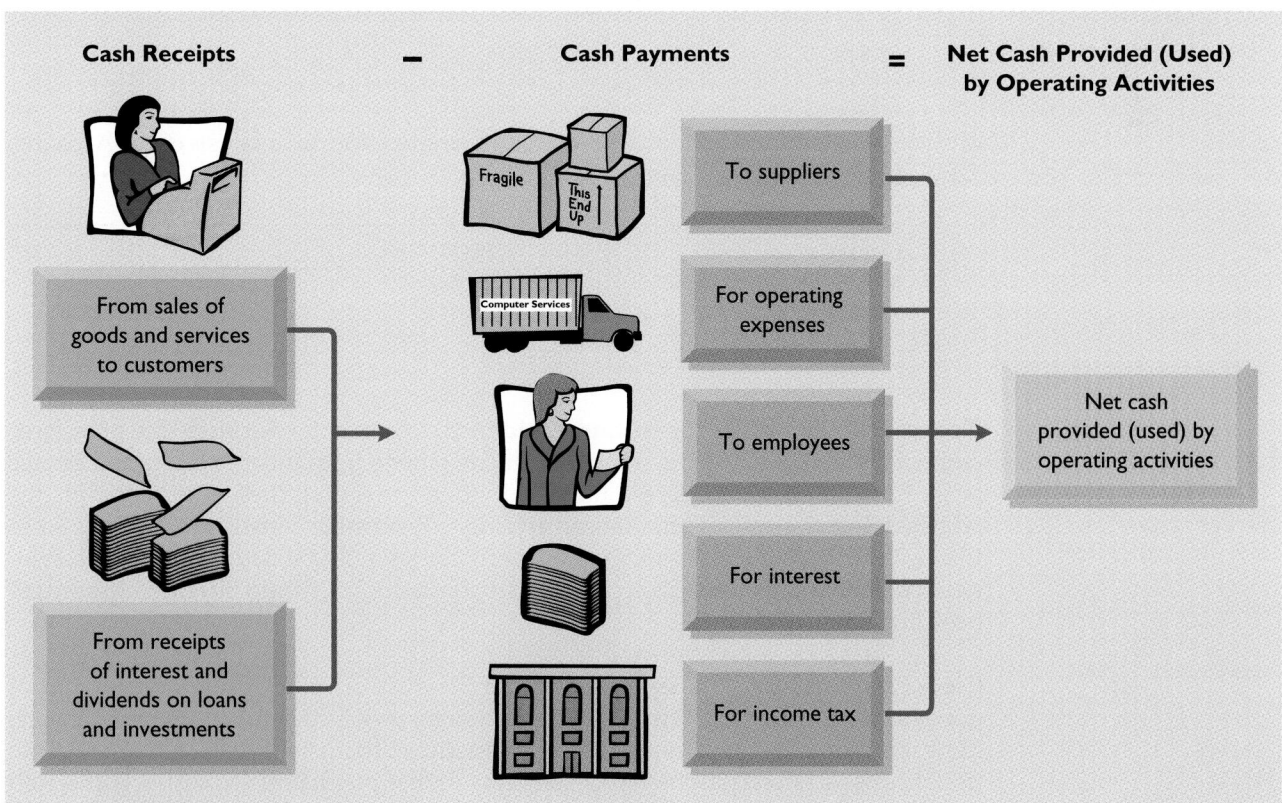

An efficient way to apply the direct method is to analyse the items reported in the income statement in the order in which they are listed. Cash receipts and cash payments related to these revenues and expenses are then determined by adjusting for changes in the related current balance sheet accounts. For example, **increases in current asset accounts are deducted from revenues and added to expenses to convert accrual-based income statement amounts to cash-based amounts. Conversely, decreases in current asset accounts are added to revenues and deducted from expenses. Increases in current liability accounts are added to revenues and deducted from expenses to convert accrual-based income statement amounts to cash-based amounts. Conversely, decreases in current liability accounts are deducted from revenues and added to expenses.**

We explain the reasoning behind these adjustments for Computer Services Corporation in 2002, in the following sections:

Cash Receipts from Customers.   The income statement for Computer Services Corporation reported revenues from customers of $150,000. How much of that was cash receipts? To answer that, it is necessary to consider the change in accounts receivable during the year. When accounts receivable increase during the year, revenues on an accrual basis are higher than cash receipts from customers. Operations lead to increased revenues, but not all of these revenues result in cash receipts. To determine the amount of cash receipts, the increase in accounts receivable is deducted from sales revenues. On the other hand, there may be a decrease in accounts receivable. That would occur if cash receipts from customers exceeded sales revenues. In that case, the decrease in accounts receivable is added to sales revenues.

For Computer Services Corporation, accounts receivable increased by $30,000. Thus, cash receipts from customers were $120,000, calculated as in Illustration 18-18:

Illustration 18-18

Formula to calculate cash receipts from customers— direct method

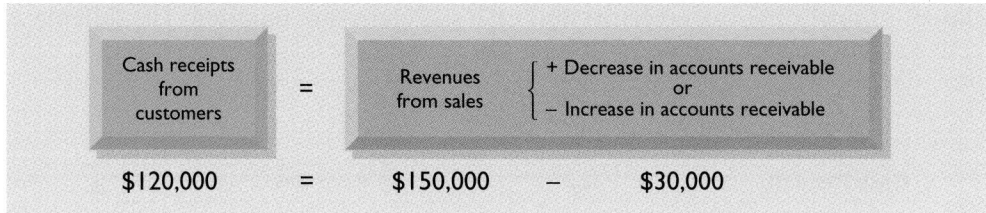

Cash receipts from customers can also be determined from an analysis of the Accounts Receivable account, as shown below.

Accounts Receivable			
1/1/02	Balance	0	
	Revenues from sales	150,000	Receipts from customers 120,000
12/31/02	Balance	30,000	

$30,000 net increase

Cash Receipts from Interest and Dividends.   Computer Services does not have cash receipts from any source other than customers. If an income statement details other revenue such as interest and/or dividend revenue, these amounts must be adjusted for any accrued amounts receivable to determine actual cash receipts. As in Illustration 18-18, increases in accrued receivables would be deducted from accrual-based revenues. Decreases in accrued receivable accounts would be added to accrual-based revenues.

Cash Payments to Suppliers.   Computer Services Corporation reported a cost of goods sold, using the perpetual inventory system, of $65,000 on its income statement. How much of that was cash payments to suppliers? To answer that, it is necessary to find the cost of goods purchased for the year. To find purchases, the cost of goods sold is adjusted for the change in inventory. When inventory increases during the year, the cost of goods purchased exceeds the cost of goods sold. To determine the cost of goods purchased, the increase in inventory is added to the cost of goods sold. Any decrease in inventory would be deducted from the cost of goods sold. Computer Services cost of goods purchased is $90,000 ($65,000 + $25,000).

After the cost of goods purchased is calculated, cash payments to suppliers can be determined. This is done by adjusting the cost of goods purchased for the change in accounts payable. When accounts payable increase during the year, purchases on an accrual basis are higher than they are on a cash basis. To determine cash payments to suppliers, an increase in accounts payable is deducted from the cost of goods purchased. On the other hand, there may be a decrease in accounts payable. That would occur if cash payments to suppliers exceeded purchases. In that case, the decrease in accounts payable is added to the cost of goods purchased.

For Computer Services Corporation, cash payments to suppliers were $75,000 ($90,000 − $15,000), calculated as follows:

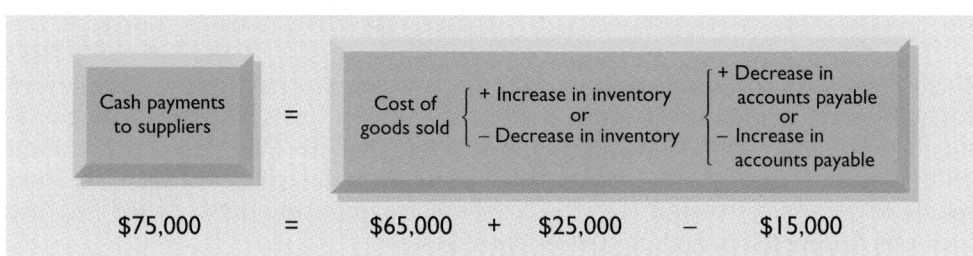

Illustration 18-19

Formula to calculate cash payments to suppliers— direct method

Cash payments to suppliers (also known as creditors) can also be determined from an analysis of the Inventory and Accounts Payable accounts below:

Inventory			
1/1/02 Balance	0		
Purchases	90,000	Cost of goods sold	65,000
12/31/02 Balance	25,000		

Accounts Payable			
		1/1/02 Balance	0
Payments to suppliers	75,000	Purchases	90,000
		12/31/02 Balance	15,000

Cash Payments for Operating Expenses. Operating expenses of $40,000 were reported on Computer Services' income statement. To determine the cash paid for operating expenses, we need to adjust this amount for any changes in prepaid expenses and accrued liabilities.

If prepaid expenses increase during the year, cash paid for operating expenses will be higher than operating expenses reported on the income statement. To adjust operating expenses to cash payments for services, the increase in any prepaids must be added to operating expenses. On the other hand, if prepaid expenses decrease during the year, the decrease must be deducted from operating expenses.

Operating expenses must also be adjusted for changes in accrued liability accounts (e.g., accrued expenses payable). While some companies record accrued liabilities separately, others combine them with accounts payable. In a merchandising company, such as Computer Services, the Accounts Payable account is often used only for purchases of merchandise inventory on account. Accrued liability accounts are used for all other payables.

When accrued expenses payable increase during the year, operating expenses on an accrual basis are higher than they are on a cash basis. To determine cash payments for operating expenses, an increase in accrued expenses payable is deducted from operating expenses. On the other hand, a decrease in accrued expenses payable is added to operating expenses because cash payments exceed operating expenses.

Computer Services' cash payments for operating expenses were $36,000, calculated as in Illustration 18-20.

Illustration 18-20

Formula to calculate cash payments for operating expenses—direct method

Cash payments for operating expenses can also be determined from an analysis of the Accrued Expenses Payable account, as shown below:

Accrued Expenses Payable			
Payments for operating expenses	36,000	1/1/02 Balance	0
		Operating expenses	40,000
		12/31/02 Balance	4,000

$4,000 net increase

Cash Payments to Employees. Some companies report payments to employees separately, removing these payments from operating expenses. To determine payments to employees, you would have to know the Salary (or Wage) Expense amount on the income statement and any Salaries Payable on the balance sheet. Cash payments to employees would equal Salary Expense, plus any decrease (or less any increase) during the period in Salaries Payable.

Other companies condense their income statements in such a manner that cash payments to suppliers and employees cannot be separated from cash payments for operating expenses (i.e., they do not disclose cost of goods sold or salary expense separately). Although the disclosure will not be as informative, it is acceptable to combine these sources of cash payments for reporting purposes.

Cash Payments for Interest and Income Tax. Computer Services has no interest expense. The income statement for Computer Services does show an income tax expense of $10,000. This amount equals the cash paid. The comparative balance sheet indicated no income tax payable at either the beginning or the end of the year.

The relationship among cash payments for income tax, income tax expense, and changes in income tax payable (if any) is shown in Illustration 18-21:

Illustration 18-21

Formula to calculate cash payments for income tax—direct method

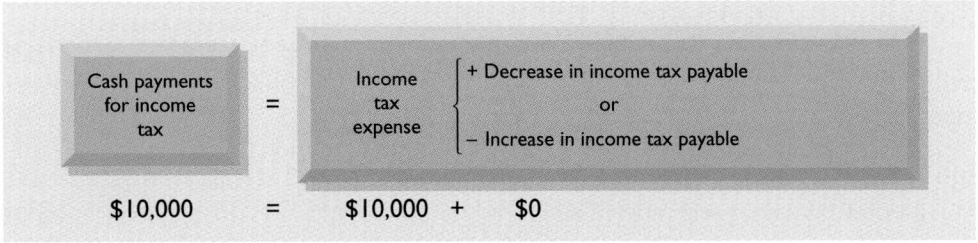

A similar formula can be used for interest expense, if there is any. Amounts for income tax and interest, if any, should be reported separately.

All of the revenues and expenses in the 2002 income statement have now been adjusted to a cash basis. The operating activities section of the cash flow statement is shown in Illustration 18-22:

Illustration 18-22

Operating activities section—direct method

COMPUTER SERVICES CORPORATION
Cash Flow Statement—Direct Method (partial)
For the Year Ended December 31, 2002

Cash flows from operating activities		
Cash receipts from customers		$120,000
Cash payments		
To suppliers	($75,000)	
For operating expenses	(36,000)	
For income tax	(10,000)	(121,000)
Net cash used by operating activities		(1,000)

Helpful hint Whether the direct or indirect method (Section 1) is used, net cash provided by operating activities will be the same.

Step 3: Determine Net Cash Provided (Used) by Investing and Financing Activities

Preparing the investing and financing activities sections of the cash flow statement begins by determining the changes in noncurrent accounts reported in the comparative balance sheets. The change in each account is then analysed to determine the effect, if any, of the change on cash.

Helpful hint Investing and financing activities are measured and reported in the same way under the direct and indirect methods.

Increase in Equipment. No additional information is given for the increase in equipment. In such cases, you should assume that the increase affected cash. In solving assignments, you should assume that **any unexplained differences in noncurrent accounts involve cash.** The purchase of equipment is an investing activity. Thus, an outflow of cash of $10,000 for the purchase of equipment should be reported in the investing activities section.

Increase in Common Shares. The increase in common shares resulted from the issue of common shares for $60,000 cash. It is reported as an inflow of cash in the financing activities section.

Increase in Retained Earnings. What caused the net increase of $20,000 in the Retained Earnings account? First, net income increased retained earnings by $35,000. Second, the additional information section indicates that a cash dividend of $15,000 was declared and paid. The adjustment of revenues and expenses to arrive at net cash provided by operating activities was done in Step 2. The cash dividend paid is reported as an outflow of cash in the financing activities section.

Helpful hint It is the **payment** of dividends, not the declaration, that appears on the cash flow statement.

The $20,000 increase in Retained Earnings in 2002 is a net change. When a net change in a noncurrent balance sheet account has occurred during the year, it is necessary to report the individual items that caused the net change.

This analysis can also be made directly from the Retained Earnings account in the ledger of Computer Services Corporation, as shown below:

Retained Earnings				
		1/1/02	Balance	0
Cash dividend	15,000		Net income	35,000
		12/31/02	Balance	20,000

} $20,000 net increase

Cash Flow Statement

We can now prepare the cash flow statement. The operating activities section is reported first, followed by the investing and financing activities sections. The cash flow statement for Computer Services Corporation for 2002 is shown in Illustration 18-23.

Illustration 18-23

*Cash flow statement,
2002—direct method*

COMPUTER SERVICES CORPORATION
Cash Flow Statement—Direct Method
For the Year Ended December 31, 2002

Cash flows from operating activities		
Cash receipts from customers		$120,000
Cash payments:		
To suppliers	$(75,000)	
For operating expenses	(36,000)	
For income tax	(10,000)	(121,000)
Net cash used by operating activities		(1,000)
Cash flows from investing activities		
Purchase of equipment	$(10,000)	
Net cash used by investing activities		(10,000)
Cash flows from financing activities		
Issue of common shares	$ 60,000	
Payment of cash dividend	(15,000)	
Net cash provided by financing activities		45,000
Net increase in cash		34,000
Cash, January 1		0
Cash, December 31		$34,000

Helpful hint Note that in
the investing and financing
activities sections, positive
numbers indicate cash inflows
(receipts) and negative numbers indicate cash outflows
(payments).

The cash flow statement shows the following: Operating activities **used** $1,000 of the net increase in cash. Investing activities **used** $10,000 of cash. Financing activities **provided** $45,000 of cash. The $34,000 net increase in cash agrees with the increase in cash of $34,000 reported in the comparative balance sheet.

Second Year of Operations—2003

Illustrations 18-24 and 18-25 present information related to the second year of operations for Computer Services Corporation.

Illustration 18-24

*Comparative balance sheet,
2002 and 2003*

COMPUTER SERVICES CORPORATION
Balance Sheet
December 31

Assets	2003	2002	Change Increase/Decrease
Cash	$ 56,000	$34,000	$ 22,000 Increase
Accounts receivable	20,000	30,000	10,000 Decrease
Inventory	75,000	25,000	50,000 Increase
Prepaid expenses	4,000	0	4,000 Increase
Land	130,000	0	130,000 Increase
Building	160,000	0	160,000 Increase
Accumulated amortization—building	(11,000)	0	11,000 Increase
Equipment	27,000	10,000	17,000 Increase
Accumulated amortization—equipment	(3,000)	0	3,000 Increase
Total	$458,000	$99,000	
Liabilities and Shareholders' Equity			
Accounts payable	$115,000	$15,000	$100,000 Increase
Accrued expenses payable	9,000	4,000	5,000 Increase
Bonds payable	130,000	0	130,000 Increase
Common shares	60,000	60,000	0
Retained earnings	144,000	20,000	124,000 Increase
Total	$458,000	$99,000	

Illustration 18-25

Income statement and additional information, 2003

COMPUTER SERVICES CORPORATION
Income Statement
For the Year Ended December 31, 2003

Revenues		$900,000
Cost of goods sold		393,000
Gross profit		507,000
Operating expenses (excluding amortization)	$261,000	
Amortization expense	15,000	
Loss on sale of equipment	3,000	279,000
Income from operations		228,000
Income tax expense		89,000
Net income		$139,000

Additional information:
1. In 2003, the company declared and paid a $15,000 cash dividend.
2. The company obtained land through the issue of $130,000 of long-term bonds.
3. A building costing $160,000 was purchased for cash. Equipment costing $25,000 was also purchased for cash.
4. During 2003, the company sold equipment with a net book value of $7,000 (cost of $8,000 less accumulated amortization of $1,000) for $4,000 cash.

Step 1: Determine the Net Increase (Decrease) in Cash

The comparative balance sheet shows a beginning cash balance of $34,000 and an ending cash balance of $56,000. Thus, there was a net increase of $22,000 in cash in 2003.

Step 2: Determine Net Cash Provided (Used) by Operating Activities

Cash Receipts from Customers. Revenues from sales were $900,000. Since accounts receivable decreased by $10,000, cash receipts from customers were greater than sales revenues. Cash receipts from customers were $910,000, calculated as in Illustration 18-26.

Illustration 18-26

Calculation of cash receipts from customers

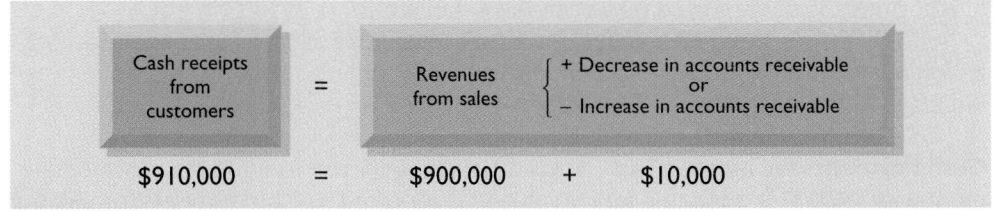

Cash Payments to Suppliers. The conversion of (1) the cost of goods sold to the cost of goods purchased, and (2) the cost of goods purchased to cash payments to suppliers is similar to the calculations made in 2002. For 2003, the cost of goods purchased is calculated using the cost of goods sold of $393,000 from the income statement and the increase in inventory of $50,000 from the comparative balance sheet. The cost of goods purchased of $443,000 ($393,000 + $50,000) is then adjusted by the $100,000 increase in accounts payable. Cash payments to suppliers were $343,000 ($443,000 − $100,000), calculated as in Illustration 18-27.

Illustration 18-27

Calculation of cash payments to suppliers

Cash Payments for Operating Expenses.   Operating expenses for 2003 (exclusive of amortization expense) were reported at $261,000. This amount is then adjusted for changes in prepaid expenses and accrued expenses payable to arrive at cash payments for operating expenses.

As shown in the comparative balance sheet, prepaid expenses increased by $4,000 during the year. This means that cash payments for expenses were greater than the operating expense amount shown (cash was paid for both operating and prepaid expenses). To determine cash payments for operating expenses, the increase in prepaid expenses is added to operating expenses.

Accrued expenses payable increased by $5,000 during the period. As a result, cash payments were $5,000 less, than the amount reported for operating expenses. The increase in accrued expenses payable is deducted from operating expenses. Cash payments for operating expenses were $260,000, calculated as in Illustration 18-28.

Illustration 18-28

Calculation of cash payments for operating expenses

Amortization Expense and Loss on Sale of Equipment.   Operating expenses are shown without amortization. Amortization expense in 2003 was $15,000. Amortization expense is not shown on a cash flow statement because it is a noncash charge. If the amount for operating expenses includes amortization expense, operating expenses must be reduced by the amount of amortization to determine the cash payments for operating expenses.

The loss on sale of equipment of $3,000 is also a noncash charge. The loss on sale of equipment reduces net income, but it does not reduce cash. Thus, the loss on sale of equipment is not reported on a cash flow statement.

Other charges to expense that do not require the use of cash, such as the amortization of a bond discount, are treated in the same manner as the amortization of capital assets.

Cash Payments for Income Tax.   Income tax expense reported on the income statement was $89,000. No income tax payable was reported. Cash payments for income tax were, therefore, $89,000, as shown below:

Illustration 18-29

Calculation of cash payments for income tax

Summary of Conversion to Net Cash Provided by Operating Activities—Direct Method.   The direct method classifies operating activities into major categories of cash receipts (e.g., from customers, from investments) and cash payments (e.g., to suppliers, for operating expenses, to employees, for interest, for income tax). To find cash receipts and payments, accrual-based revenues and expenses must be adjusted for changes in noncash current asset and current liability accounts.

Increases in related current liability accounts and decreases in related current asset accounts are added to accrual-based revenues to determine cash receipts. Increases in related current asset accounts and decreases in related current liability accounts are added to accrual-based expenses to determine cash payments. Noncash items, such as amortization, do not affect cash and are therefore excluded from the cash flow statement.

Step 3: Determine Net Cash Provided (Used) by Investing and Financing Activities

Increase in Land. Land increased by $130,000. The additional information section indicates that bonds were issued to purchase the land. The issue of bonds for land has no effect on cash. But, it is a **significant noncash investing and financing transaction.** This transaction must be disclosed in a note to the cash flow statement.

Increase in Building. As specified in the additional data, a building was acquired using cash of $160,000. This transaction is a cash outflow reported in the investing section.

Increase in Equipment. The comparative balance sheet shows that equipment increased by $17,000 in 2003. The additional information in Illustration 18-25 indicates that the increase resulted from two investing transactions: (1) Equipment costing $25,000 was purchased for cash. (2) Equipment costing $8,000 was sold for $4,000 cash when its net book value was $7,000 (cost of $8,000 less accumulated amortization of $1,000).

The relevant data for the cash flow statement are the cash paid for the purchase and the cash proceeds from the sale. For Computer Services, the investing activities section will show the following: the $25,000 purchase of equipment as an outflow of cash, and the $4,000 sale of equipment as an inflow of cash. **The two amounts should not be offset,** because one is an outflow of cash and the other is an inflow of cash. **Both individual outflows and inflows of cash should be shown.**

The analysis of the changes in equipment should include the related Accumulated Amortization account. These two accounts for Computer Services are shown below:

Equipment				
1/1/03 Balance	10,000			
Purchase of equipment	25,000	Cost of equipment sold	8,000	} $17,000 net increase
12/31/03 Balance	27,000			

Accumulated Amortization—Equipment				
Accumulated amortization on equipment sold	1,000	1/1/03 Balance	0	
		Amortization expense	4,000	} $3,000 net increase
		12/31/03 Balance	3,000	

The following entries reconstruct the details of the equipment transactions:

Equipment	25,000		
Cash		25,000	
To record purchase of equipment.			

A	=	L	+	SE
+25,000				
−25,000				

Cash	4,000		
Accumulated Amortization	1,000		
Loss on Sale of Equipment	3,000		
Equipment		8,000	
To record sale of equipment.			

A	=	L	+	SE
+4,000				−3,000
+1,000				
−8,000				

Increase in Bonds Payable. Bonds Payable increased by $130,000. The additional information indicates that bonds were issued in exchange for land. As noted previously, this transaction is a **significant noncash investing and financing transaction.** It must be reported in a note to the statement.

Increase in Retained Earnings. The $124,000 net increase in Retained Earnings resulted from net income of $139,000 and the declaration and payment of a cash dividend of $15,000. **Net income is not reported in the cash flow statement under the direct method.** Instead, the individual components that make up net income are reported when they affect cash flows. The cash dividend paid of $15,000 is reported in the financing activities section as an outflow of cash.

Cash Flow Statement

The cash flow statement for Computer Services Corporation is shown in Illustration 18-30.

Illustration 18-30

Cash flow statement, 2003—direct method

COMPUTER SERVICES CORPORATION Cash Flow Statement—Direct Method For the Year Ended December 31, 2003		
Cash flows from operating activities		
Cash receipts from customers		$910,000
Cash payments		
To suppliers	$(343,000)	
For operating expenses	(260,000)	
For income tax	(89,000)	(692,000)
Net cash provided by operating activities		218,000
Cash flows from investing activities		
Purchase of building	$(160,000)	
Purchase of equipment	(25,000)	
Sale of equipment	4,000	
Net cash used by investing activities		(181,000)
Cash flows from financing activities		
Payment of cash dividend	$ (15,000)	
Net cash used by financing activities		(15,000)
Net increase in cash		22,000
Cash, January 1		34,000
Cash, December 31		$ 56,000
Note x: Noncash investing and financing activities		
Issue of bonds payable to purchase land		$130,000

Before You Go On .

▸*Review It*

1. What is the format of the operating activities section of the cash flow statement using the direct method?
2. Where is amortization expense shown on a cash flow statement using the direct method?
3. Where are significant noncash investing and financing activities shown on a cash flow statement? Give some examples.

4. Which method of calculating net cash provided by operating activities does The Second Cup use? Does The Second Cup use cash or cash and cash equivalents in its statement? If the latter, what is included in cash equivalents? The answer to these questions is provided at the end of this chapter.

►*Do It*

Presented below is information related to Reynolds Company. Use the direct method to prepare a cash flow statement.

REYNOLDS COMPANY LTD.
Balance Sheet
December 31

Assets	2003	2002	Change Increase/Decrease
Cash	$ 54,000	$ 37,000	$ 17,000 Increase
Accounts receivable	68,000	26,000	42,000 Increase
Inventories	54,000	0	54,000 Increase
Prepaid expenses	4,000	6,000	2,000 Decrease
Land	45,000	70,000	25,000 Decrease
Buildings	200,000	200,000	0
Accumulated amortization—buildings	(21,000)	(11,000)	10,000 Increase
Equipment	193,000	68,000	125,000 Increase
Accumulated amortization—equipment	(28,000)	(10,000)	18,000 Increase
Totals	$569,000	$386,000	

Liabilities and Shareholders' Equity			
Accounts payable	$ 23,000	$ 40,000	$ 17,000 Decrease
Accrued expenses payable	10,000	0	10,000 Increase
Bonds payable	110,000	150,000	40,000 Decrease
Common shares	220,000	60,000	160,000 Increase
Retained earnings	206,000	136,000	70,000 Increase
Totals	$569,000	$386,000	

REYNOLDS COMPANY LTD.
Income Statement
For the Year Ended December 31, 2003

Revenues		$890,000
Cost of goods sold	$465,000	
Operating expenses	221,000	
Interest expense	12,000	
Loss on sale of equipment	2,000	700,000
Income from operations		190,000
Income tax expense		65,000
Net income		$125,000

Additional information:
1. Operating expenses include amortization expense of $33,000.
2. $25,000 of land was sold for cash.
3. Cash dividends of $55,000 were declared and paid in 2003.
4. Interest expense of $12,000 was paid in cash.
5. Equipment with a cost of $166,000 was purchased for cash. Equipment with a cost of $41,000 and a net book value of $36,000 was sold for $34,000 cash.
6. Bonds of $40,000 were redeemed at their face value for cash.
7. Common shares of $160,000 were issued for cash.
8. Accounts payable pertain to merchandise suppliers.

Action Plan

• Determine the net increase (decrease) in cash.
• Determine the net cash provided (used) by operating activities. Operating activities generally relate to cash receipts and cash payments from operations (shown on the income statement).
• Determine the net cash provided (used) by investing and financing activities. Investing activities generally relate to changes in noncurrent assets. Financing activities generally relate to changes in noncurrent liabilities and shareholders' equity accounts.

Solution

REYNOLDS COMPANY LTD.
Cash Flow Statement—Direct Method
For the Year Ended December 31, 2003

Cash flows from operating activities		
Cash receipts from customers		$848,000[a]
Cash payments		
To suppliers	$(536,000)[b]	
For operating expenses	(176,000)[c]	
For interest	(12,000)	
For income tax	(65,000)	(789,000)
Net cash provided by operating activities		59,000
Cash flows from investing activities		
Sale of land	$ 25,000	
Sale of equipment	34,000	
Purchase of equipment	(166,000)	
Net cash used by investing activities		(107,000)
Cash flows from financing activities		
Redemption of bonds	$ (40,000)	
Sale of common shares	160,000	
Payment of dividends	(55,000)	
Net cash provided by financing activities		65,000
Net increase in cash		17,000
Cash, January 1		37,000
Cash, December 31		$ 54,000

Calculations:
[a] Cash receipts from customers: $848,000 = $890,000 – $42,000
[b] Payments to suppliers: $536,000 = $465,000 + $54,000 + $17,000
[c] Payments for operating expenses: $176,000 = $221,000 – $33,000 – $2,000 – $10,000

THE NAVIGATOR

Related exercise material: BE18–7, BE18–8, BE18–9, BE18–10, E18–6, E18–7, E18–8, and E18–9.

Note: This concludes Section 2 on the preparation of the cash flow statement using the direct method. You should now continue with the next—and concluding—section of the chapter, "Using the Information in the Financial Statements."

Using the Information in the Financial Statements

STUDY OBJECTIVE

5

Analyse the cash flow statement.

The cash flow statement provides information about a company's financial health that is not evident from an analysis of the balance sheet or the income statement. Bankers, creditors, and other users of the cash flow statement are often more concerned with cash flow from operating activities than they are with net income, because they are interested in a company's ability to pay its bills.

As with the balance sheet and income statement, a ratio analysis of the cash flow statement can evaluate liquidity, profitability, and solvency. Four cash flow ratios that contribute to this evaluation are (1) the cash current debt coverage, (2) the cash return on sales, (3) the cash flow per share, and (4) the cash total debt coverage.

►Accounting in Action ► *Business Insight*

Analysts from investment houses say that they are using cash flow figures instead of, or in addition to, net income because they have lost faith in accrual accounting numbers. They suggest that accrual-based net income is losing its usefulness because companies take advantage of generally accepted accounting principles to report net income figures that meet management's goals. Evidence of this shift toward cash flows is found in the fact that 72% of brokerage firm reports now use a cash flow earnings multiple. An increasing number of companies report cash-based income numbers as supplemental information in their annual report.

Source: "Analysts Increasingly Favour Using Cash Flow Over Reported Earnings in Stock Valuations." *The Wall Street Journal*, April 1, 1999, C1.

Cash Current Debt Coverage

A disadvantage of the **current ratio**, introduced in Chapter 4, is that it employs year-end balances of current asset and current liability accounts. These year-end balances may not be representative of what the company's position was during most of the year. A ratio that partially corrects for this problem is the ratio of net cash provided by operating activities to average current liabilities, referred to as cash current debt coverage. Because it uses net cash provided by operating activities during the period, rather than a balance at a point in time, it may provide a better picture of liquidity. Using The Second Cup's financial data, the cash current debt coverage ratio is calculated as in Illustration 18-31:

Illustration 18-31

Cash current debt coverage

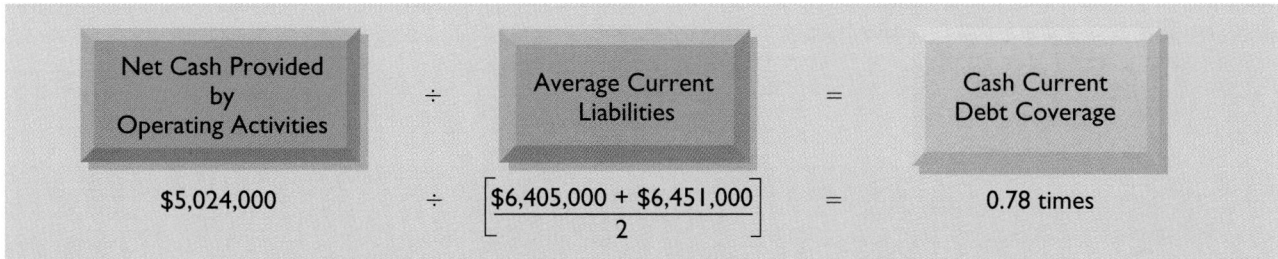

This ratio indicates that for every dollar of debt due during the year, $0.78 of cash was generated from operating activities to pay that debt.

Cash Return on Sales

One measure of profitability under accrual accounting is the **profit margin ratio**. This ratio is defined as net income divided by net sales. It measures the net income generated by each dollar of sales. The cash-based counterpart to this ratio is the cash return on sales. It is calculated by dividing net cash provided by operating activities by net sales. For The Second Cup, this ratio is calculated as in Illustration 18-32:

Illustration 18-32

Cash return on sales

Some difference is to be expected between cash and accrual accounting ratios. But significant differences should be investigated. The Second Cup's cash return on sales of 24% is much higher than its profit margin of 4.7% ($972,000 ÷ $20,844,000). It appears that The Second Cup is efficient at turning sales into cash, since its cash return on sales is greater than its profit margin.

Cash Flow Per Share

Because of the importance of the cash flow statement to a wide variety of users, many people have recommended that the statement include cash flow per share data, just as the income statement includes **earnings per share** data. Both are additional measures of profitability. Although the CICA does not require the inclusion of cash flow per share data, it does say that this information may be disclosed and provides some guidance on its calculation and presentation. Companies can include cash flow per share on the cash flow statement, or in a note to the financial statements cross-referenced to this statement. Cash flow per share information is not a substitute for earnings per share. It should not be presented on the income statement.

Cash flow per share can be calculated in a number of different ways. One way is to divide cash flow from operating, investing, and financing activities by the number of common shares. This is similar to how earnings per share is calculated (see Illustration 15-19) except that cash flow replaces net income. Both the cash flow per share and EPS calculations must be refined if complex capital structures exist. These calculations are learned in an intermediate accounting course.

The following illustration demonstrates the calculation of cash flow per share for The Second Cup Ltd.:

Illustration 18-33

Cash flow per share

The Second Cup's cash flow per share is less than its earnings per share of $0.10. It is interesting to compare cash flow per share to earnings per share for selected companies in a recent year, as shown in Illustration 18-34. Neither statistic on its own provides sufficient information for decision-makers. However, taken together, earnings and cash flow per share provide two significant pieces of information needed to predict a company's future viability.

Illustration 18-34

Comparison of cash flow and earnings per share for selected companies

Company	Cash Flow Per Share	Earnings Per Share
Cott	$(0.43)	$0.31
Maple Leaf Foods	0.02	0.77
Molson	(0.29)	0.74
MP3.Com	3.44	(3.97)

Cash Total Debt Coverage

One measure of long-term solvency is **debt to total assets**, introduced in Chapter 16. Its cash basis counterpart is cash total debt coverage. It is the ratio of net cash provided by operating activities to average total liabilities. This ratio demonstrates a company's ability to repay its liabilities from net cash provided by operating activities without having to liquidate the assets used in its operations. The Second Cup's cash total debt coverage is calculated as in Illustration 18-35.

Illustration 18-35

Cash total debt coverage

$$\text{Net Cash Provided by Operating Activities} \div \text{Average Total Liabilities} = \text{Cash Total Debt Coverage}$$

$$\$5,024,000 \div \left[\frac{(\$6,405,000 + \$10,250,000 + \$212,000) + (\$6,451,000 + \$19,300,000 + \$219,000)}{2} \right] = 0.23 \text{ times}$$

This ratio indicates that for every dollar of total debt, $0.23 of cash was generated from operating activities to pay that debt.

The four cash-based ratios presented here show that The Second Cup Ltd. is efficiently generating cash. These ratios indicate that the company is liquid, profitable, and solvent.

Before You Go On . . .

►*Review It*

1. Why might an analyst want to supplement accrual-based ratios with cash-based ratios?
2. What cash basis ratios may be prepared to evaluate liquidity, profitability, and solvency? What are their accrual-based counterparts?

Related exercise material: BE18–11, E18–10, and E18–11.

THE NAVIGATOR

►*A Look Back at Our Feature Story*

Refer to the opening story about TD Canada Trust's small business loans, and answer the following questions:
1. Explain what information the balance sheet, income statement, and cash flow statement provide that help Ms. LeBrun decide whether or not to grant a loan.
2. How would the loan proceeds and later repayment be reported on the borrower's cash flow statement? Interest payments?

Solution

1. The balance sheet provides information about the amount of cash on hand, the current asset and current liability (working capital) position, and the amount of debt the company currently has. The cash flow statement would provide information about the ending cash position on the balance sheet, explaining where cash came from and where cash went. This information is useful, in combination with net income presented on the income statement, for predicting future cash flows. Future cash inflows and outflows are essential to ensure that loan and interest payments can be paid.
2. The loan proceeds would be reported as a cash inflow in the financing activities section of the cash flow statement. The repayment of the loan would be reported as a cash outflow in the financing activities section. Interest expense, adjusted for any changes in interest payable to determine interest payments, would be reported as a cash outflow in the operating activities section of the cash flow statement.

THE NAVIGATOR

DEMONSTRATION PROBLEM

**Additional
Demonstration Problem**

The income statement for the year ended December 31, 2003, for Kosinski Manufacturing Company Ltd. contains the following condensed information:

KOSINSKI MANUFACTURING COMPANY LTD.
Income Statement
For the Year Ended December 31, 2003

Revenues		$6,583,000
Cost of goods sold	$3,427,000	
Operating expenses (excluding amortization)	1,469,000	
Amortization expense	880,000	
Loss on sale of machinery	24,000	5,800,000
Income before income tax		783,000
Income tax expense		353,000
Net income		$ 430,000

The following balances are reported on Kosinski's comparative balance sheet at December 31:

KOSINSKI MANUFACTURING COMPANY LTD.
Balance Sheet (partial)
December 31

	2002	2003
Cash	$672,000	$130,000
Accounts receivable	775,000	610,000
Inventories	834,000	867,000
Accounts payable	521,000	501,000

Additional information:

1. Machinery was sold for $270,000 cash at a loss of $24,000. Other machinery was purchased at a cost of $750,000.
2. Income tax expense of $353,000 equals the amount paid in 2002.
3. Dividends declared and paid in 2003 totalled $200,000.

Instructions

(a) Prepare the cash flow statement using the indirect method.
(b) Prepare the cash flow statement using the direct method.

Solution to Demonstration Problem

(a)

KOSINSKI MANUFACTURING COMPANY LTD.
Cash Flow Statement—Indirect Method
For the Year Ended December 31, 2003

Cash flows from operating activities		
Net income		$ 430,000
Adjustments to reconcile net income to net cash provided by operating activities:		
Amortization expense	$880,000	
Loss on sale of machinery	24,000	
Increase in accounts receivable	(165,000)	
Decrease in inventories	33,000	
Increase in accounts payable	20,000	792,000
Net cash provided by operating activities		1,222,000
Cash flows from investing activities		
Sale of machinery	$270,000	
Purchase of machinery	(750,000)	
Net cash used by investing activities		(480,000)
Cash flows from financing activities		
Payment of cash dividends		(200,000)
Net increase in cash		542,000
Cash, January 1, 2003		130,000
Cash, December 31, 2003		$ 672,000

(b)

KOSINSKI MANUFACTURING COMPANY LTD.
Cash Flow Statement—Direct Method
For the Year Ended December 31, 2003

Cash flows from operating activities		
Cash collections from customers		$6,418,000 [a]
Cash payments to suppliers		(3,374,000) [b]
Cash payments for operating expenses		(1,469,000)
Cash payment for income tax		(353,000)
Net cash provided by operating activities		1,222,000
Cash flows from investing activities		
Sale of machinery	$270,000	
Purchase of machinery	(750,000)	
Net cash used by investing activities		(480,000)
Cash flows from financing activities		
Payment of cash dividends		(200,000)
Net increase in cash		542,000
Cash, January 1, 2003		130,000
Cash, December 31, 2003		$ 672,000

Direct Method Calculations:

[a] Cash collections from customers:

Revenues per the income statement	$6,583,000
Deduct increase in accounts receivable	165,000
Cash collections from customers	$6,418,000

[b] Cash payments to suppliers:

Cost of goods sold per the income statement	$3,427,000
Deduct decrease in inventories	33,000
Deduct increase in accounts payable	20,000
Cash payments for operating expenses	$3,374,000

THE
NAVIGATOR

APPENDIX 18A ▸ Using a Work Sheet to Prepare the Cash Flow Statement—Indirect Method

STUDY OBJECTIVE
··········**6**··········

Explain and apply the procedural steps in using a work sheet to prepare the cash flow statement using the indirect method.

When preparing a cash flow statement, many adjustments of net income may be necessary. In such cases, **a work sheet is often used to assemble and classify the data that will appear on the statement.** The work sheet merely helps prepare the statement. Using it is optional.

The skeleton format of a work sheet for preparation of the cash flow statement is shown in Illustration 18A-1.

Illustration 18A-1

Format of work sheet

	End of Last Year	Reconciling Items		End of Current Year
HILL COMPANY LTD.				
Cash Flow Statement Work Sheet—Indirect Method				
For the Year Ended....				
Balance Sheet Accounts	Balances	Debits	Credits	Balances
Debit balance accounts	XX	XX	XX	XX
	XX	XX	XX	XX
Totals	XXX			XXX
Credit balance accounts	XX	XX	XX	XX
	XX	XX	XX	XX
Totals	XXX			XXX
Cash Flow Statement Effects				
Operating activities				
Net income		XX		
Adjustments to net income		XX	XX	
Investing activities				
Receipts and payments		XX	XX	
Financing activities				
Receipts and payments		XX	XX	
Totals		XXX	XXX	
Increase (decrease) in cash		XX	XX	
Totals		XXX	XXX	

The following guidelines are important in using a work sheet:

1. In the balance sheet section, **accounts with debit balances are listed separately from those with credit balances**. This means, for example, that Accumulated Amortization is listed under credit balances, not as a contra asset account under debit balances. The beginning and ending balances of each account are entered in the appropriate columns. The transactions that caused the change in the account balance during the year are entered as reconciling items in the two middle columns.

   After all reconciling items have been entered, each line related to a balance sheet account should add across. That is, the beginning balance plus or minus the reconciling item(s) must equal the ending balance. When all balance sheet accounts agree, all changes in account balances have been reconciled.

2. The bottom portion of the work sheet consists of the operating, investing, and financing activities sections. It provides the information necessary to prepare the formal cash flow statement. **Inflows of cash are entered as debits in the reconciling columns. Outflows of cash are entered as credits in the reconciling columns.** Thus, in this section the sale of equipment for cash at book value is

entered as a debit under investing activities. Similarly, the purchase of land for cash is entered as a credit under investing activities.

3. **The reconciling items shown in the work sheet are not entered in any journal or posted to any account.** They do not represent either adjustments or corrections of the balance sheet accounts. They are used only to simplify the preparation of the cash flow statement.

Preparing the Work Sheet

As illustrated in earlier chapters, the preparation of a work sheet involves a series of steps. The steps in this case are as follows:

1. Enter the balance sheet accounts and their beginning and ending balances in the balance sheet accounts section.
2. Enter the data that explain the changes in all balance sheet accounts other than cash—and their effects on the cash flow statement—in the reconciling columns of the work sheet.
3. Enter the increase or decrease in cash on the cash line and at the bottom of the work sheet. This entry ensures that the totals of the reconciling columns are in agreement.

The work sheet can be used for either the indirect method or the direct method of determining operating activities. You will remember that use of the indirect or direct methods affects only the calculation and presentation of individual operating cash flows, not investing and financing cash flows. To illustrate the preparation of a work sheet, we will use the 2003 data for Computer Services Corporation and the indirect method. Your familiarity with these data should help you understand the use of a work sheet. Refer to Illustrations 18-9 and 18-10 for the comparative balance sheet, income statement, and selected data for 2003.

The work sheet for Computer Services Corporation is shown in Illustration 18A-2. The work sheet illustrates how easy it is to generate a cash flow statement using a computer. The computer output must be carefully analysed, to ensure that changes in noncurrent balance sheet accounts are not netted (that is, that increases have not been offset against decreases).

Determining the Reconciling Items

Several approaches may be used to determine the reconciling items. For example, the changes that affect net cash provided by operating activities can be completed first. Then the effects of financing and investing transactions can be calculated. Or the balance sheet accounts could be analysed in the order in which they are listed on the work sheet. We will follow this latter approach for Computer Services, except for cash. As indicated above, **cash is handled last**.

COMPUTER SERVICES CORPORATION
Cash Flow Statement Work Sheet—Indirect Method
For the Year Ended December 31, 2003

Balance Sheet Accounts	Balance 12/31/02		Reconciling Items Debit		Credit	Balance 12/31/03
Debits						
Cash	34,000	(n)	22,000			56,000
Accounts receivable	30,000			(a)	10,000	20,000
Inventory	25,000	(b)	50,000			75,000
Prepaid expenses	0	(c)	4,000*			4,000
Land	0	(d)	130,000			130,000
Building	0	(e)	160,000			160,000
Equipment	10,000	(f)	25,000	(g)	8,000	27,000
Total	99,000					472,000
Credits						
Accounts payable	15,000			(h)	100,000	115,000
Accrued expenses payable	4,000			(i)	5,000	9,000
Bonds payable	0			(d)	130,000*	130,000
Accumulated amortization—building	0			(j)	11,000	11,000
Accumulated amortization—equipment	0	(g)	1,000	(k)	4,000	3,000
Common shares	60,000					60,000
Retained earnings	20,000	(m)	15,000	(l)	139,000	144,000
Total	99,000					472,000
Cash Flow Statement Effects						
Operating activities						
Net income		(l)	139,000			
Decrease in accounts receivable		(a)	10,000			
Increase in inventory				(b)	50,000	
Increase in prepaid expenses				(c)	4,000	
Increase in accounts payable		(h)	100,000			
Increase in accrued expenses payable		(i)	5,000			
Amortization expense—building		(j)	11,000			
Amortization expense—equipment		(k)	4,000			
Loss on sale of equipment		(g)	3,000			
Investing activities						
Purchase of building				(e)	160,000	
Purchase of equipment				(f)	25,000	
Sale of equipment		(g)	4,000			
Financing activities						
Payment of dividend				(m)	15,000	
Totals			683,000		661,000	
Increase in cash				(n)	22,000	
Totals			683,000		683,000	

* Significant noncash investing and financing activity.

Illustration 18A-2

Completed work sheet—indirect method

Accounts Receivable.   The $10,000 decrease in accounts receivable means that cash collections from revenues are higher than the revenues reported in the income statement. To convert net income to net cash provided by operating activities, the decrease of $10,000 is added to net income. The entry in the reconciling columns of the work sheet follows:

| (a) | Operating Activity—Decrease in Accounts Receivable | 10,000 | |
| | Accounts Receivable | | 10,000 |

Inventory. A $50,000 increase in inventory means that the expense recorded for merchandise sold is less than the cost of merchandise purchased. The increase of $50,000 must be deducted from net income in determining net cash provided by operating activities. The work sheet entry follows:

| (b) | Inventory | 50,000 | |
| | Operating Activity—Increase in Inventory | | 50,000 |

Helpful hint Note that the decrease in accounts receivable represents an inflow/increase in cash, and is therefore logically recorded as a debit.

Helpful hint The increase in inventory represents an outflow/decrease in cash, and is therefore logically recorded as a credit.

Prepaid Expenses. An increase of $4,000 in prepaid expenses means that expenses deducted in determining net income are less than expenses that were paid in cash. The $4,000 increase must be deducted from net income in determining net cash provided by operating activities. The work sheet entry follows:

| (c) | Prepaid Expenses | 4,000 | |
| | Operating Activity—Increase in Prepaid Expenses | | 4,000 |

Land. The increase in land of $130,000 resulted from a purchase through the issue of long-term bonds. This transaction should be reported as a significant noncash investing (land) and financing (bonds) activity. The work sheet entry follows:

| (d) | Land | 130,000 | |
| | Bonds Payable | | 130,000 |

Building. The cash purchase of a building for $160,000 is an investing activity cash outflow. The entry in the reconciling columns of the work sheet follows:

| (e) | Building | 160,000 | |
| | Investing Activity—Purchase of Building | | 160,000 |

Equipment. The $17,000 increase in equipment resulted from a cash purchase of $25,000 and the sale of equipment costing $8,000. The net book value of the equipment was $7,000, the cash proceeds were $4,000, and a loss of $3,000 was recorded. The work sheet entries follow:

(f)	Equipment	25,000	
	Investing Activity—Purchase of Equipment		25,000
(g)	Investing Activity—Sale of Equipment	4,000	
	Operating Activity—Loss on Sale of Equipment	3,000	
	Accumulated Amortization—Equipment	1,000	
	Equipment		8,000

Helpful hint Note that, in each case, we are reconstructing journal entries—except that cash is replaced by the appropriate activity (operating, investing, or financing).

Accounts Payable. The increase of $100,000 in accounts payable indicates that cash payments for merchandise were less than the cost of merchandise purchased. This increase must be added to net income to obtain net cash provided by operating activities. The work sheet entry follows:

| (h) | Operating Activity—Increase in Accounts Payable | 100,000 | |
| | Accounts Payable | | 100,000 |

Accrued Expenses Payable. The $5,000 increase of in accrued expenses payable must be added to net income to obtain net cash provided by operating activities. The work sheet entry follows:

| (i) | Operating Activity—Increase in Accrued Expenses Payable | 5,000 | |
| | Accrued Expenses Payable | | 5,000 |

Bonds Payable. The $130,000 increase in this account resulted from the issue of bonds for land. This has already been dealt with in work sheet entry (d).

Accumulated Amortization—Building, and Accumulated Amortization—Equipment. The increases in these accounts of $11,000 and $4,000, respectively, resulted from amortization expense. Amortization expense is a noncash charge that must be added to net income to determine net cash provided by operating activities. The work sheet entries follow:

(j)	Operating Activity—Amortization Expense—Building	11,000	
	Accumulated Amortization—Building		11,000
(k)	Operating Activity—Amortization Expense—		
	Equipment	4,000	
	Accumulated Amortization—Equipment		4,000

Retained Earnings. The $124,000 increase in retained earnings resulted from net income of $139,000 and the declaration and payment of a $15,000 cash dividend. Net income is included in net cash provided by operating activities, and the dividend is a financing activity cash outflow. The entries in the reconciling columns of the work sheet follow:

(l)	Operating Activity—Net Income	139,000	
	Retained Earnings		139,000
(m)	Retained Earnings	15,000	
	Financing Activity—Payment of Dividend		15,000

Disposition of Change in Cash. The firm's cash increased by $22,000 in 2003. The final entry on the work sheet, therefore, is as follows:

(n)	Cash	22,000	
	Increase in Cash		22,000

As shown in the work sheet, the increase in cash is entered in the reconciling credit column as a **balancing** amount. This entry should complete the reconciliation of the changes in the balance sheet accounts. It should also ensure that the totals of the reconciling columns agree. When all changes have been explained and the reconciling columns agree, the reconciling columns are ruled to complete the work sheet.

Preparing the Statement

The cash flow statement is prepared directly from the data that appear in the work sheet under cash flow statement effects. The reconciling columns should also be scanned for any asterisked items that designate significant noncash activities. The formal statement was shown in Illustration 18-14.

Before You Go On . . .
▸*Review It*

1. Explain how the work sheet facilitates the preparation of the cash flow statement.

Related exercise material: *BE18–12 and *E18–12.

THE
NAVIGATOR

Summary of Study Objectives

1. *Describe the primary purpose of the cash flow statement.* The primary purpose of the cash flow statement is to provide information about the cash receipts and cash payments of an entity during a period. A secondary objective is to provide information about the operating, investing, and financing activities of the entity during the period.

2. *Distinguish among operating, investing, and financing activities.* Operating activities include the cash effects of transactions that affect net income. Investing activities involve cash flows resulting from changes in investments and long-term asset items. Financing activities involve cash flows resulting from changes in long-term liability and shareholders' equity items.

3. *Prepare a cash flow statement using the indirect method.* The preparation of a cash flow statement involves three major steps: (1) determining the net increase or decrease in cash, (2) determining net cash provided (used) by operating activities, and (3) determining net cash flows provided (used) by investing and financing activities. Under the indirect method, accrual-based net income is adjusted to net cash provided by operating activities.

4. *Prepare a cash flow statement using the direct method.* The preparation of the cash flow statement involves three major steps: (1) determining the net increase or decrease in cash, (2) determining net cash provided (used) by operating activities, and (3) determining net cash flows provided (used) by investing and financing activities. The direct method reports cash receipts less cash payments to arrive at net cash provided by operating activities.

5. *Analyse the cash flow statement.* The cash current debt coverage ratio measures liquidity and is a counterpart to the accrual-based current ratio. The cash return on sales ratio, in addition to cash flow per share, measures profitability. Their accrual-based counterparts are the profit margin and earnings per share. The cash total debt coverage ratio measures solvency and is a counterpart to the accrual-based debt to total assets ratio.

6. *Explain and apply the procedural steps in using a work sheet to prepare the cash flow statement using the indirect method (Appendix 18A).* When there are numerous adjustments, a work sheet can be a helpful tool in preparing the cash flow statement. Key guidelines for using a work sheet are as follows: (1) List accounts with debit balances separately from those with credit balances. (2) In the reconciling columns in the bottom portion of the work sheet, show cash inflows as debits and cash outflows as credits. (3) Do not enter reconciling items in any journal or ledger. Use them only to help prepare the cash flow statement.

The steps in preparing the work sheet are as follows: (1) Enter the beginning and ending balances of balance sheet accounts. (2) Enter debits and credits in reconciling columns. (3) Enter the increase or decrease in cash in two places as a balancing amount.

THE NAVIGATOR

GLOSSARY

 Key Term Matching Activity

Cash current debt coverage—A cash-based measure of liquidity. It is calculated as net cash provided by operating activities divided by average current liabilities. (p. 855)

Cash flow per share—A cash-based measure of profitability. It can be calculated as net cash provided by all activities (operating, investing, and financing) divided by the number of common shares. (p. 856)

Cash flow statement—A financial statement that provides information about the cash receipts and cash payments of an entity during a period, classified as operating, investing, and financing activities, in a format that reconciles the beginning and ending cash balances. (p. 823)

Cash return on sales—A cash-based measure of profitability. It is calculated as net cash provided by operating activities divided by net sales. (p. 855)

Cash total debt coverage—A cash-based measure of solvency. It is calculated as net cash provided by operating activities divided by average total liabilities. (p. 857)

Direct method—A method of determining the net cash provided by operating activities by adjusting each item in the income statement from the accrual basis to the cash basis. (p. 843)

Financing activities—Cash flow activities from noncurrent liability and equity items. These include (a) obtaining cash from issuing debt and repaying the amounts borrowed, and (b) obtaining cash from shareholders and providing them with a return on their investment. (p. 823)

Indirect method—A method of preparing a cash flow statement in which net income is adjusted for items that did not affect cash, to determine net cash provided by operating activities. (p. 830)

Investing activities—Cash flow activities from noncurrent assets. These include (a) acquiring and disposing of investments and productive long-lived assets, and (b) lending money and collecting on those loans. (p. 823)

Operating activities—Cash flow activities that include the cash effects of transactions that create revenues and expenses, and thus affect net income. (p. 823)

Note: All **asterisked** Questions, Exercises, and Problems below relate to material contained in the appendix to the chapter.

SELF-STUDY QUESTIONS

 Chapter 18 Self-Test

(SO 1) K   Answers are at the end of the chapter.

1. Which of the following remarks about the cash flow statement is *incorrect*?
   a. It is a fourth basic financial statement.
   b. It provides information about the cash receipts and cash payments of an entity during a period.
   c. It reconciles the ending cash account balance to the bank statement balance.
   d. It provides information about the operating, investing, and financing activities of the business.

(SO 2) K   2. The cash flow statement classifies cash receipts and cash payments by the following activities:
   a. operating and non-operating.
   b. operating, investing, and financing.
   c. financing, operating, and non-operating.
   d. investing, financing, and non-operating.

(SO 2) K   3. An example of a cash flow from an operating activity is:
   a. a payment of cash to lenders for interest.
   b. a receipt of cash from the sale of share capital.
   c. a payment of cash dividends to the company's shareholders.
   d. None of the above

(SO 2) K   4. An example of a cash flow from an investing activity is:
   a. a receipt of cash from the issue of bonds payable.
   b. a payment of cash to repurchase share capital.
   c. a receipt of cash from the sale of equipment.
   d. a payment of cash to suppliers for inventory.

(SO 2) K   5. An example of a cash flow from a financing activity is:
   a. a receipt of cash from the sale of land.
   b. an issue of debt for cash.
   c. a purchase of equipment for cash.
   d. None of the above

(SO 2) K   6. Cash dividends paid to shareholders are classified on the cash flow statement as:
   a. operating activities.
   b. investing activities.
   c. financing activities.
   d. Cash dividends are reported on the statement of retained earnings, not the cash flow statement.

(SO 2) K   7. Which of the following remarks about the cash flow statement is *incorrect*?
   a. The direct method may be used to report cash provided by operating activities.
   b. The statement shows the cash provided (used) for three categories of activity.
   c. The operating section is the last section of the statement.
   d. The indirect method may be used to report cash provided by operating activities.

Questions 8 and 9 apply only to the indirect method.

8. Net income is $132,000. During the year, accounts   (SO 3) AP
   payable increased by $10,000, inventory decreased by $6,000, and accounts receivable increased by $12,000. Under the indirect method, net cash provided by operating activities is:
   a. $102,000.
   b. $112,000.
   c. $124,000.
   d. $136,000.

9. In determining cash provided by operating activities   (SO 3) K
   under the indirect method, noncash charges that are added to net income do not include:
   a. the amortization of capital assets.
   b. a gain on the sale of equipment.
   c. the amortization of a bond discount.
   d. a loss on the sale of equipment.

Questions 10 and 11 apply only to the direct method.

10. The beginning balance in accounts receivable is   (SO 4) AP
    $44,000. The ending balance is $42,000. Sales during the period are $129,000. Cash receipts from customers are:
    a. $127,000.
    b. $129,000.
    c. $131,000.
    d. $141,000.

11. Which of the following items is reported on a cash   (SO 4) K
    flow statement prepared by using the direct method?
    a. a loss on the sale of a building.
    b. an increase in accounts receivable.
    c. amortization expense.
    d. cash payments to suppliers.

12. The cash flow statement should not be used to evalu-   (SO 5) K
    ate an entity's ability to:
    a. earn net income.
    b. generate future cash flows.
    c. pay dividends.
    d. meet obligations.

13. Which of the following ratios provides a useful coun-   (SO 5) K
    terpart to the accrual-based current ratio?
    a. Cash return on sales
    b. Cash current debt coverage
    c. Cash total debt coverage
    d. Cash flow per share

*14. In a work sheet for the cash flow statement, a decrease   (SO 6) K
    in accounts receivable is entered in the reconciling columns as a credit to Accounts Receivable and a debit in the:
    a. investing activities section.
    b. operating activities section.
    c. financing activities section.
    d. none of the above.

THE NAVIGATOR

QUESTIONS

(SO 1) C 1. (a) What is the cash flow statement?
(b) Isabelle Moreau maintains that the cash flow statement is an optional financial statement. Do you agree? Explain.

(SO 1) C 2. What questions about cash are answered by the cash flow statement?

(SO 1) C 3. What are "cash equivalents"? How do cash equivalents affect the cash flow statement?

(SO 1) C 4. Distinguish among the three types of activities reported in the cash flow statement.

(SO 2) K 5. What are the major inflows of cash in a cash flow statement? What are the major outflows of cash?

(SO 2) C 6. Why is it important to disclose significant noncash transactions? How should they be disclosed?

(SO 2) C 7. Wilma Flintstone and Barney Kublestone were discussing the presentation format of the cash flow statement of Stone Candy Co. Cross-referenced to Stone Candy's cash flow statement was a note entitled "Noncash investing and financing activities." Give three examples of significant noncash transactions that might be reported in this note.

(SO 2) C 8. Why is it necessary to use a comparative balance sheet, a current income statement, and certain transaction data in preparing a cash flow statement?

(SO 2) C 9. Contrast the advantages and disadvantages of the direct and indirect methods and answer the following questions:
(a) Are both methods acceptable?
(b) Which method is preferred by the CICA?
(c) Why do most companies favour the indirect method?

(SO 2) C 10. When the total cash inflows exceed the total cash outflows in the cash flow statement, how and where is this excess identified?

(SO 2) C 11. Why is it necessary to convert accrual-based net income to cash-based income when preparing a cash flow statement?

(SO 2) C 12. The president of Pets.com Company is puzzled. During the year, the company experienced a net loss of $800,000, yet its cash increased by $300,000 during the same period. Explain to the president how this situation could occur.

(SO 2) C 13. Why is the cash flow statement useful?

(SO 3) C 14. Describe the indirect method for determining net cash provided by operating activities.

(SO 3) K 15. Identify five items under the indirect method that could be adjustments to reconcile net income to net cash provided by operating activities.

(SO 3) C 16. Why and how is amortization expense reported in a statement prepared using the indirect method?

(SO 4) C 17. Describe the direct method for determining net cash provided by operating activities.

(SO 4) K 18. Give the formulas under the direct method for calculating (a) cash receipts from customers, and (b) cash payments to suppliers.

(SO 4) AP 19. Crawford Inc. reported sales of $2 million for 2003. Accounts receivable decreased by $200,000 and accounts payable increased by $300,000. Calculate cash receipts from customers, assuming that the receivable and payable transactions related to operating activities.

(SO 4) C 20. Under the direct method, why is amortization expense not reported in the cash flow from operating activities section?

(SO 5) C 21. Give an example of one accrual-based ratio and one cash-based ratio to measure these characteristics of a company:
(a) Liquidity
(b) Solvency
(c) Profitability

(SO 6) C *22. Why is it advantageous to use a work sheet when preparing a cash flow statement? Is a work sheet required in preparing a cash flow statement?

BRIEF EXERCISES

••

Indicate statement presentation.
(SO 2) AP

BE18–1   Each of the following items must be considered in preparing a cash flow statement for Survivor Corp. for the year ended December 31, 2003. For each item, state how it should be shown in the cash flow statement:
(a) Issued bonds for $200,000 cash.
(b) Purchased equipment for $150,000 cash.
(c) Sold land costing $20,000 for $30,000 cash.
(d) Declared and paid a $50,000 cash dividend.

Classify transactions by activity.
(SO 2) AP

BE18–2   Classify the following items as an operating, investing, or financing activity. Assume all items involve cash.
(a) Purchase of equipment
(b) Sale of building
(c) Retired bonds
(d) Payment of dividends
(e) Issue of share capital

Identify financing activities.
(SO 2) AP

BE18–3   The following T account is a summary of the cash account of Baker Company:

Cash (Summary Form)

Balance, 1/1/03	8,000		
Receipts from customers	364,000	Payments to suppliers	200,000
Dividends on equity investments	6,000	Payments for operating expenses	140,000
Proceeds from sale of equipment	36,000	Interest paid	10,000
Proceeds from issue of bonds		Income tax paid	8,000
payable	200,000	Dividends paid	45,000
Balance, 12/31/03	211,000		

For Baker Company, what amount of net cash provided (used) by financing activities should be reported in the cash flow statement?

Calculate cash from operating activities—indirect method.
(SO 3) AP

BE18–4   Dressmart.com, Inc., reported net income of $2.5 million in 2003. Amortization expense for the year was $280,000, accounts receivable decreased by $350,000, and accounts payable decreased by $310,000. Calculate net cash provided by operating activities using the indirect method.

Calculate cash from operating activities—indirect method.
(SO 3) AP

BE18–5   The net income for Sterling Engineering Co. for 2003 was $250,000. For 2003, amortization expense on capital assets was $60,000, and the company incurred a loss on the sale of capital assets of $9,000. Calculate net cash provided by operating activities under the indirect method.

Calculate cash from operating activities—indirect method.
(SO 3) AP

BE18–6   The comparative balance sheet for the Harden Company shows the following changes in noncash current asset accounts: Accounts Receivable decrease of $75,000, Prepaid Expenses increase of $12,000, and Inventories increase of $30,000. Calculate net cash provided by operating activities using the indirect method. Assume that net income is $220,000 for the year ended December 31, 2003.

Determine cash received from sale of equipment.
(SO 3, 4) AN

BE18–7   The T accounts for Equipment and the related Accumulated Amortization for Trevis Company at the end of 2003 are as follows:

Equipment				Accumulated Amortization			
Beg. bal.	80,000	Disposals	22,000	Disposals	5,500	Beg. bal.	44,500
Acquisitions	41,600					Amort.	12,000
End. bal.	99,600					End. bal.	51,000

In addition, Trevis Company's income statement reported a loss on the sale of equipment of $4,900. What amount was reported on the cash flow statement as "cash flow from sale of equipment"?

Calculate cash receipts from customers—direct method.
(SO 4) AP

BE18–8   Westcoast Corporation has accounts receivable of $14,000 at January 1, 2003, and of $24,000 at December 31, 2003. Sales revenues were $470,000 for the year. What is the amount of cash receipts from customers in 2003?

Calculate cash payments for income tax—direct method.
(SO 4) AP

BE18–9   Home Grocery Corporation reported income tax expense of $90,000 in its 2003 income statement, and income tax payable of $14,000 at December 31, 2002, and of $9,000 at December 31, 2003. What was the amount of cash payments made for income tax during 2003?

BE18–10 Linux Corporation reports operating expenses of $100,000, excluding amortization expense of $15,000, for 2003. During the year, prepaid expenses decreased by $6,600 and accrued expenses payable increased by $2,400. Calculate the cash payments for operating expenses in 2003.

Calculate cash payments for operating expenses—direct method.
(SO 4) AP

BE18–11 For the year ended March 31, 2000, **Alliance Atlantis Communications Inc.** reported (in millions) cash provided by operating activities of $558.2; cash used by investing activities of $666.2; and cash provided by financing activities of $52.5. In addition, average current liabilities were $581.6; average total liabilities were $884.6; net sales and net income available to common shareholders were $771.6 and $37.0, respectively. The number of shares was 28.2. Calculate these values: (a) cash current debt coverage, (b) cash return on sales, (c) cash flow per share, and (d) cash total debt coverage.

Calculate cash-based ratios.
(SO 5) AN

***BE18–12** Fill in the missing amounts in Wetaskiwin Corporation's work sheet.

Indicate cash flow work sheet amounts.
(SO 6) AP

WETASKIWIN CORPORATION
Cash Flow Statement Work Sheet
For the Year Ended June 30, 2003

Balance Sheet Accounts	Balance July 1, 2002	Reconciling Items Debits	Reconciling Items Credits	Balance June 30, 2003
Debits				
Cash	25,000	(i) _____		65,000
Accounts receivable	45,000	(a) 8,000		53,000
Equipment	131,000	(b) _____		140,000
Total	201,000			258,000
Credits				
Accumulated amortization—equipment	81,000		(c) 14,000	95,000
Accounts payable	15,000	(d)		12,000
Common shares	45,000		(e) 35,000	80,000
Retained earnings	60,000	(g)	(f) 31,000	71,000
Total	201,000			258,000
Cash Flow Statement Effects				
Operating activities				
Net income		(f) 31,000		
Increase in accounts receivable			(a) 8,000	
Amortization expense		(c) 14,000		
Decrease in accounts payable			(d)	
Investing activities				
Purchase of equipment			(b)	
Financing activities				
Payment of dividend			(g)	
Issue of common shares		(e) 35,000	_____	
Total		160,000	(h)	
Increase in cash		_____	(i) _____	
Total		160,000	160,000	

EXERCISES

E18–1 Eng Corporation had the following transactions during 2003:
1. Purchased a machine for $30,000, giving a long-term note in exchange.
2. Issued common shares for cash, $50,000.
3. Collected $16,000 of accounts receivable.
4. Declared and paid a cash dividend of $25,000.
5. Sold a long-term investment with a cost of $15,000 for $10,000 cash.
6. Retired bonds having a carrying value of $200,000 for $175,000.

Classify transactions by activity.
(SO 2) AP

Instructions

Analyse the transactions above and indicate whether each transaction resulted in a cash inflow or cash outflow from (a) operating activities, (b) investing activities, (c) financing activities, or (d) non-cash investing and financing activities.

Classify transactions by type of activity—indirect method.
(SO 2) AP

E18–2   An analysis of the comparative balance sheet, the current year's income statement, and the general ledger accounts of Fisher Corp. uncovered the following items. Assume all items involve cash unless there is information to the contrary.

(a) Purchase of land
(b) Payment of dividends
(c) Sale of building at a gain
(d) Exchange of land for patent
(e) Redemption of bonds at carrying value
(f) Receipt of interest on notes receivable

(g) Issue of share capital
(h) Amortization of patent
(i) Issue of bonds for land
(j) Payment of interest on notes payable
(k) Sale of land at a loss
(l) Receipt of dividends on investment in pre-ferred shares

Instructions

Indicate how the above items should be classified in the cash flow statement using these major classifications: operating activity (indirect method), investing activity, financing activity, and noncash investing and financing activity.

Prepare operating activities section—indirect method.
(SO 3) AP

E18–3   Pesci Company reported net income of $195,000 for the year ended July 31, 2003. Pesci also reported an amortization expense of $45,000 and a loss of $5,000 on the sale of equipment. The comparative balance sheet shows an increase in accounts receivable of $15,000 for the year, an $8,000 increase in accounts payable, and a decrease in prepaid expenses of $4,000.

Instructions

Prepare the operating activities section of the cash flow statement for 2003. Use the indirect method.

Prepare operating activities section—indirect method.
(SO 3) AP

E18–4   The current sections of Invest.com Inc.'s balance sheets at December 31, 2002 and 2003, are presented below.

INVEST.COM INC.
Balance Sheet (partial)
December 31

	2003	2002
Current assets		
Cash	$105,000	$ 99,000
Accounts receivable	110,000	89,000
Inventory	171,000	186,000
Prepaid expenses	27,000	32,000
Total current assets	$413,000	$406,000
Current liabilities		
Accrued expenses payable	$ 15,000	$ 5,000
Accounts payable	85,000	92,000
Total current liabilities	$100,000	$ 97,000

Invest.com's net income for 2003 was $163,000. Amortization expense was $30,000.

Instructions

Prepare the operating activities section of Invest.com Inc.'s cash flow statement for the year ended December 31, 2003, using the indirect method.

Prepare partial cash flow statement—indirect method.
(SO 3) AP

E18–5   Presented below are three accounts that appear in the general ledger of Dupré Corp. during 2003:

Equipment

Date		Debit	Credit	Balance
Jan. 1	Balance			160,000
July 31	Purchase of equipment	70,000		230,000
Sept. 2	Cost of equipment constructed	53,000		283,000
Nov. 10	Cost of equipment sold		45,000	238,000

Accumulated Amortization—Equipment

Date		Debit	Credit	Balance
Jan. 1	Balance			71,000
Nov. 10	Accumulated amortization on equipment sold	30,000		41,000
Dec. 31	Amortization expense		24,000	65,000

Retained Earnings

Date		Debit	Credit	Balance
Jan. 1	Balance			105,000
Aug. 23	Dividends (cash)	14,000		91,000
Dec. 31	Net income		57,000	148,000

Instructions

From the postings in the accounts above, indicate how the information is reported by preparing a partial cash flow statement using the indirect method. The loss on the sale of equipment was $4,000.

E18–6 McGillis Company has just completed its first year of operations on December 31, 2003. Its initial income statement showed that McGillis had revenues of $137,000 and operating expenses of $88,000. Accounts receivable at year end were $42,000. Accounts payable at year end were $33,000. Assume that accounts payable related to operating expenses. There was no income tax paid or payable.

Calculate cash from operating activities—direct method.
(SO 4) AP

Instructions

Calculate net cash provided (used) by operating activities using the direct method.

E18–7 The income statement for the Nickerson Company shows a cost of goods sold of $325,000 and operating expenses (exclusive of amortization) of $250,000. The comparative balance sheet for the year shows that inventory increased by $6,000, prepaid expenses decreased by $6,000, accounts payable (merchandise suppliers) decreased by $8,000, and accrued expenses payable increased by $4,000.

Calculate cash payments—direct method.
(SO 4) AP

Instructions

Using the direct method, calculate (a) cash payments to suppliers and (b) cash payments for operating expenses.

E18–8 The following information is taken from the general ledger of Robinson Company:

Rent:	Rent expense	$ 33,000
	Prepaid rent, January 1	7,900
	Prepaid rent, December 31	3,000
Salaries:	Salaries expense	$ 54,000
	Salaries payable, January 1	5,000
	Salaries payable, December 31	8,000
Sales:	Revenue from sales	$180,000
	Accounts receivable, January 1	12,000
	Accounts receivable, December 31	7,000

Calculate operating cash flows—direct method.
(SO 4) AP

Instructions

In each of the above cases, calculate the amount that should be reported in the operating activities section of the cash flow statement using the direct method.

E18–9 The year 2003 accounting records of Frontier Airlines reveal the following transactions and events:

Prepare operating activities section—direct method.
(SO 4) AP

Payment of interest	$ 6,000	Collection of accounts receivable	$180,000
Cash sales	38,000	Payment of salaries and wages	65,000
Receipt of dividend revenue	14,000	Amortization expense	18,000
Payment of income tax	15,000	Proceeds from sale of aircraft	812,000
Net income	38,000	Purchase of equipment for cash	22,000
Payment of accounts payable		Loss on sale of aircraft	3,000
for merchandise	90,000	Payment of dividends	14,000
Payment for land	74,000	Payment of other expenses	20,000

Instructions

Prepare the operating activities section of the cash flow statement, using the direct method. (Note: Not all of the above items will be used.)

Prepare cash flow statement—
indirect method
(SO 3, 5) AP

E18–10   The comparative balance sheet for Véfour Company is presented below:

VÉFOUR COMPANY
Balance Sheet
December 31, 2003

Assets	2003	2002
Cash	$ 63,000	$ 22,000
Accounts receivable	85,000	76,000
Inventories	180,000	189,000
Land	75,000	100,000
Equipment	260,000	200,000
Accumulated amortization	(66,000)	(42,000)
Total	$597,000	$545,000

Liabilities and Shareholders' Equity	2003	2002
Accounts payable	$ 34,000	$ 47,000
Bonds payable	150,000	200,000
Common shares	214,000	164,000
Retained earnings	199,000	134,000
Total	$597,000	$545,000

Additional information:

1. Net income for 2003 was $125,000.
2. Cash dividends of $60,000 were declared and paid.
3. Bonds payable with a carrying value of $50,000 were redeemed for $50,000 cash.
4. Common shares were issued for $50,000 cash.
5. Land was sold at a gain of $5,000.
6. Net sales for the year were $978,000.

Instructions

(a) Prepare a cash flow statement for 2003 using the indirect method.
(b) Calculate the following cash-based ratios:
    1. Cash current debt coverage
    2. Cash return on sales
    3. Cash total debt coverage

Prepare cash-based ratios.
(SO 5) AN

E18–11   Presented here is selected information (in thousands) for **Reitmans (Canada) Limited** and **La Senza** for the year ended January 29, 2000.

	Reitmans	La Senza
Cash provided by operating activities	$ 32,548	$ 24,784
Cash provided by all activities	33,810	3,584
Average current liabilities	65,521	50,576
Average total liabilities	65,689	106,480
Sales	477,730	354,279
Number of shares	8,764	9,338

Instructions

Using the cash-based ratios presented in this chapter, compare (a) the liquidity, (b) the profitability, and (c) the solvency of the two companies.

Prepare cash flow work sheet—
indirect method.
(SO 6) AP

*E18–12   Use the data in E18–10 (for Véfour Company) to prepare a work sheet for a cash flow statement for 2003. Enter the reconciling items directly on the work sheet and identify the entries alphabetically.

PROBLEMS: SET A

P18–1A You are provided with the following transactions that took place during a recent fiscal year:

Classify transactions by activity.
(SO 2) AP

Transaction	Classification	Cash Inflow or Outflow?
(a) Recorded amortization expense on the capital assets.		
(b) Sold a capital asset for cash, at a price above net book value.		
(c) Sold a capital asset for cash, at a price below net book value.		
(d) Acquired a building by paying 10% in cash and signing a mortgage payable for the balance.		
(e) Made principal repayments on the mortgage.		
(f) Issued common shares for cash.		
(g) Purchased shares of another company for cash, to be held as a long-term equity investment.		
(h) Paid cash dividends to common shareholders.		
(i) Distributed stock dividends to common shareholders.		
(j) Sold inventory on credit. The company uses a perpetual inventory system.		
(k) Purchased inventory on credit.		
(l) Paid wages owing to employees.		

Instructions

Complete the table indicating whether each transaction (1) should be classified as an operating activity, investing activity, financing activity, or noncash transaction, and (2) represents a cash inflow or cash outflow. If the transaction does not affect the statement or notes in any way, state that there is no effect.

P18–2A Snair Limited's comparative balance sheet at December 31, 2003 and 2002, and its income statement for the year ended December 31, 2003, are as follows:

Prepare operating activities section—indirect method.
(SO 3) AP

SNAIR LIMITED
Balance Sheet
December 31

Assets	2003	2002
Cash	$ 164,000	$ 85,000
Accounts receivable	750,000	600,000
Inventory	500,000	330,000
Prepaid advertising	18,000	25,000
Equipment and vehicles (net of accumulated amortization)	650,000	720,000
Total assets	$2,082,000	$1,760,000
Liabilities and Shareholders' Equity		
Accounts payable	$ 226,000	$ 200,000
Salaries payable	30,000	40,000
Interest payable	26,000	20,000
Notes payable	500,000	400,000
Common shares	400,000	400,000
Retained earnings	900,000	700,000
Total liabilities and shareholders' equity	$2,082,000	$1,760,000

SNAIR LIMITED
Income Statement
For the Year Ended December 31, 2003

Sales		$4,000,000
Expenses		
Cost of goods sold	$2,100,000	
Salaries expense	400,000	
Amortization expense	70,000	
Advertising expense	150,000	
Interest expense	80,000	
Other expenses	1,000,000	3,800,000
Net income		$ 200,000

Instructions

Using the indirect method of presentation, prepare the cash flows from operating activities section of the cash flow statement.

Source: Adapted from Certified General Accountants Association of Canada, *Financial Accounting 1 Examination,* December 1999, Question 7.

Prepare cash flow statement—indirect method.
(SO 3) AP

P18–3A   Presented below is the comparative balance sheet for Cousin Tommy's Toy Company as of December 31:

COUSIN TOMMY'S TOY COMPANY
Balance Sheet
December 31

Assets	2003	2002
Cash	$ 39,000	$ 45,000
Accounts receivable	49,500	52,000
Inventory	151,450	142,000
Prepaid expenses	16,780	21,000
Land	100,000	130,000
Equipment	228,000	155,000
Accumulated amortization—equipment	(45,000)	(35,000)
Building	200,000	200,000
Accumulated amortization—building	(60,000)	(40,000)
	$679,730	$670,000
Liabilities and Shareholders' Equity		
Accounts payable	$ 38,730	$ 40,000
Bonds payable	250,000	300,000
Common shares	200,000	150,000
Retained earnings	191,000	180,000
	$679,730	$670,000

Additional information:

1. Operating expenses include amortization expense of $42,000.
2. Land was sold for cash at cost.
3. Cash dividends of $27,000 were paid.
4. Equipment was purchased for $95,000 cash. In addition, equipment costing $22,000 with a net book value of $10,000 was sold for $8,100 cash.
5. Bonds were redeemed at face value by issuing common shares.

Instructions

Prepare a cash flow statement for the year ended December 31, 2003, using the indirect method.

P18–4A The following selected account balances relate to the capital asset accounts of Trudeau Inc. at year end:

Determine cash flow effects of changes in capital asset accounts.
(SO 3, 4) AP

	2003	2002
Accumulated amortization—buildings	$337,500	$300,000
Accumulated amortization—equipment	144,000	96,000
Amortization expense	101,500	85,500
Buildings	750,000	750,000
Equipment	300,000	240,000
Land	100,000	70,000
Loss on sale of equipment	2,000	0

Additional information:

Trudeau purchased $80,000 of equipment and $30,000 of land for cash in 2003. Trudeau also sold equipment in 2003.

Instructions

(a) Determine the amounts of any cash inflows or outflows related to the capital asset accounts in 2003.
(b) Indicate where each of the cash inflows or outflows identified in (a) would be classified on the cash flow statement.

P18–5A The income statement of Oak Island Company is shown below:

Prepare operating activities section—indirect method and direct method.
(SO 3, 4) AP

OAK ISLAND COMPANY
Income Statement
For the Year Ended November 30, 2003

Sales		$6,900,000
Cost of goods sold		
Beginning inventory	$2,000,000	
Purchases	4,300,000	
Goods available for sale	6,300,000	
Ending inventory	1,600,000	
Cost of goods sold		4,700,000
Gross profit		2,200,000
Operating expenses		
Selling expenses	$ 450,000	
Administrative expenses	700,000	1,150,000
Net income		$1,050,000

Additional information:
1. Accounts receivable decreased by $280,000 during the year.
2. Prepaid expenses increased by $150,000 during the year.
3. Accounts payable to suppliers of merchandise decreased by $200,000 during the year.
4. Accrued expenses payable decreased by $100,000 during the year.
5. Administrative expenses include an amortization expense of $70,000.

Instructions

(a) Prepare the operating activities section of the cash flow statement for the year ended November 30, 2003, using the indirect method.
(b) Prepare the operating activities section of the cash flow statement for the year ended November 30, 2003, using the direct method.

P18–6A The income statement of Hanalei International Inc. for the year ended December 31, 2003, reported the following condensed information:

Prepare operating activities section—direct method.
(SO 4) AP

HANALEI INTERNATIONAL INC.
Income Statement
For the Year Ended December 31, 2003

Revenue from fees	$470,000
Operating expenses	280,000
Income from operations	190,000
Income tax expense	47,000
Net income	$143,000

Hanalei's balance sheet contained the following comparative data at December 31:

	2003	2002
Accounts receivable	$55,000	$40,000
Accounts payable	32,000	41,000
Income tax payable	6,000	4,000

Hanalei has no amortizable assets. Accounts payable relate to operating expenses.

Instructions

Prepare the operating activities section of the cash flow statement using the direct method.

Prepare cash flow statement—
direct method
(SO 4) AP

P18–7A Condensed financial data of e-Perform.com Ltd. appear below:

E-PERFORM.COM LTD.
Balance Sheet
December 31

Assets	2003	2002
Cash	$ 92,700	$ 47,250
Accounts receivable	90,800	57,000
Inventories	121,900	102,650
Investments	84,500	87,000
Capital assets	250,000	205,000
Accumulated amortization	(49,500)	(40,000)
	$590,400	$458,900

Liabilities and Shareholders' Equity	2003	2002
Accounts payable	$ 57,700	$ 48,280
Accrued expenses payable	12,100	18,830
Bonds payable	100,000	70,000
Common shares	250,000	200,000
Retained earnings	170,600	121,790
	$590,400	$458,900

E-PERFORM.COM LTD.
Income Statement
For the Year Ended December 31, 2003

Revenues		
Sales	$297,500	
Gain on sale of capital assets	8,750	$306,250
Expenses		
Cost of goods sold	$ 99,460	
Operating expenses	14,670	
Amortization expense	49,700	
Income tax expense	7,270	
Interest expense	2,940	174,040
Net income		$132,210

Additional information:

1. New capital assets costing $92,000 were purchased for cash during the year.
2. Investments were sold at cost.
3. Capital assets costing $47,000 were sold for $15,550.
4. A cash dividend of $83,400 was declared and paid during the year.
5. Accounts payable relate only to merchandise creditors.

Instructions

Prepare a cash flow statement using the direct method.

TORAM LTD.
Income Statement
For the Year Ended December 31, 2003

Sales		$900,000
Cost of goods sold		600,000
Gross profit		300,000
Operating expenses	$157,000	
Amortization expense	43,000	
Loss on sale of equipment	4,000	
Gain on sale of long-term investment	(12,000)	192,000
Net income		$108,000

Instructions

Prepare the operating activities section of Toram's cash flow statement using the indirect method. Toram defines its "cash" as cash plus temporary marketable investments, for the purpose of this statement.

Source: Adapted from Certified General Accountants of Canada, *Financial Accounting 1 Examination*, June 1999, Question 8.

P18–3B Presented below is the comparative balance sheet for SoftWorld Company at December 31:

Prepare cash flow statement — indirect method.
(SO 3) AP

SOFTWORLD COMPANY
Balance Sheet
December 31

Assets	2003	2002
Cash and cash equivalents	$ 45,000	$ 57,000
Accounts receivable	72,000	64,000
Inventory	132,000	140,000
Prepaid expenses	12,140	16,540
Land	125,000	150,000
Equipment	200,000	175,000
Accumulated amortization—equipment	(60,000)	(42,000)
Building	250,000	250,000
Accumulated amortization—building	(75,000)	(50,000)
	$701,140	$760,540

Liabilities and Shareholders' Equity		
Accounts payable	$ 38,000	$ 45,000
Bonds payable	235,000	265,000
Common shares	280,000	250,000
Retained earnings	148,140	200,540
	$701,140	$760,540

Additional information:

1. Net income for 2003 was $26,890.
2. Operating expenses include an amortization expense of $70,000.
3. Equipment was purchased by issuing common shares. In addition, equipment costing $40,000 with a net book value of $13,000 was sold for $14,000 cash.
4. Land was sold for cash at cost.
5. Bonds were redeemed for cash equal to their face value.
6. Cash dividends were paid during the year.

Instructions

Prepare a cash flow statement for 2003 using the indirect method.

Determine cash flow effects of changes in equity accounts.
(SO 3, 4) AP

P18–4B   The following selected account balances relate to the shareholders' equity accounts of Valerio Corp. at year end:

	2003	2002
Common shares, no par value, 10,500 and 10,000 shares respectively	$160,000	$140,000
Cash dividends	10,000	10,000
Preferred shares, no par value, 5,000 shares	125,000	125,000
Stock dividends	10,500	0
Retained earnings	300,000	240,000

Instructions

(a)   What was the amount of net income reported by Valerio Corp. in 2003?

(b)   Determine the amounts of any cash inflows or outflows related to the shareholders' equity accounts in 2003.

(c)   Indicate where each of the cash inflows or outflows identified in (b) would be classified on the cash flow statement.

Prepare operating activities section—indirect method and direct method.
(SO 3, 4) AP

P18–5B   The income statement of Ski-Board.com is shown below:

SKI-BOARD.COM
Income Statement
For the Year Ended April 30, 2003

Sales		$7,100,000
Cost of goods sold		5,600,000
Gross profit		1,500,000
Operating expenses		
Selling	$750,000	
Administrative	725,000	
Amortization	205,000	1,680,000
Net loss		$ 180,000

Additional information:

1.   Accounts receivable increased by $490,000 during the year.
2.   Inventory increased by $220,000 during the year.
3.   Prepaid expenses increased by $170,000 during the year.
4.   Accounts payable to merchandise suppliers increased by $40,000 during the year.
5.   Accrued expenses payable decreased by $180,000 during the year.

Instructions

(a)   Prepare the operating activities section of the cash flow statement for the year ended April 30, 2003, using the indirect method.

(b)   Prepare the operating activities section of the cash flow statement for the year ended April 30, 2003, using the direct method.

Prepare operating activities section—direct method.
(SO 4) AP

P18–6B   Sable Island Company Ltd.'s income statement for the year ended December 31, 2003, contained the following condensed information:

SABLE ISLAND COMPANY LTD.
Income Statement
For the Year Ended December 31, 2003

Revenue from fees		$900,000
Operating expenses	$624,000	
Amortization expense	60,000	
Loss on sale of equipment	26,000	710,000
Income before income tax		190,000
Income tax expense		40,000
Net income		$150,000

Sable Island's balance sheet contained the following comparative data at December 31:

	2003	2002
Accounts receivable	$47,000	$57,000
Accounts payable	41,000	36,000
Income tax payable	4,000	9,000

Accounts payable relate to operating expenses.

Instructions

Prepare the operating activities section of the cash flow statement using the direct method.

P18–7B Condensed financial data of Galenti, Inc., appear below:

Prepare cash flow statement—direct method.

(SO 4) AP

GALENTI, INC.
Balance Sheet
December 31

Assets	2003	2002
Cash	$ 93,800	$ 38,400
Accounts receivable	90,800	33,000
Inventories	116,500	102,850
Prepaid expenses	18,400	16,000
Investments	108,000	94,000
Capital assets	270,000	242,500
Accumulated amortization	(50,000)	(52,000)
	$647,500	$474,750

Liabilities and Shareholders' Equity		
Accounts payable	$ 82,000	$ 67,300
Accrued expenses payable	16,500	17,000
Bonds payable	95,000	110,000
Common shares	220,000	175,000
Retained earnings	234,000	105,450
	$647,500	$474,750

GALENTI, INC.
Income Statement
For the Year Ended December 31, 2003

Sales		$342,080
Expenses		
Cost of goods sold	$115,460	
Operating expenses	12,410	
Amortization expense	46,500	
Interest expense	2,730	
Loss on sale of capital assets	7,150	184,250
Income before income tax		157,830
Income tax expense		7,280
Net income		$150,550

Additional information:
1. New capital assets costing $85,000 were purchased for cash during the year.
2. Old capital assets with an original cost of $57,500 were sold.
3. Bonds matured and were retired at face value for cash.
4. A cash dividend of $22,000 was declared and paid during the year.
5. Accounts payable relate only to merchandise creditors.

Instructions

Prepare a cash flow statement using the direct method.

Prepare a cash flow statement—
indirect method and direct
method. Calculate cash-based
ratios.
(SO 3, 4, 5) AP

P18–8B The financial statements of Kit-n-Kaboodle Company Ltd. appear below:

KIT-N-KABOODLE COMPANY LTD.
Balance Sheet
December 31

Assets	2003	2002
Cash	$ 19,000	$ 5,000
Temporary investments	10,000	8,000
Accounts receivable	28,000	14,000
Merchandise inventory	25,000	35,000
Capital assets	60,000	78,000
Accumulated amortization	(20,000)	(24,000)
Total	$122,000	$116,000

Liabilities and Shareholders' Equity		
Accounts payable	$ 27,000	$ 23,000
Income taxes payable	5,000	8,000
Bonds payable	27,000	33,000
Common shares	18,000	14,000
Retained earnings	45,000	38,000
Total	$122,000	$116,000

KIT-N-KABOODLE COMPANY LTD.
Income Statement
For the Year Ended December 31, 2003

Sales		$220,000
Cost of goods sold		180,000
Gross profit		40,000
Selling expenses	$14,000	
Administrative expenses	10,000	24,000
Income from operations		16,000
Interest expense		2,000
Income before income tax		14,000
Income tax expense		4,000
Net income		$ 10,000

Additional information:

1. Dividends declared and paid were $3,000.
2. During the year, equipment was sold for $8,500 cash. This equipment had cost $18,000 originally and had a net book value of $8,500 at the time of sale.
3. All amortization expenses are in the selling expenses category.
4. All sales and purchases are on account.
5. The number of common shares was 13,000.
6. Kit-n-Kaboodle's temporary investments are highly liquid and should be combined with cash
   for this statement.

Instructions

(a) Prepare a cash flow statement using the indirect method.
(b) Further analysis reveals the following:
   1. All accounts payable relate to merchandise suppliers.
   2. All operating expenses except for amortization were paid in cash.
   Prepare a cash flow statement using the direct method.
(c) Calculate the following cash-based ratios:
   1. Cash current debt coverage
   2. Cash return on sales
   3. Cash flow per share
   4. Cash total debt coverage

Prepare cash flow work sheet—
indirect method.
(SO 6) AP

*P18–9B Refer to Problem 18–3B (for SoftWorld Company) and use these data to prepare a work
sheet for a cash flow statement. Enter the reconciling entries directly on the work sheet, and identify the entries alphabetically.

*B*roadening Your Perspective

FINANCIAL REPORTING AND ANALYSIS

Financial Reporting Problem

BYP18–1 Refer to the consolidated financial statements for The Second Cup Ltd., which are reproduced in Appendix A at the end of the textbook.

Instructions

(a) 1. What was the amount of net cash provided by operating activities for fiscal 2000? For the pro forma results in fiscal 1999?
2. How much interest did The Second Cup pay in 2000? Income tax?
3. Refer to the line in the Operating Activities section of the statement that reads "Loss (Gain) on Disposal of Capital Assets and Investments." Explain why the gain in fiscal 2000 was subtracted in calculating the cash provided by operating activities.

(b) Compare the company's cash flows related to Investing Activities during fiscal 2000 to those of 1999. Comment upon anything significant that you observe.

(c) Compare the company's cash flows related to Financing Activities during fiscal 2000 to those of 1999. Comment upon anything significant that you observe.

(d) Notice the large decrease in cash and cash equivalents that occurred during 1999. What was the primary cause of this decrease?

Interpreting Financial Statements

BYP18–2 For several years, Chapters and Indigo Books fought for market dominance in the book industry in Canada. Late in December 2000, Indigo (through Trilogy Retail Enterprises) launched a hostile takeover bid for Chapters; it gained control of it in February 2001. The following selected financial information is taken from the interim financial statements of Chapters Inc. at the end of December, immediately before the takeover:

Additional Cases

CHAPTERS INC.
Selected Information From Statements of Earnings and Cash Flows
13 weeks ended December 31
(in thousands)

	2000	1999
Cash provided by operating activities	$ 82,048	$ 52,300
Cash used by investing activities	11,056	(15,124)
Cash used by financing activities	(79,181)	(39,719)
Net increase (decrease) in cash during the period	13,923	(2,543)
Cash, end of period	16,474	51,965
Revenue	247,550	234,695
Net earnings	8,996	9,733
Number of common shares	11,375	11,343

Instructions

(a) Calculate (1) the earnings per share and cash flow per share, and (2) the profit margin and cash return on sales for each interim period. Discuss the company's ability to finance future growth for Indigo from internally generated cash.

(b) Discuss any potential implications of the change in Chapters' cash during the period.

BYP18–3   Sleeman Breweries Ltd. is the largest craft brewer in Canada and the country's leading brewer of premium beers. In 1999, Sleeman purchased the Shaftebury Brewing Company for $10 million. This move gave Sleeman national distribution in Canada's beer markets.

The 2000 balance sheet of Sleeman Breweries showed current assets of $38 million and current liabilities of $39.8 million, including bank indebtedness (negative cash balance) of $9.9 million. On a more positive note, Sleeman nearly doubled its earnings in 2000, from $6.5 million in 1999 to $9 million in 2000. In addition, its cash flow statement indicates that it generated $12.4 million of cash from operating activities in 2000.

Instructions

(a) Do you believe that Sleeman's creditors should be worried about its lack of cash? Explain why or why not.

(b) If you were a creditor of Sleeman, and noted that it did not have enough current assets to cover its current liabilities, what additional information might you request to help you assess its solvency?

(c) Why do you think Sleeman generated $12.4 million of cash from operating activities but has no cash?

Accounting on the Web

BYP18–4   The software industry presents some unique challenges regarding cash flow. The industry is highly competitive, with a practice of providing free, or heavily discounted, products as a market-entry technique. This case reviews the cash flows of a company in the software industry. The changing share price of this company is evaluated against its cash and income (loss) position.

Instructions

Specific requirements of this Internet case are available on the Weygandt website.

CRITICAL THINKING

••

Collaborative Learning Activity

BYP18–5   Greg Rhoda and Debra Sondgeroth are examining the following cash flow statement for Tuktoyaktuk Trading Company for the year ended January 31, 2004:

TUKTOYAKTUK TRADING COMPANY
Cash Flow Statement
For the Year Ended January 31, 2004

Cash inflows		
From sale of merchandise	$390,000	
From sale of common shares	420,000	
From sale of investment (purchased below)	80,000	
From amortization	55,000	
From issue of note for truck	20,000	
From interest on investment	6,000	
Total sources of cash		$971,000
Cash outflows		
For purchase of fixtures and equipment	$340,000	
For merchandise purchased for resale	268,000	
For operating expenses	160,000	
For purchase of investment	75,000	
For purchase of truck by issue of note	20,000	
For interest on note payable	3,000	
Total uses of cash		866,000
Net increase in cash		$105,000

Greg claims that Tuktoyaktuk's cash flow statement is an excellent example of a superb first year, because cash increased by $105,000. Debra replies that it was not a superb first year. The year was an operating failure. She says that the statement is incorrectly presented, and that $105,000 is not the actual increase in cash. The cash balance at the beginning of the year was $140,000.

Instructions

With the class divided into groups, answer the following:
(a) With whom do you agree, Greg or Debra? Explain your position.
(b) Using the data provided, prepare a cash flow statement in proper form using the indirect method. The only noncash items in the income statement are amortization expense and the gain from the sale of the investment. There were no changes in any current accounts other than cash.
(c) Prepare the operating activities section of the cash flow statement using the direct method.
(d) Would you recommend the payment of a cash dividend this year?

Communication Activity

BYP18–6 Arnold Byte, the president of Computer Services Corporation, is unfamiliar with the cash flow statement which you prepared, as his accountant. He finds it very confusing to understand, especially when the indirect method is used to prepare the operating activities section. He asks for further explanation.

Instructions

Write Mr. Byte a brief memo explaining the form and content of the cash flow statement for Computer Services Corporation.

Ethics Case

BYP18–7 Paradis Corporation is a wholesaler of automotive parts. It has 10 shareholders who have been paid a total of $1 million in cash dividends for eight consecutive years. The Board of Directors' policy requires that in order for this dividend to be declared, net cash provided by operating activities, as reported in Paradis's current year cash flow statement, must be in excess of $1 million. President and CEO Phil Monat's job is secure so long as he produces annual operating cash flows to support the usual dividend.

At the end of the current year, controller Rick Rodgers presents president Monat with some disappointing news. The net cash provided by operating activities is only $970,000. The president says to Rick, "We must get that amount above $1 million. Isn't there some way to increase operating cash flow by another $30,000?" Rick answers, "These figures were prepared by my assistant. I'll go back to my office and see what I can do." The president replies, "I know you won't let me down, Rick."

Upon close scrutiny of the cash flow statement, Rick concludes that he can get the operating cash flows above $1 million by reclassifying a two-year $60,000 note payable that is listed in the financing activities section as "Proceeds from bank loan—$60,000." He will report the note instead in the operating activities section. He returns to the president, saying, "You can tell the Board to declare its usual dividend. Our net cash flow provided by operating activities is $1,030,000." "Good man, Rick! I knew I could count on you," exults the president.

Instructions

(a) Who are the stakeholders in this situation?
(b) Was there anything unethical about the president's actions? Was there anything unethical about the controller's actions?
(c) Are the Board members or anyone else likely to discover the misclassification?

Answers to Self-Study Questions

1. c   2. b   3. a   4. c   5. b   6. c   7. c   8. d   9. b   10. c   11. d   12. a   13. b   *14. b

Answer to Second Cup Review It Question 4

The Second Cup uses the indirect method and cash and cash equivalents in its cash flow statement. Cash equivalents include short-term investments (see Note 14).

Remember to go back to the Navigator box on the chapter-opening page to check off your completed work.

• • • • • ▶ **Concepts for Review**

Before studying this chapter, you should understand or, if necessary, review:

a. *The various types of users of financial statement information. (Ch. 1, pp. 3–5)*
b. *The content and classification of a corporate income statement. (Ch. 15, pp. 704–708)*
c. *The content and classification of a corporate balance sheet. (Ch. 17, pp. 798–799)*
d. *The ratios introduced in previous chapters: current (Ch. 4, pp. 171–172); gross profit margin, profit margin, inventory turnover, days sales in inventory (Ch. 5, pp. 224–225 and p. 229); acid test, receivables turnover, collection period (Ch. 9, pp. 438–439); asset turnover, return on assets (Ch. 10, p. 487); return on equity, book value (Ch. 14, pp. 667–669); earnings per share, price-earnings, payout, dividend yield (Ch. 15, pp. 709–712); debt to total assets, interest coverage, cash interest coverage (Ch. 16, pp. 759–760); and cash current debt coverage, cash return on sales, cash flow per share, and cash total debt coverage (Ch. 18, pp. 855–857).*

THE
NAVIGATOR

Just Fooling Around?

Few people predicted how dramatically the Internet would change the investment world. For example, individuals used to put their savings into mutual funds, relying on professionals to decide which shares to buy and sell. Now, many people spurn investment professionals and make their own investment decisions. In fact, a whole new breed of investors, known as "day traders," has arisen. These are people—from doctors to mechanics—who spend hours a day trading their shares over the Internet.

What has caused this change? The Internet. It has empowered individuals by providing access to information that was never available before.

Two early pioneers in this area are Tom and David Gardner. They created an on-line investor service called The Motley Fool. Tom and David view themselves as 20th-century "fools," revealing the "truths" of the stock markets to the small investor, who they feel has been taken advantage of by insiders. Their on-line discussion boards enable investors to exchange information and insights about companies.

Critics of these discussion boards or chat rooms contend that they are nothing more than high-tech rumour mills that are largely responsible for building a speculative house of cards. There is little to stop people from putting misinformation on the board to influence a share's price in the desired direction. Some observers are concerned that small investors—ironically, the very people the Gardner brothers are trying to help—are hurt the most by misinformation and intentional scams.

So, how should you decide what shares to buy? Rather than getting swept away by rumours, investors must sort out the good information from the bad. Learning how to properly evaluate financial information is a start. One thing is for certain, as information services such as The Motley Fool increase in number, gathering information will become even easier, and evaluating it will become the harder task.

www.fool.com

THE
NAVIGATOR

THE NAVIGATOR ✓

- Understand *Concepts for Review* ☐
- Read *Feature Story* ☐
- Scan *Study Objectives* ☐
- Read *Preview* ☐
- Read text and answer *Before You Go On*
  p. 897 ☐ p. 916 ☐ p. 918 ☐
- Work *Demonstration Problems* ☐
- Review *Summary of Study Objectives* ☐
- Answer *Self-Study Questions* ☐
- Complete assignments ☐

CHAPTER • 19

FINANCIAL STATEMENT ANALYSIS

▶ **STUDY OBJECTIVES** ◀

After studying this chapter, you should be able to:

1. *Discuss the need for comparative analysis.*
2. *Discuss the tools of financial statement analysis.*
3. *Explain and apply horizontal analysis.*
4. *Explain and apply vertical analysis.*
5. *Identify and calculate ratios and describe their purpose and use in analysing a firm's liquidity, profitability, and solvency.*
6. *Recognize and illustrate the limitations of financial statement analysis.*

THE
NAVIGATOR

An important lesson can be learned from the feature story: Financial information must be gathered and evaluated carefully. If you are thinking of purchasing shares of a company—say, Sears Canada—how can you determine the value of the shares? How can you determine the company's financial soundness, or its profitability? How does Sears compare financially with other companies in the retail industry? To answer these types of questions, we need to know how to analyse financial statement information.

In making decisions about a company, financial statement analysis, the topic of this chapter, adds to the usefulness of published financial statements.

The chapter is organized as follows:

THE NAVIGATOR

Basics of Financial Statement Analysis

Analysing financial statements involves evaluating three characteristics of a company: its liquidity, its profitability, and its solvency. A **short-term creditor**, such as a bank, is mostly interested in the ability of the borrower to pay obligations when they come due. The liquidity of the borrower is important because it helps the bank evaluate the safety of a loan. A **long-term creditor**, such as a bondholder, looks to measures of profitability and solvency that indicate the firm's ability to survive over a long period of time. Long-term creditors consider such measures as the amount of debt in the company's capital structure and its ability to meet interest payments. Similarly, **shareholders** are interested in the profitability and solvency of the enterprise. They want to assess the likelihood of dividends and the growth potential of the shares.

STUDY OBJECTIVE

Discuss the need for comparative analysis.

Need for Comparative Analysis

Every item reported in a financial statement has significance. When Sears reports cash and temporary investments of $135.5 million on its balance sheet, we know that the company had that amount of cash and temporary investments on the balance sheet date. However, we do not know whether the amount represents an increase over prior years, or whether it is adequate for the company's cash needs. To obtain such information, it is necessary to compare the amount of cash with other financial statement data.

Comparisons can be made on a number of different bases. The following three are illustrated in this chapter.

1. **Intracompany basis.** This basis compares an item or financial relationship **within a company** in the current year with the same item or relationship in one or more prior years. For example, Sears can compare its cash and temporary investments balance at the end of the current year with last year's balance to find the amount of the increase or decrease. Likewise, Sears can compare the percentage of cash and temporary investments to current assets at the end of the current year with the percentage in one or more prior years. Intracompany comparisons are useful for detecting changes in financial relationships and significant trends.

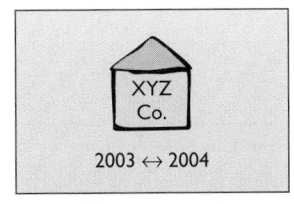

2. **Intercompany basis.** This basis compares an item or financial relationship of one company with the same item or relationship in **one or more competing companies**. The comparisons are made on the basis of the published financial statements of the individual companies. For example, Sears' total sales for the year can be compared with the total sales of one of its major competitors, such as The Bay. Intercompany comparisons are useful for understanding a company's competitive position.

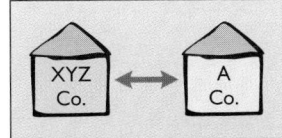

3. **Industry averages.** This basis compares an item or financial relationship of a company with **industry averages** (or **norms**). These averages are found in annual publications, such as Dun & Bradstreet Canada's *Duns Financial Profile*, *The Financial Post's Industry Reports*, and Statistics Canada's *Financial Performance Indicators for Canadian Business*. Comparisons with industry averages provide information about a company's relative performance within the industry. For example, Sears' net income can be compared with the average net income of all companies in the retail industry.

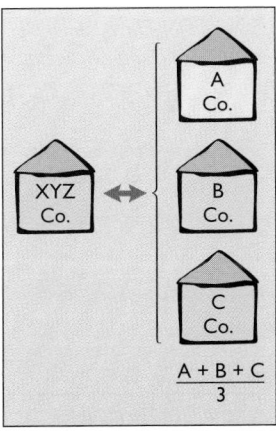

Tools of Financial Statement Analysis

Various tools are used to evaluate the significance of financial statement data. Three commonly used tools follow:

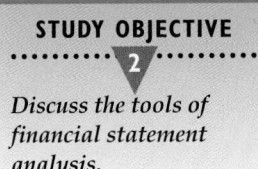

*   **Horizontal analysis** evaluates a series of financial statement data over a period of time.
*   **Vertical analysis** evaluates financial statement data by expressing each item in a financial statement as a percentage of a base amount for the same period of time.
*   **Ratio analysis** expresses the relationship among selected items of financial statement data.

Horizontal analysis is used primarily in intracompany comparisons. Two features in published financial statements make this type of comparison easier. First, each of the basic financial statements is presented on a comparative basis for a minimum of two years. Second, a summary of selected financial data is presented for a series of five to ten years or more.

Vertical analysis is used in both intracompany and intercompany comparisons. Ratio analysis is used in all three types of comparison. In the following sections, we will explain and illustrate each of the three types of analysis.

Horizontal Analysis

STUDY OBJECTIVE

· · · · · · · · · **3** · · · · · · · · ·

Explain and apply horizontal analysis.

Illustration 19-1

Sears' revenues

Horizontal analysis, also called **trend analysis,** is a technique for evaluating a series of financial statement data over a period of time. Its purpose is to determine the increase or decrease that has taken place. This change may be expressed as either an amount or a percentage. For example, recent revenue figures for Sears are as in Illustration 19-1:

SEARS CANADA INC.				
Revenues (in millions)				
For the Year Ended December 31				
2000	1999	1998	1997	1996
$6,355.8	$5,776.5	$5,481.4	$4,583.5	$3,955.9

If we assume that 1996 is the base year, we can measure all percentage increases or decreases from this base period amount as shown in Illustration 19-2:

Illustration 19-2

Formula for horizontal analysis of changes since base period

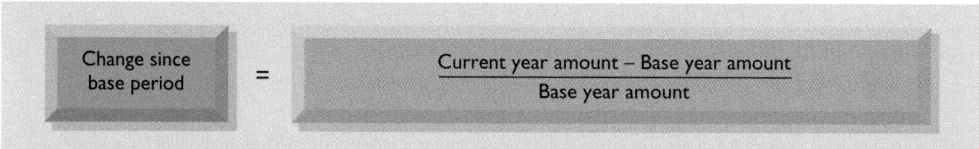

$$\text{Change since base period} = \frac{\text{Current year amount} - \text{Base year amount}}{\text{Base year amount}}$$

For example, we can determine that revenues for Sears increased by approximately 16% [($4,583.5 − $3,955.9) ÷ $3,955.9] from 1996 to 1997. Similarly, we can determine that net sales increased by 61% [($6,355.8 − $3,955.9) ÷ $3,955.9] from 1996 to 2000.

Alternatively, we can express current year sales as a percentage of the base period amount. This is done by dividing the current year amount by the base year amount, as shown in Illustration 19-3:

Illustration 19-3

Formula for horizontal analysis of current year in relation to base year

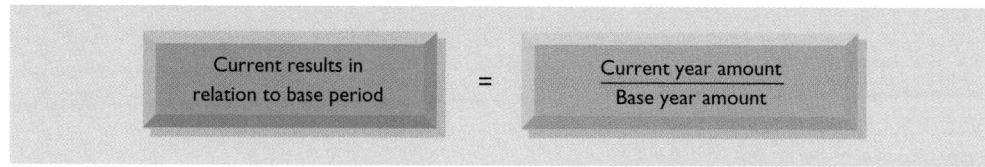

$$\text{Current results in relation to base period} = \frac{\text{Current year amount}}{\text{Base year amount}}$$

Illustration 19-4 presents this analysis for Sears for a five-year period using 1996 as the base period.

Illustration 19-4

Horizontal analysis of Sears' revenues

SEARS CANADA INC.				
Revenues (in millions)				
For the Year Ended December 31				
2000	1999	1998	1997	1996
$6,355.8	$5,776.5	$5,481.4	$4,583.5	$3,955.9
161%	146%	139%	116%	100%

▸Accounting in Action ▸ *Business Insight*

Investors are focusing on revenue trends, rather than income trends, lately. There are two reasons for this. One is a concern that net income in recent years has been improved by cost-cutting and productivity gains that are no longer sustainable. Another is skepticism about the reliability of the income figure, which is often distorted by accounting changes. Revenue usually gives a better picture of a company's financial health, especially in technology industries.

Balance Sheet

To further illustrate horizontal analysis, we will use the financial statements of Quality Department Store. It is a fictitious full-line department store located in a small city. Its two-year condensed balance sheet, showing dollar and percentage changes, are presented in Illustration 19-5.

QUALITY DEPARTMENT STORE INC. Balance Sheet December 31				
			Increase (Decrease) during 2000	
	2000	1999	Amount	Percentage
Assets				
Current assets	$1,020,000	$ 945,000	$ 75,000	7.9%
Capital assets (net)	815,000	650,000	165,000	25.4%
Total assets	$1,835,000	$1,595,000	$240,000	15.0%
Liabilities				
Current liabilities	$ 344,500	$ 303,000	$ 41,500	13.7%
Long-term liabilities	487,500	497,000	(9,500)	(1.9%)
Total liabilities	832,000	800,000	32,000	4.0%
Shareholders' Equity				
Common shares	275,400	270,000	5,400	2.0%
Retained earnings	727,600	525,000	202,600	38.6%
Total shareholders' equity	1,003,000	795,000	208,000	26.2%
Total liabilities and shareholders' equity	$1,835,000	$1,595,000	$240,000	15.0%

Illustration 19-5

Horizontal analysis of balance sheet

Helpful hint It is difficult to understand how significant a change is when only the dollar amount of the change is examined. When the change is expressed as a percentage, it is easier to grasp its true size.

The comparative balance sheet in Illustration 19-5 shows that a number of significant changes have occurred in Quality Department Store's financial structure from 1999 to 2000. In the assets section, capital assets increased by $165,000, or 25.4%. In the liabilities section, current liabilities increased by $41,500, or 13.7%. In the shareholders' equity section, retained earnings increased by $202,600, or 38.6%. This suggests that the company expanded its asset base during 2000. It did this by retaining income, rather than by assuming additional long-term debt.

Income Statement

Illustration 19-6 presents a horizontal analysis of the two-year condensed income statement for Quality Department Store for the years 2000 and 1999.

Horizontal analysis of the income statement shows the following changes:

1. Net sales increased by $260,000, or 14.2% ($260,000 ÷ $1,837,000).
2. Cost of goods sold increased by $141,000, or 12.4% ($141,000 ÷ $1,140,000).
3. Total operating expenses increased by $37,000, or 11.6% ($37,000 ÷ $320,000).

Overall, gross profit and net income were up substantially. Gross profit increased by 17.1%, and net income by 26.5%. Quality's profit trend appears favourable.

Illustration 19-6

*Horizontal analysis of
income statement*

Helpful hint   Note that
while the amount column is
additive (the total is $55,300),
the percentage column is not
additive (the total is not 26.5%).
A separate percentage has been
calculated for each item.

QUALITY DEPARTMENT STORE INC.
Income Statement
For the Year Ended December 31

	2000	1999	Increase (Decrease) during 2000 Amount	Percentage
Sales	$2,195,000	$1,960,000	$235,000	12.0%
Sales returns and allowances	98,000	123,000	(25,000)	(20.3%)
Net sales	2,097,000	1,837,000	260,000	14.2%
Cost of goods sold	1,281,000	1,140,000	141,000	12.4%
Gross profit	816,000	697,000	119,000	17.1%
Selling expenses	253,000	211,500	41,500	19.6%
Administrative expenses	104,000	108,500	(4,500)	(4.1%)
Total operating expenses	357,000	320,000	37,000	11.6%
Income from operations	459,000	377,000	82,000	21.8%
Other revenues and gains				
Interest and dividends	9,000	11,000	(2,000)	(18.2%)
Other expenses and losses				
Interest expense	36,000	40,500	(4,500)	(11.1%)
Income before income tax	432,000	347,500	84,500	24.3%
Income tax expense	168,200	139,000	29,200	21.0%
Net income	$ 263,800	$ 208,500	$ 55,300	26.5%

Statement of Retained Earnings

A horizontal analysis of Quality Department Store's comparative statement of retained earnings is presented in Illustration 19-7. Analysed horizontally, net income increased by $55,300, or 26.5%. This is consistent with that shown in the horizontal analysis of the income statement above. Dividends increased by only $1,200, or 2%. Ending retained earnings, as also shown in the horizontal analysis of the balance sheet on the previous page, increased by 38.6%. As indicated earlier, the company retained a significant portion of net income to finance additional capital assets.

Illustration 19-7

*Horizontal analysis of
statement of retained
earnings*

QUALITY DEPARTMENT STORE INC.
Statement of Retained Earnings
For the Year Ended December 31

	2000	1999	Increase (Decrease) during 2000 Amount	Percentage
Retained earnings, Jan. 1	$525,000	$376,500	$148,500	39.4%
Add: Net income	263,800	208,500	55,300	26.5%
	788,800	585,000	203,800	34.8%
Less: Dividends	61,200	60,000	1,200	2.0%
Retained earnings, Dec. 31	$727,600	$525,000	$202,600	38.6%

A horizontal analysis of changes from period to period is relatively straightforward and is quite useful. But complications can occur in making the calculations. If an item has no value in a base year or preceding year and a value in the next year, no percentage change can be calculated. Similarly, if a negative amount appears in the base or preceding period and a positive amount exists the following year, or vice versa, no percentage change can be calculated.

We have not included a horizontal analysis of Quality Department Store's cash flow statement. Such an analysis is not as useful as the horizontal analyses performed on the balance sheet and income statement. The amounts presented in the cash flow statement (except in the operating activities section) detail the changes between two periods (opening and ending balance sheets). The value of this statement comes from the analysis of where cash came from and what it was used for rather than from comparing these changes to a base amount.

Vertical Analysis

Vertical analysis, also called **common size analysis**, is a technique for evaluating financial statement data that expresses each item within a financial statement as a percentage of a base amount. On a balance sheet, we might say that current assets are 56% of total assets (total assets being the base amount). Or, on an income statement, we might say that selling expenses are 12% of net sales (net sales being the base amount).

STUDY OBJECTIVE
·········· 4 ··········
Explain and apply vertical analysis.

Balance Sheet

Presented in Illustration 19-8 is the vertical analysis of Quality Department Store's comparative balance sheet. The base amount for the asset items is **total assets**. The base amount for the liability and shareholders' equity items is **total liabilities and shareholders' equity, which equals total assets**.

Alternative terminology
Horizontal analysis is also known as *dynamic analysis*, since it spans years. Vertical analysis is also known as *static analysis*, since it incorporates only one year.

Illustration 19-8
Vertical analysis of balance sheet

QUALITY DEPARTMENT STORE INC. Condensed Balance Sheet December 31				
	2000		1999	
Assets	Amount	Percentage	Amount	Percentage
Current assets	$1,020,000	55.6%	$ 945,000	59.2%
Capital assets (net)	815,000	44.4%	650,000	40.8%
Total assets	$1,835,000	100.0%	$1,595,000	100.0%
Liabilities				
Current liabilities	$ 344,500	18.8%	$ 303,000	19.0%
Long-term liabilities	487,500	26.5%	497,000	31.2%
Total liabilities	832,000	45.3%	800,000	50.2%
Shareholders' Equity				
Common shares	275,400	15.0%	270,000	16.9%
Retained earnings	727,600	39.7%	525,000	32.9%
Total shareholders' equity	1,003,000	54.7%	795,000	49.8%
Total liabilities and shareholders' equity	$1,835,000	100.0%	$1,595,000	100.0%

Helpful hint The formula for calculating these balance sheet percentages follows:
$$\frac{\text{Each item on B/S}}{\text{Total assets}} = \%$$

Vertical analysis shows the relative size of each category in the balance sheet. It can also show the **percentage change** in the individual asset, liability, and shareholders' equity items. For example, we can see that current assets decreased from 59.2% of total assets in 1999 to 55.6% in 2000, even though the absolute dollar amount increased by $75,000 in that time. Capital assets increased from 40.8% to 44.4% of total assets. Retained earnings increased from 32.9% to 39.7% of total liabilities and shareholders' equity. These results reinforce the earlier observation that

Quality is financing its growth by retaining earnings, rather than by issuing additional debt.

Income Statement

Vertical analysis of Quality's income statement is shown in Illustration 19-9. The base amount is usually **net sales** on the income statement. We see that cost of goods sold as a percentage of net sales declined by 1% (62.1% versus 61.1%) and that total operating expenses declined by 0.4% (17.4% versus 17.0%). As a result, it is not surprising to see income from operations as a percentage of net sales increase from 20.5% to 21.9%. Quality appears to be a profitable enterprise that is becoming even more successful.

Illustration 19-9

Vertical analysis of income statement

Helpful hint The formula for calculating these income statement percentages follows:

$$\frac{\text{Each item on I/S}}{\text{Net sales}} = \%$$

	2000		1999	
QUALITY DEPARTMENT STORE INC. Income Statement For the Year Ended December 31				
	Amount	Percentage	Amount	Percentage
Sales	$2,195,000	104.7%	$1,960,000	106.7%
Sales returns and allowances	98,000	4.7%	123,000	6.7%
Net sales	2,097,000	100.0%	1,837,000	100.0%
Cost of goods sold	1,281,000	61.1%	1,140,000	62.1%
Gross profit	816,000	38.9%	697,000	37.9%
Selling expenses	253,000	12.0%	211,500	11.5%
Administrative expenses	104,000	5.0%	108,500	5.9%
Total operating expenses	357,000	17.0%	320,000	17.4%
Income from operations	459,000	21.9%	377,000	20.5%
Other revenues and gains				
Interest and dividends	9,000	0.4%	11,000	0.6%
Other expenses and losses				
Interest expense	36,000	1.7%	40,500	2.2%
Income before income tax	432,000	20.6%	347,500	18.9%
Income tax expense	168,200	8.0%	139,000	7.5%
Net income	$ 263,800	12.6%	$ 208,500	11.4%

Vertical analysis can also be performed on the statement of retained earnings and cash flow statement. However, this is seldom done, since each statement already provides comparative detail of the change between two periods (opening and ending balance sheets).

Intercompany Comparisons

Another benefit of vertical analysis is that it enables you to compare companies of different sizes. For example, Quality's main competitor is Sears. Using vertical analysis, the condensed balance sheet (or the income statement) of the local retail enterprise Quality Department Store can be more meaningfully compared with the balance sheet (or respective financial statement) of the giant retailer Sears Canada, as shown in Illustration 19-10 which follows:

Illustration 19-10

Intercompany balance sheet comparison—vertical analysis

	Quality Department Store Inc.		Sears Canada Inc.	
Condensed Balance Sheets (in thousands)				
Assets	Dollars	Percentage	Dollars	Percentage
Current assets	$1,020.0	55.6%	$2,416,800	61.1%
Investments and other assets		0.0%	339,000	8.6%
Capital assets (net)	815.0	44.4%	1,199,200	30.3%
Total assets	$1,835.0	100.0%	$3,955,000	100.0%
Liabilities				
Current liabilities	$ 344.5	18.8%	$1,730,000	43.7%
Long-term liabilities	487.5	26.5%	675,700	17.1%
Total liabilities	832.0	45.3%	2,405,700	60.8%
Shareholders' Equity				
Common shares	275.4	15.0%	455,600	11.5%
Retained earnings	727.6	39.7%	1,093,700	27.7%
Total shareholders' equity	1,003.0	54.7%	1,549,300	39.2%
Total liabilities and shareholders' equity	$1,835.0	100.0%	$3,955,000	100.0%

Sears' total assets are 2,155 times greater than the total assets of the smaller Quality Department Store. But vertical analysis eliminates this difference in size. The percentages show that Quality's and Sears' current assets are different, but not significantly so, at 55.6% and 61.1% of total assets.

The percentages related to capital assets are also different, at 44.4% and 30.3%. A number of factors contribute to this disparity. For example, Quality owns its own facilities, whereas Sears often leases facilities in malls or elsewhere. Sears also generates a significant portion of its revenues from catalogue sales. Although Sears has 116 department stores it has more than 2,000 catalogue pick-up locations. These operations do not require capital-intensive facilities. Sears also has 114 independent, locally owned and operated stores, which generate additional revenue.

While Sears' retained earnings are 1,503 times larger than those for Quality, Sears' retained earnings as a percentage of total liabilities and shareholders' equity (27.7%) are much lower than Quality's (39.7%). However, Sears' total liabilities (60.8%) are also much higher than Quality's (45.3%).

Before You Go On . . .

▶ Review It

1. What are the different tools that might be used to compare financial information?
2. What is horizontal analysis?
3. What is vertical analysis?
4. Identify the specific sections in The Second Cup Ltd.'s 2000 annual report where horizontal and vertical analysis of financial data is presented. The answer to this question is provided at the end of this chapter.

▶ Do It

Summary financial information for Bonora Company is as follows:

	December 31, 2003	December 31, 2002
Current assets	$234,000	$180,000
Capital assets (net)	756,000	420,000
Total assets	$990,000	$600,000

Calculate the amount and percentage changes in 2003, using (a) horizontal analysis, assuming 2002 is the base year, and (b) vertical analysis, assuming total assets is the base.

Action Plan

- Horizontal analysis: Find the percentage change by dividing the amount of the increase by the 2002 amount (base year).
- Vertical analysis: Find the percentage change by dividing the specific asset amount by total assets, for each of 2003 and 2002.

Solution

		Increase in 2003	
(a) Horizontal analysis:	Amount	Percentage	
Current assets	$ 54,000	30%	[($234,000 − $180,000) ÷ $180,000]
Capital assets (net)	336,000	80%	[($756,000 − $420,000) ÷ $420,000]
Total assets	$ 390,000	65%	[($990,000 − $600,000) ÷ $600,000]

(b) Vertical analysis:	2003		2002	
Current assets	23.6%	($234,000 ÷ $990,000)	30%	($180,000 ÷ $600,000)
Capital assets (net)	76.4%	($756,000 ÷ $990,000)	70%	($420,000 ÷ $600,000)
Total assets	100.0%		100%	

THE NAVIGATOR

Related exercise material: BE19–1, BE19–2, BE19–3, BE19–4, BE19–5, BE19–6, E19–1, E19–2, E19–3, and E19–4.

Ratio Analysis

STUDY OBJECTIVE
5

Identify and calculate ratios and describe their purpose and use in analysing a firm's liquidity, profitability, and solvency.

Ratio analysis expresses the relationships between selected items of financial statement data. A **ratio** expresses the mathematical relationship between one quantity and another. The relationship is expressed as either a percentage, a rate, or a simple proportion. To illustrate, Le Château had current assets of $33.4 million and current liabilities of $13.8 million in 2000. The relationship is determined by dividing current assets by current liabilities. The different ways of expressing the relationship follow:

Percentage: Current assets are 242% of current liabilities.
Rate: Current assets are 2.42 times greater than current liabilities.
Proportion: The relationship of current assets to liabilities is 2.42:1.

Many computer programs routinely generate financial ratios. All the ratio calculations presented in this chapter can be done with electronic spreadsheets or manually. Also, many software programs are written specifically for financial statement analysis. These packages are written both for general purpose use and for use in specific industries. For example, financial institutions routinely use over 60 ratios, intended specifically for the banking industry.

For an analysis of the primary financial statements, ratios can be used to evaluate liquidity, profitability, and solvency. These classifications are described and shown in Illustration 19-11.

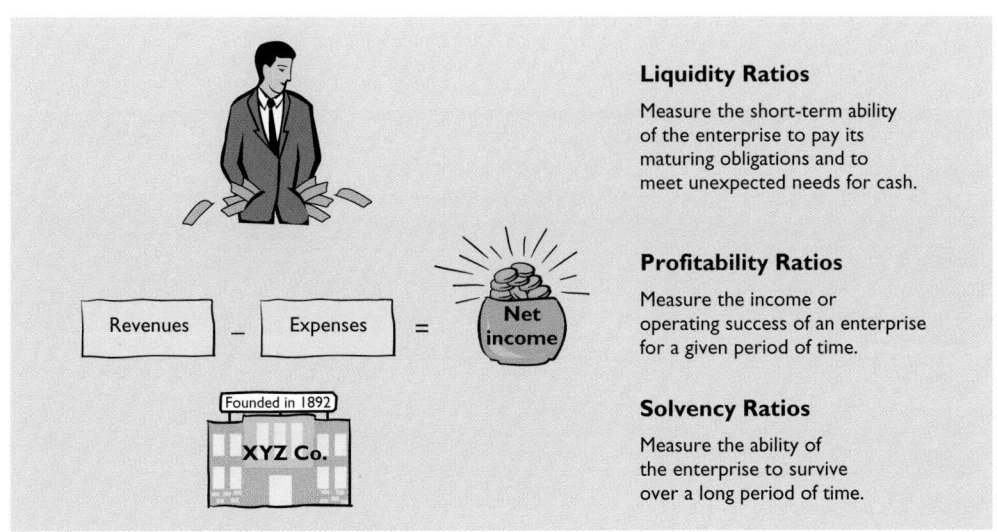

Liquidity Ratios

Measure the short-term ability of the enterprise to pay its maturing obligations and to meet unexpected needs for cash.

Profitability Ratios

Measure the income or operating success of an enterprise for a given period of time.

Solvency Ratios

Measure the ability of the enterprise to survive over a long period of time.

Ratios can provide clues about underlying conditions that may not be apparent from individual financial statement components. However, a single ratio by itself is not very meaningful. Accordingly, in the discussion below we will use the following types of comparisons:

1. **Intracompany comparisons** for two years for Quality Department Store.
2. **Intercompany comparisons** of Quality Department Store and Sears Canada, Quality's principal competitor.
3. **Industry average comparisons** for the retail industry. (For some of the ratios that we use, industry comparisons are not available. These are identified with "n/a.")

Liquidity Ratios

Liquidity ratios measure the short-term ability of the enterprise to pay its maturing obligations and to meet unexpected needs for cash. Short-term creditors such as bankers and suppliers are particularly interested in assessing **liquidity**. The ratios that can be used to determine the enterprise's short-term debt-paying ability are the current ratio, acid test ratio, cash current debt coverage, receivables turnover, and inventory turnover.

Current Ratio

The current ratio is a widely used measure of a company's liquidity and short-term debt-paying ability. The ratio is calculated by dividing current assets by current liabilities. The 2000 and 1999 current ratios for Quality Department Store and comparative data are shown in Illustration 19-12.

What does the ratio actually mean? The 2000 ratio of 3.0:1 means that for every dollar of current liabilities, Quality has $3 of current assets. Quality's current ratio has decreased slightly in the current year. However, compared to the industry average and Sears Canada's 1.4:1 current ratio, Quality appears to be highly liquid.

The current ratio is sometimes referred to as the **working capital ratio** because **working capital** is the excess of current assets over current liabilities. The current ratio is a more dependable indicator of liquidity than working capital. Two companies with the same amount of working capital may have significantly different current ratios.

Illustration 19-12

Current ratio

$$\text{CURRENT RATIO} = \frac{\text{CURRENT ASSETS}}{\text{CURRENT LIABILITIES}}$$

Quality Department Store

2000	1999
$\frac{\$1,020,000}{\$344,500} = 3.0:1$	$\frac{\$945,000}{\$303,000} = 3.1:1$
Industry average 1.2:1	Sears Canada 1.4:1

Helpful hint

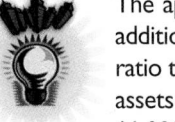

	Co. A	Co. B
Current assets	$100,000	$500,000
Current liabilities	50,000	450,000
Working capital	$ 50,000	$ 50,000
Current ratio	2.0:1	1.1:1

The current ratio is only one measure of liquidity. It does not take into account the composition of the current assets. For example, a satisfactory current ratio does not disclose the fact that a portion of the current assets may be tied up in uncollectible accounts receivable or in slow-moving inventory. A dollar of cash is more available to pay the bills than a dollar of slow-moving inventory that has yet to be sold and paid for.

▶Accounting in Action ▸ *Business Insight*

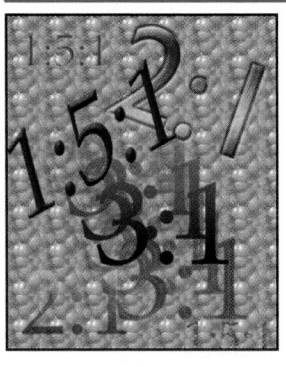

The apparent simplicity of the current ratio can have real-world limitations. An addition of equal amounts to both the numerator and the denominator causes the ratio to decrease. Assume, for example, that a company has $2,000,000 of current assets and $1,000,000 of current liabilities. Its current ratio is 2:1. If it purchases $1,000,000 of inventory on account, it will have $3,000,000 of current assets and $2,000,000 of current liabilities. Its current ratio will decrease to 1.5:1. If, instead, the company pays off $500,000 of its current liabilities, it will have $1,500,000 of current assets and $500,000 of current liabilities. Its current ratio will increase to 3:1. Any trend analysis should be done with care, since the ratio is susceptible to quick changes and is easily influenced by management.

Acid Test Ratio

Alternative terminology
The acid test ratio is also called the *quick ratio*.

The **acid test ratio** is a measure of a company's immediate short-term liquidity. It is calculated by dividing the sum of cash, temporary investments, and net receivables by current liabilities. It is an important complement to the current ratio. For example, assume that the current assets of Quality Department Store for 2000 and 1999 consist of the following items:

Illustration 19-13

Current assets of Quality Department Store

QUALITY DEPARTMENT STORE INC. Balance Sheet (partial) December 31		
	2000	1999
Current assets		
Cash	$ 100,000	$155,000
Temporary investments	20,000	70,000
Receivables (net)	230,000	180,000
Inventory	620,000	500,000
Prepaid expenses	50,000	40,000
Total current assets	$1,020,000	$945,000

Cash, temporary investments, and receivables are highly liquid compared to inventory and prepaid expenses. The inventory may not be readily saleable, and the prepaid expenses may not be recoverable. Thus, the acid test ratio measures **immediate** liquidity. The 2000 and 1999 acid test ratios for Quality Department Store and comparative data are as follows in Illustration 19-14:

Illustration 19-14

Acid test ratio

$$\text{ACID TEST RATIO} = \frac{\text{CASH + TEMPORARY INVESTMENTS + RECEIVABLES (NET)}}{\text{CURRENT LIABILITIES}}$$

Quality Department Store

2000	1999
$\dfrac{\$100{,}000 + \$20{,}000 + \$230{,}000}{\$344{,}500} = 1.0{:}1$	$\dfrac{\$155{,}000 + \$70{,}000 + \$180{,}000}{\$303{,}000} = 1.3{:}1$
Industry average 0.3:1	Sears Canada 0.6:1

The ratio declined in 2000. Is an acid test ratio of 1.0:1 adequate? When compared to the industry median of 0.3:1 and Sears 0.6:1, Quality's acid test ratio appears more than adequate. It has sufficient short-term liquidity to fully satisfy all current obligations.

Cash Current Debt Coverage

A disadvantage of the current and acid test ratios is that they use year-end balances of current assets and current liability accounts. These balances may not represent the company's current position during most of the year. A ratio that partially corrects for this problem is the cash current debt coverage ratio. It is calculated by dividing net cash provided by operating activities by average current liabilities. Because it uses net cash provided by operating activities and an average of the current liabilities, rather than a balance at a point in time, it may provide a better idea of a company's liquidity.

Assume that Quality Department Store's net cash provided by operating activities was $125,300 in 2000 and $151,500 in 1999. Current liabilities at January 1, 1999, were $290,000. The cash current debt coverage ratio for Quality Department Store and comparative data are as in Illustration 19-15:

Illustration 19-15

Cash current debt coverage

$$\text{CASH CURRENT DEBT COVERAGE} = \frac{\text{NET CASH PROVIDED BY OPERATING ACTIVITIES}}{\text{AVERAGE CURRENT LIABILITIES}}$$

Quality Department Store

2000	1999
$\dfrac{\$125{,}300}{\left[\dfrac{\$303{,}000 + \$344{,}500}{2}\right]} = 0.4 \text{ times}$	$\dfrac{\$151{,}500}{\left[\dfrac{\$290{,}000 + \$303{,}000}{2}\right]} = 0.5 \text{ times}$
Industry average 1.1 times	Sears Canada 0.3 times

Helpful hint Whenever an end-of-period (e.g., balance sheet) figure is compared to a period figure (e.g., income statement or cash flow statement), the end-of-period figure must be averaged so that it approximates the same period of time. Comparisons of end-of-period figures to end-of-period figures, or period figures to period figures, do not require averaging.

The ratio has declined slightly in 2000. Is the coverage adequate? It is difficult to say. Quality's operating cash flow coverage of average current liabilities is not as good as its acid test ratio or the industry average, but it is slightly better than Sears'.

Receivables Turnover

Liquidity may be measured by how quickly certain assets can be converted to cash. How liquid, for example, are the receivables? The ratio used to assess the liquidity of the receivables is receivables turnover. It measures the number of times, on average, receivables are collected during the period. Receivables turnover is calculated by dividing net credit sales (net sales less cash sales) by the average net receivables. Unless seasonal factors are significant, average net receivables outstanding can be calculated from the beginning and ending balances of the net receivables.[1]

Assuming that all sales are credit sales and the balance of accounts receivable (net) at the beginning of 1999 is $200,000, the receivables turnover for Quality Department Store and comparative data are shown in Illustration 19-16.

Illustration 19-16

Receivables turnover

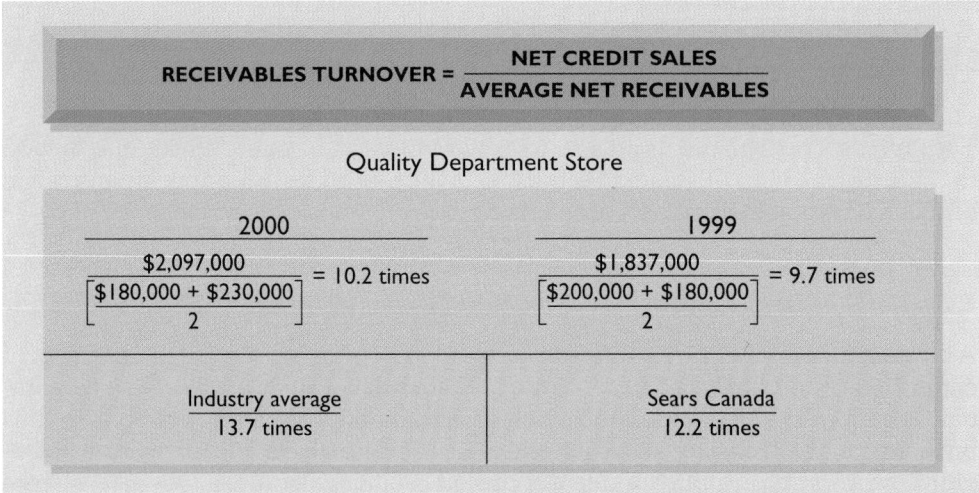

RECEIVABLES TURNOVER = $\dfrac{\text{NET CREDIT SALES}}{\text{AVERAGE NET RECEIVABLES}}$

Quality Department Store

2000	1999
$\dfrac{\$2,097,000}{\left[\dfrac{\$180,000 + \$230,000}{2}\right]}$ = 10.2 times	$\dfrac{\$1,837,000}{\left[\dfrac{\$200,000 + \$180,000}{2}\right]}$ = 9.7 times
Industry average 13.7 times	Sears Canada 12.2 times

Quality's receivables turnover improved in 2000. The turnover of 10.2 times is still not as high as Sears' 12.2 times, or the industry's mean of 13.7 times. In general, the faster the turnover, the greater the reliability of the current and acid test ratios for assessing liquidity.

Care must also be taken in interpreting this ratio, as credit sales were assumed to equal net sales. Although this was an assumption (and likely a wrong one, since many department stores do have a significant amount of cash sales), intracompany, intercompany, and industry comparisons can still be made, as the same assumption (total sales approximates credit sales) was applied to Sears and the industry average.

A popular variant of the receivables turnover ratio is to convert it to an average collection period in days. This is done by dividing 365 days by the receivables turnover. For example, in 2000 the receivables turnover of 10.2 times for Quality is divided into 365 days to obtain 35.8 days. This means that receivables are collected, on average, every 36 days. The average collection period is frequently used to assess the effectiveness of a company's credit and collection policies. The general rule is that the collection period should not greatly exceed the credit term period (the time allowed for payment).

▶**International note**

Average collection periods are usually longer in Japan than in other countries. Due dates are frequently extended during business downturns to ensure that a stable workforce can be maintained.

[1] If seasonal factors are significant, the average receivables balance might be determined by using monthly amounts.

Inventory Turnover

Inventory turnover measures the average number of times the inventory is sold during the period. Its purpose is to measure the liquidity of the inventory. The inventory turnover is calculated by dividing cost of goods sold by the average inventory. Unless seasonal factors are significant, average inventory can be calculated from the beginning and ending inventory balances.

Assuming that the inventory balance for Quality Department Store at the beginning of 1999 was $450,000, its inventory turnover and comparative data are shown in Illustration 19-17.

Helpful hint Inventory is compared to cost of goods sold, not sales, because inventory is recorded at cost.

Illustration 19-17

Inventory turnover

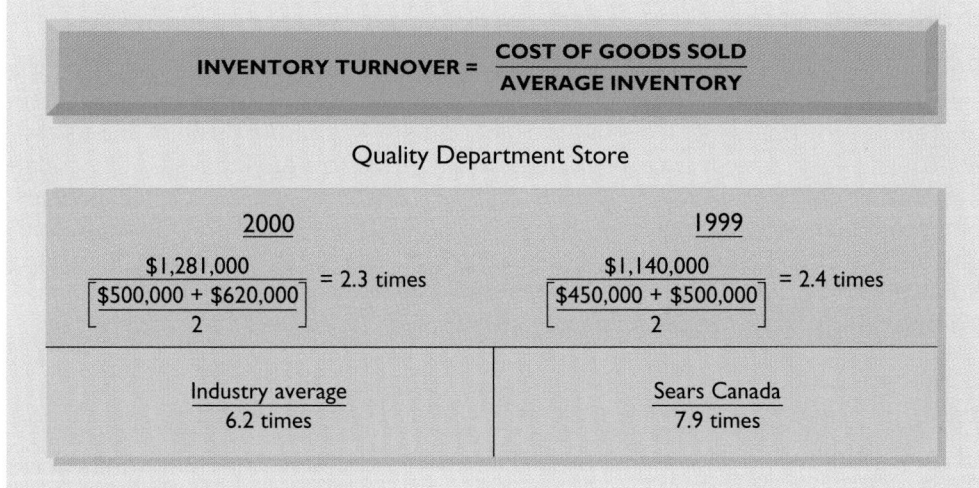

Quality's inventory turnover declined slightly in 2000. The turnover ratio of 2.3 times is low compared to the industry average of 6.2 and Sears' inventory turnover of 7.9. Generally, the faster the inventory turnover, the less cash that is tied up in inventory and the less chance of inventory obsolescence. As mentioned before, however, it is important to use judgement in interpreting these ratios. Remember that Quality is only one store, while Sears consists of hundreds.

A variant of inventory turnover is the average days sales in inventory. This is calculated by dividing the inventory turnover into 365 days. For example, Quality's 2000 inventory turnover of 2.3 times divided into 365 days is approximately 159 days. An average selling time of 159 days is very slow compared to the industry average of 59 days (365 ÷ 6.2) and Sears' rapid average of 46 days (365 ÷ 7.9).

One possible explanation for the significant variance between Sears and the industry ratios is that the industry ratios are greatly affected by giant retailers such as Wal-Mart and The Bay, in addition to Sears, which are large enough to take advantage of just-in-time or other computerized inventory management techniques. Sears' year-end inventory balance, for example, is only 42.0% of its total current assets, whereas Quality's is 60.8%. Quality, as an independent department store, may not have access to many sophisticated inventory options. Nonetheless, Quality must keep a close eye on its inventory. It runs the risk of being left with unsaleable inventory that is out of season or out of fashion, not to mention the additional costs of financing and carrying this inventory for an extended period of time.

▶Accounting in Action ▸ *Business Insight*

Inventory turnover ratios vary considerably among industries. For example, grocery store chains have a turnover of eight times and an average selling period of 46 days. In contrast, jewellery stores have an average turnover of 1.7 times and an average selling period of 215 days. Even within a company, there may be significant differences in inventory turnover among different types of products. Thus, in a grocery store, the turnover of perishable items such as produce, meats, and dairy products will be faster than the turnover of soaps and detergents.

Profitability Ratios

Profitability ratios measure the income or operating success of an enterprise for a specific period of time. Income, or the lack of it, affects the company's ability to obtain debt and equity financing. It also affects the company's liquidity position and its ability to grow. As a consequence, both creditors and investors are interested in evaluating earning power (profitability). Profitability is frequently used as the ultimate test of management's operating effectiveness. Profitability ratios include the profit margin, cash return on sales, asset turnover, return on assets, return on common shareholders' equity, book value per share, cash flow per share, earnings per share, price-earnings, payout, and dividend yield ratios.

Profit Margin

Alternative terminology
Profit margin is also called the *return on sales.*

Profit margin is a measure of the percentage of each dollar of sales that results in net income. It is calculated by dividing net income by net sales. Quality Department Store's profit margin and comparative data are shown in Illustration 19-18.

Illustration 19-18

Profit margin

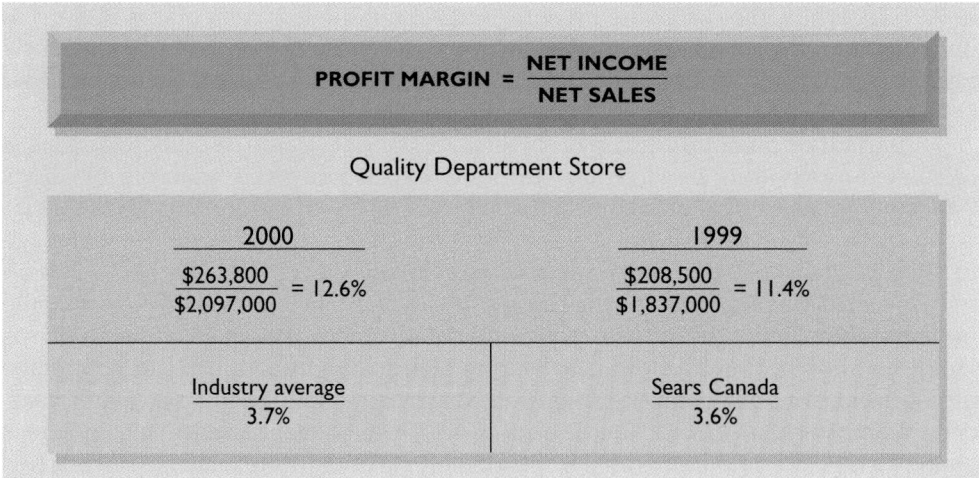

$$\text{PROFIT MARGIN} = \frac{\text{NET INCOME}}{\text{NET SALES}}$$

Quality Department Store

2000	1999
$\frac{\$263,800}{\$2,097,000} = 12.6\%$	$\frac{\$208,500}{\$1,837,000} = 11.4\%$
Industry average 3.7%	Sears Canada 3.6%

Quality experienced an increase in its profit margin from 1999 to 2000. Its profit margin is unusually high in comparison with the industry average of 3.7% and Sears' 3.6%. One possible explanation for this is that Quality may sell higher-quality merchandise, with higher prices and higher margins, than other companies such as Sears.

One way to investigate this is to calculate the gross profit margin. The gross profit margin is determined by dividing gross profit (net sales less cost of goods sold) by net sales. Gross profit indicates a company's ability to maintain its selling price above its cost of goods sold. Quality's gross profit margin is 38.9% ($816,000 ÷ $2,097,000). Sears does not separately disclose its cost of goods sold, so we are unable to calculate Sears' gross profit margin. The industry average is 35.6%. As we speculated previously, Quality appears to sell merchandise with higher prices and margins than the industry.

High-volume (high inventory turnover) enterprises such as grocery stores (Loblaw or Sobeys) and discount stores (Zellers or Wal-Mart) generally experience low profit margins. In contrast, low-volume enterprises such as jewellery stores (Birks) or airplane manufacturers (Bombardier) have high profit margins.

Cash Return on Sales

The profit margin ratio discussed above is an accrual-based ratio, which uses net income as the numerator. The cash basis counterpart is cash return on sales. It uses net cash provided by operating activities (from the cash flow statement) as the numerator and net sales as the denominator. The difference between these two ratios relates to differences between accrual basis accounting and cash basis accounting (that is, differences in the timing of revenue and expense recognition). Using net cash provided by operating activities of $125,300 in 2000 and $151,500 in 1999, Quality Department Store's cash return on sales is calculated in Illustration 19-19:

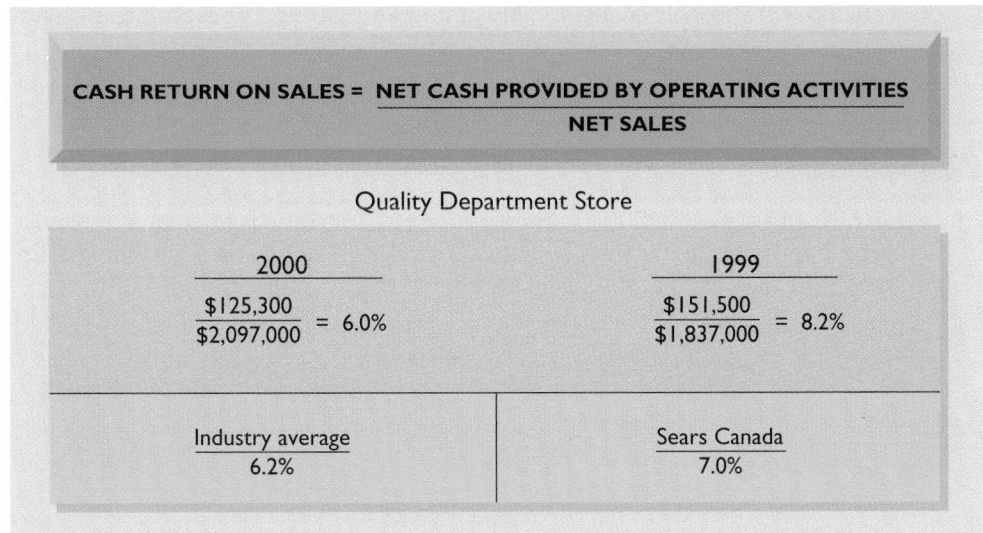

Illustration 19-19

Cash return on sales

Quality's cash return on sales (6.0%) is considerably lower than its profit margin on sales (12.6%). The primary difference between net income and cash provided by operating activities was caused by increased receivables (which increased accrual-based sales but not cash receipts from customers).

Compared to its competition, Quality appears to have a reasonable, although declining, cash return on sales.

Asset Turnover

Asset turnover measures how efficiently a company uses its assets to generate sales. It is determined by dividing net sales by average total assets. The resulting number shows the dollars of sales produced by each dollar of assets. Unless seasonal factors are significant, average total assets can be calculated from the beginning and ending balances of total assets. Assuming that total assets at the beginning of 1999 were $1,446,000, the 2000 and 1999 asset turnover ratios for Quality Department Store and comparative data are as in Illustration 19-20:

Illustration 19-20

Asset turnover

In 2000, Quality generated $1.20 of sales for each dollar it had invested in assets. The ratio is unchanged from 1999 to 2000. Quality's asset turnover ratio is somewhat below Sears' ratio of 1.6 times and the industry's ratio of 2.3 times.

Asset turnover ratios vary considerably among industries. For example, the average asset turnover for utility companies is 0.4, while the grocery store industry has an average asset turnover of 3.5.

Return on Assets

An overall measure of profitability is return on assets. This ratio is calculated by dividing net income by average total assets. The 2000 and 1999 return on assets for Quality Department Store and comparative data are shown below in Illustration 19-21:

Illustration 19-21

Return on assets

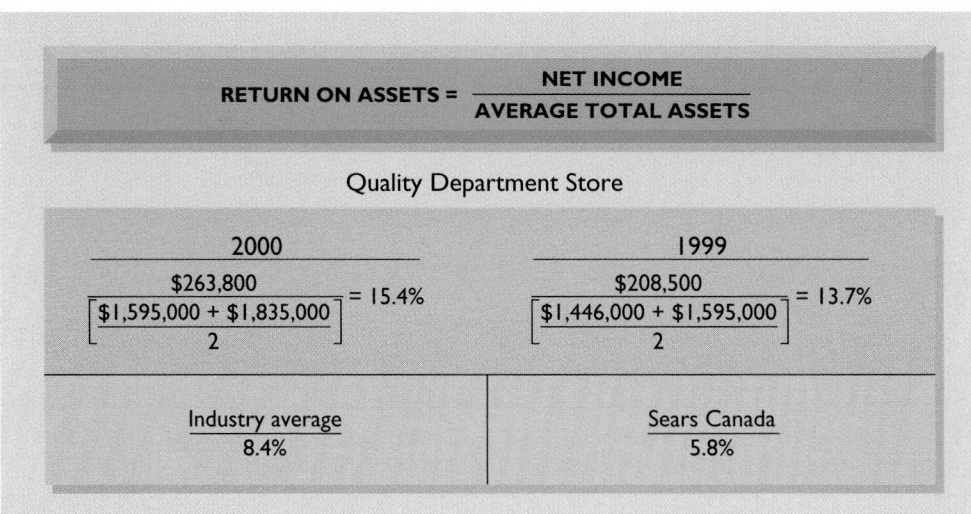

Quality's return on assets improved from 1999 to 2000. Its return of 15.4% is very high compared to the industry average of 8.4% and Sears' 5.8%. Although the percentage is high, it must be analysed in perspective. Quality's earnings improved, and they were strong to begin with. However, they are being compared to a relatively small asset base, so small dollar increases result in large percentage increases.

Return on Common Shareholders' Equity

In Chapter 14, we learned about return on equity, a widely used profitability ratio. This ratio calculates a return using total shareholders' equity, which is the same as common shareholders' equity if only one class of shares is issued. This ratio is commonly called the return on common shareholders' equity. It is calculated by dividing net income by average common shareholders' equity. Assuming that common shareholders' equity at the beginning of 1999 was $667,000, the 2000 and 1999 ratios for Quality Department Store and comparative data are shown in Illustration 19-22.

Alternative terminology
Return on equity is also known as *return on investment.*

Illustration 19-22
Return on common shareholders' equity—no preferred shares

When **preferred shares** are present, preferred dividend requirements are deducted from net income to calculate the income available to common shareholders. Similarly, the legal capital of preferred shares must be deducted from total shareholders' equity to determine the amount of common shareholders' equity used in this ratio.

Quality's return on common shareholders' equity is unusually high, at 29.3%, considering an industry average of 12.9% and a rate of 15.6% for Sears.

Note that Quality's return on common shareholders' equity (29.3%) is much higher than its return on assets (15.4%). The reason is that Quality has made effective use of leveraging or trading on the equity. Trading on the equity means that the company can earn a higher rate of interest by using the borrowed money than it has to pay on the borrowed money. This enables Quality Department Store to use money supplied by non-owners to increase the return to the owners.

Alternative terminology
Trading on the equity is also called *leveraging.*

A comparison of the rate of return on total assets to the rate of interest paid for borrowed money indicates the profitability of trading on the equity. Note, however, that trading on the equity is a two-way street. For example, if you borrow money at 7% and earn only 4% on it, you are trading on the equity at a loss rather than a gain. Quality Department Store earns more on its borrowed funds than it has to pay in the form of interest. Thus, the return to shareholders exceeds the return on assets, which indicates that shareholders are benefiting from positive leveraging or trading on the equity.

▶Accounting in Action ▶ *@ -Business Insight*

Gary Meehan, president of Onvia.com Canada, believes that e-commerce companies should focus on return on investment. Onvia.com is a leading business-to-business e-marketplace for small-business buyers and sellers. "Our own product teams have become much more ROI (return on investment) focused," says Meehan. "Not only are we talking about ROI a lot more in the high-tech sector, but we're trying to be a lot more accurate" as investors want to know what their return will be.

Source: "E-commerce Companies Should Stay Focused on More ROI." *The Globe and Mail,* March 19, 2001, C4.

Book Value Per Share

Book value per share represents **the equity a common shareholder has in the net assets of the corporation** from owning one share. Assuming that the number of common shares for Quality Department Store at December 31 was 272,700 for 2000 and 270,000 for 1999, the book value per share is calculated as in Illustration 19-23:

Illustration 19-23

Book value per share—no preferred shares

If there are **preferred shares**, their equity (legal capital) must be deducted from total shareholders' equity to determine the shareholders' equity that applies to the common shareholders.

Quality's book value per share has increased, reflecting the company's increased retention of earnings. Remember, however, that book value per share is not a measure of the worth of a company. It reflects historical costs, not anticipated earnings.

Note that no industry data are presented. In addition, the Sears book value per share amount is presented for information only. Such comparisons are not meaningful because of the wide variations in the number of shares among companies.

Cash Flow Per Share

Cash flow per share is an important measure of performance for companies. There is currently no one prescribed method to calculate this ratio. However, the CICA has a project under way that will eventually guide the calculation and presentation of the cash flow ratio. In the interim, one common way of calculating this ratio is by dividing the cash flow from operating, investing, and financing activities by the number of common shares issued. The 2000 and 1999 ratios for Quality Department Store and comparative data are shown in Illustration 19-24. Cash and temporary investments were combined for the purposes of the cash flow statement and an opening balance of $141,500 was assumed for January 1, 1999.

When the term cash flow per share is used, it refers to the amount of cash flow applicable to each **common share**.

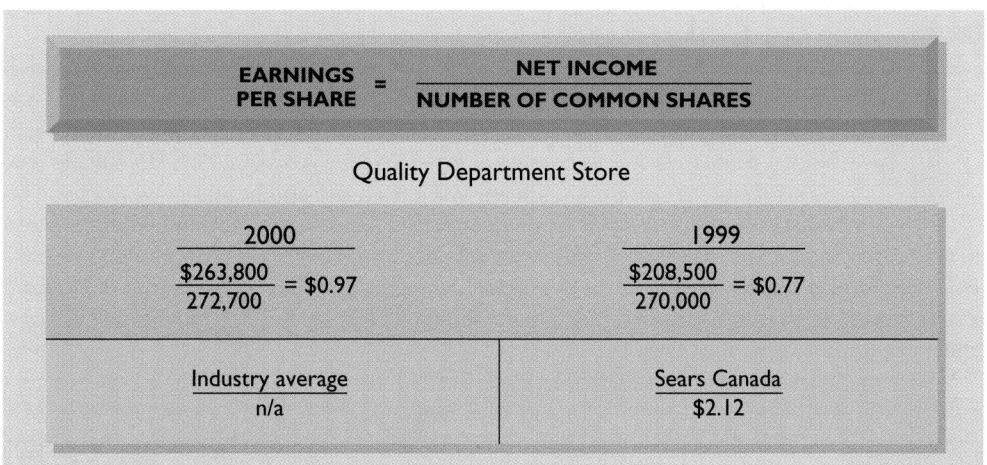

Illustration 19-24

Cash flow per share

One might conclude that while Quality's profitability is stronger than Sears', Sears' cash flow is better than Quality's (even though negative). However, such comparisons are not meaningful—again due to the wide variations in the number of shares issued.

Earnings Per Share (EPS)

Earnings per share is a measure of the net income earned on each common share. It is calculated by dividing net income by the number of common shares issued.

Shareholders usually think in terms of the number of shares they own or plan to buy or sell. Reducing net income earned to a per share basis provides a useful measure of profitability. This measure is widely used and reported. Because of the importance of the earnings per share ratio, most companies are required to present it directly on the income statement.

The net income per share for Quality Department Store for 2000 and 1999 is calculated as shown in Illustration 19-25.

▶ **International note**

The most quoted measure of shareholder profitability is earnings per share. Only in a few countries, such as Germany and Italy, is EPS not disclosed.

Illustration 19-25

Earnings per share—no preferred shares

$$\text{EARNINGS PER SHARE} = \frac{\text{NET INCOME}}{\text{NUMBER OF COMMON SHARES}}$$

Quality Department Store

2000	1999
$\dfrac{\$263,800}{272,700} = \$0.97$	$\dfrac{\$208,500}{270,000} = \$0.77$
Industry average	Sears Canada
n/a	$2.12

Quality's earnings per share increased by $0.20 per share in 2000. This represents a 26% increase over the 1999 earnings per share of $0.77. Comparisons to the industry average or Sears are not meaningful because of the wide variations in the number of shares among companies. The only meaningful EPS comparison is an intracompany one.

As with return on common shareholders' equity, preferred dividends must be deducted from net income to arrive at the income available to the common shareholders. In addition, if common shares are issued throughout the period, a weighted average number of shares must be determined. Calculating earnings per share can be complex. These intricacies are studied in an intermediate accounting course.

Price-Earnings (PE) Ratio

The price-earnings (PE) ratio is an often-quoted measure of the ratio of the market price of each common share to the earnings per share. The price-earnings ratio reflects investors' assessments of a company's future earnings. It is calculated by dividing the market price per share by earnings per share. Assuming that the market price of Quality Department Store common shares was $12 in 2000 and $8 in 1999, the price-earnings ratio is calculated as in Illustration 19-26:

Illustration 19-26

Price-earnings ratio

$$\text{PRICE-EARNINGS RATIO} = \frac{\text{SHARE PRICE}}{\text{EARNINGS PER SHARE}}$$

Quality Department Store

2000	1999
$\dfrac{\$12.00}{\$0.97} = 12.4$ times	$\dfrac{\$8.00}{\$0.77} = 10.4$ times
Industry average 32 times	Sears Canada 10 times

In 2000, each Quality share sold for 12.4 times the amount that was earned on each share. Quality's and Sears's price-earnings ratios are still much lower than the industry average.

▶Accounting in Action ▸ *Business Insight*

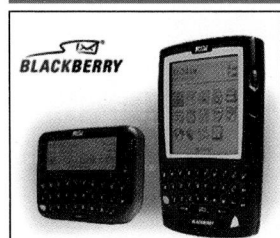

The price-earnings ratio is a user-friendly yardstick that even a novice investor can use to help gauge whether a share is outrageously pricey or sitting in the bargain bin. If a company's shares have great prospects for growth, a high PE multiple may be justified—because the company will earn more and because investors will be willing to pay more for those earnings. Take Research in Motion Limited, located in Waterloo, Ontario, the maker of BlackBerry, a wireless e-mail pager. BlackBerry won the 2000 PC World World Class Award for Best Wireless Communication Device. Research in Motion's shares traded at an outrageously high PE multiple of 1,227 in early 2001, indicating investors' cheery optimism about the company's future.

High multiples, however, can also mean high risk. To determine when to buy or sell at a certain price, many investors study a company's PE ratio over time. If the highs and lows of a particular share's PE ratio remain constant over several stock market cycles, then these highs and lows can indicate selling and buying points for the shares. Studying the PE ratios of competing companies and the industry index can also put the movements into perspective.

Payout Ratio

The payout ratio measures the percentage of earnings distributed as cash dividends. It is calculated by dividing cash dividends by net income. Companies that have high growth rates usually have low payout ratios, because they reinvest most of their net income in the business. The 2000 and 1999 payout ratios for Quality Department Store are calculated as in Illustration 19-27:

Helpful hint Companies must be cautious about changing their payout ratio too dramatically. Why? Because shareholders buy and hold shares based on the company's historical and expected dividend-paying practices.

$$\text{PAYOUT RATIO} = \frac{\text{CASH DIVIDENDS}}{\text{NET INCOME}}$$

Quality Department Store

2000	1999
$\dfrac{\$61,200}{\$263,800} = 23.2\%$	$\dfrac{\$60,000}{\$208,500} = 28.8\%$

Industry average	Sears Canada
n/a	11.3%

Illustration 19-27

Payout ratio

Quality's payout ratio is more than double Sears' payout ratio of 11.3%. Many companies with stable earnings have high payout ratios. For example, BCE has an 81% payout ratio. Conversely, companies that are expanding rapidly, such as Alliance Atlantis Communications, Biochem Pharma, and Corel, have never paid cash dividend.

Dividend Yield

Another measure, the dividend yield, supplements the payout ratio. The dividend yield reports the rate of return a shareholder earned from dividends during the year. It is calculated by dividing cash dividends per share by the share price, as shown in Illustration 19-28.

Illustration 19-28

Dividend yield

$$\text{DIVIDEND YIELD} = \frac{\text{CASH DIVIDENDS PER SHARE}}{\text{SHARE PRICE}}$$

Quality Department Store

2000	1999
$\dfrac{\$61,200 \div 272,700}{\$12} = 1.9\%$	$\dfrac{\$60,000 \div 270,000}{\$8} = 2.8\%$

Industry average	Sears Canada
n/a	1.1%

Assuming share prices of $12 for 2000 and $8 for 1999, Quality's dividend yield has declined. However, it is still substantially above Sears'. A dividend yield is not available for the industry as share prices aren't comparable. As with the payout ratio, companies that are expanding rapidly can be expected to have low dividend yields.

Solvency Ratios

Solvency ratios measure the ability of the enterprise to survive over a long period of time. Long-term creditors and shareholders are particularly interested in a company's ability to pay interest as it comes due and to repay the face value of debt at maturity. Debt to total assets, interest coverage, cash interest coverage, and cash total debt coverage are four ratios that provide information about debt-paying ability.

Debt to Total Assets

Helpful hint A popular variant of this ratio is the debt to equity ratio. It is calculated by dividing total debt by shareholders' equity. It compares the percentage of assets provided by creditors to that provided by shareholders.

Debt to total assets measures the percentage of the total assets provided by creditors. It is calculated by dividing total debt (both current and long-term liabilities) by total assets. This ratio indicates the company's degree of leverage or trading on the equity. It also provides some indication of the company's ability to absorb losses without hurting the interests of creditors. The higher the percentage of total debt to total assets, the greater the risk that the company may be unable to meet its maturing obligations. The 2000 and 1999 ratios for Quality Department Store and comparative data are as in Illustration 19-29:

Illustration 19-29

Debt to total assets

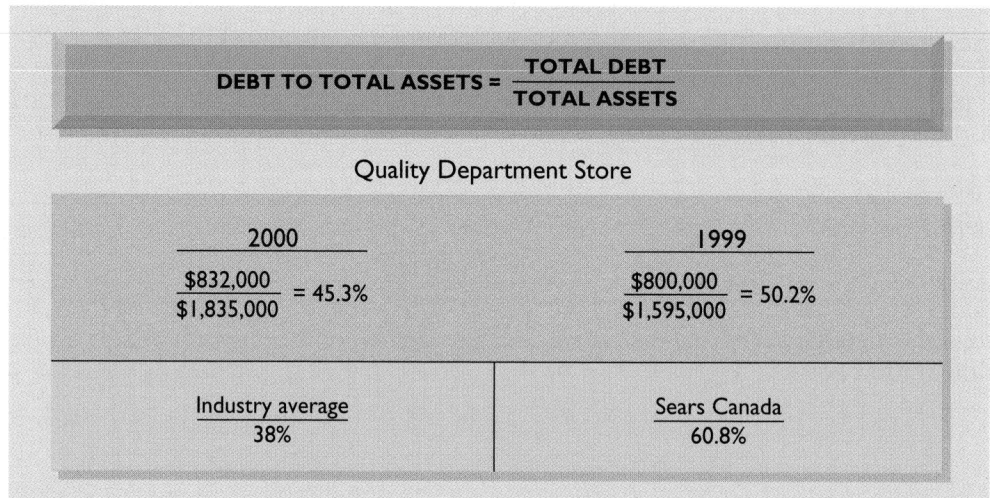

A ratio of 45.3% means that creditors have provided 45.3% of Quality Department Store's total assets. Or, conversely, that shareholders have financed 54.7% (100% − 45.3%) of the total assets. Quality's 45.3% is below Sears's ratio of 60.8%. The lower the ratio, the more equity "buffer" there is for creditors. Thus, from the creditors' point of view, a low ratio of debt to total assets is usually desirable.

The adequacy of this ratio is often judged according to the company's earnings. Generally, companies with relatively stable earnings (such as utilities) have higher debt to total assets ratios than cyclical companies with widely fluctuating earnings (such as many high-tech companies).

Interest Coverage

Alternative terminology The interest coverage ratio is also called the *times interest earned ratio.*

The interest coverage ratio provides an indication of the company's ability to meet interest payments as they come due. It is calculated by dividing **income before interest expense and income tax expense** by interest expense. Note that the interest coverage ratio uses income before interest expense and income tax expense. As we learned in Chapter 16, this is often abbreviated as EBIT, earnings before interest and tax. EBIT represents the amount available to cover interest.

The 2000 and 1999 ratios for Quality Department Store and comparative data are shown in Illustration 19-30.

Illustration 19-30

Interest coverage

$$\text{INTEREST COVERAGE} = \frac{\text{INCOME BEFORE INTEREST EXPENSE AND INCOME TAX EXPENSE}}{\text{INTEREST EXPENSE}}$$

Quality Department Store

2000	1999
$\dfrac{(\$263,800 + \$36,000 + \$168,200)}{\$36,000} = 13.0$ times	$\dfrac{(\$208,500 + \$40,500 + \$139,000)}{\$40,500} = 9.6$ times
Industry average 8.2 times	Sears Canada 6.0 times

Quality's interest expense is very well covered, at 13 times, relative to Sears at 6.0 times, and the industry at 8.2 times.

Cash Interest Coverage

The interest coverage ratio is an accrual-based measure. It does not necessarily indicate whether the company has the cash available to pay the interest. Cash interest coverage is the cash-based counterpart to interest coverage. It is calculated by dividing **income before interest expense, income tax expense, and amortization expense** by interest expense. As we learned in Chapter 16, this numerator is often abbreviated as EBITDA, earnings before interest, tax, depreciation, and amortization.

Assume that Quality's amortization expense (reported within administrative expenses) is $40,000 in 2000 and $32,000 in 1999. The 2000 and 1999 ratios for Quality Department Store and comparative data are shown in Illustration 19-31.

Illustration 19-31

Cash interest coverage

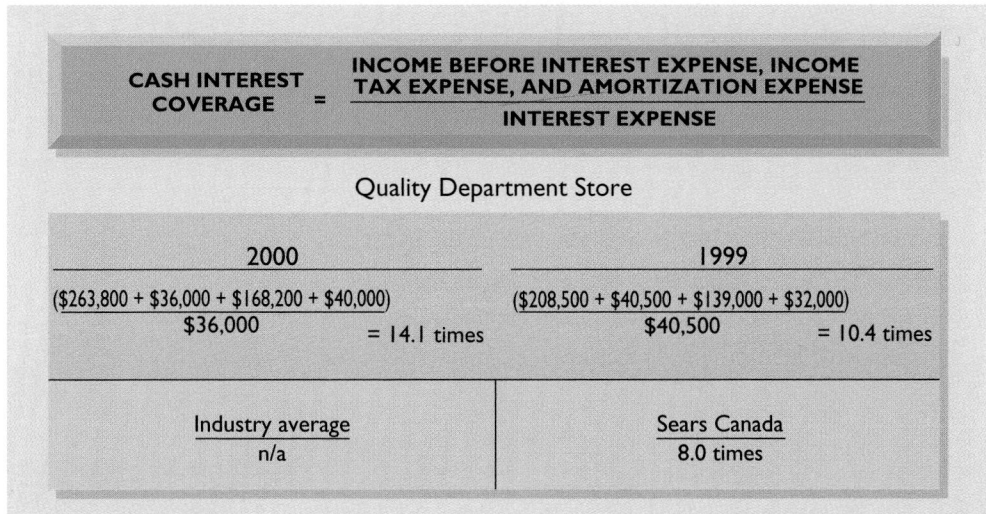

$$\text{CASH INTEREST COVERAGE} = \frac{\text{INCOME BEFORE INTEREST EXPENSE, INCOME TAX EXPENSE, AND AMORTIZATION EXPENSE}}{\text{INTEREST EXPENSE}}$$

Quality Department Store

2000	1999
$\dfrac{(\$263,800 + \$36,000 + \$168,200 + \$40,000)}{\$36,000} = 14.1$ times	$\dfrac{(\$208,500 + \$40,500 + \$139,000 + \$32,000)}{\$40,500} = 10.4$ times
Industry average n/a	Sears Canada 8.0 times

As with the interest coverage ratio, Quality is in a strong position to meet its interest payments.

Cash Total Debt Coverage

The ratio of net cash provided by operating activities to average total liabilities is referred to as the cash total debt coverage. As you learned in Chapter 18, this ratio is a cash-based measure of solvency. Earlier, we calculated a short-term version of this ratio using *current* liabilities. We now use *total* liabilities to expand the horizon.

This ratio demonstrates a company's ability to repay its liabilities from cash generated by operating activities, without having to liquidate assets. Using Quality's net cash provided by operating activities of $125,300 in 2000 and $151,500 in 1999, and assuming total liabilities of $779,000 on January 1, 1999, the cash total debt coverage ratios are calculated as follows in Illustration 19-32:

Illustration 19-32

Cash total debt coverage

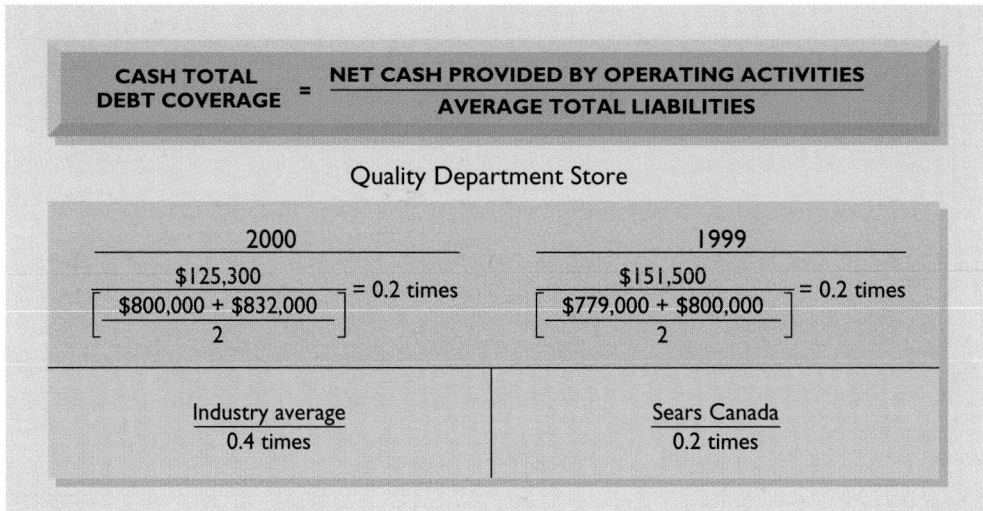

Based on net cash generated by operating activities in 2000, it would take Quality five years (1 ÷ 0.2) to generate enough cash to pay off all its liabilities. This assumes that all of the net cash generated is used for that purpose only. Quality's cash total debt coverage ratio is comparable to Sears'.

Summary of Ratios

Illustration 19-33

Summary of liquidity, profitability, and solvency ratios

A summary of the ratios discussed in the chapter is presented in Illustration 19-33, including the formula and purpose or use of each.

Ratio	Formula	Purpose or Use
Liquidity Ratios		
Current ratio	$\dfrac{\text{Current assets}}{\text{Current liabilities}}$	Measures short-term debt-paying ability.
Acid test (quick) ratio	$\dfrac{\text{Cash + temporary investments + receivables (net)}}{\text{Current liabilities}}$	Measures immediate short-term liquidity.
Cash current debt coverage	$\dfrac{\text{Net cash provided by operating activities}}{\text{Average current liabilities}}$	Measures short-term debt-paying ability (cash basis).
Receivables turnover	$\dfrac{\text{Net credit sales}}{\text{Average net receivables}}$	Measures liquidity of receivables.

Collection period	$\dfrac{365 \text{ days}}{\text{Receivables turnover}}$	Measures number of days receivables are outstanding.
Inventory turnover	$\dfrac{\text{Cost of goods sold}}{\text{Average inventory}}$	Measures liquidity of inventory.
Days sales in inventory	$\dfrac{365 \text{ days}}{\text{Inventory turnover}}$	Measures number of days stock is on hand.

Profitability Ratios

Profit margin	$\dfrac{\text{Net income}}{\text{Net sales}}$	Measures net income generated by each dollar of sales.
Gross profit margin	$\dfrac{\text{Gross profit}}{\text{Net sales}}$	Measures gross profit generated by each dollar of sales.
Cash return on sales	$\dfrac{\text{Net cash provided by operating activities}}{\text{Net sales}}$	Measures the net cash flow generated by each dollar of sales.
Asset turnover	$\dfrac{\text{Net sales}}{\text{Average total assets}}$	Measures how efficiently assets are used to generate sales.
Return on assets	$\dfrac{\text{Net income}}{\text{Average total assets}}$	Measures overall profitability of assets.
Return on common shareholders' equity	$\dfrac{\text{Net income}}{\text{Average common shareholders' equity}}$	Measures profitability of shareholders' investment.
Book value per share	$\dfrac{\text{Total shareholders' equity}}{\text{Number of common shares}}$	Measures the equity in net assets of each common share.
Cash flow per share	$\dfrac{\text{Net cash provided by all activities}}{\text{Number of common shares}}$	Measures the amount of cash flow generated on each common share.
Earnings per share (EPS)	$\dfrac{\text{Net income}}{\text{Number of common shares}}$	Measures net income earned on each common share.
Price-earnings (PE) ratio	$\dfrac{\text{Share price}}{\text{Earnings per share}}$	Measures ratio of the share price to earnings per share.
Payout ratio	$\dfrac{\text{Cash dividends}}{\text{Net income}}$	Measures percentage of earnings distributed in the form of cash dividends.
Dividend yield	$\dfrac{\text{Cash dividends per share}}{\text{Share price}}$	Measures rate of return earned from dividends.

Solvency Ratios

Debt to total assets	$\dfrac{\text{Total debt}}{\text{Total assets}}$	Measures percentage of total assets provided by creditors.
Interest coverage	$\dfrac{\text{Income before interest expense and income tax expense (EBIT)}}{\text{Interest expense}}$	Measures ability to meet interest payments as they come due.
Cash interest coverage	$\dfrac{\text{Income before interest expense, income tax expense, and amortization expense (EBITDA)}}{\text{Interest expense}}$	Measures ability to meet interest payments as they come due (cash basis).
Cash total debt coverage	$\dfrac{\text{Net cash provided by operating activities}}{\text{Average total liabilities}}$	Measures long-term debt-paying ability (cash basis).

▶Accounting in Action ▸ *e-Business Insight*

Today, investors have access to information provided by corporate managers that used to be available only to professional analysts. Corporate managers have always made themselves available to security analysts for questions at the end of every quarter. Now, because of new corporate disclosure requirements and technologies that make communication to large numbers of people possible at a very low price, the average investor can listen in on these discussions.

For example, one individual investor, Matthew Johnson, a Nortel Networks local area network engineer in Belfast, Northern Ireland, stayed up past midnight to listen to Apple Computer's recent Internet conference call. Hearing the company's news "from the dog's mouth," he says, "gave me better information than hunting through chat-rooms."

Source: Jeff D. Opdyke, "Individuals Pick Up On Conference Calls." *The Wall Street Journal*, November 20, 2000, C1.

Before You Go On . . .

▶Review It

1. What are liquidity ratios? Explain the current, acid test, cash current debt coverage, receivables turnover, and inventory turnover ratios.
2. What are profitability ratios? Explain the profit margin, gross profit margin, cash return on sales, asset turnover, return on assets, return on common shareholders' equity, book value per share, cash flow per share, earnings per share, price-earnings, payout, and dividend yield ratios.
3. What are solvency ratios? Explain the debt to total assets, interest coverage, cash interest coverage, and cash total debt coverage ratios.

▶Do It

Selected financial data for Drummond Company at December 31, 2003, are as follows: net cash provided by operating activities $315; total assets $2,350; total liabilities $1,300. Total liabilities at December 31, 2002, were $1,500. Calculate the debt to total assets and cash total debt coverage ratios.

Action Plan

- Use the formula for the debt to total assets ratio: Total debt 4 total assets.
- Use the formula for the cash total debt coverage ratio: Net cash provided by operating activities ÷ average total liabilities.

Solution

Debt to total assets = 55.3% ($1,300 ÷ $2,350)
Cash total debt coverage = 22.5% [$315 ÷ (($1,300 + $1,500) ÷ 2)]

Related exercise material: BE19–7, BE19–8, BE19–9, BE19–10, BE19–11, BE19–12, E19–5, E19–6, E19–7, E19–8, E19–9, and E19–10.

▶Limitations of Financial Analysis

STUDY OBJECTIVE

•••••••••▼•••••••••
6

Recognize and illustrate the limitations of financial statement analysis.

Significant business decisions are frequently made by using one or more of the analytical tools illustrated in this chapter. But you should be aware of the limitations of these tools and of the financial statements they are based on.

Estimates

Financial statements contain many estimates. For example, estimates are used to determine the allowance for uncollectible receivables, periodic amortization, the costs of warranties, and contingencies. To the extent that these estimates are inaccurate or biased, the financial ratios and percentages are inaccurate or biased.

Cost

Traditional financial statements are based on cost. They are not adjusted for price-level changes. Comparisons of unadjusted financial data from different periods may be invalid due to inflation or deflation. For example, a five-year comparison of Sears' revenues might show growth of 161%. But this growth trend would be misleading if the general price-level had increased or decreased significantly during the same period.

Alternative Accounting Methods

Companies vary in the generally accepted accounting principles they use. Such variations may reduce comparability. For example, one company may use the FIFO method of inventory costing. Another company in the same industry may use average. If inventory is a significant asset to both companies, it is unlikely that their current ratios are comparable.

Also, in an increasing number of industries, competition is global. To evaluate a company's standing, an investor or analyst must make comparisons to companies from other countries. However, due to the many differences in accounting practices, these comparisons can be both difficult and misleading. Although differences in accounting methods might be detectable from reading the notes to the financial statements, adjusting the financial data to compensate for the different methods is difficult, if not impossible, in some cases.

Atypical Data

Fiscal year-end data may not be typical of the financial condition during the year. Firms frequently establish a fiscal year end that coincides with the low point in operating activity or in inventory levels. Therefore, certain account balances (cash, receivables, payables, and inventories) at year end may not represent the balances in the accounts during the year.

Diversification of Firms

Diversification in Canadian industry also limits the usefulness of financial analysis. Many firms today are so diversified that they cannot be classified by industry. Bombardier, for example, operates in the rail transportation equipment, recreational product, aerospace, and financial services fields. Consequently, deciding what industry a company is in is actually one of the main challenges to an effective evaluation of its results.

Other companies may appear to be comparable but are not. McCain Foods and Irving-owned Cavendish Farms compete in the frozen potato product field. Yet McCain produces other food products besides french fries, and Irving has many other interests, including oil, newspapers, tissue products, transportation, and shipbuilding.

Helpful hint *Financial Reporting in Canada* reported that 95% of the companies it surveyed in 1999 disclosed segment information.

When companies have significant operations in different lines of business, they are required to report additional disclosures in a **segment information** note to their financial statements. Segment information includes the following: services or product lines, foreign geographic segments, and export sales. Foreign operating income, revenues, and identifiable assets are also reported. Many analysts say that segment information is the most important data in the financial statements. Without it, a comparison of diversified companies is very difficult.

▶Accounting in Action ▶ *Business Insight*

Many people would argue that non-financial performance measures are more important than financial measures in assessing success. Financial measures can evaluate only past performance. Non-financial measures may be better predictors of future performance. Non-financial performance measures include factors such as customer service, customer satisfaction, and market performance. Knowledge resources also contribute to a firm's success. These include innovation, information systems, employee satisfaction and abilities, and company and product reputation.

Before You Go On . . .
▶*Review It*

THE
NAVIGATOR

1. What are some limitations of financial analysis?
2. Give examples of alternative accounting methods that reduce comparability.
3. In what way does diversification limit the usefulness of financial statement analysis?

▶*A Look Back at Our Feature Story*

Refer to the opening story and answer the following questions:
1. What makes The Motley Fool on-line discussion boards attractive to day traders?
2. What are the dangers of using discussion boards or chat rooms for investment purposes?

Solution

1. The Motley Fool on-line discussion boards allow subscribers to exchange information and insights about companies of interest to investors and potential investors. The information sources are endless (grassroots, insiders, anyone), worldwide, and nearly costless.
2. Critics contend that discussion boards or chat rooms are nothing more than high-tech rumour mills that tend to build a speculative house of cards. Participants do not have to give their identities. Consequently, there is little to stop people from putting misinformation on-line to influence share prices in the direction they want. Much of the information is soft and stands in sharp contract to the data and ratios provided by the analysis of financial statements illustrated in this chapter.

DEMONSTRATION PROBLEM

The condensed financial statements of Mark's Work Wearhouse for the years 2001 and 2000 are presented below:

**Additional
Demonstration Problem**

MARK'S WORK WEARHOUSE LTD.
Condensed Balance Sheet
January 31
(in thousands)

	2001	2000	1999
Assets			
Current assets			
Cash and cash equivalents	$ 6,993	$ 1,774	$ 2,710
Accounts receivable	13,998	15,010	13,364
Merchandise inventories	84,483	81,468	76,982
Other current assets	4,913	3,223	3,304
	110,387	101,475	96,360
Capital assets (net)	42,620	36,969	32,244
Other assets	4,053	4,640	4,388
Total assets	$157,060	$143,084	$132,992
Liabilities and Shareholders' Equity			
Liabilities			
Current liabilities	$ 63,222	$ 57,296	$ 56,525
Long-term liabilities	29,117	26,217	23,161
Total liabilities	92,339	83,513	79,686
Shareholders' equity			
Share capital	31,228	32,715	32,696
Retained earnings	33,493	26,856	20,610
Total shareholders' equity	64,721	59,571	53,306
Total liabilities and shareholders' equity	$157,060	$143,084	$132,992

MARK'S WORK WEARHOUSE LTD.
Condensed Statement of Earnings
52 Weeks Ended January 31
(in thousands)

	2001	2000
Sales	$363,870	$314,547
Cost of sales	214,361	186,723
Gross margin	149,509	127,824
Front-line expenses	104,690	89,567
Back-line expenses	27,745	25,572
Earnings before income taxes	17,074	12,685
Income taxes	8,346	5,923
Net earnings before goodwill amortization	8,728	6,762
Goodwill amortization	548	375
Net earnings	$ 8,180	$ 6,387

Action Plan
• Remember that the current ratio includes all current assets. The acid test ratio uses only cash, temporary investments, and receivables.
• Remember that interest coverage uses EBIT as its numerator.
• Use average balances whenever an end-of-period figure (balance sheet) is compared to a period figure (income or cash flow statement).

Additional information (all numbers in thousands):
1. There are no preferred shares.
2. Interest expense was $3,978 in 2001; $4,017 in 2000.
3. Cash flow generated by operating activities in 2001 was $21,140; in 2000 it was $10,299.

Instructions

Calculate the following selected ratios for Mark's Work Wearhouse for 2001 and 2000. Comment on the results.
1. Liquidity
   (a) Current ratio
   (b) Cash current debt coverage
   (c) Inventory turnover
   (d) Days sales in inventory
2. Profitability
   (a) Profit margin
   (b) Cash return on sales
   (c) Asset turnover
3. Solvency
   (a) Debt to total assets
   (b) Interest coverage
   (c) Cash total debt coverage

Solution to Demonstration Problem

1. Liquidity
   (a) Current ratio:
      2001: $110,387 ÷ $63,222 = 1.7:1
      2000: $101,475 ÷ $57,296 = 1.8:1

   (b) Cash current debt coverage:
      2001: $21,140 ÷ [($63,222 + $57,296) ÷ 2] = 0.4 times
      2000: $10,299 ÷ [($57,296 + $56,525) ÷ 2] = 0.2 times

   (c) Inventory turnover:
      2001: $214,361 ÷ [($84,483 + $81,468) ÷ 2] = 2.6 times
      2000: $186,723 ÷ [($81,468 + $76,982) ÷ 2] = 2.4 times

   (d) Days sales in inventory:
      2001: 365 ÷ 2.6 = 140 days
      2000: 365 ÷ 2.4 = 152 days

Mark's Work Wearhouse's current ratio declined marginally in 2001. However, its inventory turnover improved, as did its cash current debt coverage ratio. A quick calculation of the receivables turnover shows improvement in that area as well, so Mark's should have no worries about the slight decline in its current ratio. This decline apparently relates only to an increase in other current assets, such as prepaids and the like.

2. Profitability
   (a) Profit margin:
      2001: $8,180 ÷ $363,870 = 2.2%
      2000: $6,387 ÷ $314,547 = 2.0%

   (b) Cash return on sales:
      2001: $21,140 ÷ $363,870 = 5.8%
      2000: $10,299 ÷ $314,547 = 3.3%

   (c) Asset turnover:
      2001: $363,870 ÷ [($157,060 + $143,084) ÷ 2] = 2.4 times
      2000: $314,547 ÷ [($143,084 + $132,992) ÷ 2] = 2.3 times

Mark's Work Wearhouse's profit margin and asset turnover improved slightly in 2001. Its cash return on sales improved at an even greater rate. Mark's appears to have no concerns with regard to its profitability.

3. Solvency
 (a) Debt to total assets:
  2001: $92,339 ÷ $157,060 = 58.8%
  2000: $83,513 ÷ $143,084 = 58.4%
 (b) Interest coverage:
  2001: ($8,180 + $8,346 + $3,978) ÷ $3,978 = 5.2 times
  2000: ($6,387 + $5,923 + $4,017) ÷ $4,017 = 4.1 times
 (c) Cash total debt coverage:
  2001: $21,140 ÷ [($92,339 + $83,513) ÷ 2] = 0.2 times
  2000: $10,299 ÷ [($83,513 + $79,686) ÷ 2] = 0.1 times

Mark's Work Wearhouse's proportion of debt financed by creditors rose marginally (to 58.8% from 58.4%) in 2001. However, its ability to pay interest improved, as did its cash coverage of its debt.

THE
NAVIGATOR

Summary of Study Objectives

1. Discuss the need for comparative analysis. There are three bases of comparison: (1) intracompany, which compares an item or financial relationship to other data within a company; (2) intercompany, which compares an item or financial relationship of a company to data of one or more competing companies; (3) industry, which compares company data to industry averages.

2. Discuss the tools of financial statement analysis. Financial statements may be analysed horizontally, vertically, and with ratios.

3. Explain and apply horizontal analysis. Horizontal analysis is a technique for evaluating a series of data over a period of time. The increase or decrease that has taken place is determined, and expressed as either an amount or a percentage.

4. Explain and apply vertical analysis. Vertical analysis is a technique for expressing each item within a financial statement as a percentage of a relevant total (base amount).

5. Identify and calculate ratios and describe their purpose and use in analysing a firm's liquidity, profitability, and solvency. The formula and purpose of each ratio are presented in Illustration 19-33.

6. Recognize and illustrate the limitations of financial statement analysis. The usefulness of analytical tools is limited by the use of estimates, the cost basis of accounting, the application of alternative accounting methods, atypical data at year end, and the diversification of firms.

THE
NAVIGATOR

GLOSSARY

 Key Term Matching Activity

Acid test (quick) ratio   A measure of a company's immediate short-term liquidity. It is calculated by dividing the sum of cash, temporary investments, and (net) receivables by current liabilities. (p. 900)

Asset turnover   A measure of how efficiently a company uses its assets to generate sales. It is calculated by dividing net sales by average total assets. (p. 906)

Book value per share   The equity a common shareholder has in the net assets of the corporation from owning one share. It is calculated by dividing shareholders' equity by the number of common shares. (p. 908)

Cash current debt coverage   A cash basis measure of short-term debt-paying ability. It is calculated by dividing net cash provided by operating activities by average current liabilities. (p. 901)

Cash flow per share   The cash flow produced by each common share. It is calculated by dividing net cash provided by operating, investing, and financing activities by the number of common shares. (p. 908)

Cash interest coverage   A cash-based measure of a company's ability to meet interest payments as they come due. It is calculated by dividing income before interest expense, income tax expense, and amortization expense (EBITDA) by interest expense. (p. 913)

Cash return on sales   A measure of the cash generated by every dollar of sales. It is calculated by dividing net cash provided by operating activities by net sales. (p. 905)

Cash total debt coverage   A cash-based measure of total debt-paying ability. It is calculated by dividing net cash provided by operating activities by average total liabilities. (p. 914)

Collection period   The result of 365 days divided by the receivables turnover. Determines the average number of days that receivables are outstanding. (p. 903)

Current ratio   A measure of a company's liquidity and short-term debt-paying ability. It is calculated by dividing current assets by current liabilities. (p. 899)

Days sales in inventory   The number of days that merchandise inventory is on hand, calculated by dividing 365 days by the inventory turnover ratio. (p. 903)

Debt to total assets   A measure of the percentage of total assets provided by creditors. It is calculated by dividing total debt by total assets. (p. 912)

Dividend yield   A measure of the rate of return a shareholder earned from dividends during the year. It is calculated by dividing cash dividends per share by the share price. (p. 911)

Earnings per share (EPS)   The net income earned by each common share. It is calculated by dividing net income by the number of common shares. (p. 909)

Gross profit margin   Measures the gross profit (net sales less cost of goods sold) earned for each dollar of sales. It is calculated by dividing gross profit by net sales. (p. 905)

Horizontal analysis   A technique for evaluating a series of financial statement data over a period of time to determine the increase (decrease) that has taken place. This increase (decrease) is expressed as either an amount or a percentage. (p. 892)

Interest coverage   A measure of a company's ability to meet interest payments as they come due. It is calculated by dividing income before interest expense and income tax expense (EBIT) by interest expense. (p. 913)

Inventory turnover   A measure of the liquidity of inventory. It is calculated by dividing cost of goods sold by average inventory. (p. 903)

Leverage   See trading on the equity. (p. 907)

Liquidity ratios   Measures of the short-term ability of the enterprise to pay its maturing obligations and to meet unexpected needs for cash. (p. 899)

Payout ratio   A measure of the percentage of earnings distributed as cash dividends. It is calculated by dividing cash dividends by net income. (p. 911)

Price-earnings (PE) ratio   The ratio of the market price of each common share to the earnings per share. It is calculated by dividing the share price by earnings per share. (p. 910)

Profit margin   A measure of the percentage of each dollar of sales that results in net income. It is calculated by dividing net income by net sales. (p. 904)

Profitability ratios   Measures of the income or operating success of an enterprise for a specific period of time. (p. 904)

Ratio analysis   A technique for evaluating financial statements that expresses the relationship between selected financial statement data. (p. 898)

Receivables turnover—A measure of the liquidity of receivables. It is calculated by dividing net credit sales by average net receivables. (p. 902)

Return on assets   An overall measure of profitability. It is calculated by dividing net income by average total assets. (p. 906)

Return on common shareholders' equity   A measure of the dollars of net income earned for each dollar invested by the owners. It is calculated by dividing net income by average common shareholders' equity. (p. 907)

Solvency ratios   Measures of the ability of the enterprise to survive over a long period of time. (p. 912)

Trading on the equity (leverage)   Borrowing money at a lower rate of interest than can be earned by using the borrowed money. (p. 907)

Vertical analysis   A technique for evaluating financial statement data that expresses each item within a financial statement as a percentage of a base amount. (p. 895)

SELF-STUDY QUESTIONS

Chapter 19 Self-Test

Answers are at the end of the chapter.

(SO 1) K
1. Comparisons of data within a company are an example of the following comparative basis:
   a. Industry averages
   b. Intracompany
   c. Intercompany
   d. Both (b) and (c)

(SO 3) K
2. In horizontal analysis, each item is expressed as a percentage of the:
   a. net sales amount.
   b. shareholders' equity amount.
   c. total assets amount.
   d. base year amount.

(SO 3) AP
3. Rankin Inlet Corporation reported net sales of $300,000, $330,000, and $360,000 in the years 2001, 2002, and 2003, respectively. If 2001 is the base year, what is the trend percentage for 2003?
   a. 77%
   b. 108%
   c. 120%
   d. 130%

(SO 4) K
4. In vertical analysis, the base amount for amortization expense is generally:
   a. net sales.
   b. amortization expense in a previous year.
   c. gross profit.
   d. net income.

(SO 4) K
5. The following schedule is a display of what type of analysis?

	Amount	Percentage
Current assets	$200,000	25%
Capital assets	600,000	75%
Total assets	$800,000	100%

   a. Horizontal analysis
   b. Differential analysis
   c. Vertical analysis
   d. Ratio analysis

(SO 5) K
6. Which of the following measures is an evaluation of a firm's ability to pay current liabilities?
   a. Debt to total assets
   b. Current ratio
   c. Cash interest coverage
   d. None of the above

(SO 5) K
7. A measure that is useful for evaluating the efficiency in managing inventories is:
   a. inventory turnover.
   b. days sales in inventory.
   c. Both (a) and (b)
   d. None of the above

(SO 5) K
8. Which of the following is not a liquidity ratio?
   a. Current ratio
   b. Asset turnover
   c. Inventory turnover
   d. Receivables turnover

(SO 5) AP
9. Dion Corporation reported net income of $24,000, net sales of $400,000, and average assets of $600,000 for 2003. The 2003 profit margin was:
   a. 6%.
   b. 12%.
   c. 40%.
   d. 200%.

(SO 6) K
10. Which of the following is generally not considered to be a limitation of financial analysis?
   a. Use of estimates
   b. Use of ratio analysis
   c. Use of cost
   d. Use of alternative accounting methods

THE NAVIGATOR

QUESTIONS

(SO 1) C
1. (a) Kim Sung believes that the analysis of financial statements is directed at two characteristics of a company: liquidity and profitability. Is Kim correct? Explain.
   (b) Are short-term creditors, long-term creditors, and shareholders mainly interested in the same company ratios? Explain.

(SO 1) C
2. Distinguish among the following bases of comparison: (1) intracompany, (2) intercompany, and (3) industry averages.

(SO 3, 4) C
3. Two popular methods of financial statement analysis are horizontal analysis and vertical analysis. Explain the difference between these two methods.

(SO 3, 4) AP
4. (a) If Liong Company had net income of $480,000 in 2002 and it experienced a 24.5% increase in net income for 2003, what is its net income for 2003?

   (b) If six cents of every dollar of Liong's revenue is net income in 2002, what is the dollar amount of 2002 revenue?

(SO 5) C
5. What is a ratio? What are the different ways of expressing the relationship of two amounts? What information does a ratio provide?

(SO 5) K
6. What do the following classes of ratios measure: (a) liquidity ratios, (b) profitability ratios, and (c) solvency ratios?

(SO 5) C
7. What is the difference between the current and acid test ratios? The interest coverage and cash interest coverage ratios?

(SO 5) C
8. Seneca Company, a retail store, has a receivables turnover of 4.5 times. The industry average is 12.5 times. Does Seneca have a collection problem with its receivables?

(SO 5) C   9. Loren Foelske is puzzled. His company had a gross profit margin of 40% and a profit margin of 10% in 2003. He feels that this is an indication that the company is doing well. Joan Graham, his accountant, says that more information is needed to determine the firm's financial well-being. Who is correct? Why?

(SO 5) C   10. Recently, the price-earnings ratio of **Future Shop Ltd.** was 9.2. The price-earnings ratio of **Staples Inc.** was 22.4. Which company did investors favour? Explain.

(SO 5) C   11. Which ratios should be used to help answer the following questions?
(a) Is the company efficient at using its assets to produce sales?
(b) How near to sale is the inventory on hand?
(c) How many dollars of net income were earned for each dollar invested by the owners?
(d) Is the company able to meet interest charges as they come due?

(SO 5) K   12. What ratios are dependent on cash-based data? That is, what ratios use data from the cash flow statement?

(SO 5) C   13. What is the formula for calculating the payout ratio? The dividend yield? Would you expect these ratios to be high or low for a growth company?

(SO 5) C   14. With all other factors constant, indicate whether each of the following changes generally signals good or bad news about a company:
(a) Increase in profit margin
(b) Decrease in inventory turnover
(c) Increase in current ratio
(d) Decrease in earnings per share
(e) Increase in price-earnings ratio
(f) Increase in debt to total assets ratio
(g) Decrease in interest coverage
(h) Increase in cash return on sales

(SO 5) C   15. The return on total assets for Windsor Corporation is 7.6%. During the same year, Windsor's return on shareholders' equity is 12.8%. What is the explanation for the difference in the two ratios?

(SO 5) C   16. Which two ratios do you think should be of greatest interest to:
(a) a pension fund considering the purchase of 20-year bonds?
(b) a bank contemplating a short-term loan?
(c) a common shareholder?

(SO 5) C   17. (a) What is meant by trading on the equity?
(b) How would you determine the profitability of trading on the equity?

(SO 5) AP   18. (a) Nanaimo Inc. has net income of $270,000 and 50,000 common shares. What is Nanaimo's earnings per share?
(b) The market price of Nanaimo's common shares is $108 per share. What is the company's price-earnings ratio?
(c) Phil Remmers, the president of Nanaimo Inc., believes the price-earnings ratio of the company is high. Is a high PE ratio always a good sign?

(SO 5) C   19. Identify and briefly explain the limitations of financial analysis.

(SO 6) AN   20. Unlike most retailers, whose fiscal year ends a month into the following year, Sears' year end is December 31.
(a) What effect does Sears' nonstandard year end (for a retailer) have on the comparability of Sears' ratios to those of other large retailers?
(b) What effect does Sears' year end have on the inventory turnover and receivables turnover ratios?

(SO 6) AP   21. Explain how the choice of one of the following accounting principles over the other raises or lowers a company's net income during a period of continuing inflation (rising prices):
(a) Use of FIFO instead of average for inventory costing
(b) Use of a three-year life for machinery instead of a five-year life
(c) Use of straight-line amortization instead of declining-balance amortization

BRIEF EXERCISES

Calculate percentage change.
(SO 3) AP

BE19–1   Net income was $500,000 in 2001, $400,000 in 2002, and $504,000 in 2003. What is the percentage change from (1) 2001 to 2002, (2) 2002 to 2003, and (3) 2001 to 2003? Is the change an increase or a decrease?

Prepare horizontal analysis.
(SO 3) AP

BE19–2   Using the following data from the comparative balance sheet of Yanthe Company, prepare a horizontal analysis:

	December 31, 2003	December 31, 2002
Accounts receivable	$520,000	$400,000
Inventory	840,000	600,000
Total assets	3,500,000	2,800,000

Use horizontal analysis to calculate net income.
(SO 3) AP

BE19–3   Cavalier Company had net income of $700,000 in 2003. It experienced a 25% increase in net income over 2002. What was its 2002 net income?

BE19–4 Horizontal analysis percentages for Cho Company's sales, cost of goods sold, and operating expenses are shown below:

Use horizontal analysis to determine change in net income.
(SO 3) AP

Horizontal Analysis	2003	2002	2001
Sales	96.2%	106.8%	100.0%
Cost of goods sold	102.0	97.0	100.0
Operating expenses	110.6	95.4	100.0

Did Cho's net income increase, decrease, or remain unchanged over the three-year period?

BE19–5 Using the same data presented earlier in BE19–2 for Yanthe Company, prepare a vertical analysis.

Prepare vertical analysis.
(SO 4) AP

BE19–6 Vertical analysis percentages for Waubons Company's sales, cost of goods sold, and operating expenses are shown below:

Use vertical analysis to determine change in net income.
(SO 4) AP

Vertical Analysis	2003	2002	2001
Sales	100.0%	100.0%	100.0%
Cost of goods sold	58.2	62.4	64.5
Operating expenses	25.0	26.6	28.5

Did Waubons' net income as a percentage of sales increase, decrease, or remain unchanged over the three-year period? Use numbers to support your answer.

BE19–7 **The Arctic Group Inc.**, based in Manitoba, operates in the packaged ice industry. From a recent balance sheet, selected condensed financial data are shown below:

Calculate liquidity ratios.
(SO 5) AP

THE ARCTIC GROUP INC.
Balance Sheet (partial)
December 31, 2000
(in thousands)

Current assets	
Cash and cash equivalents	$ 2,214
Accounts receivable	8,377
Inventories	3,126
Prepaid expenses	1,569
Total current assets	15,286
Total current liabilities	16,626

What are (a) working capital, (b) the current ratio, and (b) the acid test ratio?

BE19–8 The following data are taken from the quarterly report of Maple Leaf Foods Inc.:

Evaluate management of accounts receivable.
(SO 5) AP

MAPLE LEAF FOODS INC.
September 30
(in thousands)

	2000	1999	1998
Accounts receivable	$ 241,527	$ 209,890	$ 205,641
Sales (assume on account)	2,874,808	2,631,748	2,398,635

Calculate, for each of 2000 and 1999, (a) the receivables turnover and (b) the collection period. Assume terms for all sales are n/45. What conclusion about the management of accounts receivable can be drawn from these data?

BE19–9 The following data are taken from the income statements of Clearwater Company:

Evaluate management of inventory.
(SO 5) AN

	2003	2002
Sales	$6,420,000	$6,240,000
Beginning inventory	980,000	837,000
Purchases	4,640,000	4,661,000
Ending inventory	1,020,000	980,000

Calculate for each year (a) the inventory turnover, and (b) the days sales in inventory. What conclusion concerning the management of the inventory can be drawn from these data?

BE19–10 Staples, Inc. is a large supplier of office products in Canada, the U.S., the UK, Germany, the Netherlands, and Portugal. The company had net income of $315.0 million and net revenue of $8,936.8 million in 2000. Its total assets were $3,179.3 million at the beginning of the year and $3,846.1 million at the end of the year. What are Staples, Inc.'s (a) asset turnover ratio and (b) profit margin ratio?

Calculate profitability ratios.
(SO 5) AP

Use profitability ratios to calcu-late amounts.
(SO 5) AP

BE19–11   La Pointe Products Company has shareholders' equity of $200,000 and net income of $50,000. It has a payout ratio of 10% and a rate of return on assets of 6%. How much did La Pointe Products pay in cash dividends? What were its average assets?

Calculate cash-based liquidity, profitability, and solvency ratios.
(SO 5) AP

BE19–12   Topps Company, Inc. is a trading-card company, whose products (including Star Wars and Pokémon cards) are sold in more than 50 countries. Selected data taken from the 2000 financial statements are as follows (US$ in millions):

Net sales	$374.2
Current liabilities, February 27, 1999	68.6
Current liabilities, February 26, 2000	86.2
Net cash provided by operating activities	58.9
Total liabilities, February 27, 1999	86.8
Total liabilities, February 26, 2000	97.8

Calculate these ratios at February 26, 2000: (a) cash current debt coverage, (b) cash return on sales, and (c) cash total debt coverage.

EXERCISES

Prepare horizontal analysis.
(SO 3) AP

E19–1   Financial information for Dressaire Inc. is presented below:

	December 31, 2003	December 31, 2002
Current assets	$125,000	$100,000
Capital assets (net)	400,000	330,000
Current liabilities	91,000	70,000
Long-term liabilities	144,000	95,000
Common shares	155,000	115,000
Retained earnings	135,000	150,000

Instructions
Prepare a schedule showing a horizontal analysis for 2003, using 2002 as the base year.

Prepare vertical analysis.
(SO 4) AP

E19–2   Operating data for Gear.com Corporation are presented below:

	2003	2002
Sales	$800,000	$600,000
Cost of goods sold	464,000	378,000
Selling expenses	120,000	72,000
Administrative expenses	80,000	54,000
Income tax expense	38,400	25,200
Net income	97,600	70,800

Instructions
Prepare a schedule showing a vertical analysis for the years ended December 31, 2003 and 2002.

Prepare horizontal and vertical analyses.
(SO 3, 4) AP

E19–3   The comparative balance sheet of Kouri Corporation is presented below:

KOURI CORPORATION
Balance Sheet
December 31

	2003	2002
Assets		
Current assets	$ 76,000	$ 80,000
Capital assets (net)	124,000	130,000
Total assets	$200,000	$210,000
Liabilities and Shareholders' Equity		
Current liabilities	$ 45,800	$ 48,000
Long-term liabilities	138,000	150,000
Shareholders' equity	16,200	12,000
Total liabilities and shareholders' equity	$200,000	$210,000

Instructions

(a) Prepare a horizontal analysis of the balance sheet data for Kouri Corporation using 2002 as the base year. (Show the amount of increase or decrease as well.)

(b) Prepare a vertical analysis of the balance sheet data for Kouri Corporation for 2003.

E19–4 The condensed comparative balance sheet of **Mountain Equipment Co-operative**, an outdoor equipment supplier, is presented here:

Prepare horizontal and vertical analyses.
(SO 3, 4) AP

MOUNTAIN EQUIPMENT CO-OPERATIVE
Balance Sheet
December 31
(in thousands)

	2000	1999
Assets		
Current assets	$31,117	$30,656
Investment and advances	233	288
Capital assets	37,123	29,215
Total assets	$68,473	$60,159
Liabilities and Members' Equity		
Current liabilities	$12,096	$10,567
Long-term liabilities	6,069	6,329
Total liabilities	18,165	16,896
Members' equity	50,308	43,263
Total liabilities and members' equity	$68,473	$60,159

Instructions

(a) Prepare a horizontal analysis of the balance sheet for Mountain Equipment Co-op using 1999 as the base year. Show the amount of increase or decrease as well.

(b) Prepare a vertical analysis of the balance sheet data for Mountain Equipment Co-op for 2000 and 1999, using total assets as the base amount.

(c) Comment on any significant trends.

E19–5 Nordstar, Inc., operates department stores in several provinces. Selected financial statement data for a recent year are as follows:

Calculate liquidity ratios and compare results.
(SO 5) AN

NORDSTAR, INC.
Balance Sheet (partial)
December 31
(in millions)

	End of Year	Beginning of Year
Cash and cash equivalents	$ 33	$ 91
Receivables (net)	676	586
Merchandise inventory	628	586
Prepaid expenses	61	52
Total current assets	$1,398	$1,315
Total current liabilities	$ 690	$ 627

For the year, net sales were $3,894 million and cost of goods sold was $2,600 million. The net cash provided by operating activities during the year was $500 million.

Instructions

(a) Calculate the liquidity ratios at the end of the current year.

(b) Using the data in the chapter, compare Nordstar's liquidity to the liquidity of (1) Sears Canada Inc., and (2) the industry averages for the retail industry.

*Determine effects of transactions
on current and acid test ratios.*
(SO 5) AP

E19–6 Warrakah Incorporated had the following transactions, involving current assets and current liabilities, during February 2003:

Feb. 3 Accounts receivable of $15,000 are collected.
  7 Equipment is purchased for $25,000 cash.
 11 The amount of $3,000 is paid for a one-year insurance policy.
 14 Accounts payable of $12,000 are paid.
 18 Cash dividends of $6,000 are declared.

Additional information:

As at February 1, 2003, current assets were $120,000 and current liabilities were $50,000. Current assets included $15,000 of inventory and $5,000 of prepaid expenses.

Instructions

(a) Calculate the current ratio at the beginning of the month and after each transaction.
(b) Calculate the acid test ratio at the beginning of the month and after each transaction.

Calculate selected ratios.
(SO 5) AP

E19–7 Mwanaki Company has the following comparative balance sheet data at December 31:

MWANAKI COMPANY.
Balance Sheet
December 31

	2003	2002
Assets		
Cash	$ 15,000	$ 30,000
Receivables (net)	65,000	60,000
Inventories	60,000	50,000
Capital assets (net)	205,000	180,000
	$345,000	$320,000
Liabilities and Shareholders' Equity		
Accounts payable	$ 50,000	$ 60,000
Mortgage payable	100,000	100,000
Common shares	140,000	120,000
Retained earnings	55,000	40,000
	$345,000	$320,000

Additional information for 2003:

1. Net income was $25,000.
2. Sales on account were $420,000. Sales returns and allowances were $20,000.
3. Cost of goods sold was $198,000.
4. Net cash provided by operating activities was $33,000.

Instructions

Calculate the following ratios at December 31, 2003:

(a) Current
(b) Acid test
(c) Receivables turnover
(d) Inventory turnover
(e) Cash return on sales
(f) Cash total debt coverage
(g) Debt to total assets
(h) Asset turnover

Calculate selected ratios.
(SO 5) AN

E19–8 Selected comparative financial data of Canada's #1 bookseller, **Chapters Inc.**, before it was acquired by Indigo Books, are presented here (in thousands):

	March 31		
	2000	1999	1998
Revenue	$660,309	$577,880	$456,611
Interest expense	6,117	3,785	2,627
Income tax expense (recovery)	(7,619)	9,202	
Net income	17,195	10,301	8,420
Accounts receivable	15,224	7,636	6,117
Inventories	269,316	224,606	142,103
Total assets	495,310	345,485	219,410
Total common shareholders' equity	165,173	115,222	104,433
Cash provided (used) by operating activities	(43,551)	6,265	16,815

Instructions

(a) Calculate the following ratios for 2000 and 1999:
  1. Profit margin
  2. Asset turnover
  3. Return on assets
  4. Return on common shareholders' equity
  5. Cash return on sales
  6. Interest coverage

(b) Indicate whether each ratio improved or deteriorated in 2000.

E19–9 The income statement for the year ended December 31, 2003, of LeFay, Inc., appears below: *Calculate selected ratios.* (SO 5) AP

LEFAY INC.
Income Statement
For the Year Ended December 31, 2003

Sales	$400,000
Cost of goods sold	230,000
Gross profit	170,000
Expenses (including $15,000 amortization, $20,000 interest, and $24,000 income tax)	100,000
Net income	$ 70,000

Additional information:
1. Number of common shares, 40,000.
2. The market price of LeFay, Inc., shares was $15 at the end of 2003.
3. Cash dividends of $21,000 were paid.
4. Net cash provided by operating activities was $98,000.

Instructions

Calculate the following ratios for 2003:
(a) Earnings per share
(b) Price-earnings
(c) Payout
(d) Dividend yield
(e) Interest coverage
(f) Cash interest coverage
(g) Cash return on sales
(h) Gross profit margin

E19–10 Cougar Corporation experienced a fire on December 31, 2003, in which its financial records were partially destroyed. It salvaged some of the records and has figured out the following balances as at December 31: *Calculate amounts from ratios.* (SO 5) AP

	2003	2002
Cash	$ 30,000	$ 10,000
Receivables (net)	72,500	126,000
Inventory	200,000	180,000
Accounts payable	50,000	90,000
Notes payable	30,000	60,000
Common shares	400,000	400,000
Retained earnings	115,000	101,000

Additional information:
1. The inventory turnover is 3.8 times.
2. The return on common shareholders' equity is 22%. The company only has one class of shares.
3. The receivables turnover is 8.4 times.
4. The return on assets is 20%.
5. Total assets at December 31, 2002, were $605,000.

Instructions

Calculate the following for Cougar Corporation:
(a) Cost of goods sold for 2003
(b) Net sales for 2003
(c) Net income for 2003
(d) Total assets at December 31, 2003

PROBLEMS: SET A

••

Prepare vertical analysis, calculate profitability ratios, and comment on profitability.
(SO 4, 5) AN

P19–1A Comparative statement data for Chen Company and Couric Company, two competitors, appear below. All balance sheet data are as at December 31.

	Chen Company		Couric Company	
	2003	2002	2003	2002
Net sales	$1,549,035		$339,038	
Cost of goods sold	1,080,490		238,006	
Operating expenses	292,275		79,000	
Interest expense	6,800		2,252	
Income tax expense	41,230		6,650	
Current assets	325,975	$312,410	83,336	$ 79,467
Capital assets (net)	521,310	500,000	139,728	125,812
Current liabilities	66,325	75,815	35,348	30,281
Long-term liabilities	108,500	90,000	29,620	25,000
Common shares	500,000	500,000	120,000	120,000
Retained earnings	172,460	146,595	38,096	29,998

Instructions

(a) Prepare a vertical analysis of the 2003 income statement data for Chen Company and Couric Company.

(b) Calculate the gross profit margin, profit margin, return on assets, asset turnover, and return on common shareholders' equity ratios for both companies.

(c) Comment on the relative profitability of the companies.

Calculate ratios.
(SO 5) AP

P19–2A The comparative statements of Westphal Tool Company are presented below.

WESTPHAL TOOL COMPANY
Income Statement
For the Year Ended December 31

	2003	2002
Net sales (all on account)	$1,818,500	$1,750,500
Cost of goods sold	1,005,500	996,000
Gross profit	813,000	754,500
Selling and administrative expense (including $60,000 and $50,000, respectively, of amortization expense)	506,000	479,000
Income from operations	307,000	275,500
Interest expense	27,000	19,000
Income before income tax	280,000	256,500
Income tax expense	84,000	77,000
Net income	$ 196,000	$ 179,500

WESTPHAL TOOL COMPANY
Balance Sheet
December 31

Assets	2003	2002
Current assets		
Cash	$ 60,100	$ 64,200
Temporary investments	54,000	50,000
Accounts receivable (net)	107,800	102,800
Inventory	123,000	115,500
Total current assets	344,900	332,500
Capital assets (net)	625,300	520,300
Total assets	$970,200	$852,800
Liabilities and Shareholders' Equity		
Current liabilities		
Accounts payable	$160,000	$145,400
Income tax payable	43,500	42,000
Total current liabilities	203,500	187,400
Bonds payable	200,000	200,000
Total liabilities	403,500	387,400
Shareholders' equity		
Common shares	280,000	300,000
Retained earnings	286,700	165,400
Total shareholders' equity	566,700	465,400
Total liabilities and shareholders' equity	$970,200	$852,800

There were 60,000 common shares on December 31, 2003. Net cash provided by operating activities for 2003 was $270,000.

Instructions

Calculate the following ratios for 2003:

(a) Current ratio
(b) Acid test ratio
(c) Cash current debt coverage
(d) Receivables turnover
(e) Inventory turnover
(f) Cash return on sales
(g) Asset turnover

(h) Return on assets
(i) Return on common shareholders' equity
(j) Earnings per share
(k) Debt to total assets
(l) Interest coverage
(m) Cash interest coverage
(n) Cash total debt coverage

P19–3A Condensed balance sheet and income statement data for Pitka Corporation appear below:

Perform ratio analysis and evaluate financial position and operating results.
(SO 5) AN

PITKA CORPORATION
Balance Sheet
December 31

Assets	2003	2002	2001
Cash	$ 25,000	$ 20,000	$ 18,000
Receivables (net)	50,000	45,000	48,000
Merchandise inventory	90,000	85,000	64,000
Investments	75,000	70,000	45,000
Capital assets (net)	400,000	370,000	358,000
	$640,000	$590,000	$533,000
Liabilities and Shareholders' Equity			
Current liabilities	$ 75,000	$ 80,000	$ 70,000
Long-term debt	80,000	85,000	50,000
Common shares	340,000	300,000	300,000
Retained earnings	145,000	125,000	113,000
	$640,000	$590,000	$533,000

PITKA CORPORATION
Income Statement
For the Year Ended December 31

	2003	2002
Sales	$740,000	$700,000
Less: Sales returns and allowances	40,000	50,000
Net sales	700,000	650,000
Cost of goods sold	420,000	400,000
Gross profit	280,000	250,000
Operating expenses (including income tax)	230,000	215,000
Net income	$ 50,000	$ 35,000

Additional information:
1. All sales were on account.
2. All dividends were paid in cash.
3. Net cash flow from all activities was $5,000 in 2003 and $2,000 in 2002.
4. There were 30,000 common shares throughout 2001 and 2002. On January 1, 2003, 4,000 common shares were issued.
5. The market prices of Pitka's common shares were $4.00, $5.00, and $7.95 for 2001, 2002, and 2003, respectively.

Instructions

(a) Calculate the following ratios for 2002 and 2003:

1. Receivables turnover	8. Cash flow per share
2. Inventory turnover	9. Earnings per share
3. Profit margin	10. Price-earnings
4. Gross profit margin	11. Payout ratio
5. Asset turnover	12. Dividend yield
6. Return on assets	13. Debt to total assets
7. Book value per share	

(b) Based on the ratios calculated, briefly discuss the changes in financial position and operating results of Pitka Corporation from 2002 to 2003.

Calculate ratios and effects of selected transactions.
(SO 5) AN

P19–4A   Financial information for Insider.com Company is presented below:

INSIDER.COM COMPANY
Balance Sheet
December 31

Assets	2003	2002
Cash	$ 60,000	$ 55,000
Temporary investments	45,000	40,000
Receivables (net)	94,000	90,000
Inventories	130,000	125,000
Prepaid expenses	25,000	23,000
Land	140,000	140,000
Building and equipment (net)	190,000	175,000
	$684,000	$648,000
Liabilities and Shareholders' Equity		
Notes payable	$100,000	$100,000
Accounts payable	45,000	42,000
Accrued liabilities	40,000	40,000
Bonds payable, due 2009	150,000	150,000
Common shares (20,000 shares)	200,000	200,000
Retained earnings	149,000	116,000
	$684,000	$648,000

INSIDER.COM COMPANY
Income Statement
For the Year Ended December 31

	2003	2002
Sales	$850,000	$790,000
Cost of goods sold	610,000	570,000
Gross profit	240,000	220,000
Operating expenses	194,000	180,000
Net income	$ 46,000	$ 40,000

Additional information:

1. All sales were on account.
3. Inventory at the beginning of 2002 was $115,000.
2. Receivables at the beginning of 2002 were $88,000.
4. Total assets at the beginning of 2002 were $630,000.

Instructions

(a) Indicate, by using ratios, the change in liquidity and profitability of Insider.com Company from 2002 to 2003. (*Note*: Not all ratios can be calculated.)

(b) Below, there are three *independent* situations and a ratio that may be affected. For each situation, calculate the affected ratio (1) as at December 31, 2003, and (2) as at December 31, 2004. Net income for 2004 was $48,000. Total assets on December 31, 2004, were $700,000.

Situation	Ratio
1. 18,000 common shares were issued at $10 each on January 1, 2004.	Return on common shareholders' equity
2. All of the notes payable were paid in 2004.	Debt to total assets
3. The market prices of the common shares were $9.00 and $12.80 on December 31, 2003 and 2004, respectively.	Price-earnings

P19–5A Future Shop sells computers, office equipment, and other electronic products in more than 90 stores throughout Canada. **InterTan** owns 1,500 Radio Shack and Tandy stores in Canada, Australia, and the UK. Selected financial data of these two close competitors are presented here (in millions) for a recent year:

Calculate selected ratios and compare liquidity, profitability, and solvency for two companies. (SO 5) AN

	FUTURE SHOP LTD.	INTERTAN, INC.
	Income Statement Data for Year	
Sales	$1,960.3	$500.1
Cost of sales	1,546.7	280.9
Gross profit	413.6	219.2
Selling, general, administrative, and other expenses	432.5	180.7
Interest expense	0	3.3
Unusual item	83.8	35.1
Total expenses	516.3	219.1
Income (loss) before income tax	(102.7)	0.1
Income tax recovery (expense)	20.5	(24.7)
Net income (loss)	$ (82.2)	$ (24.6)
	Balance Sheet Data (End of Year)	
Current assets	$ 221.3	$174.0
Capital and other assets	117.2	24.3
Total assets	$ 338.5	$198.3
Current liabilities	$ 253.9	$ 77.0
Long-term liabilities	28.3	10.5
Total liabilities	282.2	87.5
Shareholders' equity	56.3	110.8
Total liabilities and shareholders' equity	$ 338.5	$198.3

	Other Data	
Average net receivables	$ 20.1	$ 9.1
Average inventories	207.4	130.1
Average total assets	389.9	210.9
Average total shareholders' equity	73.1	98.4
Net cash provided (used) by operating activities	(49.2)	25.9

The unusual items related to the closure of Future Shop's U.S. operations and InterTan's UK operations.

Instructions

(a) For each company, calculate the following ratios. Industry averages are provided in parentheses following each ratio, where available.

1. Current (1.58:1)
2. Receivables turnover (28.13)
3. Collection period (13 days)
4. Inventory turnover (4.93)
5. Days sales in inventory (74 days)
6. Profit margin (1.5%)
7. Gross profit margin (27.3%)
8. Asset turnover (3.23)
9. Return on assets (4.7%)
10. Return on common shareholders' equity (11.5%)
11. Debt to total assets (61%)
12. Interest coverage (6.93)
13. Cash current debt coverage (n/a)
14. Cash return on sales (n/a)
15. Cash total debt coverage (n/a)

(b) Compare the liquidity, solvency, and profitability of the two companies.

Evaluate impact of transactions on ratios.
(SO 5) AN

P19–6A   Mahat Corporation started the year with the following ratios:

Current ratio	1.5:1
Cash current debt coverage	40%
Debt to total assets	30%
Return on assets	20%

Instructions

Determine the effect each of the following independent transactions has on these ratios. Indicate whether the transaction would cause each ratio to improve (I), deteriorate (D), or if there would be no effect (NE).

(a) Mahat purchased merchandise inventory on account from a supplier. Mahat uses a perpetual inventory system.
(b) The company paid an account payable.
(c) Mahat sold merchandise on account to a customer.
(d) A customer paid an account receivable.
(e) Mahat purchased capital assets, issuing a long-term note payable in payment.
(f) Mahat paid interest expense and a portion of the principal due on the note payable.

Use ratios to calculate missing data.
(SO 5) AN

P19–7A   Presented below is an incomplete income statement and an incomplete comparative balance sheet of Resolute Corporation:

RESOLUTE CORPORATION
Income Statement
For the Year Ended December 31, 2003

Sales	$	(a)
Cost of goods sold		6,960,000
Gross profit		(b)
Operating expenses		1,665,000
Income from operations		(c)
Interest expense		(d)
Income before income tax		(e)
Income tax expense		580,000
Net income	$	(f)

RESOLUTE CORPORATION
Balance Sheet
December 31

Assets	2003	2002
Current assets		
Cash	$ (g)	$ 375,000
Accounts receivable (net)	1,250,000	950,000
Inventory	(h)	1,720,000
Total current assets	(i)	3,045,000
Capital assets (net)	4,600,000	3,955,000
Total assets	$ (j)	$7,000,000
Liabilities and Shareholders' Equity		
Current liabilities	$ (k)	$ 825,000
Long-term notes payable	(l)	2,800,000
Total liabilities	(m)	3,625,000
Common shares	3,200,000	3,000,000
Retained earnings	400,000	375,000
Total shareholders' equity	3,600,000	3,375,000
Total liabilities and shareholders' equity	$ (n)	$7,000,000

Additional information:
1. The receivables turnover for 2003 is 10 times.
2. All sales are on account.
3. The profit margin for 2003 is 14.5%.
4. The return on assets is 22% for 2003.
5. The current ratio on December 31, 2003, is 3.2:1.
6. The inventory turnover for 2003 is 4.8 times.

Instructions

Use the ratios above to calculate the missing information. Show your calculations. (*Note*: Start with one ratio and get as much information as possible from it before trying another ratio. You will not be able to calculate the missing amounts in the same sequence as they are presented above.)

P19–8A Nextec Corp. has been in business for five years. Nextec has plans to create a new software package intended to allow users with limited computer knowledge to easily navigate the Internet by using their television sets and a control box that plugs into the cable jack.

    You are the loan officer at a Canadian chartered bank. The manager has asked you to analyse Nextec's financial statements and recommend whether or not the bank should lend Nextec additional funds for the project, based on its historical financial statements. Comparative financial statements follow:

Interpret company and industry ratios.
(SO 5, 6) AN

NEXTEC CORP.
Balance Sheet
March 31

Assets	2003	2002
Cash	$ 45,000	$ 0
Accounts receivable	510,000	470,000
Inventory	50,000	40,000
Prepaid expenses	5,000	10,000
Patents	38,000	0
	$648,000	$520,000
Liabilities and Shareholders' Equity		
Bank overdraft	$ 0	$ 20,000
Accounts payable	50,000	60,000
Current portion of long-term debt	60,000	50,000
Long-term debt	100,000	160,000
Common shares	100,000	100,000
Retained earnings	338,000	130,000
	$648,000	$520,000

NEXTEC CORP.
Income Statement
For the Year Ended March 31

	2003	2002
Sales (all on credit)	$1,600,000	$1,400,000
Cost of goods sold	300,000	200,000
Gross profit	1,300,000	1,200,000
Operating expenses		
Salaries	870,000	940,000
Office	20,000	20,000
Rent	40,000	40,000
Interest	20,000	30,000
Amortization expense	2,000	0
	952,000	1,030,000
Income before income tax	348,000	170,000
Income tax (40%)	139,200	68,000
Net income	$ 208,800	$ 102,000

Selected comparative ratios and industry averages follow:

	2003	2002	Industry Average
Current ratio	5.5:1	4:1	2:1
Collection period	112 days	120 days	45 days
Inventory turnover	6.7×	5.7×	5×
Return on shareholders' equity	63%	44%	40%
Debt to total assets	32%	56%	50%

Instructions

(a) Indicate whether the 2003 ratios presented above are favourable or unfavourable compared to the industry average.

(b) Based on a comparison of Nextec Corp.'s ratios to the industry average, identify *one* significant area that Nextec Corp. must improve and what it should do to improve it.

(c) The President of Nextec Corp. estimates that the company needs $1,000,000 to ensure the new software project's success. Based on the ratios given, and the financial statements presented, determine whether or not you would lend $1,000,000 to Nextec Corp. Explain your decision.

(d) Identify one additional thing Nextec could do (other than borrow) to raise the money it needs.

(e) In addition to the financial statements of Nextec Corp., list two other non-financial factors that should be considered when evaluating that company.

PROBLEMS: SET B

P19–1B Comparative statement data for Breau Company and Shields Company, two competitors, appear below. All balance sheet data are as at December 31, 2003, and December 31, 2002.

Prepare vertical analysis, calculate profitability ratios, and comment on profitability.
(SO 4, 5) AN

	Breau Company		Shields Company	
	2003	2002	2003	2002
Net sales	$250,000		$1,200,000	
Cost of goods sold	160,000		720,000	
Operating expenses	51,000		252,000	
Interest expense	3,000		10,000	
Income tax expense	11,000		65,000	
Net cash provided by operating activities	30,000		175,000	
Current assets	140,000	$110,000	700,000	$650,000
Capital assets (net)	305,000	270,000	928,000	750,000
Current liabilities	60,000	52,000	250,000	275,000
Long-term liabilities	50,000	68,000	200,000	150,000
Common shares	260,000	210,000	750,000	700,000
Retained earnings	75,000	50,000	428,000	275,000

Instructions

(a) Prepare a vertical analysis of the 2003 income statement data for Breau Company and Shields Company.

(b) Calculate the gross profit margin, profit margin, cash return on sales, return on assets, asset turnover, and return on common shareholders' equity ratios for both companies.

(c) Comment on the relative profitability of these companies.

(d) Identify two main reasons for the difference in profitability.

P19–2B The comparative statements of Rosen Company Inc. are presented here:

Calculate ratios.
(SO 5) AP

ROSEN COMPANY INC.
Income Statement
For the Year Ended December 31

	2003	2002
Net sales	$660,000	624,000
Cost of goods sold	440,000	405,600
Gross profit	220,000	218,400
Selling and administrative expenses (including amortization expense of $46,000 and $45,000, respectively)	143,880	149,760
Income from operations	76,120	68,640
Other expenses and losses		
Interest expense	7,920	7,200
Income before income tax	68,200	61,440
Income tax expense	25,300	24,000
Net income	$ 42,900	$ 37,440

ROSEN COMPANY INC.
Balance Sheet
December 31

Assets	2003	2002
Current assets		
Cash	$ 23,100	$ 21,600
Short-term investments	34,800	33,000
Accounts receivable (net)	106,200	93,800
Inventory	72,400	64,000
Total current assets	236,500	212,400
Capital assets (net)	465,300	459,600
Total assets	$701,800	$672,000
Liabilities and Shareholders' Equity		
Current liabilities		
Accounts payable	$134,200	$132,000
Income tax payable	25,300	24,000
Total current liabilities	159,500	156,000
Bonds payable	132,000	120,000
Total liabilities	291,500	276,000
Shareholders' equity		
Common shares (15,000 shares)	150,000	150,000
Retained earnings	260,300	246,000
Total shareholders' equity	410,300	396,000
Total liabilities and shareholders' equity	$701,800	$672,000

All sales were on account. Net cash provided by operating activities was $36,000.

Instructions

Calculate the following ratios for 2003:

(a) Earnings per share
(b) Return on common shareholders' equity
(c) Return on assets
(d) Current ratio
(e) Acid test ratio
(f) Receivables turnover
(g) Collection period
(h) Inventory turnover

(i) Days sales in inventory
(j) Interest coverage
(k) Asset turnover
(l) Debt to total assets
(m) Cash current debt coverage
(n) Cash return on sales
(o) Cash total debt coverage
(p) Cash interest coverage

Perform ratio analysis and evaluate financial position and operating results.
(SO 5) AN

P19–3B Condensed balance sheet and income statement data for Colinas Corporation appear below:

COLINAS CORPORATION
Balance Sheet
December 31

Assets	2003	2002	2001
Cash	$ 40,000	$ 24,000	$ 20,000
Receivables (net)	70,000	45,000	48,000
Inventory	80,000	75,000	62,000
Investments	90,000	70,000	50,000
Capital assets (net)	450,000	400,000	360,000
	$730,000	$614,000	$540,000
Liabilities and Shareholders' Equity			
Current liabilities	$ 98,000	$ 75,000	$ 70,000
Long-term debt	97,000	75,000	65,000
Common shares	400,000	340,000	300,000
Retained earnings	135,000	124,000	105,000
	$730,000	$614,000	$540,000

COLINAS CORPORATION
Income Statement
For the Year Ended December 31

	2003	2002
Sales	$700,000	$750,000
Less: Sales returns and allowances	40,000	50,000
Net sales	660,000	700,000
Cost of goods sold	420,000	400,000
Gross profit	240,000	300,000
Operating expenses (including $45,000 and $40,000, respectively, of amortization expense)	194,000	237,000
Interest expense	10,000	9,000
Income before income tax	36,000	54,000
Income tax expense	14,000	21,000
Net income	$ 22,000	$ 33,000

Additional information:

1. All sales were on account.
2. Cash provided by operating activities was $15,000 in 2002 and $25,000 in 2003.
3. All dividends were paid in cash.
4. There were 30,000 common shares on December 31, 2001; 34,000 on December 31, 2002; and 40,000 on December 31, 2003.
5. The market prices of Colinas's common shares were $5.00, $4.50, and $2.30 for 2001, 2002, and 2003, respectively.

Instructions

(a) Calculate the following ratios for 2002 and 2003:

1. Collection period	7. Price-earnings
2. Days sales in inventory	8. Payout ratio
3. Cash return on sales	9. Dividend yield
4. Asset turnover	10. Debt to total assets
5. Return on common shareholders' equity	11. Cash interest coverage
6. Earnings per share	

(b) Based on the ratios calculated, briefly discuss the changes in financial position and operating results of Colinas Corporation from 2002 to 2003.

P19–4B Financial information for Track.com Company Ltd. is presented here:

Calculate ratios and effects of selected transactions.
(SO 5) AN

TRACK.COM COMPANY LTD.
Balance Sheet
December 31

Assets	2003	2002
Cash	$ 50,000	$ 42,000
Temporary investments	80,000	100,000
Receivables (net)	100,000	87,000
Inventories	440,000	400,000
Prepaid expenses	25,000	31,000
Land	75,000	75,000
Building and equipment (net)	570,000	500,000
Total assets	$1,340,000	$1,235,000
Liabilities and Shareholders' Equity		
Notes payable	$ 125,000	$ 125,000
Accounts payable	160,000	140,000
Accrued liabilities	50,000	50,000
Bonds payable, due 2006	200,000	200,000
Common shares (100,000 shares)	500,000	500,000
Retained earnings	305,000	220,000
Total liabilities and shareholders' equity	$1,340,000	$1,235,000

TRACK.COM COMPANY LTD.
Income Statement
For the Year Ended December 31

	2003	2002
Sales	$1,000,000	$940,000
Cost of goods sold	650,000	$635,000
Gross profit	350,000	305,000
Operating expenses	235,000	215,000
Net income	$ 115,000	$ 90,000

Additional information:

1. Inventory at the beginning of 2002 was $350,000.
2. Receivables at the beginning of 2002 were $80,000.
3. Total assets at the beginning of 2002 were $1,175,000.
4. Current liabilities at the beginning of 2002 were $300,000.
5. Total shareholders' equity at the beginning of 2002 was $740,000.
6. All sales were on account.
7. Cash provided by operating activities was $80,000 in 2003 and $65,000 in 2002.

Instructions

(a) Indicate, by using ratios, the change in liquidity and profitability of Track.com Company from 2002 to 2003. (*Note*: Not all ratios can be calculated.)

(b) Below, there are three independent situations and a ratio that may be affected. For each situation, calculate the affected ratio at December 31, 2003 (1) before the transaction, and (2) after the transaction occurred.

Situation	Ratio
1. Sold merchandise on account for $50,000. The cost of the sale was $30,000. Track.com uses a perpetual inventory system.	Current ratio
2. Operating expenses of $25,000 were incurred on account.	Profit margin
3. The account receivable incurred in situation 1 above was collected.	Cash return on sales

Calculate selected ratios, and compare liquidity, profitability, and solvency for two companies. (SO 5) AN

P19–5B   Inco Limited is the Western world's top producer of nickel, and mines and processes other precious minerals and metals throughout the world. **Falconbridge Limited** is also one of the world's leading producers of nickel, among other metals and minerals. Both companies are headquartered in Toronto. Selected financial data of these two close competitors are presented here (in millions) for a recent year:

	INCO LIMITED	**FALCONBRIDGE LIMITED**
	Income Statement Data for Year	
Net sales	$1,766	$1,674
Cost of sales and operating expenses	1,735	1,359
Selling, general, and administrative expenses	96	86
Interest expense	86	54
Other expenses	55	250
Income (loss) before income tax	(206)	(75)
Income and mining tax recovery	94	39
Income (loss) from continuing operations	(112)	(36)
Income from discontinued operations	36	0
Net income (loss)	$ (76)	$ (36)
Earnings (loss) per share	$(0.63)	$(0.24)

Balance Sheet Data at End of Year

Current assets		
Cash and cash equivalents	$ 82	$ 100
Accounts receivable	256	294
Inventories	473	372
Other current assets	63	0
Total current assets	874	766
Capital and other assets	6,468	4,033
Total assets	$7,342	$4,799
Current liabilities	$ 560	$ 340
Long-term liabilities	2,424	2,141
Total liabilities	2,984	2,481
Shareholders' equity	4,358	2,318
Total liabilities and shareholders' equity	$7,342	$4,799

Other Data

Average net receivables	$ 323.5	$ 336.7
Average inventories	634.5	349.0
Average total assets	7,557.0	4,556.3
Average total shareholders' equity	4,414.5	2,319.0
Net cash provided (used) by operating activities	174.0	176.9
Dividends paid	44.0	76.7

Instructions

(a) Calculate the liquidity, solvency, and profitability ratios, as appropriate, for each company.

(b) Compare the liquidity, solvency, and profitability of each company to those of its competitor and of the industry. Selected industry averages are available for the following ratios:

Current ratio	1.7:1
Acid test ratio	0.7:1
Receivables turnover	9.7×
Inventory turnover	4.1×
Interest coverage	1.8×
Profit margin	1.7%
Return on assets	1.1%

P19–6B Bowen Corporation started the year with the following ratios:

Evaluate impact of transactions on ratios.
(SO 5) AN

Acid test ratio	1.0:1
Inventory turnover	10×
Debt to total assets	30%
Asset turnover	2×
Cash return on sales	20%

Instructions

Determine the effect each of the following independent transactions has on these ratios. Indicate whether the transaction would cause each ratio to improve (I), deteriorate (D), or if there would be no effect (NE).

(a) Bowen purchased merchandise inventory on account. Bowen uses a perpetual inventory system.

(b) The company paid an account payable.

(c) Bowen sold merchandise on account to a customer at a price higher than its cost.

(d) A customer paid an account receivable.

(e) Bowen purchased capital assets, issuing a long-term note payable in payment.

(f) Bowen earned (and received) interest income from a temporary investment.

Use ratios to calculate misssing data.
(SO 5) AN

P19–7B Presented here are an incomplete income statement and an incomplete comparative balance sheet of Vienna Corporation:

VIENNA CORPORATION
Income Statement
For the Year Ended December 31, 2003

Sales	$11,000,000
Cost of goods sold	(a)
Gross profit	(b)
Operating expenses	1,665,000
Income from operations	(c)
Interest expense	(d)
Income before income tax	(e)
Income tax expense	560,000
Net income	$ (f)

VIENNA CORPORATION
Balance Sheet
December 31, 2003

Assets

Current assets	
Cash	$ 450,000
Accounts receivable (net)	(g)
Inventory	(h)
Total current assets	(i)
Capital assets (net)	4,620,000
Total assets	$ (j)

Liabilities

Current liabilities	$ (k)
Long-term liabilities	(l)
Total liabilities	(m)

Shareholders' Equity

Common shares	3,000,000
Retained earnings	400,000
Total shareholders' equity	3,400,000
Total liabilities and shareholders' equity	$ (n)

Additional information:

1. The receivables turnover for 2003 is 10 times.
2. All sales are on account.
3. The gross profit margin is 36.73%.
4. The profit margin for 2003 is 14.5%.
5. The return on assets is 22%.
6. The current ratio on December 31, 2003, is 3:1.
7. The inventory turnover for 2003 is 6.444 times.

Instructions

Calculate the missing information using the ratios. Round your answers to the nearest thousand dollars. Use ending balances instead of average balances where averages are required for ratio calculations. Show your calculations. (*Hint*: Start with one ratio and get as much information as possible from it before trying another ratio. You will not be able to calculate the missing amounts in the same sequence as they are presented above.)

Interpret company and industry ratios.
(SO 5, 6) AN

P19–8B Selected ratios for two companies operating in the beverage industry follow, in alphabetical order, for the year ended December 31, 2003. Industry ratios, where available, have also been included ("n/a" indicates that the ratio was not available).

Ratio	Refresh Corp.	Taste.Com	Industry
Acid test (quick) ratio	0.4:1.0	0.7:1.0	0.4:1.0
Asset turnover	1.0 times	1.0 times	0.9 times
Cash flow per share	$1.56	$2.12	$1.87
Cash total debt coverage	0.3 times	0.2 times	n/a
Current ratio	0.6:1.0	1.1:1.0	0.8:1.0
Debt to total assets	56%	72%	n/a
Earnings per share	$0.98	$1.37	$1.08
Gross profit margin	73.8%	60.0%	57.7%
Inventory turnover	5.8 times	9.9 times	8.3 times
Price-earnings	50.3 times	24.3 times	32.2 times
Profit margin	12.3%	11.2%	8.1%
Receivables turnover	11.4 times	9.8 times	9.3 times
Return on assets	11.2%	9.3%	7.2%
Return on common shareholders' equity	25.7%	29.8%	26.4%
Interest coverage	15.3 times	7.9 times	5.3 times

Instructions

Answer the following questions, refering to appropriate ratios to justify your answer:

(a) Which company appears to be the most liquid? Explain.

(b) As a potential investor, are you concerned with the debt levels of either company? Why or why not?

(c) Which company is the most profitable? Explain.

(d) One should always be cautious in interpreting ratios. Identify any two facts that you should keep in mind about the limitations of ratio analysis as you interpret the ratios in this question.

Broadening Your Perspective

FINANCIAL REPORTING AND ANALYSIS

••

Financial Reporting Problem

BYP19–1   Refer to the 2000 annual report and consolidated financial statements for **The Second Cup Ltd.**, which are reproduced in Appendix A at the end of this textbook.

Instructions

(a) Prepare vertical analysis balance sheets and income statements for The Second Cup for fiscal years 2000 and pro forma 1999. Comment on any significant features that you observe in these. (*Hint*: Use the Total Revenue figures as the base amount for your income statement calculations. Systemwide Sales includes the revenues of all Second Cup franchises.)

(b) Prepare a ratio analysis of the company's financial statements, and comment on any significant results that you observe. (You may recall that many of these ratios have already been calculated in previous chapters.) For some of the ratio calculations, you will also need to refer to the following balance sheet amounts (in thousands of dollars) which the company reported for its fiscal year ended June 27, 1998:

THE SECOND CUP LTD.
Balance Sheet
June 27, 1998
(in thousands)

Assets

Current assets

Cash and short-term investments	$26,236
Accounts receivable	3,127
Inventories	168
Prepaid expenses and sundry assets	118
	29,649
Capital assets	1,662
Investment in Diedrich Coffee, Inc.	5,960
Deferred income taxes	628
Goodwill, less accumulated amortization	9,049
	$46,948

Liabilities

Current liabilities

Accounts payable and accrued liabilities	$ 2,289
Current portion, long-term debt	3,000
Deposits	574
Income taxes payable (receivable)	(1,102)
	4,761
Long-term liabilities	31,237
	35,998

Shareholders' Equity

Share capital (9,309,840 shares issued)	61,447
Retained earnings (deficit)	(50,497)
	$46,948

(c) Review the section of the report titled "Management's Discussion and Analysis of Operating Results." Using management's comments provided in this section, plus the points you noted in parts (a) and (b) above, write a report summarizing your views regarding The Second Cup's financial position and performance. (Hint: You should refer to qualitative information—such as the general state of the economy, the competitive environment in the industry, etc.—at the same time as you interpret the quantitative data.)

Interpreting Financial Statements

Additional Cases

BYP19–2   **Canadian National Railway (CN)**   is the only railroad in North America to cross the continent from east to west and north to south, serving ports on the Atlantic, Pacific and Gulf coasts. CN's revenue is derived 52% from the U.S., 24% from Canada, and 24% internationally. Its primary North American competitor is Burlington Northern Santa Fe Corporation. These two companies have called off a proposed merger, which would have created the largest railroad in North America, because of a U.S. moratorium on rail mergers.

The following data were taken from the financial statements for the December 31, 2000, fiscal years of each company. All data are in millions, except for per share data.

BURLINGTON NORTHERN   CANADIAN NATIONAL

Financial Highlights	(in millions of US$)		(in millions of CDN$)	
	2000	1999	2000	1999
Cash and cash equivalents	$ 11	$ 22	$ 19	$ 307
Net receivables	314	397	737	803
Inventories	220	255	110	116
Other current assets	431	392	259	301
Total current assets	976	1,066	1,125	1,527
Total assets	24,375	23,700	15,196	14,757
Current liabilities	2,186	2,075	1,903	1,777
Total liabilities	16,895	15,528	9,498	9,251
Total shareholders' equity	7,480	8,172	5,698	5,506
Revenues	$ 9,205	$ 9,189	$ 5,446	$ 5,261
Operating expenses	6,272	6,086	3,525	3,582
Amortization expense	895	897	412	400
Interest expense	453	387	295	308
Income tax expense	605	682	442	369
Net income	$ 980	$ 1,137	$ 772	$ 602
Earnings per share	$ 2.36	$ 2.44	$ 3.90	$ 3.02
Cash provided by operating activities	$ 2,317	$ 2,424	$ 1,128	$ 962
Cash provided (used) by all activities	(11)	(3)	(288)	(10)
Dividends paid	197	222	136	118

Where available, industry averages for the North American railroad industry are shown in parentheses next to each ratio below.

Instructions

(a) Calculate the following liquidity ratios for 2000. Discuss the relative liquidity of the two companies and of the railroad industry.
1. Current (0.7:1)
2. Acid test (0.5:1)
3. Cash current debt coverage (n/a)
4. Receivables turnover (9.73)

(b) Calculate the following profitability ratios for 2000. Discuss the relative profitability of the two companies and of the railroad industry.
1. Profit margin (8.7%)
2. Cash return on sales (n/a)
3. Asset turnover (0.43)
4. Return on assets (3.7%)
5. Return on common shareholders' equity (11.3%)
6. Payout ratio (n/a)

(c) Calculate the following solvency ratios for 2000. Discuss the relative solvency of the two companies and of the railroad industry.
1. Debt to total assets (n/a)
2. Interest coverage (3.43)
3. Cash interest coverage (n/a)
4. Cash total debt coverage (n/a)

Accounting on the Web

BYP19–3   Once upon a time, there were two brothers, David and Tom Gardner. They were interested in investing and created a light-hearted website called The Motley Fool (see the opening story to this chapter). The Motley Fool's motto is "to educate, amuse and enrich" and it has become one of the most popular sites on the Internet. This case uses The Motley Fool website to look at the basics of the stock market, what corporate financial information is useful when assessing shares, and a model portfolio.

Instructions

Specific requirements of this Internet case can be found on the Weygandt website.

BYP19–4   Besides earnings per share, the price-earnings ratio (PE) is a popular analysis tool used to form an opinion as to whether a share is a good buy. This case will review several Canadian corporations to evaluate their PEs.

Instructions

Specific requirements of this Internet case can be found on the Weygandt website.

CRITICAL THINKING

Collaborative Learning Activity

BYP19–5   As the accountant for Martinez Manufacturing Inc., you have been asked to develop some key ratios from the comparative financial statements. This information is to be used to convince creditors that Martinez Manufacturing Inc. is solvent and will continue as a going concern. The data requested and the calculations developed from the financial statements follow:

	2003	2002
Current ratio	3.1:1	2.1:1
Acid test ratio	0.8:1	1.4:1
Asset turnover	2.8 times	2.2 times
Net income	Up 32%	Down 8%
Earnings per share	$3.30	$2.50
Book value per share	Up 8%	Up 11%
Return on common shareholders' equity	23%	27%

Instructions

With the class divided into groups, answer the following:

(a) Martinez Manufacturing Inc. asks you to comment on how each of these items supports the company's solvency and going-concern potential. The company wants to use your comments to support its presentation of data to its creditors. Prepare the comments as requested, giving the implications and the limitations of each item separately. Then prepare the general conclusion that may be drawn from the individual items about Martinez's solvency and going-concern potential.

(b) What warnings should you offer these creditors about the limitations of ratio analysis for the purposes stated here?

Communication Activity

BYP19–6   Sari Jahe is the Chief Executive Officer of Ranger Electronics. Jahe is an expert engineer but a novice in accounting. Jahe asks you, as an accounting student, to explain (1) the bases for comparison in analysing Ranger's financial statements, and (2) the limitations, if any, of financial statement analysis.

Instructions

Write a letter to Sari Jahe explaining the bases for comparison and the limitations of financial statement analysis.

Ethics Case

BYP19–7   Sabra Surkis, president of Surkis Industries, wishes to issue a press release to improve her company's image and the share price, which has been gradually falling. As controller, you have been asked to provide a list of 20 financial ratios along with some other operating statistics relative to Surkis Industries' first quarter financials and operations.

Two days after you provide the ratios and data requested, Carol Dunn, the public relations director of Surkis, asks you to prove the accuracy of the financial and operating data contained in the press release written by the president and edited by Carol. In the news release, the president highlights the sales increase of 25% over last year's first quarter and the positive change in the current ratio from 1.5:1 last year to 3:1 this year. She also emphasizes that production was up 50% over the prior year's first quarter.

You note that the release contains only positive or improved ratios, and none of the negative or weakened ratios. For instance, there is no mention that the debt to total assets ratio has increased from 35% to 55%. Nor was it mentioned that inventories are up 89%, and that, while the current ratio improved, the acid test ratio fell from 1:1 to 0.5:1.

Instructions

(a) Who are the stakeholders in this situation?

(b) Is there anything unethical in president Surkis's actions?

(c) Should you as controller remain silent? Does Carol have any responsibility?

Answers to Self-Study Questions

1. b   2. d   3. c   4. a   5. c   6. b   7. c   8. b   9. a   10. b

Answer to Second Cup Review It Question 4

The Second Cup does not present any vertical analysis in its annual report. It does use horizontal analysis in its "To Our Shareholders" letter and "Management's Discussion and Analysis of Operating Results" sections of its report.

Remember to go back to the Navigator box on the chapter-opening page to check off your completed work.

SPECIMEN FINANCIAL STATEMENTS:
The Second Cup Ltd.

www.secondcup.com

The Annual Report

Once each year, corporations communicate to shareholders and other interested parties by issuing audited financial statements and other financial information. The **annual report**, as this communication is called, summarizes the financial results of the company's operations for the year and presents its plans for the future.

Most annual reports are attractive, effectively designed communication vehicles. They not only inform readers about financial information, but also about more qualitative information such as the company's strategic vision and its goals and objectives. Annual reports also usually include information about how the company is governed, its assumed social responsibilities, and details about its products, people, and geographic areas of operation. While qualitative information helps provide a useful context for the understanding and interpretation of the financial information, the basic function of every annual report is to report financial information.

The content and organization of corporate annual reports have become fairly standardized. Excluding the non-financial part of the report (pictures and products), the following items are the traditional financial portions of the annual report:

Financial Highlights
Letter to Shareholders
Management's Discussion and Analysis of Operating Results
Comparative Financial Statements
    Management's Responsibility for Financial Reporting
    Auditors' Report
    Balance Sheet
    Income Statement
    Statement of Retained Earnings
    Cash Flow Statement
    Notes to the Financial Statements
Five-Year Financial Review

In this appendix, we illustrate current financial reporting with a comprehensive set of corporate financial statements. These statements have been prepared in accordance with generally accepted accounting principles and audited by an independent chartered accounting firm. We are grateful for permission to use the actual financial statements and other accompanying financial information from the annual report of The Second Cup Ltd.

Financial Highlights

The financial highlights section of an annual report is usually presented inside the front cover or on the first page of the annual report. This section generally reports the total or per share amounts for selected financial items for the current year and one or more previous years.

Financial items from the income statement and the balance sheet usually include sales, income from continuing operations, net income (or loss), earnings (or loss) per share, dividends per share, capital expenditures, and the amount of cash flow from operating activities.

The financial highlights section from The Second Cup Ltd.'s 2000 annual report is shown below:

	Audited		Pro Forma (unaudited)
(millions of Canadian dollars, except per share amounts and store numbers)	**2000**	1999	1999
OPERATING RESULTS AND FINANCIAL POSITION			
Systemwide sales	**$159.2**	$340.8	$149.0
Revenue	**20.8**	105.4	21.5
EBITDA*	**10.1**	10.4	8.2
Write down of investment	**(4.1)**	—	—
Loss on disposition of investments	—	(16.2)	—
Net earnings (loss)	**1.0**	(10.1)	3.8
EARNINGS (LOSS) PER SHARE	**$ 0.10**	$ (0.72)	$ 0.41
NET DEBT**	**$ 11.8**	$ 25.0	$ 1.4
STORES AT END OF PERIOD			
Franchised	**392**	374	374
Corporate	**6**	6	6
Total	**398**	380	380

* EBITDA represents earnings before interest, taxes, depreciation, amortization, minority interest, write down of investment and gains or losses on disposition of investments.
** Total debt net of cash.

In its financial highlights, The Second Cup includes a column headed "Pro Forma (unaudited) 1999." In 1999, The Second Cup sold its non-core businesses—Coffee People and The Great Canadian Bagel—as part of a strategic realignment. Since the 1999 financial statements include a portion of the results of these operations, management adjusted the 1999 financial results to remove the effects of this divestiture. This makes the 1999 results easier to compare to the 2000 results.

Letter to Shareholders

Nearly every annual report contains a letter to the shareholders from the Chair of the Board of Directors or the President of the company. This letter typically discusses the company's accomplishments during the preceding year. It also highlights significant events such as acquisitions and divestitures, new products, operating achievements, business philosophy, changes in officers or directors, financing commitments, expansion plans, and future prospects. The letter to the shareholders of The Second Cup Ltd., signed by Randy Powell, President and Chief Executive Officer, is shown below and continues on the next page:

TO OUR SHAREHOLDERS

Brand power, strong growth opportunities and exceptional people will continue to drive our future success.

As we look back at fiscal 2000, we do so with a great deal of pride. Our results, particularly in the areas of increased operating earnings and store expansion, were strong. However, the true source of our pride is the fact that these results were achieved during such challenging times. Our industry and our Company have faced shifting consumer retail shopping habits and an aggressive competitive climate. During the past year, we also engaged in a comprehensive review of shareholder value creation alternatives. It was the conclusion of the Board of Directors that it was not advantageous to pursue these alternatives at this time and that the best course of action was to remain focused on Second Cup's core coffee business.

The Company's earnings before interest, taxes, depreciation, amortization and write down of investment ("EBITDA") totaled $10.1 million, an increase of 23% over the previous year's pro forma results. However, the Company recorded net income of $1.0 million, or 10 cents per share, due to a $4.1 million non-cash charge for the write down of our investment in Diedrich Coffee, Inc. This investment now reflects its current market value. Excluding the Diedrich Coffee, Inc. non-cash share write down, Second Cup earnings per share were 54 cents in 2000, 32% higher than prior year's pro forma earnings per share of 41 cents.

Systemwide sales in Canada rose by 7% or $10.2 million to $159.2 million, while same store sales grew by 0.8%. We are pleased to report that the fourth quarter of fiscal 2000 represents our 27th consecutive quarter of positive same store sales growth; a rare and admired accomplishment in Canadian retailing. Excluding the Diedrich Coffee, Inc. write down the Company's return on capital employed increased to 52% in 2000, from 43% in the previous year's pro forma results.

In our business, opportunities abound, but the most exciting progress in fiscal 2000 involved our café expansion initiatives. This year we opened 50 new cafés, and closed 32 cafés bringing our system total to 398. These store closures reflect our commitment to world class operations delivered through a modern real estate portfolio. We continue to be Canada's largest specialty coffee retailer.

At Second Cup, our focus has been and always will be to build long term and sustainable shareholder value increases. To that end, on June 11, 1999 we completed a major buyback of five million Second Cup shares at $16 per share.

Randy Powell,
President and
Chief Executive Officer

1

Furthermore, on April 26, 2000, the Board of Directors approved the payment on May 31, 2000 of a special dividend of $2 per share. These two initiatives saw the Company return close to $100 million to shareholders, once again demonstrating Second Cup's effective balance sheet management and the cash generative nature of our business model.

In fiscal 2000, we also made some important organizational decisions to drive efficiencies. The consolidation and downsizing of our corporate infrastructure will reduce overhead costs going forward.

Plus 23% EBITDA growth over the previous year's pro forma results, continued café expansion, and positive same store and systemwide sales, have not positively impacted our stock price. That said, we believe that over the long term, strong financial performance can not be ignored and will ultimately be reflected in our share price.

What does the future hold for Second Cup and why do we look forward with such confidence and optimism? We are extremely excited about the long-term growth potential for the Second Cup Coffee Co. The success we have enjoyed over the past 25 years can be attributed to three key factors:

- Brand Power
- Strong Growth Opportunities
- Exceptional People

This year we opened 50 new cafés, bringing our total to 398 across Canada.

Second Cup returned close to $100 million to shareholders over a one year period.

It is these attributes that will continue to drive our success for the next 25 years. It is my pleasure to further expand on each of these key factors in the pages that follow.

At the conclusion of fiscal 2000, my predecessor as CEO, Michael Bregman changed his role with the restructuring to become Chairman of Second Cup without operating responsibility. It is with sincere gratitude that we thank Michael for his visionary leadership over the years. It is under his guidance and direction that Second Cup has become a force in Canadian retailing. We are very pleased that we still have opportunity to draw upon his many years of experience as we move forward.

Let me conclude by thanking our shareholders for their continued support; our Directors for their advice and counsel; and our franchising partners, managers and employees for their hard work and dedication. It is because of you that fiscal 2000 is a year in which we all can be proud.

Randy Powell,
President and
Chief Executive Officer

Management's Discussion and Analysis of Operating Results

The **management discussion and analysis (MD&A)** section covers three financial aspects of a company: its results of operations, its ability to pay near-term obligations, and its capacity to fund operations and expansion. Management identifies favourable and unfavourable trends and significant events and uncertainties that affect these three factors. This discussion involves a number of estimates and opinions.

The MD&A section of The Second Cup's annual report is presented on the following pages:

MANAGEMENT'S DISCUSSION AND ANALYSIS OF OPERATING RESULTS

This discussion and analysis should be read in conjunction with the consolidated financial statements and the pro forma financial statements and related notes included in the Annual Report to Shareholders of The Second Cup Ltd. ("Second Cup" or the "Company"). "2000" and "1999" refer to the fiscal years ended June 24, 2000 and June 30, 1999 respectively.

CURRENT YEAR AND PRIOR YEAR'S PRO FORMA RESULTS OF OPERATIONS

The operating results of the Second Cup in 2000 reflect those of the Canadian business. In 1999, the Company underwent a strategic realignment that saw it eliminate non-core business activities and focus on the strengths of its established, growing Canadian coffee business. Specifically, Second Cup sold its investment in Coffee People, Inc. ("Coffee People") in exchange for cash and shares in Diedrich Coffee, Inc. ("Diedrich Coffee"). It also sold its investment in The Great Canadian Bagel, Ltd. for cash, and curtailed immediate acquisition activities by returning surplus funds to shareholders by repurchasing for cancellation five million shares.

Given the material impact of the realignment on the Company, pro forma financial statements for 1999 were prepared using assumptions as if the strategic realignment of the Company had been completed immediately prior to the commencement of 1999. The pro forma financial statements are presented as supplementary information to the audited consolidated financial statements (refer to Note 1 to the Consolidated Financial Statements). It is management's opinion that the current year's results are best understood by comparison to the 1999 pro forma financial statements. Accordingly, all 1999 comparisons in this section below are to the pro forma financial statements.

Second Cup leveraged its core Canadian coffee business, maximizing earnings before interest, taxes, depreciation, amortization, minority interest, write down of investment and gains or losses on disposition of investments ("EBITDA") despite a decline in total revenues. EBITDA increased 23% in 2000 as compared to 1999.

Systemwide sales grew 7% to $159.2 million in 2000 from $149 million the previous year. The increase in systemwide sales is due to the increasing number of new cafés opened. Same store sales grew by 0.8% in 2000 (5.5% in 1999). In fiscal 2000, Second Cup added a net of 18 stores for a total of 398 stores open. 50 new stores were opened including 47 traditional stores and three new sites opened under the Cara license agreement (1999 – 43 traditional store openings and 13 new sites opened under the Cara license agreement). 32 stores, including nine units in former Eaton's department stores, were closed in 2000. With the exception of the nine Eaton's stores, these closures were largely part of an ongoing process to maintain a high quality and modern portfolio of stores.

Total revenues declined 3%. The overall decline in total revenues was largely due to sales from corporate stores where there were fewer corporate stores operating in 2000 than in 1999. Also declining were product sales in 2000 as 1999 included one time fees received under a master license agreement.

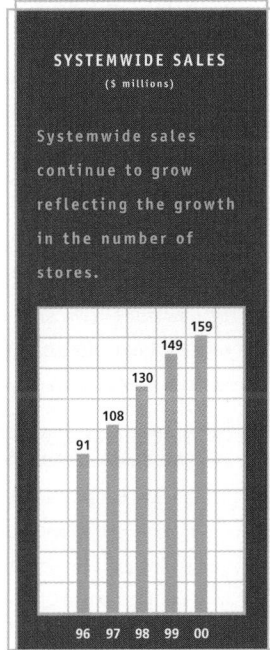

SYSTEMWIDE SALES
(\$ millions)

Systemwide sales continue to grow reflecting the growth in the number of stores.

96	97	98	99	00
91	108	130	149	159

Franchise revenue lessened the impact of these declines by increasing $1.4 million or 8% to $19 million in 2000 from $17.6 million a year ago. The increase is substantially due to growth in retail sales of franchises upon which royalties are collected.

EBITDA was $10.1 million in 2000, up 23% from $8.2 million in 1999. EBITDA growth was delivered through a combination of the previous discussed franchise revenue growth and as well from cost reductions. Cost reductions were principally related to non-recurring lease termination charges recorded in 1999 as well as reductions in general and administrative expenses.

Depreciation of capital assets was higher in 2000 due to it including a provision for impairment in net book value of specific corporate store assets.

A portion of the proceeds received in 1999 by Second Cup upon the divestiture of Coffee People was 1.0 million shares in Diedrich Coffee. At that time Second Cup recorded its best estimate of the fair value of these common shares. The Company reviewed this estimate again in 2000 and has reduced the carrying value by $4.1 million which has been reflected in the Statement of Operations and Deficit in the current year. 2000 earnings per share without this non-cash charge for the write down in the Diedrich Coffee investment was $0.54 ($0.41 – 1999).

NUMBER OF STORES – NATIONAL

Second Cup will celebrate the opening of its 400th store in fiscal 2001.

96	97	98	99	00
243	299	354	380	398

CURRENT YEAR AND PRIOR YEAR'S CONSOLIDATED RESULTS OF OPERATIONS

The audited Consolidated Statement of Operations for 2000 includes The Second Cup Ltd., the operator of the core Canadian coffee business and its wholly-owned subsidiary, a company holding the investment in Diedrich Coffee. The comparable statement for 1999 includes The Second Cup Ltd., its wholly-owned subsidiary, the strategic realignment expenses of $0.9 million eliminated in the 1999 pro forma statements, and the 1999 operating results for Second Cup's U.S. business which was divested as at June 30, 1999.

Accordingly, 2000 systemwide sales were $181.6 million less than those in 1999. Total revenues declined to $20.8 million in 2000 from $105.4 million in 1999 consolidated results. These declines are due solely to the divestiture of Coffee People.

EBITDA declined $0.3 million in 2000 as compared to 1999. The Second Cup Ltd., unconsolidated, experienced EBITDA growth of 39% to $10.1 million in 2000 from $7.3 million in 1999. This growth substantially offset the loss of Coffee People's contribution to EBITDA following its divestiture.

INTEREST AND OTHER INVESTMENT INCOME

In 2000 interest income declined to nil compared with 1999 net interest and other investment income of $3.4 million. In October of 1999, the Company retained an advisor to explore ways to further enhance shareholder value. Until this process was terminated in April 2000, the Company maintained significant cash balances and bank debt to allow maximum flexibility. A special dividend totaling $18.7 million was paid on May 31, 2000. For the year Second Cup maintained average cash balances of $23.2 million and average bank debt balances of $19.4 million.

The 1999 consolidated net interest and other investment income included $4.0 million earned prior to the $80.0 million repurchase for cancellation of five million common shares on June 11, 1999.

INCOME TAXES

The Company's consolidated effective tax rate for 2000 rose to 44.3% from 43.3% in 1999.

Second Cup has capital losses of approximately $24.0 million available for application against future capital gains. The value of these losses has not been recognized in the financial statements.

The Company changed its method of accounting for income taxes from the deferral method to the asset and liability method. The cumulative effect of this change was immaterial and is accounted for in the current year's income tax expense.

LIQUIDITY AND CAPITAL RESOURCES

During 2000 and 1999 Second Cup returned $99.1 million to its shareholders. The return was accomplished in three manners:

(1) A special dividend of $2.00 per common share was paid May 31, 2000 to shareholders of record May 19, 2000. This special dividend amounted to $18.7 million;

(2) Five million common shares were repurchased for cancellation on June 11, 1999 for $80.0 million; and

(3) During 1999 a Normal Course Issuer Bid saw the Company repurchase $0.4 million of its common shares in the market.

Second Cup's cash flow from Canadian operations was $6.6 million in 2000 and $3.8 million in 1999 on a pro forma basis ($8.8 million in 1999 when the operating results of Coffee People are considered). The significant increase in cash flow over 1999 pro forma results is mostly attributable to the 23% EBITDA improvement recorded by the Company in fiscal 2000. Cash flow from operations was used primarily to pay down debt and as well to finance capital expenditures. The Company's fiscal 2000 capital expenditures of $0.8 million were significantly lower than 1999 pro forma expenditures – 1999 expenditures included costs for expanded Coffee Central offices and Coffee College training facilities in addition to the build out of three store locations in advance of franchising. Fiscal 2000 capital expenditures related to Coffee Central systems development projects and the build out of one store location in advance of franchising.

Fiscal 2000 non-operating cash flow was significantly impacted by the expected receipt of $23 million proceeds due from the sale of Coffee People in 1999 as well as the receipt of $3.5 million due from the sale of the Company's investment in The Great Canadian Bagel, Ltd. In compliance with the terms of our non-revolving credit facility, proceeds from the sale of The Great Canadian Bagel, Ltd. investments were applied to pay down debt. Proceeds from the sale of Coffee People were used to fund payment of the above mentioned special dividend payment and as well to pay down long-term debt. In aggregate the Company paid down $12.6 million of debt in fiscal 2000.

EBITDA*
CANADIAN COMPANY
($ millions)

The Second Cup Ltd. unconsolidated continues to leverage its earnings.

96	97	98	99	00
5.7	6.7	7.3	7.3	10.1

Earnings before interest, income taxes, depreciation and amortization, write down of investment and gains or losses on disposition of investments.

Fiscal 2000 working capital was significantly lower than both 1999 consolidated and pro forma working capital balances. The reduction against both 1999 consolidated and pro forma results is primarily due to the special dividend payment made May 31, 2000.

At June 24, 2000 the Company had outstanding borrowings of $13.3 million. These borrowings represent the remaining facility of committed term debt of $25 million established and fully drawn upon in 1999. This facility requires equal quarterly repayments of $0.75 million, with the balance due June 7, 2004 and carries interest at 1.375% over the lender's cost of funds. Also available to the Company is a floating rate $10 million revolving/term credit facility that can be used for general corporate purposes. This facility is extendable annually, and if not extended is convertible into a term facility that matures June 7, 2004. This facility was not used at June 24, 2000 (June 30, 1999 – $0.8 million).

The Company expects that existing external credit sources and internally generated cash flows will be sufficient for future internal and external cash requirements.

RISKS AND UNCERTAINTIES

The Company's core specialty coffee retailing business is highly competitive. Competitors are not considered a threat to Second Cup's position as the market leader due to the established operating system, high quality products and well-known brand of Second Cup.

Coffee is a commodity whose market price fluctuates with worldwide demand and supply. Second Cup moderates the risk of price fluctuations by entering into forward commodity contracts. Further diminishing this risk is the fact that the cost of coffee is relatively modest compared to the overall cost of sales and thus has a limited impact on overall store profitability. Second Cup generates the majority of its income from royalties based on systemwide sales, which do not correlate directly to changes in coffee commodity prices.

Second Cup is the head tenant on the leases which it in turn subleases to its franchisees. If a franchisee is unable to pay the lease obligation on its sublease, then the obligation becomes that of the Company. Second Cup minimizes its risk by carefully selecting its sites and its franchisees. Should a lease obligation fall to Second Cup, then it either negotiates an end to the lease, operates it corporately or re-franchises the site. Sites revert to the Company infrequently.

OUTLOOK

Second Cup has completed its first year after the strategic realignment undertaken in 1999. Within the Canadian operations EBITDA has grown 23% when compared to 1999 pro forma results. Management has plans to continue growing the Second Cup brand and expand profitably in Canada through continued focus on new store expansion and growth in sales per unit.

Comparative Financial Statements

Management's Responsibility for Financial Reporting

An important inclusion in corporate annual reports is the statement made by management about its responsibility for, and its role in assuring, the accuracy and integrity of the financial statements. In The Second Cup's statement of **Management's Responsibility for Financial Reporting**, the Chairman and the President do the following: (1) They assume primary responsibility for the financial statements and the related notes. (2) They outline and assess the company's internal control system. (3) They declare the financial statements in conformity with generally accepted accounting principles. (4) They comment on the audit and the composition and role of the Audit Committee of the Board of Directors.

    The Second Cup's statement of management's responsibility is presented below:

MANAGEMENT'S RESPONSIBILITY FOR FINANCIAL REPORTING

The management of The Second Cup Ltd. is responsible for the integrity of the financial statements and all other information, including the pro forma financial statements, contained within this annual report. The financial statements were prepared by management in accordance with Canadian generally accepted accounting principles which involve the use of informed judgements and estimates. All financial information in the annual report is consistent with the financial statements.

The Company maintains systems of internal control which have been designed to provide reasonable assurance that accounting records are reliable and assets are safeguarded. The independent audit firm of PricewaterhouseCoopers LLP have audited the financial statements on behalf of the shareholders and have expressed an opinion based upon their audits which were conducted in accordance with Canadian generally accepted auditing standards.

The Board of Directors oversees management's responsibility for financial reporting primarily through its Audit Committee, the majority of the members of which are outside directors, and to which the independent auditors have free access.

Michael Bregman
Chairman

Randy Powell
President
and Chief Executive Officer

Toronto, Canada
August 4, 2000

13

Auditors' Report

All publicly held corporations, as well as many other companies, hire independent public accountants to provide an objective report on their financial statements. After a comprehensive examination of the company's accounting system, records, and financial statements, the external auditors issue the auditors' report.

The standard auditors' report consists of three paragraphs: an introductory paragraph, a scope paragraph, and an opinion paragraph. In the **introductory paragraph**, the auditors identify who and what was audited. They indicate the responsibilities of management and the auditors relative to the financial statements. In the **scope paragraph**, the auditors state that the audit was conducted in accordance with generally accepted auditing standards. They also discuss the nature and limitations of the audit. In the **opinion paragraph**, the auditors express an informed opinion as to (1) the fairness of the financial statements and (2) their conformity with generally accepted accounting principles.

The Auditors' Report of PricewaterhouseCoopers LLP, Chartered Accountants, addressed to the shareholders of The Second Cup Ltd., is shown below:

AUDITORS' REPORT

TO THE SHAREHOLDERS OF THE SECOND CUP LTD.

We have audited the consolidated balance sheets of The Second Cup Ltd. as at June 24, 2000 and June 30, 1999 and the consolidated statements of operations and deficit and cash flows for the fiscal periods then ended. These financial statements are the responsibility of the Company's management. Our responsibility is to express an opinion on these financial statements based on our audits.

We conducted our audits in accordance with Canadian generally accepted auditing standards. Those standards require that we plan and perform an audit to obtain reasonable assurance whether the financial statements are free of material misstatement. An audit includes examining, on a test basis, evidence supporting the amounts and disclosures in the financial statements. An audit also includes assessing the accounting principles used and significant estimates made by management, as well as evaluating the overall financial statement presentation.

In our opinion, these consolidated financial statements present fairly, in all material respects, the financial position of the Company as at June 24, 2000 and June 30, 1999 and the results of its operations and the changes in its cash flows for the fiscal periods then ended in accordance with Canadian generally accepted accounting principles.

PricewaterhouseCoopers LLP

Toronto, Canada   PricewaterhouseCoopers LLP
August 4, 2000   *Chartered Accountants*

The auditors' report issued on The Second Cup's financial statements is unqualified (or clean). It contains no qualifications or exceptions. In other words, the auditors conformed completely with generally accepted auditing standards in performing the audit. And the financial statements conformed in all material respects with generally accepted accounting principles.

If the financial statements do not conform with generally accepted accounting principles, or if the scope of the audit has been restricted, the auditors must issue a **qualified** opinion and describe the exception. If the lack of conformity with GAAP is significant, the auditors are obliged to issue an **adverse** opinion or denial. An adverse opinion means that the financial statements do not fairly present the company's financial condition and/or the results of the company's operations.

Companies do their best to obtain an unqualified auditors' report. You will rarely encounter anything other than this type of opinion on the financial statements.

Financial Statements and Accompanying Notes

The standard set of financial statements consists of the following: (1) a comparative balance sheet for two years, (2) a comparative income statement for two years (called a statement of operations by The Second Cup), (3) a statement of retained earnings or deficit for two years (sometimes combined with the income statement or statement of operations as The Second Cup has done), (4) a comparative cash flow statement for two years, and (5) a set of accompanying notes that are considered an integral part of the financial statements. Some companies present comparative figures for three years.

The financial statements and accompanying notes for The Second Cup for the years ended June 24, 2000, and June 30, 1999, appear on the following pages. They are **consolidated financial statements** which means that the statements include the financial results for The Second Cup and its subsidiary company, Diedrich Coffee.

CONSOLIDATED BALANCE SHEETS

As at June 24, 2000 and June 30, 1999 (thousands of dollars)	2000	1999	Pro Forma (Note 1) (unaudited) 1999
ASSETS			
Current assets			
Cash and cash equivalents	$ 1,446	$ 822	$ 20,942
Accounts receivable (Note 3)	2,294	25,525	2,494
Inventories (Note 4)	107	103	103
Prepaid expenses and sundry assets (Note 13)	419	934	934
Income taxes receivable	1,150	—	517
	5,416	27,384	24,990
Capital assets (Note 6)	1,768	2,308	2,308
Deferred financing charges (Note 7)	125	235	235
Loans to directors and officers (Note 13)	674	753	753
Investment in Diedrich Coffee, Inc. (Note 3)	1,838	5,960	5,960
Investment in The Great Canadian Bagel, Ltd. (Note 5)	—	3,495	—
Future income taxes (Note 10)	295	700	700
Goodwill, less accumulated amortization of $3,304 (1999 – $3,004)	8,449	8,749	8,749
	$ 18,565	$ 49,584	$ 43,695
LIABILITIES			
Current liabilities			
Accounts payable and accrued liabilities	$ 2,718	$ 3,415	$ 2,528
Current portion, long-term debt (Note 7)	3,000	6,500	3,000
Deposits	687	923	923
Income taxes payable	—	467	—
	6,405	11,305	6,451
Long-term debt (Note 7)	10,250	19,300	19,300
Other deferred liabilities	212	219	219
SHAREHOLDERS' EQUITY			
Share capital (Note 8)	62,355	61,670	61,670
Deficit	(60,657)	(42,910)	(43,945)
	1,698	18,760	17,725
	$ 18,565	$ 49,584	$ 43,695

See accompanying notes to Consolidated Financial Statements.

Approved by the Board

Michael Bregman, *Chairman*   Roy Sugden, *Director*

CONSOLIDATED STATEMENTS OF OPERATIONS AND DEFICIT

For the Fiscal Years Ended June 24, 2000 and June 30, 1999 (thousands of dollars, except per share data)	2000	1999	Pro Forma (Note 1) (unaudited) 1999
Systemwide sales	$159,198	$340,753	$148,970
Revenue			
Franchise revenue	$ 19,021	$ 28,163	$ 17,573
Sales from corporate stores	1,750	51,645	3,507
Product sales	73	25,549	385
Total revenue	$ 20,844	$105,357	$ 21,465
EBITDA*	$ 10,086	$ 10,395	$ 8,180
Depreciation of capital assets	621	1,897	430
Amortization of goodwill	300	1,490	300
Earnings before the undernoted	9,165	7,008	7,450
Write down of investment (Note 3)	(4,122)	—	—
Loss on disposition of investments (Notes 3 and 5)	—	(16,233)	—
Earnings (loss) before interest, taxes and minority interest	5,043	(9,225)	7,450
Net interest and other investment income (expense) (Note 9)	(13)	3,350	(557)
Earnings (loss) before income taxes and minority interest	5,030	(5,875)	6,893
Income taxes (Note 10)	4,058	4,249	3,102
Earnings (loss) before minority interest	972	(10,124)	3,791
Minority interest	—	29	—
Net earnings (loss)	972	(10,095)	3,791
Retained earnings (deficit), beginning of period	(42,910)	14,875	(47,736)
Special dividend (Note 8)	(18,719)	—	—
Share repurchase in excess of book value (Note 8)	—	(47,690)	—
Deficit, end of period	$ (60,657)	$ (42,910)	$ (43,945)
Weighted average shares outstanding during the fiscal period	9,347,389	13,944,989	9,329,604
Earnings (loss) per share	$0.10	$(0.72)	$0.41

* EBITDA represents earnings before interest, taxes, depreciation, amortization, minority interest, write down of investment and gains or losses on disposition of investments.

See accompanying notes to Consolidated Financial Statements.

CONSOLIDATED STATEMENTS OF CASH FLOWS

For the Fiscal Years Ended June 24, 2000 and June 30, 1999 (thousands of dollars)	2000	1999	Pro Forma (Note 1) (unaudited) 1999
CASH PROVIDED BY (USED IN)			
Operating activities			
Net earnings (loss) for the fiscal period	$ 972	$(10,095)	$ 3,791
Items not involving cash:			
Amortization and depreciation	921	3,387	730
Minority interest	—	(29)	—
Future income taxes	154	(99)	(72)
Loss (gain) on disposal of capital assets and investments	(120)	15,293	(940)
Shares reserved for issue to directors	172	81	81
Forgiveness of loan to officer	250	250	250
Amortization of deferred financing charges	110	—	—
Write down of investment (Note 3)	4,122	—	—
Cash flow from operations	6,581	8,788	3,840
Increase in non-cash working capital items related to operations	(1,557)	(2,335)	(1,055)
	5,024	6,453	2,785
Investing activities			
Purchase of capital assets	(727)	(3,503)	(2,078)
Proceeds from disposal of capital assets	766	3,455	1,943
Proceeds from The Great Canadian Bagel, Ltd. debenture (Note 5)	3,495	1,550	—
Proceeds from the sale of Coffee People, Inc. (Note 3)	23,000	—	—
Net cash position divested on sale of Coffee People, Inc. (Note 3)	—	(1,954)	—
Cumulative foreign exchange translation adjustments	—	(13)	—
	26,534	(465)	(135)
Financing activities			
Repurchase of common shares (Note 8)	—	(81,078)	—
Payment of special dividend (Note 8)	(18,719)	—	—
Proceeds from issuance (repayment) of long-term debt	(12,550)	24,742	(26,921)
Proceeds on issuance of shares (Note 8)	513	143	(63)
Loans to directors and officers (Note 13)	(171)	(654)	(988)
Other deferred liabilities	(7)	(89)	(7)
	(30,934)	(56,936)	(27,979)
Increase (decrease) in cash and cash equivalents during the fiscal period	624	(50,948)	(25,329)
Cash and cash equivalents, beginning of fiscal period	822	51,770	46,271
Cash and cash equivalents, end of fiscal period	$ 1,446	$ 822	$ 20,942

Supplemental disclosure of cash flow information (Note 14)

See accompanying notes to Consolidated Financial Statements.

1. BASIS OF PRESENTATION OF PRO FORMA FINANCIAL INFORMATION (UNAUDITED)

Due to the material nature of the fiscal 1999 strategic realignment of the Company, pro forma financial information has been compiled to reflect the Consolidated Balance Sheet, Statement of Operations and Deficit and Statement of Cash Flows for the fiscal year ended June 30, 1999 as if:

(i)   The merger of Gloria Jean's Inc. with Coffee People, Inc. and the subsequent sale of Coffee People, Inc. to Diedrich Coffee, Inc. had been completed at the end of the previous fiscal year. Cash proceeds of $23,000 from the sale of the Company's investment in Coffee People, Inc. earned interest at 5%.

(ii)   The Company repurchased five million of its common shares for $80,650, including transaction costs, at the end of the preceding fiscal year. Debt incurred as a result of the repurchase bore interest at 6.5%.

(iii)   The Company divested its investment in The Great Canadian Bagel, Ltd. for proceeds of $5,050 at the end of the preceding fiscal year. These proceeds were used to retire debt.

(iv)   Expenses in the fiscal year ended June 30, 1999 were reduced by $930 attributable to costs associated with the strategic realignment of the Company.

(v)   An average income tax rate of 45% had been applied to all interest and expense adjustments.

2. SUMMARY OF SIGNIFICANT ACCOUNTING POLICIES

PRINCIPLES OF CONSOLIDATION

The consolidated financial statements include the accounts of the Company and its subsidiary. All significant intercompany accounts and transactions have been eliminated on consolidation.

CASH AND CASH EQUIVALENTS

Cash and cash equivalents consist of cash on hand, balances with banks, and investments in short-term money market instruments. Investments in short-term money market instruments are recorded at the lower of cost and estimated market value and consist substantially of highly liquid investments.

INVENTORIES

Inventories are valued at the lower of cost and net realizable value with cost being determined substantially on a first-in, first-out basis.

CAPITAL ASSETS

Capital assets are recorded at cost. Depreciation is calculated using the straight-line basis at the following rates, which are based on the expected useful life of the asset:

Computer software and hardware	3 years
Equipment, furniture, fixtures and other	7 years
Leasehold improvements	lesser of 10 years and the remaining term of the lease

GOODWILL

The excess of the purchase price over the estimated fair value of identifiable net assets acquired represents goodwill. Goodwill is amortized over 40 years on a straight-line basis.

The Company reviews the carrying value of goodwill on an annual basis to determine if an impairment in value has occurred. The Company measures the potential impairment of goodwill by comparing the undiscounted value of expected future earnings before income taxes, interest and amortization of goodwill to the current carrying value of goodwill. Any permanent impairment in the value of goodwill is written off against earnings. The Company is of the opinion that there has been no permanent impairment in the value of goodwill.

FOREIGN CURRENCY TRANSLATION

The accounts of the Company's foreign subsidiaries operating in the United States have been translated using the current rate method. Under this method, assets and liabilities have been translated into Canadian dollars at the year-end exchange rate. Revenue and expenses have been translated at the average exchange rates in effect during the year. Exchange gains or losses on translation were deferred and included as a separate component of shareholders' equity.

FINANCIAL INSTRUMENTS

Financial instruments are initially recorded at historical cost. If subsequent circumstances indicate a decline in fair value is other than temporary, the financial asset is written down to fair value. Unless otherwise indicated, the fair value of financial instruments approximate recorded amounts. The fair value of cash equivalents, accounts receivable, accounts payable and accrued liabilities approximate recorded amounts because of the short-term period to receipt or payment of cash.

USE OF ESTIMATES

The preparation of financial statements in conformity with Canadian generally accepted accounting principles requires the Company to make estimates and assumptions that affect the reported amounts of assets and liabilities and the disclosure of contingent assets and liabilities at the date of the financial statements and the amounts of revenues and expenses for the reported years. Actual results may differ from those estimates.

SYSTEMWIDE SALES

Systemwide sales includes retail sales of all corporate and franchised stores, based on sales information reported by store operators.

FRANCHISE REVENUE

Initial franchise fees for stores are recognized as income when the store has opened. Master franchise fees are recognized as income when the agreement has been signed and any material conditions have been met. Franchise royalties are recognized as earned.

STORE PRE-OPENING COSTS

Certain costs incurred in connection with the opening of new corporate-owned stores are capitalized and expensed during the stores' first year of operation.

FISCAL YEAR END

Ordinarily, the Company's fiscal year end is the last Saturday in June. In fiscal 1999, the fiscal year was extended to Wednesday, June 30, 1999, in order to reflect the disposition of the Company's investment in Coffee People, Inc.

FUTURE INCOME TAX ASSETS

Future income tax assets are recognized for deductible temporary differences and operating loss or tax credit carryforwards, and future income tax liabilities are recognized for taxable temporary differences. Temporary differences are the differences between the amounts of assets and liabilities recorded for income tax and financial reporting purposes. The income tax expense or benefit is the income tax payable or refundable for the year plus or minus the change in future income tax assets and liabilities during the year. In 1999, the value of the future income tax asset was determined using the deferral basis.

STOCK-BASED COMPENSATION PLANS

The Company has three stock-based compensation plans, which are described in Note 8. Compensation expense is not recognized when stock or stock options are issued under the Amended Directors, Officers and Employees Stock Option Plan or the Share Purchase Plan. Compensation expense is recognized when stock is issued or reserved for future issue under the Directors Share Plan. Any consideration received on exercise of stock options or purchase of stock under all plans is credited to share capital. If stock or stock options issued under these plans are repurchased, the excess of consideration paid over the carrying amount of the stock or stock option canceled is charged to retained earnings.

COMPARATIVE FIGURES

Certain comparative figures have been reclassified to conform with the financial statement presentation adopted in the current year. The Consolidated Statement of Cash Flows has been restated to comply with new accounting requirements. As well during the current year, the Company adopted the asset and liability method of accounting for income taxes on a prospective basis.

3. ACQUISITION AND DIVESTITURE

On March 16, 1999, the Company's subsidiary, Coffee People, Inc. ("Coffee People") executed an agreement and plan of merger with Diedrich Coffee, Inc. ("Diedrich Coffee"), a NASDAQ listed company, pursuant to which Diedrich Coffee would purchase all of the issued and outstanding shares of Coffee People for consideration of cash and Diedrich Coffee common shares. The transaction was completed, subject to receipt of final funds, on June 30, 1999, following approval by the shareholders of the two companies and the successful placement of 4.6 million common shares by Diedrich Coffee.

The Company divested its investment in Coffee People, pursuant to this transaction for cash proceeds of $23,000 and 1,044,495 common shares of Diedrich Coffee, valued at $6,000. These shares represent approximately 8% of the issued and outstanding common shares of Diedrich Coffee and are subject to a one year lock-up agreement and certain share registration requirements. The value ascribed to these common shares at June 30, 1999 reflected the Company's best estimate of the fair value taking into consideration current trading values, liquidity of the stock, the size of the Company's investment relative to the public float and the restrictions on trading these shares.

The total cash consideration of $23,000 is included in "Accounts receivable" as at June 30, 1999 and was received during the current year. This transaction gave rise to a $14,700 loss which is included in "Loss on disposition of investments" for the year ended June 30, 1999.

In accordance with Canadian generally accepted accounting principles, because this divestiture occurred on the last day of the Company's fiscal year, the Consolidated Statement of Operations and Consolidated Statement of Cash Flows include the activities of Coffee People for the year ended June 30, 1999. However, the Consolidated Balance Sheet as at June 30, 1999 reflects the divestiture and consequently, excludes Coffee People assets and liabilities.

During the year the Company reviewed the carrying value of its investment in Diedrich Coffee using the same criteria as at June 30, 1999. It was determined that there had been a permanent impairment in value of $4,122 which has been reflected in the Consolidated Statement of Operations and Deficit in the current year.

4. INVENTORIES

	2000	1999
Merchandise held for resale	$ 96	$ 93
Supplies	11	10
	$107	$103

5. INVESTMENT IN THE GREAT CANADIAN BAGEL, LTD.

On October 4, 1996, the Company invested $6,495 in The Great Canadian Bagel, Ltd. The investment consisted of a 5% equity interest and a $5,695 subordinated convertible debenture bearing interest at 10%, payable quarterly in arrears. The Company also held warrants to purchase additional shares of The Great Canadian Bagel, Ltd. which expired on October 4, 1998 and October 4, 1997. During the period of this investment the Company earned and received cumulative interest and other investment income of $1,624 pre-tax to June 30, 1999. These receipts were reported in the relevant fiscal year. During the year ended June 30, 1999, the Company also received a $500 prepayment of the debenture from The Great Canadian Bagel, Ltd. and sold $1,050 of the remaining debenture to The Great Canadian Bagel, Ltd.'s majority shareholders at face value. On August 4, 1999, the Company sold its remaining investment in The Great Canadian Bagel, Ltd. to these shareholders for proceeds of $3,495. The transaction, net of costs, resulted in a loss of $1,487 which was accrued in fiscal 1999.

6. CAPITAL ASSETS

	2000	1999
Cost		
Leasehold improvements	$1,157	$1,294
Equipment, furniture, fixtures and other	1,099	1,020
Computer software and hardware	757	664
	3,013	2,978
Accumulated depreciation		
Leasehold improvements	402	190
Equipment, furniture, fixtures and other	474	279
Computer software and hardware	369	201
	1,245	670
Net book value	$1,768	$2,308

Depreciation of capital assets for the fiscal period ended June 24, 2000 was $621 (June 30, 1999 – $1,897). Included in this charge is a provision for impairment in net book value of corporate store leasehold improvements, equipment, furniture, fixtures and other of $193 (1999 – nil).

7. LONG-TERM DEBT

	2000	1999
Non-revolving term facility maturing June 7, 2004	$13,250	$25,000
$10 million revolving/non-revolving credit facility, maturing June 5, 2001		
(June 30, 1999 – maturing June 6, 2000).	—	800
	13,250	25,800
Less: Current portion	(3,000)	(6,500)
	$10,250	$19,300

The Company's non-revolving term facility requires quarterly payments of $750 plus the proceeds received from the liquidation of the Company's investment in The Great Canadian Bagel, Ltd. The revolving/non-revolving facility contains a convertible option whereby on each anniversary date, if the option is not extended, payment could be made in full or in installments equal to $2^{1}/_{2}\%$ of the outstanding balance on a quarterly basis. Any remaining balance would be due on June 7, 2004. On June 6, 2000 the option was extended for another year.

These facilities are secured by the Company's investment in Diedrich Coffee, Inc. and provide that the Company may borrow using Prime, Bankers Acceptances or LIBOR based loans plus interest spreads which vary within a range depending upon a ratio of total debt to EBITDA. Borrowings currently bear interest at the lender's cost of funds plus 1.375%. Deferred financing charges of $125 ($235 at June 30, 1999) incurred by the Company in securing these facilities will continue to be amortized over the term of the loan based on the repayment of the facility. Management considers the carrying value of long-term debt to be fair market value.

8. SHARE CAPITAL

Authorized share capital consists of an unlimited number of common shares and an unlimited number of first preference shares issuable in one or more series of which none are issued.

Details of share transactions during the year are as follows:

	Common Shares	
	Shares	Amount
Balance as at June 27, 1998	14,329,590	$ 94,833
Issued for cash to employees and directors	16,599	143
6,441 shares reserved for issue to directors	—	81
Repurchase of shares	(5,035,800)	(33,387)
Balance as at June 30, 1999	9,310,389	$ 61,670
Issued for cash to employees and directors	49,170	513
14,480 shares reserved for issue to directors	—	172
Balance as at June 24, 2000	9,359,559	$ 62,355

On April 26, 2000, the Company declared a special dividend of $2.00. This dividend was paid on May 31, 2000 to shareholders of record on May 19, 2000.

On May 14, 1999, the Company offered to purchase for cancellation a maximum of five million of its then issued and outstanding common shares at a price of $16.00 per common share. Five million common shares were tendered by shareholders prior to the June 7, 1999 expiration of the offer and on June 11, 1999, the Company purchased and cancelled these shares at a cost of $80,700, including transaction costs. The common stock account of the Company was reduced by the weighted average original issue cost of the purchased common shares and the balance of the transaction cost was applied to retained earnings.

On September 18, 1998, The Toronto Stock Exchange approved the Company's Notice of Intention to make a Normal Course Issuer Bid. This Bid permitted the Company to repurchase, for cancellation, through the facilities of the Exchange up to a total of 716,522 common shares, representing approximately 5% of the outstanding common shares. During the year ended June 30, 1999, 35,800 common shares were repurchased and cancelled at a cost of $429. The Toronto Stock Exchange's approval for the Company to make a Normal Course Issuer Bid expired September 21, 1999. No common shares were repurchased and cancelled in fiscal 2000 prior to the expiration date.

The Company has a Directors Share Plan, an Amended Director, Officer and Employee Stock Option Plan, and a Share Purchase Plan under which shares are reserved for future issue.

Up to 147,876 shares may be issued under the Directors Share Plan, which was approved by the shareholders at the October 16, 1996 Annual and Special Meeting. During the year ended June 24, 2000, 3,399 shares at prices ranging from $7.21 to $14.09 were issued to directors of the Company under this Plan. Also during the current fiscal year, 14,480 shares have been allotted for future issue to directors at prices ranging from $7.21 to $15.12. Under the Directors Share Plan at June 24, 2000, a total of 10,984 shares have been issued and 35,272 shares have been reserved for issue, and 101,620 shares remain available for future issue or allotment. The compensation liability related to shares allotted and reserved for issue is recorded in share capital.

Up to 1,360,775 shares have been authorized for issue under the Amended Director, Officer and Employee Stock Option Plan (the "Option Plan"). To June 24, 2000, 141,475 shares have been issued upon exercise of stock options under the Option Plan. Options granted under the Option Plan prior to June 24, 1998 are exercisable commencing three years after the date granted and expire seven years thereafter. Options granted on or after June 24, 1998 vest in equal annual installments over three years following the date of grant and expire ten years from the grant date. Options to purchase 524,513 shares remain available to be granted in the future. During the current year the exercise price of all outstanding share options was reduced by $1.03. This was done in consideration of the impact of the special dividend of $2.00 per common share paid May 31, 2000. Details of the Option Plan activity are as follows:

	Number	Exercise Option Price	Weighted Average Exercise Price
Outstanding at June 27, 1998	554,907	$ 6.75 – $17.19	$10.26
Issued	242,819	$11.35 – $15.97	$13.20
Cancelled	(78,825)	$ 9.97 – $15.97	$11.12
Exercised	(12,300)	$ 6.75 – $ 8.00	$ 7.17
Outstanding at June 30, 1999	706,601	$ 6.75 – $17.19	$11.60
Issued	99,561	$ 7.21 – $14.09	$12.66
Cancelled	(66,100)	$ 6.97 – $16.16	$13.13
Exercised	(45,275)	$ 5.72 – $12.50	$10.01
Outstanding at June 24, 2000	694,787	$ 5.72 – $16.16	$10.67

The details of share options outstanding at June 24, 2000 are as follows:

	Vested		Non-Vested	
Fiscal Year of Expiry	Weighted Average Exercise Price	Number of Shares	Weighted Average Exercise Price	Number of Shares
2003	$ 5.97	65,000	—	—
2004	$ 5.72	12,400	—	—
2005	$ 6.81	16,000	—	—
2006	$10.97	15,000	—	—
2007	$10.54	59,594	$ 9.98	535
2008	—	—	$ 9.73	235,978
2009	$13.04	67,947	$13.04	135,272
2010	—	—	$12.63	87,061
Total	$ 9.52	235,941	$11.26	458,846
Total number of vested and non-vested shares and weighted average exercise price	$10.67	694,787		

Under the Share Purchase Plan, which was approved by the Board of Directors on October 16, 1996, employees have an opportunity from time-to-time to elect to purchase shares at fair market value from treasury. Up to 415,588 shares are reserved for future issue. To June 24, 2000, 500 shares have been issued (June 30, 1999 – 500) under the Share Purchase Plan.

9. INTEREST AND OTHER INVESTMENT INCOME

	2000	1999
Interest and other investment income	$ 1,380	$ 4,111
Interest expense		
Long-term debt	(1,299)	(752)
Other	(94)	(9)
	$ (13)	$ 3,350

10. INCOME TAXES

	2000	1999
Combined Canadian approximate income tax rates	45%	45%
Income taxes at combined Canadian statutory rates	$ 4,118	$(2,644)
Non-deductible losses on disposition of investment	—	7,056
Non-taxable gain	—	(83)
Expenses not deductible for tax purposes	122	—
Manufacturing and processing profits reduction	(80)	(72)
Adoption of new accounting standard for income taxes	(24)	—
Other	(78)	(8)
	$ 4,058	$ 4,249

Effective, July 1, 1999, the Company changed its method of accounting for income taxes to the asset and liability method. Previously, income taxes were accounted for by the deferral method. The cumulative effect of this change has been accounted for in the current year. The prior period comparatives remain unchanged.

As of June 24, 2000, the Company has available capital losses for tax purposes of approximately $24,000 that may be used to reduce its capital gains for income tax purposes in future years. The benefits of these losses have not been recognized in these financial statements.

The significant components of future income tax assets and liabilities are summarized as follows:

	2000	1999
Capital loss carryforwards	$ 7,095	$ —
Write down of investment	1,243	—
Amortization	(25)	(116)
Reserves	313	633
Share issue costs	—	311
Deferred financing costs	7	(102)
Other	—	(26)
	8,633	700
Valuation allowance	(8,338)	—
Net future income tax asset	$ 295	$ 700

The Company has recorded a valuation allowance against its capital loss carryforwards and the investment write down because it believes it will likely not generate sufficient capital gains in the future to utilize these future tax assets. Realization of the future tax benefit is dependent upon many factors, including the Company's ability to generate capital gains in the future.

11. CASH HELD IN TRUST

Cash held in trust on behalf of franchisees at June 24, 2000 amounted to $2,302 (June 30, 1999 – $4,462) and is not recorded on the Company's balance sheet.

12. MINIMUM LEASE COMMITMENTS AND CONTINGENT LIABILITIES

The Company has lease commitments for corporate-owned stores and office premises. The Company also, as the franchisor, is the lessee in most of the franchisees' lease agreements. The Company enters into sublease agreements with the individual franchisee, whereby the franchisee assumes responsibility for and makes lease payments directly to the landlord.

The Company's minimum lease commitments and contingent liabilities for any leases subject to a sublease agreement between the Company and a franchisee at June 24, 2000 are approximately as follows:

	Minimum Lease Commitments	Contingent Liabilities
2001	$ 577	$14,070
2002	586	13,585
2003	535	12,868
2004	513	12,182
2005	511	10,945
Thereafter	1,039	32,109
	$3,761	$95,759

13. RELATED PARTY TRANSACTIONS

Included in "Loans to directors and officers" are loans due from directors totaling $674 (June 30, 1999 – $503) that were made under the Director Share Loan Plan (the "Loan Plan") which was approved by the Board of Directors on June 24, 1998. The loans are secured by promissory notes and bear interest equal to the amount of any ordinary dividends declared and paid on the common shares by the Company. Common shares purchased pursuant to the Loan Plan are pledged by the director to the Company as additional security for the repayment of the loan and all interest thereon. Repayment can be made at any time, but in any case no later than three months subsequent to the point in time at which the director ceases, for any reason, to be a director of the Company. As at June 24, 2000 the market value of the common shares pledged as security was less than the amount of the outstanding loans. As at June 30, 1999 the market value of the common shares pledged as security exceeded the amount of the outstanding loans.

As at June 24, 2000, a non-interest-bearing loan totaling $250 (June 30, 1999 – $500) was due from an officer of the Company; this amount is included in "Prepaid expenses and sundry assets". $250 of the loan balance outstanding at June 30, 1999 was forgiven by the Company on June 26, 2000, and has been expensed in the fiscal 2000 year. The remaining $250 will be forgiven by the Company on July 2, 2001 providing that the officer is in the employ of the Company on that date. The outstanding loan balance is immediately repayable when the officer ceases, for any reason, to be an employee of the Company.

During the year ended June 24, 2000, the Company recorded franchise income of $455 (June 30, 1999 – $462) from Cara Operations Limited, which owns approximately 39% of the Company's issued and outstanding common shares. The franchise income was earned in the normal course of business pursuant to the license agreement signed July 2, 1996.

During the year ended June 30, 1999, the Company loaned some of its excess cash to Cara Operations Limited on a short-term basis at prevailing market rates. Total interest earned on the loans made during the year ended June 30, 1999 was $114. At June 30, 1999 there were no loans outstanding.

14. SUPPLEMENTAL DISCLOSURE OF CASH FLOW INFORMATION

	2000	1999
Interest paid	$1,029	$1,012
Taxes paid	$5,436	$4,374

CASH AND CASH EQUIVALENTS

Cash and cash equivalents included in the cash flow statements comprise the following:

	2000	1999
Cash on hand and balances with banks	$ 448	$ 822
Short-term investments	998	—
Total cash and cash equivalents	$1,446	$ 822

The following is a summary of the Company's operations and assets by geographic area:

	Canada		United States		Consolidated	
	June 24 **2000**	June 30 1999	**June 24** **2000**	June 30 1999	**June 24** **2000**	June 30 1999
Systemwide sales	**$159,198**	$148,970	—	$191,783	**$159,198**	$340,753
Revenue:						
Franchise revenue	**$ 19,021**	$ 17,573	—	$ 10,590	**$ 19,021**	$ 28,163
Sales from corporate stores	**1,750**	3,507	—	48,138	**1,750**	51,645
Product sales	**73**	385	—	25,164	**73**	25,549
Total revenue	**$ 20,844**	$ 21,465	—	$ 83,892	**$ 20,844**	$105,357
EBITDA – operations	**$ 11,814**	$ 9,549	—	$ 3,145	**$ 11,814**	$ 12,694
Corporate office administration	**(1,728)**	(2,299)	—	—	**(1,728)**	(2,299)
EBITDA	**$ 10,086**	$ 7,250	—	$ 3,145	**$ 10,086**	$ 10,395
Depreciation and amortization	**921**	730	—	2,657	**921**	3,387
Earnings before the undernoted	**$ 9,165**	$ 6,520	—	$ 488	**$ 9,165**	$ 7,008
Write down of investment					**(4,122)**	—
Loss on disposition of investments					—	(16,233)
Earnings (loss) before interest, taxes and minority interest					**$ 5,043**	$ (9,225)
Interest and other investment income (expense)					**(13)**	3,350
Income taxes					**(4,058)**	(4,249)
Minority interest					—	29
Net earnings (loss)					**972**	(10,095)
Total assets	**$ 18,565**	$ 49,584	—	—	**$ 18,565**	$ 49,584
Number of stores:						
Franchised	**392**	374	—	—	**392**	374
Corporate	**6**	6	—	—	**6**	6
Total number of stores	**398**	380	—	—	**398**	380

Five-Year Financial Review

A five- or ten-year summary of selected financial data is usually presented close to the audited financial statements. The summary makes it possible to see trends and growth patterns over a fairly long period of time.

The Second Cup presented the following five-year financial review that includes operating results, financial position data, and selected operating statistics:

FIVE-YEAR FINANCIAL REVIEW

(thousands of dollars, except per share amounts and number of stores)	2000	1999	1998	1997	1996
OPERATING RESULTS					
Systemwide sales	$159,198	$340,753	$283,256	$260,375	$213,488
Revenue	20,844	105,357	69,922	73,063	63,302
EBITDA	10,086	10,395	12,649	6,055	8,221
Earnings before income taxes and minority interest	5,030	(5,875)	12,744	6,786	66
Net earnings (loss) for the period	972	(10,095)	9,100	2,981	(2,366)
Cash flow from operations	6,581	8,788	11,452	5,079	5,721
Earnings (loss) per share	$0.10	$(0.72)	$0.64	$0.21	$(0.25)
FINANCIAL POSITION					
Cash and short-term investments	$ 1,446	$ 822	$ 51,170	$ 46,083	$ 35,760
Total assets	18,565	49,584	153,106	112,389	104,751
Total debt	13,250	25,800	7,458	—	—
Shareholders' equity	1,698	18,760	113,004	101,216	97,372
OPERATING STATISTICS					
Number of stores opened in the period	50	56	102	91	58
Number of stores closed/disposed in the period	32	30	39	36	12
Number of stores acquired in the period	—	—	39	—	236
Number of stores at end of period	398	380	669	567	512

PRESENT VALUE CONCEPTS

Business enterprises borrow and invest large sums of money. Both of these types of transactions involve the use of **present value calculations**. A present value calculation is based on the concept of the **time value of money**. Would you rather be given $1,000 today or $1,000 a year from today? If you get the $1,000 today and invest it to earn 5% per year, the $1,000 will accumulate to $1,050 ($1,000 plus the $50 interest) one year from today. The $1,000 received today is the present value amount that is equivalent to the future amount of $1,050 one year from now.

Before we turn to a discussion of present value concepts, let's first refresh our knowledge about the nature of interest.

Nature of Interest

Interest is payment for the use of money. It is the difference between the amount borrowed or invested (called the principal) and the amount repaid or collected. The amount of interest to be paid or collected is usually stated as a rate over a specific period of time. The rate of interest is generally stated as an annual rate.

The amount of interest involved in any financing transaction is based on three elements:

1. **Principal (p)**: The original amount borrowed or invested
2. **Interest Rate (i)**: An annual percentage of the principal
3. **Number of periods (n)**: The time period that the principal is borrowed or invested

Simple Interest

Simple interest is calculated on the principal amount only. It is the return on the principal for one period. Simple interest is usually expressed as shown in Illustration B-1.

Illustration B-1

Simple interest formula

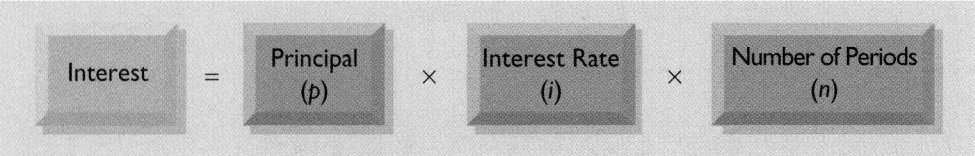

For example, if you borrowed $1,000 for 3 years at a simple interest rate of 9% annually, you would pay $270 in total interest, calculated as follows:

$$
\begin{aligned}
\text{Interest} &= p \times i \times n \\
&= \$1{,}000 \times 9\% \times 3 \\
&= \$270
\end{aligned}
$$

Compound Interest

Compound interest is the return on (or growth of) the principal for two or more time periods. Compounding calculates interest not only on the principal but also on the interest earned to date on that principal, assuming the interest is left on deposit.

To illustrate the difference between simple and compound interest, assume that you deposit $1,000 in the Last Canadian Bank, where it will earn simple interest of 9% per year, and you deposit another $1,000 in the First Canadian Bank, where it will earn interest of 9% per year compounded annually. Also assume that in both cases you will not withdraw any interest until three years from the date of deposit. The calculation of interest to be received and the accumulated year-end balances are given in Illustration B-2.

Illustration B-2

Simple versus compound interest

Last Canadian Bank				First Canadian Bank		
Simple Interest Calculation	Simple Interest	Accumulated Year-End Balance		Compound Interest Calculation	Compound Interest	Accumulated Year-End Balance
Year 1 $1,000.00 × 9%	$ 90.00	$1,090.00		Year 1 $1,000.00 × 9%	$ 90.00	$1,090.00
Year 2 $1,000.00 × 9%	90.00	$1,180.00		Year 2 $1,090.00 × 9%	98.10	$1,188.10
Year 3 $1,000.00 × 9%	90.00	$1,270.00		Year 2 $1,188.10 × 9%	106.93	$1,295.03
	$270.00		$25.03 Difference		$295.03	

Note in Illustration B-2 that simple interest uses the initial principal of $1,000 to calculate the interest in all three years. Compound interest uses the accumulated balance (principal plus interest to date) at each year end to calculate interest in the succeeding year—which explains why your compound interest account is larger. For practical purposes, compounding assumes that unpaid interest earned becomes a part of the principal. The accumulated balance at the end of each year becomes the new principal on which interest is earned during the next year.

Obviously, if you had a choice between investing your money at simple interest or at compound interest, you would choose compound interest, if all other things—especially risk—are equal. In the example, compounding provides $25.03 of additional interest income.

Compound interest is used in most business situations. Simple interest is generally applicable only to short-term situations of one year or less. Present value concepts use compound interest.

Present Value Variables

The present value is based on three variables: (1) the dollar amount to be received (the future amount), (2) the length of time until the amount is received (the number of periods), and (3) the interest rate (the discount rate). The process of determining the present value is referred to as **discounting the future amount**. The word **discount** has many meanings in accounting, each of which varies with the context in which it is being used. Be careful not to confuse the use of this word.

In this textbook, present value calculations are used to measure several items. For example, in Chapter 16 we determine the market price of a bond by calculating the present value of the principal and interest payments. Calculating the amount to be reported for notes payable, pension, and capital lease liabilities also involves present value calculations.

Present Value of a Single Future Amount

To illustrate present value concepts, assume that you want to invest a sum of money that will yield $1,000 at the end of one year. The question, therefore, is what amount do you need to invest today to have $1,000 one year from now? If you want a 5% rate of return, the investment or present value is $952.38 ($1,000 ÷ 1.05). This amount may also be determined by formula as shown in Illustration B-3.

$$\text{Present value } (PV) = \frac{\text{Future value } (FV)}{(1 + i)^n}$$
$$= \$1,000 \div (1 + 5\%)^1$$
$$= \$1,000 \div 1.05$$
$$= \$952.38$$

Illustration B-3

Present value of 1 formula

The future amount ($1,000), the discount rate (5%), and the number of periods (one) are known. The variables in this situation are shown in the time diagram in Illustration B-4.

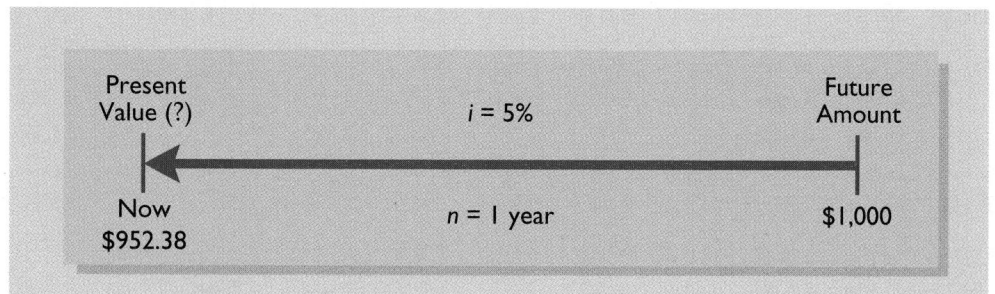

Illustration B-4

Time diagram for the present value of $1,000 discounted for one period at 5%

If the single future amount of $1,000 is to be received in two years and discounted at 5%, its present value is $907.03 [$1,000 ÷ (1 + 5%)² or ($1,000 ÷ 1.05) ÷ 1.05], as shown in Illustration B-5 as follows:

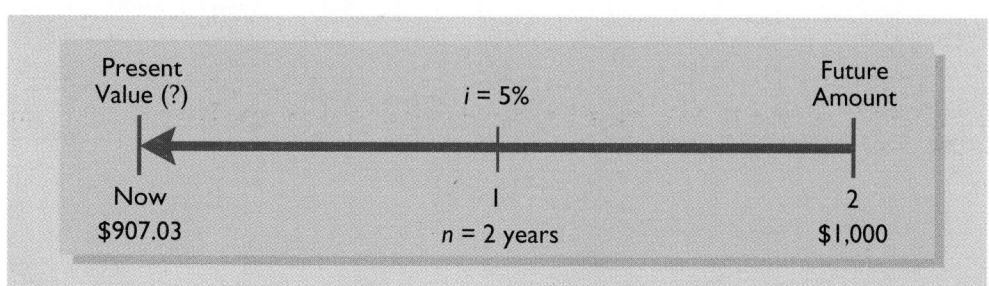

Illustration B-5

Time diagram for present value of $1,000 discounted for two periods at 5%

The present value may also be determined through tables that show the present value of 1 for *n* periods. In Table B-1, *n* is the number of discounting periods involved. The percentages are the periodic interest rates or discount rates. The five-digit decimal numbers in the respective columns are the factors for the present value of 1.

When Table B-1 is used, the future amount is multiplied by the present value factor specified at the intersection of the number of periods and the discount rate. For example, the present value factor for 1 period at a discount rate of 5% is 0.95238, which equals the $952.38 ($1,000 × 0.95238) calculated in Illustration B-3. For two periods at a discount rate of 5%, the present value factor is 0.90703, which equals the $907.03 ($1,000 × 0.90703) calculated in Illustration B-5.

Helpful hint
$PV = FV \times PV$ factor
$FV = PV \div PV$ factor

What if you know the present value and wish to determine the future amount? The present value amount can be *divided* by the present value factor specified at the intersection of the number of periods and the discount rate in Table B-1. For example, it can easily be determined that an initial investment of $907.03 will grow to yield a future amount of $1,000 in two periods, at an annual discount rate of 5% ($1,000 = $907.03 ÷ 0.90703).

A higher discount rate produces a smaller present value. For example, using an 8% discount rate, the present value of $1,000 due one year from now is $925.93 versus $952.38 at 5%. It should also be recognized that **the further away from the present the future amount is, the smaller the present value.** For example, using the same discount rate of 5%, the present value of $1,000 due **in five years** is $783.53. The present value of $1,000 due in one year is $952.38.

TABLE B-1
PRESENT VALUE OF 1

$$PV = \frac{1}{(1 + i)^n}$$

(n) Periods	2%	2½%	3%	4%	5%	6%	7%	8%	9%	10%	11%	12%	15%
1	0.98039	0.97561	0.97087	0.96154	0.95238	0.94340	0.93458	0.92593	0.91743	0.90909	0.90090	0.89286	0.86957
2	0.96117	0.95181	0.94260	0.92456	0.90703	0.89000	0.87344	0.85734	0.84168	0.82645	0.81162	0.79719	0.75614
3	0.94232	0.92860	0.91514	0.88900	0.86384	0.83962	0.81630	0.79383	0.77218	0.75131	0.73119	0.71178	0.65752
4	0.92385	0.90595	0.88849	0.85480	0.82270	0.79209	0.76290	0.73503	0.70843	0.68301	0.65873	0.63552	0.57175
5	0.90573	0.88385	0.86261	0.82193	0.78353	0.74726	0.71299	0.68058	0.64993	0.62092	0.59345	0.56743	0.49718
6	0.88797	0.86230	0.83748	0.79031	0.74622	0.70496	0.66634	0.63017	0.59627	0.56447	0.53464	0.50663	0.43233
7	0.87056	0.84127	0.81309	0.75992	0.71068	0.66506	0.62275	0.58349	0.54703	0.51316	0.48166	0.45235	0.37594
8	0.85349	0.82075	0.78941	0.73069	0.67684	0.62741	0.58201	0.54027	0.50187	0.46651	0.43393	0.40388	0.32690
9	0.83676	0.80073	0.76642	0.70259	0.64461	0.59190	0.54393	0.50025	0.46043	0.42410	0.39092	0.36061	0.28426
10	0.82035	0.78120	0.74409	0.67556	0.61391	0.55839	0.50835	0.46319	0.42241	0.38554	0.35218	0.32197	0.24718
11	0.80426	0.76214	0.72242	0.64958	0.58468	0.52679	0.47509	0.42888	0.38753	0.35049	0.31728	0.28748	0.21494
12	0.78849	0.74356	0.70138	0.62460	0.55684	0.49697	0.44401	0.39711	0.35553	0.31863	0.28584	0.25668	0.18691
13	0.77303	0.72542	0.68095	0.60057	0.53032	0.46884	0.41496	0.36770	0.32618	0.28966	0.25751	0.22917	0.16253
14	0.75788	0.70773	0.66112	0.57748	0.50507	0.44230	0.38782	0.34046	0.29925	0.26333	0.23199	0.20462	0.14133
15	0.74301	0.69047	0.64186	0.55526	0.48102	0.41727	0.36245	0.31524	0.27454	0.23939	0.20900	0.18270	0.12289
16	0.72845	0.67362	0.62317	0.53391	0.45811	0.39365	0.33873	0.29189	0.25187	0.21763	0.18829	0.16312	0.10686
17	0.71416	0.65720	0.60502	0.51337	0.43630	0.37136	0.31657	0.27027	0.23107	0.19784	0.16963	0.14564	0.09293
18	0.70016	0.64117	0.58739	0.49363	0.41552	0.35034	0.29586	0.25025	0.21199	0.17986	0.15282	0.13004	0.08081
19	0.68643	0.62553	0.57029	0.47464	0.39573	0.33051	0.27651	0.23171	0.19449	0.16351	0.13768	0.11611	0.07027
20	0.67297	0.61027	0.55368	0.45639	0.37689	0.31180	0.25842	0.21455	0.17843	0.14864	0.12403	0.10367	0.06110

Before You Go On . . .

►Review It

1. How is Table B-1 used to calculate the present value of a single future amount?
2. How can Table B-1 be used to calculate the future amount of a single present value?

►Do It

Suppose you have a winning lottery ticket and the lottery commission gives you the option of taking $10,000 three years from now, or taking the present value of $10,000 now. An 8% discount rate is used. How much will you receive if you accept your winnings now?

Action Plan

• Use Table B-1 to determine the present value of 1 for $n = 3$ and $i = 8\%$.

Solution

The present value factor from Table B-1 is 0.79383 (three periods at 8%). The present value of $10,000 to be received in three years, discounted at 8%, is $7,938.30 ($10,000 × 0.79383).

►Do It Again

Determine the amount you must deposit now in your savings account, paying 3% interest, in order to accumulate $5,000 for a down payment on a Ford Focus four years from now, when you graduate.

Action Plan

• Use of Table B-1 to determine the present value of 1 for $n = 4$ and $i = 3\%$.

Solution

The present value factor from Table B-1 is 0.88849 (four periods at 3%). The present value of $5,000 to be received in four years, discounted at 3%, is $4,442.45 ($5,000 × 0.88849).

Related exercise material: BEB–1, BEB–2, BEB–3, BEB–4, BEB–5, BEB–6, BEB–7, and BEB–8.

Present Value of a Series of Future Amounts (Annuities)

Alternative terminology
Payments at the end of each period are known as an *ordinary annuity* or *annuity in arrears*. Payments at the beginning of each period are known as an *annuity due* or *annuity in advance*. Unless otherwise indicated, this text assumes that all payments are made or received at the end of each period.

The preceding discussion was for the discounting of only a single future amount. Businesses and individuals frequently engage in transactions in which a series of equal dollar amounts are to be received or paid periodically. Examples of a series of periodic receipts or payments are loan agreements, instalment sales, mortgage notes, lease (rental) contracts, and pension obligations. These series of periodic receipts or payments are called **annuities**. In calculating the present value of an annuity, it is necessary to know (1) the discount rate (i), (2) the number of discount periods (n), and (3) the amount of the periodic receipts or payments (FV).

To illustrate the calculation of the present value of an annuity, assume that you will receive $1,000 cash annually for three years, and that the discount rate is 4%. This situation is shown in the time diagram in Illustration B-6.

Illustration B-6

Time diagram for a three-year annuity

The present value in this situation may be calculated as in illustration B-7:

Illustration B-7

Present value of a series of future amounts

Future Value	×	Present Value of 1 Factor at 4%	=	Present Value
$1,000 (one year away)		0.96154		$ 961.54
1,000 (two years away)		0.92456		924.56
1,000 (three years away)		0.88900		889.00
		2.77510		$2,775.10

This method of calculation is required when the periodic cash flows are not the same in each period. When the future receipts are the same in each period, there are two other ways to calculate present value. First, the annual cash flow can be multiplied by the sum of the three present value factors. In the example above, $1,000 × 2.77510 equals $2,775.10. This can be expressed as a formula, shown in Illustration B-8.

Illustration B-8

Present value of an ordinary annuity of 1 formula

$$\text{Present value } (PV) = \text{ Future value } (FV) \times \left[\frac{1 - \dfrac{1}{(1 + i)^n}}{i} \right]$$

$$= \$1,000 \times [(1 - (1 \div (1 + 4\%)^3)) \div 4\%]$$
$$= \$1,000 \times [(1 - (1 \div (1.04)^3)) \div 0.04]$$
$$= \$1,000 \times [(1 - (1 \div 1.124864)) \div 0.04]$$
$$= \$1,000 \times [(1 - 0.888996358) \div 0.04]$$
$$= \$1,000 \times 2.77509$$
$$= \$2,775.09$$

TABLE B-2
PRESENT VALUE OF AN ANNUITY OF I

$$PV = \dfrac{1 - \dfrac{1}{(1+i)^n}}{i}$$

(n) Periods	2%	2½%	3%	4%	5%	6%	7%	8%	9%	10%	11%	12%	15%
1	0.98039	0.97561	0.97087	0.96154	0.95238	0.94340	0.93458	0.92593	0.91743	0.90909	0.90090	0.89286	0.86957
2	1.94156	1.92742	1.91347	1.88609	1.85941	1.83339	1.80802	1.78326	1.75911	1.73554	1.71252	1.69005	1.62571
3	2.88388	2.85602	2.82861	2.77509	2.72325	2.67301	2.62432	2.57710	2.53129	2.48685	2.44371	2.40183	2.28323
4	3.80773	3.76197	3.71710	3.62990	3.54595	3.46511	3.38721	3.31213	3.23972	3.16987	3.10245	3.03735	2.85498
5	4.71346	4.64583	4.57971	4.45182	4.32948	4.21236	4.10020	3.99271	3.88965	3.79079	3.69590	3.60478	3.35216
6	5.60143	5.50813	5.41719	5.24214	5.07569	4.91732	4.76654	4.62288	4.48592	4.35526	4.23054	4.11141	3.78448
7	6.47199	6.34939	6.23028	6.00205	5.78637	5.58238	5.38929	5.20637	5.03295	4.86842	4.71220	4.56376	4.16042
8	7.32548	7.17014	7.01969	6.73274	6.46321	6.20979	5.97130	5.74664	5.53482	5.33493	5.14612	4.96764	4.48732
9	8.16224	7.97087	7.78611	7.43533	7.10782	6.80169	6.51523	6.24689	5.99525	5.75902	5.53705	5.32825	4.77158
10	8.98259	8.75206	8.53020	8.11090	7.72173	7.36009	7.02358	6.71008	6.41766	6.14457	5.88923	5.65022	5.01877
11	9.78685	9.51421	9.25262	8.76048	8.30641	7.88687	7.49867	7.13896	6.80519	6.49506	6.20652	5.93770	5.23371
12	10.57534	10.25776	9.95400	9.38507	8.86325	8.38384	7.94269	7.53608	7.16073	6.81369	6.49236	6.19437	5.42062
13	11.34837	10.98319	10.63496	9.98565	9.39357	8.85268	8.35765	7.90378	7.48690	7.10336	6.74987	6.42355	5.58315
14	12.10625	11.69091	11.29607	10.56312	9.89864	9.29498	8.74547	8.24424	7.78615	7.36669	6.98187	6.62817	5.72448
15	12.84926	12.38138	11.93794	11.11839	10.37966	9.71225	9.10791	8.55948	8.06069	7.60608	7.19087	6.81086	5.84737
16	13.57771	13.05500	12.56110	11.65230	10.83777	10.10590	9.44665	8.85137	8.31256	7.82371	7.37916	6.97399	5.95423
17	14.29187	13.71220	13.16612	12.16567	11.27407	10.47726	9.76322	9.12164	8.54363	8.02155	7.54879	7.11963	6.04716
18	14.99203	14.35336	13.75351	12.65930	11.68959	10.82760	10.05909	9.37189	8.75563	8.20141	7.70162	7.24967	6.12797
19	15.67846	14.97889	14.32380	13.13394	12.08532	11.15812	10.33560	9.60360	8.95011	8.36492	7.83929	7.36578	6.19823
20	16.35143	15.58916	14.87747	13.59033	12.46221	11.46992	10.59401	9.81815	9.12855	8.51356	7.96333	7.46944	6.25933

Second, annuity tables may be used. As illustrated in Table B-2 , these tables show the present value of 1 to be received periodically for a given number of periods. From Table B-2, it can be seen that the present value factor of an annuity of 1 for three periods at 4% is 2.77509. This present value factor is the total of the three individual present value factors, as shown in Illustration B-7.[1] Applying this amount to the annual cash flow of $1,000 produces a present value of $2,775.09.

Interest Rates and Time Periods

In the preceding calculations, the discounting has been done on an annual basis using an annual interest rate obtained from a table. There are two situations where adjustments may be required to the interest rate, the time period, or both.

Interpolation

In situations where the factor for a certain interest rate is not available, it can be deduced or **interpolated** from the tables. For example, if you wished to find the factor to determine the present value of 1 for a 3½% interest rate and five periods, it

---

[1] The difference of .00001 between 2.77509 and 2.77510 is due to rounding.

would be difficult to use Table B-1 to do so. Table B-1 (or Table B-2 for that matter) does not have a 3½% interest rate column. We can, however, average the factors for the 3% and 4% interest rates to approximate the factor for a 3½% interest rate.

Illustration B-9

Interpolation of 3½% interest rate factor

Factor, $n = 5, i = 3\%$	0.86261
Factor, $n = 5, i = 4\%$	+ 0.82193
Sum of two factors	= 1.68454
Average two factors	÷ 2
Factor, $n = 5, i = 3\frac{1}{2}\%$	= 0.84227

Using Time Periods of Less Than One Year

Discounting may be done over shorter periods of time than one year—such as monthly, quarterly, or semi-annually. When the time frame is less than one year, it is necessary to convert the annual interest rate to the applicable time frame. Assume, for example, that the investor in Illustration B-7 received $500 **semi-annually** for three years instead of $1,000 annually. In this case, the number of periods (n) becomes six (three annual periods × 2), the discount rate (i) is 2% (4% × $^6/_{12}$ mos.). The present value factor from Table B-2 is 5.60143, and the present value of the future cash flows is $2,800.72 (5.60143 × $500). This amount is slightly higher than the $2,775.09 calculated in Illustration B-8 because interest is calculated twice during the same year. Thus interest is compounded on the first half-year's interest.

Before You Go On . . .

▶Review It

1. What is an annuity?
2. How is Table B-2 used to calculate the present value of an annuity?
3. How do you interpolate an interest rate?

▶Do It

Corkum Company has just signed a capital lease contract for equipment that requires rental payments of $6,000 each, to be paid at the end of each of the next five years. The appropriate discount rate is 6%. What is the present value of the rental payments—that is, the amount used to capitalize the leased equipment?

Action Plan

• Use Table B-2 to determine the present value of an annuity of 1 for $i = 6\%$ and $n = 5$.

Solution

The present value factor from Table B-2 is 4.21236 (five periods at 6%). The present value of five payments of $6,000 each, discounted at 6%, is $25,274.16 ($6,000 × 4.21236).

Related exercise material: BEB–9, BEB–10, BEB–11, BEB–12, BEB–13, BEB–14, BEB–15, and BEB–16.

Calculating the Present Value of a Bond

The present value (or market price) of a bond is a function of three variables: (1) the payment amounts, (2) the length of time until the amounts are paid, and (3) the market interest rate, also known as the discount rate.

The first variable (dollars to be paid) is made up of two elements: (1) the principal amount (a single sum), and (2) a series of interest payments (an annuity). To calculate the present value of the bond, both the principal amount and the interest payments must be discounted—which requires two different calculations.

When the investor's market interest rate is equal to the bond's contractual interest rate, the present value of the bonds will equal the face value of the bonds. To illustrate, assume there is a bond issue of five-year 6% bonds with a face value of $100,000. Interest is payable **semi-annually** on January 1 and July 1. If the market rate is the same as the contractual rate, the bonds will sell at face value. In this case, the investor will receive (1) $100,000 at maturity, and (2) a series of ten $3,000 interest payments [($100,000 × 6%) × $\frac{6}{12}$ mos.] over the term of the bonds. The length of time is expressed in terms of interest periods (n), in this case ten, and the discount rate per semi-annual interest period (i), 3%. The time diagram in Illustration B-10 shows the variables involved in this discounting situation.

Illustration B-10

Time diagram for the present value of a 5-year 6%, bond paying interest semi-annually

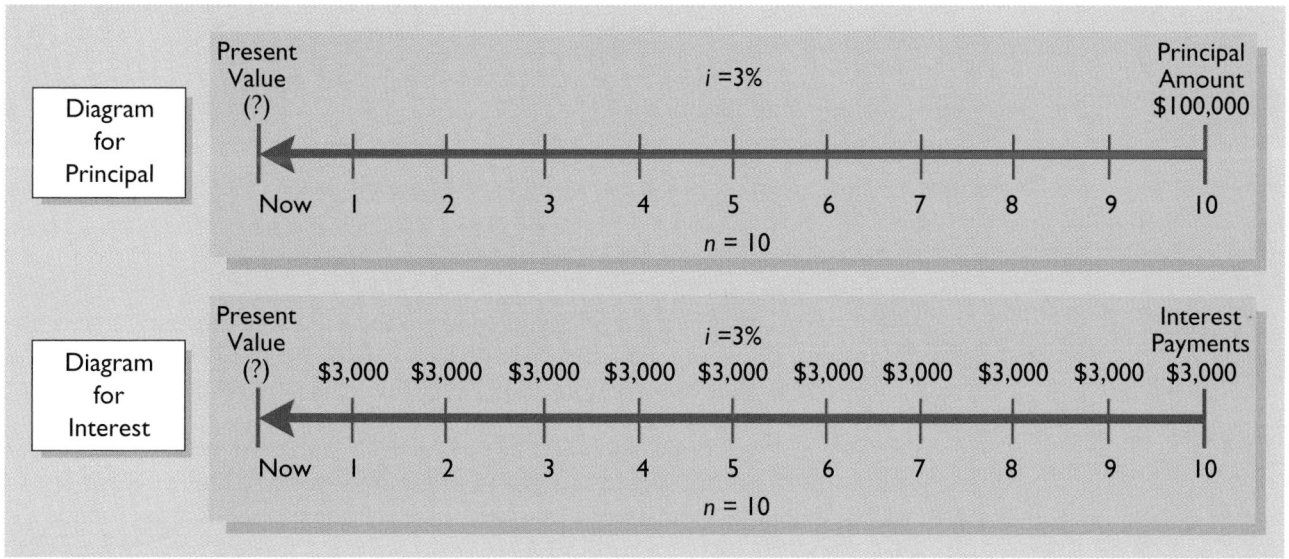

The calculation of the present value of these bonds is shown in Illustration B-11:

Illustration B-11

Present value of principal and interest (face value)

6% Contractual Rate and 6% Market Rate	
Present value of principal to be received at maturity	
$100,000 × PV of 1 due in 10 periods (n) at 3% (i)	
$100,000 × 0.74409 (Table B-1)	$ 74,409
Present value of interest to be received periodically over the term of the bonds	
$3,000 × PV of 1 due periodically for 10 periods (n) at 3% (i)	
$3,000 × 8.53020 (Table B-2)	25,591*
Present value of bonds	$100,000

* Rounded

Now assume that the investor's market rate of return is 8%, not 6%. The future amounts are again $100,000 and $3,000, respectively. **These amounts are based on the bond contract and do not vary with the investor's rate of return.** What does vary is the investor's rate of return, depending on available rates in the marketplace. In this case, a market interest rate of 4% (8% × ⁶⁄₁₂ mos.) will be used. The present value of the bonds is $91,889, as calculated in Illustration B-12.

Illustration B-12

Present value of principal and interest (discount)

6% Contractual Rate and 8% Market Rate	
Present value of principal to be received at maturity	
$100,000 × PV of 1 due in 10 periods (*n*) at 4% (*i*)	
$100,000 × 0.67556 (Table B-1)	$67,556
Present value of interest to be received periodically	
over the term of the bonds	
$3,000 × PV of 1 due periodically for 10 periods (*n*) at 4% (*i*)	
$3,000 × 8.11090 (Table B-2)	24,333
Present value of bonds	$91,889

In this situation, the bonds will sell for $91,889, at a discount of $8,111.

Conversely, if the market rate is 5% and the contractual rate is 6%, the present value of the bonds is $104,376, calculated as in Illustration B-13.

Illustration B-13

Present value of principal and interest (premium)

6% Contractual Rate and 5% Market Rate	
Present value of principal to be received at maturity	
$100,000 × PV of 1 due in 10 periods (*n*) at 2.5% (*i*)	
$100,000 × 0.78120 (Table B-1)	$ 78,120
Present value of interest to be received periodically	
over the term of the bonds	
$3,000 × PV of 1 due periodically for 10 periods (*n*) at 2.5% (*i*)	
$3,000 × 8.75206 (Table B-2)	26,256
Present value of bonds	$104,376

These bonds will sell for $104,376, at a $4,376 premium.

The above discussion relied on present value tables to solve present value problems. Electronic calculators may also be used to calculate present values without the use of these tables. Some calculators, especially financial calculators, have present value and future value functions that allow you to calculate the desired value by inputting the proper amount, discount rate, and periods, and then pressing the appropriate key. Most computer spreadsheets and programs also have built-in formulas to perform the discounting functions if the basic information of the situation is entered.

Before You Go On . . .

►*Review It*

1. Explain how the present value of a bond is determined.
2. If the bonds have interest payable semi-annually, should the *i* used to determine the appropriate discount factor be doubled or halved? The *n*?
3. What table is used to determine the present value of the bond principal? The bond interest?

Related exercise material: BEB–17, BEB–18, BEB–19, BEB–20, and BEB–21.

BRIEF EXERCISES

••

BEB–1 Determine the amount of interest that will be earned on each of the following investments:

Calculate simple and compound interest.

	Investment	(*i*) Interest Rate	(*n*) Number of Periods	Type of Interest
(a)	$100	5%	1	Simple
(b)	$500	6%	2	Simple
(c)	$500	6%	2	Compound

BEB–2 Smolinski Company is considering an investment that will return a lump sum of $500,000 five years from now. What amount should Smolinski Company pay for this investment in order to earn a 7% return?

Calculate present value of single-sum investment.

BEB–3 Levesque Company earns 8% on an investment that will return $875,000 six years from now. What is the amount Levesque should invest now in order to earn this rate of return?

Calculate present value of single-sum investment.

BEB–4 On the joyous occasion of their granddaughter's birth, Kailynn's doting grandparents invest $7,000 in a five-year guaranteed investment certificate (GIC) in her name. If the investment pays 6% annually, how much will the GIC yield when it matures five years from now? (*Hint*: FV = PV ÷ PV factor.)

Calculate future value of single-sum investment, interest compounded annually.

BEB–5 Assume the same information as BEB–4, except that interest on the investment is compounded semi-annually. How much will the GIC yield when it matures five years from now?

Calculate future value of single-sum investment, interest compounded semi-annually.

BEB–6 Chang Company is considering purchasing equipment. The equipment will produce the following cash flows: Year 1, $35,000; Year 2, $45,000; Year 3, $55,000. Chang requires a minimum rate of return of 10%. What is the maximum price Chang should pay for this equipment?

Calculate maximum price to pay for machine.

BEB–7 If Kerry Dahl invests $2,090 now, she will receive $10,000 at the end of 15 years. What annual rate of interest will Kerry earn on her investment? (*Hint*: Use Table B-1.)

Calculate interest rate on single sum.

BEB–8 Maloney Cork has been offered the opportunity to invest $43,233 now. The investment will earn 15% per year, and at the end of that time will return Maloney $100,000. How many years must Maloney wait to receive $100,000? (*Hint*: Use Table B-1.)

Calculate number of periods of single-investment sum.

BEB–9 For each of the following cases, indicate the appropriate discount rate. Identify (a) the interest rate columns, and (b) the number of periods you used in looking up the discount rate.

Use present value tables.

(a) In Table B-1 (present value of 1):

	(*i*) Interest Rate	(*n*) Number of Years Involved	Frequency of Payments
1.	8%	3	Quarterly
2.	5%	4	Semi-annually
3.	4%	5	Annually

(b) In Table B-2 (present value of an annuity of 1):

	(*i*) Interest Rate	(*n*) Number of Years Involved	Frequency of Payments
1.	8%	3	Quarterly
2.	6%	6	Semi-annually
3.	4%	15	Annually

BEB–10
(a) What is the present value of $10,000 due eight periods from now and discounted at 10%?
(b) What is the present value of $10,000 to be received at the end of each of six periods and discounted at 8%?

Determine present values.

BEB–11 Kilarny Company is considering investing in an annuity contract that will return $25,000 at the end of each year for 15 years. What amount should Kilarny Company pay for this investment if it earns a 6% return?

Calculate present value of annuity investment.

Calculate present value of annuity investment.

BEB–12   Deutsch Enterprises earns 9% on an investment that pays back $100,000 at the end of each of the next four years. What is the amount Deutsch Enterprises invested to earn the 9% rate of return?

Calculate value of machine for purchase decision.

BEB–13   Barney Googal owns a garage and is contemplating purchasing a tire retreading machine for $16,100. After estimating costs and revenues, Barney projects a net cash flow from the retreading machine of $2,690 annually for eight years. Barney hopes to earn a return of 11% on such investments. What is the present value of the retreading operation? Should Barney Googal purchase the retreading machine?

Calculate interest rate on annuity.

BEB–14   Annie Dublin purchased an investment for $9,818.15. From this investment, she will receive $1,000 annually for the next 20 years, starting one year from now. What rate of interest will Annie's investment be earning for her? (*Hint*: Use Table B-2.)

Calculate number of periods of annuity.

BEB–15   André Bourque invests $7,786.15 now for a series of $1,000 annual returns, beginning one year from now. André will earn a return of 9% on the initial investment. How many annual payments of $1,000 will André receive? (*Hint*: Use Table B-2.)

Interpolate discount factors.

BEB–16   Insert the appropriate discount factor in to the table below for each of the situations given. These factors have to be interpolated from Tables B-1 and B-2.

	PV of 1 (Table B-1)	PV of an Annuity of 1 (Table B-2)
(a) $n = 4, i = 4\frac{1}{2}\%$		
(b) $n = 6, i = 6\frac{1}{2}\%$		

Calculate present value of bonds.

BEB–17   Cross Country Railroad Co. is about to issue $100,000 of 10-year bonds that pay a 6% annual interest rate, with interest payable semi-annually. The market interest rate is 5%. How much can Cross Country expect to receive for the sale of these bonds?

Calculate present value of bonds.

BEB–18   Assume the same information as BEB–17, except that the market interest rate is 7% instead of 5%. In this case, how much can Cross Country expect to receive from the sale of these bonds?

Calculate present value of bonds.

BEB–19   Thibodeau Enterprises issued $2,000,000 of eight-year 8% bonds that pay interest semi-annually on October 1 and April 1. The bonds are dated April 1, 2003, and are issued on that date. The market rate of interest for such bonds on April 1, 2003, is 10%. What cash proceeds did Thibodeau receive from the issue of the bonds?

Calculate present value of note.

BEB–20   Caledonian Company receives a six-year $50,000 note that bears interest at 8% (paid annually) from a customer at a time when the discount rate is 7%. What is the present value of the note received by Caledonian? (*Hint*: Calculate the present value of the principal and interest separately, similar to bonds.)

Calculate present value of note.

BEB–21   Hung-Chao Yu Company issues a five-year 10% mortgage note on January 1, 2003, to obtain financing for new equipment. The terms provide for semi-annual instalment payments of $112,825. What were the cash proceeds received from the issue of the note?

*B*roadening Your Perspective

Accounting on the Web

BYPB–1   This problem illustrates the time value of money. The "Investing for Kids Java Goals Calculator" is used to see how long it will take to reach financial goals, using standard rates of return for bank deposits, T-bills, bonds, and shares.

Instructions

Specific requirements of this Internet case are available on the Weygandt website.

COMPANY INDEX

Abitibi Consolidated, 281
Advanced Micro Corp., 654
Agra Inc., 663
Air Canada, 1, 208, 267, 461, 515, 522, 586, 675
Alberta Natural Gas, 281
Alcan Aluminium Limited, 13, 254
Alcatel, 785
Aliant, 168
Alliance Atlantis Communications, 869
Alteon WebSystems, 785
American Airlines, 522
Andrés Wines, Ltd., 103, 170, 281, 395, 486, 487, 516
Apple Computer, 916
Atlantic Lotteries, 649
Ault Foods, 281

Bank of Montreal, 208, 721
BC Ferries, 649
BCE, 168, 649, 785
BCT Telus, 417, 461
Bell Canada, 13, 468
Berkshire Hathaway, 697
Best Buy, 208
Big Brothers/Big Sisters, 648
Boise Cascade, 470
Bombardier, 12, 468, 740, 741
Boston Celtics Limited Partnership, 638
Bre-X, 651
Bridgestone/Firestone Inc., 552
Bruncor, 168
Bryony House, 320
Burlington Northern Sante Fe Corporation, 944, 945

Calgary Flames Limited Partnership, 635
Canada Post, 167, 208, 649
Canadian Chamber of Commerce, 648
Canadian National Institute for the Blind, 648
Canadian National Railway Company (CN), 451, 725, 944, 945
Canadian Occidental Petroleum, 661
Canadian Pacific, 461, 468, 476, 649
Canadian Tire, 281, 297, 469, 826
Canadian Utilities Limited, 461
Cara Operations, 1, 13, 103, 469, 785, 792, 794

Carrefour, 259
Casino Windsor, 574
Cavendish Farms, 917
Centennial College, 586
Ceridian Canada Ltd., 531
CertaPay Inc., 379
Chapters Inc., 214, 669, 673, 883, 928
Chrysler, 466
CHUM Limited, 662
CIBC, 103
Cineplex Odeon Corp., 648
Cinnamon Toast Records, 602
Cisco Systems, 162
Citizens Bank of Canada, 385
Coca-Cola, 468
College Pro Painters, 208
Cominco Ltd., 281, 526
Concordia University Bookstore, 262
Corel Corporation, 48, 416, 648
Corus Entertainment, 706
Cott Corporation, 149, 555
Cypost Corp., 718

Danier Leather, 289
Deloitte & Touche, 8
DelSecur Corp., 656
Delta Hotels, 1
Diedrich Coffee, 568
Dominion Bond Rating Service, 739
Donahue Ernst & Young, 607
Dun & Bradstreet Canada, 891

Eastman Kodak, 482
eBay, 484
EcomCard Inc., 433
Ernst & Young, 8
Estée Lauder, 218, 427

Fairfax Financial, 579
Falconbridge Limited, 940
Financial Post, 891
Finning Tractor, 281
Ford Motor Company, 13, 466
Forster's Restaurants, 51
Forzani Group, 168, 169
Future Electronics Inc., 288
Future Shop, 696, 924, 933

Ganong Bros., Limited, 597

Gap, Inc., 11, 588
General Motors (GM), 109, 317, 466
George Weston, 13
Goran Capital, 667
Grant Thornton, 8
Great Canadian Bagel, 785
Greyhound, 11, 12
GUARD, Inc., 688

Harry Rosen, 264
High Liner Foods, 455
Hollinger Inc., 667
Hudson's Bay Company, 94, 208, 265, 650,
    690, 794, 804, 806, 826

Imax Corporation, 498
Imperial Metals, 470
Imperial Oil, 470
Imperial Tobacco Canada, 525
Inco Limited, 461, 940
Independent Weekly, 420
Indigo Books, 883
Indigo.ca, 208
ING Direct, 385
International Olympic Committee (IOC),
    9
InterTan, 933
Intrawest Corporation, 579, 674, 730
IPSCO Inc., 250
Irkutsk Energo, 5
Irving Oil, 14

JDS Uniphase, 485, 592
Journey's End, 607

Kmart, 806
Kodak, 482
KPMG, 8
Kraft Canada, 1

La Senza Corporation, 555
Lafarge Canada Inc., 574
Laidlaw, 663
Le Château, 469
Le Groupe Vidéotron Ltée, 708
Leon's Furniture, 211, 586, 684
Loblaw Companies, 13, 468, 476, 669, 773
Loew's Cineplex Entertainment Corpo-
    ration, 545
Luby's, Inc., 650

Maclean Hunter, 469
Macleans, 520
MacMillan Bloedel, 817
Maple Leaf Foods, 508, 648

Marina Limited Partnership, 640
Mark's Work Wearhouse, 103, 258, 438,
    588, 669, 919
McCain Foods, 14, 917
McDonald's, 11
McGill University, 782
Metfin Properties Limited Partnership,
    637
Microsoft, Inc., 11, 417
Molson Inc., 768
Moody's Investors Service, 739
Mortgage.com Inc., 755
Moulé, 153
Mountain Equipment Co-op, 206, 281,
    927
MP3.com, 483
MT&T, 168
Mug and Musket, 51

Nestlé S.A., 597
Net Nanny Software International Inc.,
    588, 685
Newbridge Networks, 785
NHC Communications, 674
Nike, 11
Nortel Networks, 13, 168, 468, 485, 579,
    669, 674, 729, 785
Northwest Sports Enterprises, 498

Occidental Petroleum, 662
Ontario Hydro, 649
Ontario Securities Commission (OSC),
    570
Open Text, 674
OpenAir.com, 429

Palliser Furniture, 14
Pan-Canadian, 470
Pegasus, 214
Polaroid, 482
Portfolio Management Foundation
    (PMF), 782
PricewaterhouseCoopers, 8, 607, 642
Procter & Gamble, 109
Proxy Monitor, 650

RBC Dominion Securities, 654
RBC Financial Group, 586
Red Cross, 648
Reitmans, 555, 680, 710
Research In Motion (RIM), 646, 649, 655,
    675, 910
Rocky Mountain Bicycle, 648
Rogers Communication, 822
Royal Bank, 389

SAMsports.com Inc., 255
Samsung, 11
Scotiabank, 436
ScotiaMcleod, 654
Seagram, 785
Sears Canada, 169, 586, 596, 649, 656, 683, 771, 826, 892, 897, 900-914
Second Cup, Ltd., 1, 13, 47, 96, 103, 148, 171, 225, 229, 258, 316, 367, 416, 439, 455, 487, 508, 555, 564, 568, 570, 575, 597, 648, 649, 655, 667, 668, 684, 703, 705, 711, 712, 729, 755, 759, 760, 785, 792, 794, 817, 855-857, 883, 943, A1-A25
Seneca College, 100, 103
Shaw Communications, 706
Sideware Systems Inc., 198
Siemens Canada Limited, 515
Sleeman Breweries, 169, 170, 191, 649, 884
SNC-Lavalin Group, 663
Sobeys Inc., 197, 281, 691, 776
Society for Prevention of Cruelty to Animals, 648
Sony of Canada, 427
Southern Alberta Institute of Technology (SAIT), 458, 599
Sports Chek, 168
Sports Experts, 168
SPS Technologies, 817
Standard and Poor's, 739
Staples Inc., 924, 925
Starbucks, 317, 578
Stephanie's Gourmet Coffee and More, 370
Straight Crossing Development, 569, 734
Straight Crossing Financial, 734
Sun Ice, 103, 664
Suncor, 281
Suzy Shier (Canada) Limited, 555
Swiss Chalet, 13

T.Eaton Co. Ltd., 427
TCE Capital, 431
TD Canada Trust, 820
TD Evergreen, 656
Teleglobe, 168, 785
Telus Corporation, 417, 461, 690, 729
The Arctic Group, 925
The Gap, 11, 588
The Motley Fool, 888
Tommy Hilfiger Canada, 427
Topps Company, 926
Toronto Blue Jays, 586, 822
Toronto Stock Exchange (TSE), 685
Toyota, 11
Toys "R" Us, 208
TransCanada PipeLines, 461, 664
Twentieth Century Fox, 569

United Grain Growers (UGG), 96, 103
University of British Columbia, 782

Vivendi, 785

Wal-Mart, 11, 259
West Edmonton Mall, 14, 512
Weyerhaeuser, 817
WestJet, 520
Willamette Industries, 473

Zellers, 297, 794, 806

SUBJECT INDEX

Accelerated amortization method, 469
Account, 54
Accounting
    bookkeeping, distinguished, 6
    defined, 2
    history of, 5, 6
    users of accounting information, 3, 4
    uses of, in other careers, 6, 7
Accounting assumptions, 11, 12
    economic entity assumption, 12, 568
    going concern assumption, 12, 567
    monetary unit assumption, 12, 568
    time period assumption, 103, 568
Accounting cycle
    adjusted trial balance, 120-122
    adjusting entries. *See Adjusting entries*
    analyse business transactions, 59
    closing entries, 158-162
    financial statements. *See Financial statements*
    journalizing, 60-62
    post-closing trial balance, 163
    posting, 64, 65
    steps in process, 164
    trial balance, 73-75
Accounting information, characteristics, 564-566
Accounting information systems, 8, 322-324
Accounting principles
    cost principle, 11, 575
    full disclosure principle, 284, 574, 575
    matching principle, 104, 573, 574
    revenue recognition principle, 103, 569-573
Accounting profession, 7, 8
Accounting software packages, 324, 325
Accounting Standards Board (AcSB), 562
Accounting Standards Oversight Council (AcSOC), 562
Accounts payable ledger, 325
Accounts receivable, 423-438
    ageing, 428
    allowance method, 425-430
    bad debts expense, 424-430
    balance sheet presentation, 438
    credit card sales, 431-433
    debit card sales, 433
    direct write-off method, 424, 425
    disposing of, 431-433
    factoring, 431
    loans secured by, 433
    notes receivable, compared, 434
    percentage of receivables basis, 428, 429
    percentage of sales basis, 428
    recognizing, 423
    recording estimated uncollectibles, 425
    recording write-off of uncollectible, 426
    recovery of uncollectible, 427
    valuing, 424-431
Accounts receivable ledger, 325
ACCPAC for Windows, 156, 324
Accrual basis of accounting, 104, 105
Accrued expenses, 113-115
Accrued interest, 113, 114
Accrued liabilities, 114
Accrued revenues, 112, 113
Accrued salaries, 114, 115
Accumulated amortization—office equipment, 117
Acid test ratio, 438, 900, 901
AcSB, 562
AcSOC, 562
Additional contributed capital, 666
Additions and improvements, 474
Adjusted trial balance, 120-122
Adjusting entries
    accruals, 111-115
    accrued expenses, 113-115
    accrued revenues, 112, 113
    amortization, 116, 117
    estimates, 116
    merchandising company (inventory), 220
    prepaid expenses, 108-110, 124, 125
    prepayment, 107-110
    types, 106
    unearned revenues, 110, 111, 126
    when needed, 106
Adjusting the accounts, 101-152
    accrual vs. cash basis of accounting, 104, 105
    adjusted trial balance, 120-122
    adjusting entries. *See Adjusting entries*
    timing issues, 102
Administrative expenses, 225
Admission by investment, 617
Admission by purchase of an interest,

616, 617
Advertising supplies, 108, 109
Ageing the accounts receivable, 428
Allowance for doubtful accounts, 425-429
Allowance for doubtful notes, 437
Allowance to reduce cost to market value, 797
Allowance method, 425-430
Amortizable cost, 467
Amortization
    adjusting entries, 116, 117
    bonds, 744-751
    comparison of amortization methods, 471, 472
    declining-balance method, 468, 469
    defined, 464-473
    effective interest method, 746-751
    factors in calculating, 465, 466
    intangible assets, 486
    natural resources, 479
    periodic revisions, 473
    straight-line method, 466-468, 744-746, 748, 749, 751
    units-of-activity method, 469, 470, 479
Amortization schedule, 467, 469, 470
Analysing financial statements. *See Financial statement analysis*
Anderson, Tanis, 51
Annual report, 27
Annual report (Second Cup), A1-A25
    auditors' reports, A10, A11
    comparative financial statements, A9-A24
    financial highlights, A2
    financial statements/accompanying notes, A11-A24
    five-year financial review, A25
    letter to shareholders, A2-A4
    management's responsibility for financial reporting, A9
    MD&A, A4-A8
Annuity, B6, B7
Annuity due, B6
Annuity in advance, B6
Annuity in arrears, B6
Articles of incorporation, 652
Asset turnover, 487, 905, 906
Assets, 14
Assumptions. *See Accounting assumptions*
Auditing, 7
Authorization of transactions and activities, 373
Authorized shares, 654
Average cost method, 279, 280

Bad debts expense, 424-430
Balance sheet, 25, 26
    account form, 170
    capital assets, 168, 486
    classified, 167
    current assets, 167
    current liabilities, 169, 526, 527
    equity, 170
    inventory, 289
    inventory cost flow methods, 283
    inventory errors, 286, 287
    long-term investments, 168
    long-term liabilities, 169
    receivables, 438
    report form, 170, 171
Balchen, Paul, 512
Banerjee, Neela, 5
Bank, 385-393
    cheques, 386-388
    deposits, 386
    EFT, 386
    reconciliation, 390-393
    statement, 388, 389
Bank advances, 516
Bank credit cards, 432
Bank deposits, 386
Bank indebtedness, 516
Bank memoranda, 391
Bank overdraft, 394, 516
Bank reconciliation, 390-393
Bank service charge, 389
Bank statement, 388, 389
Bar codes, 210
Basic accounting equation, 14
Basket purchase, 463
Bearer bonds, 738
Belford, Terrence, 431
Big Five accounting firms, 8
Big GAAP-little GAAP controversy, 577
Bill of lading, 214
Bond certificate, 739, 740
Bond indenture, 739
Bond issue costs, 739
Bond ratings, 739
Bonding, 377
Bonds, 736-754
    advantages/disadvantages, 736, 737
    amortization, 744-751
    discount/premium, 743
    investments, as, 787-789
    issuing procedures, 739, 740
    issuing, at discount, 744-748
    issuing, at face value, 742, 743
    issuing, at premium, 748-751
    issuing, between interest dates, 751, 752

market value, 741, 742, B9-B11
present value, 741, 742, B9-B11
ratings, 739
redemption/retirement of, 753, 754
trading, 740, 741
types, 738
Bonus, 532
Book value per share, 668, 669, 908
Bookkeeping, 6
Bourgeois, Pierre, 233
BPI Accounting, 324
Bregman, Michael, 1
Brisebois, Diane, 220
Budgeting, 8
Buildings, 463
Bullock, James, 663
Burkhead, J. Gary, 75
Business advisory services, 8
Business document, 59

CA, 7
Calendar year, 103
Callable bonds, 738
Callable preferred shares, 665
Canada Business Corporations Act, 650
Canada Pension Plan (CPP), 532, 534
Canadian Institute of Chartered Accountants (CICA), 10, 560, 562
Capital assets, 459-510
    intangible, 481-486. *See also Intangible capital assets*
    natural resources, 478-481
    PP&E. *See Property, plant, and equipment*
    ratio analysis, 487
    statement presentation, 487
    tangible, 461
Capital cost allowance (CCA), 472
Capital deficiency, 626, 627
Capital expenditures, 475
Capital lease, 758
Carter, Larry, 162
Cash
    defined, 379
    internal control over disbursements, 382-384
    internal control over receipts, 379-382
    reporting, 394, 395
Cash basis of accounting, 104, 105
Cash basis of revenue recognition, 572
Cash count sheet, 381
Cash current debt coverage, 855, 901
Cash disbursements, 382-384
Cash disbursements journal, 337
Cash dividend, 691-693
Cash equivalents, 394

Cash flow per share, 856, 908, 909
Cash flow statement, 25, 26, 821-886
    cash flow, defined, 823
    classification of cash flows, 823, 824
    direct method, 842-854
    format, 825
    indirect method, 829-842
    preparation, 826, 827
    purpose, 823
    ratio analysis, 855-857
    significant noncash activities, 824
    usefulness, 825, 826
Cash interest coverage, 760, 913
Cash return on sales, 855, 856, 905
Cash total debt coverage, 857, 914
Cash payments journal, 337-339
    journalizing, 338, 339
    posting, 339
    proving the ledger, 339
    sales taxes, 346
Cash receipts, 379-382
Cash receipts journal
    journalizing, 332-334
    posting, 335
    proving the ledgers, 335
    sales taxes, 346
Cash register tapes, 216
CCA, 472
Certified general accountant (CGA), 7
Certified management accountant (CMA), 7
CGA, 7
Change in accounting principle, 700
Chart of accounts, 65, 66
Chartered accountant (CA), 7
Chase, Steven, 483
Cheque, 386-388
CICA, 10, 560, 562
CICA Handbook, 10, 562
CIF, 214
Classified balance sheet, 167
Classified financial statements, 166
Closely held corporation, 649
Closing entries, 158-162, 221, 273, 274
Closing the books, 158-162
CMA, 7
Cogan, Ellen, 560
Collateral, 515
Collection period, 439, 902
Collusion, 377
Common shares, 652, 659-661
Common size analysis, 895
Common stock dividends distributable, 695
Comparability, 565

Comparative analysis. *See Financial statement analysis*
Compensating balances, 395
Completed-contract method, 572
Compound entry, 62
Compound interest, B2
Computer fraud, 378
Computerized accounting system, 324
Conceptual framework, 563, 578
Conservatism, 287, 565
Consigned goods, 267
Consistency, 565
Consolidated financial statements, 794
Constraints, 576, 577
Contingent liabilities, 525, 526
Contra account, 117
Contra asset account, 117
Contra liability account, 117, 744
Contra revenue account, 218
Contractual interest rate, 739
Contractual restrictions, 698
Control account, 213, 325
Controlling interest, 794
Convertible bonds, 738
Convertible preferred shares, 664, 665
Copyrights, 483
Corporate capital, 657, 658
Corporation, 13, 14, 647-732
    advantages/disadvantages, 652
    authorized shares, 654
    characteristics, 649-652
    common shares, 652
    corporate capital, 657, 658
    corporate name, 652
    Crown, 649
    defined, 648
    dividends, 690-696
    formation, 652
    income statement, 704-709
    income tax, 651, 704-706
    issue of shares, 654, 655, 659-661
    market value of shares, 655, 656
    preferred shares, 663-666
    prior period adjustments, 699, 700
    privately held, 649
    profit/not-for-profit, 648
    publicly held, 648, 649
    ratio analysis, 667-669
    reacquisition of shares, 661, 662
    regulations, 650
    retained earnings, 698-704
    shareholders' equity, 657, 658, 666, 667, 703
    shareholders' rights, 652, 653
Correcting entries, 165, 166

Correction of prior period error, 699, 700
Cost accounting, 8
Cost-benefit, 577
Cost method, 791, 792, 794
Cost of goods available for sale, 271
Cost of goods on hand, 271
Cost of goods purchased, 271
Cost of goods sold, 208, 270-272
Cost principle, 11, 575
Coupon bonds, 738
Coupon interest rate, 739
Cox, Brian, 688
CPP, 532, 534
CPT, 214
Craig, Suzanne, 656
Credit, 55
Credit balance, 55
Credit card sales, 431-433
Credit cards, 379
Credit memorandum, 389
Credit purchase, 19
Credit terms, 215
Crediting the account, 55
Creditors, 4, 15
Crown corporation, 649
Culligan, Tom, 1
Cumulative dividend, 664
Current assets, 167
Current liabilities, 169, 513-558
    contingent liabilities, 525, 526
    current maturities of long-term debt, 521
    estimated liabilities, 522-524
    financial statement presentation, 526, 527
    key features, 514
    notes payable, 516, 517
    operating line of credit, 515, 516
    product warranties, 523, 524
    property taxes, 522, 523
    sales taxes payable, 517, 518
    unearned revenues, 520
Current maturities of long-term debt, 521
Current ratio, 171, 172, 438, 899, 900
Currie, Ron, 100
Customers, 4

DacEasy, 156
Day traders, 888
Days sales in inventory, 229, 903
Debenture bonds, 738
Debit, 55
Debit balance, 55
Debit card sales, 433
Debit cards, 379

Debit-credit rules, 55-58
   assets/liabilities, 56
   normal account balances, 58
   owner's capital, 56
   owner's drawings, 57
   revenues/expenses, 57
Debit memorandum, 389
Debiting the account, 55
Debt investments, 787-789
Debt to equity ratio, 912
Debt to total assets, 759, 760, 912
Declaration date, 692
Declining-balance method, 468, 469
Deferred charges, 485
Deferred income taxes, 705
Deferred revenues, 110
Deficit, 698
Definitely determinable liabilities, 515-522
Deposit slips, 386, 387
Deposits in transit, 391
Depreciation, 117. *See also Amortization*
Digital cash, 379
Direct method (cash flow statement), 842-854
Direct write-off method, 424, 425
Discontinued operations, 706, 707
Discount (on bonds payable), 743
Discounting, 437
Discounting the future amount, B3
Discounts
   purchases, 215, 216
   sales, 218
Dishonoured note, 436
Dividend yield, 712, 911
Dividends, 16, 690-697
   cash, 691-693
   declaration of, 691
   liquidating, 691
   ratio analysis, 711, 712
   stock, 693-695
   stock split, 695, 696
Dividends in arrears, 664
Documentation procedures, 374, 375
Domain names, 483
Double declining-balance method, 468
Double-entry system, 55
Doubtful accounts expense, 425
Dow Jones Industrial Average, 796
Drawings, 15
Duggan, Shawn, 602
Duns Financial Profile, 891
Dynamic analysis, 895

Earnings per share (EPS), 710, 711, 909, 910
EBIT, 760
EBITDA, 760
Economic entity assumption, 12, 568
Economic events, 2
Economic planners, 4
Edur, Olev, 211
Effective interest method of amortization, 746-751
Effective interest rate, 741, 746
EFILE, 705
EFT, 386
EI, 532, 533, 535
El-Raheb, S., 211
Electronic funds transfer (EFT), 386
Elements of financial statements, 566
Elmasry, Mohamed, 646
Elstein, Aaron, 650, 755
Employee benefits, 520, 534, 535
Employee deductions. *See Payroll accounting*
Employee earnings record, 535, 536
Employment Insurance (EI), 532, 533, 535
Entity income tax, 651
EPS, 710, 711, 909, 910
Equation analyses, 60
Equipment, 463
Equity investments, 790-794
   defined, 790
   holdings of between 20/50%, 792-794
   holdings of less than 20%, 791, 792
   holdings of more than 50%, 794
Equity method, 792-794
Error, 74
Estimated liabilities, 522-524
Estimating inventories, 296-298
Ethics, 9, 10
   amortization, 472
   errors vs. irregularity, 74
eTransact, 325
Excel, 156
Expanded basic equation, 58
Expense recognition, 573, 574
Expenses, 15
Expired costs, 573
External auditors, 377
External transactions, 17
External users, 4
External verification, 377
Extraordinary items, 707, 708

Face value, 435, 739
Factor, 431
Factored receivables, 431
Faithful representation, 564

FCA, 214
Feedback value, 564
FIFO
    balance sheet effects, 283
    income statement effects, 282
    periodic inventory system, 278, 279
    perpetual inventory system, 292
Financial instruments, 665, 739
Financial Performance Indicators for Canadian Business, 891
Financial ratios. *See Ratio analysis*
Financial statement analysis, 889-947
    horizontal analysis, 892-895
    limitations, 916-918
    need for comparative analysis, 890, 891
    ratio analysis, 898-915. *See also Ratio analysis*
    vertical analysis, 895-897
Financial statements
    balance sheet. See Balance sheet
    cash flow statement. *See Cash flow statement*
    classified, 166
    consolidated, 794
    income statement. *See Income statement*
    merchandising operations, 223-229
    preparing, from work sheet, 177-179
    samples. *See Annual report (Second Cup)*
    statement of owner's equity, 25, 26
Financing activities, 823, 824
Finished goods, 289
First-in first-out. *See FIFO*
Fiscal year, 103
Fixed assets. *See Property, plant, and equipment*
Floating (variable) interest rate, 755
FOB destination, 214
FOB shipping point, 214
Forms of business organization, 13
Forsyth, Walter, 602
Franchise, 484
Francis, Diane, 651
Fregin, Douglas, 646
Freight costs
    purchases, 214, 269
    sales, 218
Frequent flyer program, 522
Full disclosure principle, 284, 565
Fully diluted earnings per share, 711
Future income taxes, 705
Future revenues, 110

GAAP, 10, 562
Gain on disposal, 476, 477
Gain or loss on realization, 624

Gardner, Tom and David, 888
General accounting, 8
General expenses, 225
General journal, 60, 340
General ledger, 63
General partner, 607
General partnership, 607
Generally accepted accounting principles (GAAP), 10, 562
Gerstner, Lou, 7
Going concern assumption, 12, 567
Goods and services tax (GST), 233. *See also Sales taxes*
Goods in transit, 266
Goodwill, 484, 485
Gorenstein, Laurie, 153
Gray, Robin, 288
Great salad oil swindle, 266
Gross earnings, 531
Gross margin, 209
Gross profit, 208, 224
Gross profit margin, 224, 573, 904
Gross profit method, 296, 297
GST, 233. *See also Sales taxes*
GST payable, 235

Harmonized sales tax (HST), 233
Heard, James, 650
Heinzl, John, 427
History of accounting, 5, 6
Honouring of notes receivable, 436
Horizontal acquisition, 785
Horizontal analysis, 892-895
Howlett, Karen, 379
HST, 233
Hughes, John, 575

IASB, 11, 579
Impairment loss, 462
Imprest system, 383
Income from operations, 227
Income ratio, 610-612
Income statement, 24, 25
    corporations, 704-709
    gross profit, 224
    inventory cost flow methods, 282
    inventory errors, 285, 286
    multi-step, 223-227
    net income, 225
    net sales, 224
    non-operating activities, 225-227
    operating expenses, 225
    periodic inventory system, 272, 273
    single-step, 227, 228
Income summary, 158

Income tax
    amortization, 472
    corporations, 651, 704-706
    personal taxes (employee deductions), 533
Income tax accounting, 8
Independent verification, 376, 377
Indirect method (cash flow statement), 829-842
Industry Reports, 891
Initial public offering (IPO), 654
Input tax credit, 235
Instalment method, 572
Instalment notes payable, 755-757
Intangible capital assets, 481-486
    amortization, 486
    copyrights, 483
    franchises/licences, 484
    goodwill, 484, 485
    other assets, 485
    patents, 482
    R&D costs, 485
    trademarks (trade names), 483
Interest, B1
Interest coverage, 760, 912, 913
Interim periods, 103
Internal auditing, 8
Internal auditors, 376, 377
Internal control, 372-378
    authorization of transactions and activities, 373
    bonding, 377
    cash disbursements, 382-384
    cash receipts, 379-382
    documentation procedures, 374, 375
    independent verification, 376, 377
    limitations, 377, 378
    payroll accounting, 529-531
    rotating employees' duties, 377
    safeguarding assets/records, 375
    segregation of duties, 374
Internal reports, 4
Internal transactions, 17
Internal users, 3, 4
Internal verification, 376, 377
International accounting standards, 578, 579
International Accounting Standards Board (IASB), 11, 579
Internet banking, 385, 389
Interperiod tax allocation, 705, 706
Interpolation, B7, B8
Intraperiod tax allocation, 706
Inventory
    balance sheet presentation, 289

    classifying, 289
    cost flow assumptions. *See Inventory cost flow methods*
    determining quantities, 265-268
    estimating, 296-298
    LCM, 287, 288
    ownership of goods, 266, 267
    periodic inventory system, 211. *See also Periodic inventory system*
    perpetual inventory system, 210. *See also Perpetual inventory system*
    ratios, 229
Inventory cost flow methods
    average cost method, 279, 280
    balance sheet effects, 283
    consistent usage, 284
    FIFO, 278, 279, 282, 283, 292
    financial statement effects, 283
    income statement effects, 282
    LIFO, 280-283, 293, 294
    moving average cost method, 292, 293
    periodic inventory system, 275-284
    perpetual inventory system, 291-294
    selection of method, 283, 284
    specific identification method, 277
    usage, 281
Inventory errors, 285-287
Inventory losses, 220
Inventory turnover, 229, 903, 904
Investee, 787
Investing activities, 823, 824
Investment portfolio, 786
Investments, 168, 783-819
    equity, 790-794
    financial statement presentation, 797-800
    LCM rule, 796
    temporary. *See also Temporary investments*
    valuation, 796, 797
    why corporations invest, 784-786
Investor, 787
Investments by owner, 15
Investors, 4
IPO, 654
Irregularity, 74
Issued shares, 662

Johnson, Matthew, 916
Joint and several liability, 606
Journal, 60
Journal entries, 60
Journalizing
    cash payments, 338
    cash receipts, 332-334

credit purchases, 336
credit sales, 329, 330
recording process, as part of, 60, 61
Jumani, Fara, 206

Kalawsky, Keith, 662
Keebler, Karen, 458
King, Chad, 734

Labour unions, 4
Land, 462
Land improvements, 462
Last-in first-out. *See LIFO*
Laurer, George, 210
Lazaridis, Mike, 646
LCM, 287, 288, 796
Lease liabilities, 757
LeBrun, Shelley, 820
Ledger, 63
Legal capital, 656
Legal title to inventory, 266, 267
Lessee, 757
Lessor, 757
Lever, Rob, 385
Leveraging, 907
Lewandowski, René, 233
Lewis, Michael, 288
Liabilities, 15. *See also Current liabilities, Long-term liabilities*
Licences, 484
LIFO
    balance sheet effects, 283
    income statement effects, 282
    periodic inventory system, 280, 281
    perpetual inventory system, 293, 294
Limited liability, 13
Limited liability partnership (LLP), 607
Limited partner, 607
Limited partnership, 607
Line of credit, 515, 516
Lipscombe, Lena, 262
Liquidating dividend, 691
Liquidity, 171
Liquidity ratios, 899-903
LLP, 607
Long-term debt investments, 788, 789
Long-term investments, 168, 787
    debt investments, 788, 789
    financial statement presentation, 798
    valuation, 797
Long-term liabilities, 169, 170, 735-780
    bonds. *See Bonds*
    leases, 757-759
    notes payable, 755-757
    ratio analysis, 759, 760

Long-term notes payable, 755-757
Long-term notes receivable, 436
Loss on disposal, 477
Love, Cathy, 320
Lower of cost and market (LCM), 287, 288, 796
Lump-sum purchase, 463

MacKenzie, Colin, 602
Mail receipts, 381
Maintenance expense, 474
Maker, 386
Management discussion and analysis (MD&A), A4-A8
Managerial accounting, 8
Manual accounting system, 324
Manufacturing company, 289
Market interest rate, 741
Market value per share, 655, 656, 669
Marketable securities. *See Temporary investments*
Matching principle, 104, 573, 574
Maturity value, 739
McArthur, Keith, 522
McCutcheon, Catherine, 518
McFarland, Janet, 570
McHardie, Daniel, 433
McInnis, Joe, 782
McNall, Bruce, 13
MD&A, A4-A8
MDP, 607
Measurement criteria, 566
Mechanical and electronic controls, 375
Meehan, Gary, 908
Merchandising operations, 207-261
    adjusting entry, 220
    closing entry, 221
    financial statements, 223-229
    inventory, 289
    multi-step income statement, 223-227
    operating cycles, 209
    periodic inventory system, 211
    perpetual inventory system, 210
    post-closing trial balance, 222
    purchases of merchandise, 212-215. *See also Purchases of merchandise*
    sales of merchandise, 216-218. *See also Sales of merchandise*
    single-step income statement, 227, 228
    worksheet, 237-239
Mintenko, Stephanie, 370
Monetary unit assumption, 12, 568
Mortgage bond, 738
Mortgage note payable, 755
Moving average cost method, 292, 293

Multidisciplinary practice (MDP), 607
Multinational corporations, 578
Multiple-step income statement, 223-227
Mutual agency, 605
MYOB Accounting, 324

Natural resources, 478-481
Net book value, 117, 465
Net income, 16, 225
Net loss, 16
Net pay, 534
Net purchases, 271
Net realizable value, 287, 425, 435
Net sales, 224
Neutrality, 564
Newcomb, Brook, 385
No capital deficiency, 624, 625
No par value share, 656
Non-operating activities, 225-227
Nonbank credit cards, 432, 433
Noncumulative preferred shares, 664
Not-for-profit accounting, 8
Not-for-profit corporation, 648
Notes payable, 516, 517, 755-757
Notes receivable
    accounts receivable, compared, 134
    dishonoured note, 436
    disposing of, 436, 437
    honouring, 436
    interest calculations, 435
    long-term, 436
    promissory notes, 434
    recognizing, 435
    sale of, 437
    valuing, 435
NSF cheque, 389

O'Dea, Frank, 1
Objective of financial reporting, 563
Objectivity, 565
Obsolescence, 465
Off balance sheet financing, 759
Oldford, Glenn, 420
1/10, n/30, 215
One-write system, 328
Online banking, 385, 389
Opdyke, Jeff D., 916
Operating activities, 823, 824
Operating cycles, 167, 209
Operating expenditures, 474
Operating expenses, 208, 225, 484
Operating lease, 757
Operating line of credit, 433, 515, 516
Ordinary annuity, B6
Ordinary repairs, 474

Organization costs, 652
Other expenses and losses, 226
Other intangible assets, 485
Other receivables, 422
Other revenues and gains, 225
Outstanding cheques, 391
Outstanding shares, 662
Over-the-counter receipts, 380, 381
Owner's deficiency, 15
Owner's equity, 15, 16, 170, 614
Ownership of goods, 266, 267

Pacioli, Luca, 5
Padding the payroll, 530
Paid absences, 535
Par value, 739
Par value share, 656
Parent company, 794
Partners' equity, 16, 170, 614
Partnership Act, 604
Partnership agreement, 608
Partnership liquidation, 624
Partnerships, 16, 603-644
    admission of partner, 616-620
    advantages/disadvantages, 608
    characteristics, 604-606
    closing entries, 610, 611
    defined, 604
    dissolution, 606
    dividing income/loss, 610-614
    financial statements, 614
    formation, 609, 610
    general, 607
    income ratios, 610-612
    investment of assets, 617-620
    liability of partners, 606
    limited, 607
    liquidation, 624-627
    LLPs, 607
    MDPs, 607
    partnership agreement, 608
    withdrawal of partner, 620-622
Partridge, John, 390
Patents, 482
Payee, 386
Payer, 386
Payment date, 692
Payout ratio, 711, 712, 911
Payroll accounting, 518-520, 529
    CPP, 532, 534
    EI, 532, 533, 535
    employer payroll costs, 534, 535
    filing/remitting payroll deductions, 538
    gross earnings, 531, 532

internal control, 529-531
not pay, 534
paid absences, 535
payroll deductions, 532-534
payroll department records, 535, 536
personal income tax, 533
post-employment benefits, 535
recognizing payroll expenses/liabilities, 536, 537
recording payment of payroll, 537, 538
voluntary deductions, 534
workers' compensation, 535, 538
Payroll deductions, 532-534
Payroll deductions tables, 533
Payroll register, 536
PE ratio, 711, 910
Percentage-of-completion method, 571, 572
Percentage of receivables basis, 428, 429
Percentage of sales basis, 428
Periodic inventory system
    closing entries, 273, 274
    cost of goods sold, 270-272
    income statement presentation, 272, 273
    overview, 211
    perpetual inventory system, compared, 268, 270
    physical count, 265
    purchases of merchandise, 269
    sales of merchandise, 268, 269
    special journals, 343
Permanent accounts, 158
Perpetual inventory system
    overview, 210
    periodic inventory system, compared, 268, 270
    physical inventory count, 220
    purchases of merchandise, 212-215
    sales of merchandise, 216-218
    subsidiary account, 213
Personal income tax, 533
Personal Tax Credits Return (TD1), 533
Petty cash fund, 383, 384
Physical controls, 375
Physical inventory count, 211, 220, 265
Plant assets. *See Property, plant, and equipment*
Point of sale, 570
Post-closing trial balance, 163
Post-employment benefits, 535
Posting
    cash payments journal, 339
    cash receipts journal, 335
    purchases journal, 336

recording process, as part of, 64, 65
sales journal, 330
PP&E. *See Property, plant, and equipment*
Predictive value, 564
Preemptive right, 653
Preferred shares, 663-666
    convertible, 664, 665
    dividend preference, 664
    liquidation preference, 666
    redeemable/retractable, 665
Premium (on bonds payable), 743
Prenumbering, 375
Prepaid expenses, 108-110, 124, 125
Prepaid insurance, 109, 110
Present value, 741, 742, B1-B13
    annuities, B6, B7
    bonds, 741, 742, B9-B11
    compounding, B2
    interpolation, B7, B8
    single future amount, B3, B4
    tables, B4, B6
    time periods of less than one year, B8
    variables, B3
Present value tables, B4, B7
Price-earnings (PE) ratio, 711, 910
Prime rate, 755
Principal value, 435
Principles. *See Accounting principles*
Prior period adjustments, 699, 700
Private accounting, 8
Private corporations, 14
Privately held corporation, 649
Product warranties, 523, 524
Profit and loss ratio, 610
Profit margin, 225, 904, 905
Profit margin ratio, 855
Profitability ratios, 904-912
Program controls, 375
Promissory note, 434
Property taxes, 522, 523
Property, plant, and equipment, 461-478
    amortization, 464-473. *See also Amortization*
    basket purchase, 463
    buildings, 463
    cost, 461-464
    disposals of, 475
    equipment, 463
    exchanges of, 477, 478
    expenditures during useful life, 474, 475
    land, 462
    land improvements, 462
    retirement of, 475, 476
    sale of, 476, 477

Proprietorship, 13
Provincial sales tax (PST), 233. *See also Sales taxes*
Provincial sales tax rates, 517
Proving the ledgers
    cash payments journal, 339
    cash receipts journal, 335
    purchases journal, 337
    sales journal, 331
Provision for uncollectibles, 425
PST, 233. *See also Sales taxes*
Public accounting, 7, 8
Public corporations, 14
Publicly held corporation, 648, 649
Purchase allowance, 215
Purchase discounts, 215
Purchase invoice, 212
Purchase on account, 19
Purchase order, 212
Purchase return, 215
Purchase returns and allowances, 215, 269
Purchases journal, 335-337
    expanding the journal, 337
    journalizing, 336
    posting, 336
    proving the ledgers, 337
    sales taxes, 346
Purchases of merchandise, 212-215
    discounts, 215, 216
    freight costs, 214
    periodic inventory system, 269
    purchase returns and allowances, 215
    sales taxes, 236
    subsidiary inventory records, 213

QPP, 532
Quantity discount, 215
Quattro Pro, 156
Quebec Pension Plan (QPP), 532
Quick ratio, 438, 900
QuickBooks, 156, 324

R&D costs, 485
Ratio, 898
Ratio analysis, 898-915
    cash flow statement, 855-857
    dividend record, 711, 712
    earnings performance, 710, 711
    liquidity ratios, 899-903
    long-term liabilities, 759, 760
    profitability ratios, 904-912
    shareholders' equity, 667-669
    solvency ratios, 912-914
    summary of ratios, 914, 915
Raw materials, 289

Reacquisition of shares, 661, 662
Realization, 624
Receivables, 421-456
    accounts. *See Accounts receivable*
    notes. *See Notes receivable*
    other, 422
    ratio analysis, 438, 439
    statement presentation, 438
    trade, 422
Receivables turnover, 439, 902
Receiver General, 532
Recognition criteria, 566
Reconciling the bank account, 390-393
Record date, 692
Recording process, 53-99
    chart of accounts, 65, 66
    debit/credit rules, 55-58
    illustration, 66-72
    journalizing, 60-62
    ledger, 63
    posting, 64, 65
    steps in process, 59
    use of dollars/cents, 75
Recourse, 431
Redeemable bonds, 738
Redeemable preferred shares, 665
Reference column
    journal, 64
    ledger account, 64
Registered bonds, 738
Regulatory agencies, 4
Relevance, 564
Reliability, 564
Repair expense, 474
Replacement cost, 287
Research and development costs, 485
Residual claim, 653
Residual equity, 15
Restrictive endorsement, 381
Retail inventory method, 297, 298
Retailers, 208
Retained earnings, 16, 657, 698-704
Retained earnings restrictions, 698, 699
Retractable bonds, 738
Retractable preferred shares, 665
Return on assets, 487, 906
Return on common shareholders' equity, 907
Return on equity, 667
Return on investment, 667, 907
Return on sales, 904
Revenue recognition principle, 103, 569-573
Revenues, 15
Reverse stock split, 696

Reversing entry, 164, 179, 180
Rosen, Al, 579
Rotating employees' duties, 377
Roy, Piali, 264
Royalties, 484

Safeguarding assets/records, 375
Salaries expense, 114, 115
Salary, 532
Sales, 216, 217
Sales invoice, 212, 216
Sales journal
    advantages, 332
    journalizing, 329, 330
    posting, 330
    proving the ledgers, 331
    sales taxes, 345, 346
Sales of merchandise, 216-218
    discounts, 218
    freight costs, 218
    periodic inventory system, 268
    sales, 216, 217
    sales returns and allowances, 217, 218
    sales taxes, 217, 233-235
Sales returns and allowances, 217, 218, 268
Sales revenue, 208
Sales taxes, 217, 233-237
    amount payable, 517, 518
    disbursements, on, 235-237
    operating expenses, 236, 237
    purchase returns and allowances, 236
    purchases, 236
    receipts, on, 233-235
    sales returns and allowances, 235
    special journals, 344-346
Sales taxes payable, 517, 518
Schwill, Robin, 565
Secondary market, 654
Secured bonds, 738
Securities exchanges, 655
SEDAR, 731
Segregation of duties, 374
Selling expenses, 225
Serial bonds, 738
Service companies, 208
Share capital, 16, 666
Share certificate, 652, 653
Shareholders' equity, 16, 170, 657, 658, 666, 667, 703
Shaw, Jim, 532
Shoniker, Jim, 431
Shoplifting, 220
Short-term investments. *See Temporary investments*
Signature card, 386

Simple interest, B1
Simply Accounting, 156, 320, 324
Single-step income statement, 227, 228
Solvency ratios, 912-914
Special journals, 328-340
    cash payments journal, 337-339, 346
    cash receipts journal, 332-335, 346
    general journal, and, 340
    periodic inventory system, 343
    purchases journal, 335-337, 346
    sales journal, 329-332, 345
    sales taxes, 344-346
Specific identification method, 277
Standard form of account, 63, 64
Stated interest rate, 739
Stated value, 656
Statement of cash flows. *See Cash flow statement*
Statement of changes in financial position, 25, 26
Statement of earnings, 537. *See also Income statement*
Statement of financial position. *See Balance sheet*
Statement of operations. *See Income statement*
Statement of owner's equity, 25, 26
Statement of partners' capital, 614
Statement of retained earnings, 701-704
Static analysis, 895
Stock dividend, 693-695
Stock option plans, 532
Stock split, 695, 696
Straight-line method of amortization, 466-468, 744-746, 748, 749, 751
Strauss, Marina, 427
Subsidiary account, 213
Subsidiary company, 794
Subsidiary ledger, 325-328
Summa de Arithmetica, Geometrica, Proportioni et Proportionalita (Pacioli), 5
Supplies, 108, 109

T account, 54
Take-home pay, 534
Taxation, 8
Taxing authorities, 4
TD1, 533
Temporary accounts, 158
Temporary debt investments, 787, 788
Temporary investments
    characteristics, 786
    defined, 786
    financial statement presentation, 797, 798

valuation, 796, 797
Term bonds, 738
Thomas, David, 663
Three-column form of account, 63, 64
Time-clock procedures, 530
Time period assumption, 103, 568
Time value of money, 741, B1. *See also Present value*
Timeliness, 564
Times interest earned ratio, 760, 912
Trade name, 483
Trade receivables, 422
Trademark, 483
Trading on the equity, 907
Transaction analysis
    investment by owner, 18, 19
    payment of accounts payable, 21
    payment of expenses, 21
    purchase of advertising on credit, 20
    purchase of equipment for cash, 19
    purchase of supplies on credit, 19
    receipt of cash on account, 22
    services provided for cash, 20
    services rendered for cash and credit, 20, 21
    withdrawal of cash by owner, 22
Transactions, 17
Transposition error, 75
Treasury shares, 662
Trend analysis, 892
Trustee, 739
Trial balance, 73-75
    adjusted, 120-122
    limitations, 74
    locating errors, 74, 75
    post-closing, 163
Trites, Gerald, 27

Uncollectible accounts, 424-430
Understandability, 564
Unearned revenues, 110, 111, 126, 520
Unexpired costs, 574
Units-of-activity method, 469, 470, 479
Units-of-production method, 469
Universal product code (UPC), 210
Unlimited liability, 606
Unsecured bonds, 738
Useful life, 116
Users of accounting information, 3, 4

Variable interest rate, 755
Verifiability, 564
Vertical acquisition, 785
Vertical analysis, 895-897
Voluntary restrictions, 698

Wages, 531
Warranties, 523, 524
Wasting assets, 479
Weber, Juergen, 433
Withdrawal by payment from partners' personal assets, 620, 621
Withdrawal by payment from partnership assets, 621, 622
Work in process, 289
Work sheet
    electronic, 156
    merchandising companies, 237-239
    preparing financial statements from, 177-179
    steps in preparing, 175-177
    using, 156, 157
Working capital, 899
Working capital ratio, 899
Workers' compensation, 535, 538
Workers' Compensation Board, 538
Working capital, 171
Workplace Health, Safety and Compensation Commission, 538
Workplace Health, Safety and Compensation Plan, 535

Yield, 741

PHOTO CREDITS

Chapter 1
OPENER: The Second Cup Ltd. Page 48: Corel Corporation.

Chapter 2
OPENER: Anthony Fast. Page 57: Totonto Blue Jays Baseball Club. Page 65: The Goodyear Tire & Rubber Co. Page 96: United Grain Growers Limited.

Chapter 3
OPENER: Seneca College. Page 109: Procter & Gamble.

Chapter 4
OPENER: Moulé. Page 167: Canada Post Corporation. Page 168: BCE Inc. Page 169: The Forzani Group Ltd. Sears Canada Inc. Page 170: Sleeman Breweries Ltd. Andrés Wines Ltd. Page 202: Future Shop Ltd. Fisheries Products International Limited.

Chapter 5
OPENER: Mountain Equipment Co-op. Page 258: Mark's Work Wearhouse Ltd.

Chapter 6
OPENER: Concordia University. Page 264: Michael Schellenberg. Page 289: Danier Leather Inc.

Chapter 7
Page 379: CertaPay Inc.

Chapter 8
OPENER: Stephanie's Gourmet Coffee and More. Page 385: ING Direct. Page 388: Bank of Montreal. Page 390: Scotiabank. Page 392: Bank of Canada. Page 395: Andrés Wines Ltd. Page 416: Corel Corporation. Page 417: Telus Corporation.

Chapter 9
OPENER: *The Independent Weekly.* T. Eaton Co. Records, Archives of Ontario, F229-308-463. Page 438: Mark's Work Wearhouse Ltd. Page 455: High Liner Foods Incorporated

Chapter 10
OPENER: Southern Alberta Institute of Technology. Page 483: eBay Inc. Page 487: Andrés Wines Ltd. Page 508: Maple Leaf Foods.

Chapter 11
OPENER: West Edmonton Mall. Page 516: Andrés Wines Ltd. Pages 526 & 537: Cominco Ltd. Page 531: Ceridian Canada Ltd. Page 532: Shaw Communications. Page 555: La Senza Corporation. Reitmans (Canada) Limited.

Chapter 12
OPENER: Canadian Institute of Chartered Accountants. Page 574: Casino Windsor. Page 575: Ontario Securities Commission. Page 599: Southern Alberta Institute of Technology.

Chapter 13
OPENER: Cinnamon Toast Records. Pages 607 & 642: PricewaterhouseCoopers.

Chapter 14
OPENER: Research In Motion. Page 650: Yahoo. Page 663: Laidlaw Inc. Page 685: Net Nanny Software International.

Chapter 15
OPENER: GUARD Inc. Page 706: Canada Customs and Revenue Agency. Page 710: Reitmans. Page 729: Nortel Networks. Page 730: Intrawest Coporation.

Chapter 16
OPENER: John Sylvester. Page 740: Bombardier Inc. Page 777: Reitmans & La Senza Corporation. Page 778: RBC Dominion Securities.

Chapter 17
OPENER: University of British Columbia. Page 817: Weyerhaeuser & SPS Technologies Inc.

Chapter 18
OPENER: TD Canada Trust. Page 883: Chapters. Page 884: Sleeman Breweries Ltd.

Chapter 19
OPENER: The Motley Fool. Page 892: Sears Canada Inc. Page 910: Research In Motion. Page 919: Mark's Work Wearhouse. Page 945: Canadian National